International Conference on Automation, Computing and Communication (ICACC-2020)

ITM Web of Conferences Volume 32 (2020)

Navi Mumbai, India
27 – 28 June 2020

Editors:

Mukesh D. Patil
Vishwesh A. Vyawahare

ISBN: 978-1-7138-1414-6

Printed from e-media with permission by:

Curran Associates, Inc.
57 Morehouse Lane
Red Hook, NY 12571

proceedings.com

Some format issues inherent in the e-media version may also appear in this print version.

For additional information, please contact EDP Sciences – Web of Conferences
at the address below.

EDP Sciences – Web of Conferences
17, Avenue du Hoggar
Parc d'Activité de Courtabœuf
BP 112
F-91944 Les Ulis Cedex A
France

Phone: +33 (0) 1 69 18 75 75
Fax: +33 (0) 1 69 28 84 91

contact-edps@webofconferences.org

Additional copies of this publication are available from:

Curran Associates, Inc.
57 Morehouse Lane
Red Hook, NY 12571 USA
Phone: 845-758-0400
Fax: 845-758-2633
Email: curran@proceedings.com
Web: www.proceedings.com

TABLE OF CONTENTS

https://doi.org/10.1051/itmconf/20203200001

Preface

The first International Conference on Automation, Computing and Communication (ICACC-2020) was organized by Ramrao Adik Institute of Technology (affiliated to DY Patil deemed to be University), Nerul, Navi Mumbai, India, between June 27-28, 2020. It was co-sponsored by the IEEE Bombay Section. Due to the COVID 19 pandemic, the conference was conducted online.

ICACC-2020 was organized with a motivation to provide a platform for researchers working in the areas of automation, computing and communication to showcase their research and to create a strong community which thrive on the frontier of technology.

The conference received overwhelming response from the research community for its call for papers. We received 253 submissions. These were checked for plagiarism and the submissions who passed this check were sent for rigorous review. The experts from academia and industry were assigned as reviewers. Only 75 submissions with quality and originality of work were accepted (approx. 30% acceptance ratio). The accepted papers are from a broad spectrum of fields like control systems, signal and image processing, AI and ML applications, intelligent systems, PV cell technology, Deep Learning, Blockchain, virtual reality and many more. The keynote speakers and authors presented their work online. The sessions were interactive and brainstorming.

We would like to take this opportunity to express our deep sense of gratitude towards our management, especially Hon. Dr D Y Patil (Founder President), Hon. Dr Vijay Patil (President), and Hon. Mrs Shivani Patil (Managing Trustee) for the encouragement and support. We sincerely thank Dr Shirish Patil, Hon. VC, DY Patil deemed to be University for his guidance. We put on record our sincere thanks to the members of international programme committee and technical programme committee, keynote speakers, reviewers, session chairs, session coordinators, authors and participants for making this conference a grand success. Thanks are due to our colleagues in the institute for supporting us. The tireless efforts and meticulous planning by the organizing team to make this event successful deserve special appreciation. We would also like to acknowledge the cooperation and support by the teams at Easychair conference management system and ITM, Web of Conferences.

We sincerely hope that research community will be truly benefitted by the ICACC-2020 contributions.

We look forward to welcome all in ICACC-2021.

Prof. Mukesh D. Patil, Conference Chair, ICACC-2020

Prof Vishwesh A. Vyawahare, Convener, ICACC-2020

June 2020.

Statement of Peer review

In submitting conference proceedings to *Web of Conferences*, the editors of the proceedings certify to the Publisher that

1. They adhere to its **Policy on Publishing Integrity** in order to safeguard good scientific practice in publishing.
2. All articles have been subjected to peer review administered by the proceedings editors.
3. Reviews have been conducted by expert referees, who have been requested to provide unbiased and constructive comments aimed, whenever possible, at improving the work.
4. Proceedings editors have taken all reasonable steps to ensure the quality of the materials they publish and their decision to accept or reject a paper for publication has been based only on the merits of the work and the relevance to the journal.

Title, date and place of the conference

International Conference on Automation, Computing and Communication, June 27-28, 2020
Ramrao Adik Institute of Technology, Nerul, Navi Mumbai, India

Proceedings editor(s):

Dr. Mukesh D Patil,
Dr. Vishwesh A Vyawahare

Date and editor's signature

July 10, 2020

ITM Web of Conferences **32**, 01001 (2020) https://doi.org/10.1051/itmconf/20203201001
ICACC-2020

Rubble Assistant Robot using SLAM

Priyal Patil[1,*], *Jayraj* Pol[2,**], and *Amarkant* Roy[3,***] *Dr. Sharmila* Petkar[4,****]

[1]Department of Electronics Engineering, Ramrao Adik Institute Of Technology, Nerul, Navi Mumbai, India

Abstract. In this paper, we are going to present an implementation of SLAM. This SLAM technology is used for creating a map of an unknown environment by placing a robot. Robot will be interfaced and controlled using Robot Operating System (ROS). We are aiming to create a map of a region where disaster has taken place. It can be used to create a map of the regions where humans cannot reach. In the disaster prone areas it is not possible for humans to check the location of survivors. Our robot will help to amplify low human noise to detect presence of humans under the rubble and to detect them using sensors and then we can mark that location so that rescue team would quickly reach to that location for their rescue, also simultaneous live feed/streaming using normal camera to monitor the area. Here main part is odometry of robot. To calculate odometry, camera and encoders are used. So, SLAM based robots can help in mapping their locations digitally.

1 Introduction

Mapping a territory has always been an essential topic in science and technology, especially in robotics. Different types of methods have been developed, since one of the problem that has been developed and is still being solved is the SLAM. SLAM refers to Simultaneous Localization and Mapping. SLAM is a challenge of putting a robot in an unknown region which maps its surroundings with respect to its own position [1]. In this project our model will be interfaced with Robot Operating System (ROS). Mechanism of our robot will be a Rocker Bogie Mechanism. We are going to use Tiva C launchpad for interfacing the sensors, motors. We are going to create a map which requires various parameters which would be obtained from various sensors. As the robot moves around the area, it uses ultrasonic sensors to detect and avoid obstacles. DC encoder motors are used to provide mobility. MPU 6050 is used for calculating odometry of robot along with encoders. Mapping needs 3D vision camera to sense the surrounding objects and maps them in 3D. In this project we are using xbox kinect 360, which is a depth sensor mostly used for detecting gestures/motion for gaming purpose.

2 Literature Survey

The industrial revolution lead the advancement in science and technology. Through robotics it becomes easier to solve the problems with more accuracy and with more efficiency as compared to the manual method to solve any problem.Earlier in robotics, it was mandatory that an individual team should monitor the and give commands to the robot using communication interfaced with robot. The historical review of the first 20 years of the SLAM problem is given by Durrant–Whyte and Bailey in two surveys. (1986–2004) the classical age saw the introduction of the main probabilistic formulations for SLAM, including approaches based on Extended Kalman filters (EKF), Rao–Blackwellized particle filters, and maximum likelihood estimation; moreover, it describes the basic challenges connected to efficiency and robust data collection [1]. The marketability of the SLAM problem is related with the emergence of indoor applications of mobile robotics. Indoor operation removes the use of GPS to limit the localization error; furthermore, SLAM provides an appealing alternative to user-defined maps, showing that robot operation is possible in the absence of an Ad-HOC localization infrastructure [1].

Figure 1. NASA's Mars Pathfinder.

*e-mail: priyalpatil98@gmail.com
**e-mail: jayraj.pol@gmail.com
***e-mail: roy.amarkant@gmail.com
****e-mail: profsjpetkar@gmail.com

Hardware implementation of our robot is based on Rocker-Bogie mechanism. NASA developed rocker-bogie suspension system for their rovers and was implemented in Mars Pathfinder and Sojourner rover [2]. This system maintains all wheels in contact with ground even in rough terrains.

Robots in the field of disaster management are rarely seen. Researchers at IIT-Istituto Italiano di Tecnologia developed, assembled a new disaster response robot called the Centauro [3]. Even few robots are being developed to control fire.

3 Software Implementation

The software designing of our robot model consist of number of implementation steps. These steps include ROS implementation, Programming Tiva C launchpad using Energia IDE, Gazebo simulation using rviz package of ROS. This simulation helps us to know whether the robot is working properly before actually implementing on hardware.

3.1 Introduction to ROS

The Robot Operating System (ROS) is a open-source platform and a flexible robotics framework. The autonomous mobile robot using multi-sensor data deals with various sensors functioning simultaneously.

ROS provides different software tools to visualize and debug robot data. The core of the ROS framework is a message-passing middle-ware in which processes can communicate and exchange data with each other even when running from different machines.Using the ROS developers can create many of robotic capabilities, such as mapping and navigation in mobile robots [4].

In our project, we used "ROS-Kinetic" framework running in Ubuntu operating system (16.04).

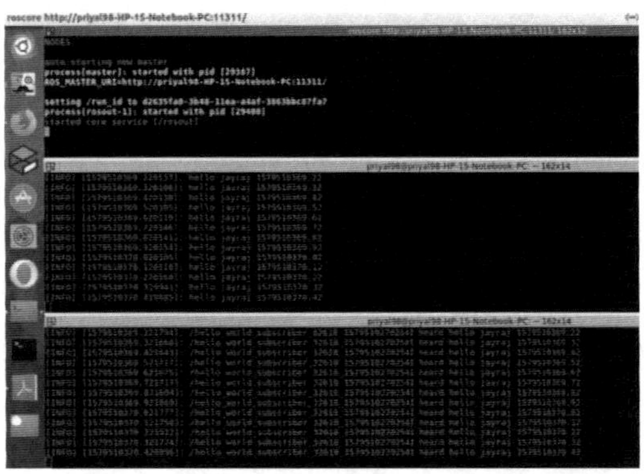

Figure 2. Basic ROS Program.

3.2 Creating Robot model

- Creating URDF File of Robot URDF is a Unified Robot Description Format which is used to create programmed representation of a mobile robot in Gazebo. It is an XML format for robot boundaries representation. The .urdf file consist of links and joints of the robot model. Every link and joint is described explicitly which increases redundancy [5].

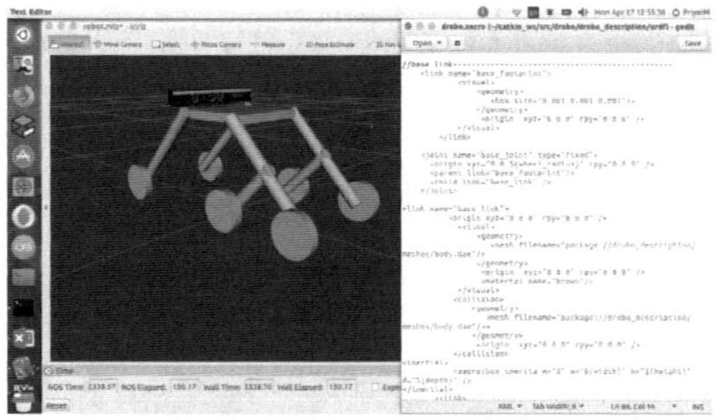

Figure 3. Rviz visualization of Drobo.

- Creating a XACRO File XACRO file is a XML Macro Language. It is used to simplify the URDF file which reduces the redundancy of programming. It uses parameterized entities like shapes, collision parameters, weight for defining robot attributes [5].

3.3 Simulating Robot on Gazebo

Gazebo is a software to simulate the robot model before implementing it on hardware. It is used to create a virtual world where we can test work-ability of our robot.It provides a easy programming interface and good quality graphics [6].

Figure 4. Gazebo simulation of Drobo.

3.4 Kinect's Depth Sensor Operation

Microsoft Kinect Sensor consist of visual camera, 3D depth sensor, microphone array, motorized tilt. Depth Sensor mainly consist of IR projector along with CMOS Infrared camera(IR Camera). We are using it for mapping purpose in which robot is capable of creating a map of its surrounding environment. Kinect sensor was mostly used for tracking human actions for gaming purpose [7].

Depth sensor transmits infrared rays and measures the distance of each node points of the object by measuring the reflected rays from the objects (time of flight). Kinect consists of array of four microphones which enables to conduct ambient noise suppression which helps us to amplify low voice of humans under the rubble.

OpenNI package of ROS is used for kinect's integration. It also supports freenect package.

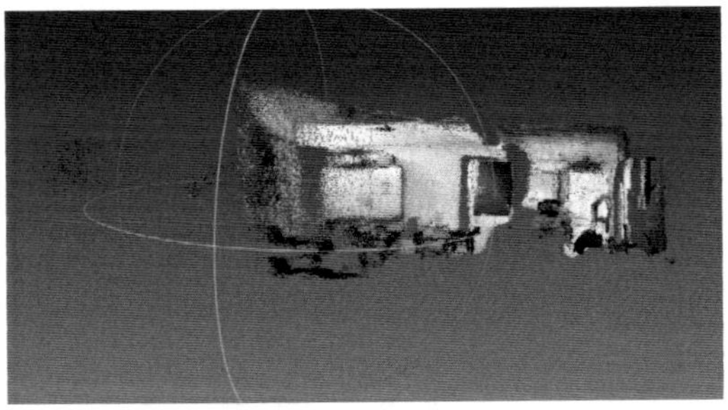

Figure 5. 3D Map obtained through Kinect sensor.

3.5 Introduction to SLAM

SLAM is a simultaneous operation of localization and mapping. While mapping, landmark objects are recognized using robot's odometry and also while localization the position of robot is measured with respect to the objects in the surrounding [8]. In fig.2 we have shown

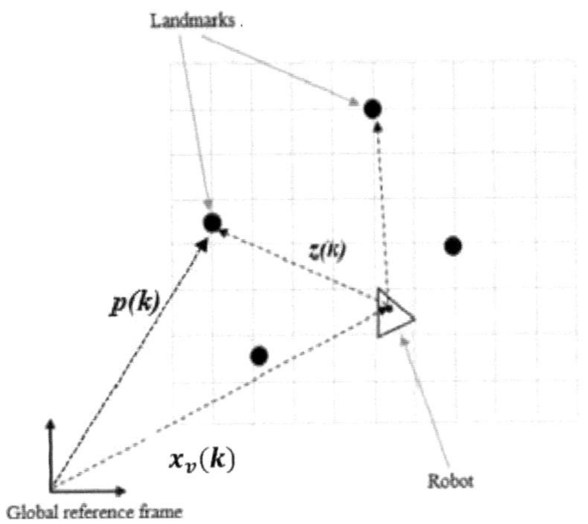

Figure 6. SLAM

the slam parameters which explain the localization of the robot. While creating a map, robot position is considered as X(k). z(k) is considered as the landmark location with respect to robot. p(k) denotes landmark location with respect to global reference point. While updating the map, robot is located using landmarks and the data which has been collected. The uncertainty of data (errors) involved in this process can be removed using filters [9].

The gmapping, rtabmap, and cartographer packages are widely used for implementing SLAM. Cartographer package is developed by google. In this project, we have used the gmapping package.

3.6 Simultaneous Localization and Mapping

- **Mapping (gmapping):** GMapping is a Rao-Blackwellized particle filter (RBPF) which is highly efficient to learn grid maps from data of laser range. Using this package we can create a 2D grid map from data (laser and position) collected by mobile robot. The graphical representation of a map can be visualized using Rviz (ROS Visualizer) package of ROS [10].
- **Localization (amcl):** Localization is achieved using Monte Carlo Localization, which uses particle filtering to navigate the robot. We used amcl (Adaptive Monte Carlo Localization) package of ROS. Amcl transforms kinect sensor's data into odometry frame which is combined with the real time position [10].
- **Using the Odometry Data:** Odometry of robot is obtained through IMU data and motor encoders. This is important to obtain the exact locations of robot in surrounding, which helps to obtain precise map of the area.
- **Interfacing Tiva C Launchpad:** Tiva C Launchpad is similar to arduino which acts as a bridge between ground sensors and processing computer. This is used to acquire sensor data as well as controlling motors. It is programmed using Energia IDE which provides user-friendly programming environment [11].

4 Hardware Implementation

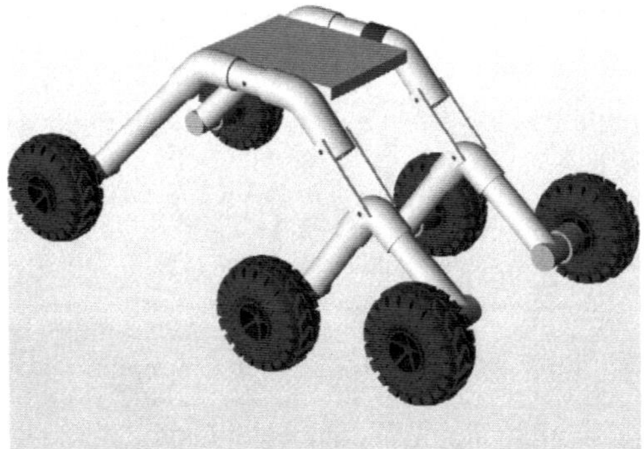

Figure 7. Rocker-Bogie Mechanism

We have implemented a Rocker-Bogie Mechanism as a hardware design. Our objective behind this is to design a robot for working on different landscapes like rough terrain, plain surfaces,and also overcoming obstacles as well as climbing over obstacles of certain height.

One of the biggest challenges was to use pipes for our hardware implementation. We cut those pipes in proper

https://doi.org/10.1051/itmconf/20203201001

dimension and used various hardware tools to assemble them together. PVC pipes are easily available in the market and plus they are light-weighted. Due to these factors, we choose PVC pipes as a material to build our robot.

Various hardware components are used such as motors, sensors, embedded boards, batteries etc; they need to be integrated together. First, we tested each component individually such as working of motors, observed readings of different sensors such as ultrasonic sensor, IMU sensor interfaced with Tiva C Launchpad. Kinect sensor calibration was conducted using OpenNi package of ROS. Integrating all these components together was the last step of the project.

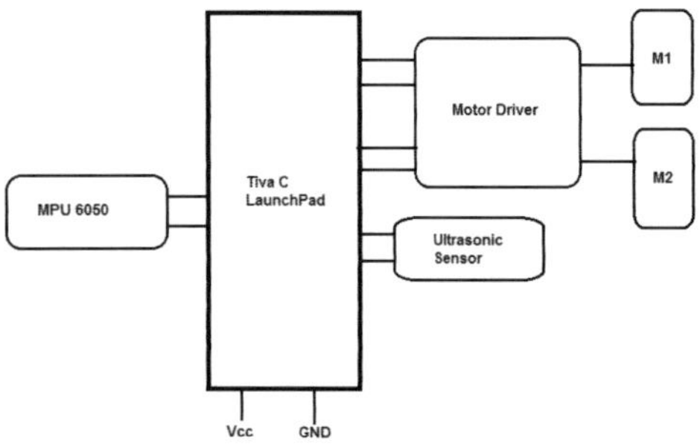

Figure 8. Block Diagram

5 Results

5.1 Robot Model Simulation

This model simulation contains kinect sensor, motors, actuators defined according to gazebo syntax. Due to this gazebo identifies various sensors and function accordingly.

A node running in terminal is a keyboard teleop node (teleoperation) which gives velocity commands on press of respective key from keyboard to the wheels attached to robot.

On applying velocity commands to robot, it moves accordingly in the world. Even we can increase/decrease speed of rotation from this teleop node [12].

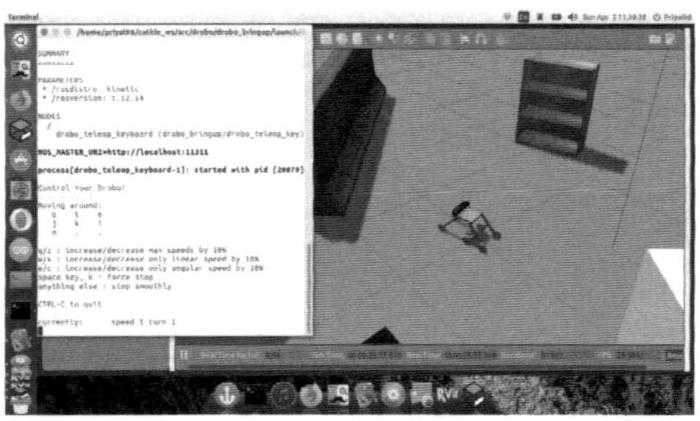

Figure 9. Drobo Model Simulation

5.2 Mapping

Rviz helps to visualize map generated by robot of a certain unknown world [13]. This generated map can be saved and used for navigation autonomously afterwards. Package used to generate map is gmapping package. Topics such as /scan of laserscan node and /map of gmapping node is used prominently.

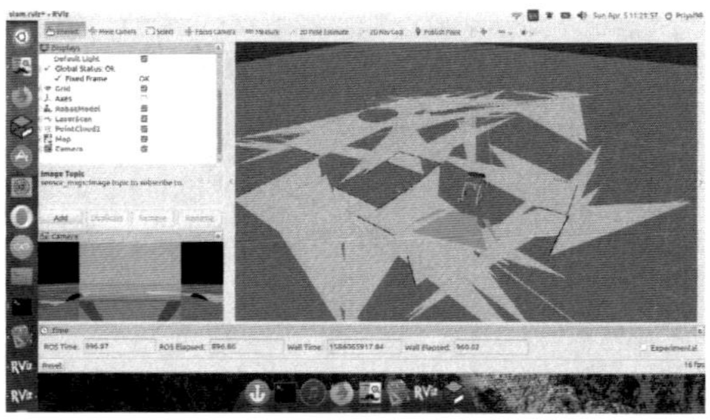

Figure 10. Map generation using gmapping package

5.3 Localization

Rviz also helps in navigating robot through a map generated through gmapping package earlier. To navigate robot without colliding is main task which is carried out through amcl package. We can set goal to our robot and our robot will reach the goal by planning its own path avoiding the obstacles placed in between [14].

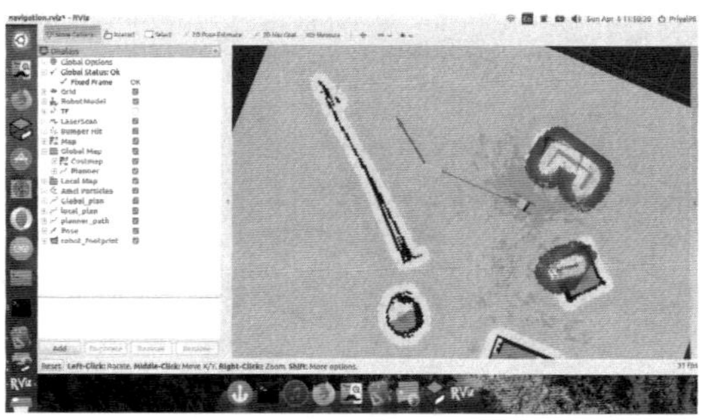

Figure 11. Robot reaching goal through amcl package

6 Applications and Future Scope

- Medical Assistant Robot which will assist doctors while surgery.
- Underwater implementation of SLAM based robot will help to map area underwater and to study and to collect data marine life.
- Underground monitoring robot based on SLAM will help to monitor and survey area under the ground such as Oil pipeline, Tunnels, Mining Area, Underground Metro tracks.

https://doi.org/10.1051/itmconf/20203201001

- Hotel Assistant Robot which will act as laundry service/ room service or it will act as a waiter which will serve food to the tables.
- Space Robots can be implemented which will map the unknown planets and can monitor the surface of that planet.
- Unmanned Air-Vehicle (UAV) can be used for surveillance around the specific area. Using SLAM, it will be useful during wars for navigating enemy's territory from air.

7 Conclusion

Generally we cannot conclude our work right here as SLAM is still an area of research. Many ROS developers are still exploring this field of robotics and there are areas that have not even been touched yet.

In our project, we were able to assemble Drobo (Short for Disaster robot) and were able to map area of its surrounding. In this year we were able to map an indoor area. In next stages of our research, we will be extending its reach and ability to map larger areas with outdoor locations. We also plan to extend path planning to uneven 3D terrains as disaster-prone area won't be plain surface at all.

Simultaneous Localization and Mapping (SLAM) is a technology which helps to build a map of an unknown location and simultaneously keeping track of it. Kinect used, which guarantees the precision of mapping environment. This kind of robot is beneficial in many applications. Our work will be helpful for further reference or study in SLAM. Despite of having complex structure, this technology will be a leading technology in near future.

Acknowledgment

Our first and sincere appreciation goes to our honourable Principal of RAIT, Nerul, Navi Mumbai, Dr. Mukesh D Patil and Head of Department for Electronics Engineering Dr. Vishwesh Vyawahare for helping and providing better environment to work on our dissertation.

We would like to thank our mentor and guide Dr. Sharmila Petkar whose guidance and support was invaluable to us, which helped us to overcome all the difficulties faced.

References

[1] SLAM for Dummies A Tutorial Approach to Simultaneous Localization and Mapping By the 'dummies'.

[2] https://mars.nasa.gov/mars-exploration/missions/pathfinder/

[3] Centauro-https://spectrum.ieee.org/automaton/robotics/industrial-robots/centauro-a-new-disaster-response-robot-from-iit

[4] http://wiki.ros.org/Documentation

[5] https://ni.www.techfak.uni-bielefeld.de/files/URDF-XACRO.pdf.

[6] Gazebo robot simulator, www.gazebosim.org

[7] https://www.choitek.com/uploads/5/0/8/4/50842795/ros-kinect.pdf

[8] G. Dissanayake, S.B. Williams, H. Durrant-Whyte, T. Bailey: Map management for efficient simultaneous localization and mapping (SLAM), Autonom. Robot. 12, 267–286 (2002)

[9] Weerasinghe, K.K.D.K.U., Silva, L.C.J., Basnayake, B.M.S.S., Sandanayaka, S.D.M., Kumarawadu, S.P., Chandima, D.P. and Jayasekara, A.G.B.P., 2016, December. Mapping and path planning for long distance autonomous navigation using multisensory data. In 2016 Electrical Engineering Conference (EECon) (pp. 1-6). IEEE.

[10] Nieto, T. Bailey, E. Nebot: Scan-SLAM: Combining ekf-slam and scan correlation, Proc. IEEE Int. Conf. Robotics and Automation (Barcelona 2005)

[11] Tiva C Launchpad- http://www.ti.com/tool/EK-TM4C123GXL.

[12] http://wiki.ros.org/teleop-twist-keyboard

[13] RViz -3D visualization tool for ROS, wiki.ros.org/rviz

[14] Joseph, Lentin. Mastering ROS for robotics programming. Packet Publishing Ltd, 2015.

[15] Quigley, M., Gerkey, B. and Smart, W.D., 2015. Programming Robots with ROS: a practical introduction to the Robot Operating System. " O'Reilly Media, Inc.".

ITM Web of Conferences **32**, 01002 (2020) https://doi.org/10.1051/itmconf/20203201002
ICACC-2020

Home Automation Using Chatbot and Voice Assistant

Bhavyasri Kadali[1,*], *Neha* Prasad[1,**], *Pranaya* Kudav[1,***], and *Manoj* Deshpande[1,****]

[1]Department of Computer Engineering A.C. Patil College of Engineering.

Abstract. In a world with ever increasing needs for comfort, human race is relying more and more on technological advancements to find solutions to their problems. Home Automation Systems have become a go-to arena in the recent years. In the following paper, we propose a Home Automation system that uses a wholesome blending of some technologies like Internet of Things, Natural Language Processing and Machine Learning. The prime feature of this system is that, it provides two modes of communication to the user : Text and Voice. The text input from the user will be given via a Chatbot Application and the voice input from the user will be given via a voice assistant. The input will undergo Natural Language Processing to find the action that the user wants the system to perform. The IoT component, Raspberry Pi would perform the actuations in the form of switching On or Off of Lights and Fans of a room in the house.

1 Introduction

We live in a rapidly evolving environment. With advancement in technology fields, humans needs w. r. t. to efficiency and comfort are reaching a new high every day. People are leaving behind the conventional methods of operation and opting for Smart solutions, not only in industrial zones but also for the domestic environment.

Home Automation seems like a perfect solution for the current scenario where we want every small task to happen with a click of a button. The need for a centralized system which could remotely monitor home appliances is arising with the increase in the working population of nations. We have to consciously take efforts to move towards a sustainable future where technology meets the need to make use of resources, sustainably. Our project is a small attempt towards an affordable and efficient home automation system which specifically focuses on the switching on and off of electrical appliances like fans and lights of a house.

Home Automation with Chatbot Application and Voice Assistance - Our project intends to allow users to control electric home appliances, over internet using Internet of Things (IoT), thus increasing the efficiency and ease of use. We intend to make efficient use of Internet of Things (IoT) to provide a congruent zone for a two way conversation between the user and the system.

The proposed system will take input query from the user in the form of :

- Text (via the Chatbot Application)
- Voice (via Voice Assistant)

The input will be processed in the IoT component (Raspberry Pi) leading to actuation based on the decision formulated. The Proposed system will give outputs to the user after actuating as per the processed query, in the form of text message or voice reply. The user will be given the flexibility of using the Chatbot Application for controlling the appliances (fans and lights) remotely, and/or to use a voice command when in vicinity.

2 Literature Review

Home Automation systems have been implemented earlier using different technologies like GSM, Bluetooth and Internet. Having a higher rate of power consumption, Bluetooth based system requires each component to have a Bluetooth adapter for communication, but its limitation lies in the minimum range of 100 meters. GSM based system involves transducers to take inputs (mostly physical quantities) via sensors and convert them into understandable commands using microcontrollers. But DTMF processing, one of the communication method used in GSM based system is susceptible to fuzzing attacks. Using a Internet based system via a Web browser opens up the possibilities of numerous browser based security issues.[1]

A Chatbot is an artificial intelligence (AI) software that can simulate a conversation (or a chat) with a user in natural language through messaging applications, websites, mobile apps or through the telephone. Ideal chatbots are expected to understand context of a conversation, learn from the conversations and improve themselves over time. This can be achieved through various machine learning

*e-mail: bhavyakadali21@gmail.com
**e-mail: nehaprasad2912@gmail.com
***e-mail: pran12698@gmail.com
****e-mail: mmdeshpande@acpce.ac.in

and deep learning techniques. Chatbots provide a medium to remotely access the Automation system while giving the end user a visual interface to maintain ease of use. This technology is experiencing an exponential growth since it is also inclusive of multi-language support.[2]

Voice assistants react to voice commands and give the user relevant information about his/her inquiry. Voice assistants use natural language processing (NLP) to match user voice input to executable commands.Use of both, Chatbot Application and Voice Assistant reduces single input dependency to a considerable extent. The entire framework can be extended further, in future to reach out to the needs of the differently abled section of the society.[3]

Natural Language Processing is the processing of natural language in order to derive meaning from it. In the proposed system, some basic techniques of Natural Language Processing like tokenization, removal of stop-words and lemmatization are used.

3 Proposed system

3.1 Architecture

The following architecture diagram shows the integrated working of all the modules in the Home Automation System : Chatbot module, Voice assistant module, Speech Recognition which is inclusive in the former module, and the NLP module. The Chatbot module provides input in

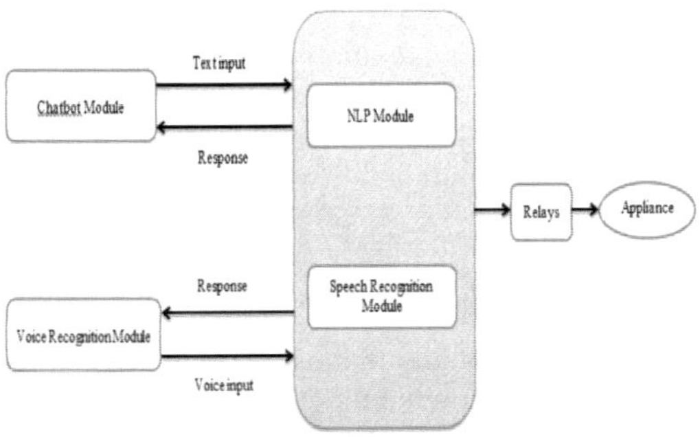

Figure 1: Architecture of the proposed system

textual format whereas the Voice Assistant module will provide the input as a voice command. These inputs will be sent to the Internet of Things (IoT) component, Raspberry Pi. The entire processing of the acquired input happens in this unit. The Raspberry Pi unit contains Natural Language Processing (NLP) unit. This unit is responsible for processing the textual input to find the intent. The speech input from the Voice Assistant module will undergo speech-to-text processing, hence providing a text input to the NLP module.

Inside the NLP module, the intent generated acts as the deciding factor for defining the actuations based on the rules and/or constraints defined.
The NLP module leads two processes simultaneously :

- Actuation based on evaluation of input.
- The output response generated for the user

The output signals regarding the actions that need to be performed on the electronic devices are sent to them through the relays.

3.2 Components

3.2.1 Hardware requirements

- Raspberry Pi 3B+
- Relays
- Microphone
- Speaker

3.2.2 Software requirements

- **Python NLTK library** : Natural Language Toolkit is a free and open source platform for building Python programs to work with human language data. It provides easy-to-use interfaces along with a suite of text processing libraries for classification, tokenization, stemming, tagging, parsing, and semantic reasoning and wrappers for industrial-strength NLP libraries.[2]
- **Python Pyaudio library** : PyAudio provides Python bindings for PortAudio, the cross-platform audio I/O library. PyAudio uses Python to play and record audio on a variety of platforms.
- **Python GPIO library** : Used to control General Purpose Input Output devices using Python.
- **Raspbian OS** : Raspbian is a free operating system based on Debian, optimised for the Raspberry Pi hardware.
- **Telegram Bot API** : The Bot API is an HTTP-based interface created for developers to build bots for Telegram.[3]

3.3 Implementation

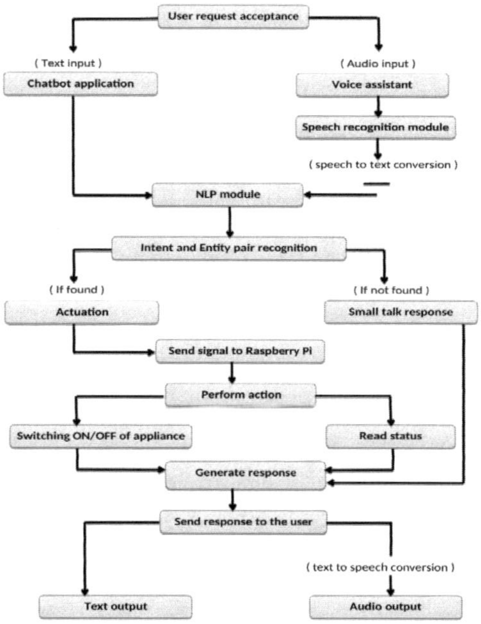

Figure 2: Flow Chart of the system

Step1 : Setup and Installation of Raspberry Pi. This is followed by installing some necessary tools and libraries : Telepot required to build application for Telegram Bot API for to and fro of messages. NLTK (Natural Language Tool Kit) is a suite of libraries required for natural language processing. The working of Voice Assistant makes use of Speech Recognition, pyttsx/gTTS. Some of the machine learning techniques used require the installation of Scikit Learn.

- Telepot
- Speech Recognition
- NLTK
- scikit-learn
- pyttsx/gTTs

Step 2 : Implementation of a chatbot using Telegram server to control the home appliances via GUI(custom keyboard) and/or sending a sentential input.

Step 3 : Implementation of a voice recognition module to accept voice input via microphone. Convert this speech input to textual format via Speech recognition module which will undergo NLP processing to find intent. Output generated as a response to the input query will be converted from text to speech using pyttsx/gTTs.

Step 4 : Input from the user undergoes NLP processing as shown in figure 3 .

Step 5 : Establishing connections between Raspberry Pi and home appliances.

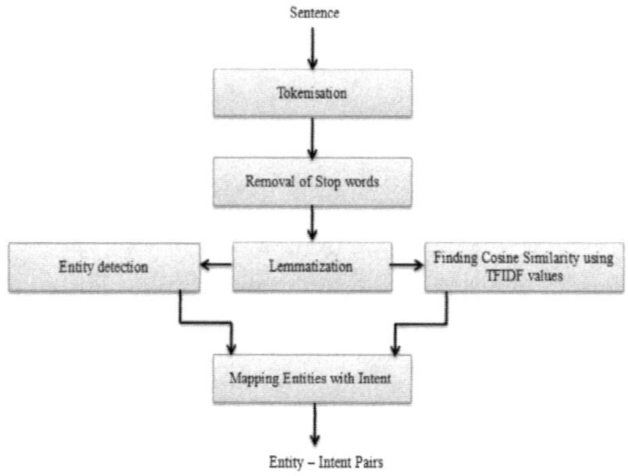

Figure 3: Block diagram of NLP Module

4 Result and Analysis

The testing and result analysis includes the following Three interfaces :

- Chatbot Interface
- Terminal Interface (for Voice Assistant)
- Working Model Interface

The system is currently customized for three rooms : Living Room, Kitchen, Bedroom.

Each of the aforementioned rooms have four appliances each, namely : Fan, LED, Bulb, TubeLight.
As far as the model is concerned, it uses LEDs to represent all the appliances hence, providing the visuals for Switching On and Off actions.

The following images show the Switching On of LED in Bedroom using Chatbot.
The initial state of all appliances is considered to be Switched Off.

Figure 4.1: Chatbot interface

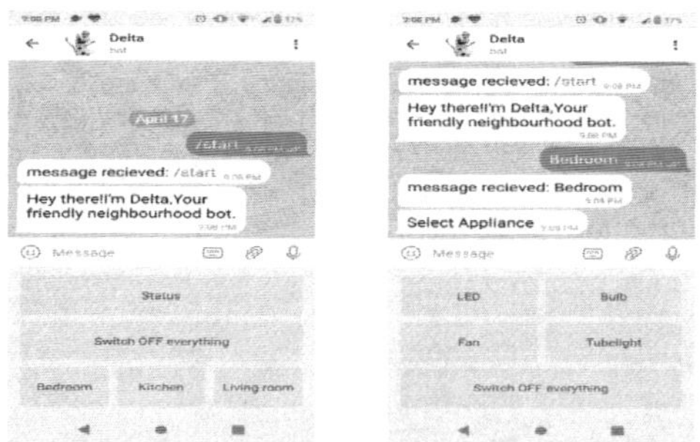

(a) Custom keyboard interface (b) Room selected: Bedroom

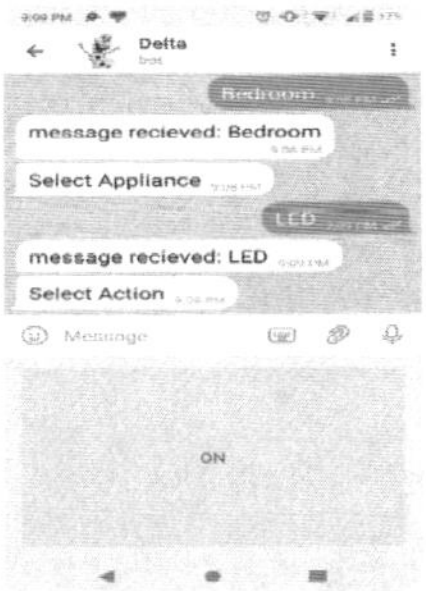

(c) Appliance selected: LED

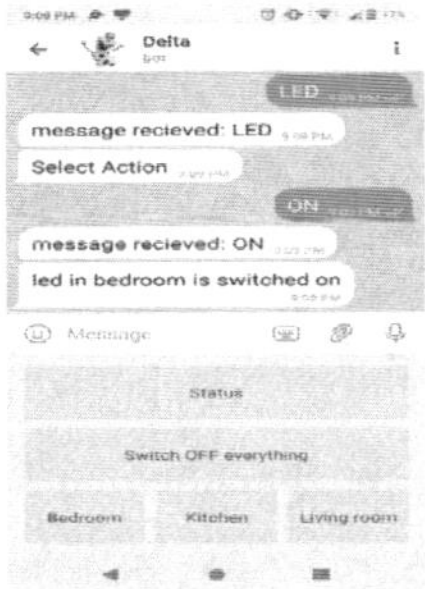

(d) Action selected: ON

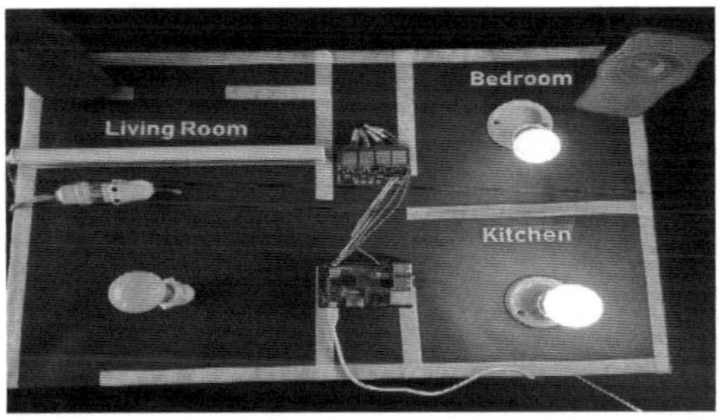

Figure 5.2: Bulb in Kitchen is turned ON and LED in bedroom is turned ON

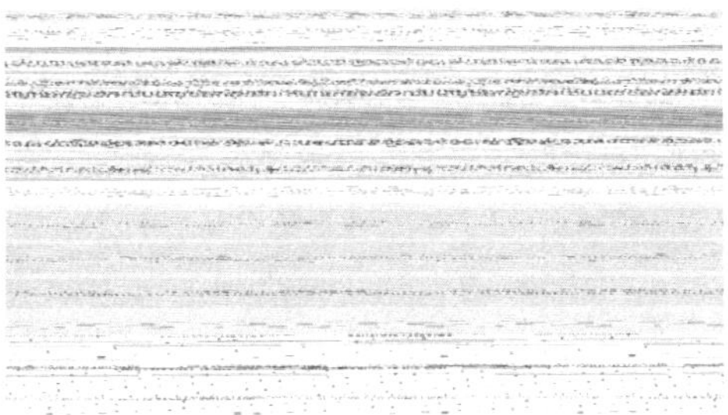

Figure 4.2: LED in bedroom is switched ON

The functionality for Switching OFF of all the Appliances at once, using a custom keyboard button :

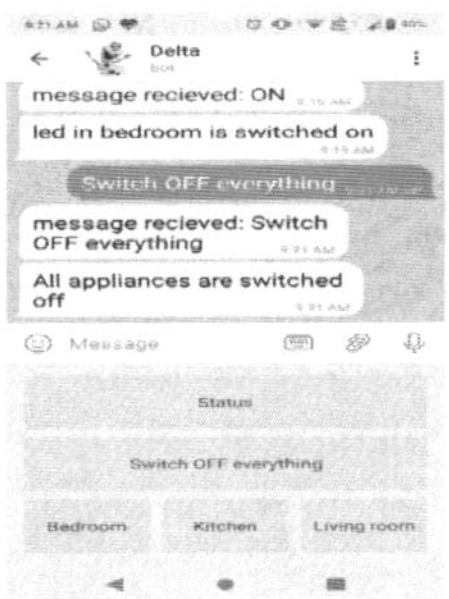

Figure 6.1: Sentential input to switch OFF everything

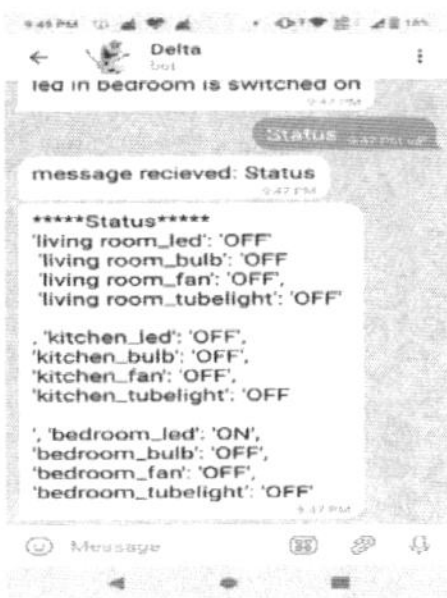

Figure 4.3: Status changed is reflected

Figure 6.2: All Appliances turned OFF

The following images show the Switching On of Bulb in Kitchen by providing input in Sentential form.

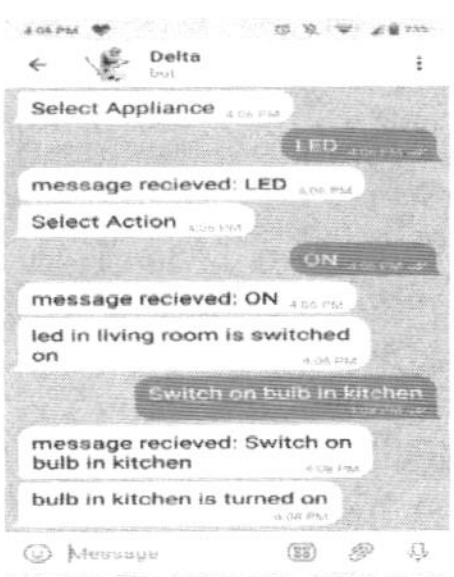

Figure 5.1: Sentential input to turn ON the Kitchen bulb

Figure 6.3: Status changed is reflected

https://doi.org/10.1051/itmconf/20203201002

Interaction Via Voice Assistant :

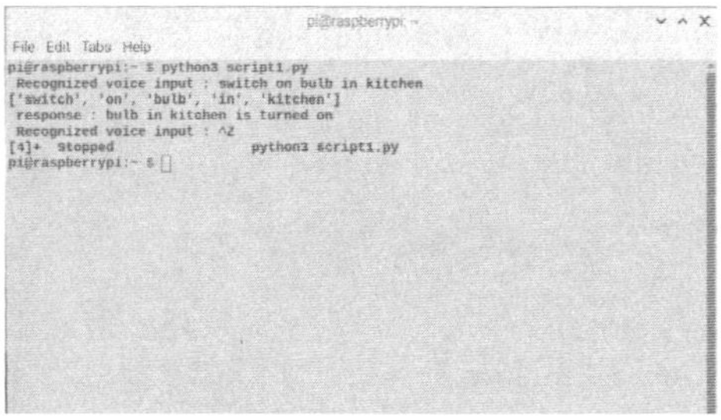

Figure 7.1: Terminal interface when command for Switching ON the Kitchen bulb is given via voice

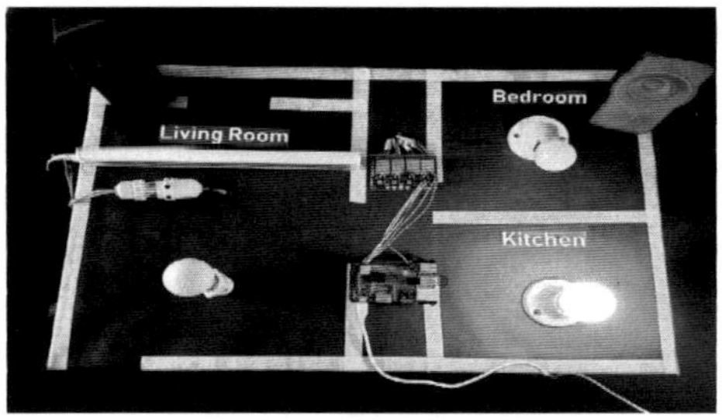

Figure 7.2: Kitchen bulb turned ON

Small talk response in the Chatbot :

Figure 8: Responses when the user intends to have a small talk with the bot

5 Conclusion and Future Work

This project is a small attempt at delivering an efficient but affordable Home Automation System with a flexibility to acquire input through two means alternatively, text and speech. This will contribute in removing the dependency on either forms of input i.e speech and text.

The system can be further made inclusive of extensions such as attaching of email services as an alternate form of message delivery, in situations of utmost importance. The number of devices that can be connected to the system can be expanded to a larger range. The proposed system is based on the inputs in English language, which could further be expanded to accommodate several other regional languages as well.

This would also prove to be a small step in consideration of ease in access of modern technology for the differently abled section of the society as well.

References

[1] Ronik Dhakar. *"Comparison of Various Technologies for Home Automation System"*. International Journal of Research and Scientific Innovation (IJRSI),2017.

[2] AM Rahman , Abdullah Al Mamun , Alma Islam *"Programming challenges of Chatbot: Current and Future Prospective"*. 2017 IEEE Region 10 Humanitarian Technology Conference (R10-HTC)21 - 23 Dec 2017, Dhaka, Bangladesh.

[3] Polyakov E.V., Mazhanov M.S., Rolich A.Y., Voskov L.S., Kachalova M.V., Polyakov S.V. *Investigation and Development of the Intelligent Voice Assistant for the Internet of Things Using Machine Learning* 2018 Moscow Workshop on Electronic and Networking Technologies (MWENT)

[4] https://www.nltk.org/index.html

[5] https://core.telegram.org/bots/ap

Demand side management based charging strategy for fleet of plug-in hybrid electric vehicles

Sachpreet Kaur[1,*], *Ravtej Singh* Sandhu[2], *Tarlochan* Kaur[1], and *Rintu* Khanna[1]

[1]Punjab Engineering College, Electrical Department, Chandigarh, India
[2]Symbiosis Institute of Business Management, Pune, India

Abstract. In coming years, the widespread use of Plug-in Hybrid Electric Vehicles (PHEVs) will impose a significant burden on the existing electric grid. The situation may worsen due to uncontrolled charging strategies adopted for PHEVs. On the other hand, these PHEVs, if charged through proper control mechanisms may reduce additional dynamic load demands. Also, if utilized properly, they may provide significant support to electric grid from time to time. The entire process of regulating the power exchanged with PHEVs w.r.t the existing grid conditions is well known as Demand Side Management (DSM). To indulge PHEVs in DSM, an accurate estimate of characteristics of PHEVs, both on-road and off-road, is necessary. Thus, this study aims to mathematically model the behaviour of four imperative parameters of PHEVs. These are dynamic travel behaviour, battery state-of-charge (SOC) requirements, the energy demands of PHEVs and, total power exchanged by PHEVs with the electric grid. In addition to this, a smart charging strategy is proposed and tested to verify the ability of PHEVs for participating in DSM for peak load management. The impacts of uncontrolled charging and smart charging of PHEVs on grid power demands are also discussed.

1 Introduction

The random charging of Plug-in Hybrid Electric Vehicles (PHEVs) may impose severe load demands on distribution networks, thus causing various harmful effects. The major effects include transformer overloading, frequency deviations, and voltage fluctuations [1]. On the other hand, charging PHEVs through smart control techniques allows them to exploit their potential to provide grid ancillary services. Also, the controlled charging reduces the burden on the electric grid significantly. The process of regulating load demands on the distribution side is known as Demand-Side Management (DSM) [2]. DSM techniques inhibit different behaviors during contingency and non-contingency events. The main motive for DSM is to utilize existing grid infrastructure efficiently for handling increased electricity load demand, without the need to install additional generation units. So far, the techniques suggested for DSM majorly aim at proposing incentive-based actions to control electricity usage effectively. Some widely adopted economic incentives include real-time pricing, peak time rebate, and critical peak pricing [3].

The increasing penetration of PHEVs in electric grids day by day, demands a particular interest in integrating DSM techniques with charging infrastructures. A statistical analysis conducted in [4] revealed that the probability of PHEVs staying at home is 0.5 and for staying at home during mid-day is 0.9. Thus, there is significant scope for participating PHEVs in DSM. The usage of a PHEV for DSM is highly dependent upon its user's convenience and travel schedule. In addition, to indulge PHEVs in DSM, proper control strategies incorporated with correct information regarding PHEV's travel behavior, battery rating, energy demand, and initial state-of-charge are required [4]. Moreover, since the management of a fleet of PHEVs is a highly complex process, an accurate estimate of the availability of PHEVs off-road for charging is required at all instants of time. Previously, some studies have been conducted to estimate the effect of PHEVs on the existing electric grid [5]. The authors in [5] observed that wide-scale adoption of EVs will have a significant impact on power generation capacities and residential distribution systems. The study conducted in [6], revealed the harmonic distortion effects of PHEV charging loads on the distribution system. Authors in [7], discussed in detail the technical specifications involved for the adoption of PHEVs. In recent years, the literature is witnessing a continuous drift towards the decentralized approach for PHEV charging. In this approach, PHEVs owners have complete involvement in charging decisions [8]. The authors in [9] coordinated the aggregate of PHEVs for participation in frequency regulation. They investigated the role of PHEVs in fulfilling grid power requirements using a suitable Fuzzy Logic Controller (FLC). The authors in [10] proposed an adaptive controller for managing power requirements of PHEVs for load management in microgrids. However, the authors lack in discussing the role of incentives in smart charging. Several price-based charging frameworks have been proposed in the literature for volunteer participation of PHEV users in DSM [11]. In comparison to existing flat-rate pricing incentive, the real-time pricing incentives has been

* Corresponding author: sachpreetkaur.phdele16@pec.edu.in

considered as the finest cost-effective alternative for both PHEV users and utility. It prevents overcharging of PHEVs during peak hours [12]. Another useful work reported in [13] discussed the optimized charging of PHEVs, in order to reduce their usage cost. In [14], the authors proposed an energy cost-sharing model based on game theory to encourage PHEV owners to participate in coordinated charging and discharging.

Summarizing the above, it has been observed that the major portion of literature focuses on the study of harmful effects of integrating PHEVs with existing electric grids. Some researchers emphasized the need for DSM using PHEVs. However, in order to achieve optimal scheduling of PHEVs and to effectively indulge them in DSM, the government organizations and utilities must be able to forecast total charging load demands of PHEVs, at all instants of time. Also, since the adoption of PHEVs on a wide scale is a futuristic approach, accurate modelling of PHEV load demand is desired. Keeping in concern the above, this study aims to model mathematically the four imperative parameters of PHEVs. These include the travel behaviour of PHEVs, energy demands of PHEVs, State-of-Charge (SOC), and total power exchanged between the PHEV and electric grid. Initially, statistical tools have been designed to predict the load demands of PHEVs during different times of the day. Thereafter, a smart charging strategy has been proposed and tested to analyse the ability of PHEVs to participate in DSM. The remainder of the paper is organized in the following manner. Section 2 discusses the mathematical modelling of load demand of PHEVs, Section 3 explains two different charging scenarios of PHEVs, Section 4 compiles the results along with the discussions and Section 5 considers the conclusions observed during analysis.

2 Mathematical Modelling of Load Demand of PHEVs

The adoption of PHEVs as dynamic storage buffers in balancing load demands and power generation is gaining attention worldwide. In recent years, Nickel Metal Hydride (NiMH), lead-acid and lithium-ion have been the most widely used batteries in PHEVs. This is due to various reasons including their performance characteristics and economic profits [15]. In this study, PHEVs equipped with lithium-ion batteries are considered for analysis purposes.

In order to determine load demands by PHEVs, statistical behaviour and analysis is essential. Since the behaviour of PHEVs on-road and off-road is highly dynamic in nature, the present study assumes the plug-in time of a PHEV to be a random variable, with Probability Density Function (pdf), *f(t)*. The two important parameters: the initial SOC of battery (SOC_i) and the electricity tariff structure highly influence the randomness of plug-in time of PHEVs. Since the SOC_i of a PHEV's battery is dependent upon the travel behaviour of PHEV's users and the total distance they travel in a day, the present study also assumes the SOC_i to be a random variable varying between the range 0-100% [16]. As a result, in order to analyse SOC_i, the correct estimate of distance travelled by PHEV is required. Based on the information available in [17], a pdf of daily distance travelled in a day is obtained. As seen in the curve shown in Figure 1, it is observed that the distribution pattern is of 'lognormal type', where the probability of occurrence of negative distance is zero, and that of positive distance extends till infinity. Eq. (1) computes the pdf for the travel behaviour of PHEV w.r.t the distance travelled.

$$p(d; \mu, \sigma) = \frac{1}{d\sqrt{2\pi\sigma^2}} e^{\frac{-(\ln d-\mu)^2}{2\sigma^2}}, d > 0 \qquad (1)$$

In Eq. (1) 'd' represent the distance travelled by PHEV, μ is the mean, and σ is the standard deviation. Based on data extracted from [17], the mean and standard deviation of distance travelled are 17.89 miles and 9.86 miles respectively.

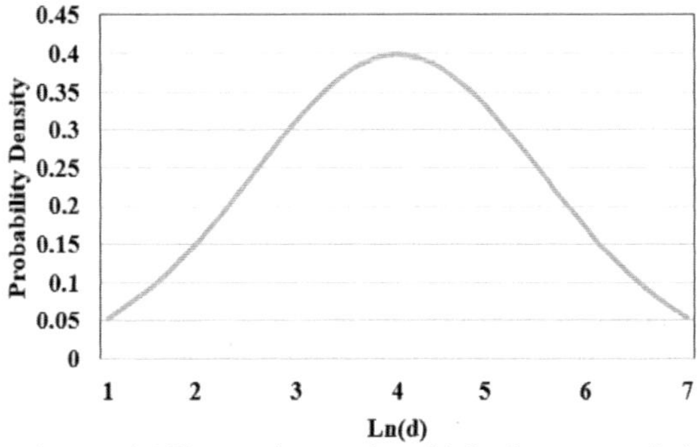

Fig.1. Probability Density Function of daily distance travelled by PHEV users

Given the statistical analysis of distance travelled 'd', the SOC_i of PHEV can be estimated using Eq. (2) as [16],

$$SOC_i = \left(1 - \frac{\alpha d}{d_m}\right) \times 100\% \qquad (2)$$

In the above-mentioned equation, 'd_m' represents the maximum range of EV and 'α' is the number of days the EV has travelled since the last plug-in (here α is assumed as 1). The pdf curve of SOC_i depicted in Figure 2 is expressed in Eq. (3) and is formulated using Eqs. (1) and (2) as,

$$s(SOC; \mu, \sigma) = \frac{1}{\frac{d_m}{\alpha}(1 - SOC)\sqrt{2\pi\sigma^2}} \times e - \frac{\left[ln(1-SOC)-\left(\mu - ln\left(\frac{d_m}{\alpha}\right)\right)\right]^2}{2\sigma^2}, 0 < SOC < 1 \qquad (3)$$

Depending upon 'SOC_i', the energy and power demands of a PHEV can be computed using Eq. (4) and Eq. (5) respectively.

$$E_i = (1 - SOC_i)E_r \qquad (4)$$

$$\int_{tp_{in}}^{tp_{out}} P_i(t)dt = (1 - SOC_i)E_r \qquad (5)$$

In the above-mentioned equations, 'tp_{in}' and 'tp_{out}' represent PHEV's plug-in and plug-out times respectively. E_i represents the energy requirements of PHEV and $'P_i(t)'$ represents the power demanded by PHEV.

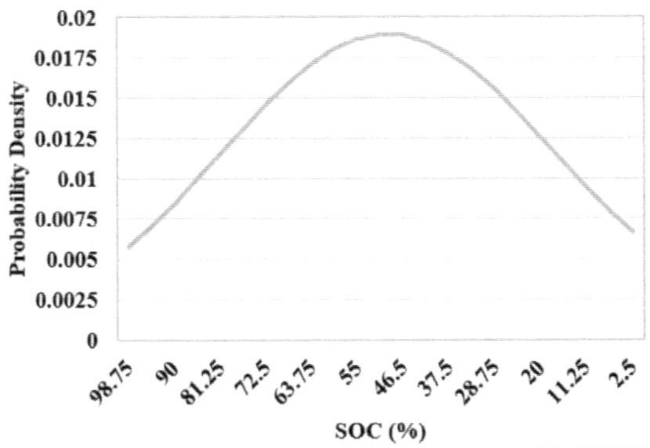

Fig.2. Probability Density Function of SOC of plugged-in PHEV

The power demand of a PHEV varies throughout the charging process according to its battery characteristics as observed in [18]. Also, the power demand occurs independently and varies irrespective of SOC_i. To conduct numerical calculations, the total power demanded by PHEV battery has been divided into $(tp_{out} - tp_{in})/2$ intervals where $(tp_{out} - tp_{in})$ represents the time required for the entire charging process. The power level P_c is then expressed as Eq. (6),

$$P_c = \frac{P((c-1)\Delta t)+P(c\Delta t)}{2} \qquad (6)$$

Where, Δt is the length of each interval (*here* Δt=0.5 and $tp_{out} - tp_{in} = 5$). The probability of PHEV charging load, operating at power P_c at time t is represented as $\emptyset(P_c, t)$. The total charging load at any load for a single PHEV is obtained using Eq. (7),

$$\mu(P) = \sum_{c=1}^{(tp_{out}-tp_{in})/2} P_c \emptyset(P_c, t) \qquad (7)$$

For multiple batteries, the overall charging demand in a system is computed as the summation of power levels of $'n'$ number of PHEVs and is expressed as Eq. (8),

$$P_n = \sum_{i=1}^{n} \sum_{c=1}^{(tp_{out}-tp_{in})/2} P_c \emptyset(P_c, t) \qquad (8)$$

3 Charging scenarios for PHEVs

In this study, two different charging scenarios i.e. Uncontrolled charging and Controlled charging are proposed. During uncontrolled charging, the PHEVs randomly plug-in to charge according to their convenience. In Controlled charging, every PHEV charges through a proper control mechanism, thus participating in DSM. To implement the two control scenarios, three tariff structures are considered. These are flat-rate tariff, time-of-use tariff, and real-time tariff. In a flat-rate tariff-based approach, energy cost/kWh remains constant throughout the day. In the time of use based approach, off-peak times, and peak times have different energy cost/kWh. Real-time tariff considers an adaptive approach that constantly monitors the tariff structure in a day depending upon the contingency and non-contingency events. Figure 3. depicts the normalized electricity tariff structure [12].

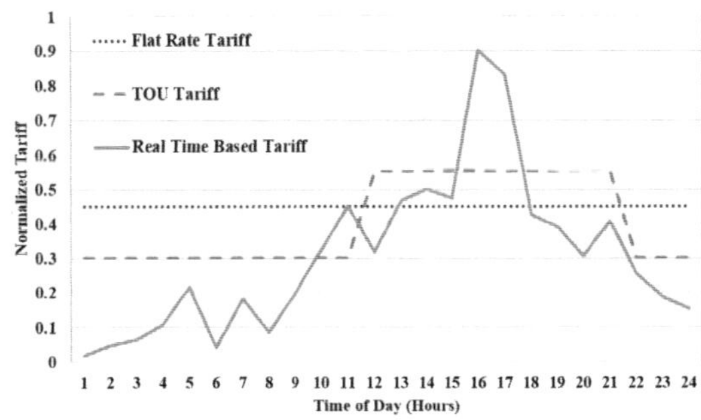

Fig.3. Electricity Tariff Structure

3.1. Uncontrolled Charging

In this scenario, a flat-rate tariff-based charging strategy is adopted i.e. government authorities do not provide any incentives to PHEV users for charging. This simply means that the PHEV users start charging anytime according to their convenience and requirement. To analyze the worst-case scenario, it is assumed that all PHEV's begin to charge simultaneously at 17:00. As a result, a uniform probability density function *pdf* $f_1(t)$ of PHEV charging start time is adopted, as described in Eq. (9),

$$f_1(x) = \begin{cases} 1.00, & t = 17 \\ 0, & t = some\ other\ time \end{cases}, (1 \leq t \leq 24) \qquad (9)$$

The total amount of load imposed by PHEVs at time *'t'* can be computed using the above equation by incorporating an appropriate battery profile and $s(SOC; \mu, \sigma)$.

3.2. Controlled Charging

In this scenario, time-of-use based or real-time tariff based PHEV charging strategy is adopted, to determine the most economic time for plugging-in PHEVs for charging. For this purpose, two main parameters i.e. real-time traffic data and real-time tariff data are required. Figure 4 shows the distribution of PHEV's initial charging time obtained by plotting the reciprocal of the product of two above mentioned parameters. It is observed that the resultant distribution of plug-in time is nearly bell-shaped with the mean around (24:00). Thus, a Gaussian distribution function has been employed to compute *'pdf'* of battery plug-in time as expressed in Eq. (10),

$$f(d; \mu, \sigma) = \frac{1}{\sqrt{2\pi\sigma^2}} e^{\frac{-(x-\mu)^2}{2\sigma^2}} \qquad (10)$$

The main focus of DSM based smart charging of PHEVs is to determine optimal charging schedules, to minimize overall economic costs required to satisfy PHEV's owners. Also, it requires effective management of available energy resources with additional monetary benefits provided to

PHEV users. The mathematical modelling of PHEV smart charging is represented in Eq. (11),

$$min \sum_{k=1}^{n} C_k(t)\, P_k(t) \quad (11)$$

Where the number of PHEVs vary from k=1...n, $C_k(t)$ is the real-time cost function and $P_k(t)$ is the PHEV load at a particular instant of time. The cost function $C_k(t)$ at any time t is expressed in Eq. (12).

$$C_k(t) = C_{grid}(t) + C_{battd}(t) \quad (12)$$

In the above-mentioned equations, $C_{grid}(t)$ refers to the grid operating cost and $C_{battd}(t)$ refers to the battery degradation cost. While allowing PHEVs for smart charging, certain uncertainties need to be considered. The charging pattern should strictly observe PHEV battery rating, charger specifications, bus voltage, and power flow constraints.

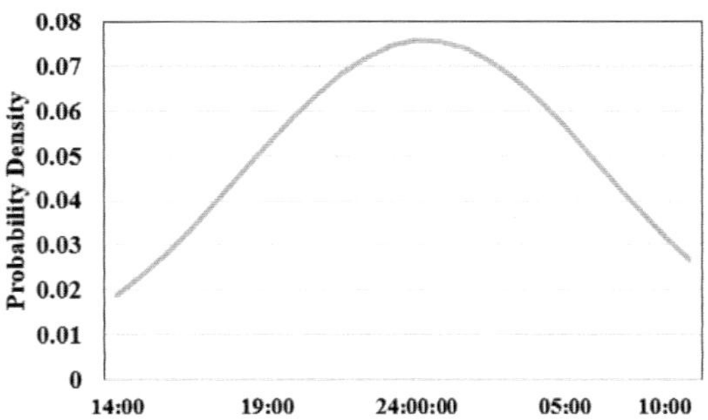

Fig.4. Gaussian Distribution of initial plug-in time of PHEVs

4 Results and Discussion

In this study, a small-scale solar-powered microgrid has been studied to determine the impact of PHEV's charging load on the system. The proposed microgrid consists of a photovoltaic power plant, diesel generation unit, and PHEV charging infrastructure The microgrid is supposed to feed residential sector load demands. The load demand data for the residential sector has been obtained from [19] and is plotted in Figure 5. It is observed from the obtained curve, that the load demand reaches it's peak in between t=17:00-19:00 h. The load curve observes off-peak behavior at t=5:00 h. The smart scheduled charging mechanism strictly monitors the peak load and off-peak load contingency events, to regulate and schedule PHEV charging. The minimization of objective function expressed in Eq. (11), acts as the base for the scheduling process during controlled charging. The PHEV charging infrastructure can integrate a total of 200 PHEVs simultaneously. However, in this study three different penetration levels of PHEVs are considered : 0% i.e. no PHEV present, 25% equivalent to 50 EVs and 50% equivalent to 100 EVs. In order to analyze load demands, charging characteristics of a 16.5 kWh lithium-ion battery has been considered [16].

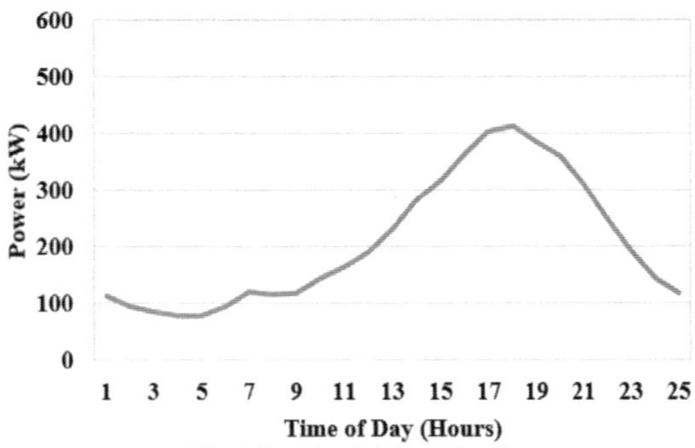

Fig.5. Residential Load Profile

The SOC_i and d charactersitics for 12.5% penetration of PHEVs have been shown in Figure 6. It is clearly observed that more the distance travelled, lesser is the SOC availability in PHEVs for grid support.

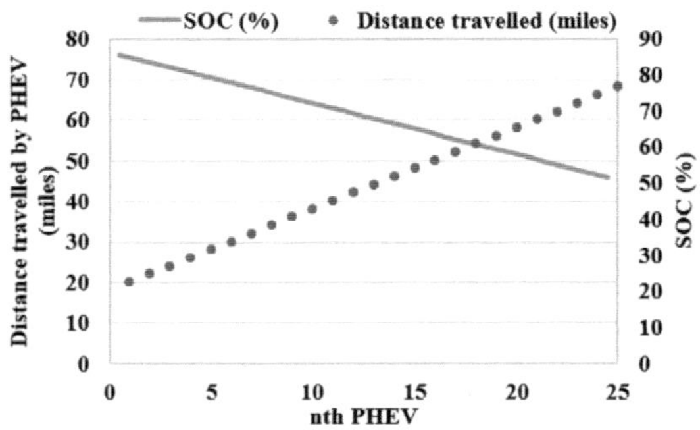

Fig.6. Relationship between SOC_i and d characteristics of $PHEV_i$

The load modelling of PHEV is done in two different scenarios: Scenario 1-Uncontrolled charging and Scenario 2-Controlled charging. Figure 7 and Figure 8 depict the load behavior of PHEV in Scenario 1 and Scenario 2 respectively. As observed in Figure 7, during uncontrolled charging, a significant additional peak load originates due to the PHEV charging load at 17:00. The impact analysis of PHEV on peak load is done for different penetration levels of vehicles. The maximum peak originates for 50% penetration of PHEV. It is clearly observed that even a portion of PHEVs i.e. 25% penetration in the electric grid, causes a significant impact on load patterns. The peak may further deteriorate with increase in number of PHEVs. The imbalance originated in load-generation may cause various effects in the grid including voltage fluctuations and frequency deviations.

On the other hand, the results obtained after applying DSM based smart charging are depicted in Figure 8. In this scenario, the PHEV power load during different instants of time is based on the optimization of objective function proposed in Eq. (11). The results obtained indicate that the PHEV charging does not generates high peak loads as seen in Scenario 1. Figure 8 reveals the results obtained during the smart charging of PHEVs. The obtained curves show the efficiency of the proposed smart strategy in coordinating EV charging. It is observed that rather than showing a single peak rise in load demand, the load demand in Scenario 2 is distributed due to PHEV scheduled charging.

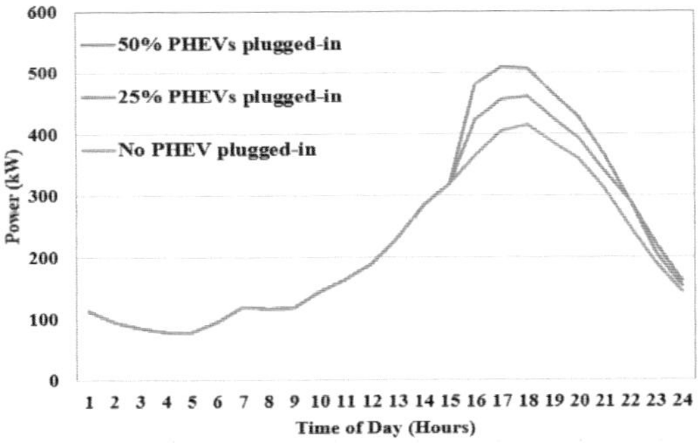

Fig.7. Uncontrolled PHEV charging

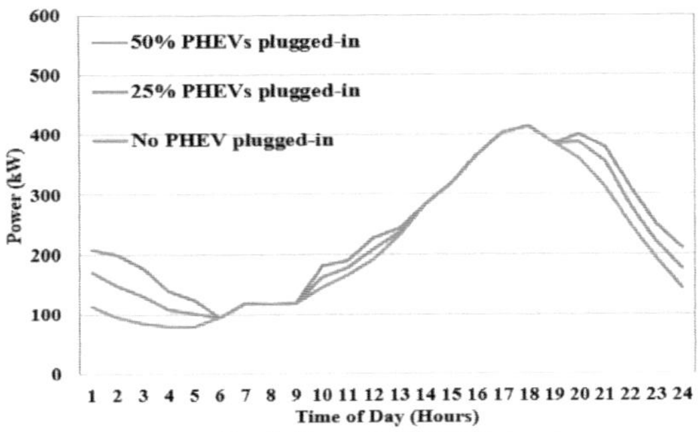

Fig. 8. Controlled PHEV charging

5 Conclusions and Future Scope

The present paper employs mathematical modelling to analyze the ability of PHEVs to participate in demand-side management. Statistical survey of behaviour of PHEVs for providing grid regulation is obtained. Further, two different charging strategies, uncontrolled charging and controlled charging, are proposed and discussed. It is observed that during uncontrolled charging, a significant peak load is observed in the distribution system. On the other hand, the proposed coordinated PHEV charging strategy helps to reduce the PHEV load burden on electric grids.

As an extension to this analysis, the influence of PHEVs on important parameters of grid like voltage and frequency could be analyzed. The obtained characteristics will be helpful to develop a suitable control algorithm for PHEVs to provide grid support.

References

[1] S. Soheil, S. Filizadeh, and E. Bibeau, "Profile of charging load on the grid due to plug-in vehicles," IEEE Trans. Smart Grid, **3**, 135–141 (2012)

[2] J. Zazo, S. Zazo, and S. V. Macua, "Robust worst case analysis of demand-side management in smart grids," IEEE Trans. Smart Grid, **8**, 662–673 (2017)

[3] Mou, Yuting, Hao Xing, Zhiyun Lin, and Minyue Fu. "Decentralized optimal demand-side management for PHEV charging in a smart grid." IEEE Transactions on Smart Grid, **6**, 726-736 (2014)

[4] Quirós-Tortós, Jairo, Luis F. Ochoa, and Becky Lees. "A statistical analysis of EV charging behavior in the UK." In *2015 IEEE PES Innovative Smart Grid Technologies Latin America (ISGT LATAM)*, 445-449 (2015)

[5] J. T. Salihi, "Energy requirements for electric cars and their impact on electric generation and distribution systems," IEEE Trans. Ind. Appl.**5**, 516–531 (1973)

[6] J. C. Gomez and M. M. Morcos, "Impact of EV battery chargers on the power quality of distribution systems," IEEE Trans. Power Del.,**18**, 975–981, (2003)

[7] Kaur, Sachpreet, Tarlochan Kaur, Rintu Khanna, and Parampal Singh. "A state of the art of DC microgrids for electric vehicle charging." *In 2017 4th International Conference on Signal Processing, Computing and Control (ISPCC)*, 381-386 (2017).

[8] M. C. Falvo, G. Graditi, and P. Siano, "Electric vehicles integration in demand response programs," in *Proc. Int. Symp. Power Electron. Elect. Drives Autom. Motion*, 548–553 (2014)

[9] Falahati, Saber, Seyed Abbas Taher, and Mohammad Shahidehpour. "Grid frequency control with electric vehicles by using of an optimized fuzzy controller." Applied energy, **178,** 918-928 (2016).

[10] Kaur, Sachpreet, Tarlochan Kaur, and Rintu Khanna. "ANFIS Based Frequency Control in an Autonomous Microgrid Integrated with PV and Battery Storage." In *2019 9th International Conference on Power and Energy Systems (ICPES)*, 1-4 (2019)

[11] Schuller, Alexander. "Charging coordination paradigms of electric vehicles." In Plug in Electric Vehicles in Smart Grids, Springer, Singapore,1-21 (2015).

[12] L. Jia and L. Tong, "Dynamic pricing and distributed energy management for demand response," IEEE Trans. Smart Grid, **7**, 1128–1136 (2016).

[13] S. Sarabi and L. Kefsi, "Electric vehicle charging strategy based on a dynamic programming algorithm," in *Proc. Int. Conf. Intell. Energy Power Syst. (IEPS)*, 1–5 (2014)

[14] Hutson, Chris, Ganesh Kumar Venayagamoorthy, and Keith A. Corzine. "Intelligent scheduling of hybrid and electric vehicle storage capacity in a parking lot for profit maximization in grid power transactions." *In 2008 IEEE Energy 2030 Conference*, 1-8 (2008)

[15] D. Linden and T. B. Reddy, *Handbook of Batteries*, 3rd ed. New York, McGraw-Hill, (2001)

[16] Qian, Kejun, Chengke Zhou, Malcolm Allan, and Yue Yuan. "Modeling of load demand due to EV battery charging in distribution systems." IEEE transactions on power systems **26**, 802-810 (2010)

[17] López, Karol Lina, Christian Gagné, and Marc-André Gardner. "Demand-side management using deep learning for smart charging of electric vehicles." IEEE Transactions on Smart Grid **10**, 2683-2691 (2018)

[18] Madrid, Christopher, Juan Argueta, and Jordan Smith. "Performance characterization—1999 Nissan Altra-EV with lithium-ion battery." Southern California EDISON (1999).

[19] System Advisory Model (SAM) [On-line] Website: https://sam.nrel.gov/ (2018)

Super-twisting Control of Magnetic Levitation System

Rupak Rokade,* and *Deepti* Khimani,**

[1]Department of Instrumentation Engineering, V.E.S.Institute of Technology, Mumbai, India.

Abstract. This article presents the implementation results of second order sliding mode control (SOSM) for magnetic levitation system. In practical systems, especially when the actuators are electro-mechanical, the conventional (first order) sliding mode control can not be used effectively as it exhibits chattering, which is highly undesirable. Therefore, for such systems, sliding mode control of higher order can be a suitable choice as the reduce the chattering significantly. In this article the super-twisting control, which isa second order sliding mode control, is designed and implemented for the experimental setup of Maglev system, Model 730 developed by ECP systems.

1 Introduction

Reduction of the friction between moving surfaces is quite important aspect in electro-mechanical designs. Magnetic levitation principle provides an option of the non-contacting motion of moving objects, which substantially reduces the resistance to the motion. This increases the overall efficiency of the system.

Many industrial applications have been found in literature to have used a magnetic levitation successfully such as high-speed train suspension [1], magnetic bearings [2], launch assistance in space missions [3], superconductor rotor suspension of gyroscopes [4] and wind turbines [5, 6].

The control objective in such systems is to design the controller that maintains levitation of an object at a desired height. In past three decades various methods for the design of control for magentic levitation (maglev) systems have been reported in literature, for example, linear and nonlinear controller designs in [7, 8] via feedback linearization [9].

As the model uncertainties or the external disturbances may cause the system to underperform, it is desirable to design the robust controller that guarantees the desired performance in presence of disturbance. Numerous methods of robust controller design for Maglev system can be found in literature. For example, adaptive robust control design against parametric uncertainties [10], robust controller based on Lyapunov's direct method [3] or two DOF controller for magnetic levitation using quantitative feedback technique [11]. A sliding mode control (SMC) is one of popular robust control design methods for simplicity in control structure and insensitivity to a matched disturbances See [12, 13]. Numerous articles on SMC design for Maglev system are found in literature. An experimental comparison of SMC and classical control has been found in [14] and that of sliding mode disturbance compensation and H−∞ in [15]. In [16], SMC has been employed to provide high performance over a wide bandwidth in tracking of piezoelectric driven devices. Recently, experimental results on sliding mode control of maglev system has been discussed in [17]. The conventional (first order) sliding mode control exhibits chattering phenomenon due to it's discontinuous nature, which often is not suitable for practical applications. For a magnetic levitation system, SMC based on input-dependent surface to reduce the chattering has been discussed with simulation results in [18]. In [19], SMC has been designed with effective switching gain that is a function of distance between trajectory and the sliding surface. Super-twisting control (STC) is well known second order SMC, which reduces the chattering effect significantly [20–23]. This paper discusses the design and implementation of the STC on experimental setup Maglev Model 730 laboratory setup from educational control products [24]. The experimental results are compared with simulation results and are found satisfactory.

2 System Description

An experimental setup ECP Model 730 Maglev system [24] consists of two electromagnetic actuator coils, one mounted at the bottom that produces repulsive magnetic force to levitate the magnet and other actuator coil is mounted at the top, which produces the attractive magnetic force to that can be used to levitate the magnet. Each coil can be energized separately to levitate one or two magnets along a glass rod. Therefore, this system can either be configured as single-input single-output (SISO) or multi-input multi-output (MIMO) or multi-input single-output (SIMO) system. Fig.1 shows the representative diagram of experimental setup.

In this paper, we consider maglev system in SISO configuration and using lower coil to produces appropriate repulsive magnetic force that levitate the magnet at desired

*e-mail: rupak.rokade@ves.ac.in
**e-mail: deepti.khimani@ves.ac.in

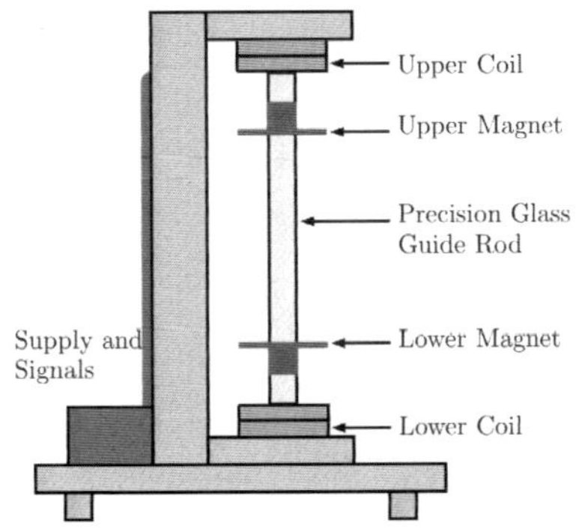

Figure 1. Maglev system, ECP-Model 730 representative diagram.

position while the upper coil is left unenergized. Fig.2 shows the free body diagram of ECP Model 730 Maglev system. The dynamical equation for the motion of the magnet with displacement $x(t)$ is given by,

$$m\ddot{x}(t) + c\dot{x}(t) = F_u(t) - mg \tag{1}$$

Where, m is mass of magnet, c is coefficient of viscous friction offered by glass rod during motion and $F_u(t)$ is repulsive force produced by the lower actuator (coil), which is nonlinear with respect to current i through the coil and it is given by,

$$F_u(t) = \frac{i(t)}{a(b + x(t))^N} \tag{2}$$

Where N, a and b are constants which can be determined via numerical approximation from the characteristics. Therefore, from (1) and (2), we get

$$m\ddot{x}(t) + c\dot{x}(t) = \frac{i(t)}{a(b + x(t))^N} - mg \tag{3}$$

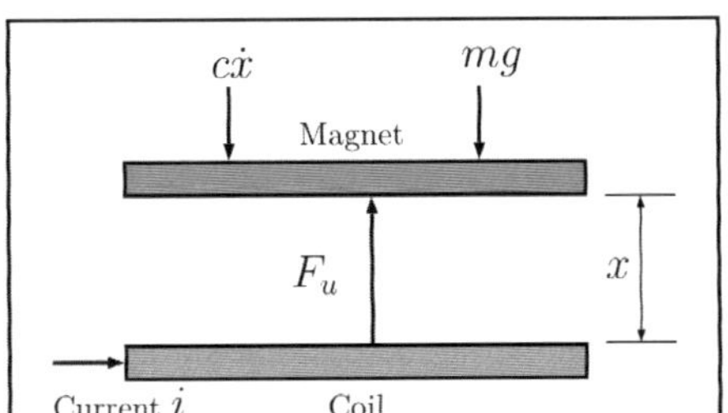

Figure 2. Free body diagram of ECP-Model 730 (SISO).

Define the state variables, $z_1 := x$, $z_2 := \dot{x}$ and control effort $u := i$. So the system (3) can be represented in state variable form as,

$$\dot{z}_1(t) = f_1(t) = z_2(t) \tag{4}$$

$$\dot{z}_2(t) = f_2(t) = -\frac{c}{m} z_2(t) + \frac{u(t)}{ma(b + z_1(t))^N} - g \tag{5}$$

$$y(t) = z_1(t) \tag{6}$$

2.1 Linearization at operating point

Let $u_0 = i_0$ be the current passes through coil that levitate the magnet at desired height x_0. Therefore, at the operating point $(z_1, z_2, u) = (x_0, \dot{x}_0, u_0) =: O$. To linearize the system we perform Jacobian linearization at operating point. Follow from (4)-(5),

$$J_z = \begin{bmatrix} \frac{\partial f_1}{\partial z_1} & \frac{\partial f_1}{\partial z_2} \\ \frac{\partial f_2}{\partial z_1} & \frac{\partial f_2}{\partial z_2} \end{bmatrix}, \quad J_u = \begin{bmatrix} \frac{\partial f_1}{\partial u} \\ \frac{\partial f_2}{\partial u} \end{bmatrix} \tag{7}$$

$$J_z = \begin{bmatrix} 0 & 1 \\ \frac{-Nu(t)}{a(b+z_1(t))^{N+1}} & -\frac{c}{m} \end{bmatrix}, \quad J_u = \begin{bmatrix} 0 \\ \frac{1}{a(b+x(t))^N} \end{bmatrix} \tag{8}$$

Then the linearized model at operating point is given by,

$$\begin{bmatrix} \dot{z}_1(t) \\ \dot{z}_2(t) \end{bmatrix} = J_z|_O \begin{bmatrix} z_1(t) \\ z_2(t) \end{bmatrix} + J_u|_O\, u(t)$$

This gives,

$$\begin{bmatrix} \dot{z}_1(t) \\ \dot{z}_2(t) \end{bmatrix} = \begin{bmatrix} A_{11} & A_{12} \\ A_{21} & A_{22} \end{bmatrix} \begin{bmatrix} z_1(t) \\ z_2(t) \end{bmatrix} + \begin{bmatrix} 0 \\ B_2 \end{bmatrix} u(t)$$

$$y = z_1(t) \tag{9}$$

Where,

$$A_{11} = 0,\ A_{12} = 1,\ A_{21} = \frac{-Nu_0}{ma(b + x_0)^{N+1}}$$

$$A_{22} = -\frac{c}{m} \text{ and } B_2 = \frac{1}{ma(b + x_0)^N} \tag{10}$$

Remark 2.1 *In ideal condition, $c = 0$ i.e there is no air resistance and no friction between glass rod and magnet, the system can be represented as,*

$$\begin{bmatrix} \dot{z}_1(t) \\ \dot{z}_2(t) \end{bmatrix} = \begin{bmatrix} 0 & 1 \\ A_{21} & 0 \end{bmatrix} \begin{bmatrix} z_1(t) \\ z_2(t) \end{bmatrix} + \begin{bmatrix} 0 \\ B_2 \end{bmatrix} u(t)$$

$$y(t) = z_1(t) \tag{11}$$

Note that, the response of the system (11) *is oscillatory about the operating point because the poles are pure imaginary at $\pm j\sqrt{|A_{21}|}$. However, practically, there exist a finite amount of resistance that can be modeled as viscous friction, though very small. This results in underdamped transient response.*

3 System identification

For the linear model (11), the mass of magnet and gravitational force are known. However, parameters a, b and N are required to compute A_{21} and B_2. For the experimental setup, the values recommended by manufacturer are $b = 6.2$ and $3 < N < 4.5$. With these values, the constant a can be computed using the curve-fitting of actuator (2) response for input u and the magnet position x. As the steady-state height of the magnet represents an equilibrium, i.e. $F_u = mg$, therefore from (2) we get,

$$a = \frac{u}{mg(b + z_1)^N} \tag{12}$$

Table 1. Parameters of Maglev system

Parameter	Quantity	Remark
m	0.12 Kg	mass of magnet
N	4	selected
b	6.2	provided by manufacturer
g	9.81	m/s^2

The value of constant a for the pair (x, u) can be computed from (12) and data in Table 1. The mean value is found to be $a = 0.99$ after curve fitting. Based on these parameters, the linear model at $x_0 = 2cm$ and $u_0 = 5000\, counts$ can be identified as,

$$\begin{aligned} \dot{x}(t) &= \begin{bmatrix} 0 & 1 \\ -313 & -6.5 \end{bmatrix} x(t) + \begin{bmatrix} 0 \\ 5000 \end{bmatrix} u(t) \\ y(t) &= z_1(t) \end{aligned} \tag{13}$$

Fig. 3 shows open loop responses of the system, obtained practically as well as via simulation.

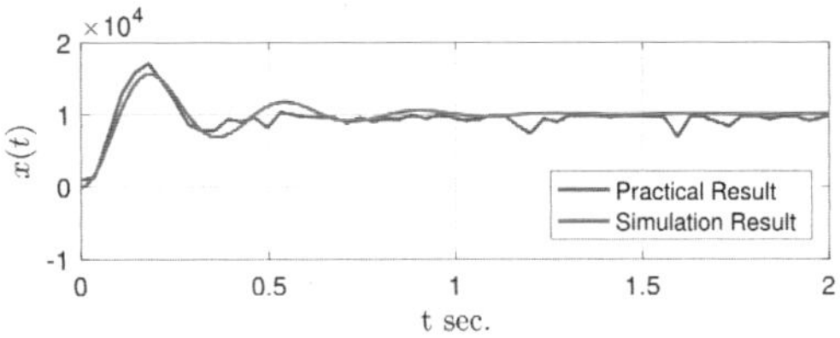

Figure 3. Open loop response of the Levitation $y(t)$ of magnet.

4 Super-twisting control

Consider a controllable system,

$$\dot{\mathbf{z}}_1(t) = A_{11}\mathbf{z}_1(t) + A_{12}z_2(t) \tag{14a}$$

$$\dot{z}_2(t) = A_{21}\mathbf{z}_1(t) + A_{22}z_2(t) + B_2u(t) + d(\mathbf{z}, t) \tag{14b}$$

where, $\mathbf{z}_1 \in \mathbf{R}^{n-1}$, $z_2 \in \mathbf{R}$, $z = [\mathbf{z}_1^\top z_2]^\top$ represent states of the system, $u \in \mathbf{R}$ and $d \in \mathbf{R}$ represent input and disturbance, respectively. Assume that, the system is controllable and observable. Also, assume that the disturbance and its rate of change with respect to time are bounded by, $|d(\mathbf{z}, t)| \le \gamma$ and $\phi(z, t) := |\dot{d}(\mathbf{z}, t)| \le \gamma_1$, respectively.

4.1 Sliding Function and Sliding Mode Control

Let there exist $c_1 \in \mathbf{R}^{1\times(n-1)}$ such that $(A_{11} - A_{12}c_1)$ is Hurwitz. Such a matrix F exists as the (A_{11}, A_{12}) pair inherits the controllability property.

Let the sliding set be,

$$\mathbf{S} = \{\mathbf{z} \in \mathbf{R} \mid s(t) := c_1\mathbf{z}_1(t) + z_2(t) = 0\} \tag{15}$$

Clearly, when the state trajectory is held on the surface $s(t) = 0$, we get $z_2 = -c_1\mathbf{z}_1$. Therefore, from (14a) we can write governing equation for sliding motion of $\mathbf{z}_1$ (and subsequently, $\mathbf{z}_2 = -c_1\mathbf{z}_1$) trajectory as

$$\dot{\mathbf{z}}_1(t) = (A_{11} - A_{12}c_1)\mathbf{z}_1(t) \tag{16}$$

As $(A_{11} - A_{12}c_1)$ is Hurwitz by design, thus when trajectory of the system is held on $s(t) = 0$, $\|\mathbf{z}_1\| \to 0$ as $t \to \infty$ and $\|z_2\| \to 0$ as $\|\mathbf{z}_1\| \to 0$.

Therefore, it is essential to design the control such that the trajectory $(\mathbf{z}_1, z_2)$ reaches the sliding surface $s(t)$ in finite time and remain on that thereafter. For such systems, the conventional sliding mode control that enforces the system trajectory on the surface in finite time and restrict them on it can be given by,

$$\begin{aligned} u(t) = -B_2^{-1}\,(c_1[A_{11}\mathbf{z}_1(t) + A_{12}z_2(t)] \\ +A_{21}\mathbf{z}_1(t) + A_{22}z_2(t) + Q\text{sgn}(s)),\ \ Q > \gamma \end{aligned} \tag{17}$$

The conventional sliding mode control (17) ensures $s(t) = 0$ in a finite time. However, the term $Q\text{sgn}(s)$ makes the control u discontinuous and may exhibit the chattering. This problem can be overcome by using second order sliding mode, in which the time derivative of the control is considered to be the new virtual control that ensures $\dot{s}(t) = 0$ in finite time as well.

From (15), we can write,

$$\begin{aligned} \dot{s}(t) &= c_1\dot{\mathbf{z}}_1(t) + \dot{z}_2(t) \\ &= c_1[A_{11}\mathbf{z}_1(t) + A_{12}z_2(t)] + A_{21}\mathbf{z}_1(t) \\ &\quad + A_{22}z_2(t) + B_2u(t) + d(\mathbf{z}, t) \end{aligned} \tag{18}$$

Define,

$$f(t) := c_1[A_{11}\mathbf{z}_1(t) + A_{12}z_2(t)] + A_{21}\mathbf{z}_1(t) + A_{22}z_2(t)$$

Therefore, from (18) we can write,

$$\dot{s}(t) = f(t) + B_2u(t) + d(\mathbf{z}, t) \tag{19}$$

Clearly, objective is to design the control such that, $s(t) = \dot{s}(t) = 0$ for all $t \ge t_r$, $t_r \in \mathbf{R}^+$.

4.2 Super-twisting Control

The first order (conventional) SMC as in (17) is discontinuous in nature. Practically such discontinuous control cannot be applied at infinite frequency, this leads to the chattering that may excite unmodelled dynamics and as a result system may under perform or may result into the actuator failure. In order to obtain the sliding motion as in (16) along with robustness properties, a super-twisting control can be used, which circumvents the chattering issue. Typically, the super-twisting structure is given by,

$$\begin{aligned} \dot{s}(t) &= -k_1|\,s\,|^{\frac{1}{2}}\text{sgn}(s) + \xi(t) \\ \dot{\xi}(t) &= -k_2\,\text{sgn}(s) + \phi(t) \end{aligned} \tag{20}$$

Then $s(t)$ and $\dot{s}(t)$ converge to zero in finite time if k_1 and k_2 are chosen as, $k_2 > \gamma_1$ and $k_1 > 1.8\sqrt{\gamma_1 + k_2}$, see [23] for proof.

Clearly, if we design a control,

$$u(t) = -B_2^{-1}\left(f(t) + k_1|s|^{\frac{1}{2}}\text{sgn}(s) + k_2\int_0^t \text{sgn}(s)d\tau\right) \quad (21)$$

Then (19) can be written as,

$$\dot{s}(t) = -k_1|s|^{\frac{1}{2}}\text{sgn}(s) - k_2\int_0^t \text{sgn}(s)d\tau + d(\mathbf{z}, t) \quad (22)$$

Define, $\xi := -k_2\int_0^t \text{sgn}(s)d\tau + d(\mathbf{z}, t)$ and $\phi(t) := \dot{d}(\mathbf{z}, t)$
Therefore (22) can be written as,

$$\begin{aligned}\dot{s}(t) &= -k_1|s|^{\frac{1}{2}}\text{sgn}(s) + \xi(t)\\ \dot{\xi}(t) &= -k_2\,\text{sgn}(s) + \phi(t)\end{aligned} \quad (23)$$

Thus, $s(t) = \dot{s}(t) = 0$ for all $t > t_r$ for some $t_r \in \mathbf{R}^+$ if we choose $k_2 > \gamma_1$ and $k_1 > 1.8\sqrt{\gamma_1 + k_2}$.

5 Sliding mode and super-twisting control for maglev system

This section demonstrates the simulation and practical responses of magnetic levitation system with sliding mode control and super-twisting control. Both the controllers are designed for the identified system as in (13).

Comparing (9) and (13), we get,

$$\begin{aligned}&A_{11} = 0,\ A_{12} = 1,\ A_{21} = -313\\ &A_{22} = -6.5 \text{ and } B_2 = 5000\end{aligned} \quad (24)$$

To track the reference input r, we transform the system to new co-ordinates that represent error between system states and the desired states. Define $e_1 := z_1 - z_{1d} = z_1 - r$, $e_2 := z_2 - z_{2d}$, and $\Delta u := u - u_d$. So the system (9) can be represented as,

$$\dot{e}_1(t) = A_{11}e_1(t) + A_{12}e_2(t) \quad (25)$$
$$\dot{e}_2(t) = A_{21}e_1(t) + A_{22}e_2 + B_2\Delta u(t) \quad (26)$$

5.1 Sliding function

From (15), we can design sliding function as,

$$s(t) = c_1e_1(t) + e_2(t) = 0 \quad (27)$$

such that the sliding motion governed by

$$\dot{z}_1(t) = (A_{11} - A_{12}c_1)z_1(t) \quad (28)$$

will exhibit the desired characteristic. We choose, $c_1 = 10$, therefore for the maglev system surface is given by

$$s(t) = 10e_1(t) + e_2(t) = 0 \quad (29)$$

5.2 Sliding mode control

Follow from (17), we can design the sliding mode control for the system (25)-(26) that initiates the sliding motion in finite time,

$$\begin{aligned}u(t) = -B_2^{-1}\,(c_1[A_{11}e_1(t) + A_{12}e_2(t)]\\ +A_{21}e_1(t) + A_{22}e_2(t) + Q\text{sgn}(s))\end{aligned} \quad (30)$$

Where Q is chosen greater than bound of the absolute value of disturbance and k is chosen to increase the speed of response during reaching phase. To check the robustness property of the sliding mode control, disturbance $d(t) = 2\sin 20t$ is introduced. Therefore, we select $Q = 5 > 2$ and $k = 40$ to speed up the response in the reaching phase. Thus, the sliding mode control is designed as,

$$\begin{aligned}u(t) &= 0.626e_1(t) - 0.0007e_2(t) - 0.008s(t)\\ &\quad -0.001\text{sgn}(s)\end{aligned} \quad (31)$$

that initiates the sliding motion

$$\dot{z}_1(t) = -10z_1(t) \quad (32)$$

in finite time. Clearly, $\|e_1\| \to 0$ as $t \to \infty$ and as $e_2(t) = -10e_1$ therefore $\|e_2\| \to 0$ as $t \to \infty$. Thus, $y = z_1$ tracks r asymptotically.

Fig.4 shows the comparison of simulation response with the response of magnet levitation performed on experimental setup ECP Maglev 730. Fig.4 shows the control efforts (31) and evolution of sliding function (29) for both simulation and practical performance.

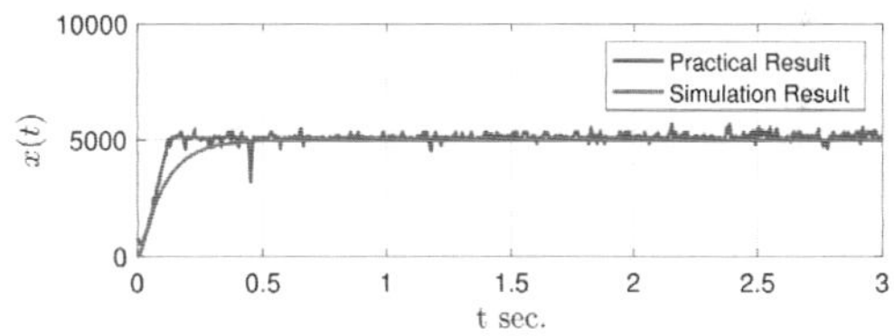

Figure 4. Levitation $x(t)$ of magnet with sliding mode control (31).

5.3 Super-twisting control

Form Fig.5 (a), it is quite evident that the applied control exhibits the chattering, therefore we design super-twisting control, which is second order continuous control as discussed in section 4.2. Follow from (21), we can write the super-twisting control for a system (25)-(25) described in error variables as,

$$u(t) = -B_2^{-1}\left(f(t) + k_1|s|^{\frac{1}{2}}\text{sgn}(s) + k_2\int_0^t \text{sgn}(s)d\tau\right) \quad (33)$$

where,

$$f(t) = c_1[A_{11}e_1(t) + A_{12}e_2(t)] + A_{21}e_1(t) + A_{22}e_2(t)$$

https://doi.org/10.1051/itmconf/20203201004

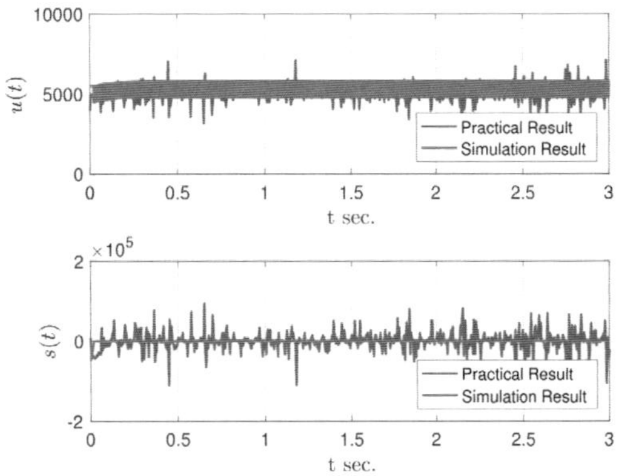

Figure 5. (a) Control input (31) to the system. (b) Evolution of sliding surface (29).

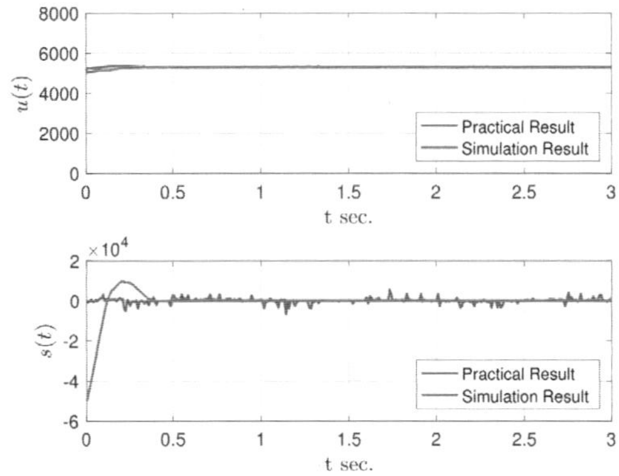

Figure 7. (a) Control input (34) to the system. (b) Evolution of sliding surface (29).

Thus, for experimental setup ECP Maglev 730 with disturbance $d(t) = 2\sin 20t$, we design a control with $k_1 = 16000$ and $k_2 = 10$ as,

$$u(t) = 0.626e_1(t) - 0.0007e_2(t) - 3.2|s|^{\frac{1}{2}}\text{sgn}(s) + 0.002\int_0^t \text{sgn}(s)d\tau \quad (34)$$

that provides the super-twisting control in terms of counts as,

$$\begin{aligned} \dot{s}(t) &= -16000|s|^{\frac{1}{2}}\text{sgn}(s) + \xi(t) \\ \dot{\xi}(t) &= -10\,\text{sgn}(s) + \phi(t) \end{aligned} \quad (35)$$

Note that, $\max|\phi(t)| = \max|\dot{d}| = 2$, therefore $k_2 > 2.2$ is satisfied and $k_1 > 1.8\sqrt{2.2+10}$ is also satisfied. As s and $\dot{s}$ both converge to 0 in finite time, sliding motion (32) is initiated. This implies, $\|e_1\| \to 0$ as $t \to \infty$ and as $e_2(t) = -10e_1$ therefore $\|e_2\| \to 0$ as $t \to \infty$. Thus, $y = z_1$ tracks r asymptotically. Fig.6 shows the comparison of simulation response and the response of magnet levitation performed on experimental setup ECP Maglev 730 with super-twisting control (34). Fig.7 shows the control efforts (34) and evolution of sliding function (29) for both simulation and practical performance. It can be seen in Fig.7(a) that control effort (34) does not exhibit chattering.

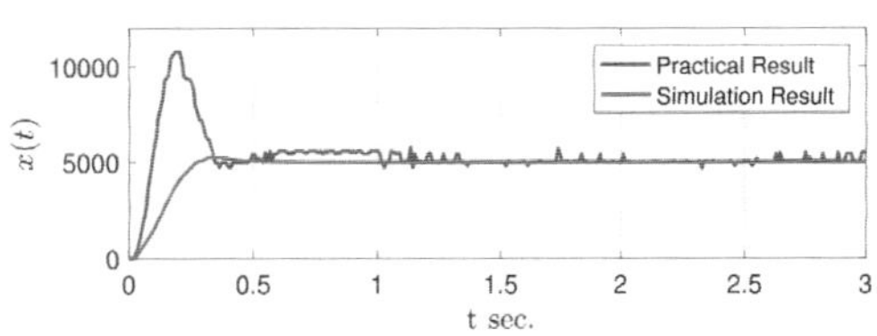

Figure 6. Levitation $x(t)$ of magnet with sliding mode control (34).

6 Conclusion

In this paper, we have designed and implemented the sliding mode (SMC) and super-twisting control (STC) for the Maglev Model 730 experimental setup manufactured by educational control products, which is an open loop underdamped system. The experimental results with SMC and STC are compared with simulation results and found satisfactory in presence of external disturbance.

It can be verified from the simulation as well as practical results that STC is continuous control and does not exhibit chattering and the manget levitation response does not hinder in presence of applied disturbance.

References

[1] B.Z. Kaplan, D. Regev, IEEE Transactions on Magnetics **12**, 556 (1976)

[2] M. Dussaux, *Status of the industrial applications of the active magnetic bearings technology*, in *ASME 1990 International Gas Turbine and Aeroengine Congress and Exposition* (American Society of Mechanical Engineers, 1990), pp. V005T14A016–V005T14A016

[3] J. Kaloust, C. Ham, J. Siehling, E. Jongekryg, Q. Han, IEE Proceedings-Control Theory and Applications **151**, 460 (2004)

[4] W.J. Bencze, Y.M. Xiao, D.N. Hipkins, G.F. Franklin, B.W. Parkinson, *Gyroscope spin axis direction control for the Gravity Probe B satellite*, in *Decision and Control, 1996., Proceedings of the 35th IEEE Conference on* (IEEE, 1996), Vol. 1, pp. 480–485

[5] S.Y. Hu, *Magnetic levitation weight reduction structure for a vertical wind turbine generator* (2008), uS Patent 7,462,950

[6] J. Kumbernuss, C. Jian, J. Wang, H. Yang, W. Fu, Applied Energy **90**, 148 (2012)

[7] W. Barie, J. Chiasson, International Journal of systems science **27**, 1153 (1996)

[8] A. El Hajjaji, M. Ouladsine, IEEE Transactions on industrial Electronics **48**, 831 (2001)

[9] A. Isidori, *Nonlinear control systems* (Springer Science & Business Media, 2013)

[10] Z.J. Yang, M. Tateishi, Automatica **37**, 1125 (2001)

[11] P. Nataraj, M.D. Patil, *Robust control design for nonlinear magnetic levitation system using quantitative feedback theory (QFT)*, in *India Conference, 2008. INDICON 2008. Annual IEEE* (IEEE, 2008), Vol. 2, pp. 365–370

[12] C. Edwards, S.K. Spurgeon, *Sliding Mode Control: Theory and Applications* (Taylor & Francis Ltd., 1998)

[13] Y. Shtessel, C. Edwards, L. Fridman, A. Levant, *Sliding mode control and observation* (Springer, 2014)

[14] D. Cho, Y. Kato, D. Spilman, IEEE control systems **13**, 42 (1993)

[15] J.C. Shen, Asian Journal of Control **4**, 333 (2002)

[16] H.M. Gutierrez, P.I. Ro, IEEE Transactions on Industrial Electronics **45**, 921 (1998)

[17] D. Khimani, R. Rokade, *Implementation of sliding mode control on magnetic levitation system*, in *Advances in Computing, Communication and Control (ICAC3), 2017 International Conference on* (IEEE, 2017), pp. 1–5

[18] N. Al-Muthairi, M. Zribi, Mathematical Problems in Engineering **2004**, 93 (2004)

[19] J. Phuah, J. Lu, T. Yahagi, IEEJ Transactions on Electronics, Information and Systems **125**, 600 (2005)

[20] A. Levant, Automatica **34**, 379 (1998)

[21] A. Polyakov, A. Poznyak, IEEE Transactions on Automatic Control **54**, 1951 (2009)

[22] J.A. Moreno, M. Osorio, IEEE Transactions on Automatic Control **57**, 1035 (2012)

[23] A.K. Behera, A. Chalanga, B. Bandyopadhyay, Automatica **87**, 437 (2018)

[24] ECP, *Operational Manual for Magnetic Levitation system-Model 730* (ECP Systems, 2015), http://www.ecpsystems.com/controls_maglevit.htm

 https://doi.org/10.1051/itmconf/20203201005

INTELLIGENT ROBOTIC ARM

Prasad Ban[1], *Shweta Desale*[2], *Revati Barge*[3] , *Pallavi Chavan*[4]

[1]Information Technology, Ramrao Adik Institute of Technology, Nerul, Navi Mumbai, MH, India

[2]Information Technology, Ramrao Adik Institute of Technology, Nerul, Navi Mumbai, MH, India

[3]Information Technology, Ramrao Adik Institute of Technology, Nerul, Navi Mumbai, MH, India

[4]Information Technology, Ramrao Adik Institute of Technology, Nerul, Navi Mumbai, MH, India

Abstract. Regardless the abundance of technological robotic equipment's present in the form of auto- mated Mechanical Robotic Arm, most of the citizens in India are not able to use those robots in their regular day to day life. This paper talks about the Intelligent robotic Arm (IRA) which is able to cook food dishes in an ordinary home environment. The robotic arm recognizes the utensils and ingredients required for the particular recipe. For object detection we have developed a system using OpenCV and Python which helps the robotic arm to recognize the correct ingredient and pick and drop it to appropriate utensil for cooking the required recipe. It involves automated tasks which the arm has to perform while commands are given to it for making the particular recipe. Our motivation is to help brilliant supplier robots that work by and large human environments ,automating continuous errands. In quest for this objective, we follow the universal apply autonomy worldview, in which savvy observation and control, are blended in with ubiquitous processing. By misusing sensors and effectors in its condition, a mechanical can work extra confused obligations other than turning out to be excessively perplexing itself. Following this understanding, we have built up a supplier automated that works independently in a sensor-prepared kitchen. The mechanical gains from exhibition, and performs refined assignments, working together with the system of gadgets in its condition. We record on the structure, usage, and utilization of this framework, which is unreservedly accessible for use, and improvement through others, in the examination network .

1. INTRODUCTION

Detecting objects and specific elements in real world by any robot itself is still a crucial task. Robots have the capability to work precisely and in almost 97% accurate form. Real time object recognition entails identification of objects by means of Computer Vision and Artificial Intelligence, it involves Machine Learning and Deep Learning concepts. Intelligent Robots can be used in day to day life of a normal middle-class person in India in fact the main objective behind the making of robots is to reduce the physical workload on Human, to automate the completion of tasks and to get more precise and accurate outcomes. [1] The system proposed is that automating and assisting in regular cooking work in a kitchen of a normal middle-class person in India by use of a Robotic Arm. Thus, the problem we define here is to design and develop an intelligent Mechanical Robotic Arm which could be used in regular home environment for the purpose of cooking meal. The system itself would be able to cook normal recipe in kitchen via a remote access to the robotic arm through a smartphone. Rather than commonplace mechanical mechanization frameworks robot ought to have the option to respond to unforeseen, questionable and obscure occasions by parameter adjustment or extra arranging exercises. The robot© capacity to gain from its n experience and through human direction is done through AI. Learning should prompt quicker issue arrangements, quicker or progressively solid arrangement executions or to the capacity to take care of issues the robot was not ready to comprehend previously. Profound learning permits robots to improve examination and recognition of unvulgar things through progressively definite and complex information. Our base approach to achieve the goal includes [a]developing a low budget affordable robotic arm and [b] system capable of recognizing and detecting objects and ingredients used in cooking meal with the use of Image Processing, Computer vision, Artificial Intelligence and Machine Learning. [c] Robotic arm capable of picking and dropping the ingredients recognized by the system. Imagine you are being offered a meal which has been taught by you to the robot, isn't it would be a great pleasure for you? This section describes the background in brief and gives the reader an overview of the problem and a better understanding of what artificial intelligence, robotics, machine learning and deep learning technology is and why it is needed. Artificial intelligence is the most growing technology. The real-world data is collected and the robotics are trained with that data through artificial intelligence technology. Robotics are manipulated with that real-world data, more the data is used, more will be the performance of robot improves. Along these things by consolidating man-made brainpower, AI and profound learning perspectives, the completely mechanized and shrewd robot can prepare home-made supper with no human intercession. It will learn plans and cook them for you.

2. LITERATURE REVIEW

The overall market changes when new technology is introduced. The technologies help speed up the processes and bring more efficiency into the market. Cooking takes a ton of time. Somebody in the family winds up going through a few hours in the kitchen every day. This ends up being an exceptionally substantial weight on family units and unhitched males/old maids. The Robotic Chef helps the weight of the cook by setting up a help in cooking by automated processes. [1] Nowadays many companies are developing robots and Robotic Arms having different use in automating the human tasks but most of the Arms and Robots are only used for industrial purpose and process automations. [2] Companies are also developing Robots for cooking meals in kitchen in replacement for human chef, some of which are being developed by Moley Robotics and Samsung Robotics, including a progressed, completely practical robot incorporated into a delightfully structured, proficient robotic kitchen setup. The complete setup is operated by a single interface on a touch screen panel integrated with the robotic setup. Moley has made the world©first automated kitchen.

 https://doi.org/10.1051/itmconf/20203201005

Highlighting a progressed, completely practical robot incorporated into a delightfully structured, proficient kitchen, it cooks with the ability and style of an ace culinary expert. The model was debuted to boundless approval at Hanover Messe, the global mechanical technology appears. [3] A Bangalore based startup also came with a modern solution for the problem of cooking. They developed a robot which can prepare a meal when pre-cut vegetables are introduced to it. Its user only needs to load in cut vegetables. The machine does the everything else and presents a delicious meal. This Cooking Robot makes numerous Indian Foods by doing 3 operations. One is, dropping – fixings into the dish being cooked; Second operation is, Heating – the dish being cooked; The third one is, Stirring – the substance. These three activities are everything necessary to get ready numerous Indian dishes. The machine as of now comes stacked with all the flavors that are required for cooking the client includes the vegetables required for the cook and the machine at that point dominates and does everything else. At the point when the client chooses what they need to cook, the machine guides them through what vegetables they have to get ready and cut, in the amounts they need. It at that point guides them through the stacking of the vegetables into the machine. The vessels that hold the vegetables and any piece of the machine that comes into contact with the nourishment can be snapped here and there, and is in this manner simple to clean. The quantity of such parts to clean is additionally limited. Individuals will incline toward the adaptability of having a cooking machine within reach that can cook for them whenever, particularly one that they can control from their telephone so it begins cooking when its clients are still on their way once more from work. In spite of the fact that this Robot does a large portion of the Cooking consequently, it despite everything has a few confinements. With the present AI Technology, it is as yet not a basic issue to fabricate cutting machines that are likewise simple to clean. Along these, a human would be expected to do the cutting and stripping. The Mechanical Chef likewise doesn©set up any dishes that require molding, for example, dosas and idli and the size of this robot is huge as it won't fit into an average sized kitchen. [4] Another one of the best inventions which we studied is Dorna robotic arm. Dorna is a quick, amazing and exact automated arm. Dorna is a modern evaluation 5-hub mechanical arm with an open source programming and firmware, and it is equipped for computerizing numerous genuine assignments. Dorna gives an ideal answer for entrepreneurs, producers, analysts, specialists and any individual who needs to quit fooling around in mechanical autonomy without spending a fortune on a modern automated arm, but again the basic problem with this arm is that Dorna is not affordable for small scale earning people.[6]Algorithms of Computer Vision and Deep Learning modules which are able to find and classify objects in the live feed from PiCam and normal USB-Camera. Some of the algorithms useful for Deep Learning, Canny Edge algorithm in OpenCv and the Cv2 libraries, CUPA toolkit for deep learning (Developed by NVDIA). [4] Canny Edge and other imutils Python libraries with CNN and TensorFlow have been successfully implemented for object detection in OpenCV. [5] The reason behind selecting this algorithm is that it is compatible with python libraries in OpenCV and works efficiently on Raspbian Operating System. PC have gigantic learning ability and have exhibited predominant insight in numerous spaces. Cooking Robots could be helpful to the individuals with serious physical incapacity. In this way, cooking includes numerous troublesome undertakings that requires physical connection like cutting, and so forth. Hence, it is as yet a moving activity for a robot to perform in typical kitchen condition. Late research have improved the robot©ability what©more, adaptability to PC vision and arranging. The utilitarian item situated system (FOON) to demonstrate the availability of the utilitarian related items and their movements in control undertakings. The graphical model FOON is learned by watching object state change and human controls with the objects. Utilizing a very much prepared FOON, robots can decode an errand objective, look for the right objects at the ideal states on which to work, and create a succession of legitimate control movements. A chart recovery approach is introduced to produce control movement groupings from the FOON to accomplish an ideal objective, showing the adaptability of FOON in making a novel and versatile methods for taking care of an issue utilizing information assembled from numerous sources. The outcomes are shown in a reproduced domain to outline the movement successions created from the FOON to complete the ideal undertakings. To remove information from instructional recordings , a four – arrange video understanding pipeline is created. This assistance to perceive all occasions in video and play out the total errand as needs be.[6] The double arm humanoid cooking robot can cook dishes like an ace culinary specialist in common home kitchens. The kinematic investigation is first done for the 6DOF arm of the robot. Organize outlines are relegated to each connection of the arm utilizing the Denavit-Hartenberg show. The dynamic conditions are then acquired utilizing the Lagrangian technique by ascertaining motor vitality and potential vitality. A reenactment for a Chinese cooking development is then done, joint torques for each joint of the robot© arm during this development are obtained. Recent inquire has been made to bring the PC insight into physical world with the goal that robots can be capable perform physical control assignments. The approach first enable robots to become familiar with the aptitudes by "viewing" on the web instructional recordings. Subsequent to looking out for 200 recordings the expertise to adjust PC knowledge is created.[7] Sereneti needs Cooki to be a piece of an environment that incorporates an assistance called Foodie, where they send you pre-bundled fixings that your robot at that point cooks for you. At this moment, Cooki can deal with up to four fixings, and the last rendition will likewise incorporate a ring over the container to include oil, salt, pepper and other spices.It© additionally be littler and particular with the goal that you can extend number of ingredients.Sereneti was focusing on a mid 2017 release.

3. INTELLIGENT ROBOTIC ARM

This paper proposed a simple robotic arm which is a 6d.o.f arm (having 6 degree of freedom). . . The main model of the robotic arm comprises the basic three components. [a]Actuators (Servos), [b]End Effector, [c]Controller (Arduino). The actuators are responsible for the movement of the robotic arm in the tri Axis coordinates. End effector is the component which grips the object which is to be picked up and the brain of the arm, the controller it controls all the movement of the complete robot and the actuators.

3.1 System Architecture

Architecture of the project provides the complete Insight of the project; this alludes the complete structure of the software and control of creating such logical and systematic structures. System architecture of this project is in figure 1.

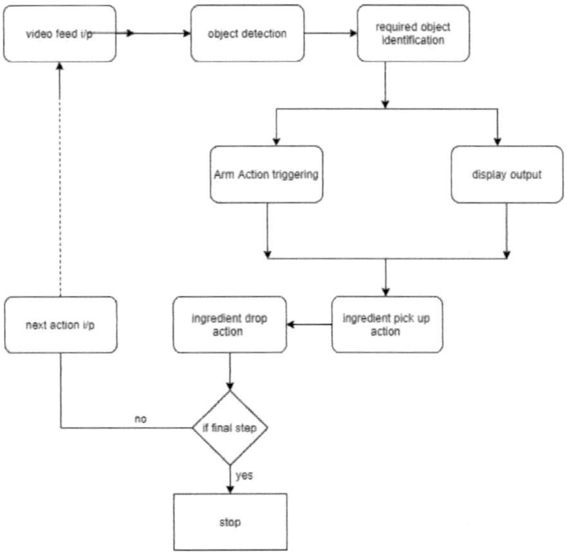

Figure 1. architecture of the proposed system

The Development process is designed in following steps:

- Live feed from PiCam to system
- Object Detection and ingredient identification
- Setting the particular recipe
- Pick and drop action by Robotic Arm

Input to the system includes the object detection and identification of the required ingredient which is first required for preparation of the particular recipe. The image processing Algorithm used for the proposed system works on LeNet – CNN (Convolutional Neural Network) and TensorFlow. The system takes live feed through the PiCam and matches the similar objects which are being found through the input using Canny-Edge algorithm for object identification. Science all edge detection outputs are easily affected by noise, to prevent the false detection a gaussian filter kernel is bonded to the image, the equation of gaussian filter kernel smoothening is given by:

$$H_{ij} = \frac{1}{2\pi\sigma^2} \exp\left(-\frac{(i-(k+1))^2 + (j-(k+1))^2}{2\sigma^2}\right); 1 \leq i, j \leq (2k+1)$$

In post processing, the output from the live feed i.e. identified ingredient triggers a signal to the script which initiates the robotic arm to pick up the particular ingredient and drop it at a particular destination which is already set. Further the mapping of the code written for particular recipe is done and next actions are taken which includes again scanning for the next ingredient required.

3.2 IMPLEMENTATION

The proposed model is a Robotic arm which is operated by Arduino UNO and Raspberry Pi for cooking which is built in low cost. The Robotic arm is capable for cooking recipe in regular home environment, for example: for the set of code written for the recipe of normal Maggie, after triggering the recipe for Maggie the Object detection algorithm will be searching for noodles and Maggie spices and after detecting the required ingredients the arm will pick up the ingredients and drop it at the required utensil. [1] Object detection and recognition is a technique to change over a video image for recognizing the particular element in the feed. For successful working of the algorithm we need to feed the model and compile a huge set of labelled data and train it accordingly. The object detection is used in many domains where the projects related to computer vision are implemented example, the automated self-driving car. Object detection also known as computer vision is a technical field that deals with searching the ways to automate all the job that a human visual system can do.[2] Taking deep learning-based object detection concept, there are three basic methods which can be used for the object detection purpose. [a]Faster R-CNN'S [b] YOLO (you only look once) and the third one is [c] Single shot Detectors. The SSD is developed by the google, SSD method stands more accurate than R-CNN and YOLO

MobileNet: Efficient deep learning neural network

MobileNet are more compatible for running on small devices like raspberry pi and any smart-phone, these are different from normal CNN because of the usage of the depth wise separable convolution. In the proposed model the base object detection is built using MobileNet SSD and the deep neural network module.

The end result of this method in deep learning-based object detection is that it can process approximately 16- 18 fps depending upon the speed of the system being used, and the output is given by checking the confidence (i.e. probability) associated with each detection because there can exist multiple similar object in the input feed provided.

TensorFlow is a free and open-source programming library for dataflow and differentiable programming over a scope of errands. It is a representative math library, and is additionally utilized for AI applications, for example, neural systems. In March 2018, Google declared TensorFlow.js adaptation 1.0 for AI in JavaScript. In Jan 2019, Google declared TensorFlow 2.0. It turned out to be authoritatively accessible in Sep 2019.In May 2019, Google declared TensorFlow Graphics for profound learning in PC graphics. TPU is a programmable AI quickening agent intended to give high throughput of low-exactness number juggling (e.g., 8-piece), and situated toward utilizing or running models as opposed to preparing them. Google declared they had been running TPUs inside their server farms for over a year, and had discovered them to convey a request for size better-advanced execution per watt for AI. Edge TPU is Google©motivation assembled ASIC chip intended to run TensorFlow Lite AI (ML) models on little customer processing gadgets, for example, smartphones known as edge figuring. among the applications for which TensorFlow is the establishment, are computerized picture inscribing programming, for example, Deep Dream. Rank Brain now handles a significant number of search inquiries, supplanting and enhancing conventional static calculation-based inquiry results.

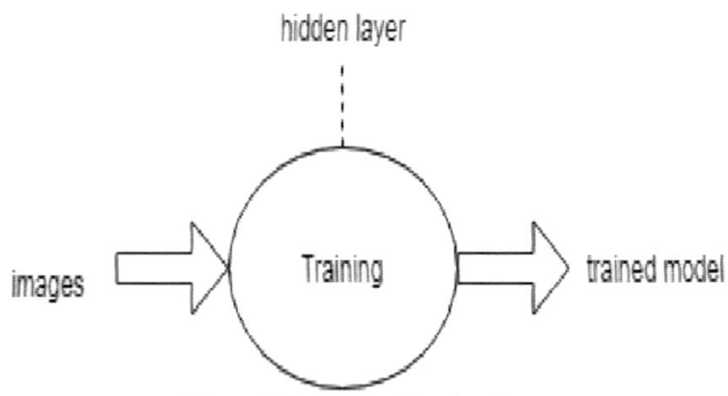

Figure 2 [Training of database]

a neural network is a mind-boggling information esteem and can be put away as a typical item. The object-situated methodology creases the most agreeable and characteristic configuration model for neural systems. In the terms of article arranged database frameworks neural systems are dealt with for the most part as mind boggling objects. These frameworks demonstrated truly important at taking care of what©more, administrating such articles in various regions, as PC supported structure, geographic databases, organization of part structures, etc. The proposed worldview permits the meaning of a solitary system up to a group of comparable systems. These are systems with comparable properties, similar to organize worldview and structure. The term comparable is not limited to arrange properties just, however covers additionally organizes, which achieve uncommon undertakings. The attributes of these systems can be totally different, yet the database input is the equivalent. The information control offices of the framework are abused to deal with the systems and their assignments inside a similar structure.

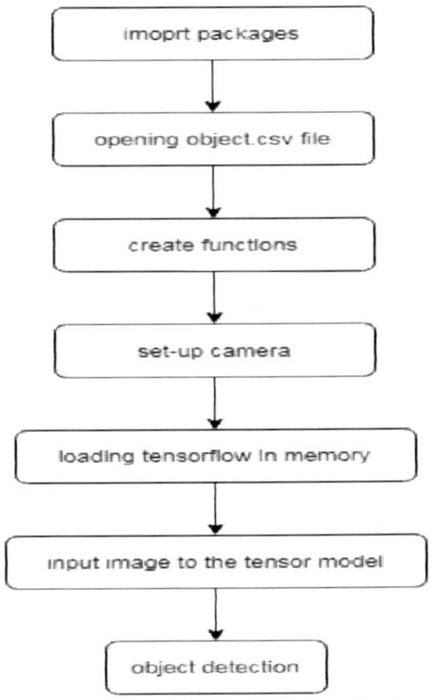

Figure 3 [TensorFlow Construction]

A neural system (NN), on account of counterfeit neurons called artificial neural system (ANN) or simulated neural system (SNN), is an interconnected gathering of natural or artificial neurons that utilizes a numerical or computational model for data preparing dependent on a connectionistic way to deal with calculation. Much of the time an ANN is a versatile framework that changes its structure dependent on outside or interior data that courses through the system. In increasingly commonsense terms neural systems are non-linear factual information displaying or dynamic devices. They can be utilized to demonstrate complex connections among information sources and yields or to discover designs in information.

Video enhancement entails removal of the different noise from the video feed. There is a need to boost the quality of the live feed which is being analyzed by the algorithm for the better outcome. The input feed is the live video which is taken by the PiCam or any other digital camera which is connected to the raspberry pi.

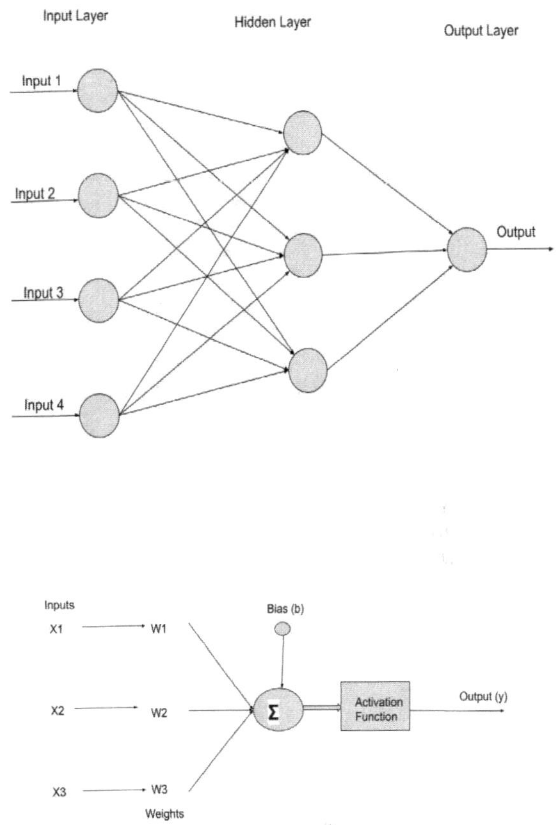

Figure 4 [Feedforward Neural Network]

The resolution of the camera is a considerable factor which captures the live feed. The credibility of the element detection depends on the resolution of the camera used.

The PiCam which we are using is shown in figure 5.

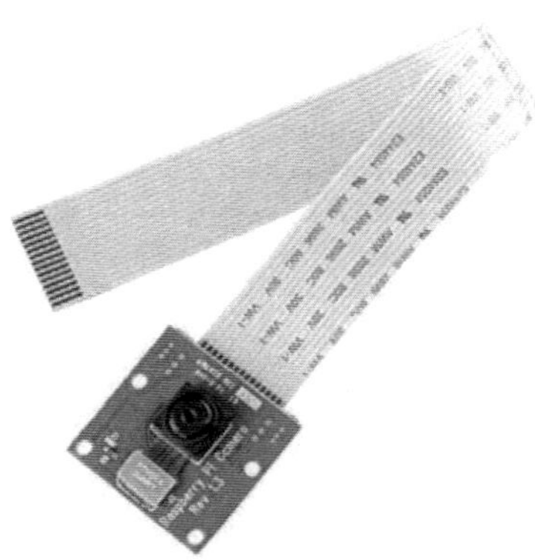

Figure 5. [PiCam]

 https://doi.org/10.1051/itmconf/20203201005

Prototype Execution

The proposed model works on then deep learning mechanism. Deep Learning and neural network-based methods have transcended traditional machine learning techniques by a vast scope in terms of accuracy in many areas of Computer Vision. The object detection is done from the live stream from the PiCam/Webcam. Depending on the recognized object the controller of the arm initiates the gripping action as they are pre-feded to the system. The End effector which is the gripper of the robotic arm hold the object to be picked up. The end Effector act as the human wrist for the pick and place work. There are numerous end effectors which can be used for the gripping purpose. The one which is used in proposed model in in figure 2.

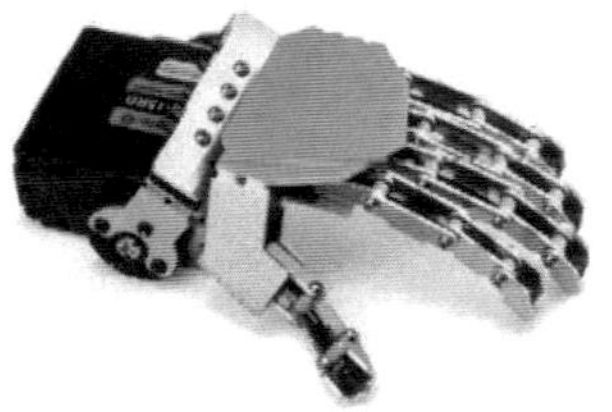

Figure 6. [Gripper]

4. RESULT

The input was provided in the form of live feed through the webcam attached at the end of the prototype robotic arm. The algorithm of object detection applied on the live stream through the web cam which works on 60fps.The object is recognized which is required for the particular search which is to be performed. The model scans the whole region which is under the frame of the webcam and detects the required object/element. The output of the process is that the required element is detected for performing the pick and place task. The prototype model grips the object and uplift it and place it at the desired destination or performs the further task as instructed by the code written for the particular recipe. Following image op1 shows how the webcam connected at the terminal of the prototype robotic arm shows the result at the monitor frame.

Figure 7- [model for prototype experimentation (without gripper)]

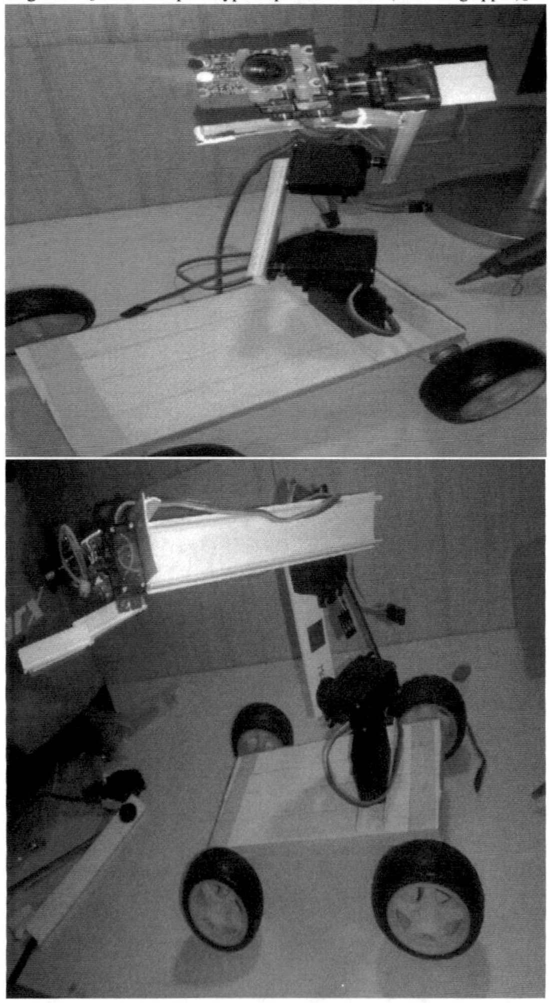

Figure 8 [web cam used for experimentation.]

After performing the algorithm for detecting a spoon in the live stream through the web can it showed the following result-

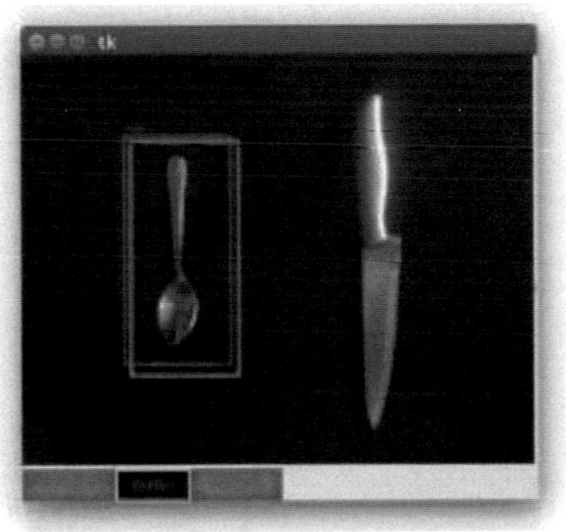

Figure 9 [Object Recognition]

5. CONCLUSION

The model automates the cooking process in normal home environment which will play an important role in helping humans to assist in cooking. After conducting survey, we found that existing cooking robots are much expensive and not portable. Since the world is rapidly changing and dive loping, there are lot of technological advancements are happening on a daily basis. Therefore, if we have something powerful and less expensive at our disposal then we need to ensure that we make use of it to full extent. An automatic cooking arm is presented which will fulfill the basic cooking tasks. A cost effective, more efficient and small size intelligent robotic arm will be developed.Moreover, the precision factor of the object detection algorithm needsto be improved. The proposed model Is not yet developed to perform for longer period on the time, as it will be working in the heat surrounding it need to get protected from the several environmental effects which can cause damage to the robot.The main aim of this system is to cook different recipe without human intervention. So, the future scope to the project is to engross and perform all the operations which are necessary for the cooking purpose and to get controlled through a remote accessible application through web or mobile phone.

References

[1] Jiaxin Zhai ; Gen Pan ; Weixin Yan ; Zhuang Fu ; Yanzheng Zhao," Dynamic analysis of a dual-arm humanoid cooking robot ", 2015 IEEE 10th Conference on Industrial Electronics and Applications (ICIEA), 10.1109/ICIEA.2015.7334226

[2] Oussam Khatib , Journal of Robotics, February 1987, "A Unified Approach for Motion and Force Control of Robot Manipulators: The Operational Space Formulation" , Vol. RA-3, NO. 1

[3] Yu Sun, "Robot Perception and Action Lab", Department of Computer Science and Engineering, University of South Florida, USA ," AI Meets Physical World Exploring Robot Cooking" arXiv: 1804.07974v1

[4] Radu Bogdan Rusua, Brian Gerkeyc, Michael Beetz — "Robots in the kitchen: Exploiting ubiquitous sensing and actuation", Researchgate2018, 10.1016/j.robot.2008.06.010

[5] raspberry-pi robotic arm with computer vision-electrom dust(youtube).https://www.youtube.com/watch?v=bL8fScdBOos&t

[6] Timothy Chen, "Cooki, A desktop robotic kitchen chef that does everything, IEEE Spectrum 2018

[7] Adrian Rosebrock. PyImageSearch" (Deep Learning and Computer Vision)

[8] Samsung bot chef(robotic kitchen by samsung)-cnet.com

[9] Michael Beetz — "Robots in the kitchen: Exploiting ubiquitous sensing and actuation".researchgate, 10.1016/j.robot.2008.06.010

[10]Dorna(high performance robot) ,dorna.ai.

PMU and DVR based Power System Monitoring, Controlling and Voltage sag Compensation.

Abhishek Chalwadi[1], *Kiruthika* M[1] and *Bindu* S[1]

[1]Department of Electrical Engineering, Agnel Charities, Fr. C. Rodrigues Institute of Technology, Vashi, Navi Mumbai

Abstract: The power system network is becoming dense and much more complex. Dynamic and continuous monitoring of the power system network is required to avoid power outages. Phasor Measurement Unit (PMU) is one such device that provides state estimation parameters of dynamic power system networks that are used for designing relays and controlling the system network. Power Quality problems such as voltage sags and swells can damage the sensitive load and cause abnormal voltage, current, and frequency conditions in a power system network. Fast and major developments in power electronics technology have made it possible to mitigate the power quality problems. Dynamic Voltage Restorer (DVR) is a voltage sag compensation device that compensates the difference in voltage avoiding interruptions and restores the voltage to the pre-fault value. This paper discusses a technique used for monitoring, protecting, and controlling the system under fault condition using PMU and compensate voltage sag for a sensitive load using DVR based on the data collected by placing PMU in an optimal location. The outcome of the above analysis is recorded which shows that effective monitoring, controlling, and voltage sag compensation can be done with less number of PMU's placed optimally in conjunction with DVR.

Keywords: PMU, DVR, Optimal Location, voltage sag.

1. Introduction

Power System outages in large power transmission lines have become more frequent and are subjected to transmission line faults at every instant. Faults can be defined as undesirable and unavoidable incidents that can disturb the stable condition of the power system network. Due to factors such as the detection of faults and abnormal conditions, there is a need for constant monitoring of power system networks [1]. Phasor Measurement Units (PMU) is a controlling and monitoring device that consistently monitors the power system network and controls the operation of circuit breakers by designing a protective relaying scheme [2]. The installation of PMU in a power system network is not feasible due to the high installation cost, the use of high precision sensors, and the development of phasor data centers. The use of PMU must be such that it should provide monitoring and controlling of the entire power system network with full observability and using the least number of PMU [3].

Power Quality problems like voltage sags, swells, dips, and harmonics create problems for both end-user customer and electrical utility. The power quality problems can be rectified using Flexible Alternating Current Transmission System (FACTS) devices. Dynamic Voltage Restorer (DVR) is a power electronic device from the FACTS family that protects the sensitive load from various disturbances in the power supply. The basic principle of DVR is to detect the voltage sag and restore the difference in voltage of desired magnitude and frequency. The advantage of DVR is that it compensates voltage sag of sensitive load with a fault current limiting capacity [4]. In a three-phase system, DVR compensates the difference in voltage with desired magnitude, frequency, and phase angle in synchronism to reshape the voltage waveform. In the distribution system, the amplitude and phase angle of the injected voltage is variable allowing the control of real and reactive power exchange, leading to improving the efficiency of the system and protecting the grid from tripping. [5]- [6].

Constant monitoring of the power system is required for the control of FACTS devices [7]. FACTS devices (thyristor based) in conjunction with PMU provides a compatible solution for uninterrupted power supply. PMU monitors the power supply network and provides data required for protection as well as it provides the state estimation parameters required for the operation of FACTS devices.[8]. Implementation of FACTS devices using the thyristor-based technique is complex, whereas implementation using MOSFET is simple in operation. Hence, in this paper an attempt has been made to implement PMU in conjunction with (MOSFET based) DVR for monitoring, controlling, and voltage sag compensation for a sensitive load. It is not advisable to place PMU on every bus.

Also, an IEEE 5 BUS System is monitored, controlled, and protected from transmission line faults by placing PMUs in optimal places. To observe the whole system, the optimal location of PMU is obtained through an Integer Programming based method. PMU data are used for fault detection and protection of transmission lines. DVR is implemented for the IEEE 5 BUS system network where it compensates the voltage sag of a sensitive load. The data obtained from PMUs are used for DVR operation.

The paper is organized as follows, In Section 2 Optimal Placement of PMU methodology is explained. Section 3 gives a brief introduction to the DVR. Section 4 includes the case study performed in MATLAB/Simulink. The paper is concluded in Section 5 and References are listed.

* Corresponding author: achalwadi49@gmail.com

2. Optimal Placement of PMU

Phasor Measurement Units provide two types of measurement; they are branch voltage phasors and branch current phasors. Installation Cost of PMU is high due to the setup of Phasor Data Centres (PDC) for controlling the transmission line remotely where the phasors are synchronized with Global Positioning System (GPS). For a wide-area measurement system (WAMS) placing PMU at every bus is not possible, hence the objective of the PMU placement problem is to render an observable system by using a minimum number of PMUs. The Optimal PMU placement problem is solved using Integer Programming based procedure. Using the numerical based method of Integer Programming based Procedure the Optimal Placement Problem is formulated [9]- [10]

For an n-bus system, the PMU placement problem can be formulated as follows:

$$f(x) = \Sigma_{k=1}^{N} x(k) \qquad (1)$$

=1

subject to $\lfloor A\rfloor * \lfloor X\rfloor \geq \lfloor b\rfloor$

where N is a number of system buses and $\lfloor A\rfloor$ is admittance matrix. Entries for Matrix $\lfloor A\rfloor$ is derived as follows:

$$[A] = \begin{cases} 1\ if\ i = j \\ 1\ if\ i\ and\ j\ are\ connected \\ 0\ if\ otherwise \end{cases} \qquad (2)$$

In equation (1), $f(x)$ is the vector function that gives the optimal number of PMU's to be used. $\lfloor X\rfloor$ is defined as a binary decision variable vector where $\lfloor X\rfloor = \lfloor x_1 x_2 x_3 x_4 \ldots xn\rfloor\ T$

$$xi = \begin{cases} 1\ if\ PMU\ is\ installed\ at\ bus\ i \\ 0\ otherwise \end{cases} \qquad (3)$$

$\lfloor b\rfloor$ is a column vector where Matrix $\lfloor b\rfloor = \lfloor 1\ 1\ 1\ 1 \ldots 1\ \rfloor^T 1 * N$

Using the admittance matrix, the optimal placement of PMU is derived. The procedure followed for calculating the bus admittance matrix is such that, the bus that has a PMU installed provides voltage and current phasor of all the buses that are connected to it using Ohm's law. Zero injection bus (ZIB) are those buses that do not have any generation or load across it. When PMU is incident to an observable ZIB, all buses are observable. Then, an unobservable system is identified by applying Kirchhoff's Current Law (KCL) at the ZIB. When PMU is placed for an unobservable ZIB, the ZIB will be identified as observable by applying the node equation. The procedure of developing the constraint functions are carried out for two possible cases in the power system network are:

1. A System with no Conventional Measurements

In this case, the ZIB buses are ignored by the test system. Initially for obtaining the constraint set of the system network the bus admittance matrix A is formed such that entries in the admittance matrix are in the form of binary form as mentioned in equation 1 and 2.

2. System with Zero Injection Bus

Zero Injection Bus (ZIB) doesn't have any generation or load unit. For ZIB in a power system network, the current phasor of all the buses can be obtained using Kirchhoff's Current Law. This reduces the number of PMUs in every case. The ZIB method is mostly used for the distribution system where voltage injection is done to the grid. Hence, a Power System Network which has Zero Injection Bus reduces the complexity in designing the admittance matrix and also reduces the number of PMUs to be placed.

A case study is performed for obtaining the optimal location of PMU for an IEEE 5 Bus System.

3. Dynamic Voltage Restorer

DVR is a compensation device used for compensating voltage sag for sensitive load where the demand for voltage is high [11]. The location of DVR is near to the load as shown in Fig.1. The components of DVR are Direct Current (DC) voltage Source, Voltage Source Inverter (VSI), DVR Control Unit, Injection Transformer, and Filters. The Control Unit of DVR detects the voltage sag and injects the difference in voltage using VSI and Injection Transformer. DVR remains in standby mode when no voltage sag is detected and is in active mode after the detection of voltage sag. The control of DVR is shown in Fig.2. The three-phase voltage of the transmission line Vsa, Vsb, and Vsc are compared continuously with a three-phase reference voltage Vra, Vrb, and Vrc to detect the voltage sag condition [11]. The Phase-Locked Loop (PLL) method is implemented to calculate phase angle, frequency, and amplitude of voltage using the Synchronous Reference Frame (SRF) theory. The advantage of using SRF theory is that it is easy to detect voltage sag of a dynamic system in a rotating reference frame and easy to implement and control reactive power flow. After detecting the voltage sag in the rotating reference frame, it is converted to the a-b-c reference frame to calculate the voltage sag.

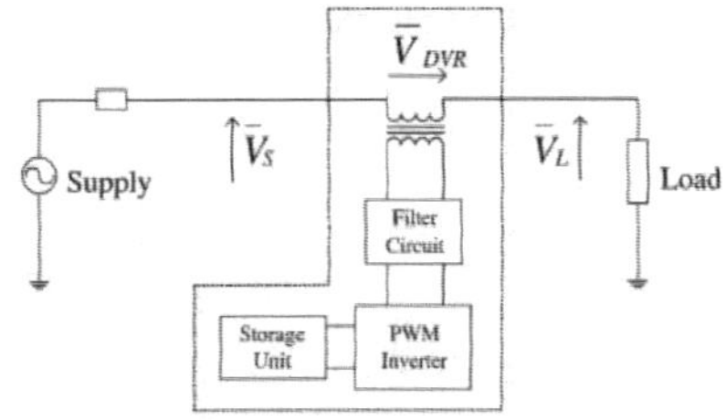

Fig.1. Block Diagram of DVR

The detected sag voltage in the a-b-c reference frame is used to generate the pulses for VSI. VSI is

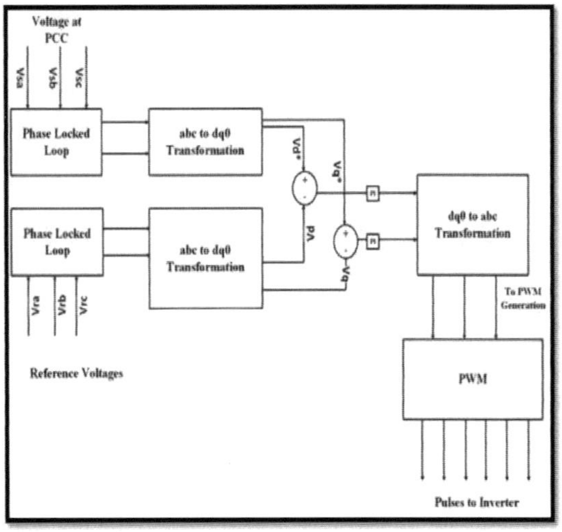

Fig.2 Control System of DVR

driven using the Sinusoidal Pulse Width Modulation technique where the pulses are generated by comparing the voltage sag sine wave with the high switching frequency wave [12]-[13]. The produced voltage is filtered out using an LC filter eliminating the harmonics and providing a smooth sinusoidal waveform. The produced difference in voltage is injected into the transmission line using injection transformers.

4. Monitoring using PMU and compensation using DVR

The case study is performed in MATLAB/Simulink for three cases.

Case1: Optimal Placement of PMU using Integer Programming based Method
Case2: Monitoring of entire IEEE 5 BUS System using PMU
Case3: Monitoring, controlling, and compensating voltage sag using PMU and DVR for one load.

Case1: The optimal placement of PMU is tested in an IEEE 5 Bus System as shown in Fig3. The Standard IEEE 5 Bus System is as follows:

1. The total number of buses are 5.
2. Two three-phase voltage sources DG1 and DG2 are placed at BUS1 and BUS2 that supply power to four loads placed at BUS2, BUS3, BUS4, and BUS5 respectively. The load at BUS5 is sensitive as mentioned in the Appendix.
3. DG1 and DG2 form a distribution network of 7.9kV which is supplying power to four identical types of load forms a ring distribution network as mentioned in the Appendix.
4. There are seven transmission lines and they are interconnected to the buses as Line 1-2, Line 2-3, Line 2-4, Line 2-5, Line 4-5, Line 3-4, and Line 1-3.

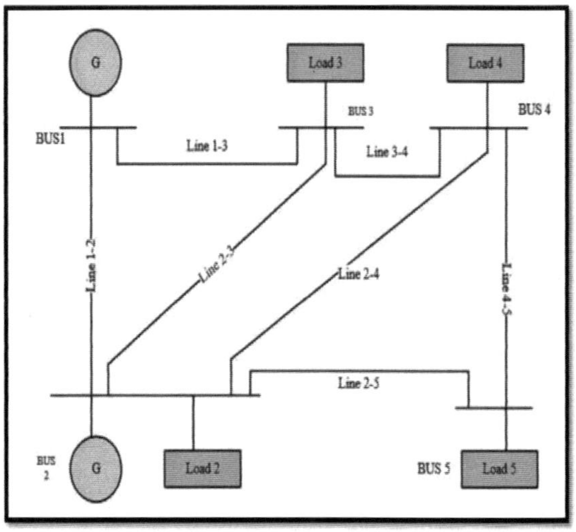

Fig.3 IEEE 5 BUS System

The Optimal Placement problem of PMU for the IEEE 5 Bus system is resolved using Integer Programming based Method.

At BUS1 if a voltage measurement block is placed, it will observe the voltage and current measurements radially of BUS 2 and BUS 3. So, if PMU is placed at BUS1 it provides the state estimation of BUS1, BUS2, and BUS3.

Similarly, if a Voltage measurement block is placed at BUS 3, it will observe the voltage and current ratings of BUS 1, BUS 2, BUS 3 and BUS 4

As mentioned in equation (1), (2) and (3), The Bus Admittance Matrix A for IEEE 5 Bus System is written as

$$A = \begin{pmatrix} 1 & 1 & 1 & 0 & 0 \\ 1 & 1 & 1 & 1 & 1 \\ 1 & 1 & 1 & 1 & 0 \\ 0 & 1 & 1 & 1 & 1 \\ 0 & 1 & 0 & 1 & 1 \end{pmatrix} \tag{4}$$

The constraints for the above case are formed as,

$$\begin{cases} f1 = x1 + x2 + x3 & \geq 1 \\ f2 \ = x1 + x2 + x3 + x4 + x5 & \geq 1 \\ f3 = x1 + x2 + x3 + x4 & \geq 1 \\ f4 = x2 + x3 + x4 + x5 & \geq 1 \\ f5 = x2 + x4 + x5 & \geq 1 \end{cases} \tag{5}$$

The operator '+' is the logical OR Operator the use of 1 on the right-hand side of the inequality ensures that at least one of the variables appearing in the sum will be non-zero. The first constraint $f1 \geq 1$ implies that one PMU must be placed at either of the buses 1,2 and 3 to make bus 1 observable. Similarly, for the second constraint $f2 \geq 1$ implies that PMU must be placed either of the buses 1,2,3,4 and 5 to make bus 2 observable. The IEEE 5 Bus System is shown in Fig.3

The Optimization of selecting the Placement of PMU is done such that, from the admittance matrix, the BUS which contains more number of binary 1s in its row is selected as an optimal placement where the system is completely observable. Hence for a Standard IEEE 5

Bus system single, PMU is placed at BUS 2(as observed from the matrix). The solution for IEEE 5 Bus system is tabulated in Table 1,

Table1 Solution for Optimal Placement Problem

System	No. of Branches	No. of PMU's	Location of PMU's
IEEE 5 BUS	7	1	Bus 2

Case2: Monitoring of entire IEEE 5 BUS System using PMU

The objective of the case study is to monitor the IEEE 5 BUS System from an optimized location of PMU. The data collected are used for:

1. Voltage sag compensation of sensitive load at BUS 5 using DVR.
2. Protection of BUS 4 from transmission line fault using PMU based impedance relay.

Observation of Case2:

The IEEE 5 BUS designed in MATLAB/Simulink is implemented as shown in Fig3. During normal conditions, the PMU at BUS 2 shows the voltage ratings as 7.07kV and current rating as 0.27A. The waveforms are shown in Fig.4 and Fig.5

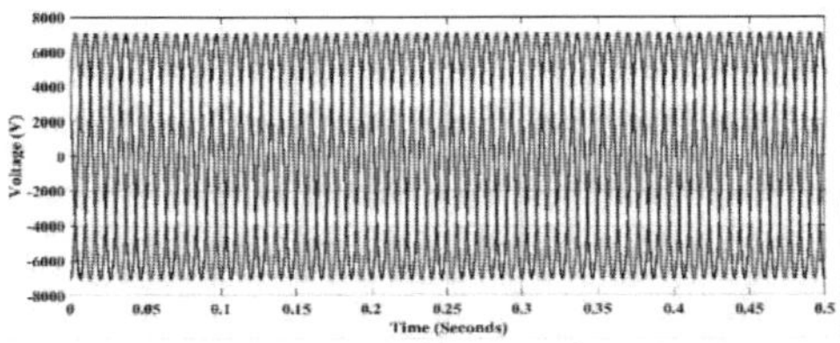

Fig.4 Voltage reading recorded by PMU from BUS2

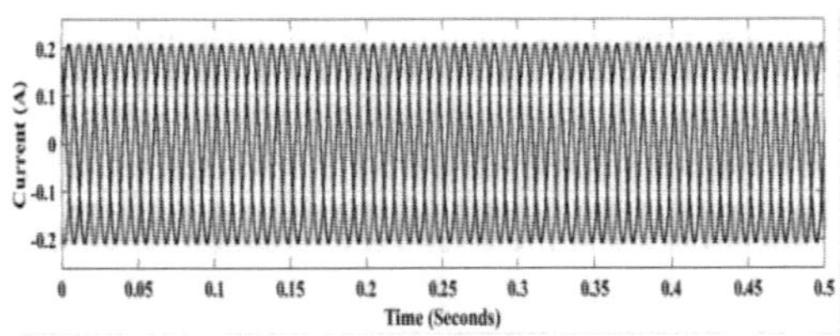

Fig.5 Current reading recorded by PMU from BUS2

The Positive sequence voltage recorded by PMU at BUS2 during normal condition was observed to be 7.07kV as shown in Fig. 6.

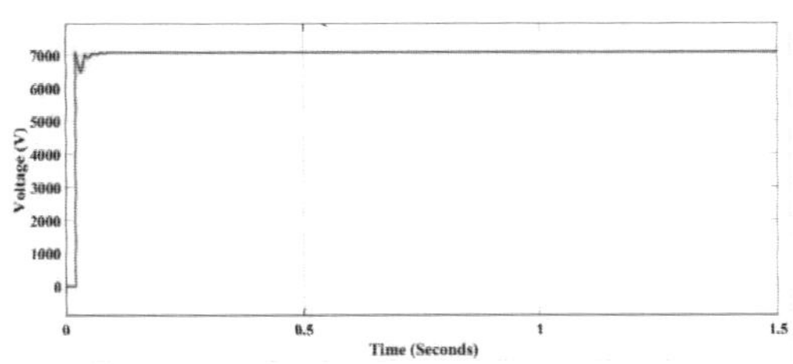

Fig.6 Positive Sequence voltage recorded by PMU from bus2

The Positive Sequence current observed by PMU at Bus 2 during normal condition is 0.2A as shown in Fig.7.

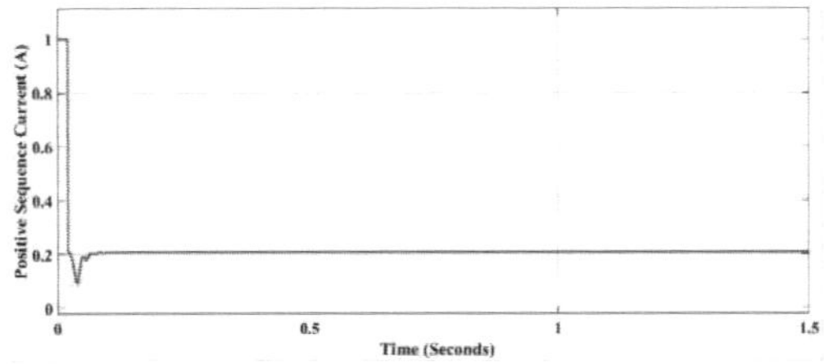

Fig.7 Positive Sequence current recorded by PMU from bus2

The impedance reading of PMU observed is 33460 ohms. The waveform is shown in Fig.8.

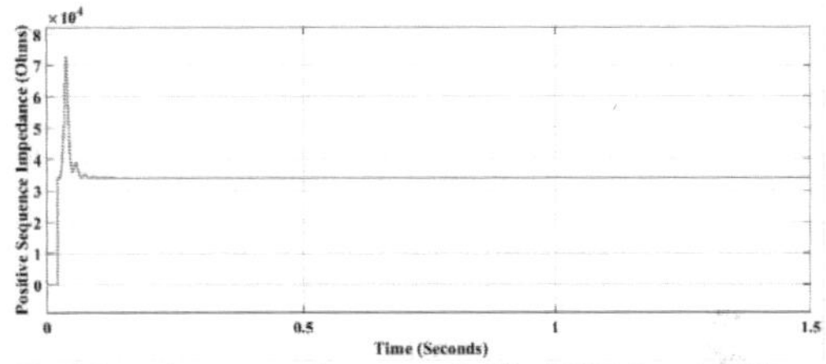

Fig.8 Impedance waveform recorded by PMU from BUS2

Case3 (a): In case3 (a), transmission line fault detection using optimized PMU location for an IEEE 5 BUS System was simulated in MATLAB/Simulink as shown in Fig 9.

In this case study for an IEEE 5 BUS system, a three-phase fault is generated at every transmission line for a specific time and the system is observed. The voltage and current readings recorded by PMU from BUS 2 are tabulated in Table 2.

Table 2 Reading recorded by PMU during faults from BUS2

Transmission Line Number	Fault Time	Voltage Readings (V)	Current Readings (A)
Line 1-2	0.1 to 0.2 sec	V1=1.9 V2=1.8 V3=-1.7	I1=828A I2=796A I3=792A
Line 1-3	0.3 to 0.4sec	V1=6.2kV V2=6.2kV V3=6.2kV	I1=52A I2=52A I3=52A
Line 2-3	0.5 to 0.6 sec	V1=6.2kV V2=6.2kV V3=6.2kV	I1=52A I2=52A I3=52A
Line 2-4	0.7 to 0.8 sec	V1=6.15kV V2=6.15kV V3=6.15kV	I1=60A I2=60A I3=60A
Line 2-5	0.9 to 1 sec	V1=1.8V V2=1.8V V3=1.7V	I1=314A I2=314A I3=314A
Line 3-4	1.1 to 1.2 sec	V1=6.2kV V2=6.2kV V3=6.2kV	I1=52A I2=52A I3=52A
Line 4-5	1.3 to 1.4 sec	V1=6.15kV V2=6.15kV V3=6.15kV	I1=60A I2=60A I3=60A

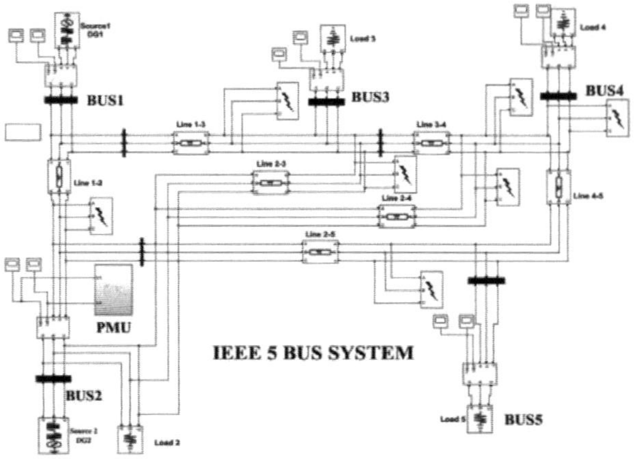

Fig.9 Transmission line fault detection using PMU

As mentioned in Table 2, PMU detects a fall in voltage ratings during the fault generated time at every transmission line. The entire system is observable with a single PMU placed at BUS 2 and the voltage waveform observed from the optimal location is shown in Fig.10.

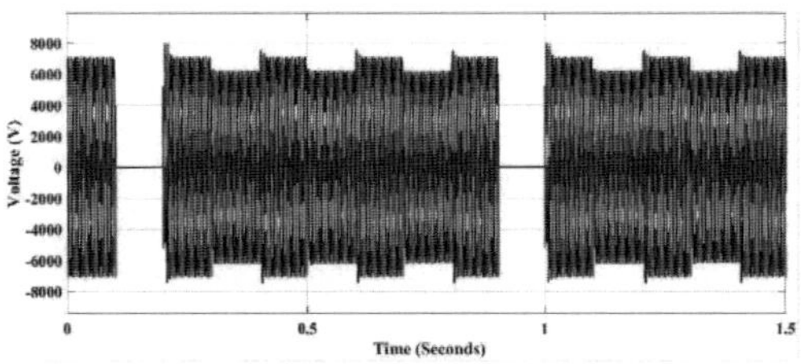

Fig.10 Voltage waveform recorded by PMU from BUS2

PMU detects the rise in current ratings from a nominal range of 0.2A whenever a fault is generated which is shown in Fig 11.

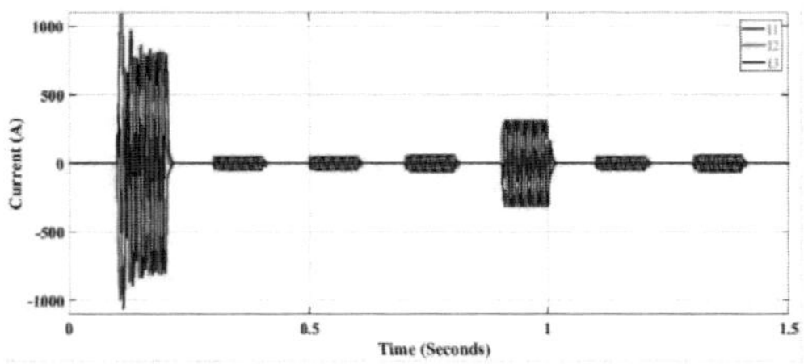

Fig.11 Current waveform recorded by PMU from Bus2

Positive sequence voltage, positive sequence current, and impedance readings recorded by PMU during fault conditions are tabulated in Table 3.

The Circuit breaker is placed on transmission line 3-4 for protection of Load at BUS4. The logic operation of the circuit breaker is designed in such a manner that whenever the impedance value goes below 2000 Ω PMU senses the fault and the impedance relay gives the trip signal command to the circuit breaker. The load connected to the faulty transmission line is isolated after detecting thc fault.

Case 3(b): Monitoring, Controlling and voltage sag compensation of a sensitive load in an IEEE 5 BUS System

For an IEEE 5 BUS System, the three-phase fault is generated at bus 4 on transmission lines 3-4 for a period of 0.3 seconds from 0.3 to 0.6 seconds causing voltage sag at Bus 5. The objective of this case study is to isolate the Bus 4 during fault conditions by sensing the fault conditions and simultaneously compensating voltage sag at BUS 5 using DVR.

Table 3 Sequence Voltage, Current Readings, and Impedance recorded by PMU

Transmission Line Number	Fault Time	Positive Sequence Voltage Readings (V)	Positive Sequence Current Readings (A)	Impedance
Line 1-2	0.1to 0.2 sec	1.7 V	828A	0.002
Line 1-3	0.3 to 0.4sec	6.2kV	52A	117
Line 2-3	0.5 to 0.6 sec	6.2kV	52A	117
Line 2-4	0.7 to 0.8 sec	6.15kV	60A	101
Line 2-5	0.9 to 1 sec	1.7V	314A	0.005
Line 3-4	1.1 to 1.2 sec	6.2kV	52A	117
Line 4-5	1.3 to 1.4 sec	6.15kV	60A	101

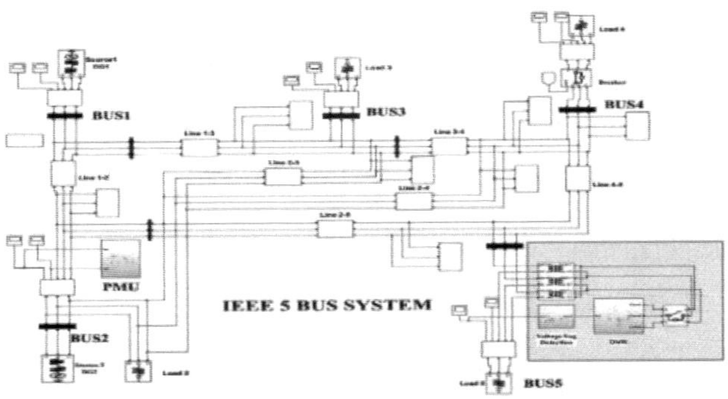

Fig12 IEEE 5 Bus System in MATLAB/Simulink

DVR is connected between BUS 4 and BUS 5. Since a three-phase fault is generated on transmission lines 3-4 which leads to voltage sag condition at BUS 5 which is a sensitive load. The block diagram of the above case study is shown in Fig. 12.

Table 4 DVR Parameters for case study 4

Block	Parameters
DC-Link Voltage	5070V
Fault Time	0.3 to 0.6 Sec
Injection Transformer ratio	1:1
PWM Inverter (SPWM)	6 Pulses 2kHz
Controller	Vector Control
Fault Location	BUS 4 Transmission line 3-4
DVR Location	At BUS 5

During the normal condition, the voltage rating is 7.07kV, and the current is 0.2A. During fault time, the PMU records drop in voltage as 6.2kV and increase in current as 60A which are the positive sequence voltage and positive sequence current. The voltage observed at Bus 2 by PMU is 6.2 kV is shown in Fig.13.

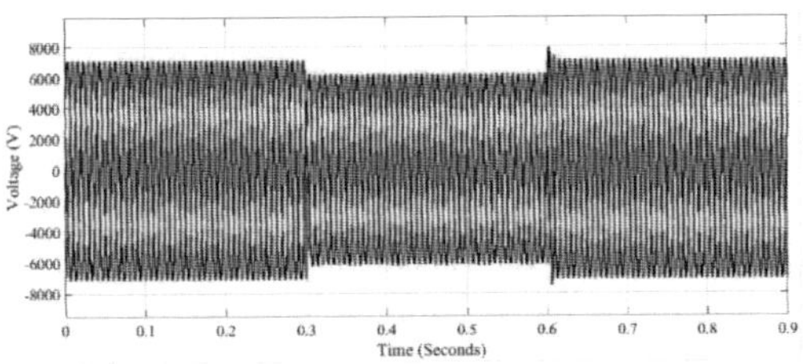

Fig.13 Voltage reading observed during fault conditions

The expanded waveform of voltage rating is shown in Fig 14.

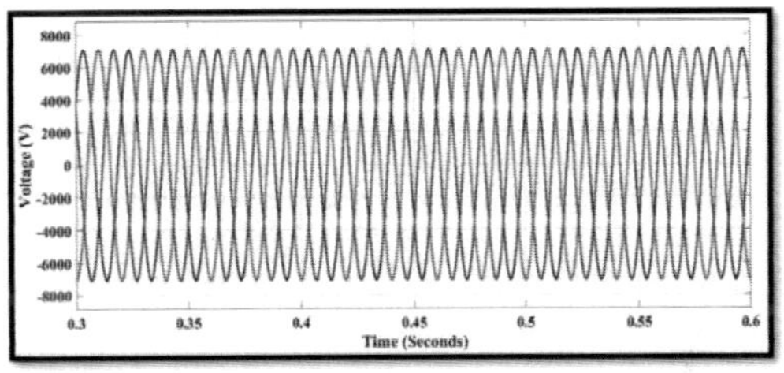

Fig14 Expanded Voltage Waveform

The current observed form Bus 2 by PMU is 60 A as shown in Fig15.

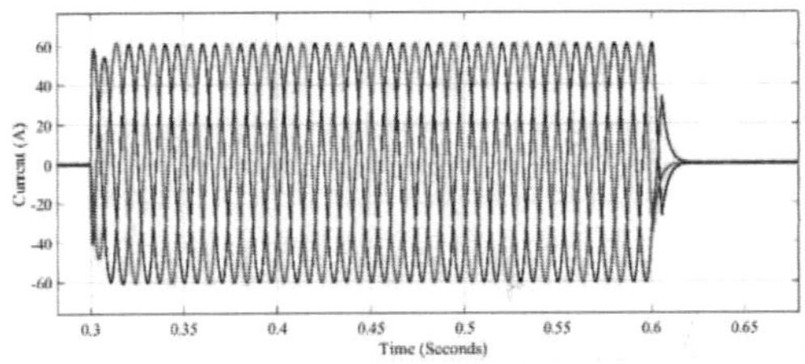

Fig.15 Current reading observed during the fault condition

The Positive Sequence Impedance during normal conditions is 33460 Ω which falls to 100 Ω during fault time.

For BUS 4, The Impedance relay is designed such that whenever the impedance falls below 33000 Ω the breaker trips. For safer limits, the value is considered as 20000 Ω where a trip signal is generated by PMU for the tripping of the circuit breaker.

The Circuit breaker at BUS 4 trips at 0.3 seconds isolating the load at BUS 5. The Current waveform of BUS 4 is shown in Fig.16.

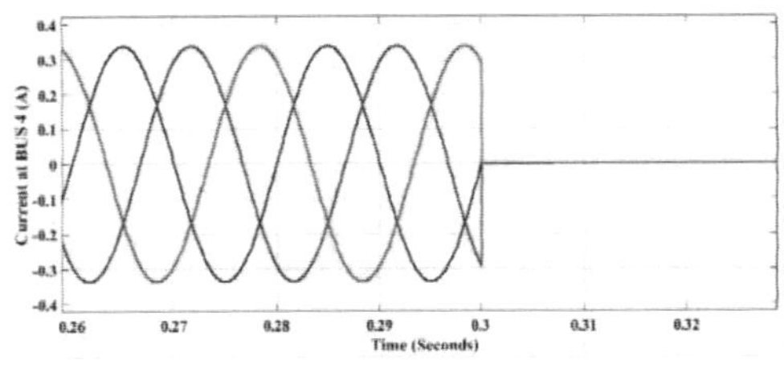

Fig.16 Breaker trips at BUS4

The Voltage Sag Compensation of Load 5 placed at BUS 5 is such that, during normal condition the voltage is 7.07kV and during fault for a period 0.3 to 0.6 sec it goes down to 4.11kV. as shown in Fig. 17.

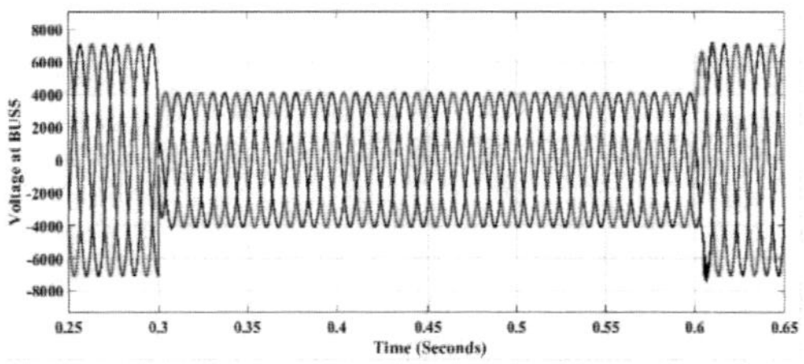

Fig.17 Voltage sag detected at BUS5

The DVR injects the difference of 2.96kV voltage into the system using Injection transformer. The Voltage at BUS5 after injection of Voltage into the system is shown in Fig.18.

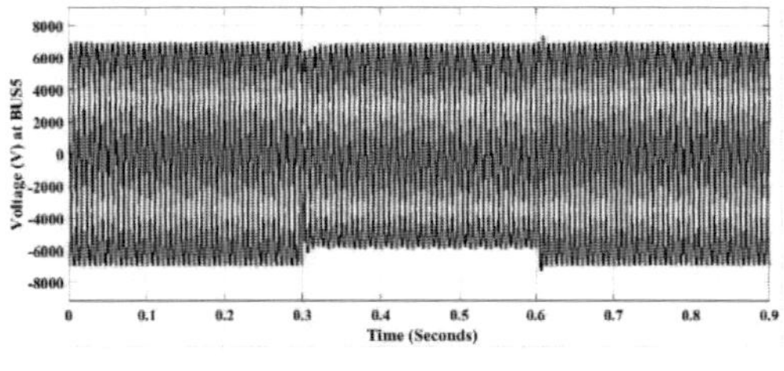

Fig.18 Voltage Sag compensated at BUS5

The faulty transmission line 3-4 is isolated at 0.3 secs, DVR compensates the voltage sag observed at load 5 due to fault at transmission line 3-4 between 0.3 to 0.6 seconds as shown in Fig 18.

5. Conclusion

PMU is used as a monitoring and controlling device for the detection of faults and protection. The above work has been carried out by considering the optimal location of PMU for an IEEE 5 BUS System. By using Integer Programming based Method the optimal location for placing PMU was obtained to be BUS 2. Several case studies have been discussed in this paper to show that a single PMU can monitor the whole system efficiently. Results have been recorded for monitoring and controlling the full system when a three-phase fault occurs, From the results, it is observed that data from a single PMU at BUS 2 is sufficient to monitor, protect and also compensate the voltage sag for a sensitive load. The MOSFET-based FACTS device (DVR) was implemented for voltage sag compensation using the data collected through PMU's. The case study performed shows that PMU in conjunction with DVR was found to be simple and easy to detect the voltage sag. It can be concluded that a power system network can be monitored, controlled, and protected using less number of PMU's. Various voltage sag compensation techniques can be implemented using PMU data for improving reliability.

6. References

[1] K. G. Nagananda, S. Kishore and R. S. Blum,("A PMU Scheduling Scheme for Transmission of Synchrophasor Data in Electric Power Systems," in *IEEE Transactions on Smart Grid*, vol. **6**, no. 5, pp. 2519-2528, Sept. 2015)

[2] G. A. Ortiz, D. G. Colomé and J. J. Q. Puma, ("State estimation of power system based on SCADA and PMU measurements," *2016 IEEE ANDESCON*, Arequipa, 2016, pp. 1-4).

[3] T. J. Overbye and J. D. Weber, ("The smart grid and PMUs: Operational challenges and opportunities," *IEEE PES General Meeting*, Providence, RI, 2010, pp. 1-5).

[4] A. V. Ital and S. A. Borakhade, ("Compensation of voltage sags and swells by using Dynamic Voltage Restorer (DVR), "*2016 International Conference on Electrical, Electronics, and Optimization Techniques (ICEEOT)*, Chennai, 2016, pp. 1515-1519)

[5] J. Kohila, S. Kannan, and V. S. Kumar, ("Control of dynamic voltage restorer for injecting active power using synchronous reference frame theory," *2015 International Conference on Circuits, Power and Computing Technologies [ICCPCT-2015]*, Nagercoil, 2015, pp. 1-6).

[6] K. S. Varaprasad, ("Comparison and Analysis on the Role of DSTATCOM and DVR with PI Controller to improve the Power Quality in Distributed Networks", *International Research Journal of Computer Science (IRJCS)*, Vol. **1** Issue **2**, October 2014).

[7] B. D. Biswal, J. K. Dash and P. K. Satpathy, ("A PMU based adaptive compensation for a transmission line using FC-TCR," *2016 International Conference on Energy Efficient Technologies for Sustainability (ICEETS)*, Nagercoil, 2016, pp. 947-951)

[8] Mohd Tauseef Khan, Anwar Shahzad Siddiqui, ("FACTS devices control strategy using PMU," *Perspective in Science,* Volume 8, pp 730-732, September 2016)

[9] H. D. Lashkari and J. B. Sarvaiya, ("Matlab based Simulink Model of Phasor Measurement Unit and Optimal Placement Strategy for PMU Placement," *International Journal for Scientific Research and Development*, vol. **2**, no. **03**, pp. 135–138, 2014).

[10] E. Khorram and M. Taleshian Jelodar, ("PMU placement considering various arrangements of lines connections at complex buses," *International Journal for Electrical and Power Energy Systems*, vol. **94**, pp. 97–103, 2018).

[11] Yash Pal, A. Swarup, Senior Member, IEEE, and Bhim Singh, Senior Member, IEEE ("A Review of Compensating Type Custom Power Devices for PowerQuality Improvement" *IEEE Power India Conference*, pp. 1-8, 2008).

[12] F. B. Ajaei, S. Afsharnia, A. Kahrobaeian, and S. Farhangi ("A fast and effective control scheme for

the dynamic voltage restorer", IEEE *Transactions on power delivery*, vol. **26**, no.**4**, pp.2398-2406, 2011).

[13] S. R. Reddy, P. V. Prasad, and G. N. Srinivas, ("Performance comparison of DVR by various compensation methods," *2014 6th IEEE Power India International Conference (PIICON)*, Delhi, 2014, pp. 1-6).

Appendix

Abbreviation

MOSFET: Metal Oxide Semi-Conductor Field Effect Transistor

IEEE 5 BUS System Parameter

The sensitive load is placed at BUS 5. The Parameters of Load and Three-phase source used in IEEE 5 Bus System is mentioned in Table 1

Table 1 Parameters in IEEE 5 BUS System

Bus Code	Assumed Bus Voltage	Generation		Load	
		Watts	vars	Watts	vars
1	5 kV	$3.9*10^3$	0	0	0
2	5 kV	$9.65*10^2$	0	0	0
3	0	0	0	$1.54*10^3$	0
4	0	0	0	$1.5*10^3$	0
5	0	0	0	$-1.5*10^3$	0

The Bus type, Initial Voltage, and angle of IEEE 5 BUS Network is shown in Table 2

Table 2 Bus Type. Initial Voltage of IEEE 5 BUS System

BUS No	1	2	3	4	5
BUS Type	PV	PV	Constant Z	Constant Z	Constant Z
Initial Voltage (Per Unit)	1	1	1	1	1
Initial Voltage Angle	0	0	0	0	0

Transmission Line Parameter is tabulated in Table 3 and Table 4

Table 3 Transmission Line Parameter of IEEE 5 BUS System per unit value

From BUS	To BUS	Transmission Line resistance	Transmission Line Reactance	Transmission line Conductance	Transmission Line Susceptance
1	2	0.02	0.06	0	0.06
1	3	0.08	0.24	0	0.05
2	3	0.06	0.18	0	0.04
2	4	0.06	0.18	0	0.04
2	5	0.04	0.12	0	0.03
3	4	0.01	0.03	0	0.02
4	5	0.08	0.24	0	0.05

Table 4 Length of Transmission Line

BUS	Length Of transmission Line
1-2	47
1-3	87
2-3	67
2-4	67
2-5	47
3-4	19
4-5	87

Hindi Language Interface to Database

Rachana Dubey[1,*], *Tejal Kawale*[2,**], *Twisha Choudhary*[3,***] and *Dr. Vaibhav Narawade*[4,****]

[1]Ramrao Adik Institute of Technology, Computer Department, Navi Mumbai, India
[2]Ramrao Adik Institute of Technology, Computer Department, Navi Mumbai, India
[3]Ramrao Adik Institute of Technology, Computer Department, Navi Mumbai, India
[4]Ramrao Adik Institute of Technology, Computer Department, Navi Mumbai, India

Abstract. In our everyday lives we require information to accomplish daily tasks. Database is one of the most important sources of information. Database systems have been widely used in data storage and retrieval. However, to extract information from databases, we need to have some knowledge of database languages like SQL. But SQL has predefined structures and format, so it is hard for the non-expert users to formulate the desired query. To override this complexity, we have turned to natural language to retrieve information from database, which can be an ideal channel between a non-technical user and the application. But the application cannot understand natural language so an interface is required. This interface is capable of converting the user's natural language query to an equivalent database language query. In this paper, we address the system architecture for translating a Hindi sentence in the form of an audio to an equivalent SQL query. The users don't need to learn any formal query language; hence it's easy to use for common people.

1. Introduction

Data is any form of information that is present in the computer memory. Database is one of the major sources of data. It is an organized collection of various types of information. In other words, database is a system that allows storage, easy access, manipulation and updating of data. We require databases for many reasons such as to manage large chunks of data, to secure the data, to maintain the accuracy and integrity of data. Mostly, a database is composed of tables containing rows and columns like a spreadsheet. Some of the famous database platforms to host or create databases are MySQL and SQLite. A database management system is interacting with the users and the database to analyze data. It is a software used to store and retrieve users' data. Users can create their own databases as per their needs using database management system. They can also perform various operations, such as adding, accessing, updating and deleting a record or the entire data. The system serves as a foundation for a database, related operations and makes it much easier to use a database and manage the data.

2. Literature Survey

Information storage in today's world is vastly dependent on relational databases. These databases offer the foundations for the systems like medical records, money markets, and electronic commerce. Using relational databases, a user can use a declarative language or Wh-type questions to describe the intended query.

The main reason behind using Natural Language Processing in any application is to make computer understand the human language either in the form of speech or text and perform the required operation. For beginners and novice who is unaware of the structure of queries and knows very little about the database query languages such as SQL, an easy approach of accessing and manipulating the data is asking questions to databases in natural language. Automatic speech recognition (ASR) [3] is becoming more famous and hence is the reason that is being used widely in many applications. It is the process and related technology used to covert the speech input into its corresponding sequence of words or transcript. The user can ask interact with the database with their voice which

*e-mail: rachanadubey.7@gmail.com
**e-mail: tejalkawale20@gmail.com
***e-mail: tc.twisha@gmail.com
****e-mail: vnarawade@gmail.com

undergoes the stages of refinement and then is passes to retrieve the details from the database. Thus, making it easier for novice user to interact with the system without having prior knowledge about the SQL queries.

Using Stanford Dependency Parser, Wibisono developed a domain-independent NLIDB as a tool in processing user input. Filbert Reinaldha and Tricya E. Widagdo [1] presents a solution to two of Wibisono's NLIDB problems, which are inability to process question-type queries and unit conversion. The major stages in processing the previous two mentioned types included Question Identification, Question Handling which again diverges to Wh-question or Yes-No type question, Tag question. Apart from this, the model also included solution for unit conversion.

Mohit Dua, Sandeep Kumar and Zorawar Singh Virk. in [2] proposed an architecture that converts the CRUD operations from text based natural language to SQL query in Hindi. The system accepts the query in the form of natural language in Hindi text, converts it into SQL query wherein the lexicon is used as a dictionary for conversion of Hindi words to equivalent English words. The system support selection, updating and deletion type of queries.

To ease the user's interaction for generation of SQL queries, Prabhdeep Kaur and Shruthi J in [3] proposed Acoustic and Language models to convert speech utterance to query in English language. The Natural Language Processing techniques were applied on English text to generate SQL query. Lexical analyzer, parser and syntax directed translation techniques were used for translation. To make use of such applications in real life, Abhilasha Kate, Satish Kamble, Aishwarya Bodkhe and Mrunal Joshi [4] proposed a system that could be used by Training and Placement cell officers who handle students' details for the placement purposes. The system proposes an architecture wherein the input can be in the form of either speech or text and after processing, it would generate the SQL query. The applications such as ATIS, Geo, Academic, Spider designs models trained on datasets that can work only for the specific database. [5] WikiSQL, a corpus of 87,000 hand-annotated instances of natural language questions, SQL queries, and SQL tables, is the task of mapping a natural language question to form a SQL query given a table from a Wikipedia article. WikiSQL consists of examples of SQL table, question, and corresponding SQL query hand-annotated by crowd workers on Amazon Mechanical Turk [6]. [7] A large-scale complex and cross-domain semantic parsing and text-to-SQL dataset annotated by 11 Yale students is Spider. The goal of the Spider challenge is to develop natural language interfaces to cross-domain databases [8]. It covers 138 different domains that consists of 10,181 questions and 5,693 unique complex SQL queries on 200 databases with multiple tables. The applications and different approaches towards processing of natural language query to SQL query were studied. LADDER, CHAT-80, NaLIX and WASP are few of the interfaces and systems which are working on NLPs [5,9].

3. Problem Statement

With the data growing exponentially day by day, there is a need to access the data in the efficient way to make the most use out of it. Natural language helps a novice to query the database in the preferred language (here, Hindi), this reduces the time and effort required to query the database such as MySQL since the person does not have to worry about the correct syntax behind a correct SQL query. Thus, we aim at developing an application that would provide a dialogue- based environment for the users to use Hindi language as in voice command to query the required information from the database.

4. Architecture

The user is able to give command Hindi language which would be further processed through speech recognition. The data is extracted from the text and then it undergoes Lexical Analysis, Syntax Analysis and Semantic Analysis. This results in a SQL query which could be further refined (if necessary), the resulting SQL query will be fired on the database and the output will then be displayed to the user.

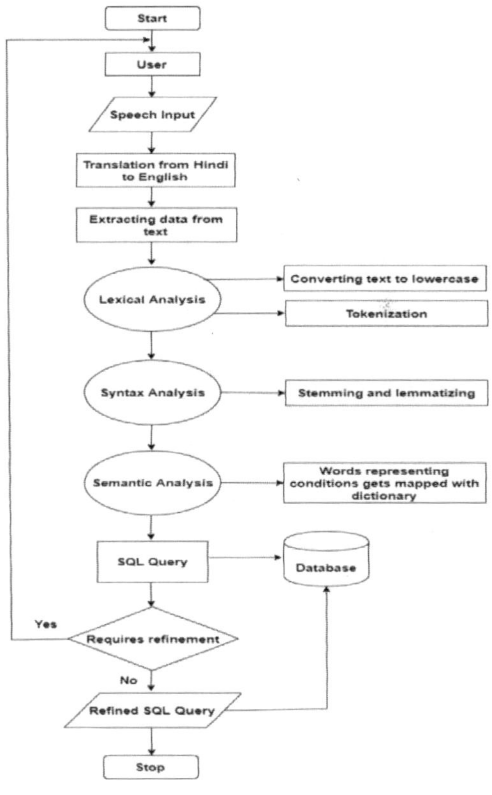

Fig. 1. Architecture of the system

5. Components of HLIDB

5.1. Linguistic Component

The linguistic component of the application handles the speech input by the user in Hindi language. The input could be of declarative type or Wh-type. It would then translate the sentence and form the intermediate SQL query which could be refined (if required) by the user. This component performs morphological analysis and syntax-level analysis to generate the SQL query.

5.2. Database Component

It is responsible to perform traditional database management functions. It executes the query and provides the result of query.

6. Methodology

The proposed method makes use of python language with MySql as a database NLTK (Natural Language Toolkit) library, Speech recognition library, CORE NLP library, PY audio library.

Following are the stages onto which the proposed methodology is based:

i. Natural Language Query

In this step, the user can query the system in Hindi language. The functioning of the system has been explained using an example:

उस विद्यार्थी का नाम और अंक बताइये जिनका अनुक्रमांक १५ है

There could be similar sentences as mentioned above, thus multiple inputs of similar kind would be mapped to the same outputs.

The sentences could be as:

उस विद्यार्थी का नाम और अंक बताइये जिनका अनुक्रमांक १५ है

उस विद्यार्थी का नाम और अंक बताओ जिसका अनुक्रमांक १५ है

उस विद्यार्थी का नाम और अंक दिखाइए जिसका अनुक्रमांक १५ है

उस छात्र का नाम और अंक बताओ जिसका अनुक्रमांक १५ है

ii. Tokenize Query

User provides input to the system in the form of simple sentence in Hindi Language. The system tokenizes that sentence and produce tokens that are to be searched in the system dictionary for mapping. The tokens for the input sentence are as follows:

उस, विद्यार्थी, का, नाम, और, अंक, बताइये, जिनका, अनुक्रमांक, १५, है

iii. Finding English words of Hindi tokens:

Using a system dictionary, the tokens are mapped to their respective English words. It only works on logical word in input sentence. So, we neglect the few words in the query that are present in the system's ignore list. The English words are then generated by the dictionary for input sentence as below:

उस- neglect

विद्यार्थी - Student

का - from

नाम - name

अंक - marks

बताइए - select

जिनका - where

अनुक्रमांक- roll_no

१५ - 15

है – neglect

iv. Map tokens for operations

After finding all the tokens, their corresponding English words are found from the system dictionary which contain the Hindi and English words. All the words of input sentences except proper noun are stored in the dictionary. After finding the English words from the dictionary, input sentence is analysed so that system understands the type of the query entered, i.e., information retrieval, update, insert or delete query.

- If the input sentence contains words like "करो", "कीजिए", "बदलिए", "कर, system interprets it is as "update" and forwards the processed input for the query formulation.
- If the input sentence contains words like "हटाइए", "हटाओ", "रद्द", "निकालये", "निकालो", system interprets it is as "delete" and forwards the processed input for the query formulation.
- If the input sentence contains words like "बताओ", "बताइए", "दिखाइए", "दिखाओ", system interprets it is as "select" and forwards the processed input for the query formulation.

v. Syntactic parsing (Map tokens for table name, columns name, conditions and operators)

The system contains the tables like TABLE-NAME, COLUMN-NAME, CONDITIONS and OPERATORS. TABLE-NAME, COLUMNS-NAME table contains the data required to map table name and column name that are found in Hindi sentence onto their corresponding English words.

vi. Generate SQL Query

After the tokens are mapped, SQL query is generated according to the type of the input Hindi sentence. After that if the input sentence provided by the user contains ambiguity the system will recommend few alternate queries from which the user has to choose one so that he gets the correct information he demanded for. After that, the query is executed on the database. The SQL query generated by this function for input sentence.

Query: Select name, marks from student where roll_no = 15.

vii. Execute the SQL query:

The SQL query is executed on the database. The retrieved data from the database is displayed to the user as the output.

7. Implementation

This application accepts query in Hindi language which is an audio, parses, translates and tokenizes the sentence using GoogleTrans library and maps the Hindi words with their corresponding English words using maintained dictionary. Currently, the system supports single table named as 'Student' with basic attributes. For better accuracy, POS tagging is also applied to the translated sentence. By analyzing the combination of both, the Hindi input sentence and the translated sentence, it is tested the sentence form is of which type. The type could be of selection, insertion, count, conditional selection or deletion and is understood by a set of predefined words. After this, the table names, column names and conditions are searched in the database table's list. The tokens are then mapped with the database values. After mapping an intermediate SQL query is generated. Finally, a SQL query is generated and executed and the result is presented to the user.

8. Results

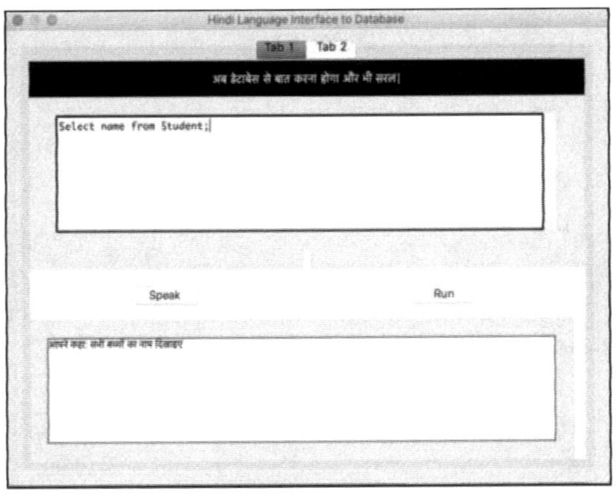

Fig. 2. Select record(s) from the database.

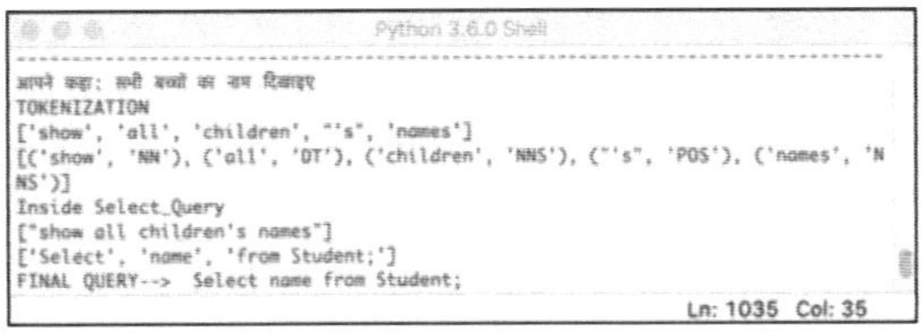

Fig. 3. Pre-processing of data.

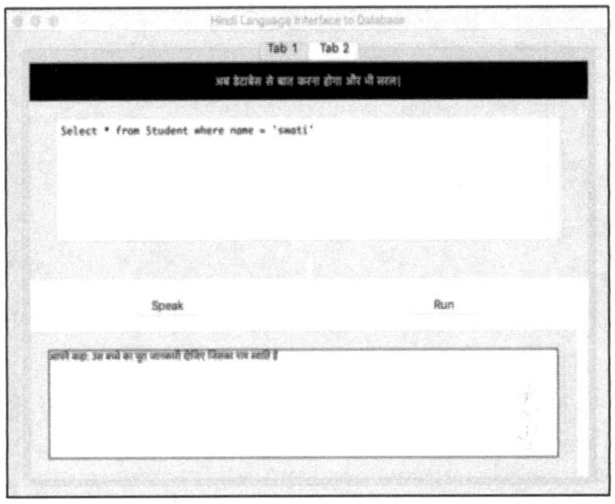

Fig. 4. Query with 'where' clause.

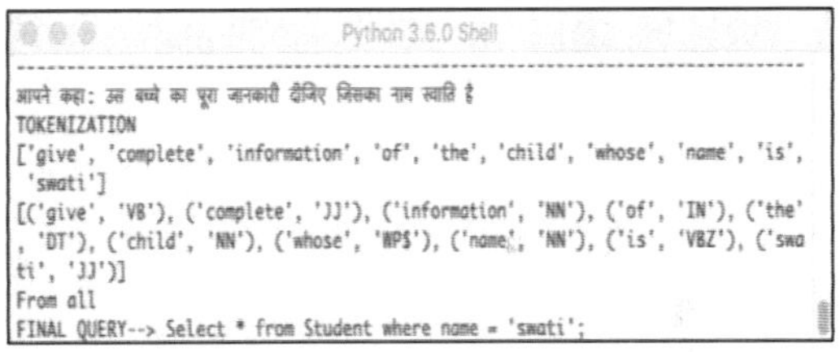

Fig. 5. Query formulation (step by step).

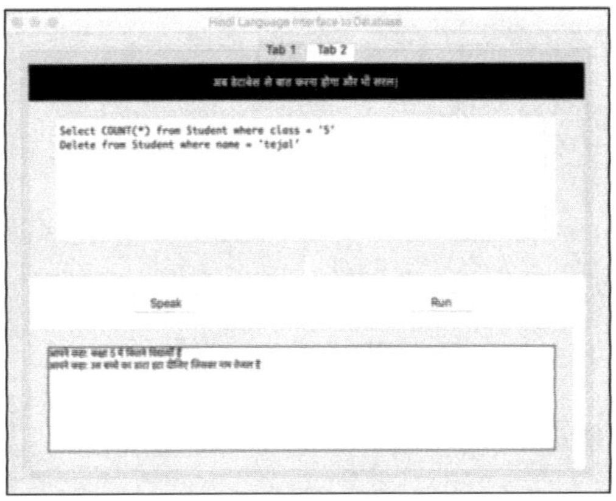

Fig. 6. Count and Delete query

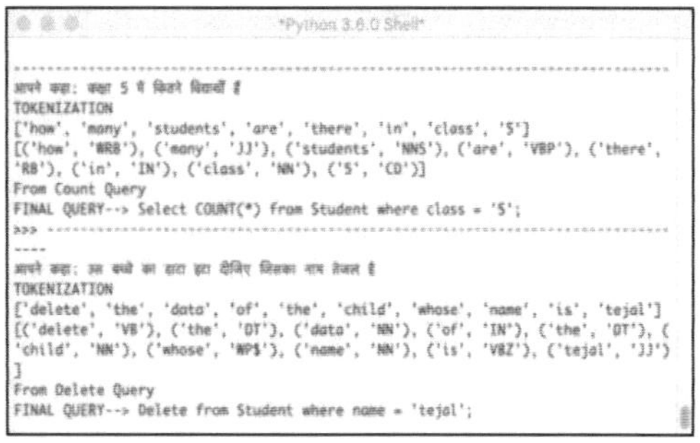

Fig. 7. Query formulation (step by step).

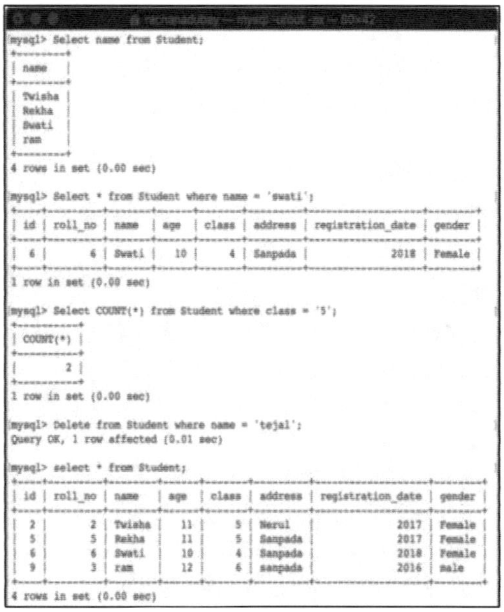

Fig. 8. Results of the final queries.

9. Future Work

We further suggest a framework that could support complex queries like GROUP BY and HAVING which require access to more than one table to get the result. The GROUP BY clause is used to gather rows of similar data into groups. The HAVING clause is used to impose restriction(s) on the results based on certain criteria.

10. Conclusion

Through the discussed methodology we present an approach that would use speech recognition, natural language processing and SQL query generation. The user asks for an operation to be executed on relational databases in natural language which is then processed and converted to the corresponding SQL query and is fired on the database based upon the existing table names and attribute names. To make the system user-friendly and simple enough to understand, interactive environment is created through dialogue-based process.

REFERENCES

[1] Filbert Reinaldha and Tricya E. Widagdo. Natural language interfaces to database (nlidb): question handling and unit conversion. International Conference on Data and Software Engineering (ICODSE) (2014).

[2] Mohit Dua, Sandeep Kumar, and Zorawar Singh Virk. Hindi language graphical user interface to database management system. 12th International Conference on Machine Learning and Applications, IEEE (2013).

[3] Prabhdeep Kaur and Shruthi J. Conversion of natural language query to sql. 12th International Conference on Machine Learning and Applications(2016).

[4] Abhilasha Kate, Satish Kamble, Aishwarya Bodkhe, and Mrunal Joshi. Conversion of natural language query to sql. Second International Conference on Electronics, Communication and Aerospace Technology (ICECA), IEEE (2018).

[5] Victor Zhong. How to talk to your database. https://blog.einstein.ai/how-to-talk-to-your-database.

[6] Abhijeet R. Sontakke and Prof. Amit Pimpalkar. A review paper on hindi language graphical user interface to relational database using nlp. International Journal of Advanced Research in Computer Engineering & Technology (IJARCET), **Volume 3 Issue 10** (2014).

[7] https://yale-lily.github.io/spider

[8] E U Reshma and P C Remya. A review of different approaches in natural languages interfaces to databases. International Conference on Intelligent Systems (ICISS), IEEE (2017).

[9] Tao Yu. Spider: One more step towards natural language interfaces to databases. https://medium.com/@tao.yu/spider-one-more-step-towards-natural-language-interfaces-to-databases-62298dc6df3c (2018).

 https://doi.org/10.1051/itmconf/20203201008

Design and Development of Solar Powered Intelligent Irrigation & Water Management System using Data Science

Atharva Saney; *Ayush* Guha; *Amey* Parulekar & *Sharad* Jadhav

E–mail: atharva.saney1998@gmail.com, ayush.guha23@gmail.com, ameyparulekar123@gmail.com, hodin@rait.ac.in.

Department of Instrumentation Engineering, Ramrao Adik Institute of Technology, Dr. D.Y. Patil Vidyanagar, Nerul, Navi Mumbai, Maharashtra – 400706, India.

Abstract: India is an agricultural country. Agriculture and its allied activities act as main source of livelihood for more than 80 percent population of rural India. Available irrigation systems are not efficient and lead to wastage of water. Literature revels that there is need to develop automated irrigation system with latest technology. In this paper we are proposing a system which will detect the moisture percentage of the respective farmland and compare it with the provided set point. Based on the difference our machine learning algorithms will decide how long the water pump will remain switched on, it will then close the pump after that particular time and give out final moisture percentage reading and final water level of the water storage tank. Also, there will be a website provided which will continuously show current moisture percentage, amount of water present in the tank, how long water in the tank will last, the usage statistics and predict preferred and non- preferred crop to grow in that particular season. Plus a manual override will be provided for all systems.Usage statistics will consist of a graph showing water usage vs day. System display will show amount of water used vs date and below that the median and mode of the outcomes will also be indicated. Proposed in-house designed system has potential to provide the list of preferred and non-preferred crops.

1. Introduction

Water is one of the precious natural resources which is depleting severely in India. The past few decades we have witnessed a significant increase in demand for water across various sectors, thus facing the worst water crisis in history. Intelligent Irrigation System is the systematic approach to conserve existing water resources and efficiently managing them for agricultural usage with the latest technology. Data Science/ Machine Learning is one of such new techniques which can help our country to reduce the overall impact of faulty water management in agricultural sector. Many farms across India and the world still depend on manual gauges and minimal level of automation for executing this process. This leads to inefficiency and wastage. Hence if proper automated machines are implemented with latest technology, we can make amends to all the problems and make sure the deficit is minimum. In this paper, we are proposing to design and develop a prototype of Intelligent Irrigation and Water Management System for agriculture. Machine learning technology plays a vital role in the system. It is a data analytic technique which has different types of algorithms and models to learn information directly from data. For example, it optimizes water usage and provides essential amount of water and fertility to the field and hence improves yield production, reduces manual intervention (man hours), and also suggests or predicts preferred crop based on availability of water and available data. This system will be helpful for farmer to improve the productivity and adapt suitable system according to their requirements.

We are proposing a real time monitoring system for water usage during farming practices. The

https://doi.org/10.1051/itmconf/20203201008

paper consists of two main parts hardware and software. The hardware is a basic implementation of any irrigation practice as it suits the user for eg. Sprinklers or drip irrigation methods. However, the control module used will be a Raspberry Pi based control circuit [6]. In this system the user will be able to monitor the water usage on a daily basis and also the whole system will be automated for the purpose of minimizing errors. The hardware part is basic and easy to understand but the software part is the heart of this system. Data science will be done by Data Analysis practices using Pandas. The website will consist of graphical representation of water usage vs time (days). The prediction of how long water in the tank will last, will be done based on previous data.

The hardware that we are going to use will vary from farm to farm depending upon the area. Thus enabling the scope of this system to higher levels. The machine learning algorithms are of various types; however, in this paper we are mainly going to focus on Supervised Learning and Associative Learning to get the desired outputs [3]. In Supervised Learning we are going to work with Linear Regression mainly and in some cases where the input/output curve may not be a straight line then we are going to choose Stochastic Gradient Descent (SGD) which is used for nonlinear parameters. Finally, in order to verify the output of the system to be genuine, we will be plotting a graph of usage vs day for the amount of water, using Matplotlib function in python. We can plot a graph with any desired input-outputs. We are also going to use Associative Learning to develop similarities between parameters of the system and we will be able to train it to provide the maximum duration, water inside the tank will last considering the use of water in the farm.

We cannot ignore the fact that farmers are the backbone of this country, so it is our duty to not only be grateful to them but also be able to share their load in any way possible. So we have decided to create a low budget system so that even farmers with low financial resourced could afford this system. There are regions in our country where water abundance is a major issue, as a measure to conserve water this system can be handy as it only uses the amount that is required. In our paper we are trying to create a solar powered electronic system which can be used for smart irrigation. Our main goal is to make this system user friendly so that even a non-technical person can operate it with ease. Easy use of website can help people understand its working without understanding the science behind it.

The rest of the paper is organized as follows: in the next section the block diagram and description of complete system is explained. Then we will look at the design and development section which further elucidates the working of the model for both hardware and software aspects after assembly. Here we will also learn in detail the learning process of machine learning in the system. Following this we will study the implementation of the model which provides insight on practical application on the system on a pre-decided test crop and the use case for this proposed system. The last section presents conclusion and the future scope for further advancements in the model.

2. Proposed system's block diagram & description

Fig 2.1 shows the entire block diagram for the system which consists of the following:

- **Raspberry Pi**: it is a credit card sized minicomputer which can be used for many small computing tasks and IoT's (Internet of Things).
- **FC28 moisture sensor**; which is an easy to use digital soil moisture sensor. It has two electrodes and the amount of current passing through them is proportional to the amount of moisture in the soil. Now since Raspberry Pi only has digital pins and we need an output in analog, we are using an ADC (Analog to Digital Convertor).

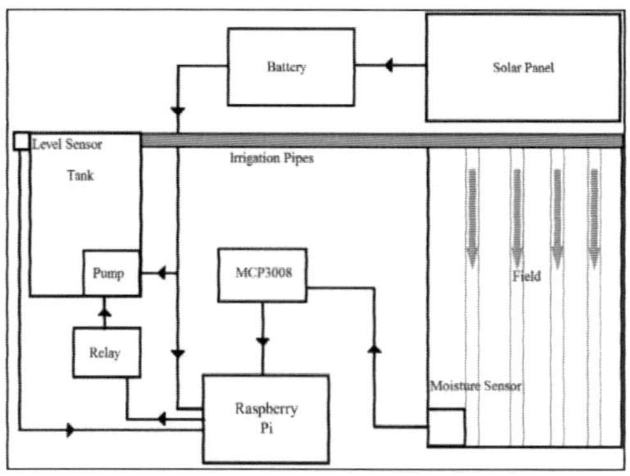

Fig 2.1: Proposed System's Block Diagram

- **A pump motor:** It will be used to move water from storage tank to field. Although

 https://doi.org/10.1051/itmconf/20203201008

since Raspberry Pi cannot sustain enough power required for the pump to function, a **Relay module** will be used and an external battery connected to the solar panel will be used. Generally for Drip irrigation a 0.5 kW, 2-5 HP, 3-phase induction motor is used which gives a flow rate of about 100-500 LPM.

- **Ultrasonic sensors:** They will be used for measuring the level of water in the tank. Since different tanks will be of different sizes and shapes proper calibration will be done.
- **A Battery:** Specification of battery will depend on the field into consideration. Although, a 1800 W battery is generally preferred for large scale applications.
- **Solar panels**: They will be our primary source of energy. We will be using 4 panels of 250W each [1]. In normal conditions, minimum to no external supply will be needed as this assembly can charge a 1800 W battery (preferable) in about 2-3 hours.
- **MCP3008:** This is an Analog to Digital Convertor used in the system because Raspberry pi only has digital pins but we need the output from moisture sensor to be analog.

3. Design and development

The whole system has been divided into three essential parts such as:

(a) Moisture calibration and analysis.

(b) Prediction of how long water in tank will last, usage statistics and preferred crop prediction on the given Website (using Machine Learning).

(c) Storage of data on firebase for back end purposes.

3.1 Hardware working

Fig. 3.1 shows the proposed design of the entire system. The pump connected to Raspberry Pi 3 is the output of this system. Raspberry Pi is the CPU for the system [6].

Moisture sensors will be placed in the field to sense moisture content present in the soil [1, 6]. This reading will be processed further by machine learning algorithms. Train test split method will predict the duration of the pump running.

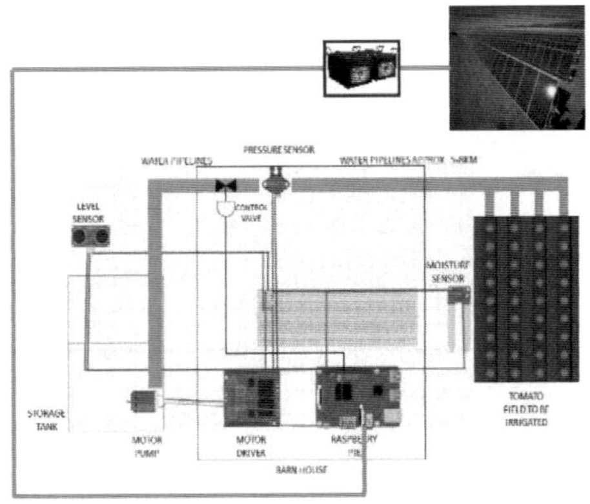

Fig. 3.1: Proposed Design

The Ultrasonic sensor will continuously provide signals in the form of pulses. The amount of water in the tank can be calculated using:

$$D = S * T \quad \ldots (1)$$

Where,

S = speed of ultrasonic waves in air

D = distance travelled by ultrasonic waves

T = time take by ultrasonic waves to reach the receiver

Hence as given in Eqn. (1) by calculating D, we will get the level of water in the tank as ultrasonic waves will be reflected from the surface of water. The level before and after the use of system will be stored and its difference will give the amount of water used in one cycle. The outputs of average moisture and daily water requirements will be stored in a database which will be updated regularly. This database will be used to display a graph using python library matplotlib. It helps in understanding further the use of various hardware with its placement and also the working of system.

3.2 Software working

Supervised and Associative Learning are being used in the system [3]. The pump will be controlled by a relay which will be given some delay by using Linear Regression. We have created a dataset after calculating the flow rate of the pump, thereby collecting the time intervals for particular moisture levels to reach the desired value.

Train_Test_Split is the model from Scikit-Learn library that will be used to train the data. For crop prediction we have decided to use Associative Learning model.

For our prototype we provided the data set given in the Table No. 3.1 below. The set point considered is 80%. The actual values can be calibrated depending on application. Once calibrated, values do not need to be recalibrated.

Fig 3.2 shows the representation of website consisting of 3 pages. On the first page level of water in the tank, current moisture percentage, No. of days water in the tank will last and pressure (if needed) is displayed. Two buttons are also provided on the same page; one for pump manual override and another for usage statistics.

Clicking on usage statistics will redirect user to the 2nd page which is a calendar, and selecting a particular month will redirect user to the 3rd page which consists of the graph mentioned above. Below the graph will be the median and mode values. On scrolling down a list of preferred and non-preferred crop will be given.

3.2.1 Learning process in machine learning

Supervised learning is used in our paper to determine the time for which pump stays on for that particular amount of moisture content [3]. The data set for this purpose is predominantly linear in nature so Linear Regression is being used. The dataset contains set of percentages of moisture level that have been converted using interp function and the time intervals that are provided to the relay. The time interval vs moisture percentage is calibrated manually. For example: if value of moisture is 30% and set point is 70%, the time pump takes to increase moisture level to 70% is recorded and thus added to the dataset against that particular level. The whole dataset consists of percentages from 0-70, divided by an interval of 10. Now the role of linear regression algorithm is to analyse the dataset. Train_Test_Split algorithm will divide the dataset in provided ratio for eg. 80:20. The dataset is split randomly into training (80) and testing (20). Training is when model uses the given data set to get answers, whereas Testing is when model uses the gained knowledge to predict answer. Now when any specific percentage of moisture content is sensed by the sensor and passed to the model to predict the time interval, the algorithm will go through the dataset in the training model and find a correlation between them. This value is compared with testing model and a linear result is provided as output. The linearity of the model can be checked by plotting a graph using matplotlib function.

Associative learning is used to predict preferred crops. Prediction will depend on water usage, moisture content and soil testing results [2].

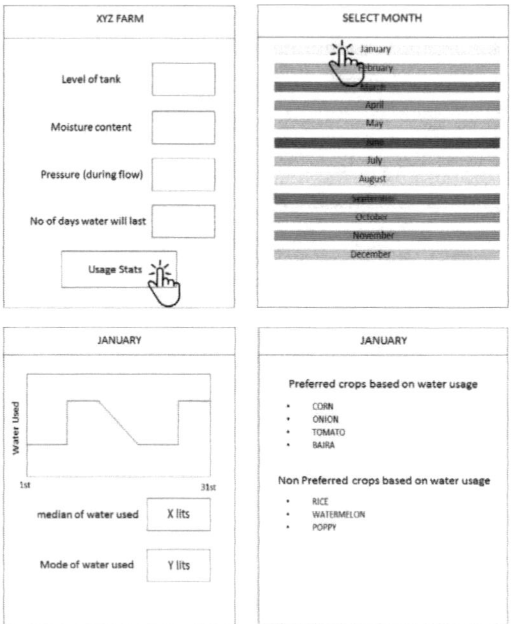

Fig 3.2 : Represensation of the Website

Table No. 3.1: Dataset for mustard crop in Black soil [5].

Sr No.	Set point (%)	Current moisture content (%)	Time for which pump will remain on (seconds)
1	80	10	21.8
2	80	20	18.7
3	80	30	15.8
4	80	40	12.2
5	80	50	9.5
6	80	60	6.2
7	80	70	3.4
8	80	80	0

4. Prototype Implementation

This section explains the complete prototype of the proposed system shown in Fig. 4.1. Also, it presents the detailed explanation of each and every block. This proposed prototype consists of number of field devices, and the collected data from all devices is gathered at the core controller i.e. Raspberry Pi3. Then according to gathered data, control action takes place directed by machine learning algorithms.

Test crop selected is Mustard. It requires black or alluvial soil to grow, germinates in 5-6 days and requires no fertilizer if soil quality is optimum. Black soil is used in this prototype because of its ease of availability and low cost. Mustard ideally requires about 2 inches of water per week, which is approximately equal to 5 mL/sq. cm per week. Also it is essential to provide regular water per day twice. Since our considered field is of about 345 sq. cm, amount of water ideally required should be 1.725 liters per week, which is 246.43 milliliters per day [4]. Although ideal conditions do not exist in real life, the readings received were quite representative of the Fig. , keeping weather conditions constant, as shown in Table 4.1. Since continuous water flow is not needed, a delay of one day (24 hours) is provided between two cycles. Irrigation control center (ICC) also called irrigation shop, is a housing setup where CPU and other electronic circuitry is housed. In actual practice irrigation control center is isolated near a field. In the prototype the Irrigation Control Center (ICC) is shown in Fig. 4.2.

Also we have developed the use case diagram for the system as shown in figure 4.3. A use case is a methodology used in system analysis to identify, clarify, and organize system requirements. It also helps us understand the various inputs and outputs for all the considered elements. As is depicted in the use case: a farmer, Firebase, and Agricultural department are the main elements of the use case. All actions that can be performed by the elements in regard to our proposed system are joined the respective element with the use of arrows. The headings (intelligent irrigation and website) show the domain in which the actions will take place. The function <<includes>> is used to extract common parts of the respective element or action, whereas the function <<extends>> is used to show optional actions after performing the given action.

Table No. 4.1: Output after the implementation

Sr. No.	Days	Water used (mL)
1	1	251.35
2	2	242.11
3	3	235.56
4	4	246.43
5	5	247.76
6	6	239.96
7	7	256.67
8	8	240.07
9	9	238.84
10	10	246.55

Fig. 4.1: Prototype of the system

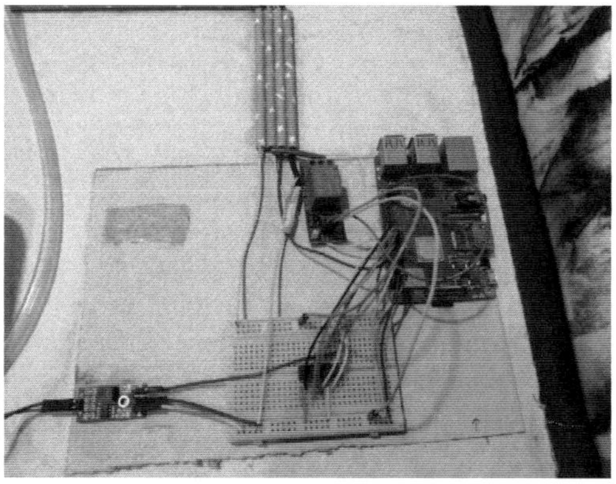

Fig. 4.2: Irrigation Control Center (ICC) of Prototype

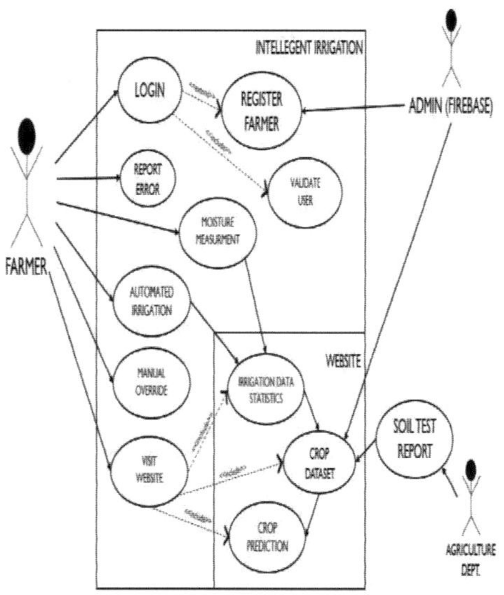

Fig. 4.3: Use Case diagram.

6. Conclusion

This system can be used by farmers for achieving optimum results in agriculture. Papers similar to this concept exist but none are implementable for various reasons. However, this system is both fully implementable and economically sustainable. It is a great step towards conservation of water and smart irrigation especially in the areas where rainfall is scarce [2]. The website part of this paper is easy to understand and can be accessible through the user's personal device from any location. This system can be further advanced by adding a few more sensors such as temperature and pressure sensor. The proposed system can be used in any type of irrigation such as sprinkler or drip. Also this system provides extra information regarding which crops to be grown by the farmer for better yield.

5.1 Future scope

This proposed system mentioned is fully implementable and works its basic purpose. However, certain advancements can be made, some of which are:

- Multilingual website: since most farmers in India are not well versed in English. A setup of multilingual website consisting of the respective local language can alleviate any discrepancies by overcoming the language barrier
- Use of neural networks: implementation of neural networks can help in detecting diseases in plants, soil productivity and contamination warning [2].
- Addition of fertilizer/pesticide channel: in the same piping which moves water from reservoir to field, a fertilizer and/or pesticide flow can be added which would require separate calculations, calibration and installation of various sensors.

7. References

1. S. Harishankar, R. Sathish Kumar, Sudharsan K.P, U. Vignesh and T.Viveknath, Solar Powered Smart Irrigation System. **Volume 4**, Number 4, pp. 341-346, (2014).
2. K. Jha San, A. Doshi, P. Patel, Intelligent irrigation system using artificial intelligence and machine learning: a comprehensive review. Article DOI: 10.21474/IJAR01/7959, (2018).

3. M. Janani and R. Jebakumar, A Study on Smart Irrigation Using Machine Learning. Article DOI: 10.23880/cclsj-16000141, (2019).
4. https://www.ikisan.com/up-mustard-water-management.
5. https://www.agrifarming.in/mustard-farming information.
6. Ms. S. Pawar, Prof. P. Rajput, Prof. A. Shaikh, Smart Irrigation System Using IOT and Raspberry Pi. **Volume 05,** Issue: 08, pp. 1163-1166, (2018).

Electronic Stability Control of Vehicles

Suryakant Gupta[1,*], *Nidhi* Hiremath[2,**], *Samiksha* Raut[2,***], *Gaurav* Datkhile[3,****], and *Prasiddh* Trivedi[3,†]

[1]Ramrao Adik Institute of Technology, Navi Mumbai, Nerul.

Abstract. The paper presents the Electronic Control Unit of vehicles with the main focus on Anti-lock braking system. ABS is used in traction control and to maintain vehicle stability. The paper describes the detail study of CarSim model and it gives us the most accurate and efficient method to simulate the performance of vehicle and how ABS can be used in different scenarios. The result of vehicular model without and with ABS for different test cases is presented in the paper. The vehicular model is implemented on MATLAB Simulink environment and the corresponding results are presented.

1 Introduction

Electronic control unit recently has become an essential part of the vehicles as it helps prevent accidents and gives more control to the vehicle. ABS is a part of Electronic stability control. Here it plays a vital role where brakes are used in the case of emergencies by maintaining the stability of the vehicle. Hence designing a proper ABS controller is particularly important as safety of the driver is of the cardinal aspect. Testing the vehicle manually with real-time responses is not economically feasible and hence virtual environment comes into picture. The results can be thus observed by simulation[11].

CarSim by Mechanical Simulations provides the users, the environment to get responses for any type of scenarios for the vehicle. The Software can be used to customize vehicles by entering their parameters and create a path for vehicles to run. The Animator output of Carsim helps to study the vehicle movement, forces and its measurements. They can also be precisely plotted on the graph and observed[10].

2 Description of vehicle model

Carsim has datasets for some standard vehicles, hence from that we have a used B-class hatchback for our study but there is an option to make a vehicle from scratch in CarSim provided the parameters and dynamics of the vehicle are known. For our study we have used the same car with and without an ABS and observed the different responses[9][10].

*e-mail: suryakantgupta66@gmail.com
**e-mail: nidhihiremath@gmail.com
***e-mail: samuraut8@gmail.com
****e-mail: gaurav.datkhile@rait.ac.in
†e-mail: prasiddh.trivedi@rait.ac.in

2.1 B-Class Hatchback Without ABS

Generic B-Class (Compact) hatchback with Strut front and 5-Link rear suspension. B-Class vehicles include the Citroen C3, Ford Fiesta, Opal Corsa, and Volkswagen Polo. Compared to some of the other B-Class vehicle examples, the following has the CarSim without ABS selected on the Brakes data screen[9][10].

2.2 B-Class Hatchback With ABS

Generic B-Class (Compact) hatchback with Strut front and 5-Link rear suspension. B-Class vehicles include the Citroen C3, Ford Fiesta, Opal Corsa, and Volkswagen Polo. Compared to some of the other B-Class vehicle examples, the following has the CarSim ABS selected on the Brakes data screen[9][10].

3 Literature Survey

The friction coefficient can be expressed as an empirical function, where the wheel slip is a function argument:

$$\mu = A.(B.(1 - e^{-Cs}) - D.s) \tag{1}$$

Table 1. Empirical coefficient for different road type

	Road Type			
Empirical coefficient	Dry Concrete	Wet Concrete	Snow	Ice
A	0.9	0.7	0.3	0.1
B	1.07	1.07	1.07	1.07
C	0.2773	0.5	0.1773	0.38
D	0.0026	0.003	0.006	0.007

Anti-lock braking systems (ABS) are meant to control the wheel slip in order to maintain the friction coefficient close to the optimal value[3][11]. Wheel slip is defined as the relative motion between a wheel (tire) and the surface of the road, during vehicle movement. Wheel slip occurs when the angular speed of the wheel (tire) is greater or less compared to it's free-rolling speed[7][8].

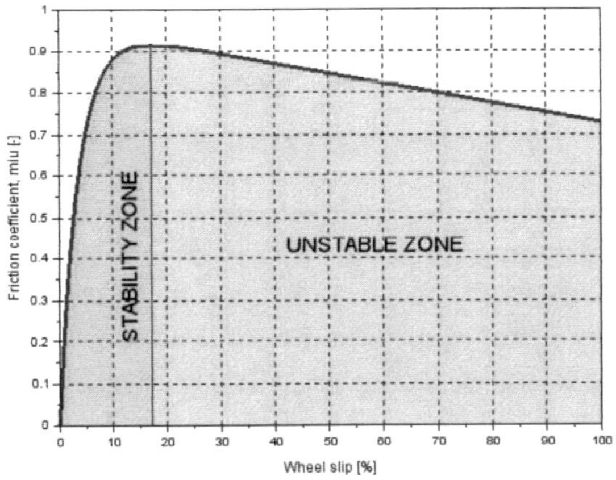

Figure 1. mu vs slip on concrete surface.[8]

During braking, if the wheel slip is 100 % the wheel is locked but the vehicle is still moving. At 0 % slip, the wheel and vehicle have e the same speed.

In Figure 1 the optimum friction coefficient (highest value) is obtained when the wheel slip is around 20 %. As you can see, the friction coefficient curve is split into two areas:

- stability zone: where the friction coefficient increases with the increase in wheel slip[8].
- unstable zone: where the friction coefficient decreases with the increase in wheel slip[8].

If the wheel slip enters an unstable area, the friction coefficient will decrease and the wheel will lock causing skid and vehicle instability.

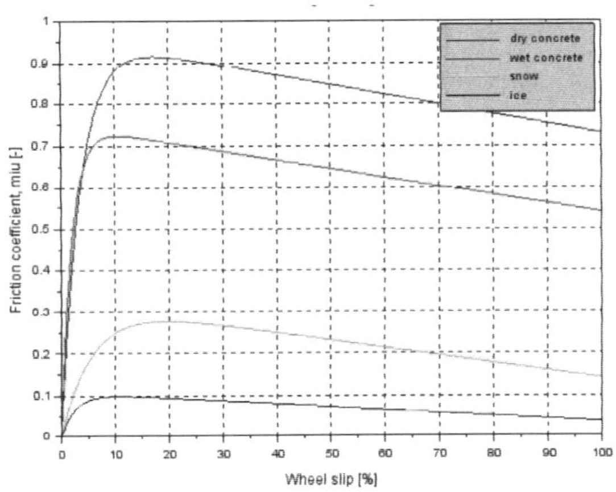

Figure 2. mu vs slip on different surface.[8]

In Figure 2, it can be seen that the maximum value of the friction coefficient decreases sharply for a road covered by snow or ice. Even if the value of the friction coefficient is not significantly lower for 100 % slip, preventing wheel lock improves vehicle maneuverability (steering)[1][3].

4 Electronic Stability Control

An electronic control unit of the vehicle is responsible to maintain the stability, traction of vehicle with the road, to prevent roll-over and to reduce side slip. This will be helpful in dangerous scenarios like slippery roads or braking during a steep turn at a very high speed[2].

4.1 Antilock Braking System

ABS is the system which assists the driver while applying a brake. For our study to tune the ABS controller for better efficiency, we have worked on three parameters of ABS given by CarSim - Slip ON , Slip OFF and Cut-off speed[7][8][9].

- Slip ON : This is the wheel slip condition at which brakes are turned ON by the ABS controller where '0' slip represents free rolling and '1' represents full lock-up[7][8][9].
- Slip OFF : This is the wheel slip condition at which brakes are turned OFF by the ABS controller where '0' slip represents free rolling and '1' represents full lock-up[7][8][9].
- Cut-OFF speed : It is the minimum wheel speed for the built in ABS controller. When absolute vehicle speed drops below this level the ABS controller is turned off and wheel lockup is allowed. [7][8][9]

4.2 Analysis and Physics

$$w_v = \frac{V}{R} \tag{2}$$

V = Vehicle linear velocity
R = Wheel Radius
w_v = Vehicle speed divided by wheel radius from (Equation 2)
w_w = wheel angular velocity

$$slip = 1 - \frac{w_w}{w_v} \tag{3}$$

5 Test Cases

In our test we have used the same vehicle as given in section 2 with and without ABS controller for two scenarios. The two situations are as follows:-

 https://doi.org/10.1051/itmconf/20203201009

5.1 Split mu

In this case there are two different coefficients of friction on the same road. Hence wheels of vehicle can lose traction and make the vehicle unstable which can lead to accidents. These situations can occur if the roads are not constructed properly or there is oil on certain parts of the road, or during rainy days as given in Equation 1, Table 1 [4][5].

Figure 3. On Road Split-mu

5.2 Tight turning point of the road

This is a situation where tight turns are involved and brakes are applied to prevent the vehicle from going off the road[2][5].

Figure 4. Tight turning point of the road

6 Results

We are testing this vehicle for 2 conditions on the road from section 5. First is Split-mu condition from Figure 3. In this condition the coefficient of friction is different for different wheels in the vehicle and the condition can be a case when oil is spilled on the road or road is slippery on some parts so all the wheels do not get proper traction. Hence we have simulated this condition using Carsim and the results are given below with and without Abs system from section 2, 4, 5.

6.1 Split-mu Results

In the Figure 5 the misbalance of the vehicle can be clearly observed. As ABS is not present in the vehicle in this particular scenario hence as we can observe from graph the movement of center of gravity of the vehicle is not linear and it depicts that the vehicle is not stable and in spinning motion.

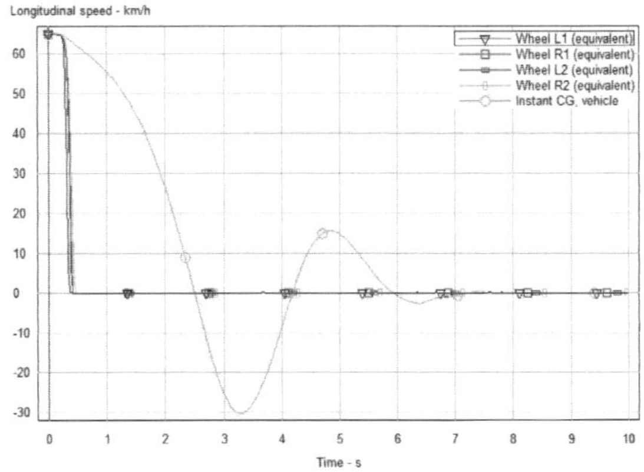

Figure 5. Center of Gravity of the vehicle without ABS.

From Figure 6 when it is compared to previous response of Figure 5 with no ABS it has a better stability and has thus prevented the misbalance of Center of Gravity of the vehicle. This is concluded on the basis of linear motion of Center of Gravity of the vehicle.

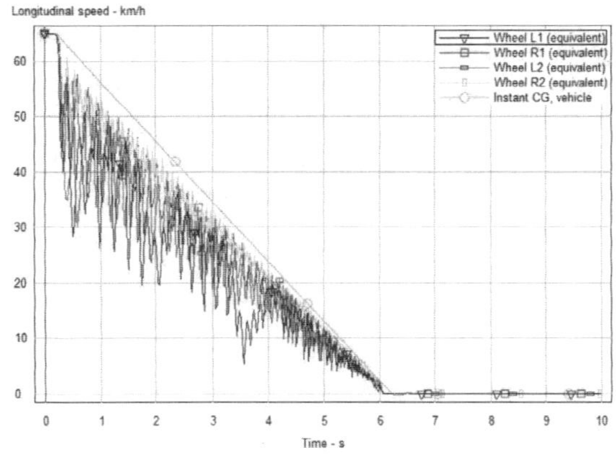

Figure 6. Center of Gravity of the vehicle with Abs.

In the Figure 7 it can be clearly seen that without ABS, brake pressure on wheels becomes constant and wheels gets locked which lead to wheel slip from section 3 this results in the misbalance of the vehicle and it may lead to accidents[3].

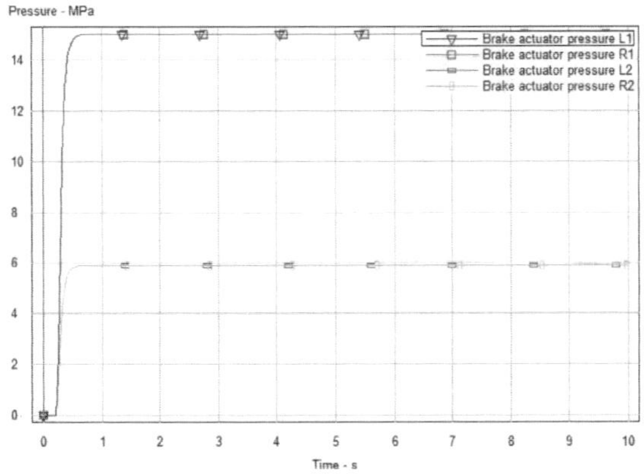

Figure 7. Brake Pressure on the brake cylinders of the wheels without ABS.

In Figure 8 we can observe that vehicle with ABS controller, controls the brake pressure and prevents the wheels from getting locked. From section 3 and from Figure 8 it is concluded that ABS has maintained slip around 20% and thus it has maintained the stability of the vehicle and the value of maintaining slip at 20 % was refered from Figure 1.

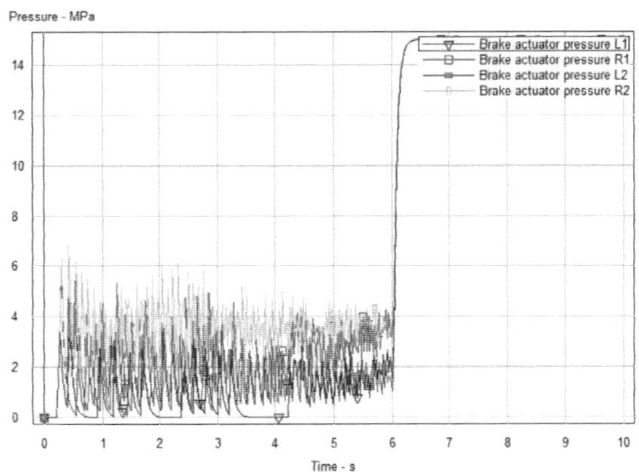

Figure 8. Brake Pressure on the brake cylinders of the wheels with ABS.

From the Figure 9 vehicle without ABS controller, a slip is observed in both the directions as from Figure 5 it gave us the response for the spining motion. As the plot shows slip value to be '1' it indicates the full lock-up of the wheels and negative and positive sign just indicates at the direction of slip, thus it lead to instability and may cause accidents[8].

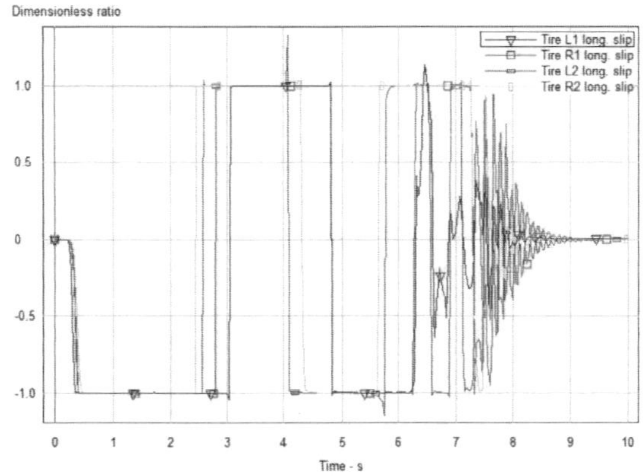

Figure 9. Tire Slip without ABS.

In the Figure 10 , vehicle with a ABS controller, slip is maintained around 0.2 ie 20 % of wheel slip from Figure 1, until the speed of the vehicle does not come below the threshold value to prevent full lock-up off the wheels so that vehicle stability is maintained[8].

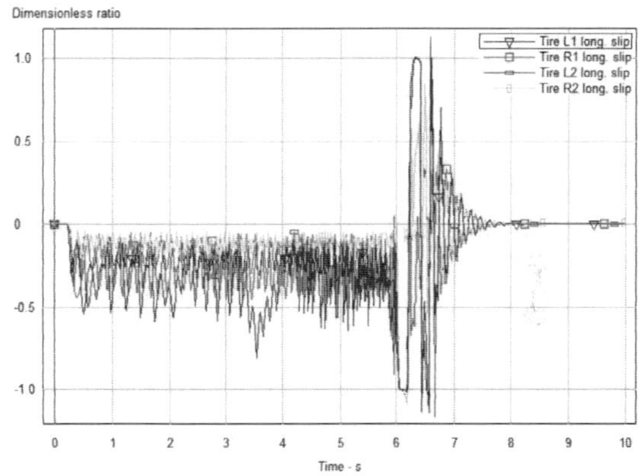

Figure 10. Tire Slip with ABS.

6.2 Simulink Interface

The Vehicle model has been implemented on MATLAB simulink interface and the corresponding results can be observed from Figure 12, 14. The model is in Simulink can be interfaced with various external hardwares and it increases the scope of development which make CarSim more powerfull along with Matlab Simulink.[9][10].

In Figure 11 the simulink model is shown where CarSim S-function block is given by Carsim software which has all the parameters of vehicle and as Figure 11 is the model that represent without ABS there is no ABS controller block and at the Brake Actuator Block control mode input is constant 1. This mean that full brake pressure is applied and as we have seen in section 3 this condition leads to wheel lock.

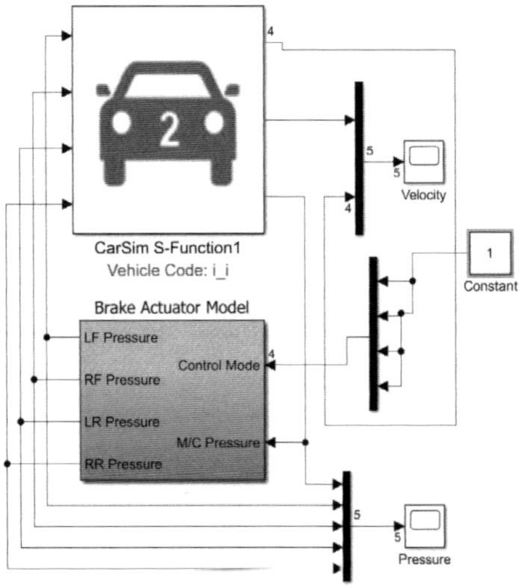

Figure 11. Simulink Model Without ABS Controller.

From Figure 12 the corressponding response of Center of Gravity of the Vehicle is scene which is same as observed in Figure 5 and it has been explained in section 6 both of the results are same because ABS was not present in both condition just the difference is that Figure 5 is from CarSim and Figure 12 is from simulink scope.

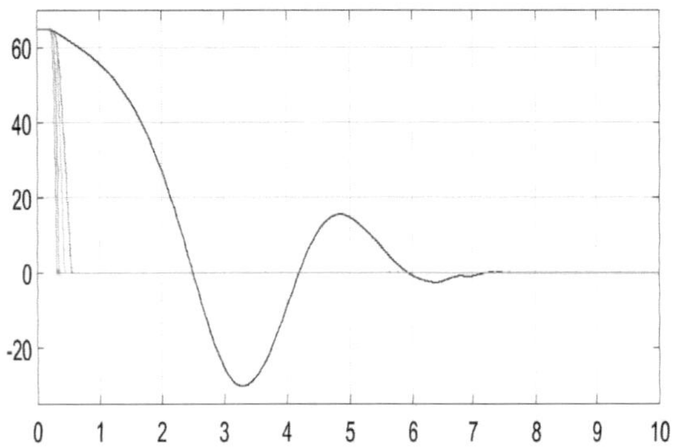

Figure 12. CG of Vehicle Observed in Simulink.

From Figure 13 as you compare it with Figure 11 you can see the presence of ABS controller block which has the data of slip on, off and cut-off as given in section 4. This block work towards maintaining stability as per Figure 2 and controls the slip of the wheels.

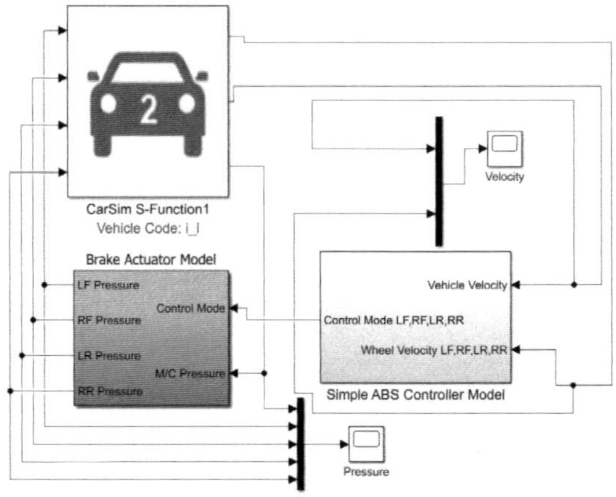

Figure 13. Simulink Model With ABS Controller.

From Figure 14 the corressponding response of Center of Gravity of the Vehicle is scene which is same as observed in Figure 6 and it has been explained in section 6 both of the results are same because ABS is present in both condition just the difference is that Figure 6 is from CarSim and Figure 14 is from simulink scope.

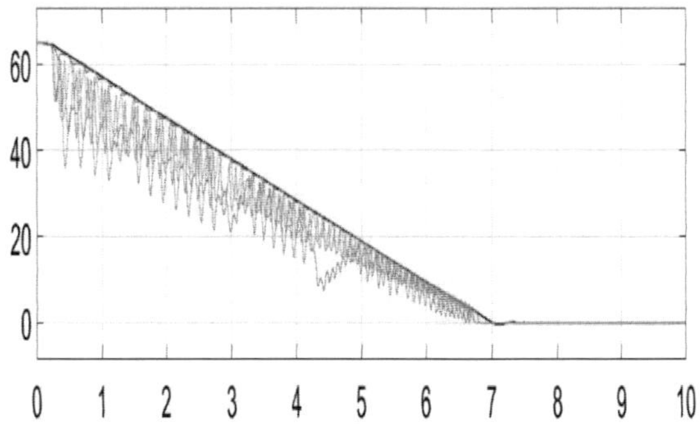

Figure 14. CG of Vehicle Observed in Simulink.

6.3 Results of tight turning point on the road

We are testing this vehicle for 2 conditions on the road as given in section 5. Second is Tight turning point of the road condition as shown in Figure 4. In this condition at high speed there are chances of vehicle Rollover[1][6] .This can be the condition where driver takes the sudden turn and applies brake to stop the vehicle if it becomes unstable. Hence we have simulated this condition using Carsim and the results are given below with and without Abs system using section 2, 4, 5.

In Figure 15 the Center of gravity of the vehicle seems to be linear but as we can observed wheel longitudinal speed has suddenly came to 0 which means that the wheels are getting locked and as per section 3 wheels are now slipping and it can take the vehicle off the road

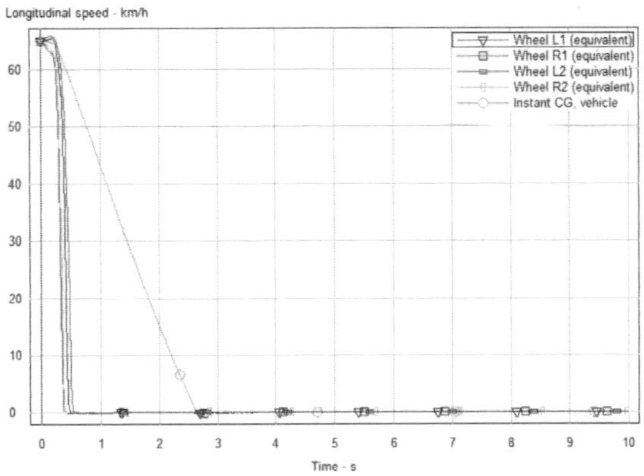

Figure 15. Vehicle Center of Gravity without Abs.

From Figure 16 as we compare it with Figure 15 here the Center of Gravity of the vehicle also seems to be linear but as you can observe the response of the wheels it is not getting locked and as per section 3 vehicle stability is maintained by ABS as it is controlling the slip of the wheels

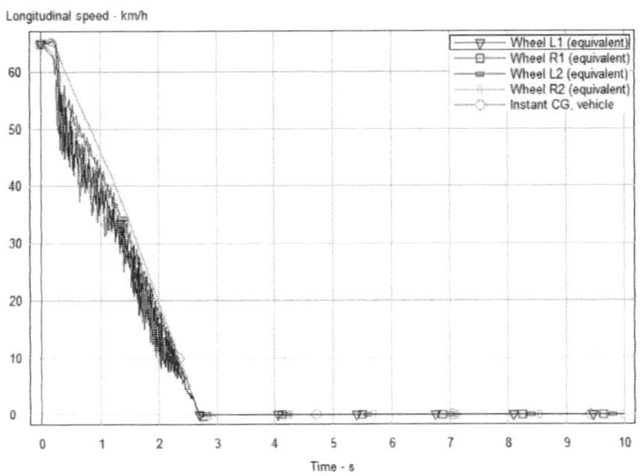

Figure 16. Vehicle Center of Gravity with Abs.

From Figure 15 it was observed that wheels were getting locked which was leading to instability of the vehicle and the reason was that constant brake pressure is applied in the vehicle without ABS which can be observed in Figure 17 and as per section 3 these are the condition for instability

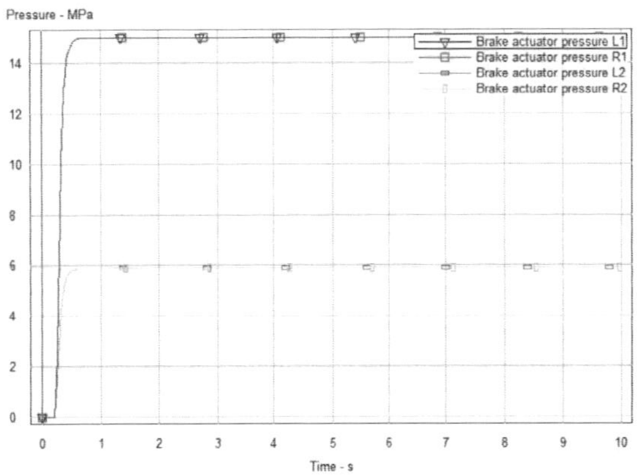

Figure 17. Brake Pressure on the brake cylinders of the wheels without Abs.

From Figure 16 it was observed that wheels were prevented from getting locked which has lead to the stability of the vehicle and the reason was that the brake pressure is controled by ABS according to section 4. The vehicle brakes with ABS response can be observed in Figure 18 this response is trying to maintain wheel slip around 20% and as per section 3 these are the condition for stability[4]

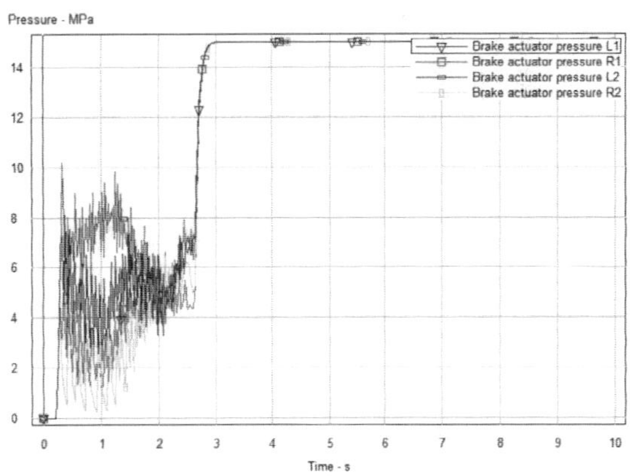

Figure 18. Brake Pressure on the brake cylinders of the wheels With Abs.

In the Figure 19 the complete slip of the tire is observed as the value reaches '1' when the brakes are applied. The negative and positive sign indicates the direction and as slip is reaching 1 it means wheels are getting locked and this is leading to the instability of vehicle as per section 3[4].

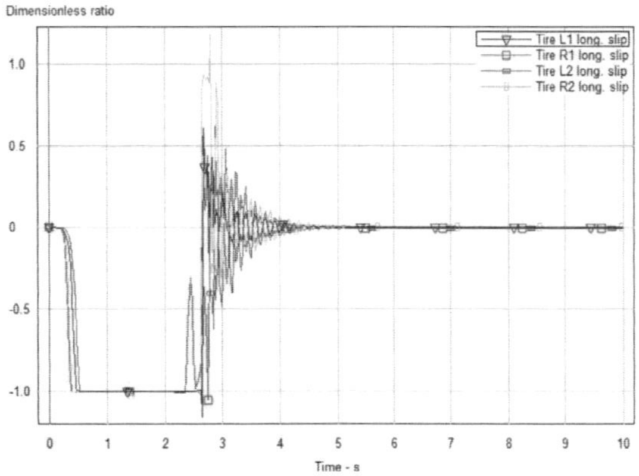

Figure 19. Tire Slip without ABS.

In the Figure 20 the slip of the tire is observed and the value is maintained around 0.2 ie 20% wheel slip. The negative and positive sign indicates the direction and as vehicle speed decreases considerably and it goes below threshold speed at which wheel lock is safe ie from section 4.1 the Cut-Off speed is that threshold parameter and as wheel lock is allowed it makes the vehicle stationary and keeps the vehicle stable 3[4].

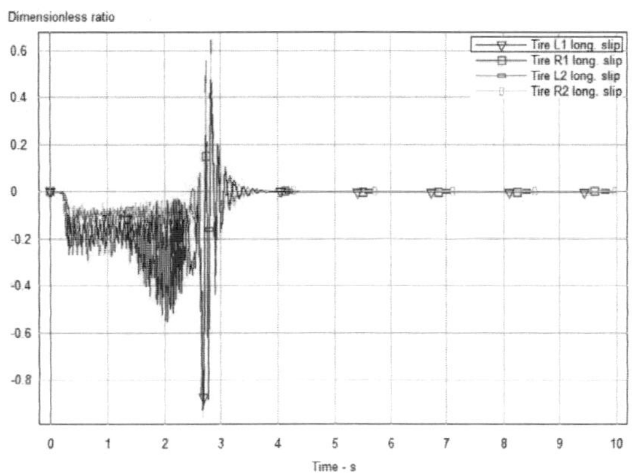

Figure 20. Tire Slip with ABS.

7 Conclusion

Carsim can be used for wide variety of simulation and realistic response can be observed using it. The analysis of Electronic Control Unit has been done using Carsim and Simulink. Hence using the tools provided by CarSim all parameters of the vehicle can be studied and system with best effeciency can be developed and this makes it easier to understand dynamics of the vehicle without having a deep mathematical knowledge of it.

8 Future Scope

The Hardware-in-the-Loop (HIL) simulation of corresponding vehicle model can be implemented using dSPACE and DSP processor.The vehicle model can be implemented on dSPACE and implementation of controller on DSP processor.

References

[1] Model-Based Design of a SUV Anti-Rollover Control System https://www.mathworks.com/matlabcentral/fileexchange/23622-model based-design-of-a-suv-anti-rollover-control-system, MATLAB Central File Exchange.

[2] Observer-Based Robust Control of Vehicle Dynamics for Rollover Mitigation in Critical Situations Hamid Dahmani, Olivier Pagès, Ahmed El Hajjaji, and Nawal Daraoui

[3] New Paradigms for the Integration of Yaw Stability and Rollover Prevention Functions in Vehicle Stability Control Rajesh Rajamani, Senior Member, IEEE, and Damrongrit (Neng) Piyabongkarn, Member, IEEE

[4] Switched stable control design methodology applied to vehicle rollover prevention based on switched suspension settings

[5] Driving Control Algorithm for Maneuverability, Lateral Stability, and Rollover Prevention of 4WD Electric Vehicles With Independently Driven Front and Rear Wheels Juyong Kang, Jinho Yoo, and Kyongsu Yi

[6] A Three-Dimensional Dynamics Control Framework of Vehicle Lateral Stability and Rollover Prevention via Active Braking With MPC Liang Li, Member, IEEE, Yishi Lu, Rongrong Wang, and Jie Chen

[7] Modeling an Anti-Lock Braking System https://www.mathworks.com/help/simulink/slref/modeling-an-anti-lock-braking-system.html

[8] https://x-engineer.org/projects/anti-lock-braking-system-abs-modeling-simulation-xcos

[9] https://www.carsim.com/downloads/pdf/CarSim_Math_Models.pdf

[10] https://www.carsim.com/products/supporting/simulink/index.php

[11] An empirical study of the effectiveness of electronic stability control system in reducing loss of vehicle control Yiannis E. Papelis ,1, Ginger S.Watson2, Timothy L. Brown The University of Iowa, Iowa City, IA 52242, United States

Indian Language Identification using Deep Learning

Shubham Godbole[1,*], *Vaishnavi* Jadhav[2,**], and *Gajanan* Birajdar[3,***]

[1]Department of Electronics Engineering, Ramrao Adik Institute of Technology, Nerul, Navi Mumbai, India

Abstract. Spoken language is the most regular method of correspondence in this day and age. Endeavours to create language recognizable proof frameworks for Indian dialects have been very restricted because of the issue of speaker accessibility and language readability. However, the necessity of SLID is expanding for common and safeguard applications day by day. Feature extraction is a basic and important procedure performed in LID. A sound example is changed over into a spectrogram visual portrayal which describes a range of frequencies in regard with time. Three such spectrogram visuals were generated namely Log Spectrogram, Gammatonegram and IIR-CQT Spectrogram for audio samples from the standardized IIIT-H Indic Speech Database. These visual representations depict language specific details and the nature of each language. These spectrograms images were then used as an input to the CNN. Classification accuracy of 98.86% was obtained using the proposed methodology.

Index Terms: Convolutional Neural Network (CNN), Spoken Indian Language Identification (SLID), Log Spectrogram, gammatonegram, IIR-CQT Spectrogram, Artificial Neural Network (ANN), Deep Learning

1 Introduction

Inventive systems like Siri and Google Assistant depend on Automatic Speech Recognition (ASR). In order to work appropriately the ASR frameworks expect users to manually indicate the proper input language. Traditional Language Identification (LID) systems use area explicit information for extracting hand-made features from sound samples[4].

Recently, Deep Learning and Artificial Neural Networks (ANN) are been considered the best in class for pattern recognition issues[25]. A variety of computer vision tasks like Image Classification, display better performance using Deep Neural Networks. LID can be characterized as the task of recognizing the spoken language in any given utterance.

As research in ASR advances, a LID system would be important for any multi-lingual speech recognition system. In case of multi-lingual speech recognition, the accuracy of the speech recognizer system can be improved by using LID setup at the front-end. It reduces complication by directly processing the speech over the identified language rather than running over several languages.

Particularly, in an Indian scenario where nearly every state has its very own language and each language having many lingos, designing LID system becomes vital. The languages and dialects used in India are categorized into distinct families: the significant ones are Indo-Aryan, Dravidian, Sino-Tibetan, Austroasiatic, Tai–Kadai and Great Andamanese languages [16]. This experimental study involves languages from two of the family groups. Marathi, Hindi, Bengali belong to the Indo-Aryan family whereas Tamil, Telugu, Kannada and Malayalam belong to the Dravidian family[4].

Neural networks are used to classify the different languages. The issue regarding LID can also be modeled as a pattern recognition task. Patterns from the given spectrogram can be identified by the trained ANN which helps it to classify the unfamiliar language specimen into a known category. Seven languages from IIIT-H Indic speech databases are used for evaluation[1].

In our methodology, WAV files from the database were converted into spectrogram visuals. Each sample is represented by separate visuals viz. Log Spectrogram, Infinite Impulse Response Constant-Q Transform (IIR-CQT) Spectrogram and Gammatonegram. Convolutional Neural Network (CNN) is used for classification of different languages. The classification accuracy rate obtained using CNN is 98.86%.

Formulation of the paper is done in the following manner: In section II wide range of methodologies and approaches for LID are summarized. Section 3 presents the architecture for LID using spectrogram visuals. Simulation results and comparison between the proposed method and available techniques are introduced in Section 4. Section 5 concludes the article.

2 Literature Survey

In LID various features and methods such as acoustic, phonotactic and prosodic along with different classifiers are used to differentiate the languages. In one of the previous works, sound samples from the dataset [1] were converted into spectrogram visuals which were then classi-

*e-mail: godboleshubham2@gmail.com
**e-mail: vaishnavijadhav1998@gmail.com
***e-mail: gajanan.birajdar@rait.ac.in

 https://doi.org/10.1051/itmconf/20203201010

fied using CNNs. Considerable results were obtained using this methodology with an accuracy of 95.52% which was highest in comparison to different works done till date [2].

An approach based on Grey Wolf Optimizer (GWO) feature selection and ANN classifier was applied for LID. For extracting features from the spectrogram image LBPHF, CLBP and Wavelet are used. The GWO algorithm helps in extracting only the optimal features from the spectrogram. The ANN classifier then differentiates between languages using results obtained from the GWO algorithm. An accuracy of 97% was achieved using this approach [3].

Deepti Deshwal et al. [5] carried out research demonstrating feature extraction methods in LID. This article classifies multiple feature extraction approaches based on various highlights, the human speech production framework, spectral or cepstral research and also on the basis of different transforms. In addition, various techniques including noise compensation have also been mentioned. The study additionally exhibits that Mel-Frequency Cepstral Coefficients (MFCCs) intertwined with other features vectors and cleansing approaches gives better performance as in comparison with pure MFCC based feature extraction.

With a lot of languages spoken in India, building speech applications becomes a difficult task. For building a speech-based application, recognition of the language being spoken is one of the foremost steps. Bakshi Aarti et al. [4] have summarized the acoustic, phonetic and prosodic features used for SLID specifically for Indian Languages.

A study of acoustic features and different classifiers proposed by S. Jothilakshmi et al. [16] features a hierarchical approach to distinguish between 9 Indian Languages. The language is identified at first by segregating it to the family it belongs and then recognizing it from its' corresponding family. This approach is carried out using GMM based LID system using MFCC with delta and acceleration coefficients which results in the accuracy of 80.56%.

Another method for speech classification uses the human auditory system along with spectrogram features proposed by A.F.Pour et al. [7] clarifies that the basilar membrane filters are generally represented by a gammatone function which provides good approximation about the predecided responses.

A study represented by Nadia Jmour et al.[9] describes a learning approach on training CNNs for Image Classification. Here, Traffic Sign Image Classification System was developed with a total of 360 images, each of the neural network layers was considered and fine-tuning technique was used for experiments varying in the number of epochs. The highest accuracy of 93.33% was achieved by running 6 epochs.

Another analysis conducted by Raj Kumar G.A et al. [11] broadens the idea of a CNN. The algorithm proposes the use of CNN for recognition of Facial Emotions. A CNN Architecture designed for this problem results in a staggering accuracy of 90+% compared to other studies which could only give up to 48%.

Earlier, Automatic SLID systems were built using language dependent speech to-text synthesizers. Saikia R. et al. [17] presents the response of Language Independent speech to text transcribers for various Indian languages. This closely relates to the need for deep learning in order to overcome the lack of accuracy in traditional LID systems.

[15] Examines the use of spectral features that are extracted using conventional block processing, pitch synchronous analysis and glottal closure regions for Language Recognition Performance. The spectral features extracted from PSA and GC based regions showed better results on both IITKGP-MLILSC (27 Indian Languages) and OGI-MLTS speech databases.

The study by C. Madhu et al. [14] uses language dependent phonotactic features and prosodic information along with a multilayer feed forward neural network classifier for LID. Phonotactic feature vectors are obtained by numerically representing two consecutive syllables whereas Prosodic feature vectors are obtained by concatenating features of three consecutive syllables resulting into an accuracy of 72% and 68% respectively.

3 Proposed LID Algorithm using Deep Learning

3.1 Proposed Method

The process of taking an input and yeilding a class or a probability that the input belongs to a specific class is known as Image Classification. CNN is a part of Deep learning neural networks. They are normally used to examine images and are more often used in image classification. CNNs' are preferred over other image classification algorithms due to its' requirement of very less processing. In the convolution layer, the neurons get input from only a specific area of the preceding layer. Neurons in the dense layer receive input from every input in the earlier layer. The main function of CNN is to extract features from the images, this makes feature extraction by manual methods a redundant task. These features are learned on a set of training images and make the model very accurate for image classification tasks[11]. Algorithm for CNN:-

1. Initialization of the filters and weights with arbitrary values.

2. The training image is then sent as input to the network and it follows the forward propagation phase (i.e the convolution layer, pooling layer, and the fully connected layer) and gives the output chances for different classes.

3. Calculation of the absolute error at the output layer is computed.

4. Gradient descent helps calculate the error for the weights of the network. All the filter values, parameter values and weights are updated to reduce the

output error. The weights are then adjusted in such a way so as to influence the network in reducing the gross error. After updating the values, the network can now categorize the image accurately.

3.2 Log Spectrogram

A spectrogram is a visual portrayal representing a range of frequencies as they differ in time. When correlated with an audio signal, at times they are also called sonographs or voice grams. Music, sonar, radar are the fields which highly utilize the use of Spectrogram. These Spectrograms can be utilized to recognize speech. Various methods such as an optical spectrometer, use of bandpass filters, Fourier or wavelet transform are used to create a Spectrogram. The classic format of a graph represents time on one axis while the other axis represents frequency; the amplitude of a specific frequency at a particular time is denoted by colour which can also be called as the third dimension. There are numerous varieties of format, at times the vertical and horizontal axes are switched which can be either linear or logarithmic. Short Time Fourier transform was used to generate the spectrogram and the frequency axis was scaled logarithmically. Short Time Fourier Transform can be mathematically represented by the equation: [8]

$$X(l,w) = \sum_{a=-\infty}^{\infty} x[a]w[a-l]e^{-jwa} \tag{1}$$

Where w[l]: a specified window. l(time): Discrete variable, w(freq): Continuous variable. Typical graphical representation of Short Time Fourier transform is a Spectrogram which is characterized as follows:

$$Spectrogram = |X(l,w)|^2 \tag{2}$$

3.3 Gammatonegram

Gammatone filters resemble closely to the refining performed by our ear. These filters help in generating time-frequency surfaces dependent on a gammatone study, which may be utilized as a substitution for a traditional spectrogram. While spectrogram is conventionally used as a time-frequency interpretation, it has many differences in the methodology by which the ear perceives and analyzes the information and the approach by which the spectrogram does it[7]. The gammatone function is given as follows:

$$g(t) = t^{N-1}e^{-at}Cosw_0tu(t) \tag{3}$$

Where a:bandwidth parameter, w_0: center frequency, N: order of gammatone function.[6]

3.4 IIR CQT Spectrogram

3.4.1 Implementation of IIR CQT

Constant-Q transform (CQT) refers to a method that transforms a time-domain signal x(n) into time-frequency domain so as to obtain the middle frequencies of the frequency bins which are geometrically distributed and the Q-factors are equal. Although these are wavelet transforms due to comparitively high values of Q-factor the term CQT is preferred. The CQT transform X^{CQ} (l,m) of a discrete time-domain signal x(m) is given by:

$$X^{CQ}(l,m) = \sum_{j=m-\lfloor \frac{N_k}{2} \rfloor}^{m+\lfloor \frac{N_k}{2} \rfloor} x(j)a*_l(j-m+\frac{N_k}{2}) \tag{4}$$

where l = 1, 2, . . . , K: indexes related to frequency bins which denote rounding towards negative infinity, $a*_l$(m): complex conjugate of a_l(m).

IIR filter with one zero and one pole is used on the spectrum of the signal. The zero is positioned at -1 in the Z-plane so as to force a time window that is zero in its extremes. The position of the pole is different for each frequency bin so as to obtain distinct time window widths. The recursive equation of the filter is:

$$y[l] = x[l] + x[l+1] + poles[l] * y[l-1] \tag{5}$$

3.5 Convolutional Neural Network

Convolutional Networks (ConvNets) are at present the most competent deep learning models for classifying image data. They are closely related to the neural network system from the human body. These models learn invariant features heirarchically. They initially differentiate low-level features and afterwards figure out how to perceive and merge these features to learn progressively convoluted examples. Distinctive levels of features are extracted by the various layers of the network. Neurons in each layer are are represented in 3 dimensions namely height, width, depth. An input image is generally represented as a matrix of pixels. A grayscale image has 2 measurements height and width. The color of the image is represented by depth.

3.5.1 Convolutional Layer

The convolutional layer is always the initial phase of a CNN. Extraction of features from the input image is the main function of the convolution layer. Convolution maps are generated by passing the input image through convolution kernels. Convolution layer needs a 3D input generally represented as [w1xh1xd1] where w1: width, h1: height and d1: depth, the outputs of neurons in this layers are determined by multiplying the weights and the regional matrix they are associated to in the input volume . The convolution maps now have new volume [w2xh2xd2] where, w2: new width, h2: new height and d2: new depth[9].

$$w2 = \frac{w1 - f + 2*p}{s} + 1 \tag{6}$$

$$h2 = \frac{h1 - f + 2*p}{s} + 1 \tag{7}$$

$$d2 = k \tag{8}$$

f : spatial extend of the filter. k : number of filters. p : zero padding. s : stride.

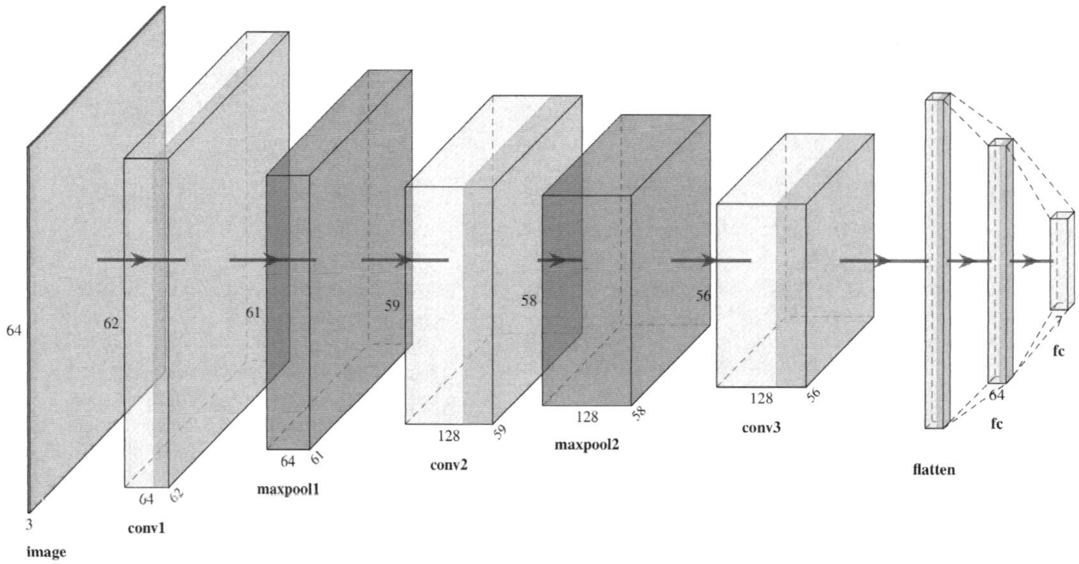

Figure 1: Architecture of Deep CNN.

3.5.2 Max Pooling Layer

Pooling dynamically reduces the size of the input representation. It helps to reduce the required parameters thereby reducing the computation power. This layer additionally helps to control over-fitting. Pool layer is embedded in the middle of two consecutive Conv layers, reducing the spatial dimensions of width and height.

Generally max pooling is used, the input image to this layer is subdivided into a set of areas that don't overrun on each other. The outputs are the maximum value of each area. They are obtained using MAX operation which reduces the number of parameters as well as optimzes the spatial dimensions. The volume of the Pool layer is [w2xh2xd2] and given by:

$$w2 = \frac{w1 - f}{s} + 1 \tag{9}$$

$$h2 = \frac{h1 - f}{s} + 1 \tag{10}$$

$$d2 = d1 \tag{11}$$

3.5.3 Flatten Layer

Flattening transforms a two-dimensional matrix of features into a single vector that can be further connected to the dense layer of the neural network.

3.5.4 Fully Connected Layer

The output from the earlier Layer is applied as an input to the fully connected layers. It combines the characteristics of CNN to categorize the image. It decides the classes introducing it in an output volume size of (1x1xk). As the name suggests each of the output neurons are connected to the earlier layer which results in classification of a particular category.

4 Experimental Results

4.1 Dataset

At present, the IIIT-H Indic speech database comprises of text and speech information in Bengali, Hindi, Kannada, Malayalam, Marathi, Tamil and Telugu. These languages were picked, as the absolute number of articles in every one of these languages sums up to be more than 10,000 and the speakers of these local languages were easily accessible. Every one of these dialects has a few lingos. As an underlying estimation, the discourse was recorded in the lingo in which the local speaker was comfortable with [1]. The samples in the dataset were converted into different spectrogram visuals viz. Log Spectrogram, Gammatonegram and IIR-CQT Spectrogram.

A key principle followed in developing a CNN is to manage the features spaced widely in the initial stage and then make it precise and deeper at the end. Generally, the number of channels are the same or increase while we advance through the layers in the CNN. The Activation shape can be calculated as (ceil(N+f-1)/s, ceil(N+f-1)/s, Number of filters), where 'N': input dimensions, 'f': filter size and 's': stride length. Activation value is calculated by taking the product of all the values in the dimensions of Activation Shape. The model used for CNN classification (Table 2) is as given below:

The performance of the proposed model can be evaluated from the confusion matrix (Table 1). It can be in-

https://doi.org/10.1051/itmconf/20203201010

Table 1: Confusion Matrix

	Bengali	Marathi	Telugu	Tamil	Malayalam	Kannada	Hindi
Bengali	2953	10	5	6	7	6	13
Marathi	7	2972	2	3	4	3	9
Telugu	1	2	2974	9	5	7	2
Tamil	2	3	9	2966	9	7	4
Malayalam	3	1	9	7	2972	7	1
Kannada	1	3	7	5	8	2974	2
Hindi	12	13	4	4	6	6	2955

Table 2: Architecture

Layer(type)	Output Shape	Parameters
conv2d_15 (Conv2D)	(None, 298, 138, 64)	1792
max_pooling2d_10 (MaxPooling)	(None, 149, 69, 64)	0
conv2d_16 (Conv2D)	(None, 147, 67,128)	73856
max_pooling2d_11 (MaxPooling)	(None, 73, 33, 128)	0
conv2d_17 (Conv2D)	(None, 71, 31, 128)	147584
flatten_5 (Flatten)	(None, 281728)	0
dense_10 (Dense)	(None, 64)	18030656
dense_11	(None, 7)	455
Total parameters: 18,254,343		
Trainable parameters: 18,254,343		
Non-Trainable parameters: 0		

ferred from the false positive values that Bengali, Marathi and Hindi share a common family and Kannada, Tamil, Telugu and Malayalam belong to the Dravidian family.

4.2 Results and Discussion

Using the CNN approach an accuracy of 98.86% is obtained.

Following are the graphs (fig.1 and fig.2) for the accuracy and loss of the model. Previous research on Indian LID demonstrates feature extraction and the use of different classifiers. Making modifications to the previous work and designing a CNN architecture that is deeper and which has an increased number of filters with a smaller filter size, exhibited better results.

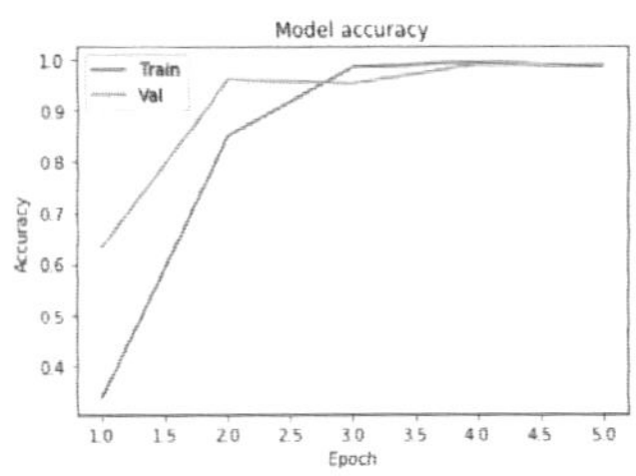

Figure 2: Model Accuracy

The Accuracy Graph (fig-1)initially demonstrates that the model is undergoing training. The training and validation datasets overlap at the end which determines that the model has a proper fit.

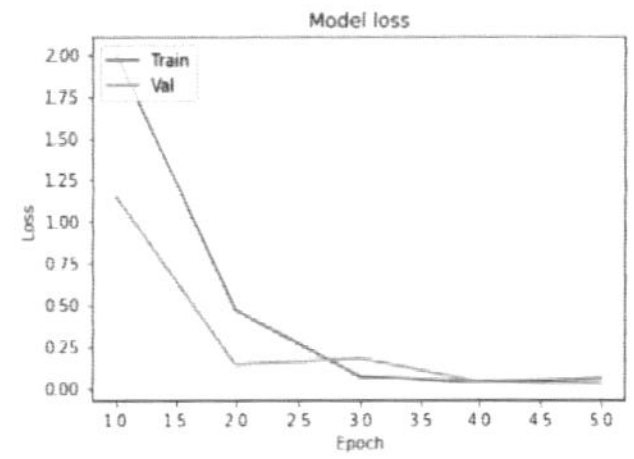

Figure 3: Model Loss

The Loss Graph (fig-2) depicts that the model has comparable performance on both training and validation datasets. Although, the model shows a high learning rate during the initial epochs, it settles to a point of stability with a minimal gap between the two final loss values.

5 Conclusion and Future Work

Identification of Language becomes a crucial part of Speech Recognition, especially in multilingual scenario. This article proposes an approach which works by visualizing the audio samples of each language with the help of spectrogram and a Deep Learning based LID system. The analysis was performed on seven Indian languages from the standardized dataset obtained from IIIT-H database . The experimental results demonstrate the classification accuracy using CNN to be 98.86%. A comparison between existing methods and studies was made depicting the proposed method (Table 3) to give the highest accuracy. As an extension to our work, a plan to implement the proposed method on a different dataset containing multiple languages can be executed. The languages can also be distinguished using a Multiview Deep Learning approach.

Table 3: Comparison of the proposed approach with existing algorithms.

Algorithm	Features	Languages	Accuracy
Verma et al.[12]	SVM	3	81%
Gupta et al.[13]	MFCC with random forest and SVM	4	92.6%
Madhu et al. [14]	Phonotactic and Prosodic	7	72% and 68%
Rao et al.[15]	MFCC,GMM	27	58.14%
S. Palanivel et al.[16]	MFCC,GMM,HMM and ANN	9	80.56%
Saikia et al.[17]	Transcription-based	7	96%
Himadri M et al.[2]	CNN	7	95.52%
Proposed	CNN	7	98.86%

References

[1] "IIIT-H Indic Speech Databases, IIIT Hyderabad, India", *http://festvox.org/databases/iiit_voices/*

[2] Himadri Mukherjee, Subhankar Ghosh,Shibaprasad Sen, Obaidullah Sk Md, K. C. Santosh, Santanu Phadikar, Kaushik Roy, Neural Computing and Applications **31**, pp. 8483-8501 (2019)

[3] Amit A. Chowdhury, Vaibhav S. Borkar and Gajanan K. Birajdar, Journal of Experimental and Theoretical Artificial Intelligence **32**, pp. 111-132 (2019)

[4] Bakshi Aarti and Sunil Kumar Kopparapu, Sādhanā **43**, (2018)

[5] Deepti Deshwal, Pardeep Sangwan and Divya Kumar, Wireless Personal Communications **107**, pp. 2071–2103 (2019)

[6] A. Venkitaraman, A. Adiga, C. S. Seelamantula, Signal Processing (Elsevier) **94**, pp. 608-619 (2014)

[7] Aref Farhadi Pour, Mohammad Asgari and Mohammad Reza Hasanabadi, 4th International Conference on Computer and Knowledge Engineering (ICCKE), pp. 1-4 (2014)

[8] E. Jacobsen and R. Lyons, IEEE Signal Processing Magazine **20**, pp. 74-80 (2003)

[9] Nadia Jmour, Sehla Zayen, Afef Abdelkrim, International Conference on Advanced Systems and Electric Technologies (IC_ASET), pp. 1-6 (2018)

[10] Y. LeCun, B. Boser, J. S. Denker, Henderson, R. E. Howard, W. Hubbard, L. D. Jackel, Neural Computation **1**, pp. 541-551 (1989)

[11] Rajesh Kumar G A, Ravi Kant Kumar, Gaotam Sanyal, International Conference on Signal Processing and Communication (ICSPC), pp. 1-6 (2017)

[12] Verma, V.k., Khanna ,N., IEEE Students Conference on Engineering and Systems (SCES), pp. 1-5 (2013)

[13] Manish Gupta, Shambhu Shankar Bharti, Suneeta Agarwal, 4th International Conference on Power, Control and Embedded Systems (ICPCES), pp. 1-6 (2017)

[14] Madhu, C.,George, A. and Mary, L., IEEE International Conference on Signal Processing, Informatics, Communication and Energy Systems (SPICES), pp. 1-6 (2017)

[15] Rao, K. S., Maity, S. Â. V., Reddy, R., International Journal of Speech Technology **16**, pp. 413-430 (2013)

[16] S. Jothilakshmi, V. Ramalingam, S. Palanivel, Digital Signal Processing (Elsevier) **22**, pp. 544-553 (2012)

[17] Saikia R, Singh SR, Sarmah P, International conference on Asian language processing (IALP), pp. 1-4 (2014)

[18] Neha Sharma, Vibhor Jain, Anju Mishra, Procedia Computer Science **132**, pp. 377-384 (2018)

[19] Paolo Arena, Adriano Basile, Maide Bucolo, Luigi Fortuna, Nuclear Instruments and Methods in Physics Research Section **497**, pp.174-178 (2003)

[20] Jaromir Przybyło, Mirosław Jabłoński, Computers and Electronics in Agriculture (Elsevier) **156**, pp. 490-499 (2019)

[21] Maier, A., Syben, C., Lasser, T., and Riess, C., Zeitschrift für Medizinische Physik **29**, pp. 86-101 (2019)

[22] Rashid, H., Zafar, N., Iqbal, M. J., Dawood, H., and Dawood, H., Procedia Computer Science (Elsevier) **147**, pp. 124-130 (2019)

[23] Liu, S., Wang, Y., Yang, X., Lei, B., Liu, L., Xiang Li, S., Wang, T, Environmental Science and Technology **53**, pp. 4128-4139 (2019)

[24] Pan Zhou and Jiashi Feng., International Conference on Machine Learning (ICML), pp.1-10 (2018)

[25] Kim, T., Information Security and Assurance - 4th International Conference (ISA), CCIS **76** pp. 138-148 (2010)

ROS based SLAM implementation for Autonomous navigation using Turtlebot

Sumegh Pramod Thale[1], Mihir Mangesh Prabhu[2], Pranjali Vinod Thakur[3], Pratik kadam[4]
Dept.of Electronics Engg,
Ramrao Adik Institute of Technology, Navi Mumbai, India
[1]*thalesumegh@gmail.com*

***Abstract*—This paper presents the autonomous navigation of a robot using SLAM algorithm.The proposed work uses Robot Operating system as a framework.The robot is simulated in gazebo and Rviz used for data visualization.Gmapping package is used for mapping by utilizing laser and odometry data from various sensors.The Turtlebot provides open source software to perform navigation.**

***Index Terms*—Robot Operating System (ROS),Simultaneous localization and mapping (SLAM), Adaptive Monte Carlo Localization (AMCL) Kinect, Rviz, Gazebo, Gmapping, Turtlebot, URDF, Odometry**

I. Introduction

Autonomous navigation is a research field that has seen incredible advances for the past few years.In this well researched domain of autonomous navigation our main area of interest is indoor office like environment. In industrial applications the use of autonomous robots is increasing, the main cost associated with manual material handling is labour.The plant's material handling cost can be reduced up to 30 per cent by the use of autonomous robotic vehicles.These autonomous robots can navigate in locations dangerous to workers with minimum human intervention.Various issues in autonomous navigation like mapping,localization and path planning can be solved using different approaches.The purpose of this paper is to discuss and demonstrate the concept of designing and simulating a mobile robot capable of visually detecting and avoiding static obstacles using SLAM and reaching the desired location autonomously.

A. Related work

In the research paper [1] the authors have discussed various methods to implement SLAM through the use of Extended Kalman filter and Rao-Blackwellized Filter.The authors of paper [1]have incorporated autonomous navigation for moving obstacles and outdoor vision based navigation.Various SLAM algorithms like CoreSLAM, Gmapping, and HectorSLAM have been evaluated in the paper [2].The authors of the paper [3] made use of a kinect sensor and rviz to implement autonomous navigation on turtlebot 2.The utilization of compact RF ID sensor for the object level mapping of indoor environment has has been briefly explained by the authors of [4].

B. Solution

For implementing autonomous navigation SLAM algorithm can be used. SLAM is used for estimating the position of the robot by moving it along the unknown area. More the number of attempts of exploring the unknown area, the more is the quality of the generated map. SLAM algorithm is implemented using GMapping Tool. GMapping Tool requires odometry data (encoder data from the wheels) and laser data (kinect data) . slam_gmapping is used to create 2-D occupancy grid map which is like a building floor plan.

The robot software development is done in ROS (Robot Operating System). ROS provides services like message passing between processes and package,low level device control, implementation of common functions. In ROS the process are shown in graph format and the processing happens in nodes.

All the complex 3D simulations are done in GAZEBO. Models, GZ Sever, GZ Client and GZ Web are the main components of it. GAZEBO has features like built in robot models, cloud simulation,dynamics simulation, advanced 3D graphics, command line tools and TCP IP transport. With the help of GAZEBO we can conceptualize Inertia, Forces and Sensor Information.

C. Objectives

- Manually mapping the environment.
- To locate the robot in the generated map.
- Autonomously moving the robot.

D. Organization

Section 2 gives a brief information about the simulation environment and how the system is implemented in it. Section 3 consists of a theoretical explanation of SLAM and Section 4 has map generation and SLAM implementation.

II. Simulation Environment

A. What is ROS?

Robot operating system is an open source meta operating system under BSD (Berkeley Software Distribution) license. Code can be written, built and tested across various computers using the inbuilt tools and libraries provided in ROS. Various services like controlling low level devices, implementing generally used functionality, exchanging messages between various processes and management of packages are provided in

https://doi.org/10.1051/itmconf/20203201011

ROS [5]. ROS enables us to use already created packages like Gmapping and teleop_key which reduces development time. In this paper ROS is used to publish messages in the form of topics between different nodes. ROS is also used to create a virtual environment, generate robot model, implement the algorithms and visualize it in the virtual world rather than implementing the whole system in the hardware itself. The creation of the virtual environment is done using Gazebo and rviz.

B. What is Gazebo?

Gazebo is a 3D dynamic simulator used for simulating complex robotic models in indoor and outdoor environments.It provides with the ability to test the robotic model in the simulated environment and incorporate the data from the sensors.Gazebo allows to test the performance of the robotic model in extreme conditions without damaging the hardware.It uses an physical engine for illumination,inertia,gravity,etc.An XML file called the (URDF) Universal Robotic Description Format is used to describe different elements of the robot. The "Fig. 1" shows the 3D model of turtlebot simulated in gazebo.The robotic model is tested in the environment shown in the "Fig. 2".

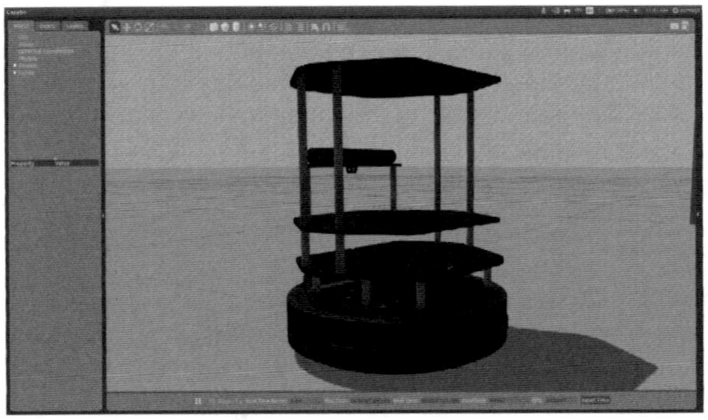

Fig. 1: Turtlebot model in gazebo

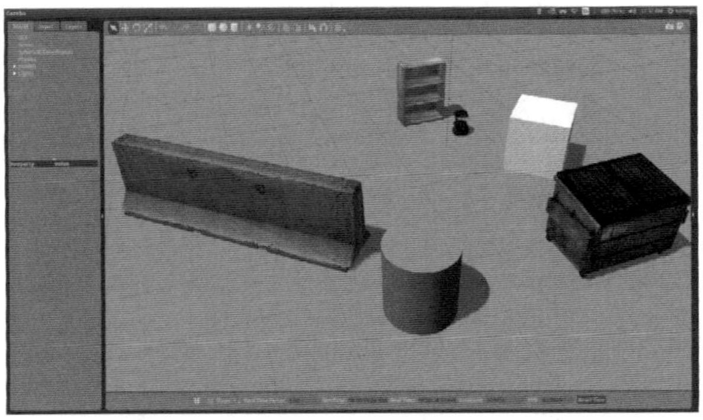

Fig. 2: Simulated environment in gazebo

C. What is Rviz?

Rviz is an acronym for ROS visualization, is a effective 3D visualization tool for ROS. It permits the user to see the simulated robot model, log sensor data from the robot's sensors, and replay the logged sensor data. By visualizing what the robot is seeing, thinking, and doing, the user can debug a robot application from sensor inputs to planned (or unplanned) actions.

Rviz exhibits 3D sensor data from stereo cameras, lasers, Kinects, and other devices in the form of point clouds. 2D sensor data from webcams, RGB cameras can be viewed in rviz as image data.

III. SLAM ALGORITHM

Autonomous robots are able to navigate indoors and outdoors without colliding with obstacles in its environment. Simultaneous localization and mapping is a technique used for the purpose of making a map, updating it and to estimate the position of the robot. Some of the algorithms that are used to solve it include particle filter, Extended Kalman filter, FastSLAM, Covariance intersection and Graph based SLAM. SLAM algorithm is a combination of Mapping, Sensing, Kinematic modeling, Multiple Objects, Multiple Cameras, Moving Objects, Loop closure, Exploration, Complexity. The main part of SLAM is a range measurement device which is used for observing the environment. The range measurement device depends on different variables. The robot uses landmarks to determine its location using measuring devices and sensors. When the robot has sensed a landmark it extracts the input and identifies the environment. Some types of SLAM algorithm that exist are CoreSLAM, Gmapping, KartoSLAM, Lago SLAM and HectorSLAM. In this paper the SLAM algorithm used is Gmapping which relies on Particle filter. The Objective of the particle filter is to compute the posterior distributions of the states of a Markov process, if there are some noisy and partial observations. Particle filter uses approximate prediction and updates. The samples from the distribution are given in the form of particles, each particle has a weight assigned to it which represents the probability of particles being sampled.

Gmapping is a profoundly proficient Rao-Blackwellized particle filter that creates grid maps from laser data [6]. This package contains a ROS wrapper for OpenSlam's Gmapping. The gmapping package provides laser-based SLAM, as a ROS node called slam_gmapping. Utilizing slam_gmapping, you can create a 2-D occupancy grid map from laser and pose data gathered by a mobile robot .

SLAM algorithm is implemented in various applications such as self driving cars, underwater reef monitoring, mine explorations and unmanned aircrafts. SLAM algorithms are implemented using an open source ROS.

IV. Adaptive Monte Carlo Localization

A key issue with particle filter is keeping up random distribution of particles all through the state space, which gets complicated if the problem is of high magnitude.Because of these reasons it is preferred to utilize an adaptive particle filter which merges a lot quicker and is computationally considerably more effective than a primitive particle filter.

AMCL is a probabilistic localization system, which is used in robots moving in 2D. It performs the adaptive Monte Carlo localization approach, which utilizes a particle filter to follow the position of a robot against a previously known map.

The first step to utilize adaptive particle filter for localization is generate the map of the environment. The robot can be set to a random location or it could start from no initial estimate of its position. After the robot moves forward the generation of new sample starts that will predict the robots position after the command. Random uniformly distributed samples can be added as the robot recovers if it losses track of its position.

V. SLAM implementation

A. Map Generation

The map generation is carried out by first generating the environment and importing turtlebot in Gazebo.The robot model consists of two wheels and a kinect sensor is mounted inside the frame.The mapping process in this paper is implemented using the gmapping package.To use gmapping the robot model must provide odometry data and should be equipped with a horizontally-mounted, fixed, laser range-finder.The kinect captures the depth image of the environment using Infrared sensors and acts as a range finder device.It takes 16 bits per pixel infrared data with a resolution of 640 x 480 as an color image format.This depth image is converted into a 3d point cloud using the depth_image_proc package in ROS.Further this 3d point cloud data is converted into 2d laserscan using pointcloud_to_laserscan package.By providing all the required parameters to the packages in gmapping a map is created in rviz.The "Fig. 3" shows the generated map.Initially the robot is moved in the simulated environment using the teleop_key package in ROS by sending velocity commands via keyboard.The "Fig. 5" shows the rqt graph of gmapping.The gmapping package provides /map topic which can be used by the map_server package to save the generated map.The map is now ready to be utilized for autonomous navigation.

B. Localization

Localization estimates the position and pose of the robot with respect to the environment.To localize the robot laser data, odometry data and the map of environment are essential.The turlebot uses AMCL (Adaptive Monte Carlo Localization) for localization.It follows an probabilistic localization approach for robots in 2 dimensions.In AMCL the pose of the robot is tracked against the known map of the environment using a particle filter.To reduce the computational requirement KLD (Kullback-Leibler divergence) sampling is utilized to automatically adapt for sample size [7].The "Fig. 4" shows the self localized robot rviz.

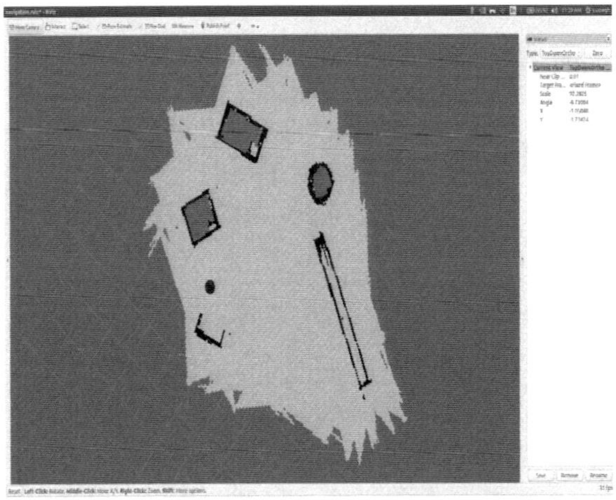

Fig. 3: Visualizing map in rviz

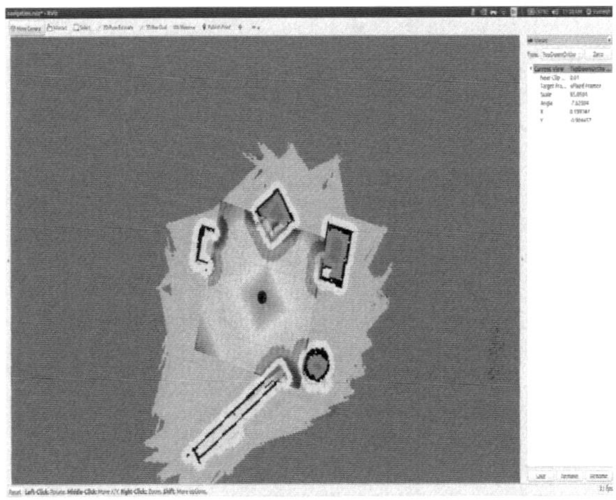

Fig. 4: Localized robot in rviz

C. Rqt graph

The Rqt tool suite in ROS provides a GUI plugon called Rqt graph.The rqt graph is a tool used to visualize all the running nodes and processes as well as the communication between them.The rqt graph can provide a global overview of the system.Rqt can be used as a debugging tool for the system.

D. Autonomous navigation

The autonomous navigation can be performed once the mapping and localization is completed.The ROS navigation stack packages are used to implement AMCL.The node to perform localization on a static map is provided by ROS AMCL package.This node subscribes to the TF data,2D laser

 https://doi.org/10.1051/itmconf/20203201011

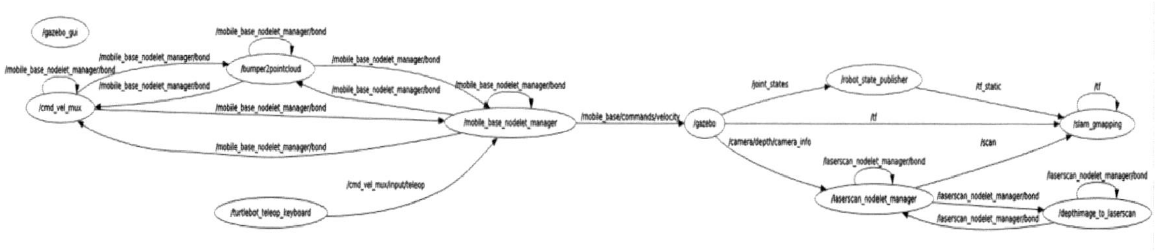

Fig. 5: Rqt graph gmapping

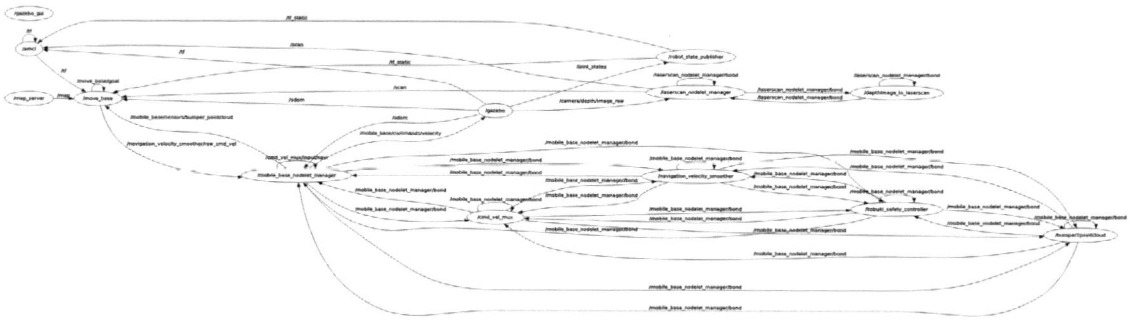

Fig. 6: Rqt graph AMCL

scan data provided by the robot and the previously generated static map.The pose of the robot and its estimated position with respect to the map is published by the AMCL node.The "Fig. 6" shows the rqt_graph of the AMCL.The information about the obstacles in the simulated world is stored in two costmaps.Global costmap is used for global path planning,it makes a long term path plan over the map.The local costmap is used for obstacle avoidance and local path planning.The Rviz visualizes the global and local costmap. The robot can be now moved autonomously .The 2D nav goal in Rviz is used to assign a destination goal to the robot in the map along with its orientation.The path to the desired destination is planned by the robot and velocity commands are given to the robot controller. The "Fig. 7" shows the path followed by the robot to navigate from its initial position to the desired destination goal assigned.

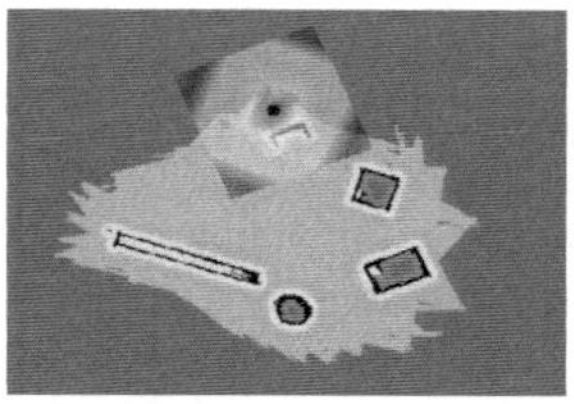
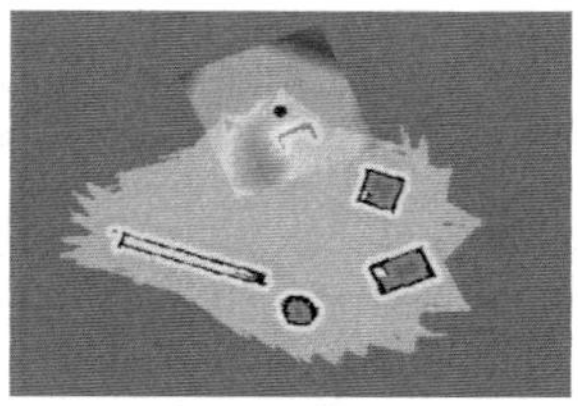

(a) First (b) Second

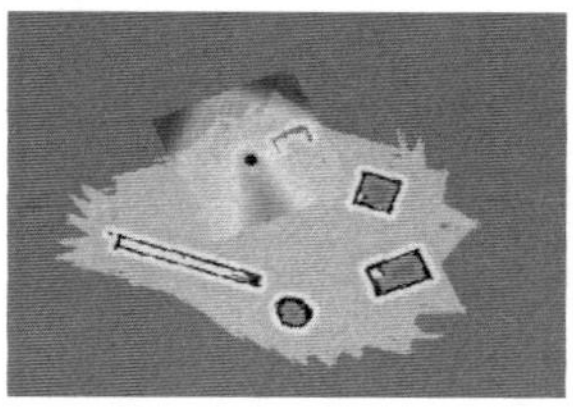
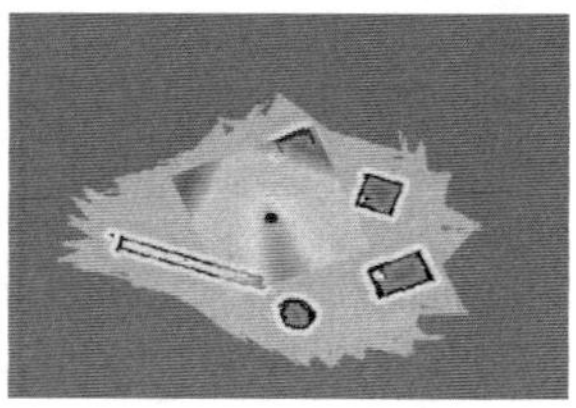

(c) Third (d) Forth

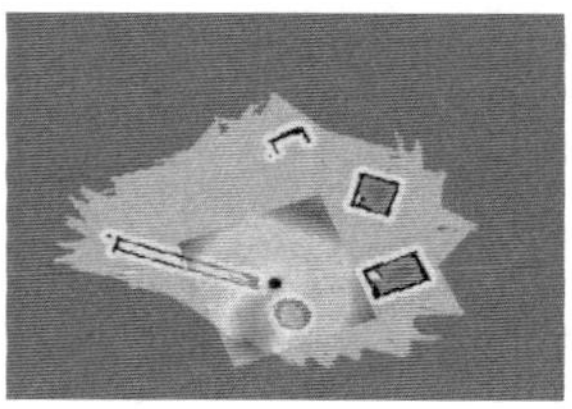
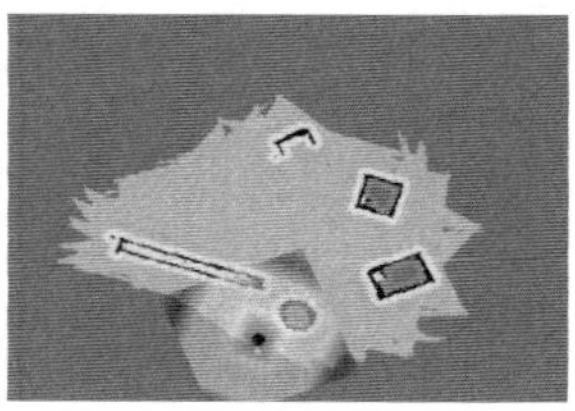

(e) Fifth (f) Sixth

Fig. 7: Autonomous navigation

VI. Conclusion

In this paper, we have analyzed and successfully executed an autonomous navigation system using ROS. The software and hardware of the system are described in the above section. Turtle bot was used in a simulated environment created with the help of Gazebo for experimenting and implementing autonomous navigation. Methods used for navigation are SLAM and path planning algorithms. As shown in the above section of the map was successfully generated by robot and managed to reach the assigned destination without colliding.

The current work can achieve more precision in navigation through more software development and analysis. The full hardware implementation and calibration for achieving more precision remains for future work.

References

[1] Cherubini, A., Spindler, F. and Chaumette, F., 2014. Autonomous visual navigation and laser-based moving obstacle avoidance. IEEE Transactions on Intelligent Transportation Systems, 15(5), pp.2101-2110.

[2] Turnage, D.M., 2016, December. Simulation results for localization and mapping algorithms. In 2016 Winter Simulation Conference (WSC) (pp. 3040-3051). IEEE.

[3] Omara, H.I.M.A. and Sahari, K.S.M., 2015, August. Indoor mapping using kinect and ROS. In 2015 International Symposium on Agents, Multi-Agent Systems and Robotics (ISAMSR) (pp. 110-116). IEEE.

[4] Malla, H., Purushothaman, P., Rajan, S.V. and Balasubramanian, V., 2014, November. Object level mapping of an indoor environment using RFID. In 2014 Ubiquitous Positioning Indoor Navigation and Location Based Service (UPINLBS) (pp. 203-212). IEEE.

[5] Amanda Dattalo, "Introduction," ros.wiki.org.

[6] Grisetti, G., Stachniss, C. and Burgard, W., 2007. Improved techniques for grid mapping with rao-blackwellized particle filters. IEEE transactions on Robotics, 23(1), pp.34-46.

[7] Zaman, S., Slany, W. and Steinbauer, G., 2011, April. ROS-based mapping, localization and autonomous navigation using a Pioneer 3-DX robot and their relevant issues. In 2011 Saudi International Electronics, Communications and Photonics Conference (SIECPC) (pp. 1-5). IEEE.

Diabetic Retinopathy Severity Detection using Convolutional Neural Network

Mayank Shete[1,*], *Saahil* Sabnis[2,**] *Srijan* Rai[3,***], and *Gajanan* Birajdar[4,****]

[1]Department of Electronics Engineering, Ramrao Adik Institute of Technology
Nerul, Navi Mumbai, Maharashtra, India
400706

Abstract. Diabetic Retinopathy is one of the most prominent eye diseases and is the leading cause of blindness amongst adults. Automatic detection of Diabetic Retinopathy is important to prevent irreversible damage to the eye-sight. Existing feature learning methods have a lesser accuracy rate in computer aided diagnostics; this paper proposes a method to further increase the accuracy. Machine learning can be used effectively for the diagnosis of this disease. CNN and transfer learning are used for the severity classification and have achieved an accuracy of 73.9 percent. The use of XGBoost classifier yielded an accuracy of 76.5 percent.

Keywords: Convolutional Neural Networks, Hypertensive Retinopathy, Arteriosclerotic Retinopathy, Machine learning, Transfer Learning, EyePacs

1 Introduction

Diabetic Retinopathy (DR) is a disease which occurs due to damage to the retina. It is a leading cause of blindness [15]. Diabetic Retinopathy has different levels of severity. Severity level is a crucial aspect in Diabetic Retinopathy. It not only tells us about the risk of blindness but also dictates whether it can be cured or not. People diagnosed with diabetes have a higher probability of getting diagnosed with DR. Hence regular screening of diabetic patients for DR helps in early detection and therefore treatment.

Early detection is an important aspect in Diabetic Retinopathy. Diabetic retinopathy affects up to 80 percent of those who have had diabetes for 20 years [1] or more. It often has no early warning signs, but if detected early it can be cured 90 percent of the time [15]. DR can be classified into three categories [3]: 1.Hypertensive Retinopathy 2.Arteriosclerotic Retinopathy 3.Retinopathy of prematurity

This paper focuses on Hypertensive and Arteriosclerotic retinopathy. Hypertensive retinopathy is caused by high blood pressure [3]. The high blood pressure causes damage to blood vessels in the retina. This puts pressure on the optic nerve which can limit the retina function leading to blindness. Arteriosclerotic retinopathy is caused by Arteriosclerosis [4]. Thickening of walls of arteries in the eye occurs in this condition. Hence the blood flow is partially blocked which causes vision impairment. If this condition remains untreated can cause swelling or even bursting of blood vessels. Hence the early detection and treatment of Diabetic Retinopathy is necessary.

In hospitals and clinics the analysis is performed by an ophthalmologist manually. The retina scan is captured by retinal scanners. These scans are observed and analyzed. The ophthalmologist looks for signs such as hemorrhages, swelling of blood vessels, clots, the color of the retina and many more [5]. This entire process is manual and thus takes a significant amount of time. Besides this there's always the element of human error which cannot be predicted. These factors can collectively lead to misdiagnosis.

If Diabetic Retinopathy is misdiagnosed and accurate treatment isn't provided it can cause irreversible damage to the retina and might result in permanent blindness. Thus an accurate diagnosis is necessary. Computerizing the whole detection is one way to prevent misdiagnosis.

A neural network is a set of algorithms loosely modeled after the structure of the human brain [16]. Neural networks are designed to recognize patterns. Hence we can make such a network that'll help us identify the cases of diabetic retinopathy. A tool to determine the severity of the DR would be incredibly useful so doctors can diagnose it faster and more accurately.

Several algorithms have been proposed for DR detection and severity analysis. However these algorithms have a lower rate of correct diagnosis. To address this low accuracy problem, we used different neural networks but mainly Convolutional Neural Network (CNN). CNN is a type of neural network mostly used to analyze visual imagery. CNNs consist of multilayer perceptrons [16]. Multilayer perceptrons are fully connected networks. The name 'Convolutional Neural Network' implies that the network is performing convolution function. In CNN

*e-mail: mayankshete9@gmail.com
**e-mail: saahilsabnis@gmail.com
***e-mail: raisrijan5@gmail.com
****e-mail: gajanan.birajdar@rait.ac.in

the input is a tensor with a definite shape. This shape is 'number of images x image width x image height x image depth' After the image passes through these layers a feature map is created. This way each layer performs convolution and passes the result to the next layer.

Our dataset was created using retinal scans provided by EyePacs. This dataset contained normal retina scans as well as retina scans of people diagnosed with DR. The dataset had retinal scans with varying severity of DR. The severity of Diabetic Retinopathy was on a scale of 0 to 4, 0 being the absence of DR and 4 being proliferative DR. Using these images neural network was trained to look for features such as shape, size, color etc. Using these parameters the network gave the result. The output of CNN was the indication of the severity of the DR.

Firstly, pre-processing was performed in order to fine tune the dataset. This included cropping of the retinal scan, suppressing the noise etc. We make use of VggNet, ResNet and inception V3 to obtain a more accurate result. The use of XGBoost trainer classifier further increased the accuracy.

We illustrated dataset, pre-processing and algorithm in section 3 and in section 4 we illustrated the testing results and accuracy of the various models.

2 Literature Survey

In the (DRSS) Diabetic Retinopathy Severity Score manual [14], Bob Wilkes explains how diabetic retinopathy is detected from retina scans of the eyes. The manual explains how the early signs of diabetic retinopathy which are abnormal blood vessels, retinal detachment and swelling of the retina. These signs are looked for in a patient's retinal scans to check if there is any danger to the patient's eyesight. Bio-inspired nano-sensor-enhanced CNN visual computer, elaborated on image recognition, stabilization, and pattern detection can be done using a CNN [12]. In [15] demonstrates the effectiveness in the detection of lesions in retinal images using CNNs.

In [13], the resourcefulness of transfer learning models was illustrated. Google's inception V3 has been used after cleaning the dataset via transfer learning. While training a validation split of 0.1 was introduced and the model used the Softmax classifier and Inception v3 is a widely-used image recognition model that has been shown to attain greater than 78.1 percent accuracy on the ImageNet dataset.

The use of a combination of datasets is explained in [6], and one of those was maintained by EyePacs. The other dataset was named Messidor-2 and is publicly available. While training the model, Pre-initialization and batch normalization was used to improve training speed and accuracy. The model used 80 percent of the images for optimizing network weights and 20 percent to optimize hyperparameters. The model accuracy was 70.7 percent.

In [7], during their pre-processing stage they performed color normalization using the OpenCV package. They trained the network using stochastic gradient descent with Nesterov momentum. They performed analysis to grade the severity of Diabetic Retinopathy and validated their result by verifying from an expert ophthalmologist. [9] explained the advantages of GoogleNet, ResNet, AlexNet etc. The accuracy of the used VggNet-s model classification was 95.68 percent.

Pires et al. in their research have demonstrated how a multi-resolution training approach works [10]. In this model the weights from the previously trained network can be utilised in order to increase accuracy and boost the efficiency. So this used multiple CNNs. The weights from the first CNN at the end were used as the initial weights of the second CNN. In "Modified Alexnet architecture for classification of diabetic retinopathy images" the images were split in RGB channels [11]. Using these channels the images were refined. As different channels have different advantages their added collective benefit increased the model accuracy to 96 percent. By reading all these papers on Diabetic Retinopathy detection using the Convolutional Neural Network we created our own model based on that knowledge.

3 Proposed Algorithm

The retinal scans we used in the dataset were maintained by EyePacs, a California based foundation that actively works on Diabetic Retinopathy screening programs. There were a total of 35126 retinal scans in the training data. These images were in pairs having a left and right retinal images of every subject and it was named accordingly. A trained clinician-rated the presence of Diabetic Retinopathy and included the same for every individual image in a .csv file. The CSV file contained the severity graded from 0-4 of its corresponding retinal image.

Class Name	Degree of DR	Numbers
Class 0	Normal	25810
Class 1	Mild	2443
Class 2	Moderate	5292
Class 3	Severe	873
Class 4	Proliferative	708

Since the images had a different resolution we had to reshape them to a standard resolution to make the dataset. The standard resolution we chose was 1024x1024. So keeping that in mind we resized all the images to that resolution. While doing so we changed the aspect ratio of all images to 1:1. This made the dataset more uniform. The image below shows the difference between a normal retina and a retina of a person diagnosed with Diabetes.

Hemorrhages, Aneurysm and abnormal growth of blood vessels can be observed in the second retina scan. We pre-processed our data to enhance these features of the retina scan so that they can be easily detected. We tried Ben Graham's insightful way of improving lighting in the images so that the lesions, hemorrhaging are visible clearly in the image.

In this method we convert the image into gray-scale to reduce the layers of the image to reduce computing time. Next we add another image to the image, this added image is called the Gaussian Blur effect. It adds an image

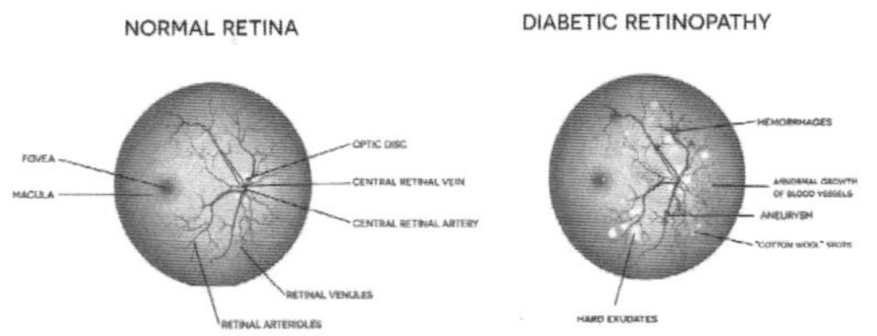

Figure 1. Normal eye vs affected eye

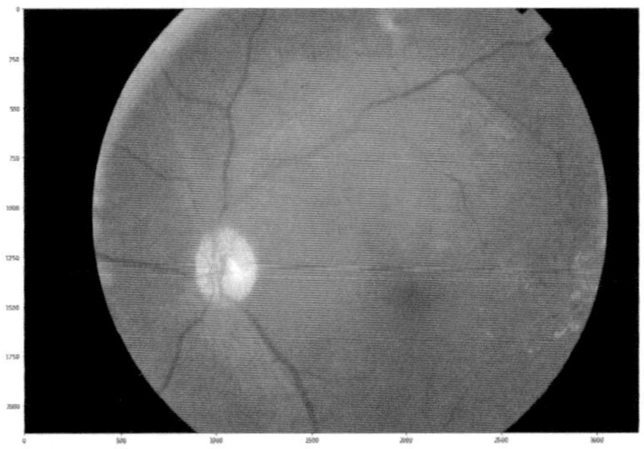

Figure 2. Gray scale image

which is considered as white Gaussian Noise which suppresses the non-vital regions in the image. It has its own sigma level adjustments and alpha-beta-gamma filter levels to adjust the levels of the Gaussian Blur.

We have also cropped out the non relevant black areas in the background of the scans by using a cropping algorithm that crops out the areas without any information and keeps only the areas which contain the retinal scans. However the method used by us is applicable only for gray-scale images.The preprocessed images were then converted to datasets to be used by the models that will be further developed by us.

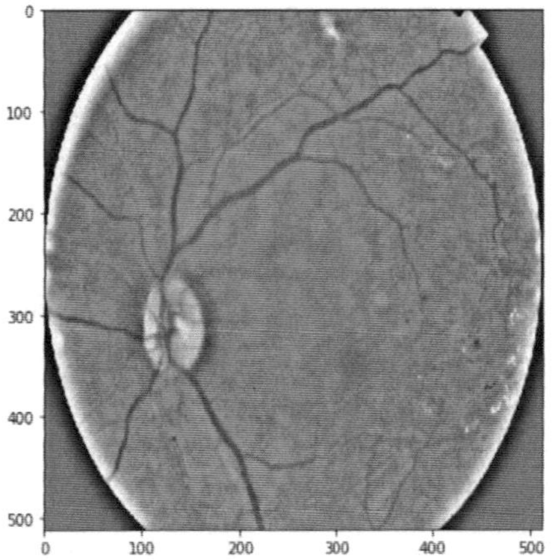

Figure 3. Image with Gaussian Blur

We have developed a Convolutional Neural Network of 7 layers that extract the features from the images and help the network to classify the images more accurately. The network runs for 10 epochs and gives accuracy in the range of 70-80 percent. Another method used in this paper is the XGBoost library which uses Booster models for classification problems. This method works very well for imbalanced datasets like the ones used for this problem. They have block structure implementation to support parallelization of tree structure. This ensures a very high accuracy in the training process.

We have employed two transfer learning models as well to gauge the accuracy of the detection under some of the established learning algorithms. Transfer learning is an approach that involves storing knowledge acquired from solving a problem and using that knowledge to solve another pertinent problem. For instance, the knowledge gained while learning to identify cars could be used to design a model that would recognize trucks.

From a practical standpoint, transferring information from previously trained models or tasks for the learning of distinct and newer tasks has the potential to significantly boost the performance of a reinforcement learning agent. Three possible benefits to look for when using transfer learning as stated by Lisa Torrey and Jude Shavlik in their book under the chapter of transfer learning are [20]: "Higher start. The initial skill (before refining the model) on the source model is higher than it otherwise would be. Higher slope. The rate of improvement of skill during the training of the source model is steeper than it otherwise would be. Higher asymptote." The overall capability of the the transferred model is better than a model that would be designed from scratch.

We have used the following three pre-trained models to implement transfer learning: Google's Inception V3 model and Microsoft's ResNet

4 Results

Vision loss can be prevented if diabetic retinopathy is diagnosed at an early stage.The algorithm proposed focuses on developing an accurate model to detect the severity of the disease. Deep learning is one of the most widely used techniques for countering classification problems with higher efficiency. Meticulously designed Convolution Neural Networks providing accurate classification will be helpful in the diagnosis. The class with the highest probability score is called the winning class.

Algorithm	Classifier	Performance
CNN	Sigmoid	73.9%
ResNet50	Relu	73.9%
InceptionV3	Relu	73.9%
XGBoost	XGBClassifier	76.5%

There were a total of 35126 images available for training. The CNN Model developed by us yields an accuracy of 73.9 percent , whereas th e value accuracy for the model is 75.1 percent. The XGBoost classifier trainer gives us a

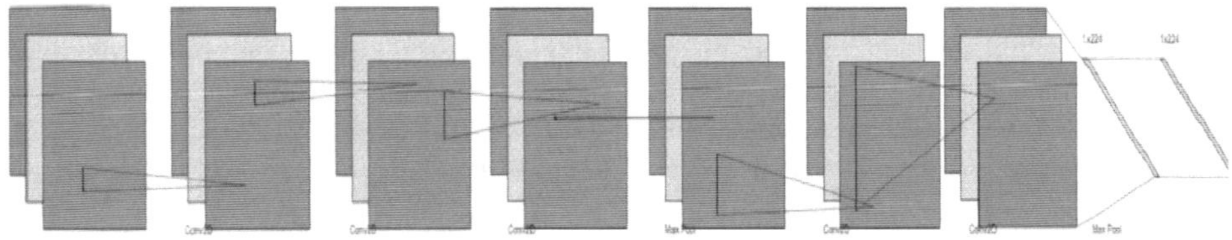

Figure 4. CNN Architecture

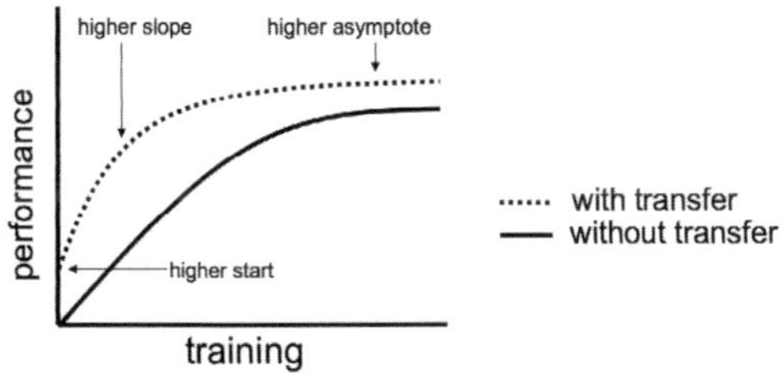

Figure 5. Advantages of transfer learning

better accuracy of 76.5 percent since it uses a scaling tree boosting system which uses a recursive learning system to rectify the errors. The ResNet50 model yielded a 75.3 percent accuracy and uses around 24,113,421 total parameters out of which 24,060,541 are trainable and 53,120 are non-trainable parameters. The Inception V3 is the algorithm developed by Google which is widely used for image recognition and gives us an accuracy of 76.2 percent.

Name	Technique	Accuracy
Xiaoling Wang et. al. [17]	Inception V3	63.23%
Kwasigroch et. al. [18]	CNN	51%
Hare S.S. et. al. [19]	CNN	74.04%
Proposed	XGBoost	76.5%

5 Conclusion

In this paper we introduced a CNN architecture designed to detect and identify the cases of Diabetic Retinopathy. This method was used to classify a retina scan into different classes from 0 to 4, class 0 indicating absence of DR and class 4 being proliferative DR. This architecture yielded an accuracy of 73.9 percent, and on using XGBoost the accuracy rose to 76.5 per cent. Further research can improve the accuracy.

References

[1] Kertes PJ, Johnson TM, eds. (2007). Evidence Based Eye Care. Philadelphia, PA: Lippincott Williams and Wilkins. ISBN 978-0-7817-6964-8.

[2] Tapp RJ, Shaw JE, Harper CA, de Courten MP, Balkau B, McCarty DJ, Taylor HR, Welborn TA, Zimmet PZ (June 2003). "The prevalence of and factors associated with diabetic retinopathy in the Australian population". Diabetes Care. 26 (6): 1731–7. doi:10.2337/diacare.26.6.1731

[3] EverydayHealth.com. (2020). Diabetic Retinopathy - Types, Symptoms, Causes and Complications | Everyday Health. [online] Available at: https://www.everydayhealth.com/diabetic-retinopathy/guide/

[4] MedicineNet. (2020). Definition of Arteriosclerotic retinopathy. [online] Available at: https://www.medicinenet.com/script/main/art.asp?articlekey=24652

[5] Cold, F., Health, E., Disease, H., Disease, L., Management, P., Conditions, S., Problems, S., Disorders, S., Checker, S., Blogs, W., Boards, M., Answers, Q., Guide, I., Doctor, F., A-Z, C., A-Z, S., Medications, M., Identifier, P., Interactions, C., Drugs, C., Pregnant, T., Management, D., Obesity, W., Recipes, F., Exercise, F., Beauty, H., Balance, H., Relationships, S., Care, O., Health, W., Health, M., Well, A., Sleep, H., Teens, H., Pregnant, G., Trimester, F., Trimester, S., Trimester, T., Baby, N., Health, C., Vaccines, C., Kids, R., Cats, H., Dogs, H., Updates, C., Untreatable, C., Back, I., Play Golf, L., Peak, F., Boards, M., Blogs, W. and Center, N. (2020). Diabetic Retinopathy: Risks, Treatments, Prevention. [online] WebMD. Available at: https://www.webmd.com/diabetes/diabetic-retinopathy1

[6] Gulshan, V., Peng, L., Coram, M., Stumpe, M., Wu, D., Narayanaswamy, A., Venugopalan, S., Widner, K., Madams, T., Cuadros, J., Kim, R., Raman, R., Nelson, P., Mega, J. and Webster, D. (2016). Development and Validation of a Deep Learning Algorithm for Detection of Diabetic Retinopathy in Retinal Fundus Photographs. JAMA, 316(22), p.2402.

[7] Pratt, H., Coenen, F., Broadbent, D., Harding, S. and Zheng, Y. (2016). Convolutional Neural Networks for Diabetic Retinopathy. Procedia Computer Science, 90, pp.200-205.

[8] Triwijoyo, B., Budiharto, W. and Abdurachman, E. (2017). The Classification of Hypertensive Retinopathy using Convolutional Neural Network. Procedia Computer Science, 116, pp.166-173.

[9] Wan, S., Liang, Y. and Zhang, Y. (2018). Deep convolutional neural networks for diabetic retinopathy detection by image classification. Computers and Electrical Engineering, 72, pp.274-282.

[10] Pires, R., Avila, S., Wainer, J., Valle, E., Abramoff, M. and Rocha, A. (2019). A data-driven approach to referable diabetic retinopathy detection. Artificial Intelligence in Medicine, 96, pp.93-106.

[11] Shanthi, T. and Sabeenian, R. (2019). Modified Alexnet architecture for classification of diabetic retinopathy images. Computers and Electrical Engineering, 76, pp.56-64.

[12] Porod, Wolfgang and Werblin, Frank and Chua, Leon and Roska, Tamas and Rodriguez-Vazquez, Angel and Roska, Botond and Fay, Patrick and Bernstein, Gary and Huang, Yih-Fang and Csurgay, Árpád. (2004). Bio-Inspired Nano-Sensor-Enhanced CNN Visual Computer. Annals of the New York Academy of Sciences. 1013. 92-109. 10.1196/annals.1305.011.

[13] S. Srivastava, S. Prabhu, S. Ramesh, S. Pratapneni, A. Abraham and S. V Bhandary, "Visualizing the Indicators of Diabetic Retinopathy Learnt by Convolutional Neural Networks," 2017 IEEE International Conference on Computational Intelligence and Computing Research (ICCIC), Coimbatore, 2017, pp. 1-3.

[14] Wilkes, B. (2009). Central Mersey Diabetic Retinopathy Screening Programme. [online] pp.45-50.

[15] DocShop. (2020). Diabetic Retinopathy - Causes, Diagnosis, Symptoms, Risks. [online] Available at: https://www.docshop.com/education/vision/eye-diseases/diabetic-retinopathy.

[16] DeMuro, J. (2020). What is a neural network?. [online] TechRadar. Available at: https://www.techradar.com/news/what-is-a-neural-network.

[17] X. Wang, Y. Lu, Y. Wang and W. Chen, "Diabetic Retinopathy Stage Classification Using Convolutional Neural Networks," 2018 IEEE International Conference on Information Reuse and Integration (IRI), Salt Lake City, UT, 2018, pp. 465-471.

[18] Kwasigroch, Arkadiusz, Bartlomiej Jarzembinski, and Michal Grochowski. "Deep CNN based decision support system for detection and assessing the stage of diabetic retinopathy." 2018 International Interdisciplinary PhD Workshop (IIPhDW). IEEE, 2018

[19] Sharma, H., Singh, A., Chandel, A., Singh, P. and Sapkal, P. (2019). Detection of Diabetic Retinopathy Using Convolutional Neural Network. SSRN Electronic Journal.

[20] Torrey, Lisa and Jude Shavlik. "Transfer Learning." Handbook of Research on Machine Learning Applications and Trends: Algorithms, Methods, and Techniques. IGI Global, 2010. 242-264.

Class Attendance Management System using Facial Recognition

Clyde Gomes[1,4,*], *Sagar* Chanchal[2,**], *Tanmay* Desai[3,***], and *Dipti*Jadhav[4,****]

[1]Department of Computer Engineering
[2]Premier Automobiles Road Kurla(W)
[3]Mumbai - 400700

Abstract. Attendance marking in a classroom during a lecture is not only a onerous task but also a time consuming one at that. Due to an unusually high number of students present during the lecture there will always be a probability of proxy attendance(s).Attendance marking with conventional methods has been an area of challenge. The growing need of efficient and automatic techniques of marking attendance is a growing challenge in the area of face recognition. In recent years, the problem of automatic attendance marking has been widely addressed through the use of standard biometrics like fingerprint and Radio frequency Identification tags etc., However,these techniques lack the element of reliability. In this proposed project an automated attendance marking and management system is proposed by making use of face detection and recognition algorithms. Instead of using the conventional methods, this proposed system aims to develop an automated system that records the student's attendance by using facial recognition technology. The main objective of this work is to make the attendance marking and management system efficient, time saving, simple and easy. Here faces will be recognized using face recognition algorithms. The processed image will then be compared against the existing stored record and then attendance is marked in the database accordingly. Compared to existing system traditional attendance marking system, this system reduces the workload of people. This proposed system will be implemented with 4 phases such as Image Capturing, Segmentation of group image and Face Detection, Face comparison and Recognition, Updating of Attendance in database.
Keywords- Attendance, Facial recognition and detection, Haar cascade, LBPH, OpenCV-Python.

1 Introduction

At present facial recognition and image processing is a very interesting topic that has only had its surface scratched, facial recognition is quickly surpassing other forms of biometrics (Fingerprints, RFID etc) as facial recognition systems use a set of features distinct to one person. This proposed project can be applied to create an attendance system using facial recognition as the traditional method i.e., pen and paper is not only time consuming and burdensome it is also prone to proxies and manipulation, our aim in developing this project is to make the attendance system efficient, stop methods and means of proxies and to save time that would otherwise be lost in the lecture.

The idea for this project came to us in class as we saw the amount of time that has to be skipped for attendance and the nonchalance of students who had already marked their attendance which leads to the method being delayed further, we then decided that this would be a good and interesting field to delve into for our Project as the field of Image processing, recognition etc; has a world of scope and would help us inculcate our skills and make us a tad bit ready for any or most challenges ahead.

2 Related Work

The are a number of existing systems closely related to the proposed idea of marking attendance in a class by making use of facial recognition techniques and algorithms.To analyze these systems a literature survey of the proposed systems was done. The proposed case study was designed around certain relevant sources related to facial recognition and image processing.A descriptive framework was designed using the other design approaches. [1]

This system makes use of DNN to detect the faces of students and PCA and LDA algorithm for image matching and a SVM classifier and CNN, they achieved a accuracy of 86 percent with a database containing eleven images, the database was created by extracting frames from a video recording of a student and those respective frames were then stored in the database .[1]

The authors developed a system using a raspberry pi camera module which is installed on the door,and the database is connected to a web management server system. When the raspberry pi captures an image, Local Binary pattern algorithm is applied to it, if it matches the

*e-mail: clyde9gomes@gmail.com
**e-mail: sagarr2112@gmail.com
***e-mail: desaitanmay200@gmail.com
****e-mail: dipti.dbit@dbclmumbai.org

image stored in the database, a servo motor opens the door for the student. This implemented system has an accuracy of 95 percent with a dataset of 11 images.[2]

The authors main aim here is to develop a face recognition algorithm with OpenCV 2.4.8 by using an attendance system as their case study, here the authors have compared two famous face recognition algorithms i.e., PCA(Eigenface) LDA(Fisherface)using a ROC curve on their training set, the result was Eigenface out performed Fisherface and got an accuracy of 70 percent to 90 percent similarity for genuine faces.[3]

The authors here propose a method of reducing the candidate gallery set and employing facial component classification, so as to enhance facial recognition, the authors performed experiments on CMU-PIE image database and PCA(Principal Component Analysis) algorithm, a success rate of 91.7 , the main aim of this system is to try and get down the processing time as much as possible.[4]

The authors here have made use of CNN(Convolutional Neural Networks) to detect and extract features from the captured images that contain the faces of the students. They have also made use of CNN to train their model and a SVM(Support Vector Machine) classifier to classify the trained images. They achieved an accuracy rate of 95 percent accuracy.[5]

The authors here have developed an application that makes use of mobile terminals and also the students GPS location to mark attendance and perform other activities. The app also has many functionalities that make interaction easier. [6]

The authors here have conducted research on how distance and slope between facial features affects facial recognition, an increase in the facial features of a face the recognition rate increases, the highest accuracy obtained was 94.60 percent with the MLP classifier, thereby showing that the higher the number of facial features the better is the recognition rate.[7]

The authors here have made use of a NFC(Near field communications) card, the faculty must have a mobile device with NFC, so that they can then scan the NFC card of a student, the device will also have a camera so that they can capture the images of the students present. The attendance is then uploaded to the main server.[8]

Here the authors have made use of Eigen face database along with Principal Component Analysis and integrate them with Matlab GUI, this system was developed to overcome the issues of image quality, image size and varying intensities of light etc. [9]

Here the authors have created a facial image recognition system making use of a correlation image sensor. Differential geometry and vector maps are used to find the key points of the face, a 3D real time facial imaging system was built using the correlation image sensor.[10]

3 Existing System

Traditional attendance marking techniques i.e, pen and paper or signing attendance sheets are easy to bypass and trick as giving proxies or false signatures is a common practice among students nowadays, students take an unfair advantage of this at most times. But a facial recognition system is unassailable and cannot be fooled as each person has a set of unique and individual features common to that person and cannot be replicated or changed, it all comes down to one simple truth that is, unless you are physically present in the lecture your attendance will not get marked.

Table 1. Existing systems and their limitations.

Existing system	Limitations
Pen and paper	False signatures and proxies
RFID tags	Can be used by anybody, no guarantee.
Biometric, fingerprint	Is a costlier approach.

3.1 Current Scenario : Challenges in images going unrecognized

Now the attendance systems that we have gone through in the literature survey have one aspect crucial to attendance marking that they do not take into account and that is what if a students attendance is not marked, because his face is not recognized or processed, in such a case the unrecognized image will be stored in a secondary database and an alert will be generated for the admin who then can manually add the attendance for said student.

4 Research methodology

This sections deals primarily with proposed techniques, methodologies and concepts relevant to facial recognition and image processing which is more specific and niche to a single process which uses facial recognition algorithms image processing techniques.

The proposed project includes four sequential phases; namely capture ,detection, image matching and attendance marking.

4.1 Primary database creation and training

The original database containing the images of the students is created by taking a live real time video of the students, and splitting the video into thirty frames, converting them to gray scale and storing only the faces of the students as images, then we will be training the respective images using the LBPH algorithm all the while storing their respective histogram value's and then comparing the stored and trained images against the captured images to mark the attendance. The software used for splitting the video into frames is Open-CV.

Figure 1. Primary database creation.

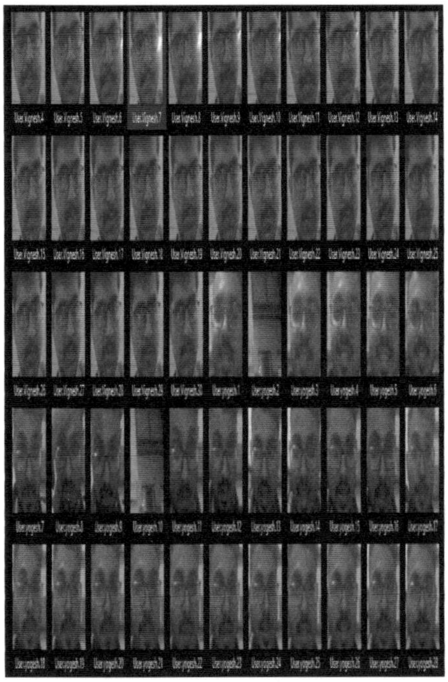

Figure 2. Images stored in the database.

4.2 Image Capturing Phase

In this phase the professor will capture a real time video of the class room or lecture hall by means of their own mobile device and making use of the DroidCam application which links the system that is running on your laptop to your mobile device and lets you use your mobile camera to capture the students present in the class room, the system can be accessed by the professors by accessing the laptop where all the data is stored.

4.3 Image Detection Phase

In this second phase once the video has begun capturing, simultaneously the Haar Cascade algorithm is applied to the video to get individual faces of the students and obtaining the distinct features of their face(eyes, nose, ears

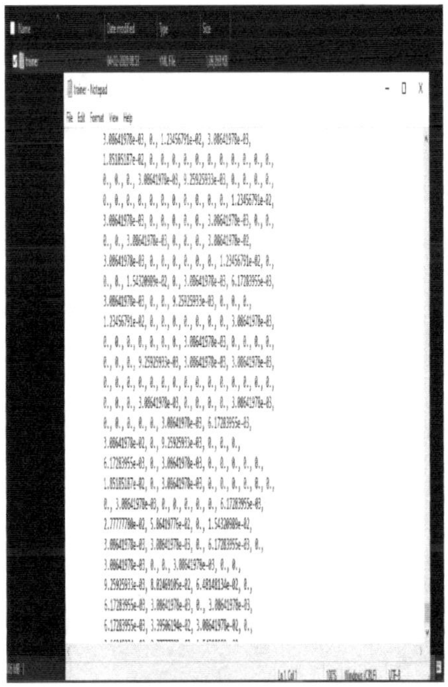

Figure 3. Trained values of the data-set.

and lips) by making use of line features and edge features, the Haar cascade algorithm basically works by giving us the parts of the face that are needed most for detection i.e, the ROI (Region of Interest) and processing and cropping out other regions of the face that do not play a role in the image processing and matching part. Once the faces are detected they are extracted and stored.

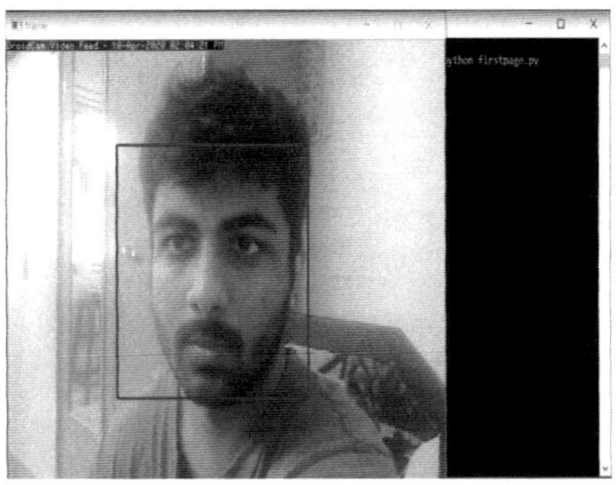

Figure 4. First detection of image using haar cascade algorithm.

4.4 Image Matching Phase

In this third and most crucial phase of recognising the student, that is comparing captured image against the stored images in the database, this method is done by making use of the LBPH algorithm(Local Binary Pattern Histogram), each image stored in the database has it's histogram value calculated and is cross checked against the calculated Histogram value of the images extracted from the captured video feed.

The name of the student appears above and the number indicates the confidence.

Note: Lower the confidence number higher is the accuracy.

As we can see from Fig. 5, the system not only detects just one face of a single student, but of multiple students or faces. As the system works for three faces at once by law of induction we can say that it will work for at least more than 15 faces at a single time.

Figure 5. Detection of Multiple faces.

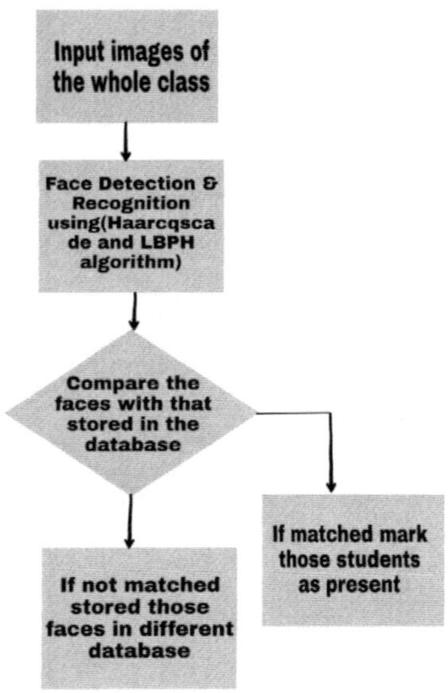

Figure 6. Image matching and verification.

4.5 Attendance Marking Phase

In this phase the attendance is marked, if the uploaded image matches the image stored in the database, then the attendance is marked present for that lecture and saved, but if any student goes unrecognized then that particular image is stored in the secondary database and an alert is generated for the admin.

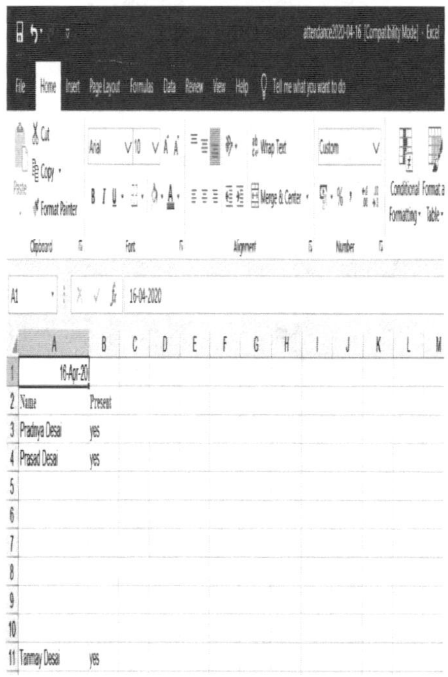

Figure 7. Attendance being marked using excel sheets.

4.6 Proposed Architecture

The architecture for the proposed system has been designed to keep it pretty straightforward and easy to understand. The steps that have to be undertaken to reach the final end step of the system which is making sure the attendance of the student is updated correctly and timely.
The system can easily be accessed by anyone, where attendance of the students can easily be checked and maintained by the faculty as when required. The DroidCam ap will allow easy use for capturing live video feeds of the class and simultaneously perform recognition for the students.
OpenCV-Python will be used to access the Haar Cascade and LBPH algorithms and their libraries that are required for training, recognition and matching of the captured images against the stored images available in the previously acquired data sets.

Algorithms being used:

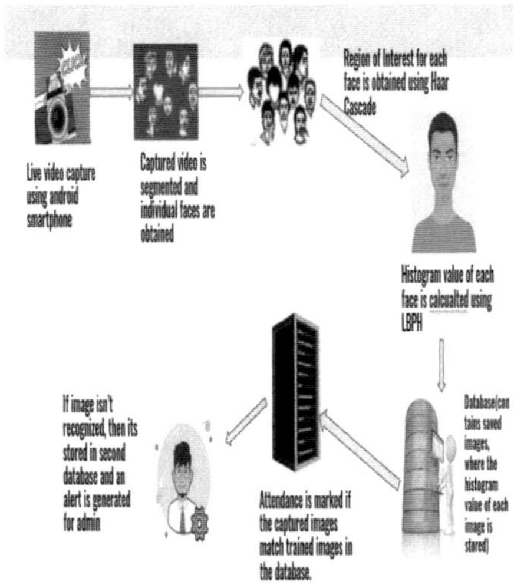

Figure 8. Proposed workflow and architecture

4.6.1 Haar Cascade

The Haar Cascade algorithm is a set of classifiers used for object detection. Haar Cascade is a machine learning-based approach where a lot of positive and negative images are used to train the classifier. The images which we would like to be classified by the classifier are known as positive images and the images we would not want our classifier to classify are known as negative images.

4.6.2 Local Binary Pattern Histogram

The Local Binary Pattern is used for face recognition, which means identifying the captured image against the image already stored in the database. The algorithm makes use of four main parameters to recognise a face. The Local Binary Pattern is applied to the image and compared against the central pixel of the image, then we calculate the histogram value for the said lbp image. The value of the newly calculated histogram is then compared against the already pre-processed histogram value of the already stored image in the database. This is how the Local Binary Pattern Histogram carries out facial identification of images.

4.7 Benefits of Proposed system

4.7.1 Foolproof

Attendance marking becomes foolproof in nature, students cannot carry out the previous means of false proxies for their friends as the system needs faces of the students and nothing else.

4.7.2 Time saving

Helps save time that at moments can get lost due to students disrupting the normal attendance marking method.

4.7.3 Efficient

Instead of teachers manually updating attendance to the college servers, the system will itself calculate attendance of students beforehand. [11]

5 Further Work

To improve the functionality and reliability of the system in the future we can add some of the following enhancements:

1. Add a self generating defaulter list, that is created after a certain amount of fixed time has passed for any student whose attendance is below seventy five percent.
2. The System will have to separate between recognised and unrecognised faces, faces that go unrecognised can be stored in a secondary database.

6 Conclusions

This paper presents a simple yet efficient approach to calculate the attendance in a class by employing facial recognition techniques. The output of this system can be outlined as follows:

As is seen in Fig. 6, the system not only detects just one face of a single student, but successfully detects multiple students or faces. As the system works for three faces at once by law of induction we can say that it will work for at least more than 15 faces at a single time.
The system also successfully recognises and marks the attendance of the detected students.
We wish to implement an efficient, time saving and easy to operate system which will in turn benefit both faculty and students.

References

[1] Radhika C.Damale, Prof.Bageshree.V.Pathak. *"Face Recognition Based Attendance System Using Machine Learning Algorithms."* Proceedings of the Second International Conference on Intelligent Computing and Control Systems (ICICCS 2018) IEEE Xplore Compliant Part Number: CFP18K74-ART; ISBN:978-1-5386-2842-3. IEEE 2018

[2] Omar Abdul, Rhman Salim, Rashidah Funke Olanrewaju, Wasiu Adebayo Balogun. *" Class Attendance Management System Using Face Recognition."* 2018 7th International Conference on Computer and Communication Engineering (ICCCE) IEEE 2018.

[3] Adrian Rhesa Septian Siswanto, Anto Satriyo Nugroho, Maulahikmah Galinium. *"Implementation of Face Recognition Algorithm for Biometrics Based Time Attendance System"* Center for Information Communication Technology Agency for the Assessment Application of Technology (PTIK-BPPT) Teknologi 3 Bld., 3F, PUSPIPTEK Serpong, Tangerang, INDONESIA, 15314.

[4] Jinsu Kim, Usman Cheema, Seungbin Moon. *",Face Recognition Enhancement by Employing Facial Component Classification and Reducing the Candidate Gallery Set.* Department of Computer Engineering, Sejong University, Seoul, 143-747, Korea (sbmoon@sejong.ac.kr).

[5] Nusrat Mubin Ara, Nishikanto Sarkar Simul, Md. Saiful Islam.*" "Convolutional Neural Network(CNN) Approach for Vision Based Student Recognition System."* 2017 20th International Conference of Computer and Information Technology (ICCIT), 22-24 December, 2017.

[6] Xinxiong Liu, Wanru Wang *"User Centered Design of Attendance Record System Based on Mobile Terminals"* 2017 International Symposium on Computer Science and Intelligent Controls.

[7] Turgut Özseven, Muharrem Düenci *"Face Recognition by Distance and Slope between Facial Landmarks"* Gaziosmanpaúa University Turkey, Tokat ; Karabuk University, Turkey, Karabük.

[8] Savitra Paharekari, Chaitali Jadhav, Surabhi Nilangekar, Jitesh Padwal *"Automated Attendance System in College Using Face Recognition and NFC"*International Journal of Computer Science and Mobile Computing A Monthly Journal of Computer Science and Information Technology ISSN 2320–088X IMPACT FACTOR: 6.017 IJCSMC, Vol. 6, Issue. 6, June 2017, pg.14 – 21

[9] Rekha.E, Dr. Ramaprasad.P *"An Efficient Automated Attendance Management System based on Eigen Face Recognition"*Department of Electrical Engineering, Amity University, Dubai UAE

[10] Shu Zhan Toru Kuriharak, Shigeru Ando *"Facial Authentication System Based on Real-Time 3D Facial Imaging By Using Correlation Image Sensor"* School of Computer and Information Department of Information Physics and Computing Hefei University of Technology The University of Tokyo Hefei, Anhui, 230009, China 7-3-1 Bunkyo-Ku, Tokyo 113-8656, Japan shu$_z$*han@hfut.edu.cnzhan, bond, ando@alab.t.u – tokyo.ac.jp*

Lossless and Reversible Data Hiding using Public Key Cryptography

POOJA SHETYE{e-mail: pooja.shetye118@gmail.com}, *SRUSHTI* VAREKAR, *MANALI* ZAJAM, and *MONIKA* PAWAR *SUJATA* KADAM{e-mail: sujatakadam7890@gmail.com}

[1]R.A.I.T, DEPARTMENT OF EXTC ENGG.

Abstract. - In today's world, the internet is a platform, where large amount of data can be obtained and transferred. Different technologies and internet access are used to transfer the data which can be accessed by authorized and unauthorized users.The major drawback of these technologies are that any unauthorized person can access it.Hence encryption and decryption is perform on Message/Data .In encryption the plain text/image is converted into cipher text/image.The technique of data hiding is used to hide the data that has to be transferred from the source to the destination.The process involves insertion of secret message in the cover image which is encrypted with the help of AES algorithm. This algorithm generates public/private key. All this process can be performed in lossless and reversible manner.

Keywords- Data hiding,lossless,reversible,algorithm

1 Introduction

Day by day with the rapid advancement of information technology enormous images and data are available on the internet.It alarms for a need to provide some kind of certification on such significant data. when we transfer any image,data to the receiver there might be possibility that any intruder is present and may obtain the confidential data .After apprehending the image, the trespasser may view the meaningful subject in the image. This may not matter in some cases. But in medical and military field images with distortion is unacceptable. This process involves embedding of some secret information in carrier signal. For copyright protection and covert communication the properties of less importance are changed. Generally,the data hiding process will result in degradation of properties in host signal. Application like law enforcement, system of medical images expects to reverse the the modified image back to original image for legal reasons ,whereas in application like remote sensing and military imaging high precision is expected. In some scientific research, practical data are expected to be obtained. In these situations, the reversibility of the image is expected. This technology is used in many application like in certification, military, medical and law enforcement.

CRYPTOGRAPHY

Cryptography is a worldwide well-known process in which plain text is encrypted to generate cipher (encrypted) text. Plain text is data that can be read and understood easily without any special measures. When plain text is encrypted unreadable text is generated called as cipher text. In short cryptography converts data to make sure of secrecy as genuine nature of information and data is transmitted through insecure networks .it facilitates the secure transfer to authorized recipient. Cryptography consists of two branches cryptolog and cryptanalysis. Cryptology aims at keeping plain text secret from impertinent person, while cryptanalysis creates such techniques to recover original information which is considered authentic. Basically, all cryptographic processes have four basic parts.

- Plain text - Untangled information for example sensitive information like a credit card number, password, a bank account number, pay-roll data, personnel information, or a secret formula is transmitted between organizations.
- Cipher text- Mathematical algorithm renders plain text into unintelligible Cipher text.This encrypted plain text is transported to receiver.
- Key- A mathematical value, formula, or process decides how a plain text message is encrypted or decrypted . The key is the only way to work out the secret information.
- Cryptographic Algorithm – This is a mathematical method which is used to convert the data from plain text form to cipher text form.By using the cryptographic algorithm we convert plain text form to cipher text form which is referred as encryption and the process of converting cipher text form back to plain text form by using the same technique reversibly is called as decryption.To make secure communication there's illustration of steps below for secret key cryptography

The technique of cryptographic system which uses both the keys namely public key and private key is known as technique of public-key cryptography or asymmetric cryptography. Such keys are generated by mathematical problem based cryptographic algorithm. For efficient security only private key is expected to kept private whereas public key can be disclosed without hesitation.Due to which the receiver is able to receive the message but while decryption is not possible to access because the private key is kept secret. Sometimes combining a message with private key i.e a short digital signature on message is generated. To verify validity of signature the corresponding public key is combined message with digital signature and authenticated using known public key. This is process involved in robust authentication The applications and protocols of public key algorithm assuring the secretiveness, certification and non-contradiction of electronics communications and data storage makes it prime element in modern cryptosystems.Various internet standards underpinned by public key algorithm are Transport Layer Security (TLS), S/MIME, PGP, and GPG. All in all public key provides, key distribution and confidentiality and digital signature.

1.2 Fundamentals of Reversible Data Hiding (RDH):

Following are the approaches used in RDH:

1] After encryption little space is vacated to hide the data.

2] First room is vacated in original media and then the encrpytion technique is processed for image encryption.

As in the first approach due to encryption modification of image takes place makes it difficult to vacate room for hiding data whereas in second approach no difficulty is faced and procedure is carried on efficiently.

1.3 To measure the performance of the RDH techniques following parameters :

To measure the performance of RDH technique following are the steps taken :

There are various methods of hiding data reversibly in an image. Any one among them expected to benefit us. The parameters are as follows:

- Quantity of Data: It facilitates hiding of maximum amount of data in the image.
- Complexity of technique: usability of technique depend on simpler and complex nature of technique.
- Quality of cover image: it suggest the quality of image is significant because if the quality of original image is spoiled after extracting message it will not tolerated in RDH.

2 LITERATURE SURVEY

Lichin Huang[8] proposed the histogram shift method for reversible data hiding from all the various data embedding techniques.

The histogram shift method is done by shifting the histogram in a fix direction, where there are two important points which are peak and zero point. The peak point resembles to grey scale value's maximum pixel number in image and the zero-point, minimum pixel value that is zero in the given histogram image. At the embedding process, in this histogram shift-based algorithm, the pixel in peak and zero point are modified in such a way that the pixel in the peak point carries a bit of secret message while the other doesn't carry any secret data.

For increasing the embedding capacity, Yeh[4] proposed a predict error method for data embedding. In this method, the cover image is divided in two block and a center point is obtained and prediction error value is obtained between it and its surrounding pixel values. The predict error value histogram is drawn and is peak value is found while the secret data in embedded a two side of peak point.

Intended on further better hiding capacity, J. Tian[5] has presented a Difference Expansion (DE) technique which gives an added storage space for dismissal of any useless content in image. In this, difference between the adjacent pixel is collected and some values are selected for further DE process. This method is best for visual quality and capacity limit.

In this paper we have anticipated lossless and reversible data hiding technique using public key cryptography which is further explained.

3 DATA HIDING USING ENCRYPTION

Reversible data hiding and visual crptography methods are included in the encryption process where the text is hide in reversible manner. The Tian's paper has proposed the scheme of difference expansion which is only applicable for gray scale images where,it gives an extra storage space by exploring the dismissal in the image media.In our approach we have personalized this method for colour images by reversibly data hiding in each colour component individually, which also increases the space to hide data. Basic technique for obtaining the reversed data is by selecting an area from an image, where this image is first converted into binary format to form a pixel matrix. Then the binary value of LSB that is the unit place value of selected matrix are interchanged with the binary value of data. Similarly all binary bits of the data to be hidden are embedded on image through same bit value change technique. By using this technique the data is divided and separately inserted at each pixel of matrix. This will help to sustain the quality and intensity of the cover image in which secret message or data is hidden. The PSNR value can be used to differentiate the feature of cover and original image. For protection of cover image instead of using pattern cipher,we used public or private key (i.e. the password of certain length is entered for obtaining the data). This method is plain and the output obtained will be initial image with the hidden data. The PSNR of the output image is kept to infinity which imports that the image is same as the initial image.

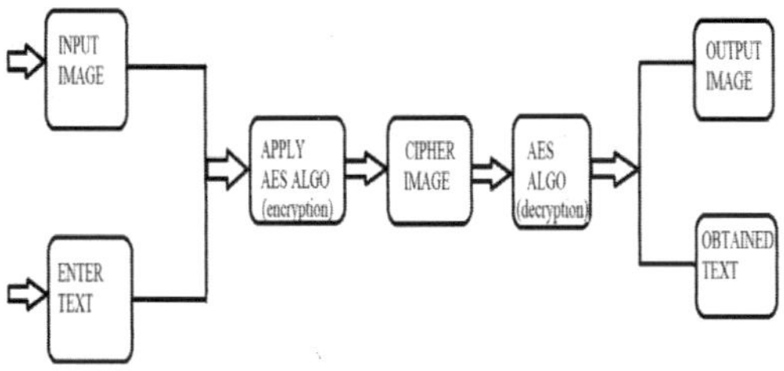

Figure 1. DATA HIDING PROCESS

4 ALGORITHM:

AES ALGORITHM

The Advanced Encryption Standard (AES) is a symmetric-key block cipher algorithm. The AES has three exact 128-bit block ciphers with secret key sizes are 128, 192 and 256 bits. Key extent is infinite, whereas the maximum block size is 256 bits.Substitution-permutation network (SPN) is used while plaining AES whereas the Data Encryption Standard (DES) Feistel network is not used.

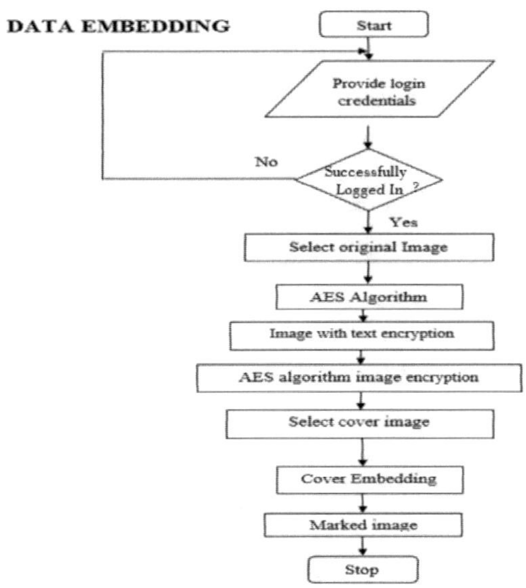

Figure 2. ENCRYPTION FLOWCHART

• Key Expansions:AES consists of a distinct 128-bitround key chunk for every another chunk.This technique of key expansion algorithm takes an input of a four-word key and the product obtained is a lined array of 44 words i.e.176 bytes.

• Opening Step

Data Extraction:

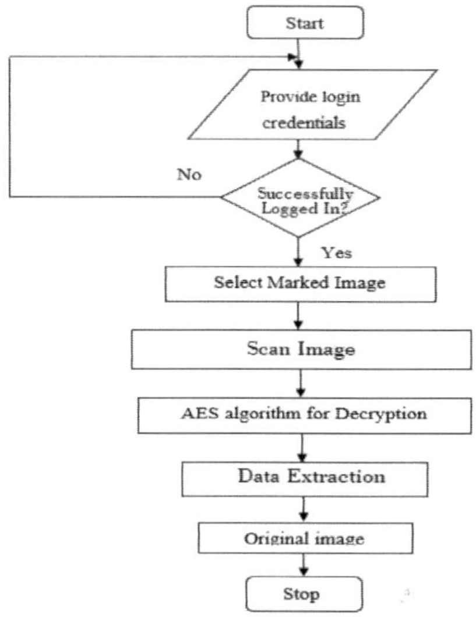

Figure 3. DECRYPTION FLOWCHART

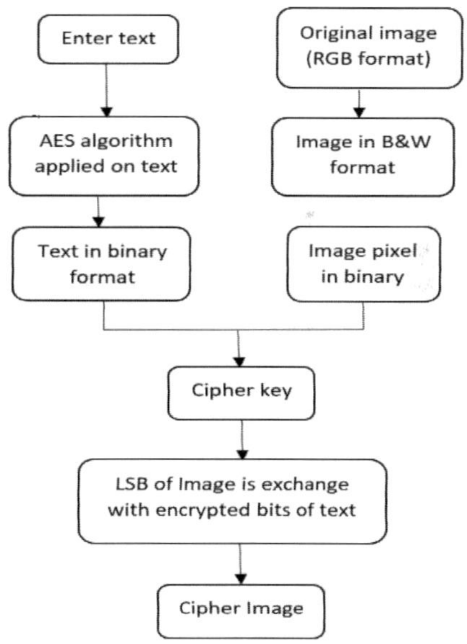

Figure 4. ENCRYPTION PROCESS

o Add Round Key:Every byte is united with a block of a round key, this is done by using bitwise xor.

• What are Rounds?

o Sub Bytes—Each byte is interchanged with another byte according to a lookup table.

o Shift Rows—The last three rows of the state are shifted cyclically to a firm number of steps.

o Mix Columns—In this step a mixture of columns occurs and the output is a four byte in every column.

https://doi.org/10.1051/itmconf/20203202002

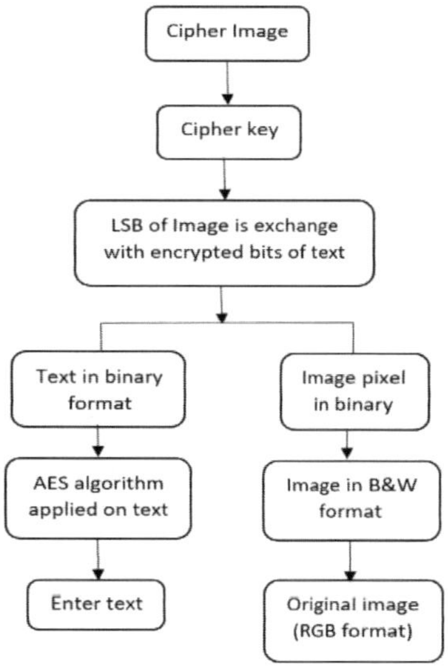

Figure 5. DECRYPTION PROCESS

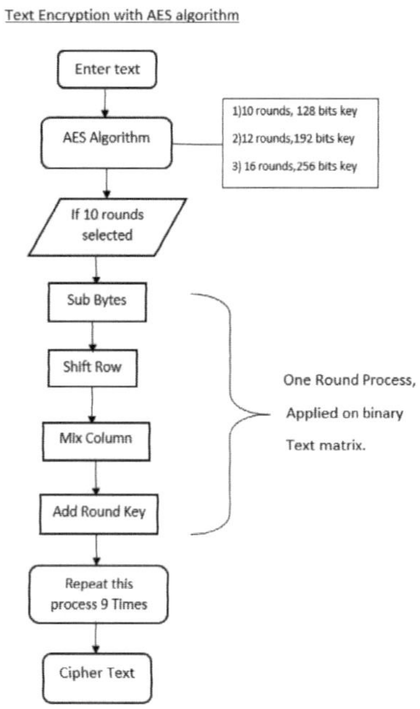

Figure 6. TEXT ENCRYPTION

o Further add the RoundKey

• Last Step (no compound Columns)

This is also similar to upper one just the one step is not required in it. The steps involved in it are sub byte, shift row and add round key.

Encryption with AES:

AES (Advanced Encryption Standard)

Nowadays largely adopted uniform encryption algorithm fitting to be encountered (AES). Its six time faster than tripple DES

As key size was much smaller it led to replacement of DES. Due to greater computing power , it is specified as sensitve towards intensive attack of key search. to overcome this shortcoming led to invention of tripple DES which was discovered to be slow.

Following are features of AES –

1] Software implementable in C and Java

2] 128-bit data, 128/192/256-bit keys

3] Provide full specification and design details

4] Symmetric key block cipher

5] Stronger and faster than Triple-DES

5 RESULT

Figure 7. Original image of Lena - size 28.7 KB

Figure 8. Encrypted image of Lena - size 174 KB

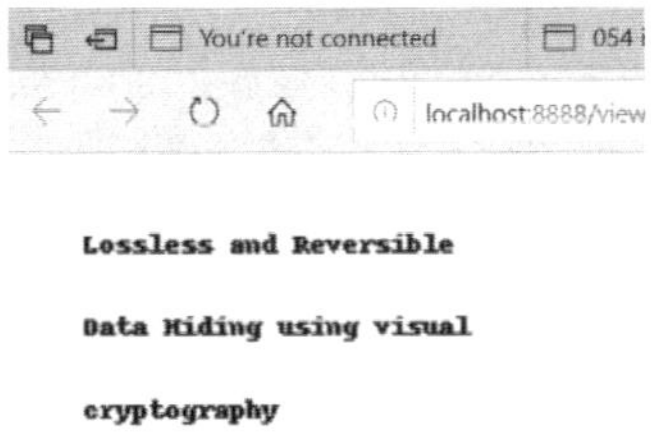

Figure 9. Decoded message after decryption process

Figure 10. Decoded image of Lena after decryption process - size 27.9 KB

The first image taken, which is the original image (fig 4)of size 28.7KB with pixel resolution of 550X824. The input text which has to be hidden is encrypted in image. The encrypted image obtain by interchanging 8 bit pixel value with the binary value of data which is called as cipher image(fig 5). Here the size of image gets increase and can go to 174KB but the pixel resolution remains unchanged. The data is hided in the image by using encryption algorithm and thus forms a cipher image. The last image shows decoded image (fig 6) where the data is remove from the cipher image,whose size is similar to the original size. Histogram graph and PSNR value are used to compare the quality and noise between original image and encoded image.Here the histogram of original and encoded image has some minute differences such as the colour of graph but overall both histogram are similar.

Figure 11. (a)LENA (b)BEACH (c)CAMERA (d)SUNSET

Table 1. Comparison of images with different parameters

Image name	PSNR value	Original size (KB)	Encrypted size (KB)	Decrypted size (KB)
LENA	8.308	28.7	174	27.9
BEACH	6.057	74	219.3	73.5
CAMERA	4.760	51	196.3	50.3
SUNSET	7.160	44.7	190	44.1

6 HISTOGRAM

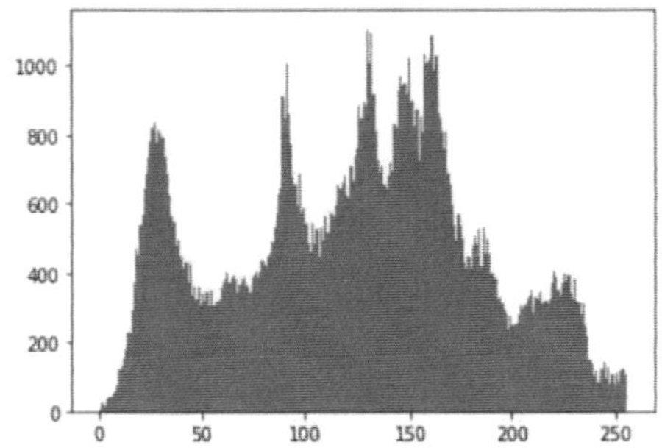

Figure 12. Histogram of original image of LENA

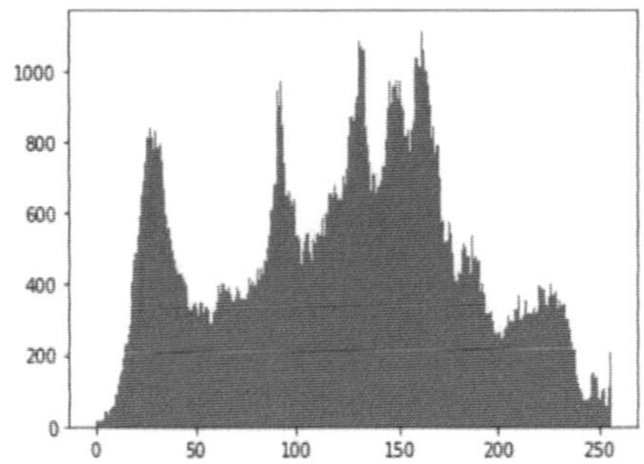

Figure 13. Histogram of encoded image of LENA

7 ADVANTAGES

1.A prediction method which is smarter, is fully used to make the estimated errors almost zero, the performance achieved will be much better, but because of prediction the computation complexity will be higher.

2. The twist or deformation performance of the proposed scheme is superb.

3.A number of subsets are formed by dividing the "input image" and then in the estimated errors of the next subset, the reserved information of a subset is always implanted.

4. This method implant secret data successfully and get the original data in the subsets inversely.

5. Using this technique one can solve the issue of key distribution in the algorithms of symmetric key.

6. The technique of public key cryptography is not used to replace the technique of secret key cryptography, but rather it is used as a complementary technique, to make the data more secured.

7. The security level of data is increased by using the two keys.

8. Refused digital signatures are provided by this technique.

8 DISADVANTAGES

1) Hiding capacity is low

2) Data compression is not enough.

3) The image quality of the decrypted images decreases.

4) Speed is one of the disadvantage of public key cryptography technique for encryption; there are many famous encryption techniques based on the secret key cryptography which are much faster and better than the ones, currently used as the encryption techniques for the public key.

5) For imitation the technique of public key cryptography may be not efficient, even if the private key of user is not available.

9 APPLICATIONS

1) This technique provides secrecy to the data, especially for confidential data or secret data in defence forces during communication as most essential thing in this field is to keep the secrecy level of embedded data as high as possible.

2)The cryptography technique provide us the following benefits:

a. Potential to hide the existence of secret data.

b. Due to encryption technique, the difficulty level of detecting the hidden data is high.

c. To enhance the security level of encrypted data.

3) Protects the altered data:

a. In this application area we take the advantage of embedded data's fragility.

b. The data embedded should be more fragile.

4)Biological data safekeeping:

In this, either your eye or finger is scanned and their specific features are saved. Further when you scan your finger it matches the pattern of previously saved image and scanned image. In this,the image of fingerprint is not saved, instead series of binary codes are saved for the verification.

5)Bank customer Credentials:

While visiting a bank website, this website displays cipher text and images. When logged in, bank sends a message to the customer i.e. the OTP. Again, the transaction key i.e.captcha: random alphanumeric, entered for logging in.

10 CONCLUSION

The technique of reversible data hiding that we used, is able to encrypt upto 80KB of image where it's resolution is upto "600 x 600 x 8 gray scale image". Various type of images are encrypted using this algorithm which has profitably applied to often used images such as medical, texture, aerial, and all of the CorelDraw database images. Besides, this algorithm is very simple and the time required to complete this process is short and faster which makes this algorithm best within any other reversible data hiding algorithm.

11 REFERENCES

[1]W. Su, Z. Ni, N. Ansari, and , Y.-Q. Shi , "Reversible Data Hiding,"IEEE Trans. on Circuits and Systems for Video Technology, 16(3),pp. 354-362, 2006.

[2]Hang Cheng,Xinpeng Zhang, Zichi Wang, , Jing Long and , "Lossless and Reversible Data Hiding in Encrypted Images with Public Key Cryptography", in IEEE Transactions on Circuits and Systems for Video Technology.

[3International Journal of Advanced Research in Computer and Communication Engineering ISO 3297:2007 Certified Vol. 5, Issue 7,July 2016 Copyright to IJARCCE DOI 10.17148/IJARCCE.2016.5764 321 Lossless and Reversible Data Hiding Mayuri B. Lokhande1,Prof. N. G. Pardeshi.

[4]Yeh, "Reversible data hiding scheme based on prediction error".

[5] J. Tian, "Reversible data embedding using a difference expansion," IEEE Trans. Circuits Syst. Video Technol., vol. 13, no. 8, pp. 890-896, 2003.

[6] X. Zhang, "Separable Reversible Data Hiding in Encrypted Image," IEEE Trans. Information Forensics Security, 7(2), pp. 526-532,2012.

[7] X. Zhang, "Reversible Data Hiding with Optimal Value Transfer," IEEE Trans. on Multimedia, 15(2), 316-325, 2013.

[8]Lichin Huang has proposed the method for reversibly hiding the data inthe image using histogram shift method.

[9]A. M. Darwish, N. A. Saleh, S. I. Shaheen, H. N. Boghdad , "High Capacity Lossless Data Embedding Technique for Palette Images Based on Histogram Analysis," Digital SignalProcessing, 20, pp. 1629-1636, 2010.

A Novel Communication System For Deaf And Dumb People using gesture

Pritesh Ambavane[1,*], *Rahul* Karjavkar[2,**], *Hemant* Pathare[3,***], *Shubham* Relekar[4,****], *Bhavana* Alte[5,†], and *Neeraj Kumar* Sharma[6,‡]

[1]Dept. of Computer Engineering Ramrao Adik Institute of Technology, Nerul, India.

Abstract. Human Beings know each other and contact with themselves through thoughts and ideas.The best way to present our idea is through speech. Some people don't have the power of speech; the only way they communicate with others is through sign language. Now a days technology has reduced the gap through systems which can be used to change the sign language used by these people to speech. Sign language recognition (SLR) and gesture-based control are two major applications used for hand gesture recognition technologies. On the other side the controller converts the sign language in to the text and speech which gets converted with the help of text to speech conversion and analog to digital conversion. A Dumb person throughout the world uses sign language for the communication.The best way to present our idea is through speech. Some people don't have the power of speech; the only way they communicate with others is through sign language. Now a days technology has reduced the gap through systems which can be used to change the sign language used by these people to speech. Sign language recognition (SLR) and gesture-based control are two major applications used for hand gesture recognition technologies. On the other side the controller converts the sign language in to the text and speech which gets converted with the help of text to speech conversion and analog to digital conversion. A Dumb person throughout the world uses sign language for the communication.

Keywords: Microprocessors, Flex sensor, Arduino board, Accelerometer, Microcontroller, Bluetooth module, Analog signal, Digital signal, Transformer, Rectifier, Filter, Regulator

1 Introduction

In today's world dumb and deaf people face a lot of difficulties in day to day life to communicate with the normal people. To ease their communication problem, we design and develop a communication system that will convert their sign language into the speech and text. As the name suggests, this system gives voice to voiceless i.e. voice is given to the person who is not able to speak. Dumb people use signs to communicate with the people. This sign includes different forms which are made with hand to understand what the person wants to say. This sign language includes different types of hand gestures such as, different facial movements which express the feelings of the persons. In our proposed system flex sensors (mounted on gloves) plays an important role. These flex sensors are attached to the gloves using a thread. Flex sensors are those which carry a certain amount of current which flows through the flex sensors. Further, AVR (Alf and Vegard's RISC processor) controller (mounted on gloves) takes the input signal in analog form from the flex sensors which is further converted into digital form by using inbuilt microcontroller. Further, digitally converted data is transferred to the android device from microcontroller to the android device wirelessly using Bluetooth chip. Hence, this digital signal (user instruction) is sensed by the android device and will speak according to the character generated.

The existing system dealt with similar problems has some drawbacks and used video devices such as camera for processing data [4]. But the key limitations of the existing system are lack of feasibility (not robust for the use), portability, and accuracy [5]. Further, in the existing system author used contact sensors, image processing are used which makes the project complex in nature. The other limitations of the existing project were limited number of letters can be implemented (American sign language only) [1], unable to display or recognize the sentences, special gestures/patterns are not included, and help message is not implemented.

The key motivation of the proposed IOT based device is to ease the day to day life of disable people who face problems in communication. They face many difficulties in their day to day life because of communication gap with other people. This project will help them to easily communicate with the other people with just their hand gestures. The overall idea of the proposed work in this paper is describe as in sensor-based system, the values which are stored in the microcontroller are transferred to the mobile device wirelessly. After the data stored in the device is

*e-mail: priteshambavane5@gmail.com
**e-mail: karjavkar.rahul.16ce5003@gmail.com
***e-mail: hemantpathare007@gmail.com
****e-mail: relekarshubham00@gmail.com
†e-mail: bhavana.alte@gmail.com
‡e-mail: neeraj16ks@gmail.com

matched with the corresponding values it displays the respected text. This text is also converted in to speech by text to speech conversion. Hence, the key contributions of the proposed work in this paper are described as follows:
1. To design and develop a robust and low-cost communication system for deaf and dumb people
2. To design a portable and high accuracy system.
3. To design and develop a low maintenance a low maintenance system using lithium battery.

The reminder of this paper is organised as follows: Literature survey with reference to novel communication system for deaf and dumb people is given in section II. Section III provides proposed work. Experimental setup, results and analysis are described in section IV. Section V presents the conclusion and future work.

2 Literature Survey

The existing work of the IOT based gesture recognition system is described as follows: W. Jingqiu et al [1], suggests design and develop a communication system through an fusing of manual as well as non-manual signals. Manual signals basically refer to hand posturing and hand motions, whereas non-manual signals resemble to an external appearance. The main limitation of the proposed system is lack of device mobility due to wired signal. A. Z. Shukor et al [2] authors used their own sign language in place of generalized sign language for example (American Sign Language (ASL) and Germany Sign Language (GSL)). However, there are similar sign languages for each country but slightly change version of sign languages in different regions of same country. Therefore, it is a challenge to implement a universal sign language used worldwide.

N. Sriram et al [3] study, used sign languages which is used for recognizing by using two different methods that is vision and non-vision approaches. But the key limitation of the proposed work is lots of miss interpretation of data.

To resolve the problem with vision approach S. V. Matiwade et al [4] designed and developed a system which uses a camera to observe the information received through finger and hand movement is the most widely adopted visual-based approach. But the key limitation of the proposed work was lack of portable in nature. A similar Approach was used by More and Sattar S et al [6] using SIFT algorithm, that further lowered dimensions of the feature vector by using Principal Component Analysis (PCA) algorithm to speed up the time of processing. Since the key limitation of the proposed work was author used storage space to store the database which requires lot of external storage space. To recognize dynamic hand movements used in Japanese Sign Language (JSL),Murakami and Taguchi [7] proposed utilizing the recurrent neural systems fit for perceiving the JSL finger letters in order, which comprise of 42 gestures. Neural network was used by author for the gesture reorganization which increase the complexity of the system.

In variation, Chowdary et al. [8] has used a basic checking approach to calculate the movement and fingers orientation in binary that transform images which are captured from a web camera. More sophisticated recognition of gesture system was proposed by Khan and Pathan [9] making use of digital images, that includes filtering of image(pre-processing), segmentation of image, color segmentation of, detection of skin(detecting hand and finger by using binary images), and matching the template. For the time being, an indirect method recognizes fingers and hand gestures on the basis of the RGB color spaces divided based on various hue for each finger by making use of a data glove.

An achievable division strategy utilizing RGB shading spaces utilizing a hand glove for seeing motion was proposed by Siby et al. [10]. This method utilizes estimations of RGB shading space drawn out from a hand signal picture caught from information glove, and contrasts those qualities and the one those put away in database.Further, Lamberti and Camastra [11] a continuous hand motion acknowledgment framework was proposed utilizing a learning vector quantization classifier for separating three shades of wool glove comparing to the fingers, palm and remaining parts of glove from image that are captured.

The limitation of a vision-based technique is enormously influenced by the processing of t images, likely background cancellation, image filtering, detection of boundary and color segmentation, for example, uncontrolled and diverse images of background can influence color of the skin segmentation or detection of movement. In fact, many researchers have failed to address such complications, and no strong solutions are yet been proposed. As a result, a non-vision-based technique is an alternative approach. This method typically utilizes motion and flex sensors to calculate the fingers flexion and the orientation of hand, separately.

The summary of existing work with their limitations is described in Table 1.

Table 1. Summary of Existing Work

Sr no	Existing System	Proposed system
1	Use of Video devices such as camera[4]	No use of video devices
2	Feasibility(real time) is less in existing.[5]	Feasibility(real time) is more in existing.
3	Help message is not implemented[14]	Help message is broadcasted on internet just with hand gestures
4	Limited number of letters can be implemented (American sign language). [1]	Large set of letters and words are implemented (Indian Sign Language).
5	Unable to display or recognize sentences[15]	Few daily needed sentences can be recognized by hand gestures.

https://doi.org/10.1051/itmconf/20203202003

3 Proposed Work

In our proposed work in this paper we designed and develop a data glove for communication of dumb and deaf people. The flow chart of the proposed system is shown in figure 1. In the our proposed system we used Arduinoboard, Flex sensors, Accelerometer, Bluetooth module and Android Mobile.

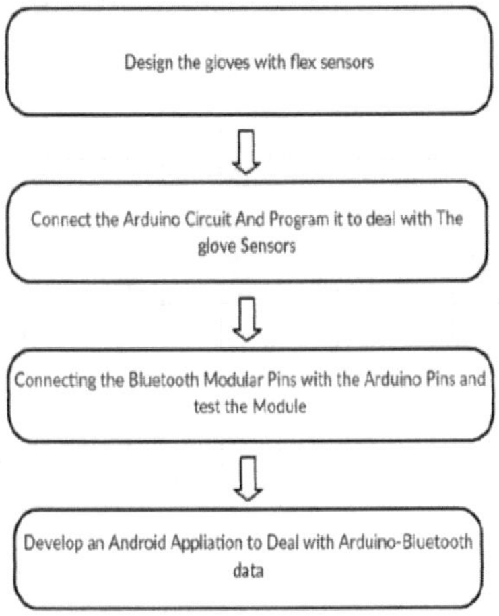

Figure 1: Flow of Chart of the Proposed System.

To recognize the hand movement first of all we design a glove by mounting the flex sensors, PCB circuit, components on PCB circuit such as (microcontroller, accelerometer, battery, Bluetooth module and voltage regulator). The Changes in hand movement will generate a voltage drop in flex sensors in analog form will be forwarded to microcontroller. After receiving the analog signal microcontroller converts the analog signal to digital signal. The digital signal via Bluetooth module send to android user. The second stage is to write and install the program on microcontroller for gesture reorganization. After that develop an android app for communication and we used Bluetooth for the interfacing. Once the values are send to the mobile device it maps the word or letter matching to that value and display that letter or word. Once the hand moment gets matched with the value in mobile device it prints the particular word or letter and also voice is generated in mobile device.

Figure 2 shows the block diagram of the components mounted on data glove. The detailed descriptions of the different components are described are as follows:

Flex sensors :
Flex sensors are attached to the gloves. These flex sensors contains the continuous flow of current voltage. These sensors when bend creates a drop in voltage which in turn is recorded in microcontroller.

Accelerometer sensor :
Accelerometer sensor measures the dynamic acceleration.

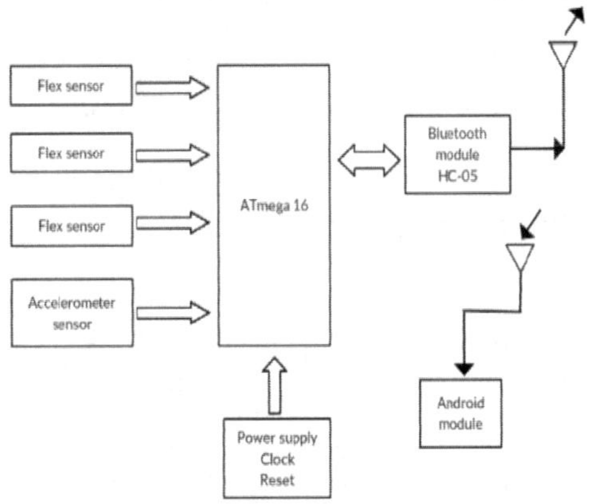

Figure 2: Block Diagram of the Components Mounted on Glove.

When we attach a accelerometer then we get a axis which can be used for every finger direction.

Micro controller :
This is the heart of the complete system. Here AVR ATmega16 microcontroller is used. It has in built ADC. The analogue input data from flex sensors is converted to digital form by micro controller.

Bluetooth Module :
Microcontroller sends the digital data to the mobile device using Bluetooth module wirelessly.The Bluetooth module used in this system is HC-05.

Android Mobile :
The digital signal which is transferred from the microprocessor is recorded in the android device.There is the fix algorithm for every input and according to the input the output is generated in the device.

Power Supply :
An AVR microcontroller and flex sensor needs 5V DC voltage whereas operating voltage of Bluetooth module is 3.3V. Power supply consists of transformer, rectifier, filter and regulator. The rectifier used here is a Bridge Rectifier which converts 230V AC into desired DC voltage.

Figure 3 shows the actual image of hardware setup of the proposed data glove:

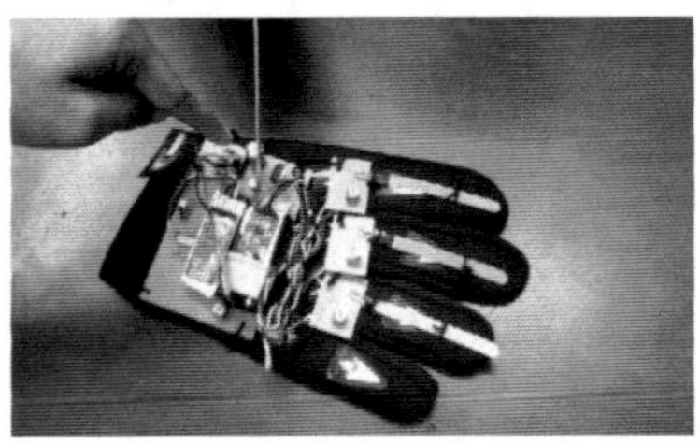

Figure 3: Hardware setup of the Proposed System.

4 Result And Discussion

To check the performance of our proposed data glove we set the experimental setup. We used Bluetooth connectivity for transferring the data from microcontroller to android device. We designed an android app using basic for android software (B4A) which is based on c language. After setting the detailed hardware setup user generates the input signal by bending the wrist movement and finger movements. On the basis of all the movements of data gloves the out will generates in the form of digital signal. Then we map the voltage value with the alphabets implemented in the program. And then after it will display the recognized alphabets with its sound. Hence, by this way we can generate the word and sentences. Further, theses word and sentences will be used for the communication of deaf and dump people. Hence, by this way we can provide a strong communication media to deaf and dump people for their communication and makes their life easy.

Figure 4 shows the voltage graph at the initial stage when no hand gestures are made in idle state. We can see in the graph the voltage line is constant with respect to time in all the images in figure 4. The main reason of constant voltage line is because of no hand movements are generated. And no hand movement their is no voltage variation. .

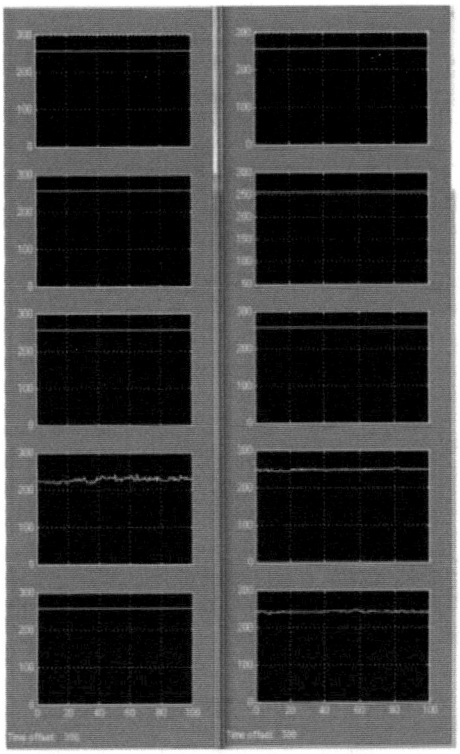

Figure 4: Voltage levels for idle state of the glove.

Figure 5 shows the changing voltage levels in the proposed system. The variation in the voltage with reference to time is because of hand movement. The hand movement will generate.

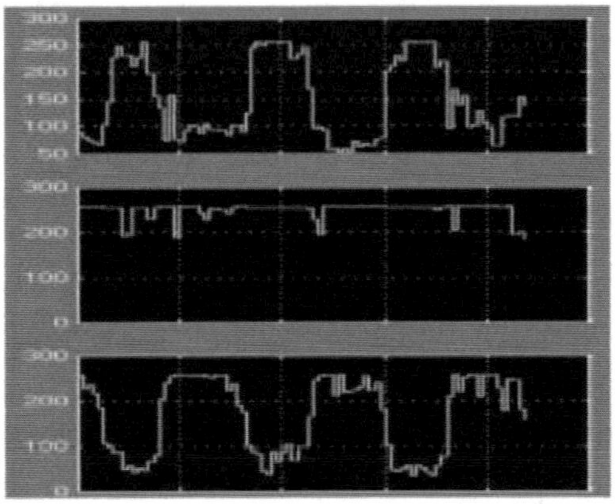

Figure 5: Voltage levels for bending of fingers.

the different voltage values. Hence, the voltage value is changing according to finger and wrist movements as we can see in figure5 the voltage is varying with reference to time.

Figure 6 shows the plot when the glove is held as a fist. In this position, all the voltages are low as can be seen below.

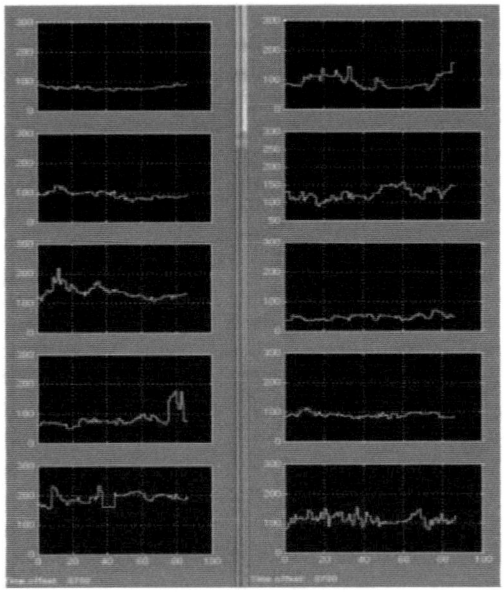

Figure 6: Final Voltage levels.

Below Figure 7 shows the hand gestures that represents 26 characters from A to Z and also some sentences which are used in daily life for deaf and dumb people.

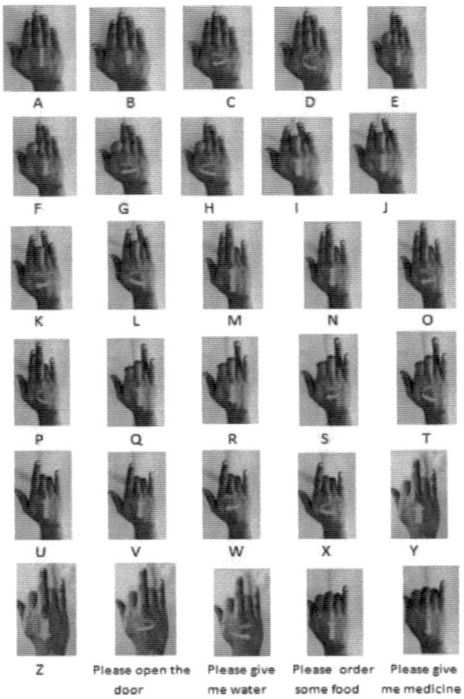

Figure 7: Hand Gestures

Table 2 describes the voltage value of each character in the alphabet from a to z. These different voltage values we got from three flax sensors and theses values used for character reorganization.

Table 2. Voltage values for Characters

CHARACTERS	F1	F2	F3	X-axis	Y-Axis	Z-axis
A	295	351	394	516	514	507
B	393	348	395	515	514	507
C	330	282	375	515	513	507
D	344	413	354	515	513	507
E	334	352	416	492	509	507
F	351	367	424	493	508	506
G	349	288	387	492	509	507
H	350	411	360	491	509	507
I	319	338	410	514	492	506
J	401	362	381	513	492	505
K	338	281	373	513	491	505
L	359	411	350	513	491	504
M	285	347	382	514	509	490
N	396	352	394	514	513	491
O	335	281	373	513	514	491
P	351	414	353	514	514	490
Q	302	339	396	493	492	508
R	400	355	383	495	492	507
S	333	283	380	495	491	507
T	360	411	360	494	492	507
U	291	357	385	514	492	492
V	403	353	381	514	492	492
W	336	283	378	514	492	492
X	357	410	364	513	491	491
Y	291	345	396	492	512	491
Z	400	354	386	492	514	491

5 Conclusions And Future Work

This paper highlights the to reduce the communication gap between deaf or mute community and normal people. The proposed system in this paper will improve dumb/ deaf person's lifestyle. Even it will be beneficial for the communication between the blind person and the dumb person. Overall System is effective and efficient because the use of AVR microcontroller and android phone. The system can be extended to support more number of signs and different languages mode.

In future work we will implement different day to day life activities with the help of different sensors

6 References

[1] W. Jingqiu and Z. Ting, "An ARM-based embedded gesture recognition system using a data glove," presented at the 26th Chinese Control Decision Conf., Changsha, China, May/Jun. 2014.

[2] A. Z. Shukor, M. F. Miskon, M. H. Jamaluddin, F. A. Ibrahim, M. F. Asyraf, and M. B. Bahar, "A new data glove approach for Malaysian sign language detection," Procedia Comput. Sci., vol. 76, no. 1, pp. 60–67, Dec. 2015.

[3] N. Sriram and M. Nithiyanandham, "A hand gesture recognition based communication system for silent speakers," presented at the Int. Conf. Hum. Comput. Interact., Chennai, India, Aug. 2013.

[4] S. V. Matiwade and M. R. Dixit, "Electronic support system for deaf and dumb to interpret sign language of communication," Int. J. Innov. Res. Sci., Eng. Technol., vol. 5, no. 5, pp. 8683–8689, May 2016.

[5] S. Goyal, I. Sharma, and S. Sharma, "Sign language recognition system for deaf and dumb people," Int. J. Eng. Res. Technol., vol. 2, no. 4, pp. 382–387, Apr. 2013.

[6] S. P. More and A. Sattar, "Hand gesture recognition system using image processing," presented at the Int. Conf. Elect., Electron., Opt. Techn., Chennai, India, Mar. 2016.

[7] K. Murakami and H. Taguchi, "Gesture recognition using recurrent neural networks," in Proc. SIGCHI Conf. Hum. Factors Comput. Syst., New York, NY, USA, 1991, pp. 237–242.

[8] P. R. V. Chowdary, M. N. Babu, T. V. Subbareddy, B. M. Reddy, and V. Elamaran, "Image processing algorithms for gesture recognition using MATLAB," presented at the Int. Conf. Adv. Commun. Control Comput. Technol., Ramanathapuram, India, Jan. 2015.

[9] T. Khan and A. H. Pathan, "Hand gesture recognition based on digital image processing using MATLAB," Int. J. Sci. Eng. Res., vol. 6, no. 9, pp. 338–346, Sep. 2015.

[10] J. Siby, H. Kader, and J. Jose, "Hand gesture recognition," Int. J. Innov. Technol. Res., vol. 3, no. 2, pp. 1946–1949, Mar. 2015.

[11] L. Lamberti and F. Camastra, "Real-time hand gesture recognition using a color glove," presented at the

Int. Conf. Image Anal. Process., Ravenna, Italy, Sep. 2011.

[12] Y. Iwai, K. Watanabe, Y. Yagi, and M. Yachida, "Gesture recognition using colored gloves," in Proc. 13th Int. Conf. Pattern Recognit., Vienna, Austria, Aug. 1996, pp. 662–666.

[13] S. P. Dawane and H. G. A. Sayyed, "Hand gesture recognition for deaf and dumb people using GSM module," Int. J. Sci. Res., vol. 6, no. 5, pp. 2226–2230, May 2017.

[14] C. Preetham, G. Ramakrishnan, S. Kumar, and A. Tamse, "Hand talkimplementation of a gesture recognizing glove," presented at the Texas Instrum. India Edu. Conf., Bengaluru, India, Apr. 2013.

Anonymous De-centralized Ephemeral Chat Application using Interplanetary File System

Faraz Khan[1], *Niraj* Mantri[2], *Sagar* Rajput[3], *Dhananjay* Dhakane[4], *Puja* Padiya[5,*]

[1]Department of Computer Engineering, Ramrao Adik Institute Of Technology, Nerul, Navi Mumbai, India
[2]Department of Computer Engineering, Ramrao Adik Institute Of Technology, Nerul, Navi Mumbai, India
[3]Department of Computer Engineering, Ramrao Adik Institute Of Technology, Nerul, Navi Mumbai, India
[4]Department of Computer Engineering, Ramrao Adik Institute Of Technology, Nerul, Navi Mumbai, India
[5]Department of Computer Engineering, Ramrao Adik Institute Of Technology, Nerul, Navi Mumbai, India

Abstract— Communication is essential for human beings and we communicate globally with the means of internet every day. Internet is an interconnected mesh of networks where our data is transferred through hundreds of nodes before reaching its destination. As the intermediary network node increases, the risk of losing confidentiality and integrity is also affected. Decentralized Chat (DChat) is a chat service on the Interplanetary File System (IPFS) peer-to-peer protocol where users can communicate with ephemeral chats under any anonymous alias. The users are not aware of real identity of each other and the chats are lost from the service once the node is disconnected. The data is tamper-resistant because to alter it would change the hash and invalidate it from the network. Here we aim to develop a secure chat service that provides anonymity and ephemeral chats using cost-effective IPFS technology.

Keywords— decentralized, anonymous, peer-to-peer, tamper-resistant, ephemeral, chat.

1. Introduction

We use internet a lot, maily for communication. We rely on applications like Facebook, Twitter, Whatsapp. We use them to connect with our family, friends and colleagues but unfortunately these applications are not ephemeral, meaning they leave an electronic trace of ours online which can be easily tracked down to us by a proper cyber forensic team or some skilled individual.

We use chat applications often without knowing that we could under surveillance which could back fire us in an unexpected way in the future. Privacy has value to democracy, liberty and basic human rights. This has to be solved by voluntarily safeguarding and making the conversations ephemeral.

Today when we visit a website, browser sends a GET request to the server and connects to a system that hosts website. The request is routed through the internet and if the servers are at far away distance, the process may take a really longtime and requires intermediate nodes to be involved in it.

Hackers are becoming more prominent today making internet security a major issue. Open and free Wi-Fi may be a threat to one's personal data. It is easier for the hacker to enter into the system and access personal information or other devices connected via open Wi-Fi. Research suggests some of the ways to protect from online threats. One must turn off file sharing before using free public networks. One must avoid signing any site that requires password. Another public but distributed technology that prevents data from being modified is blockchain technology [1].

A blockchain is a database accessed over a computer netw ork. It is very difficult to change when a record has been attached to the chain. The data approved by the network is attached to a chain. A unique code called a hash is contained in each node. It also includes the hash of the chain's previous node.

IPFS [2] is a modern peer-to-peer hypermedia protocol intended at supplementing the Hypertext Transfer Protocol now controlling the Network, or perhaps even replacement. An unique fingerprint, called a cryptographic hash, is given in IPFS to each file and to all blocks. IPFS prevents network-wide duplicates. Each network node only stores content it needs and some indexing information helps find out who stores what. You ask the network to find nodes that store content behind a specific hash while searching data.

* Corresponding author: puja.padiya05@gmail.com

 https://doi.org/10.1051/itmconf/20203202004

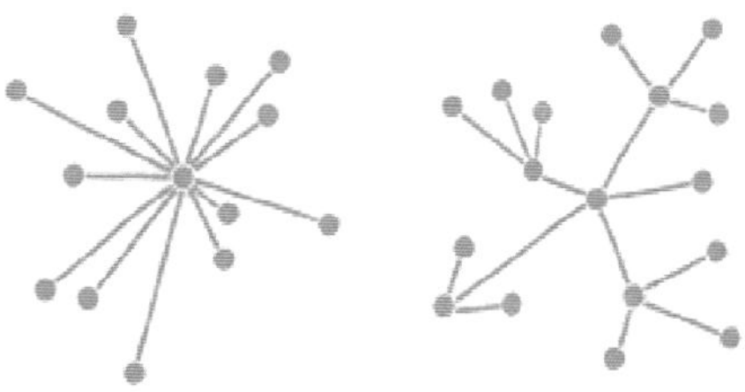

Fig.1 Centralized and Decentralized nature

The focus of our research is to build a decentralized anonymous and tamper-proof cross platform communication system with user friendly interface, that provides integrity and availability and to overcome the demerits of having a central server which loses access to data on failure of single point.

The paper is organized as follows: in section 2 the motivation and approach towards the research is described, section 3 describes the literature survey, problem definition is stated in section 4, and section 5 describes the proposed system followed by results in section 6. Section 7 concludes the paper along with section 8 which describes the future work.

2. Motivation

Everyone likes their own personal space and likewise some people likes being anonymous on the internet. Anonymity has certain benefits for individuals and the environment, such as creating a sense of protection. If they are anonymous, some people may feel safer online. Anonymity is preferred when someone gives their opinion on controversial topics. Anonymity ensures privacy, facilitates freedom of speech, preserves the identity of the individual from public and decreases self-awareness. In addition to anonymity, it is necessary to provide ephemeral chat to prevent those records from haunting us in future. This violates the basics of cyber security, i.e. integrity of the messages are getting intercepted and manipulated during the transmission. To resolve this, there is a need of trustworthy mechanism to disallow validation and acceptance of intercepted and manipulated messages. The concept of key value is something that can bridge the gap. This mechanism uses the concept of a key-value data store. If the value of the hash changes then we can say that the data is invalid.

3. Literature Survey

Most popular online chat sites used by millions of users are Whatsapp [3] and Snapchat [4]. As per recent news of August 2018, WhatsApp was vulnerable to let hackers intercept personal and group messages and manipulate messages.

Here are the few takeaways from the article:

1. The vulnerability concerns WhatsApp's encryption process, which is meant to protect every 2message, picture, call, video or other content sent in chats.

2. However when decrypted, the Check Point team realized that the protocols being used by WhatsApp could be converted and accessed, allowing them to see exactly what rules were being used, and also to change them to their liking.

3. This may allow hackers to modify a group chat text by putting words or using the quote feature in a chat group discus sion to modify the sender's identity.

4. Hackers could also send a personal message to another group participant posing as a public message for all so that wh en the person in question answers, he is visible to all.

The similarities of the system can be related to how Snapchat works on the frontend. By default upon the chat window is closed everyone message in the conversation is deleted from the user's device. This makes the idea rather confusing to naive users. This idea makes more sense in a scenario where the privacy of the conversation is really important. The message is deleted from the conversation the companies claim that the information is deleted off the companies' servers unless the conversation is reported for violating the policies of the application. In that case the conversation is reviewed before it is deleted from the company servers. In either case the integrity of privacy is often affected in some way of the other.

These messaging systems never function on a peer-to-peer basis. There is no relation to each computer of your friends (from your device). You attach your computer to your server instead. You can then use a custom TCP protocol to send your communications to the server, or perhaps to HTTP.

The procedure of visiting a website is firstly your browser requests the server upon which the web service is running on. Even in case in which these servers are far remotely across the world. This is location based reference. This process is bandwidth heavy and thus making it a disadvantage relatively. Also the contents are retrieved from a single data source this is prone to attacks as the availability of the content is at risk. In comparison IPFS downloads the content from multiple sources.

Having a centralized server means the data access to the content can very well be easily blocked by governments and etc. Browser data may expose your device to virtual threats. This information can be the name of your computer, your IP address, the operating system you use, and any other details you request from your website.

All the existing systems [5], [6], [7], suffer from the drawback of centralization of information. They still rely on

* Corresponding author: puja.padiya05@gmail.com

 https://doi.org/10.1051/itmconf/20203202004

traditional centralized technologies exposing them to attacks concentrated on the central server. Our research aims to overcome this drawback of centralization by using decentralized storage for storing the chat messages securely on IPFS network. Some of the surveys related to IPFS tecnology are as follows:

Youn Chen in [1] introduced blockchain to combine IPFS with the zig-zag storage model. To facilitate permanence and collaboration in web archives, Salwood Alam Mat in [2] had built Interplanetary Wayback to disseminate the contents of WARC files into the IPFS network. S. Muralidharann and Heedong Ko in [8] proposed IoT framework in a P2P decentralized storage infrastructure using IPFS. From the survey we conclude that IPFS technology will be the future for decentralized communication reducing the burden of centralized system [9].

The focus of our research is to build a secure communication application with respect to concepts of security, demolishing the centralized monopoly built by tech giants, having more control over our data as we have clear transparent information on how it is stored and passed on, maintaining integrity of transferred data and anonymity without gathering any user personal data.

4. Proposed System

We are proposing a Secure Distributed Chat application for users that can be used as an alternative to the current Centralized server chat applications. The proposed system uses the advantages of IPFS [9] technology to improve the reliability of the communication applications respecting the privacy of customers.

The user communicates under a fake alias which can be changed anytime during the conversation in the chatroom. This gives complete anonymity and flexibility to the users of the Dchat application. Our system not only provides a means of anonymous communicating, but also follows the cybersecurity basics and promotes them. Also the messages during the conversation are ephemeral [10] messages and are destroyed upon disconnect of the user.

IPFS uses the concept of pinning. Since IPFS is a file system the data may be needed to store for a long time. You can pin your own information or use some third party services to pin it for a small amount of monthly fee depending on the service used. Since we do not want our chat to be persisted, we are transmitting the communicational information only in real time and since we do not pin these information the information gets lost and this achieves ephemerality.

Security in this implementation is IPFS dependent, meaning every information can be accessed by anyone if they're the hash of the information this can be seen as a security risk at first but IPFS hashes are of 32 bytes hash with SHA256. So it is impossible for anyone to guess the hash of any information exchanged and even if they manage to guess it correctly. It is only one message out of the many from the conversation and since the chat is ephemeral the hash must be referred to, as the communication is taking place as the information will be wiped from the IPFS File system by not pinning it. The only way for a third party to intercept the communication is by knowing the chat room ID of the communication which is taking place and actively being listening in real time. So it is recommended to use long and complicated chatroom names to avoid security breaches.

4.1 Interplanetary File System (IPFS):

IPFS establishes a permanent distributed network by using content-based reference. This is different as compared to the usual location based reference of traditional protocols like HTTP.

To compare the structure of a request of HTTP with IPFS.

HTTP request

https://192.168.0.125/files/resume.pdf

IPFS request

/ipfs/QmjY8F0C3Onu/files/resume.pdf

IPFS [11], [12], [13], [14] uses the hash of the file itself to be used as a reference. This hash is the result of a cryptographic cipher which makes sure that only one copy of the file exists on the IPFS network which in results avoids duplications across the network.

IPFS uses peer to peer technology. Hence making a direct communication of two peers possible. This is possible due to the ipfs pubsub-room. Upon receiving a connection request the browser initiates an IPFS node in the client's browser and connects it to a room. LibP2P protocol is used is to emit membership events, listen for incoming messages and broadcasts and directly messaging to the peers on the network. Upon sending a message the message gets routed through the IPFS network to the receiver with the correct PeerID. Likewise upon receiving a text-message the network(IPFS) checks the peerID from the metadata of the message it is specified for and thus completing the communication process.

A broadcast room is a chatroom where multiple people are communicating at the same time therefore broadcasting messages to everyone connected in the IPFS room. Users have to visit the DChat web application for the first time The IPFS Server initializes a new node for the current user. Upon initialization is completed the user is now connected to the IPFS server chat room. The chat room has a new unique name on which the clients send and listen for new messages

User selects an alias name for the messages on the application Throughout the conversation the user has the flexibility to change his alias to any other name When the chat

* Corresponding author: puja.padiya05@gmail.com

https://doi.org/10.1051/itmconf/20203202004

room detects a new message event the message is returned to all connected nodes Someone can choose to either connect to someone from the chat room for a private peer to peer chat or create their own custom chat room.

The browser uses ipfs-js package for instantiating a node in the browser, the node of ipfs-js is then passed on to a ipfs-pubsub service which allows the possibility of using IPFS as a potential chat application with web sockets like functionalities to connect and subscribe to messages in real time.

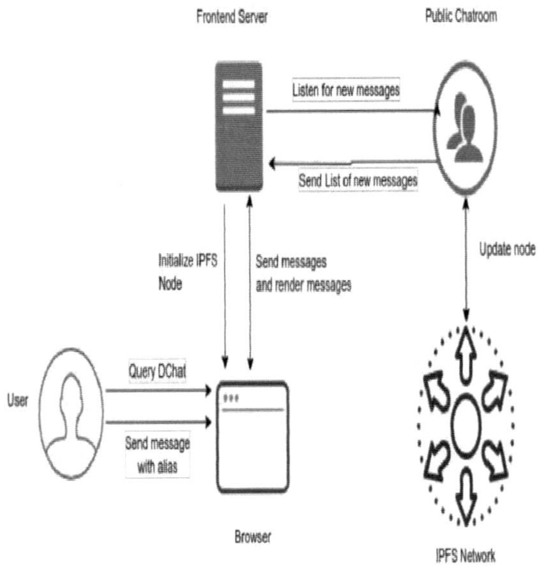

Fig.2. System Architecture

Users have to visit the DChatwebapp for the first time The IPFS Server initializes a new node for the current user. Upon initialization is completed the user is now connected to the IPFS 7server chatroom. The chatroom has a new unique name on which the clients send and listen for new messages.

4.2 Design of the System:

User selects an alias name for the messages on the application. Throughout the conversation the user has the flexibility to change his alias to any other name When the chatroom detects a new message event the message is returned to all connected nodes. Someone can choose to either connect to someone from the chatroom for a private peer to peer chat or create their own custom chat room. When the connection to the IPFS node is lost, the connection is dropped and the addresses to the previous messages are lost.

The user initializes an IPFS node and once the initialization is completed user gets connected to the chatroom using IPFS technology and if not it throws a error "try again".

Once the user is connected to the chatroom it broadcasts a message to all the users in the chatroom under an alias. The alias as is, is anonymous. Everyone in the chatroom receives the message.

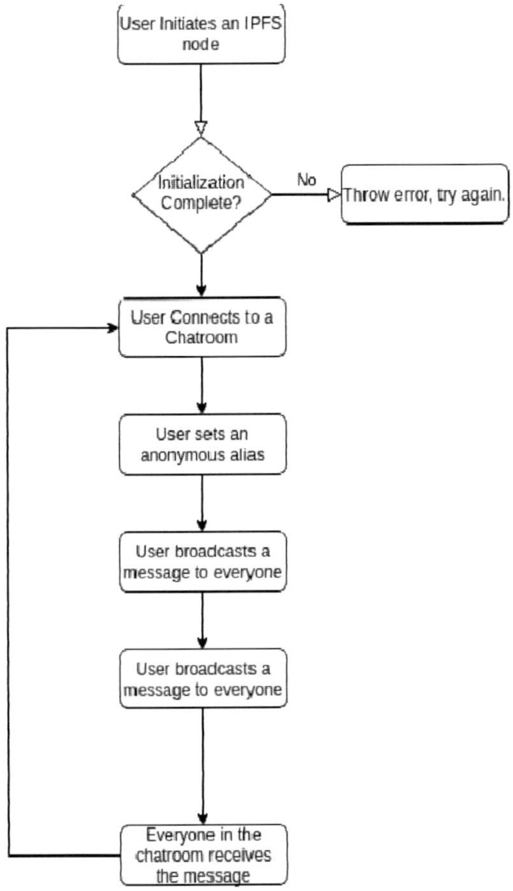

Fig. 3. Flow Diagram

The particular person who wants to communicate with the user sends a message back and after some verification they can communicate secretly or one can create their own custom chat room. Once the chat ends and they exit the chat gets deleted permanently and as there is no record of chat it is completely secure.

The major components of the system consist of the core blocks:

* Corresponding author: puja.padiya05@gmail.com

1. User Interface - User Interface Design is important because it can make or break your customer base. It creates fewer problems, increases user involvement, perfects functionality and creates a strong link between your customers and your application. The user interface for the DChat application is a simple responsive Chat interface with options for user to send a message under a random and flexible alias name.

2. Storage the new list of messages received on the Chatroom are temporarily stored in the volatile storage object of the React server which upon reload or refresh is lost

3. IPFS node each user on the network connected to the website gets their own instance of an IPFS node through which they can send and receive messages

4.Chatroom IPFS can store all type of information, In this case we store a chatroom data which consist of the name of the chatroom and the hashes of user connected, hashes of messages and etc.

5. Results

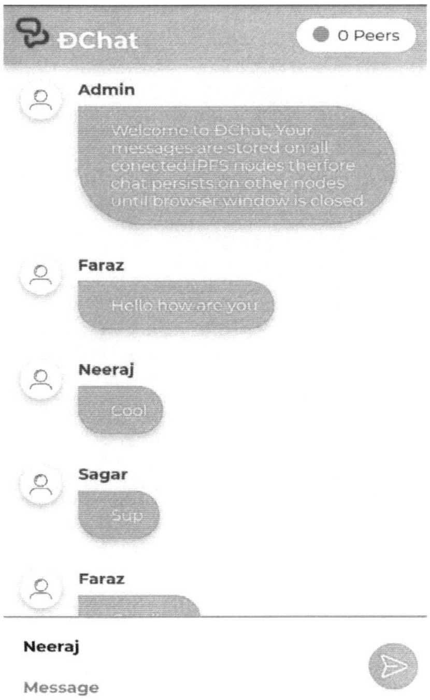

Fig. 4. Snapshot of the developed DChat application

Users have to visit the webapp.

2. The IPFS Server initializes a new node for the current user.

3. Upon initialization is completed the user is now connected to the IPFS server chatroom.

4. The chatroom has a new unique name on which the clients send and listen for new messages.

5. User selects an alias name for the messages on the application.

6. Throughout the conversation the user has the flexibility to change his alias to any other name.

7. When the public chatroom detects a new message event the message is displayed onto all the 9 nodes which are connected to the public chatroom.

8. When the connection to the IPFS node is lost, the connection is dropped and the address to the previous messages is lost.

The new proposed system uses the advantages of IPFS technology to improve the reliability of the communication applications respecting the privacy of customers. Confidentiality refers to protecting information from being accessed by unauthorized parties. Proposed Dchat does not disclose the identity of the user and the only way user is recognized on the network is their IPFS node hash. Integrity refers to ensuring the authenticity of information that information is not altered. Dchat uses technology of IPFS where the data is tamper-resistant as to alter any information it would change the hash. Availability means that information is accessible by authorized users. We achieve it through the help of IPFS peer to peer architecture where the same data is stored on each node connected on the network. Therefore the data is always available until at least one node is available on the network. Dchat provides anonymity as throughout the conversation the user has the flexibility to change his alias to any other name. When the connection to the IPFS node is lost, the connection is dropped and the addresses to the previous messages are lost and all the chat are cleared. The chat communications provided by Dchat are ephemeral.

6. Conclusion

We conclude that the Decentralized Chat (Dchat) is a cross-platform application, an anonymous and tamper-proof communication system with user friendly interface which follows integrity and availability concepts of cyber security, with ephemeral communication and overcomes the demerits of having a central chat server. Thus, redefining the concept of secure chat app on the internet.

7. Future Work

Proposed Dchat is a text messaging application that uses IPFS technology for decentralized anonymous and tamper-proof cross platform communication system with user friendly interface. It provides integrity and makes sure that the

* Corresponding author: puja.padiya05@gmail.com

communication is ephemeral communication. In future, newer version of Dchat application will provide images and videos to be communicated along with the text messages.

References

1. Y. Chen, H. Li, K. Li and J. Zhang, "An improved P2P file system scheme based on IPFS and Blockchain," 2017 IEEE International Conference on Big Data (Big Data), Boston, MA, pp. 2652-2657, (2007)
2. S. Alam, M. Kelly and M. L. Nelson, "Interplanetary Wayback: The permanent web archive," 2016 IEEE/ACM Joint Conference on Digital Libraries (JCDL), Newark, NJ, pp. 273-274, (2016)
3. S. Patmanthara, D. Febiharsa and F. A. Dwiyanto, "Social Media as a Learning Media: A Comparative Analysis of Youtube, WhatsApp, Facebook and Instagram Utillization," 2019 International Conference on Electrical, Electronics and Information Engineering (ICEEIE), Denpasar, Bali, Indonesia, pp. 183-186, (2019)
4. N. S. Al-Saqer and M. E. Seliaman, "The Impact of Privacy Policies Awareness on Snapchat Saudi users Discontinuous Usage Intention," 2018 21st Saudi Computer Society National Computer Conference (NCC), Riyadh, pp. 1-6, (2018)
5. D. Henriyan, Devie Pratama Subiyanti, R. Fauzian, D. Anggraini, M. Vicky Ghani Aziz and Ary Setijadi Prihatmanto, "Design and implementation of web based real time chat interfacing server," 2016 6th International Conference on System Engineering and Technology (ICSET), Bandung, pp. 83-87, (2016)
6. I. Karabey and G. Akman, "A cryptographic approach for secure client - server chat application using public key infrastructure (PKI)," 2016 11th International Conference for Internet Technology and Secured Transactions (ICITST), Barcelona, 2016, pp. 442-446, (2016)
7. R. Sanjaya and A. S. Girsang, "Implementation application internal chat messenger using android system," 2017 International Conference on Applied Computer and Communication Technologies (ComCom), Jakarta, pp. 1-4, (2017)
8. S. Muralidharan and H. Ko, "An InterPlanetary File System (IPFS) based IoT framework," 2019 IEEE International Conference on Consumer Electronics (ICCE), Las Vegas, NV, USA, pp. 1-2, (2019)
9. R. Kumar and R. Tripathi, "Implementation of Distributed File Storage and Access Framework using IPFS and Blockchain," 2019 Fifth International Conference on Image Information Processing (ICIIP), Shimla, India, pp. 246-251, (2019)
10. A. Malhotra, V. Sharma, P. Gandhi and N. Purohit, "UDP based chat application," 2010 2nd International Conference on Computer Engineering and Technology, Chengdu, pp. V6-374-V6-377, (2010)
11. Teixeira Pedro, "*Professional Node.js: Building Javascript Based Scalable Software Kindle Edition*", (Wrox, 2012)
12. Online: https://ipfs.io/ [Accessed: 15-09-2019]
13. Online: https://github.com/ipfs-shipyard/ipfs-pubsub-room [Accessed: 27-09-2019]
14. Online: https://github.com/ipfs-shipyard/ipfs-pubsub-1on1 [Accessed: 04-10-2019]

* Corresponding author: puja.padiya05@gmail.com

Spectrum Sensing Using Energy Detector in Rayleigh Fading Channel

Hemlata Patil[1*], *Sai Vennela* Nekkanti[1], *Disha* Negi[1], *Nikita* Masanagi[1], and *Sakshi* More[1]

[1]EXTC Department, RAIT, Nerul, India.

Abstract. Cognitive Radio, which is an adaptive and intelligent radio has an important feature called spectrum sensing. It monitors the presence or absence of the authorized users in a fixed or licensed spectrum. There is a rise in the use of wireless communications in recent times, which has led to the underutilization of the available bandwidth. This problem can be solved to some extent by using cognitive radio technology. Cognitive radio gives an opportunity for unauthorized users to use the licensed spectrum, resourcefully, when not in use. Using spectrum sensing energy detection methods, the existence of authorized users, in various fading channels can be done. The operating characteristics of the receiver can be analyzed using parameters of performance like signal to noise ratio, probability of false-alarm, probability of detection. In this paper we assess Rayleigh fading channel and compare with AWGN (non- fading) channel. Theoretical and simulated results are compared, and observations are being made.

1 Introduction

The conventional wireless networks use constant policies for spectrum allocation for authorized users. Current studies show that spectrum utilization is very inefficient using conventional spectrum allocation policies. This inefficiency arises because of the fact that authorized users do not exploit the available spectrum completely. Therefore, in order to satisfy the growing demand for communication and wireless application, the requirements for a flexible spectrum management approach are emerging to reflect the efficacy of the band. Cognitive radio is a powerful tool that can allow a dynamic approach to spectrum access and address the present inadequacy issues. It can allow unauthorized users to gain access to the available spectrum left unused by the authorized user[2].

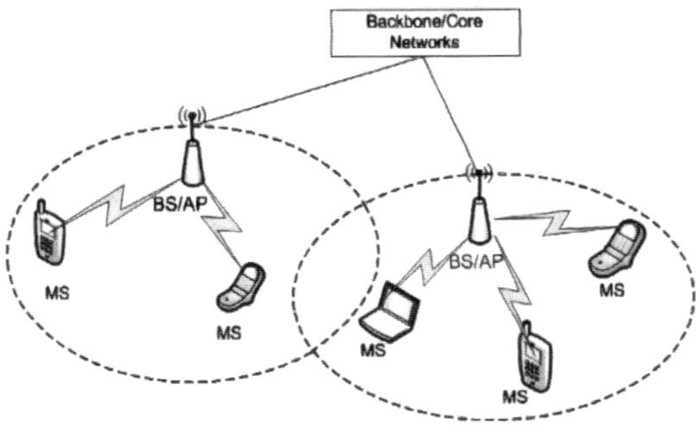

Figure 1. Cognitive Radio fundamental block diagram

Cognitive Radio technique is introduced to occupy the holes in the spectrum when it is not fully utilized and segment the spectrum avoiding damaging interference resourcefully. Hence, continued sensing of the spectrum is a significant job for sensing the existence of authorized users by CR as shown in Figure 1. Here, energy detectors are used for the measurement of received signal energy for a fixed interval of time [1].

J.Mitola. established a unique approach to the entire world about the term CR which can be used for enhancing the utilization of a valuable resource, the electromagnetic radio spectrum [1]. The idea of SDR and the abridged way to execute it was characterized by Simon Haykin. He declared that software radios are advancing stages for multimode communications [2]. Diverse spectrum sensing methods were proposed by Fabrício B. S. de Carvalho. In his theory, he explained the concept of CR along with the analysis of CR spectrum sensing using ED for various fading channels [3].The authors investigated the spectrum sensing method of CR rooting ED. While fulfilling dependability limitations and giving a throughput to SUs an optimization issue occurs reducing the energy utilized in sensing the spectrum. To unravel this issue an arrangement is generated to decide the ideal sensing, informing and transmission period [4]. Evaluation and simulation outcomes proclaimed the esteem value sensing, informing, and transmission period to attain the top leading trade-off amidst the consumption of energy and throughput for SUs [5]. The issue of energy detection of obscured deterministic signals of the authorized users across the Nakagami-m fading channel and presuming ECG method is examined by Herath et al [6]. The authors in analyzed the performance of ED across different fading channels like rayleigh, rician, and nakagami using diversity reception. The authors obtained theoretical results and practical results for probability detection and

*Corresponding author - hema.patil08@gmail.com

false alarm in terms of various channels [7].The authors concluded their observations that Cognitive Radio Network with low computational complications, can detect the existence of primary user signal which is the easiest job via ED based Spectrum sensing technique [8][9]. There are some limited theories on the working of ED spectrum sensing for composite multipath fading [10][11].

In this paper, we discuss spectrum-sensing techniques via energy detectors for Rayleigh fading channels and study the ability to detect signals. The mathematical expressions for Rayleigh and non-fading AWGN channels are derived including false alarm probability and the detection-probability in correlation with a signal to noise ratio.

A simulation model has been established using MATLAB aimed at spectrum sensing based on energy detection. The theoretical results are precisely synchronized with the simulated results of the Rayleigh channel and AWGN channel. Various parameters like the value of SNR, different fading parameters for different fading channels have been analyzed.

2 System Model

One of the significant functions for discerning wireless network communication is spectrum sensing. Continuous sensing is required for assigning cognitive radio users with the unoccupied spectrum bands. Mainly, there are 3 detection methods, to recognize the unused band which is vacant. They are namely, a) Matched-filter-detector, b) Cyclostationary-detector and c) Energy-detector [8]. Among these, the most widely used method is an energy detector, because it does not need previous information of the main signal and is less complex than other methods.

In ED, the received signal is observed and the existence or absence of primary signal is decided. This is done by assuming that the primary signal is noise. Energy-detectors are robust to the variations in the main signal. Furthermore, it has low complexity because it does not require tedious signal processing. It is preferable for wider-band spectrum sensing. The functional block diagram of ED is given in Figure 2 which consists of four main parts [9].

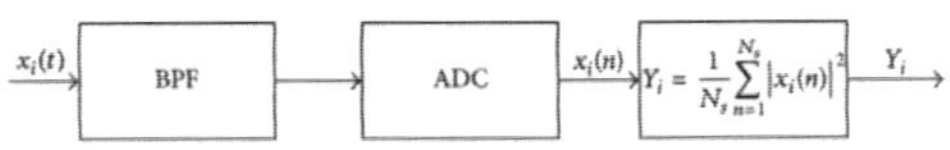

Figure 2. Functional diagram of Energy Detector

The input signal is first sent through the bandpass filter that is then sent to the squaring device and integrator.The output from the integrator is the signal which is received at the 'T' time interval. This yield is then passed through the threshold device and tested for 2 hypotheses (H_0H_1)

H_0 refers to the presence of only noise and absence of the signal and H_1 refers to the existence of both signal and noise.

Hence the significant cases for two-state hypothesis are [9]:-

Y(m) = W(m) : H_0

Y(m) = X(m) + X(m) : H_1

Here, X(m) is the Input signal, Y(m) is the output, and W(m) is the noise.

a)H_1 becomes true when the authorized user is not present that is nothing but false alarm probability (P_F) [P(H_1 /H_0)] b)H_1 is true when the authorized user is present that is called detection-probability (P_D) [P(H_1/ H_1)]. c)H_0 is true when the authorized user is available is called the missed-detection probability (P_m) [P(H_0/ H_1)] [7]

2.1 Decision Statistic

Decision theory or decision statistics is the part of statistics that deals with making optimal decisions, using quantitative methods in uncertain times. Let us consider the subsequent representations:

x_i (t) is the input signal which is the waveform which is transmitted, y_i (t) is the output signal which is the waveform received, pq(t) is quadrature phase component, pi(t) is in phase-noise component. BW_N is noise-bandwidth, N_0 is two-sided power spectral density, N is one-sided power spectral-density, E_s is the signal energy is the sampling interval, Λ is decision threshold. The received-signal is filtered by a band-pass filter which is the pre-filter. The signal which is filtered is sent to the A/D converter and is converted to samples [7].

The decision-statistics can be or any value. Let us take Y' as a decision-statistic [10].

$$Y' = \frac{1}{N_0}\int_0^T y_i^2(t)\; dt \tag{1}$$

Where,

$$\gamma = \frac{E_s}{N} = \frac{E_5}{2N_0} = \frac{\lambda}{2} \tag{2}$$

2.2 AWGN Channel's detection probability

The preset value of an energy detector is also called threshold energy defined by λ [8]. With this λ we can evaluate 3 factors and analyze the detector performance: a) probability of missed-detection, b) the probability of false-alarm and c) the probability of detection.

The detection-probability P_D and false-alarm probability P_F are given by

https://doi.org/10.1051/itmconf/20203202005

$$P_D = P(Y^{'} > \Lambda \mid H_1) \tag{3}$$

$$P_F = P(Y^{'} > \Lambda \mid H_0) \tag{4}$$

Here Λ is the threshold of detection. P_F can be written in the form of Probability density function (PDF),

$$P_F = \int_{\Lambda}^{\infty} f_{Y'}(y)\ dy \tag{5}$$

$$P_F = \frac{1}{2^d \Gamma(d)} \int_{\Lambda}^{\infty} y^{d-1} e^{-(\frac{y}{2})}\ dy \tag{6}$$

By changing the limits and substituting we get,

$$P_F = \frac{1}{2\Gamma(d)} \int_{\frac{\Lambda}{2}}^{\infty} t^{d-1}\ e^{-(t)}\ dt \tag{7}$$

Or

$$P_F = \frac{\Gamma(\mathrm{d}, \frac{\Lambda}{2})}{\Gamma(d)} \tag{8}$$

$\Gamma(.)$, defined as an incomplete-gamma-function. Subsequently, P_D can be defined by using Cumulative-Distribution-Function (CDF).

$$P_D = 1 - F_{Y'}(\Lambda) \tag{9}$$

CDF of Y' can be obtained by [9],

$$F_{Y'}(y) = 1 - Q_d(\sqrt{\lambda}\ ,\ \sqrt{\Lambda}) \tag{10}$$

Using above two equations, the P_D for AWGN is [11]

$$P_D = Q_d(\sqrt{\lambda}\ ,\ \sqrt{\Lambda}) \tag{11}$$

$$P_D = Q_d(\sqrt{2\gamma}\ ,\ \sqrt{\Lambda}) \tag{12}$$

Here $Q_d(...)$ is called the generalized Marcum-Q function. In this manner, we can calculate P_D of AWGN using the expression above.

2.3 Probability of detection for Rayleigh Channel

The amplitude of signal follows a Rayleigh distribution when they exists in the environment enormous number of plane waves and few types of scattering. In such cases, the SNR γ has a PDF which is exponentially given by,

$$f(\gamma) = \frac{1}{\bar{\gamma}} exp^{(\frac{-\gamma}{\bar{\gamma}})} \qquad \gamma > 0 \tag{13}$$

We can obtain detection-probability, P_D for Rayleigh Channel by averaging their probability-density-function (PDF) over detection-probability for AWGN Channel,

$$P_{d,R} = \int_{0}^{\infty} P_d f(\gamma)\, \mathrm{d}\gamma \tag{14}$$

Here $P_{D,R}$is the probability of detection for Rayleigh Channel.

$$P_{D,R} = \frac{1}{\bar{\gamma}} Q_d\left(\sqrt{2\gamma},\ \sqrt{\Lambda}\right) \mathrm{d}\gamma \tag{15}$$

Simplifying[11],

$$P_{D,R} = e^{(-\frac{\Lambda}{2})} \sum_{n=0}^{d-2} \frac{1}{n!}\left(\frac{\Lambda}{2}\right)^n +$$

$$\left(\frac{1+\bar{\gamma}}{\bar{\gamma}}\right)\left[exp^{(-\frac{\Lambda}{2(1+\bar{\gamma})})} - exp^{(-\frac{\Lambda}{2})} \sum_{n=0}^{d-2} \frac{1}{n!}\left(\frac{\Lambda}{2(1+\bar{\gamma})}\right)^n\right] \tag{16}$$

The expression above gives detection-probability (P_D)for spectrum-sensing over Rayleigh Channel based on energy detection[8].

3 Result

Using MATLAB for simulation purposes for various channels (fading and non- fading) the output which was received was noted. In order to evaluate which spectrum sensing method is better various parameters are taken into accounts such as missed-detection-probability (P_m), detection-probability (P_D), and false-alarm-probability (P_F). ROC curve is been plotted of (P_m) versus PF and (P_F) versus (P_F) through which the performance can be distinguished, of various spectrum methods.

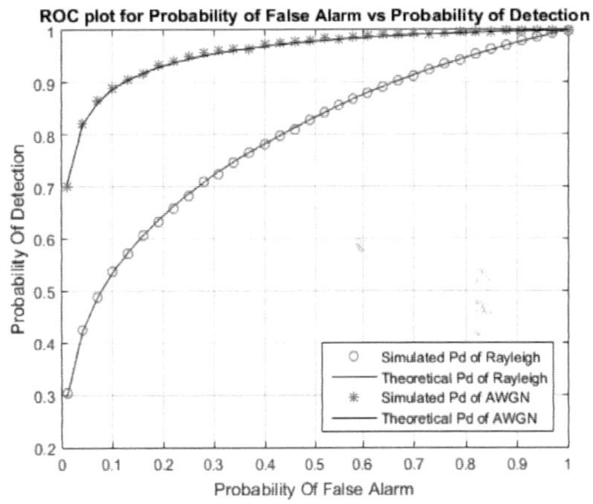

Figure 3. P_D versus P_F of fading and non -fading channels

From the Figure 3 it is clear that the detection-probability (PD) of fading channel (Rayleigh) is less than the non-fading channel (AWGN). This graph clearly gives the idea that the usage of the spectrum band is less when the fading is taken into consideration. The results obtained after simulation and the theoretical ones are matched approximately.

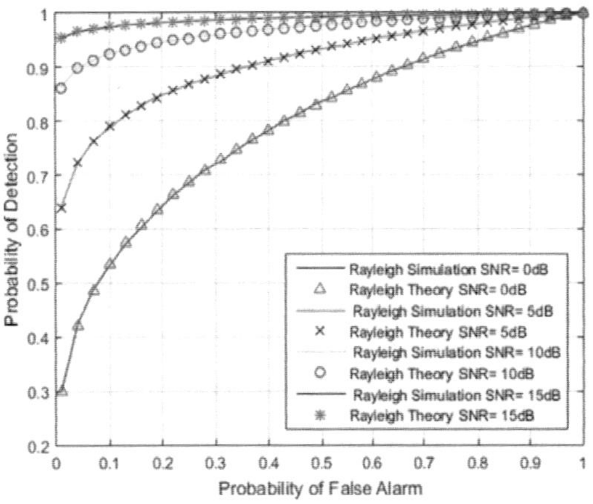

Figure 4. P_D versus P_F of fading channel (Rayleigh)

As from the above Figure 4 it is evident that when the energy detector is being used in such conditions that the SNR values are varied from -30 - 10 dB the Rayleigh fading channel efficiency gets decreased accordingly. This shows that the probability detection values get increased when the signal to noise ratio increases.

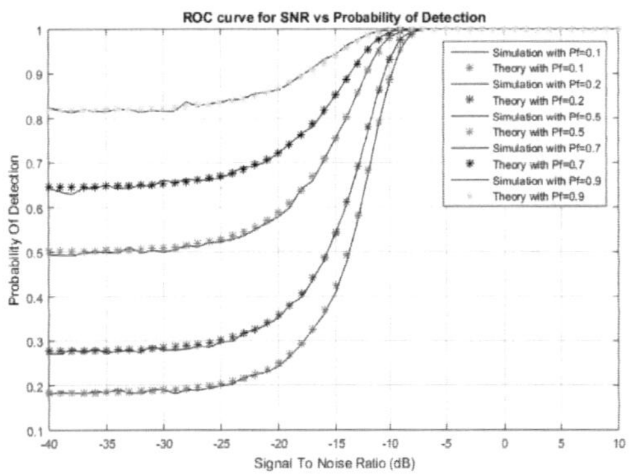

Figure 5. P_D versus SNR of fading channel (Rayleigh)

The above Figure 5 is evident that when the probability of the false-alarm values is varied from 0.1-1 an upgrade or improvement is observed in the probability of detection.

4 Conclusion

In this paper, the nuts and bolts of cognitive radio have been discussed including spectrum management and performance of energy detector-based detection techniques. The closed-form expression of detection-probability and false-alarm probability over Rayleigh channel and the non-fading channel has been discussed. Different ROC curves have been plotted and the values of parameters of fading such as SNR values, false alarm probability cause a significant change in the corresponding detection probability and hence affect the overall performance. Rayleigh channel is observed in contrast with the AWGN channel. Various fading channels have varied impacts on the signal.

References

[1] J. Mitola, Cognitive radio: making software radios more personal- **Volume: 6**, Page numbers: 13-18, Year (1999)

[2] Simon Haykin, Cognitive radio: brain-empowered wireless communications- **Volume: 23**, Page numbers: 201 - 220, Year FEBRUARY(1999)

[3] Carvalho, Fabrício B S DeLopes, Waslon T Alencar, Marcelo S,"Performance of Cognitive Spectrum Sensing Based on Energy Detector in Fading Channels", Procedia Computer Science 65, 2015.

[4] Zhang S, Bao Z. Linear combination-based energy detection algorithm in low signal-to noise ratio for cognitive radios. Eur trans Telecommunication 2011;211-17.

[5] TevfikYucek and HuseyArslam,"A Survey of Spectrum Sensing Algorithms for Cognitive Radio Applications", IEEE, vol. 97,2009.

[6] Herath S, Rajatheva N, TellamburaC.Energy detection of unknown signals in fading and diversity reception. IEEE Trans communication 2007;55(1):21-4.

[7] F.F. Digham, M.S. Alouini and M.K. Simon, "Energy Detection of unknown signals over fading channels", IEEE Transactions on Communications, Vol. 5, No.1, pp. 21- 24, 2007 .

[8] M. Ranjeeth, S. Anuradha, Performance of Fading Channels on Energy Detection Based Spectrum Sensing, Procedia Materials Volume 10, 2015,Pages 361-370..

[9] Patil, Vilaskumar M. et al. "Signal Detection in Cognitive Radio Networks over AWGN and Fading Channels." International Journal of Wireless Information Networks 25 (2018): 79-86.

[10] S. Atapattu, C. Tellambura and H. Jiang, "Analysis of Area under ROC curve of energy detection" IEEE Transactions On Wireless Communications, Vol. 9, 2010.

[11] Ibrahem E. Atawi, Osamah S. Badarneh, Mohammed S. Aloqlah, and Raed Mesleh. 2016. Spectrum-sensing in cognitive radio networks over composite multipath/shadowed fading channels. Comput. Electr. Eng. 52, 337–348, (May 2016).

Performance analysis of Strain sensor based on Fiber Bragg Grating

Aniket Shivram More[1], *Pritam sanjay Lad*[2], *Shivram RamnarayananKrishnan*[3], and *Savita R. Bhosale*[4*]

[1]Department of Electronics, Ramrao Adik Institute of Technology,Navi Mumbai India
[2]Department of Electronics, Ramrao Adik Institute of Technology, Navi Mumbai India
[3]Department of Electronics, Ramrao Adik Institute of Technology, Navi Mumbai India
[4]Department of Electronics, Ramrao Adik Institute of Technology, Navi Mumbai India

Abstract: A fiber Bragg grating can be worked as reflector, it is constructed in a short section of optical fiber that reflects light of specific wavelength and allow to pass remaining wavelengths. This is possible by creating a periodic change in refractive index within the fiber core. The change in the modal index of fiber caused due to strain results in a Bragg wavelength. This work describes performance of Fiber Bragg Gratings as a strain sensor at 1550nm wavelength is considered for simulation, corresponding dynamic strain and wavelength shifts are analysed. This performance analysis is useful especially for intrusion detection system where environments are harsh. This sensor is compatible with data communication system and can be used for remote sensing.

Keywords: Fiber Bragg Grating, Optical sensors, Strain, Wavelength

1 Introduction

The Optical fiber supported sensors gaining attention due to its advantages than existing sensing technologies with improved sensitivity. FBG sensors are not affected by electromagnetic interference, this characteristics improves accuracy of the intrusion detection system. The uses of Optical fiber sensors are receiving attention to deploy traditional electrical and mechanical sensors for monitoring parameters. In FBG based sensors the core of single mode fiber is exposed to a periodic pattern the exposure creates variation in refractive index of fibers core which results in fixed index modulation called grating. The working principle of FBG is wavelengths of the output signal shifted with change in strain [1-2].
Fibers explored many applications in remote sensing. In few applications, optical fiber itself can act as sensor.
Fiber optics based sensors are popular because of its small size, light weight and free from electromagnetic and electrical interference.
The basic principle of working of FBG sensors are change in the field of the grating or the change in the refractive index directly proportional to the change in the Bragg wavelength. Thus physical parameter change can be sensed using a FBG, by measuring the change in the Bragg wavelength or the change in reflection coefficient of a particular wavelength [3]. ER-FBGs sensor with different diameters build good strain sensor for high temperature environments strain sensor like aerospace engines, and high temperature pipelines in the oil and gas industry[4].
A FBG strain sensors network can be used for security purpose on railway track. FBG sensors do not need electrical power. These sensors have multiplexing capability. Due to this characteristic it offers cost effective solution to security systems. A high intrinsic sensitivity FBG sensor configuration offers many advantages whenever simultaneous measurements are required. FBG sensors are cost effective and easy to fabricate [5-6].

2 Literature Survey

An optical fiber sensor has the potential to overcome drawbacks of conventional electric sensors. A variety of of optical fiber sensors based FBG have been proposed based on incident lights modulation parameters.
A PS-FBG sensor system with high-sensitivity ultrasonic was proposed and demonstrated. The variable wavelength of the TLS were used, the reflected and transmitted optical powers of the sensor was balanced.
The Fiber Bragg Gratings (FBGs) sensors have ability to look after big areas to secure from unauthorized actions in railway scenarios.This broad-bandwidth quasi-static FBG strain sensor with dual-comb spectroscopy was

* Corresponding author: savita.bhosale@rait.ac.in

proposed. This 1-THz bandwidth sensor can be used for geophysics applications.

There are various sensing techniques explored depending on different systems such as transmitting systems, such as wired security systems and optical fiber security systems. Earlier wired security systems were considered the most reasonable and consistent systems, although they usually have to be set by expert to make sure wires, run from each sensor to the control panel,

The advantage offered by wired systems is they can be effortlessly linked to a display device using a telephone line.

A sensitivity-enhanced fiber-optic based strain sensor with an etched and regenerated FBG (ER-FBG) was shown experimentally which can be used for temperature measurements. The processes of chemical etching provide regenerated gratings.

Optical fiber based security system gives many advantages where as optical fiber can act not only transmission medium but also sensor. It is lightweight, very small size, ability to work in rough environment, immune to radio frequency interference, electromagnetic interference, requires low power, having large bandwidth, its capability to interface data communication system and much more sensitive than traditional sensors. This work focuses on how FBG can be used as strain sensor. The FBG based sensor especially more sensitive to strain variation.

A new sensing configuration was proposed for parallel measurement of strain and temperature based on a Bragg grating duo, with one grating in the etched and the other in un-etched region of polymer fibre. This sensor configuration recommends a number of advantages over earlier reported techniques, including high intrinsic sensitivity, low cost and eases in fabrication.

The FBGs are highly sensitive towards various ecological parameters, considering physical, chemical, biomedical, electrical parameter and these sensors can be used for monitoring structural health in civil infrastructure and interrogation techniques.

A high-resolution concurrent strain and temperature measurement system using π -phase-shifted fiber Bragg grating was proposed and designed.

3 Theory and Working Principle

The Fig. 1 shows Fiber Bragg Gratings with refractive index n0, n1, n2 and n3.Spectral response of input, transmitted signal and reflected is also illustrated.

The general equation of the FBG is

$$\lambda B = 2\eta eff\,\Lambda \quad (1)$$

Where

λB is Bragg wavelength

ηeff is effective refractive index of the core

Λ is the grating period.

If Fiber Bragg condition is not satisfied, the light from each subsequent plane in the grating will be out of phase and cancel.

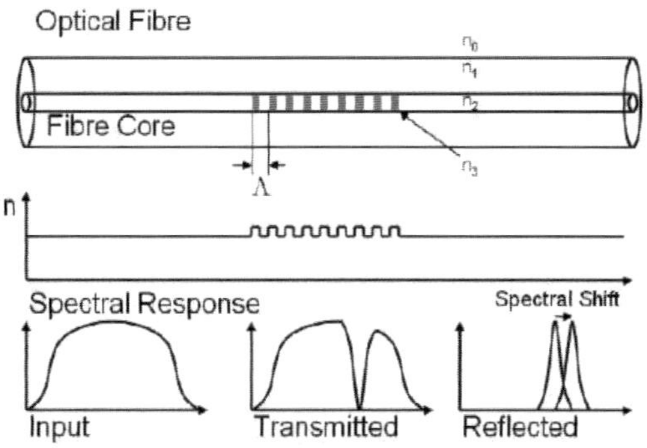

Fig. 1. Fiber Bragg Grating

The sensitivity of the Bragg wavelength strain can be calculated as below

$$\Delta\lambda_{B=} \left[\lambda \frac{\delta n}{\delta t} + n \frac{\delta\Lambda}{\delta x}\right] \Delta l \quad (2)$$

Δl is differences of Fiber Bragg Gratings length affected by strain[7-8].

4 Sensing Principle

The Fiber Bragg grating is widely employed for sensing applications. The main principle used in FBG based sensor is to analyse the shift in Bragg wavelength. The Bragg wavelength of an optical fiber grating is depends on function of grating period Λ.

Thus any change in refractive index directly proportional the Fiber Bragg wavelength and this change can be obsereved in display of transmitted or reflected signals spectrum, also any change in the grating period due to external strain will change Bragg wavelength.

The basic principle of FBG is measurement of the peak wavelength shift due to applied strain. Single mode FBG at 1550nm is used for analysis of strain performance. The selected wavelength of 1550nm offers less attenuation and absorption losses. The proposed system is designed and its performance is analyzed by using Optisystem software [9-10].

5 Block Diagram

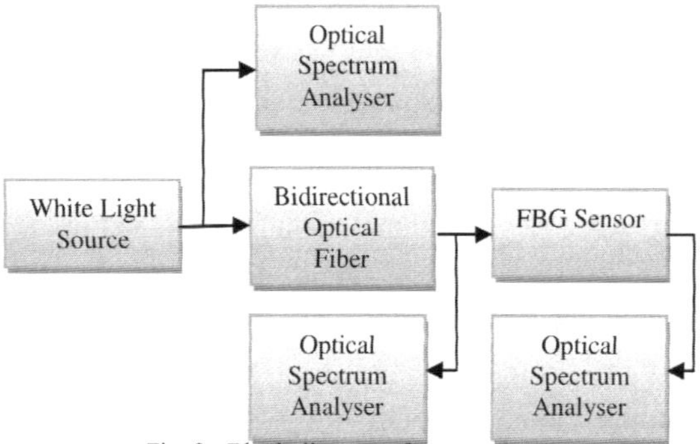

Fig. 2. Block diagram of sensor system

The block diagram of sensor system is as depicted in Fig.2.

The design consists of white light source, Fiber Bragg grating sensor, Optical delay and Spectrum analyzer.
A white light source is selected because as light source it has broad optical bandwidth and emits visible white light. Optical delay is used to provide precision optical path variation, it controls the delay through the device by varying the distance the light travels between the input and output power. To measure and display the distribution of power of an optical source Optical spectrum analyzer is used. Optical power is displayed on vertical axis while frequency is displayed along horizontal axis.

5.1 Parameter selection

The parameter selection is as shown in Table 1.

Table 1. Parameter Selection

Name	Specification
White light source	Frequency 193.1THz and Power -130dBm
Bidirectional Optical Fiber length	0.002Km
Uniform FBG sensor	at 1550nm
Optical Null	One
Optical Spectral Analyzer	Three

The parameters are selected as mentioned in Table 1. White light source at frequency of 193.1 THz and of power -130dBm is used as optical source. Bidirectional Optical fiber is of length 0.002Km is used.
FBG sensor is used at 1550nm.Optical null is used for accuracy measurement. Optical spectral analyzers are used for spectrum analysis of input signal, transmitted signal and reflected signal. Optical null is used to improve the accuracy of optical measurement.
A simplified architecture of fiber optic sensor system based on FBG is illustrated in Fig.3.
The simulations are carried out as per selected blocks and design parameters.

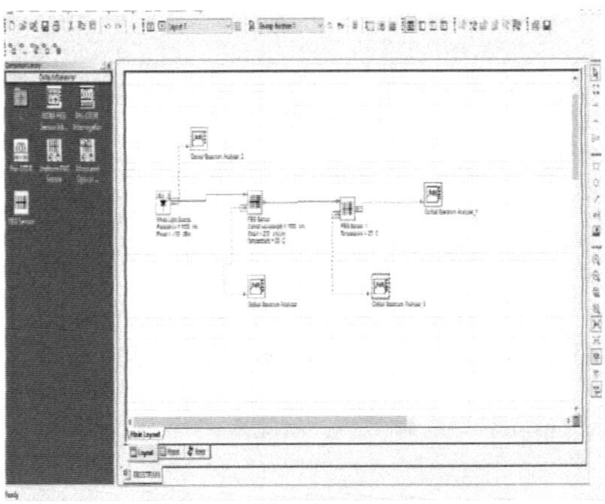

Fig. 3. A simplified architecture of fiber optic sensor

6 Results and Discussion

Total six simulations for six different values of strain are carried out to analyse the performance of FBG based sensor and corresponding wavelength shifts using Optisystem software. Power spectrum of input signal is depicted in Fig.4

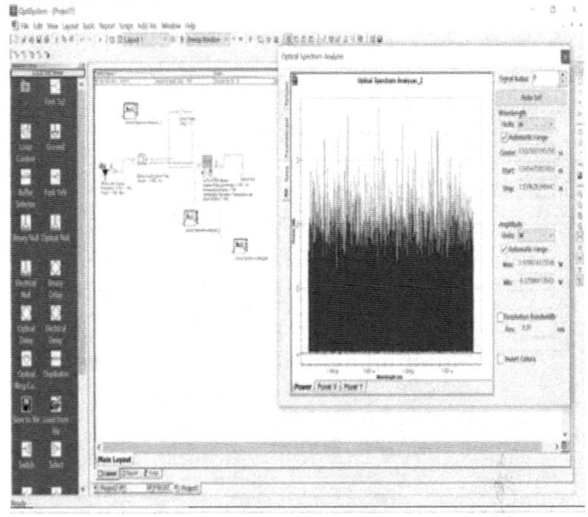

Fig. 4. Power spectrum of Input signal

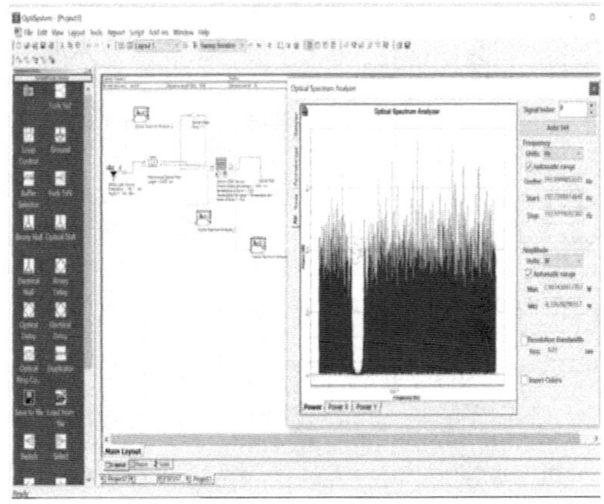

Fig. 5. Power spectrum of transmitted signal

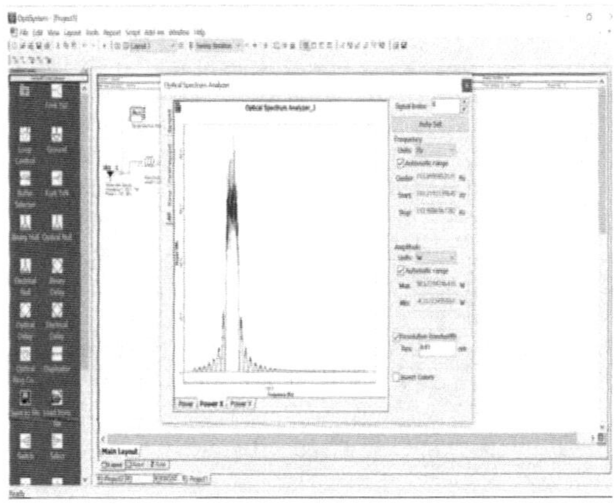

Fig. 6. Power spectrum of reflected signal

The transmitted signals and reflected signal power spectrum is depicted in Fig. 5 and Fig. 6

Table 2. Wavelength shifting (Theoretical result)

Initial Wavelength λB (nm)	Temperature in ^{0}C	Strain Experienced by FBG	Wavelength Shifted Δλ in (μm)
1550	20	0.005	0.01010
1550	20	0.006	0.01134
1550	20	0.007	0.01258
1550	20	0.008	0.01382
1550	20	0.009	0.01506
1550	20	0.001	0.01630

Table 3. Wavelength shifting (simulation result)

Initial Wavelength λB (nm)	Temperature in ^{0}C	Strain Experienced by FBG	Wavelength Shifted Δλ in (μm)
1550	20	0.005	0.0101
1550	20	0.006	0.01142
1550	20	0.007	0.01235
1550	20	0.008	0.0136
1550	20	0.009	0.0142
1550	20	0.001	0.01520

The initial wavelength is considered as 1550nm and temperature is considered as 20^{0}C.The wavelength shifting for theoretical result and the wavelength shifted simulation result are illustrated in Table 2 and Table 3. The theoretical and simulated results are closure. The proposed system is simulated at constant temperature.

7 Conclusion

Simulation of FBG based sensor system is successfully demonstrated, it has been observed that FBG sensor can be used to measure strain analysis. A Fiber Bragg Grating based sensors can be used for strain analysis. The wavelength of FBG sensors changes with change in the refractive index. Thus any physical parameter can be sensed by using FBG, the simulation tool can provide valuable inputs ahead of essentially engraving the grating in the fiber, in optimizing the design parameters of FBG based sensors. The FBG based sensors has capability to replace existing traditional sensors.

References

1. O. Andreas, K. Kyriacos, Fiber Bragg Grating. Fundamentals and Applications in Telecommunications and Sensing, Artech House (1999).
2. Yu, F.T.S. Yin, S. Fiber Optic Sensors Marcel Dekker Ltd.: New York, NY, USA(2002).
3. G. Wild S. Hinckley and P. Jansz, A transmit reflectdetection system for fiber Bragg grating hotonicsensors, Proc. SPIE,**20** 6801(2008).
4. K.S.Khaled, M.Zafrullah; S.M.Bilal,M.A.Merza, Analysis of Gaussian Apodized Fiber Bragg Grating Sensor, Journal of Optical Technology, **79**, 77-85(2012).
5. Kuse, N. Ozawa, A.; Kobayashi, Y. Static FBG strain sensor with high resolution and large dynamic range by dual-comb spectroscopy. Opt. Express, **21**, 11141(2013).
6. Wang, Y., Qiao, X.; Yang, H., Su, D. Li, L. Guo, T. Sensitivity-Improved Strain Sensor over a Large Range of Temperatures Using an Etched and Regenerated Fiber Bragg Grating. Sensors **14,** 18575–18582(2014).
7. Catalano, A., Bruno, F.; Pisco, M., Cutolo, A. Cusano, A. An Intrusion Detection System for the Protection of Railway Assets Using Fiber Bragg Grating Sensors. Sensors **14**, 18268–18285(2014).
8. Bhowmik, K.; Peng, G.D.; Luo, Y.; Ambikairajah, E.; Lovric, V., Walsh, W.R.; Rajan, G. High Intrinsic Sensitivity Etched Polymer Fiber Bragg Grating Pair for Simultaneous Strain and Temperature Measurements. IEEE Sens. J., **16**, 2453-2459(2016).
9. Chen, J. Liu, Q. He Z. High-Resolution Simultaneous Measurement of Strain and Temperature Using pi-Phase-Shifted FBG in Polarization Maintaining Fiber. J. Lightw. Technol. , **35**, 4838–4844(2017).
10. Joe, H.E. Yun, H. Jo, S.H. Jun, M.B. Min, B.K. A review on optical fiber sensors for environmental monitoring. Int. J. Precis. Eng. Manuf. Green Technology. 2018, 5, 173–191(2018).

Traffic Avoidance System for High Priority Vehicles

Ashly Sara Roy*, *Merin* Jose, *Sreya* Thomas, *Shweta* Dalvi, and *Manita* Rajput

Department of Electronics and Telecommunication Engineering, Fr.C.R.I.T Vashi, Navi Mumbai, Maharashtra, India

Abstract. India and most of the developing countries have unplanned cities in which roads are narrow and unkempt. Due to increasing vehicular density, repair of roads and traffic rules violation, traffic congestion is increasing at an alarming rate. Delay in arrival of High Priority Vehicles (HPV) like ambulances and fire engines cause severe loss to life and property. Although most HPVs are equipped with sirens, it is not efficient to guarantee a clear road to HPVs due to its audibility range. Hence, we propose a system by which the vehicles near the traffic junction will be alerted about the oncoming of HPV much in advance of its arrival so that they can make way for the HPV. In this system, every HPV is provided with an active RFID tag. Few kilometers before the main signal, an active RFID reader would be placed which would detect the vehicle and send this information to the display screen placed near the traffic junction signal via LoRa wirelessly, starting to make way for the HPV. Therefore, this project proposes to streamline the traffic and allow HPV to pass easily.

1 Introduction

With increasing vehicular density day by day on our roads, traffic jams have become a very common problem in metropolitan cities. Traffic congestion has always been a hindrance in everybody's normal life routine. However, efficiently synchronizing traffic at multiple junctions is complex. Conventional control systems do not handle the dynamic flow of traffic which results in chaos. Vehicles lie stagnant on the road for hours and for High Priority Vehicles (HPV) such as ambulances and fire engines, it is nearly impossible to pass through the traffic congestion. Delay in the arrival of HPVs causes a lot of damage to properties and loss of human life. Most of the 'declared dead' and 'died on road' scenarios happen where there is a time lag in moving the critical patients from one place to another due to traffic congestion. Even though the siren of HPV alerts the drivers in a traffic jam, they can't do much as less space is there for them to give way. This project develops a system that will recognize a HPV by detecting the active RFID tag allotted to it by the active RFID reader placed a few kilometers before the main traffic signal. Reader then sends the information of oncoming HPV to the traffic signal at a junction via LoRa transceiver modules. The information that the HPV is on its way will be displayed on the display screen at the junction well in advance before the HPV reaches the junction thereby alerting all the other vehicle drivers which will make it easier for them to give way by eventually streamlining the flow of traffic.

Section 2 discusses about all the literature survey that was done in the pre planning stage of the system. Section 3 discusses the functional block diagram of the system. Section 4 elaborates on the hardware modules used in the project, while section 5 gives details about the software. The implementation is discussed in section 6. Section 7 contains the results and lastly, section 8 concludes the paper and gives future scope.

2 Literature survey

In [1], R.Want discusses RFID and its applications and the challenges faced while deploying this technology. He further discusses Active and Passive tags and different design approaches that exist for transferring power from the reader to the tag. The tag antenna captures the energy and transfers it to the tag's ID. The tag's integrity and the antenna remains protected due to encapsulation from environmental conditions or reagents. The near-and far-field based signals also transmit and receive data by various modulation techniques

An effective application of RFID technology can be seen in [2], where students in a classroom are provided

*Corresponding author: ashly1598@gmail.com

with RFID tags attached to their ID cards which makes the process of taking attendance more secure and faster as compared to existing conventional methods. The passive RFID reader generates radio frequency which is transmitted to the surrounding using the antenna of the reader. If there is an RFID tag near the reader, a small power will be induced from the radio wave to the tag and allow a modulated electromagnetic wave to be sent back to the reader which uniquely detects the tag. The performance of RFID based attendance systems has been evaluated on different tag positions and distance.

In [3], the authors have mentioned the application of RFID in healthcare. This technology can be applied to collecting sensor derived data and doing computation by extending the chip's interface capability to a sensor. In hospitals, temperature sensing makes it very convenient to track tainted blood to aid in protecting a hospital's blood supply, chemical sensing can support advanced medical monitoring. It can also be used for retrieving patient information and patient location in hospitals to increase the accuracy of patient identification. Asset and equipment tracking is yet another field where this technology is widely used.

The authors in [4] discuss the security-related aspect of RFID technology. Here in this paper, there are various attacks mentioned on the RFID tag and reader. One of them in which cloning of the tag takes place where information received can be used for further attacks. Eavesdropping is one of the most widely deployed threats due to the wireless nature of RFID In eavesdropping, unauthorized individuals use an antenna to communicate between legitimate RFID tags and readers. This attack can take place both ways: tag to reader and reader to tag. Various algorithms are devised on securing communication between tag and reader.

Emerging transmission technologies dedicated to IoT networks are explained by Umber Noreen and Ahcene Bounceur in [5].The performance of LoRa is based on three basic parameters: Code Rate, Spreading Factor, and Bandwidth. LoRa becomes resistant to channel noise, long term relative frequency, Doppler effects, and fading due to usage of the wider band. Here in this paper, the performance of LoRa based on three basic parameters: Code Rate, Spreading Factor, and Bandwidth are analyzed. A decrease in data rate is due to the increase in the value of the code rate and the spreading factor which causes an increase in time for LoRa to reach its destination. The choice of bandwidth also influences data rate and time on the air of a packet.

An investigation is carried out in [6] between LoRa and IEEE 802.15.4g networks to measure the interference between them.CSS(Chirp Spread Spectrum) modulation is used by LoRa in contrast to GFSK(Gaussian Shift Keying) used by IEEE 802.15.4g. GFSK concentrates the energy on two-shift frequencies making 802.15.4g more sensitive to narrowband interference while CSS spreads the energy of the symbol across the whole bandwidth. LoRa is much more tolerant than IEEE 802.15.4g under interference and LoRa's radio configuration is important to the degree of tolerance. LoRa can tolerate interference power that is 6 dB higher for a high data rate setting, than the actual LoRa receiving power and for the low data rate, it can tolerate up to 16 dB.

In [7], the signal propagation measurement of LoRa devices that was observed in an indoor environment is depicted. The measurements were performed in the building of a university with 12 floors. To measure signal propagation in the indoor environment, a LoRa gateway is set up at the rooftop of the building and the end nodes are placed at six different locations of each floor. After processing the signals that are collected from the end node, the gateway will provide useful information such as Received Signal Strength Indicator (RSSI), Signal Noise Ratio (SNR), Received Frequency. From these data, the ability to communicate in an indoor environment where there are many obstacles can be confirmed.

3 Block diagram of the system

Fig. 1. shows the sequence of steps involved in the proposed system.

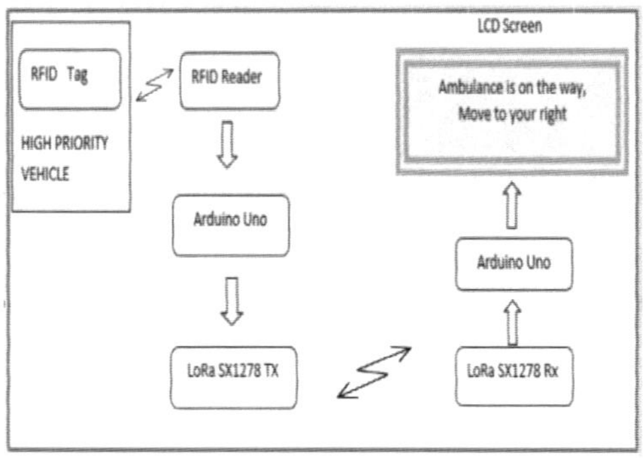

Fig. 1. Block diagram of the proposed system

The detailed step by step working of the system is explained as follows:

3.1 RFID detection

The reader is placed on a lamp post which will be at some distance above the ground. The RFID reader will be kept at a distance of 2 kilometers from the main traffic junction.

https://doi.org/10.1051/itmconf/20203202007

All the HPVs will be given an active RFID tag which has a unique ID linked to it. As soon as an HPV comes within the reading range of the reader, the tag is detected within a few milliseconds.

3.2 Authentication of the tag values

The Arduino has a database of all the RFID tag values allotted to the HPVs stored in its internal memory. When the tag value of the HPV matches with any of the tag values in the database, the data pin of the Arduino is enabled and passes signal to LoRa receiver, placed at the main traffic junction, which is connected to another Arduino.

3.3. Activation of LoRa - transmitting side

LoRa used in this project is of 433MHz frequency. The LoRa module is interfaced to Arduino and is placed with the RFID reader. When the LoRa is on, it starts to transmit tag value through its antenna. Both the transmitting and the receiving antenna are kept in Line of Sight.

3.4 Activation of LoRa - receiving side

LoRa receiver, which is placed at the main traffic junction, is connected to another Arduino. When the message packets are received, it is displayed on the LCD screen.

3.5 LCD screen display

The LCD is placed in such a way that it is visible to all the automobile drivers. It displays a message stating "HPV on its way, move to your right" which will alert the drivers and they can make way for the HPV much in advance by moving to their right leaving the left lane empty for HPV to pass. If the tag value doesn't match the database, the input is ignored and the reader waits for another valid tag.

Fig. 2. gives the functional flow diagram of the proposed system as explained above.

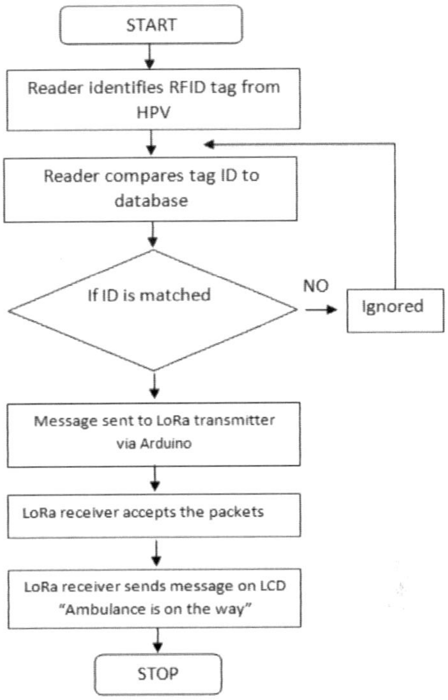

Fig. 2. Functional flow diagram of the proposed system

4 Hardware used

The hardware used in this system consists of SAAT-F520 Active RFID reader, active RFID tags, SX1278 LoRa transceiver modules, Arduino Uno board for interface, and a 16x2 Liquid Crystal Display (LCD). The antenna used for LoRa is a 433 MHz with IPEX connector.

4.1 SAAT-F520 RFID reader

RFID is a form of wireless communication that uses electromagnetic coupling for uniquely identifying a tag. There is an internal battery that enables the tag to have extremely long read ranges [8]. The operating frequency of active RFID is 2.45 GHz. It supports RS-232,10/100M Adaptive Ethernet and also supports active and passive reading, multi-reading, timing trigger, command trigger, external trigger and other modes, to meet users' various integration needs [9].

4.2 SX 1278 LoRa module

LoRa is a wireless network technology that offers long range, low power and secure data transmission. LoRa stands for Long Range devices. It uses unlicensed frequency bands of 433MHz, 868MHz and 916MHz. LoRa SX1278 is an ultra-low power long range Wireless Transceiver. It supports FSK, GFSK, MSK, GMSK, LoRa and OOK modulations. SX1278 has a programmable rate up to 300kbps. It supports half-duplex SPI (Serial Peripheral Interface) communication. The operating voltage of LoRa SX1278 is 1.8v - 3.7v. The Line of Sight (LOS) range of LoRa is 20 kilometers and Non Line of Sight (NLOS) range is 3kms.

The antennas used for LoRa are Omni directional antennas. These antennas can transmit electromagnetic waves in all directions equally. IPEX connectors are used to connect the antenna to the ground (antenna pin) of the LoRa module. It has a frequency range of 433MHz and maximum range of 2.9dB [10].

4.3 Arduino UNO

Arduino is the microcontroller board used in this project because of its ease to use. It has 16 MHz quartz crystal, USB connection, 6 analog inputs and 6 PWM outputs, reset button and its operating voltage is 5V. It reads input and shows output by turning on LED [11].

4.4 LCD screen

The LCD (Liquid Crystal Display) used in this project is a 16x2 size display. 16 characters per line can be displayed in this LCD and there are 2 such lines. In this LCD each character is displayed in a 5x7 pixel matrix [12].

5 Software used

The RFID reader uses a software SAAT-520 series to read the tag values. The reader is interfaced with a pc using RS-232. Since Active tags are used, once the COM port is selected, the carrier is opened and the reader is set up to read the tags. A text file is generated with the tag value and the time of the detection of the ambulance. This text file is then read by the Arduino which detects the tag value and compares it to the database. Fig. 3. shows the GUI of SAAT-520.exe application file.

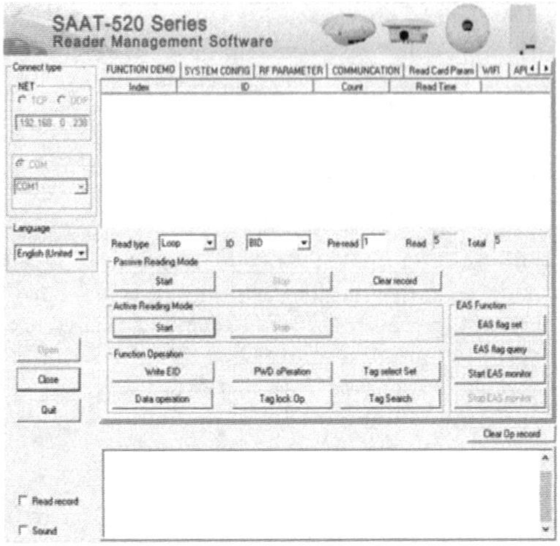

Fig. 3. SAAT-F520 series reader software

It has options to select COM port, the transport layer protocols, and also required language. It can be used for both passive as well as active tag detection. It also displays a list of tag values read along with the read time and number of repetitions.

6 Implementation

6.1 LoRa transmission

The project started with interfacing the Lora SX1278 with the Arduino. The Arduino database consists of tag values of all HPVs. Once the tag value detected matches with the database, it initializes the counter for the packets to be sent. The baud rate is set at 9600bps. The LoRa library installed checks if the frequency is equal to 433 MHz and will start the transmission of packets only if it matches. Fig. 4 shows the steps of LoRa transmission through the Arduino.

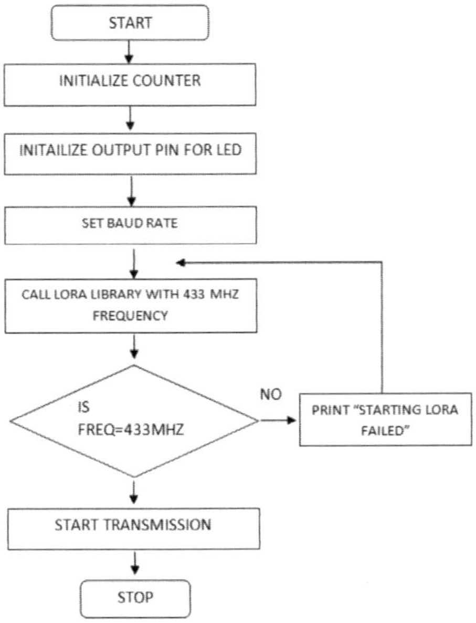

Fig. 4. Steps for LoRa transmission

6.2 LoRa reception

The receiver LoRa is also set at the same baud rate and frequency as that of the sender. It waits for the message packets to arrive. Once the message is received, it is displayed on the LCD. The steps for reception of LoRa are explained in fig. 5.

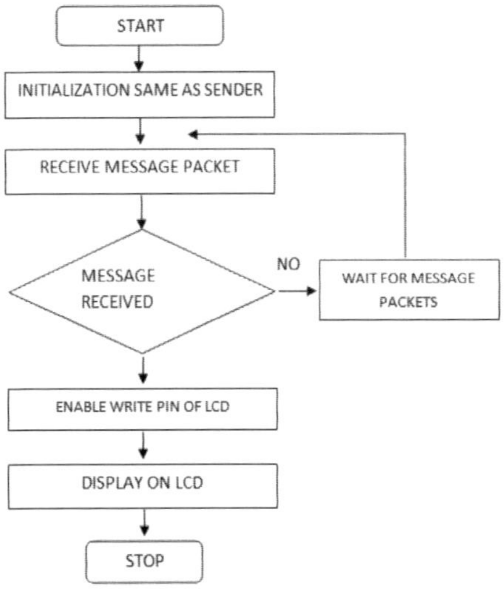

Fig. 5. Steps for LoRa reception

7 Result

Fig. 6. shows the tags detected by the SAAT-520 software.

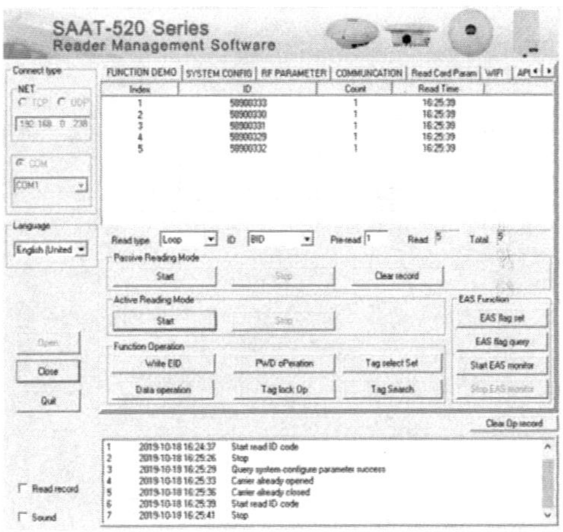

Fig. 6. RFID tags detected by SAAT-520

Number of times the tags are detected and the time at which the tags are detected are also shown in the display window. As shown, 5 tag values were detected and displayed on the SAAT application.

The results obtained on the serial monitor of Arduino IDE of the LoRa transmitter are shown in the following fig. 7.

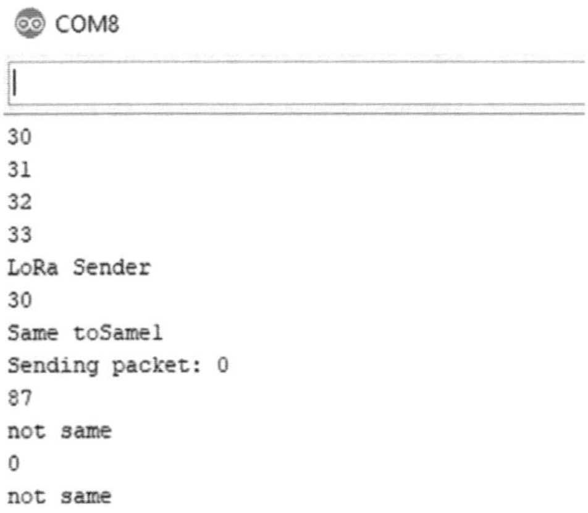

Fig. 7. LoRa sender output display on the Arduino IDE

The values given on the first four lines are the last two digits of the 8 digit RFID tag IDs stored in the Arduino database. When the read tag ID matches with the database, message packets are transmitted otherwise it is ignored.

The message sent by the transmitter is received by the receiver along with the packet number and the RSSI (Received Signal Strength Indicator) value is shown in the fig. 8.

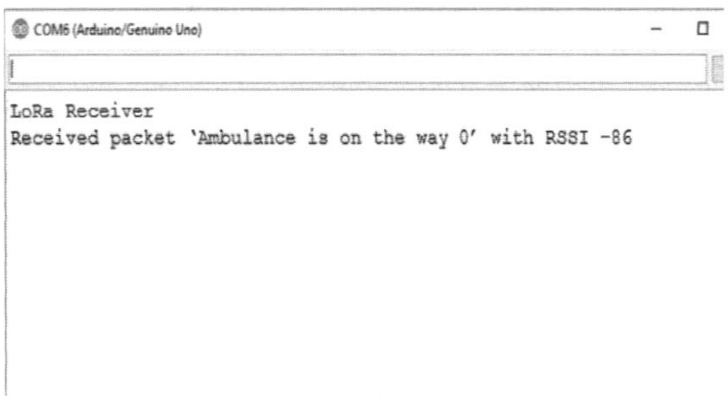

Fig. 8. LoRa receiver output display on Arduino IDE

The LCD screen will display the message received as shown in fig. 9.

Fig. 9. Message displayed on LCD screen

Table 1. Read range testing of RFID reader

DISTANCE (m)	LOS/NLOS	TAG DETECTED OR NOT
10	NLOS	YES
10	LOS	YES
25	NLOS	YES
25	LOS	YES
30	NLOS	NO
50	LOS	YES
75	LOS	YES
90	LOS	NO

The Range testing was performed at distances mentioned in Table 1. under both LOS and NLOS conditions. Since the road varies from one lane road to a six lane expressway, the tags getting detected at these distances are tabulated. The test was carried out indoors. The RFID reader was kept stationary and the tags were placed at specific marked distances to measure the reading range. Proper detection of tags were observed.

Table 2. Range Testing of LoRa transceiver module

DISTANCE (in m)	LOS/NLOS	PACKET LOSS OBSERVED
22	LOS	NO
22	NLOS	NO
44	LOS	NO
44	NLOS	NO
66	LOS	NO
66	NLOS	YES
88	LOS	NO
120	LOS	YES

The LoRa range testing was carried out outdoors at the distances mentioned in Table 2. One LoRa module was kept stationary and the other was moved in both LOS and NLOS directions. It was placed at specific marked distances to measure the reading range. The packets were transmitted and received efficiently without any loss observed. The loss was observed only after 100 meters for LOS and after 60 meters for NLOS.

8 Conclusion and future scope

The proposed system for High Priority Vehicles to avoid the traffic has been successfully developed. The aim of this project was to reduce the road time of the HPV. This system compared to the conventional methods in use has several advantages. It will act like an efficient alert system and thus save lives.

The drawback is that the theoretical range of LoRa is given to be 20 km LOS, and practically it was found that it doesn't cover a long range when configured with Arduino Uno. Hence in real time implementation, the number of LoRa modules will increase. As an alternative either LoRa gateways can be configured or microprocessors with higher output power can be used to increase the communication range of the network. In the future, the system is still to be tested in real time scenarios. The proposed system works with RFID and LoRa being put in Active mode always hence, increases power. If the microprocessors like Raspberry Pi are used, then LoRa can be put into sleep mode which gets activated only when required.

References

[1] R.Want, "An introduction to RFID technology," in IEEE Pervasive Computing, vol. 5, no. 1, pp. 25-33, Jan.-March (2006), doi: 10.1109/MPRV.2006.2.

[2] T. S. Lim, S. C. Sim and M. M. Mansor, "RFID based attendance system," 2009 IEEE Symposium on Industrial Electronics & Applications, Kuala Lumpur, (2009), pp. 778-782.

[3] W. Yao, C.Chu and Z. Li, "The use of RFID in healthcare: Benefits and barriers," IEEE International Conference on RFID-Technology and Applications, Guangzhou, (2010), pp. 128-134, doi: 10.1109/RFID-TA.2010.5529874.

[4] N. Kannouf, Y. Douzi, M. Benabdellah and A. Azizi, "Security on RFID technology," International Conference on Cloud Technologies and Applications (CloudTech), Marrakech, (2015), pp. 1-5, doi: 10.1109/CloudTech.2015.7336997.

[5] U. Noreen, A. Bounceur and L. Clavier, "A study of LoRa low power and wide area network technology," 2017 International Conference on Advanced Technologies for Signal and Image Processing (ATSIP), Fez, 2017, pp. 1-6.

[6] C. Orfanidis, L. M. Feeney, M. Jacobsson and P. Gunningberg, "Investigating interference between LoRa and IEEE 802.15.4g networks," IEEE 13th International Conference on Wireless and Mobile Computing, Networking and Communications (WiMob), Rome, (2017), pp. 1-8.

[7] L. H. Trinh, V. X. Bui, F. Ferrero, T. Q. K. Nguyen and M. H. Le, "Signal propagation of LoRa technology using for smart building applications," IEEE Conference on Antenna Measurements & Applications (CAMA), Tsukuba, (2017), pp. 381-384, doi: 10.1109/CAMA.2017.8273458.

[8] https://internetofthingsagenda.techtarget.com/definition/RFID-radio-frequency-identification

[9] https://www.fastprorfid.com/pro-rfid-readers-active-directional-reader.php

[10] https://www.everythingrf.com/community/what-is-lora

[11] https://www.coursehero.com/file/28669168/Arduino-Unotxt/

[12] https://www.elprocus.com/lcd-16x2-pin-configuration-and-its-working

Epileptic Seizure Detection Using Artifact Reduction and HOS Features of WPD

Meenal Vijay Kakade
Department of EXTC
RAIT, Navi Mumbai, India
meenalkakade1@gmail.com

Chandrakant J. Gaikwad
Department of EXTC
RAIT, Navi Mumbai, India
cjgaikwad@gmail.com

Vijay R. Dahake
Department of EXTC
RAIT, Navi Mumbai, India
vijayr_dahake@rediffmail.com

***Abstract*—The use of computer aided diagnosis systems for disease identifiscation, based on signal processing, image processing and video processing terminologies is common due to emerging technologies in medical field. The detection of epilepsy seizures using EEG recordings is done by different signal processing techniques. To reduce the disability caused by the uncertainty of the occurrence of seizures, a recording system which shall result accurate and early detection of seizure with quick warning is greatly desired. To optimize the performance of EEG based epilepsy seizures detection, in this work we are presenting a method based on two key algorithms. Here, we propose unique algorithm based on SWT (Stationary Wavelet Transform), for easier seizure analysis process, along with improved performance of the application of seizure detection algorithms. Then, we propose the algorithm for feature extraction that makes use of Higher Order Statistics of the coefficients that are calculated using Wavelet Packet Decomposition (WPD).This helps in improving the epilepsy seizures detection performance. The proposed methods helps to improve the overall efficiency and robustness of EEG based epilepsy seizures detection system.**

***Index Terms*—Artifacts, EEG, Feature Extraction, Higher Order Statistics, Stationary Wavelet Transform, Seizure, Wavelet Packet Decomposition.**

I. Introduction

Epilepsy characterize a disorder of brain, which can occur to people with any age. One of the main symptoms of epilepsy is the occurrence of the epileptic seizure. Reason for occurrence of seizure may be hereditary or due to some brain injury. Epilepsy can show symptoms through any neurological part of the body, but the mostly affected organ is the brain. Due to this, the diagnostic equipment which can help in the detection and further help in the treatment of the epilepsy is the Electroencephalogram (EEG). The main issue while detecting the epilepsy with the help of EEG is that, the artifacts mix with the seizure signals and can appear as seizure which can result in the misdiagnosis in the level of the disease. These artifacts can be system generated as well as can be generated by the human body due to various factors such as blinking of eye, body movement,etc[1]. So, the purpose of this work is to remove artifacts effectively so as enhance the seizure detection due to epilepsy.

There are many acknowledged systems working for this purpose[3]-[13], but there are some or the other drawbacks or issues related to it like some systems can detect only particuar type of artifacts, some algorithms are complex affecting the effectiveness and the usefulness of the system. There are also some feature extraction methods mentioned in the literature[14]-[15], but resuts in less efficient output.In this work, we try to overcome the issues by using the methods which can perform well and will give effective results in terms of accuracy and also in terms of number of false positive. Here, we use SWT for the process of seizure analysis, and for better detection of epilepsy seizure, we propose a feature extraction method that makes use of Higher Order Statistics (HOS) of WPD coefficients.

II. Proposed Classification System

SWT in addition with denoising process helps us to abolish the artifacts. The bandwidth of the EEG signal is 0.05Hz to 128Hz, whereas the seizure activities occur in the range of 0.5 Hz to 29 Hz. Depending on this frequency band, the level of decomposition of the EEG can be decided. The decomposition of the EEG using SWT results in the approximate and the detailed coefficients. These coefficients are denoised to discard the artifacts that are incorporated in the EEG signal. Figure 1 imitate the layout for the proposed system. Non-negative garrote shrinkage function is availed to discard the artifacts as it is less sensitive to the change in the input[10]. For denoising the coefficients, we make use of the universal threshold which is given by[8] :

$$T_H = T_P \mu_{j,l} \sqrt{2lnL} \qquad (1)$$

Here, L denote the epoch duration and $\mu_{j,l}$ denote noise variance and is represented as $\delta_{j,l}$ which can be calculated by the formula give below:

$$\mu_{j,l} = \frac{median(|\delta_{j,l}|)}{0.6745} \qquad (2)$$

$\delta_{j,l}$ is the coefficient of the wavelet for l th level of decomposition. A new parameter T_P is observed for thresholding the coefficients. $(T_P)_A$ is used for thresholding the approximate coefficients and $(T_P)_D$ is used for thresholding the detailed coefficients.

The features represent the nature of the EEG signal. So here we make use of the feature extraction methods for the effective seizure detection. Feature extraction method includes calculation of the HOS of the WPD Coefficients.

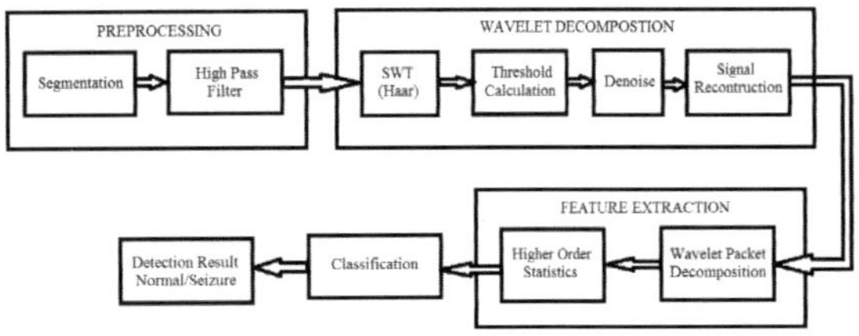

Fig. 1. Block Diagram

A. *Wavelet Packet Decomposition*

WPD is a Wavelet Transform which decomposes signal as low pass approximation coefficients and high pass detailed coefficients[19]. These coefficients are further decomposed into respective approximate and detailed coefficients creating a full binary tree as shown in the figure 2. The main advantage of WPD over Discrete Wavelet Transform (DWT) is that, DWT only break down the low frequency approximate coefficients which can result in the loss of data from the detailed co-efficients. WPD decomposes both approximate as well as the detailed coefficients, helping us to extract more features further increasing the accuracy in seizure detection.

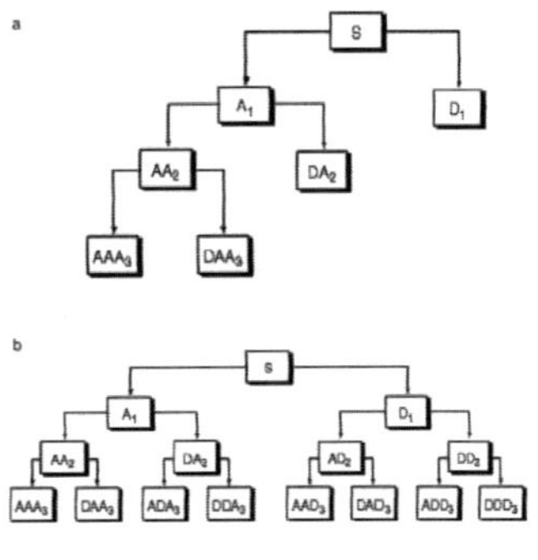

Fig. 2. (a) DWT and (b) WPD[19]

B. *Higher Order Statistics*

Higher Order Statistics (HOS) is used when we deal with nonlinear signals, and most of the applications are based on nonlinear signals. And in our work, we work on EEG which is a nonlinear signal. The initial two order statistics consists of the mean as well as the variance whereas, HOS consists of the cumulants and moments. The 2nd, 3rd and 4th order cumulants are determined considering a lag 0. These cumulants are given paarticular names, viz, variance for the second order cumulants, and Skewness and Kurtosis for third and fourth order cumulants repectively. Higher Order Statistics generate 30 sub-bands for 4 level. From each sub-band, 3 features are extracted which results in total of 90 features for all the levels of Wavelet Packet Decomposition as shown in figure 3. Although, the lower order statistics consists and works on variance and mean; HOS focuses on cummulants and moments[19].

$$\varphi(t) = E[exp(ktx)] \qquad (3)$$

For digitalized signal with zero cummulants, moments and mean, can be shown as:

$$m_2(p) = E[X(L), X(l+p)]$$

$$m_3(p,q) = E[X(L), X(l+p).X(l+q)]$$

$$m_4(p,q,r) = E[X(L), X(l+p).X(l+q).X(l+r)]$$

Here $E[\cdot]$ denotes operation of Expectation where as $X(\cdot)$ represents a random process. Also $X(l)$, which is the second characteristic function is given as:

$$X(t)ln\varphi(t) = E[exp(ktx)] \qquad (4)$$

and this is also called as cummulant generating function

$$c_2(p) = m_2(p)$$

$$c_3(p,q) = m_3(p,q)$$

$$c_4(p,q,r) = m_4(p,q,r) - m_2(p)m_2(q-r) - m_2(q)m_2(r-p) - m_2(r)m_2(p-q)$$

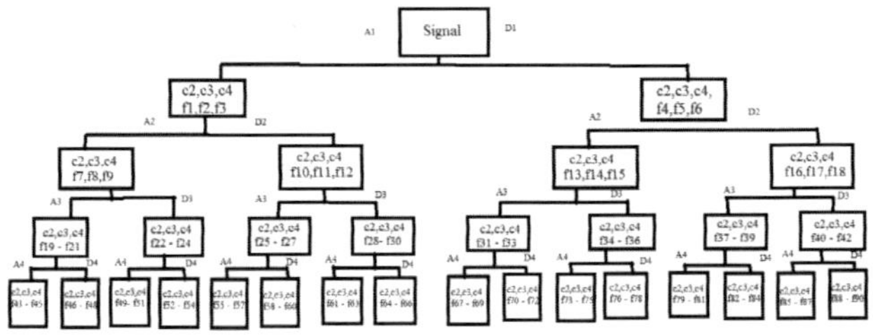

Fig. 3. Extraction of 90 HOS features from the fourth level of WPD[19]

Hence, the HOS methods are used for the extraction of new and less features from WPD coefficients. Cumulants for decomposition level are calculated using HOS methods. As mentioned previously, there are 30 subbands for the 4 levels. 3 features are derived for each decomposition level by using HOS. 90 features are acquired as shown in fig (fig 3) for all levels of WPD.

C. *Data Normalization*

Data normalization is used to reduce data redundancy and which results in the improvement of the data integrity. It converts the data in the range of -1 to 1.

$$Y(n) = 2[\frac{X(n) - X(n)_{min}}{X(n)_{max} - X(n)_{min}}] - 1 \qquad (5)$$

 https://doi.org/10.1051/itmconf/20203200005

The above expression gives normalized matrix,
Here $X(n)$ represents the nth sample vector.

III. Performance Evaluation and Simulation Results

To evaluate the performance of the above method, here we calculate the metrics so as to verify and quantify the efficiency of the work.

A. *Performance Metrics and Evaluation*

1)η: Artifact Reduction is given by:

$$\eta = 100(1 - \frac{C_R - C_{RC}}{C_R - C_A}) \qquad (6)$$

Where,
C_R : Coefficient of autocorrelation of the reference signal for a time lag 1
C_A : crosscorrelation coefficients among reference and artifactual signal.
C_{RC} : crosscorrelation coefficients among reference and reconstructed signals

2) $\triangle SNR$: Considering that the signals posses zero mean, then $\triangle SNR$ is calculated as the difference in SNR prior and after artifact removal:

$$\triangle SNR = 10log_{10}(\frac{\sigma^2_{X_R}}{\sigma^2_{e_{br}}}) - 10log_{10}(\frac{\sigma^2_{X_R}}{\sigma^2_{e_{ar}}}) \qquad (7)$$

where
$\sigma^2_{X_R}$: reference signal variance
$\sigma^2_{e_{br}}$: error signal prior artifact removal
$\sigma^2_{e_{ar}}$ error signal after artifact removal

3) Spectral Distortion P_{sd}:

Let
$P_{ref}(f)$: PSD for Reference Signal
$P_{art}(f)$: PSD for artifactual signal, and
$P_{rec}(f)$:PSD for reconstructed signal, PSD- Power Spectral Density then P_{sd} is calculated as follows:

$$P_{sd} = \frac{\sum_{f=1}^{\frac{F_s}{2}}[(P_{rec}(f))^2}{\sum_{f=1}^{\frac{F_s}{2}}[(P_{ref}(f))^2} \qquad (8)$$

4) $\triangle Cor$: Correlation helps in determining the similarity between two signals in time domain. The improvement in correlation $\triangle Cor$ caused due to the removal of artifact can be given by :

$$\triangle Cor(\%) = \frac{C_{RC} - C_A}{C_A} 100 \qquad (9)$$

where
C_A:cross correlation coefficients among ref and artifact consisting signal and
C_{RC} : cross correlation coefficient among reference and reconstructed signals

5) $\triangle Coh$: Coherence helps in determining the analogy among signals in frequency domain. It is characterized among two signals $p(t)$ and $q(t)$ as

$$\triangle Coh = \frac{|SD_{pq}|^2}{SD_{pp}G_{qq}} \qquad (10)$$

where $|SD_{xy}|$: cross-spectral density , and
SD_{xx} and $SD_{yy}$are the autospectral density.
$\triangle Coh$ is calculated by:

$$\triangle Coh = \frac{Coh_{aft} - Coh_{bef}}{Coh_{bef}} \qquad (11)$$

6) SNR_{art}: For calculating SNR Artifact, Let, artifact be the signal and reference neural signal be noise, hence,

$$SNR_{art} = 10log_{10}\frac{\sigma^2{}_{e_{br}}}{\sigma^2{}_{x_{ref}}} \qquad (12)$$

7)$\triangle T_{art}$: It represents the percentage of the duration of the artifact out of the total length of the signal.

$$\triangle T_{art}(\%) = \frac{T_{art}}{T_{total}} * 100 \qquad (13)$$

TABLE I
Results for Artifact Removal Based on Different Artifact SNR (SNR_{Art})

SNR_{Art}	η	$\triangle SNR$	$\triangle PDS_{dis}$	$\triangle Corr(\%)$	$\triangle Coher(\%)$
3.50	51.59	0.05	98.00	90.47	40.98
14.60	44.22	0.27	98.00	42.26	44.99
16.85	39.26	0.18	97.00	39.00	34.99

TABLE II
Results for Artifact Removal Based on Different Artifact Durations ($\triangle T_{Art}$)

$\triangle T_{Art}$	η	$\triangle SNR$	$\triangle PDS_{dis}$	$\triangle Corr(\%)$	$\triangle Coher(\%)$
31.00	37.88	4.77	98.00	37.60	42.00
32.00	46.37	6.46	96.00	46.82	44.00

https://doi.org/10.1051/itmconf/20203200005

B. Simulation Results

The images below show the signals prior and after abolishing the artifacts from the signal, the artifact signal in the EEG, and the coefficients for the four level decomposition

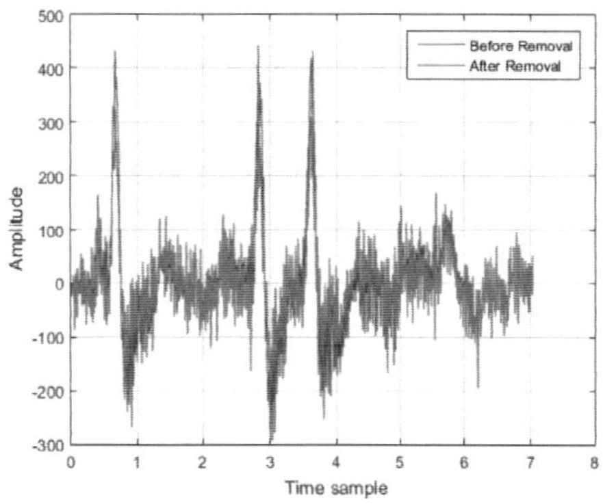

Fig. 4. Artifactual Data and Reconstructed Data

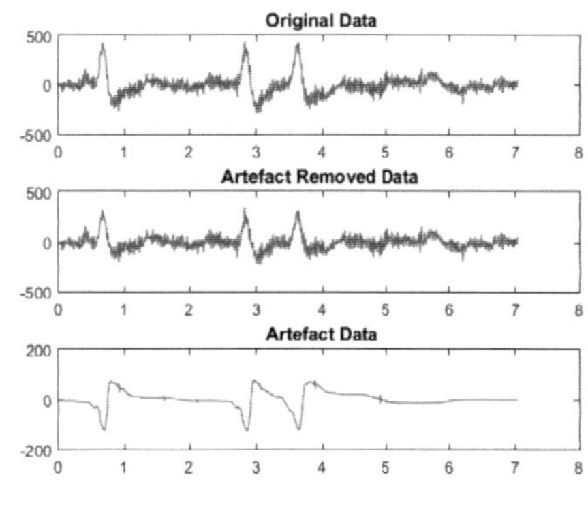

Fig. 5. Original Data, Artifact Removed Data and Artifact Data

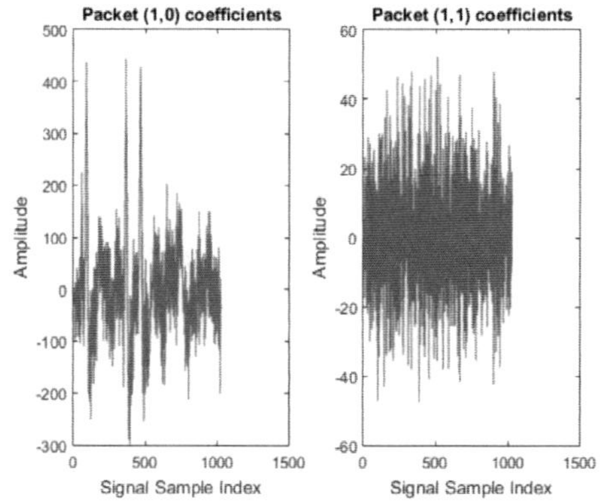

Fig. 6. 1st level decomposition coefficients

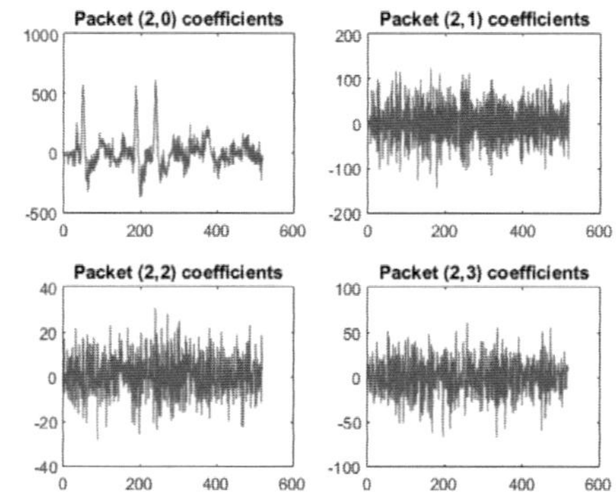

Fig. 7. 2nd level decomposition coefficients

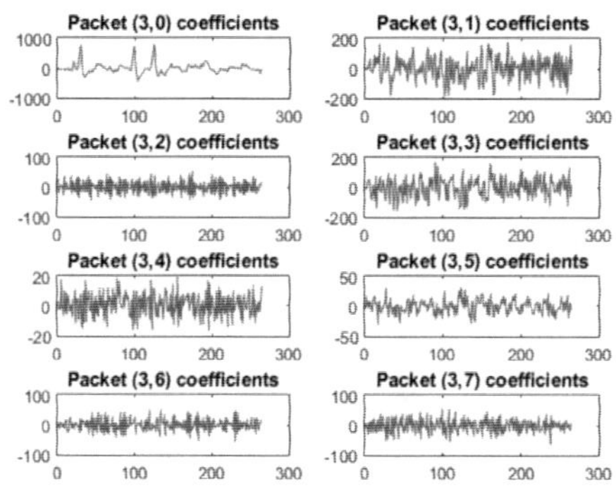

Fig. 8. 3rd level decomposition coefficients

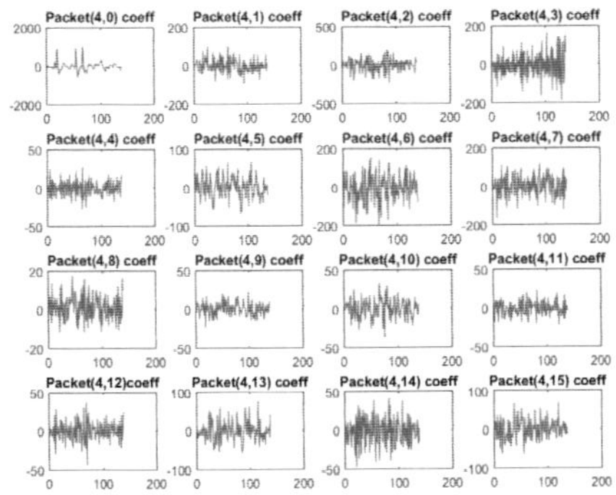

Fig. 9. 4th level decomposition coefficients

TABLE III
CLASSIFICATION PERFORMANCE MEASURES

Performance Measures	Using Sample Entropy(%)	Using WPD and HOS(%)
Detection Accuracy	83.26	90.44
Improvement in Seizure Detetction	69.78	84.04

IV. CONCLUSION

In this work, EEG artifact removal is analyzed and used to enhance the seizure detection process. Sationary Wavelet transform is used for artifact removal which also retaines the signal of interest or the events that represented a seizure activity. In the proposed work, seizure detection performance is enhanced using the Wavelet Packet Decomposition and Higher Order Statistics of it. The proposed method based on WPD and its HOS features excels as compared to the methods available in the literature in terms of detection accuracy and the improvement seizure detection as shown in the table 3.

REFERENCES

[1] Islam, Md Kafiul, Amir Rastegarnia, and Zhi Yang. "A wavelet-based artifact reduction from scalp EEG for epileptic seizure detection." IEEE journal of biomedical and health informatics 20.5 (2016): 1321-1332.
[2] Fisher, Robert S., et al. "The impact of epilepsy from the patients perspective I. Descriptions and subjective perceptions." Epilepsy research 41.1 (2000): 39-51.
[3] ORegan, Simon, Stephen Faul, and William Marnane. "Automatic detection of EEG artefacts arising from head movements using EEG and gyroscope signals." Medical engineering physics 35.7 (2013): 867-874.
[4] Gwin, Joseph Toliver, et al. "Removal of movement artifact from high-density EEG recorded during walking and running." American Journal of Physiology-Heart and Circulatory Physiology (2010).
[5] Saab, M. E., and Jean Gotman. "A system to detect the onset of epileptic seizures in scalp EEG." Clinical Neurophysiology 116.2 (2005): 427-442.
[6] Teplan, Michal. "Fundamentals of EEG measurement." Measurement science review 2.2 (2002): 1-11.
[7] Bowman, James, F. Edward Dudek, and Mark Spitz. "Epilepsy is a chronic neurological disorder characterized by recurrent epileptic seizures. Brain injury and genetic abnormalities underlie this disorder."
[8] Islam, Md Kafiul, et al. "Artifact characterization and removal for in vivo neural recording." Journal of neuroscience methods 226 (2014): 110-123.
[9] Coifman, Ronald R., and David L. Donoho. "Translation-invariant denoising." Wavelets and statistics. Springer, New York, NY, 1995. 125-150.
[10] Gao, Hong-Ye. "Wavelet shrinkage denoising using the non-negative garrote." Journal of Computational and Graphical Statistics 7.4 (1998): 469-488.
[11] Flexer, Arthur, et al. "Using ICA for removal of ocular artifacts in EEG recorded from blind subjects." Neural Networks 18.7 (2005): 998-1005.
[12] Joyce, Carrie A., Irina F. Gorodnitsky, and Marta Kutas. "Automatic removal of eye movement and blink artifacts from EEG data using blind component separation." Psychophysiology 41.2 (2004): 313-325.
[13] Hallez, Hans, et al. "Removing muscle and eye artifacts using blind source separation techniques in ictal EEG source imaging." Clinical Neurophysiology 120.7 (2009): 1262-1272.
[14] Esteller, Rosana, et al. "Line length: an efficient feature for seizure onset detection." 2001 Conference Proceedings of the 23rd Annual International Conference of the IEEE Engineering in Medicine and Biology Society. Vol. 2. IEEE, 2001.
[15] Rafiuddin, Nidal, Yusuf Uzzaman Khan, and Omar Farooq. "Feature extraction and classification of EEG for automatic seizure detection." 2011 International Conference on Multimedia, Signal Processing and Communication Technologies. IEEE, 2011.
[16] Song, Yuedong, Jon Crowcroft, and Jiaxiang Zhang. "Automatic epileptic seizure detection in EEGs based on optimized sample entropy and extreme learning machine." Journal of neuroscience methods 210.2 (2012): 132-146.
[17] Misiti, M., et al. "Wavelet toolbox for use with Matlab, Users Guide, Ver. 3., The MathWorks." Inc. Users Guide (2004).
[18] (2014, Nov. 21). [Online]. Available: http://physionet.nlm.nih.gov/pn6/chbmit/
[19] Kutlu, Yakup, and Damla Kuntalp. "Feature extraction for ECG heartbeats using higher order statistics of WPD coefficients." Computer methods and programs in biomedicine 105.3 (2012): 257-267.

 https://doi.org/10.1051/itmconf/20203203001

Blockchain technology based e-voting system.

Prof. Anita A. Lahane[1,*], *Junaid* Patel[1,**] , *Talif* Pathan[1,***] and *Prathmesh* Potdar[1,****].

[1]Juhu Versova Link Rd, behind HDFC Bank, Gharkul Society, Bharat Nagar, Versova, Andheri West, Mumbai, Maharashtra 400053.

Abstract.
Election could be a important event during a trendy democracy however massive sections of society round the world don't trust their election system that is major concern for the democracy. Even the world's largest democracies like Republic of India, us, and Japan still suffer from a blemished legal system. Vote rigging, hacking of the EVM (Electronic vote machine), election manipulation, and booth capturing square measure the key problems within the current electoral system. during this system, we tend to square measure work the problems|the problems within the election vote systems and attempting to propose the E-voting model which might resolve these issues. The system can highlight a number of the popular blockchain frameworks that provide blockchain as a service and associated electronic E-voting system that is predicated on blockchain that addresses all limitations severally, it additionally preserve participant's obscurity whereas still being hospitable public examination.
Building Associate in Nursing electronic electoral system that satisfies the legal necessities of legislators has been a challenge for an extended time. Distributed ledger technologies is Associate in Nursing exciting technological advancement within the info technology world. Blockchain technologies supply Associate in Nursing infinite vary of applications cashing in on sharing economies.
Blockchain could be a unquiet technology of current era and guarantees to enhance the resilience of e-voting systems. this technique presents a shot to leverage edges of blockchain like cryptological foundations and transparency to attain an efficient theme for e-voting. The projected theme conforms to the elemental necessities for e-voting schemes and achieves end-to-end verifiability. The system presents in-depth analysis of the theme that with success demonstrates its effectiveness to attain Associate in Nursing end-to-end verifiable e-voting theme.

Keywords.
Blockchain, Electronic Voting System and E-voting.

1 Introduction

In each democracy, the protection of AN election may be a matter of national security. the pc security field has for a decade studied the probabilities of electronic choice systems, with the goal of minimizing the price of getting a national election, whereas fulfilling ANd increasing the protection conditions of an election. From the dawn of democratically electing candidates, the legal system has been supported pen and paper. commutation the normal pen and paper theme with a replacement election system is essential to limit fraud and having the choice method traceable and verifiable. Electronic choice machines are viewed as blemished, by the protection community, based totally on physical security considerations. Anyone with physical access to such machine will sabotage the machine, thereby moving all votes run up the said machine. Enter blockchain technology.

A blockchain could be a distributed, immutable, incontrovertible, public ledger. This new technology works through four main features:

1. The ledger exists in many different locations: No single point of failure in the maintenance of the distributed ledger.
2. There is distributed management over United Nations agency will append new transactions to the ledger.
3. Any projected "new block" to the ledger should reference the previous version of the ledger, making a changeless chain from wherever the blockchain gets its name, and so preventing meddling with the integrity of previous entries.
4. A majority of the network nodes must reach a consensus before a proposed new block of entries becomes a permanent part of the ledger.

These technological options operate through advanced cryptography, providing a security level equal and/or bigger than any antecedently notable information. The

*e-mail: anita.lahane@mctrgit.ac.in
**e-mail: junaidpatel1998@gmail.com
***e-mail: talifpathan13@gmail.com
****e-mail: prathmeshpotdar08@gmail.com

blockchain technology is thus thought of by several, together with America, to be the best tool, to be accustomed produce the new fashionable democratic ballot method. This paper evaluates the employment of blockchain as a service to implement associate degree electronic ballot (e-voting) system. The system makes the subsequent original contributions:

1. research existing blockchain frameworks suited to constructing blockchain primarily based e-voting system,
2. propose a blockchain-based e-voting system that uses "permissioned blockchain" to alter liquid democracy.[4]

2 Literature Survey

2.1 Survey Existing system

1. Adida, B., Helios (2008).**"Web-based open-audit voting."**, in Proceedings of the 17th Conference on Security Symposium, ser. SS'08. Berkeley, CA, USA: USENIX Association, 2008.

   This paper proposes associated justify an adequate security model and criteria to judge comprehensibility. It additionally describe a web ballot theme, Pretty graspable Democracy, show that it satisfies the adequate security model which it's a lot of graspable than Pretty smart Democracy, presently the sole theme that additionally satisfies the planned security model.

2. Chaum, D., Essex, A., Carback, R., Clark, J., Popoveniuc, S., Sherman, A. and Vora, P. (2008).**"Scantegrity: End-to-end voter-veriable optical- scan voting."**, IEEE Security Privacy, vol. 6, no. 3, pp. 40-46, May 2008.

   This paper describes Scantegrity that minimally impacts election procedures and is the first independent E2E verification mechanism that preserves optical scan as the underlying voting system and doesn't interfere with a manual recount.

3. Dalia, K., Ben, R. , Peter Y. A, and Feng, H. (2012). **"A fair and robust voting system by broadcast."**, 5th International Conference on E-voting, 2012.

   This paper proposes a recovery round to enable the election result to be announced if voters abort and also added a commitment round to ensure fairness. In addition, it also provided a computational security proof of ballot secrecy.

4. Bell, S., Benaloh, J., Byrne, M. D., Debeauvoir, D., Eakin, B., Kortum, P., McBurnett, N., Pereira, O., Stark, P. B., Wallach, D. S., Fisher, G., Montoya, J., Parker, M. and Winn, M. (2013).**"Star-vote: A secure, transparent, auditable, and reliable voting system."**, in 2013 Electronic Voting Technology Workshop/Workshop on Trustworthy Elections (EVT/WOTE 13). Washington, D.C.: USENIX Association, 2013.

   This paper describes the STAR-Vote design, that may preferably be the next-generation electoral system for Travis County and maybe elsewhere.

Recent major technical challenges relating to e-voting systems embrace, however not restricted to secure digital identity management. Any potential citizen ought to are registered to the electoral system before the elections. Their data ought to be in a very digitally processable format. Besides, their identity data ought to be unbroken personal in any involving information. ancient E-voting system could face following problems:

- Anonymous vote-casting.
- Individualized ballot processes.
- Ballot casting verifiability by (and only by) the voter.
- High initial setup costs.
- Increasing security problems.
- Lack of transparency and trust.
- Voting delays or inefficiencies related to remote/absentee voting.[7]

2.2 Limitations of Existing system or Research gap

Recent major technical challenges relating to e-voting systems embody, however not restricted to secure digital identity management. Any potential citizen ought to are registered to the electoral system before the elections. Their data ought to be during a digitally processable format. Besides, their identity data ought to be unbroken non-public in any involving info. ancient E-voting system might face following problems:

- **Anonymous vote-casting:** Each vote may or may not contain any choice per candidate, should be anonymous to everyone including the system administrators, after the vote is submitted through the system.
- **Individualized ballot processes:** How a vote are depicted within the involving net applications or databases continues to be AN open discussion. whereas a transparent text message is that the worst plan, a hashed token is wont to offer obscurity and integrity. Meanwhile, the vote ought to be non-reputable, that can't be bonded by the token resolution.
- **Ballot casting verifiability by (and only by) the voter:** The elector ought to be ready to see and verify his/her own vote, when he/she submitted the vote. this is often vital to realize so as to forestall, or a minimum of to note, any potential malicious activity. This counter live, except for providing suggests that of non-repudiation, can sure boost the sensation of trust of the voters. These issues area unit partly self-addressed in some recent applications. Yet, suggests that of e-voting is presently in use in many countries together with Brazil, uk, Japan, and Republic of Estonia. Republic of Estonia

ought to be evaluated otherwise than the others, since they supply a full e-voting resolution that's, said to be, equivalent of ancient paper-based elections.

- **High initial setup costs:** Though sustaining and maintaining on-line selection systems is way cheaper than ancient elections, initial deployments could be pricy, particularly for businesses.
- **Increasing security problems:**Cyber attacks cause an excellent threat to the general public polls. nobody would settle for the responsibility if associate degreey hacking try succeeds throughout an election. The DDoS attacks ar documented and largely not the case within the elections. The citizen integrity commission of the u. s. gave an affidavit concerning the state of the elections within the North American country recently. Accordingly; Ronald Rivest explicit that "hackers have myriad ways in which of assaultive pick machines". As associate degree example; barcodes on ballots and smartphones in pick locations may be utilized in the hacking method. Apple explicit that we tend to mustn't ignore the actual fact that computers ar hackable, and also the evidences will simply be deleted. Double-voting or voters from the opposite regions also are some common issues.[8]

To mitigate these threats, software mechanisms which promise the following should be deployed:

1. Prevention of evidence deletion.
2. Transparency with privacy.
   - **Lack of transparency and trust:** How can people surely trust the results, when everything is done online? Perceptual problems cannot be ignored.
   - **Voting delays or inefficiencies related to remote voting:** Timing is very important in voting schemes; technical capabilities and the infrastructures should be reliable and run at the highest possible performance to let remote voting be synchronous.[5]

2.2.1 Problem Statement and objectives

Our objective is to solve the issues of digital voting by using blockchain technology.Blockchain enabled e-voting could reduce viter fraud and increase voter access.

2.3 Objectives

Thus, the voting system that is hereby conceived must satisfy the following requirements:

1. The election system must be openly verifiable and transparent.
2. The election system must ensure that the vote cast by the voter has been recorded.
3. Only eligible voters must be allowed to vote.
4. The election system should be tamper-proof.
5. No power-hungry organization must be able to manipulate and rig the election process.

Using a Blockchain, the most important requirements are satisfied :

- **Authentication:** Only registered voters will be allowed to vote.
- **Anonymity:** The system prevents any interaction between the votes casted by the voters and their identities.
- **Accuracy:** Votes once cast are permanently recorded and cannot be modified or changed under any circumstances.
- **Verifiability:** The system will be verifiable such that the number of votes is accounted for.[6]

3 Proposed System

The simple rationalization could be a 'chain' of blocks. A block is associate degree mass set of information. knowledge square measure collected and methoded to suit in an exceedingly block through a process known as mining. every block may be known employing a science hash (also referred to as a digital fingerprint). The block shaped can contain a hash of the previous block, so blocks will kind a sequence from the primary block ever (known because the Genesis Block) to the shaped block. during this method, all the information may be connected via a connected list structure.

3.1 Analysis/Framework/Algorithm

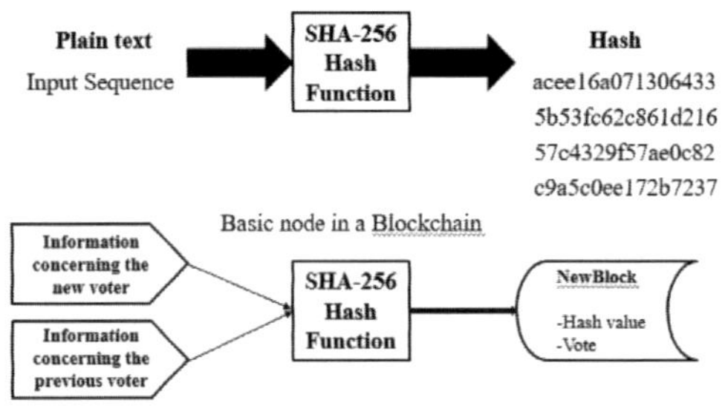

Figure 1. SHA-256 Algorithm Working

Working:

- The SHA-256 algorithm takes an input of any random length and produces an output of a fixed length(256 bits).
- In the case of SHA-256 algorithm no matter how big or small is the input, the output is of fixed length(256 bits).

A cryptographic hash function has the following properties:

1. **Deterministic:**This means that no matter how many times we enter the same input we will get te sam e result.
2. **Quick Computation:**This means that the result is generated quickly and this leads to an increase in the system effiency.
3. **Pre-Image resistance:**Suppose we are rolling a dot(1-6) and instead of getting a specific number we get the hash vaalue.Now we calculate the hash value of each number and then compare it with the result.And for a larger data sets it is possible to break pre-Image resistance by brute force method and this takes too long that it does not matter.
4. **Small changes in Input change the whole Output:** A minor change in the input significantly changes the whole output.
5. **Collision Resistant:**Every input will have a unique hash value.
6. **Puzzle friendly:**The combination of two values gives the hash value of new variable.

The need of hashing in blockchain:

- The blockchain is a sequence of blocks that contain data.
- Each block has a hash pointer that contains previous block's data.
- So if a hacker tries to attack a particular block, the changes will be reflected to the entire chain of blocks.
- Therefore, the blockchain concept is so revolutionary.

3.2 Details of Hardware and Software

3.2.1 Software Requirements

- **OS:** Windows 10.
- **Framework:** Visual Studio.
- **Server:** Localhost.
- **Database:** MS-SQL Server 2012/2014.

3.2.2 Hardware Requirements

- **Processor:** Intel Quad core 1.7 GHZ Processor or above.
- **HD:** Minimum 10 GB of HD.
- **RAM:** Minimum 8 GB of RAM.

3.3 Design Details

The .NET Framework is Microsoft's Managed Code programming model for building applications on Windows shoppers, servers, and mobile or embedded devices. Microsoft's .NET Framework could be a computer code technology that's on the market with many Microsoft Windows operative systems. within the following sections describes

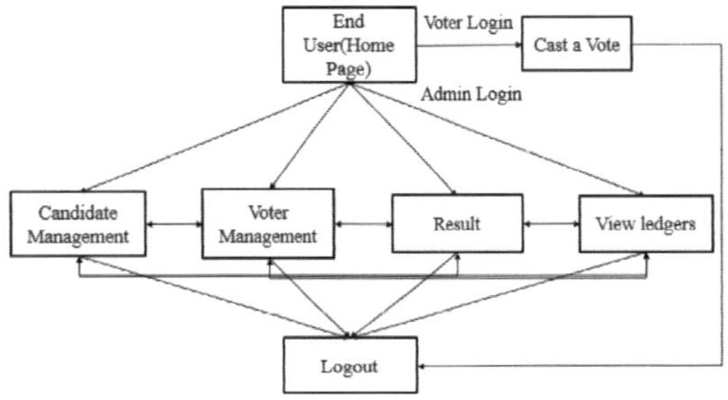

Figure 2. The Proposed System/System Architecture

, the fundamentals of Microsoft .Net Frame work Technology and its connected programming models.

C# may be a language for skilled programming. C# (pronounced C sharp) may be a programing language designed for building a large vary of enterprise applications that run on the .NET Framework. The goal of C# is to produce a straightforward, safe, modern, object-oriented, superior and sturdy language.

.NET development. conjointly it allows developers to make solutions for the broadest vary of purchasers, as well as net applications, Microsoft Windows Forms-based applications, and thin- and smart-client devices.[4]

- **Microsoft SQL Server 2008:**

Business nowadays demands a special quite knowledge management resolution. Performance measurability, and dependability ar essential, however businesses currently expect additional from their key IT investment.

SQL Server 2008 exceeds reliableness necessities and provides innovative capabilities that increase worker effectiveness, integrate heterogeneous IT ecosystems, and maximize capital and operative budgets. SQL Server 2008 provides the enterprise knowledge management platform your organization has to adapt quickly in an exceedingly quick ever-changing surroundings.

Benchmarked for scalability, speed, and performance, SQL Server 2008 is a fully enterprise-class database product, providing core support for Extensible Mark-up Language (XML) and Internet queries.[4]

- **Easy-to-use Business Intelligence(BI) Tools:**

Through wealthy information analysis and data processing capabilities that integrate with acquainted applications like Microsoft workplace, SQL Server 2008 permits you to produce all of your staff with vital, timely business data tailored to their specific data desires. each copy of SQL Server 2008 ships with a collection of metallic element services.[4]

- **Self-Tuning and Management Capabilities:**

Revolutionary self-tuning and dynamic self-config uring options optimize info performance, whereas man agement tools automatise customary activities. Graphical tools and performance, wizards change setup, info style, and performance watching, permitting info directors to tar get meeting strategic business desires.[4]

3.3.1 Detailed Design

The following usecase diagram explains the flow of the project from user end and backend.

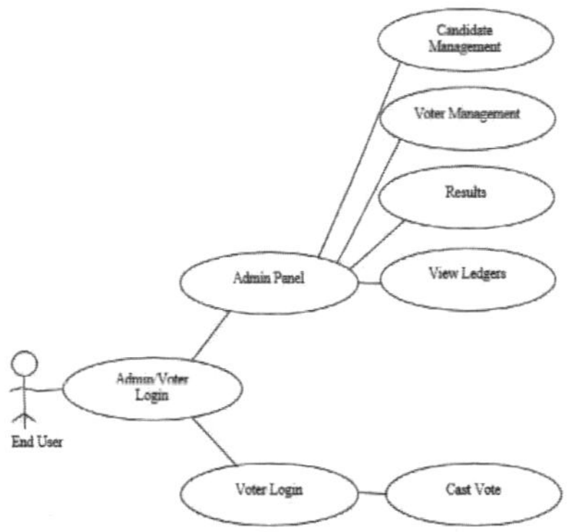

Figure 3. Use Case Diagram

The user firstly need to register to the website.Then the user can go to the voting page where he/she enters the OTP that they have received through e-mail blockchainev@gmail.com. Once the user enters the OTP, then he will be get access to cast a vote.After, the user casts a vote they will be acknowledged by a prompt stating that successfully voted.Finally, the user can logout after voting.

3.4 Methodology/Procedures(Approach to solve the problem)

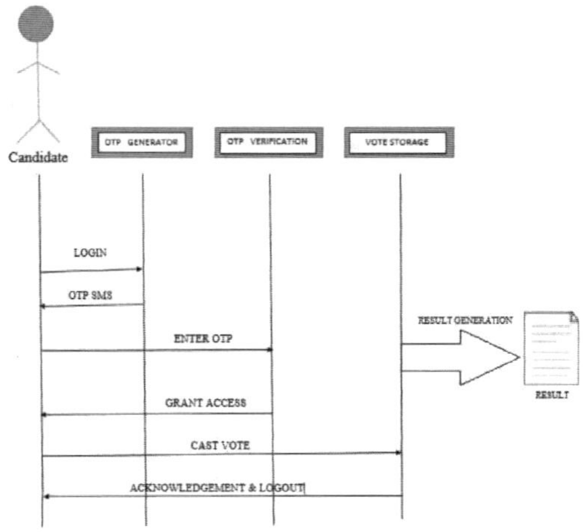

Figure 4. Sequence Diagram

4 Results

This is the home page that consists of different parties.

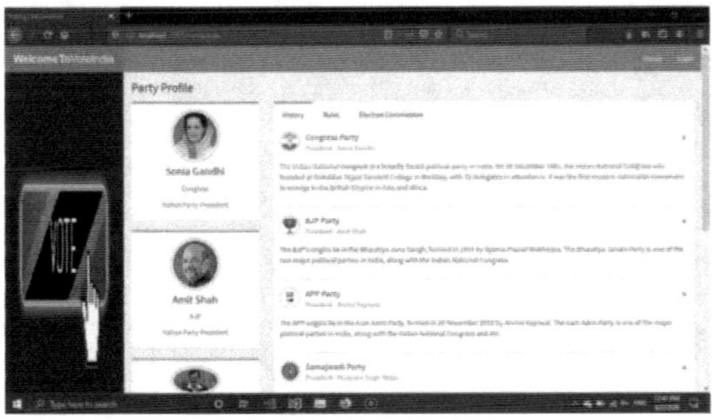

Figure 5. Home Page

This page allows the admin or voter to login(Admin).

Figure 6. Admin or Voter Login

This page allows to view,add or edit new candidate.

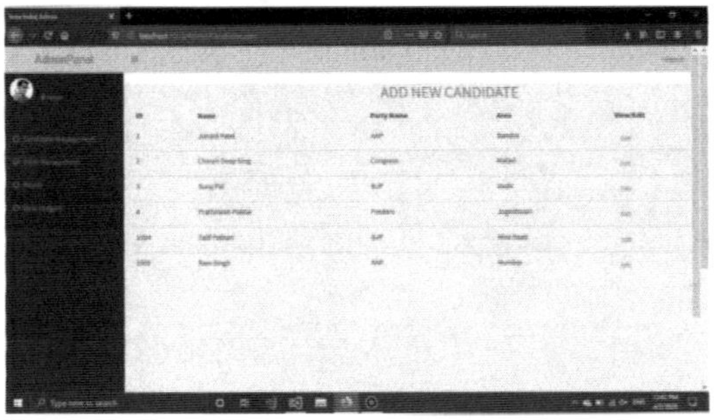

Figure 7. Candidate Management Page

This page allow a new candidate to register.

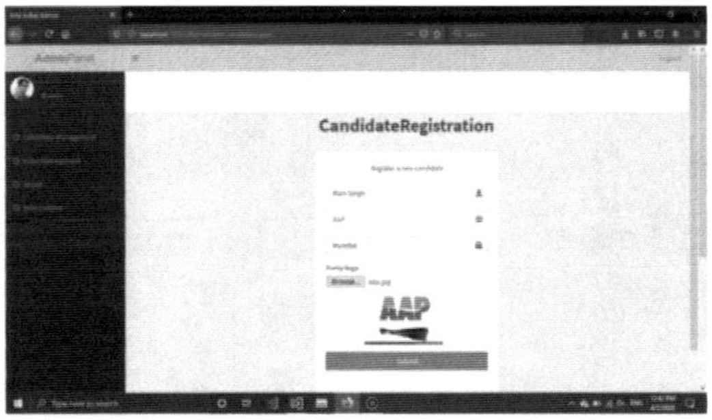

Figure 8. Candidate Registration Page

This page allows a new voter to register.

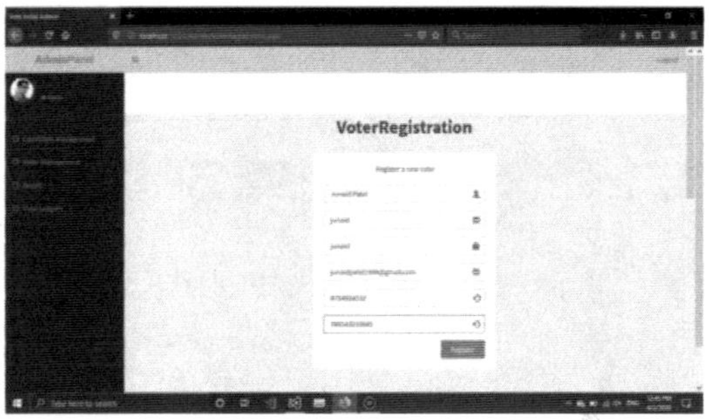

Figure 9. Voter Registration Page

This prompt shows that a new voter is successfully registered.

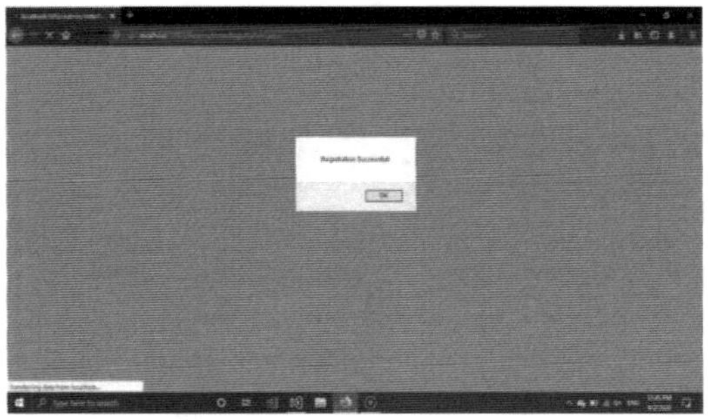

Figure 10. Voter Registration Prompt

This is the result page that displays the winner of the election.

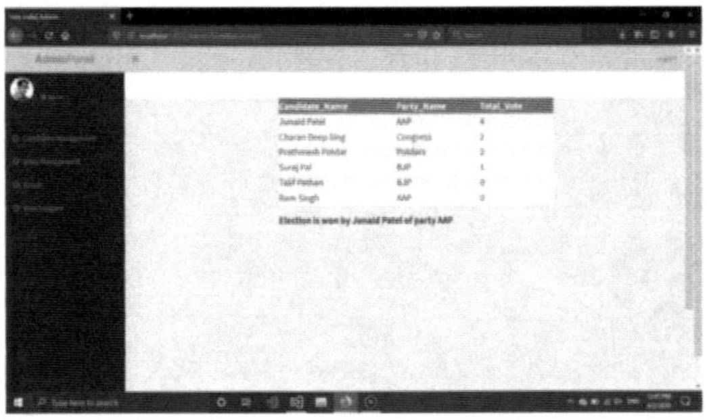

Figure 11. Result Page

This page shows the blockchain implementation for a particular candidate.

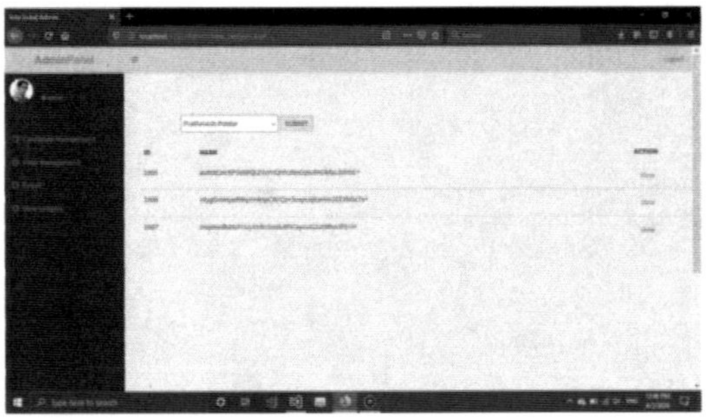

Figure 12. View Ledgers

This page allows the voter to cast a vote.

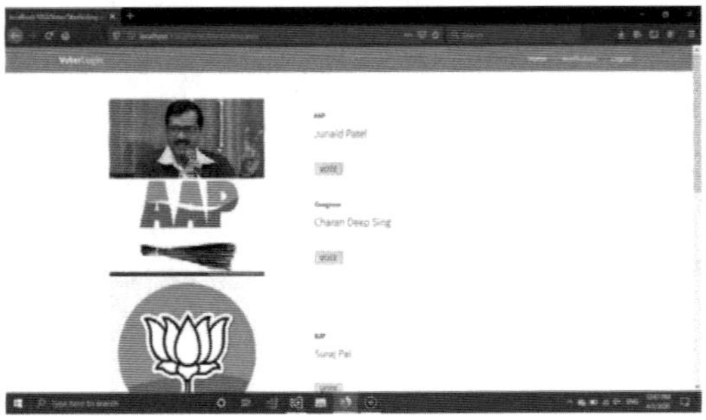

Figure 13. Voting Page

This prompt shows that the voter has successfully voted.

Figure 14. Vote Saved Prompt

This message tells that the voter has already voted.

Figure 15. Already Voted Message

5 Discussion-Comparative study/Analysis

Table 1. Results Calculated Using Proposed Voting System

No of voters	Correct verification	Correct voting count	Accuracy
3	3	3	100%
5	5	5	100%
10	10	10	100%
30	30	30	100%

6 Conclusion

The transparency of the block-chain allows additional auditing and understanding of elections. These attributes square measure a number of the wants of a legal system.

These characteristics come back from redistributed network, and may bring additional democratic processes to elections, particularly to direct election systems. For e-voting to become additional open, clear, and severally auditable, a possible answer would bc basc it on blockchain technology. This paper explores the potential of the blockchain technology and its quality within the e-voting theme. The blockchain are going to be in public verifiable and distributed during a manner that nobody are going to be able to corrupt it.

The idea of adapting digital selection systems to create the general public electoral method cheaper, quicker and easier, could be a compelling one in trendy society. creating the electoral method low cost and fast, normalizes it within the eyes of the voters, removes an explicit power barrier between the elector and therefore the functionary and puts an explicit quantity of pressure on the functionary. It additionally opens the door for a additional direct sort of democracy, permitting voters to precise their can on individual bills and propositions.[5]

7 Scope

The following improvements can be made to the system,

- Adding Aadhar number verification system.
- Linking application with Government voting system data.
- Making the system more secure.
- Enhnacing the Graphical User Interface(GUI) of the application.
- Local languages can be included which will play a vital role for people living in rural areas as well as uneducated people.
- A Candidate's earlier social work and candidate qualification's can be added for a voter to have better choice.
- Also, adding suggestion system for voters that enables the public to give suggestions to the current winner.
- A complaint system can be included, that allows the people to file complaint against a candidate.

References

[1] Bell, S., Benaloh, J., Byrne, M. D., Debeauvoir, D., Eakin, B., Kortum, P., McBurnett, N., Pereira, O., Stark, P. B., Wallach, D. S., Fisher, G., Montoya, J., Parker, M. and Winn, M. (2013). "**Star-vote: A secure, transparent, auditable, and reliable voting system.**", in 2013 Electronic Voting Technology Workshop/Workshop on Trustworthy Elections (EVT/WOTE 13). Washington, D.C.: USENIX Association, 2013.

[2] Dalia, K., Ben, R. , Peter Y. A, and Feng, H. (2012). "**A fair and robust voting system.**" by broadcast, 5th International Conference on E-voting, 2012.

[3] Adida, B.; 'Helios (2008). "**Web-based open-audit voting.**", in Proceedings of the 17th Conference on Security Symposium, ser. SS'08. Berkeley, CA, USA: USENIX Association, 2008, pp. 335348.

[4] Chaum, D., Essex, A., Carback, R., Clark, J., Popoveniuc, S., Sherman, A. and Vora, P. (2008). "**Scantegrity: End-to-end voter-veriable optical-scan voting.**" , IEEE Security Privacy, vol. 6, no. 3, pp. 40-46, May 2008.

[5] Bohli, J. M., Muller-Quade, J. and Rohrich, S. (2007). "**Bingo voting: Secure and coercion- free voting using a trusted random number generator.**", in Proceedings of the 1st International Conference on E-voting and Identity, ser. VOTE-ID'07. Berlin, Heidelberg: Springer-Verlag, 2007, pp. 111-124.

[6] Adida B. and Rivest, R. L. (2006). "**Scratch and vote: Self-contained paper-based cryptographic voting.**", in Proceedings of the 5th ACM Workshop on Privacy in Electronic Society, ser. WPES '06. New York, NY, USA: ACM, 2006, pp. 29-40.

[7] Chaum, D., Ryan, P. Y. A. and Schneider, P. Y. A. (2005). "**A practical voter-verifiable election scheme.**", in Proceedings of the 10th European Conference on Research in Computer Security, ser. ESORICS'05. Berlin, Heidelberg: Springer-Verlag, 2005, pp. 118-139.

[8] Chaum, D. (2004)."**Secret-ballot receipts: True voter-verifiable elections.**" , IEEE Security Privacy, vol. 2, no. 1, pp. 38-47, Jan 2004.

[9] Chaum, D. (1981)."**Untraceable electronic mail, return addresses, and digital pseudonym.**", Commun. ACM, vol. 24, no. 2, pp. 84-90, Feb.

Indoor Navigation in Stadium using Virtual Reality

Swaleha Khan[1], *Ashwini* Patil[2], *Gauri* Kadam[3], and *Dr.Ashish* Jadhav[4,*]

[1]Ramrao Adik Institute of Technology, Nerul, Navi Mumbai
[2]Ramrao Adik Institute of Technology, Nerul, Navi Mumbai
[3]Ramrao Adik Institute of Technology, Nerul, Navi Mumbai
[4]Ramrao Adik Institute of Technology, Nerul, Navi Mumbai

Abstract. Virtual Reality is a computer generated scenario that simulates a realistic experience. Current popular online maps majorly provide two-dimensional upper views of buildings. It becomes difficult to visualize the interiors of a place. Indoor navigation using VR technology addresses the problem of visualizing the interior infrastructure of huge complex buildings like stadium. This paper 'Indoor Navigation in Stadium using Virtual Reality' aims to provide highly realistic and immersive experience by incorporating an app that uses 360 degree images to serve the purpose. The paper explains how WebVR technology can be used effectively in order to provide a three dimensional view of the stadium with navigation functionalities to the users.

1 Introduction

Navigation systems have been extensively used in outdoor environments, but indoor navigation systems are still in initial development stages. Modern navigation systems use electronic devices to determine user's current location, find the best possible routes, and in some cases also independently guide users to the destination. Presently, most navigation systems use signals from Global Positioning System (GPS), which works in outdoor environments but has difficulty indoors due to reduced signal strength. Complementary technologies such as Wi-Fi-based and code-based methods have been proposed for indoor navigation; though, a definite solution for the industry has not been established. As the popularity of mobile devices and location-aware applications has increased, indoor navigation systems have become highly beneficial for both personal use and applications in many industries such as retail, entertainment, healthcare, and manufacturing. Some indoor navigation systems provide 360-degree panoramic photos of a location, but do not provide an inside view of some huge complex buildings. Thus, it becomes difficult to visualize the interiors of a place.

Virtual reality technology can be efficiently used in indoor navigation systems. One of the technique of virtual reality is Window on World (WoW), also known as "Desktop VR" or "WebVR", which provides the three-dimensional view of world to users through the 'window' of the computer monitor and navigates users through the space with control devices such as mouse or keyboard. The computer monitor screen is used to display virtual reality applications and provides graphical interface to users. Additionally, this concept can be extended to Smartphone or tablet screens too.

*e-mail: ashish.jadhav@rait.ac.in

However, WebVR apps are not graphic intensive. The complexity of the 3D scene has to be planned carefully. Building an application that is technically as well as socially robust is a lot of work. Sensible planning of the application such that it supports a bigger number of devices is required.

Virtual reality-based solutions can be productively used in entertainment industry as Virtual reality completely engages the user into simulated and interactive environment to provide more enhanced experience. Fans in massive Entertainment Complex like stadium want to be entertained in ways outside of the event itself and in a streamlined, engaging manner. The focus has shifted from a purely "game-focused" experience to more of a "well Enhanced" experience. One of the core expectations from the modern fan is an exciting atmosphere within the Entertainment Complexes. The Virtual Reality centered solution presented in this paper provides indoor navigation facility to enhance fan's experience.

2 Related work

The paper on the Introduction to Virtual Reality and its Challenges [1] explains what VR is and its principles. It states how VR is used to simulate real world experiences for its users to get an immersive experience and how the technology gives enormous scope to explore the world of 3D and your imagination. Its applications spread wide from product development to entertainment. However, its challenges include creating a convincing 3D virtual environment - the more realistic the environment, the longer it takes to make it. Thus, it gets tedious too. Many systems rely on hardware that encumbers a user or limits his options through physical tethers.

https://doi.org/10.1051/itmconf/20203203002

The paper on Hyper-navigation [2] shows how agents can be used to guide the user in virtual world about actions they can take in their virtual environment, thus helping them escape the virtual world. The interior of buildings and rooms within it are demonstrated for navigation. This is done with the help of task-oriented agents. Another paper referred for navigation [3] proposes view-based navigation system for performing indoor navigation. The navigation to a destination is provided with the help of a single monocular camera wherein having of a smartphone with a good quality camera is a necessity. Thus, it has been observed that indoor navigation can be provided with different ways which can prove beneficial to a number of users.

Ibrahim Arda Cankaya et al. proposed the paper [4] that uses Augmented Reality for the navigation system. This paper introduces the pedometer algorithm that first filters the data according to the axis and also considers the variations that come forth according to the gender. This is done by utilizing smart phone's accelerometer as the pedometer, compass and camera features with augmented reality. Another paper titled Combination of Real and Virtual World for Indoor Navigation using Mobile Application [5] also uses Augmented Reality for performing navigation However, the approach is different. It uses ARCoreSDK that has an inbuilt property called Area Learning which is similar to machine learning that helps to learn the present scenario features which in turn facilitate indoor navigation. Thus, it has been observed that using of Augmented Reality imposes the use of additional hardware or software requirements. Using of Virtual Reality technology cuts down the need of such additional requirements. DesktopVR thus facilitates the combination of Virtual Reality with web development. The JavaScript enabled web browser can be used for virtual navigation.

Quan Ye et al. proposed the paper [6] that talks about VR Interactive Feature of HTML5-based WebVR Control Laboratory by Using Head-mounted Display. It uses Three.js graphic engine based on Web Graphics Library (WebGL) to implement the feature. In order to illustrate the operational approach, a ball and beam system is used. It also explains the concept of 3D modeling, data communication that takes place in virtual reality and lastly a case study on the NCSLab and how they enhanced the experience of the online laboratory using virtual reality. Another paper titled 'Virtual Reality Websites' [7] explains the current SaaS technologies used for Virtual Reality (VR). Thus these papers prove helpful in understanding how VR can be implemented by using WebVR.

QR code technique can be advantageous in navigating the path from current source. In [8], each geographical area is assigned rooms for efficient working of the algorithm implemented. It consists of partition, functional and connectivity number attached to it for precise routing to desired destination. Similarly, another paper [9] used the concept of QR codes to help blind people navigate within huge buildings. Thus, an inference is that QR codes can be used to store location details of a particular place such as the QR code on stadium tickets can be used to retrieve the seat location of the user and help him navigate accordingly.

3 Proposed Methodology

3.1 Problem Definition

Most maps do provide a navigation system but what is lacking is the detailed indoor navigation for a particular place. The navigation can be provided with the help of location of the person. However, this might fail when the person enters huge buildings or areas where tracking of the location becomes difficult. Also, the floor level and rooms inside the building couldn't be tracked with the help of GPS. Indoor navigation gives an immersive experience to the user with the help of images. These images are enhanced 360 degree images which give better viewer experience than 2D images. The 360 degree images provide a 360 view from any location captured. Therefore, to guide or navigate visitors in the stadium to their seat they will be given a virtual tour of the stadium by designing a 360 degree interior map of the stadium.

3.2 System Architecture

The system is a web application which is divided into 3 major parts: The Front-End, The Middleware and The Back-End. The user interacts with the front-end, which sends requests to the back-end and gets back some response. This is how a typical web VR application works.

Figure 1 below shows what the architecture consists of. The user may or may not have a ticket with a QR code. The user then access the webapp which consists of a MapsServer with the database. The input from the user is assessed and data is retrieved after which the business logic is applied considering the input. The renderer is then used to render the final map back to the user's web browser.

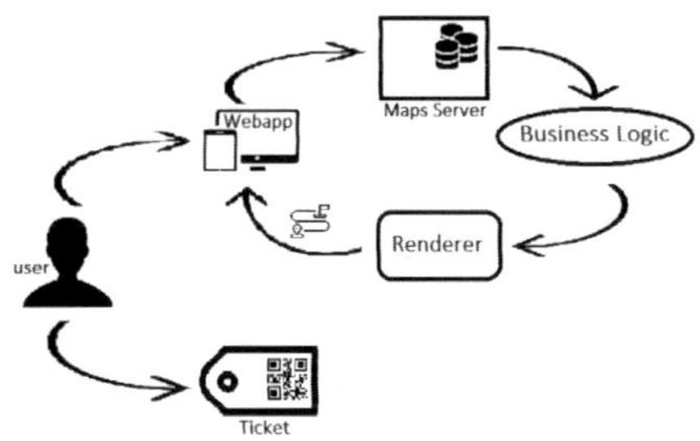

Figure 1. System Architecture.

The Front-End framework used is Angular 4 which is a JavaScript framework along with PhotoSphereViewerJS for rendering the panoramic photo. It sends HTTP Requests to the middleware. Node.js is an application server that serves as the middleware here whereas MongoDB is the NoSQL database daemon process that serves the Back-End. With the help of Node.js, the requests are being sent to the database to which the database responds accordingly. The images along with marker data are then loaded to the frontend.

 https://doi.org/10.1051/itmconf/20203203002

3.3 System Design

The core of the system is built using MEAN stack. Users can find the optional route by providing their current location and destination. The 360 degree panoramas are viewed inside PhotoSphereViewer which can be panned or zoomed in any direction. The map of the stadium is represented as a Graph structure where pictures are nodes and the edges represent adjacency. The system then calculates the minimum hops to load an image with the help of Adjacency matrix and accordingly provides virtual directions to reach from source to destination.

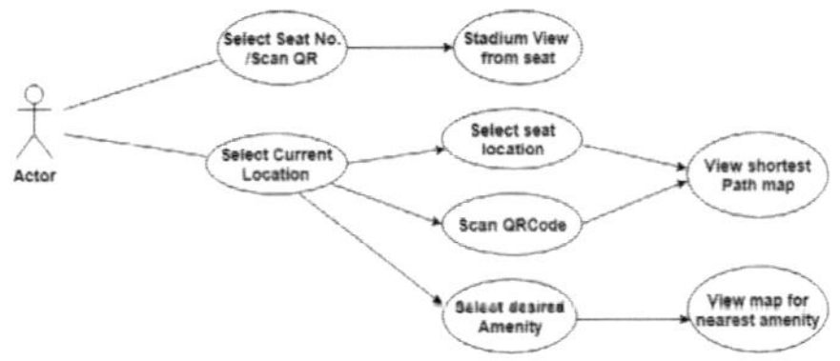

Figure 2. Use Case Diagram.

Use Case Diagram in Figure 2 shows in detail the varied options available for the user to perform as the webapp loads as well as the expected outputs received depending on the input.

Upon initialization of web application, the user has following options:

- The user can also search for a specific location with the help of a search box provided.
- Enter any gate number as source and then scan the QR code which recognizes the seat number or enter the destination manually.
- Autoplay the desired path from the source or use markers that will have tooltip which will hint the user about the next path that will be loaded.
- Get the path from any particular location to any stadium amenity nearest to him.

Data flow diagram in Figure 3 describes the data flow of proposed system in detail wherein four inputs are taken from the user and accordingly the backend processes the request. The output received from the system helps navigate the user to the destination.

3.4 Implementation

- **Capturing panoramic photos:**

  360 degree photographs of each node are captured for each node. The camera used for this purpose is Samsung gear 360. ActionDirector is used to get a complete photo sphere.

- **Storing panorama data and marker:** data into database:

  Every node's data is stored in MongoDB which is NoSQL database. The markers present in each photo sphere with Latitude and Longitude of the marker and tooltip data are stored in the database.

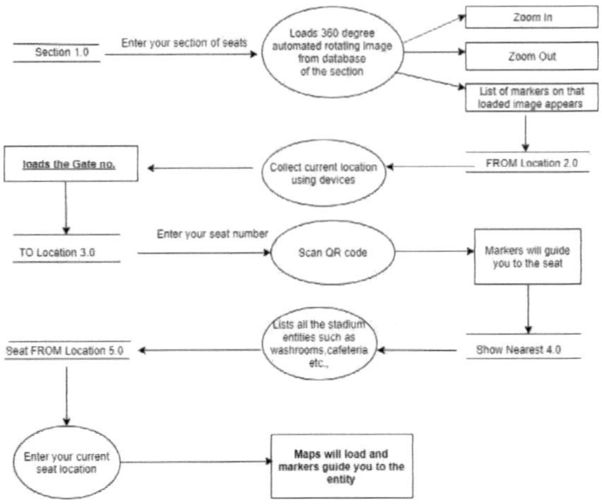

Figure 3. Data Flow Diagram.

- **Creating graph data structure:**

  There is a need to find the shortest path between two nodes for which a JS script is used for creating a graph data structure and making inter-connections between nodes.

- **Developing web Application.**

  The system is a web application which the user can access using any modern JavaScript enabled web browser.

4 Results and Discussions

Figure 4 shows the first page that loads when you open the Webapp.

Figure 4. System User Interface.

As explained through Figure 2, the closer look to the interface shown in Figure 5 shows the varied options available to the user for navigating in the stadium.

The 'View from seat' section lets the user get an entire 360 degree view from any particular seat and helps the user to decide during seat booking. The 'Get Path' section is the one which helps navigate by providing a map to the user along with markers. The source and destination for navigation to a particular seat can either be manually entered or user's location can be detected for getting

Figure 5. Options available.

source information and QR on the ticket can be scanned for seat information. The subsection of Get Path is to show path for the nearest desired amenity from a source that can again be detected from user's location or be manually entered.

The three buttons at the bottom are submit buttons that send request to the server. The Show Path renders the map to the user along with markers that help users reach the destination. The Autoplay Path too renders the map but autoplays the entire path to the user without having the user to click on markers. The Clear Path button clears the fields entered above and refreshes back to the start page of the webapp.

Figure 6. Marker

Figure 6 shows how the marker appears on an image along with the tooltip information on the marker. The system loads the first image with markers. Further, if a marker is clicked upon, it will load the next image that is linked to that particular marker. This process can continue even if the fields on the left are not entered. Also, this way the system can support large number of users since every mobile phone is running their own instance of the webapp locally and accordingly the map is rendered.

Parameter	2D image	360 degree image
Total number of images for the stadium	*360-400*	*90-100*
Approximate size of each image	*50 -80 KB*	*8-10 MB*
Load on database wrt size of image	*Low*	*High*
Load on database wrt number of images	*High*	*Low*
Markers per image	*1*	*2-4*
Response time for navigation in the map rendered on the app	*Fast*	*Fast*
Worst case number of images to be downloaded to the app for navigation	*30*	*20*
Best case number of images to be downloaded to the app for navigation	*4*	*1*
User Experience rating according to survey taken	*3*	*9*

Figure 7. 2D vs 360

The webapp includes 360 degree images instead of simple 2D images. A con of using the 360 degree images is the image size since 360 degree images are large in size. However, there are many pros with respect to the user experience. Markers can be embedded on 2D images as well but the number of images will increase with 2D images since a 2D image cannot show every route or turn possible from any particular position the user is at. Thus, even though the size of images is reduced with 2D images, the number of images increase. This has been explained in Figure 7 through a table which also shows the rating for the user experience. The survey was conducted among the students of RAIT, Nerul wherein the average score on 10 is calculated and shown in the table. The numbers given in the table are approximate.

The traditional alternative to indoor navigation is by following the sign boards in the stadium or by asking other individuals present in there. However, both are inconvenient since they waste time of the user. With a VR-based Indoor Navigation, the user can not only plan their day beforehand and utilise time for a better purpose but also get an immersive experience of the interiors of a stadium. The manpower required for guiding the spectators also reduces.

The system runs in its worst case when the source is at one end of the stadium and the destination is at the other opposite end. In this case, quite a lot number of markers have to be traversed and clicked upon to reach to the destination which at times may seem cumbersome to the user. The system runs in its best case when the destination is adjacent to the source with respect to the adjacency matrix.

5 Conclusion

This paper proposes an indoor navigation for stadium using The WebVR technology providing the user with a complete riveting experience. The feature of QR code scanning on the ticket brings an effortless solution to the user thus increasing feasibility. The virtual shortest path to the destination is shown with the help of 360 degree images. This is achieved by calculating adjacency matrix between the images. The proposed system works even on simple low end devices like mobile phones or even a low end desktop PC. Virtual reality is traditionally associated with high end computing for which a wide range of hardware and software is being used. However, a serious concern about this technology is related to the issue of privacy. A stranger knowing so many things about your indoor infrastructure might become a security issue. The security issues need to be addressed before implementing applications that involve covering the secured infrastructure.

Acknowledgment

We thank The D.Y. Group for the constant cooperation by giving us the permission to click images and to access the infrastructure of The D. Y. Patil Stadium as and when required for the project.

References

[1] Sharmistha Mandal, Brief Introduction of Virtual Reality and its Challenges **4**, (2013)

[2] J. Emhardt , J. Semmler and T. Strothotte, Hypernavigation in virtual buildings **6**, (2002)

[3] Mitsuaki Nozawa , Yoshinobu Hagiwara and Yongwoon Choi, Indoor human navigation system on smartphones using view-based navigation, 1916-1919 (2012)

[4] Ibrahim Arda Cankaya, Arif Koyun, Tuncay Yigit and Asim Sinan Yuksel, Mobile Indoor Navigation System in iOS Platform Using Augmented Reality, (2015)

[5] Vidhyavani.A, StephinStanly, Ankit Kumar Pandey and Shivam Choudhury, Combination Of Real And Virtual World For Indoor Navigation using Mobile Application **8**, (2019)

[6] Quan Ye, Wenshan Hu, Hong Zhou, Zhongcheng Lei, Shiqi Guan, VR Interactive Feature of HTML5-based WebVR Control Laboratory by Using Head-mounted Display **14**, (2018)

[7] Vinit Sathe , Piyush Gupta , Karan Kaushik , Suvarna Bhat and Sachin Deshpande, Virtual reality websites(VR WEB) **1**, 647-652 (2017)

[8] Ying Zhuang , Yuhao Kang , Lina Huang and Zhixiang Fang, A Geocoding Framework for Indoor Navigation based on the QR Code, 1-4 (2018)

[9] Affan Idrees , Zahid Iqbal and Maria Ishfaq, An efficient indoor navigation technique to find optimal route for blinds using QR codes, 690-695 (2015)

A novel approach to ensemble MLP and random forest for network security

Bhushan Deore[1], *Aditya* Kyatham[1] *and Shubham* Narkhede[1]

[1]Electronics and Telecommunication, Ramrao Adik Institute of Technology, Nerul-400706, Navi Mumbai, India

Abstract. The following paper provides a novel approach for Network Intrusion Detection System using Machine Learning and Deep Learning. This approach uses two MLP (Multi-Layer Perceptron) models one having 3 layers and other having 6 layers. Random Forest is also used for classification. These models are ensembled in such a way that the final accuracy is boosted and also the testing time is reduced. Researchers have implemented various ways for the ensemble of multiple models but we are using contradiction management concept to ensemble machine learning models. Contradiction Management concept means if two machine learning models are contradicting in their decisions (in our case 3-layer MLP and Random Forest), then the third model's (6-layer MLP) decision is considered whose accuracy is higher than the previous models. The third model is only used for testing when the previous two models contradict in their decision because the testing time of third model is higher than the two previous models as the third model has complex architecture. This approach increased the final accuracy as ensemble of multiple models is done and also testing time has reduced. The novelty of this paper is the choice and the combination of the models for the purpose of Network security.

1. Introduction

Today, use of Internet has drastically increased. In future, every person on the earth would be a part of network. Many internet users are not aware about the hacking techniques. So, there is high probability of intrusion of a black hat hacker into a personal network of various devices. Many companies are using cloud technology for their system operations. If an unauthorized intruder gets access to the private data of the company, then the intruder could use the data for gaining money.

Network Intrusion Detection system (NIDS) is a very important part of a network. Along with the firewall, NIDS has to be deployed because firewall blocks a particular website only if the website is blacklisted in the database. But NIDS works on the packet data. It traces the packet and uses anomaly detector to detect the intruder.

In this approach, we used Machine Learning models to detect the intruder. The decisions of multiple machine learning models are considered and using the proposed approach decision is finalized. The packet will be captured by the packet capturer and then the packet is tested on the trained Machine Learning models. The model gives its decision. If the decision is positive i.e. the packet is anomaly, then the system administrator is alerted about the packet. This approach also decreases the packet waiting time. Packet waiting time means the time for which the packet is tested by the NIDS.

The main goal of the paper is to boost the accuracy of NIDS using multiple machine learning models and also to reduce the packet waiting time. We have used CIC (Canadian Institute of Cybersecurity) dataset for training the model. The packet analyzer used is CIC-Flow-Meter.

2. Related Work

YONG ZHANG et al [1] introduced a new network intrusion detection model named the deep hierarchical network, that combines LeNet-5 and LSTM Neural networks.

Meng Wang et al [2] proposed a method to choose optimal feature for detecting DDoS attack using sequential feature selection with MLP.

Yi Yi Aung et al [3] explained the method of applying Random Forest for Network Intrusion Detection System.

Prachi Barapatre et al [4] used MLP with back-propagation algorithm to classify attacks. Dataset used was KDD99 dataset. They analysed the working of MLP model and studied the advantages and disadvantages of MLP model. The main goal was to decrease false alarms.

Dimitra Chamou et al [5] used Deep Neural Networks for classification of DDoS attacks and Malware attacks. They used 5-layer which are fully-connected layers of neural network.

Vinayakumar et al [6] explained the working of Convolutional Neural Networks (CNN) in Network Intrusion Detection System. They applied the data on various models having various layers.

3. PROPOSED APPROACH

3.1 Dataset Introduction: -

We trained our algorithm on the CIC (Canadian Institute for Cyber Security) datasets of 5 days. The network data has been captured using the CICFlowMeter which is a packet capturer developed by CIC. This dataset has updated attacks compared to NSL-KDD dataset. The data was captured in 2017 by CIC.

This dataset is built on the abstract behaviour of 25 users based on HTTP, HTTPS, FTP, SSH and email protocols. The capturing of the network data started from 9 am Monday July 3rd 2017, and ended on Friday 7th July,2017 at 5 pm. Monday was a normal traffic so we didn't use it for training. We used the dataset of the other 4 days. On Tuesday = SSH-Patator and FTP-Patator, Wednesday=DoS/DDOS, Thursday=Infiltration, Friday =Portscan, DDOS, Bot attacks were done. For more information about dataset and packet capturer refer [13].

All the datasets contain 79 features including label column and samples are over 50000, non-null and data types consist of int, float and object. The final dataset consists of packets from all the 4 days with labels as Anomaly and Normal which basically can be used for Anomaly Detector.

3.2 Feature Engineering: -

In feature engineering, we need to select the important features which are responsible for classification. Because some features are not relevant to the output label which decreases accuracy. Those irrelevant features should be dropped out from the dataset. To calculate the relevance of the features with the output label, we should calculate correlation of each and every feature with the output label. If the correlation of a particular feature is less, then those particular features should be dropped off from the dataset. Feature importance in the features of CIC Dataset (top 25 are shown but top 58 were considered for training) shown in Fig. 1.

After feature reduction or dimensionality reduction, the data should be split into training, testing and validation sets. The splitting ratio was 80% training, 10% testing and 10% validation. Now, the data should be label encoded. Label encoding is a process in which the character type features or features containing character type data, should be converted to categorical data

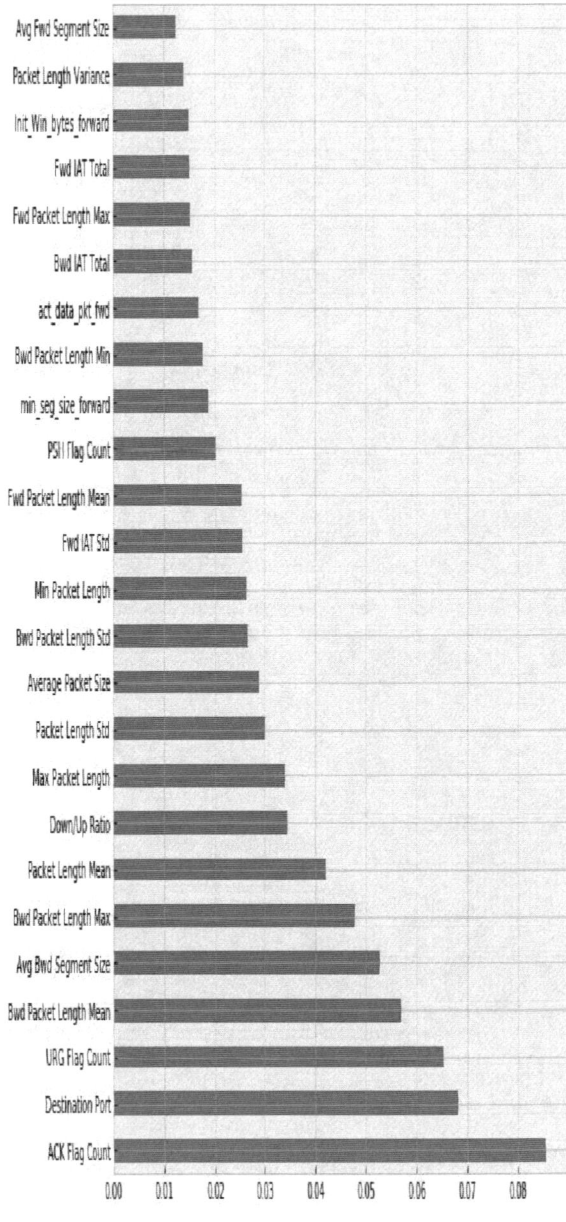

Fig. 1. Feature Importances

Now, the data has to be normalized to prevent biasing condition and then it has to be reshaped to a particular array which can be fed to Neural Networks.

3.3 Model Building: -

The CIC dataset is used to train three models. Three models are: - MLP (Multi-Layer Perceptron) with 3-layer, 6-layer MLP and Random Forest. After training, the packet will be sent to Random Forest and 3-layer MLP for testing. Both the models will give their decisions. Now, both the decisions are compared and if there is contradiction then that particular packet is sent to 6-layer MLP. This 6-layer MLP has more accuracy than Random Forest and 3-layer MLP but more testing time than the both. So, as the 6-layer MLP has more testing time, testing all the packets on 6-layer MLP would increase packet waiting time which is not desirable. There is no need to test a packet on 6-layer MLP if the 3-layer MLP and Random Forest both are giving same decision because this shows that the probability of decision being correct is high as both the models gave same decision.

If all the packets are tested on 6-layer MLP then the testing time will be high but, in our approach, we found out that only few samples (<5 %) are sent to 6-layer MLP which decreases the overall testing time. The 3-layer MLP has 128 neurons in 1st and 3rd layer and then 64 neurons in 2nd layer with 'relu' activation and output activation as 'sigmoid'. The dropout is 1%. Similar, configuration is there for 6-layer MLP with alternate layers of 128 and 64 neurons. Architecture is shown in Fig. 4.

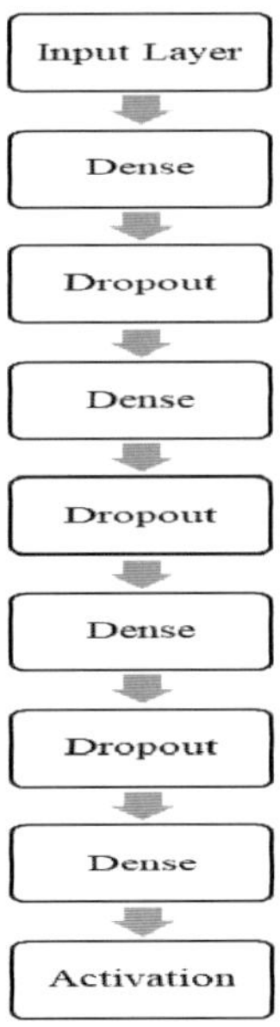

Fig. 2 3-Layer Multi-Layer Perceptron (MLP) Model

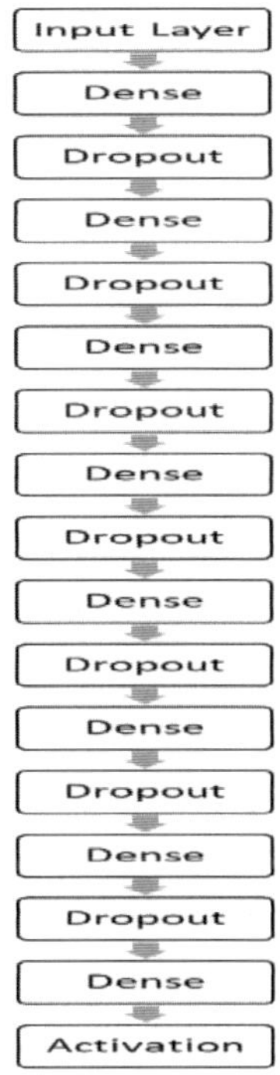

Fig. 3 6-Layer MLP Model

For Random Forest, we used 50 estimators and the criterion used was entropy. Rest of the parameters were set to default.

Below is the architecture of the proposed approach:

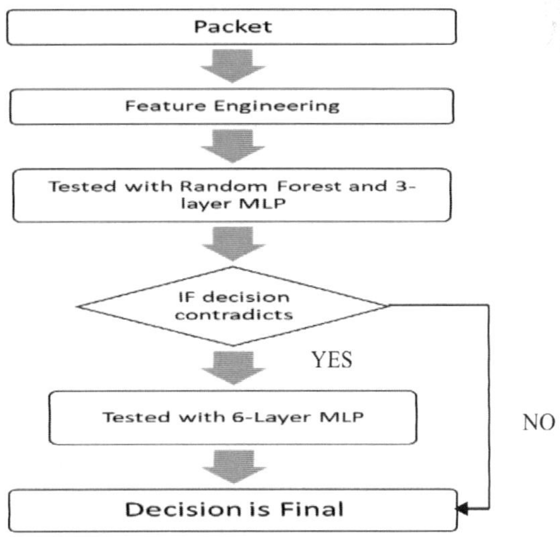

Fig. 4 Proposed Model Architecture of an Anomaly Detector.

4. RESULT ANALYSIS

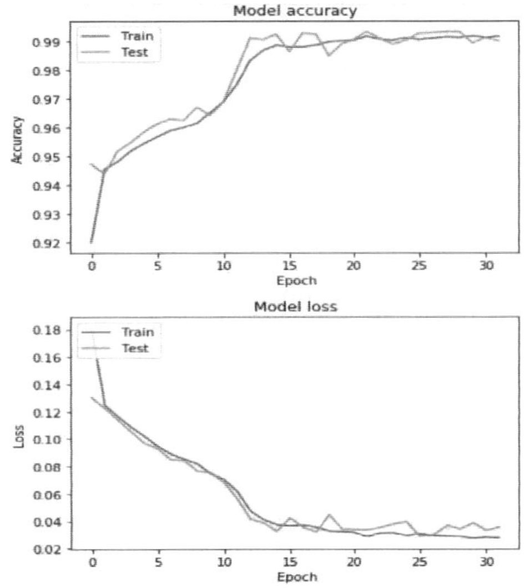

Fig. 5 Loss and Accuracy graph of 3-layer MLP

Fig. 5 & 6 shows the graph of loss decreasing and accuracy increasing which states that the model is successfully learning. There are some ripples during the learning process but ultimately the ripples decrease signifying that the model is learning with stable state.

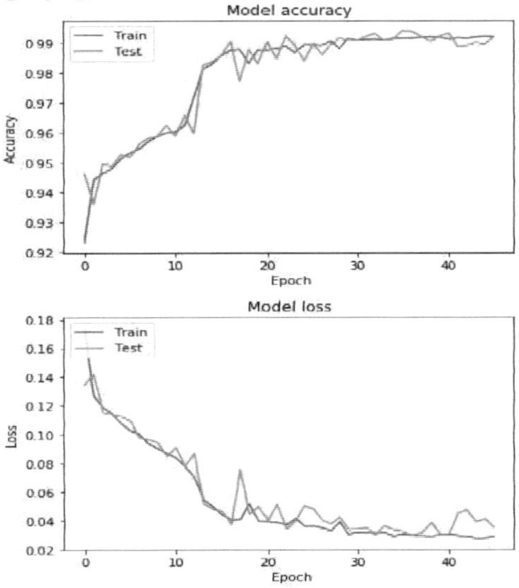

Fig. 6 6-Layer MLP Loss & Accuracy Graph

TABLE I. 3-layer MLP Metrics

Labels	Accuracy	Precision	Recall	F1 score
ANOMALY	98.87	97.00	99.00	98.00
NORMAL		100.00	99.00	99.00

TABLE. II. Random Forest Metrics

Labels	Accuracy	Precision	Recall	F1 score
ANOMALY	85.32	100.00	51.00	68.00
NORMAL		83.00	100.00	91.00

TABLE III. 6-Layer MLP Metrics

Labels	Accuracy	Precision	Recall	F1 score
ANOMALY	99.12	99.00	98.00	99.00
NORMAL		99.00	99.00	99.00

TABLE IV. Proposed Approach Metrics

Labels	Accuracy	Precision	Recall	F1 score
ANOMALY	99.31	99.00	99.00	99.00
NORMAL		100.00	100.00	100.00

From the above metrics, we can see that proposed approach metrics has more accuracy than the other models as it boosted the accuracy by ensemble of the above existing models. Table I is the result, when the dataset is tested only on 3-Layer MLP, which tells us that it gives a pretty good metrics. As the dataset is little imbalanced with respect to the labels, we also considered the precision, recall and F1-score. Table II is for Random Forest in which metrics are lower than 3-layer MLP but can be used as a validation model for 3-layer MLP. Table III is for 6-layer MLP, as layers are more the learning is more accurate, so in this case the metrics are higher. Now, using the models in the table I, II and III in the proposed manner, the results show that the metrics are boosted. The testing time is also found less when the packet is tested with Random Forest and 3- Layer MLP as compared to 6-Layer MLP as more the layers, more will be the mathematical calculations and thus more testing time is needed. The drawback would be when the packet has to be tested for all the 3 models, but the probability of that happening is found to be very less i.e. 5%.

Following are the testing times:

Models	Testing Time (seconds)
Random Forest + 3-layer MLP	0.256
6- Layer MLP	0.264

Comparison of different algorithms

Sr. No	Algorithm	Accuracy	Precision	Recall	F1 Score
1	Nathan Shone's algorithm	91.13	89.00	91.00	90.00
2	Auto Encoder with Neural Network	90.15	91.85	90.64	88.97
3	Adaboost with Neural Network	94.08	95.05	94.08	94.42
4	Bagging Neural Network	95.56	95.81	95.56	95.48
5	Random Forest	94.58	94.00	95.00	94.00
6	LDA (Linear Discriminant Analysis)	96.05	96.00	96.00	96.00
7	QDA (Quadratic Discriminant Analysis)	93.10	92.00	93.00	93.00
8	Linear SVC	94.08	94.00	94.00	94.00
9	Simple RNN (Recurrent Neural Network)	95.07	96.42	95.82	96.11
10	RNN-LSTM	97.04	96.41	94.39	95.38
11	GRU	94.09	97.00	96.00	97.00
12	Simple CNN	96.07	97.00	96.00	97.00
13	KNN	94.11	93.00	94.00	94.00
14	**The proposed Model**	99.31	99.50	99.50	99.50

We used ensembled algorithm i.e. Random Forest and Neural Network that's why our metrics is higher than others.

5. Conclusion

We can conclude that, by considering decisions of multiple models and if the decisions contradict, then that decision will be taken by another Neural Network model which has complex architecture but has high accuracy. In this way, the resulting model will have high accuracy and low testing time. In the future work, there is scope of developing new techniques for ensemble modelling

References

[1] Zhang, Yong, et al. "Network intrusion detection: Based on deep hierarchical network and original flow data." *IEEE Access* 7 (2019): 37004-37016.

[2] Wang, Meng, Yiqin Lu, and Jiancheng Qin. "A dynamic MLP-based DDoS attack detection method using feature selection and feedback." *Computers & Security* 88 (2020): 101645.

[3] Yi, Y. A., and Myat Myat Min. "An analysis of random forest algorithm based network intrusion detection system." *Proceedings of the International Conference on Software Engineering, Artificial Intelligence, Networking and Parallel/Distributed Computing, Kanazawa, Japan*. 2017.

[4] Barapatre, Prachi, et al. "Training MLP neural network to reduce false alerts in IDS." *2008 International Conference on Computing, Communication and Networking*. IEEE, 2008.

[5] Chamou, Dimitra, et al. "Intrusion Detection System Based on Network Traffic Using Deep Neural Networks." *2019 IEEE 24th International Workshop on Computer Aided Modeling and Design of Communication Links and Networks (CAMAD)*. IEEE, 2019.

[6] Vinayakumar, R., K. P. Soman, and Prabaharan Poornachandran. "Applying convolutional neural network for network intrusion detection." *2017 International Conference on Advances in Computing, Communications and Informatics (ICACCI)*. IEEE, 2017.

[7] Ertam, Fatih, and Orhan Yaman. "Intrusion detection in computer networks via machine learning algorithms." *2017 International Artificial Intelligence and Data Processing Symposium (IDAP)*. IEEE, 2017.

[8] Esmaily, Jamal, Reza Moradinezhad, and Jamal Ghasemi. "Intrusion detection system based on multi-layer perceptron neural networks and decision tree." *2015 7th Conference on Information and Knowledge Technology (IKT)*. IEEE, 2015.

[9] Ahmad, Iftikhar, et al. "Intrusion detection using feature subset selection based on MLP." *Sci Res Essays* 6.34 (2011): 6804-6810.

[10] Yulianto, Arif, Parman Sukarno, and Novian Anggis Suwastika. "Improving adaboost-based intrusion detection system (IDS) performance on CIC IDS 2017 dataset." *Journal of Physics: Conference Series*. Vol. 1192. No. 1. IOP Publishing, 2019.

[11] Sathesh, A. "ENHANCED SOFT COMPUTING APPROACHES FOR INTRUSION DETECTION SCHEMES IN SOCIAL MEDIA NETWORKS." *Journal of Soft Computing Paradigm (JSCP)* 1.02 (2019): 69-79.

[12] Anguraj, Dinesh Kumar, and S. Smys. "Trust-based intrusion detection and clustering approach for wireless body area networks." *Wireless Personal Communications* 104.1 (2019): 1-20.

[13] Dhanabal, L., and S. P. Shantharajah. "A study on NSL-KDD dataset for intrusion detection system based on classification algorithms." *International Journal of Advanced Research in Computer and Communication Engineering* 4.6 (2015): 446-452.

[14] Shone, Nathan, et al. "A deep learning approach to network intrusion detection." *IEEE Transactions on Emerging Topics in Computational Intelligence* 2.1 (2018): 41-50.

[15] CIC dataset :https://www.unb.ca/cic/datasets/ids-2017.htm

Phishing-Inspector: Detection & Prevention of Phishing Websites

Tanmay Doke, Pranav Khismatrao, Vaibhav Jambhale and Mr. Nilesh Marathe.

Department of Information Technology, Ramrao Adik Institute of Technology, Dr. D.Y. Patil Vidyanagar, Nerul, Navi Mumbai, Maharashtra – 400706, India

Abstract — With a tremendous boost in technologies & available learning material developing any website has become very easy. Due to this the number of websites are exponentially growing day by day. The traditional approach of comparing websites with Blacklist and whitelist is not so efficient. As attackers have become more intelligent regarding hiding and redirecting of the URL and thereby tricking the user into phishing attack without been getting detected. So there's a need to have a novel approaches based on Machine learning (ML) which would expose this phishing websites. In this paper, the proposed system is an extension to web browser which made use of ML algorithm to extract various features and thereby helping the user to distinguish between Legitimate website and Phishing website.

Keywords — phishing websites, machine learning, blacklist, whitelist, phishing attacks, anti-phishing extension, SSL certificate, classification, legitimate, security.

I. INTRODUCTION

Phishing is a social engineering attack or fraudulent attempt to steal user's identity & private information. Personal details such as credit card number and login credentials are often stealing from the user by sending an email from trusted looking dummy site. User's been unaware of such activities tends to open the link which is sent by the attacker and ends up giving their login credentials. Once the login credentials are exposed to the attacker, various activities such as removal of money from bank account or using fake identity to do various illegal things are encouraged to be done by attacker.

Websites are also designed in such a way that they tend to appear exactly similar with the legitimate site. Displaying some URL and redirecting to some other URL is so common nowadays. In today's scenario many users prefer to do online shopping. As online transactions are increasing day-by-day identifying such phishing websites is so important. About 42% of phishing attack is been observed in payment sector.

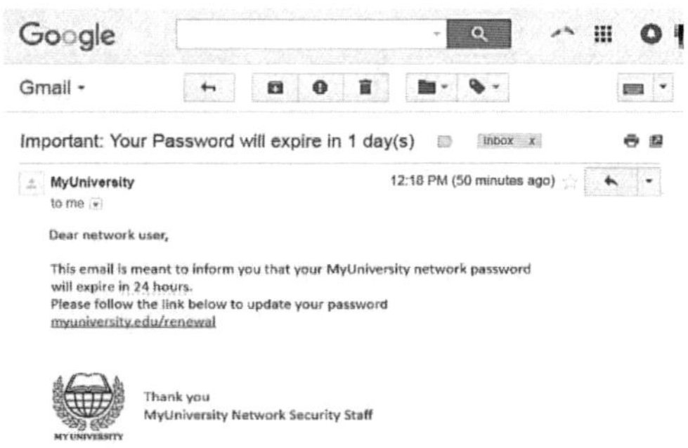

Fig.1 Web spoofing attack performed by attacker

Fig.1 depicts how a fake website which is been designed professionally like a legitimate website is accessed by the user. Thinking it as a legitimate website user will share his login credentials by clicking on that link, which may cause in installing some malware into his system. Once the attacker gets the credentials it can be used for any illegal purposes. There are many targets where phishing is done on large scale such as Facebook, Paytm, PayPal, Bank accounts, etc.

The remainder of this paper is structured as follows: in section II, survey on related work is reviewed. In section III, detailed explanation of proposed methodology along with system flow diagram and analysis is described. In section IV, results are displayed. In section V, overall understanding and outcomes are summarized and concluded. In section VI, references are mentioned.

II. RELATED WORK

This section reviews various research done in order to detect and prevent phishing websites. Many researchers have applied different methods and algorithm in process to make their system more accurate. We have reviewed various work and gathered information which could help our system to result in more accurate results.

Jhen-Hao Li et al. [1] they have proposed an approach called Phish-Box to effectively collect phishing data and generate models for phishing validation and detection. It is a Two Staged Detection Model in which first data is collected from databases using ETL approach. Blacklist from Phish Tank is extracted and Alexa Toplist is extracted to check whether site is Phish site or legit site. Various features or parameters are considered like Host information, URL, Content, Screenshot. Second Stage is Voting Module.

Samuel Marchal et al. [2] they have designed a distinct concept explaining Intra-URL relatedness which is then carefully evaluated using a Features extraction from the letters and words that form a URL. The features extracted are then analyzed by using them as input in a machine learning Classification Model. 12 features are extracted from an individual URL based on Random Forest Classifier. A score is generated for every URL. It has accurate classification rate of 94.90.

P.A. Barraclough et al. [3] they have proposed an approach filed Online Phishing Detection. The entire system is made up 4 components: Six sets of data inputs, Algorithm to extract features, Website to be checked, An result phase. The 6 set of data inputs is applied to fuzzy if-then extractor algorithm. If the presence of phishing site is detected, a voice generating user warning signals are generated to alert the user of the website. User is alerted by giving red color dialogue box and notified by green color dialogue box.

Samuel Marchal et al. [4] this application was designed to be Client-Side only for Enhanced Privacy and extra protection. Resilience to dynamic Phish are some of the important features. The various data sources collected for the detection purpose are: Starting URL, Redirection Chain Landing URL, Logged Links and Webpage Contents. It is a Bowser Add-On and Brand Independent Application.

M. Zabihimayvan et al. [7] they have proposed a Fuzzy Rough Set theory tool to select most effective features from 3 data sets. For evaluating the FRS Feature Selection, they developed a generalizable phishing detection model in which the classifiers are trained by a separate data set consisting of 14000 website samples. 95% is the maximum F-measure gained by FRS Feature Selection.

III. PROPOSED WORK

A. Overview of our approach

The overall approach of our system is depicted in the figure. 1. The system is an Extension to the Web browser. The system initially extract's the URL of the website from the browser. Then the extracted URL is checked in dataset, which contains list of phishing website and legitimate website. If the URL is found in dataset labeled as legitimate website then the current website is declared as Legitimate site, but if the URL is found in dataset as phishing site then the current website is declared as phishing website. Same is the process for suspicious website. If the URL is not found in dataset lists, then the URL is passed as an input to the Phishing Detector machine learning algorithm. The algorithm used is Random forest algorithm and it uses 13 different kinds of features for decision making. The output of the ML algorithm is then given to the SSL certificate checker which checks the SSL certificate of the website After that output of SSL certificate is given to Domain creation and expiration date checker which checks for how much period the webpage is active. Based on the results the website is detected as Legitimate or Suspicious or Phishing.

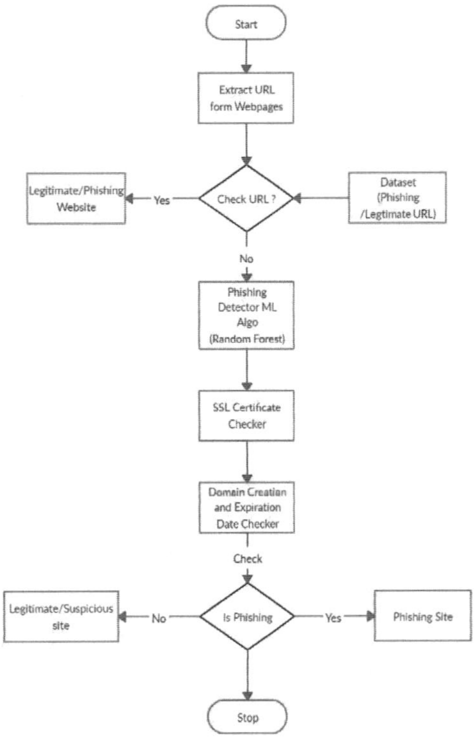

Fig 2. Architecture

B. Requirement Analysis

In order for the system to work smoothly the user's machine should satisfy the following software and hardware requirements.

1. Software Requirements

- Python 3.6 or above: Higher level language used for backend.
- Beautiful Soup: A package in python which is used for web scrapping.
- Scikit-learn: A package in python which has libraries for machine learning.
- JavaScript: Used for getting URL from the extension.
- Browser: A Google Chrome browser.

2. Hardware Requirements

- Hard disk with minimum of 250 GB.
- Minimum 4 GB RAM.
- Windows 7, 8, 8.1, 10.
- System Type: 32-bit Operating System and above.

C. Design Phase

1. Design Goals

- The system created should not be dependent on features specific to a target.
- To reduce the number of phishing attacks thereby helping the user to preserve confidential information.
- To detect real time generated phishing websites.
- To maintain privacy of user by not asking them their browsing history.
- The system can be used by business organization to conduct phishing campaigns.
- The warning messages generated by the system must be clear and easy to understand.

2. Design Choices

- The system made is totally client-side. It uses the URL features and domain information to compute the decision.
- The system uses some static and some non-static features for the detection purpose.
- The created system also relies on some predefined feature characteristics which are bound to present in most of the phishing websites.

3. Architecture and Implementation

The system is developed as an add-on to a web browser like chrome and is suitable windows operating system.

The add-on is created using JavaScript. When the user clicks on the icon on the navigation bar, a popup is displayed as shown in figure. Once the user clicks the check button the JavaScript method collects the URL of the current website. This URL is then passed to PHP file which executes the python file. This add-on is used to display the result.

The background process is developed in python. The main reason to use python is because of the availability of machine learning libraries. The python code does the following functionality:

Checking the website in the available dataset: The dataset has websites labeled as 1, 0, -1. Here '1' stands for phishing website, '0' stands for legitimate website and '-1' stands for suspicious website. This functionality is first executed on execution of python file. The extracted URL is searched in the dataset and the label of the matched URL is returned. If the URL is not found in the dataset, then the other functions are executed else only this function is executed.

Phishing detection ML Algorithm: If the URL is not found in the dataset then the URL is passed to machine learning algorithm. The machine learning algorithm is used to compute the decision based on the features which are extracted from the URL. Random Forest Algorithm is used for this purpose. Total 13 features are extracted from the particular URL which are then used by the ML algorithm. The result is then used for further decision making process.

SSL Certificate Checker: This function is used to get the SSL certificate of the particular website. The function takes the hostname of the website and fetches the respective SSL certificate. Python inbuilt method of 'ssl.get_server_certificate' is used for this purpose. The result is again forwarded for decision making purpose.

Domain Creation and Expiration Date checker: This function is used to get the creation date and the expiration date of the domain used in the particular URL. Using these parameters, the period remaining for the domain to expire and the period for which the domain is active till current date is calculated. If both the period calculated comes to less than 1 year, then the chances of the website being a phishing or suspicious website is more. The age of domain is also calculated i.e. the period for which the domain is registered. If it is less than 1½ years than the result is more aligned towards the website being a phishing website. This is because the attackers mostly take domains with less period, as the websites get banned once found out to be phishing websites. Python inbuilt method 'whois' is used for this purpose.

Final Decision Making: The final decision of the website being a phishing website or legitimate website or suspicious website is taken based on following table

Table 1 Implementation Logic

ML Output	SSL Certificate	Domain Duration	Result
Phishing	Not Present	-	Phishing Site
Legitimate	Not Present	-	Phishing Site
Phishing	Present	Less	Phishing Site
Legitimate	Present	Less	Suspicious Site
Phishing	Present	More	Suspicious Site
Legitimate	Present	More	Legitimate Site

4. User Interface

The user interface is used to check the legitimacy of the website and the result is displayed through it. The user interface is simple and has minimal text. The navigation bar icon is the logo of the developed system. This icon is always present on the browser.

5. Machine Learning Algorithm

To differentiate between a legitimate and phishing website we use machine learning technique. The attackers always have some limitations while creating a phishing URL, this is because a URL is composed of registered domain and free URL. Registered domain has to be used as it, but the attackers can modify the free URL as they want. So machine learning approach is used to differentiate the legitimate and phishing sites. We have used supervised learning technique. In supervised learning the model is trained used labeled dataset. The dataset which is used to train the model consists of different classes for different values. Once the model is trained, it can be used to predict the class of the unlabeled data which is given as an input to the model.

For the training purpose we are using Random Forest algorithm. In this algorithm random

https://doi.org/10.1051/itmconf/20203203004

samples of data are selected from the dataset, using these samples separate decision trees are created for each and every sample. After this, prediction result for every decision tree is generated and the best decision tree is used for training the model. The reason for using random forest algorithm is the minimum overfitting risk and also it takes less time to train. Another advantage is the efficiency of the algorithm for large datasets and its high accuracy.

For the training purpose different features are extracted from the URL. A total of 13 features are generated.

- No of dots: It tells the count of the dots used in the URL.
- No of delimiters: It counts the different kinds of delimiters in the URL.
- Presence of '-', '@', '//': It checks the presence of these parameters in the URL.
- Count of sub-directory, sub-domain and queries: It counts the number of times the mentioned parameters used in the URL.
- Length of the URL, whether shortening service is used and whether IP address is used as URL are the other features being used for the training purpose of the model.

D. Analysis Phase

1. Dataset

The dataset which is used for the training purpose consists of 7030 URLs. These 7030 URLs consists of both legitimate as well as phishing URLs. The count of phishing URLs is 3536 and the count of legitimate URLs is 3494. A new dataset is created for the newly tested URLs. This dataset is different from the dataset which is used during the training of the model. The model can be trained using this newly generated dataset after some amount of time when the URL count in the dataset reaches a certain value.

2. Accuracy for phishing websites

Phishing websites were correctly predicted with accuracy of 93.16%. It had false positive rate of 7.38%.

3. Accuracy for legitimate websites.

Legitimate websites were correctly predicted with accuracy of 92.62%. False positive rate of 6.84% was observed.

Table 2 Classification Results for Random Forest

URL	Phishing Class	Legitimate Class	Precision	F-1 Score	Accuracy
Phishing	93.16% (TP)	6.84% (FN)	93%	93 %	93%
Legitimate	7.38 % (FP)	92.62 % (TN)			

4. Accuracy of the System

Accuracy of the system is defined as the count of the legitimate and phishing URLs which are correctly classified over total number of URLs present in the dataset. The calculated accuracy of the system is **93%**. True Positive Rate: It is defined as the percentage of phishing websites which are correctly classified. False Positive Rate: It is defined as the percentage of phishing websites which are incorrectly classified.

5. Feature Analysis

Fig 3. Displays various classification results for 6 classifiers. But accuracy percentage, TN rate and TP rate of Random forest is greater other classifiers.

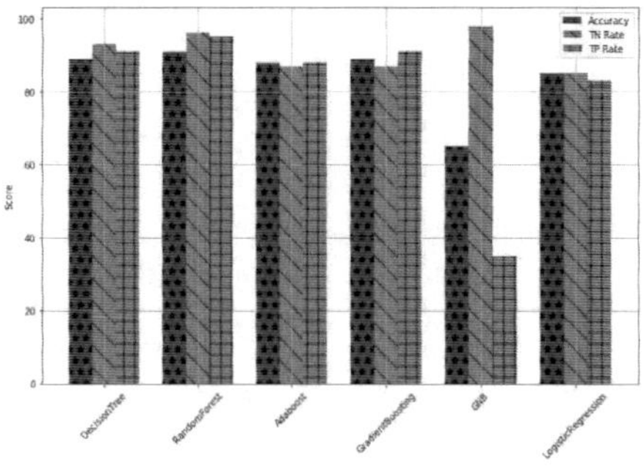

Fig 3. Classification Results for 6 Classifiers

https://doi.org/10.1051/itmconf/20203203004

IV. RESULT

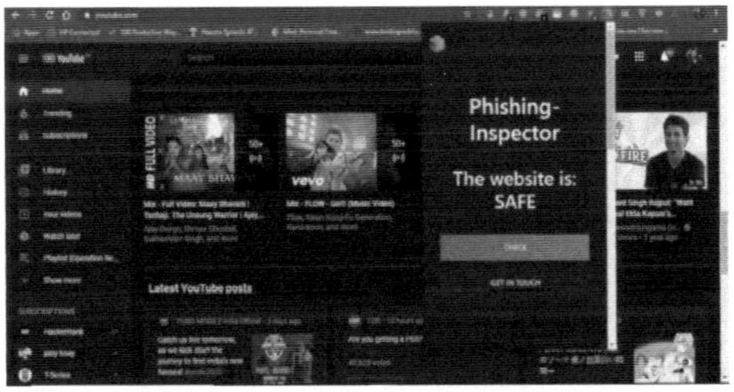

Fig 4. Safe Website

Fig 5. Phishing Website

Fig 4. Depicts the safe website. Fig 5. Depicts the phishing website which is caught by our phishing inspector. This website was not blocked by google chrome but here our system has detected it successfully. Such websites are fake as they try to trick the user to fall into their hands to perform illegal activities.

V. CONCLUSION

With the percentage of phishing attacks increasing this proposed system will enable the user for safe browsing and also for making safe transactions. It will also prevent sharing of confidential information of the user. Proposed system is able to differentiate between legitimate site and phishing site with ease so that anyone can use it without any hesitation. Education awareness should be spread across everyone so that there are less victims to such attack. Internet experts provides various security guidelines which must be followed while surfing on the internet. Users should not blind fondly open any URL link to encourage such attack. One must check the URL carefully and then only processed for further interaction where sensitive information is being asked.

VI. REFERENCES

[1] Jhen-Hao Li , Sheng-De Wang. PhishBox: An Approach for Phishing Validation and Detection. 2017 IEEE 15th Intl Conf on Dependable, Autonomic and Secure Computing, 15th Intl Conf on Pervasive Intelligence and Computing, 3rd Intl Conf on Big Data Intelligence and Computing and Cyber Science and Technology Congress(DASC/PiCom/DataCom/CyberSciTec)

[2] Samuel Marchal , Jérôme François , Radu State , Thomas Engel.] PhishStorm: Detecting Phishing With Streaming Analytics. Engel IEEE Transactions on Network and Service ManagementYear: 2014 , Volume: 11

[3] P.A. Barraclough, G. Sexton & N. Aslam. Online Phishing Detection Toolbar for Transactions. Science and Information Conference 2015 July 28-30 2015 | London, UK Computer Science and Digital Technology University of Northumbria Newcastle Upon Tyne, NE 18ST, United Kingdom.

[4] Samuel Marchal ; Giovanni Armano ; Tommi Gröndahl ; Kalle Saari ; Nidhi Singh ; N. Asokan. Off-the-Hook: An Efficient and Usable Client-Side Phishing Prevention Application. IEEE Transactions on ComputersYear: 2017 , Volume: 66.

[5] Ludl, C., McAllister, S., Kirda, E., & Kruegel, C. (2007). On the effectiveness of techniques to detect phishing sites.In Detection of Intrusions and Malware, and Vulnerability Assessment (pp. 20-39). Springer Berlin Heidelberg.

[6] Y. Pan, X. Ding, "Anomaly based web phishing page detection", Proc. 22nd Annu. Comput. Security Appl. Conf., pp. 381-392, 2006.

[7] M. Zabihimayvan and D. Doran, "Fuzzy Rough Set Feature Selection to Enhance Phishing Attack Detection," 2019 IEEE International Conference on Fuzzy Systems (FUZZ-IEEE), New Orleans, LA, USA, 2019, pp. 1-6

 https://doi.org/10.1051/itmconf/20203203005

Fraudulent Face Image Detection

Rahul Awhad[1,*], *Saurabh* Jayswal[1,**], *Adesh* More[1,***], and *Jyoti* Kundale[1,****]

[1]Ramrao Adik Institute of Technology, Dept. of Information Technology, Mumbai, India

Abstract. Due to the growing advancements in technology, many software applications are being developed to modify and edit images. Such software can be used to alter images. Nowadays, an altered image is so realistic that it becomes too difficult for a person to identify whether the image is fake or real. Such software applications can be used to alter the image of a person's face also. So, it becomes very difficult to identify whether the image of the face is real or not. Our proposed system is used to identify whether the image of a face is fake or real. The proposed system makes use of machine learning. The system makes use of a convolution neural network and support vector classifier. Both these machine learning models are trained using real as well as fake images. Both these trained models will take an image as an input and will determine whether the image is fake or real.

1 Introduction

Many available software applications in the market can be used to modify and edit images. Some advanced software is capable of making an altered image which can seem to be realistic. Hence such alterations affect the authenticity and originality of the image and it becomes very difficult for a person to identify whether an image is altered or not. Such altered images can be of a person's face also. Altered images of the face can be used to create fake profile images on social media platforms and can be used to deceive other people. There are now emerging new technologies for solving such problems. Such technology is machine learning. Machine learning is a technique used to train a system and make a prediction for a problem-based on the trained system. Our proposed system is an attempt to check the originality of the image of a face. Our proposed system will help in identifying whether the face in the image is spliced or not.

2 Review of Literature

Fake Colorized Image Detection: Guo, Cao, Zhang, and Wang in the year 2018 have proposed that there are many techniques used for coloring gray-scale images. In this paper, they have used histogram-based fake colorized detection and encoding based fake colorized image detection techniques to identify whether the image is a colorized image or not. The histogram-based detection uses the hue and saturation channel of an image. The histogram for the hue channel of fake images is generally smooth while the histogram for the saturation channel for fake images shows different peak values. Their proposed system observes the statistical inconsistencies in the bright and dark channels of the image [1].

Detection of GAN-generated Fake Images Over Social Networks: Marra, Gragnaniello, Cozzolino, and Verdoliva in the year 2018 have proposed that generative adversarial network allows one to modify the image in a very realistic way. In this paper, they have studied the performance of many forgery detectors. The detection accuracy can be achieved by up to 95% by the use of conventional and deep learning detectors [2].

Fake Colorized Image Detection with Channel-wise Convolution based Deep-learning Framework: Zhuo, Tan, Zeng, and Lit in the year 2018 have proposed a system to identify a fake colorized image. They have introduced a Wider separate-then-reunion network, a deep learning-based data-driven color image steganalyzer to detect fake colorized images [3].

Image Splicing Detection Through Illumination Inconsistencies and Deep Learning: Pomari, Ruppert, Rezende, Rocha, and Carvalho in the year 2018 have proposed a system for detecting spliced images. They have made use of illuminant maps and deep neural network for training data to find hints of forgery. The system makes use of the deep neural network as well as the transfer learning process. The transfer learning process uses an already trained machine learning model for training the data for the required application. The proposed system eliminates the tedious engineering process and provides an accuracy of more than 96% [4].

Digital image tampering detection and localization using singular value decomposition technique: Mall, Roy, and Mitra in the year 2013 have proposed a way to identify the integrity of the digital images. The proposed

*e-mail: rahul.awhad28@gmail.com
**e-mail: srsjayswal@gmail.com
***e-mail: adeshmore98@gmail.com
****e-mail: jyoti.jadhav@rait.ac.in

https://doi.org/10.1051/itmconf/20203203005

system is based on the generation of a hash of the image using singular value decomposition. The generated hash value will be affected if any tampering is done on the image. Such a hash vector will help in localizing image tampering [5].

Fake Face Detection Based on Radiometric Distributions: Edmunds and Caplier in the year 2016 have proposed a method for fake face detection using radiometric distortions. In this paper, the modeling of radiometric distortions arising in the recapturing process is done to solve the crisis of fake image detection. In this technique, the detection process occurs after the face identification process. Based on twelve features, differentiation between real and fake faces is done [6].

Learning to detect fake face images in the wild: Hsu, Lee, and Zhuang in the year 2018 have proposed a system to detect computer-generated images. In this paper, a deep forgery discriminator is developed to detect computer-generated images. The system is trained using fake images with the help of a deep neural network. Fake images generated by (GAN) Generative Adversarial Network are successfully detected. This was the first work to solve problems of detecting fake images. The system successfully detected 94.7% of the fake images created by GAN techniques [7].

Detecting Both Machine and Human Created Fake Face Images In the Wild: Tariq, Lee, Kim, Shin, and Woo in the year 2018 has proposed a system to detect fake face images generated by both machine and human effort. Machine created images are GAN-created images. Human created fake images are images which are edited in software like Adobe Photoshop. For detecting GAN-created images, they have created a neural network model by training real and fake images of varying sizes from 64X64 to 1024X1024 pixel size images. For detecting human-created fake face images, they distinguish real ad fake images by using RGB channel information [8].

Image forgery detection based on physics and pixels: Kumar and Srivastava in the year 2017 have made a detailed discussion about various passive forgery detection techniques. The techniques discussed are copy-move based forgery detection, resampling-based forgery detection techniques, forgery detection based on splicing, and physics/lighting-based forgery detection techniques [9].

Classifying Genuine Face images from Disguised Face Images: Kim, Han, and Woo in the year 2019 have proposed a system for classifying fake face images. Their proposed system makes use of face detection classifiers like ShallowNet, VGG-16 and, Xception. The Xception model from the proposed system is giving an accuracy of 62% [10].

3 Background Study

3.1 Convolution Neural Network

Convolution Neural Network is a category of neural networks. It is mostly used for image recognition or image classification. The first layer in CNN is the convolution layer which is responsible for feature extraction. Then pooling is performed to reduce the dimensional size. The output in the vector form is then fed into the fully connected layer. The output of a fully connected layer classifies the image.

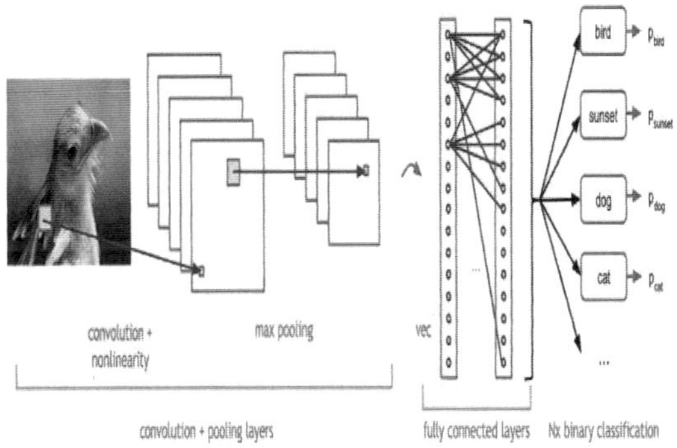

Figure 1. Working of Convolution Neural Network

3.2 Support Vector Classifier

Support Vector Classifier is a technique used in Support Vector Machine to classify the training data as per the labels. This technique is used in supervised learning. SVC algorithm classifies given training data with the help of a hyper-plane. Hyper-plane is a line that divides a plane into two parts thus separating data into different classes.

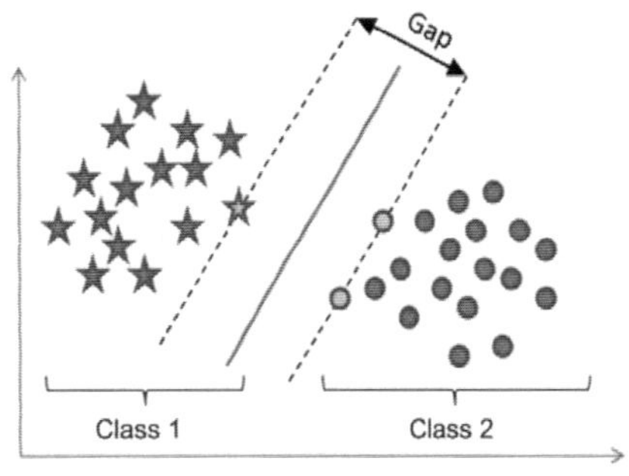

Figure 2. Classification Example

4 Proposed Method

The proposed system utilizes the concept of machine learning. There are various machine learning models available for different applications. The proposed system makes use of a convolution neural network and support vector classifier. Both models give their results for the input image. The proposed system makes use of a convolution neural network and supports vector classifier models. The working of our proposed system is as follows:

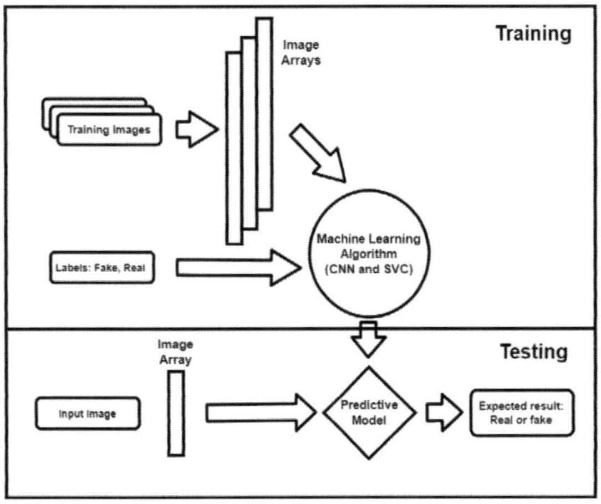

Figure 3. Block Diagram of the Proposed System

- The first step in the system involves collecting the training images and converting then into image arrays.
- Each fake or real image is labeled accordingly.
- The next step involves feeding the training data-set and the labels to the machine learning algorithm to form a model.
- After the model is created, an input image that is to be tested is taken and it is converted into an image array.
- The image array of the input image is then fed into the machine learning model to do the prediction.
- The model gives a label as a result of the prediction which is real or fake.

4.1 Data Collection

The data consists of images of different faces. Real as well as fake images are collected for training. The data can be obtained by manually altering images or by obtaining through online available sources.

4.2 Data Preparation

The images are resized to a fixed dimension. The images are resized to 50X50 pixel size to decrease the overall size and space required to train the data. Images are then stored in an array format for data training. After the model is created, the input image for testing is also resized to 50X50 pixel size.

4.3 Choosing a Model

The proposed system makes use of a convolution neural network and an SVC-based machine learning model. CNN model is generally used for image recognition and processing pixel data. The proposed neural network uses two activation functions. The two activation functions used are the ReLu and the Sigmoid activation function. The SVC classifier classifies the data into two classes. The two classes are "real" and "fake".

4.4 Sigmoid Activation Function

The curve of the Sigmoid function appears as an S-shape. The main reason we use sigmoid is that its value lies between 0 and 1.

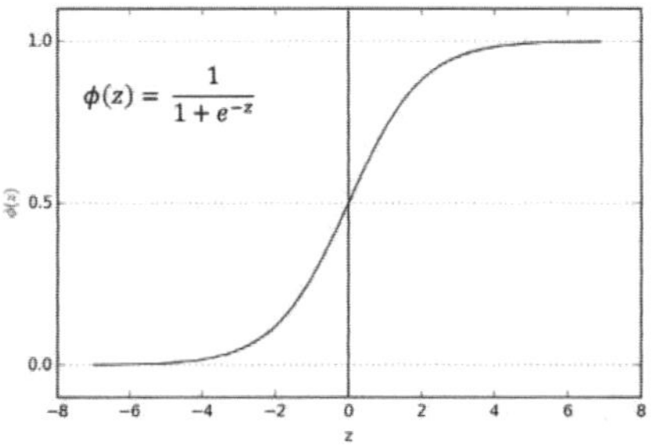

Figure 4. Sigmoid Graph

The curve is given by the following formula:

$$f(x) = \frac{L}{1 + e^{-k(x-x_0)}} \tag{1}$$

where:
L = Curve's maximum value
k = Steepness of the curve
x_0 = x value of sigmoid's midpoint

It is therefore often used in models where we have to estimate the likelihood of an output. Since the probability of the output or prediction lies only between the range of 0 and 1, the sigmoid activation function is preferred for classification.

4.5 ReLU Activation Function

ReLU stands for the Rectified Linear Unit. It is the most used activation function in many machine learning applications. Hence it is almost used in all convolution neural networks and deep learning. The ReLU function is halfway rectified from the bottom. The value of a function is zero when z is less than 0 and the value of a function is z if the value of z is above or equal to zero. The equation for the ReLu function can be given as:

$$f(z) = max(0, z) \tag{2}$$

https://doi.org/10.1051/itmconf/20203203005

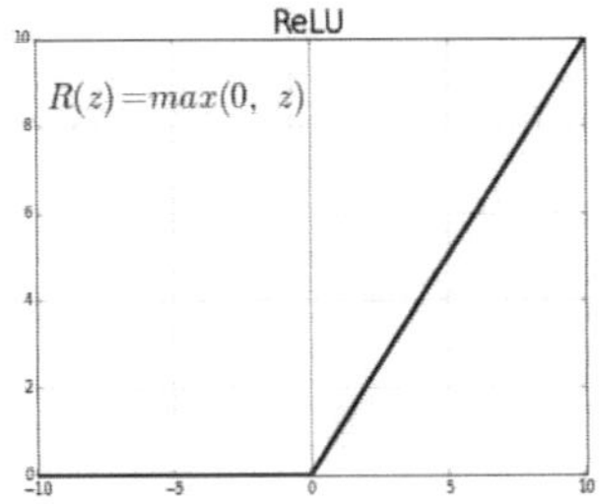

Figure 5. ReLU Graph

4.6 Training Model and Predicting

The convolution neural network is trained using the collected images using the above activation functions. The proposed system's code is written in python language. For training the data we used python's "sklearn" and "tensorflow" module. After the model is trained, it can be used to test the input images. The model will predict whether the input image is fake or real.

4.7 Training and Working of the CNN-Based Model

The training data consist of real and fake images. All the images are converted into gray-scale images. All the images are then resized into 50X50 pixel size images. This will reduce the size and space of data for training purposes. All the images are shuffled before giving input for the training. The machine learning model is created using the python module called "tensorflow".

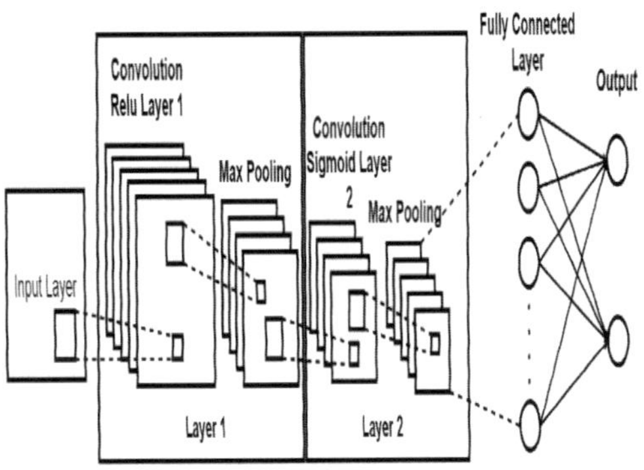

Figure 6. Training of CNN model

For the proposed system, the neural network model used is called the Sequential model. This model has two main layers. There are two types of activation functions used which are "ReLU" and "Sigmoid". Each layer consists of a finite number of neurons. These neurons hold different values after the training process. When the test image is input to the model, the model identifies the pattern for a real or a fake image using the values stored in the neural network model. The last layer will give the value which is used to determine the result.

4.8 Training and Working of the SVC-Based Model

SVC machine learning model is created using python's "sklearn" module. This model is also trained using 50X50 pixel-sized and gray-scale images. This model creates a graph of points and one or more hyper-plane that classifies these points in the graph. This model can classify the points linearly or non-linearly which depends on the application. For the proposed system, classification is done non-linearly. We can specify the way in which we want to classify the data in the kernel parameter. We have used the "rbf" type of non-linear classification which is specified in the kernel parameter. After creating the model, the input image is classified as per the graph formed from the trained data.

5 Results

The proposed system is trained using 2041 images out of which 960 are fake images and 1081 are real images. Figure 7 and figure 8 display the result of the prediction done by the SVC and neural network model for the real and fake image. We have tested the proposed system for 409 images. The SVC-Based model is giving an accuracy of 65% and the CNN-Based model is giving an accuracy of 94%. The 409 tested images include both real and fake images. Figure 6 represents opening an image from the graphical user interface of the system. The 'Open' button will open a window from where you can select an image from your computer to be checked. Figure 7 displays the result of the proposed system for a real image. The 'Check' button will run the script for checking the image. Figure 8 displays the process of splicing an image. Here, the term splicing

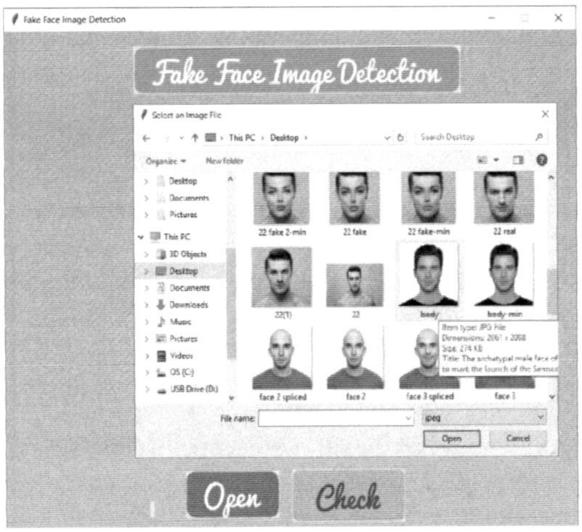

Figure 7. Graphical user interface of the proposed system

https://doi.org/10.1051/itmconf/20203203005

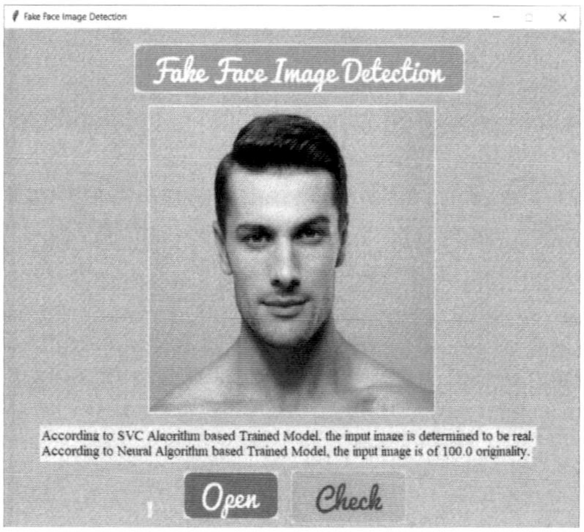

Figure 8. Result of a real image

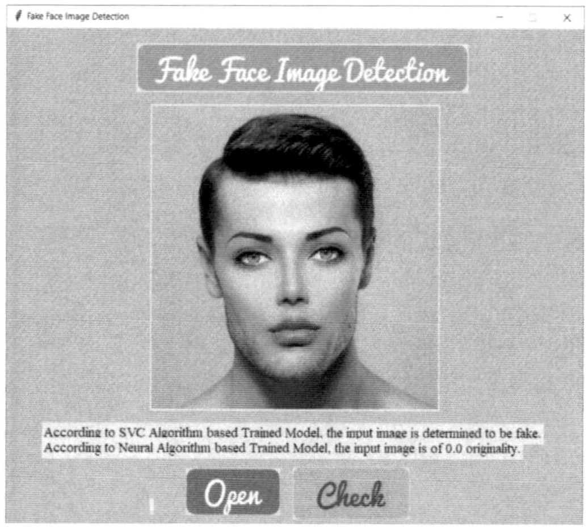

Figure 10. Result of a fake image

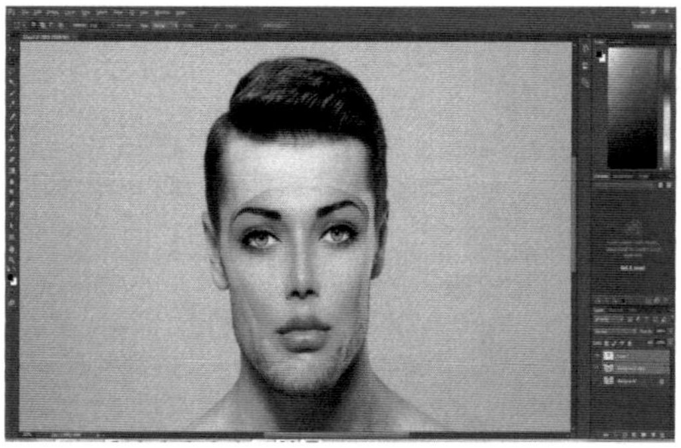

Figure 9. Process of splicing an image

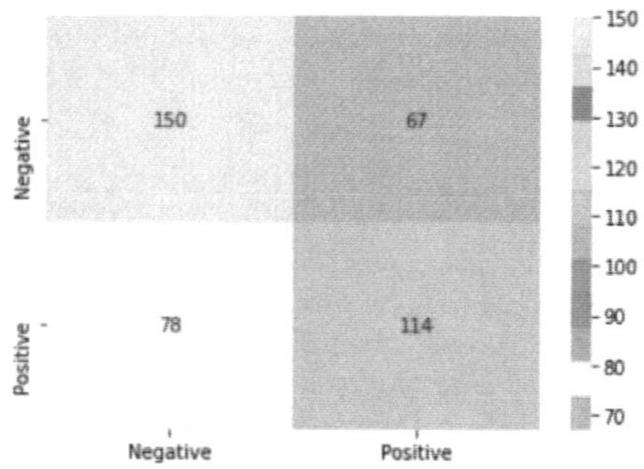

Figure 11. Confusion matrix for the SVC-based model

	precision	recall	f1-score	support
0	0.66	0.69	0.67	217
1	0.63	0.59	0.61	192
accuracy			0.65	409
macro avg	0.64	0.64	0.64	409
weighted avg	0.64	0.65	0.64	409

Figure 12. Classification report for the SVC-based model

means taking a part of the image from any other resource and replacing it on to the target image. Figure 9 displays the result of a fake image that is given as input to the system. The confusion matrix for the SVC-based model is shown in Figure 11. The classification report for the SVC-based algorithm is shown in Figure 12. The confusion matrix for the Neural Network based model is shown in Figure 13. The classification report for the Neural Network algorithm is shown in Figure 14.

6 Comparison with a Existing System

Our proposed system is similar to Pomari et.al's [4] method of determining inconsistencies in an image. Pomari et.al's [4] system makes use of a deep neural network and a transfer learning process whereas our proposed system makes use of a convolutional neural network. Pomari et.al's [4] system utilizes the ReLu activation function while our proposed system makes use of ReLu as well as Sigmoid activation function. Pomari et.al's [4] system trains the data using the transfer learning process which involves an already trained model for a different application. Our proposed system trains the data from scratch without the help of a pre-built machine learning model. Pomari et.al's [4] system finds inconsistencies in all types of images whereas our proposed system focuses on the images consisting of a single face of a person. Pomari et.al's [4] system gives a classification accuracy of 96%. Our proposed system has an accuracy of 65% for the SVC-based model and accuracy of 94% for the CNN-based model.

7 Conclusion

The proposed system determines whether the image of a face is real or fake. The fake image can be a spliced image in which some part of a face is replaced with a part from another face. The proposed system makes use of a convo-

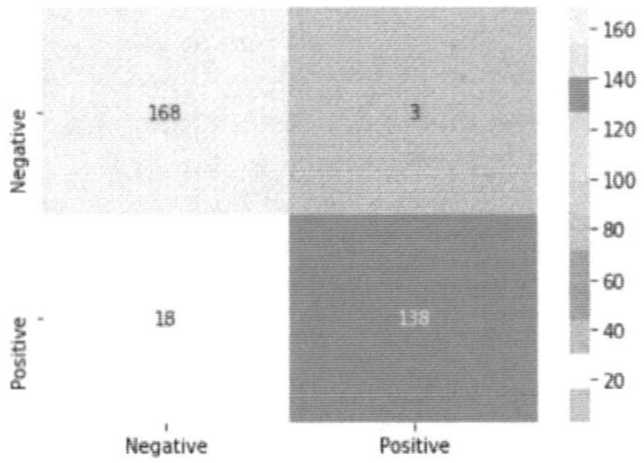

Figure 13. Confusion matrix for the CNN-based model

	precision	recall	f1-score	support
0	0.90	0.98	0.94	171
1	0.98	0.88	0.93	156
accuracy			0.94	327
macro avg	0.94	0.93	0.94	327
weighted avg	0.94	0.94	0.94	327

Figure 14. Classification report for the CNN-based model

lution neural network and support vector classifier. Both these algorithms extract the features from training images and forms two models. One model is based on CNN and the other is based on the support vector classifier. Both of these models predict their own results. The proposed system displays result from both the models. The currently proposed system has an accuracy of 65% for the SVC-based model and 94% for the CNN-based model used in the proposed system. Hence, the proposed system can play an important role in identifying any altered face image which can help people from getting misguided on social media platforms.

8 Future Scope

The proposed system can be included with a face recognition algorithm to identify the presence of any face before checking the image. The accuracy of the system can be increased by providing more data-set of real and fake images. The accuracy can also be increased by altering the parameters used for training the data. The parameters include the number of layers of neurons, activation functions, etc. The proposed system can be applied to social media platforms to check the authenticity of a facial image. Hence, the proposed system can help people to identify if any facial image is altered or not on social media platforms.

References

[1] Y. Guo, X. Cao, W. Zhang and R. Wang, "Fake Colorized Image Detection," in IEEE Transactions on Information Forensics and Security, vol. 13, no. 8, pp. 1932-1944, August 2018.

[2] F. Marra, D. Gragnaniello, D. Cozzolino and L. Verdoliva, "Detection of GAN-Generated Fake Images over Social Networks," 2018 IEEE Conference on Multimedia Information Processing and Retrieval (MIPR), Miami, FL, pp. 384-389, 2018.

[3] L. Zhuo, S. Tan, J. Zeng and B. Lit, "Fake Colorized Image Detection with Channel-wise Convolution based Deep-learning Framework," 2018 Asia-Pacific Signal and Information Processing Association Annual Summit and Conference (APSIPA ASC), Honolulu, HI, USA, pp. 733-736, 2018.

[4] T. Pomari, G. Ruppert, E. Rezende, A. Rocha and T. Carvalho, "Image Splicing Detection Through Illumination Inconsistencies and Deep Learning," 2018 25th IEEE International Conference on Image Processing (ICIP), Athens, pp. 3788-3792, 2018.

[5] V. Mall, A. K. Roy and S. K. Mitra, "Digital image tampering detection and localization using singular value decomposition technique," 2013 Fourth National Conference on Computer Vision, Pattern Recognition, Image Processing and Graphics (NCVPRIPG), Jodhpur, pp. 1-4, 2013.

[6] T. Edmunds and A. Caplier, "Fake face detection based on radiometric distortions," 2016 Sixth International Conference on Image Processing Theory, Tools and Applications (IPTA), Oulu, pp. 1-6, 2016.

[7] C. Hsu, C. Lee and Y. Zhuang, "Learning to Detect Fake Face Images in the Wild," 2018 International Symposium on Computer, Consumer and Control (IS3C), Taichung, Taiwan, pp. 388-391, 2018.

[8] Tariq, Shahroz Lee, Sangyup Kim, Hoyoung Shin, Youjin Woo, Simon. (2018). Detecting Both Machine and Human Created Fake Face Images In the Wild. 81-87. 10.1145/3267357.3267367.

[9] Kumar, Manoj Srivastava, Sangeet. (2017). Image forgery detection based on physics and pixels: a study. Australian Journal of Forensic Sciences. 51. 1-16. 10.1080/00450618.2017.1356868.

[10] J. Kim, S. Han and S. S.Woo, "Classifying Genuine Face images from Disguised Face Images," 2019 IEEE International Conference on Big Data (Big Data), Los Angeles, CA, USA, 2019, pp. 6248-6250.

A Compression Algorithm for DNA Palindrome Compression Technique

Dr.D.Suneetha ,Dr.D.Rathna Kishore,Mr.P.Narendra Babu

Professor, Department of CSE, NRIIT, Vijayawada, A.P, India.
Professor, Department of CSE, NRIIT, Vijayawada, A.P, India.
Associate Professor, Department of CSE, NRIIT, Vijayawada, A.P, India

Abstract:

Data Compression in Cryptography is one of the interesting research topic. The compression process reduces the amount of transferring data as well as storage space which in turn effects the usage of bandwidth. Further, when a plain text is converted to cipher text, the length of the cipher text becomes large. This adds up to tremendous information storing. It is extremely important to address the storage capacity issue along with the security issues of exponentially developing information. This problem can be resolved by compressing the ciphertext based on a some compression algorithm. In this proposed work used the compression technique called palindrome compression technique. The compression ratio of the proposed method is better than the standard method for both colored and gray scaled images. An experimental result for the proposed methods is better than existing methods for different types of image.

Keywords: DNA Cryptography, Plaindrome, Data Compression, Encryption, Decryption

Introduction:

The cryptography plays a vital role to provide security in the field of network or any storage media. There are various cryptographic techniques available now a days. Out of which, DNA cryptography is new born field in the field of Cryptography. While encrypting the cipher text using DNA, one will get very long length sequences of ciphertext. In order to provide efficient storage for the ciphertext there is a need to compress the generated DNA sequences[1]. The compression process reduces the amount of transferring data as well as storage space which in turn effects the usage of bandwidth. Reducing the size of data leads to reduction in the transmission time of data in a network. There are two types of data compression techniques available. One is Lossless and Lossy Compression techniques. Examples of Lossless Compression are Runlength Coding, Huffman Coding and LZ77[3]. Examples of Lossy Compression techniques are picture transformation, picture resizing and quantization. This chapter discuss the compression technique which will be used for providing efficient storage for cipher text.

Related Work:

Amikov proposed compression algorithm based on the tree modelling for color map images. It works with the phenomena of n ary context free model with complex binary tree structures of n color map images. The major thing present in this is it is suitable for the color images only with

72 colors only[5]. Improvement in LZC[7] command of unix operating system proposed a new method in compression algorithm based on the dictionary and it is suitable for textual patterns not for the images.

Cuitex propsed a new compression algorithm with increase in throughput and compression ratio. The design principal of this algorithm is based on the adaptive pre-processor which will reduce the coorelation ratio between the blocks[8]. VLSI architecture is used for reducing compression ratio. Moreover this algorithm have high redundancy of data when compared to other existing algorithms like LZW[9].

Increase the bandwidth speed by reducing the size of the transmitted data on a network. Decrease the size of the data without loss of information is called Lossless Compression. Lossy compression can be done on images[4]. In Lossless Compression, RLE, Huffman Coding, LZW77 and PPM are familiar methods. In RLE, note down the occurrences of same sequence consequently[2].

LZ77 was implemented based on search buffer and look ahead buffer. It is also called as Sliding window Compression. Search buffer is used as dictionary and look ahead buffer is used to find the matches which are search buffer[6].

Proposed Method:

DESIGN AND IMPLEMENTATION

It is used the compression technique called palindrome compression technique. Palindrome means the original sequence is equal to the reverse of the sequence.

For eg., Consider a sequence S=CGTTTTGC.

The reverse of the sequence is R=CGTTTTGC which is same as the original sequence. The palindrome compression technique includes storing of half of the string instead of storing full length string. In decompression process, the string already stored is reversed and added at the end of the same string to get the final string.

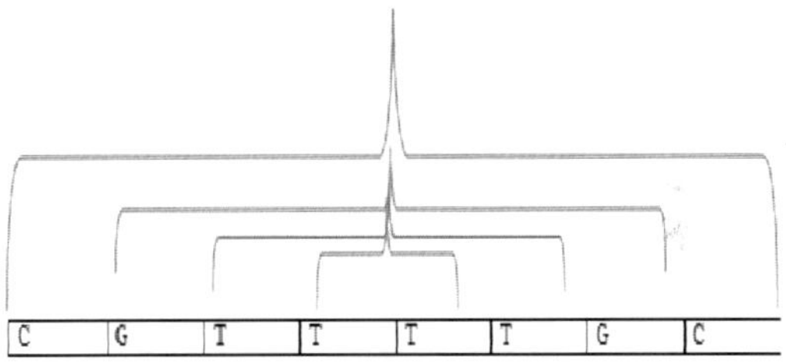

Figure 1.Palindrome Technique

Compression Algorithm:

Algorithm PalinCompress(C, length)

C is the Ciphertext in the form of DNA Sequences and length is used to divide the DNA sequence into number of specified length strings.

BEGIN

1. Split the DNA strand into number of substrings based on the given length
2. Check whether each substring is palindrome or not. If the substring is palindrome then store half of the string.
3. If it is not palindrome, continue with the same string.
4. Repeat step 2 & 3 for all the substrings.
5. Revrse the obtain string and divide into equal parts

 https://doi.org/10.1051/itmconf/20203203006

6. Repeat step 2&3 for the substrings

END

Decompression Algorithm

Algorithm PalinDeCompress(D)

D is the Decompressed DNA strand.

BEGIN

1. Read the DNA strand until you find the digit.
2. When the digit is found, count the number of characters equal to the digit, that are immediately presented the digit and add the same characters in reverse order from the location where the digit is found that is the digit is replaced by the first character.

END

Empirical Analysis

For example take a DNA Strand

Best Case:

C=AGGTTGGAACGTTGCAAAAAAAAATTGGGGTT and Length=8

Divide the DNA strand into 8 length substrings then

C1=AGGTTGGA

C2=ACGTTGCA

C3=AAAAAAAA

C4=TTGGGGTT

Find each substring is palindrome or not, if yes then store half of the string and the number of leftover characters of the substring. Here, all four strings are palindromes then store half of the strings and the lengths then the compressed string is

C=AGGTACGTAAAATTGG

Compression Ratio=Number of Sequences After Compression/Number of Sequences

Before Compression,

Compression Ratio=16/32=0.5. In this case, the transmitted date rate reduced to half.

C=GGTTAAAATGCATGGA

C1=GGTT

C2=AAAA

C3=TGCA

C4=TGGA

Find each substring is palindrome or not, if yes then store half of the string and the number of leftover characters of the substring.

C=GGTTAATGCATGGA

Compression Ratio=14/32=0.43.

Worst Case:

Consider the Sequence

S=ACGTACGTAAAAAGTAAATTATATTCCTTCCC and take the length as 8

S1=ACGTACGT

S2=AAAAAGTA

S3=AATTATAT

S4= TCCTTCCC

Here no substring is palindrome so compression ratio is 32/32=1. When the compression ratio is one then compression will not be helpful.

Results:

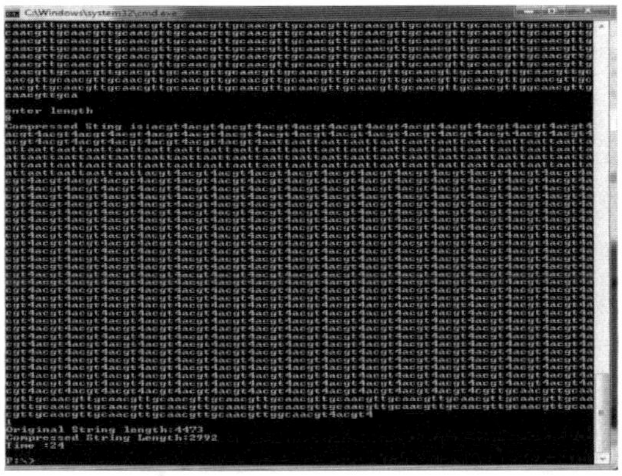

Figure 2 Compression of DNA sequences

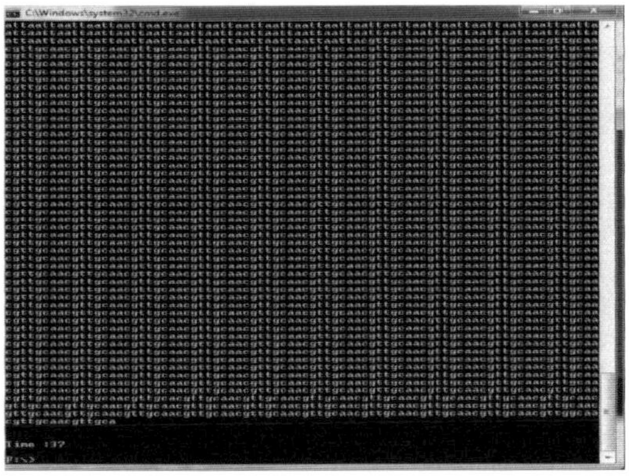

Figure 3 Decompressing DNA sequences

PERFORMANCE ANALYSIS

The analysis of an algorithm measured in Intel i3 processor in jdk1.8.0-131 environment with 4GB RAMS in Window7 Platform for various text documents. The following table showed that the compression and Decompression time taken to compress various DNA Sequences which were stored in various text documents.

Table 1. Performance Measurement for Compression and Decompression of various text documents.

Text Documents in terms KB	Original DNA Sequence	Compressed DNA Sequence	Compression Ratio	Compression Time(ms)	Decompressioi Time(ms)
1	169	109	0.644	3	3
2	417	284	0.68	4	4
3	1251	1120	0.895	11	10
4	2048	1876	0.916	15	17
5	4393	2645	0.602	23	22
6	6425	4654	0.7214	41	38

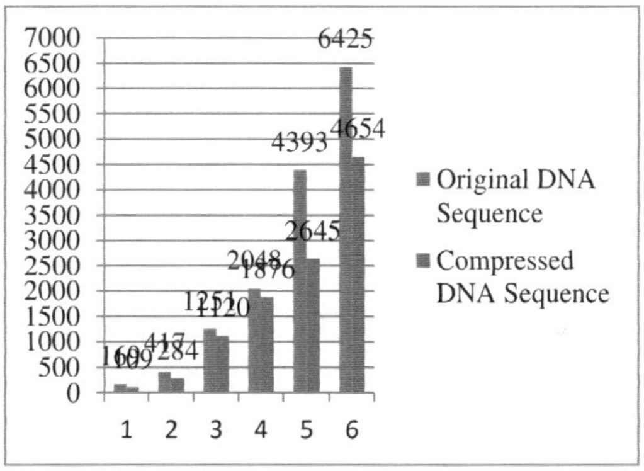

Figure 4 : Comparison of Conversion of Compressed to Original sequences with the time

CONCLUSION

Several methods are available to compress the DNA sequences which are stored in GeneBank. The compression algorithm which is implemented here used the palindrome technique which is meant to reduce the storage space as well as bandwidth while transmitting the data. Thus it gave rise to a lossless compression reducing more than 50% of space. Further it is easy to implement with less computational complexity.

REFERENCES:

1. https://en.wikipedia.org/wiki/Run-length_encoding visited on 12.06.2017.
2. [Ziv, J.1978] Lempel, "Compression of Individual Sequences via Variable-Rate Coding". IEEE Transactions on Information Theory, Vol.24, Issue 5,pp. 530-536.
3. Xin Chen 1," A Compression Algorithm for DNA Sequences and Its Applications in Genome Comparison"
4. Nour Bakr," DNA Lossless Compression Algorithms: Review, Reserch gate Vol 24.
[5] AkimA[1], KolenikovA, FraäntiP." Lossless compression of color map images by context tree modeling",IEEE Transction Image Process,2007,Jan;16(1);114-20.
[6] Ammit Makar, 2Gurit Singh, 3Rajneesh Narula," Improving LZW Compression", IJCST Vol. 3, Issue 1, Jan. - March 2012.
[7] Jing-Yu Cui,∗ Saurabh Mathur, Michele Covell, Vivek Kwatra, Mci Han," Example Based Image Compression", Google Research, Google Inc., Mountain View CA 94043.
[8] Madhu Sunil Dalal," Review Paper on Image Compression Using Lossless and Lossy Technique", International Journal of Advance Research , Ideas and Innovations in Technology, ISSN: 2454-132X Impact factor: 4.295 (Volume3, Issue2).
[9] Pankaj R. Parwe1 , Prof. Nitin N. Mandaogade2," A Review on Image Compression Techniques", International Journal of Computer Science and Mobile Computing, Vol. 4, Issue. 2, February2015,pg.198–201

Online Payment Using Blockchain

Karthikeya Thanapal, *Dhiraj* Mehta, *Karthik* Mudaliar, and *Bushra* Shaikh
SIES Graduate School of Technology,
University of Mumbai,
Maharashtra, India.

Abstract. **Increasing list of records is with blockchain where each record is linked with the help of cryptography. Every block in the chain contains timestamp, transaction details and hash of a previous block, hash is cryptographic hash. This is a secured system, which we plan to replace the current online payment system. A current online payment gateway is prone to hackers where the attacker can tamper into the network, thus creating money loss. And not only this but also the transaction has to go through multiple payment systems which consumes time, also creating a risk of transaction getting failed. So, our system would be using blockchain that allows online transactions which would allow online payments to be sent directly from one party to another without going through a financial institution and in a secured way. This system allows online transactions between two parties based on cryptographic proof without relying and trusting for a third party. To record transactions, we use proof of work algorithm which makes computationally impractical for an attacker to change. Digital signatures provide part of the solution for ensuring the security and integrity of the data that is recorded onto a blockchain.**

I. INTRODUCTION

A blockchain is a public ledger of information collected through a network that sits on top of the internet. It is how this information is recorded that gives blockchain its groundbreaking potential.

Blockchain [1], as its name suggests, consists of multiple blocks strung together. The words "block" (digital pieces of information) and "chain" (stored in a public database). Each block in the network containing the data is secured and connected to each other with the help of cryptography principles Data cannot be changed or altered once recorded in a block, making it impossible to do so without it being seen by the other participants on the network

A node can be any electronic device, including a computer, phone, a printer or even a fridge, as long as it is connected to the internet. All nodes are equal in importance on a blockchain, but a node can have different roles in making a blockchain work. In comparison to the normal network, the blockchain network is completely different having no central point that stores and controls information. Instead, the responsibility to look after the network and store information is shared by different devices, known as peers, on that network. This is why a blockchain network is known as a peer-to-peer network. Instead, information is being constantly recorded and interchanged between all of the participants on the network.

Cryptography is used in blockchain as a means of ensuring transactions are done safely, while securing all information and storages of value. Therefore, anyone using blockchain can have complete confidence that once something is recorded on a blockchain, it is done so legitimately and in a manner that preserves security. Integrity of the data is ensured using digital signature, which is the main aspect of data recorded in blockchain Genesis block is the first block of blockchain, contains its transactions that, when combined and validated, produce a unique hash. This hash and all the new transactions that are being processed are then used as input to create a unique hash that is used in the next block in the chain. This ensures that each block links to its previous block through its hash, forming a chain back to the genesis block, so the name blockchain.

Online transaction has gained a huge market for payment and hence becomes important to look into its cons as well as flaws. The current payment gateway systems include various third party system, which is time consuming because it happens that the transaction has to go through multiple third parties which also creates the risk of transaction getting failed. The very next important factor is security, where the current system is not fulfilling the expectations of the customer. This is because there are various cases breaking the security of the transaction where the attacker tampers into the network and leading to money loss and also the faith of the customers is lost. Then there comes additional transactional charges which is point to be looked upon from the customer's point of view which can be reduced using blockchain. Again, improving financial management is a need which can be accomplished using blockchain where we look upon to create a decentralized application. Blockchain makes it easy to maintain the transactions on a whole, and also fastens the transactions where the current system fails i.e. it is much slower compared to blockchain.

So we plan at introducing blockchain for online payment. Each node i.e. customer side transaction would be recorded in the blockchain. The current public blockchains available are Ethereum, Bitcoin etc. Though Ethereum provides a platform to create our own smart contracts, but since it is a public network the transaction details get visible to all rather than just showing it to a sub-network where only respective people get to view their transactions.

We aim at creating our own public network where MongoDB acts as the blockchain database. All the transactions would be first validated through miners and then stored as a chain in MongoDB. Every time a user tries to have a transaction first its been shared with the miners. There would be specific number of miners who would be using of proof of work for validation and then their results will be shared with each other to finally validate the transaction and then added to the chain in the MongoDB.

II. LITERATURE SURVEY

Nakamoto, Satoshi [2]. In this paper, the complete mechanism of blockchain technology for a electronic cash system that basically allows online payments to be sent directly from one party to another without going through a financial institution is presented. It explains a network system which is distributed i.e. peer to peer network which resulted to be a solution for double spending and the Proof of Work algorithm for carrying out safe and secure transactions.

Judmayer, Aljosha et.al [3] presented an overview of blockchain technology in technical point of view also introduced the concepts of cryptographic currencies and the consensus ledgers. This paper mainly focused on the Bitcoin cryptographic currencies saying that the current scientific community is relatively slowly to this emerging and fast-moving field of blockchain technology reason as not sufficient resources available other than bitcoin. It explained deeply about bitcoin and why it has gained a huge market and interest in today's technology and also highlights the challenges in the area of digital assets management and presents a discussion of Bitcoin usability, privacy, and security challenges from the user's perspective, the concept, characteristics, need of Blockchain and how Bitcoin works. It attempts to highlights role of Blockchain in shaping the future of banking, financial institutions.

Zibin Zheng et al. [4] provided an overview of blockchain architecture firstly and compared some typical consensus algorithms used in different blockchains. Also discussed various blockchain based applications that are covering numerous fields like financial services, reputation system, IOT so on. Furthermore, technical challenges of blockchain technology such as scalability of security problems waiting to be overcome and recent advances are briefly listed and possible future trends for blockchain.

III. SYSTEM DESIGN

Fig 1. explains the workflow of usage of Blockchain in Online payment system. When the user initializes a transaction, a block is been created which is sent for the confirmation or verified using the consensus algorithm. After the successful verification the block gets added in the chain and transaction is done.

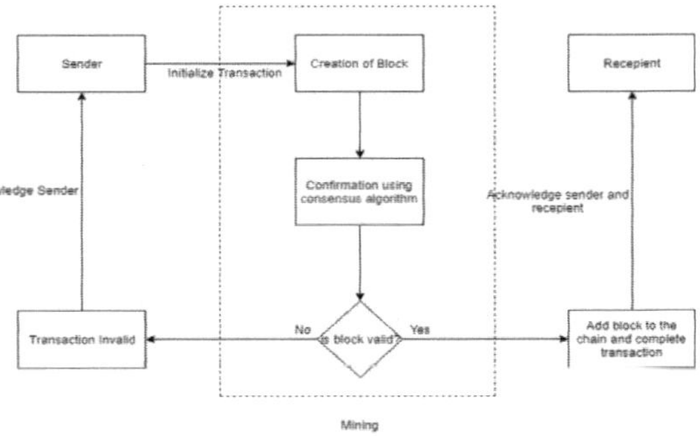

Fig 1. System Design

A. *METHODOLOGY*

Every time a new user starts with our application, he/she has to register in the application with the account details. As soon as the user registers himself/herself a private key is generated for account recovery. This private key is generated using random-words npm package which generates a 12-words private key. And the input to this random-words package is the account details added by the user. This private key has to be privately stored by the user for account recovery in the future, and also this secures the user account from being compromised.

After successful registration, the user can login into the application using the username and password, where each user is uniquely identified by his/her username. Post successful login the user can initiate the transaction, where he/she can send the money to the other users with in the application. Once user initiates the transaction, it is been shared with all the miners. Initially, a hash value is generated for the transaction using the sender's username, receiver's username, the amount and timestamp. Timestamp parameter makes sure that each block is unique which in turn generates a unique hash value.

Now in the MongoDB we have 3 collections. One is the user collection having all the user account details. Then we have transaction collection which contains the validated transactions. Here, the UserID is considered as the key, and the value is transaction ID and its relevant details. And the third table is the validation table, where after a transaction is initiated it is been added to the table. UserID again remains key and value for this key is again the transaction ID and the hash value generated after transaction initialization.

As soon as transaction is initiated, the transaction details are updated in a real time database which then triggers the miner's application. Now we have 5 predetermined miners, where we have a NodeJS application running in the system. The application here uses proof of work as the consensus algorithm to validate the transaction.

User chain is the complete transaction details which is been encrypted using user's private key and distributed among all the miners. Once the transaction is initiated by the user, his/her user chain is validated. Here validation is done by first checking the encrypted chain stored at the miner side with the user's current chain in the blockchain. If yes, then transactions proceeds for further validation using proof of work algorithm. If the user chain with in the miner is not same then it may be a case of some attack or malicious activity and the transaction is failed. Our system has 5 miners, so if suppose there are 2 miners who have a different user chain, then we take those encrypted user chain, and try decrypting it using user's private key. If its getting decrypted than that user chain is correct and others are being the wrong ones, so accordingly we update the correct user chain among the miners and roll back the transaction. After the chain validation, we go with proof of work.

Going deeper, proof of work is a requirement to define an expensive computer calculation, also called mining, that needs to be performed in order to create a new group of trustless transactions (the so-called block) on a distributed ledger called blockchain.
Mining serves as two purposes:

1. To verify the legitimacy of a transaction, or avoiding the so-called double-spending;
2. To create new digital currencies by rewarding miners for performing the previous task.

So in our application the difficulty level is set to 4. So the hash value must have four zeros in the start and then the algorithm tries to find the nonce value. For example if this is our hash is 4dd3426129639082239efd583b5273b1bd75e8d78ff2e8d then the miner tries to find the nonce value where after appending random value if the resultant hash has four zeros in the start then that value is considered as the nonce value. Once nonce value is determined, the value is shared between the miners. We again have a database, where for each transaction we have the miner and their nonce value. If the maximum number of miners have the same nonce value then the transaction is validated or it is rejected. The difficulty level is set to 4 precisely because if it is kept more than 4, the time consumption would be more and if set less than 4 probability of finding the nonce value becomes easy.

Now, the hash sent by the user is encrypted using the generated nonce value. Then at the server side, we try to decrypt the hash value using the nonce value sent by the miners. This is just to confirm that, no attack is been performed or data is been manipulated while sharing it between the users and miners. So if we are able to decrypt the hash value using the nonce value the transaction is added to the transaction table with respect to the particular UserID as the key who initiated the transaction. And these transactions are fetched and viewed in the application. Else the transaction is failed. This way we can also tackle the 51% attack.

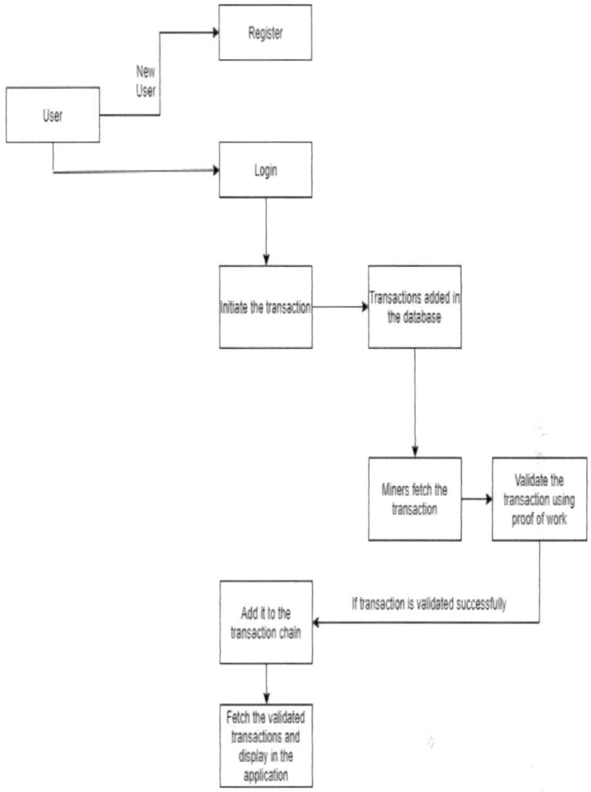

Fig 2. Workflow

B .RESULTS AND DISCUSSIONS

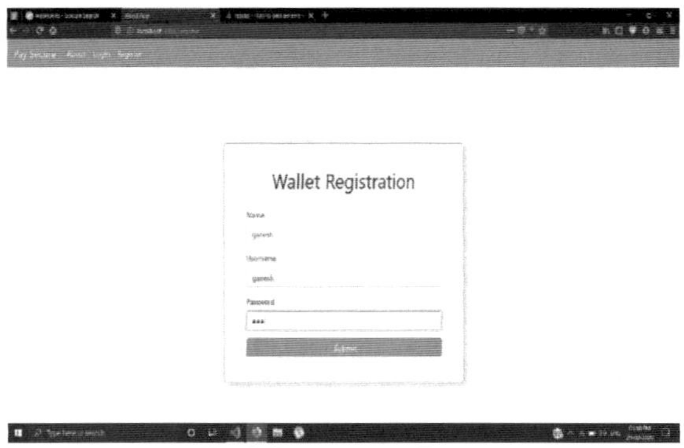

Fig 3. Registration Page

As shown in Fig 3. The user registers himself/herself first where the following details are mandatory and then the private key is generated. Here the username has to be unique, as the user is identified by the username.

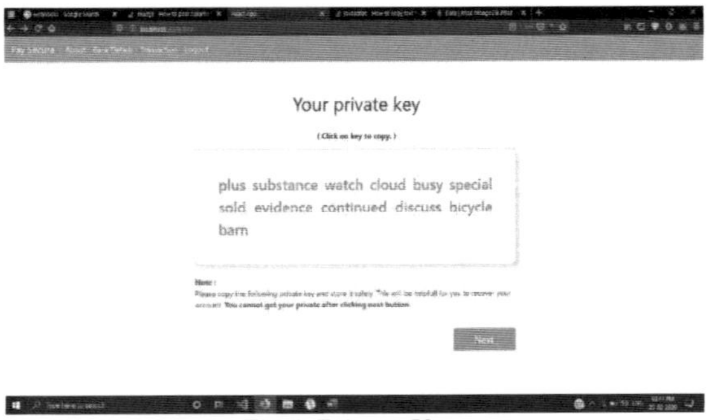

Fig 4. Private Key

In Fig 4. The Private key has to be stored separately by the user, as this private key is used for account recovery.

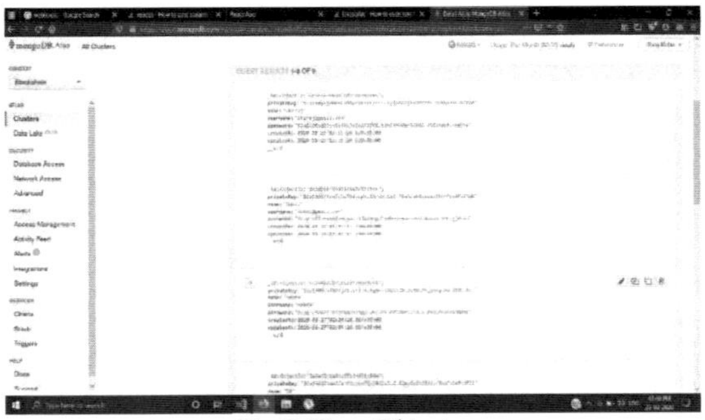

Fig 5. User Objects

The user details are added into collections shown in Fig 5.

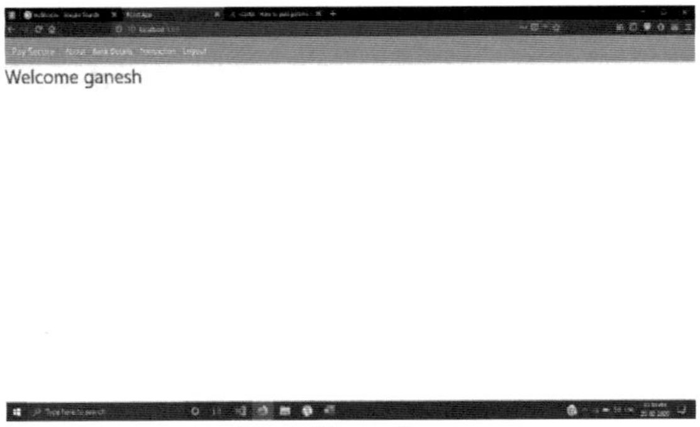

Fig 6. Home Page

Once the user is logged in successfully he/she is redirected to the homepage as shown in Fig 6. Here the user can link the virtual bank account or perform the transactions.

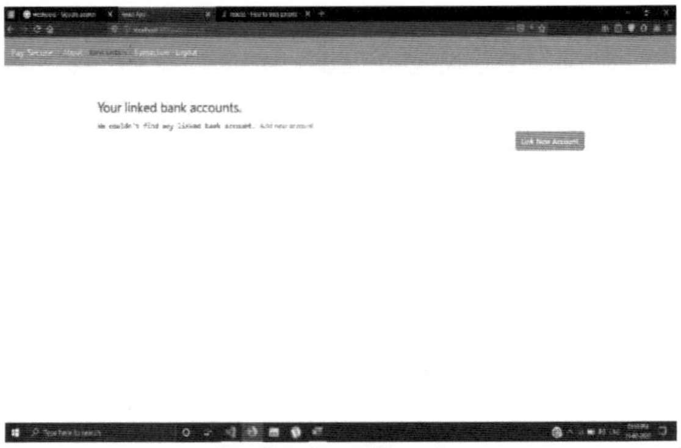

Fig 7.1. Bank Details

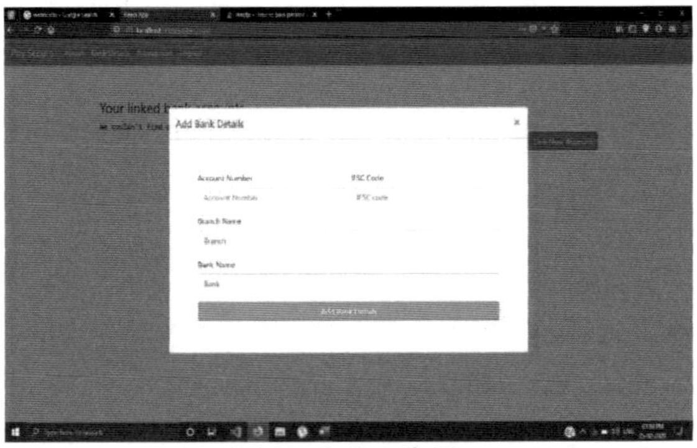

Fig 7.2. Bank Details Form

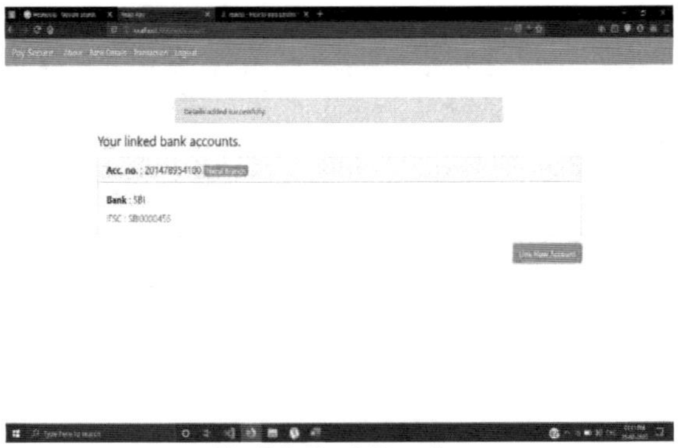

Fig 7.3. Bank Details

The above Fig 7.1,2,3 shows how the user can link to the virtual bank account which can be considered as wallet through which money would be detected or added.

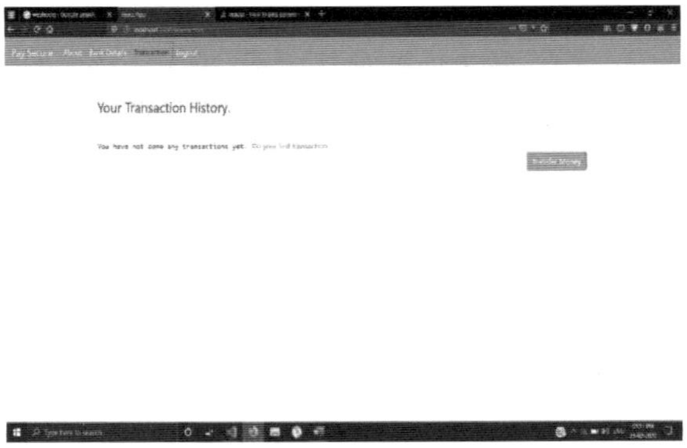

Fig 8.1. Transaction Page

Here the valid transactions from the Transaction chain is fetch according to respective UserID and displayed in this page in Fig 8.1.

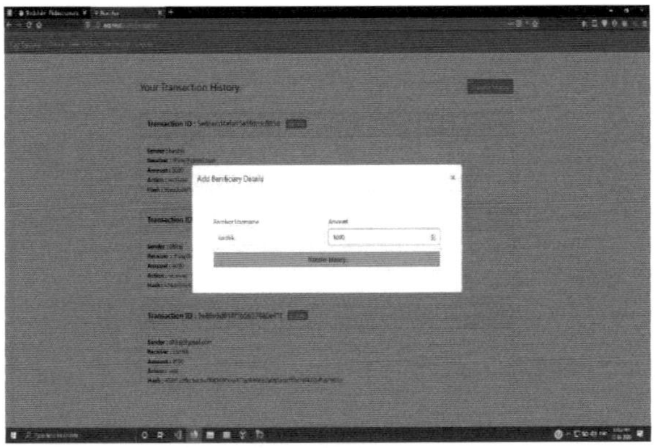

Fig 8.2. Transactions Form

In Fig 8.2. The user may mention the beneficiary's username and amount to be added and then the transaction would be initiated. Post this the user transaction chain at each miner is validated.

Fig 9. Encrypted chain saved on miner's side

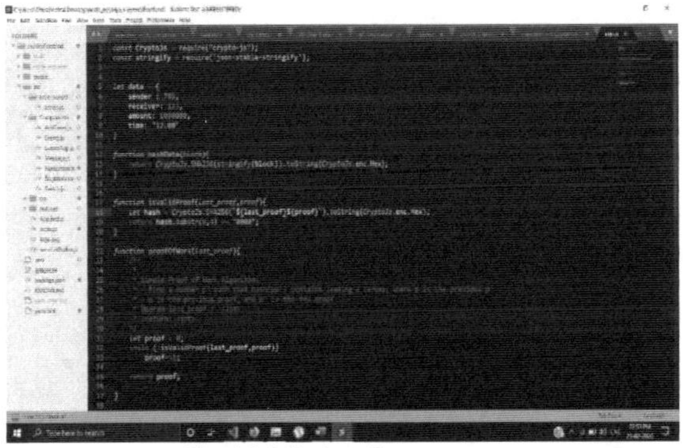

Fig 10. Mining Consensus

Fig 9&10. Explains the proof of work algorithm used by the miners to validate the transactions. Every time it generates the nonce value based on the difficulty value set. The nonce value from the different miners are checked and if the maximum number of nonce value is same, then the transaction is validated.

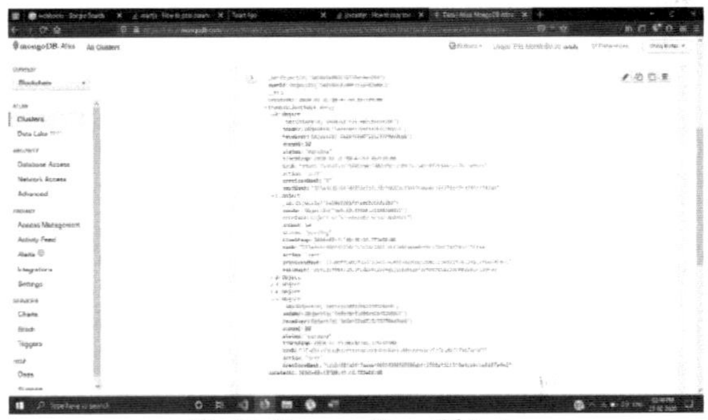

Fig 11. Transactions Object

In Fig 11. The validated transactions are added into the chain and then fetched and displayed to the user .

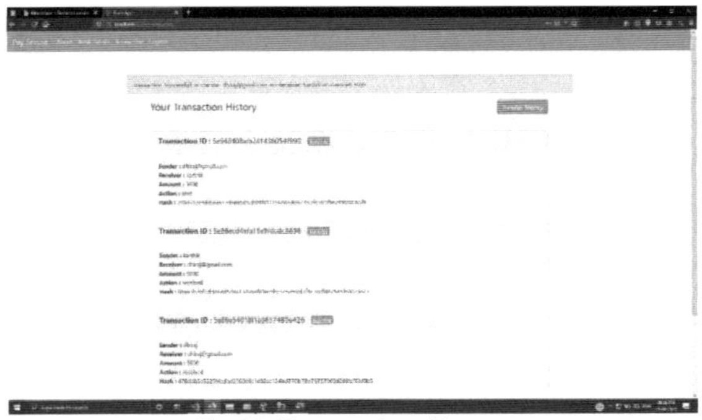

Fig 12. Transactions Page

Fig 12. shows that after successful validation and mining the transaction is successfully added to the user's transaction chain.

Also post transaction initialization when the attack is performed the transaction completely fails and it is not been added to the user's transaction chain.

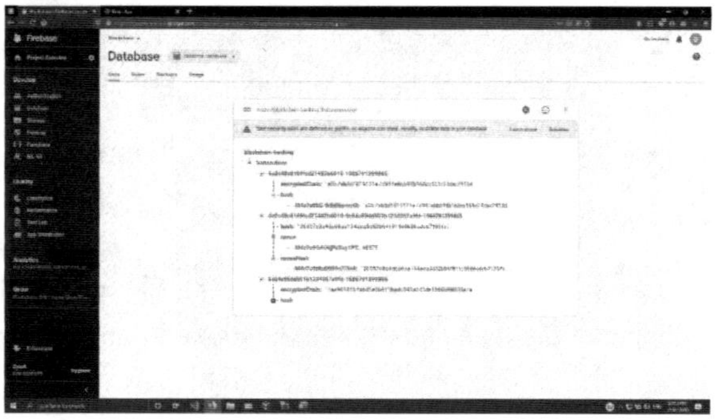

Fig 13.1 Data uploaded by server and updated by miners

After validation and performing consensus algorithm. Miners update the nonce values and encrypted hash values into the server as in Fig 13.2.

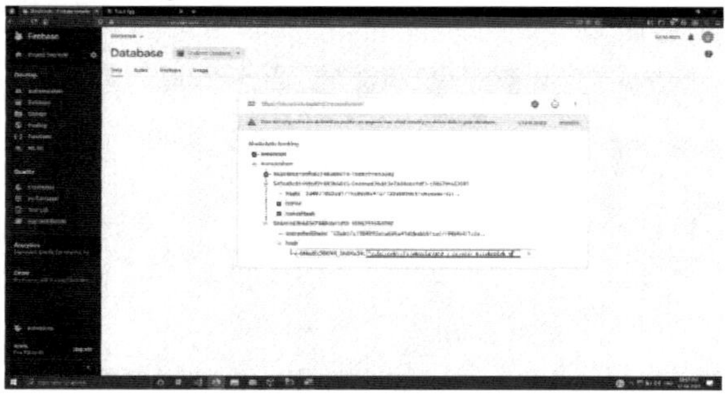

Figure 13.2 Data tampering in database

When some malicious attack is been performed, like here the database is been tampered by changing the value updated by user, the transaction fails which is shown in Fig 13.3.

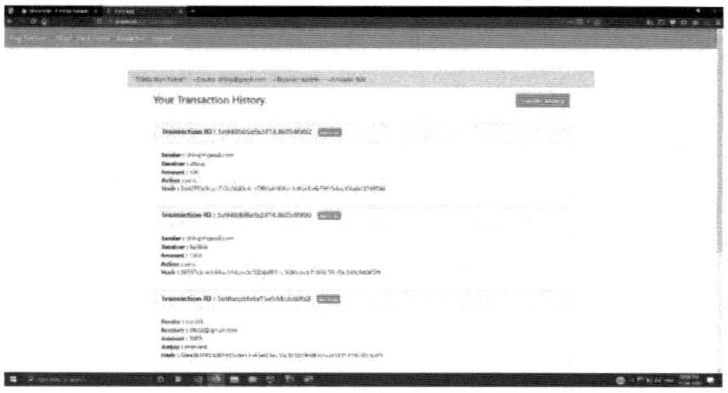

Figure 13.3 Transaction failed on data tampering

Thus, as we can see performing any attacks or malicious activities make transaction fail and hence creating a secured system for online transactions. Thus, we had complete white box testing checking the system's internal functionalities thoroughly whether it is securing the transactions properly

IV. Conclusion

Thus, we have successfully implemented the online payment transactions using blockchain, which aims at securing the complete process. The use of one-way hashing algorithm helps in securely sending the data to the miners and further the miners use the proof of work algorithm to validate the transactions using the hash value sent. The validated transactions are then stored into the blockchain and once stored the transactions in the chain cannot be tampered. Thus, the application aims at giving a secure process for online transactions by overcoming the attacks such as man-in-the-middle attack and also eliminates third-party gateways which makes the entire process of online money transfer faster.

References

[1] What is Blockchain Technology? A Step-by-Step Guide For Beginners. Available Online: https://blockgeeks.com/guides/ is-blockchain-technology/

[2] Nakamoto, Satoshi. "Bitcoin: A peer-to-peer electronic cash system." (2008). Available Online: https://bitcoin.org/bitcoi

[3] Judmayer, Aljosha, Nicholas Stifter, Katharina Krombholz, and Edgar Weippl. "Blocks and chains: introduction to bitcoin, cryptocurrencies, and their consensus mechanisms." Synthesis Lectures on Information Security, Privacy, & Trust 9, no. 1 (2017): 1-123.

[4] Zheng, Zibin, Shaoan Xie, Hongning Dai, Xiangping Chen, and Huaimin Wang. "An overview of blockchain technology: Architecture, consensus, and future trends." In 2017 IEEE International Congress on Big Data (BigData Congress), pp. 557-564. IEEE, 2017.

ITM Web of Conferences **32**, 03008 (2020) https://doi.org/10.1051/itmconf/20203203008
ICACC-2020

MoView Engine : An Open Source Movie Recommender

Vallari Manavi[1], *Anjali* Diwate[2], *Priyanka* Korade[3], and Mrs. *Anita* Senathi[1*]

[1] Ramrao Adik Institute of Technology Nerul, Information Technology Department, India
[2] Ramrao Adik Institute of Technology Nerul, Information Technology Department, India
[3] Ramrao Adik Institute of Technology Nerul, Information Technology Department, India
[1*] Ramrao Adik Institute of Technology Nerul, Information Technology Department, India

Abstract- Recommendation is an ideology that works as choice-based system for the end users. Users are recommended with their favorite movies based on history of other watched movies or based on the category of the movies. These types of recommendations are becoming popular because of their ability to think and react as human brain. For this purpose, deep learning or artificial intelligence comes into picture. It is the ability to think as a human brain as give the output best suited to the end users liking. This paper focuses on implementing the recommendation system of movies using deep learning with neural network model using the activation function of SoftMax to give an experience to users as friendly recommendation. Moreover, this paper focuses on different scenarios of recommendation like the recommendation based on history, genre of the movie etc.

I. INTRODUCTION

Recommendation systems are highly popular in the field of entertainment like movies, songs, clothes, accessories, food, restaurants etc. The increasing popularity is due to the accuracy in prediction. Even before a person can imagine about the next similar movie or song, it is recommended under the section of "you may also like". The prediction of movies or songs of user interest has boosted the gain of companies and profit of such predicting systems. Predictions are generally done on the basis of human interests, behavior, personality etc. For any recommendation system to work properly it should know its audience. Some of such highly popular recommendation websites are Netflix, YouTube, Amazon, Flip kart, Hulu etc. These systems have taken user understanding and prediction to a great level.
Recommendations are generally classified in two types – Collaborative filtering and Content based filtering. In collaborative filtering user with similar interests are found out from a large group of users. Then the user is recommended with items based on the items liked or used by similar users. In content-based filtering, liking of only one particular user is taken into consideration. The formerly liked items by the user are collected and based on the similarity between these items new items are recommended. Some websites also using hybrid filtering, which combines the collaborative filtering and the content-based filtering. Netflix and Amazon Prime is an example of such a hybrid system.
In this paper, content-based filtering is applied using Python and tensorflow as backend. The recommendations done in this paper are made using deep learning that considers a favorite movie of the user and recommends similar ten movies based on keywords, cast, director, genre and popularity of the movie. It also recommends the top ten movies based on the genre (or category) of the movie which uses popularity as the major aspect to recommend the movies.

II. PROBLEM DEFINITION

There are lot of alternatives available on internet when user wants to search for something of his interest. But to choose from such a wide area is very puzzling and frustrating as it is not probable that the user will acquire the information which he wants. Now-a-days there is a need of recommendation system that can think as a human brain. Just like Netflix where even the user is not aware of his favorite movies or series, Netflix suggests the user with what should be watched next. Netflix uses the hybrid method (content-based + collaborative filtering) with deep learning. This project recommends the user with movies of his choice using the deep learning neural network model and content based filtering. This system specifically focuses on the recommendation of movies.
The user will enter his favorite movie and based on the similarity between that movie and other movies, user will be suggested top ten movies. Similarity is checked on the basis of parameters such as popularity, genre, cast, director, keywords. It uses DNN model which is trained on the basis of the mentioned parameters and one hot encoding is performed on those parameters. The concept of model training reduces the time required for prediction and ultimately provides parallel processing.

III. RELATED WORK

[1] An improved approach for Movie Recommendation System includes the hybrid version of traditional methods. The system includes both Content based filtering and Collaborative filtering method. Hybrid method is specially used for improving quality of the recommendation system. Improved version of recommendation uses Genetic Methodology for implementation and Support Vector Machine as a classifier. Hybrid approach helps to get advantages from both the methods as well as removes the drawbacks of both methods. Due to combination of the two methodologies, the proposed approach shows an

improvement in accuracy, scalability and quality of recommendation.

[2] Recommendation using Collaborative Filtering is the main approach of the above system. Collaborative filtering systems analyses the user's behavior and preferences and predict what they would like based on similarity with other users. The system is implementation of Collaborative Filtering algorithm using Apache Mahout. Apache Mahout is Big Data component which provides machine learning libraries. Matplotlib is one of the Python libraries used for machine learning. The entire system is implemented using the combination of Collaborative filtering and Apache Mahout.

[3] Movie Recommendation system is based on the Collaborative Filtering method. The paper focuses on how to design reliable and highly accurate algorithm for movie recommendation. Java Language on a Ubuntu System is specially used for recommendation. The system also uses MapReduce Framework of Big Data, which can easily handle large data sets. By using MapReduce framework, the result shows that the system can achieve high efficiency and reliability in case of large data sets.

[4] In this paper, they have proposed a deep learning approach based on auto encoders to produce a collaborative filtering system which predicts movie ratings for a user based on a large database of ratings from other users. Using the Movie Lens dataset, they have predicted users' ratings on new movies, thereby enabling movie recommendations using a neural network model which performs well in terms of root mean squared error for collaborative filtering. Further the system uses regularization to reduce recommendation errors.

[5] A model combining a collaborative filtering recommendation algorithm using deep learning technology is proposed in two parts. First, the model uses a feature representation method based on a quadric polynomial regression model, which obtains the latent features more accurately by improving upon the traditional matrix factorization algorithm. Then, these latent features are regarded as the input data of the deep neural network model, which is the second part of the proposed model and is used to predict the rating scores. Finally, by comparing with other recommendation algorithms on three public datasets, it is verified that the recommendation.
Performance can be effectively improved by this model.

[6] This paper introduces content-based recommender system for the movie website of VionLabs. There are a lot of features extracted from the movie by analyzing the text information, they are diversity and unique, which is also the difference from other recommender systems. They used these features to construct movie model and calculate similarity to recommend movies and introduced a new approach for setting weight of features, which improves the representative of movies

VI. PROPOSED WORK

A. Overview of our Approach

The proposed framework is an online website. The system initially contains a movies dataset consisting of 40,000 records. When user enters a movie of his choice one hot encoding is performed on the parameters of the movie such as *cast, genre, director, keywords*. The given movie by the user is parsed through the neural network model and the model is trained with all the words containing the parameters of the movies.
Based on similarity between the parameters of the movies, top 10 movies are recommended to the user. Probability of similarity between the movies is calculated using the softmax activation function. Similarity matrix is calculated in descending order to generate a list of top 10 similar movies. User can also enter the category of the movie he is interested in, for example, comedy movies. Then based on the *popularity* of the comedy movies the system produces top ten movies as a result. You can view the movie details by clicking on the movie name you wish to watch from the recommended list.

The system uses tensorflow as backend and flask framework to generate a user-friendly website. Tensorflow is used in order to support neural network. Along with ternsorflow library, NLTK library is also used for natural language processing of the movie parameters. Natural language processing is required in order to find out the similarity percentage between all the movies. Tokenization of these parameters is done using NLTK to perform one hot encoding. Based on the result of one hot encoding a bag of words is made which contains the result which specifies whether the word is present (1) or absent (0). This bag of words is then given as input to the neural network model to train itself. The output of the model is the similarity probability.
The figure 1 shows a workflow model of the proposed recommendation system. The figure 2 shows how the deep learning model works internally with input layers, hidden layers and output layer.

https://doi.org/10.1051/itmconf/20203203008

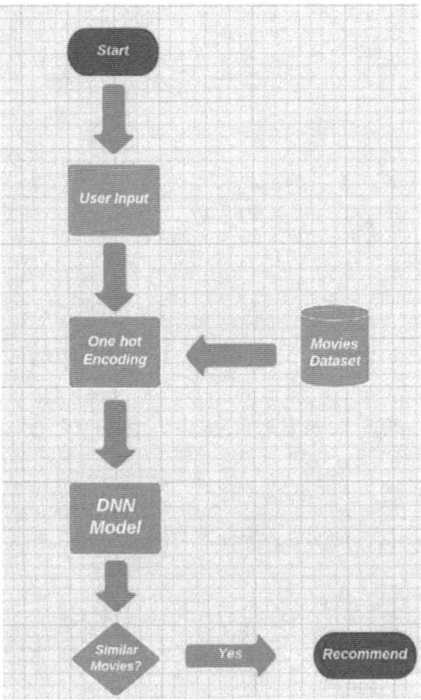

Fig 1. Workflow Chart

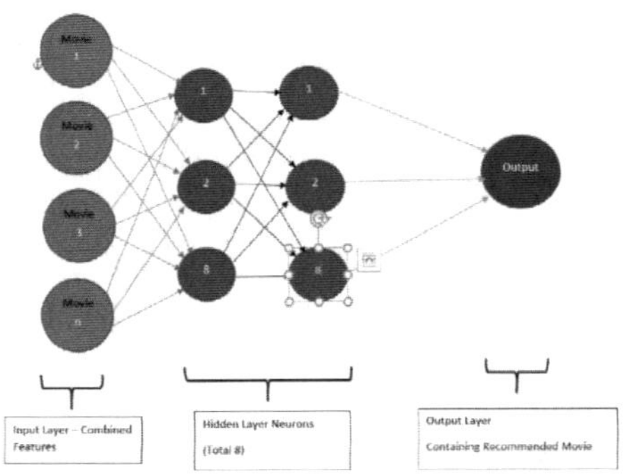

Fig 2. Neural Network Model

B. System Architecture

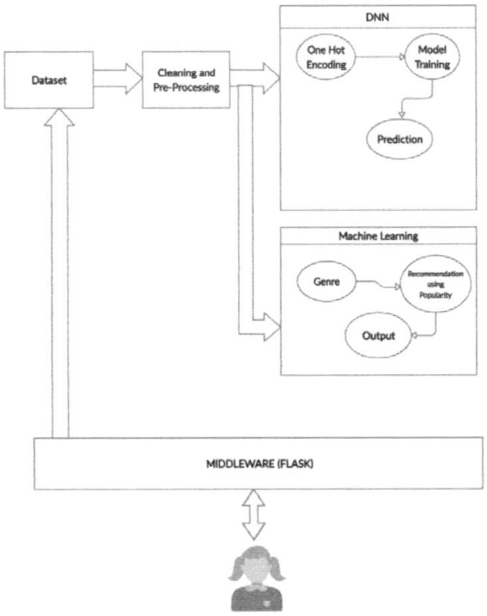

C. Implementation

At first the dataset of almost 40,000 Hollywood movies consisting of release date, popularity, cast, director, genre, title and many more columns is processed to remove all the ambiguities and impurities present in the data. Data processing occurs in order for the data to be transmitted should be clean and error-free. After the data processing and data cleaning is done, one more column known as "combined_features" is added to the existing dataset. In this column all the data for four columns, namely, genre, title, cast, director is combined. Later one hot encoding is performed on this column and a "bag_of_words" is formed which contains either 1 or 0. 1 resembling the presence while 0 resembling the absence. A DNN model is created with output activation function as softmax and the bag of words and one result in predicted by the model. The model is trained with 150 epochs and 7342 steps.

After the processing is completed on the dataset, input from the user is accepted. User is prompted to enter his favorite movie. When the user enters the title of his favorite movie corresponding row from the combined_features column is searched and again one hot encoding is performed where categorical variables are assigned binary representation. This calls the DNN trained model and a list of result is given as output by the model which specifies the probabilities of similarities with all the movies. By arranging the top 10 similar movies the title of those top 10 movies is generated as the output and shown to the user.

The movies are not only generated based on the combined features after user enters the title of the movie, but the movies are also generated based on the popularity aspect of the movie. When an user enters only the genre of the

movie (say comedy) then based on the popularity top 10 movies are generated.
For the implementation of system these basic requirements are needed to be satisfied.

1. Software Requirements
   a. Python 3.7.2 – Used for backend as high level language.
   b. An IDE that supports Python. (For this project PyCharm is used).
   c. Tensorflow – Package in Python used for deep learning.
   d. Flask – A Python framework used for hosting the website.

2. Hardware Requirements
   a. System with minimum 6 GB RAM.
   b. I5 processor or above.
   c. System type – 32 bit operating system and above.
   d. Hard disk with minimum of 250 GB.

D. Deep Learning Algorithm

The deep learning model used for this system is the basic DNN algorithm. Deep learning is all about the use of Neural Networks. Neural networks is based on the neuron system of the human brain. It analyses the input deeply and finally provides an output.
There are many activation functions and types of neural network models. For this system the basics are used. A simple DNN model with 8 nodes in the hidden layer and an activation function of SoftMax. This SoftMax activation function is used only while calculating the output or we can say the result matrix. At first the DNN model is trained using the existing dataset to generate the result. Then the input of the user is applied over the trained DNN model to generate a result matrix. This result matrix is a list in python which contains the percentage of similarity between the entered movie and the movies present in the database. This percentage of similarity is calculated by the SoftMax function.
The figure shows the general working of the DNN model and the SoftMax activation func

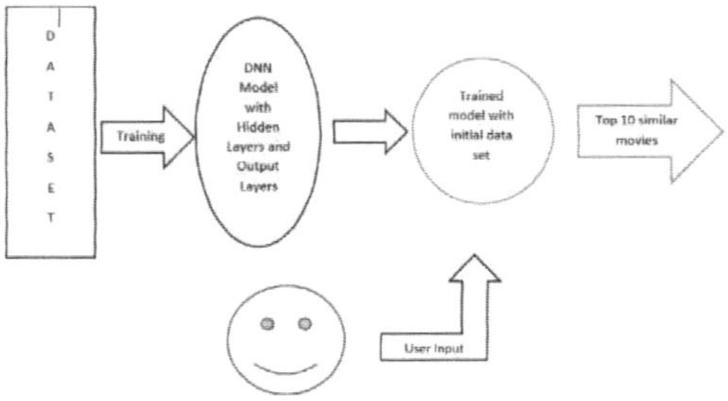

Fig 3. Implementation Analysis

E. User Interface

User interface is the middleware through which users communicate with the system. For the proposed framework user interface is created through a Flask framework of Python. It gives the ability to associate HTML, CSS and JavaScript in the Python environment. A flask website can be personalized as per users need and requirements. For this project, a simple UI has been maintained with a text box hinting the user to enter his favorite movie.
While entering the favorite movie user is also provided with some auto suggestions emerging from the database using JavaScript. This reduces the efforts and time of the user to enter the entire movie name also it becomes easy for the backend code to directly fetch the movie title. Recommendation based on genre of the movie gives the user a broader view of movies if he is not sure about any particular movie. These all things are provided in the user interface which is created using the Flask framework.

V. RESULTS AND ANALYSIS DATASET

The dataset used for this project consists of 40,000 Hollywood movie records consisting of the attributes such as *ID, Title, Release_Date, Director, Cast, Popularity, Keywords, Genre* and many more attributes. The attributes used for this project are popularity, genre, title, director and keywords.

ACCURACY BASED ON USER HISTORY
For recommending the movies based on history of movies by user is based on the DNN model training. The accuracy at the end when the model is trained is 91% with a loss of 9%. For model training attributes such as keywords, title, genre, cast and director are used.

ACCURACY BASED ON GENRE
The user enters the type of the movie that are to be suggested. The type of the movies can be of any kind, such as, Comedy, Action, Sci-Fi, Adventure etc. This recommendation is done on the basis of popularity attribute from the dataset. The accuracy for this is of 94% with a loss of 6% and a Mean Square Error of 0.034.

Table 1. Table shows the summarized content of the accuracy, loss and MSE.

Based On	% Success	% Loss	Mean Square Error
History of movies	91%	9%	0.018
Genre	94%	6%	0.0034

 https://doi.org/10.1051/itmconf/20203203008

Fig 4. Flask UI

The figure shows the basic user interface created using the Flask framework which acts as a combiner for Machine Learning and HTML. Flask is easily manageable and can be developed according to the user needs. Flask is a direct framework provided by Python.

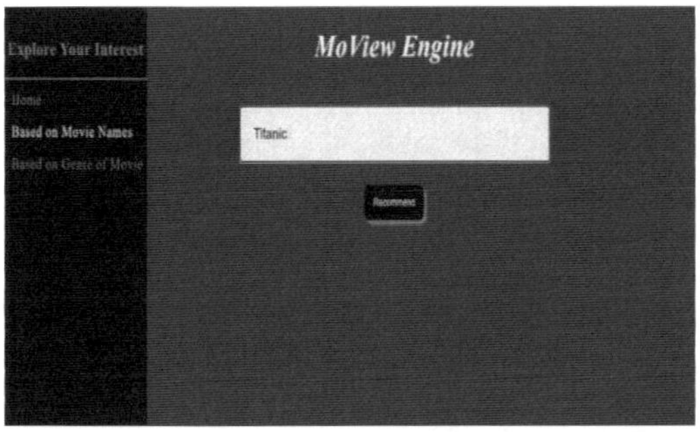

Fig 5. Input by user-1 (based on movie name)

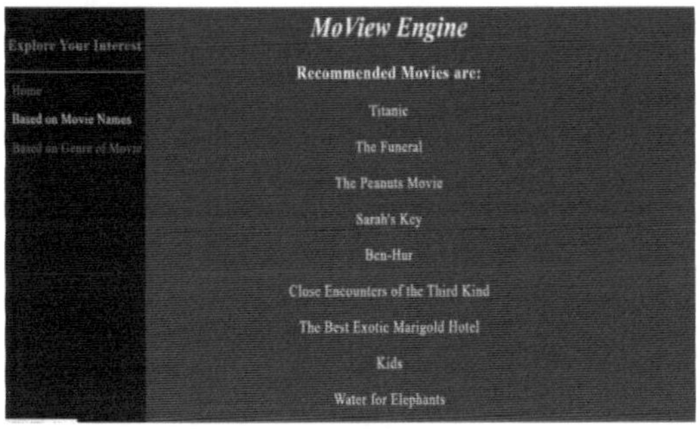

Fig 6. Top ten recommended movies

The figure specifies the input given by the user. Input -1 shows the movie name entered by the user. This name is given as input to the DNN model for fetching the closely related movies based on Neural Networks. The corresponding attributes of the entered movie are fetched and then passed to the trained DNN model.
The next figure shows the top ten recommended movies similar to the input.

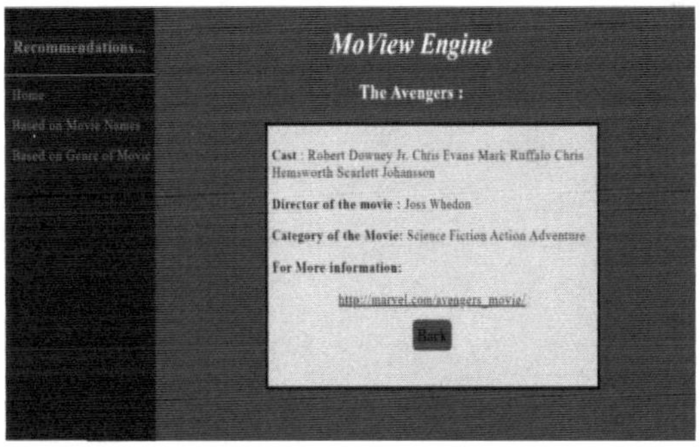

Fig 7. Details of the movie

Above figure shows the details of the movie such as cast, director of the movie, category of the movie and URL for more information selected by the user from the recommended list.

Fig 8. Genre of movie

The figure shows the genre of the movie (in this case comedy). All the comedy movies based on their popularity are suggested to the end user. User can enter any genre of the movie and then the output is generated.

VI. CONCLUSION

The most important thing that any user wishes, is to have the information that he truly desires, to be available at any given time. If the user has to search for some information by devoting his valuable time, it becomes tedious. To avoid this recommendation systems were built. This recommendation system completely focuses on recommending best top 10 movies to the user based on his choice thus saving his time.

VII. REFERENCES

[1] Shreya Agarwal, CSE ME, Indore, India.
An Improved Approach for Movie Recommendation System.

[2] Ching-Seh (Mike) Wu Dept. of Computer Science San Jose State University, Deepti Garg Dept. of Computer Science San Jose State University, Unnathi Bhandary Dept. of Computer Science San Jose State University.
Movie Recommendation System Using Collaborative Filtering

[3] Tianqi Zhou, Lina Chen, Jian Shen. Movie Recommendation System Employing the User-based CF in Cloud Computing

[4] Jeffrey Lund Computer Science Department Brigham Young University Provo, Utah 84602, USA jeflund@byu.edu
Yiu-Kai Ng Computer Science Department Brigham Young University Provo, Utah 84602,
USA ng@compsci.byu.edu
Movie Recommendations Using the Deep Learning Approach

[5] Libo Zhang 1, Tiejian Luo2, Fei Zhang2,
And Yanjun Wu1
1 Institute of Software, Chinese Academy of Sciences, Beijing 100190, China.
2. University of Chinese Academy of Sciences, Beijing 101408, China. A Recommendation Model Based on Deep Neural Network

[6] KE MA: Master's Thesis at VionLabs Supervisor: Chang Gao Examiner: Mihhail Matskin.
Content-based Recommender System for Movie Website

 https://doi.org/10.1051/itmconf/20203203009

Hybrid Image Encryption Technique Using Genetic Algorithm and Lorenz Chaotic System

Vishwanath Chikkareddi[1,*], *Anurag* Ghosh[2,**], *Preksha* Jagtap[3,***], *Sahil* Joshi[4,****], and *Jeel* Kanzaria[5,†]

[1]Ramrao Adik Institute of Technology
[2]Navi Mumbai
[3]Maharashta

Abstract. One of the important application of image encryption is storing confidential and important images on a local device or a database in such a way that only the authorized party can view or perceive it. The current image encryption technique employs the genetic algorithm to increase confusion in the image, but compromises in time and space complexity. The other method employs chaos or pseudo random number generating systems which have fast and highly sensitive keys but fails to make the image sufficiently noisy and is risky due to its deterministic nature. We propose a technique which employs the non-deterministic, optimizing power of genetic algorithm and the space efficiency and key sensitivity of chaotic systems into a unified, efficient algorithm which will retain the merits of both the methods whereas tries to minimize their demerits in a software system. The encryption process proceeds in two steps, generating two keys. First, an encryption sequence is generated using Lorenz Chaotic system of differential equation. The seed values used are the user's actual key having key sensitivity of 10^{-14}. Second, the encrypted image's genetic encryption sequence is generated which will result in an encrypted image with entropy value greater than 7.999 thus ensuring the image is very noisy. Proposed technique uses variations of Lorenz system seed sets to generate all random mutations and candidate solutions in Genetic encryption. Since only the seed sets leading to desired solution is stored, space efficiency is higher compared to storing the entire sequences. Using this image encryption technique we will ensure that the images are hidden securely under two layers of security, one chaotic and other non-deterministic.

1 Introduction

Nowadays, the concern of information security is gaining immense importance, hence the security of confidential information and data in the field of Computer Science is crucial. In the 21th century, images have become an integral part of digital information hence maintaining the integrity, access control and confidentiality of image data from unauthorized users are essential. Cryptography is a vital tool for guarding such information in computer systems. It refers to secure information and communication techniques that descended from mathematical concepts along with a set of algorithms to reconstruct messages in ways that are hard to decipher. Encryption is translation of data into another form, or code so that only people with access to a decryption key or password can access it. Image encryption plays a crucial role in the field of information security and makes the information in the image unreadable. Consequently, no third party can decrypt and retrieve information from this image, thus ensuring complete privacy for the users. In the past years, a lot of research has been made into refining algorithms that deal with data encryption. The genetic algorithm is one such type of non-deterministic evolutionary algorithm which uses its powerful features like crossover and mutation to generate a symmetric key which also augments the entropy furthermore the noise of the resulting encrypted image [4]. Chaos-based cryptographic systems have become an important part of data encryption techniques because of their excellent performance in generating highly sensitive keys and prompt results [1]. Our aim is to propose an integrated algorithm which employs the agility, efficiency and high key sensitivity of chaotic systems and the optimizing power of the genetic algorithm. In this paper, a novel method of image encryption is introduced and the aim to design a system for optimizing and analyzing the whole process of image encryption wherein Lorenz Chaotic System and Genetic Algorithm are employed to encrypt and store the image data securely is achieved.

*e-mail: vishwa.chikareddy@gmail.com
**e-mail: ghoshanurag99@gmail.com
***e-mail: prekshajagtap@gmail.com
****e-mail: joshi.k.sahil@gmail.com
†e-mail: jeelkanzaria1997@gmail.com

2 Literature Survey

Encryption is a process of encoding the data to prevent unauthorized access. With the rapid growth of computer networks, the world we live in sharing images has become a major part of our lives. Privacy is of utmost importance. Hence we need image encryption to secure the image for unauthorized use. Different papers to propose an efficient method for image encryption have been referred.

The paper[1] proposed a inventive chaotic picture encryption method dependent on the opposite fractal insertion function. This framework is connected to produce clamorous arrangements. The groupings inferred are then used to permute the pixel positions to get the rearranged picture by disorganized succession arranging. To upgrade the security the acquired chaotic sequences are then evaluated and used to perform dissemination. A new scheme based on mixed chaotic map and Josephus traversing is being proposed in methodology [2]. The proposed technique comprises three procedures. Initially a key stream generator is structured dependent on another proposed plan of chaotic frameworks. At that point Josephus traversing is utilized in scrambling, next, the segments and the columns of the pixels are traded in extent to characterized guidelines lastly the chaotic coordinates are utilized to exchange the places of every pixel. In the last advance the picture information and four disordered maps are utilized to change the pixel gray level values and break the solid relationships between neighboring pixels of the picture at the same time. The consequences of this technique and security investigation affirm that the framework proposed has better execution. A picture cryptography framework dependent on a chaotic True Random Bit Generator (TRBG) is anticipated in method [3]. The chaotic generator might be a nonlinear electronic circuit that produces twofold parchment chaotic attractors. The estimations of the underlying conditions rationale entryway parameters are the keys of the cryptological framework. Since the dynamic conduct of the circuit is incredibly unusual, a genuine arbitrary bits succession is made through perceived procedure. Likewise, the assurance investigation of the scrambled picture represents the high security of the anticipated topic. A hybridized model for encoding pictures through a blend of hereditary calculation and DNA Sequence was anticipated in procedure [4]. The encoding method comprises two stages Transportation and Scrambling area and Substitution stage. In the initial stage, the pixel areas are modified by utilizing GA to curtail the relationship among nearby pixels. In the substitution part, pixels are supplanted by utilizing XOR activity between the pixel esteems redesigned into double strings and DNA corrosive sub-strings got from an irregular DNA string. The DNA sub-strings are utilized as keys for picture encryption. The exploratory result approves that the calculation is direct, quick and conceivable. A usage of computerized picture encoding framework utilizing the Lorenz chaotic framework is anticipated in strategy [5]. Subsequent to creating a disorganized key stream, the hash estimation of plain picture is inserted to change the initial secret keys progressively to help security. The anticipated digital picture cryptography calculation basically contains two stages. In the primary stage we will in general create secret keys utilizing 256-piece hash estimation of plain picture and furthermore the strategic guide. Inside the second segment the plain picture is encoded by utilizing Lorenz confused arrangements with the key keys from the past segment. The projected method [6] uses adjustive Genetic algorithm to create an efficient variety of optimum clusters centers in real time pictures. Genetic operators like mutation and crossover are done and are enforced with an adjustive nature to try and do work expeditiously to decide the cluster heads. By using this data K-means clustering rule is applied. The output is a clustered medical look. Through the results it may be concluded that the projected technique of clustering of medical pictures using genetic rule is effective. Segmentation is needed to dis-join a complete image into tiny segments such that they collectively cover the complete image. This was planned in approach [7]. within the planned system, we tend to begin by taking a gray image. Noise is introduced during this image using numerous noise models. Afterwards Genetic algorithm is applied for segmentation of the obtained image. Thus, the final segmented image is obtained and at last we tend to confirm the peak Signal to Noise ratio and Mean square Error for noisy image and metameric image. The values obtained are compared with alternative image segmentation algorithmic programs like OSTU and Watershed and it's concluded that Genetic algorithm works best for segmentation of noisy image. An investigation on the employment of other kinds of sequences referred to as chaotic sequences for DS-SS system is planned in procedure [8]. It also thinks about the execution of picture encoding utilizing run of the mill pseudo irregular code generators thereto utilizing new confused sequence generator. A buildup arithmetic number is added to the framework; this strategy is assessed and thought about thereto of non residue numeration framework and it quantifies its execution. To add a great deal of highlights to the riotous correspondence framework Residue numeration framework (RNF) is included. The creators of [9] propose a standard for pseudo irregular range arrangement generator utilizing tests of Chen chaotic framework. This procedure explains the matter of the non-uniform possibility dispersion of grouping created specifically by the Chen disordered framework. The varied applied arithmetic tests check that the arrangements created by our anticipated framework have reasonable factual properties. The test consequences of the security examination approve the high ability of the anticipated system to oppose changed assaults. Further depictions of the use of pseudo random number generators in the domain of image encryption techniques with the incorporation of a perceptron model within a neural network proposed in [10] and the used of transposition and substitution techniques in [11] is used to further the encryption efforts to ensure the abstraction of the information to a great extent. The proposed methodology in the work in [13] features the uses of multiple pseudo random generator techniques in various steps of the mentioned encryption technique which are the chaotic map functions. The used functions being Cubic Map, Henon Map, Quadratic Map, Logistic Map. The work has as mentioned in the paper proved to have better encryption quality in terms of entropy and correlation than the compared works.

3 Proposed Methodology

In the proposed methodology, image encryption algorithm takes part in two major phases using two different techniques of random sequence generation and genetic algorithm (G.A.) to optimize/improve image noise. They are encryption using Lorenz chaotic system and noise enhancement using genetic algorithm. In the first phase we generate a random sequence of integers $K_c = \{k_{c_0}, k_{c_1}, k_{c_2}, k_{c_3}, ..., k_{c_n}\}$ whose values range form [0...255] corresponding to the first layer of encryption. This sequence K_c is generated using Lorenz Chaotic system of Differential equations. The length of sequence K_c i.e. n will be equal to the number of pixels in the image. Each pixel in the original image I is traversed and sequentially XORed with the values in the sequence K_c generating an intermediate encrypted image I_{en_1}. The next phase takes the image I_{en_1} as input to the Genetic algorithm and generates a genetic encryption sequence $K_g = \{k_{g_0}, k_{g_1}, k_{g_2}, k_{g_3}, ..., k_{g_n}\}$ which is another sequence of integral values where individual value ranges from [0...255] having length equal to the number of pixels in the image. These values are again sequentially XORed onto each pixel of the image I_{en_1} and the final encrypted image I_{en_2} is generated. For decryption the sequences K_c and K_g are regenerated, whose individual values are sequentially XORed to each image pixel of image I_{en_2} to decrypt and regenerate the original image I.

3.1 Encryption Process With Lorenz Chaotic System:

The Lorenz system, first studied by Edward Lorenz around 1960, is a dynamical system described by the following nonlinear system of ordinary differential equations:

$$\frac{dx}{dt} = a(y - x), \quad (1)$$

$$\frac{dy}{dt} = (c - z)x - y, \quad (2)$$

$$\frac{dz}{dt} = xy - bz \quad (3)$$

The real numbers given by a, b, c are the control parameters, whereas real values given by x, y, z are called the state variables, and the given equations 1, 2 and 3 are for the time derivatives of the variables x, y and z. For a given set of control parameters and initial set of values x_0, y_0 and z_0 which are the initial state variables are provided. All these values are seed values and combined form a sets call as the seed set which is the encryption, decryption key for this phase. The system is non linear , non periodic. It does not repeat its values over a time period and takes three input variables x y and z. This implies that the system is three dimensional and deterministic thus from a given current state and inputs, it can always be determined what the next state will be.

Step 1: The generation of the random sequence is done by first defining a key /seed set containing the seed values for the Lorenz system as follows:

$$x_0 = 15 + random(-1, 1) * random(10^{-14}, 10^{-2}) \quad (4)$$

$$y_0 = 28 + random(-1, 1) * random(10^{-14}, 10^{-2}) \quad (5)$$

$$z_0 = 8/3 + random(-1, 1) * random(10^{-14}, 10^{-2}) \quad (6)$$

Here the random() function takes two real numbers as parameters random(m,n) where m is the lower limit and n is the higher limit, random() generates a real number v such that, m ≤ v ≤ n. Similarly we consider control parameters as

$$a = 22 + random(-1, 1) * random(10^{-14}, 10^{-2}) \quad (7)$$

$$b = 9.0 + random(-1, 1) * random(10^{-14}, 10^{-2}) \quad (8)$$

$$c = 12 + random(-1, 1) * random(10^{-14}, 10^{-2}) \quad (9)$$

Also, initially we have to define the number of steps after which we will extract values from the Lorenz system

$$dt = 0.01 + random(-1, 1) * random(10^{-14}, 10^{-4}) \quad (10)$$

Step 2: These values a, b, c, x_0, y_0, z_0 and dt are the seed values and the set of values that users needs to store for generating encryption sequence K_c instead of storing the entirety of K_c. Once these parameters are set i.e. a user key is defined, we begin our iteration to generate sequence K_c. Consider an image I having height H and width W that means H pixels in a row and W pixels in a column respectively, the number of random numbers to be generated are H * W. That means H * W values or samples of x , y and z are considered.

Let x_{i-1}, y_{i-1} and z_{i-1} be the values of x, y and z at iteration i-1 respectively. The values for x, y and z in the next iteration is given by:

$$x_i = x_{i-1} + dx_i, \quad (11)$$

$$y_i = y_{i-1} + dy_i, \quad (12)$$

$$z_i = z_{i-1} + dz_i, \quad (13)$$

Substituting the values of dx, dy and dz from equations 1, 2 and 3 we get

$$x_i = x_{i-1} + a(y_{i-1} - x_{i-1})dt, \quad (14)$$

$$y_i = y_{i-1} + ((c - z_{i-1})x_{i-1} - y_{i-1})dt, \quad (15)$$

$$z_i = z_{i-1} + (x_{i-1} - b * z_{i-1})dt \quad (16)$$

To generate random whole number less than K. Let S be a key set such that

$$S = \{s_0, s_1, s_2, s_3, s_4, s_5, s_6, s_7, s_8, s_9\} \quad (17)$$

Here s_0 = x, s_1 = y, s_2 = z, s_3 = a, s_4 = b, s_5 = c, s_6 = dt, $s_7 = x_0$ $s_8 = y_0$ and $s_9 = z_0$. Initially $s_0 = s_7$, $s_1 = s_8$ and $s_2 = s_9$

Algorithm 1: The algorithm to generate random whole number less than K using user key/ seed set S:
RandomInt(K, S):

dx = s_3 * (s_1 - s_0) * s_6
dy = ((s_5 - s_2) * s_0 - s_1) * s_6
dz = (s_0 - s_4 * s_2) * s_6
$s_0 = s_0 + dx$
$s_1 = s_1 + dy$
$s_2 = s_2 + dz$
return $|([s_0 * 10^{12}] \oplus [s_1 * 10^{12}] \oplus [s_2 * 10^{12}])|$ % K

The square brackets in the above equation represents rounding off operation to its nearest integral value.

Algorithm 2: To generate random double between 0 to 1 using user key S:
Random(S):
dx = s_3 (s_1 - s_0) * s_6
dy = ((s_5 - s_2) * s_0 - s_1) * s_6
dz = (s_0 - s_4 * s_2) * s_6
$s_0 = s_0 + dx$
$s_1 = s_1 + dy$
$s_2 = s_2 + dz$
return $|fractional(s_0 * 10^{12} + s_1 * 10^{12} + s_2 * 10^{12})|$

Therefore $K_c = \{k_{c_0}, k_{c_1}, k_{c_2}...k_{c_{L*W-1}}\}$ is generated as follows.

for i in range(0, H * W):
k_{c_i} = Random(256, S)

Step 3:To encrypt, every pixel of the image is traversed. Let I_{ij} represent pixel at row i and column j of the image matrix and the encryption sequence be K_c.

Algorithm 3: The algorithm for encrypting the image I using sequence K_c:
Encrypt(I, K_c):
for i in range(0, H):
for j in range(0, W):
$I_{ij} = I_{ij} \oplus k_{c_{i*W+j}}$

Every pixel I_{ij} will be XORed with $k_{c_{i*W+j}}$ i.e (i * W + j)th value the in the sequence K_c. This produces a new encrypted image matrix I_{en_1}.

3.2 Encryption Process With Genetic Algorithm:

The genetic algorithm is an adaptive heuristic search algorithm. It is an soft computing technique which is used to implement artificial intelligence. For a particular problem to be solved we first start with the initial generation of candidate solutions and a function that evaluates how good is the solution based on some fixed parameters called as fitness function. The attributes of the candidate solution which define how the candidate solved the problem is called the chromosome of that solution. Through the stochastic process of G.A., the proposed technique tries to improve these chromosomes. Out of the initial candidate solutions a set of solutions is selected as parents by some stochastic selection process giving greater priority to fitter parents. They are then used to develop a fresh generation of candidate solutions via the operations of crossover and mutation to bring diversity in the solutions. This process is continued and new generations are generated from the previous ones until a stopping condition is reached. The candidate solutions over the generations become more tuned, optimal and better for the given problem.

In the following approach Lorenz chaotic system itself is used to generate all the initial random candidate solutions and introduce the mutations to the selected parents in the heuristic search process of Genetic Algorithm. This therefore helps us surf and eventually discover the locations in the search space where the solution is reasonably optimized i.e. the key sequence gives considerably enhanced entropy/noise after encrypting the image.

In current phase the proposed technique generates another encryption sequence $k_{g_0}, k_{g_1}, k_{g_2}, k_{g_3}..., k_{g_n}$ and genetic key A. Every value k_{g_i} in K_g is an integer ranging from 0 to 255 and the length of the sequence is equal to the number of pixels in the image I. This sequence is called as genetic encryption sequence K_g. The purpose of K_g is to increase the noise in the image I_{en_1} resulting from the chaotic encryption process and also add another layer of security to the image so that the encryption is stochastic.

Step 1: First, an initial population that is a set of 20 such random sequences are spawned $K^0_{g_0}, K^0_{g_1}, K^0_{g_2}, K^0_{g_3}, ..., K^0_{g_{19}}$ and each of this sequence is generated by Lorenz system similarly to how K_c was generated previously thus each sequence $K^0_{g_i}$ uses a set of Lorenz seed values. Let the seed set corresponding to the ith sequence be denoted as $S^0_{g_i}$ where

$$S^0_{g_i} = \{x_0, y_0, z_0, a + a^0_{g_i}, b + b^0_{g_i}, c + c^0_{g_i}, dt + t^0_{g_i}\} \quad (18)$$

For every set $S^0_{g_i}$ initial Lorenz's state values x_0, y_0 and z_0 remains the same as used by the user in the Lorenz encryption process, only the sampling gap or time step dt and control parameters a, b and c differs by a value of $t^0_{g_i}$, $a^0_{g_i}$, $b^0_{g_i}$, $c^0_{g_i}$ respectively. They are generated randomly such that $10^{-14} \leq t^0_{g_i}, a^0_{g_i}, b^0_{g_i}, c^0_{g_i} \leq 10^{-6}$.
The superscript 0 represents the generation, in this case initial generation. Thus we generate 20 sets $S^0_{g_0}$, $S^0_{g_1}$, $S^0_{g_2}$, $S^0_{g_3}$,...,$S^0_{g_{19}}$ using which we generate 20 keys $K^0_{g_0}, K^0_{g_1}, K^0_{g_2}, K^0_{g_3}, ..., K^0_{g_{19}}$. Now with respect to each sequence $K^0_{g_i}$ of the 20 new sequences we encrypt the image I_{en_1} to generate their corresponding encrypted image $I^0_{g_i}$.
Algorithm 4: The algorithm to obtain the encrypted image using original image I of size H * W and encryption sequence K = $\{k_0, k_1, K_2, ..., k_{H*W}\}$is as follows:
Step 2: Encrypt(I, k):
for i in range(0, H):
for j in range(0, W):
$I_{ij} = I_{ij} \oplus k_{i*W+j}$

Step 3: For the resulting image from each sequence it's respective fitness is calculated as per the following function:

$$I_{fitness} = I_{entropy} = \sum_{i=0}^{255} p(i) * log_2(1/p(i)) \quad (19)$$

here, in equation 19, $I_{fitness}$ is the fitness the resulting image equal to the $I_{entropy}$ i.e. the entropy of the resulting image. p(i) in equation 19 is the probability of a shade i such that $0 \leq i \leq 255$ in the resulting image given as:

$$p(i) = \frac{freq(i)}{H * W} \quad (20)$$

$freq(i)$ is the frequency or the number of times the shade i occurs in the image I. The greater the value of $I_{entropy}$ the more even is the frequency distribution of the shades in the image and more the noise. For maximum entropy the value freq(i) of every shade i should be:

$$freq(i) \approx \frac{L * W}{256} \quad (21)$$

This state of maxi-ma in the final encrypted image I_{en_2} is what the proposed system tries to achieve via the heuristic search process of genetic algorithm.

Step 4: Of these 20 sequences $K^0_{g_0}, K^0_{g_1}, K^0_{g_2}, K^0_{g_3}, ..., K^0_{g_{19}}$ The parent is selected via Elitism selection process i.e. the parent giving best fitness and a new generation of 20 sequences via mutation process is spawned. Lets say $K^0_{g_i}$ is the selected parent. Values $t^0_{g_i} * 10^{12}$, $a^0_{g_i} * 10^{12}$, $b^0_{g_i} * 10^{12}$ and $c^0_{g_i} * 10^{12}$ are appended to the solution array/ Genetic Key A and the value of it's fitness is stored in global best fitness G and a variable g (generations computed) is set to one i.e. g = 1.

Step 5: After initial population generation and parent selection, mutation is performed in the rest of the generations. In the mutation process first a mutation rate lets say m is set and 20 Lorenz seed sets $S^j_{g_0}, S^j_{g_1}, S^j_{g_2}, S^j_{g_3}, ..., S^j_{g_{19}}$ are generated where:

$$S^j_{g_i} = \{x_0, y_0, z_0, a, b, c, dt + t^j_{g_i}\} \quad (22)$$

Here in above set equation 22 j represents the current iteration or the generation we are on and $t^j_{g_i}$ is a small randomly generated number added to dt of set $S^j_{g_i}$ such that $10^{-14} \leq t^j_{g_i} \leq 10^{-6}$. The values of x_0, y_0, z_0, a, b, c and dt are the same values used in the Lorenz encryption process in user key or seed set. Now suppose the generation is j and selected best parent from the previous generation is K^{j-1}_g.

Algorithm 5: Mutation of parent encryption sequence $K^{j-1}_{g_i}$ to generate i^{th} candidate sequence $K^j_{g_i}$ for j^{th} generation and mutation rate m is as follows:

Mutation($K^j_{g_i}$, $K^{j-1}_{g_i}$, $t^j_{g_i}$, m):
  $S^j_{g_i}$={x_0, y_0, z_0, a, b, c, dt+$t^j_{g_i}$}
  for k in range(0, H * W):
    r = Random($S^j_{g_i}$):
    if r ≤ m :
      $K^j_{g_i}$[k] = $K^{j-1}_{g_i}$[k] + RandomInt(256, $S^j_{g_i}$)
    else:
      $K^j_{g_i}$[k] = $K^{j-1}_{g_i}$[k]

Here $K^{j-1}_{g_i}$[k] and $K^j_{g_i}$[k] represents the kth value in the sequence $K^{j-1}_{g_i}$ and $K^j_{g_i}$ respectively.

Step 6: Thus 20 independent mutations are performed on selected parent sequence K^{j-1}_g to generate 20 separate candidate sequences $K^j_{g_0}, K^j_{g_1}, K^j_{g_2}, K^j_{g_3}, ..., K^j_{g_{19}}$ and with respect to each the image I_{en_1} is encrypted using the Encrypt algorithm shown before to generate $I^j_{g_0}, I^j_{g_1}, I^j_{g_2}, ..., I^j_{g_{19}}$ respectively. Calculate the fitness of each of these images and the sequence which gives the image with fitness greater than G after encryption is selected via elitism selection process, lets say $K^j_{g_i}$, this is passed on to the next generation as parent and its corresponding value of $t^j_{g_i} * 10^{12}$ is appended to the solution array A. Update G as fitness of image $I^j_{g_i}$. If none of the child candidates in the current generation are able to perform better than current G, the entire generation is discarded and the process is repeated. For every computed generation set g = g + 1. These operations are performed unless a stopping condition is reached. The stopping condition being that G ≤ 7.9997 or g ≤ 200 whichever comes first. Finally a solution array A = $a_0, a_1, a_2, ..., a_l$ is generated which is our genetic key and will be an array of values where $3 \leq l \leq 203$ and the image with entropy G is our final encrypted image I_{en_2}.

3.3 Decryption Process:

The decryption process consists of the following steps.

Step 1: The chaotic encryption sequence $K_c = \{k_{c_0}, k_{c_1}, k_{c_2}, k_{c_3}, ..., k_{c_n}\}$ is regenerated using the values a, b, c, x_0, y_0, z_0 and dt that are entered by the user that is the user key.

Step 2: For genetic decryption we first generate the initial sequence K form the Lorenz seed set S_0 derived from the genetic key A as follows

$$S_0 = \{x_0, y_0, z_0, a+A[0], b+A[1], c+A[2], dt+A[3]\} \quad (23)$$

Step 3: Then perform mutation on the key sequence K:
Algorithm 6: Mutation on key sequence K using seed set S and genetic key A and mutation rate m:

Mutation(S, A, K, m):
  for j in range(4, l + 1):
    S_{j-3}={x_0, y_0, z_0, a, b, c, dt + A[j]}
    for i in range(0, H * W):
      r := Random(S_{j-3})
      if r ≤ m:
        K[i] = K[i] ⊕ RandomInt(256, S_{j-3})

Thus K is mutated into the genetic encryption sequence K_g

Step 4: Using the generated keys in the above process $K_g=\{k_{g_0}, k_{g_1}, k_{g_2}, ..., k_{g_n}\}$ and $K_c=\{k_{c_0}, k_{c_1}, k_{c_2}, ..., k_{c_n}\}$ to decrypt image I_{en_2}

Algorithm 7: Decryption of image I_{en_2} using encryption sequences K_g and K_c is as follows:
Decrypt(I_{en2}, K_g, K_c):
    for m in range(0, H):
        for n in range(0, W):
            $I_{mn} := I_{mn} \oplus k_{g_{m*W+n}} \oplus k_{c_{m*W+n}}$

Where I_{mn} represents pixel at position (m,n) of image I_{en_2}. This will thus help us the original image I. Once the Genetic key A for the image is obtained, it can be used for both future encryption and decryption rapidly.

4 Results And Discussion

This chapter provides us with the detailed analysis and outcome of the proposed image encryption technique in terms of image entropy, standard deviation of pixel states and time. It also analyses the Lorenz sequence sensitivity with respect to the initial seed values(user's key).

4.1 Results

Through the proposed work the following are the outcomes.

• The first stage involves using Lorenz chaotic system which generates a sequence K_c XORed onto the original image figure 1 Cameraman of size 256x256. Applying the Chaotic encryption process we get the encrypted figure 2. This is the intermediate encrypted image denoted as I_{en_1} in the proposed methodology. I_{en_1} has an image Entropy of 7.99691 and the control parameters a, b and c, initially x, y, and z state values i.e.: x_0, y_0 and z_0 and sampling gap/step size dt in they user key are as follows

Figure 1. Original Image

$$a = 14.996842793294382,\ b = 27.999174693379107,\ c = 2.656926910693863,$$
$$x_0 = 21.991698467920756,\ y_0 = 11.993968326510558,$$
$$z_0 = 8.998217020214971,$$
$$dt = 0.010007020214971$$

• The part following this is the generation of genetic key and encryption sequence to add the second layer of security which adds stochastic elements to the encryption process and enhances the image noise. Here new Lorenz seeds sets are generated from seed values used in the previous process to generate random initial population of candidate solutions and the best are selected by Elitism selection. Then again new seed sets are used to generate random sequence to mutate the parent and next generation is generated. Mutation rate of 0.5% i.e. m = 0.005 was chosen. Described operations are carried out for over 200 iterations or till the an image with entropy greater than 7.99971 is reached which ever comes first. Thus out our final encryption sequence K_g, genetic key A and final encrypted image I_{en_2} figure 3 is obtained.

Figure 2. Encrypted Image after first stage

Figure 3. Encrypted Image after final stage

The figure 4 demonstrates the gradual improvement in the encrypted image fitness as the whole G.A. process progresses. Chaotic encryption gave an image noise of 7.99691 which was improved by genetic Key to 7.9997. All of these methods have image entropy greater than 7.9997 which means information leakage in the encryption scheme is negligible.

• Now if we change the value of dt during the decryption process by adding 10^{-14} and then try to decrypt the image:

Thus the proposed system has demonstrated the high sensitivity of the user key and decryption process to the initial parameters. Changing even one of the parameters by a factor of 10^{-14} will lead to a completely different sequence hence failing to successfully decrypt the image. This is because Lyapunov exponents are a measure that is

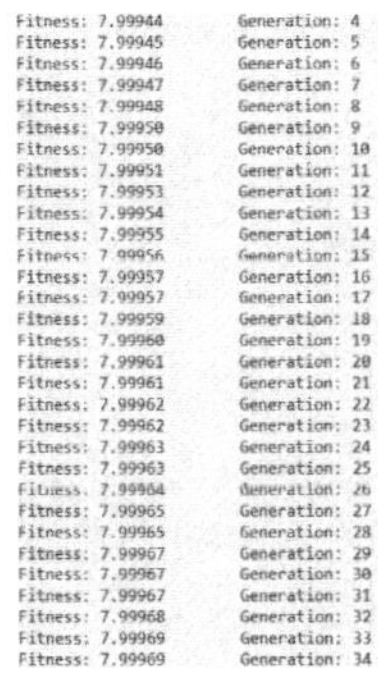

Figure 4. Genetic Optimization

Figure 5. Failed decryption using wrong key

used to quantify the sensitivity of system to initial state or condition. Such chaotic systems or Lorenz system in particular that exhibit chaos have positive Lyapunov exponents.

4.2 Evaluation Parameters

The evaluation parameters taken into consideration for analysis are as follows:

• Key Space Analysis: In order to review the proposed image encryption design, the key analysis is very essential. In this analysis, the key space is required to be sufficiently large to make the brute-force attack unattainable.

• Histogram Analysis: Histogram analysis shows the unique distribution of plain image. For good encryption design, encrypted image should attempt to erase the traces of the plain image. In order to safeguard the information of the original image, it is imperative for the encrypted image to exhibit no statistical similarity with the original image.

• Entropy Analysis: The entropy analysis is practiced to assess the randomness of an image. If an image has an excellent random property, it determines that the entropy score is close to the maximum entropy value. Its value can be computed by the following equation:

$$I_{entropy} = \sum_{i=0}^{255} p(i) * log_2(1/p(i)) \quad (24)$$

where p(i) is the probability of a shade i such that $0 \leq i \leq 255$ in the resulting image. The greater the value of $I_{entropy}$ the more even is the frequency distribution of the shades in the image and more the noise. For maximum entropy the value p(i) of every shade i should be:

$$p(i) \approx \frac{L * W}{256} \quad (25)$$

• Correlation Coefficient Analysis: The security level of cryptography system is also commonly measured in terms of diffusion and confusion. Therefore, statistical analysis is conducted on the image by testing the correlation 10,000 randomly selected pairs of two adjacent pixels in the original image and encrypted image. Next, the correlation of each pair is calculated using the following equations:

$$r_{xy} = \frac{cov(x, y)}{(\sqrt{D(x)})(\sqrt{D(y)})} \quad (26)$$

where,

$$cov(x, y) = \frac{1}{N}\sum_{i=1}^{N}(x_i - (\frac{1}{N}\sum_{i=1}^{N} x_i))(y_i - (\frac{1}{N}\sum_{i=1}^{N} y_i)) \quad (27)$$

$$D(x) = \frac{1}{N}\sum_{i=1}^{N}(x_i - (\frac{1}{N}\sum_{i=1}^{N} x_i))^2 \quad (28)$$

Where x_i and y_i are random selected pair pixels.

4.3 Key Space Analysis

In the proposed algorithm, the initial conditions of the Lorenz Chaotic System have been employed as the secret keys with the precision of 10^{-14}.

An efficient chaotic system is distinguished for its high sensitivity to the initial conditions. In the proposed algorithm, the initial control parameters 'a', 'b', 'c' and the sampling interval 'dt' each of 14 digit precision post-decimal points is the user secret key or password. The key length is 56 digit, hence 56! i.e (7.1099859e + 74) combinations are possible. The key space of our proposed system is 10^{56}. Ideally, the key space should be more than 2^{100} to provide adequate security in order to evade brute-force attacks. According to this, the key space is large enough for the secret keys and to withstand all kinds of brute-force attacks.

In the proposed algorithm, the initial control parameters 'a', 'b', 'c' and the sampling interval 'dt' each of 14 digit precision post-decimal point is the user secret key or password.

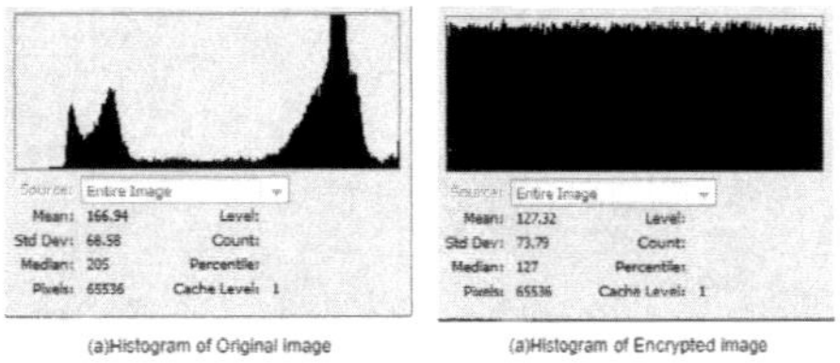

Figure 6. Histograms of the Lena image (a) Original images (b) Encrypted image

4.4 Histogram Analysis

Figure 6 shows the histogram of the original image Lena with the size of 256 x 256 and its corresponding encrypted image. It is observed that histogram of encrypted image is very uniform, and the regularity of plain image is not bought into the encrypted image. The domain of the histogram are discrete integers ranging from 0 to 255 representing pixel shades. The Y axis also contains integers representing the number of occurrences.

4.5 Entropy Analysis

The below Table I shows the entropy of two different images Lena and Cameraman.The table addresses the entropy value for the plain input image and encrypted image. Lena and Cameraman image are of size 256x256

Table 1. Entropy Of Images

Images	Lena	Camera Man
Plain Image	7.575	7.0710
Encrypted Image	7.99965	7.9997

4.6 Correlation Coefficient Analysis

The correlation coefficient between adjacent pixels of original image and encrypted image are given in Table II. The experimental results show that the correlation coefficient between adjacent pixels are high in plain original image and being greatly weakened in the encrypted image Ref [14].The proposed encryption scheme is perfect for coefficient analysis. Lena and Cameraman image are of size 256x256

Table 2. Correlation Coefficient Of Cameraman Image after and before encryption

Criterion	Lena	Cameraman
Input Image	0.9268	0.9567
Encrypted Image	0.00548	0.00145

The comparison of correlation coefficient and entropy of proposed method with Cameraman image 256*256 with other methods is shown in the below table 3.

It is observed in the table above that the entropy and correlation coefficient of proposed method is better than the referred methods. In figure 7 we can see that the disorder brought about in the encrypted image by the proposed method is more than that brought about by the individual methods. Similarly figure 8 shows that the encrypted image produced by the proposed method has least correlation to the original image in comparison to the other methods.

Table 3. Correlation Coefficient Of Cameraman Image after and before encryption

Method	Correlation	Entropy
Lorenz Chaotic System Ref[14]	0.0054	7.9971
Genetic Algorithm Ref[12]	0.0048	7.9904

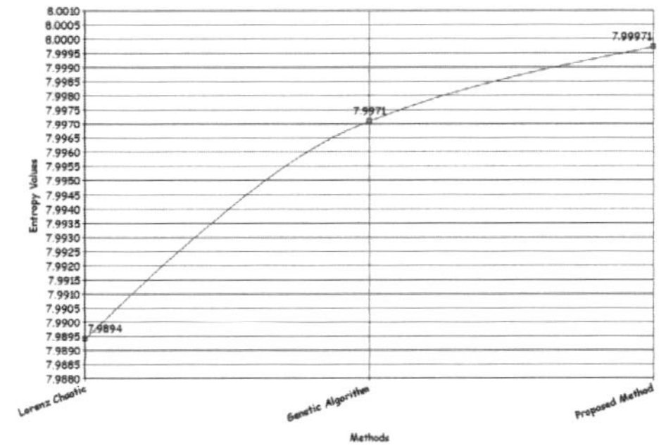

Figure 7. Entropy analysis of Cameraman Image

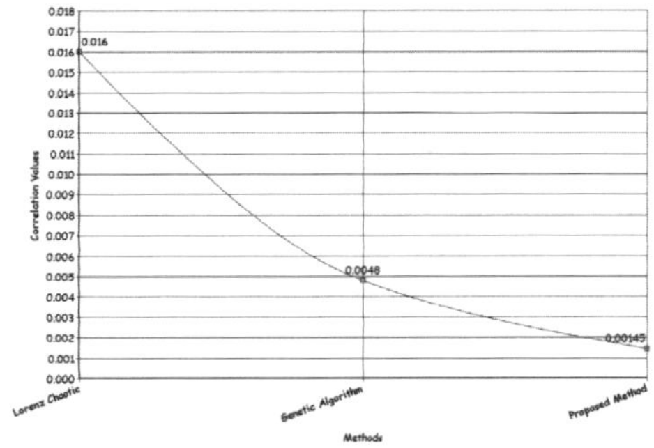

Figure 8. Correlation analysis of Cameraman Image

5 Conclusion

Proposed system has shown an easy and highly optimized way of encrypting images which has been clarified by our design and methodology. Technique first utilizes Lorenz chaotic system of differential equation to generate a random sequence of integers ranging from 0 to 255 which are highly dependent on the initial values, time step and control parameters which form a key that generates sequence K_c to achieve the first level of encryption and a noisy image. Given that the whole sequence can be generated using just the initial parameters the whole sequences need not be stored apart from those initial parameters that are the seed values making it space efficient. Also these values should be accurate up to 10^{-14} decimal place ensuring high key sensitivity, changing those values even slightly will give a completely different image during decryption. Following Lorenz encryption, Genetic algorithm used hence is used to optimize the noise in the encrypted image I_{en_1} generated by the Lorenz System even further making it more random and chaotic giving us a second layer of security to nullify the deterministic nature of Lorenz system and an image entropy close to or over 7.9997 with adequately small pixel correlation of the final encrypted image I_{en_2}. We have hereby demonstrated a way to use Lorenz system to generate the candidate solutions and introduce random mutations in the heuristic search process of Genetic Algorithm to eventually locate the optimum solution in the search space. The merit of our proposed system lies in the fact that our genetic sequence K_g i.e. the solution once generated can be regenerated easily by the genetic key A of length 200 or less for both encryption and decryption process, thus is space efficient because only this array needs to be stored and not the entire sequence.

References

[1] Ruisong Ye, Yinhua Li, Yajuan Li *An Image Encryption Scheme Based on Fractal Interpolation ACM 2018.*.Department of Mathematics, Shantou University Shantou, Guangdong, 515063, China e-mail: rsye@stu.edu.cn

[2] Xingyuan Wamg , Xiaoqiang Zhu , and Yingqian Zhang *"An Image Encryption Algorithm Based on Josephus Traversing and Mixed Chaotic Map" IEEE 2018...School of Information Science and Technology, Dalian Maritime University, Dalian 116026*

[3] Ch. K. Volos, I. M. Kyprianidis, I. N. Stouboulos *"Image encryption process based on a Chaotic True Random Bit Generator" IEEE 2009...Department of Physics, Aristotle University of Thessaloniki*

[4] Saswat Pujari, Gargi Bhattacharjee, Sumyakanta Bhoi *"Hybridized Model For Image Encryption Through Genetic Algorithm And DNA Sequence"*...Tata Consultancy Mumbai, Department of Information Technology, Veer Surendra Sai University of Technology, Burla, Odisha, India Elsevier-2018.

[5] Obaida M. Al-Hazaimeh1, Mohammad F. Al-Jamal2, Nouh Alhindawi3, Abedalkareem Omari *"Image encryption algorithm based on Lorenz chaotic map with dynamic secret keys" SPRINGER 2017*...The Natural Computing Applications Forum 2017

[6] P.Rajkumar, V.Balamurgan, Priyanka Mishra *"Adaptive Genetic Algorithm for a Real Time Medical Images"*...Faculty of Electrical and Electronics Sathyabama university Sathyabama University Chennai-600119... IEEE 2016

[7] Shikha Pathak, Vikas Sejwar *"Optimized Noisy Image Segmentation Using Genetic Algorithm"*Department of CSE and IT Madhav Institute of Technology and Science Gwalior, India...IEEE 2017.

[8] M. I. YOUSSEF, M. ZAHARA, A. E. EMAM, and M. ABD ELGHANY *"Image Encryption Using Pseudo Random Number and Chaotic Sequence Generators"*Al-Azhar University - Cairo - Egypt.

[9] Rafik Hamza *"A novel pseudo random sequence generator for image-cryptographic applications"*LAMIE Laboratory, Department of Computer Science, University of Batna 2, Batna, Algeria...Elsevier 2017

[10] Xing-YuanWang · Lei Yang · Rong Liu · *"A chaotic image encryption algorithm based on perceptron model"*Faculty of Electronic Information and Electrical Engineering, Dalian University of Technology, Dalian 116024, China...Springer 2010

[11] Ashwin Ramesh,Akash Jain *"Hybrid Image Encryption using Pseudo Random Number Generators, and Transposition and Substitution Techniques"*Department of CSE MIT, Manipal...IEEE 2015

[12] Saeed Mozaffari· *"Parallel image encryption with bitplane decomposition and genetic algorithm"*Faculty of Electrical and Computer Engineering, Semnan University, Semnan, Iran...Springer 2018

[13] Mohamed A. Mokhtar1, Nayra M.Sadek2, Amira G. Mohamed3· *"Design of Image Encryption Algorithm Based on Different Chaotic Mapping"* Faculty of Engineering, Alexandria University, Alexandria, Egypt...IEEE 2017

[14] Obaida M. Al-Hazaimeh, Mohammad F. Al-Jamal, Nouh Alhindawi, Abedalkareem Omari· *"Image encryption algorithm based on Lorenz chaotic map with dynamic secret keys"*Department of Computer Science, Al-Balqa' Applied University, Al-Huson University College, P. O. Box 50, Al-Huson, Irbid, Jordan...Springer 2017

Imputation of missing data in time series by different computation methods in various data set applications

Dhiraj Magare[1,*], *Sushil Labde*[2], *Manoj Gofane*[3] *and Vishwesh Vyawahare*[4]

[1,2,3,4] Ramrao Adik Institute of Technology, D.Y. Patil Group, Nerul, Navi Mumbai-400 706, India

Abstract. In a modern technology generation, big volumes of data are evolved under numerous operations compared to an earlier era. However, collection of data without missing single value, is a great challenge ahead. In practice, there are many solutions suggested to avoid the missing values in time series applications. The existing methods used in imputation and their prediction with time series, varies with applications. The existing methods mostly available for imputation are least squares support vector machine (LSSVM), autoregressive integrated moving average models (ARIMA), Artificial Neural Network (ANN), Artificial Intelligence (AI) techniques, state space models, Kalman filtering and fuzzy model. The extensive experimental application data is used to analyze these methods. In addition, a synthetic set of data can also be used to forecast missing value, which improves performance of imputation methods in time series. In this paper, predominantly used imputation methods have been listed with their fundamental computational information along with their verification on set of data mentioned.

1 INTRODUCTION

A time series observations are the observations that have been taken successfully at an equal time interval. The main objective of time series forecast solely depends on the past recorded data. In case the historical data recorded includes few hours or days or months, of missing data, the parameter prediction increases the complexity. This missing data of various real time applications, influences the deviation in the actual output. Thus, this missing data plays an imperative task in many decision-making applications. The applications are monitoring the industrial activities, financial analysis, business resources, and power plant with grid control.

It would create a loss in prediction in different aspects. There are two different types of methods available for evaluation of missing data in multiple steps. Those are direct method and iterative method. The direct method evaluates the forecasting result in multiple step and reaches towards the final value while, iterative method evaluates the forecasted value iteratively until it matches the required step value. In multi-variable time series, various methods are proposed in the literature.

The various methods are such as linear interpolations, Stineman interpolations, Kalman filtering with structural model and smoothing, weighted moving average are used for estimation of missing values for solar irradiance data [1]. Further, time-series forecasting explained in [2]. In this, author had adopted wavelet model technique. The suggested methods might be infeasible to particular set of application or inefficient to predict missing data in real time. Thus, still there is a scope of improvement to exiting proposed methods, and their verification on various data sets.

As the forecasting of time series data plays a vital role, it is very important to find the accuracy of these different forecasting techniques. Different applications use different parameters for the measurement of the accuracy of these forecasting techniques. Shin-Fu Wu et al. [3] used normalized root mean squared error (NRMSE), performance measurement parameter for defining the accuracy of (LSSVM) forecasting technique of time series data. Root mean square error (RMSE) is used to evaluate the performance of the proposed algorithm for missing data estimation of synthetic multivariate time series data [4, 5, 6].

2 Methodology

In this section, most commonly used and advanced imputation methods are briefly described.

2.1. ARIMA (Autoregressive Integrated Moving Average)

ARIMA is Autoregressive Integrated Moving Average models. With the help of time-series data, statistical modeling technique predicts the future values, so this model is used in the field where short term forecasting is needed. It needs minimum 40 past data points. If the data is reasonably extended and the correlation between the past data points is steady, ARIMA model is more efficient compared to the exponential smoothing. Flowchart of Autoregressive Integrated Moving Average

* Corresponding author: dhiraj.magare@rait.ac.in

model shown in Fig. 1. With the help of ARIMA model, stationary time series data can be described as a function of auto regression and moving average parameters.
In flowchart p, d, q are order of AR model, order of MA model, and order of difference respectively (to make non stationary data to stationary data).
AR model is represented by:

$$Z(t) = C(1) *Z(t-1) + G(t) \quad (1)$$

MA model is represented by:

$$Z(t) = D(1) *G(t-1) + G(t) \quad (2)$$

where, G(t) = error parameter, Z(t) is time series data C and D are constants.
Vichaya L. et al. [7] proposed forecasting technique namely, seasonal autoregressive integrated moving average (SARIMA), for missing data imputation, which uses mean value of the global horizontal irradiance (GHI) averages over data. A comparative study of different forecasting models such as neural network (NN), autoregressive and moving average (ARMA), coupled autoregressive and dynamical system (CARDS) is done for forecasting of 1 to 6 hr ahead [8].

2.2 Support Vector Machine (SVM)

Support Vector Machine (SVM) is effective Deep Learning method. The theory of statistics is the basis of machine learning. It is basically used for classification problems and forecasting of time series data. SVM was first developed at AT&T Bell Laboratory in 1970 by Vapnik and colleagues. Forecasting of time series data is difficult with the missing data. Replacing missing data with values obtained by imputation method and ignoring missing data, will affect the performance of forecasting of time series data. The principle of SVM is to discover function which establishes a relationship between input P and output Q.Q=f(P) from set of data points.
Consider input data points

$$F = \{(P_i, (Q_i)\} \in R \qquad i=1: n \quad (3)$$

$$f(x) = w\Phi(x) + b \qquad b \in R \quad (4)$$

F:time series data
R: Real set
W: Noise Matrix
b: Constant
$\Phi(x)$ is nonlinearly mapped higher dimensional feature space from input space

Shin-Fu Wu et al. [3] suggested a machine-learning tool LSSVM (Least square support vector machine). It is applied to time series forecasting with missing data. For forecasting, time series data and local time indexes (LTI) are fed to LSSVM. The results so obtained are compared with the forecasting performance of other imputation methods.

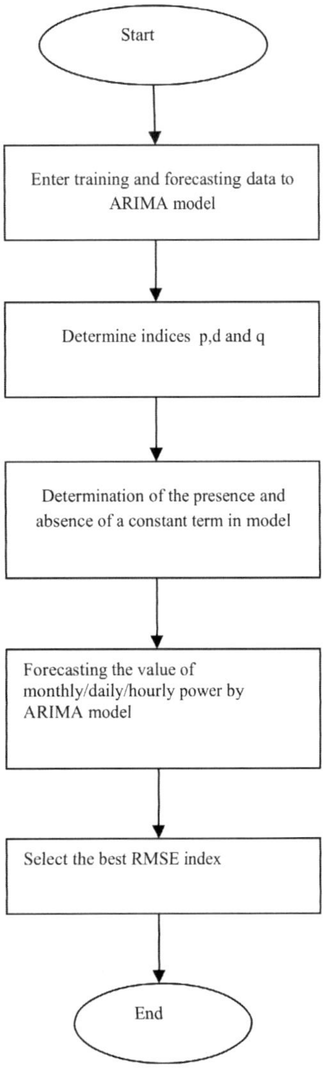

Fig. 1 Flowchart of Autoregressive Integrated Moving Average model

2.3 ANN (artificial neural network)

Recently, ANN (artificial neural network) is most widely used machine learning algorithm that is based on biological nervous systems. Neural network consist of elements called neutron operating in parallel. Flowchart of artificial neural network shown in Fig. 3. Neuron is a fundamental information processing part of neural network. It consists of three basic elements; a set of weights, an adder for adding the inputs, and activation function for limiting the amplitude. The neural network is getting rapid importance because of its capability to offer solution to variety of problems. Flowchart of artificial neural network shown in Fig. 3. Badia Amrouche et al. [9] proposed novel approach, which is combination of artificial neural network and spatial modeling for forecasting global solar irradiance.

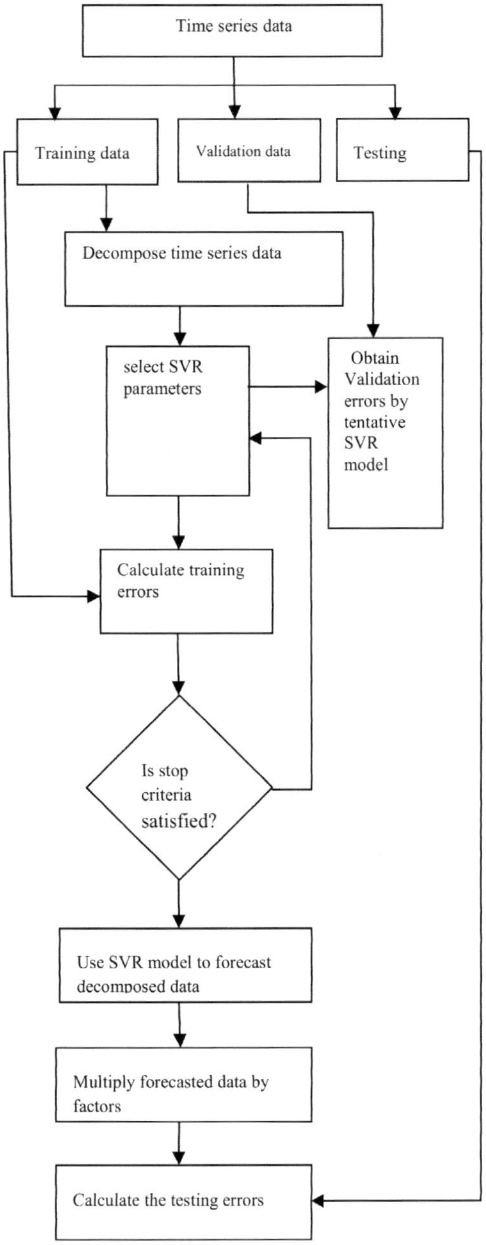

Fig. 2 Flowchart of support vector machine

The application area of ANN is very wide. MLP (Multi-layer-Perceptron) is one type of such neural technique. MLP with back propagation ANN model is mostly applied in various types of real time examples. MLP Model does not assume any prior information regarding data distribution as many statistical models do.

The model consists of a system of interconnected nodes or neurons and weights; it represents the non-linear relationship between input and output. A MLP may have one or more hidden output of a neuron. The model is trained to perform the particular function by adjusting the weights between the elements. Neural networks are trained or re-estimated in such a type that the specific input leads to specific output target. An ANN model consists of input, output layer, and hidden layers. The layers may vary for different applications. The model has capability to learn through training. Training needs a set of data. To minimize the error, training is done to find the different combination of weights. Adel Mellit a, et al. [2] proposed a practical method for forecasting the time series data of solar radiation using ANN. Further, ANN used in forecast irradiance [10].

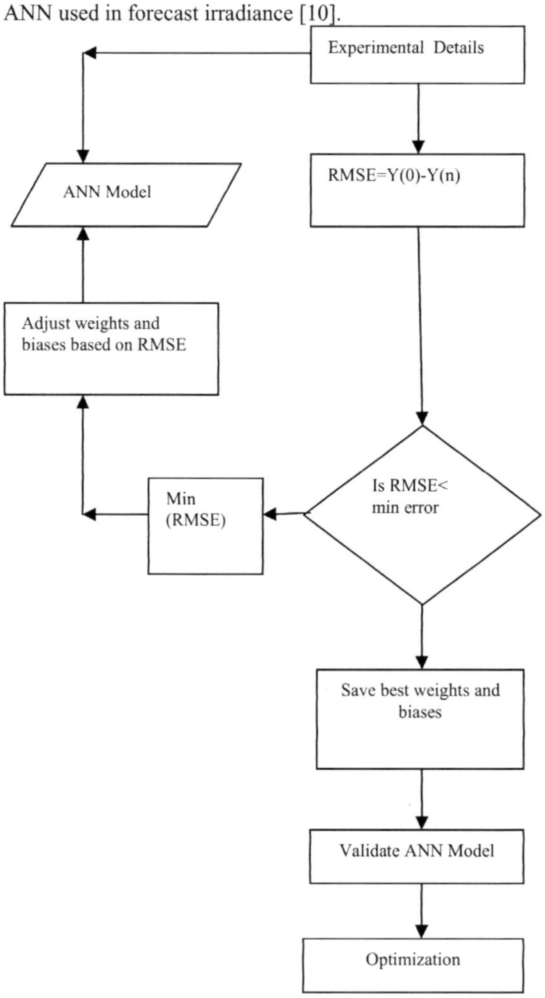

Fig. 3 Flowchart of artificial neural network.

2.4 KALMAN FILTER

The optimal estimation of states of the system can be implemented by kalman filtering algorithm, with the help of least squares approximation or maximum likelihood estimation. Due to this, the accuracy of time series forecasting improves. Flowchart of generalised kalman filter shown in Fig. 4.

The algorithm is based on the discretization of linear dynamic system. It has capability to predict the current state with the help of measurement and with predicted state from previous time step. The model can be mathematically represented as :

$$X_t = A_t X_{t-1} + W_t \quad (5)$$

$$Y_t = H_t X_t + V_t \quad (6)$$

where X_t : State vector at time t.

A_t: State transition matrix.

Y_t: The vector of measurement.

H_t: Transformation matrix.

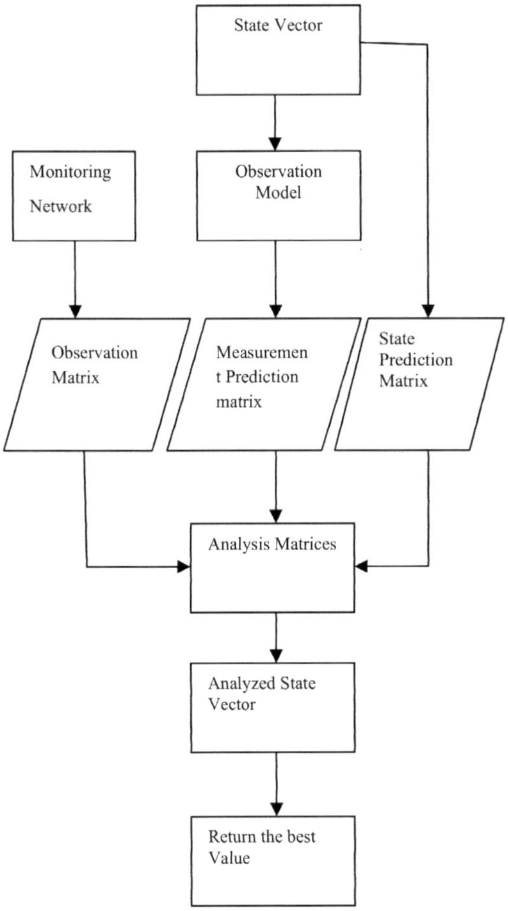

Fig. 4 Flowchart of generalised kalman filter.

3 Results and Discussion

In this section, mostly used important imputation methods have been briefly explained. Imputation methods along with data used in that particular method have been list out in Table 1. The performance parameter also is incorporated in Table 1.

Wu et. al. [3] discussed that LTI offers comparable or even better NRMSE values. Furthermore, LTI runs much faster, compared with other imputation methods, including mean, hot deck and auto regression (AR). Shi. et. al. [4] infers that even for high (90%) missing ratio the RMSE calculated would be small using proposed methods. Hence, this proposed method can be an alternative model to find the missing values in time series under large scaled multivariable system. The suggested method can be used in various applications such as, electric equipment monitoring, climate or financial forecasting. The environment state monitoring, security inspection etc. are some of the applications. Mellit et. al. [2] proposed prediction of 24 hour in advance of solar irradiance is possible with Multi layer Perceptron model with consideration of mean value of solar irradiance. The air temperature, as well as day of month also been included in forecasting. The MLP-forecaster finds application in GCPV plant, solar irradiance forecasting of (24 hour in advance), renewable systems etc. Gao et. al. [11] discussed methods for estimating missing data in case of sensor failures. Guo et. al. [12] discussed that the published algorithm proved with considerable performance. The verification had been applied on the missing data, which is at random fashion. This algorithm is more appropriate for applications with high computational error requirements. Demirhan et. al. [1] showed in case when the rate of missingness is enlarged to 50 %, the special forecasting algorithm needed to follow. For solar radiation forecasting, non-seasonal Stineman interpolation, Kalman filtering in addion of ARIMA, and smoothing work with good agreements. ARIMA can also been used in marine [11, 13]. Anava Oren et. al. [14] discussed model which is used in biomedical application. Application of adaptive wavelet network architecture for forecasting solar radiation on daily basis explained in [2, 15]. Akarslan et. al. [16] showed the predictions possibility with linear prediction filters over the measured values. The prediction of in-plane irradiation with a neural network approach has been most common [17, 18].

Table 1 Imputation methods along with data set and performance parameter.

Ref. no.	Methods	Data set used	Performance parameter
[1]	linear and Stineman interpolations and Kalman filtering with structural model and smoothing, weighted moving average	short to mid-term horizontal solar irradiance data	Not Applicable
[2]	Multilayer Perceptron MLP-model	Solar irradiance. Air temperature. These data covers July 1st 2008 to May 23rd 2009. Also, November 23rd 2009 to January 24th 2010. Both have been used.	MAE: < 5% verified on the correlation coefficients arranged from 90-92%

[3]	Least squares support vector machine (LSSVM).	They are tested on 3 generated datasets (sine function, sinc function, and Mackey-Glass chaotic time series) and 4 benchmark datasets Poland electricity load, Sunspot, Jenkins-Box, and EUNITE competition).	Not Applicable
[4]	Improved matrix factorization techniques. : 1) MFS: Matrix Factorization with Smoothness constraints; 2) CSM: Correlated Sensors based Matrix factorization; 3) USM: Uncorrelated Sensors based Matrix factorization; 4) CSMS: Correlated Sensors based Matrix factorization with Smoothness constraints; 5) USMS: Uncorrelated Sensors based Matrix factorization with Smoothness constraints;	Synthetic multivariate time series data.	NRMSE:0.01-0.2 for LTI & hot deck
[6]	Multivariate Imputation by Chained Equations (MICE)	Central Marine Fisheries Research Institute (CMFRI) is the source of past data. Data as old as 20 years may be collected.	MSE: 0.042 verified on ARIMA model.
[7]	seasonal autoregressive integrated moving average models (SARIMA)	Not Applicable	RMSE:0.86 Verified on proposed method II, MAE: 0.57
[8]	MTSDI(multi variate time series data imputation)	The daily concentrations of particulate matter with an aerodynamic volume up to 10 mg/m3 was collected for 366 days (PM10), which were measured at ten monitoring stations in the city of Brazil.	Not Applicable
[9]	Permutation of spatial modelling. Also, Artificial neural networks (ANNs) method	GHI data	highest MSE: 53.97 W/m2 ,lowest MSE: 16.46 W/m2 VERIFIED on GHI
[10]	fuzzy and neural networks, stochastic models: : AR, ARMA, ARIMA and Markov chain , (AI) techniques (ANN), fuzzy model	solar radiation data	MAPE: 6.03%-9.65%. These were checked on proposed method. Those included fuzzy and neural network scheme.
[11]	Gaussian function as well as Cosine function used. ANN with feed-forward.	Solar radiation and indoor temperature of tertiary buildings	MRE(%): 8 Gaussian approach
[12]	Kronecker Compressive Sensing theory.	MOTES, GSA and SST	RMSE: 0.005 Verified on gas sensor array dataset, ARTS: 0.05 verified on MOTES dataset (back propagation method)

[13]	LMQR, weighted quantile regression. (WQR) . Quantile regression neural network (QRNN). Recursive generalized AR conditional hetero-skedasticity (GARCHrls).	Not Applicable	Not Applicable
[14]	Yule-Walker, EM (Kalman filter),	Not Applicable	MSE:0.0979for 10% missing data verified on proposed algorithm
[15]	adaptive wavelet-network architecture	Solar-radiation data from Algeria. meteorological station 1981 - 2001	MSE:0.05 structure 5 (for wavelet 5x12x1)
[16]	Linear prediction filters & empirical model method used.	solar radiation data	RMSE (%) :34.86 Verified on Proposed Adaptive Approach
[17]	Neural networks.	Datasets available from meteorological lab.	MBE(%): 0.8, and energy output 0.9 verified on In-plane irradiation low as 0.9
[18]	Back-filling of missing data.	Synthetic dataset	RMSE (%): 2.8, MBE (%):1.5 verified on horizontal irradiation.

4 Conclusions

LSSVM is used in different fields of applications, such as time series prediction and financial forecasting [3]. Mellit et. al. [2] proposed MLP forecaster which finds application in GCPV plant, solar irradiance forecasting of (24h ahead) and, renewable systems etc. Junger et. al. [8] discussed an imputation based method. This method, when compared with GAM method (GAM is based on use of ARIMA) gave good results. ARIMA can also been used in marine [11, 13]. Anava Oren et. al. [14] discussed model that applied to various applications. Such as, in DNA microarray, market analysis as well as noise uncertainty reduction. Amrouche et. al. [9] proposed a novel technique. This technique applied to predict daywise global horizontal radiation.

Thus, there is still a scope of improvement in the existing proposed methods. A new proposed method when verified on existing data sets may give better results for a particular application.

References

1. H. Demirhan, Z. Renwick, Missing value imputation for short to mid-term horizontal solar irradiance data. Appl Energy, vol. **225**, pp. 998–1012, (2018). 10.1016/j.apenergy.2018.05.054.
2. A. Mellit, A.M. Pavan, A 24-h forecast of solar irradiance using artificial neural network: application for performance prediction of a grid-connected PV plant at Trieste, Italy. Solar Energy, vol. **84(5)**, pp. 807-821, (2010). 10.1016/j.solener.2010.02.006.
3. S. Wu, C. Chang, S. Lee, Time Series Forecasting with Missing Values, *1st Int. Conf. Ind. Networks Intell. Syst.*, pp. 151-156, *(2015)*. 10.4108/icst.iniscom.2015.258269.
4. W. Shi et al., Effective prediction of missing data on Apache Spark over multivariable time series", *IEEE Trans. Big Data, vol.* ***6****, pp. 57239-27248,* (2017). 10.1109/TBDATA.2017.2719703.
5. Yanjie Wei et al., Any-time Methods For Time-series Prediction With Missing Observations, *IEEE International Congress on Big Data (BigData Congress)*, (2017). 10.1109/BigDataCongress.2017.62.
6. M.O.D. Rizwan et al., A Novel Approach For Time Series Data Forecasting Based On Arima Model For Marine Fishes, International Conference on Algorithms, Methodology, Models and Applications in Emerging Technologies (ICAMMAET), (2017). 10.1109/ICAMMAET.2017.8186707.
7. V. Layanun, S. Suksamosorn, J. Songsiri, Missing-data Imputation for Solar Irradiance Forecasting in Thailand. *In: Proceedings of the SICE Annual Conference 2017 September 19–22, Kanazawa University, Kanazawa, Japan*, (2017). 10.23919/SICE.2017.8105472.
8. W.L. Junger, A.P. de Leon, Imputation of missing data in time series for air pollutants, Atmospheric Environment, vol. **102**, pp. 96-104, (2015). 10.1016/j.atmosenv.2014.11.049.
9. B. Amrouche, X. Pivert Le, Artificial neural network based daily local forecasting for global solar radiation. Appl Energy vol. **130**, pp. 333–341, (2014) 10.1016/j.apenergy.2014.05.055.
10. S.X. Chen, H.B. Gooi, M. Wang. Solar radiation forecast based on fuzzy logic and neural networks. Renew Energy, vol. **60**, pp. 195–201, (2013). 10.1016/j.renene.2013.05.011.
11. Z. Gao, W. Cheng, X. Qiu, L. Meng, A Missing Sensor Data Estimation Algorithm Based on Temporal and Spatial Correlation, *International Journal of Distributed Sensor Networks*, vol. **2015**, pp. 1-10, (2015). 10.1155/2015/435391.

12. Y. Guo , X. Song , D. Fang, An Efficient Missing Data Prediction Method Based on Kronecker Compressive Sensing in Multivariable Time Series.IEEE Trans, pp. 57239 – 57248, (2018). 0.1109/ACCESS.2018.2873414.
13. M. David, L. Mazorra, P. Lauret, Comparison of intraday probabilistic forecasting of solar irradiance using only endogenous data. Int J Forecast, vol. **19(4)**, pp. 299–311, (2018). 10.1016/j.ijforecast.2018.02.003 .
14. A. Oren, H.. Elad, Z Assaf, Online time series prediction with missing data. *In Proceedings of the 32nd International Conference on Machine Learning*, vol. **37**, pp. 2191–2199, (2015).
15. S.A. Kalogirou, Artificial neural networks in renewable energy systems applications: a review. Renew Sustain Energy Rev, vol. **5(4)**, pp. 373–401, (2001). 10.1016/S1364-0321(01)00006-5.
16. E. Akarslan, FO Hocaoglu. A novel adaptive approach for hourly solar radiation forecasting. Renew Energy, vol. **87**, pp. 628–633, (2016). 10.1016/j.renene.2015.10.063.
17. E. Koubli, D. Palmer, T. Betts, P. Rowley, R. Gottschalg, Inference of missing PV monitoring data using neural networks, *43rd IEEE Photovoltaic Specialists Conference, PVSC, Portland*, pp. 1-6, (2016). 10.1109/PVSC.2016.7750305 .
18. E. Koubli, D. Palmer, P. Rowley, R. Gottschalg. Inference of missing data in photovoltaic monitoring datasets, IET Renew. Power Gener., vol. **10(4)**, pp. 434-439, (2016). 10.1049/iet-rpg.2015.0355

Deep Learning- Based Surveillance System using Face Recognition

Divya Kapil[1]*, *Aishwarya Kamtam*[1]*, *Akhil Kedare*[1]*, *Smita Bharne*[1]*

[1]*Ramrao Adik Institute of Technology, Navi Mumbai, India*

Abstract. Surveillance systems are used for the monitoring the activities directly or indirectly. Most of the surveillance system uses the face recognition techniques to monitor the activities. This system builds the automated contemporary biometric surveillance system based on deep learning. The application of the system can be used in various ways. The face prints of the persons will be stored inside the database with relevant statistics and does the face recognition. When any unknown face is recognized then alarm will ring so one can alert the security systems and in addition actions will be taken. The system learns changes while detecting faces automatically using deep learning and gain correct accuracy in face recognition. A deep learning method including Convolutional Neural Network (CNN) is having great significance in the area of image processing. This system can be applicable to monitor the activities for the housing society premises.

1. Introduction

Privacy isn't the state of maintaining secrecy, is the state of being alone and not watched or disturbed by alternative people. Individuals are developing to be profoundly troubled and on edge of their surroundings attempting to guarantee that they stay secured consistently. Surveillance videos have a major contribution for the security purpose. CCTV cameras are implemented in all places where security is having much importance. A surveillance system consists of monitoring of different activities through the detection and recognition of faces. As a significant part of biometric distinguishing proof innovation, face acknowledgment innovation has the attributes of helpful procurement and high unwavering quality that has broadly utilized in the fields of data security, national security and traffic monitoring. Face recognition is the category of biometric programming that maps and people's facial highlights scientifically and stores the information as face print [3].

Hence the surveillance system which captures the individual user face, detect and compare with the existing user is the utmost requirement while monitoring. Thus, the face recognition techniques having great importance while monitoring through the surveillance system. The technique like Deep Convolutional Neural Network (CNN) algorithm is used to compare a live capture or digital image to the stored face print in order to verify an individual's identity. The convolution neural system can communicate the qualities of the chain of importance and can communicate the attributes of the picture well. The present convolution neural system has been applied to protest classification, picture division, and video recovery and different fields.

In the profundity of learning, the convolution neural system is the best application. It can utilize an enormous number of labelled data, extract the attributes of various levelled structure, and can get the profundity of the picture articulation qualities, can be communicated all the more distinctive picture features [4].

2. Literature Survey

In paper [1] Xiujie Qu, et.al, proposed "Fast Face Recognition System" using Field Programmable Gate Array board with the help of Convolutional Neural Network that could recognize face instantly. It helped in increasing the computational speed of the network in real time processing system to give accurate results. Power consumption was more in Field Programmable Gate Array (FPGA) and the programmers did not have control over the optimization of code and the system was appropriately only for low quantity production.

In paper [2] Zhiming Li, et.al proposed "Double Supervision Face Recognition Based on Deep Learning" with the help of double supervised full convolution neural network to identify face. It was implemented using python and resulted in good practical value that could be applied in industrial fields. With the help of this system faces could be classified and then verified for the purpose of identification. It can extract many features of face and is superior compared to traditional method. This system consumed large amount of power which resulted in lowering the processing speed.

* Corresponding author: divyakapil98@gmail.com, aishu.kamtam@gmail.com, akhil.kedare@gmail.com, smita.bharne@rait.ac.in

In paper [3] Aniwat Juhong, et.al proposed "Face Recognition on Facial Landmark Detection" using Supervised learning with human annotated data which was used in detecting the facial landmarks and recognizing face. It was implemented using python to provide robust, fast processing system and less expensive. This system could not provide accuracy since it used very less database.

In paper [4] Sanjay Thakre, et.al, proposed "Secure Reliable Multimodal Biometric Face Recognition" using Principal Component Analysis for multimodal feature extraction to integrate the face image pixels intensity and local entropy of the image. The advantage of the system is for a static database is proven as an efficient application with very lower, negligible percentage of false acceptance and rejection rate.

From literature survey, it has been understood that the various systems are proposed along with the usage of one-of-the-kind algorithms with some advantages and limitations. The recent paper said that the system was made using Field-Programmable Gate Array (FPGA) which helped in determining the face pixels but due to this large amount of power was consumed. In paper [2] used double supervised full convolution neural network to identify face but it could work accurately and also it was good only for low quantity of production. In paper [3] used Supervised Learning with human annotated data to achieve the best classification but the results were always not accurate. In paper [4] used multimodal feature extraction to integrate the face image pixels intensity and local entropy of image but it resulted in inaccurate results. Considering all the above methods this system is generated using the FaceNet Model.

3. Proposed Methodology

3.1 System Design

Figure 1 shows the flow of proposed system. The user face is scanned and stored in the database. We first train the data set for our surveillance system using one shot learning using FaceNet[7][11]. The matches the faces and based on FaceNet is a pre-trained CNN which embeds the input image into a 128-dimensional vector encoding. It is trained on several images of the face of different people. Although this model is pre-trained. But it still struggles to output usable encoding for unseen data. We want this model to generate encoding such that there is less distance between encoding of the images of same person, and more distance between encoding of the different persons.

To achieve this goal images, we will train FaceNet model on Triplet Loss function [7][11]. This function takes three images as anchor points as positive and negative. and Positive means images of same person whereas negative means the image of a different person.
Now when a user tries to pass through the surveillance system his face image is captured. Then the image is fed into the Deep learning CNN architecture. The output is 128D vector encoding. This output is then matched with the data set if it matches the user is allowed through the surveillance system else his entry is rejected.

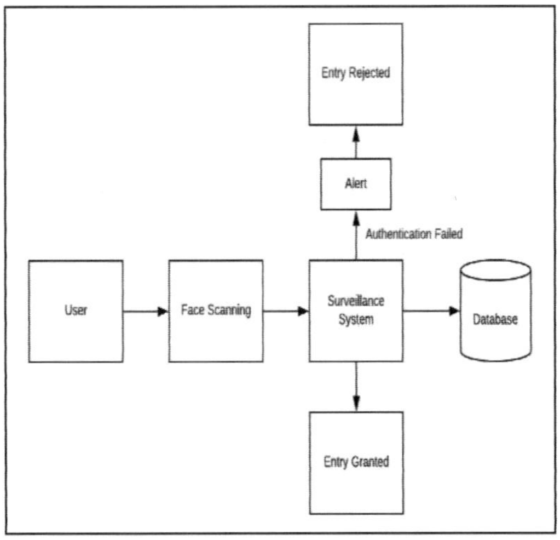

Fig. 1. Proposed System Design

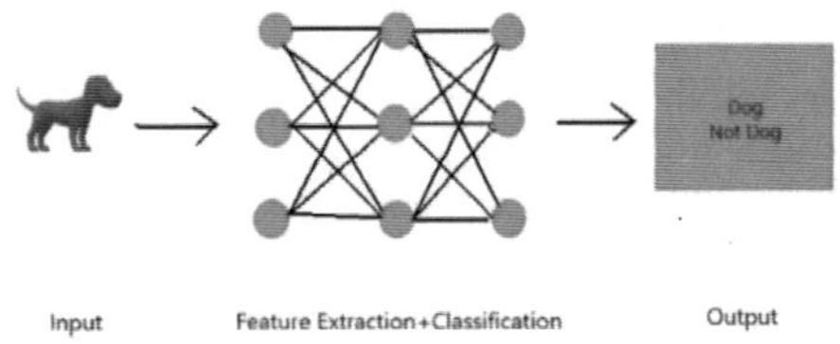

Fig. 2 : Deep Learning

Figure 2 shows the concept of deep Learning. A deep CNN algorithm is used to compare images stored in a face prints to verify individuals. stored in a face prints to verify individuals. The extracted features from these images can be used to train a classifier which can be verify the individual person's identity. While registration it takes 50 images per person. This model takes 50 images for the purpose f registration. While capturing image of the user it gets train with FaceNet model. The FaceNet model extracts the features of the registered image and then gives to the CNN module for face recognition. CNN module will match the images with the registered images in the database and then identify whether the person is authenticated user or not.

3.2 FaceNet and Feature Extraction

The model utilized in our assessment is the FaceNet [7], which changes the face into 128D Euclidean space like word implanting. FaceNet is the pre-prepared CNN model. The FaceNet model having been prepared with triplet misfortune for various classes of countenances to catch the similitudes and contrasts between them, the 128-

dimensional installing returned by the FaceNet model can be utilized to groups faces successfully. It can be used to clusters faces effectively. Vectors of the space are created for recognition, verification and clustering may be easily implemented with the use of standard strategies with FaceNet. Smaller distance indicates closer for similar faces and similarly away for non-similar faces.[11] FaceNet utilizes a particular misfortune strategy called Triplet Loss to compute loss. Triplet Loss limits the separation between a grapple and a positive, pictures that contain the same personality, and expands the separation between the stay and a pessimistic, pictures that contain various characters.

Figure 3 shows the triplet loss mechanism. The triplet-based loss function used to learn the mapping of a classifier with same or different persons. It uses the network trained using aggregate of classification and verification loss. The verification loss they use is much like the triplet loss used to examine the mapping utilized by FaceNet in that it minimizes squared L2 distances between snapshots of faces from the same person and enforces a margin separating photographs of faces from a unique individual, however its unique in that only pairs of photographs are compared, whereas the triplet loss encourages a relative distance constraint by searching at three at a time[7][11]. We want to ensure that an image x(a) of a specific person is closer to all images x(p)of that same person than is closer to all other images x(p)of that same person than it is to any image x(n)of any other person by a margin where x(a) is the anchor point of the input image , x(p) is the positive point of the image which is similar or close to the input image and x(n) is the negative point which is the dissimilar image.

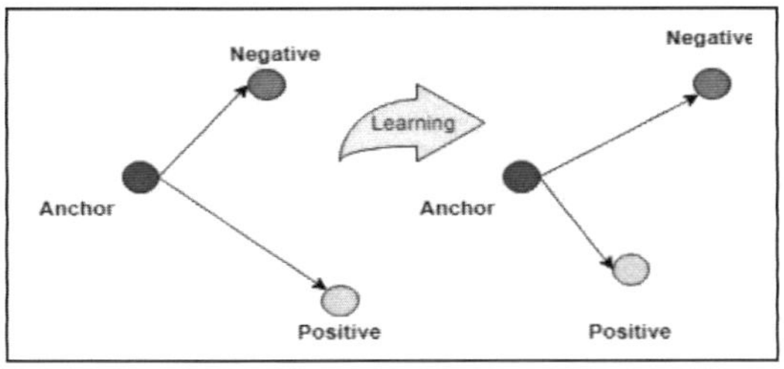

Fig. 3 : Triplet Loss

4. Results Analysis and Discussion

The dataset is used by the system where in one shot 50 frames per user is captured and then feed to the system. The sample images of some users are shown in fig 4(a). Total 2000 images were taken of 50 users and then trained into the model i.e. 4 classes were generated. The images of user2 were trained with spectacles

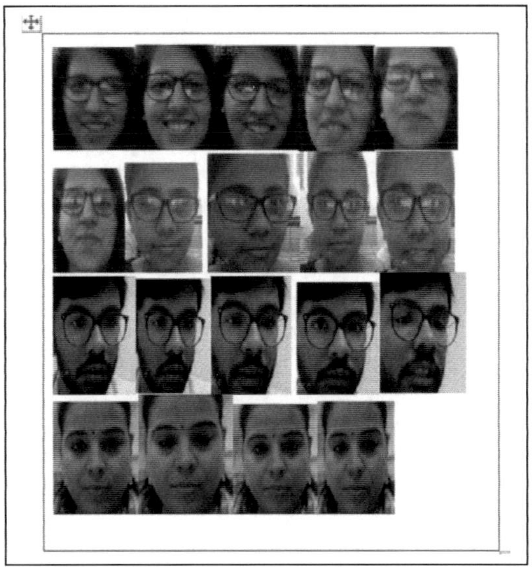

Fig. 4(a) : Input Data (Training data -Sample Images)

The images of user2 were then tested with different specifications such as with spectacles and without spectacles. The system is able to identify the faces with the learned specifications. Also using deep learning system is able to identify the faces with the variations of feature points.

Fig. 5(a) : Test case1 with Glasses

Fig. 5(b) : Test case1 without Glasses

The images of user-2 have been tested with different specifications such as with spectacles and without spectacles. Figure 5(a) and 5(b) shows the test case with glasses and without glasses respectively. Table 1 shows the accuracy results with glasses.

Table 1. Results for Facial recognition of User-2 with Glasses.

Test Cases	User1	User2	User3	User4	Accuracy
1.	0.03367	0.87418	0.06516	0.02698	87%
2.	0.03937	0.85495	0.06732	0.03833	85%
3.	0.04253	0.84192	0.07869	0.03685	84%
4.	0.04634	0.82040	0.10254	0.03071	82%
5.	0.03270	0.85782	0.07884	0.03062	85%

The results of the table 1 shows an average of 84.6% accuracy where the user-2 was with spectacles.

Table 2 shows an average of 68% accuracy where the user-2 was without spectacles.

Figure 7 shows the accuracy graph of the system. Results generated results by the proposed system is able to detect the faces with the different complexities. This feature makes our system more robust comparing with existing system. Literature survey shows the accuracy of existing system from 80 to 85 % [7][5]. In our system we are achieving accuracy up to 87% and also with the complex-additive features for same user up to 68%. For same user feature mention in table 1 and table 2 makes our system differentiable from the existing system.

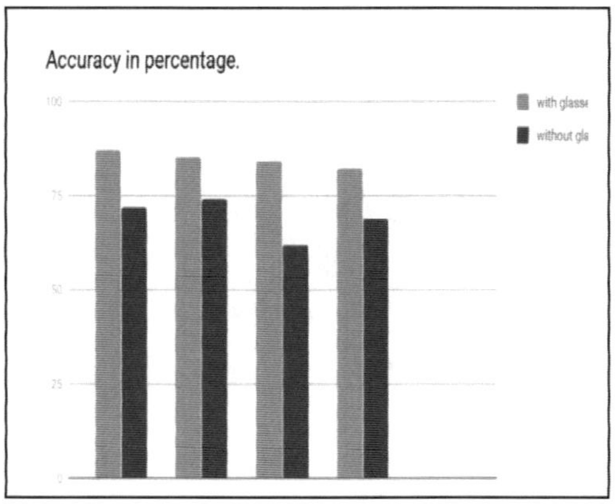

Fig 7: Accuracy Graph

Table 2. Results for Facial recognition of User2 without glasses

Test Cases	User-1	User-2	User-3	User-4	Accuracy
1.	0.0574	0.72486	0.0509	0.1667	72%
2.	0.0670	0.74153	0.0591	0.1323	74%
3.	0.0940	0.64932	0.0509	0.2056	64%
4.	0.0586	0.69176	0.0533	0.1963	69%
5.	0.0710	0.61811	0.0565	0.2602	61%

Fig 8: Surveillance system detecting multiple faces

Figure 8 shows the frame which is captured from a live surveillance system detecting and identifying authorised users.
The proposed system uses images of face from different angles to train the model giving it an upper edge over existing systems. The proposed system can work with normal CPU but can give better performance with GPU.

5. Conclusion

This work has been carried for recognizing facial images which can be used in different real time applications like forensics analysis, residential, system security etc. The photo can be highly contrasting or conceal for the above-built up usage. Considering housing society most of the information stored manually can be altered which leads to misleading actions. Thus, the system uses the deep learning which identifies unknown faces entering into the residential and maintain proper data regarding relevant information of the visitors and people residing in it. The proposed method tries to provide better solutions and helpful towards the betterment of the people

References

[1] Xiujie Qu, Tianbo Wei, Cheng Peng, Peng Du, "A Fast Face Recognition System Based On Deep Learning", 2018 11th International Symposium on Computational Intelligence and Design.
[2] Zhiming Li, Yongzhong Tang, " Double Supervision Face Recognition Based on Deep Learning", 2017 International Conference on Computer Systems, Electronics and Control (ICC- SEC)
[3] Aniwat Juhong, C. Pintavirooj, "Face Recognition Based on Facial Landmark Detection", The 2017 Biomedical Engineering International Conference (BMEiCON-2017)
[4] Sanjay Thakre, Ambikesh Kumar Gupta, Shilpi Sharma, "Secure Reliable Multimodel Biometric Fingerprint and Face Recognition", 2017 International Conference on Computer Communication and Informatics (ICCCI -2017).
[5] Umme Aiman, Virendra P. Vishwakarma, "Face Recognition using modified deep learning neural network", IEEE – 40222, July 2017.
[6] Virendra P. Vishwakarma, "Deterministic Learning Machine for Face Recognition with Multi-model Feature Extraction", 2016 Ninth International Conference on Contemporary Computing (IC3), Aug 2016.
[7] "FaceNet Based Face Sketch Recognition",2017 International Conference on Computational Science and Computational Intelligence (CSCI) by Hyo Jong Lee,Weiguo Wan, Dec 2017.
[8] Phat Nguyen Huu, Loc Hoang Bao, Hoang Lai The. "Proposing an Image Enhancemen Algorithm Using CNN for Applications of Face Recognition System", Journal of Advances in Mathematics and Computer Science, 2020
[9] Thida Nyein, Aung Nway Oo. "University Classroom Attendance System Using FaceNet and Support Vector Machine", 201 International Conference on Advanced Information Technologies (ICAIT), 2019
[10] P. Jothi Thilaga, B. Arshath Khan, A.A. Jones N. Krishna Kumar. "Modern Face Recognition with Deep Learning", 2018 Second International Conference on Inventive Communication and Computational Technologies (ICICCT), 2018

[11] Guodong Guo, Na Zhang,"A Survey on Deep Learning Based Face Recognition"2019 Computer Vision and Image Understanding 189(2019) 102805.
[12] by Qiangchang Wang, Guodong Guo. Benchmarking deep learning techniques for face recognition", J.Vis. Commun. Image R.65 (2019)102663.

 https://doi.org/10.1051/itmconf/20203203012

Association Mining for Super Market Sales using UP Growth and Top-K Algorithm

Harshal Bhope[1,*], *Yash* Mahajan[2,**], *Swapnil* Deore[3,***], and *Vimla* Jethani[4,****]

[1]Ramrao Adik Institute of Technology,Nerul,Navi Mumbai
[2]Ramrao Adik Institute of Technology,Nerul,Navi Mumbai
[3]Ramrao Adik Institute of Technology,Nerul,Navi Mumbai
[4]Ramrao Adik Institute of Technology,Nerul,Navi Mumbai

Abstract. Frequent itemsets(HUIs) mining is an evolving field in data mining, that centers around finding itemsets having a utility that meets a user-specified minimum utility by finding all the itemsets. A problem arises in setting up minimum utility exactly which causes difficulties for users. By setting minimum utility underneath average, too many incessant itemsets will be generated, which in turn will make the mining process quite inefficient. No frequent itemsets will be found if the minimum utility is set too huge. The research focuses on generating frequent itemsets by using the transaction weighted utility of each product. While using UP growth methodology for discovering high utility items from large datasets it takes more time and consumes more memory due to which it is less efficient. So to overcome these drawbacks of UP growth we use the Top-K algorithm which makes it more scalable and efficient. Therefore, we use the Top-K algorithm which does not require a minimum threshold.

1 Introduction

In day to day transactions, High utility mining is used for generating frequent items and existing patterns in user database. Predefined thresholds for measures like support and confidence are used for detection of user interestedness in utility mining. The utiity value of each item is not appropriately determined due to use of these approaches. In business world real time request and frequent itemset mining is in trend these days. Algorithms like aproiri and FP growth seem quite familiar in the transactional system. The above stated methodologies states the frequent items without taking acquisition weights of item into consideration. Finding higher utilities in business decision plays a vital role and helps in earning profits.

Business analytics in research stresses more on FIM these days. The sets with low prioritized value which are frequently repeated are viewed in huge amount by major FIM approaches. The loss of data occurs due to sets with less selling frequencies. Therefore, it can't fulfill client necessity who needs high utilization, for example, more benefits. It comprises of amount as item utility and unit benefit as number of event tally in every dataset. As per client determination the utilization of set constitute to as far as transaction weighted utility, tally , limit or other information. On the other side,it is possible that utility of HUI is more than client minimum value, at that point sets are called as high utility item set and accordingly it has critical job in market analysis.

Mining high frequent items prompts the revelation of connection among items in huge value based or social datasets. With large amount of information being constantly gathered and saved numerous industries are getting keen on mining such examples from their databases. The disclosure of compulsive connection among large amount of transaction record can help in numerous business decision making procedure, for example, customer shopping behaviour analysis. The disclosure of these fascinating relation can assist retailers with creating business advertising systems by picking up information into which items are habitually bought together by clients.

2 Literature Survey

Ameena Aiman and Raafiya Gulmeher[1],"Efficient Algorithms for Mining Top-K High Utlity Itemsets" They proposed TKU(Top-k Utility Itemsets) and TKO(Top-K utility itemsets in one phase) algorithms without the need to set minimum utility.

Myneni Madhu Bala and Rahit Dandamudi[2],"Efficient High Utility Pattern Mining Algorithm for E-Business" by analysis of market behaviour and customer interests of transactional data. This technique uses UP growth strategy(UP tree) and TKU method and discovering top-k utility in one phase approach with TKO method to mine frequent without any presumptions of minimum limit threshold which increases performance and scalability.

*e-mail: harshalbhope67@gmail.com
**e-mail: mahajanprajwal@gmail.com
***e-mail: mahajanswapnil31@gmail.com
****e-mail: vimlajethani@gmail.com

Serin Lee and Jong Soo Park[5],"High Utility Itemset Mining based on Utility-List Structures". They proposed a new strategy TKUL-miner, to draw top-k high utility items efficietly. It utilizies another utility list structure which stores fundamental data at every hub(node) on the queue tree for mining the itemsets. This strategy has a technique utilizing search request for specific region to raise the outskirt least utility threshold value.

V.Kavitha and B.G.Geetha[6],"Review on High Utility Itemset Mining Algorithms". They have discussed a comparative study of three mining approaches such as FHM, HUI Miner and Two phase miner.

Junqiang Liu, Ke Wang and Benjamin C.M. Fung[7],"Mining High Utility Patterns in one phase without generating candidates". This paper introduces Utility Pattern Growth approach. This model developement approach is to draw a reverse set enumeration tree and to prune search tree by utility upper bounding.

3 Proposed Work

In this research, we are discussing different kind of data mining approaches, that is, Top-K(TKU and TKO) and UP growth algorithms in order to obtain frequent itemsets from large datasets. The first stage involves TKO Algorithm, the process of generating Utility List Structure using Transaction Utility(TU) and Transaction Weighted Utility(TWU)[3]. After generating utility list structure, we obtain the base value called Threshold. The second involves the TKU Algorithm, which is the process of constructing UP Tree and generates PKMUIs. At last we obtain two tables, Minimum Utility of an Item Table(MIU) and Maximum Utility of an Item Table(MAU), which provides us the range to generate frequent Itemsets.

So,we are doing the comparative study of two algorithms which are Top-k and UP growth.

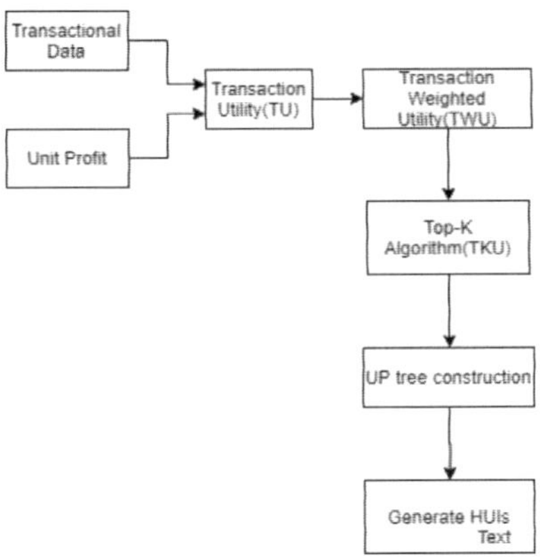

Figure 1. Flow Diagram

4 Methodology

4.1 UP Growth

We outline the feature of UP-growth for effectively producing PHUIs(Potentially high utility itemset) from the UP-tree with two techniques, in particular DLU (Discarding nearby unpromising thing) and DLN (Decreasing neighborhood hub utilities). By utilizing these two strategies, the unpromising set of items having least utility are disposed of from utility at the instant of building a basic UP-Tree. The general methodology of mining utility example is to count every subset of and text if X has utility over the limit. Anyway a comprehensive count is infeasible because of large number of subsets of J and thus it is analytical to utilize tough pruning procedures.

Transaction Utility(TU):

$$\sum_{i\epsilon n} unit\ profit(t) * quantities(c)$$

Transaction weighted Utility(TWU):

$$\sum_{i=1}^{n} TU$$

Full Prefix Expression of an Item(fpe):

$$\sum u(fpe(X,t)t)$$

Let J be the set of items. Let B be a sets of transactions (t1, t2, t3,..tn) where each transaction tj belongs to J. Each item in a transaction is allocated a non-zero value. Each clear-cut item has a benefit self-sufficient of any transaction, given by an Internal and External Utility Table (UT). The issue is to discover all high utility patterns.

Table 1. Transaction Table

Transactions		
TID	**Items**	**Product Utility**
T1	(k,2),(m,2),(o,2)	12
T2	(k,7),(l,3),(m,3),(p,5)	38
T3	(k,2),(l,2),(m,3),(n,3),(o,6),(q,6)	57
T4	(k,4),(l,3),(n,4),(o,3)	35
T5	(k,3),(l,2),(n,3),(p,3)	25

Consider the information or model of a supermarket.Quantity ,that is, value of each product is listed in Table 1 for each shopping transaction where J= k,l,m,n,o,p,q and B= t1, t2, t3, t4, t5 and Table 2 lists the profit of each product. For transaction t2 = k, l, m, p, we have iu(k, t2)= 7, iu(l,t2)= 3, iu(m,t2)= 3, iu(p,t2)= 5, eu(k)= 1, eu(l)= 2, eu(m)= 5, and eu(p)= 2. Here, u(j, t) is the product of iu(j, t) and eu(j). Thus, u(k, t2)= 7, u(l,t2)= 6, u(m,t2)= 15, u(p,t2)= 10, and so on.

Now, we will construct the tree by considering count(s), utility(u), TWU, Ufpe respectively. As, it is not

Table 2. Items with Profit

Item	Profit
K	1
L	2
M	5
N	4
O	3
P	2
Q	1

Table 3. Utilities(minU=45)

utility table for root node				
Item	**count(s)**	**u**	**twu**	**ufpe**
K	5	18	167	18
L	4	20	155	36
M	3	40	107	61
N	3	40	105	78
O	3	33	104	86
P	2	16	63	55
Q	1	6	57	57

possible to show entire tree together because it requires wide space. So we are going node by node.

Step 1:- By taking threshold=45,we will compare utility of full prefix expression(Ufpe) of each node with threshold. If Ufpe>threshold, then the nodes have greater utility as compared to threshold will consider that nodes such as nodes M,N,O,P,Q have Ufpe>30.

Step 2:- Here, First we are going with Node M.

Table 4. After comparing with threshold expanding node have ufpe>threshold

Node M				
Item	**count(s)**	**u**	**twu**	**ufpe**
K	3	51	61	44
L	2	49	49	49

Step 3:- Compare Ufpe values of K and L with threshold. As Ufpe(B)>30. Therefore,

Table 5. K is High Utility Item

Item	count(s)	u	twu	ufpe
K	2	49	49	49

We will repeat the above process until we get the high utility itemset for all node which have ufpe greater than minU(threshold).

4.2 Top-K

The proposed algorithm improves the efficiency of the process by reducing the low utility items. The enormous value-based database is taken by applying TKU strategy. TWU is determined depending on unit benefit and amount. At some point, large tallies of each set is recognized, and UP tree is developed dependent on Top-K high utility item set. A top-k high utility mining strategy works as: First it sets an central minimum utility to 0, and begins to traverse the seek space. At some point, when k high utility itemsets are discovered, the central minimum utility is raised to the utility of the example having the most minimal utility among the present top-k models. Then, the seeking proceeds and for every high utility itemset found, the set of the present top-k sample is revised just like the minimum limit.

Transaction Utility(TU):

$$\sum_{i\epsilon n} unit\ profit(t) * quantities(c)$$

Transaction weighted Utility(TWU):

$$\sum_{i=1}^{n} TU$$

Table 6. Transaction Table

Transactions		
TID	**Items**	**Product Utility**
T1	(k,2),(m,2),(o,2)	12
T2	(k,7),(l,3),(m,3),(p,5)	38
T3	(k,2),(l,2),(m,3),(n,3),(o,6),(q,6)	57
T4	(k,4),(l,3),(n,4),(o,3)	35
T5	(k,3),(l,2),(n,3),(p,3)	25

Table 7. Items with Profit

External Utility	
Item	**Profit**
K	1
L	2
M	5
N	4
O	3
P	2
Q	1

In table 8, we have shown calculated TWU of items with their respective count.

Table 8. Transaction Weighted Utility

TWU		
Item	**Count**	**TWU**
K	5	167
L	4	155
M	3	107
N	3	105
O	3	104
P	1	63
Q	1	57

Now, we construct UP tree taking first node as a root node depending upon count of items and transaction wise.

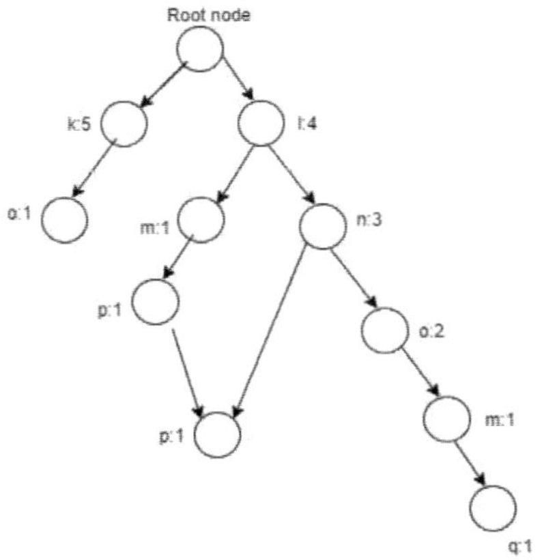

Figure 2. UP tree based on counts of respective items transaction wise.

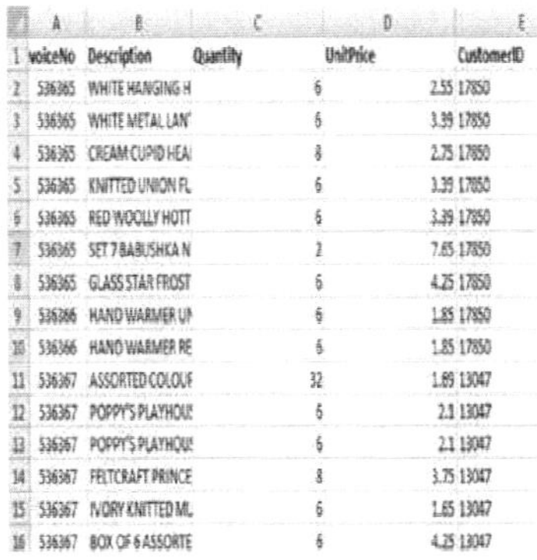

	A	B	C	D	E
1	voiceNo	Description	Quantity	UnitPrice	CustomerID
2	536365	WHITE HANGING H	6	2.55	17850
3	536365	WHITE METAL LAN'	6	3.39	17850
4	536365	CREAM CUPID HEA	8	2.75	17850
5	536365	KNITTED UNION FL	6	3.39	17850
6	536365	RED WOOLLY HOTT	6	3.39	17850
7	536365	SET 7 BABUSHKA N	2	7.65	17850
8	536365	GLASS STAR FROST	6	4.25	17850
9	536366	HAND WARMER U	6	1.85	17850
10	536366	HAND WARMER RE	6	1.85	17850
11	536367	ASSORTED COLOUI	32	1.69	13047
12	536367	POPPY'S PLAYHOU	6	2.1	13047
13	536367	POPPY'S PLAYHOU	6	2.1	13047
14	536367	FELTCRAFT PRINCE	8	3.75	13047
15	536367	IVORY KNITTED ML	6	1.65	13047
16	536367	BOX OF 6 ASSORTE	6	4.25	13047

Figure 3. Optimal Attributes of SuperMarket Datasets[8]

Table 9. Comparison of UP and Top-k

Comparison		
Parameters	**UP Growth**	**Top-K**
Method	1.Construction of UP tree. 2.Generates Potential High Utility Itemsets. 3.Identify high utility items using PHUI values.	1.TKO(Top-K in One phase). 2. TKU(Top-K Utility Patterns)
Strategy	1.Discarding Global Unpromising Item(DGU Strategy) is used for contruction of UP tree. 2.Discarding Global Node Utilities(DGN strategy)	1.TU and TWU are calculated . 2.UP tree is constructed in TKO. 3.TKU is used to generate High Utility items.
Time Taken	More as compared to Top-k.	Less as compared to UP growth.
Memory Consumption	More as compared to Top-K.	Less as compared to UP growth.

5 Results and Analysis

The experimented results were conducted on SuperMarket Datasets. The dataset is collected from online Kaggle datasets repository(https://www.kaggle.com/jihyeseo/online-retail-data-set-from-uci-ml-repo/data)[8]. The attributes taken from the datasets are shown below in figure 3.

The complete evaluation of UP Growth and Top-K(TKU) is with UP tree. To contrast UP tree client has to pick ideal and separate parameters. Super Market is the only dataset which incorporates both buy amount and unit benefit. Here, Super Market dataset has been considered for performance evaluation of UP growth and Top-k(TKU).

Table 10. Time Taken Values

Time		
HUIs	**Top-K**	**UP Growth**
5	0.2635s	0.567s
10	0.187s	0.364s
15	0.094s	0.183s
20	0.109	0.204s

In figure 4, we can see that the two algorithms UP growth and Top-K are compared on the basis of time consumption. In below graph, it visible that Top-K takes less time to generate high utility items as compared to UP growth algorithm. The graph generated shows that with respect to time Top-K is more scalable than UP growth.

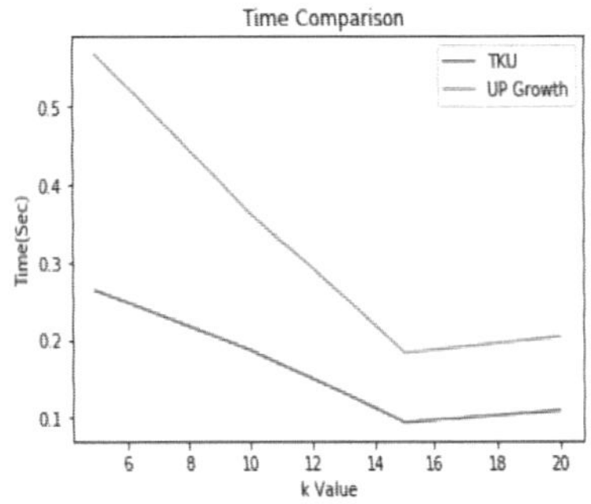

Figure 4. (a)Graph showing comparative study of UP growth and TKU based on Time.

In figure 5, The two algorithms TKU and UP growth are compared on the basis of memory usage. As we can see, UP growth consumps more memory as compared to TKU due to which less efficient.

Table 11. Memory Consumption values

Memory		
HUIs	**Top-K**	**UP Growth**
5	22.7492 MB	22.285 MB
10	29.7471 MB	31.747 MB
15	42.5744 MB	43.310 MB
20	42.59 MB	43.0742 MB

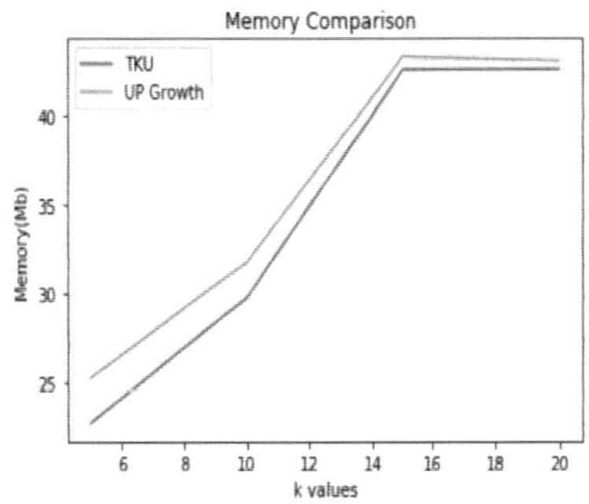

Figure 5. (b)Graph showing comparative study of UP growth and TKU based on Memory Consumption.

6 Conclusion

In this research, the high utility mining issue is resolve by utilization of weighted utility without considering threshold values. For that the proposed strategy Top-K having two periods of execution TKU and TKO. TKU calculation gives UP tree using count and TWU. From the normal outcomes, the proposed method is productive to mine the high utility models with more utilization of items without considering any base utility that is minutil. This assessment of procedure gives great versatile and productive execution on large and dense data.

References

[1] A. Aiman , R. Gulmeher, "Efficient Algorithms for Mining Top-K High Utility Itemsets" at *International Journal of Computer Science and engineering*, July (2018).

[2] M. M. Bala and R. Dandamudi, " HUPM: Efficient High Utility Pattern Mining Algorithm for E-Business" at *8th International Advance Computing Conference(IACC)*, (2018).

[3] S. D. Ambulkar and Dr. P. N. Chatur,"Efficient Algorithms for mining High Utility Itemset" at *International Conference on Recent Trends in Electrical, Electronics and Computing Technologies* ,(2017).

[4] V. S. Tseng, Cheng Wei Wu, P. Fourier-Viger, and Philip S. Yu, "Efficient Algorithms for Mining Top-K High Utility Itemsets" at *IEEE Transactions On Knowledge And Data Engineering*, January (2016).

[5] S. Lee and Jong Soo Park, "Top-K High Utlity Itemset Mining Based on Utility-List Structues" at *International Conference on Big Data and Smart Computing (BigComp)*, January (2016).

[6] V.Kavitha and Prof. B.G.Geetha."Review on High Utility Itemset Mining Algorithms", at *IEEE Sponsored World Conference on Futuristic Trends in Research and Innovation for Social Welfare*, (2016).

[7] Junqiang Liu, Ke Wang and Benjamin C.M. Fung, "Mining High Utility Patterns In One Phase without Generating Candidates " at *IEEE Transactions On Knowledge And Data Engineering*, (2015).

[8] https://www.kaggle.com/jihyeseo/online-retail-dataset-from-uci-ml-repo/data.

ITM Web of Conferences **32**, 03013 (2020) https://doi.org/10.1051/itmconf/20203203013
ICACC-2020

Efficient pothole detection using smartphone sensors

Kshitij Pawar[1,*], *Siddhi* Jagtap[2,**], and *Smita* Bhoir[3,***]

[1]Department of Computer Engineering, Ramrao Adik Institute of Technology, India
[2]Department of Computer Engineering, Ramrao Adik Institute of Technology, India
[3]Department of Computer Engineering, Ramrao Adik Institute of Technology, India

Abstract. Road safety remains a casualty in India, with potholes wrecking asphalt pavements by the dozens. A study in 2017 recorded that potholes caused the budget for road safety to increase by a whopping 100.4 per cent, and even doubled the death toll from that of the year prior. To address this situation, an effective solution is required that ensures the drivers' safety and can prove beneficial for long term measures. This can be established by employing an apt pothole detection system which is simple yet functional. In this paper, the method for such a system is described which uses accelerometer and gyroscope, both built in the modern day smartphones, to sense potholes. Pothole induced vibrations can be measured on the axis reading, making them distinguishable. Our proposed Neural Network model is trained and evaluated on the data acquired from the sensors and classifies the potholes from the non-potholes. The neural network gives a classification accuracy of 94.78 per cent. It also presents a solid precision-recall trade-off with 0.71 precision and 0.81 recall, considerably high for a problem with class imbalance. The results indicate that the method is suitable for creating an accurate and sensitive supervised model for pothole detection.

1 Introduction

Roads with potholes have become nearly universal in India [1]. In fact, it has become second nature for drivers to swerve through lanes to avoid potholes, which causes nearby vehicles and other road users to panic as well. The sizes of these undesirable potholes may vary with location, but the damaged caused is just as severe. Potholes have the capability of causing accidents that may be serious or even fatal. The sudden, jarring hits against potholes affect the efficiency of the vehicles and impact the tyres, wheels, and drivers alike.

The government has mandated Road Safety Audit to provide safer transportation to road users [2]. Concerned directors inspect and take suitable short term and long term measures to ensure that the roads are pothole free. But these manual detection measures are not enough; establishment of a real-time pothole detection system is crucial for swift and effective pothole recognition.

With essentially this in mind, the pothole detection model is trained that uses the data acquired from the smartphone sensors, namely the accelerometer and the gyroscope, to classify the real instances of potholes. The accelerometer measures vibrations or inclination in the three directions, X, Y, and Z axes, and can help characterize the pothole on the basis of the magnitude of change in its reading. The gyroscope adds an additional dimension to the information supplied by the accelerometer by tracking rotation or twist. This vibrations based approach gives low response time, processing time and maintenance cost of the device.

Using these readings, our neural network model is trained and tested to accurately classify the potholes. For the purpose of the paper and the research, work has been done on a sufficiently large pre-existing dataset instead of gathering and modifying a dataset ourselves. The prime goal was to create an improved model from the ones already designed, that shows higher performance measures for categorization. Successful implementation has been done to increase the accuracy as well as sensitivity (recall) of the prototype, making the model highly suitable for a real-time pothole recognition system.

The rest of the paper is organized as follows. Section 2 gives a review of the related work. Section 3 explores the proposed methodology, and Section 4 evaluates and illustrates model metrics such as Accuracy, Precision, and Recall. Finally the paper is concluded in Section 5.

2 Literature Survey

Several pothole detection methods have been put forward, a few of which make use of the data obtained from the inbuilt smartphone accelerometer to discern potholes.

2.1 Existing Work

The undermentioned research papers related to work have been surveyed and inspected as follows.

*e-mail: kshitijvijay271199@gmail.com
**e-mail: siddhijagtap63@gmail.com
***e-mail: smitapatilbe@gmail.com

2.1.1 *Real time pothole detection using Android smartphones with accelerometers [3]*

Mednis et al proposed four pothole detection approaches in their paper to process the accelerometer data acquired using different Android OS based smart-phones. The performance analysis in context of different road irregularity classes showed true positive rates as high as 90%. The best results, displayed by the Z-DIFF approach, are however reliant on frequency and timing.

2.1.2 *Pothole Detection System using Machine Learning on Android [4]*

Kulkarni et al, in their paper describe a system using accelerometer sensor for detection and GPS for plotting. The algorithm assumes some threshold values on x-axis and z-axis, justified using a neural network technique which translates to an accuracy of 90%-95%, but bares no detail on other performance metrics.

2.1.3 *A Real-Time Pothole Detection Approach for Intelligent Transportation System [5]*

Wang et al overcame the high false-positives predicament faced by single threshold approaches by combining and improving the Z-THRESH and G-ZERO approaches as depicted in the fifth approach of their paper. Although the algorithm gives an accuracy of 100%, the limitation of this study is the sample size.

2.1.4 *Intelligent Pothole Detection and Road Condition Assessment [6]*

Bhatt et al, in their paper provide a solution to detect road conditions by capturing data on a car's movement from accelerometer and gyroscope sensors in the phone. They trained several classifiers on aggregate metrics from which the best performing classifier, support vector machine (SVM), achieved the highest test accuracy of 92.9%. Adjusting the classification threshold improved the precision-recall trade off to give a precision of 0.74 and a recall of 0.42.

2.1.5 *Pothole Detection using Machine Learning [7]*

Song et al, describe the process for their approach in their paper, which includes acquiring road status information using gyroscope and accelerate sensors, and data pre-processing for a restrained Inception V3 and Transfer Learning. The model showed 100% classification rate but the consideration of only five real instances for each class, collected 20 times for each instance, might suggest overfitting.

2.2 Analysis of Literature Survey

An analysis of various papers on pothole detection methods by considering the type of equipment and methods employed has been done and the research gaps are identified.

After analysing Table 1, it has been observed that while accuracy is high, the recall score is low and potholes are relatively misclassified as compared to non-potholes.

Table 1. Analysis of Literature Survey

Authors	**Year**	**Equipment & Methods**	**Research Gaps Identified**
Mednis et al [3]	2011	4 Android OS based smart-phones	Best results are reliant on frequency and timing
Kulkarni et al [4]	2014	Threshold values on x-axis and z-axis have been taken for the neutral network	Other performance metrics not mentioned
Wang et al [5]	2015	Combining the Z-THRESH and G-ZERO approaches	Limitation of the study is the small sample size
Bhatt et al [6]	2017	SVM classifier, improved using a threshold	Recall of 0.42
Song et al [7]	2018	Data pre-processing done for a restrained Inception V3 and Transfer Learning	Considered only five real instances, collected 20 times for each instance, suggesting overfitting

3 Proposed Work

The proposed work focuses on building an efficient pothole detection system, that is a classifier with increased accuracy, while also ensuring that the process is not too complex and time-consuming. Figure 1 presents the proposed architecture.

Figure 1. Proposed Architecture

The architecture has four major stages: data collection, pre-processing of data, building the model, and evaluating the classifier. The raw data was collected from the smartphone's in-built sensors: accelerometer and gyroscope. After the data was cleaned and transformed to

https://doi.org/10.1051/itmconf/20203203013

improve its quality, it was fed to the proposed model, that is the neural network. Finally, model was evaluated on a number of evaluation metrics to make out its performance.

3.1 Data Collection & Pre-processing

The dataset is primarily the vibration based sensor readings collected from a smartphone's in-built sensors, that is, the accelerometer and gyroscope (Figure 2), as the phone was mounted on the windshield of the vehicle to detect said vibrations.

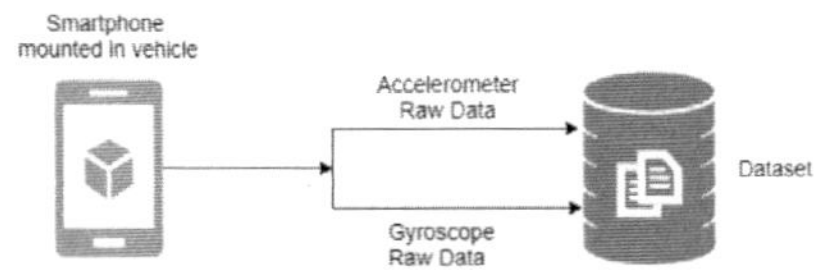

Figure 2. Raw Data Collection

The corpus of data is the result of five trips over a selected road with sufficient instances of potholes to make inferences. It consists of a total twenty-four input features and the target feature which labels the instance as pothole or not. The inputs are essentially the minimum, maximum, mean and standard deviation values of the x, y and z directions of the accelerometer as well as the gyroscope.

Figure 3 and and Figure 4 show the plots [6] for the normalised accelerometer values of the x, y and z directions for both the Good Road Points (the non-pothole occurrences) as well as the Bad Road Points (the pothole occurrences).

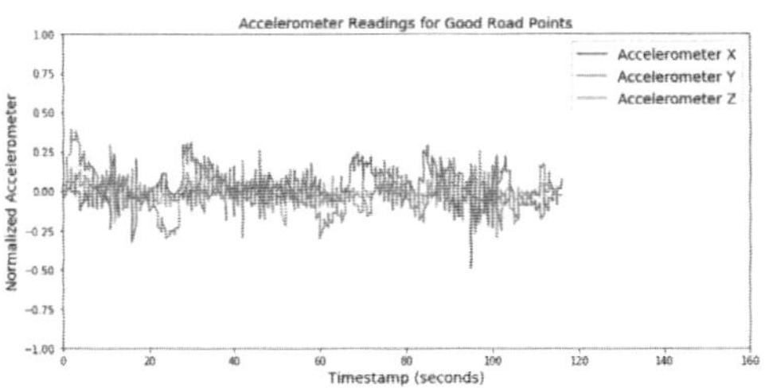

Figure 3. Accelerometer Readings for Good Road Points

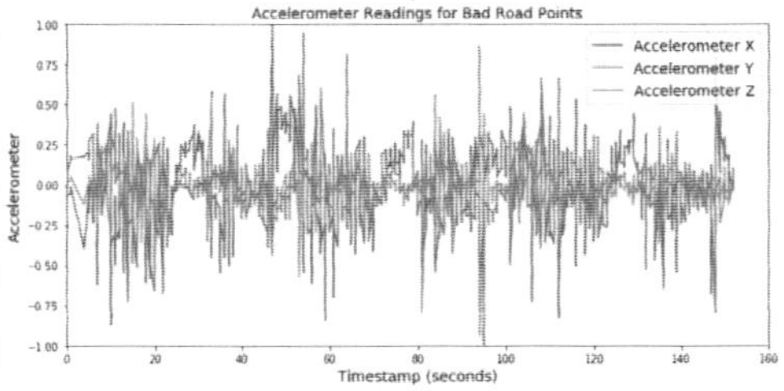

Figure 4. Accelerometer Readings for Bad Road Points

It can be clearly seen that instances of potholes have high variations compared to that of the non-potholes and this disparity benefits the model greatly.

The normalized gyroscope readings also indicate this variance and are thus instrumental features together with the accelerometer readings.

3.2 Feature Engineering

3.2.1 Grouping

Each instance of the dataset was originally taken every fifth of a second, which resulted in turbulent fluctuations. Hence, in an attempt to counter this the instances were grouped by intervals of two seconds each, in order to make better sense of the data points.

3.2.2 Scaling

The features did not have a certain range and differed from each other, hence scaling was applied to each. Standardization (or z-score normalization) scales the values by the mean while taking into account standard deviation, consequently reducing the effect of the outliers in the features.

$$x = (x - mean(x))/std(x)$$

This aggregation provides a finer signal for pothole classification as can be seen in Figure 5 and Figure 6. The plots show the accelerometer standard deviations for the Good Road and Bad Road Intervals. The sharp spikes for the pothole occurrences can now be better perceived.

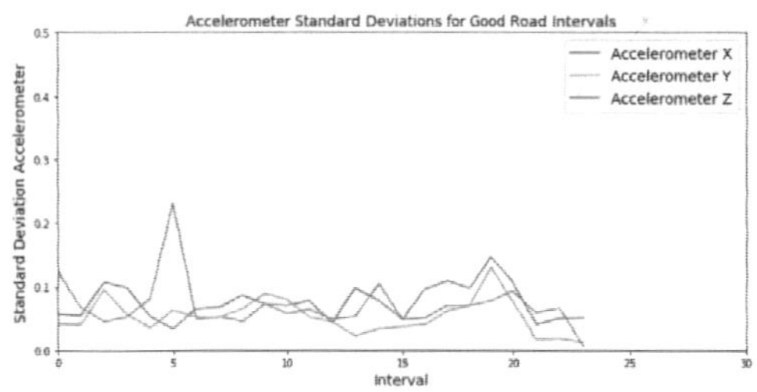

Figure 5. Accelerometer Standard Deviations of Good Road Intervals

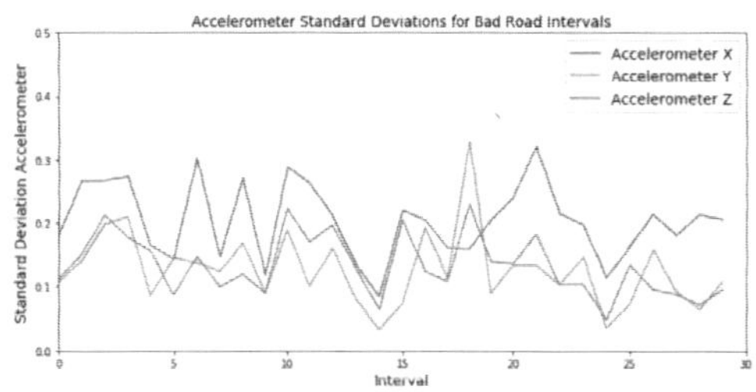

Figure 6. Accelerometer Standard Deviations of Bad Road Intervals

3.3 Proposed Model

The proposed model is a Neural Network, comprising of two hidden layers and one output layer. Each hidden layer has a dense layer with ReLU activation function, allowing faster backpropagation, and a dropout layer, to prevent overfitting, by randomly setting a fraction rate of input units to zero at each update.

The output layer, on the other hand, employs the sigmoid activation function in order to attain the probabilities to define the class of each input (pothole or not).

Further, the model uses the binary cross entropy loss function to compile, and trains over 140 epochs with a batch size of three.

4 Results and Discussions

A total of seven tests were implemented for refining the model by changing a number of parameters and measures. The different test cases along with the various hyperparameters used to tune the respective neural network are given in Table 2. The test cases are nothing but experimental trials of neural networks, each leading to better or worse results, in an attempt to find the model parameters suited best for the problem. The SMOTE case was also implemented as a solution to counter the class imbalance problem.

The pothole detection problem, like many problems, is one of severe class imbalance. The instances of potholes are very few compared to the instances of non-potholes. Synthetic Minority Oversampling Technique, or SMOTE, is an algorithm used to tackle the underlying class imbalance of the dataset by simply oversampling the instances of the minority class. The new examples are then randomly changed to create synthetic but reliable records, reducing the class disparity.

Table 2. Test Models

Test Case	Dense Layers	Dropout Layers	Epochs	Batch Size
1	1	1	700	9
2	4	1	700	12
3	3	2	100	1
4	3	2	100	2
5	3	2	100	5
6	3	2	300	3
Proposed Model	**3**	**2**	**140**	**3**
SMOTE	3	2	40	32

Ultimately, among the eight cases implemented, the seventh case which is the proposed model gave the best results, with sufficiently high classification metrics as required for the problem.

4.1 Results

The results obtained from the different test cases are shown in Table 3. The proposed model gives a high accuracy of 0.9478 and a prominent precision-recall trade-off, with 0.7105 precision and 0.8181 recall.

Table 3. Results

Case	Accuracy	Precision	Recall	F1 Score
Baseline	**89.877**	**1**	**0**	**0**
1	0.9141	0.6315	0.3636	0.4615
2	0.9018	0.5217	0.3636	0.4285
3	0.9171	0.6071	0.5151	0.5573
4	0.9171	0.6667	0.3636	0.4705
5	0.9141	0.5806	0.5454	0.5625
6	0.9018	0.5172	0.4545	0.4838
Proposed Model	**0.9478**	**0.7105**	**0.8181**	**0.7605**
Expected	**0.9263**	**0.7368**	**0.4242**	**0.5384**
SMOTE	0.8957	0.4864	0.5454	0.5142

The comparison between model evaluation metrics of our proposed model with that of the Bhatt et al support vector machine (SVM) model are illustrated in Figure 7. It is observed that our proposed model achieved significantly better recall, implying that the model is able to recognize the actual potholes adequately well.

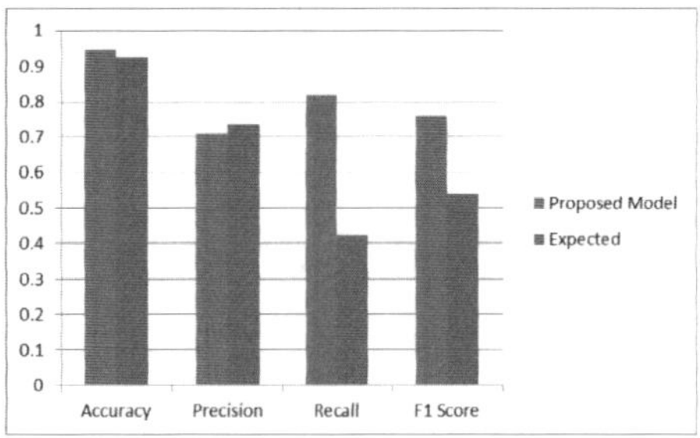

Figure 7. Comparison of expected and proposed model

For this specific problem with class imbalance it is observed that neural networks are better equipped for the job and give better results due to scarcity of dataset and large number of input features i.e., 24. Several key parameters about the structure of the input data are required to be set in case of SVM, which leads to it being a stiff and inflexible architecture. However, in case of neural networks loss is automatically minimized using Gradient Descent without any special configurations. SVM can also suffer during scaling i.e., when the size of the dataset increases on being deployed in production, whereas neural networks do not suffer from the increased size of dataset and scale quite efficiently too.

4.2 Analysis

The seventh test gave the best results with high train and test accuracy over passing epochs, as well as low output loss.

Figure 8 and Figure 9 explore the values of accuracy and loss over epochs for the train and test sets respectively.

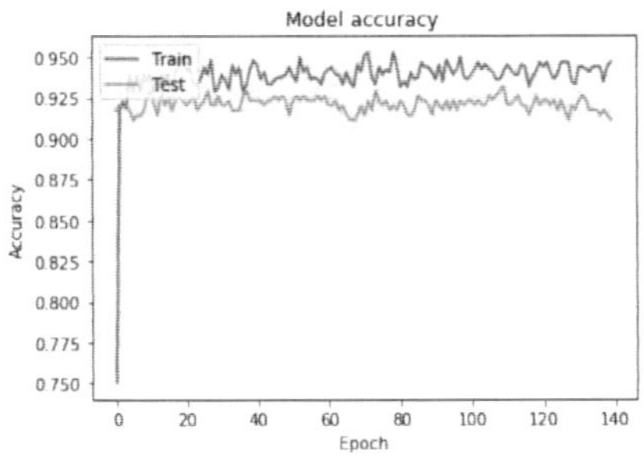

Figure 8. Epoch vs. Accuracy

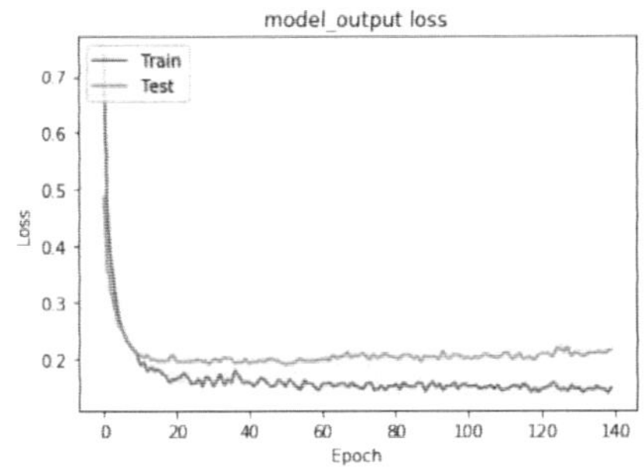

Figure 9. Epoch vs. Loss

4.2.1 Accuracy Metrics

The model shows an accuracy of 0.9478 which is higher than the baseline considered. Not only that, the precision-recall trade-off too is quite high with a precision of 0.71 and a recall of 0.81, accounting to a F1-score of 0.76.

Precision is the ratio of correctly predicted pothole observations to the total observations predicted as potholes. Recall (Sensitivity) is the ratio of correctly predicted potholes to all the observations that are actually potholes.

F1 Score is the weighted average of Precision and Recall. Therefore, this score takes both false positives and false negatives into account. F1 is more useful than accuracy, for a problem of uneven class distribution. Hence a high F1 score of 0.76 shows the superior skills of the classifier.

4.2.2 ROC-AUC Curve

Another evaluation metric considerd for the class imbalance is the ROC-AUC Curve.

ROC (Receiver Operating Characteristics) is a probability curve and AUC (Area Under the Curve) represents degree or measure of separability. The x-axis of the plot indicates the False Positive Rate and the y-axis indicates the True Positive Rate. It tells how much the model is capable of distinguishing between the binary classes. Higher the AUC, better the model is at predicting the positive classes.

The neural network gives an AUC of 0.972 for the training data, as shown in Figure 10. This indicates that there is a 97.2% chance that the model will be able to distinguish between the pothole class and the non-pothole class.

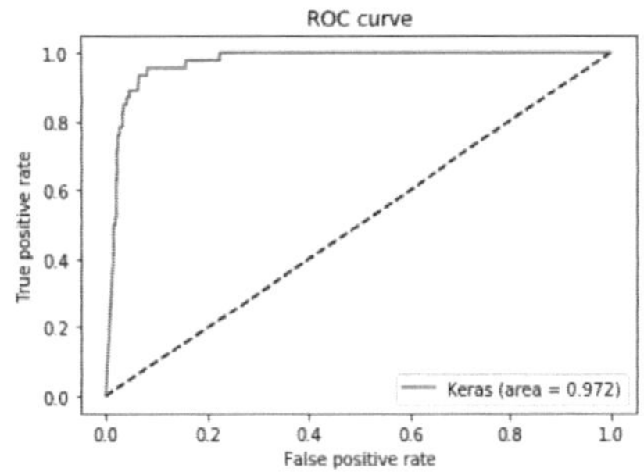

Figure 10. ROC Curve

5 Conclusion and Future Work

By crowd sourcing, one can map locations of potholes and provide such information to authorities and develop more detailed maps for safe travel.

In this paper, a coherent approach is proposed to recognize and detect a pothole on the road. The data was acquired from the smartphone sensors, making the approach cost-effective. A simple yet functional Neural Network for the class imbalance classification problem is utilized, improving the accuracy measures seen previously. The proposed model gives a sufficiently high accuracy of 0.94 and a significant recall of 0.81, making the model suitable for real-time systems.

Further improvement in model accuracy can be increased by collecting more sensor data over different sized potholes to better represent the variety in depths of potholes. Scope can be expanded to classify different types of potholes as well.

References

[1] A. Sherrif, "How Difficult Is It to Keep Our Roads Pothole Free" (2018)
[2] V. Singh, "The pothole problem in India" (2018)

[3] A. Mednis, G. Strazdins, R. Zviedris, G. Kanonirs, L. Selavo, "Real time pothole detection using Android smartphones with accelerometers", Int. Conf. DCOSS, 1-6 (2011)

[4] A. Kulkarni, N. Mhalgi, S. Gurnani, N. Giri, "Pothole Detection System using Machine Learning on Android", Int. Jou. Em. Tech. Adv. Eng. **14**, 7 (2014)

[5] H. Wang, C. Chen, D. Cheng, C. Lin, C. Lo, "A Real-Time Pothole Detection Approach for Intelligent Transportation System", Math. Prob. in Eng. **2015**, 1-7 (2015)

[6] U. Bhatt, S. Mani, E. Xi, J.Z. Kolter, "Intelligent Pothole Detection and Road Condition Assessment", ArXiv **abs/1710.02595** (2017)

[7] H. Song, K. Baek, Y. Byun, "Pothole Detection using Machine Learning", Adv. Sci. Tech. Let. **150**, 151-155 (2018)

Violence Detection using Embedded GPU

Sagar R. Tharali, Gaurav S. Wakchaure, Durvesh S. Shirsat, Navin G. Singhaniya
Department of Electronics Engineering
Ramrao Adik Institute of Technology
Nerul, Navi Mumbai
Email: sagart2207@gmail.com, gauravwakchaure1998@gmail.com, durvesh301198@gmail.com, navin.singhaniya@rait.ac.in

***Abstract*—Since the CCTV cameras been introduced in this world, society has started to depend heavily on the usage of this technology for the high security purposes in most of the public and private areas. It is convenient to use these CCTV footages in courts as evidence and has been beneficial many times. But these footages are given priority and checked later when the incident has already taken place and that too after some period of time and not in real-time of happening. The screening of the multiple CCTV footages on a single monitor is done with very less efficiency as the ratio of number of CCTV footages to that of number of surveillance staff is very high. Also, the human unreliable supervision due to many reasons like tiredness from physical or mental effort, worker boredom, or discontinuous observation make the surveillance more inefficient. To address the issue and automatically detect the violent scenes using surveillance cameras and Embedded GPU in real-time we have developed this project for the benefit of our society. As the alert is generated in real-time, the security can take action immediately to prevent any further damage or mishappening in the crowd. Our primary objective is to automatically differentiate between violent activities and non-violent activities through CCTV surveillance cameras and automatically display the security alert on the screen as soon as any violent activity is captured and thus ensuring the safety of our society.**

I. Introduction

Violence is any intentional act causing injury to another person by way of bodily contact. It can be domestic violence or workplace aggression. These crimes may happen in any crowded places like schools, hospitals, courts, malls, offices, religious places or any other public place. For ensuring the security in these places we heavily depend on the usage of CCTV cameras. In most places, we have the facilities to install CCTV cameras but do they really prove useful to avoid unusual activity eventhough they might be small like hitting one another. CCTV footages are used as an evidence in court but not often. It is also not considered in real-time at the time of happening. The footages are observed and assessed by humans but due to many worker's weariness, boredom, or discontinuous observation makes the scrutiny unreliable. We check footages after everything has happened. This can be avoided if we get an alert and take an action while happening these incidents.

The latest report on annual crime data of India, Crime in India 2017 by the National Crime Records bureau has revealed that there has been an increase of 3.6 % in criminal cases in 2017 as compared to that of 2016 when 50 lakhs of cognisable offences were lodged across the India. There was a 9 % raise in kidnapping and abduction cases in 2017, with 95,893 cases registered against 88,008 in 2016, declared by NCRB. Giving growth to the need of surveillance cameras there has been increase of manufacturing CCTV. According to industrial experts, it is estimated that over a million of surveillance systems were sold every month a couple of years ago. But now it has increased to two million. The Indian market is continuously making the growth of around 20-25% annually. Industries sources have estimated that the security and surveillance market was worth Rs 8,200 crore in year 2017, which reached 11,000 crore in year 2018 and it is expected that it may even touch to Rs 20,000 by the year 2020. But was installing the cameras has solved the problem completely? Although there has been decrease but still many incidents have been encountered and actions were taken after everything has happened. An issue with having so much of data of cameras is that they have captured too much of data for effective human observations. Due to daily increase of this data it becomes difficult for human observer to detect interested scenes from video frames. Thus limiting the benefits of recordings of surveillance cameras.

To address this issue and automatically detect the violent scenes using surveillance cameras and Embedded GPU we are aiming to develop and apply Openpose[9] and real time action recognition algorithm[1] in this project for the benefit of our society. Our idea is based on capturing crowded scenes and extracting the visual data and feeding the collected data to action recognition algorithm[1]. Our primary objective is that by using visual surveillance CCTV cameras we can ensure the maximum safety of our society by giving an alert only if any violent activities are happening avoiding the regular human actions which are not threatening to human life. The appearance of human body and behaviour of the people is different for violent activities when compared to that of people exhibiting normal activities. We would be taking live video frames captured by CCTV and extract some features. This extracted data will be compared with our database which will consist of classified frames representing both violent and non-violent behaviour. As soon as result falls in violent category a popup alert will be displayed on surveillance screen. Hence to develop a model that is based on action recognition[1] which can learn the human behaviour and actions through sequences of poses and classifying them into violent and non-violent activity is the sole purpose of this project.

II. Graphical Processing Unit

GPU can render images more quickly as compared to that of CPU because of its capability to do parallel computing at the same time since it has been featured with parallel processing architecture. A CPU also has a higher clock speed, which means it can perform any task or calculations faster than a GPU so it is often better equipped to perform basic computing tasks but not for image processing. CPU and GPU architectures also differ in their number of cores. The core is basically the processor within the processor. Each core processes its own tasks or threads. While CPUs can run only two threads per core whereas GPUs can run four to ten thread per core. Due to the available feature of massive parallel construction, GPUs can run a software algorithm much faster than any other processor could do. As the performance of hardware partially depends on software, the speed and controllability of the hardware is also increased by the use of GPUs as its software support. GPUs also give good results in floating-point operations. A GPU with 384 cores can perform 384 floating-point operations per cycle. Hence, for applications consisting of intensive image processing, GPU is considered as an ideal processing unit. GPUs also offer better backward compatibility. Nowadays, many latest signal and image processing algorithms considers GPUs for computation. Designing with Direct Memory Access (DMA) and very fast memory techniques enabled it to stream high volume data to GPU without consuming clock cycles. Further, GPUs are supported with a wide variety and wide array of free math function libraries and open development tools.

III. TensorFlow OpenPose Algorithm

Pose Estimation is the process of detecting position and orientation of a object. In case of human body detection the prime focus is on the major joints/parts of the body(Ears, Eyes, Nose, Neck, Shoulders, Wrists, Elbows, Hip, Knees, Ankles). In case of a single person pose detection it is comparatively easy process where localizing keypoints and joining the pairs of relatable parts. When there are multiple people in a image frame, the algorithm produces keypoints for each individual. The next step is to figure out which keypoints belong to which individual. The database used by the Openpose algorithm[8] is based model trained on the COCO dataset which uses 18 point skeleton. The keypoints representation is given as below:

Point	*Body Part*
0	Nose
1	Neck
2	Right Shoulder
3	Right Elbow
4	Right Wrist
5	Left Shoulder
6	Left Elbow
7	Left Wrist
8	Right Hip
9	Right Knee
10	Right Ankle
11	Left Hip
12	Left Knee
13	Left Ankle
14	Right Eye
15	Left Eye
16	Right Ear
17	Left Ear
18	Background

Fig. 1. COCO keypoints. [8]

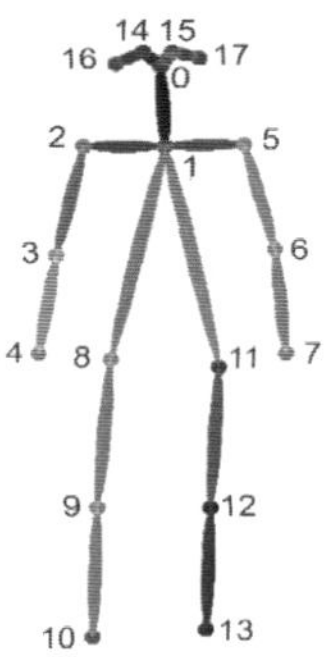

Fig. 2. OpenPose skeleton. [9]

The Openpose model takes a color image as input and produces a confidence map array for each keypoint alongwith Part Affinity Heatmaps for each key-point pair.[26] The algorithm is further divided into stages as explained below:

1) Stage 0: This stage is for creation of feature maps for each input image and consists of ten layers of VGG network. [8]
2) Stage 1:This stage uses 2-branch CNN where each branch does the following:
   a) Predicting the set of 2-D confidence maps of body parts is the main objective of this branch. It is a grayscale image which depicts high value at the prominent position of a body part. In this project the first 5 frames correspond to confidence map's matrices.[8]
   b) Predicting the set of vector fields for respective Part Affinity Fields is the objective of this branch. It illustrates the association between different body parts.[3]

IV. Design Algorithm

The Real Time Action Recognition[1] algorithm divides the process into Preprocessing, Feature Extraction, ML algorithm. Initially the video inputs from camera module are provided which needs to be converted to images. Those images contain certain series of images which define the required action. Only those are considered and OpenPose[8] algorithm is applied.

A. Preprocessing

The skeleton data obtained is stored as a raw data. It must be preprocessed before extracting the features. The following steps are to be followed to process the raw data:

1) Scaling of the coordinates
   The output obtained from Openpose algorithm has different unit for x and y coordinates. It is necessary that these units are scaled to same units. The value of height to width ratio is different for each frames. Scaling helps to obtain regular pattern in further processing.[1]

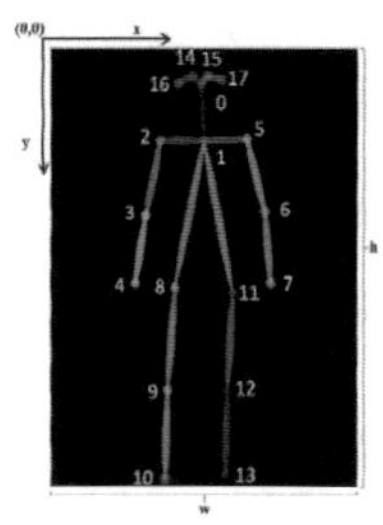

Fig. 3. Scaling of coordinates. [1]

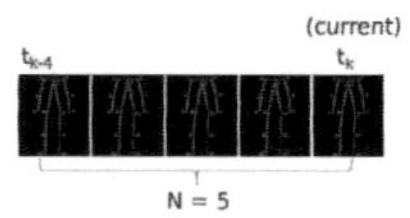

Fig. 4. Concatenation of frames. [1]

2) Remove all invalid joints
   The purpose of this project work is to classify between normal activities and violent activities. Initial classification will not require some joints in the skeleton (for example head joints). Those joints must be manually removed to make meaningful feature extraction.[1]

3) Discarding invalid frames
During the frames extraction there are chance of getting frames with no openpose skeleton or highly distorted skeleton output. Such frames are invalid for future processsing and would cause deflections in desired model designing.[1]
4) Filling up of useful missing joints
In some frames the Openpose algorithm might fail to detect a complete human skeleton. It may cause blanks in the joint positions. These values has to be filled with some valid values in order to maintain a fixed-size feature for Classification procedure. One of the solutions is to discard the frame which can cause the algorithm to not detect the person if it not facing the camera or standing sideways. The algorithm uses relative positions from previous frame that was detected. With this method the missing positions can be filled.[1]

B. Feature Extraction

At the end of the previous steps the joint positions are ready to use for feature extracting[1]. According to the application of our project following features must be computed:

1) Concatenation of Joints in N frames
This feature gives out the possible action formation with N frames concatenated altogether.
2) Average Skeleton Height
Due to removal of invalid joints in the previous steps the height of the skeleton frames may vary in height. This step helps it to normalize into average height.
3) Velocity of Body to Neck
It provides the velocity of complete body within the frame.
4) Normalized positions
The position of the subject in the skeleton frames may vary and hence a normalized position frames are extracted for better results.
5) Velocity of joints
Basic human actions can be easily classified by tracking the movements of the limbs. This feature helps extract the velocity of the joints with normalized coordinates.
6) Joint Angles
This will extract the Joint angles required for classification purpose.
7) Limb Lengths
This will extract the Limb lengths required for classification purpose.

C. Neural Networks(NN)

Neural networks consist of neurons with weight and prejudices learned. Each neuron receives several entries, take a weighted sum on them, pass it through a activation function and respond with an output. There are several layers of input and output on NN. The hidden neurons enable the network to learn complex tasks by progressively extracting more meaningful features from input patterns. The basic building block of NN is the convolution layer, which applies the convolution operation as input and passes it to the next layer. Humans can merely recognize any action which come in their sight. Though the same action may be recognized in multiple ways but atlast the action may remain the same as recognized by everyone. The task of recognizing will done using computer vision in case of computers. Computer vision depends on the images captured with certain pixel resolution. In this project approach we obtained the skeleton image data and skeleton text data of violent and non-violent actions. Neural Networks begins with taking a skeleton image with certain pixels that represent a bunch of neurons correponding the pixels sizes. Each neuron holds the number value, ranging from 0(background) to 1(skeleton limbs). This forms the first layer of neural networks. The last layer here is the activity is violent or non-violent that is two neurons. In the middle there are hidden layers which get activated depending upon the preceding layer. Such a structure helps in training the dataset to classify the activities.

V. Implementation

We created our dataset of images by recording action videos. Images containing the precise action postures were sorted manually and fed to the Openpose algorithm[8] followed by the real time action recognition algorithm[1].

- Obtain joints position from OpenPose algorithm.[9]
- Tracing each person in the image frame and distance between the joints of two skeletons is used for differentiating two skeletons.[1]
- Filling in a person's joints on the basis of previous frame or series of frames.[1]
- Extract features according to the (x,y) joint positions.Uses 5 frames(0.5s window size) for this purpose.[1]
- Extract features such as body velocity, normalized joint positions and joint velocities.[1]
- Apply PCA technique to reduce feature dimension. Classify by various machine learning algorithms.[1]
- Filtering the prediction scores between two frames and add appropriate label to the person if the score is greater than 0.8.

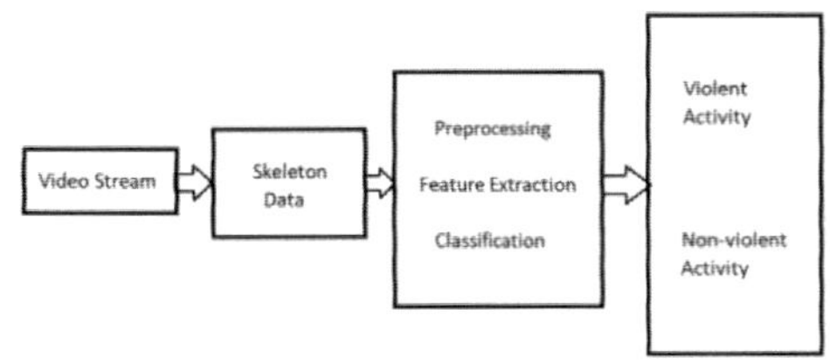

Fig. 5. Workflow.

The obtained model design will be saved as pickle file. The creation of portable and size restricted model design was fulfilled by pickle file. The overall process consisted of many objects and classes which were successfully calibrated and decalibrated with this module. Such file occupies vey less space on a disk. Merits of Pickle Module:

- Same attributes for different Classes
  It has ability to keep a track of data that has been already serialized. So this is helpful for referencing for future use.
- Object Sharing
  Pickle file stores the object once and makes sure that the references are pointing towards master copy. It proves useful for objects that are mutable.
- On-the-go defined classes
  Defining the user needed functions and classes and placing them in the correct module where its objects are located.

VI. Results

The final recognition accuracies for a selective features extracted is shown in the table below. The result shows that the accuracy of all 5 models are higher than 90%. The speed

TABLE I. Recognition Accuracy of five models.

Method	*Training Accuracy*	*Testing Accuracy*
Deep Neural Networks	100%	97%
Decision Tree	93%	92%
k-Nearest Neighbors	96%	93%
Linear SVM	92%	90%
Random Forests	100%	96%

of the algorithms was tested on a laptop with a Geforce MX 150 GPU. The project framerate runs at about 7 fps when the image is resized to 432x368. The fps is seen to decrease for high resize values. The time cost for feature extraction and classification is less than 0.01s per frame for all classifiers, since the models are all relative shallow.

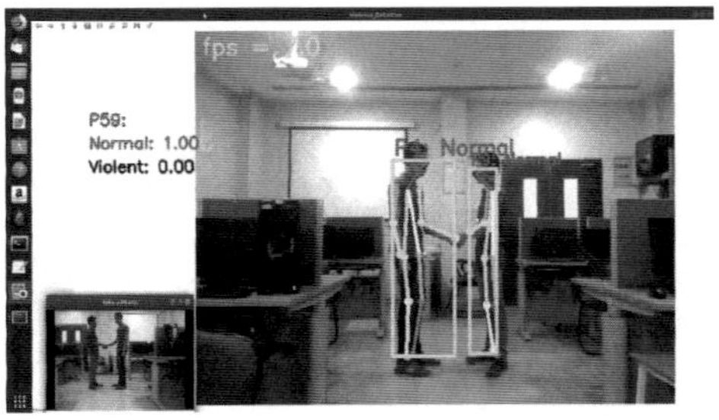

Fig. 6. Action: Non-violent

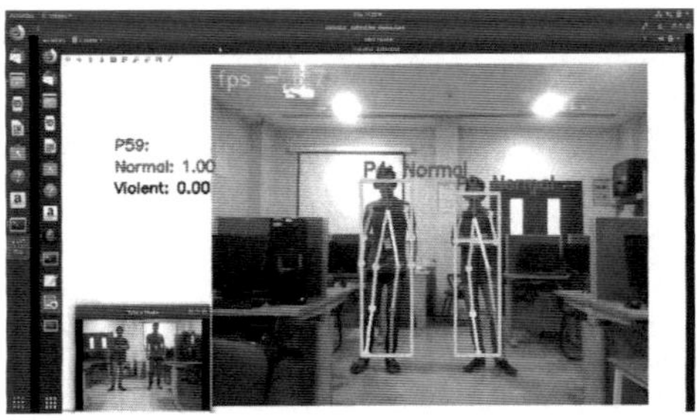

Fig. 7. Action: Non-violent

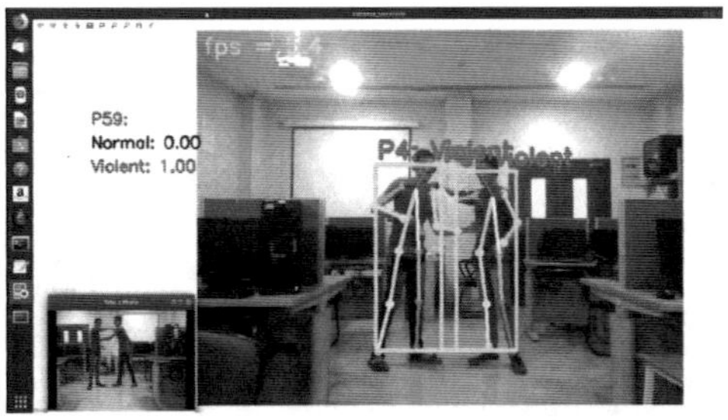

Fig. 8. Action: Violent

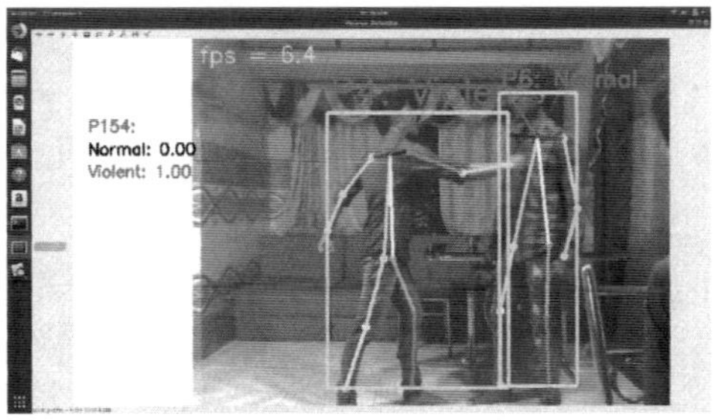

Fig. 9. Action: Violent

VII. Conclusion

We implemented a Violence Detection system that can detect types of actions as Violent and Non-violent. We obtained satisfactory results on our dataset which comprised of violent and non-violent activities. The recognition accuracy was up to 97% on the training set composed of more than 10000 samples. This detection system was then tested on real world videos captured through camera modules. It achieved stable and accurate recognition performance on a video similar to the training set and achieved relatively good result on other videos. Considering realistic issues like surveillance, human-computer interaction, the approach towards building a complex dataset is a state of art application with its broad range of applications. All the small steps taken in this field would lead to robust automatic human actions recognition system in future.

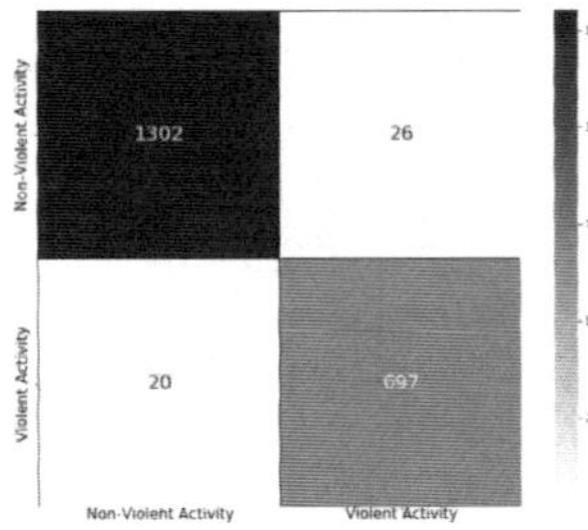

Fig. 10. Confusion Matrix.

REFERENCES

[1] Feiyu Chen, Real-time Action Recognition Based on Human Skeleton in Video, Final Project of EECS-433 Pattern Recognition, Teacher: Prof. YingWu,https://github.com/felixchenfy/Data-Storage/blob/master/EECS-433-Pattern-Recognition/FeiyuChen_Report_EECS433.pdf

[2] R. C. Gonzalez and R. E. Woods, Digital Image Processing, 3rd Edition, Prentice Hall, 2008, ISBN-13: 9780131687288.

[3] Z. Cao, T. Simon, S.-E. Wei, and Y. Sheikh, Realtime multi-person 2d pose estimation using part affinity fields, in CVPR, 2017.

[4] Lillo, I., Soto, A., and Niebles, J. C. (2014). Discriminative hierarchical modeling of spatio-temporally composable human activities, in Proc. IEEE Computer Society Conference on Computer Vision and Pattern Recognition (Columbus, OH), 812819.

[5] Yang, W., Wang, Y., and Mori, G. (2010). Recognizing human actions from still images with latent poses, in Proc. IEEE Computer Society Conference on Computer Vision and Pattern Recognition (San Francisco, CA), 20302037.

[6] Thurau, C., and Hlavac, V. (2008). Pose primitive based human action recognition in videos or still images, in Proc. IEEE Computer Society Conference on Computer Vision and Pattern Recognition (Anchorage, AK), 18.

[7] Tran, K. N., Kakadiaris, I. A., and Shah, S. K. (2012). Part-based motion descriptor image for human action recognition. Pattern Recognit. 45, 25622572. doi:10.1016/j.patcog.2011.12.028

[8] An example of the skeleton representation obtained using the OpenPose library www.researchgate.com

[9] Z. Cao, T. Simon, S.-E. Wei, and Y. Sheikh, Realtime multi-person 2d pose estimation using part affinity fields, in CVPR, 2017.

[10] Deep Neural Network for Image Classification www.datascience-enthusiast.com

[11] Sedai, S., Bennamoun, M., and Huynh, D. Q. (2013a). Discriminative fusion of shape and appearance features for human pose estimation. Pattern Recognit. 46, 32233237.doi:10.1016/j.patcog.2013.05.019

[12] Rodriguez, M. D., Ahmed, J., and Shah, M. (2008). Action MACH: a spatio-temporal maximum average correlation height filter for action recognition, in Proc. IEEE Computer Society Conference on Computer Vision and Pattern Recognition (Anchorage,AK), 18.

[13] Chaitra B H, Anupama H S, Cauvery N K "Human Action Recognition using Image Processing and Artificial Neural Networks" International Journal of Computer Applications (0975 8887) Volume 80 No.9, October 2013

[14] Maji, S., Bourdev, L. D., and Malik, J. (2011). Action recognition from a distributed representation of pose and appearance, in Proc. IEEE Computer Society Conference on Computer Vision and Pattern Recognition (Colorado Springs, CO), 31773184.

[15] L. Weilun, H. Jungong, and P. With, Flexible human behavior analysis framework for video surveillance applications, Int. J. Digital Multimedia Broadcast., vol. 2010, pp.920121-1920121-9, Jan. 2010.

[16] T. Kohonen, Self-Organizing Maps, Springer, Berlin, Heidelberg, 1995.

[17] G.Strang, The discrete cosine transform, SIAM Review, vol. 41, No.1, pp.135 - 147, 1999.

[18] Sigal, L., Isard, M., Haussecker, H. W., and Black, M. J. (2012a). Loose-limbed people: estimating 3D human pose and motion using non-parametric belief propagation. Int. J. Comput. Vis. 98, 1548. doi:10.1007/s11263-011-0493-4

[19] A tutorial on principal component analysis J Shlens - arXiv preprint arXiv:1404.1100, 2014

[20] Classification of Knowledge Based Image using Decision Tree Algorithm Vadthe Narasimha, B.Satyanarayana, K. Krishnaiah, International Journal of Recent Technology and Engineering (IJRTE) ISSN: 2277-3878,Volume-8, Issue- 1C2, May 2019

[21] RGBD Human Action Recognition using Multi-Features Combination and K-Nearest Neighbors Classification www.researchgate.net/publication/320804220

[22] Human Action Recognition using SVM and KNN Classifiers International Journal of Innovations & Advancement in Computer Science IJIACS ISSN 2347 8616 Volume 5, Issue 8 August 2016

[23] R. Poppe, A survey on vision-based human action recognition, Image and Vision Computing, vol. 28, pp. 976990, 2010.

[24] R. Messing, C. Pal, and H. Kautz, Activity recognition using the velocity histories of tracked keypoints, in ICCV, 2009.

[25] 2017 CVPR: Quo vadis, action recognition? a new model and the kinetics dataset

[26] 2017 CVPR: Realtime Multi-Person 2D Pose Estimation using Part Affinity Fields 2007.

 https://doi.org/10.1051/itmconf/20203203015

A Parallel Environment Designing for OWL Thinking

Ms. Sanjana C Madargi[1,3,*] and *Dr. Leena R* Ragha[2]*Mrs. Vanita M* Mane[3]

[1]Department of Computer Engineering R.A.I.T Nerul, Navi Mumbai, 400706.
[2]Department of Computer Engineering R.A.I.T Nerul, Navi Mumbai, 400706
[3]Department of Computer Engineering R.A.I.T Nerul, Navi Mumbai, 400706

Abstract. A huge volume of information available today is in the form of images and searching the wanted images is very difficult and highly time-consuming. The search may take longer periods as the search volume on the internet is very huge and also the relevance of extracted images is still not up to the mark. The technologies like ontology and languages like OWL help us to tag the images that describe the semantic of the images. Hence, it helps in faster searching of the wanted images. Also, another challenge with OWL and Semantic web is the speed in which one can derive the relationships between various objects extracted from the images. The challenge is to extract the semantic from the images more efficiently using a parallel approach. In this paper, we explore the different techniques for generating semantic knowledge using parallel approaches like the T-box approach, merge classification, extract concept for matching ontology. We propose an enhanced method to speed-up the computation by combining T-box and merge classification techniques.

Keywords: OWL, Multiple-threading, Merge sort, Ontology.

1 Introduction

With technology growth, everything is getting automated these days at a faster pace. Human adopts to the technologies that give him the best results. Nowadays we communicate with each other on the web. Thus, a lot of data is generated in the form of text and images. As a human, it is quite simple to understand the natural language but it is a challenging task for a system, thus natural language processing is required. A picture worth a thousand words. And hence, communication through images has taken over the world. There is a need for categorization of these images for faster searching from the huge volume of various categories and domains of images. Traditional co-ordination frameworks have essentially focused on syntactic organization and concentrated less on the semantic information. Given the dynamic and complex environment, where data from the scope of heterogeneous spaces is traded, it is critical to think about the natural significance of data.

The understanding of ontology procedure requires a detailed examination of ideas, terms, and connections in different areas of interest. It requests a minute exchange of information related to ideas since it is conveyed for an away from the area. Ontology learning is beginning to develop as a sub-area of ontology designing because of the fast increment of web archives and the propelled methods shared by the data recovery, AI, regular language preparation, and artificial intelligence networks.

*e-mail: sanjanacmadargi@gmail.com

Philosophy portrays an area, while an information base (given ontology) depicts a specific situation. The conceptualization portrays information about the area in the form of objects and not about the specific situation in the space. Also, the conceptualization does not change or changes once in a while. Philosophy is then the determination of this conceptualization and is indicated by utilizing a specific display of dialect and specific terms. Formal determination is required to have the capacity to process ontology and work on object identification simultaneously.

Therefore, looking through the immense volume of data as pictures extracting the needed pictures that too in real-time is a challenge and we propose to work on this front. The paper explores the parallel technologies used by different researchers in this domain of image information retrieval in section 2 as part of a literature survey. Section 3 concentrates on the proposed method and applies it to an example to demonstrate how it works. The practical implementation of it in the distributed environment and the time complexity analysis is beyond the scope of the paper.

2 Literature Review

We surveyed research work based on parallel computing techniques and algorithms. The overall methodology applied by different researchers is explained below:
Gauthami Latha [1] et.al. the author explain about semantic-based inquiry gives suitable and applicable outcomes than those of conventional watchword based hunt. The effectiveness of the semantic-put together pursuit depends with respect to utilizing the properties and connections among the pictures are named "Ontology" and it is built by thinking about the degree of human

comprehension. Ontology is developed by utilizing the low-level highlights like surface, shading, and state of pictures which duplicates human comprehension. In this way, philosophy is viewed as progressively helpful for the recovery of pictures that are semantic-based. The picture recovery strategy named Content-based low-level highlights of the picture than the whole picture. The other option for picture recovery is supposed to be proficient as it considers low-level highlights of the picture than the whole picture. Another option for the picture recovery process is performed utilizing philosophy based portrayals named Ontology-based picture recovery which utilized the information portrayals that incorporate the setting of substance based picture recovery with the content-based picture recovery highlights. The key thought of philosophy is to introduce the picture in semantic documentation which is interpret able for the machine prompting the effective recovery of results. The Ontology gives the portrayal of information utilizing the elements indicating the OWL with the development of classes, relations, characteristics and occasions among area people which is upheld consistently as Rules.

Zixi Quan et.al. [2, 3] the author described novel parallel OWL classification architecture. They have proposed a random division strategy for good speed- up and scalable for ontology's of large sizes and in end group division strategy to complete T-box classification. In this paper, it is compared with sequential classification methods and limitations of parallel approaches. It deals with extensive scale ontology to show signs of improvement execution contrasted with existing consecutive methods. The plan is to accomplish a superior load balance answer for the two parallel phrases. By parallel T-box classification, technique demonstrates promising outcomes that influence to trust it could be connected to ontology's with a lot bigger size and confounded ontology with promising run time and a superior speed-up. Parallel T-box classification approach, in which it concentrates on parallelism on basis of threading. By multiple threads co-exists and based on randomizing distribution on a given data set. For example, an image is given in which describes fruit, vehicle, chocolate, and animal. To classify that which set will give the exact match with refined meaning. Consider some sets of threads present splitting sub-parts as P, Q, R, S for testing for the similarities. And assume the categories as C1 as Fruits, C2 as Cars, C3 as Chocolate and C4 as Dogs.

Step 1: Consider the below database of the objects as shown:
S_P = {Apple, SUV}
S_Q = {Orange, Cadbury, Peach, Sedan}
S_R = {Mango, i20, Audi, Snickers, Poodle, Pug}
S_S = {Honda city, German shepherd, Banana, Kit-kat, Water Melon}.
Step 2: As per the above given categories for each data which is fetched from the dictionary, groups will be generated as given below:
Fruit: Group 1: C_1 = {Apple, Orange, Peach, Mango, Banana, Water Melon}
Car: Group 2: C_2 = {SUV, Audi, i20, Honda city, Sedan}
Chocolate: Group 3: C_3 = {Cadbury, Kit-kat, Snickers}
Dog: Group 4: C_4 = {German shepherd, Poodle, Pug}.
Step 3: Four groups {tt_1, tt_2, tt_3, tt_4} are created from above categorization as below:
tt_1: {1,2}
tt_2: {1,3,1,2}
tt_3: {1,2,2,3,4,4}
tt_4: {2,4,2,1,3,2}.
Step 4: Finally, suppose S_X ={Apple, Sedan, Pug}. The possible sets from above sets are: tt_1 = {1}, tt_2 = {1,2}, tt_3 = {1,3}, tt_4 = {1,4}, tt_5 = {1,2,3}, tt_6 = {1,2,4}, tt_7 = {1,3,4}, tt_8= {1,2,3,4}. The result of image is group 6(tt_6) contains the set of {1,2,4} which match with {Apple, Sedan, Pug}.

Kejia Wu et.al. [4] provides exploration is motivated by the ubiquitous accessibility of multiprocessor PCs and the perception that accessible Web Ontology Language (OWL) reasoners just make utilization of a solitary processor. This much work has only researched the performance of the concurrent merge classification. Parallel merge classification uses merge sort, data set will be divided into n different parts, each part sorted and operated on a given part of data by a particular processing unit.

Mina Aslani et.al. [5] described an architecture for parallelism well-known algorithm for T-box classification. Work was focused on ontology's where free partitions cannot be effortlessly built; in this way did not utilize the recently referenced approaches in the system. Also plan to implement and test approach in a multi-center and multiprocessor condition.

Mina Aslani et.al. [6] one of the most frequently used inference services of description logic of reasoners is the classification of T-boxes with a subsumption pecking order of all named ideas as the outcome.

Markus Fronk et.al. [7] introduced a path to explaining services utilizing OWL- DL standard reasoners. The solution described in this paper especially versatile for the robotizing of the revelation and the arrangement of web services.

Alaa Qassim et.al. [8] this paper gives a depiction of the plan of the automatic annotation system. The design phase of any exploration is the most significant part as it depicts how the framework will be organized to meet the prerequisites. Matching ontology on the semantic web of documents briefly and expressly through separating just the related resultant semantics from the document. For example, Mississippi the state, from Mississippi the stream, narrow searching of the word from the dictionary which defines the meaning recognize the various words. It can resolve the ambiguity of all the contexts on which it is referred.

Andreas Steigmiller et.al. [9] presents Konclude, a high performance reasoned for the description logic SROIQV. The supported ontology language is a super-set of the logic fundamental OWL 2 reached out by nominal schemas, which takes into consideration communicating discretionary DL-safe standards. Konclude's thinking center is fundamentally founded on the well-known tableau calculus for expressive description logic. This paper depicts Konclude's interface choices, reasoner design, preparing the work process, and key improvements.

We have studied the techniques which are related to the computation work and semantics related to OWL ontology and semantics of image too. The precision of ontology classification in this context is that semantic labeling helps in arranging the general pictures, for quicker inquiry and specific individual's pictures can be understood deeply. The parallel T-box classification contains several subsumption sets due to which the performance of the overall classification of ontology gets lowered and parallel merge classification is applied to the larger samples will consume more amount of time. So, we propose to address these issues in the proposed method section below with some data-set to understand it.

3 Proposed Method

The proposed solution aims to overcome the individual drawbacks of parallel T- box and merge classification approaches. The strategy is to mix various threading and consolidation sort technique. The benefits compared to sequential execution with parallelization is that the task can be done concurrently with interaction on similar processors between them which leads to time-saving and easily share data-sets.

Working on the proposed technique and its flow is shown in Figure 1. From examples, we obtained constraints of individual techniques Parallel T-box classification approach and parallel merge classification. The proposed technique defeats the confinement of calculation. In merge-sort, multiple threading is used where each part would be operated simultaneously by a particular thread. The basic idea is to produce multiple threads that may exploit a system with a single processor with multiple cores or a multi-processor system. In a single processor system with multi-threading, context switching would be faster, the thread can easily share their data sets and stay away from conceivable race conditions for updates of shared information. Merge sort algorithm helps in better context switching and threads can easily share data by dividing and sorting. Hence improving the efficiency of computation can be achieved. For parallel computing, we require a multi-core processor with OpenMP or MPI techniques to support computing.

The steps followed are as follows:

Step 1: Loading the text or images and content is stored in the distributed memory so that work can be done at a concurrent time. As to fetch information in detail have dictionary-engine in which it has two parts. First is a tag and second are tittles which will be pointing to the keywords, so that feature extraction becomes easier.

Step 2: Dividing tasks into equal numbers that are waiting to get completed their jobs in the queue.

Step 3: Categorize the components according to who comes before the execution time slice. As the number of tasks is waiting for their execution, this helps to take concurrent work and to improve the speed-up factor.

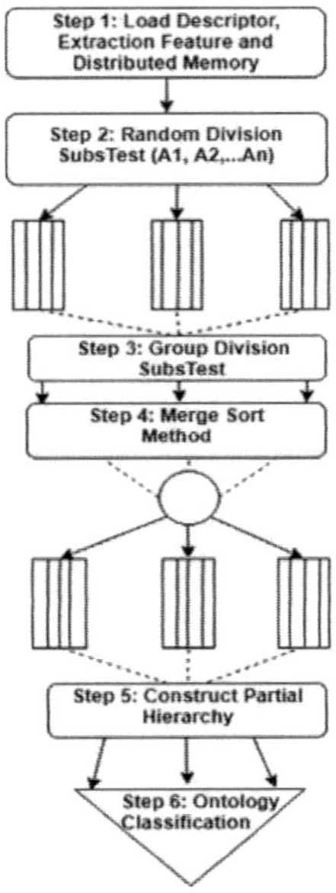

Figure 1. Generalized Working of Proposed Method

Step 4: This step is where the merge sort is to be applied. It takes the sets from the above step, divides the sets by $n1$ number of tasks of the same type, from that divide the sets by $n2$ number of sub-tasks for the total number of tasks until we get the last sub-parts separately.

Step 5: After the task is divided, fragmented order for the same sets of data will be constructed and stored to create an ontology.

Step 6: Finally, the ontology will be classified which narrows down the search process. Here we achieve the feasible solution with the finer meaning of the individual identified objects.

The whole process is demonstrated using data-set to conclude about the given proposed method the following example.

Example: The image will have objects that describe the lifestyle of a person. It is required to identify the different objects and group them to label the image in the end w.r.t. the lifestyle of a person. Here we assume that the objects are extracted from the image and are associated with object names. Also, let us assume the universal dictionary has the following groups.

Fruit: Group 1: G1 = {Apple, Orange, Peach, Mango, Banana, Water Melon}

Car: Group 2: G2 = {SUV, Audi, i20, Honda city, Sedan}

Scenery: Group 3: G3 = {Cloudy Sky, Sleepy, Snow, Sports ground, Forest}

Step 1: Divide the given sets randomly as the task is dispatched and then merge them to form groups based on the predefined Categories they belong to in the dictionary database.

Step 2: Form the local group of sets with similar context as of dictionary.
C1 = Fruit = Banana, Apple, Mango,
C2 = Car = SUV, Audi, i20,
C3 – Scenery = Cloudy Sky, Sleepy, Snow, Sports ground, Forest.
Step 3: Merge the above groups based on the relations we want between the different sets using the categorized words to form a tree as shown in Figure 2.
Step 4: In this step, Hierarchy is constructed with the help of the above tree and the lifestyle which is person-related can be further divided into with other entities like rich, poor, lavish, religious, balanced, sportsman, trekker, etc and again it gets divided accordingly to get the semantic ontology for the given image.
Step 5: Ontology of the images thus extracted is classified with this context-based interpretation.

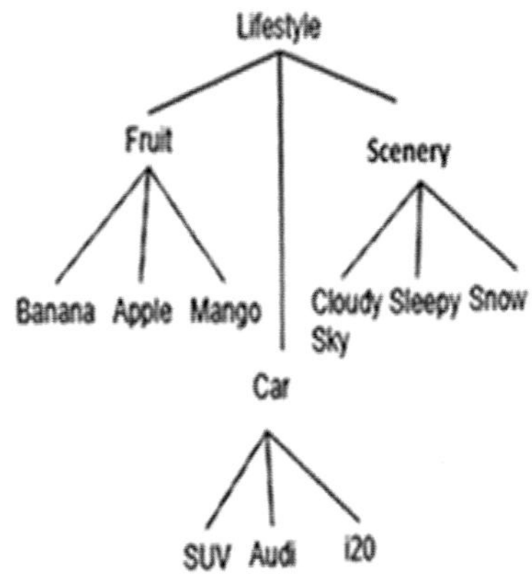

Figure 2. Result produced in Step 4

4 Results and conclusions

This kind of semantic tagging helps in categorizing the general images, for faster search. It also helps to track a particular person's images to extract the lifestyle of the person.
For an input image with objects like a person with SUV, Apple, and Snow the result will be a trekker.

One can also go beyond the lifestyle to identify his spending habits and economic status. Thus, the tree starts becoming deeper in levels. Based on the expressions given in their evaluation by the reasoning of a standard reasoner and behavioral aspects of a web application service, the request can be automatically executed to generate the semantics.

References

[1] Gauthami Latha, Ch. Satyanarayana, Y. Srinivas.: Semantic Image Annotation using Ontology And SPARQL. Web Semantics: Science, Services and Agents on the World Wide Web 2728, 2014. International Journal of Innovative Technology and Exploring Engineering (IJITEE) ISSN: 2278-3075, Volume-9 Issue-3, January 2020.

[2] Zixi Quan, Volker Haarslev.: A parallel computing architecture for high-performance OWL reasoning. Parallel Computing, 2018.

[3] Z Quan, V.Haarslev.: A Parallel Shared-Memory Architecture for OWL Ontology Classification. 46th International Conference on Parallel Processing Workshops, IEEE, 2017.

[4] Kejia Wu, V. Haarslev.: Parallel OWL Reasoning: Merge Classification. JIST, Revised Selected Papers of the Third Joint International Conference on Semantic Technology, 2013.

[5] Mina Aslani, V. Haarslev.: Parallel T-box Classification in Description Logic's First Experimental Results. Proceedings of the 2010 conference on ECAI: 19th European Conference on Artificial Intelligence, 2010.

[6] Mina Aslani, V. Haarslev.: Towards Parallel Classification of T-boxes. Proceedings of the 21st International Workshop on Description Logic's (DL 2008), Dresden, Germany, May 13-16, 2008.

[7] Markus Fronk, Jens Lemcke.: Expressing Semantic Web Service Behavior using Description Logic's, 2006.

[8] Alaa Qassim, Al-Namiy.: Algorithm to Match Ontology's on the Semantic Web. (IJACSA) International Journal of Advanced Computer Science and Applications, Vol. 4, No.3, 2013.

[9] Andreas Steigmiller, Thorsten Liebig, Birte Glimm.: Konclude: System description. Web Semantics: Science, Services and Agents on the World Wide Web 2728, 2014.

The Implementation of Covert Channel in IPV6 using Linux Kernel

Simran D Munot[1,], Mitali J Yevale [1], Nikhil M Raut [1], and Dhananjay M Dakhane[2]*

[1] Department of Computer Engg, Ramrao Adik Institute of Technology, Nerul, Navi-Mumbai, India
[2] Professor, Department of Computer Engg, Ramrao Adik Institute of Technology, Nerul, Navi-Mumbai, India

Abstract. Nowadays indirect communication is used as a mechanism to bypass the direct communication network channel. Such indirect communication channels prove as a threat to information-sensitive systems that don't allow leakage of information like Military communication. Developing a covert channel in the network requires some carriers like TCP Headers or Protocols. The only challenge is that it possesses strict semantics. If it is manipulated by even a single bit, the entire semantics will change. The packet will be considered as a forged packet and will get rejected automatically by a firewall. To avoid this, we have proposed a unique way of covert communication - TCP and IPv6 Referencing Model. In our proposed referencing model, instead of embedding any bit and destroying the semantics of the header, we are going to use the referencing method to send the covert bit from sender to receiver end. Thus the packet will appear a part of normal distribution and gets transmitted securely within the channel. Here we are using the TCP Sequence Number (SQN) to make this possible.

1 INTRODUCTION

The communication channel is defined as a mechanism to transmit any message from the sender device to the predetermined host device. Currently, the communication channels can be categorised into two: Overt and covert communication channels. The overt communication channel is defined as the mechanism which is followed ethically to establish communication between two communication devices. The covert communication channel is defined as the false mechanism that is followed by the devices to establish a communication channel between them. Today, a plethora of devices are now internet protocol (IP) enabled. Increased complexity in communication has made the task challenging for the network administrators to define a security policy that ensures an ethical way of communication between the host and the destination. Defining a new and own proprietary protocol will open up the possibilities of a security breach. As stated by Zander and Van Horenbeek in their respective studies - The real-world applications and the academic research on this topic has a huge gap; the current academic research is uncertain due to the applicability of some of the approaches on detection of such unethical communication channels. Now the question is which carrier to utilize for covert communications? Given in the present era, the choice of protocols, Internet Protocol version 4 (IPv4) currently, is one of the most pervasive protocols in deployment. It has become a good carrier for covert channel exploits because of its use in most of the communication over the globe. The IPv6 is designed for the successor of IPV4. As IPv4 is exhausting its address space for future use. It is very obvious that the focus will shift towards the IPv6 as a carrier for network covert channels. The covert channel in IPv6 is more secure like buffer overflow attacks

2 RELATED WORK

To identify the possible covert channels, R.Kemmerer in 1983 shared a resource matrix methodology that was used to analyse a constructed resource matrix. [13]

In a network environment in an OSI ISO framework, Girling, on a local area network (LAN) in 1987 first studied covert channels. He identified two storage covert channels and one covert timing channel on the LAN environment. [12]

In this protocol there are some reserved, padding and undefined fields which are used in TCP/IP protocol, In 1989 Wolf implemented the covert channels in LAN protocols. [15]
For a different TCP/IP to tunnel through, T. Handel of Stanford University in 1996 permitted a proprietary protocol that could open a security breach. The real-world applications and the academic research on this topic has a gap as pointed out by Zander [1] and Van Horenbeeck [2]; the current academic research is uncertain due to the applicability of some of the approaches on detection. Now the question is which carrier to utilize for covert communications? Given in

* Corresponding author: dhananjay.dakhane@rait.ac.in

the present era, the choice of protocols, Internet Protocol version 4 (IPv4) currently, is one of the most pervasive protocols in deployment. It has become a good carrier for covert channel exploits because of its uses in most of the communication over the globe. The IPv6 is designed for the successor of IPV4. As IPv4 is exhausting its address space for future use. It is very obvious that the focus will shift towards the IPv6 as a carrier for network covert channel. The covert channel in IPv6 is more secure like buffer overflow attacks. It stated his work on Hiding the Data in the OSI Network Model. All the possible loopholes in the OSI layers were analysed by him. It also stated that for implementing covert channels for exploiting hidden channels within the standard design of network communications protocols, this paper gave a basis to the development of a tool kit.

'Covert_tcp.c' scheme was proposed by C.H. Rowland in 1997 in which he gave the three methods which revolve around the IP-ID exploitation of IPv4 header, the sequence number and acknowledgement fields of the TCP header.

As it is a simple embedding method in these fields for covert communication which can be easily identified by SVMs and achieved a classification accuracy of up to 99% [4].

The practical techniques and uses of internet photography were investigated by Kamran Ahsan in 2002. To covertly communicate supplementary data, Internet steganography is the exploitation of Internet elements and protocols. For a demonstration of this theory, he worked on the Network layer of TCP/IP stack and analysed the two existing covert channels. He also studied the relation of bandwidth with covert communication by violating the systems security policy. This indeed increased the performance of the network applications [8].

In 2011, Grzegorz Lewandowski started his work in the paper "Network-aware Active Wardens in IPv6". The main focus of the paper was the answers to the important questions of covert channel theory. The answers were about the possibility of the existence of the covert channel in the IPv6 protocol and the counter security measures to prevent such unethical channels. [16]

Using the "IP Next Generation Protocol", widely referred to as IPv6, as well as its associated protocol ICMPv6, Geoffrey Ackerman, Daryl Johnson and Bill Stackpole in 2015 proposed a covert channel in a paper titled "Covert Channel Using ICMPv6 and IPv6 Addressing." [17]

3 PROPOSED REFERENCE MODEL

Our aim is to establish a connection over the network by creating a covert channel using TCP and IPv6 Header and decrease the asynchronous command channels between the compromised system and its master.

Every data packet is associated with a solitary 4-byte Sequence Number which is present in the TCP header. The main objective of this field is to identify the sequence of the data packets and redirect them to the proper destination host. At the receiver end, this number is also used for reassembling the data packets.

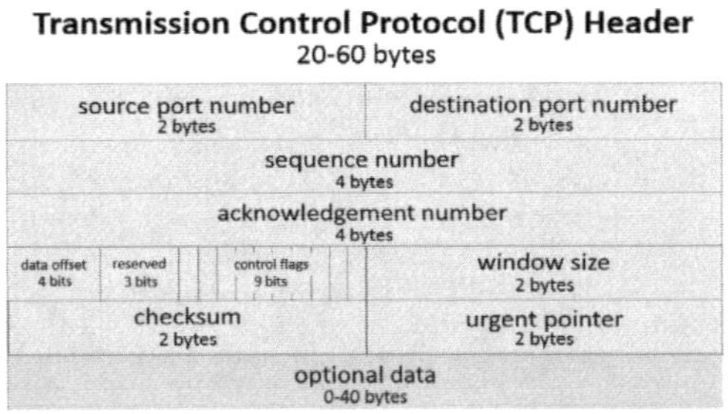

The possible combinations for the Sequence number of TCP headers are around 4294967296 values. The operating system must have a particular mechanism for the identification and generation of Sequence Number.

For implementation purposes, we propose to develop a Linux Kernel Module(LKM) at the sender's as well as the receiver's side.

As the packet enters the transport layer the programs can register with the Netfilter hooks (five predefined hooks). As the packet progresses through the stackn(Fig 3.1), it triggers the kernel modules and registers itself with the required hook. Depending upon the state of the packet (incoming or outgoing), the hooks will get triggered.

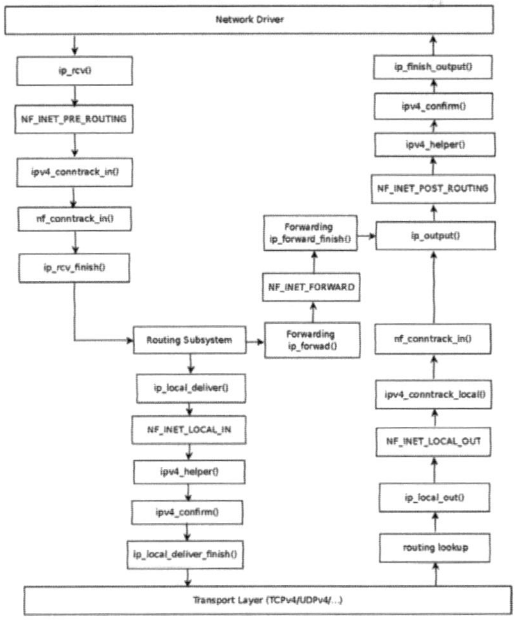

Fig.3.1: Flow of Data Packet From Network Layer to Transport layer.

The five pre-defined Netfilter hooks have well-defined points within the networking stack. They are as follows:

- NF_IP_PRE_ROUTING: Before making any routing decision (destination address), this hook gets triggered.
- NF_IP_LOCAL_IN: If the incoming data packet has the destination address of the local system then only the hook is triggered, otherwise the data packet is passed to the next hook.
- NF_IP_FORWARD: When an incoming packet is being forwarded to another host, this hook gets triggered.
- NF_IP_LOCAL_OUT: As soon as the packet enters the network stack, this hook gets triggered to create outbound traffic.
- NF_IP_POST_ROUTING: After routing takes place, this hook is triggered by any outgoing data packet or network traffic.

The order in which the hooks get triggered is determined by the priority number which is assigned to the kernel modules which wish to register themself in any of the five mentioned hooks.

A. Sender-Module

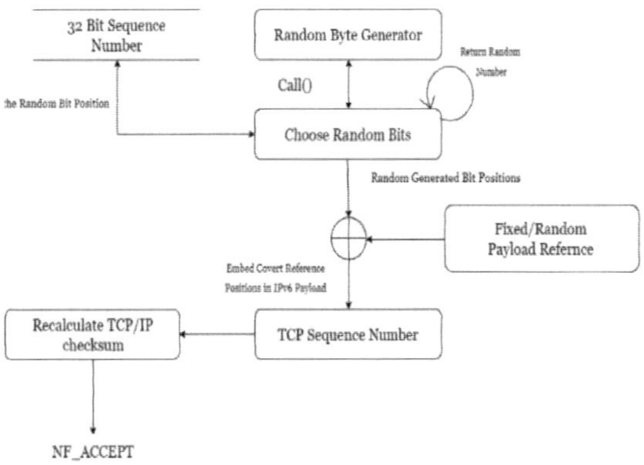

Fig 3.2: Reference Module - Sender Module.

The receiver receives covert messages from the sender through the sender module which is designed in our proposed system. Using the 32-bit Sequence Number field of TCP Header in this module, the referencing technique is used for the covert message. The architecture of the sender module is shown in Figure 3.2. In order to select the reference bit positions and embed these positions into the corresponding IPv6 payload, the Sequence Number field of TCP Header is taken into consideration. Instead of a simulated covert channel, an active covert channel is our proposed model.

32 bits per packet. i.e. total length of covert data to be sent per packet is the bandwidth of our proposed model. To elaborate, the entire 32-bits can be used as a maximum bandwidth.

Here, for all the possible bandwidths the procedure and base principles for covert information transmission are almost the same. In regards to the active covert channel, the intended process can be exploited.

B. Receiver Module

The receiving module will be similar to the sender module concerning the working mechanism. The receiver module is first initiated initially by registering itself inside the Linux kernel. As the data packet arrives at the sender end, travels through the application layer and enters the kernel level our Linux Kernel Model hook gets executed. With the help of the symbol table, the covert bits embedded in the Payload of the IPv6 Header is extracted. The bits are then converted into the actual message by the application level program.

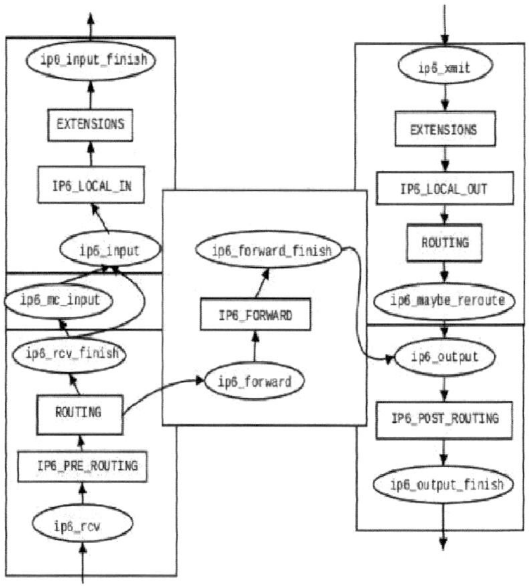

Fig 3.3: IP Routing inside the Linux Kernel.

4. RESULT

Consider the sender and Alice and receiver as Bob. Alice here wants to communicate with Bob covertly and send secure data to Bob. Suppose Alice (Sender) and Bob (Receiver) agree to use our proposed model for Communication, for sending Alice makes use of the CovertSender.ko while Bob uses CovertReceiver.ko

The table below describes the experimental results taken between Alice and Bob during their covert communication. The proposed model can be analysed using different bit sizes and different types of data used during communication.

Table No 1 contains the experimental result of covert communication when the sender sends 8-bit text data per packet, using our proposed model.

Covert Message	Text Data
File Size	2048 bytes
TCP Data Bytes	466944
Packet Received	2056
Covert Data	2048 bytes
Capacity = (Covert Data/TCP Data)	2048/466944 = 0.00438596
Bandwidth per packet	8 bit
Packet Loss	0.00%

Table 1. Results

Table No 2 contains the experimental result of covert communication when the sender sends 16-bit covert text data per packet, using our proposed model.

Covert Message	Text Data
File Size	2048 Bytes
TCP Data Bytes	233472
Packet Received	1026
Covert Data	2048 bytes
Capacity = (Covert Data/TCP Data)	2048/233472 = 0.00877193
Bandwidth per packet	16 bit
Packet Loss	0.00%

Table 2: Results

Table No 3 contains the experimental result of covert communication when the sender sends 32-bit covert text data per packet, using our proposed model.

Covert Message	Text Data
File Size	2048 bytes
TCP Data Bytes	116736
Packet Received	513
Covert Data	2048 bytes
Capacity = (Covert Data/TCP Data)	2048/116736 = 0.01754386
Bandwidth per packet	32 bits
Packet Loss	0.00%

Table 3: Results

5 CONCLUSION

While establishing a covert communication, one doesn't need to embed the data inside the TCP and IPv6 Header. Neither any bit of the TCP Header nor IPv6 Header has been modified in our proposed system. The syntax and semantics of TCP sequence number of overt communication are not altered to make it possible for covert communication. So that our covert communication is treated as overt communication. So that it will nullify the possibility of detection for passive as well as for active wardens. Hence we claim that our proposed model fulfils the criteria for "Legal and Implementation supported" type of covert channel.

That is the Network cannot distinguish between the covert and overt data packer. Hence the "Indistinguishability" characteristic has been achieved in our proposed system.

The covert channels bandwidth is an important characteristic of communication channels. Since communication is established using a single connection, there is no change in the bandwidth of the communication channel and a single persistent connection is used for communication.

6 References

[1] S. Zander, G. Armitage, P. Branch. Covert Channels and Countermeasures in Computer Network Protocols. IEEE Communications Magazine, December 2007.

[2] M. Van Horenbeeck. "Deception on the Network: Thinking Differently About Covert Channels," in Proceedings of 7th Australian Information Warfare and Security Conference, Decem- ber 2006.

[3] J. Postel, "Internet Protocol," RFC 0791, IETF, Sept. 1981.

[4] C. H. Rowland, "Covert Channels in the TCP/IP Protocol Suite," First Monday, Peer-Reviewed Journal on the Internet, July 1997.

[5] T. Sohn, J. Seo, and J. Moon, "A Study on the Covert Channel Detection of TCP/IP Header Using Support Vector Machine," Proc. 5th Int'l. Conf. Info. and Commun. Security, Oct. 2003, pp. 313–24.

[6] Fyodor: Idle scanning and related IP-ID games (2001). http://www.insecure.org/nmap/idlescan.html

[7] R. E. Best, Phase-locked loops: Design, simulation and applications. McGraw Hill Professional, 5th ed., 2003.

[8] K. Ahsan and D. Kundur, "Practical Data Hiding in TCP/IP," Proc. ACM Wksp. Multimedia Security, Dec. 2002.

[9] S. J. Murdoch and S. Lewis, "Embedding Covert Channels into TCP/IP," Proc. 7th Information Hiding Wksp., June 2005.

[10] E. Cauich, R. Gomez Cardenas, and R. Watanabe, "Data Hiding in Identification and Offset IP Fields," Proc. 5th Int'l. School and Symp. Advanced Distributed Systems (ISSADS), Jan2005, pp. 118–25.

[11] G. Danezis, "Covert Communications despite Traffic Data Retention", tech. rep., ESAT, University of Leuven, Jan.2005, http://homes.esat.kuleuven.be/ gdanezis/cover.pdf.

[12] C. G. Girling, "Covert channels in LAN's," IEEE Transactions on Software Engineering, vol. SE-13 of 2, February 1987.

[13] R. A. Kemmerer, "Shared Resource Matrix Methodology: an IEEE Communications Surveys & Tutorials • 3rd Quarter 2007 57 Approach to Identifying Storage and Timing Channels," ACM Transactions on Computer Systems (TOCS), vol. 1, no. 3, Aug. 1983, pp. 256–77.

https://doi.org/10.1051/itmconf/20203203016

[14] T. Handel and M. Sandford, "Hiding Data in the OSI Network Model," Proc. 1st Int'l. Wksp. Information Hiding, 1996 pp.23–38

[15] M. Wolf, "Covert Channels in LAN Protocols," Proc. Wksp. Local Area Network Security (LANSEC), 1989, pp. 91–101.

[16] Grzegorz Lewandowski, Syracuse University, Network-aware Active Wardens in IPv6, 2011.

[17] Georey Ackerman, Daryl Johnson, and Bill Stackpole, Covert channel using icmpv6 and ipv6 addressing, in Proceedings of the International Conference on Security and Management (SAM). 2015, p. 63, The Steering Committee of The World Congress in Computer Science, Computer Engineering and Applied Computing (WorldComp).

Web Traffic Time Series Forecasting using ARIMA and LSTM RNN

Tejas Shelatkar[1,*], *Stephen* Tondale[2,**], *Swaraj* Yadav[3,***], and *Sheetal* Ahir[4,****]

[1]Ramrao Adik Institute of Technology, Nerul
[2]Ramrao Adik Institute of Technology, Nerul
[3]Ramrao Adik Institute of Technology, Nerul
[4]Ramrao Adik Institute of Technology, Nerul

Abstract.
Nowadays, web traffic forecasting is a major problem as this can cause setbacks to the workings of major websites. Time-series forecasting has been a hot topic for research. Predicting future time series values is one of the most difficult problems in the industry. The time series field encompasses many different issues, ranging from inference and analysis to forecasting and classification. Forecasting the network traffic and displaying it in a dashboard that updates in real-time would be the most efficient way to convey the information. Creating a Dashboard would help in monitoring and analyzing real-time data. In this day and age, we are too dependent on Google server but if we want to host a server for large users we could have predicted the number of users from previous years to avoid server breakdown. Time Series forecasting is crucial to multiple domains.
ARIMA; LSTM RNN; web traffic; prediction;time series;

1 Introduction

Recently, more and more people are getting access to the internet all over the world, the rise in traffic for almost all websites are inevitable. The increase in traffic for the websites could cause a lot of problems and the company which manages to cope with the traffic changes in the most efficient way is going to succeed.[7] As most of the people may have encountered a crashed site or very slow loading time for a website when there are a a lot of people using it, like when various shopping websites may crash just before festivals as more people try to log into the website than it was originally capable of which causes a a lot of inconveniences for the users and as a result of that it could decrease the user's ratings of the site and instead use another site, therefore, reducing their business. Therefore, a traffic management technique or plan should be put in place to reduce the risk of such mishaps which could be detrimental to the existence of the company. Until recently, there wasn't a need for such tools as most servers could handle the traffic influx but the smartphone age has increased the demand to such a high level for some websites that companies could not have reacted quickly enough to maintain their regular customer service level.
Within the literature many methods have been proposed for forecasting web traffic. They can be classified broadly into two groups based on the analysed models: nonlinear prediction and linear prediction. The most widely used models Linear forecast models are: i) HoltWinters Algorithm ii) AR Model iii) MA Model. The forecasting focused on recurring neural networks is commonly used for nonlinear prediction. Discrete wavelet transform (DWT) divides the data into linear and non-linear components that help improve forecast accuracy.[1]
ES-RNN increases performance by using GPU computing to train the dataset.

*e-mail: iamtejasshelatkar@gmail.com
**e-mail: stephentondale7@gmail.com
***e-mail: swarajy26@gmail.com
****e-mail: sheetal.ahir@rait.ac.in

2 Literature Survey

Here, we explain the existing technology in the field of web traffic time series forecasting and also the data set that has been used for our prediction model.

2.1 Web Traffic Time Series Dataset

Wikipedia's pageview API is the data used for this project.That data contains daily page visits as a time series to any post. Latest data is obtained through this API. The data is returned in JSON format. The fields extracted from this data are the recorded Dates and Visits on that date. It converts this data into a data frame and fits into the predictive model. [7,8]

2.2 DWT

Discrete Wavelet Transform is used to divide the data vector by two sections into precise coefficients and approximate coefficient. A sequence of low pass filter and high pass filter are used to evaluate the DWT. This filtering produces Data Thorough and Approximate, a low frequency component, and a high frequency. After this step the two components are reconstructed by passing D and A through the inverse discrete wavelet transformation (iDWT).[1]

2.3 ARIMA MODEL

ARIMA (Auto-Regressive Integrated Moving Average) the model has a huge advantage in univariate time series forecasting. ARIMA model attempts to describe the trends and seasonality in time series as a function of lagged values(Auto Regressive parameter) and Averages changing over time intervals(Moving Averages). The model includes differencing (Integrating) the original time series data. Differencing time-series means forming a new time series by subtracting the previous observation from the current time. The point of this is to remove certain trends, such as seasonality, trends, or inconsistent variance in time series data.[5] The ARIMA equation has two important components Auto-Regressive (AR) part and the Moving Average (MA) part.

2.4 LSTM RNN

Our proposed methodology uses Long Short Term Memory (LSTM) RNN.To add a piece of new information to RNN, it completely transforms the existing information by adding a function. As a result, the whole information is updated, i.e. there is no respect for ' important ' information and ' not so important ' information in general.
Both RNNs have the recurrent layer of feedback loops. It allows them to keep information and data in' memory' over time. Nonetheless, it may be difficult to train standard RNNs to solve problems requiring long-term temporal dependencies to understand. This is because the loss function gradient decays exponentially over time (called the problem of the vanishing gradient). LSTM networks are a type of RNN that uses besides standard units, special units[3]. LSTM systems include a ' memory cell ' which can hold data in memory for long periods of time. As information enters the memory when it is output and when it is lost a series of gates is used to track it. This architecture helps them to understand longer-term dependencies. GRUs are similar to LSTMs but are structurally simplified. They also use a series of gates to control information flow, but do not use different memory cells, and use less gates. We use LSTM RNN for this effect to have more memory than conventional RNN.[2]

3 Problem Statement

The problem of forecasting the future values of time series has always been one of the most challenging problems in the field. Real time dashboard is a dashboard that contains visualizations that are automatically updated with the most current data available. These data visualizations offer a combination of historic data and real-time information that is useful for identifying emerging trends and monitoring efficiency. Real time dashboards usually contain data that is time-sensitive.

4 Proposed Methodology

Discrete wavelet Transform breaks down data signals into basic wavelet functions. Since the time-series data procured for investigation is noisy in nature it is very important to complete pre-processing of the data. Here the DWT splits down the data into pieces of low frequency and high frequency. So for best results, we can apply the algorithm to the segments. Since the data must be fixed in ARIMA henceforth we use high-frequency data as a predictive contribution. RNN uses data from low frequencies as input. It was later observed that this technique yields palatable results for less and more knowledge that is not the independently implemented situation for ARIMA and RNN.

In the following steps the proposed network traffic prediction methodology based on DWT, ARIMA, and LSTM RNN may be shown.
1. Load the time series for network traffic into a Xin vector.
2. Apply DWT to and decompose input variable. The DWT is determined via a series of low pass filter and high pass filter. This filtering produces data components of low frequency and high frequency called Detailed(D) and Approximate(A).
3. After this step, the two components are reconstructed via inverse discrete wavelet transformation (iDWT) by passing D and A.[1].
4. The ARIMA model is applied to the D component to produce forecast. BY compPicture1Residual Sum of Squares (RSS) of AR, MA, and ARIMA defines the vector-specific ARIMA model (p, d, q). Using ARIMA to estimate the linear component Yfor1 = forecast1('ARIMA model', Xd(eff)) / Xd(eff) is obtained by subtracting from the training set (p+d+q).
5. We use a Vanilla LSTM which has only a single hidden layer. We apply it to the A part. As input, forget, output get are fed then for cell state tanh activation function is used and also for the final output.
6. Combining forecasts from linear and nonlinear sections to get the final data forecast. This data can be compared with the actual data so we get errors for each algorithm.
,2 The system flow diagram is depicted in Figure 2. The figure indicates that the dataset will go through DWT to give output as linear and non-linear components. The ARIMA model will forecast for linear component and the LSTM-RNN will roll out forecasts for non-linear component. These forecasts will be combined using iDWT to provide a final forecast.

5 Implementation and Results

The dataset was analyzed and the sample data used was 'India'. Further, the dataset was divided into training and testing sets. For the time series, we plotted the number of hits vs. days along with real values and forecasts for the article 'India' during the testing period. The x-axis represents the Time Interval and the y-axis represents the page visits in powers of 10. The monthly forecast results

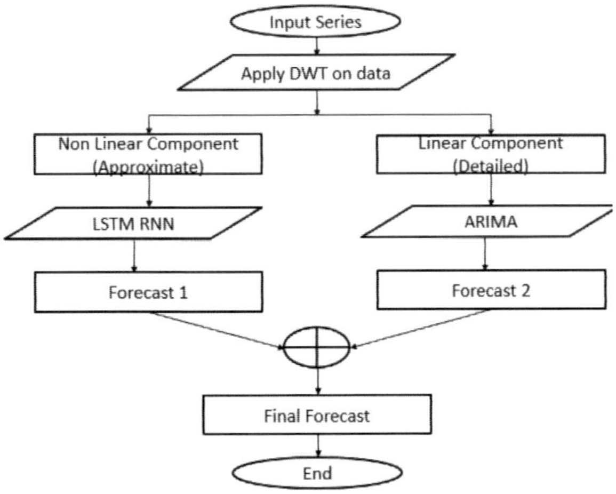

Figure 1. System Flowchart.

for languages obtained as per the proposed methods are as follows:

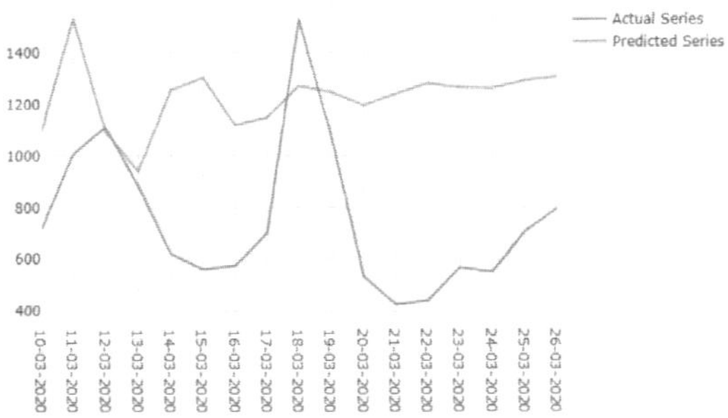

Figure 2. Forecast results for ARIMA

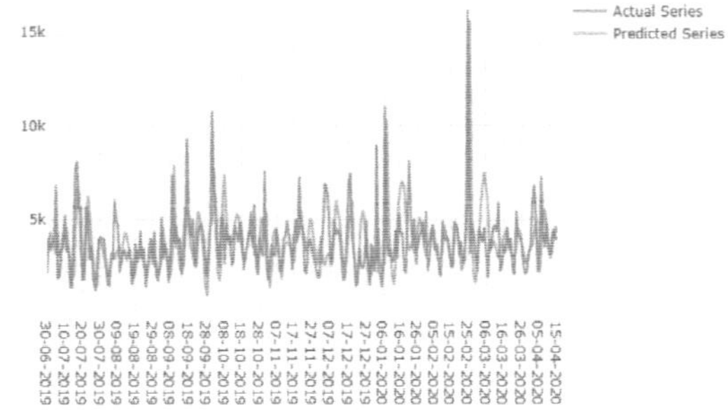

Figure 3. Forecast results for LSTM-RNN

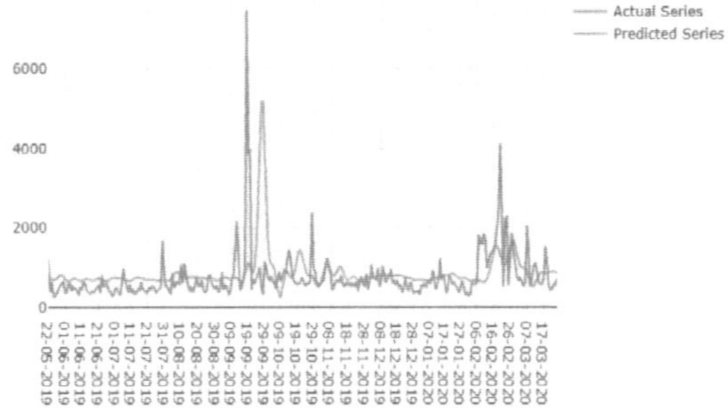

Figure 4. Forecast results after using DWT

The forecast results obtained in Figure 2 are for ARIMA model. There is a clear trend over the time interval and the forecast replicates the same. In Figure 3, the forecast results for RNN show a pattern which detects spikes accurately. Figure 4 depicts the use of DWT which combines results of ARIMA and RNN to provide more accurate results.

6 Conclusion

Web traffic Time series prediction can be carried out using Long Short Term Memory Recurrent Neural Network and Autoregressive integrated moving average more efficiently and accurately. Prediction of the number of users will access the website in the future is possible. The proposed will keep on improving as more user data is fed. Our system can be used across all websites for improving their web traffic load management and business analysis[5]. LSTM RNN brings more efficiency to our system. Our system effectively captures seasonal patterns and long-term trends Including information about holidays, day of week, language, region might help our model to capture more correctly the highs and lows.

7 Future Work

Time Series Forecasting is one of the least explored areas and various models are evaluated to improve the accuracy of the forecast. The main focus of the proposal is to predict future web traffic to make decisions for better congestion control. Past Values are considered to predict future values. We will also seek to explore multivariate time series and offer suggestions for simplifying the decision-making process in real-time.

References

[1] "Predicting Computer Network Traffic: A Time Series Forecasting Approach using DWT, ARIMA and RNN" by Rishabh Madan, 2018.
[2] "Fast ES-RNN: A GPU Implementation of the ES-RNN algorithm " by Andrew Redd and Kaung Khin, 2019.
[3] "Time Series Forecasting Based on Complex Network Analysis" by SHENGZHONG MAO AND FUYUAN XIAO, 2019.
[4] "Web Traffic Prediction of Wikipedia Pages" by Navyasree Petluri, Eyhab Al-Masri, 2019.
[5] "Time series forecasting using improved ARIMA" by Soheila Mehrmolaei,2016.
[6] "Efficient Prediction ofy Network Traffic for Real-Time Applications" by Muhammad Faisal Iqbal , Muhammad Zahid, Durdana Habib, and Lizy Kurian John, 2019.
[7] https://wikitech.wikimedia.org/wiki/Analytics/AQS/Pageviews
[8] https://towardsdatascience.com/3-facts-about-time-series-forecasting-that-surprise-experienced-machine-learning-practitioners-69c18ee89387.
[9] "Temporal Pattern Attention for Multivariate Time Series Forecasting" by Shun-Yao Shih Fan-Keng Sun Hung-yi Lee, 2018.
[10]"Time series forecasting using improved ARIMA" by Soheila Mehrmolaei,2016.
[11] "Efficient Prediction of Network Traffic for Real-Time Applications" by Muhammad Faisal Iqbal , Muhammad Zahid, Durdana Habib, and Lizy Kurian John, 2019.
[12] "Modelling Approaches for Time Series Forecasting and Anomaly Detection" by Shuyang Du , Madhulima Pandey, and Cuiqun Xing, 2018.
[13] "Neural Decomposition of Time-Series Data for Effective Generalization" by Luke B. Godfrey and Michael S. Gashler, 2017

Blockchain Enabled Online-Voting System

Akhil Shah
Ramrao Adik Institute of Technology
Mumbai University
Navi Mumbai, India
akhilhshah04@gmail.com

Nishita Sodhia
Ramrao Adik Institute of Technology
Mumbai University
Navi Mumbai, India
sodhiablue@gmail.com

Shruti Saha
Ramrao Adik Institute of Technology
Mumbai University
Navi Mumbai, India
shrutisaha96@gmail.com

Soumi Banerjee
Ramrao Adik Institute of Technology
Mumbai University
Navi Mumbai, India
soumi.banerjee@rait.ac.in

Madhuri Chavan
Ramrao Adik Institute of Technology
Mumbai University
Navi Mumbai, India
madhuri.chavan@rait.ac.in

***Abstract*—A blockchain-enabled online-voting system is being proposed in this following paper. Blockchain technologies deliver an endless variety of applications that benefit from distributed economies. The proposed model is an android application that has enhanced security features which includes both authentication and authorization. Authentication is incorporated by using a unique identification key and authorization is done by using fingerprint. Voters are also being verified by One-time password. The security in this project is implemented by using a 128 bit AES encryption algorithm and SHA-256 along with blockchain. The vote is casted in the form of transaction, where a blockchain is created, which keeps track of tallies of votes. Through this atomicity and integrity are maintained. [4]**

***Index Terms*—Voting System , Blockchain , SHA-256, Security, AES-128, Ballot**

I. Introduction

Election has a very major role in democracy because it is the deciding factor of the future of a country but the major concern is that society doesn't trust the election system. Flawed electoral system is the issue faced by even the world's largest democracies like India, United States, and Japan. Overtime, the voting systems have evolved and the breach of security has evolved. The major issues that need to be addressed in the current voting system are vote rigging, EVM hacking, polling booth capture and election manipulation.

The problems were investigated in the voting systems in this project and attempting to propose the online-voting model that can solve these problems. Using an efficient hashing algorithm technique, block formation and sealing, data collection and result declaration by versatile blockchain method is needed to solve the issue a high-end to end system that ensures security and privacy. This project proposes an online-voting system that uses the Blockchain Ethereum to create a wallet with the credentials of the user. The elector will obtain an authenticated and tamper-proof personal ID. The voter will be getting the chance to vote in the form of token which would be transferred anonymously from voter's wallet to candidate's wallet. The vote can be casted from any geographical area for voter's allotted constituency. Blockchain also helps to preserve voters's anonymity while still being open to public inspection.

The proposed voting system uses more stable, tamperproof blockchain (unchanged from voting modifications either by the voter or by any other third party) and cost-effective. We would also extend the constraints of structure, engineering, design and implementation in our society of the voting mechanism.

II. Literature Survey

A. Online Voting System For India Based on AADHAR ID - Himanshu Agarwal, G. N. Pandey in the year 2013 [5]

A high security password is checked in the main database before voting is allowed. The voter will be able to confirm if the vote is transferred to the correct candidate or party. A person from his or her allocated constituency may also vote. The tallying of the votes can be done manually, thus saving the data.

B. Biometric voting system using aadhar card in india - S Chakraborty, S Mukherjee in the year 2016 [6]

The main goal of this venture is to build a safe electronic voting machine using Finger printing technique that distinguishes evidence, so that we can use the Aadhar card database for specific marks. The online-voting confirmation process should be possible during the race voting season using finger vein detection, which enables the electronic poll reset to allow voters to cast their votes.

C. Trustworthy Electronic Voting Using Adjusted Blockchain Technology - Basit Shahzad Raju, Jon Crowcroft in the year 2019 [7]

This paper suggests a system that makes use of appropriate hashing methods to ensure data security. This paper introduces the concept of block-creation and block sealing. The implementation of a block sealing principle helps to make the blockchain flexible to meet polling process requirements.

D. Security Analysis of India's Voting Machine - Hari K. Prasad, Arun Kankipati, Sai Krishna Sakhamuri in the year 2010 [8]

A Real Indian EVM Security Review is taken from anonymous source. The paper states that EVM is vulnerable to extreme attacks that may alter the outcome and breach the ballot's confidentiality. Use custom hardware, two attacks have been demonstrated.

III. Proposed System

We are proposing a system which has greater accessibility as it is an android application and possess greater security as authentication, authorisation and verification. In this system the voter/user has to first register themselves using a registration form available within the android application and once the registration form is being submitted, an entry is being made in the centralized database. After the registration the user can log into the application and be a part of the polling process. The user with its valid credentials can log into the system and verify them by entering the one-time-password which is valid for a limited period of time. Once the user is logged into their respective account the dashboard contains all the information which is retrieved from the centralized database. After the user logs into the account the user is being authenticated using fingerprint. Each account is provided with a single token which he will use to cast a vote, casting of vote will take place by transferring the token from the respective user account to the candidate's wallet. A web application is being developed to measure the majority of votes which has the details about the total number of voters, the number of votes cast and the percentage of votes cast. Only one vote can be casted from one account and once a vote is being casted from an account the account is disabled from current voting process.

IV. Proposed Methodology

A. BLOCKCHAIN

Blockchain is a decentralized, distributed, public leadger. [4]Blockchain is of three different types, i.e. public, private, and consortium blockchain. Ethereum and Bitcoin are examples of a public blockchain. This is proofed by the complex mathematical functions. This research uses public blockchain (Ethereum). Blockchain basically consists of a chain of blocks where a block is the primary component of the blockchain. A block is the header and the body, the block body contains the transactions that are being written to the network. The block header contains the block information which includes previous hash, nonce value and difficulty, block timestamp and transactions. [7] Each block also stores information about the person participating in the transaction. The block length is variable, and is estimated to be about 1 and 8 MB in size. The block header uniquely defines the block which should be put.

1) Working of Blockchain: Blockchain is a system that is built around peer to peer system that can be shared openly among the users to generate record of transaction that is immutable. In order to generate a block, a transaction needs to occur, after that the legitimacy of transaction needs to be verified. The transaction will then be stored in the block and a hash value must be given to the block for sealing. Thus a block is created and sealed.

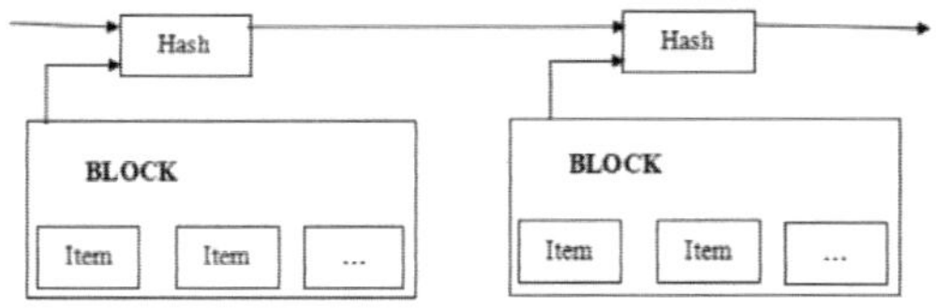

Fig. 1. Blockchain

B. ETHEREUM

Complex legal and financial applications such as Smart contract can be built and deployed using Ethereum as an open platform. Ethereum can be imagined as a programmable Bitcoin in which the underlying blockchain can be used by developers to build markets, mutual ledgers, digital associations and other endless possibilities involving unchanging data and agreements, all without the need for a middleman.Released in 2015, Ethereum is the brainchild of prodigious Vitalik Buterin who saw the possible applications of Bitcoins by Blockchain technologies as the next move in furthering the growth of the Blockchain culture. Ethereum is now the cryptocurrency with the second-highest coin market cap and is projected to overtake Bitcoin as both a valued investment and as the most common cryptocurrency in the world. [1]

C. HASHING

Hashing is the method of adjusting the arbitrary and variable input size to a fixed output size. There are various functions which perform different levels of hashing. We have implemented security by using SHA-256. SHA-256 is one of the SHA-1 (collectively referred to as SHA-2) successor hash functions and is one of the strongest hash functions available. SHA-256 is not much more difficult to code than SHA-1 and is in no way corrupted yet. [3] The 256-bit key makes AES a good partner feature which is a symmetrical key encryption cipher, meaning that the same key is used for encryption and decryption. Unlike its other predecessors, the algorithm's versatility is that it embraces any input length and produces an arbitrary output length, whilst all other algorithms generate a set output length.

D. Registration Module

The client or an individual will fill out the registration form in the registration module of the process after which their entry will be registered in the database and they are now eligible to vote for their preferred candidate. Registration form filling is mandatory without which the person is not allowed or is not eligible to vote. The registration form includes the voter information and also some documents have to be uploaded once it is done the form is submitted and the entry is reflected in the database. After the registration form is submitted the phone number and the email id given by the user is verified and the registration process is completed.

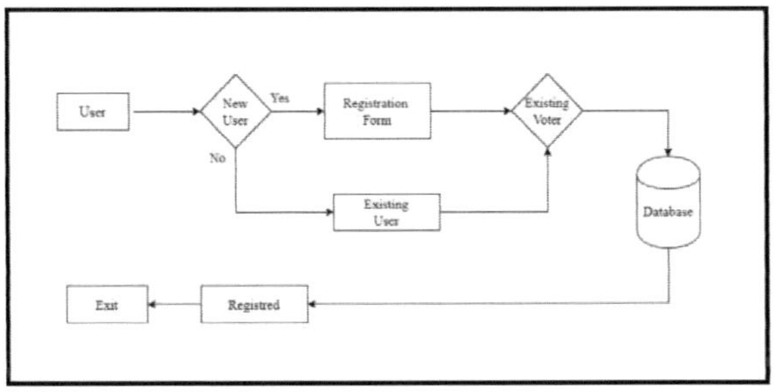

Fig. 2. Registration Module

E. Login Module

Once the registration form is submitted, the person is now eligible to vote. The user will sign in to the credentials in the authentication module and after which credentials will be checked and the user will only be able to access the dashboard after the verification has been completed. The first process in the dashboard is the OTP Verification. Once the user is verified then the user is authenticated with their fingerprint only after which the voter wallet is generated and a token is provided to the voter which will be used to cast their vote. The votes are casted by transferring the token from the voter's wallet to the respective candidate's wallet.

V. Result

In Fig 3, the login screen is being displayed wherein if a person is a new user the person can register itself with the application and if the user is an existing one they can login with valid user-id and password and thus login for the further process. The user will sign in to the credentials in the authentication module and after which credentials will be checked and the user will only be able to access the dashboard after the verification has been completed. The first process in the dashboard is the OTP Verification. Once the user is verified then the user is authenticated with their fingerprint only after which the voter wallet is generated and a token is provided to the voter which will be used to cast their vote. The votes are casted by transferring the token from the voter's wallet to the respective candidate's wallet

The above figure 4, displays the registration module wherein a new user can register oneself for the process and make a favourable vote. The users are allowed to register only once and cannot re-register thus avoiding repetitions.

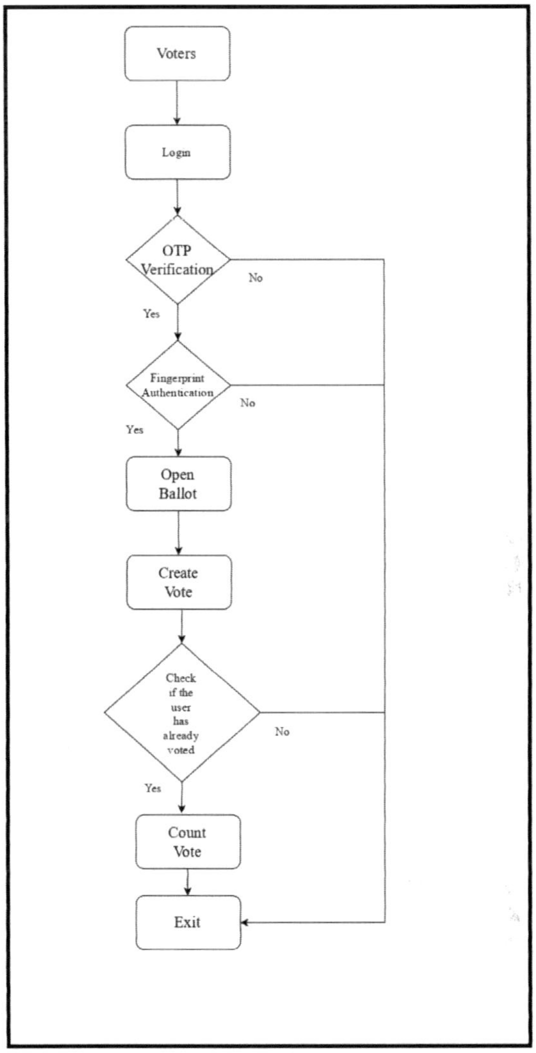

Fig. 3. Flowchart

The registration form contains various details which are to be filled by the user such as name, phone number, email-id, password, Aadhar card number etc.

In Fig 5 the verification module is being displayed in which as soon as the person logs in, the user receives a One-time password on the registered phone number. The person is logged into its respective dashboard only after the OTP is verified.

The above figure 6 displays the fingerprint authorisation

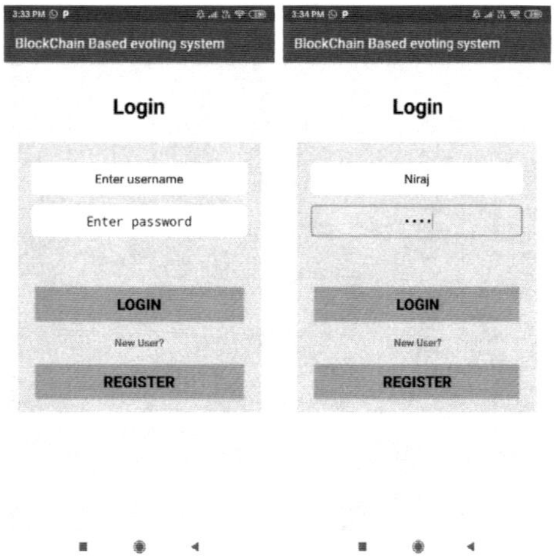

Fig. 4. Login Module

Fig. 5. Registration Module

module which enables only authorised users to login and be a part of the voting process.

Figure 7 depicts the dashboard screen where the electoral symbol of participating parties are displayed, which on click casts a vote to the respective party and once a vote is being casted the voter is not allowed to cast a vote again and after some time the user is automatically logged out to avoid multiple casting of vote from an individual.

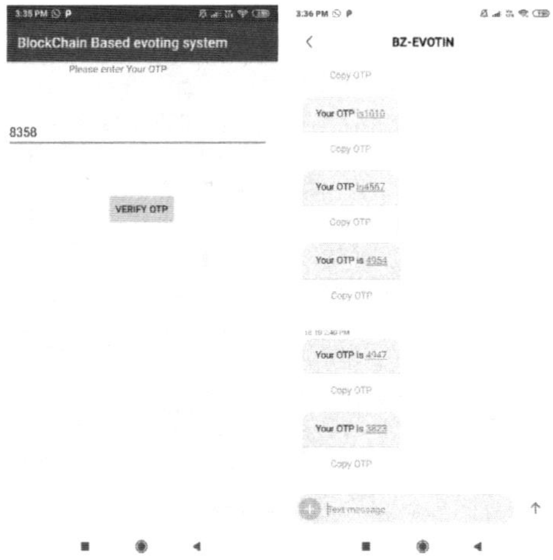

Fig. 6. Verification Module

Fig. 7. Authorisation Module

Figure 8 depicts the admin module where the process of vote counting takes place.

Figure 9 depicts creation of new blocks. New blocks are added and sealed, the blocks are sealed using SHA-256 along with AES-128 algorithm.

https://doi.org/10.1051/itmconf/20203203018

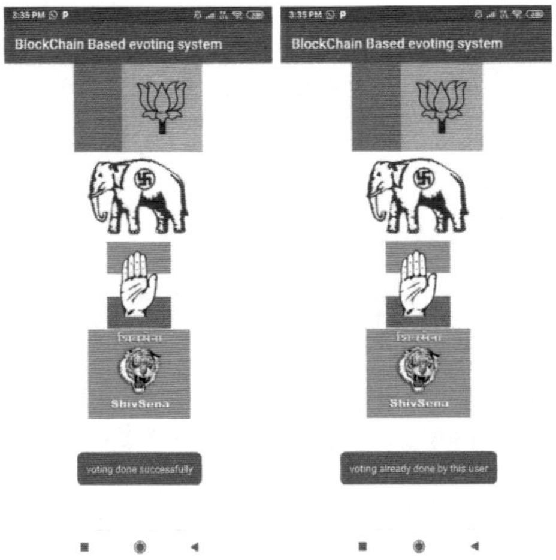

Fig. 8. Dashboard

Fig. 9. Admin

VI. Conclusion

The concept of incorporating online voting systems to make the public election process cheaper, quicker and easier is a compelling one in modern society.Having the electoral process cheap and fast, normalizing it in the electorate's eyes, removing a certain control barrier between the elector and the elected official and putting some pressure on the elected official. It also opens the door to a more transparent type of democracy that requires electors to speak their will on specific bills and initiatives.

We have deployed online-based blockchain voting framework in this project where smart contracts are used to allow secure and cost-effective election while preserving the secrecy of the voters. Compared with previous research, we have shown that the blockchain technology provides a new opportunity for democratic countries to move from the pen and paper election scheme and paperless direct-recording electronic voting machine (DRE) to a more cost-effective and time-efficient election scheme, thus mounting the security measures of the current scheme and offering new accessibility.

VII. Comparative Study

A. Online Voting System For India Based on AADHAR ID - Himanshu Agarwal, G. N. Pandey in the year 2013 [5]

A high security password is confirmed before the vote is accepted in the main database and authentication is done by incorporating fingerprint module. The voter will be able to confirm if the vote is transferred to the correct candidate or party .The tallying of the votes can be done manually, whereas in this system the vote count is done directly ensuring that each vote is counted and no vote is misinterpreted.

B. Biometric voting system using aadhar card in india - S Chakraborty, S Mukherjee in the year 2016 [6]

An electronic voting machine utilizing Finger print is developed to build a safe voting machine with distinguishing proof technique to get unique mark as Aadhar card database is utilized. But it consists of same threat faced by any other EVM such as physical security of machines, secure storage of vote, and software could be tampered.

C. Trustworthy Electronic Voting Using Adjusted Blockchain Technology - Basit Shahzad Raju, Jon Crowcroft in the year 2019 [7]

A framework is suggested that uses effective hashing techniques that ensure the security of the data. In this paper the concept of block creation and block sealing is introduced. The block sealing concept helps blockchain to be adjustable meeting the need of polling process.

D. Security Analysis of India's Voting Machine - Hari K. Prasad, Arun Kankipati, Sai Krishna Sakhamuri in the year 2010 [8]

Security Analysis was performed on real Indian EVM system. This paper states that EVM can be tampered in many ways such as, tampering with software before CPU manufacture, tampering with machine state, substituting a look a-like CPU and/or a unit and thus secrecy of the ballot can be violated. The proposed voting system does not have any major hardware requirements, thus elimination all the above disadvantages of EVM. Also the proposed model uses blockchain which ensures that the vote transfer to candidate's ballot is easy and secure.

VIII. Future Scope

The current system uses ethereum which is public blockchain. It is permissionless in nature as nothing is standing in the way of participation and anyone is able to engage with consensus mechanism, scaling obstacles have been encountered and throughput is relatively weak. [2] To avoid such issues consortium blockchain can be used which combines elements from both public as well as private blockchain.

The current project is built for small organization, but in future we would build it as a national voting system. In addition to the present fingerprint module which is used for authorization a facial recognition module would be incorporated for better security.

REFERENCES

[1] The ethos blog. https://www.ethos.io/cryptocurrency-news-ethos-blog. Accessed: 2020-01-27.
[2] Private, public, and consortium blockchains - what's the difference? https://www.binance.vision/blockchain/private-public-and-consortium-blockchains-whats-the-difference. Accessed: 2020-01-24.
[3] Sha-256 hashing algorithm. https://www.movable-type.co.uk/scripts/sha256.html. Accessed: 2020-01-27.
[4] What is blockchain. https://www.investopedia.com/terms/b/blockchain.asp. Accessed: 2020-01-24.
[5] Himanshu Agarwal and GN Pandey. Online voting system for india based on aadhaar id. In *2013 Eleventh International Conference on ICT and Knowledge Engineering*, pages 1–4. IEEE, 2013.
[6] Soumyajit Chakraborty, Siddhartha Mukherjee, Bhaswati Sadhukhan, and Kazi Tanvi Yasmin. Biometric voting system using aadhar card in india. *International journal of Innovative research in Computer and Communication Engineering*, 4(4), 2016.
[7] Basit Shahzad and Jon Crowcroft. Trustworthy electronic voting using adjusted blockchain technology. *IEEE Access*, 7:24477–24488, 2019.
[8] Scott Wolchok, Eric Wustrow, J Alex Halderman, Hari K Prasad, Arun Kankipati, Sai Krishna Sakhamuri, Vasavya Yagati, and Rop Gonggrijp. Security analysis of india's electronic voting machines. In *Proceedings of the 17th ACM conference on Computer and communications security*, pages 1–14, 2010.

ITM Web of Conferences **32**, 03019 (2020) https://doi.org/10.1051/itmconf/20203203019
ICACC-2020

Detection of Keratoconus Disease

Hitesh Sonar[1,*], *Ankit* Kadam[2,**], *Prasad* Bhoir[3,***], and *Dr. Bharti* Joshi[4,****]

[1]Ramrao Adik Institue of Technology, Nerul, Navi Mumbai, Maharastra
[2]Ramrao Adik Institue of Technology, Nerul, Navi Mumbai, Maharastra
[3]Ramrao Adik Institue of Technology, Nerul, Navi Mumbai, Maharastra
[4]Ramrao Adik Institue of Technology, Nerul, Navi Mumbai, Maharastra

Abstract. It has described that the development of an application which is used to detect Keratoconus disease is based on the photographs of the eyes. At the heart of the application is an algorithm that acquires the features of an eye, then classify the affected and healthy eye. Firstly, It has proposed a basic identification of keratoconus disease using supervised learning. Described method obtains better results in comparison with other existing methods with the same dataset. The algorithm which used in this method is trained against several samples of healthy and affected eyes and then used to classify unknown sample of eyes. This algorithm analyzes the eye's corneal curvature and topography using a convolutional neural network (CNN), capable of extracting and understanding an eye's features. This algorithm is very successful in properly classifying images contained in the training library. The aim of this study is to characterize another arrangement technique to recognize keratoconus based on statistical analysis, and to understand the forecast with insightful systems of these organized facts. The purpose of this study is to define another grouping strategy to differentiate keratoconus based on statistical analysis and to understand the expectations.

1 Introduction

Keratoconus is a condition that makes the cornea flimsy and lump out like a cone over time. The cornea is the clear window in the front of the eye. At the point when the state of the cornea changes, your eye can't center too and vision gets foggy and contorted. Its population occurrence is 500 in million. Keratoconus is viewed as a visual incapacity and requires clinical treatment. In the beginning periods of the sickness, it might be treated with contact focal points, yet in the most extreme cases a corneal transplant can be vital. The pathological mechanisms of this situation have been explored for quite a while. As of late, this infection has gone to the consideration of many research places on the grounds that the quantity of individuals determined to have keratoconus is on the ascent. Right now, that encourages both the symptomatic and treatment choices are immediately required. The existing mechanisms or devices used for detecting keratoconus disease are very expensive and not available in rural areas. Though these devices have accuracy yet it is not useful for everyone.

The exponential development of advanced cameras and smart phones has made another chance to devise a picture-based device for identifying the illness as ahead of schedule as could be expected under the circumstances.Proposed system examines the corneal topography and curvature and flow of an eye utilizing a convolutional neural network (CNN) that can separate and become familiar with the highlights of eyes. The point of this examination is to characterize another order strategy for identifying keratoconus dependent on factual investigation and to understand the expectation of these arranged information with intelligent systems. Results show that the developed algorithm guarantees an elite just as precision. The proposed framework can help the ophthalmologist in fast screening of its patients, subsequently decreasing demonstrative errors and encouraging treatment.

*e-mail: shitesh039@gmail.com
**e-mail: ankit.kadam9454@gmail.com
***e-mail: prasadbhoir6786@gmail.com
****e-mail: bharti.joshi@rait.ac.in

2 Literature Survey

1. Alexandru Lavric et al.[1] proposed information about detection of keratoconus using CNN. The main advantage is that it helps to obtain better accuracy of result. The algorithm implemented analyzes the eye's corneal topography, and then extracts and learns keratoconus eye characteristics.But the main disadvantage is it requires very large dataset and not suitable for small dataset.Proposed work is not open source.

https://doi.org/10.1051/itmconf/20203203019

2. Murat et al.[2] proposed method based on statistical analysis, authors proposed a new classification system for detecting keratoconus. The classification of statistical databases was used to identify all the assessed values to control patient progress in a healthier manner.

3. Filippo Castiglione et al.[3] proposed a new semi-automatic method for measuring the Keratoconus from the ultrasound images, thus eliminating errors in manual measurements. The algorithm used is useful for speeding up the manual measurements of corneal thinning and Keratoconus computing.But the drawback is it requires ultrasonic equipments which are costly.

4. Geethu S.S. et al.[4] proposed a method to convert the 2D eye image into 3D image as the 3D image provide more information than a 2D image. The existed 2D content doesn't provide depth information. The computation is very complex.

5. Valter Wellington et al.[5] described model that shows the best measure of assessment to be adopted by the GAADT for evolutionary process considering some metrics. Imaging devices analyze cornea in a static way while the Ocular Response Analyser uses a dynamic evaluation.

6. Maolong Tang et al.[6] describe model that uses the application of mean curvature mapping as an alternate description of the topography of the cornea. The goal is to enhance the identification of keratoconus and other diseases marked by local corneal curvature increases.

7. Naoyuki Maeda et al.[7] proposed system that can be used to differentiate clinical keratoconus from other corneal topographies as a screening technique. This method of quantitative classification may also help to improve the clinical understanding of topographical maps

3 Proposed Methodology

3.1 CNN

CNNs have wide applications in the area of image and video recognition, recommendation systems and natural language handling. Same as NNs, CNNs are made up of neurons which have learnable weights. Each neuron gets different data input, expect authority over them a weighted aggregate. The entire framework has a component of setback and all the tips and misleads we worked for neural frameworks regardless of everything apply on CNN. Architecture of CNN is shown in Figure 1.

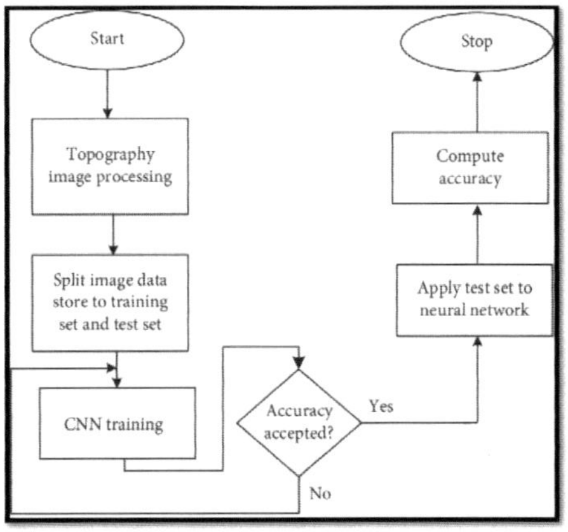

Figure 1. Flowchart of CNN Architecture

3.2 CNN operates over volume

Not at all like neural systems where input information is a vector, here the input information is a multi-channel picture shown in Figure 2. There are likewise different varieties. Before we go further, let's first comprehend what convolution suggests.

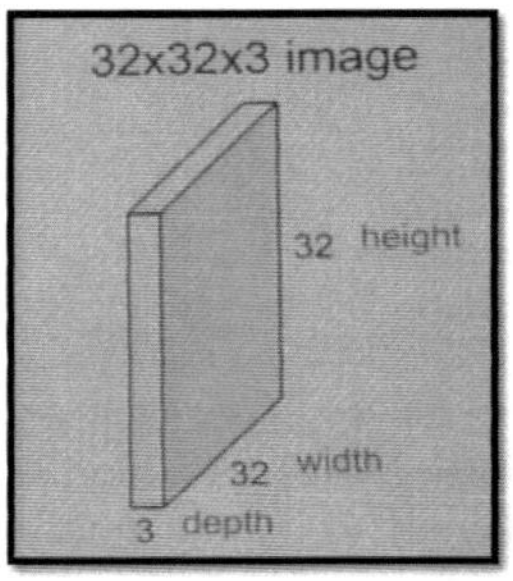

Figure 2. Convolution of multi-channeled image

3.3 Convolution

We took 5*5*3 kernel filter and apply it over the picture and along way performed product between the kernel filter and pieces of the given image shown in Figure 3. For each product, the result is a level up.

The convolution layer is the principle element of a CNN system. The convolution layer includes a lot of free filters. Each filter is autonomously convolved with the picture. All filters are instated arbitrarily and turn into our parameters which will be found out by the system in this manner.

https://doi.org/10.1051/itmconf/20203203019

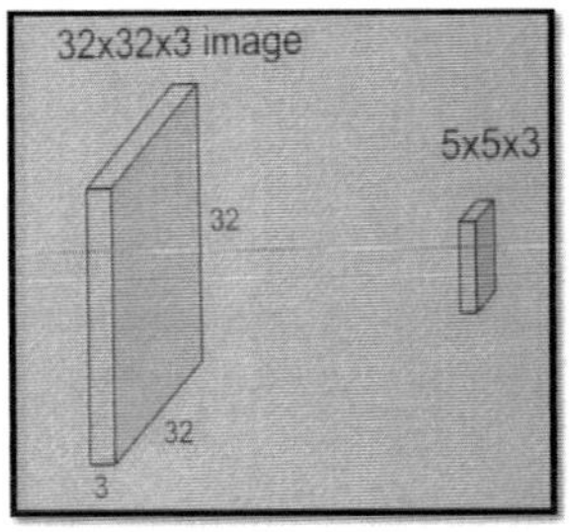

Figure 3. Convolution

3.4 Pooling

A pooling layer is also main element of a CNN. Its capacity is to dynamically lessen the spatial size of the portrayal to decrease the measure of parameters and calculation in the system. The Pooling layer works on each component map independently. The most normal methodology utilized in pooling is max pooling which is shown in Figure 4.

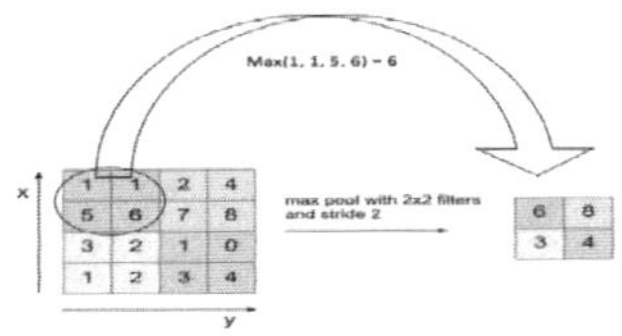

Figure 4. Max pooling

3.5 RELU

RELU is only a non-linearity which is applied comparative to neural systems. The FC is the completely associated layer of neurons toward the end of CNN. Neurons in a completely associated layer have full associations with all activations in the past layer, as found in normal Neural Systems and work in a comparative way.

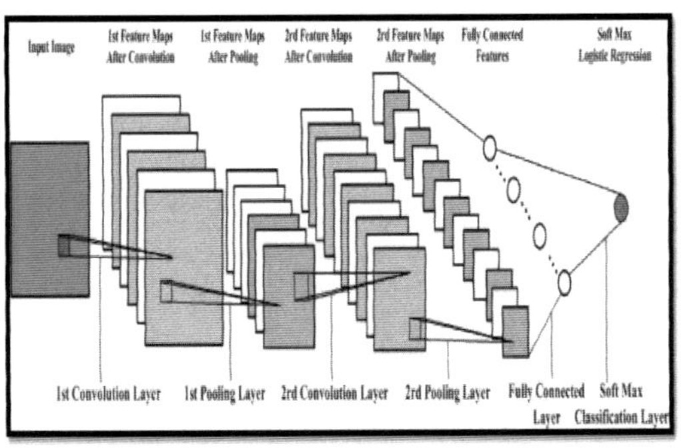

Figure 5. CNN

4 Algorithm used

4.1 Inception

Inception is latest classification algorithm. It is faster than existing algorithms. Saves memory and perform faster computation.

Inception v3 is widely used for image classification with a pretrained deep neural network.Transfer learning from Inception V3 allows retraining the existing neural network in order to use it for solving custom image classification tasks, To add new classes of data to the pretrained Inception V3 model. we use the tensorflow-image-classifier repository. This repository contains a set of scripts to download the default version of the Inception V3 model and retrain it for classifying a new set of images.

Inception V3 is consisted of inception blocks. In each inception block, convolution filters of various dimensions and pooling are used on the input in parallel. They are concatenated along their channels just before providing output. Three types of inception blocks have been used in this architecture refer Figure.6.

To reduce number of parameters, often 1×1× (no. of input channels) sized 3D filters are used before any other operation on the input. Although the architecture is quite deep, the model has only about 25 million parameters. 1×1 filters also reduce the computation cost. The larger filters capture high abstract features, and the smaller ones capture local features. Inception is latest CNN algorithm. It is faster than existing algorith. Saves memory and perform faster computation.

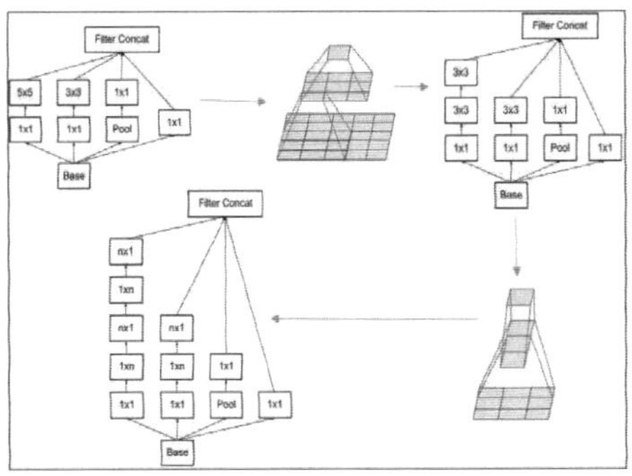

Figure 6. Blocks of Inception Algo

5 System Design

The first step is to provide image to the system as an input. In next step, there are two phases training and testing phase respectively. At training phase, input image is given to the Expert Knowledge of the proposed system which contains labeled dataset. Features of the labeled image is extracted with the help of convolution and pooling and activation functions. Based on these features CNN based feature learning network is created which can be used in testing phase.

In testing or application phase, input image is provided to trained network. Trained CNN learning network extracts and analyses features of input and assign label to the input based on features and approximations. Result provided to the user.

System Design is shown in Figure 7

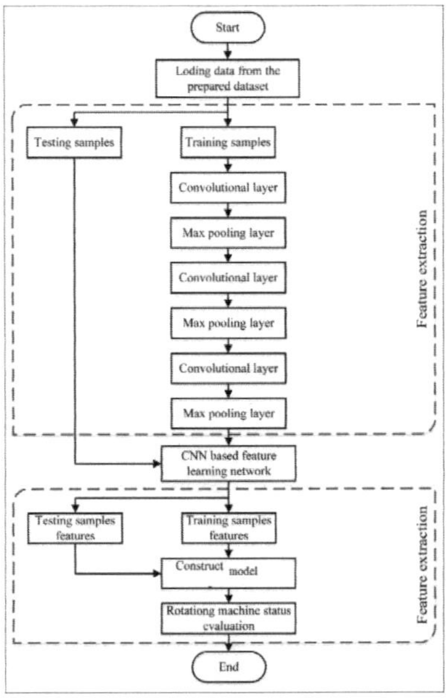

Figure 7. Flowchart of System

Result

Name	Label	Samples	Accuracy
Healthy	0	15	73.33
Keratoconus	1	10	60

Conclusion

A real time detection system with Image Processing and Machine Learning technology may help in detecting Keratoconus disease. It can be concluded that a fast and efficient disease detection system which can replace a manual system. The Proposed system overcomes many limitations incorporated in existing system like time consumption, cost etc. The proposed system is user friendly, saves great amount of time and reduces human efforts. It can be useful in rural areas where people finds hard to identify what they are affected with.

Future Work

The first changes that need to be made are further testing with the improved dataset.

The dataset itself can be further improved by adding images, removing undesired ones, apply some image preprocessing techniques to improve images or by making the image content more specific.

References

[1] Alexandru Lavric, Popa Valentin;"KeratoDetect: Keratoconus Detection Algorithm Using Convolutional Neural Networks" Hindawi Computational Intelligence and Neuroscience 2019

[2] Murat, Baha Sen, Hasan Basri Cakmak; "A Novel Classification and Estimation Approach for Detecting Keratoconus Disease with Intelligent system"

[3] Filippo Castiglione Fr. Castiglione; "Estimating the Keratoconus Index from Ultrasound Images of the Human Cornea" IEEE TRANSACTIONS ON MEDICAL IMAGING, VOL. 19, NO. 12, DECEMBER 2000

[4] Geethu S.S., Sreeletha S.H.; "A Survey on 2D to 3D Conversion Techniques" Volume 3, Issue 6, June 2016

[5] Valter Wellington, Ramos Junior;"Application of Algorithm Based on Abstract Data Types to the Keratoconus Diagnosis"

[6] Maolong Tang,Raj Shekhar, David Huang; "Mean Curvature Mapping for Detection of Corneal Shape Abnormality" IEEE TRANSACTIONS ON MEDICAL IMAGING, VOL. 24, NO. 3, MARCH 2005

[7] Naoyuki Maeda, Stephen D. Klyce, Michael K. Smolek, Hilary W. Thompson; "Automated Keratoconus Screening With Corneal Topography Analysis"

[8] https://en.wikipedia.org/wiki/Keratoconus

[9] https://www.researchgate.net/

[10] https://journals.plos.org/

[11] https://ieeexplore.ieee.org/

[12] https://towardsdatascience.com/a-simple-guideto-the-versions-of-theinception-network

An Approach To Predict Software Application Success Using Voting Ensemble Method

Sangeeta Rathod[1,*], *Prajakta* Ugalmugle[2,**], and *Ruchita* Waghmare[3,***] *Tabassum* Maktum[4,****]

[1]Department of Computer Engineering
[2]Ramrao Adik Institute of Technology
[3]Nerul, Navi Mumbai-400706,
[4]Maharashtra, India.

Abstract. Mobile app distribution platform consisting of Google play store and Apple Store gets covered with several hundreds of new apps every day with many more enthusiastic developers working independently or in a crew to make them successful. With huge competition from all over the world, it is vital for a developer to recognize if he is proceeding in the proper direction or not. It is not like making a film wherein presence of famous celebrities increase the chance of success even earlier than the movie is released, it is not the case with developing apps. Since maximum Play Store apps are free, the revenue version is pretty unknown and unavailable as to how the in-app purchases, in- app advertisements and subscriptions make a contribution to the fulfillment of an app. Thus, a software's success is normally decided through the wide variety of installs and the star ratings that it has acquired over its lifetime in place of the sales it generated. So in order to test if the app is assembly the expectancy of human beings we need a software that will check that apps evolved are successful or not. The framework for predicting success of software application is proposed in this paper. It is a software which will provide the achievement of app/software program relying not only on number of install and star rating but will consider all the factors of an application description and customers reviews. The exploratory data analysis to jump in deeper into the Google Play Store information is performed. The relationships with specific functions inclusive of how the wide variety of phrases in an app call for instance, affect installs are used to use them to find out which apps are much more likely to succeed. Using those extracted functions and the of sentiment of customers the proposed method will predict the "success" of an application using Google Play Store Data. The algorithm applied are Support Vector Machine, K-Nearest Neighbour, Decision Tree and Random Forest. In order to improve accuracy the Voting Ensemble technique is applied in proposed method. The accuracy of various algorithm is compared to judge the performance of proposed method.
Keywords : hyperplane, dataset, Support Vector Machine, Exploratory Data Analysis, voting ensemble

1 Introduction

Software industry is at its peak in this era. It has been discovered that the giant growth of the mobile application marketplace has an outstanding impact on digital technology. With huge competition from all around the world, it is vital for a developer to realize that if he is going in the perfect direction. The Google Play Store is found to be the largest app market in the world. It has been observed that although it generates more than double the downloads than the Apple App Store but makes only half the money compared to the App Store. An application's success is generally determined by the number of downloads and the user ratings that it has received over its lifespan rather than the profit it generates and rest features on which applications success depends. Two app market places which saw a hockey stick curve in their business were the following:

- The Google Play Store
- The Apple App store

These became home to millions of apps which were accessible worldwide. The access to these apps led to increase in the use of apps. More apps were needed for people who were spending increasing amount of time on their smart phones. This gave developers an opportunity to develop android and iOS applications for smart phones. The app market is estimated to cross 77 billion dollars in revenue. Looking at this lucrative opportunity, many developers jumped into app development. But, now the market place is over saturated. There are millions of apps in a single category. What once started as a blue ocean is now turned into a bloody red ocean, which is how things were predicted to be and does not really come as a surprise. There still needs to be some work around for the developers who are enthusiastic about the app market because we never know, the next company grossing the trillion dollar mark might be an app launched in the saturated app market, but which was solving a problem

*e-mail: sararathod000@gmail.com
**e-mail: prajaktaugalmugle7@gmail.com
***e-mail: ruchi.r.c.777@gmail.com
****e-mail: tabmaktum@gmail.com

or providing a service which no one else looked at. So developers still need to have an opportunity to try their hand out at the next idea of the app they have. But the reality is that app development is time-consuming. A developer might spend 4 months developing an application, which when launched on the app store would hardly have 500 users. To avoid this scenario the proposed method is given in this paper for predicting whether the developer is creating an application needed in the market place and will be successful or which will fail in the market. To check the success rate of any software application the data from the store should be collected where the app is being uploaded and made available to user. Depending on a single prediction algorithm will tend to give inaccurate result. The proposed method given in this paper uses four algorithm Support Vector Machine, K-Nearest Neighbour, Decision Tree and Random Forest to predict success rate of an application. In order to approve accuracy the Voting Ensemble Technique is applied in proposed method.

The paper is organized as follows- section 2 is literature survey on the Software Application Success Predictor which summarizes all the existing approaches and papers. Section 3 presents the information about the proposed method used in this paper. The detail methodology/techniques is discussed in this section. Section 4 presents Experiments and Results of the System which gives the details of observations, results and model outcomes. Further conclusion is given this paper.

2 Literature Survey

This section reviews some of the existing techniques for predicting the success rate of any applications. The algorithms and techniques used by diverse papers are elaborated in subsequent section In paper [3], the author scraped information from the Google Play Store to extract as many capabilities as viable the use of an internet crawler 'scrapy' and used the statistics to train three models to predict the success of an application. To predict success metrics of an app, revenue must be the key feature however as it isn't always located publicly, the author used the number of installations and average user score, skilled linear model to categorize whether an app might be a successful or not and moreover used linear regression to predict the average rating of a system. The principal factor evaluation was performed in order to focus on variation and create strong styles of the dataset by the use of inputs of GLM and Linear regression models. Using these models, the author concluded that approximately 35% of total successful applications has the word 'photo' within the description and approximately 31% has the word 'share', the usage of these models, the developer can be cited the genres of application which are primarily liked by end users. For future work, the author suggested using the revenue to predict success metrics and referred agencies like App Annie to accumulate such data. From the defined success metric, a developer may be capable of find the economic achievement of an application. This paper acted as our reference paper, we got the idea of how the wide variety of downloads and average rating can play the crucial role at the same time as defining success metric and to find the success rate of any application.

Further more in paper[4], the authors tried to represent the review-rating mismatch, through establishing multiple systems which can routinely hit upon the inconsistency between these two, to show this mismatch they carried out two machine learning approaches, it included different classifiers like Naive Bayes Classifier, Decision tree, Decision stump, Decision table, and few other algorithms, and the other approach centered on deep gaining knowledge of techniques. They also hosted numerous surveys with the intention to research the opinion of end customers and builders concerning this mismatch. The outcome of the survey was pretty expected, each the developers and end users of android app agreed that rating of an app should match with its corresponding review, and they also asserted to have an automated device to detect the mismatch between rating and review if there is any. This paper proposed a notable way to symbolize the review-rating mismatch, we got inspired by way of their work and gave an effort to create a feature based on the review and rating mismatch and remove the ones which has a better distinction in mismatch but because of time constraint three of our members could manually annotate only 2000 reviews out of 199763 individually, due to this massive variance we couldn't get a proper result and dropped the idea of doing so.

Another paper working at the same aspect [5], the author states that the numeric rating as inside the stars given by users have a large distinction than in comparison to the reviews given by means of them consequently a rating system has been proposed by using the author a good way to dispose of the ambiguity created by means of the mismatch of the score and respective review by same user. It has been visible that how much we as users are dependent on others opinion while taking any decision so in accordance to the author people download the app based on the grading that is given for that particular app. Here the author describes the trouble dividing it into two subproblems. Firstly, the vagueness and secondly it's miles the biasness to the summarized rating of the users. Further explaining the problem, he brought that earlier people used to extract the rating from the remarks instead consisting of the star rating associated with it. To clear up the problems, he proposed a technique that it will initially conduct sentiment analysis on the user reviews and will generate a numeric rating from the polarity. Thus, a final rating could be the average of the rating from the sentiment analysis and the star ratings that are given through the users. This concept would reduce the confusion of the users and permit them to have a final rating primarily based on both review and star rating. This paper shows a strong relationship into the star ratings and the reviews of the users, which helped us of selecting up the idea of using the reviews of the app in our work.

Correspondingly, in paper [6], the author proposed a framework for mobile application developers with which they may be capable of bring in modification on functions the ones are located negative primarily based on the end user's evaluation in their application. Their framework consisted of three main building blocks (i)subject matter modeling, (ii)sentiment analysis and (iii)summarization interface. This body work changed into designed to make developers comprehend that sentiment rating presents an extra accurate cost of user feedback for an application than star rating and how important it's far to take account of the biasness of the capabilities that affect the overall score of an application. This paper guide us to find the sentiment mean by showing how it delivers some more accurate value than star rating.

Considering the truth that how important polarity values are, as a consequence from paper [7], it helped us to get the concept of removing the inconsistent reviews that will basically reduce noise from the dataset and give better overall performance in sentiment analysis, and consequently will generate polarity value more accurately. They proposed WisCom, a system this is able to analyze at least ten million user ratings and comments inside the app markets in three exceptional levels. The first feature of their system is to become aware of the inconsistencies in reviews; secondly, they have looked for the reasons why people do not like a selected app and the way the opinions change over the time. They prolonged their analysis to provide a valuable perception into the whole app market providing users with fundamental concerns. It generates techniques for summarizing and mining the reviews, which will help the end users to select the exceptional app that has the best experience without analyzing the comment, also app developers can then use the set of end result to apprehend why end users don't like their app which will eventually help the developers to improve their quality of app. More specifically it analyzes reviews on 3 levels which are firstly on single review (micro level) done the usage of regularized linear regression model, secondly on reviews of each app (meso level) by way of doing LDA in addition to they accomplished topic evaluation on distinctive time segments to choose how review modifications over the time, and ultimately on all the apps within the market (macro level). They highlighted all their three-level strategies and described the benefits so as to be obtained by the end-users, developers, and the entire mobile ecosystem.

In paper [8] the authors tried to symbolize the review-rating mismatch, started investigational and exploration journey with pre- processing job of two hundred random terms, taken from Indian agriculture area based guide Hindi dictionary database. Apart from English SVM successfully carried out for identification of relations in Indian Languages from the IndoWorldNet. These classified relations can be used for the generation of established hierarchical version as ontology of particular domain conforming to the idea of semantic web.

This paper [9] proposed the combination proceed towards POS tagging, SVM classifier and FCA-based domain ontology intend to increase the sentiment classification that is training the capabilities based on the supervised learning which categorised the opinions or sentiments within the reviews or comments as positive or negative on every feature. By the use of this method we can view the strength or weak point of the products in more detail. We also looked in papers which can be of different domains however of comparable work to understand better. The main assessment criterion of the overall performance is the predicting accuracy of all users in test set.

Though there are many existing system available in literature for predicting success of software application they lack in terms of accuracy and efficiency, hence an approach to accurately predict success of software application by applying four machine learning algorithm and Voting Ensemble method is proposed in this paper.

Though there are many existing system available in literature for predicting success of software application they lack in terms of accuracy and efficiency, hence an approach to accurately predict success of software application by applying four machine learning algorithm and Voting Ensemble method is proposed in this paper.

3 Methodology

The overall process of proposed system is given in figure 1. The functionality of all module is discussed below.

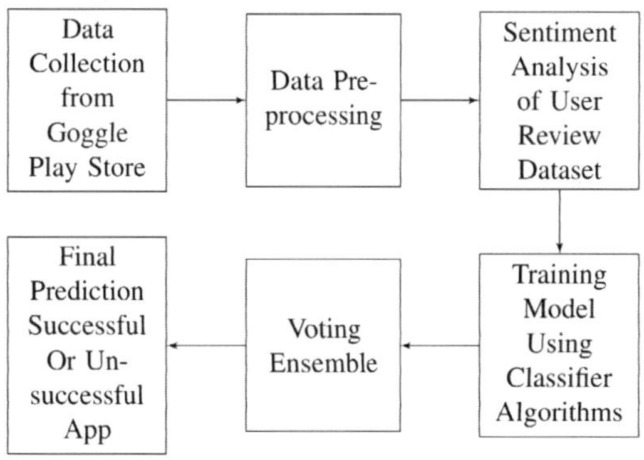

Figure 1. Block Diagram of the system

3.1 Data Collection

First of all, to gather knowledge of application with all its facts we have used Google Play Store platform. Google Play Store data can be acquired from Kaggle dataset or Web-scraping. Scraping is a technique of statistics mining from websites that uses software package to extract all the facts accessible from the targeted web site through simulating human behavior. This method largely focuses on the transformation of unstructured information (HTML format) on the websites into structured information (database or spreadsheet). The Beautiful Soup 4 (BS4) is used to extract knowledge from Play Store. Beautiful Soup 4 is a Python library for pulling knowledge out of hypertext markup language and XML files.

3.2 Data Preprocessing

All the app details have been scraped, there were no null or missing values in the dataset. Moreover, the raw in-

Table 1. features of an app

FEATURES	DESCRIPTION
name_app	This is the name of an application
cat_app	It represents the category of an app
n_review	The total number of reviews for the app given by user
rating_app	It is star rating given by user for the app
size_app	Size of an app in mb or kb
n_installs	It represents the total no of downloads for the app
type_app	It indicates whether the app is free of paid
price_app	It represents the cost for usage of the app
user_group	It represents the age group of users who are using app
genre_app	It represents genre of the app
last_updated	It is last date of updating
current_ver	It represents the current version
android_version	It is android version for the app

formation is extracted manually so there is a need of pre-processing to turn it into some utilizable information. So it is able to perform EDA and run algorithms on dataset installs, total number of ratings, rating distribution were also converted to integers. Sizes of apps having kilobyte were converted to megabytes to have consistent units. Apps with varying sizes (those that vary with device) were set to the average size of the rest of the apps. Later the categorical attributes like category or genre, content rating and type were label encoded, for instance free apps were labeled as 1 and paid apps were labeled as 0.

3.3 Feature Extraction

Feature Extraction aims to take out knowledge from the database by creating significant features from the existing ones. These new set of significant features should be able to sum up the information contained in the initial dataset. The table 1 shows the list of features in dataset.

3.4 Sentimental Analysis

Sentiment analysis is the measurement of beneficial, non beneficial and neutral language. It can evaluate how a person feels by their emotions, opinions and attitude. It can also be referred to as opinion mining. It basically inspects the issue of reading texts, like posts and thoughts uploaded by users on diverse platforms, meetings and electronic businesses regarding the 15 opinions they have about a product, service, event, man or woman or their thought by way of taking out the individual information from the source information.

3.5 Classification and Prediction Algorithm

3.5.1 K nearest neighbour Algorithm

The K nearest neighbour Algorithm is one of the frequently used classification algorithm. This algorithm divides the entire dataset into different classes and then class of any new sample can be predicted by their neighbour. It can also be used for regression output which has output in continuous domain. This value chosen is the average of the values its nearest neighbors.

3.5.2 Random Forest Algorithm

The Random forest is a ensemble model consisting of many decision trees. Random forest algorithm is prone to overfitting. Random Forest algorithm gives more accurate result than decision tree algorithm that is the reason it is widely used. It ensembles many random trees to give high accuracy. Each tree in the forest predicts the category to which the new record belongs. Finally, the new record is given to the category that wins the majority vote this is the basic task performed by random forest algorithm.

3.5.3 Support Vector Machine

The Support Vector Machine is a supervised and linear Machine Learning algorithm mostly referred as SVM. We have used SVM to train our model for predicting success of an application as SVM gives more more accuracy as compared to other algorithms such as logistic regression, Decision Tree. In SVM we have used SVC - Support Vector Classifiers which classifies apps as successful or unsuccessful by finding optimal hyperplane.

3.5.4 Decision tree

The Decision tree is a famous algorithm used for regression and classification. The model for classification is prepared in the form of tree like structure. The process of building decision tree is incremental. The leaves in the tree represents the decision for the given sample. The intermediate node contains the test for different attributes. There can be 2 or more than two branches based on the type of attributes. It accepts both numerical and categorical attributes.

3.6 Voting Ensemble

Voting Ensemble is a meta-classifiers for combining weak machine learning classifiers into one robust, accurate classifier for classification and prediction. Ensemble learning is mainly used to improve the performance of the model, or to lessen the selection of a poor one. Training a model with one algorithm will may not predict the outcome as accurate as combining two or three classifier into one meta-classifier and then training model to predict the outcome. Voting Ensemble combines different classifiers outputs and takes vote among them to predict the accurate output. Voting Ensemble prediction method is more powerful as compare to other prediction algorithm which improves precision, predictive power, accuracy and lessens error rate.

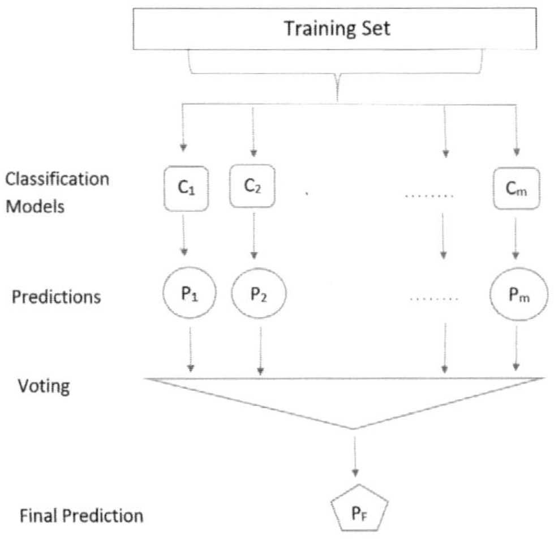

Figure 2. Voting Ensemble

3.6.1 Hard Voting Ensemble

In Hard Voting Ensemble the class which gets the highest voting is chosen. Consider that, there are n classifiers such as C1,......,Cn. The output class label l is predicted for any test data by considering the majority voting of classifiers Ci where i = 1,...,n.

$$l = mode\{C1(x), C2(x), ..., Cn(x)\} \quad (1)$$

Example : Let there be 3 classifiers the outcome given by each classifier is given below:

- C1 = 1
- C2 = 1
- C3 = 0

The output of the voting ensemble would be:

$$l = mode\{1, 1, 0\} = 1 \quad (2)$$

3.6.2 Soft Voting Ensemble

The another method for finding output class label for test data is soft voting in which rather than giving outcomes as 1 or 0, each classifiers gives probability for class 1 and 0. The output class label l for any test data is predicted by taking the average of the probabilities given by classifiers Ci where i = 1,...,n.

Example : Let there be 3 classifiers, the probabilities given by each classifier for class 1 and 0 is given below:

- classifier = [class 0, class 1]
- classifier C1 = 0.2, 0.8
- classifier C2 = 0.4, 0.6
- classifier C3 = 0.6, 0.4

Class 0 = (0.2+0.4+0.6) / 3 = 0.4

Class 1 = (0.8+0.6+0.4) / 3 = 0.6

Therefore the output of soft voting for given test data will be 1 at threshold 0.5.

Steps to develop Voting Classifier for Voting Ensemble

1. Import required classifiers and module from respective library.
2. Import VotingClassifier from sklearn.ensemble library.
3. Load the desired dataset.
4. Create classifiers Ci where i = 1,...,n.
5. create voting classifier for Ci
   voting_classifier = {
   (labels(Xn),
   (C1,C2,...Cn),
   voting=hard OR soft }
6. train and test voting classifier.

4 Experiments and Result

Dataset Description :
The proposed system is trained and tested over the dataset taken from Google Play Store. There is total 10842 application data in our dataset which is obtained from Google Play Store. After Data cleaning and pre-processing dataset was shrunk to 8892 application because of some incomplete data and null values. Among 8892 apps 4568 applications are labelled as successful after running the success matrix function and 4324 apps are labelled as unsuccessful applications.

In order to do the sentiment analysis on google play application user reviews dataset analysis was performed with two algorithm to see which gives the more accurate result.

The SVM and naive bayes algorithm are used to perform sentiment analysis. The table 3 and 4 shows the confusion matrix for both algorithm with respect to their accuracy.

	precision	recall	F1-score	support
0	0.99	0.99	0.99	12500
1	0.99	0.99	0.99	12500
micro avg	0.99	0.99	0.99	25000
macro avg	0.99	0.99	0.99	25000
weighted avg	0.99	0.99	0.99	25000
accuracy:	0.99204			

Figure 3. Confusion matrix for sentiment analysis using SVM algorithm with accuracy 99%

	precision	recall	F1-score	support
0	0.79	0.88	0.83	12500
1	0.87	0.77	0.81	12500
micro avg	0.82	0.82	0.82	25000
macro avg	0.83	0.82	0.82	25000
weighted avg	0.83	0.82	0.82	25000
accuracy:	0.825			

Figure 4. Confusion matrix of naive bayes algorithm with accuracy 82.5%

For 80/20 testing and training dataset a `train_test_split` function is used. So 7116 application are reserved for training and 1776 apps for testing purpose. Among 7116 training data 3558 apps are successful and 3558 apps are unsuccessful, and among 1776 apps 1010 apps are successful and 766 apps are unsuccessful apps. This is done in order to avoid overfitting and underfitting.

For success prediction the model is trained with four algorithms - SVM, Random Forest, K-NN algorithm, Decision Tree.

	precision	recall	F1-score	support
0	0.60	0.77	0.67	766
1	0.78	0.61	0.68	1010
macro avg	0.69	0.69	0.68	1776
weighted avg	0.70	0.68	0.68	1776
accuracy:	0.678			
AUC-ROC:	0.721			

Figure 5. Confusion matrix of SVM prediction algorithm

	precision	recall	F1-score	support
0	0.76	0.95	0.84	766
1	0.95	0.77	0.85	1010
macro avg	0.86	0.86	0.85	1776
weighted avg	0.87	0.85	0.85	1776
accuracy:	0.848			
AUC-ROC:	0.946			

Figure 6. Confusion matrix of KNN prediction algorithm

	precision	recall	F1-score	support
0	0.68	0.70	0.69	766
1	0.77	0.74	0.76	1010
macro avg	0.72	0.72	0.72	1776
weighted avg	0.73	0.73	0.73	1776
accuracy:	0.725			
AUC-ROC:	0.796			

Figure 7. Confusion matrix of Random Forest prediction algorithm

	precision	recall	F1-score	support
0	0.65	0.76	0.70	766
1	0.79	0.69	0.74	1010
macro avg	0.72	0.73	0.72	1776
weighted avg	0.73	0.73	0.72	1776
accuracy:	0.723			
AUC-ROC:	0.803			

Figure 8. Confusion matrix of Decision Tree prediction algorithm

According to table 5, 6, 7 and 8 it can be observed that the single algorithm can not predict the success of an application on his own with great accuracy. Therefor Voting Ensemble Method is proposed which is a meta classifier which will predict the final result by the method soft voting ensemble by analyzing these four algorithms.

	precision	recall	F1-score	support
0	0.93	0.97	0.95	766
1	0.97	0.95	0.96	1010
macro avg	0.95	0.96	0.95	1776
weighted avg	0.96	0.95	0.96	1776
accuracy:	0.955			
AUC-ROC:	0.991			

Figure 9. confusion matrix for Voting Ensemble prediction with accuracy of 95%

Figure 9 is the confusion matrix of voting ensemble. It can be observe that voting ensemble is the best method of predicting success of an app with as it gives 95% accuracy.

The Graph 1 shows the graph of performance comparison of SVM, KNN, Decision Tree, Random Forest with voting ensemble.

```
SVM - Support Vector Machine
KNN - K-nearest neighbor
DT - Decision Tree
RF - Random Forest
VE - Voting Ensemble
```

Graph 1. Algorithm Comparison

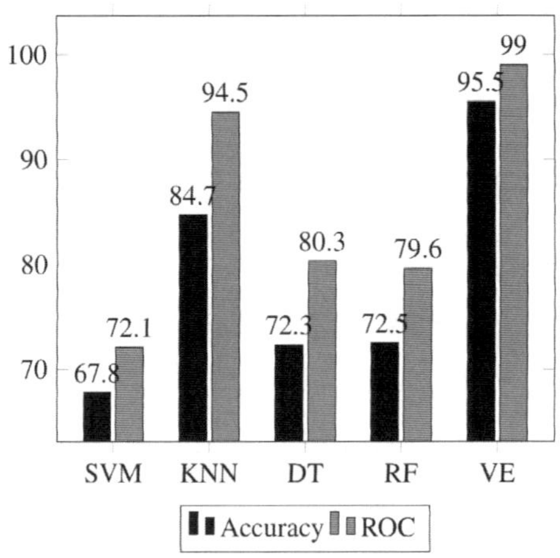

https://doi.org/10.1051/itmconf/20203203020

The accuracy of proposed model is high as compared to other models. Thus the proposed model outperforms the other algorithm. The voting ensemble method helps to correctly predict the success of any software application.

5 Conclusion

The Google Play Store is the most important app market in the world. It generates more greater number of downloads than the Apple App Store, however makes simplest half of the revenue compare to the Apple App Store. So the statistic data from the Play Store is scraped to conduct studies on it. There are a couple of troubles with the Play Store data that have been identified from exploratory data analysis. An inclusion of a function that lets users notify developers if they're unsatisfied with a new update, if they may want to go along into not plummeting an app with low installs to the ground. There is also the trouble of rating mismatch on a smaller scale. If this problem can be mitigated, the Play Store would provide an extra accurate representation of user sentiment which in turn should help developers make adjustments and update to their app accordingly. The proposed model in this paper uses Decision Tree, Support Vector Machine, k-Nearest Neighbour and Random Forest algorithm to predict the success of an application. Finally by assembling these four algorithms by Voting Ensemble Method the model predicts success rate of software application with 95% accuracy which is higher as compared to all four algorithms.

References

[1] *https://www.business2community.com/mobile-apps/2017-mobile-app-market-statistics-trends-analysis-01750346*, (2017)

[2] *https://entrepreneurscan.com/blog/help-my-ocean-is-turning-red/*, (2018)

[3] Tuckerman, C., (2014).

[4] Aralikatte, R., Sridhara, G., Gantayat, N., and Mani, S., (2018).

[5] Islam, M. R., (2014).

[6] Luiz, W., Viegas, F., Alencar, R., Mourão, F., Salles, T., Carvalho, D., Gonçalves, M. A., and Rocha, L., (2018).

[7] Fu, B., Lin, J., Li, L., Faloutsos, C., Hong, J., and Sadeh, N., (2013).

[8] Megha Garg,Bhaskar Sinha,Somnath Chandra, (2015).

[9] Khin Phyu Phyu Shein ,Thi Thi Soe Nyunt, (2010).

[10] Ziheng Wang, Yonggang Qi, Jun Liu, Zhanyu Ma, (2016).

[11] Chih-Chung Chang and Chih-Jen Lin, (2019).

[12] *https://www.kaggle.com/lava18/all-that-you-need-to-know-about-the-android-market.*

[13] *https://www.vaishalilambe.com/blog/data-science-algorithms-random-forest*

[14] *https://slideplayer.com/slide/7364467/*

[15] *https://stackabuse.com/implementing-svm-and-kernel-svm-with-pythons-scikit-learn/*

https://doi.org/10.1051/itmconf/20203203021

An ML and SMS remote access based model for Anti-theft protection of Android devices

Tanuja Sawant[1,*], *Dhrupal* Shah[2,**], *Smita* Sontakke[3,***], and *Prathmesh* Gunjgur[4,****]

[1]Department of Computer Engineering, Ramrao Adik Institute of Technology, Nerul, Navi-Mumbai, India.
[2]Department of Computer Engineering, Ramrao Adik Institute of Technology, Nerul, Navi-Mumbai, India.
[3]Department of Computer Engineering, Ramrao Adik Institute of Technology, Nerul, Navi-Mumbai, India.
[4]Department of Computer Engineering, Ramrao Adik Institute of Technology, Nerul, Navi-Mumbai, India.

Abstract. Android phones being stolen is a significant problem that causes concerns to intellectual privacy and property. Always protecting smartphones from being stolen is a problem that remains. The key findings of the survey of existing systems for theft protection are, they provide various efficient functionalities but fail when the internet is unavailable or require specialized equipment to detect thefts. Most of these solutions are not free of charge, inefficient, time-consuming, or/and inflexible. This paper puts forward a system that provides an ML-based real-time anti-theft and remote access system for android devices. It detects theft using SVM-RBF model trained on feature-set extracted from the inertial sensor's data with an accuracy of 0.76. Whereas remote access is provided using short message services (SMS). The salient feature of this system is minimal configuration without intruding human-assisted tasks. Moreover, it will be an excellent help for authentic smartphone users to realize the theft situation and utilize the remote access features.

1 Introduction

Android phones change people's way of living as they behave like a machine which is used to access data, documents, etc. and as a result, have become an essential part of their life. Android-based mobiles are ubiquitous these days as they provide a considerable number of facilities that function in a wallet as a computer. These Android phones are beneficial for doing business. It can be easily hacked since it is small in size, and any customer information or personal data stored on the phone could be revealed easily.

Theft is prohibited under normal circumstances by merely introducing application and socially embracing property law. Physical marks (license plates, name tags) also indicate ownership. When there is no clear identity of the owner and a lack of awareness, individuals may be interested in possessing the object to their benefit at the expense of the original owner (purpose and chance are elements that enable theft). While the causes for theft are diverse and intricate, and usually, victims can't control it, the majority of theft avoidance strategies focus on minimizing theft possibilities.

There is always a threat of losing data for all the users when the phone is stolen, and also forgetting your phone home can create a big hurdle. Many of the people are facing this problem, which may result in data leaks and unauthorized access to a device. If this data is confidential, it may lead to unexpected or illegal destruction, damage, modification, unlawful declaration of private data.

There are many solutions available to prevent this but failed without the internet, which led to the idea of making a system that will help users retrieve their phones and provide security even while the system has *no internet connection*. This paper presents a fast, user-friendly, android phone anti-theft system which can provide remote access to various functionalities of users phone and detect theft using ML and help the user to recover his/her device.

2 Background

Android is a collection of services and programs together to deliver results. Android phones utilize Linux kernel with few design modifications that Google makes and controls the hardware. It will serve as a middleman between the machinery and the application that handles files and passes information between both the file system and hardware. Android has given Android System Interfaces (APIs) so that the system hardware can communicate with the kernel. The Android SDK (Software Development Kit) offers resources and a lengthy collection of APIs for creating software using JAVA on an android platform. Essential components of android application [1].

- **Activity:** An activity gives a person the space to do anything and everything. For instance, any interaction like setting the pin, saving a contact, etc., is done by communicating with a screen offered by an operation.
- **Service:** Services offer no user interface and are meant to perform actions in the background regardless of what

*e-mail: sawanttanuja1998@gmail.com
**e-mail: 1289dhrupal@gmail.com
***e-mail: sontakke.smita19@gmail.com
****e-mail: prathmesh.gunjgur@rait.ac.in

the user is doing in the foreground. A good example would be short message services - the user receives SMS even if it is kept aside.

- **Content Providers:** Such modules introduce the object-oriented principles into the framework, such as data encapsulation. It provides another, serving as an interface with the content of one process. Content Provider, together with content Resolver, is used to retrieve names in a phone user's Contacts.
- **Android Intents and Broadcast Receivers:** Android Intents are the modes of communication, i.e., how components of apps interact with each other. It is used to communicate with server and trigger application on receiving SMS.

3 Literature Survey

A mobile anti-theft program is a project that helps users monitor where smartphones are located. It consists of an Android program, which sends SMS automatically when the SIM card is updated. The location tracker is operating on both GPS and GPRS. On request with specific orders, latitude and longitude coordinates will be retrieved and sent as SMS, but this information is not sufficient to identify the thief using this information.

Tiwari Mohini *et al.* [2] created a smartphone application that permits users to remotely control their access to a phone using an internet network. This application checks internet access and then executes functions accordingly.

Sainath Vitthal Pawar *et al.* [3] implemented an android application retrieving the coordinates of the lost phone using SMS facilities. This application enables people to send SMS to the stolen phone and then get the location as a response from the stolen phone, which could then be viewed utilizing Google Maps.

Onkar Mule [4] implemented an android application retrieving the coordinates of the lost phone using SMS facilities. This application enables people to send SMS to the stolen phone and then get the location as a response from the stolen phone, which could then be viewed utilizing Google Maps.

Yongqing Goa *et al.* [5] suggested a workaround that would make the subscriber identity module (SIM) card interlock. This method scans the data on the new SIM card then contrasts that to the information on the cloned SIM card. When the findings of the test are accurate, the handset will start in a usual way; otherwise, the handset will immediately run anti-theft software, and does not need to be reported to the cell phone operator, and may avoid utilizing the subscriber identity module card, the lost handset cannot be utilized by another individual to prevent the leakage of the person's confidential data.

Azeem Ush Shan Khan *et al.* [6] presented a revolutionary android-based anti-theft program. The program deploys a security solution by supplying the thief's pictures and videos, making it simple for the operator to locate the stealer and arrest that person by providing the mobile location data with the aid of texts.

Iliyasu Yahaya Adam *et al.* [7] explored the literature on trend-setting techniques used during telephone monitoring to illustrate the issues and opportunities that may emerge from this and to instill trust. It explores the consequences of different methods used, and the actions they perform to detect fraud perpetrators, emphasizing the chances of technology misuse. It concludes with some suggestions that may serve as a guide for consumers to leverage these technologies and prevent their likely pitfalls.

Shirin Salim *et al.* [8] presented the idea of a device using the GPS and WI-FI to locate the site. When the SIM is substituted, the location will be identified, and the call information will be monitored for different operations. But those activities are unaware of the thief because they are not shown in the task manager as well; they are all working in the background.

Meng Jin *et al.* [9] described a smartphone device that detects theft in real-time using distinctive data. This data is from both the sequence of movements when the smartphone is taken-out action and the output signal of every specific movement, making it easy to identify theft activity sensitively and reliably using just the built-in smartphone sensors. iGuard is reliable and sturdy in different scenarios.

Xinyu Liu *et al.* [10] showed that inertial information is adequate to identify some common types of phone theft, such as pickpocket and pick-and-run, without compromising usability by flooding users with false alarms. It was successful and can detect 100% of simulated robberies. It's because the kinds of thefts they considered here included a short jerking movement followed by the thief trying to escape, which caused a distinct pattern in the sensor data.

Many software for anti-theft has been developed, which were real-time and provided excellent data recovery methods too. They all had one thing in common that is they required the internet the whole time. They used various methods to detect theft as well as identify the thief. After studying various existing approaches and methods, few drawbacks were observed. They are as follows :

- The majority of this software is not available for free of charge.
- Using this app, it's difficult to locate the thief, and in most cases, they fail due to lack of internet or for not having another device with the same app at hand.
- The current anti-theft systems aren't getting the thief's comprehensive information for which they are made, which in most cases results in innocents being accused.
- The current system is stated to be unreliable, time-consuming, poorly managed, and lacking flexibility.

4 Proposed Methodology

4.1 Proposed Work

Because of the limitations, as mentioned above, this paper puts forward a system that deals with theft and also provides primary remote access to the user. The system starts the remote access services when it is intimated by a predefined template message and sends the data via SMS; while simultaneously working in the background to detect theft.

The whole system comprises of three major modules working hand-in-hand, as shown in Figure 1.

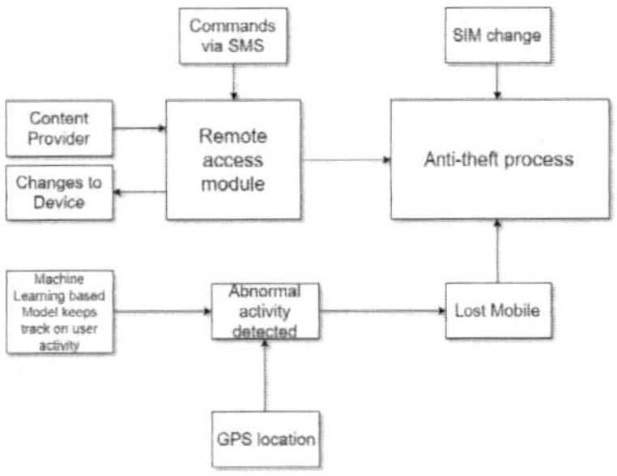

Figure 1. Architecture of proposed model

1. **Remote Access Module**

   The remote access is the module wherein the user can access remotely via other devices using SMS; the Authenticity of the user is checked based on various parameters, and if the user is authentic, it is allowed the remote access. As discussed in prerequisites, this module uses broadcasts and services, resulting in low battery consumption as the app features will be working as and when triggered.

   The SMS(s) meant for triggering the services have a predefined template, and some of its functionalities are as follows:

   - If SMS has "LOC < pin >", then the app sends location in the form of <lat, long>.
   - If SMS has "Retrieve #contact < pin >", then the app retrieves the contact and sends the number.
   - If SMS has "PROFILENAME <pin> ", then the app toggles the sound profile to the one specified in SMS.

Algorithm 1: Algorithm for location fetches

Result: Longitude and Latitude
Step 1. Start;
Step 2. Check for the SMS format;
Step 3. If format matched for location fetch;
Step 4. Turns GPS location based service is ON;
Step 5. Get the location from GPS_Provider;
Step 6. Send location information to remote user.
    Create an intent for SMS,
    Import SmsManager,
    Use SendTextMessage() for sending SMS
Step 7. End;

The Algorithm 1 shows how the SMS triggers the process and sends the location. Similarly, it works for other functionalities.

2. **Anti-theft Module**

   As the name suggests, this module deals with the anti-theft process. This module has three submodules:

   - *Machine Learning* - The sub-module requires data-set as the input, which is then filtered and then is trained with the Support Vector Machine -Radial Bias Function kernel and deployed to detect theft. The system tackles false alarms by sending a notification when theft is detected. This notification would need to be declined by the user if it's a false alarm.
   - *SIM Card Tracking* - It continuously keeps a check on SIM card bound with the phone. As soon As the SIM is changed without a proper procedure, the app triggers the anti-theft process.
   - *Remote access* - In case the application fails to recognize theft, the anti-theft process can also be triggered by sending an SMS Now, this makes the system real-time. If the theft is detected, the module runs the anti-theft process.

3. **Securing Power button options**

   Power Button is secured by depending on the external application, which protects the privacy and prevents theft by securing the power off and restart option with a password.

5 Algorithm

5.1 Support Vector Machine

Support Vector Machine (SVM) is simply scary, in any case. It turns out to be less startling once thought of it as a "road machine", which isolates the right, left-side buildings, vehicles, people on foot, and tries to make the amplest path as could reasonably be expected. What's more, those cars, buildings, truly near the road is the support vectors. The following is the detailed clarification to see how this "road-machine" works.

Back to the discussion, consider all those objects, people as points now. The yellow points represent things on the right half of the road; red points represent the ones on the left. The road becomes dashed and solid vectors. SVM works to find the decision boundary to divide the points into different classes and amplify the margin [11].

5.1.1 SVM in linearly separable cases

Endless vectors will be able to divide the red and yellow points in the example 2. Now, this is where SVM comes into working and tries to locate the ideal vector with the requirement of accurately classifying either class:

- Follow the constraint: investigate all different hyperplanes, hyperplanes that effectively classify classes.
- Conduct optimization: select the hyperplane that amplifies the margin.

Figure 2 illustrates the concept of separate hyperplane and margin.

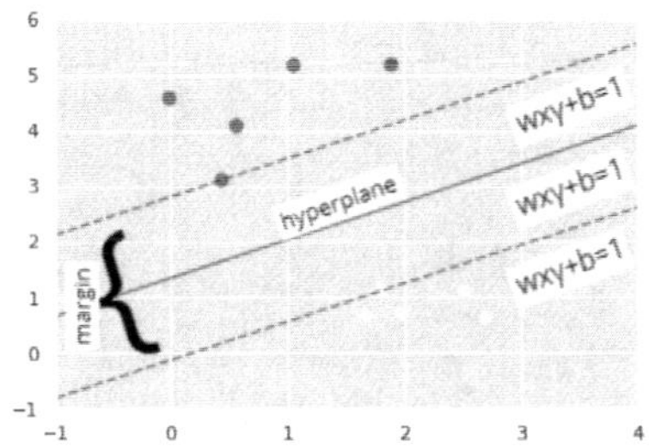

Figure 2. Linear SVM

5.1.2 SVM in linearly non-separable cases

In the cases that can be separable linearly, the goal of the SVM is to search for the hyperplane that amplifies the margin, provided that it can classify the classes effectively. But in an actual scenario, data-sets are not necessarily linearly separable, which results in not meeting the 100% effective classification criteria defined by a hyperplane. Whereas for cases that are not linearly separable, SVM deals it by presenting two ideas, which are discussed below, and flow of it is shown in Figure 3.

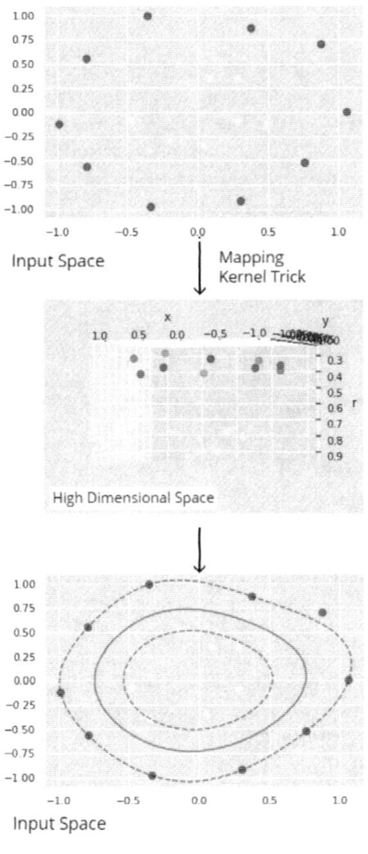

Figure 3. SVM in non-linearly separable cases

- **Soft Margin:** Using Soft Margin, SVM tries to tolerate some points to get wrongly classified and attempts to adjust balance by looking for a vector that amplifies the margin and limits the wrong classification. SVM tolerates two kinds of misclassifications under soft margin refer Figure 4 :

  - The points on the correct side of the margin but wrong side of the decision boundary (shown in first).

  - The points on the wrong side of the margin and the wrong side of the decision boundary (shown in second).

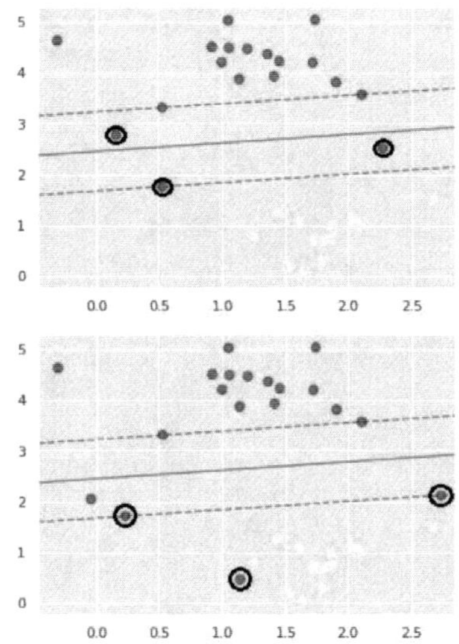

Figure 4. Soft Margin

- **Kernel Trick:** Using the existing features, Kernel Trick creates new features by applying some transformations. These transformed features are the important factors for SVM to discover the non-linear decision boundaries; refer Figure 5 for this. There are many kernel/transformations that one can choose from, for example 'RBF', 'sigmoid', 'poly', 'linear', 'precomputed'. As this system uses the Radial Basis Function (RBF), it is explained with an example below.

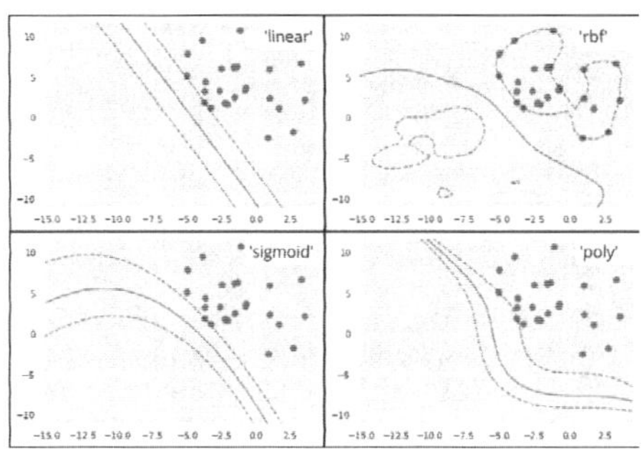

Figure 5. Kernel Trick

5.2 Radial Basis Function kernel

Radial Basis function (RBF) kernel can be imagined as a transformer/processor to produce modified features by estimating the distance between every single other point to a particular point/point-centers. The Gaussian Radial Basis Function is the most famous and simple RBF kernel. Equation 1 is the mathematical representation of RBF:

$$\phi(x, center) = exp(-\gamma\|x - centre\|^2) \quad (1)$$

Gamma(γ) decides the impact of transformed features — ϕ(x, center) on the decision boundary. As the gamma increases the impact of the features on the decision boundary also increases. To get more wiggled boundary greater gamma is required.

When using SVM with kernels, (γ), that can be tuned plays a significant role as shown in Figure 6, and its effect is summarized in Table 1.

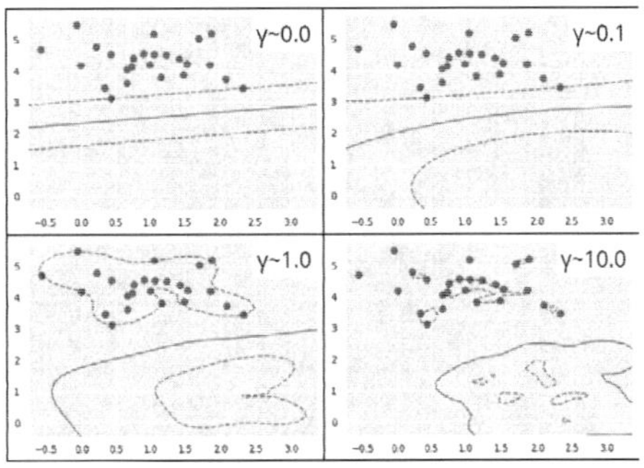

Figure 6. Illustration of how Gamma affects the Model

Table 1. Gamma results

Sr	value	impact	decision boundary
1	1E3	null	almost straight
2	0.1	small	appropriate
3	1	large	wiggled
4	10	very large	too wiggled

How applying a Gaussian rbf ((γ) = 0.1) can benefit, is illustrated in the example below:

Feature:

X = [-2,-1,0, 1,2]

Label:

Y =[0,1,1,0,0]

New Features:

X_1=[1.01, 1.00, 1.01, 1.04, 1.09]

X_2=[1.09, 1.04, 1.01, 1.00, 1.01]

ϕ(x1,center1) = 1.01

#x1=[-2,0]; #center1=[-1,0]; #gamma=0.1

As shown in Figure 7 in the first image, it isn't easy to discover a line separating the points. Nevertheless, if Gaussian RBF kernel is applied using the centers [(2,0), (-1,0)] to get transformed features, a line can be drawn that will be able to separate the red-yellow points as shown in the right.

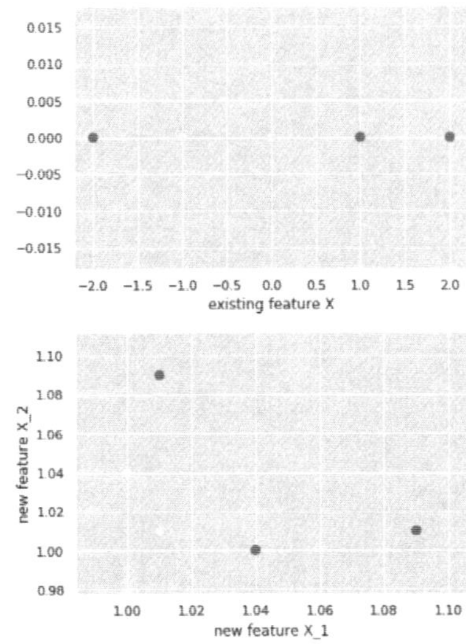

Figure 7. Transformation of Feature Set

5.3 Data-set Description

The data-set is formed from the inertial sensor readings. Classification results are much dependent on the performance of feature selection. Right now, the feature vector is extracted and chose from the time-domain velocity signal. The extraction procedure is generally straightforward. The average uniaxial velocities are investigated as the three features for classification.

Algorithm 2: How to get sensor reading

Result: Get Accelometer Reading
float x, y, z;
if *mySensor.getType()* ==
Sensor.TYPE_ACCELEROMETER **then**
x = sensorEvent.values[0];
y = sensorEvent.values[1];
z = sensorEvent.values[2];
end

The data set that is formed of inertial reading has five columns x, y, z velocities, sample number, and class. A feature-set is then formed of the above data-set that has four columns. The first three columns contain average velocities in the x-direction, y-direction, and z-direction, and 4th column is the class label for each sample. The final data-set has 350 samples.

6 Results and Discussion

For the training - testing the data-set is divided into a 70-30 ratio. The results and analysis below are based on the same.

1. **Confusion Matrix:** Confusion matrix, as shown in Table 2, is also known as an error matrix. It describes the performance of a classifier on a test dataset with known actual values and helps to visualize the performance of an algorithm.

Table 2. Confusion Matrix

	Actually Positive (1)	Actually Negative (0)
Predicted Positive (1)	33 True Positive (TP)	16 False Positive(FP)
Predicted Negative(0)	9 False Negative (FN)	47 True Negatives(TN)

2. **Accuracy:** Accuracy is the most common measure of performance and is a ratio of correctly predicted observations to total observations, refer Equation 2.

$$Accuracy = \frac{TP + TN}{TP + FP + FN + TN} \quad (2)$$

3. **Precision :** Precision is the ratio of correctly predicted positive observations to the total predicted positive observations, refer to Equation 3.

$$Precision = \frac{TP}{TP + FP} \quad (3)$$

4. **Recall:** The Recall is the ratio of correctly predicted positive observations to all observations in an actual class, refer to Equation 4.

$$Recall = \frac{TP}{TP + FN} \quad (4)$$

Table 3. Results of various SVM Kernel

Parameter	**SVM kernels**		
	Linear	**RBF**	Sigmod
Accuracy	0.68	**0.76**	0.74
Precision	0.33	**0.67**	0.63
Recall	**0.94**	0.79	0.74

Since all performance measures (as seen in Table 3) of Sigmoid kernel are low, it is not considered. The linear kernel has a high Recall but a very low Precision, which is not suitable as it would result in a low theft detection rate. Now coming to RBF even though Recall is comparatively less than that of Linear, it has a pretty high Precision. Hence RBF was selected.

7 Conclusion and Future Work

The primary goal of the implemented solution is that when an android based phone of the user is stolen, the mobile phone will automatically detect theft and start the anti-theft process if the internet is available. In case the app fails to recognize the robbery, the process can be triggered by merely sending an SMS. Since the power off and restart options are locked by the external app, mobile phones if lost/stolen, can be misused by another person and also cannot be formatted until the battery goes down, which might give users a chance to retrieve their smartphones.

The implementation of the ML model for motion detection is still on the primary stage of research and implementation. The project being on the primary stage, the training efficiency factor for algorithms is considered as their accuracy values obtained during the training phase. In the future, once the research is done, the training efficiency factor can be generated using elaborate methods to get more efficient values. For making the application more powerful, the external dependency for securing power-off and restart options would be developed. As the android only provides the image and voice-based ML models to be deployed as of now, so as further developments are made, the whole system would be able to work offline.

References

[1] Android Architechure Description [Online]. Available: https://tinyurl.com/w8b34g4

[2] Tiwari Mohini, Srivastava Kumar and Gupta Nitesh; "Review on Android and Smartphone Security" NRI Institute of Information Science and Technology, Bhopal, Madhya Pradesh, INDIA. Vol. 1(6), 12-19, November (2013).

[3] Sainath Pawar, Saiprasad Pore, Suprita Tendulkar, Vinayak Malavade "Android Application for Antitheft Security through SMS" IJSRD Vol. 4, Issue 02, 2016.

[4] Onkar Mule, Nihal Shaikh, Pratik Shinde, Amit Wagaskar, Prof. Sneha Ramtek. "Remote Access of Android Smart Phone" Volume 7, Issue 4, April 2017.

[5] Yongqing Gao, Chunlai Zhou, Dan Shang, "A Smart Phone Anti-theft Solution Based on Locking Card of Mobile Phone", International Conference on Computational and Information Sciences, 2011.

[6] Azeem Ush Shan Khan, Mohammad Naved Qureshi and Mohammed Abdul Qadeer, "Anti-Theft Application for Android-Based Devices", IEEE International Advance Computing Conference (IACC), 2014.

[7] Iliyasu Adam, Cihan Varo and Asaf Varol, "Problems and Prospects of Anti-Theft and Mobile Phone Tracking: A case in Nigeria", 7th International Symposium on Digital Forensics and Security (ISDFS), 2019.

[8] Shirin Salim "Monitoring System for detecting mobile theft" International Journal of Computational Science and Information Technology Vol.4, No.2, May 2016.

[9] Meng Jin, Yuan He, Dingyi Fang, Xiaojiang Chen, Xin Meng & Tianzhang Xing, "iGuard: A Real-Time Anti-Theft System for Smartphones", IEEE Transactions on Mobile Computing, Vol:17 Issue:10 Oct 2018.

[10] Xinyu Liu, David Wagner, Serge Egelman, "Detecting Phone Theft Using Machine Learning", 14th ICISS, 2018.

[11] Support Vector Machines Explanation [Online]. Available: https://tinyurl.com/uaouav7

ITM Web of Conferences **32**, 03022 (2020) https://doi.org/10.1051/itmconf/20203203022
ICACC-2020

Identity Theft Prediction Using Game Theory

Nikita Chorghe[1,4,*], *Akshay* Jain[2,**], *Shraddha* Mali[3,***], and *Prathmesh* Gunjgur[4,****]

[1]Department of Computer Engineering, Ramrao Adik Institute of Technology Nerul, Navi Mumbai, India.
[2]Department of Computer Engineering, Ramrao Adik Institute of Technology Nerul, Navi Mumbai, India.
[3]Department of Computer Engineering, Ramrao Adik Institute of Technology Nerul, Navi Mumbai, India.
[4]Department of Computer Engineering, Ramrao Adik Institute of Technology Nerul, Navi Mumbai, India.

Abstract. Digital devices have become an integral part of every person's life. The range of use of these devices is increasing daily. Over the decades, the number of users has increased from thousands to millions and is still increasing. Due to the multi-functional features of digital devices, their importance is now being recognized more than ever. Initially, they were used only for calling and texting; however, nowadays, they are also being used to store relevant data such as account numbers, card numbers, credentials, private pictures, passport copies, etc. The most common form of Identity Theft attack is through stealing passwords. Once the password is stolen, user privacy is lost, and the data is compromised. Thus, a system consisting of a database that comprises of leaked passwords collected from various social sites and common passwords as a part of a dictionary attack used by hackers has been created by us. When a user enters his/her password, it runs it through the database and checks for a match. This document emphasizes on how game theory can be utilized in predicting the possibility of a successful attack and discusses essential concepts such as the various components of game theory and Nash Equilibrium.

1 Introduction

With widespread digital growth occurring globally, the threats associated with these digital devices are also evolving. All digital devices are prone to cyber-attacks. With India emerging as a digital nation, the safety of digital devices can be compromised due to multiple vulnerabilities, and they can be exploited.

Mobile devices connected to a network can quickly become a target of cyber-attacks. Hence, it is vital to secure these networks. The main motive of malware is to penetrate IOS, Windows, and Android defence system. The security mechanism must be an integral part of the system and must work in coordination to identify threats and safeguard user data. Cyber-attacks are carried out in the cyber-space with social or political gains as the primary objective. Digital devices, other than being used as a means of communication, are also used for storing personal and corporate data. Viruses, malicious codes, etc. can result in disruptive consequences, which can lead to data loss and endanger the privacy of its users.

Identity theft is one of the most common attacks used by an attacker to steal user data. It is also called as Identity Fraud wherein a hacker obtains important pieces of private, confidential data such as credentials of email accounts, pan card numbers, PINs, and passwords to assume someone else's identity.

This data can serve various purposes to the hacker, such as to obtain credit, goods, or other services registered in the name of the impersonated person. The hacker can also provide false identification to the police to avoid warrants or arrests and to prevent a criminal record.

As per the latest statistics, approximately 200 billion devices will be connected to the internet by 2020. This alarming rise in the number of devices connected to the internet gives increased opportunities for attackers to steal data and infect websites. Since 2013, there has been a theft of 3,809,448 records. In 2016, 95% of the attacks were focused on government, retail, and technology industries [6].

2 Related Work

K.Veena *et.al.* have proposed a new methodology that identifies the assorted identity of any user and determines if a synthetic identity theft attack has occurred. They took three styles of information: Input, Normal, and Target data-set. They used varied identities that could be text and string information. Various identities were classified in three classes as 100% that represented high identity with accurate data, 75% that represented medium identity with partial data, and 0% that represented low identity with wrong information. The expected values were 0% or 100% for

*e-mail: nikitachorghe98@gmail.com
**e-mail: aj2812@gmail.com
***e-mail: shraddha.mali1812@gmail.com
****e-mail: prathmesh.gunjgur@rait.ac.in

the various identities, and the normal value ranged from 0% to 100%. The neural networks were trained on top of values. The progress was obtained for the epoch values, time, performance, gradient, and validation checks [1].

Sharmistha Dutta *et.al.* have proposed a method that deals with credit card application crimes. Their techniques are used to remove identity theft. They have proposed new data mining techniques. Mainly two algorithms are used they are Communal Detection and Spike Detection for fraud detection. The communal algorithm identifies the communal data, and the Spike detection algorithm is used to detect spikes in the duplicates. The system uses the resilience concept, which is a multi-layered data mining based approach [2].

Philip A.K.Lorimer *et.al.* proposed a framework that focuses on the validation of social profile. Using the proof-of-concept study, their proposed framework detects abnormal behavior in social profiles. Their numerical value results show that if the matching threshold in a decision tree is appropriately set, then the system identifies compromised accounts by avoiding the heavy central processing [3].

Very few systems have been developed for Identity Theft attack detection. The process of identification of an Identity Theft attack is based on different parameters for which various databases have been compiled. These parameters can be easily manipulated.

1. They have proposed a method that deals with credit card information theft by using two algorithms: communal data and spike detection algorithm. A major advantage is that they have used a multi-layered data mining approach [1].
2. They have also developed a framework that focuses on the validation of social platforms [2].
3. A significant drawback of all the systems is that if by chance a user's password is hacked, then using that password, data can easily be accessed. Thus, there was a need to mitigate this risk by preventing users from already using passwords that have been leaked [3].

3 Proposed Work

The objective of developing the OSI model was to provide a set of design standards for equipment manufacturers to communicate with each other. It consists of 7 layers. Attackers target the vulnerabilities present in the network and physical layers.

Over the years, many developments have been made to improve the OSI model. However, the base structure remains the same. Hence, these problems exist to date. A cyber-attack is intentional exploitation of resources, hardware/software, and networks for personal or monetary gains. Using malware, infecting systems by viruses and worms, using backdoor traps, or brute force attacks are some of the common means and methods to conduct cyber-attacks. Attackers perform these attacks to gain access to confidential information or resources of an organization or to steal data that can be later sold on the dark web.

The main motive of attackers behind Identity Theft is to steal personal or financial information of a person with the sole purpose of obtaining that person's identity and making transactions or purchases.

Table 1. Issues in Physical and Network Layers

Network layer	Physical layer
Various data routing paths for communication are provided by the Network layer.	Actual physical connectivity is defined by the Physical layer
Data is transferred in the form of packets using different logical network paths in a sequential order controlled by the network layer.	Physical layer defines the hardware equipment, cabling, wiring etc.
Network layer utilises multiple routing protocols on the network.	It majorly consists of hardware equipment such as cables, routers etc.
Various attacks such as ICMP, packet sniffing and DOS attacks are performed majorly over the Internet.	DOS attacks are performed by cutting wireless network cables.

Table 1 refers to various issues present in the Physical and Network layer of the OSI model. These vulnerabilities are exploited by the attackers to gain access to confidential data. The different types of theft are shown in Table 2.

Table 2. Different Types of Thefts [4]

Theft Type	Description
Criminal	A criminal uses the identity of other person in order to evade an arrest and conviction records.
Medical	This type of theft is usually done in order to obtain free medical services.
Financial	Among all the types of thefts, this is one of the most common and frequently committed theft. Another person's identity is used for goods, credits and services.
Child Identity Theft	The perpetrator uses the child's name and other confidential information with the intention of avoiding arrests, obtaining loan or a job etc.

Identity theft is a crime in which an attacker steals the information from a legitimate user and uses that information to impersonate someone. This leads to the immediate impact of losing something valuable like money. Identity theft victims can face abstract costs such as defamation of character, prevention in securing credit cards or position in a company, etc. There are very fewer chances of recovering from Identity theft after such circumstances.

Participation in various events is only possible because of the identities assigned to individuals and the privileges granted to them. Some of these privileges are driving, attending school, donating blood, using credits, taking loans, etc. In cases of account hacks, the hacker exploits the privileges granted to the victim by misusing resources such as writing cheques against the person's account or misusing stolen credit cards to buy utilities in the person's name. In other cases, hackers misuse an individual's identity for credit cards or loan applications. Fraudsters are coming up with new and varied methods to assume the identity of other individuals. Thus it is necessary to develop a preventive measure to reduce the disastrous effects of identity thefts [8].

Identity theft can occur in various forms, such as insurance, credit, and debit card or mortgage fraud. Most of these thefts are unreported because the victim is not aware of the occurrence of such an event. The risk to financial institutions and many such institutions continues to grow exponentially. Hence, security improvements that provide technical solutions and adjust as per human behavior are required.

Employees of businesses and organizations are targets of Identity thefts as it leads to defamation and breach of trust. Sometimes users keep a single password for multiple accounts. These can be social networking apps, email accounts, or even bank accounts. If the hacker gets access to any one of the passwords, the most common practice followed is to use the same password to hack other accounts linked to the victim. Thus, the hacker through a single password can gain access to a massive amount of personal data. Once the data is at hand, the hacker can demand a ransom or release the data on the internet. Apart from monetary loss, it can also lead to loss of life.

One of the possibilities is that the leaked passwords could be of an organization's for centralized servers. Getting access to a server's password can be troublesome for an organization. The hacker can demand a ransom, can sell all the data to the organization's competitors, or sell their client's private data on the darknet, which can put the users at risk.

The proposed framework can be used to detect attacks and, thus, mitigate such threats and secure user data. We have developed a hacked password checker, which will work as an alert system for users. The system will check whether the password has been hacked and if so, it will report to the user.

3.1 Procedure

The proposed work has a hacked password checker, which will work as an alert system for users. It will check whether the passwords have been hacked or not. It examines the password, and if that password matches the list of passwords that have been leaked, it will report to the user. Algorithm 1 provides a series of steps to be followed to prevent the user from using an already leaked password. This, in turn, will prove to be beneficial for the user by eliminating the user as a possible target of identity theft.

Algorithm 1: Identity Theft Detection

1.Start
2.Create a data set of leaked passwords.
3.Store all the entries after converting them into a hash.
4.Take a user input.
5.Convert the input into hash value.
6.Check the user input with each value stored in the database.
7.**if** *The user input matches with any of the values stored in database* **then**
  Alert the user the password has been leaked;
else
  Notify the user that the password has not been leaked;
end

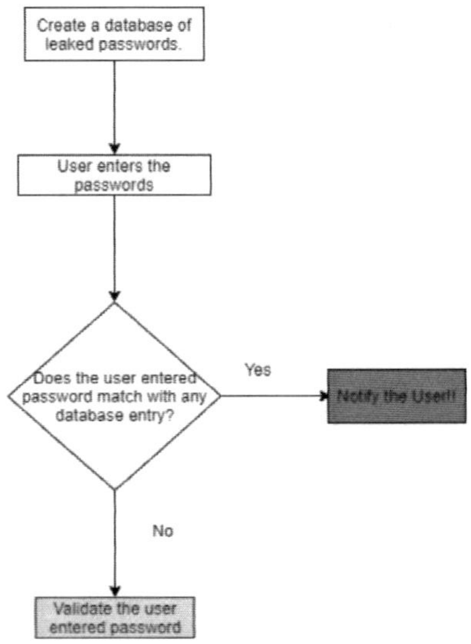

Figure 1. Identity Theft Flowchart

Figure 1 explains the flow of the prevention of Identity Theft attacks. A database of the leaked passwords is created. The user enters his/her password. The system will check if that password matches the user entered password; if that password matches the user will be notified, or else the user's password is not leaked.

3.2 Game Theory

Game theory is a theoretical framework that is used to analyze social situations among different competitors [5].

Game theory is used to study situations involving more than one participant in a scenario and in which not everything depends on one person. Game theory analyses the behavior of two or more participants involving rewards or punishments. E.g., in the game of chess, the opponent's moves continuously influence your strategy. It is also used to analyze situations in which multiple companies are competing against one another. Let us suppose if one of the competitors reduces the price of its product, other companies might be forced to do the same. The modeling of strategic interaction between multiple competitors in a scenario containing rules and outcomes is called game theory [5].

Game theory can be a useful approach to solve cybersecurity problems that require rational decision making. An assumption is made in game theory that all the participants have complete information about each other and know all the rules and regulations. Game theory enhances the ability to anticipate the actions of hackers. Recently, there were a few attacks wherein the hackers stole sensitive data and demanded Bitcoins as a ransom to maintain integrity and data security. Once the data is leaked, the hackers have complete control over it. They can compromise the security of the data by threatening the availability and confidentiality of it. Game theory is preferable as it shares similar concerns with cybersecurity in various aspects of their application. The move of the hacker with respect to the defender is not only contingent of the hacker's decision but also depends upon the defender's behavior. Thus, game theory can be used as a mathematical tool to deal with cybersecurity problems based on multi-agent behavior. Moreover, the combination of game theory and cybersecurity can be used to solve real-time problems [7].

3.2.1 Nash Equilibrium

The concept is named after the American mathematician John Nash. It is a scenario of an optimal outcome wherein the player has no motivation to change the chosen strategy. It is a concept which states that an opponent's move provides no incentive to any of the players to deviate from the initially chosen strategy. The player, even after changing the course of action, will receive no incremental benefit provided all other players do not change their methods. A game can contain multiple Nash Equilibria or none at all. It helps in determining a set of actions that all players must take to secure the best possible outcome for themselves.

To better understand Nash Equilibrium, we can consider an example. Let us suppose there are two players: A and B. In this game, players can either choose strategy 1, which can win them Rs 100, or they can choose strategy 2 wherein they lose Rs 100.

It is common sense that both players A and B will choose strategy 1. Even after revealing the strategies of players A and B to each other, the likelihood of the players changing their currently selected strategy is zero. Thus, there is no deviation from the initially chosen strategy even after knowing the opponent's move. Thus strategy 1 is Nash Equilibrium [5].

3.2.2 Components of Game theory

The Table 3 represents various components of game theory and their description.

Table 3. Components of Game Theory [5].

Components	Description
Game	Any scenario where in the result is influenced by the actions of multiple players.
Player	Any entity making deliberate decisions based upon the rules of a game.
Strategy	Series of actions that players will perform under a given circumstance, which may or may not occur in the game.
Payoff	Payoff is anything that a player incurs by arriving at a consequence. It can be in any form such as money, utility etc.
Information Set	The data available at any given point in a game.
Equilibrium	The stage where all the players have reached an outcome after making their decisions.

3.2.3 Motivation to use Game Theory

Recently, 17 million user records were stolen from Zomato's database. This information included email id's and passwords of users. This confidential data was sold on the popular Dark web for a mere $1000. [11].

In the year 2016, the Internet service company Yahoo reported two significant breaches. Both the breaches are considered as one of the most massive breaches in the history of the Internet. The first breach affected roughly 500 million Yahoo users. Yahoo confirmed that the second breach affected all 3 billion users of Yahoo. Verizon, which was to buy Yahoo for $4.8 billion, bought it for a reduced price of $350 million, proving to be a loss for Yahoo [9].

Any user can become a victim of Identity theft. As per the US Department of Justice, 17.6 million people in the United States experience some form of identity theft every year. In 2014, victims experienced a combined average loss of $1,343. In total, victims lost a massive $15.4 billion [10].

In order to reduce such catastrophic events, it is obligatory to develop a solution to prevent thefts. The methods hackers use evolves with each security system developed to prevent them. They try to expose new vulnerabilities. Thus, an ideal approach to prevent these attackers is to be used. The move of the attackers may change based on the countermeasures taken by the defense system developed to prevent such attacks. Thus, game theory proves to be the most classic approach. The game theory takes into consideration the measures to be taken by the system software or the users to prevent identity thefts and how the attackers' reactions to such countermeasures.

3.2.4 Game Theory for Identity Theft

Consider an attacker 'A' and detector 'D'. The attacker has two possibilities of either attacking or not attacking using the obtained password. The detector will detect whether the password has been leaked or not. Consider the following example. Each scenario is associated with a penalty and reward as per the action taken.

Table 4. Terminologies in an ID Theft Game

Terminology	Description
q	probability that attacker attacks
r	probability that detector detects leaked password.
U_d	Detector's Utility.
U_a	Attacker's Utility.

Table 4 represents various terminologies used in an identity theft game and its description.

Table 5. Parameter

		Attacker	
		Attack	Don't Attack
Detector	Alert	0, -2	-4, 0
	Not Alert	-6, 6	2, 0

Table 5 refers to a scenario where there are possibilities of multiple events taking place depending upon the action taken by the attacker and defender. Consider the following parameter

1. **(Alert, Attack) = (0, -2)**
   In this scenario, the attacker attacks and is detected by the detector. Here, 0 denotes the reward the detector will gain, if it successfully detects that the password has been leaked and -2 denotes the value the attacker has been penalized for being caught.

2. **(Alert, don't attack) = (-4,0)**
   In this case, the attacker does not attack even though the system denotes that the password has been leaked. -4 represents detection of leaked password even though the attacker does not attack.

3. **(Not Alert, attack) = (-6,6)**
   In this situation, the attacker is successfully able to conduct an attack without triggering the detector. -6 is penalty faced by the detector for not being able to notify about the attack and 6 represents the reward gained by the attacker for a successful attack.

4. **(Not Alert, don't attack) = (2,0)**
   In this scene, neither the attacker attacks nor the system detects anything. 2 is used to represent that password is not leaked and 0 represents that the attacker does not attack.

For this game, there is no pure Nash Equilibrium. However, we can derive a mixed strategy equilibrium.

Let us consider:
q $\Longrightarrow$ probability that attacker attacks.

For 'q' to be in equilibrium, the detector needs to be indifferent in detecting leaked and not leaked passwords. Let U_d be Detector's Utility (Expected Utility). When attacker attacks with probability 'q' and detector will detect that password is leaked.

$$U_d(q, Alert) = [q \times (0) + (1-q) \times (-4)] \quad (1)$$

$$U_d(q, Not\ Alert) = [q \times (-6) + (1-q) \times (2)] \quad (2)$$

For 'q' to be in Nash equilibrium, Equation 1 and 2 must be equal.
Thus equating both equations we get Equation 3:

$$\begin{aligned} (1-q) \times (-4) &= q \times (-6) + (1-q) \times (2) \\ -4 + 4q &= -6q + 2 - 2q \\ -4 - 2 &= -6q - 2q - 4q \\ -6 &= -12q \\ q &= 1/2 \end{aligned} \quad (3)$$

Now for attacker:
r $\Longrightarrow$ probability that detector detects leaked password.

$$\begin{aligned} U_a(Attack, r) &= [(-2) \times (r) + (1-r) \times (6)] \\ U_a &= r(-2) + (1-r)(6) \\ U_a &= -2r + 6 - 6r \\ U_a &= 6 - 8r \end{aligned} \quad (4)$$

$$U_a(Don't\ attack, r) = 0 \quad (5)$$

For r to be in Nash equilibrium, Equation 4 and 5 must be equal.
Thus equating both equations we get Equation 6:

$$\begin{aligned} 6 - 8r &= 0 \\ 6 &= 8r \\ r &= 3/4 \end{aligned} \quad (6)$$

Thus, Nash equilibrium is solved for the game. Hence, when attacker attacks 1/2 of the times, the detector alerts about leaked password for $3/4^{th}$ of the time.

4 Conclusion

Setting a password is not the only protective measure one must undertake to safeguard data. There is always a possibility of the password getting hacked or the password already being leaked. Hence, one can lower the risk of data theft by using passwords that have not been previously leaked or those which are not a part of common dictionaries used by hackers to perform brute force attacks. Thus, a system has been developed wherein a database of passwords leaked over the years from multiple social sites and those commonly used in brute force attack are compiled. This system notifies its user if their password is a part of the database. Analysis of the possibility of a successful data theft attack has been conducted with the help of Game Theory. The key concepts, such as Nash equilibrium and mixed strategy equilibrium, have been applied to predict the possibility of an attack in multiple scenarios.

References

[1] Veena, K., & Meena, K. "Determination of performance to verify the synthetic identity theft by training the neural networks," IEEE International Conference on Smart Technologies and Management for Computing, Communication, Controls, Energy and Materials (ICSTM), 2017.

[2] Sharmistha Dutta, Ankit Kumar Gupta and Neetu Narayan."Identity Crime Detection Using Data Mining," IEEE International Conference on Computational Intelligence and Networks (CINE), 2017.

[3] Philip A. K. Lorimer, Victor Ming-Fai Diec,and Burak Kantarci."Participatory detection of identity theft on mobile social platforms," IEEE Global Conference on Signal and Information Processing (GlobalSIP), 2017.

[4] Tajpour, Atefeh, "Identity Theft and Fraud Type," International Journal of Information Processing and Management (IJIPM), 2013.

[5] Raoof, Omar & Al-raweshidy, Hamed."Theory of Games: an Introduction" 10.5772/46930.(2010).

[6] Identity Theft - 1 [Online]. Available https://www.cybintsolutions.com/cyber-security-facts-stats/

[7] Annapurna P Patil, Bharath S and Nagashree M Annigeri. "Applications of Game Theory for Cyber Security System: A Survey." International Journal of Applied Engineering Research ISSN 0973-4562 Volume 13, Number 17 (2018) pp. 12987-12990, 2018.

[8] Helser, Susan, "Identity theft education: Comparison of text-based and game-based learning" (2016). Graduate Thesis and Dissertations. 15930. https://lib.dr.iastate.edu/etd/15930

[9] Identity Theft - 2 [Online]. Available: https://en.wikipedia.org/wiki/Yahoo!_data_breaches

[10] Identity Theft - 3 [Online]. Available https://www.csid.com/2016/09/real-cost-identity-theft/

[11] Identity Theft - 4 [Online]. Available bit.ly/zomatoleaks

ITM Web of Conferences **32**, 03023 (2020) https://doi.org/10.1051/itmconf/20203203023
ICACC-2020

Online Voting System using Homomorphic Encryption

Saksham Saproo[1,*], *Vedant* Warke[2,**], *Shreyas* Pote[3,***], and *Rashmi* Dhumal[4,****]

[1]Department of computer engineering,Ramrao Adik institute of Technology,Nerul

Abstract. An important part of a democratically fair society are elections. The conventional democratic framework becomes hard for the individuals who can't visit the polling stall for casting their votes. With quick advancement of data innovation, online Internet voting framework is all the more intriguing to use for the nations where vote casting cooperation is low and it is too helpful for people living far off from their homes. Security is a major worry for Internet voting system. The proposed framework guarantees security prerequisites for example, validation, precision, secrecy, receipt-freeness, unwavering quality, obviousness and reasonableness in the political race.
Keywords- Paillier algorithm; homomorphic encryption; E-voting

1 Introduction

Election are backbone of a democracy, so its important that it should be fair. The way to select your representative is by voting. In traditional voting system voters have to reach polling station and cast their vote, it gets difficult for elderly and for those living far from their homes or living in the remote locality. Voting through internet allows voters to give their votes to their representatives from anywhere through internet. online voting system is an application of cryptography. This promises an efficient and secure way of casting and calculating the votes.

Making an voting system on internet has many challenges to overcome. Some major issues are voting in a secured manner and accompanying many voters. There are some internet voting system that cannot work in situation with many voters. Our proposal uses Homomorphic encryption to over come these issues.

Homomorphic approach in Internet and systems administration applications, [8]security is significant worry in the present time of IT. The tremendous measure of data traded across the Internet is helpless against security dangers and assaults. Cryptography gives secure trade of scrambled information by shared key. The significant worry with this methodology is information protection as anyone with the key can get to the information. In addition, client loses command over information once it is transferred to the cloud Client must impart a key to play out any activities. We need to download and unscramble the information and afterward play out the activity. These methodologies lead to security issue and rehashed encryption decoding. So in this system we have decided to go for Homomorphic encryption.

A homomorphic encryption[10] strategy permits client to work on ciphertext. At the point when client decodes the resultant figure, it is same as though tasks are done on plaintext. In this manner, utilizing homomorphic encryption guarantees clients that their information is secure in all state: stockpiling, transmission and preparing. Assume if someone wants to sum two numbers together eg 10 and 20 which are stored in form on encrypted number as 98746 and 654421 respectively after that the result of addition 10+20=30 is also stored in encrypted number as 783356. In traditional way they have to first decrypt the two numbers than add them and show the results. Consider than same situation for a large set of database example salary record of all employees working in a firm , if we use the traditional way we have to decrypt all records related to salary of each and every employee , thus exposing data (salary)[11] for employees . But if we would use Homomorphic encryption we can easy compute salary on all employees without decrypting there data. The computation is done directly on the encrypted data using Homomorphic encryption .Homomorphic encryption can either be completely or halfway homomorphic encryption. A fully homomorphic encryption system provides both multiplication as well as addition of ciphertext. Partially homomorphic encryption supports either additive homomorphic or multiplicative homomorphic encryption. Such plan can perform predetermined number of activities. For instance partial homomorphic encryption plans can do multiple addition with one multiplication.

Pascal Paillier gave Paillier cryptosystem in 1999. This cryptosystem is an public key system. Paillier cryptosystem is an partial homomorphic encryption[3] scheme that can can perform addition operation on ciphered data. The properties of Paillier's system are:

*e-mail: sakshamsaproo@gmail.com
**e-mail: vedantwarke99@gmail.com
***e-mail: sap5.3.1998@gmail.com
****e-mail: rashmisalvi@gmail.com

1) It is a symmetric key cryptographic scheme[6], which encrypts message using public key and retrieve message back from ciphertext using corresponding private key.

2) Paillier has probabilistic nature[3]. Every time the ciphertext is encrypted using Pallier system a new cipher text is generated, due to which it is difficult to uniquely identify whether both the ciphertext are generated for same message or not.

3) It supports additive property of homomorphic cryptosystem[3].

The proposed online voting system is effective , robust and simple using paillier cryptosystem.Paillier cryptosystem is an additive homomorpic encryption system which enables to do operation on encrypted number without decrypting it. Thus using this property of homomorphic encryption the proposed system provides users with availability , confidentiality and integrity.

This paper is divided in to six sections , the brief introduction is given in section one, section 2 explains what is Homomorphic encryption and its properties with Pallier cryptosystem in brief with key generation , encryption , decryption algorithm, the proposed methodology is discussed in third section , the result and analysis is discussed in section four followed by conclusion in section five.

2 Homomorphic Encryption

R. Rivest, M. Dertouzos and Leo. Adleman presented the idea of Homomorphic cryptosystem, long after the development of RSA [1]. It enables to operate on encrypted data. Let E be an encryption function used to encrypt plaintext, x as plaintext and f() as operation to implement , So homomorphic encryption is defined as :

f(E(x1),E(x2)....E(xn)) = E(f(x1,x2....xn))
Additive Homomorphism :
Binary operation is denoted by + ,so additive homomorphic is described as
E(x2) + E(x1) = E(x2 + x1)
Pallier Cryptography supports additive homomorphic property.

2.1 Paillier Cryptosystem

One of the well known scheme for homomorphic cryptography is Paillier [4]. It was invented by Pascal Paillier in 1999. It can encrypt many bits in single operation with an constant factor of expansion and also an efficient decryption. Pallier cryptosystem is defined by four terms: key generation, encryption, decryption and homomorphic operation. [4].

2.2 Key generation

Consider q and p are two big random prime numbers which are mutually exclusive of one another ,that is[12] $\gcd(qp, (q-1)(p-1)) = 1$.
The above property is assured if both prime number are equal to each other in length. [3] Compute n=qp and $\lambda = \text{lcm}(q-1, p-1)$. Randomly select g as integer where g$\in \mathbb{Z}^*_{n^2}$ The existence of multiplicative inverse ensure that the order of g is divisible by n by the following equation: $\mu = (L(g^{\lambda} \bmod n^2))^{-1} \bmod n$,[18] where function L(x)=x-$1_{\frac{}{n}}$. Note that this $a_{\frac{}{b}}$ does not mean the multiplication of a times the multiplicative inverse of b, i.e., the biggest integer value v$\geq$ 0 to satisfy the relation a$\geq$ vb. The public key (encryption) is (n,g). The private key (decryption) is (λ, μ)..
If using q,p of same length, a simpler version of the key generation steps could be to set g=n+1,λ = $\varphi(n)$,, where $\varphi(n) = (p-1)(q-1)$

2.3 Encryption

Let x denote a message that we want to[4] encrypted where $0 \leq x < n$.
Select r randomly where , r$\in Z^*_{n^2}$ and 0<r<n (i.e ensure gcd(n,r)=1)
Compute ciphertext as:
c=$g^x \cdot r^n \bmod n^2$

2.4 Decryption

Let c be the encrypted text from which plaintext need to be extracted, where c$\in \mathbb{Z}^*_{n^2}$ The original message can be computed as : x=L($c^{\lambda} \bmod n^2$) $\cdot\, \mu \bmod n$ decryption is one exponentiation modulo n^2."[17]

2.5 Homomorphic characteristics

The importance of Paillier algorithm is due to its homomorphic properties and it can able to generate non-deterministic encryption.[5] As function of encryption is additive, following functions are described below:

2.6 Homomorphic addition on plaintext

The multiplication of two ciphertexts will give the addition of their corresponding plain texts when deciphered[2], $D(E(x_1, r_1) \cdot E(x_2, r_2) \bmod n^2) = x_1 + x_2 \bmod n$.[16] The product of a ciphertext with a plaintext [8][9]raising g will decrypt to the sum of the corresponding plaintexts,[13] $D(E(x_1, r_1) \cdot g^{x_2} \bmod n^2) = x_1 + x_2 \bmod n$.

2.7 Homomorphic multiplication on plaintexts

An plaintext in encrypted form when raised to the power of one another plaintext in encrypted form will give the product of the two plaintexts when decrypted, $D(E(x_2, r_2)^{x_1} \bmod n^2) = x_1 x_2 \bmod n$.)

The product of constant with plaintext in encrypted form is a decryption result of an plaintext in encrypted form is raised with a constant k.

$D(E(x_1, r_1)^k \bmod n^2) = k x_1 \bmod n$.

In any case, in the event that we are given the Paillier encryptions of two messages ,it is highly unlikely to register an encryption of the result of these messages without the utilization of private key.

3 Proposed Methodology

In today's competitive worlds most of the lot of things are created on online platform similarly in internet voting system voter can cast their votes without visiting the election booth. Online voting system utilizes homomorphic encryption to count votes. The final outcome is taken from encrypted collection of votes without decrypting them, [4]. so it remains unknown who voted whom. In this system integrity and anonymity of the voter remains hidden. The voter should have to create their own account on this portal by verified government documents. The several stages for online voting system are given below.

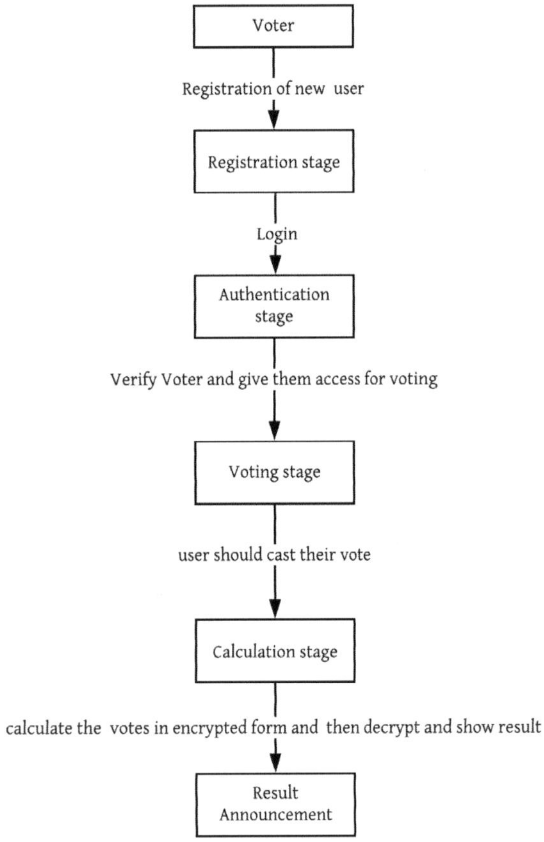

Figure 1. Flow Diagram

1) Registration stage: In this stage we can add new voter in e-voting system by authenticating voter through Election authority. The eligibility of the individual voter is verified by collecting required details about them. User will enter their basic details and will add there voter id which will be crossed checked with the election commission database. After successful registration, user will able to cast a vote through e-voting system.

2) Authentication stage: This stage comes after registration stage. In this stage user will authenticate themselves using login id(which will be there voter id) and password that was set by the user in registration phase . Thus using user id and password users can get uniquely authenticated.

3) Voting stage: In this stage voter can give their vote . They can give vote to their selected candidate . The vote given by voters to their selected candidates are then encrypted using Paillier encryption. The encrypted votes are stored in database which will be then tallied in tally stage.

4) calculation stage: In this phase Votes that are stored in encrypted (using homomorphic encyption) form in database are added to get total no of votes received by the respective parties.

Consider we have two numbers 10 and 20, we have to perform the addition on encrypted numbers by using pailliar algorithm .

Table 1. Example of Encryption

10	gANjcGhlLnBhaWxsaWVyCkVuY3J5c
20	gANjcGhlLnBhaWxsaWVyCkVuY3J
10+20=30	gANjcGhlLnBhaWxsaWVyCkVuY3

In the above mentioned example it is observed that a new ciphertext is generated for a given number whenever it is encrypted, this feature helps to maintain the integrity and enhance the complexity of computation data[15]

4 Result And Analysis

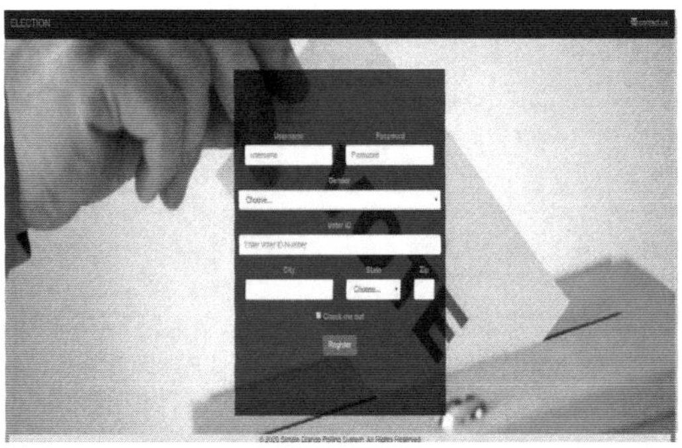

Figure 2. Registration form

Voter will Register themselves on the portal by giving some basic details as their Fullname,password, voter id, gender, state. after fill the details user's voter id will be authenticated with government database of voter id.

https://doi.org/10.1051/itmconf/20203203023

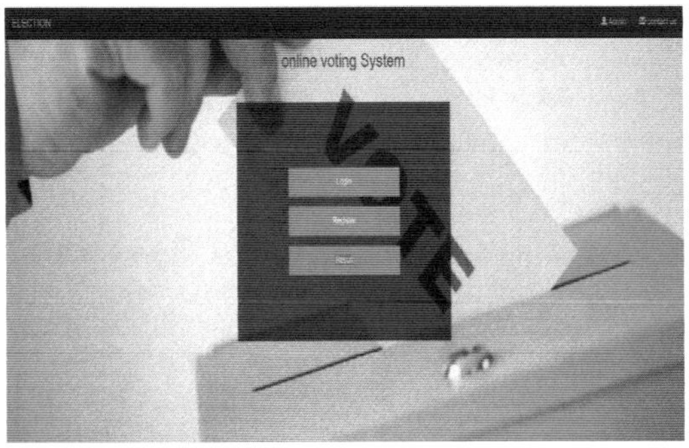

Figure 3. Home page

After successful registration stage user can login with their voterid as username and password that is set by them. Thus voters will be authenticated uniquely with the combination of voter id and password.

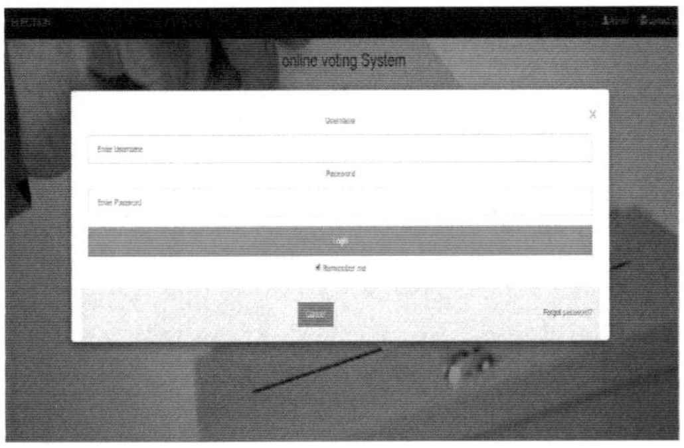

Figure 4. Login page

This is where voters will cast there vote to their choice of candidate. Candidates are denoted using there party symbol . Voter are needed to just tap on the button below the party symbol.

Figure 5. Voting Page

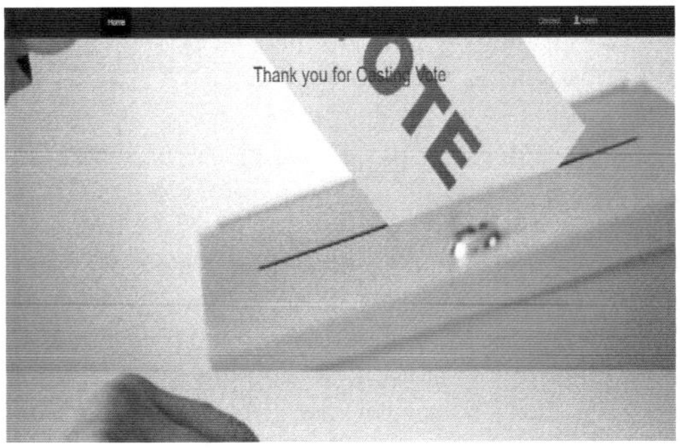

Figure 6. voting success page

After successfully casting their vote, voter's are shown a message of successfully voted and the voter are sent back to the login page and that voter cannot login again to vote. If they try to login again they will be shown a message "Already voted".

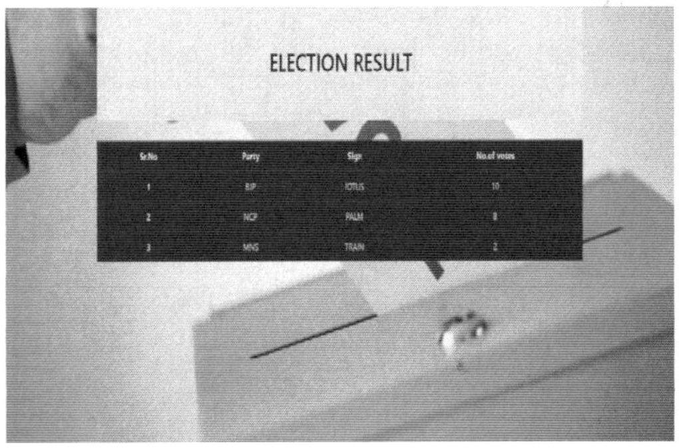

Figure 7. Polling result

In existing system, Voter cast their votes online through e-voting system and the vote is stored in encrypted form using Paillier algorithm. The ballots are shuffled and apply the rotational method on votes for storing votes in database which increase the time and space complexity so the overall cost of the system will increases. The proposed system allows voter to cast the votes and store it in encrypted form using Paillier cryptosystem for maintaining the integrity of data. When vote casted for specific candidate, votes of that candidate stored in encrypted form and null value is in encrypted form automatically set to the remaining candidates in database. This will provide more security as the vote in encrypted form is updated in database for all candidates. The attacker as well as the admin or the employees who have access to the database will not able to distinguish between the ballots stored for the candidate is a vote cast by the voter or a null value. The final count of votes for each candidate is calculated using homomorphic addition property of Paillier cryptosystem. The proposed system is more faster and provides more security as all votes are stored in encrypted form and this will help in maintaining the three traids of the cyber security i.e. Availability , Confidentiality and Integrity of the system .

5 Conclusion

Voting through internet has attracted many people specifically people living far from their homes than traditional system of voting. From past few years a lot of researchers have started seeking interest in this field due to transparency and security concern. This research paper describes the internet voting system using Paillier algorithm and its homomorphic characteristics. This system gives a assurance of data confidentiality and data integrity in which it will uses homomorphic properties for calculation of votes in there encrypted form and then decrypting them to get only total votes thus keeping it secure. This system is equivalent to system in which votes are taken in unencrypted form and then added to get then total votes received by the party. Thus it provides us with the use fullness of traditional system plus the security and modularity of modern system.

References

[1] Salavi R.R., Math M.M., Kulkarni U.P. (2019) A Survey of Various Cryptographic Techniques: From Traditional Cryptography to Fully Homomorphic Encryption. In: Saini H., Sayal R., Govardhan A., Buyya R. (eds) Innovations in Computer Science and Engineering. Lecture Notes in Networks and Systems, vol 74. Springer, Singapore

[2] K. K. Chauhan, A. K. S. Sanger and A. Verma, "Homomorphic Encryption for Data Security in Cloud Computing," 2015 International Conference on Information Technology (ICIT), Bhubaneswar, 2015, pp. 206-209.

[3] M. Nassar, A. Erradi and Q. M. Malluhi, "Paillier's encryption: Implementation and cloud applications," 2015 International Conference on Applied Research in Computer Science and Engineering (ICAR), Beirut, 2015, pp. 1-5.

[4] Shihab, T Liji, P. (2017). Simple and secure internet voting scheme using generalized paillier cryptosystem. 551-557. 10.1109/ICICICT1.2017.8342623.

[5] M. Togan and C. Pleca, *"Comparison-based computations over fully homomorphic encrypted data,"*. in Proc. 10th International Conf. Communications, pp. 1–6, 2014

[6] C. Gentry, *"Fully homomorphic encryption using ideal lattices,"*. in Proc. the 41st Annual ACM Symp. Theory of Computing, pp. 169- 178, 2009.

[7] R. L. Rivest, L. Adleman, and M. L. Dertouzos, nations where vote casting cooperation is low and it is too helpful for people living far o *"On data banks and privacy*. homomorphisms," Foundations of secure computation, vol. 4, no. 11, pp. 169–180, 1978.

[8] C. Gentry et al. , *"Fully homomorphic encryption using ideal lattices."*. in STOC, vol. 9, 2009, pp. 169–178.

[9] Z. Brakerski, C. Gentry, and V. Vaikuntanathan, *"(leveled) fully homomorphic encryption without bootstrapping,"*. in Proceedings of the 3rd Innovations in Theoretical Computer Science Conference. ACM, 2012, pp. 309–325.

[10] A. Acar, H. Aksu, A. S. Uluagac, and M. Conti, *"A survey on homomorphic encryption schemes: Theory and implementation,"*. ACM Comput. Surv., vol. 51, pp. 79:1–79:35, July 2018.

[11] P. Y. Ryan, S. Schneider, and V. Teague, "End-to-end verifiability in voting systems, from theory to practice," IEEE Security and Privacy, vol. 13, no. 3, pp. 59–62, 2015.

[12] I. Damgard, M. Jurik, and J. B. Nielsen, "A generalization of paillier's public-key system with applications to electronic voting," International Journal of Information Security, vol. 9, no. 6, pp. 371–385, 2010.

[13] P. Paillier, Public-Key Cryptosystems Based on Composite Degree Residuosity Classes. Berlin, Heidelberg: Springer Berlin Heidelberg, 1999, pp. 223–238.

[14] D. Hrestak and S. Picek, "Homomorphic encryption in the cloud," in Information and Communication Technology, Electronics and Microelectronics (MIPRO), 2014 37th International Convention on. IEEE, 2014, pp. 1400–1404.

[15] C. Ngo, "Secure voting system using paillier homomorphic encryption," Ph.D. dissertation, Texas AM University–Corpus Christi, 2014.

[16] Y. Yang, S. Zhang, J. Yang, J. Li, and Z. Li, "Targeted fully homomorphic encryption based on a double decryption algorithm for polynomials," Tsinghua science and technology, vol. 19, no. 5, pp. 478– 485, 2014.

[17] A. Snak, S. Ozkan, H. Yldrm, and S. Kiraz, "End-2-end verifiable internet voting protocol based on homomorphic encryption," International Journel Of Information Security Science, vol. 3, no. 2, pp. 165–181, 2014.

[18] A. Huszti, "A homomorphic encryption-based secure electronic voting scheme," Faculty of Informatics. University of Debrecen. Hungary, 2011.

Detection of Thoracic Diseases using Deep Learning

Salome Palani[1,*], *Arya* Kulkarni[1], *Abishai* Kochara[1], *Kiruthika* M[2,*]

[1]B.E student, Department of Computer Engineering, Agnel Charities' Fr. C. Rodrigues Institute of Technology, Vashi, Navi Mumbai, India
[2]Associate Professor, Department of Computer Engineering, Agnel Charities' Fr. C. Rodrigues Institute of Technology, Vashi, Navi Mumbai, India

Abstract— The study of using deep learning for detection of various thoracic diseases has been an active and challenging research area. Chest X-rays are currently the most common and globally used radiology practices for detecting thoracic diseases. Patients suffering from thoracic diseases need to take Chest X-Rays which are read by radiologists and a report is generated by them. However, today with the increase in the number of thoracic patients, a quick method to classify the disease and generate the report has become necessary. Also, patient history has to be considered for diagnosis. This paper offers a comparative study on the various deep learning techniques that can process chest x-rays and are capable of detecting the different thoracic diseases. Also, a technique has been proposed to classify 14 diseases namely Atelectasis, Cardiomegaly, Consolidation, Edema, Effusion, Emphysema, Fibrosis, Hernia, Infiltration, Mass, Nodule, Pneumonia, Pneumothorax, Pleural thickening based on the given X-rays using Residual Neural Network.

1. INTRODUCTION

The thorax, also called chest, is the upper part of the trunk located between the neck and the abdomen. It gets support from the rib cage, the girdle of the shoulder and the spine that also protects it. It is the region of the body formed by the sternum, the thoracic vertebrae, and the ribs. It resides between the neck and diaphragm excluding the upper limb. The heart and lungs reside in the thoracic cavity, as well as many blood vessels which play a vital role in feeding (oesophagus), breathing, and pumping the blood to all parts of the body.

Chest pain is the most frequent reason for consultation and emergency room visits. Chest radiography is the most common imaging examination globally, critical for screening, diagnosis, and management of many life-threatening thoracic diseases. Today, knowledge and observation skills of radiologists are imperative to read CXRs. However, the pathologies have complex structures, and the lesions in images of the lungs have very slight differences wherein some miniscule details can be missed out by experts. Also, there is a lack of trained and expertise radiologists. Hence, in recent years there has been a lot of research to develop systems that can detect thoracic diseases as well as generate reports. In all these researches, the researchers have used deep learning, and neural networking models. This paper aims to explore these models.

2. BACKGROUND WORK

Pranav Rajpurkar* et. al., this paper proposed the development of a deep learning algorithm called CheXNet, a 121-layer convolutional neural network trained on Chest Xray14 [7], currently the largest publicly available dataset. The model CheXNet inputs a chest X-Ray image and outputs the probability of pneumonia along with a heatmap localizing the areas of the image most indicative of pneumonia. Simple modifications to CheXNet were made to detect all 14 diseases in Chest Xray14, it was found that CheXNet outperforms results on all 14 diseases [1]. Pulkit Kumar et. al., presented a cascaded deep neural network which could diagnose 14 pathologies. [2]. Xiaosong Wang et. al., proposed a novel Text Image Embedding network (Tienet) that extracts image and text representations distinctly. [3]. Qingji Guan et. al., in this paper, a 3-branch guided CNN (AG - CNN), is used. It reduces noise and enhances the alignment of the particular affected region in the X-ray image. [4]. Imane Allaouzi et. al., this paper documents the extraction of relevant features from CXRs using pre-trained CNN and then classifying the extracted features with multi label problem transformation methods that transform the multi label problem to single-label classification [5]. Mohammad Tariqul Islam et. al., this paper detected and localized abnormalities in chest X-rays from different datasets using deep convolutional neural networks. As a measure of localization in the CXRs (Chest X-rays), heat maps are used. Trained classifiers were used to conduct localization experiments that proved to be greatly successful for abnormalities like cardiomegaly and pulmonary edema which are spread out spatially [6]. Xiaosong Wang et. al., this paper presents the chest X - Ray dataset, which comprises 108,948 frontal X - Ray images. Importantly it demonstrates the detection and localization of the commonly occurring thoracic diseases [7]. Jeremy Irvin et. al., presented CheXpert, a large dataset that contains 224,316 chest radiographs of 65,240 patients. A labeler is designed to automatically detect the presence of 14 observations in radiology reports, capturing uncertainties inherent in radiograph interpretation [8]. Juan Manuel et. al., this paper demonstrates an automatic normality/pathology classification of posteroanterior (PA) digital chest radiographs. The proposed method is not specialized in a given set of types of lesions or diseases but is able to detect anything that differs from normality [9]. Paras Lakhani et. al., recognizing the potential displayed by DCNN, a practical, result-based, statistical study was performed to determine DCNN efficiency by applying

GoogLeNet and AlexNet DCNNs in the classification of images as displaying pulmonary TB or healthy [10]. The model used by Li Yao et al. is an end-to-end, two stage neural network model. It is a combination of an image encoder with dense connections, and a decoder with recurrent neural networks [11].

3. Comparative study

Table 1. Comparative study of available literature.

Reference Paper No.	Aim/Objective	Model Used	Building Data	Target	Architecture Details	Result
1	To detect Pneumonia from Chest X-rays as well as 14 thoracic diseases at a level exceeding practicing radiologists.	121-layer Convolutional Neural Network	ChestX-ray14, National Institute of Health [7]	Thoracic Disease Label	DenseNet-121 [16] layer deep convolutional neural network replacing the fully connected network with single output.	The model was able to classify 14 different pathological diseases.
2	To build Computer Aided Diagnosis (CAD) systems by using deep convolutional neural networks.	Desnet-161 [16] Architecture with Boosted cascading	Chest X-ray14 [7]	Thoracic Disease Label	Cascaded network that uses Binary Relevance approach with Softmax loss and PWE loss.	The combination of boosted cascaded approach increased the performance compared to the single classifier for BR with cross entropy and PWE loss. However, the performance of classifier and localization needs improvements.
3	To extract the distinctive image and text representation of Chest X-rays using Text-Image Embedding network (TieNet).	CNN-RNN model (Modified Resnet 50 model), Long Short Term Memory Network	ChestX-ray14, OpenI [17], Hand-labelled data	Thoracic Disease Label	End to end trainable CNN-RNN model Attention Encoded Text Embedding. Saliency Weighted Global Average Pooling. Joint Learning. Medical Image Auto-Annotation.	An accuracy of over 0.9 on average in AUCs was seen for the assignment of labels of the disease in the evaluation dataset.
4	To perform the task of thorax disease classification using Attention Guided Convolutional Neural Network.	Attention Guided Convolutional Neural Network	ChestX-ray14 Dataset [7]	Thoracic Disease Label	Attention Guided Convolutional Neural Network (CNN) Global branch as well as the local branch make use of Resnet-50 [12]. The local branch is used to focus on the lesion.	Average AUC 0.841 with ResNet-50. [12] AUC is improved to 0.868 by AG-CNN on combining the local cues and global information. Average AUC 0.871 with DenseNet.-121 [16].
5	To improvise the performance of CAD systems for diagnosing thoracic diseases by proposing a new method comprising the use of CNNs for extracting	Convolutional Neural Network (Densenet-121 [16]) utilizing Multi-label Softmax Loss	ChestXRay14 Dataset [7], CheXpert Dataset [8]	Thoracic Disease Label	Last 14D fully connected, sigmoid activated layer removed. Adam optimizer is used.	The results show that the proposed method showed an average AUC of 0.882

	features from images as well transformation methods used in multi label classification.				
6	To localize and detect abnormalities in chest X-rays. Deep CNN is used on different datasets.	AlexNet [13], VGG-16 [15], VGG-19 [15], ResNet-50 [12], ResNet-101[12] and ResNet-152 [12]	Indiana Dataset [17], JSRT Dataset [18,19], Shenzhen Dataset [20]	Thoracic Disease Label	**DCNN Models:** AlexNet [13], VGG-Net [15] and ResNet [12]. **Localization:** Black level occlusion showed better results than the grey one as chest X-rays are grey.	Deep learning method improves the accuracy by 17 percent as compared to rule based methods. Localization of abnormalities that were spatially spread out like cardiomegaly were successful; however, it failed for features that were pointed like lung nodules.
7	To spatially locate and detect the eight common thoracic diseases.	DNorm [21], MetaMap [22], AlexNet [13], GoogleNet [14], VGGNet-16 [15], ResNet-50 [12]	ChestXray8 Dataset [7]	Thoracic Disease Label	**Unified DCNN layer -** transition layer, global pooling layer, prediction layer and loss layer. **Pre-trained models:** AlexNet [13], GoogLeNet [14], VGGNet-16 [15] and ResNet-50 [12], The FC layers and the final classification layer were left out. **Multi-label setup**.	The model used (ResNet-50 [12]) was able to classify the eight diseases. Localization was achieved by creating heatmaps with the help of transition layer's activation functions and the weights obtained by the prediction layer.
8	To present and analyse the CheXpert dataset and to design a labeler which would automatically detect the presence of 14 diseases.	Automated rule-based labeler	CheXpert Dataset [8]	Thoracic Disease Label	Uses self training approach, 3 class classification approach. Adam Optimizer is used. Labeler follows 3 distinct stages: 1) Mention extraction 2) Mention classification 3) Mention aggregation	Comparison to NIH Labeler: The labelling algorithm achieves a higher F1 score.
9	To perform an automatic normality/pathology classification of digital chest radiographs.	LBP feature extraction. GDAV, DV & CV classifiers	48 high resolution DICOM chest radiograph images (HGURS, Spain)	Thoracic Disease Label	Feature Extraction: LBP Classification: GDAV: Greater Difference in Absolute Value. DV: Discrete Voting. CV: Continuous Voting.	The CV method produces the best result among the 3 methods by giving 87% correct classifications.
10	To detect tuberculosis (TB) on chest radiographs, and thereby evaluate the efficacy of deep convolutional neural networks (DCNNs).	AlexNet [13], GoogleNet [14]	NIH ChestX-ray14 dataset[7], Shenzen dataset[20], Belarus Tuberculosis Portal[23], Thomas Jefferson University Hospital	Thoracic Disease Label	Training Augmentations: Rotations of 90°, 180°, and 270°, Contrast Limited Adaptive Histogram Equalization processing. Pre-trained networks were trained on images from ImageNet. GoogleNet [14], AlexNet [13] were used	AlexNet [13] and GoogLeNet [14] DCNNs were used together to make a classifier that had an AUC of 0.99.

					in both pre-trained and untrained forms.	

4. PROPOSED SYSTEM

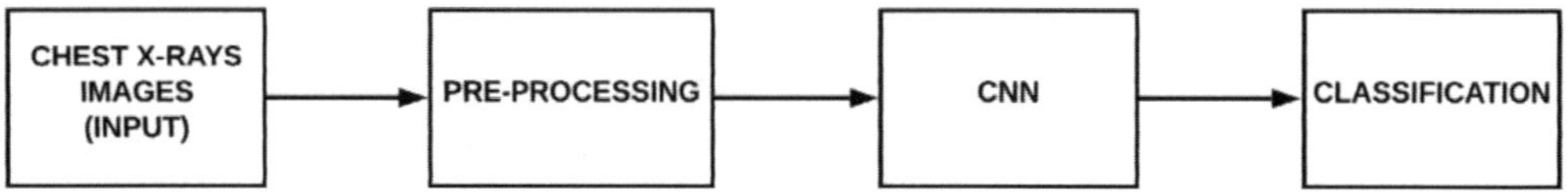

Fig. 1. Block Diagram of Proposed System.

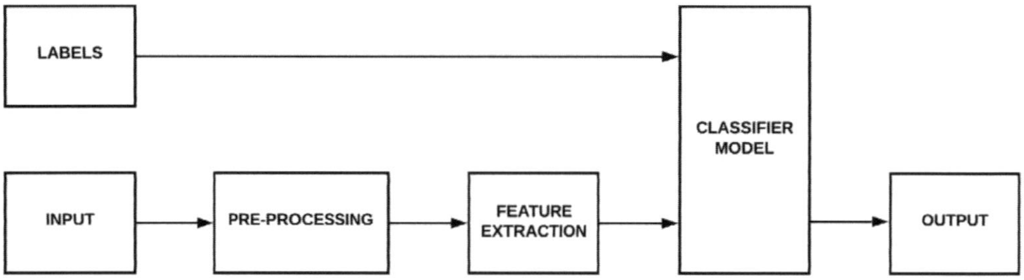

Fig. 2. Block Diagram of Training Phase.

The proposed system is designed with the aim of automating the process of detection, classification of thoracic diseases with the help of deep learning techniques.

The proposed system will involve use of deep convolutional neural networks for building a classifier that will extract and learn different features of the chest X-ray images along with their labels. Once the model is trained, it would be capable of detecting the thoracic disease given a new chest x-ray image. The system can be further extended to detect any type of thoracic disease.

The block diagram of the proposed system is shown in Fig 1 and Fig 2. and is explained as follows:

1. Input and Labels: The input of the system are frontal-view chest x-ray images with their corresponding thoracic disease as label like pneumonia, pneumothorax. The images will be fed to the convolutional neural network (CNN) in the form of batches and they will also be shuffled. This will make the model even more robust.
2. Pre-processing: The chest x-ray images will be preprocessed using various image processing techniques such as downscaling, normalization, etc. The training data can also be augmented using random horizontal flipping. This will help in improving the performance of the CNN.
3. CNN: The features of the images will be extracted using a deep convolutional neural network model consisting of convolutional layers, batch normalization, ReLU activation and max pooling layers. The final layer will be a fully connected layer with output features corresponding to the number of classes which will help in classifying the image i.e predicting the disease label.

5. IMPLEMENTATION

5.1 DATASET

The dataset used for training is the ChestX-ray14 dataset [7] which contains 112,120 frontal-view chest X-ray images of 30,805 unique patients. A smaller dataset was created by taking 100 images from each class. Hence, 1500 images along with their labels serve as input to the model.

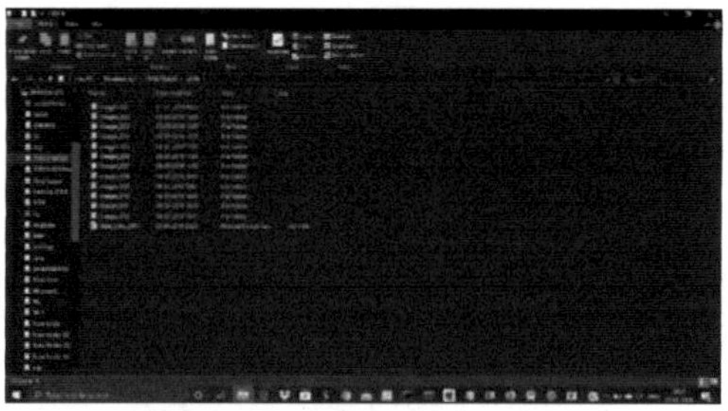

Fig. 3. The Dataset provided by NIH.

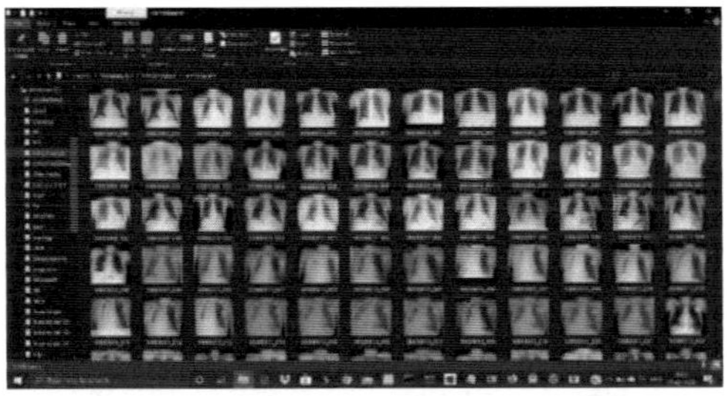

Fig. 4. Segregated images per class folders.

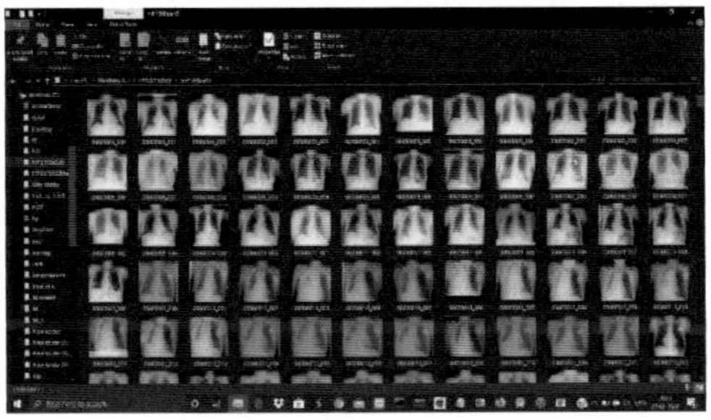

Fig. 5. 1500 images dataset(100 per class).

5.2 DATA PREPROCESSING

Input Images: The input images are downscaled to 224x224 so that it can be fed to the network. The images are also normalized based on mean and standard deviation and are also randomly horizontally flipped.

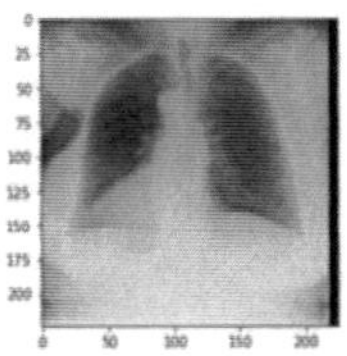

Fig. 6. Input Image.

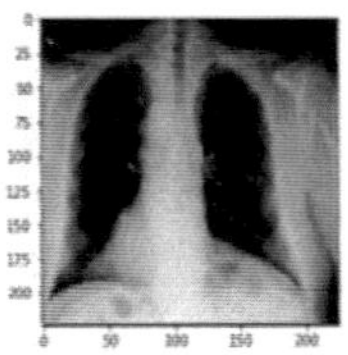

Fig. 7. Output Image after Data Preprocessing.

5.3 CLASSES (OUTPUT LABELS)

There are 15 classes(labels) out which 14 are disease labels namely Atelectasis, Cardiomegaly, Consolidation, Edema, Effusion, Emphysema, Fibrosis, Hernia, Infiltration, Mass, Nodule, Pneumonia, Pneumothorax, Pleural thickening and the last one is Normal study.

5.4 MODEL ARCHITECTURE

ResNet (Residual Neural Network) [12], is a deep neural network model architecture which uses residual blocks as a solution to vanishing gradients problem. The residual block makes use of identity mapping i.e. 'Skip Connection'. The identity mapping does not contain any parameters, it is solely used to pass the original information from one layer to another layer without being hindered. ResNet has been one of the most successful deep learning neural network architectures.

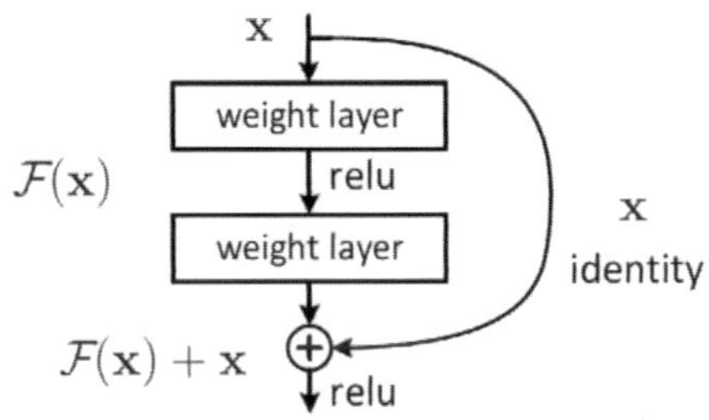

Fig. 8. Residual Learning : A building block [12].

The dataset of 1500 images is trained using ResNet -18 architecture which consists of a series of convolutional layers, batch normalization, ReLU activation layers. All these layers are then followed by an average pooling layer. The final and last layer is a fully connected layer.

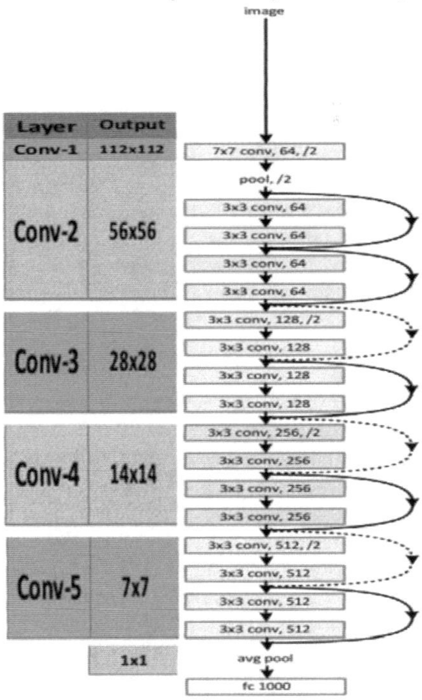

Fig. 9. Architecture of ResNet-18 [12].

5.5 Training

The first layer of the architecture is modified to accept gray-scale images as input and the number of output features in the last layer is modified to the required number of classes for output. The model has been trained from scratch, hence, the pretrained model with Imagenet weights is not used. The dataset of 1500 images is split into 70% for training.

The network is trained using Stochastic Gradient Descent as an optimizer with a learning rate of 0.001, in 4 batches for 50 epochs. A training accuracy of 97.99% is achieved.

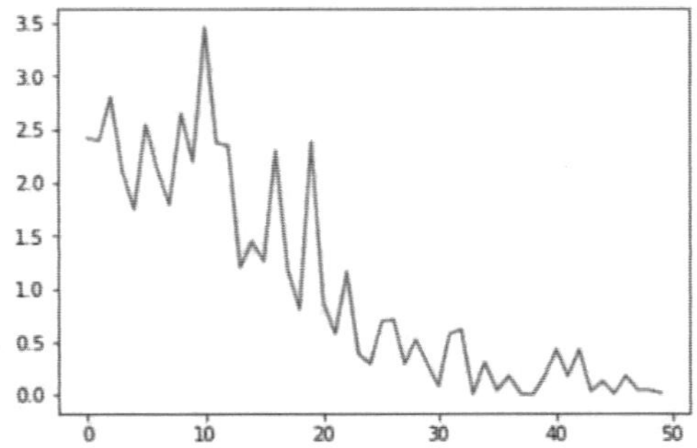

Fig. 10. Plot of loss per epoch.

6. Conclusion

The use of deep learning techniques in the field of detecting thoracic diseases from chest x-rays is still an active area of research. Thoracic diseases pose a serious, prevailing threat to the health of the global population. Hence timely diagnosis is critical. With the help of deep learning, faster and quicker diagnosis of thoracic diseases could save time. From the comparative study, the different methods used to process chest x-rays as well as detect the thoracic diseases was understood. The model proposed in the paper has been trained and the training accuracy achieved is 97.99%. Further work involves testing the model for different images belonging to each class and obtaining the results.

7. References

[1] P. Rajpurkar, J. Irvin, K. Zhu, B. Yang, H. Mehta, T. Duan, D. Ding, A. Bagul, R.L. Ball, C. Langlotz, K. Shpanskaya, M.P. Lungren, A.Y. Ng. CheXNet: Radiologist-Level Pneumonia Detection on Chest X-Rays with Deep Learning. arXiv:1711.05225v3, (2017).

[2] P. Kumar, M. Grewal, M.M. Srivastava. Boosted Cascaded Convnets for Multilabel Classification of Thoracic Diseases in Chest Radiographs. arXiv:1711.08760v1, (2017).

[3] X. Wang, Y. Peng, L. Leu, R.M. Summers . TieNet: Text-Image Embedding Network for Common Thorax Disease Classification and Reporting in Chest X-rays. arXiv:1801.04334v, (2018).

[4] Q. Guan, Y. Huang, Z. Zhong, Z. Zheng, L. Zheng, Y. Yang. Diagnose like a Radiologist: Attention Guided Convolutional Neural Network for Thorax Disease Classification. arXiv:1801.09927v1, (2018).

[5] I. Allaouzi, M. B. Ahmed.. A novel approach for multi-label Chest X-Ray classification of common Thorax Diseases. IEEEAccess.

[6] M.T. Islam, M.A. Aowal, A. T. Minhaz, K. Ashraf. Abnormality Detection and Localization in Chest X-Rays using Deep Convolutional Neural Networks. arXiv:1705.09850v3, (2017)

[7] X. Wang, Y. Peng, L. Lu, Z. Lu, M. Bagheri, R.M. Summers. ChestX-ray8: Hospital-scale Chest X-ray Database and Benchmarks on Weakly Supervised Classification and Localization of Common Thorax Diseases. arXiv:1705.02315, (2017)

[8] J. Irwin, P. Rajpurkar, M. Ko, Y. Yu, S. Ciurea-Ilcus, C. Chute, H. Marklund, B. Haghgoo, R. Ball, K. Shpanskaya, J.Seekins, D.A. Mong, S.S. Halabi, J.K. Sandberg, R. Jones, D.B. Larson, C.P. Langlotz, B.N. Patel, M.P. Lungren, A.Y. Ng . CheXpert: A Large Chest Radiograph Dataset with Uncertainty Labels and Expert Comparison. arXiv:1901.07035v1, (2019).

[9] J. M Carrillo-de-Gea, G. Garcia-Mateos, J. L. Fernandez-Aleman, J. L. Hernandez-Hernandez. A Computer-Aided Detection System for Digital Chest Radiographs. Journal of Healthcare Engineering Volume **2016**, (2016).

[10] P. Lakhani, B. Sundaram. Deep Learning at Chest Radiography: Automated Classification of Pulmonary Tuberculosis by Using Convolutional Neural Networks. Radiology: Volume **284**, (2017).

[11] L. Yao, E. Poblenz, D. Dagunts, B. Covington, D. Bernard, K. Lyman. Learning to Diagnose from Scratch by Exploiting Dependencies among Labels. arXiv:1710.10501v2, (2018).

[12] K. He, X. Zhang, S. Ren, and J. Sun, "Deep residual learning for image recognition," Conference on Computer Vision and Pattern Recognition, (2016).

[13] A. Krizhevsky, I. Sutskever, and G. E. Hinton. Imagenet classification with deep convolutional neural networks. In Advances in neural information processing systems, pages 1097–1105, (2012).

[14] C. Szegedy, W. Liu, Y. Jia, P. Sermanet, S. Reed, D. Anguelov, D. Erhan, V. Vanhoucke, and A. Rabinovich. Going deeper with convolutions. In Proceedings of the IEEE Conference on Computer Vision and Pattern Recognition, pages 1–9, (2015).

[15] K. Simonyan and A. Zisserman. Very deep convolutional networks for large-scale image recognition. arXiv preprint arXiv:1409.1556, (2014).

[16] Huang, Gao, Liu, Zhuang, Weinberger, Kilian Q, and van der Maaten, Laurens. Densely connected convolutional networks. arXiv preprint arXiv:1608.06993, (2016).

[17] D. Demner-Fushman, M. D. Kohli, M. B. Rosenman, S. E. Shooshan, L. Rodriguez, S. Antani, G. R. Thoma, and C. J. McDonald. Preparing a collection of radiology examination for distribution and retrieval. Journal of the American Medical Association, 23(2):304–310, 2015.Open-i: An open access biomedical search engine. https://openi.nlm.nih.gov.

[18] J. Shiraishi, S. Katsuragawa, J. Ikezoe, T. Matsumoto, T. Kobayashi, K.- i. Komatsu, M. Matsui, H. Fujita, Y. Kodera, and K. Doi, "Development of a digital image database for chest radiographs with and without a lung nodule: receiver operating characteristic analysis of radiologists' detection of pulmonary nodules," American Journal of Roentgenology, vol. **174**, no. 1, pp. 71–74, (2000).

[19] B. Van Ginneken, M. B. Stegmann, and M. Loog, "Segmentation of anatomical structures in chest radiographs using supervised methods: a comparative study on a public database," Medical image analysis, vol. **10**, no. 1, pp. 19–40, (2006).

[20] S. Jaeger, S. Candemir, S. Antani, Y.-X.J. Wang, P.-X. Lu, and G. Thoma, "Two public chest x-ray datasets for computer-aided screening of pulmonary diseases," Quantitative imaging in medicine and surgery, vol. **4**, no. 6, p.475, (2014).

[21] R. Leaman, R. Khare, and Z. Lu. Challenges in clinical natural language processing for automated disorder normalization. Journal of Biomedical Informatics, **57**:28–37, (2015).

[22] A. R. Aronson and F.-M. Lang. An overview of MetaMap: historical perspective and recent advances. Journal of the American Medical Informatics Association, 17(3):229–236, may (2010).

[23] Belarus Tuberculosis Portal. Belarus Public Health Website. http://obsolete.tuberculosis. Published September 1, 2011. Updated July 17, (2015). Accessed August 20, (2016).

Classifying Informatory Tweets during Disaster Using Deep Learning

Pradip Bhere [1], *Anand* Upadhyay[2], *Ketan* Chaudhari[3], and *Tushar* Ghorpade[4]

[1]Department of Computer Engineering, Ramrao Adik Institute of Technology, Nerul, Navi Mumbai, India.
[2]Department of Computer Engineering, Ramrao Adik Institute of Technology, Nerul, Navi Mumbai, India.
[3]Department of Computer Engineering, Ramrao Adik Institute of Technology, Nerul, Navi Mumbai, India.
[4]Department of Computer Engineering, Ramrao Adik Institute of Technology, Nerul, Navi Mumbai, India.

Abstract- Micro blogging platforms like Twitter generate a wealth of information during a disaster. Data can be in the form of sound, image, text, video etc. by way of tweets. Tweets produced during a disaster are not always educational. Information tweets can provide useful information about affected people, infrastructure damage, civilized organizations etc. Studies show that when it comes to sharing emergency information during a natural disaster, time is everything. Research on Twitter use during hurricanes, floods and floods provide potentially life-saving data on how information is disseminated in emergencies. The proposed system outlines how to distinguish sensitive and non-useful tweets during a disaster. The proposed method is based on the use of Word2Vec and the Convolutional Neural Network (CNN). Word2vec provides a feature vector and CNN is used to classify tweets.

1. Introduction

With the emergence of new technologies, our ability to communicate with others has increased dramatically. No longer can communities rely solely on buying traditional media, newspapers, radio, and TV news. With the emergence of smartphone technology, communities are simply an 'app' away from being able to deliver or receive information within milliseconds. Recently, Twitter has been used to spread updates/news all over the world and has been effective in emergencies during natural calamities like floods, earthquakes and wildfires. Twitter has proved that it has the potential to increase survival of a person during a Tornado related disaster. Communication forums allow for the communication of various networks that you can help officials during a disaster to make a list of victims, deceased, and contact with family and friends of all victims during the communication and planning of victims and respondents. Twitter has become an invaluable tool throughout the world, especially for spreading and discussing issues in everyday life. There are an estimated 500 million Twitter users worldwide. But the tweet generated is not always informative in nature. Thus there should be some method to classify the tweet.

Deep learning models have found great success in text processing such as text classification, natural language processing [1] etc. A major challenging task to classify the tweet in the form of text generated during disaster based on the informativeness of the tweet. Combination of deep learning models like CNN and word embedding model like Word2Vec provides functionality for classification of tweets with tremendous performance accuracy. Extracting features from the tweets generated during the disaster that are informative help in creating a model for classifying the tweet.

The rest of the paper format is as follows. The Section 2 of the paper describes the related work for the topic. Section 3 explains the proposed system. Section 4 gives analysis and experimental results. The conclusion is given in Section 5. Section 6 shows the future work.

2. Literature Survey

Several researchers are proposing strategies for classifying tweets based on the informativeness of tweets. The description of the strategies is as follows.

Deep learning has found great success in image processing and text processing. When looking for similar images, there are some articles, data of which the image and its title are not related. To address this problem paper [2] proposed a convolutional neural network model. The model proposed in this paper uses image and text features to predict similarities between them. In the model, the features of the image and text are extracted and provide opportunities for the relationship between images and text. This may have been added to the search strategy as a measure to improve search quality.

Spammers use various and advanced strategies to avoid traditional security mechanisms and create a need to come up with strong solutions that are compatible with these processes. Paper [3] proposed a method for using a low-level n-gram feature, which prevents the use of tokenizes or devices dependent on any language. Using publicly available databases they analyze the performance of several machines. This way development methods use the word n-gram from a tweet tone. They have also shown that technology can detect Spam tweets with low latency which is very important in the real Twitter scenario.

Twitter has been an important data source for many applications. That raises the popularity of tweet sentiment analysis. Paper [4] proposed a method for partial analysis of standard tweets by looking at the classification strategy with the winners. A large number of tweets contain phrases of questionable sensitivity. Thus, successfully solving specific conceptual phrases can help significantly improve the effectiveness of cognitive analysis techniques. This study establishes a method that focuses solely on the availability and behaviour of cognitive analyzes of a specific type of tweet containing phrases of positive emotion. The results indicate that the proposed method works well for both tasks.

Social media data analysis presents many challenges such as loud noises, short and formal messages, learning information categories from incoming message streams and categorizing them among others. One of the most basic requirements of these functions is the availability of information, especially human-specific information. To illustrate the use of adjectives, the proposed paper [5] has trained machine learning classifiers. In addition, the author has published the first of a large number of word2vec software trained in 52 million disaster-related tweets. To address the language problems of tweets, the author sets out common lexical resources for common lexical variants.

Paper [6] proposed a method based on the Convolution Neural Network (CNN) for determining the informative tweets and the real-time algorithm for detecting an event to find the time that occurred during a given event. In this study, the CNN model trained in recent earthquake-related tweets labelled as crowded plays a major role as the student learns to predict the twitter keyword associated with the tweet he teaches or not. Subsequently, these informative tweets were considered input data for the acquisition phase. This system with the help of the CNN module can detect earthquakes after they occur at a tolerance level and confirm prior to the announcement from the official disaster website.

From the literature search, we noted that all existing programs use a small data set or require logical variable names.

3. Problem Definition

As twitter provides connectivity to significantly active people over the globe that leads to the generation of a tremendous amount of tweets. During a disaster, proposed system can use responses generated by these active people over twitter. Since lots of spam tweets are generated, there must be an automated system for classification of the tweets. To alleviate the problem various deep neural networks are currently being used for classification. This system should provide output with very low latency and should be accessible to the officials or local NGOs for responding to the catastrophic effect of the disaster.

4. Proposed System

After analysing the existing systems, to overcome the drawbacks, the proposed system has been speculated. This project aims to classify tweet from preprocessed tweets using Convolution Neural Network and Word2Vec Model [7] and system provides the classified tweet informativeness as output. The proposed system considers the correlation between features provided by word2vec and associate tweet with it to improve the performance of tweet classification. Figure 1 describes the flow of the proposed system, it can be stated as:

Disaster tweets dataset is provided to the system

- Text preprocessing is performed to extract useful text from the tweets.
- Word embedding is performed for creating feature vectors and vocabulary list.
- Preprocessed tweets and feature vector are provided to CNN for classification.
- Classification of tweets is given as an output.

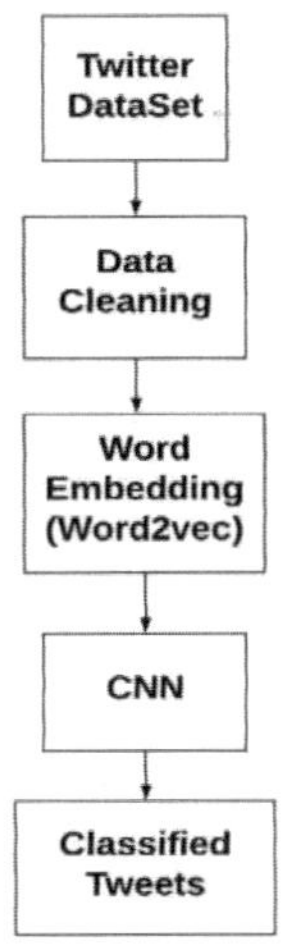

Fig 1. Flow diagram of a proposed system.

4.1 Tweet Preprocessing:

Classification on tweet focuses on textual data. The raw tweet contains text, image, gifs, emojis and HTML links etc. Preprocessing of tweet helps in removal of non-text data like images etc. It uses the regular expression for the task of removing non-text data along with URLs and hashtags if present in the data. Since creating feature vector and classification require a correlation between words, presence of pos-tags like Personal pronoun, Determiner, Coordinating conjunction, Preposition or subordinating conjunction, Possessive pronoun, no-3rd person singular present, Proper noun, singular, 3rd person singular present, Verb, base form, Modal, Adverb, past tense, Wh-pronoun, Cardinal number, Wh-adverb, Wh-determiner provides less functionality, so can be removed. Along with this, stop words are also removed. The output of this module provides only text data with specific targeted words.

4.2 Word2vec:

Word2Vec is a two dimensional non-linear network that is specially trained to reconstruct the alphabetical conditions. It takes input a large set of words and produces a vector space, usually of a size of hundred, with each different or unique word in the corpus assigned to a matching vector in space. The Word vectors are positioned in vector space in such a way that words which share common features in the corpus are built next to each other in space. Word2Vec is a very efficient predictive model for reading word embeddings from raw text. It comes with two flavour. First is the Continuous Bag-of-Words (CBOW) model and the other is the Skip-Gram model. Figure 2 shows the working of CBOW and Skip-Gram model.

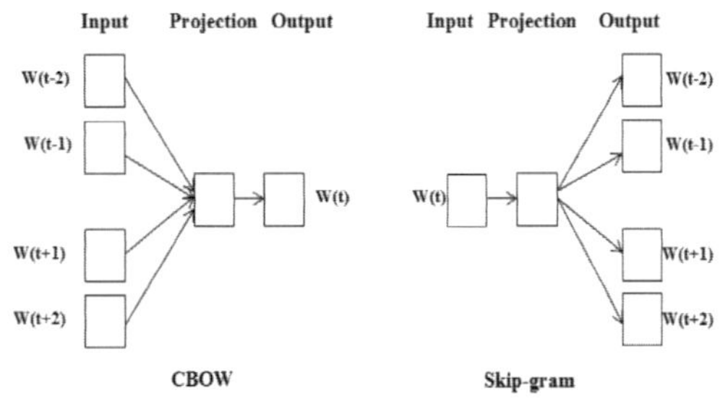

Fig 2. CBOW and Skip-Gram model [8]

• **Continuous Bag-of-Words (CBOW):** CBOW predicts target words (e.g. 'flood') in related set of words ('heavy flood prediction'). It has the effect that CBOW is smooth over most of the distribution data (by treating the whole context as a single observation).In many cases, this becomes a useful tool for small data.

• **Skip-Gram**: From target words skip-gram predicts words around context. When we deal with longer datagram treats each target based pair as a new detection.

4.3 Text to sequences:

As CNN model requires numbers or vectors to perform convolution. Textual data is converted to sequences of numbers. It uses tokenizer for creating unique indexing for the words in a tweet. This indexing is used as sequences. Further, as the CNN model requires every tweet to have a specific number of sequences. Padding is performed by appending 0 to the end of the sequences. It is shown in the figure 3 below.

Tweet	-	Rilly worried river flat flood
Sequence	-	[2791, 246, 1326, 67]
Padded Sequence	-	[2791 246 1326 67 0
		0 0 0 0 0
		0 0 0 0 0
		0 0 0 0 0
		0 0 0 0 0]

Fig 3. Converting text to sequence

4.4 Convolution Neural Network:

The Convolutional Neural Network [9] is a Deep Learning Algorithm that captures an embedded image, assigns a value (readable bits and selections) to different elements/objects in an image and is able to distinguish each other. The pre-configurations required for ConvNet are very less as compared to other classification algorithms. While using classic filtering methods is done manually, with adequate training, ConvNets has the ability to learn these filters/features. The design of ConvNet is noteworthy in common with the communication pattern of Neurons of the Human Brain. It was inspired by the Visual Cortex organization. Single neurons respond to stimuli only in the restricted region of the visual field which is known as Regency Field. A combination of such fields accumulates to cover the whole visual field.

In our proposed system, we constructed a CNN model that consists of following layers that are:

• **Input layer:** It consists of input vectors that need to be classified.

•**Embedding layer:** It contains features vectors provided by the Word2Vec model.

• **Convolution layer:** It performs convolution using 2 kernels and 100 filters.

•**Global Max Pooling layer:** It provides maximum value form area covered by the kernel.

•**Concatenate layer:** This help in connecting the pooling layers.

•**Dense layer:** Neural Network has a regular layer called dense layer. The neurons are densely connected as every neuron gets input from previous layer neurons.

• **Dropout layer:** Dropout layer works by removing inputs to a layer probabilistically, which might be input variables in the data sample or could be activations from the previous layer.

• **Activation function:** The decision regarding firing of neurons is taken on the basis of activation function. Thus we have used sigmoid activation function as output is bounded between 0 and 1.

Architecture of Convolutional Neural Network model in the proposed system can be visualized as shown in figure 4.

```
Layer (type)                      Output Shape
==============================================
embedding_4 (Embedding)           (None, 25, 200)
conv1d_6 (Conv1D)                 (None, 24, 100)
conv1d_7 (Conv1D)                 (None, 23, 100)
conv1d_8 (Conv1D)                 (None, 22, 100)
global_max_pooling1d_6 (GlobalM  (None, 100)
global_max_pooling1d_7 (GlobalM  (None, 100)
global_max_pooling1d_8 (GlobalM  (None, 100)
concatenate_2 (Concatenate)       (None, 300)
dense_7 (Dense)                   (None, 256)
dropout_2 (Dropout)               (None, 256)
dense_8 (Dense)                   (None, 1)
activation_2 (Activation)         (None, 1)
==============================================
```

Figure 4. Architecture of Convolutional Neural Network.

5. Result and Analysis

5.1 Dataset: For this system, Social Media Disaster Tweets dataset provided by Kaggle [10] is been used. It contains 10k tweets. The reason for using this dataset is that it contains tweets that are labelled as relevant or non-relevant based on keyword or type of disaster. This dataset is split in 8k tweets for training the model and 2k tweets for validation and testing of the model.

5.2 Performance Analysis: Model is been analyzed by comparing the score with CNN + Custom Weight Vocabulary, CNN + Google News Vocab, CNN + Twitter Glove Vocab. Table 1 shows the comparison of models.

Table 1. Comparison of models

Model	Accuracy (%)	Loss (%)
CNN + Custom Weight (Proposed)	84%	39%
CNN + Google News Vocab	86%	34%
CNN + Twitter Glove Vocab	81%	46%

From the above table, we can observe that due to large corpus of vocab present in Google News Vocab it generated an evaluation accuracy of 86%. Thus by increasing the size of our custom weight vocabulary, we can increase the accuracy of the model.

5.3 Confusion Matrix: After evaluation of the model. This model is been tested on 200 flood tweets that were generated during the Colorado flood in 2013. Based on the model prediction, there has been creation of a confusion matrix for the same that contains actual informative and predicted informative on these 200 tweets. Table 2 shows the confusion matrix.

Table 2. Confusion matrix

Parameters	**Predicted Informative**	**Predicted Non-Informative**
Actual Informative	61	7
Actual Non-Informative	47	85

6. Conclusion

Considering the very large number of tweets data over the internet, it is a diligent task to classify them. Because of the presence of non-textual data in tweets and the unique feature of a particular tweet, text classification has become a challenging task. This system propose a tweet classifier framework which takes in input as raw tweet and outputs are classifications of the tweet as informative or non-informative. Our model has outperformed an existing system that has used a combination of CNN + ANN. Using CBOW and Skip-Gram model of Word2Vec along with Convolution neural network, thus have achieved evaluation accuracy of 84%.

7. Future Work

As dataset was limited to 10k tweets along with particular keywords like earthquakes, floods, fire etc. In this proposed system with increase in the size of datasets and consideration of all kinds of disasters, the system will try to improve the accuracy of the model that can classify live-streamed twitter data with better performance.

References

1. Cornelia Caragea; Adrian Silvescu; Andrea H. Tapia,"Identifying Informative Messages in Disaster Events using Convolution Neural Networks",Proceedings of the ISCRAM conference,May 2016.

2. ShamikKundu;P.KSrijith; aunendraSankarDesarkar, "Classification of Short-Texts Generated During Disasters: A Deep Neural Network Based Approach" IEEE International Conference on Advances un Social Networks Analysis and Mining, 2018.

3. Mokhtar Ashour; Cherif Salama, M. W. El-Kharashi; M. W. El-Kharashi, "Detecting Spam Tweets using Character N-gram Features" ICCES'18: The thirteenth International Conference on Computer Engineering and Systems, At Cairo, Egypt, 2018.

4. Shamik Kundu ; P.K Srijith ; Maunendra Sankar Desarkar , "A Method for Detecting and Analyzing the Sentiment of Tweets Containing Fuzzy Sentiment Phrases",2019.

5. Muhammad Imran1, Prasenjit Mitra1, Carlos Castillo "Twitter as a Lifeline: Humanannotated Twitter Corpora for NLP of crisis-related Messages" 2016.

6. Van Quan Nguyen; Hyung-Jeong Yang; Kyungbaek Kim; A-Ran Oh,"Real-Time Earthquake Detection Using Convolutional Neural Network and Social Data" ,IEEE Third International Conference on Multimedia Big Data, 2017.

7. https://towardsdatascience.com/another-twitter-sentiment-analysis-with-python-part-6-doc2vec-%2012.603f11832504

8. Sreenivasulu Madichetty, Sridevi M; "Detecting Informative Tweets during Disaster using Deep Neural Networks", 11th International Conference on Communication Systems and Networks, 2019.

9. https://towardsdatascience.com/a-comprehensive-guide-to-convolutional-neural-networks-the-eli5-way-3bd2b1164a53

10. https://www.kaggle.com/jannesklaas/disasters-on-social-media

Augmented Reality based Navigation and Recognition System

Deepali Panda[1], *Gayatri Raje*[1], *and Satish Ket*[1]

[1]Department of Computer Engineering, Rajiv Gandhi Institute of Technology, Versova, Andheri(W), Mumbai, India

Abstract. The current navigation system requires the user to continuously map with the navigation application with the real-world environment. It sometimes leads to an incorrect path due to minor difference in the distance between different paths. The identification of nearby places of unknown locality is difficult as one has to ask for information and reviews which can be misleading. Recognition of unknown people for their authenticity cannot be guaranteed as one has to rely on official documents which can be fake. This paper aims to describe the design of an application that will provide the same reality-based environment as that seen through the naked eye, but it adds visual simulation or content to provide an enhanced view to the user during navigation. We will be using Augmented reality to provide users with more information, computer-assisted decision making, and interactive learning and training. The application will combine Google's existing Maps data with a live feed from your phone's camera to overlay walking directions on top of the real world and help you figure out which way you need to go. Identification of near-by places and authenticity of the unknown people can be done from the data stored on the cloud and will be augmented when scanned through the camera of the phone which is the only requirement of the application. It also enables the users to navigate indoors with the help of a radar map and arrow pointing towards the points of interest. This application enables the user to navigate using the mobile phone and get the directions augmented in the real world to take accurate decisions. The user can also navigate to different points of interest- indoor as well as outdoor. It also enables the recognition of places, as well as people and the details related to the same, get augmented.

1 Introduction

Augmented Reality is a technology that overlays the virtual graphics in the real-world [1] environment. It helps in visualization and improves user experience in applications. The current navigation system has customized road map views which are difficult for the pedestrians [2] as well as the drivers to map with the real world. Augmented Reality, when merged with the navigation system along with various Google APIs [3], provides a better user experience by augmenting the directional details. This helps the user to see the real world along with the navigational details.

In this paper, we focus on the navigation and recognition system with augmented reality integration. It uses the location and marker-based augmented reality system for navigation and recognition. The system has the recognition features which recognize objects, scenes, and people and augments their details. These details get augmented with the help of image targets [4]. The details stored in the cloud-related to the database image targets get augmented [5] on their recognition. The augmented details may include the description, ratings, reviews, etc. and can be displayed in the form of texts, images, 3d objects, and videos.

The recognition system is integrated with the navigation system to provide the pedestrians as well as the drivers with the available details [6] on their path which gets augmented on their screen. The navigation system uses Google Maps API, Google Geocoding API and Google Direction API are used to get map-based data, geolocation of the user and geo-coordinates [7-9]. The navigation system allows the user to select the source and destination points by searching the desired places for navigation. It provides an augmented route to the destination selected with various details such as the distance between the source and the destination, and the time required to cover the distance.

The system can interact with the user using voice commands and instructions [10] for giving the routing to desired locations. Along with outdoor navigation, the system also provides indoor navigation. The maps for the indoor navigation [11] can be accessed using the QR code and can be used for navigation inside the organizations with augmented details.

2 Literature Review

In the paper, "A Survey of Augmented Reality", the author R. Azuma explored six classes of potential AR applications. Author explains the characteristics [12] of the AR systems. Author describes the work performed in different sites and the issues encountered during the development. The paper summarizes the current efforts to overcome the problem of the registration and sensing errors in building effective Augmented Reality systems.

The author Ronald T. Azuma along with others, discussed in the "Recent Advances in Augmented Reality" [13] about how recent advancements in technology demand AR to be deployable on mobiles and web technologies. As to make extensive use of AR possible to maximum users. Authors discussed the research contribution of Mohring and Wagner on the usage of phones for computer vision in sensing and tracking. He studied characteristics of web 2.0 and AR 2.0 and compared them. Authors concluded how AR can be deployed with handheld devices, to generate and share information or user content with other users.

In the survey of AR navigation by Gaurav Bhorkar, he presented [14] existing research carried out in augmented reality based navigation systems. It describes the exisiting navigation systems, techniques used and problems faced. The paper concludes that augmented reality is a very powerful mechanism to provide the user with better user experience while navigating and also improves the safety of the user.

In the paper "Augmented reality as a new way of exploring the city: unified platform for data providers" [15] the authors explore Augmented Reality as a part of Location–based services. It describes a platform for the dynamic transformation of the static information obtained for the POIs. The aim was to provide the users real-time [16] updates about the POIs and to make the interface user-friendly as much as possible.

3 Methodology

For building the recognition system we have used the Wikitude SDK along with android studio which is a web application and for the outdoor navigation we have used BeyondAR SDK along with the android studio which is a native android application:

3.1 Scene and Object Recognition

In the scene recognition module, the scene is recognized with the help of image targets. These image targets are stored in the Wikitude server. Target collection is created which is a collection of targets used to recognize the scene. The live camera feed is analyzed by the image tracker and detects the targets. For each target in the target collection, the details regarding the target get augmented. The augmented details can be in the following forms:

3.1.1 Text

The textual details are augmented by converting them in the form of images. The conversion of text to image is done using the Pillow library of python. Image format to display the text is designed and is combined with the text to be augmented.

3.1.2 Image

The image resources to be augmented are passed to the AR.ImageDrawable. The ImageDrawable converts the image into a representable AR object.

3.1.3 Hyperlinks

The HTML URL are links to respective external websites. The HtmlDrawable class converts the URL that points to a particular website into an AR object that will be used for augmentation.

3.1.4 Audio

The details in the audio format can be augmented by passing the corresponding audio file to the AR.sound class. It is initialized on the recognition of the targets in the target collection and gets destroyed after the tracker is unable to track the target.

3.1.5 Video

The video related to the target is augmented with the help of VideoDrawable class. The VideoDrawable class encapsulates the video which can be used to represent the video in the form of an AR object. The VideoDrawables can be represented in the form of transparent pixels.

3.2 Navigation

In the navigation module, the start location of the user and the destination for the travel is manually taken by selecting it using the Geocoding API. The route is mapped with the help of Google Directions API which provides the map and BeyondAR SDK which recognizes the roads with the help of the neural network and augments the directional details. For the AR-based navigation, the turn by turn navigation route is given by the Directions API on top of Maps SDK by requesting the Geocoding API for source and destination. The response obtained will be the navigation route. The navigation route is displayed with the help of the virtual green spheres which get augmented along the route line with the help of BeyondAR SDK. BeyondAR SDK recognizes the road and helps in augmenting the details. The SDK helps in augmenting the start banner, green spheres along the route of navigation and stop banner on reaching the desired destination along with the time required to reach the destination and the distance to reach there.

3.2.1 BeyondAR GeoObject

A geoAR object is created with an image. This object is used to display the directional details. The world holds the information related to the objects. It helps in augmenting the objects by overlaying it with the camera frames in the application.

3.2.2 BeyondAR Google maps plugin

The google maps plugin provides an option to augment the world object on the maps view of the Map SDK provided by google. The GoogleWorldMapPlugin is used to set the geoAR object on the map view on the navigation path provided by the Directions API at specific geolocations.

3.2.3 Google Maps SDK

Google Maps SDK is used to add maps based data to the application. It handles access to Maps servers, displaying of maps on application screen, responding to the gestures and downloading map data.

3.2.4 Geocoding API

Google Geocoding API is used to get the geolocation of the start and destination place of navigation. It converts the address into geographical coordinates.

3.2.5 Directions API

The Directions API is used to get the navigation route from the source to destination. It provides the geo-coordinates along the route of navigation which in coordination with the google maps plugin is used for augmenting the world objects. It also provides the distance to the target and the time required to reach the destination.

Algorithm

```
Initialize MapActivity
Initialize Variables
Assign XML component variables
Load XML content
Load activity bindings
Check Required permissions
if internet and gps on
    pass
else
    alert user
Initialize google api client
if (googleApiClient == null)
    {googleApiClient=new
    GoogleApiClient.Builder(this)
    .addApi(LocationServices.API)
    .addConnectionCallbacks(this)
    .addOnConnectionFailedListener(this)
    .build();}
onclick()
if textfield is empty:
    report user
else:
    call geocode apigeocode()
    pass textfield string
    return latitude and longitude
    return result;
augment(directions)
    augment source to destination
    augment time
    augment distance
    augment sphere
navigation()
    geocode(start)
    geocode(destination)
    call directions api
    augment(directions)
```

4 System Architecture

The application gets the user's location with the help of GPS satellites. The Google Geocoding API provides the user's location and the Google Maps SDK and Direction API provides the map data required for the navigation module. The cloud database of Wikitude stores the image targets and provides them with the AR framework. It also stores the images, videos and other details needed to be augmented on the targets. As seen in Fig 1., the AR framework combines the real-world markers and scenes with the augmented reality world components. The AR framework provides the features of navigation and recognition. This output by the AR framework is visualized on the mobile phone screen with a camera providing the real-world environment and AR framework augmenting the AR components.

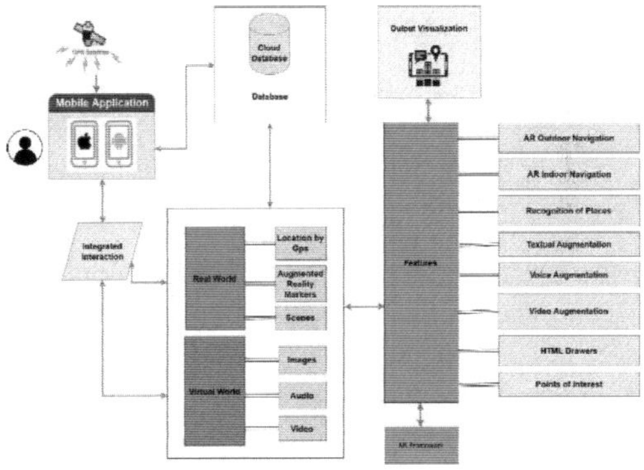

Fig. 1. System Architecture

Fig 2. depicts architecture of the Recognition system. The Wikitude SDK has been used for augmenting the details on the real-world environment. The markers are stored in the Wikitude cloud which are used to tag the real world environment and augment details on them. The AR interface data, GPS data and the compass data are given as input to the Wikitude SDK.

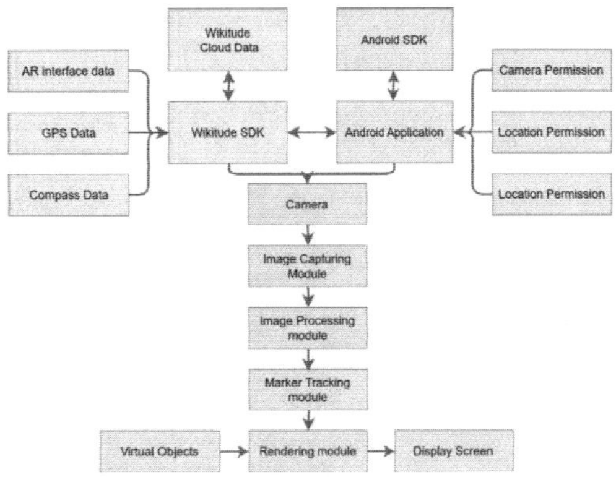

Fig. 2. Architecture of Recognition System

Fig 3. depicts the architecture of Navigation system. The BeyondAR framework contains the AR interface data, requires GPS data to augment the directional details as well as compass details for knowing the orientation of the user.

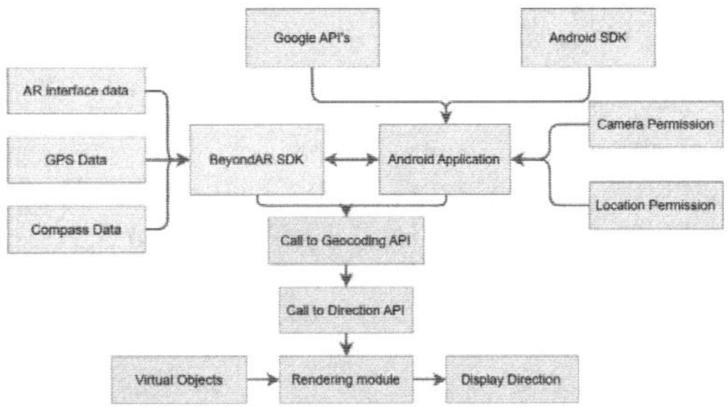

Fig. 3. Architecture of Navigation System

The android application uses the geocoding API to get the latitude and longitude values of the searched location. The user can search the source and destination for the navigation. On starting the navigation, the direction spheres get augmented along the path of the navigation.

5 Result

Outdoor navigation system assists the user in taking exact turns by augmenting the green spheres along the path of navigation. The user can follow the path along the augmented spheres which helps in tracing turns and flyovers accurately thereby avoiding ambiguity while navigating. The distance and time for navigation also gets augmented on the screen which can be seen in the Fig. 4.

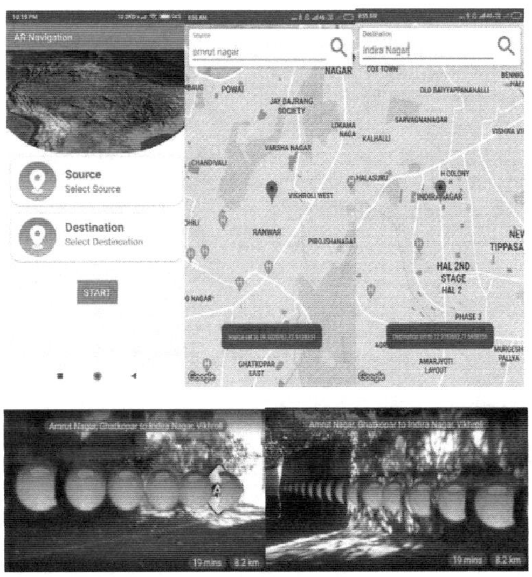

Fig. 4. Outdoor Navigation

Local Augmented Reality Navigation allows the user to view different Points of Interest in the area, navigate to them and also get additional details and distance to those places. As seen in Fig. 5., users can navigate to the points of interest by selecting them on which an arrow gets augmented on the screen which directs the user to reach the selected POI by following the path.

Fig. 5. Point of Interests

The radar on the top right corner displays the points of interest in the nearby vicinity and further helps in navigation. Users can view the description of the POIs by clicking on respective POI. This can be used to navigate indoors by placing each location with different points of interest at different latitude, longitude and altitude and adding descriptions about the same.

Fig. 6. Recognition with textual augmentation, multiple targets and audio augmentation

The Recognition module recognizes the places and the details regarding it are augmented in the form of image, audio and video which can be seen in Fig. 6. The users can also get clickable links in form of virtual buttons augmented to access the websites of the recognized place thereby reducing the effort of browsing the place explicitly. Details in the form of 3D objects as seen in Fig. 7. are also augmented with interactivity features which can be used for more realistic details and advertisement purposes.

Fig. 7. 3D model, video augmentation and website redirection

The Table 1 shows the comparison between the traditional navigation system and the augmented reality-based navigation and recognition system. The traditional navigation system results in ambiguity in turns and flyover because of custom road map view which is overcome by augmented reality-based navigation which uses camera feed and augments spheres to provide exact details of directions. Also, traditional navigation system doesn't recognize places and they need to be explicitly searched, whereas using augmented reality recognition one can get image, audio, video as well as website links augmented on the phone screen.

Table 1. Comparison between traditional navigation and augmented reality-based navigation and recognition system

Criteria	Traditional Navigation and Recognition system	AR Navigation and Recognition system
Navigation route	Custom Road Map View	Live Camera feed augmented with direction details
Turn Ambiguity	Yes	No
Flyover Ambiguity	Yes	No
Local POIs Navigation	No	Yes
Indoor Navigation	No	Yes
Add Points of Interest	No	Yes
Radar availability	No	Yes
Information about places	Needs to be search manually	Gets augmented directly on the screen
Image, Audio, Video, 3D object Details	No	Yes
Interactivity	No	Yes
HTML hyperlinks	No	Yes

6 Conclusion

In this paper, we presented an Augmented Reality based navigation and recognition system that can be run on affordable smartphones. The system designed is simple, clear, user-friendly, and provides multiple features. The user can easily select source and destination and will get a route augmented with spheres for navigation. The user will be able to view the distance between the source and destination and also the time required to reach the destination. Users can navigate indoors of organizations, historic places, institutes, etc. by using radar maps and collection of POIs. Augmented details about the nearby locations such as petrol pumps, hotels, mechanic shops, etc. during navigation based on geolocation. The details augmented can be in different forms such as text, image, audio, video, and 3D model to provide a better experience to the user. Weather details augmented for traveling pedestrians. Users can get the details augmented about a particular location along with links to their websites. Users can view POIs present within the range. Information about the selected POI can be viewed and direction to the selected POI is also provided. The application simplifies and enhances the navigation experience and provides better user experience and usability.

References

1. R. Silva, J. C. Oliveira, G. A. Giraldi, Introduction to Augmented Reality
2. S. Jang, A. Hudson-Smith, Exploring Mobile Augmented Reality Navigation System for Pedestrians
3. J. Rodriguez , Ching-Yu Huang, An Emerging Study in Augmented Reality & Geographical Information System, *International Journal of Computer Theory and Engineering*, **9**, 6, (2017)
4. J. Trojan, S. Chudacek, P. Chrastina, Augmented reality as a new way of exploring the city: unified platform for data providers, *WIT Transactions on Ecology and the Environment*, **20**, (2016)
5. S. Chanphearith, A. Santoso, Suyoto, Analysis and Implementation of Location-Based Augmented Reality Mobile Application for Searching Tourist Attractions and Culinary Places, *IJCST*, **4,** (2016)

6. H. Hile, R. Vedantham, G. Cuellar, A. Liu, N. Gelfand, R. Grzeszczuk, G. Borriello, Landmark-Based Pedestrian Navigation from Collections of Geotagged Photos, *MUM'08 - Proceedings of the 7th International Conference on Mobile and Ubiquitous Multimedia*, 145 – 152, (2008)
7. A. Pejic, S. Pletl, B. Pejic, An expert system for tourists using Google Maps API, *7th International Symposium on Intelligent Systems and Informatics*, (2009)
8. O. Aldabbagh, K. Mohsen, Design and Implementation an Online Location Based Services Using Google Maps for Android Mobile, *International Journal of Computer Networks and Communications Security*, (2014)
9. T. Michel, On mobile augmented reality applications based on geolocation, (2017)
10. D. Barclay, M. Aliasut, L. Ojeda, Augmented Reality with Location Tracking, (2017)
11. B. Parhizkar, C. Bakka, A. Pandor, N. Christian, Md. Jubair, A. Lashkari, Mobile AR GPS-Based For Navigation Purpose, (2012)
12. R. Azuma, A Survey of Augmented Reality, *In Presence: Teleoperators and Virtual Environments* (1997)
13. R. Azuma, Y. Baillot, R. Behringer, S. Feiner, S. Julier, B. Macintyre, Recent advances in augmented reality, *IEEE . Computer Graphics and Applications*, (2001)
14. G. Bhorkar, A Survey of Augmented Reality Navigation, (2017)
15. M. Williams, K. Yao, J. Nurse, ToARist: An Augmented Reality Tourism App created through User-Centred Design, *Proceedings of British HCL*, (2017)
16. B. N. Kumar1, P. Saranya, K. Bindra, Enhancement of Navigation Technology using Augmented Reality, *International Conference on Physics and Photonics Processes in Nano Sciences*, (2019)

https://doi.org/10.1051/itmconf/20203203027

Implementation of an educational model leveraging the power of incentive reward theory with Blockchain.

Rishi Gulati[1,*], *Akash* Jethi[1], *Arnab* Ghosh[1], *Abhishek* Shimpi[1], and *Ashwini* Naik[2]

[1]U.G. Student, Department of Electronics and Telecommunication, Ramrao Adik Institute of Technology, Navi Mumbai, Maharashtra, India.

[2]Professor, Department of Electronics and Telecommunication, Ramrao Adik Institute of Technology, Navi Mumbai, Maharashtra, India

Abstract. Recent studies conducted to investigate the reasons for an alarming decline in the performance of undergraduate students have thrown up a few compelling facts. These necessitate our immediate attention. Demographic shuffling along with lack of intrinsic motivation stand out as the cardinal reasons among other miscellaneous ones. There is a need to introduce programs that perk up one's persistence level and provide the missing tangible incentive for a purposeful engagement with our education system. The paper endeavours to fulfil this requirement through the use of Blockchain (cryptocurrency) guided by the principles of extrinsic motivation theory.

1 Introduction

Problem solving is commonly understood as tweaking what is wrong but an alternate approach that seeks to rectify by over emphasizing or amplifying what's right can at times be cleverly adopted. Methodology for solving a problem faced by Universities tends on similar lines. It advocates the use of Reward based Learning coupled with Aversion Theory to achieve an improved student performance.

In this approach incentives are offered to lure every individual to emulate appreciable behavioural traits. This paper proposes the use of public/ private cryptocurrency, says an ether/RAIT Coin with its scope global/ restricted inside the precincts of the University, as a reward for exemplary behaviour displayed by the students. A set of scenarios have been thought and suggested where cryptocurrency can be earned by the students while short listing the services where they could also be spent. We have further incorporated the doctrine of punishment through payment of fines in case of noncompliance by the students in our scheme of things. Students will also be able to continually monitor their rewards earned in their "Wallets" created via a webapplication. All this will positively help Universities in improving their student profiles and abate the continued pressure felt by them from state legislatures, broader public and their own placement partners to become more accountable for the performance of their students.

This paper focuses on the root concepts and their implementation to integrate the brand-new advanced model over the existing traditional model. The paper proposes a course of action for the appliance of the improved model

2 Root Concepts

2.1 Broadening the niche

The philosophy of rewarding the students for exemplary behaviour is already adopted by a few universities. These schemes have often targeted the cream students (E.g. A cash reward for the top five rank holders). This approach fizzles out and bares minimal success as it tempts to a very niche group of students and fails to captivate the interest of the average student.

The paper proposes to replace this with a new ideology revolving around the concept of setting a list of goals in compliance with the institute's guidelines. The key is to have goals for every student which he/she believes to be achievable. This ensures that the scheme gets the mass of students involved and increases the probability of success.

2.2 The stick carrot theory

The stick carrot theory is a policy which explores the use of punishments along with rewards to recondition people to a fitting behaviour. The idea is to incorporate the issuance of fines as a lenient punishment and act as a negative reinforcement.

While the use of extrinsic motivation to earn rewards is the primary arrangement the motivation to avoid being issued bills (Deterrence strategy) is of equal importance. The following diagram illustrates a very basic overview of the proposed model

*e-mail: gulatirishi29@gmail.com

https://doi.org/10.1051/itmconf/20203203027

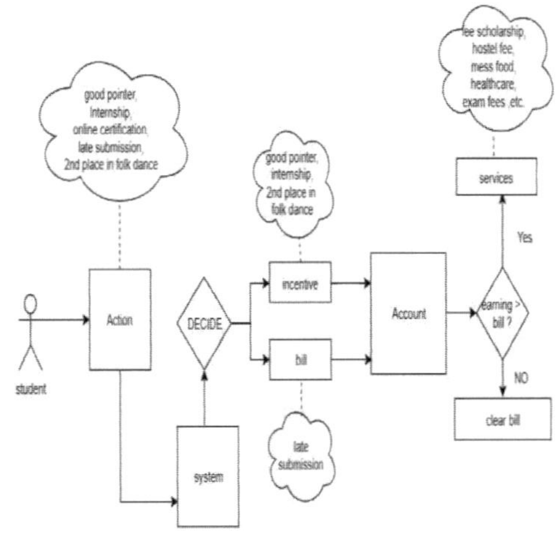

Figure 1. Overview of stick carrot model.

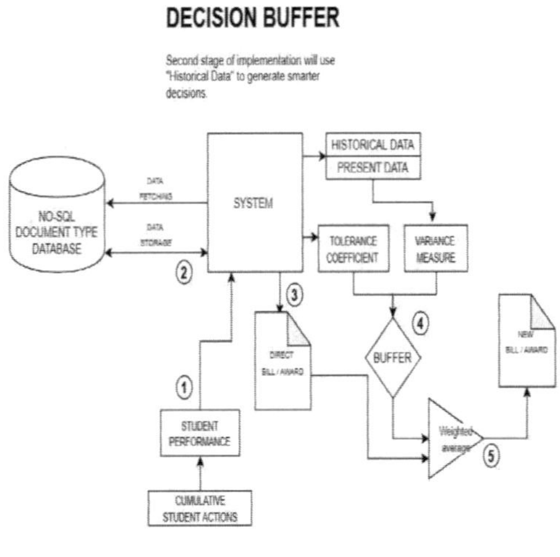

Figure 2. Overview of decision buffer system.

2.3 The Decision Buffer

The model must make some important decisions and uses specific algorithms for it. The first decision is to compare the student performance with fixed guidelines and decide upon issuing a bill or a reward. The second and the more important decision is to determine the value of bill/award to be issued.

A simpler approach would be to calculate the measure of shortcoming/ideal behaviour of student and use it to derive the value. The approach used here is a hybrid one which uses the value generated by simple approach and then modifies it depending on the modulation coefficient calculated by using the user's historical data. The coefficient value is dependent on the measure of variance between current data readings and historical data. Additional factors can be used to bias the decision.

2.4 The FPP

The FFP is an acronym for the frequent flier program but in the model it stands for the free fund program. The free fund program is inspired from the FFP which rewards user with travel miles for using the airlines. These miles can be spent by the user in exchange for other services which they desire.

Similarly under the free fund program the students can use the cryptocurrency they are awarded in exchange for various services provided by the organization. In absence of such a perk program the user will be satisfied by earning the bare minimum required to clear the bills. The FPP plays a vital role in propelling the user to earn maximum cryptocurrency. Having certain services that can be availed exclusively only by the earned cryptocurrency will further motivate the users.

2.5 The Light house effect

The extrinsic motivation and deterrence strategy certainly work however they may not be enough. The efforts and effects of the model can be compounded by use of lighthouse effect. Just like a lighthouse guides ships in storm to safe harbours, the model uses a recommendation system to guide the students. After correlating the students' performance (shortcomings and merits) with the guidelines of the university the system will generate recommendation tailored to each user.

The system operates with aim of providing the students with a gentle push in the right direction. Example of a typical recommendation generated for a student "ABC" may be 'To attend two of next three lectures of "XYZ". ' subject in the coming week as this will bolster his/her attendance above 70% and he/she will be eligible for a reward.

The following diagrams illustrates the basic operation cycle of generation of all the insights and recommendations for the end user.

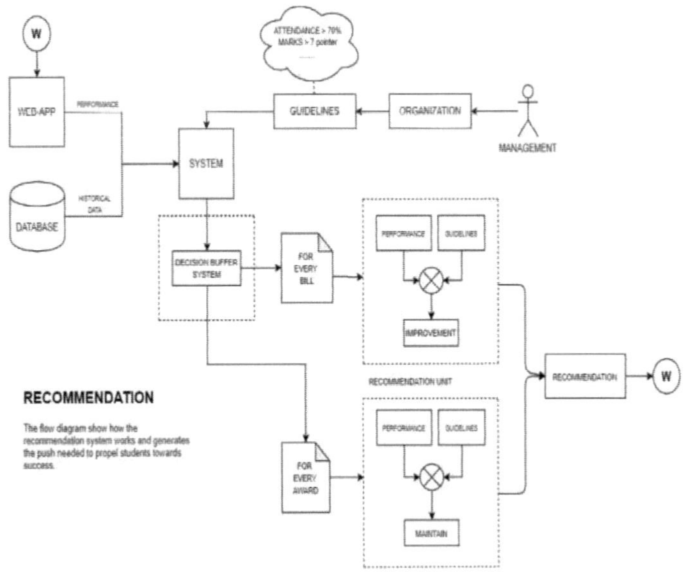

Figure 3. Overview of recommendation system

2.6 Cibil score

2.6.1 Cibil as a performance metric

Up until now the students academic success is only gauged their pointer. The pointer is a specific measure of marks scored and fails to give any other information about the student. Important parameters like attendance, timely submissions, involvement in extra-curricular activities and sports, individual achievements like winning a paper presentation competition often get neglected. The concept of maintain a Cibil score is inspired from the banks/insurance companies who maintain the credit activity of every individual to take calculated decisions. The model maintains a Cibil score with range 300 to 900 for every student which is incremented every time the student is rewarded and vice-versa. Since the awards and bills are generated for every factor of the students' performance the Cibil score acts as an overall performance metric of the student.

2.6.2 Cibil as a utility

Just as in polymorphism the Cibil score is overloaded to have more than one function. Its primary function remains to be viewed as a performance metric. The first added function is derivation of defaulter list based on Cibil. The second added function is to convert The Cibil into a utility to motivate the students to maintain a higher Cibil score. This process is carried out in steps.

1. Calculate Cibil influence factor based on the degree of variance in Cibil score over a certain period.
2. Every purchasable service will offer a discount. The discount depends on the students Cibil influence factor.
3. Every Bill payment offers "Xamount of the bill paid. The cash back percentage depends on the Cibil score.

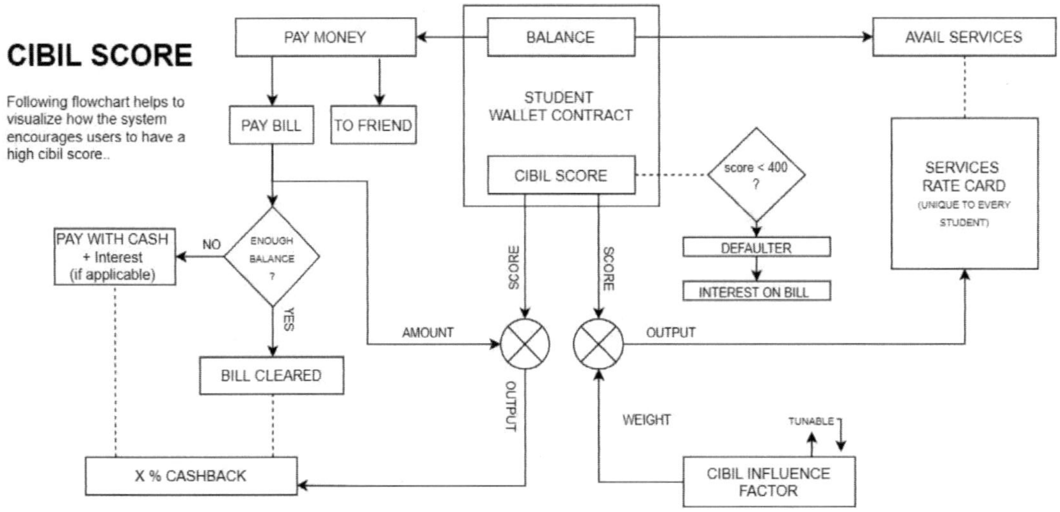

Figure 4. Overview of Cibil score's importance.

3 The Implementation blueprint

3.1 Using public Ether

If the organization decides to invest whole-heartedly in the model then a public coin like Ethereum can be used. The biggest pro of this approach is that the person being rewarded can use the reward outside the organization. The economics of this approach may make it unsuitable for many colleges. While some colleges have the resources to implement it; this approach is most suitable for commercial organizations to motivate their employees to gain advantage in today's cut-throat market. The users are expected to have a metamask account. The crypto-wallet in metamask is interfaced with web application. The system works with 3 contract types written in solidity.

The factory contract is a master contract used to deploy additional bank and wallet contracts on the Ethereum Blockchain. Every department has a bank contract assigned to it by the factory contracts constructor. On the other hand a new wallet contracts is deployed and assigned to the user by the factory each time a new user registers themselves. Each user's wallet contract has total earning, total bill, current balance and Cibil score associated with it. The transactions mostly take place between the bank and wallet contracts and are added to a block and mined on the main Ethereum network; therefore gas must be paid with each transaction. Every transaction takes about 25 seconds for completion.

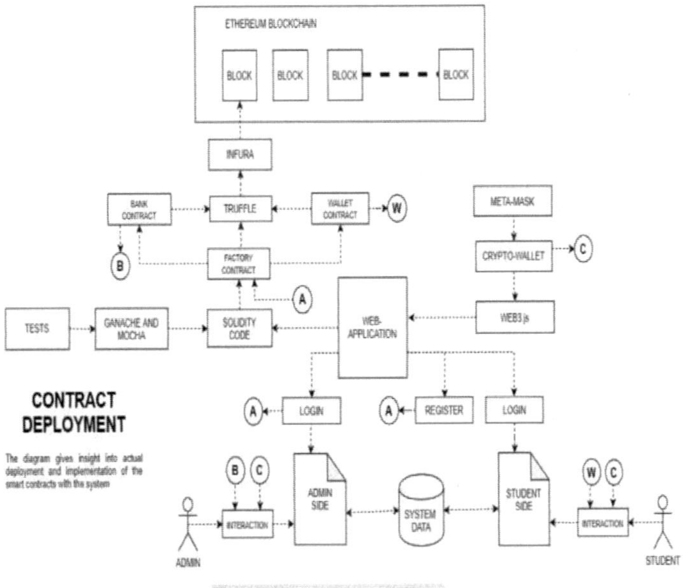

Figure 5. Public cryptocurrency blueprint

3.2 Using private cryptocurrency

For an organization with a lot of manpower (students/employees) it becomes difficult to reward with cryptocurrency because if there is a substantial difference in the currency awarded and currency recouped as bills it can drain the organization financially. To tackle this conundrum the paper proposes the creation of a private cryptocurrency with its scope restricted to the organization.

Though the rewards cannot be used outside the premises of the organization the low financial risk of this approach makes it suitable for universities and small organizations. The operational flow of student interacting with the portal remains explicitly same, though the process of making transactions strays from the original. The presence of a Metamask account which was mandatory in the first approach is no longer a necessity. The authentication and security of the whole process is monitored in three steps.

1. The verification of the transaction, relying heavily on the RSA algorithm. While sending funds the sender needs to digitally sign the transaction with their private key.

2. The authentication of the block, which involves matching the current hash of the block with previous hash. The miner involved in this process calculates the nonce and verifies the transactions by verifying the digital signature of the sender using their respective public key.

3. The authentication of the complete Blockchain. It is solely based on the concept of the consensus theory.

Private coin allows tinkering with the gas which is to be rewarded to miners. The model advocates two approaches. First approach suggests that the organization will mine every transaction involving the private coin. The second approach dictates that each individual must mine his own transactions; this approach eliminates the sending of additional gas along with transactions.

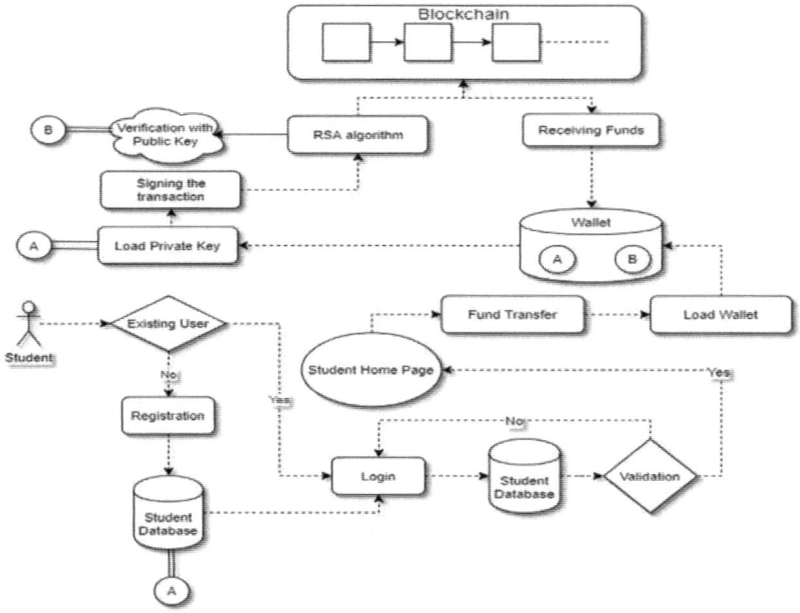

Figure 6. Private Cryptocurrency blueprint

4 Conclusion

After considering the many diverse reasons for unsatisfactory student performance and identifying the lack of intrinsic motivation as the root cause the paper proposes a new educational model. The model uses money as a tangible reward and uses cryptocurrency to carry the transactions. The paper also discusses the root concepts and strategies used by the model to alleviate probability of success. The paper further gives a blueprint to implement the model with either public cryptocurrency like Ethereum or via private cryptocurrency.

The paper focuses a lot on implementation of the model in educational institutes. The concept however can be expanded and applied across a wide array of domains ranging from Cibil score of employees in HR systems to determine appraisal, loyalty programs in gymnasiums, to an incentive system for employees in sales/marketing/trading based jobs.

References

[1] Samanez-Larkin, G.R. and Knutson, B., Decision making in the ageing brain: changes in affective and motivational circuits. Nature Reviews Neuroscience, **16(5)**, p.278.(2015)

[2] Worthy, D.A., Cooper, J.A., Byrne, K.A., Gorlick, M.A. and Maddox, W.T., State-based versus rewardbased motivation in younger and older adults. Cognitive, Affective, Behavioral Neuroscience, **14(4)**, pp.1208-1220.(2014)

[3] Eppinger, B., Walter, M., Heekeren, H.R. and Li, S.C., Of goals and habits: agerelated and individual differences in goal-directed decision-making. Frontiers in neuroscience, **7**, p.253.(2013)

[4] Wirth, C., Akrour, R., Neumann, G. and Furnkranz, J.,A survey of preference- based reinforcement learning methods. The Journal of Machine Learning Research, **18(1)**, pp.4945-4990.(2017)

[5] McGraw, K.O., 1978. The detrimental effects of reward on performance: A literature review and a prediction model. The hidden costs of reward: New perspectives on the psychology of human motivation, pp.33-60.

[6] Ellingsen, T. and Johannesson, M. ,Pride and prejudice: The human side of incentive theory. American economic review, **98(3)**, pp.990- 1008.(2008)

[7] David R. Roalf, Suzanne H. Mitchell, William T. Harbaugh, Jeri S. Janowsky, Risk, Reward, and Economic Decision Making in Aging, The Journals of Gerontology: Series B, **67B**, **Issue 3**, Pages 289– 298.(2012)

[8] Seward, J.P., Drive, incentive, and reinforcement. Psychological review, **63(3)**, p.195.(1956)

[9] Brewer, E.W., Dunn, J.O. and Olszewski, P., Extrinsic reward and intrinsic motivation: The vital link between classroom management and student performance. Journal of Education for Teaching, **14(2)**, pp.151170.(1988)

[10] Carlozo, L., What is blockchain?. Journal of Accountancy, **224(1)**, p.29.(2017)

[11] Lemieux, V.L., Trusting records: is Blockchain technology the answer?. Records Management Journal,**26(2)**, pp.110-139.(2016)

[12] Delmolino, K., Arnett, M., Kosba, A., Miller, A. and Shi, E., February. Step by step towards creating a safe smart contract: Lessons and insights from a cryptocurrency lab. In International Conference on Financial Cryptography and Data Security (pp. 79- 94). Springer, Berlin, Heidelberg (2016)

[13] Teutsch, J., Jain, S. and Saxena, P., February. When cryptocurrencies mine their own business. In International Conference on Financial Cryptography and Data Security (pp. 499-514). Springer, Berlin, Heidelberg.(2016)

[14] Stefansson, G. and Lentin, J., From Smileys to Smileycoins:Using a Cryptocurrency in Education. Ledger, 2, pp.38-54.(2017)

[15]

Density and Time based Traffic Control System using Video Processing

Tanvi Sable[1], *Nehal Parate*[1*], *Dharini Nadkar*[1], *Swapnil Shinde*[1]

[1]Department of Information Technology, Ramrao Adik Institute of Technology, Nerul, Mumbai, India

Abstract. Traffic is the serious issue which each nation faces due to the expansion in number of vehicles. One of the strategies to beat the traffic issue is to build up a smart traffic control framework which depends on computing the traffic density and about utilizing constant video and picture preparing procedures. The topic is to control the traffic by deciding the traffic density on each roadside and control the traffic signal smartly by utilizing the density data. In this paper, an automated system based on processing of real time videos is proposed for detection of vehicles and recording count of them. The System will consist of various stages which includes Object Car Detection and Signal variation based on density. Captured video will be converted into frames and which will be pre-processed for object detection using Haar-Cascade than detected object count will be used to obtain the density and manipulate the signal accordingly. The density count algorithm works by contrasting the ongoing edge of live video by the reference picture and via looking through vehicles just in the district of intrigue (for example street region). The figured vehicle thickness can be contrasted and other course of the traffic so as to perform control of the traffic flags in more smart and proficient manner.

1 Introduction

Traffic clogging has become a difficult issue in urban areas. The fundamental explanation is the increase in population in the urban area that along these lines there is high vehicular travel, which births clog issue. Because of traffic blockages there is high cost of transportation as a result of time wastage and additional fuel use [3]. For example, in the event that there is a crisis vehicle with the basic patient ready. In that circumstance if an emergency vehicle stalls out in an overwhelming congested road, at that point there are high possibilities that the patient can't arrive at the clinic on schedule. So, it is critical to structure a keen traffic framework which controls traffic brilliantly to maintain a distance from accidents, crashes and roads turned parking lots [7-8]. The most well-known explanation of traffic blockage in underdeveloped nations is a traffic signal con- trolling which influences the traffic stream. For example, if one path has less traffic and the other path has more traffic yet the green light is same then it creates problem. By considering the above model if the path with higher traffic thickness should turn on the green signal light for a longer period than the lane with lesser density. It will solve the problem. In other technique it is proposed to control the traffic signal by using image processing, in which they initially select the reference picture which is the picture without any vehicles or Less vehicles and each time they co-ordinate ongoing pictures with that reference picture, based on the level of coordinating traffic lights controlled. But in this the image matching is performed by using edge detection [3]. In this paper we propose a density-based counting of vehicles which gives us exact information for signal decision making. They are organized as follows: section II explains the review of literature. Section III shows proposed system. Section IV is with the implementation. Section V shows the result. Finally, Section VI is the conclusion of the paper followed by the key references used for the work.

[1]e-mail: tanvi291999@gmail.com
[1*]e-mail: parate860@gmail.com
[1]e-mail: dharininadkar02@gmail.com

2 Review of literature

The proposed system is aimed to give a comprehensive application to dynamically manage the traffic light systems depends on the current vehicle count. Gaussian probabilistic model is used for classification of vehicles, Kalman filter is used to detect the vehicles at the junction of the traffic light timer will be adjusted according. This proposed system will improve the traffic management system significantly by calculating accurate vehicle density on the roads. The proposed system takes the videos of all the traffic lanes at the junction as an input from the local storage of the computer and performs comparison based on the number of cars at the respective lane. The lane with the highest density will be given the priority. The scenario of the starvation of the particular lane is also taken into consideration while developing the system [1].

https://doi.org/10.1051/itmconf/20203203028

There are plenty of proposed techniques to build a wise traffic framework, for example, fluffy-based controller and morphological edge discovery. This technique is based on traffic density measurement, by relating the live traffic with an image. Other technique is proposed to design an intelligent traffic system, which is on four lanes. This also suggests identification of emergency vehicles, within a restricted scenario. Second technique is proposed based on neural networks, which analyze the traffic videos and classify the vehicles and its density. The proposed technique is based on calculating the traffic load by comparing two pictures. [2].

In this we speak about the camera-video-observation capabilities to track cross sectionally over diverse and changed street environments like vehicle discovery. The system is intended to track road and motorway wellbeing rates, it could detect the vehicles unlawful turn. The system is built using a diverse range of software's. The road intersections are the main focus of this system development. Used microcontroller is Arduino uno, used algorithm is canny. The system successfully reduces the crowd of vehicles and time of waiting through this mechanism at the traffic signals. We have coupled actual traffic images taken with microcontroller. This paper estimates the number of vehicles present, and the density is determined ac- cording to the total. This is intended to develop a system that uses camera to perform execution based on vehicle density, i.e. vehicle counting. It proves that video processing is a better option for calculating traffic density using OpenCV. It implements thickness-based operation system advancing using OpenCV video handling. The blob measurement helps to track the density of the vehicles from the live video recorded for processing. The traffic signal manipulation is successfully achieved through the count of the vehicles detected by the proposed system and reduces the traffic congestion at the intersections [3] [9].

3 Problem statement

Signals are allocated a fixed time and according to that time it will work but the problem here is even if there are no vehicles in that lane the signal will turn green according to the fixed timer statically allocated to it without any cause. We have to propose a system in which signal lights will be manipulated according to the density of the vehicles in that particular lane. The lane which has a greater number of vehicles will be given a preference. This system has been previously implemented using sensors but we are trying to substitute the whole system into video processing. The substitution results in low costs as there is no need to buy any sensors.

4 Proposed system

Proposed system is shown in figure 1 and explanation is given below.

4.1 Image Acquisition

The system starts with an image acquisition process in which the live video is taken and processed by camera, mounted on the signal stand. The video is captured lane wise, the camera shifts from one lane to another after a specific time interval.

4.2 Image cropping

The frames from the video are extracted which are processed further. The second step is the image cropping in which the focus is on region where the vehicles are present and are surrounded by noise and other data. Cropping helps to obtain the ROI for the system which can help to achieve higher accuracy.

4.3 RGB to grayscale transformation

RGB Images contains lot of data and it takes time for processing, to minimize this processing time the RGB color images are converted to gray scale and passed to next stages. The equation for rgb to gray scale conversion is given below:

$$Gray=0.2989 * R + 0.5870 * G + 0.1140 * B$$

4.4 Threshold

Thresholding is used for classifying the pixel values in an image which is done on grayscale images, which are images which have pixel values ranging from 0–255. When you threshold an image you classify these pixels into groups setting a upper and lower bound to each group. Thresholding can be performed by local methods as well as by global methods, Thresholding is one of the methods which is used to suppress the background and obtain a clear foreground. In this paper Otsu's Thresholding is ap- plied, it converts the gray scale image to binary form based on the selected threshold value.

4.5 Contour

The binarized image obtain from thresholding stage is passed to the contour step to define the contour for the detected objects. Contours can be clarified as basically as a curve joining to every single continuous point having same shade or intensity. The contours are helpful to object detection and recognition.

4.6 Calculate traffic density

In this we calculate the density of the number of vehicles present in the lanes by the camera using har cascade algorithm. Which helps to decide the changing of the signal color thus managing the traffic.
The input video provided to the system will be checked and the frames will be extracted from it. The noise and other simplifying objects like shadows will be filtered out. The conversion of the extracted frames from rgb to

grayscale will be done. After this the contours on the frames will be detected and the object will be successfully detected using Haar-Cascade algorithm.

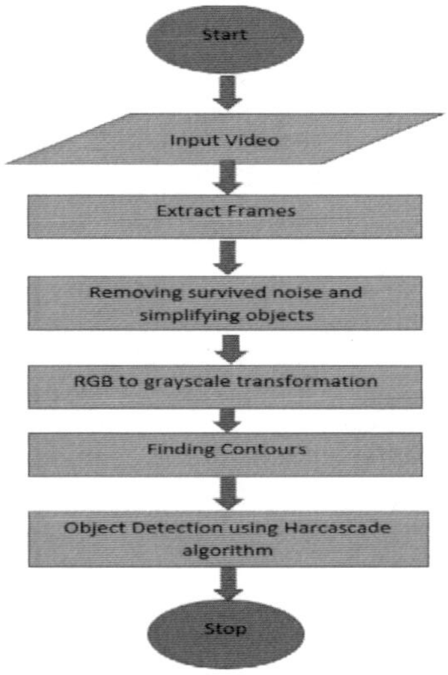

Figure 1. Video processing

1. Start
2. Give the system the input of the video to carry on further processing.
3. This step will remove the survived noise that is in the video which includes all the things other than the vehicle in the video to prevent from detection, and to simplify the video and identification of the vehicle.
4. This step will remove the survived noise that is in the video which includes all the things other than the vehicle in the video to prevent from detection, and to simplify the video and identification of the vehicle.
5. once the video is detected the video will be in colorful format that is into rgb format, so for the processing of the video the video needs to be in the grayscale format for better processing and according to the algorithm. Hence in this step we convert the RGB video into the grayscale format.
6. contours are basically the boxes formed around a detected vehicle to show that this vehicle is detected or anything that is detected comes under the counters and it gives the system a count of the detected objects.
7. finally, when the objects are countered in the previous step the object are detected with minimum error. In our case the system detects the vehicles as an object using the har cascade algorithm.

The below flowchart is for system architecture. When you turn on the system thee video processing module will open and the module will detect the number of vehicles in the particular lane where the camera is facing. If the vehicles are detected then the module will give us the count of the vehicles detected using the Haar-Cascade algorithm. Once the count is provided the signal will turn green on that particular lane for the time according to the vehicle count detected and the time allotted by the system which in our system, we have given 2 seconds for each vehicle and one extra second. If no vehicles are detected then the camera will move to the next lane to check for the vehicles and repeat the procedure.

4.7 Conventional Traffic Control System Manual Controlling:

Manual controlling refers to manual adherence for monitoring and controlling the traffic at the signals. Contingent upon the nations and states the traffic polices are allotted for a necessary region or city to control traffic. They are told to wear explicit garbs so as to control thetraffic.

4.8 Automatic Controlling:

The traffic lights are automated based on the sensor information and using clock timers for display. In rush hour gridlock light, each stage a steady numerical worth stacked in the clock. The lights are naturally jumping ON and OFF contingent upon the clock worth changes. The automated traffic signals make use of sensors to detect the vehicle availability and a flag is raised at each step, based on the above mechanism the lights turn ON and OFF automatically.

4.9 Hardware software requirements

- Power Supply
- Arduino
- Servo motor
- USB Camera
- Python 3.8
- Arduino ide
- OpenCV 3.4.9
- Ubuntu 19.04

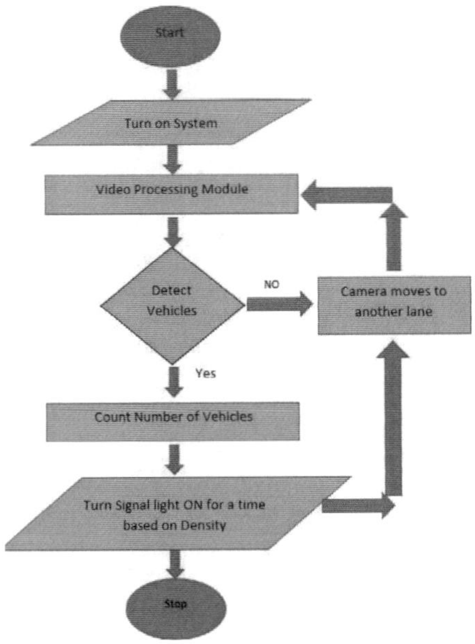

Figure 2. System Architecture

1. Start
2. Turn on the proposed system.
3. This step has the video processing module in which the methods and algorithm is present to detect the vehicles accordingly.
4. This step applies a condition in which if it detects the vehicles has a yes or no answer with the preceding step to be done.
5. If the system does detect the vehicle then it will give the total number of count of vehicles in that lane using the video processing module
6. In this step once the count is given the signal turns green for the time specified according to the algorithm based on the density or count of the vehicles in that particular lane.
7. If the camera detects no vehicle on the particular lane that he is facing then the camera will move and change its direction facing to the other lane to count the vehicle density in that particular lane and repeat from step5.
8. Stop

Figure 3. System Setup

5 Implementation

Given system uses OpenCV v3.4.9 for software, and is using the Image Processing principle. The programming language to be used will be python. In the past execution, since desktop monitor is hard to work with, we use Arduino uno micro controllers which make it easy to convert advanced digital language into a binary language. The technique that are used are blob detection and thresholding. The algo being used is Haar-Cascade. Another implementation in this project is using python. We use OpenCV due to which the project's entire cost is lessened.

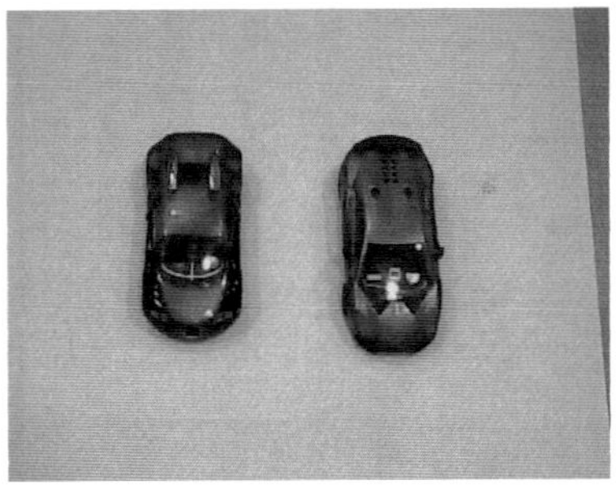

Figure 4. Image Capturing

The above figure is the image capturing done by our system.

https://doi.org/10.1051/itmconf/20203203028

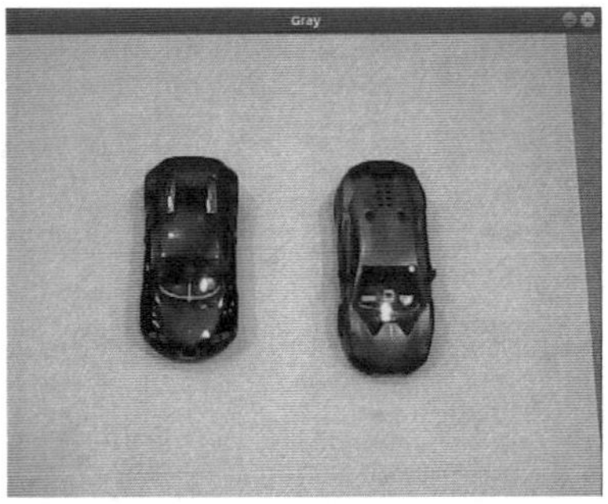

Figure 5. RGB to gray scale transformation

The above image is the transformation of the captured image from RGB to gray scale.

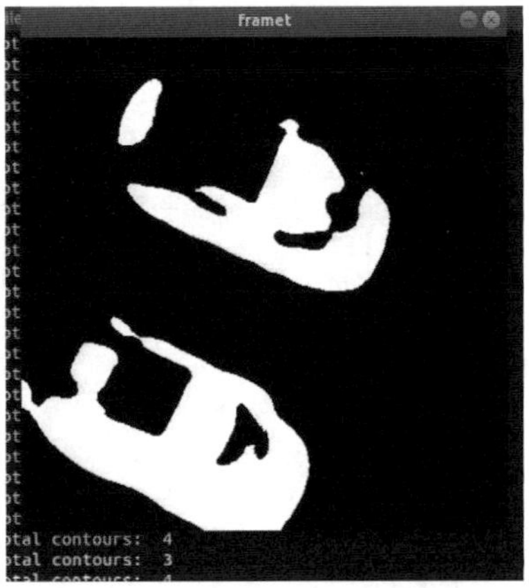

Figure 6. Threshold Image

The above image is the threshold picture of the vehicles detected by our system using Otsu thresholding.

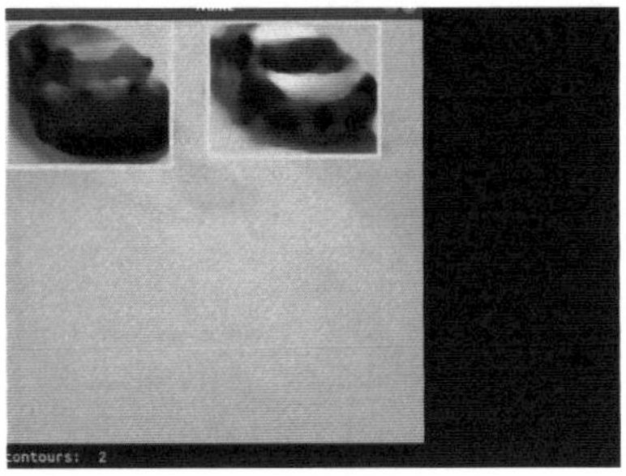

Figure 7. Car Detection by Contours

The above image is the contours detected by our system.

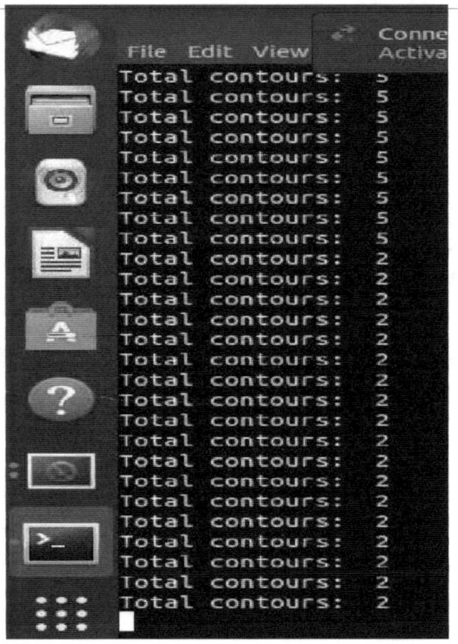

Figure 8. Density Count

The figure 8 shows the count of contours or the density of the vehicles detected by the proposed system.

6 Result

The lane number 1 has actually 5 number of vehicles present there, our system detects number of vehicles is 6 that is with the accuracy rate of 83.33. The time allotted that is number of seconds per vehicle to cross is 2 seconds and one extra second for any detection. Hence the lane 1 has 13 seconds allotted by the system. The lane 2 has actually 3 cars and our system has detected all 3 cars with the accuracy rate of 100 and the green signal is on for 7 seconds by the system.

Number of Lane	1	2
Actual Car Density	5	3
Proposed System Density	6	3
Green Signal Duration	13	7
Accuracy	83.33	100

The figure 9a and 9b below shows the number of vehicles detected by camera on two lanes having same number of vehicles. The density is same on both the lane. The lane camera is facing detects the 2 vehicles and turn the green signal ON for 5 seconds and camera rotates to other lane and on this lane, there are also 2 vehicles so the green signal turns ON for 5 seconds.

 https://doi.org/10.1051/itmconf/20203203028

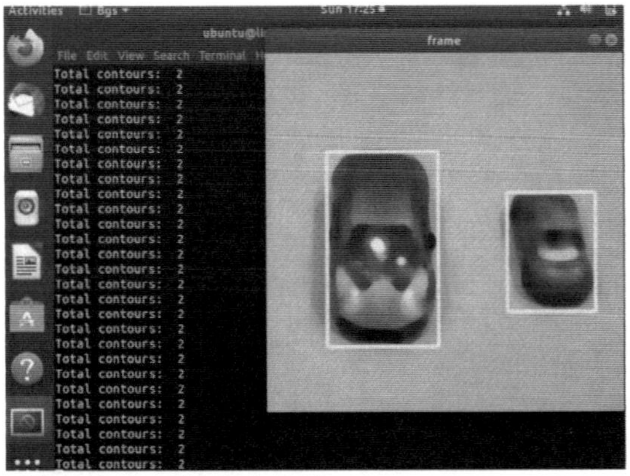

Figure 9a. Lane 1 vehicle density

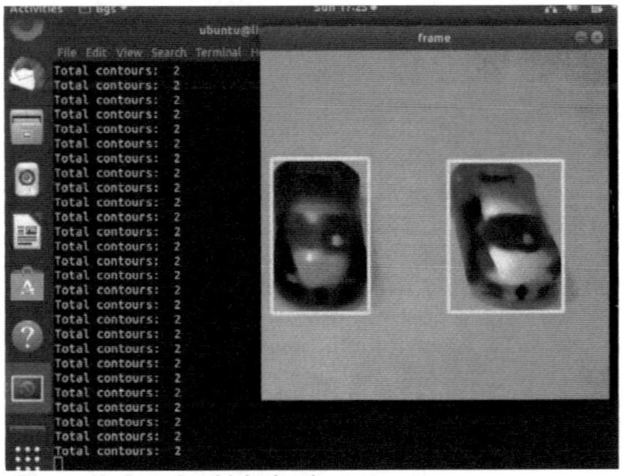

Figure 9b. Lane 2 vehicle density

On peak hours, the camera detects the number of vehicles on its range and turns the green signal ON for 2n+1 seconds. Then camera rotates to another lane.

7 CONCLUSION

The study showed that video processing is a good technique to control road congestion. It is also more consistent in detecting vehicle presence since it utilizes genuine traffic frames. It envisions the reality so it works far superior to systems which depend on the detection of vehicles. This work can be upgraded further by proposing a framework for controlling the traffic density. That will decrease our serious issue of everyday life, traffic jam. Using video processing and Object Detection mechanism, the proposed system achieves good accuracy in identifying the objects and estimating lane density. Based on lane density the traffic issue can be resolve to greater extent.

References

[1]Saraf Vaibhav, Shaikh Amaan, Mahajan Ketan, Shinde Swapnil, Sanap Varsha, Multi-Lane Dynamic Traffic Congestion Detection System using Image Processing, International Conference on ISMAC in Computational Vision and Bio-Engineering (ISMAC- IoT, Social, Mobile, Analytics and cloud) (ISMAC - CVB), March 13-14, 2019.

[2]Madhavi Arora, V. K. Banga, Real Time Traffic Light Control System, 2nd International Conference on Electrical, Electronics and Civil Engineering (ICEECE'2012), pp. 172-176, Singapore, April 28-29, 2012.

[3]Sabya sanchi kanojia, Real time Traffic light control and Congestion avoidance system, International Journal of Engineering Research and Applications (IJERA), pp.925-929, Vol. 2, Issue 2, Mar-Apr 2012.

[4]Anthony J. Venables, Evaluating Urban Transport Improvements, Journal of Transport Economics and Pol- icy, Vol. 41, No.2, pp. 173-188, May, 2007.

[5]Tommy Gerling, Geertje Schuitema, Travel Demand Management Targeting Reduced Private Car Use, Journal of Social Issues, Vol. 63, Issue 1, pp. 139153, March 2007

[6]Papageorgiou M., Diakaki C., Dinopoulou V., Kotsialos, A Review of road traffic control strategies, Proceedings of IEEE, Vol. 91, Issue 12, pp. 2043-2067, November 2004.

[7]Georgios Vigos, Markos Papageorgioua, Yibing Wangb, Real-time estimation of vehicle-count within signalized links, Journal of Transportation Research Part C: Emerging Technologies, Volume 16, Issue 1, pp.1835, February 2008.

[8]Michael W. Szeto and Denos C. Gazis, Application of Kalman Filtering to the Surveillance and Control of Traffic Systems, Journal of Transportation Science, vol.6 pp. 4419-439 , November 1972.

[9]Vikramaditya Dangi, Amol Parab, Kshitij Pawar S.S Rathod, Image Processing Based Intelligent Traffic Controller, Undergraduate Academic Research Journal (UARJ), Vol.1, Issue 1, 2012

Automated Non-invasive Diagnosis of Melanoma Skin Cancer using Dermoscopic Images

Huda Khan[1,*], *Anushka* Yadav[1], *Reha* Santiago[1], and *Sangita* Chaudhari[1]

[1]Department of Computer Engineering, Ramrao Adik Institute of Technology, Nerul, Navi Mumbai, 400706, India

Abstract. Melanoma skin cancer is one of the deadliest cancers today, the rate of which is rising exponentially. If not detected and treated early, it will most likely spread to other parts of the body. To properly detect melanoma, a skin biopsy is required. This is an invasive technique which is why the need for a diagnosis system that can eradicate the skin biopsy method arises. It is observed that the proposed method is successfully detecting and correctly classifying the malignant and non-malignant skin cancer. Finally, a neural network is used to classify benign and malignant images from the extracted features.
Keywords: Melanoma, non-invasive, skin lesion, neural network.

1 Introduction

Skin cancer is a fatal disease that is life-threatening. Recently, skin cancer has become one of the most lethal forms of cancers found in human beings. Out of all the various types of skin cancers, melanoma cell skin cancers are the most common type of skin cancer and is the most unpredictable. Malignant melanoma has become one of the most dangerous and aggressive type of skin cancer and its occurrence amongst humans has been increasing quickly. Melanoma, also known as malignant melanoma, is a variant of cancer that develops from the cells that contains a pigment known as melanocytes. These melanocytes may develop from a mole and bring about a changes that include increase in size, irregular border, and change in color, breakdown of skin or itchiness. Melanoma is usually caused by over-exposure to Ultra-Violet (UV) radiation from the sun and tanning beds. Due to this, it damages the DNA of the skin cells, and the cells can begin to grow out of control. It is one of the most unpredictable skin cancers and therefore detection of melanoma cancer at the early stages could help in curing it quickly and efficiently. Figure 1 shows a dermoscopic image of a skin melanoma.

Some of the symptoms of skin melanoma cancer is the ABCD rule which is the most common method used for detection of melanomas by doctors where the symptoms taken into consideration are:

- A - Asymmetry: The first half of a spot/lesion is not equal to the other half.
- B - Border: The edges of the lesion are ragged, irregular, or blurred.
- C - Color: The color across the lesion is not homogeneous and may include different shades of white, red, brown, blue, gray, or black.
- D - Diameter: The lesion is greater than 6 millimeters. (Albeit not all melanomas adhere to this)

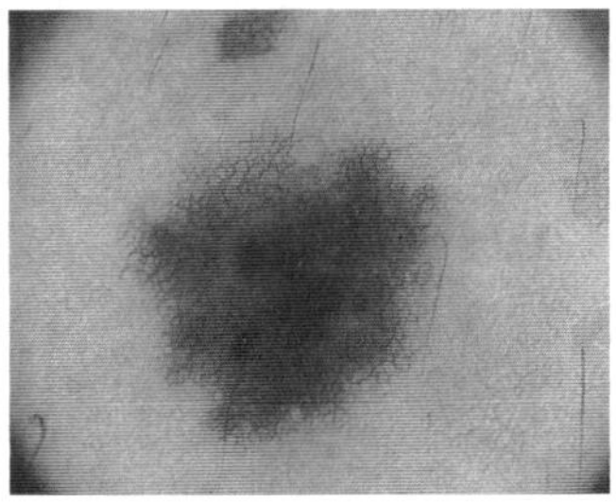

Figure 1: Dermoscopic image of a malignant melanoma

Melanoma of the skin is the 19th most commonly occurring cancer in men and women[1]. There were about 300,000 new cases of melanoma skin cancer in patients in 2018. In 2019, there were 104,350 with active melanomas which resulted in 11,650 deaths worldwide. In 2018, the highest rate of melanoma was observed in Australia followed by New Zealand. In 2018, India had about 26% of cancers reported as melanoma of the skin. Skin melanomas are treated according to the stage and location of the melanoma [2]. Most treatment operations require surgery to remove the affected area, radiation therapy, biological therapy, targeted therapy, immunotherapy, and chemotherapy. However, melanoma skin cancer can be treated easily if identified and diagnosed at an early stage. This makes the early diagnosis of melanoma as a critical part, which can be a challenging task for dermatologists since other skin lesions might have similar physical characteristics. Dermoscopic images are a widely common technique used in capturing melanomas accurately. This is done by performing an in-vivo observation of pig-

*e-mail: huda.gm.khan@gmail.com

mented skin lesions. Earlier, for the detection of malignant melanomas, dermoscopic images had great prospective, but their elucidation requires not only time but is also subjective. As a result, the necessity to construct a system that can help dermatologists in making an accurate decision for the early diagnosis of melanoma has become critical. In this paper, we are proposing an automated non-invasive diagnosis of melanoma skin cancer using dermoscopic images. Skin melanoma is represented with the help of simple yet efficient descriptors and further classified into malignant or nonmalignant melanoma cancer using neural network.

2 Literature Survey

Global warming has increased the intensity of solar radiation which has led to rise of skin melanoma cancer in human beings [2]. Melanoma, can be cured if it is detected in the early stages. Traditional approach to melanoma skin cancer detection requires biopsy- an invasive technique which can be a painful, costly and tardy procedure. Therefore, the need for an automated procedure to detect skin melanoma cancer accurately is a necessity in the medical field. Melanomas can exist in varied shapes, colors and sizes which make it difficult to detect it an early stage which is why it is essential to design a system that takes proper features into account for extraction. Diagnosis of skin melanoma cancer using an automated system includes the following steps:

- Image Acquisition: Input of data image sets is collected.
- Image Pre-processing: Removes unwanted noises and distortions in the input images.
- Image Segmentation: Involves extracting the skin lesion from the input image for further analysis.
- Feature Extraction: Selecting and extracting the relevant features from the skin lesion that is required to correctly detect skin melanoma cancer. The most common method of feature extraction is the ABCD rule where:
  - A - Asymmetry: Asymmetry specifies the axis of symmetry. Benign lesions tend to be symmetric while malignant lesions are asymmetric in shape.
  - B - Border: This is a measure of the irregular shape of the border of a lesion. Benign lesions are almost less ragged and have a smooth looking border while malignant lesions are highly irregular in nature.
  - C - Color: A color score of a lesion is a crucial feature. Benign lesions are more homogeneously colored throughout while malignant lesions could contain various undertones of brown, black, red, white or blue colors and are not uniform in color.
  - D - Diameter: A malignant melanoma tends to grow in size and surpasses its diameter of larger than 6 mm.
- Classification: The system classifies the input image as either, malignant (cancerous) or benign (non- cancerous).

Majumder and Ullah[3] proposed a system that considered more features from the fundamental ABCD rule. Image resizing and contrast adjustment were used for image pre-processing. An averaging filter was applied to the RGB input image to remove any noise like air bubbles or hair. Segmentation of the skin lesion is done by Otsu's automatic thresholding after which a gray scale masking is done to remove any small blobs present in the segmented lesion. The features that are extracted are: Asymmetry (across x and y-axis), Border Irregularity, Color Variegation, Lesion Diameter, Difference between Maximum and Minimum Feret's Diameters. On analysis, it is found that higher difference signifies the lesion is malignant and a lower difference signifies benign melanoma. These extracted features are then used to train the Back propagation Neural Network (BNN) for classification of the skin lesion as malignant or benign melanoma.

Eltayef et al.[5] proposed another system that focused on various image pre-processing and segmentation techniques. The image pre-processing in this system aimed at hair and noise detection and removal techniques. In order to eradicate any air bubbles, a thresholding method was used that used the pixel's intensity values. For the hair removal, first, the system uses a bank of 64 directional filters to detect hair in the image after which the image is filtered with the help of each of the aforementioned directional filters. Consequently, a Gaussian filter is implied by calculating each pixel's local maximum. This method of thresholding is used to differentiate between the hairs and the actual background of image. Upon detecting the hair from the image, their binary masks and gray scale image are multiplied. This system used two-step segmentation: Fuzzy c-means (FCM) and Markov Random Field (MRF).

Premaladha and Ravichandran[6] emphasizes the need for more number of features to be extracted for feature extraction. This system also uses a different image enhancement and segmentation technique. An input dataset of 992 dermoscopy images are used. It is then pre-processed of any noise, air bubbles, scars or hairs on the skin lesion. Contrast Limited Adaptive Histogram Equalization technique (CLAHE) is the preprocessing technique used to get a contrasted image which helps in accurately deriving the features. Median filtering is applied to eliminate any noise and smooth out the ragged edges of the skin lesion. Normalized Otsu's Segmentation is used for segmentation. The features extracted are: Mean, Standard deviation, Variance, Entropy, Contrast, Homogeneity, Energy, Correlation, Area, Perimeter, Diameter, Asymmetry index, Circularity index, Fractal dimension, and Compactness index. Deep learning based neural networks (DLNN) and Hybrid AdaBoost algorithms were used for classification of the skin melanomas.

Jain et al.[7] proposed a system that is so potent that it can take the input image from any camera, e.g. mobile camera. Image processing techniques like gamma correction were used that facilitated image resizing and adjustment of contrast and brightness. Image segmentation was done using Otsu's automatic thresholding, binary masking and edge detection. The features extracted in this system included geometric features of the skin lesion, they are:

Table 1: Various methods used in existing systems

Author	Pre-Processing	Segmentation	Features Extracted	Classification
Majumder and Ullah[3]	Image resizing, contrast adjustment and averaging filter to RGB input image.	Otsu's automatic thresholding method.	Asymmetry, Border Irregularity, Color Variegation, Lesion Diameter, Difference between Maximum and Minimum Feret's Diameters.	Backpropagation Neural Network (BNN).
Eltayef et al.[5]	Directional Gabor filters for hair removal.	Fuzzy C-means (FCM) and Markov Random Field (MRF).	Asymmetry, Border, Color Variegation, and Diameter.	Not specified.
Premaladha and Ravichandran[6]	Contrast Limited Adaptive Histogram Equalization (CLAHE) and Median filtering.	Normalized Otsu's Segmentation.	Mean, Standard deviation, Variance, Entropy, Contrast, Homogeneity, Energy, Correlation, Area, Perimeter, Diameter, Asymmetry index, Circularity index, Fractal dimension, Compactness index.	Deep learning based neural networks (DLNN) and Hybrid AdaBoost algorithms.
Jain et al.[7]	Image resizing, contrast and brightness adjustment.	Otsu's segmentation, 3-plane binary masking procedure and edge detection.	Area, Perimeter, Major and Minor Axis Lengths, Circularity Index, Irregularity Index.	Done by ABCD rule.
Sheha et al.[8]	Image resizing, from RGB to grey level conversion.	Uses Texture Analysis.	Contrast, Correlation, Cluster Prominence, Dissimilarity, Homogeneity, Difference variance, Difference entropy, and Inverse differences.	Multilayer Perceptron (MLP).
Isasi et al.[9]	Pattern recognition algorithms used: Globular, Reticular and Blue-vein.	Globular, Reticular and Blue-vein algorithms.	ABCD features along with features extracted from pattern recognition algorithms.	Done by the ABCD rule.
She et al.[10]	High-pass filtering and gradients in the horizontal and vertical directions are applied.	Snake-based edge detection technique.	Asymmetry, Border irregularity, Color variegation, Diameter, and one feature set is extracted from the pattern of the skin lesion.	Principal Component Analysis(PCA).

Area, Perimeter, Major Axis Length, Minor Axis Length, Circularity Index and Irregularity Indices. A pre-defined set of thresholds using the ABCD rule were set for the classification stage. The output would classify the skin melanoma as normal skin mole or melanoma skin cancer.

Sheha et al.[8] encouraged a system that uses texture analysis that eliminates the segmentation step. 102 dermoscopy images with 51 benign and 51 malignant melanomas were used on which image resizing of 512x512 is done. Additionally, features based on grey level co-occurrence matrix is carried out upon converting RGB image to gray-level. The features extracted are: Contrast, Correlation, Cluster Prominence, Dissimilarity, Homogeneity, Difference variance, Difference entropy, Information measure of correlation, Information measure of correlation, Inverse difference homogenous, Inverse difference normalized, and Inverse difference moment normalized. For classification, Multilayer Perceptron (MLP) is used.

Isasi et al.[9] proposed different pattern recognition algorithms based on the nature of the skin melanomas. Three algorithms- globular, reticulated and blue pigmentation- are proposed as these features are recurrent in malignant melanomas. Therefore, the features extracted are those from the fundamental ABCD rule in addition with the features extracted from the pattern recognition algorithms.

She et al.[10] pivots around designing a system that utilizes the ABCD rule to extract features from the skin lesion which helps improve the system's classification accuracy. High-pass filtering and gradients in the horizontal and vertical direction are applied for the image preprocessing after which a snake-based edge detection technique is used to define the lesion boundary. The features extracted are from the ABCD rule and one from the pattern of the skin lesion. Furthermore, Principal Component Analysis (PCA) is used for classification. Table 1 summarizes the various methods used in existing systems.

Table 2: Comparison of existing method and proposed method for feature extraction

Method	Features Extracted
Majumder and Ullah[3]	Asymmetry, Border Irregularity, Color Variegation, Lesion Diameter, Difference between Maximum and Minimum Feret's Diameters.
Eltayef et al.[5]	Asymmetry, Border, Color Variegation, and Diameter
Premaladha and Ravichandran[6]	Mean, Standard deviation, Variance, Entropy, Contrast, Homogeneity, Energy, Correlation, Area, Perimeter, Diameter, Asymmetry index, Circularity index, Fractal dimension, Compactness index.
Jain et al.[7]	Area, Perimeter, Major and Minor Axis Lengths, Circularity Index, Irregularity Index.
Sheha et al.[8]	Contrast, Correlation, Cluster Prominence, Dissimilarity, Homogeneity, Difference variance, Difference entropy, and Inverse differences.
Isasi et al.[9]	ABCD features along with features extracted from pattern recognition algorithms.
She et al.[10]	Asymmetry, Border irregularity, Color variegation, Diameter, Pattern of skin lesion.
Proposed System	Asymmetry along x-axis, Asymmetry along y-axis (Concept of connectivity in pixels used to evaluate principal axes for the asymmetry scores), Area to perimeter ratio, Compactness index, Product of Area and Perimeter, Color score evaluated with bitwise AND operation on the HSV image and color mask, Average of lesion diameter, Difference between the major and minor axis' lengths, and Lesion diameter.

3 Proposed System

Table 2 gives the comparison of the existing method and proposed method to extracting features. The proposed methodology comprises of the following primary steps: image acquisition, image pre-processing, image segmentation, feature extraction, and classification of the image. An input image is given to the system is a skin lesion that is to be classified as a benign or malignant melanoma. The input images are collected from PH2 database [11] and The International Skin Imaging Collaboration, ISIC. Removal of noises and hairs from the input image is crucial which is why morphological and blackhat filtering, and inpainting algorithm is implied. To segment the skin lesion from the input image, Otsu's algorithm [12] and Chan-Vese model [13] is used. This model extracts nine features according to the fundamental ABCD rule and further uses ANN classifier for classification of benign or malignant melanoma.

3.1 Image Acquisition

The PH2 database is a publicly available database of dermoscopy images provided by the Pedro Hispano Hospital. From this database, 200 melanocytic images were collected which consists of 160 benign and 40 malignant lesions. Additionally, 219 benign and 325 malignant images were collected from another publicly available database of dermosocpic images from the The International Skin Imaging Collaboration, ISIC. This totals to a dataset of 744 images.

3.2 Image Pre-processing and segmentation

The input image can contain a lot of noise and other artifacts, like air bubbles, hairs and varied textures of the skin. With all these factors, it is essential that the image is properly preprocessed and correctly segmented to increase the accuracy of the system. Image preprocessing is done by performing various morphological operations on the grayscale image. Upon applying the morphological filter on the grayscale image, a blackhat filtering operation is used that helps enhance the darkened moles on the skin lesion as the region of interest. Finally, an inpainting algorithm is used wherein a hair mask is created using thresholding that highlights the hair contours after which the original image is inpainted depending on the mask. Inpainting algorithm helps restore the background to the hairs detected in the hair mask. Suppose the hair mask, H, specifies the location of hair contours' pixels in the input image, I as follows:

$$H(x) = \begin{cases} 0, & \text{if pixel(x,y) has hair in } I \\ 1, & \text{if pixel(x,y) has no hair in } I \end{cases}$$

On locating the hairs, the pixels are then reconstructed by exploiting the information present in the regions with no hair.

Segmentation is an important step in digital image processing. The process of separating the region of interest from the skin lesion is crucial as this segmented image will further be used for feature extraction. Segmentation is performed in two steps using Otsu's thresholding method [12] and the Chan-Vese model [13]. Furthermore, morphological operations are performed to remove any more noises in the image. This allows accurate segmentation of the image. Otsu's method is used to separate the foreground and background pixels into different classes using bi-modal histogram. The algorithm then assesses the threshold that is the most optimum such that the two classes partitioned have their inter-class variance as maximum as possible. Algorithm 1 shows the Otsu's Thresholding Algorithm.

Algorithm 1: Otsu's Thresholding Algorithm

Evaluate histogram and probabilities of each intensity level.
Set the initial values of $\omega_i(0)$ and $\mu_i(0)$.
Compute class probabilities of the two classes, ω_i, and their class means, μ_i, as:
$\omega_i(t) = \sum_{0}^{t} P(i)$
$\mu_i(t) = \sum_{0}^{t} P(i)x(i)$
Step through all possible t thresholds from $t = 1$ till maximum thresholding intensity.
Update $\omega_i(t)$ and $\mu_i(t)$.
Evaluate $\sigma^2{}_b(t)$ as:
$\sigma^2{}_b(t) = \omega_2(t)\omega_2(t)[\mu_1(t) - \mu_2(t)]$
Maximum value of $\sigma^2{}_b(t)$ is the desired threshold.

The Chan-Vese model uses an active contour model. This contour must stop once it reaches the boundary separating the foreground and background. The binary output image after the Otsu's method, B, is used as an initial contour to the Chan-Vese model. The model minimizes the energy function E as given in the Equation 1:

$$\begin{aligned} E(c_1, c_2, B) = {} & \mu.\text{Length}(B) + v.\text{Area}(\text{inside}(B)) \\ & + \lambda_1 \int_{\text{inside}(B)} |u_0(x,y) - c_1|^2 dxdy \\ & + \lambda_2 \int_{\text{outside}(B)} |u_0(x,y) - c_2|^2 dxdy \end{aligned} \quad (1)$$

The values of μ, v, λ_1, λ_2 and p are $p = 1$, $v = 0$, and $\lambda_1 = \lambda_2 = 1$ according to the Mumford-Shah approach [14]. c_1 and c_2 are the averages of the given image, u_0.
After the two-step segmentation, a median filter of window size 25 and morphological closing operation is applied on the image. The preprocessed and segmented images of two sample images are shown in Figure 2.

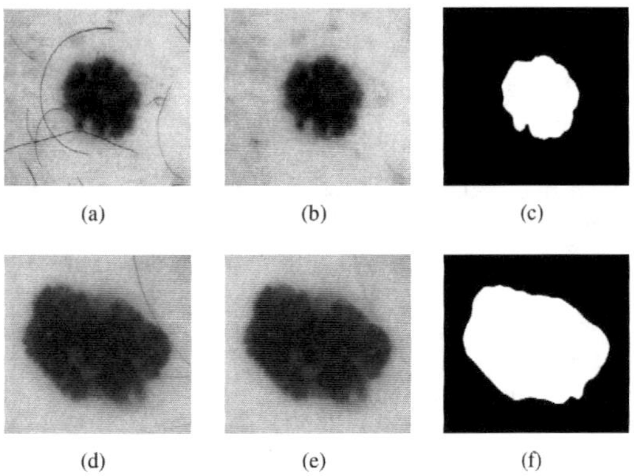

Figure 2: (a), (d) are the original images, (b), (e) are the preprocessed images, and (c), (f) are the segmented images

3.3 Feature Extraction

Once the skin lesion of interest is extracted from the source input image, we have to extract the appropriate and necessary features needed from the image. In this paper, we have heavily emphasized the accuracy of the ABCD rule, therefore, we will continue to use the fundamental rule in addition to more features. Features like Asymmetry and Diameter require principal axes for the evaluation of their scores. In order to evaluate this, the concept of connectivity in pixels in digital space has been used. A pixel p at coordinates (x, y) is connected to every other pixel horizontally, vertically, and diagonally.

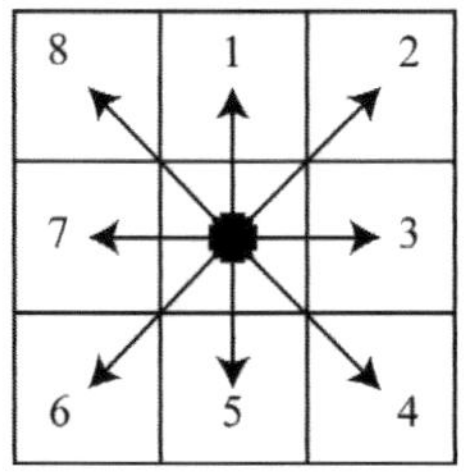

Figure 3: 8-connectivity of a pixel in digital space

As shown in the Figure 3, the pixel at the center p has 8 connected pixels. This means only four axes are possible for this pixel. Upon identifying the centroid of the skin lesion and translating it to the origin of the coordinate system, the length of the four axes passing through the centroid are evaluated and compared. The axis with the greatest length is assigned as the major axis. As principal axes are always perpendicular to each other, the corresponding minor axis of the image. For instance, in the Figure 3, if $7 - 3$ is major axis, then $1 - 5$ is assigned as the minor axis.

3.3.1 Asymmetry

Asymmetry is one of the most important features in order to classify the skin lesion as malignant or benign. It evaluates how similar one half of a region of the lesion is to the other half. A malignant melanoma will tend to be more asymmetric in nature. To calculate the asymmetry, the image obtained upon segmentation (Figure 4(a)) is made to align with the Euclidean coordinate system. The centroid of the image (Figure 4(b)) is translated into the origin of the coordinate system (Figure 4(c)). This image is then rotated with the orientation angle so that the major axis of the blob fits into the x-axis of the image, giving a lesion image, L (Figure 4(d)). This rotated image is then flipped along the x-axis, L_x (Figure 4(e)). The difference between L and L_x will give the non-overlapping region along x-axis, L'_x (Figure 4(f)). Asymmetry along y-axis is carried out in a similar fashion as shown in Figure 4(g), 4(h), and 4(i).

Asymmetry score across x-axis ($A1$) is calculated using Equations (2) and (3). Similarly, asymmetry across y-axis($A2$) is also calculated using Equations (4) and (5).

$$L'_x = L \oplus L_x \quad (2)$$

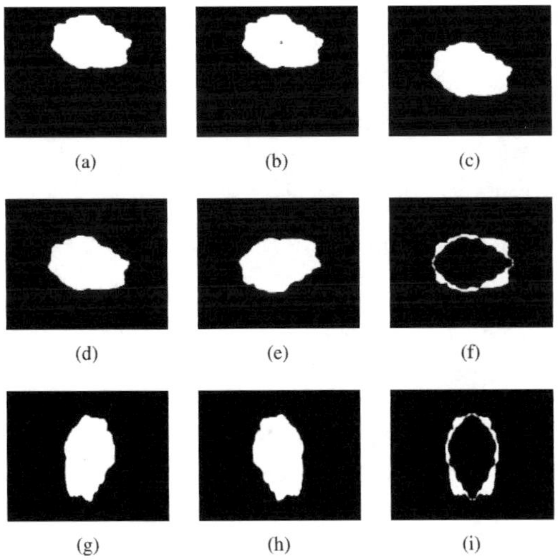

Figure 4: Evaluation of asymmetry across x and y axis

$$A1 = \frac{\text{Area of } L'_{\text{x}}}{\text{Area of } L} \quad (3)$$

$$L'_{\text{y}} = L \oplus L_{\text{y}} \quad (4)$$

$$A2 = \frac{\text{Area of } L'_{\text{y}}}{\text{Area of } L} \quad (5)$$

3.3.2 Border

Border defines the contour of the blob on the skin lesion. A malignant melanoma is highly irregular in nature and can have ragged edges to itself. The border features are $B1$, $B2$, and $B3$ which are Area to perimeter ratio, Compactness index, and Product of Area and Perimeter respectively. $B1$ and $B2$ gives smaller values in case of malignant lesions. $B2$ represents smoothness of the lesion's edges and ranges between 1 and 0. In malignant lesions, the edges are uneven and not smooth thus, giving a $B2$ score of a number closer to 0 whereas a benign lesion will have a $B2$ score of a number closer to 1. Additionally, for malignant melanomas, $B3$ tends to be of greater values. These are calculated by the equations (6), (7), and (8) respectively.

$$B1 = \frac{A}{P} \quad (6)$$

$$B2 = \frac{4\pi A}{P^2} \quad (7)$$

$$B3 = P \times A \quad (8)$$

3.3.3 Color

In determining the color score, six colors are considered important which are: black, dark brown, light brown, blue-gray, red, and white. The segmented image is used as a mask on the original RGB image to get colored segmented image. RGB threshold values for each of the six colors is initialized and the image is transformed into HSV color space. A mask is created using each corresponding color. Bitwise AND operation is performed on the HSV image in order to determine the color mask and active contours. If the length of active contours is found to be greater than zero then that color is assumed to be present in the lesion. Since there are six colors assumed to be present in the lesion, the color score, C, can range from 1 to 6. Two images having color scores 1 and 3 are shown in the Figure 5(a) and Figure 5(b).

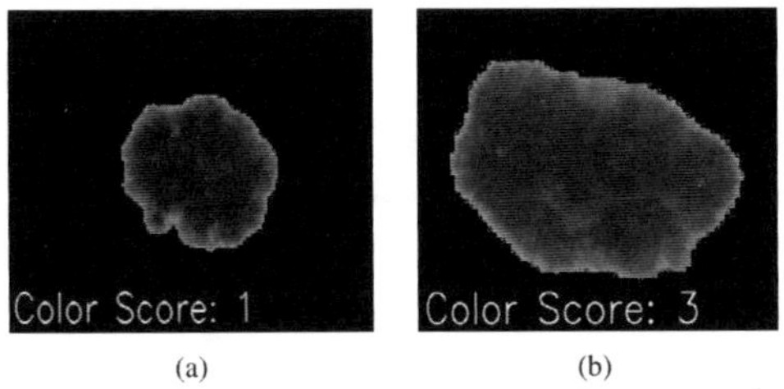

Figure 5: Color scores of two images

3.3.4 Diameter

The diameter of a malignant melanoma may grow in size of over 6mm. The diameter features are $D1$, $D2$, and $D3$ which are Average of lesion diameter, Difference between the major and minor axis' lengths, and Lesion diameter respectively. $D1$ is the average of the diameters Da and Db of the skin lesion. $D2$ is difference of the major axis, D, and minor axis, d. $D3$ is the diameter of the lesion in mm, where M is the magnification factor of the original image and 0.2645 is the factor used to convert the diameter acquired from pixels to mm. These are calculated by the equations (9), (10), and (11) as follows:

$$D1 = \frac{(Da+Db)}{2} \text{where}, Da = \sqrt{\frac{4A}{\pi}}, Db = \frac{D+d}{2} \quad (9)$$

$$D2 = D - d \quad (10)$$

$$D3 = \frac{Da}{M} \times 0.2645 \quad (11)$$

3.4 Classification

After extracting the features, a classifier is trained that uses the features extracted from the input images. Here, a sequential artificial network with four dense layers has been used. The input layer with nine input dimensions ($A1$, $A2$, $B1$, $B2$, $B3$, C, $D1$, $D2$, and $D3$) and a batch size of 10, and the second and third dense layers having a batch size of 50. The elu activation function has been used in the first two layers and the relu activation function in the third layer. The final output dense layer uses the sigmoid activation function. The classification model has been compiled used the Adam optimizer. The loss of the model has been evaluated using Mean Squared Error function.

https://doi.org/10.1051/itmconf/20203203029

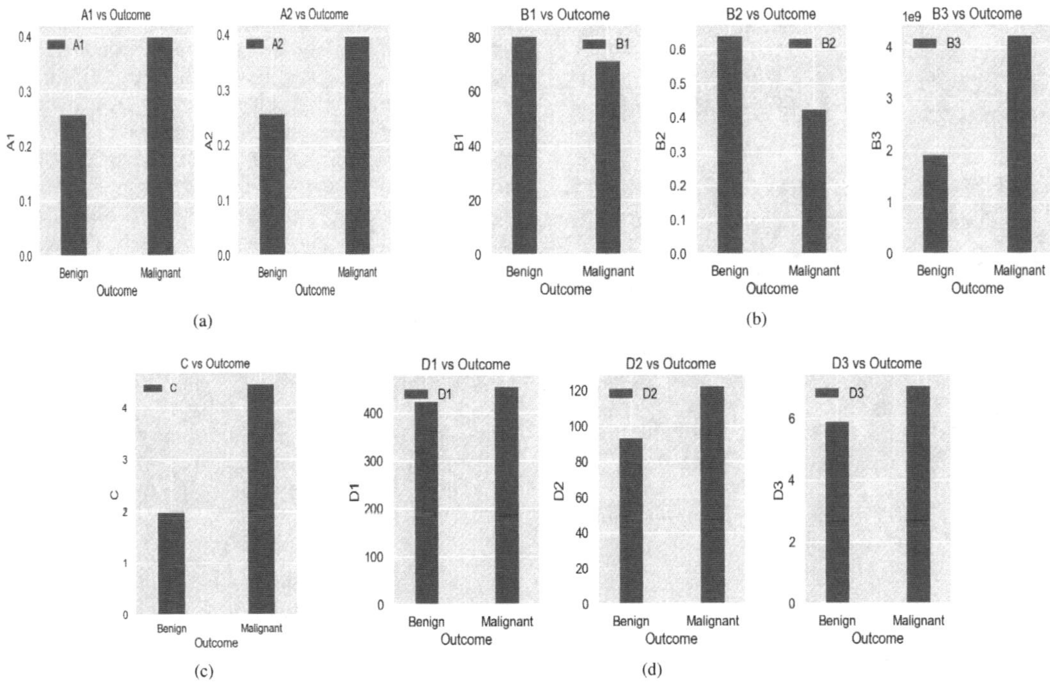

Figure 6: (a): Asymmetry Scores, (b): Border Scores, (c): Color Score, (d): Diameter Scores

4 Results

The diagnostic system proposed in this work has been implemented in Python. For the purpose of testing the system, 25 new images of lesions - 12 benign and 13 malignant - were used. The system could correctly classify the images as 'Benign' or 'Malignant'.

4.1 Feature Analysis

Figure 6(a), 6(b), 6(c), and 6(d) shows a graph representing the asymmetry scores ($A1$ and $A2$), border scores ($B1$, $B2$, and $B3$), color score, C, and diameter scores ($D1$, $D2$, and $D3$) for benign and malignant melanomas. It is observed that in case of malignant melanomas, $A1$ and $A2$ are greater for both axes, due to their asymmetric nature, $B1$ and $B2$ is smaller and $B3$ is greater, $D1$, $D2$, and $D3$ is greater, and finally, C is observed to be greater as the number of colors in them is higher when compared to benign melanomas. It is also noted that malignant melanomas tend to have 2 or more colors present in them.

4.2 System Performance

The performance measures calculated are: Accuracy, Precision, Recall, and F1-score using the Equations 12, 13, 14, and 15 respectively.

$$Accuracy = \frac{TP+TN}{TP+FN+TN+FP} \quad (12)$$

$$Precision = \frac{TP}{TP+FP} \quad (13)$$

$$Recall = \frac{TP}{TP+FN} \quad (14)$$

$$F1-score = \frac{2TP}{2TP+FP+FN} \quad (15)$$

The system gives an accuracy of 89.93% with test error rate of 0.074, precision of 95%, recall of 82.61%, and F1-score of 88.37%. Figure 7 shows the ROC curve of the ANN classifier.

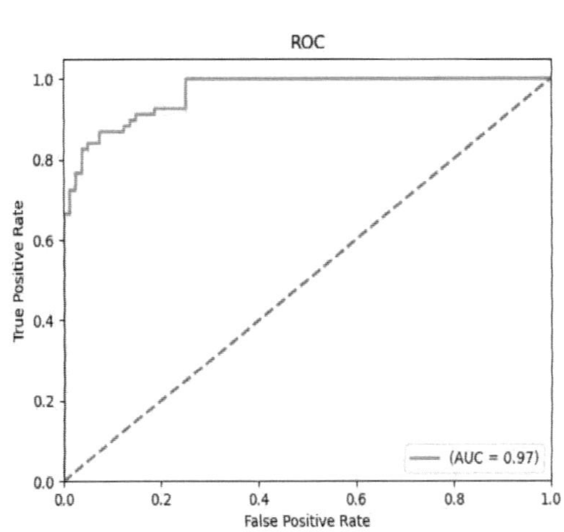

Figure 7: ROC curve of the ANN classifier

4.3 Classification with Different Classifier Models

The features extracted have also been tested with four other classifier models - Decision Tree, Random Forest, Extra Trees, and Gradient Boosting. Figure 8 shows the ROC curves of the different classifiers and Table 3 shows their performance measures.

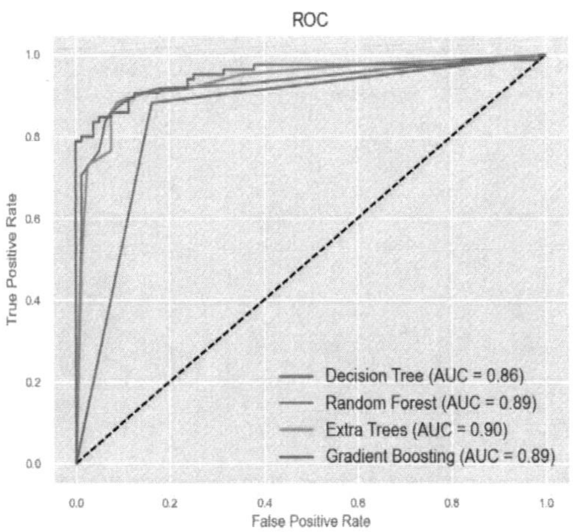

Figure 8: ROC curves of different models

Table 3: Accuracy and AUC of different classifier models

Model	Accuracy (%)	Sensitivity (%)	Specificity (%)
Decision Tree	85.98	87.4	86.8
Random Forest	89.02	87.12	92.88
Extra Trees	89.63	84.66	93.14
Gradient Boosting	88.41	86.03	93.14

It is observed that all the models have AUC of over 0.85 which is considered good for a classifier model. Also, the accuracy, sensitivity, and specificity scores of the models are also above 85% meaning that they can perform fairly well. This shows that the features extracted are appropriate and can be used to feed various classifier models to assist in classifying the skin lesions as benign or malignant.

5 Conclusion and Further Work

The exponential rise of melanoma skin cancer calls for an alternative approach to detect melanomas at an early stage so that it can be cured. The traditional approach to detecting melanomas comprise of carrying out skin biopsy. This method, although widely used, is painful, costly and time-consuming. There is a dire need of an automated process taking over the traditional method that is just as efficient, thus, making it an important area of research. The computer aided system proposed in this paper aims to do the same by using various image processing methods and machine learning algorithms that can help accurately detect melanomas. This system provides an automated system with varied methods for pre-processing, segmentation, feature extraction and classification of image. However, there is still some areas that would require further study. One instance is the segmentation of image in dark-skinned patients. Also, a large amount of image datasets would be used for further improving training the classifier neural network in the future works.

References

[1] World Cancer Research Fund on Skin Cancer Statistics. https://www.wcrf.org/dietandcancer/cancer-trends/skin-cancer-statistics. Accessed 07 Mar 2020

[2] World Health Organization on Climate Change and Human Health. https://www.who.int/globalchange/climate/summary/en/index7.html. Accessed 07 Mar 2020

[3] S. Majumder and M. A. Ullah, *Feature Extraction from Dermoscopy Images for an Effective Diagnosis of Melanoma Skin Cancer*, 2018 10th International Conference on Electrical and Computer Engineering (ICECE), 185-188 (2018). https://doi.org/10.1109/ICECE.2018.8636712

[4] T. Mendonça, P. M. Ferreira, J. S. Marques, A. R. S. Marcal, J. Rozeira, 2013 35th Annual International Conference of the IEEE Engineering in Medicine and Biology Society, 5437-5440 (2013). https://doi.org/10.1109/EMBC.2013.6610779

[5] K. Eltayef, Y. Li, X.Liu, *Detection of Melanoma Skin Cancer in Dermoscopy Images*, J. Phys.: Conf. Ser. 787 012034 (2017). https://doi.org/10.1088/1742-6596/787/1/012034

[6] J. Premaladha, K. S. Ravichandran, *Novel Approaches for Diagnosing Melanoma Skin Lesions Through Supervised and Deep Learning Algorithms*, J. Med Syst **40**, 96 (2016). https://doi.org/10.1007/s10916-016-0460-2

[7] S. Jain, V. Jagtap, N. Pise, *Computer aided Melanoma skin cancer detection using Image Processing*, J. Procedia Computer Science **48**, 735-740 (2015). https://doi.org/10.1016/j.procs.2015.04.209

[8] M. A.Sheha, M. S.Mabrouk, A. Sharawy, *Automatic Detection of Melanoma Skin Cancer using Texture Analysis*, J. Comp App (0975 – 8887) **42-No.20**, 22-26 (2012). https://doi.org/10.5120/5817-8129

[9] A. G. Isasi, B. G. Zapirain, A. Mendez *Melanomas non-invasive diagnosis application based on the ABCD rule and pattern recognition image processing algorithms*, J. Comp in Bio and Med **41, Issue 9**, 742-755, (2011). https://doi.org/10.1016/j.compbiomed.2011.06.010

[10] Z. She, Y. Liu, A. Damatoa, *Combination of features from skin pattern and ABCD analysis for lesion classification*, J. Skin Research and Tech, **13**, 25-33 (2007). https://doi.org/10.1111/j.1600-0846.2007.00181.x

[11] PH2 Database. https://www.fc.up.pt/addi/ph2\%20database.html

[12] N. Otsu, *A Threshold Selection Method from Gray-Level Histograms*, IEEE Transactions on Systems, Man, and Cybernetics, **9, no. 1**, 62-66 (1979). https://doi.org/10.1109/TSMC.1979.4310076

[13] T. F. Chan and L. A. Vese, *Active contours without edges*, IEEE Transactions on Image Processing, **10,no. 2**, 266-277, (2001). https://ieeexplore.ieee.org/document/902291

[14] D. Mumford and J. Shah, *Optimal approximation by piecewise smooth functions and associated variational problems*, Comm. Pure Appl. Math, **42**, 577-685, (1989).

Product Recommendation System based on User Trustworthiness & Sentiment Analysis

Gunjeet Kaur Soor [1*], *Amey* Morje [1*], *Rohit* Dalal [1*], and *Dr. Deepali* Vora[2]

[1]B.E., Information Technology, Vidyalankar Institute of Technology, India
[2]Professor, Information Technology, Vidyalankar Institute of Technology, India

Abstract: The current online product recommendation system based on reviews has many limitations due to randomness in the review patterns. The data which is used are the reviews and ratings from the e-commerce websites. This data might contain fake reviews that make the data uncertain. Due to this, the currently existing systems produce ambiguous results on this present data. Instead of this, the new system uses only genuine reviews, considering the trustworthiness of the user and generates the results in a more significant manner. The proposed system scrapes reviews from different online websites and performs opinion mining and sentiment analysis on it. Other factors like star ratings, the buyer's profile and previous purchases and whether the review has been given after purchasing or not are included. Based on these factors & user trustworthiness, the website from which the user should buy the product will be recommended.

1 Introduction

A product recommendation system predicts and shows the items that a user would like to purchase. It is basically a filtering system. The results might not be entirely accurate. It shows results according to your likes, and recent searches. The idea was generated on the paper which was published in 2017 in IEEE Transactions on Information Forensics and Security which was based on spam detection and fake social media reviews [1].

Recommender Systems have become more useful in recent years. They are utilized in various fields which include movies, music, news, books, research articles, search queries, social tags, and products in general. Mostly used in the digital domain, the majority of today's E-Commerce sites like eBay, Amazon, Flipkart, Alibaba, etc. make use of their proprietary recommendation algorithms in order to better serve the customers with the products they are bound to like [2].

Along with this, the product reviews are also used in the recommendation. Review helpfulness is gaining the attention of practitioners and academics. It helps in reducing risks and uncertainty faced by users in online shopping.

With the growing amount of information on the internet and with a significant rise in the number of users, it has become important for companies to search, map and according to the user's preferences and taste, it provides them with the relevant chunk of information. Chatbots also work on the same working, but they are a little smarter and learn from each product the user views or buys.

2 Literature Survey

There are a number of journals and conference papers that share information about the recommendation systems. The following table lists the key findings and algorithms used after reviewing some of the important papers. [3-11]

Table 1. Summary of Literature Survey

Sr. No.	Authors	Key Findings	Algorithm
1	K L Santhosh Kumar, Jayanti Desai, Jharna	Sentiment Analysis of reviews fetched from Amazon. Naïve Bayes algorithm shows comparatively better results than Logistic	Naïve Bayes classification, Logistic

* Corresponding author: gunjeetks@gmail.com, amey.morje@gmail.com, dalalrohit102@gmail.com

	Majumdar	Regression and SentiWordNet technique. The performance of these algorithms is measured by using quality metrics like Recall, Precision, and F-measure. [3]	Regression, SentiWordNet algorithm
2	Kai Yang, Yi Cai, Dongping Huang, et. al	A sentiment dictionary using external textual data is created and different classification models are compared along with a hybrid model. A hybrid model is made by combining Support Vector Machine (SVM) and Gradient Boosting Decision Tree (GBDT) based on Stacking approach, which is an ensemble learning approach usually used to combine different learning algorithms to get better performance. The baseline model made for verification compares between SVM, GBDT and the hybrid model, in which hybrid model is found to be the most effective. [4]	Support Vector Machine (SVM) and Gradient Boosting Decision Tree (GBDT)
3	S.A.Sadhana, L.SaiRamesh, et. al.	The proposed method based on a monolingual word alignment model (WAM) and for additionally best alignment quality, this approach uses Semi-supervised Word Alignment Model (SWAM) with supervision on alignment. The results show that the true positive rate gradually increases in prediction by the proposed SWAM technique. Experimental results also show that using the sentimental analysis the system provides the result with higher accuracy than the system without sentimental analysis. [5]	Semi- supervised Word Alignment Model
4	Prashast Kumar, Arjit Sachdeva	The process of gathering online end-user reviews for the products or services is automated. These reviews are then analyzed based on the sentiments expressed about specific features. Online product reviews from Flipkart are the inputs to this project, which the system analyzes to generate results (for reviews) which have been sorted according to various geographic regions. These results are also shared with the manufacturers to look at the sentiments and judge the improvisation and deterioration of the Product. [6]	Sentiment Analysis
5	Shaozhong Zhang and Haidong Zhong	For addressing the problem of mining users trust in an E-commerce system, the trust is divided into two categories, direct trust and propagation of trust, which represents a trust relationship between two individuals. [7]	NLProcessor linguistic parser
6	Paitoon Porntrakoon, Chayapol Moemeng	The trustworthiness of an e-vendor is measured in multiple dimensions like the product, price, and shipping. This helps the customers in making a good purchase decision from the user with a high trust score. This is analysed by using multidimensional lexicon and sentiment compensation technique. The accuracy of the proposed method (SenseComp) is compared with manual, sentiment to dimension (S2D) and dimension to sentiment (D2S) methods. The results of the experiment show that the sentiment compensation technique increases the accuracy of SenseComp in all dimensions with an overall accuracy of 93.60% as compared to S2D and D2S methods. [8]	Sentiment Compensation Technique
7	A. Angelpreethi, S. Britto Ramesh Kumar	The aim is to build a feature opinion miner which finds the important feature of the products by analyzing the review or opinion and create an opinion profile for each product which can be used by the customer. For this, the model uses a supervised syntactic approach for opinion mining. The proposed system here uses SentiWordNet for calculating the polarity of the opinion and dependency parsing is used for extracting feature matched opinion word. [9]	SentiWordNet, dependency parsing
8	Evangelos Triantaphyllou and Stuart H. Mann	The Analytic Hierarchy Process (AHP) is an effective approach in dealing with decision problems in the industry. The AHP is a decision support tool. It is used to solve complex decision problems. It works with a multi-level hierarchical structure of objectives,	Analytic Hierarchy Process (AHP)

		criteria, subcriteria, and alternatives. By using a set of pairwise comparisons, the pertinent data are derived. The reuslt of the comparisons is used to obtain the importance of the decision criteria weights, and the relative performance measures of alternative which is in terms of individual decision criterion. If the comparisons are not perfectly consistent, then it provides a mechanism for improving consistency. [10]	
9	Bilal Abu-Salih, Pornpit Wongthongtham, Kit Yan Chan, Dengya Zhu	A fine-grained users' credibility analysis framework for big social data, named CredSaT (Credibility incorporating Semantic analysis and Temporal factor) whose credibility core module is based on three main dimensions (i) distinguishing users of the various domains of knowledge; (ii) a novel metric incorporating a list of fine-grained key attributes is harnessed to create the feature-based ranking model; and (iii) the temporal factor is used to study the users' behaviour over time and reflect this behaviour by means of their domain-based credibility values. Experiments conducted to evaluate this approach validates the applicability and effectiveness of determining highly domain-based trustworthy users, as well as capturing spammers and other low trustworthy users. [11]	AlchemyAPI

2.1 Inferences from Literature Survey

From the above literature survey, it is inferred that sentiment analysis can be performed by using many algorithms but, Naïve Bayes Classifier and Logistic Regression gives optimum results. Out of the two, Logistic Regression proves to be better and works efficiently even on small datasets. For user trustworthiness, AHP is an effective approach in dealing with decision problems using a number of parameters to generate the ranking which is not possible in our case because of limited parameters. Hence, a custom scale would be used for user trustworthiness.

3 Proposed System

The following block diagram shows the flow of how the system will work. It starts with the user searching for a particular product and ends with the recommendation of the website to the user.

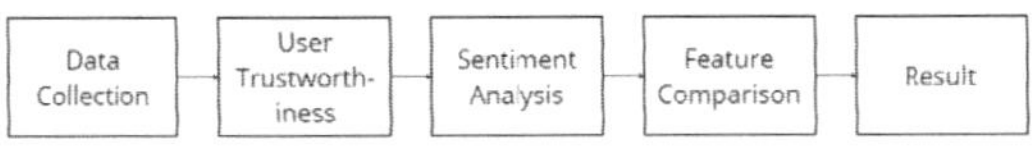

Fig. 1. Block Diagram

The above block diagram can be subdivided into five major blocks as follows:

i. **Data Scraping**
When the user enters the product, the data is collected from various E-commerce websites which are shown, viz. Amazon and Flipkart. This includes the images of the product, features of the product, product ID, star ratings and reviews from each website. All this data is obtained with scrapers which are different for different websites.

ii. **User Trustworthiness**
This block will determine whether the review given by the specific user is trusted or not. For this, various factors of the user like previous reviews, previous purchases, visits, etc. will be taken into consideration. This block is still in progress as it is facing difficulties to obtain the personal information. Rather we are trying to find a new solution.

iii. **Sentiment Analysis**
This block will perform sentiment analysis on the trusted reviews only. For this operation, we will use various python libraries out of which NLTK is an important one for Natural Language Processing. This analysis will categorize the reviews as the positive and negative using the Logistic Regression Model to produce results.

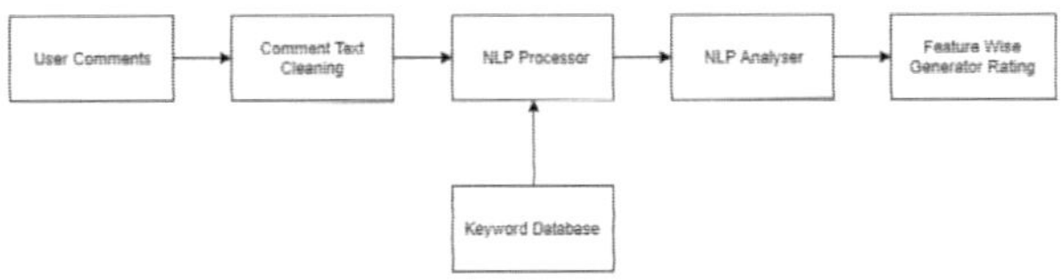

Fig. 2. Sentiment Analysis

iv. **Feature Comparison**
This block compares various other features like cost, etc. which are also collected during the scraping process. These individual run through the sentiment analysis and produce much better results.

v. **Recommendation of Website**
This block finally recommends the user the website from which the user should buy the product on the previous analysis done.

4 Design

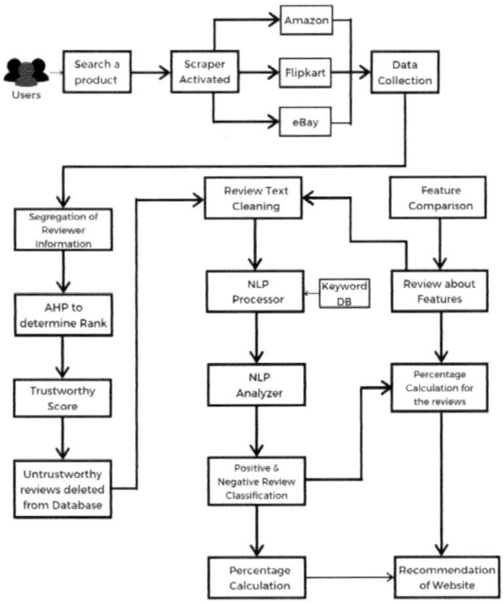

Fig. 3. Flowchart

When a user searches for a product on the web page, the reviews from the e-commerce websites are scraped. The data collected includes the reviewer's details and the review. A rank is provided to the reviewer, which is used to calculate the trustworthy score. Untrustworthy reviews/ fake reviews are removed from the database. Further, the sentiment analysis is carried on the cleaned data using NLP. Features provided by the search item are also considered to calculate the percentage for trustworthiness. All these factors combine and the website from which the user should buy is recommended.

5 Implementation

The proposed design has been implemented block-wise as scrapers for different websites, the trustworthiness model and the sentiment analysis model and in addition, an user interface is developed.

Whenever the user enters the product in the search bar, the initial scraper which is in JavaScript is activated, scrapes the relevant links of Flipkart and Amazon which are stored onto a Firebase database for further use. Now, the exclusive scrapers of Amazon and Flipkart, which are designed in Scrapy, scrape the product reviews which also include the review heading, review text, rating, author, review helpfulness count and whether the purchase is verified or not. Scrapy is a framework in Python, which is generally used for scraping. It helps in scraping large amount of data in lesser time with various features like seamless extraction with IP jumping.

The trustworthiness of the review depends on the user and certain properties of its own which could be used to decide whether they should be included for the sentiment analysis part or not. For a review to be trustworthy, some parameters like how many reviews the user has posted, how useful the reviews have been and determining the genuineness of the review i.e. whether the review is posted after purchasing or not are considered. For Amazon, only the reviews of verified purchase by the reviewer are considered and scraped. The reviews which have more than 10 helpful votes are considered. The review text length must be greater than or equal to 10. For Flipkart, the reviews with certified buyer badge are considered. The importance of the review could be assigned on the basis of likes (upvotes) and dislikes (downvotes). The review text length must be greater than or equal to 10.

The sentiment analysis on the selected reviews is performed by using python and its machine learning libraries and Logistic regression algorithm is applied on the reviews and a percentage of positive and negative reviews are obtained.

The User Interface is designed using the React.js framework and the backend is implemented using Express.js. The connection of this UI with the other elements is done with the help of Flask which is a Python framework. Flask integrates all the things into the UI and the final result is displayed which shows the product with its availability and information and the review sentiment analysis comparison on both the websites.

6 Results

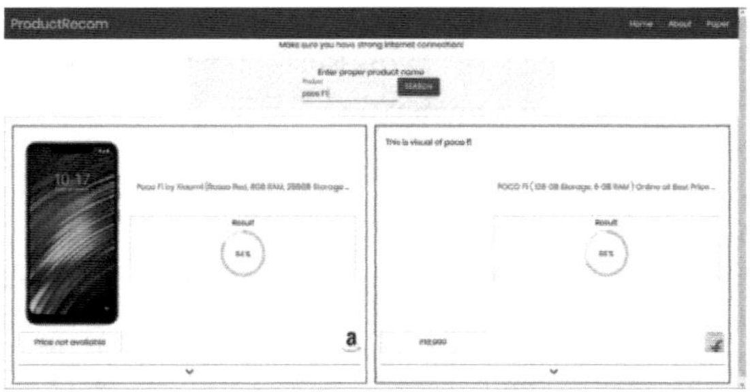

Fig. 4. Recommendation with different percentage

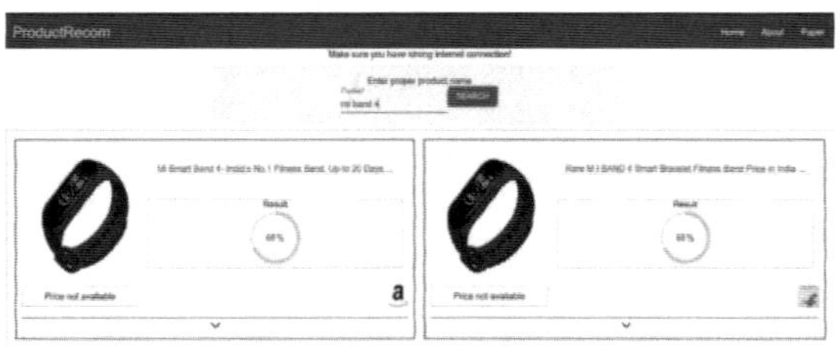

Fig. 5. Recommendation with same percentage

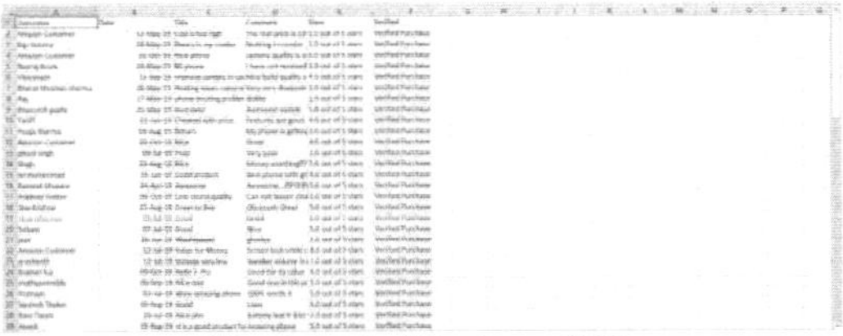

Fig. 6. Fetched Reviews (CSV)

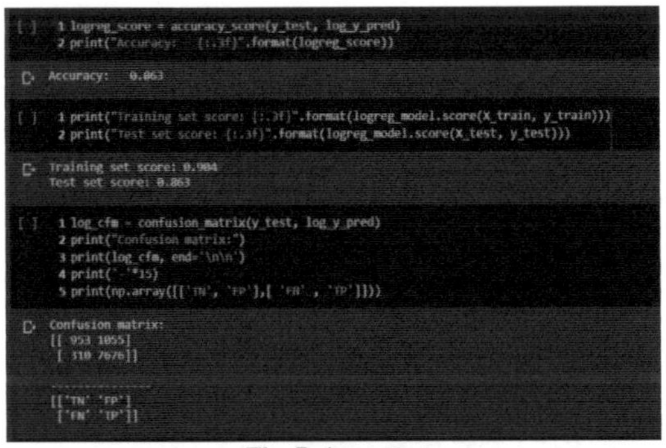

Fig. 7. Accuracy

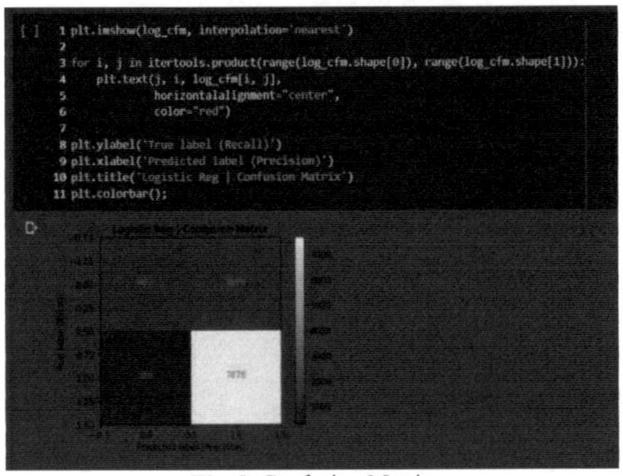

Fig. 8. Confusion Matrix

This is quite obvious that the product whose reviews are more positive will have a higher percentage and hence will be recommended to the user. The complete procedure takes about a minute or so to display the result.

In figure 4, the product Poco F1 is searched, to which the photo and other specifications from both the sites are made available. Then, the reviews from both the sites are scrapped and sentiment analysis is performed. It is seen that the Amazon reviews are 84% positive while the Flipkart reviews are 68% positive. Thus, the site recommends the Amazon website to the user which gets highlighted with a green border. It is seen that the price is not available for the Amazon site while the photo is not available for the Flipkart one. This is because sometimes the product may not be available at the moment or there might not be a fixed price of the product. While in case of Flipkart, it is observed that the website blocks the attempts to scrape after a few continuous scrape attempts are made.

It is observed that the percentage of the sentiment analysis result might be the same. At such times, if only a single website is recommended, then it could be considered that the application favours a certain website which should not be the case. So, an example of this is shown in the figure 5. The product MI Band 4 has same result percentage of 68%. Hence, it depends on the user's personal choice to buy from a specific website. For the application's recommendations, both the websites are highlighted as green and recommended.

Whenever there is huge difference between Training and Testing set, it is observed that there might be some inaccuracy in the model. The results show that the Training set accuracy is 90.4% while that of Testing set is 86.3% which is a reasonable difference.

7 Conclusion

In our work, we have covered the mining of reviews from e-commerce websites on which sentiment analysis is performed along with checking of the reviewer's trustworthiness. Many alterations and experiments were performed for Sentiment Analysis and the over-fitting difference was reduced to approximately 4%. Another option would be to adopt an approach based on neural networks to further reduce over-fitting. A dedicated user interface is developed for the execution of the tasks and to display the recommended e-commerce website to the user.

8 References

1. S. Shehnepoor, M. Salehi, R. Farahbakhsh, N. Crespi, IEEE Transactions on Information Forensics and Security, **12** (2017)
2. "Towards Data Science Blog related on Recommendation Engines", Medium Blog (2017)
3. K.L.S. Kumar, J. Desai, J. Majumdar, IEEE ICCIC, (2016)
4. K. Yang, Y. Cai, D. Huang, J. Li, Z. Zhou, X. Lei, IEEE International Conference on Big Data and Smart Computing (BigComp), (2017)
5. S.A. Sadhana, L. SaiRamesh, A. Kannan, S. Sabena, S. Ganapathy, 2nd International Conference on Recent Trends and Challenges in Computational Models (2017)
6. P. Kumar, A. Sachdeva, 5th International Conference Confluence The Next Generation Information Technology Summit (2014)
7. S. Zhang, H. Zhong, IEEE Access Volume **7** (2019)
8. P. Porntrakoon, C. Moemeng, ECTI-CON, **15** (2018)

9. A. Angelpreethi, S.B.R. Kumar, WCCCT (2017)

10. E. Triantaphyllou, S.H. Mann, International Journal of Industrial Engineering: Applications and Practice, **2**, No. 1, pp. 35-44 (1995)

11. B. Abu-Salih, P. Wongthongtham, K.Y. Chan, D. Zhu, Journal of Information Sciences (2018)

Optimization of Data using Artificial Bee Colony Optimization with Map Reduce

Parikshit Patil[1], *Hrishikesh Mhatre*[1], *Ruchita Patil1*, *Apurva Shinde*[1], *Bharti Joshi*[1]
[1]Department of Computer Engineering , Ramrao Adik Institute of Technology, Nerul.

Abstract - We are developing an idea through this paper which would give any question the perfect and best answer. Existing system is not capable of classifying according to different patterns. This compromises with efficiency of the system and quality of final result. In this project Parallel Clustering optimization method is formed by amalgamation of Map-Reduce with Ant Bee Colony Optimization Technique for improving the efficiency and success of the data science method. In addition, related running services on a Hadoop network are predicted with the help of Map Reduce algorithm.

Keywords: Map Reduce, Hadoop, Ant Bee Colony Optimization.

1. INTRODUCTION

The scope of data science and analytics is getting stronger day by day. Knowledge created by analyzing and processing data obtained from different sources can become useful in different ways. Instead of developing new and different algorithms to reach the efficient and satisfactory results, optimization of available techniques can be an option. Modification of core method used to implement those algorithms can be a better option [1]. The K-Means range algorithm is suited to e-commerce application development. The clustering algorithm works efficiently for numerical and categorical data as well as on large data sets clustering [2]. A novel hybrid optimization algorithm called BBO-PSO is proposed, which combines biogeography-based optimization with particle swarm optimization In this optimization algorithm, BBO will be used for local search while PSO will be used for mapping global data, which will allow the algorithm to have powerful search capabilities in solution space [3]. Insists strongly on increasing the convolution cycle speed but to reduce the difficulty of the convolution measurement [4]. The Particle Swarm optimization techniques instead of Ant Bee Colony Optimization with map reduce for maintaining clustering quality. New techniques need to be applied to parallel computing principles in order to be able to scale with that data set sizes [5]. Some algorithms that are capable of handling large and semi-structured data, are K-Means and ISODATA. The working analysis is carried out based on different factors, namely execution time, squared error sum, and R-square. Essentially, clustering is an unsupervised learning technique splitting into consequential groups of different similar data items. -category that is named as a cluster has similar object categories and divergent objects in other groups [6]. Sparse and compact zones should be consistent by clustering. Absolute dispersal trends and excellent collaboration lead to other areas of research such as text analysis, spatial database technology, and data extraction. Clustering was a vigorous research due to the enormous amount of data storage in databases and repositories. The experimental effects of various clustering approaches to perform reprovision of required information from massive repositories of data to make successful decisions on multiple applications. Analysis of the clusters is a difficult area. There are some distinct clustering requirements to handle high-dimensional data, user-defined limitations, noistic data, and to establish few input details by information of prior domain by using the type of attributes and the handling outliers. Our program is aimed at improving the current system while making the clustering techniques and the existing system more efficient.

2. LITERATURE SURVEY

2.1 In [4] proposed MR-CPSO algorithm increases the effectiveness of cluster quality. With growing data set sizes, it scales very well and achieves a very similar linear speed while retaining the cluster quality. The parameters focused while analyzing result of proposed system were scalability, speedup and clustering quality. In this system, on increasing number of nodes, the dataset sizes with the same ratio. But the PSO algorithm (which is the core algorithm used) is not so efficient as compared to other advance optimization algorithms like Artificial Bee Colony Optimization.

2.2 In [6] proposed the detailed analysis of performance and also the characterization of Hadoop k-means iterations by scaling different processor micro-architecture parameters. This system is based on the performance of k-means algorithm based on the hardware being used. Comparison regarding Intel and AMD processor is also discussed in this paper. The focused factors for analysis used in this paper are Total Run Time, Number of Sockets, and Number of Cores.

2.3 Authors in paper [3] proposed a winogard algorithm to improve the normal Convolution Neural Network. More precisely, it is related to the acceleration of widely used small convolution sizes. This improved algorithm is capable of reducing model sizes and increasing inference speed which leads to the increasing the ability of hardware accelerators and kernels to work with integer data. But this algorithm fails to maintain the efficiency of result with increasing data (or big dataset). Also, the quality of cluster is not guaranteed.

2.4 In paper[5] authors have derived evolutionary based clustering methods from the existing hard clustering methods. The main objective of the model was to find the optimum results. The different clustering algorithms used in this paper are ISODATA, K-means, Leader. The performance analysis of different clustering methods reveal that the rate of convergence is greater than the methods of partitioning. The different parameters used execution time, sum of squared errors, rms standard deviation. But, most important parameter like number of iterations is ignored in this evaluation. This algorithm is capable of giving better results irrespective of fitness value of different clustering algorithms Leader. The performance analysis of different clustering methods reveals that the rate of convergence is greater than the methods ofpartitioning. The different parameters used execution time, sum of squared errors, rms standard deviation. But, most important parameter like number of iterations is ignored in this evaluation. This algorithm is capable of giving better results irrespective of fitness value of different clustering algorithms.

2.5 Authors in paper [6] focused on inventing an algorithm which consists of amalgamation of Map Reduce and Artificial Bee Colony Optimization. In together the final system is called as Adaptive Artificial Bee Colony optimization. The algorithm is then compared with existing optimization algorithms like Artificial Bee Colony Optimization and particle swarm optimization. After analyzing the dataset, it is observed that new technique is very much efficient in all the fields like number of iterations required to get results, execution time. It also enhances the effectiveness of existing system. It reduces the search space thereby enhancing the time factor. The only disadvantage of this system is that there are no patterns introduced according to results we want. Thus, this leads to formation of unnecessary clusters which in turn reduces the efficiency of the system (increasing execution time, number of iterations unnecessarily). Table 1 represents the survey of Existing System done in this section.

Table 1. Survey of Existing System.

Sr. no.	Title of the paper	Algorithm	Advantages	Disadvantages	Result
1.	Parallel Particle swarm optimization algorithm [2]	PSO algorithm with Map Reduce	1. With Rising data set sizes it scales very well. 2.It achieves clustering quality.	Clustering algorithm is not so efficient and fast as compared to Artificial Bee Colony Optimization	The dataset scales with the increasing number of nodes.
2.	Performance characterizationand analysis for Hadoop K-means iteration.[4]	K-means	Data efficiency is high	Efficiency of the result is mostly affecteddue to the number of cores.	Any changes to the micro-architecture processor parameters and to estimate performance or runtime can be accepted by the model. All the test cases generate error margin of five percent
3.	A parallel optimization of fast algorithm of Convolution Neural networkon CPU.[5]	Convolution Neural Network based on winogard algorithm	1.It is more useful to speed upthealgorithm. 2.Reduces the complexity of CNN.	1. Data efficiency decreases with increasing data set sizes. 2.Quality of Cluster is not guaranteed.	Used GLOFS to increase the amount by about 30 times.
4.	Performance analysis of partition and evolutionary Clustering Methods on various Cluster Validation Criteria.[6]	K-means, Leader, ISODATA	Different performance measures like execution time, sum of squared errors, rms standard deviation are discussed.	Important measure i.e., no of iterations is ignored.	In the simulation process, the algorithm gives the better outcome in the aspect of quantization error better outcome, though the fitness value for k-means falls below the local minima.
5.	Performance measures analysis based on parallel clustered optimization techniques for I-Commerce.[7]	Map Reduce Artificial Bee Colony Optimization Particle Swarm Optimization	Enhances the effectiveness and performance of me- Commerce.	In case of large datasets, many clusters are formed thereby reducing the efficiency of algorithm.	Proposed algorithm has shorter runtime than PSO. Enhanced searching ability in solution space.

3. PROBLEM DEFINITION

The data should be used at maximum efficiency and less processing time so the map reduce technique is used with simplified datasets that is obtain by applying pattern on datasets then Artificial Bee Colony optimization is applied. To compare the performance of Artificial Bee Colony Optimization on the different datasets (Map Reduce and Non-Map Reduce datasets). Compare the different datasets according to their execution time, no of iteration, size etc. To simplify datasets according to the type of database.

4. PROPOSED METHODOLOGY

The proposed algorithm for this paper is Artificial Bee Colony Optimization using Map Reduce.

Map Reduce: Map Reduce algorithm helps for processing data in parallel manner. This reduces time by distributing data in different nodes. As its name suggests, it contains two phases. They are as follows:

Map: In this section, keys and their respective values are mapped with each other. The tasks performed in Map phase are as follows:

The data is splitted into multiple chunks and given as the input to different node for parallel processing.

In next step, each key is mapped to the respective value.

The data is then passed to the reducer phase.

4.1.2 Reduce: This phase processes the data received from Map stage and produces the final output. The tasks performed in Reduce phase are as follows:

The data received from Map phase is shuffled and then arranged in organized way.

In this step, values of same keys are added and the data is reduced.

This is the final step of Reduce phase as well as Map Reduce. In this step, final output is saved into the data block.

In this way Map Reduce helps to improve the efficiency of data by storing and representing data in the form of key-value pair.

In this paper, we have incorporated Map Reduce with patterns which will help to store and use database according to the user needs. This avoids the unnecessary cluster formation.

The dataset processed with Map Reduce is Further processed with the help of Artificial Bee Colony Optimization and the performance is measured on the basis of parameters like execution time, iterations.

Artificial honey bees is made up of three types of individuals: employees, on lookers and scouts.

The Employee Bees and Onlooker Bees exploit the nectar sources around the bee hive this corresponds to the exploitation phase while the Scout Bees explore the solution domain this is the exploration phase.

Employed bees go back to their nectar source to recruit on looker bees through the honey bee waggle dance. The number of dance repetitions performance by the worker depends on the quality of the food source.

A scout bee start searching randomly around the hive to find a new necter source around it.

The algorithm for Artificial Bee colony Optimization is as Follows:

Initialization: - Use the random distribution method to initialize all possible solutions in a search space.

Employed phase search: -Create a new solution and change the fitness number as modified solution with the greatest possible fitness for any solution.

If possibility is improved modify the solution (If fre==0: tag 2) End loop (Until exit condition) and search optimized Result.

1+(1+fre) if fre > 0 (1)

1+absolute(fre) if fre < 0 (2)

Where fitness= fi is the cost value of solution for neighboring food source

jk = yjk+r(yjk-ylk) (3)

r=any real random no [0,1] (4)

Where, yjk = yk min + rand (0,1) (yk max – yk min) j= no of ways to find solution

j= no of trails (5)

Distributions of probability: -Find potential candidate likelihood. If used bees are searched, the info of the highest hierarchy is passed. The probability of which segment depends is to find the best bees for honey.

on fitness value.

j= fitness j/j=1 n fitness (6)

Food collection by top-line bee Food from different places is scanned. Apply map reduce the cycle and produces the next nearest cluster by K-means. If quality is determined based on fitness interest, the bees test the minimum distance & quality of food

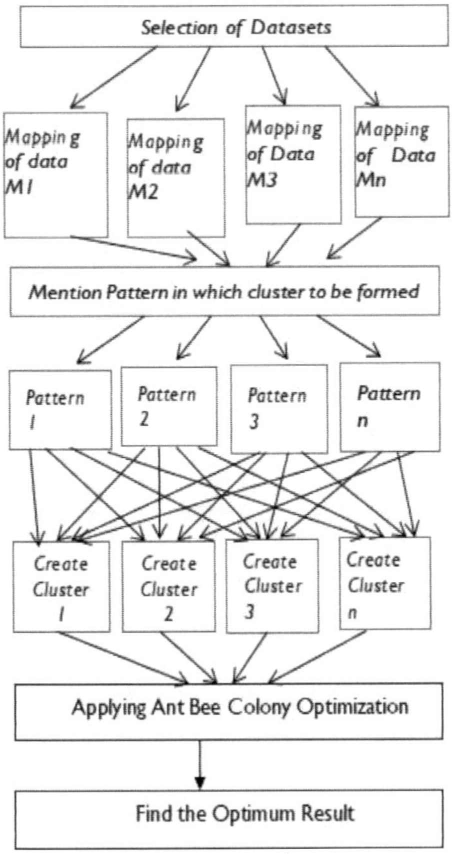

5. IMPLEMENTATION AND RESULTS

The Map Reduce algorithm with pattern has done its work flawlessly. The data sets used is the record of flights (Previous three months). The patterns apply for this data are able to find the best utilized flights where the passenger count is less than number of trips. (Patterns can be changed according to the problem statement or requirements).

The results of the map Reduce are further passed to the Artificial Bee Colony Optimization and the database is processed. The Best cost obtain in each iteration is 0 and it is consistent up to the last iteration. Also, the map reduce data is able to give results with a smaller number of iterations as compared to non-Map Reduce data. This also leads to faster processing of the data. Results are:

5.1. The data is passed through map reduce algorithm with pattern which gave value in key value pairs.

5.2. Map Reduce algorithm with pattern has done its work flawlessly.

5.3. In Map Reduce, we got specific results according to the patterns introduced. The results of the map Reduce are further passed to the Artificial Bee Colony Optimization and the data obtained is processed.

5.4. The Best cost obtain in each iteration is 0 and it is consistent up to the last iteration. Also, the no. of iteration required to process Map Reduce data are very much less than that of required to process Non-Map Reduce data. Also, the different time taken by Artificial Bee Colony to process Map Reduce data as compared to that of non-map reduce data is significant. This shows that introduced map reducing along with pattern improves time efficiency of ABC. Following table shows the effect of map reduce on various factors of ABC. Table 2 explains results obtained in this section.

Table 2 : Results obtained using ABC Algorithms.

ABC Result		
Parameters	With map reduce	Without map reduce
Time	2.15565 s	79.8255 s
Iterations	147	1000

6.CONCLUSION

In this paper, Map Reduce and other parallel cluster optimization techniques are mixed up to set up the hybrid optimization algorithm. The different techniques integrate and extract the characteristics of both the Map Reduce and a particular technique Improve the quality of the search and high local search time in global search. Also the system can be incorporated with different patterns according to the user needs which in turn increase the efficiency and quality of cluster produced. The new optimization algorithm therefore has a good solution space searching capability and pattern is used for getting optimal results with less iterations.

The Future scope can be this Paper is Compare the performance of different parallel cluster Optimization techniques using different measures like 'iterations' , 'time'. To build the system which will cluster the data set according to the patterns. To choose perfect cluster Optimization techniques for a specific data based on their performance.

REFERENCES

1. Georgios P. Papamichail, Dimitrios P. Papamichail , "The k-means range algorithm for personalized data clustering in e-commerce", European Journal of Operational Research, ELSEVIER,2007.

2. Ibrahim Aljarah and Simone A. Ludwig ,"Parallel Particle Swarm optimization Clustering Algorithm". Fourth World Congress on Nature and Biologically Inspired Computing,IEEE, 2012

3. Gang Cheng, Chao Lv, Shi Yan, Li Xu , "A Novel Hybrid Optimization Algorithm Combined with BBO and PSO",in Chinese Control and Decision Conference ,IEEE, 2016.

4. Joseph Issa, "Performance characteristics and analysis for Hadoop k-Means iteration,'Issa Journal of cloud computing:Advances, system, SpringerOpen,2016.

5. JiaHao Hunag, Tiejun wang, , Xuhui Zhu, Min Wei, Tao Wu, Xi Wu, Min Huang,"A Parallel Optimization of Fast Algorithm of convolution Neural network on CPU", 10'thInternational Conference on Measuring Technology and Mechatronics Automation,IEEE, 2018.

6. R. S. M. Lakshmi Patibandle, N. Veeranjaneyulu, 'Performance Analysis ofPartition and Evolution Clusterin

Methos on Various Cluster Validation Criteria'er Open, 2018.

7. Mr.Likhesh Kolhe, Dr. Vaishali Khairnar, Dr. Ashok kumar jetwa;' Performance Measures Analysis Using Parallel Clustered Optimization techniques For I-Commerce,"8th International Conference on cloud computing, data science Enginnering,IEEE,2018.

8. https;//drive.google.com/open?id=1rZsvBXPhl NeBMZRqKINhpGUJrYTqNqc

9. https://drive.google.com/open?id=1pkVTQCd94EA6NGuw_ WRQrOjt52b37PVu.

10. https://drive.google.com/open?id=1jBydlmonXOmr1SrhJWv c6CZgsqrnR

ITM Web of Conferences **32**, 03032 (2020) https://doi.org/10.1051/itmconf/20203203032
ICACC-2020

A Multilayer Hybrid Machine Learning Model for Diabetes Detection

Sahil Parab[1,*], *Piyush* Rathod[1,**], *Durgesh* Patil[1,***], and *Vishwanath* Chikkareddi[1,****]

[1]Ramrao Adik Institute Of Technology
Navi Mumbai
India

Abstract. Diabetes Detection has been one of the many challenges which is being faced by the medical as well as technological communities. The principles of machine learning and its algorithms is used in order to detect the possibility of a diabetic patient based on their level of glucose concentration , insulin levels and other medically point of view required test reports. The basic diabetes detection model uses Bayesian classification machine learning algorithm, but even though the model is able to detect diabetes, the efficiency is not acceptable at all times because of the drawbacks of the single algorithm of the model. A Hybrid Machine Learning Model is used to overcome the drawbacks produced by a single algorithm model. A Hybrid Model is constructed by implementing multiple applicable machine learning algorithms such as the SVM model and Bayesian's Classification model or any other models in order to overcome drawbacks faced by each other and also provide their mutually contributed efficiency. In a perfect case scenario the new hybrid machine learning model will be able to provide more efficiency as compared to the old Bayesian's classification model.

1 Introduction

Diabetes mellitus also known as diabetes, is a metabolic disorders in which high blood sugar levels are found in the patients body over prolonged period. Frequent urination, increased thirst, and increased hunger can be said to be the symptoms of suspected high sugar level in the patients body. It can lead to many complication cases and issues if the disorder is left untreated.
Diabetes as a metabolic disease have already affected strong number of people worldwide. Its incidence rates can be seen to be increasing exponentially every year. If not treated at the earliest stage of detection, diabetes-related complications and disorders in vital organs of the patients body may turn fatal. Detection of diabetes in the initial phases of the disorder is very crucial for the required treatment routine in order to prevent further complications. From healthcare perspective, machine learning is one of the attractive interest for both medical as well as pharmaceutical researchers.In medical domain where the symptoms of the disorder rely on each other, the machine learning algorithms which are optimized in interpreting the relationships between the features and outcomes is crucial. Heath care needs to understand and use machine learning as the futuristic concept and tool which needs to be deployed in real world using an incremental approach.
Inclination towards the proposed system is due to the lack of accurate and inefficient diabetes detection Systems. This inefficiency in the existing models is due to the complex symptoms that point to different diseases. The crucial part about the idea of the proposed system is that it can detect diabetes based on the probability of a symptom which uses the mathematical model for more accuracy, and the idea sought to achieve the implementation is using multiple machine learning algorithms and summarize their results using a mathematical model.

2 Literature Survey

Significant research has been done so far using the single machine learning algorithm approach in the context of diabetes diagnosis.
The discussion on finding information from medical sources and its importance in order to make an effective medical diagnosis is discussed by the Bayesian Network for Diabetes Prediction[1]. The Naive Bayes model was constructed by applying the classifier on modified preprocessed data set. Finally weka was used to do simulation, and the accuracy of the resulting model was 72.3.
The implementation of k-means dependent noise reduction technique[2] is easy to implement, but offers less productivity and needs more computational power which was observed during the study.
While the process that includes data recovery with neural network requires less computation, but offers 85 higher efficiency, the method that can be used to recover data with neural network is more acceptable.
K-means and decision tree[3] have better accuracy than other Type 2 diabetes classification frameworks. In the related studies With the rapidly increasing need for medical data processing, the proposed model can be quite helpful

*e-mail: parab.sahil.16ce1061@gmail.com
**e-mail: rathod.piyush.16ce2011@gmail.com
***e-mail: patil.durgesh.16ce6101@gmail.com
****e-mail: vishwanath.c@rait.ac.in

to physicians and doctors for decision making regarding their patients, as they can make more informed judgments by using such an efficient model.

The study carried out by Rubaiat Y.,et al.[4] uses learning algorithms and activation functions which play a crucial role in solving the neural network problem. Compared to ReLU and leaky ReLU ,the activation units show good result for the pima data set as ELU and SELU does not removes the neuronal negative outputs. Lack of adequate accuracy has been seen over some of the algorithms such as multi layer feed forward network[5] for detection of diabetes. So a bit more optimization based on curriculum learning could be applied in the future and check if that improves the outcome. On the basis of distance the data can be rearranged from classifier as rearrangement of data by probabilistic approach doesn't work well.

In Intelligible Support Vector Machines[6] for Diagnosis of Diabetes Mellitus the proposed model uses support vector machines (SVMs) along with additional explanation module for the diagnosis of diabetes mellitus. The model is a new hybrid model for diagnosis in medical, which uses various techniques of machine learning. In particular, for sampling and model building, an unsupervised and supervised learning algorithm is used, respectively, accompanied by a rule-based description section. The model used is SVMs for diabetes diagnosis and prediction, where an additional component for rule-based explanation is used to provide understanding.

The ensemble learning module[7] is used in conjunction with support vector machine[8] that converts black box of SVM decisions into clear and transparent rules. The classification system in ensemble learning utilizes Random Forest (RF) rule induction methodology[8] to establish inexpensive and feasible evaluation criteria for diabetes diagnosis. These rule sets can be considered as a diagnostic second opinion and a tool to screen individuals with undiagnosed diabetes.

M. A. Helal,et al.[9] used several classification algorithm and used them to analyze medical data in order to optimize classifier performance for diabetes and cancer prediction. The data sets used are from machine learning repository at the University of California-Irvine (UCI).The classifiers used are Ensemble Method Decision tree classifier (DTC), K- nearest neighbor (KNN), Naive Bayes(NB), Random Forest (RF), and Perceptron algorithm. For testing purpose K-fold cross validation was used with number of folds k=10. The data set is tested 10 times using K-fold cross which helps classifier to generate higher accuracy. Accuracy is calculated using the values of F-score, recall and precision which are generated using confusion matrix.

S. Lekha,et al.[10] proposes a methodology to improve the overall performance of the applications for real-time detection. This suggests an updated deep learning convolution neural network algorithm combined with vector supporting devices to address the limitations of widely implemented machine learning algorithms. The architecture of the convolution neural network is modified by replacing the multi-layer perceptron classifier fully connected with the SVM algorithm. The dividing technique of the data set into subset, made an optimal classification result. The classification done using several decision tree shows better results, when the data set is divided into subsets using technique such as K-means clustering[11]. Additionally, the classification accuracy of MLNN with LM obtained by the study presented by Temurtas,et al.[12] using correct training was better than those obtained by other studies for the conventional validation method. The multi layer neural network when used with Damped least-squares method yield better result as compared to the other validation method. The modified algorithm optimizes the overall performance and reduces computational complexity compared to the techniques already in use.

3 Working Materials And Algorithms

The data set used in order to test the proposed system is the Pima Indian Diabetes data set of National Institute of Diabetes and Digestive and Kidney Diseases.The data set is composed of total 768 instances and eight numerical attributes represents each of the patient in the data set.
These 8 attributes are:-

- Number of times pregnant
  Min Value : 0 and Max Value : 17
- Plasma glucose concentration of two hours
  Min Value : 0 and Max Value : 199
- Diastolic blood pressure
  Min Value : 0 and Max Value : 122
- Triceps skin fold thickness
  Min Value : 0 and Max Value : 99
- 2-hours Serum insulin
  Min Value : 0 and Max Value : 846
- Body mass index
  Min Value : 0 and Max Value : 67.1
- Diabetes pedigree function
  Min Value : 0.078 and Max Value : 2.42
- Age
  Min Value : 21 and Max Value : 81

The individual machine learning algorithms used as the basic building blocks for the proposed system are:

- **Naive Bayes Classifier**
  Naive Bayes is a technique of classification with a notion that describes all features as separate and unrelated to each other. It determines that the status of a specific characteristic in a class has not been impacted by the status of another characteristic in any way.
  Algorithm:-

  1.Read the training data set.

  2.Standard deviation and mean is calculated of the predictor variables in each class.

  3.Repeat:
  The Gauss density equation is used to calculate probability of fi in each class, until the probability of all predictor variables has been calculated.

  4.Calculate the probability for each class.

https://doi.org/10.1051/itmconf/20203203032

5.Fetch the greatest probability.

Mathematical equation for Naive Bayes Classifier:-

$$P(c \mid x) = \frac{P(x \mid c)P(c)}{P(x)} \tag{1}$$

Here,
P(c | x) is Posterior Probability
P(x | c) is Likelihood Probability
P(c) is Class Prior Probability
P(x) is Predictor Prior Probability

- **Decision Tree Classifier**
Decision Tree can be classified as the machine learning algorithm for the supervised classification problems.In the proposed hybrid model, the working of the decision tree is to predict required class with respect to the decision rule for the prior data.
Algorithm:-

1.Begin the tree with the root node, which contains the complete data set.

2.Find the best attribute in the data set using Attribute Selection Measure (ASM).

3.Divide the root node into subsets that contains possible values for the best attributes.

4.Generate the decision tree node, which contains the best attribute.

5.Recursively make new decision trees using the subsets of the data set created in step -3. Continue this process until a stage is reached where you cannot further classify the nodes and called the final node as a leaf node.

Mathematical equation for entropy of a specific node for Decision Tree Classifier:-

$$E(S) = -\sum_{i=1}^{n}(p_i)log(p_i) \tag{2}$$

- **K-Nearest Neighbour clustering**
KNN can be used for statistical problems both in classification and in regression. It is however more commonly used in industry classification issues.
Algorithm:-

1.Data is loaded.

2.Set the value of k.

3.Iterate from 1 to total number of training instances, in order to obtain the predicted class.

4.Euclidean Distance method is used here to calculate distance among the elements of test data and each instances of training data.

5.In ascending order sort the calculated distances based on distance values.

6.From the sorted array get top k rows.

7.Fetch thc maximum frequent class of these rows.

8.Return the predicted class.

The mathemaical equation for the euclidean distance :-

$$D(A, B) = \sqrt{\sum_{i=1}^{n}(A_i - B_i)^2} \tag{3}$$

- **Support Vector Machine**
Support Vector Machine comes under the classification-based supervised machine learning model. A SVM's objective is to find the best and the highest-margin separating hyper plane between the given two classes of the training set.
Algorithm:-

1.Load the data set.

2.Define the features and the target.

3.Before building the SVM algorithm model, Split the data set into test and training set.

4.Build the support vector machine model by importing the SVC function Sklearn SVM module.

5.Predict values using the SVM algorithm model.

6.Evaluate the Support Vector Machine model.

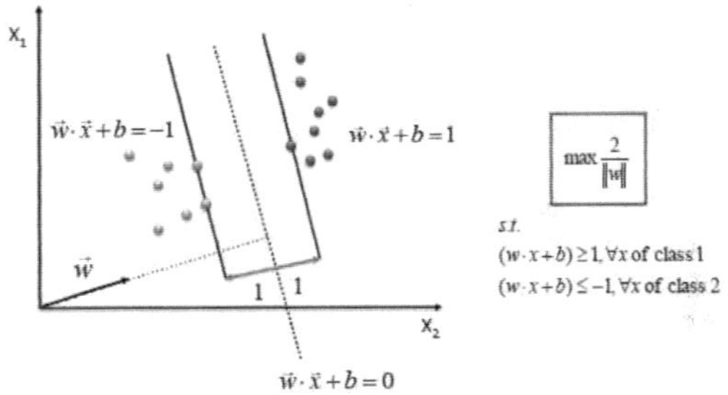

Figure 1. Optimal hyper plane to maximize the width of the margin (w)

- **Artificial Neural Networks**
The Artificial Neural Network (ANN) is known as the method of mathematically representing human neurons by expressing their learning and generalization capabilities.
Algorithm:-

1.Load the data set.

2.To compute the activation values of the Hidden nodes, the inputs from the data set and the linkages are utilized.

3.In order to compute the activation values of the output nodes, the activation values of hidden nodes found previously and linkages to output are utilized.

4.Re calibrate all the linkages between output nodes and hidden nodes to find the error rate for the output node.

5.Cascade down the errors to hidden node by using the weights and error calculated at the output node.

6.Weights among input nodes and hidden nodes are re calibrated.

7.Repeat the process till the model meets the criteria for convergence.

8.The activation rate of the output nodes is used to find linkage weights score.

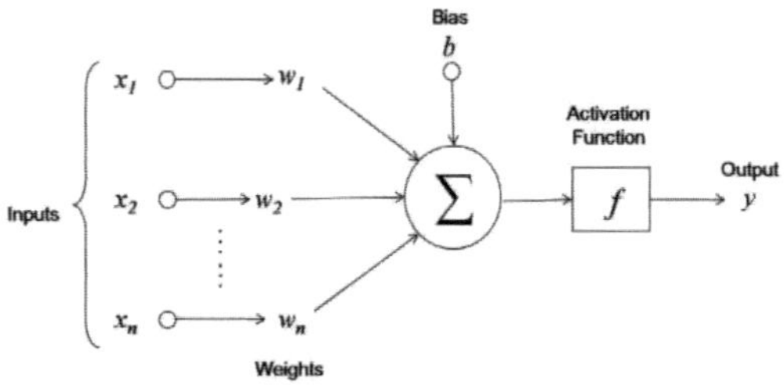

Figure 2. Artificial Neural Network Model

4 Proposed System

The Proposed model is divided into two phases i.e. Training phase and Detection phase.
In training phase, all the machine learning algorithms will be training on the given data set and will be testing their accuracy on the data set.
In detection phase, the machine learning algorithms will be using a fresh input from the data set in order to produce their own classification based on their training from the training phase. These classifications will further be summarized in order to produce final single classification of the detection phase.
It should be observed that the proposed model is not being trained directly on the data set but is indirectly relying on the individual machine learning algorithms and their training results in order to use it in its detection phase.
The basic machine learning algorithms used as the building blocks for the proposed system for our study are :

- Naive Bayes Classifier
- Decision Tree Classifier
- K-Nearest Neighbour Clustering
- Support Vector Machine
- Artificial Neural Networks

These machine learning algorithms are isolated and independent of each other i.e. the algorithms read and process the data without interfering with each other and the results generated by the algorithms does not rely on each other. The algorithms also does not have any authority to make any modifications to the data set.

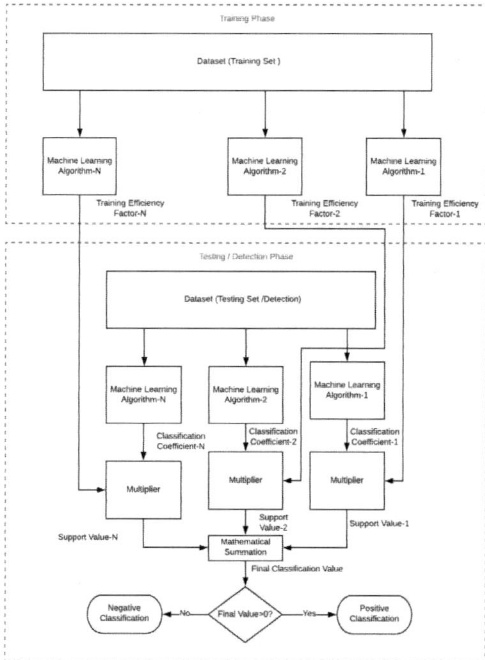

Figure 3. Phase-wise system design for the proposed model

4.1 Preparing Training and Testing data sets

Split the given pima data set into the training set and testing set as per the required distribution.Main focus will be how much training data set is acquired as the maximum training data set will generate a strong training efficiency factor required in further implementation.
The training efficiency factor is defined as the value which represents the efficiency of the algorithm on the training data set.
Consider 75:25 splitting ratio for training and testing.

4.2 Training of algorithm

Individually train every machine learning algorithm in isolation for our hybrid model to obtain the confusion matrix for every algorithm to generate an appropriate training efficiency factor.

	Actually Positive (1)	Actually Negative (0)
Predicted Positive (1)	True Positives (TPs)	False Positives (FPs)
Predicted Negative (0)	False Negatives (FNs)	True Negatives (TNs)

Figure 4. Confusion Matrix for machine learning algorithm

As mentioned above, the amount of training data set used influences the training efficiency factor. For every different split ratio of training and testing sets, the training efficiency factor generated is unique.

$$TEF = \frac{TP + TN}{TP + TN + FP + FN} \quad (4)$$

4.3 Detection by individual algorithm

In Detection/Testing Phase, every machine learning algorithm individually operates on the given input and generates a classification coefficient which is binary in nature i.e. it is either generated as +1 or -1. The classification coefficient is +1 if the classification is positive in nature or -1 if it's negative in nature.

$$CC = \begin{cases} +1 & Positive - classification \\ -1 & Negative - classification \end{cases} \quad (5)$$

For every classification coefficient generated by the machine learning algorithm, it is multiplied with corresponding training efficiency factor from training phase. The new value generated is defined as the Support Value for that algorithm for supporting whether the final classification is negative or positive classification.

$$SV = TEF \times CC \quad (6)$$

If the Support value of a algorithm is positive then it is interpreted that the algorithm is supporting the final classification as the positive classification and if it is a negative support value then it supports the final classification as negative classification. It is observed that for every algorithm there is unique support value and the efficiency of every individual algorithm in training phase will make the support value for the final classification of that algorithm either strong or weak towards its nature.

4.4 Summarization of all algorithms

A mathematical model is implemented in order to summarize the support of all the machine learning algorithms for the final classification.

$$FCV = \sum_{i=1}^{n} SV_i \quad (7)$$

As the Hybrid system idea is new and is on basic research stage it will use a summation mathematical model shown in equation (7) where all the support values of the algorithms are summed up with their nature to get a single value which is defined as the final classification value of the hybrid system for the final classification.
The final classification value has two properties: Nature and Magnitude.
The nature of the final classification value will decide the nature of final classification i.e. if the nature is negative then the final classification is negative in nature else its positive in nature.

$$Final - Classification \begin{cases} Positive & FCV > 0 \\ Negative & FCV < 0 \end{cases} \quad (8)$$

The magnitude of final classification value will give how strongly our hybrid system is confident of its classification i.e. if the magnitude is less then the system is barely able to classify and if the magnitude is greater then the system is strongly able to classify.

5 Results

In this research study, our working material was diabetes data set with 768 instances which we first of all divided into two further sets of 700 instances for training and testing of individual algorithms and remaining 68 instances to be used as the live input for the proposed model.
In Training phase of the individual algorithms, the first set of 700 instances are used to obtain TEF for the machine learning algorithms and these are shown in Table-1.

Table 1. Training Efficiency Factors for machine learning algorithms

Algorithm	TEF
Naive Bayes Classifier	0.72857
Decision Tree Classifier	0.84762
K-Nearest Neighbour	0.79048
Support Vector Machine	0.77714
Artificial Neural Network	0.90667

In the Detection phase, the remaining 68 instances used as the live input produced the confusion matrix for every individual algorithms and for the proposed system which are presented in the Table-2.

Table 2. Confusion matrix values for individual models and proposed model

Model	True Positive	True Negative	False Positive	False Negative
Naive Bayes Classifier	17	34	7	10
Decision Tree Classifier	26	1	40	1
K Nearest Neighbour	27	0	41	0
Support Vector Machine	12	13	28	15
Artificial Neural~ Network	20	16	25	7
Proposed Model	**27**	**6**	**35**	**0**

The above confusion matrix is further used to generate the following result metrics for all the individual models and the proposed model :

- **Accuracy:**
  It is the most common measure of performance for the machine learning model described as the ratio of correctly predicted observations to the total observations.

$$Accuracy = \frac{TP + TN}{TP + TN + FP + FN} \quad (9)$$

- **Precision:**
  It is described as the ratio of correctly predicted positive observations to the total predicted positive observations.

$$Precision = \frac{TP}{TP + FP} \quad (10)$$

- **Recall:**
  It is described as the ratio of correctly predicted positive observations to all observations in an actual class.

$$Recall = \frac{TP}{TP + FN} \quad (11)$$

The result metrics for all the individual models and the proposed model is presented in Table-3.

Table 3. Result metrics for individual models and proposed model in detection phase

	Result Metric		
Model	Accuracy	Precision	Recall
NB Classifier	0.750	0.708	0.629
DT Classifier	0.397	0.393	0.962
KNN Clustering	0.397	0.397	1
SVM Classifier	0.367	0.300	0.444
ANN Model	0.529	0.444	0.740
Proposed Model	**0.485**	**0.435**	**1**

The most beneficial advantage offered by the proposed system is that it is designed in such a way that it considers the classification generated by all the algorithms and not only the most efficient algorithms while discarding the less efficient algorithms during the final classification. Every algorithm is taken into consideration during the final classification based on their efficiency and accuracy in their training phase and their classification coefficient generated in their detection phase.

6 Future Work and Discussion

The hybrid machine learning model being new is still on the basic stage of research and implementation.
Being on the basic stage, the training efficiency factor for the algorithms is considered as their accuracy values obtained from the confusion matrix during the training phase. In future, once the the research on the hybrid system is in progress the training efficiency factor can be generated using complex methods to get more efficient values.
The mathematical model at the basic stage of the research is a basic summation model which directly sum up the support values of all the algorithms to get the final classification value for final classification. In future, for further stages of research a new complex mathematical model will be implemented to get more accurate final classification value for more accurate final classification.
The new hybrid system for binary classification is still in its basic theoretical stage and more research work needs to be done in order to increase its scope of binary classification and real world implementation.

7 Acknowledgment

We take this opportunity to express our profound gratitude and deep regards to our guide Mr. Chikkareddi Vishwanath S. for his exemplary guidance, monitoring and constant encouragement throughout the completion of this study.We are truly grateful to his efforts to improve our understanding towards various concepts and technical skills required in our research study. The blessing, help and guidance given by his time to time shall carry us a long way in the journey of life on which we are about to embark.
We take this privilege to express our sincere thanks to Dr. Mukesh D. Patil, Principal, RAIT for providing the much necessary facilities.We are also thankful to Dr. Leena Ragha, Head of Department of Computer Engineering, RAIT, Nerul Navi Mumbai for her generous support.
Last but not the least we would also like to thank all those who have directly or indirectly helped us in completion of this thesis.

References

[1] Mukesh kumari ,Anshul arora ,Dr.Rajan Vohra , "Prediction of Diabetes Using Bayesian Network", International Journal of Computer Science and Information Technologies ,2014.

[2] S. Wei, X. Zhao, and C. Miao, "A comprehensive exploration to the machine learning techniques for diabetes identification," 2018 IEEE 4th World Forum on Internet of Things (WFIoT), 2018.

[3] W. Chen, S. Chen, H. Zhang, and T. Wu, "A hybrid prediction model for type 2 diabetes using K-means and decision tree," 2017 8th IEEE International Conference on Software Engineering and Service Science (ICSESS), 2017.

[4] S. Y. Rubaiat, M. M. Rahman, and M. K. Hasan, "Important Feature Selection Accuracy Comparisons of Different Machine Learning Models for Early Diabetes Detection," 2018 International Conference on Innovation in Engineering and Technology (ICIET), 2018.

[5] M. Dutt, V. Nunavath, and M. Goodwin, "A Multilayer Feed Forward Neural Network Approach for Diagnosing Diabetes," 2018 11th International Conference on Developments in eSystems Engineering (DeSE), 2018.

[6] Barakat, N., Bradley, A. P., Barakat, M. N. H. "Intelligible Support Vector Machines for Diagnosis of Diabetes Mellitus". IEEE Transactions on Information Technology in Biomedicine, 14(4), 1114–1120 (2010).

[7] Han, L., Luo, S., Yu, J., Pan, L. Chen, S. "Rule Extraction From Support Vector Machines Using Ensemble Learning Approach: An Application for Diagnosis

of Diabetes ". IEEE Journal of Biomedical and Health Informatics 19, 728–734 (2015).

[8] Nongyao Nai-aruna, Rungruttikarn Moungmaia,"Comparison of Classifiers for the Risk of Diabetes Prediction" 7th International Conference on Advances in Information Technology,2015.

[9] M. A. Helal, A. I. Chowdhury, A. Islam, E. Ahmed, M. S. Mahmud, and S. Hossain, "An Optimization Approach to Improve Classification Performance in Cancer and Diabetes Prediction," 2019 International Conference on Electrical, Computer and Communication Engineering (ECCE), 2019.

[10] Lekha, S. Suchetha, M. "A Novel 1-D Convolution Neural Network With SVM Architecture for Real-Time Detection Applications". IEEE Sensors Journal 18, 724–731 (2018).

[11] Mustafa S. Kadhm,Ikhlas Watan Ghindawi,Duaa Enteesha Mhawi"An Accurate Diabetes Prediction System Based on K-means Clustering and Proposed Classification Approach" International Journal of Applied Engineering Research ISSN 0973-4562 Volume 13, Number 6 (2018)

[12] Temurtas, H., Yumusak, N. Temurtas, F. "A comparative study on diabetes disease diagnosis using neural networks". Expert Systems with Applications 36, 8610–8615 (2009).

Visualization of Droplet Dynamics in Cloud

Shubham Belgaonkar[1, *], *Bhushan* Bamble[2, **], *Amit* Barve[3, ***], *and Bipin* Kumar[4, ****]

[1,2,3] Computer Department, Ramrao Adik Institute of Technology Navi Mumbai, India
[4] HPCS, Indian Institute of Tropical Meteorology, Pune, India

Abstract. Data visualization uses charts, graphs and maps to illustrate some information. Visualizing data helps us understand information faster. The study of droplet dynamics is a critical part of cloud physics and includes studying droplet properties. The aim of this work is to visualize the droplet dynamics obtained from DNS (Direct Numerical Simulation) data due to evaporation and condensation of the droplets. This simulation contains coupled Eulerian and Lagrangian frames. Animation is created for both Eulerian grid data and Lagrangian droplet movement. Scientific visualization provides a way to analyze these turbulent properties in a part of a cloud and learn about the nature of droplets and mixing process in such highly turbulent areas.

Keywords—DNS (Direct Numerical Simulation), NetCDF (Network Common Data Form), VTK (Visualization Toolkit), HPC (High Performance Computing)

1 Introduction

Weather forecasting centers manage a large amount of meteorological data. Such data must be interpreted within short period of time. Scientific visualization can be a great help in supporting meteorological researchers and scientists. Decision-making depends on data that comes in a large quantity that it cannot be understood without some level of abstraction, such as a visual one. There are various types of meteorological data namely rainfall data, temperature data, radiation data, radar data and many more. This work involves examining various droplets' properties. It is difficult to examine the properties by just looking at Direct Numerical Simulation. Direct Numerical Simulation is method in Computational Fluid Dynamics where the range of spatial and temporal scales of the turbulence are resolved. Small scale simulation is one method in understanding the physics behind the phenomena and generate data. This work shows, the data obtained from Direct Numerical Simulation of entrainment and mixing processes in cloud affect the droplet dynamics due to condensation and evaporation. The turbulent entrainment and mixing of dry air with moist or cloudy air influences the cloud's lifespan by changing the properties. Such modifications are responsible for the droplet dynamics. This mixing process is quite complex, and it is difficult to study it during field observations. It illustrates how all of the droplets will evaporate by the same number, or the subset of the droplets evaporates entirely, while the other droplets remain intact in the cloud turbulence. However, it is not clear how the size of the droplets is influenced by the mixing process and has a major impact on the spectrum of the droplets. The types of mixing processes of the droplets are known as homogeneous mixing and in-homogeneous mixing[1]. Many visualization techniques can be used to visualize the given data[2]. This work uses ParaView for visualization because of its ability to analyze extremely large datasets rather than using expensive commercial software.

2 Literature Survey

The data formats along with the tools involved in the visualization are given below.

2.1. NetCDF File Format

NetCDF is the popular data format defined by Unidata program at the University Corporation for Atmospheric Research (UCAR), used widely in climatic, meteorological and oceanographic applications such as climate change and forecasting of weather etc. It is a data format that is created to support the array-oriented data [2]. All NetCDF formats contain a header which describing the layout of the rest of the file, particularly the data arrays. The NetCDF model of data abstraction creates scientific data set as a group of named multidimensional variables along with their coordinate systems [3]. Every NetCDF file has three components: dimensions which are used to define shape of data, variables to store the array values, and attributes to

*e-mail: shubhamb756@gmail.com
**e-mail: bhushan.bamble@gmail.com
***e-mail: barve.amit@gmail.com
****e-mail: bipink@tropmet.res.in

provide a title or this history of the data set. They help understand the data more clearly.

2.2 VTK (Visualization Toolkit)

The Visualization Toolkit offers numerous writer object with the ability to read and write standard file formats along with their own file formats. The purpose for creating other data file format is to provide a consistent data representation scheme for a number of dataset forms and to provide an easy method for transmitting data [4]. There are two file formats available in VTK, Legacy and Serial. These formats are less flexible as compared to XML file formats. While these formats are much more complicated than the Legacy format. By just providing a simple XML description any VTK source or filter can be added.

2.3 ParaView

ParaView is one of the most preferred open-source scientific visualization tools for the visualization. This software is used in many communities because of its easy to use nature to analyze and visualize large data sets. ParaView uses three steps to visualizing data: reading or loading the data files, filtering the necessary details, and then rendering the images for the given data. Reading the data involves loading the data files which creates pipelines for the loaded data, filtering the data involves creating arrays or using arrays which are necessary for the visualization and rendering involves generating and saving the images for the data set. ParaView has Python, C, C++ and Fortran bindings. In this work python shell is used for the visualization process.

3 Problem Statement

The aim of this paper is to propose a procedure for the visualization of the droplet dynamics in the cloud obtained from the DNS (Direct Numerical Simulation) data in an open-source software application, rather than expensive commercial alternatives to help the scientists and researchers to examine the properties of the droplets in cloud turbulence.

4 Data Flow Diagram

The input data consists of two datasets - Eulerian NetCDF files and Lagrangian SION files. As far as NetCDF files are concerned, there is an inbuilt NetCDF reader in ParaView software. For SION files, there are no readers as such in ParaView. So, to load SION data, SION files have to be converted into VTK format which is the default format for ParaView. Then it is to be further converted into vtkUnstructuredGrid format. The dataset forms a topologically irregular set of points and cells.
After the conversion to VTK, we extract the mixing ratio variable from the NetCDF files and create new series of NetCDF files which are smaller in size. This allows ParaView to process the files faster. Now, both the VTK and extracted NetCDF files and loaded in ParaView and visualization of the data is obtained at various time steps. The purpose of ParaView is to analyze extremely large data sets. Now these images are used for the animation purpose.

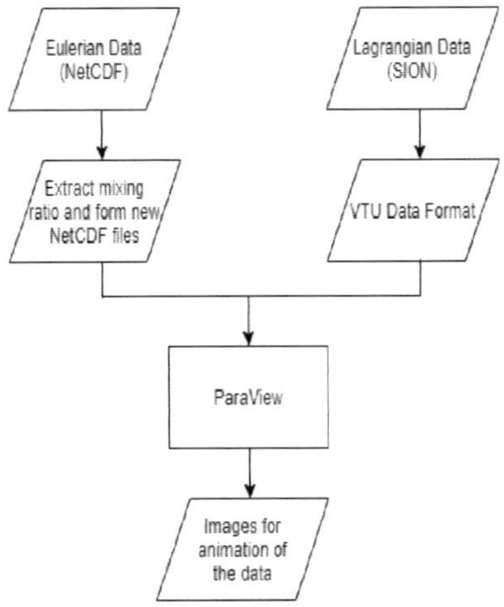

Fig. 1. Data flow Diagram

5 Process Flow Diagram

The DNS data stored in SION format could be converted to ASCII files using SIONLib [6]. ASCII files are also referred as text files that can be read easily. They often contain letters, numbers and some line separators such as comma or spaces. ASCII files may be larger in file size but the speed of writing and reading is much faster. They are efficient, but one has to specify the file's content before reading or writing the files.
So, to open and visualize the data a program must be used. There are many bindings available in all the popular languages to access these text files.
The procedure for the visualization of droplets dynamics includes extraction of the positions of the marker and radius of the droplets from the ASCII files, then preparation of data using Python script which will create series of VTK files that can be coupled with the NetCDF Eulerian grid data files and imported into open-source scientific visualization software - ParaView.
ParaView uses three steps to visualizing data: reading or loading the data files, filtering the necessary details, and then rendering the images for the given data. Data must be read in an acceptable file format into ParaView. Next, the data must be analyzed in different ways available and is to be filtered with the number of filters available. Finally, the visible image from the data is rendered and the images at different time steps can be stored. Now, these images are used to form an animation video using python script.

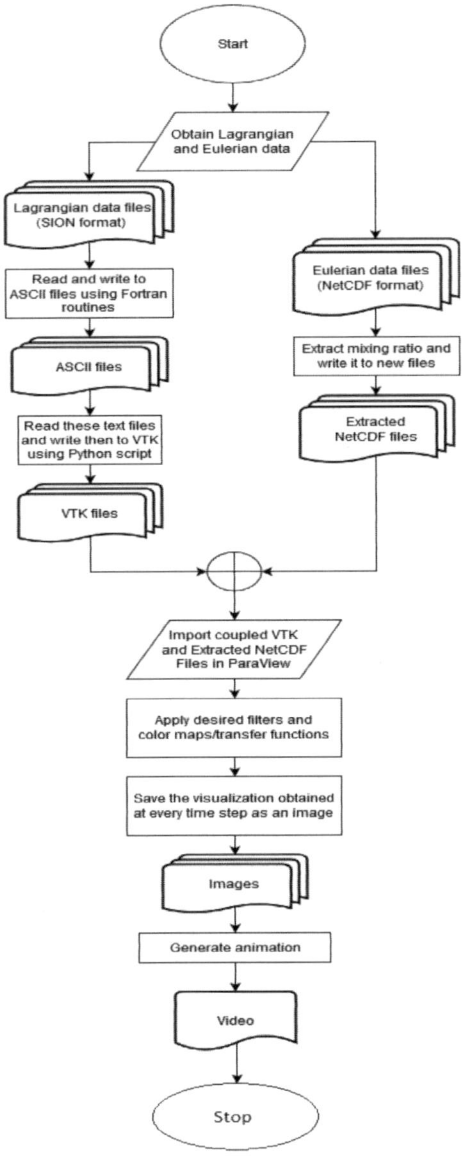

Fig. 2. Process Flow Diagram

6 Implementation

Extract the mixing ratio variable from the Eulerian data files and create series of NetCDF files containing only mixing ratio data of same dimensions x, y, z. These Eulerian data points were reduced by spacing every two grid points. We extract this variable and form new NetCDF files to reduce the memory consumption by ParaView and also to speed up the computational time. Get the Lagrangian Data files converted to ASCII text files by extracting the marker positions and radius of the droplets. Load these coupled files in ParaView by creating NetCDF Reader for extracted Eulerian data and XMLUnstructuredGrid Reader for Lagrangian data. Set scalar coloring for both and create render view with best possible resolution. Results for this paper have 2555 x 1376 pixels. Change representation type apply color maps/ transfer functions until desired visualization is obtained. Edit color legend/bar for the datasets respectively and choose the scale based on minimum and maximum values in data. Save the Screenshots of the desired visualization and run above steps in loop for each extracted Eulerian file and Lagrangian file. Use python program to animate the saved images to create an animation video.

7 Results/ Screenshots

In visualization the most important part is giving appropriate color. In ParaView, applying color map/transfer function is the part where the color is applied to the visualization. "GetColorTransferFunction('variable_name')" and "ApplyPreset('colormap_name')" functions help to apply the color map/transfer function to the variables. A gray scale color map is imported (eul_gray.8) for the visualization of cloud slab. Usually the cloud slab is represented by white coloration. The range of the mixing-ratio variable is decided to be 0 to 0.0012. For radius variable 'warm to cool' color map/transfer function is used, which is already present in ParaView. This color map is useful to highlight the contrast between smaller radii and larger radii. It would otherwise be difficult to distinguish the difference in sizes due to the high density of the data. For the desired visualization of the droplet particles, the range of the radius data was changed many times. By trying several different ranges, the desired visualization was obtained when the range was 0 to 18. These ranges were set based on the values present in the data. "RescaleTranferFunction(start_point, end_point)" function was used to set the range.

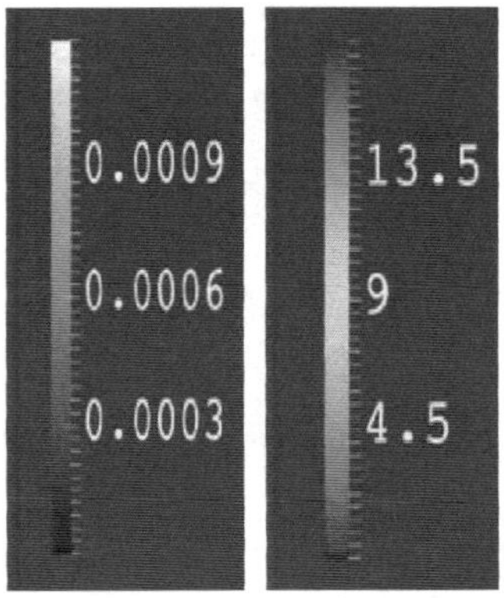

Fig. 3. Color maps/Transfer functions for mixing ratio and droplet radius respectively, Scale depends on the maximum and minimum values.

Shown in Fig. 3, is the color maps/transfer functions for mixing-ratio and droplet radius respectively. Scale of the color bar depends on the maximum and minimum values in the data. For mixing-ratio variable we use gray scale color bar and for radius variable we use 'warm to cool' color bar.

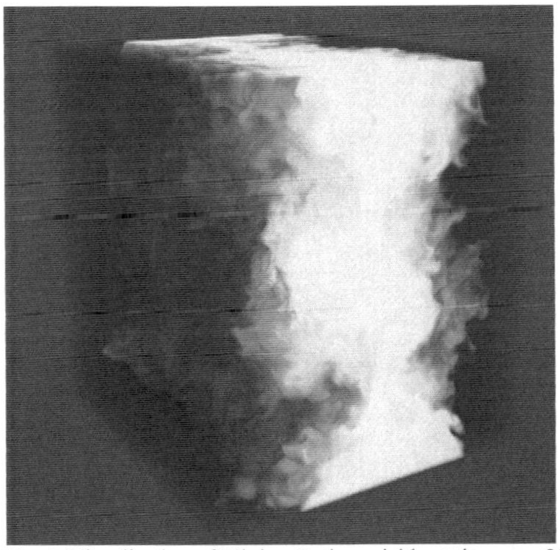

Fig. 4. Visualization of Mixing-Ratio variable at time step 20

Shown in Fig. 4, is the visualization of Eulerian gridded data colored by Mixing-Ratio variable. Central cloud slab is visible in white.

Fig. 5. Visualization of radius variable at time step 20

Shown in Fig. 5, is the visualization of Lagrangian data colored by radius variable. It shows the visualization of droplets based on their radius size. Blue droplets have larger radii and the droplets in red are with the smallest radii.

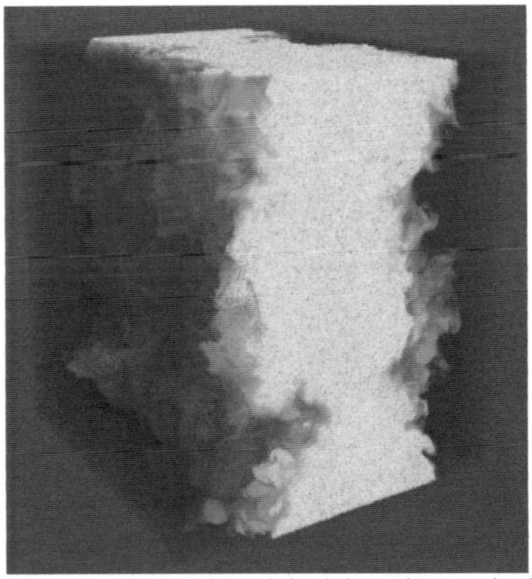

Fig. 6. Visualization of Coupled Eulerian and Lagrangian files at time step 20

Shown in Fig. 6, is the visualization of coupled Eulerian gridded data and Lagrangian data at time step 20. Both data these data files are imported simultaneously and visualized together. The droplets of different radii are visible in white cloud slab.

Fig. 7. Visualization of Coupled Eulerian and Lagrangian files at time step 80

Shown in Fig. 7, is the visualization of Eulerian gridded data and Lagrangian data together at time step 80. The droplets here evaporate and get smaller in size (red particles).

These results show the mixing process of the droplets in cloud due to evaporation and condensation. An animation is created of the visualizations obtained at every time step to help us understand the movement of droplets in the cloud turbulence.

7 Conclusion

In meteorological data analysis, visualization has emerged as a great tool to understand the data more quickly and efficiently. The results are communicated between climate researchers and scientific community. A picture is worth more than a thousand lines of numbers or words.
This visualization of droplet evolution provides the opportunity to peek inside the cloud and observe properties of individual droplets. This investigation is not possible with field observations or with traditional data analysis.

8 Future Work

This particular version of the visualization was run on an individual PC using CPU processing only. Parallel computational methods such as, GPU and multi-core processing, and those described in ParaView Visualization handbook[12] can be utilized in future studies to reduce time consumption. Due to time constraint the ASCII files were converted to VTK in this work as 'pyevtk' makes it easy to do so. In future, research can be done on how to read ASCII files directly in ParaView to avoid the step of converting them to VTK files as shown in Figure

Acknowledgement

The simulation has been carried out on a HPC facility provided by Ministry of Earth Science, Government of India at Indian Institute of Tropical Meteorology, Pune. A sincere thanks to the Institute and the scientists who contributed in this project and let us use the facility at the institute. Also, thanks to Matt Rehme, software engineer at National Centre of Atmospheric Research, who helped with his valuable inputs in the visualization with ParaView.

References

[1] B. Kumar, J. Schumacher, R. A. Shaw, Lagrangian mixing dynamics at the cloudy-clear air interface, Journal of Atmospheric Sciences 71 (7) (2014)

[2] Marc Rautenhaus, Michael Bottinger, Stephan Siemen, Robert Hoffman, Robert M Kirby, Mahsa Mirzargar, Niklas Rober, and Rudiger Westermann: Visualization in meteorology—A Survey of Techniques and Tools for Data Analysis Tasks (2017)

[3] Russ Rew and Glenn Davis: NetCDF - An Interface for Scientific Data, (1990)

[4] VTK file format: URLhttps://www.kitware.com/products/books/VTKUsersGuide.pdf

[5] S.G. Parker, D.M. Weinstein, and C.R. Johnson, "The SCIRun Computational Steering Software System," Modern Software Tools in Scientific Computing, E. Arge, A.M. Brauset, and H.P. Langtangen, pg. 5-44, (1997)

[6] Sionlib: URLhttp:/www.fzjuelich.de/ias/jsc/EN/Expertise/Support/Software/SIONlib/node.html

 https://doi.org/10.1051/itmconf/20203203034

Collaborative Recommendation System For Agriculture Sector.

Sapna Jaiswal[1,3,*], *Tejaswi* Kharade[2,**], *Nikita* Kotambe[3,***], and *Dr.Shilpa* Shinde[3,****]

[1]jsapna2011@gmail.com
[2]tejaswisampat1898@gmail.com
[3]nikitakotambe@gmail.com
[4]shilpa.shinde@rait.ac.in

Abstract. Agriculture is one of the most important sector in India and the farmers are one of the most essential members of society. The major economy of the country comes from the agricultural sector. Though there is no end to the woes of Indian Farmers. One of the major causes for the continuing Indian farmer distress is lack of knowledge and benefits of the agricultural programs and schemes proposed by the Government of India.The Collaborative Recommendation System For Agriculture Sector is one such way to solve this problem. There are various workshops conducted to create awareness about the government schemes to the farmers but still the results are not seen as expected. Even if they are aware they are not solved and hence many NGOs and Institutes have come up with various measures to solve this problem. Our research system focuses on helping the farmers by answering their agricultural queries by generating a profile of basic requirements through a web application and recommends the proposed government schemes developed to help farmers.The recommendation system also periodically update farmers with the recent trends in agricultural field, new Government schemes and programs. Keywords - agriculture, government schemes, web application, recommendation, knn algorithm, cosine similarity, CRSAS- Collaborative Recommendation System For Agriculture Sector

1 Introduction

Growth in agricultural domain are one of the main concerns to the farmers as well as to the economy of our country as it plays the major role in contribution for the same. Agriculture serves a s much as quarter of the Indian economy, employing more than 60 percent of the labour force. Despite of progress in agricultural domain, the problems faced have continued frustrating Indian farmers and the citizens. It is estimated that one-fourth of the Indian produce is lost due to inefficient methodologies used for harvesting, farming, transportation and storage of goods produced of government subsidized crops. Problems due to which farmers are lacking behind consists of Inequality in land distribution, land tenure system, sub-division and fragmentation of holdings, Cropping pattern, instability and fluctuations, and condition of labour. Poor farming technique also gives a way to different problems that ultimately affects the overall economy of the country.
The agricultural sector of India still faces a very vital issue of agricultural growth deceleration. Declining of investment in agricultural research and development stands as one of the core reasons for reduction of growth of the agriculture in India.Thus there needs some technologies and methodologies to work together and bring up a system for farmers as per their problems.

*e-mail: jsapna2011@gmail.com
**e-mail: tejaswisampat1898@gmail.com
***e-mail: nikitakotambe@gmail.com
****e-mail: shilpa.shinde@rait.ac.in

Various schemes do exist based on a single domain such as the type of soil needed for cultivation, different types of crops, other utilities required for agriculture, but there are very few such measures which guides the farmers with proper steps to be undertaken for greater yield, much more profit and also with less expenses and with a helping hand of government. We have come up with combined solution which use many technologies for getting insight of details in more depth and providing the maximum profitable solution. Surveys conducted for the betterment and educational purpose of the people will have the major usage of recommendation system.

To overcome all these problems faced by farmers and ultimately the country, Government of India has proposed and implemented a large number of welfare schemes for farmers. These schemes are to be used by farmers for their growth in agricultural domain. The schemes provide help such as financial help, marketing help, irrigation facilities, insurance to farmers crops, subsidies to farmers and their family. But these schemes need to reach every remote sector of India so that they can get benefits, since due to lack of exposure towards farmers and unawareness of different government schemes the farmers still face various problems though there are various solutions proposed by the government of India. There are various applications related to the recommendation of crops and other problem related to agriculture.[1]

There are ample amount of systems available for farmers that recommend them crops, soil quality,fertilizers to be

used, pesticides, urea for soil and also health checkup of soil. There is no such system available for farmers to help with the information of schemes and also helping them choose appropriate scheme. By working on this project we can analyse different queries imposed by farmers and recommend them different government schemes made available by Indian Government to help these farmers.
The system does query analysis from data provided by the farmers in their profile and recommends the scheme based on the feasible solution to their queries. The system also visualises the schemes proposed, implemented, number of farmer queries resolved by the available schemes.
The farmers are unaware of the different government policies/schemes that are helpful for them in various problems related to agriculture. The main objective of this project is to show the amount of queries farmers have in a particular sector such as financial help, crop detection and suggest them different government schemes so that farmers are aided with help and know the process to do so.
The structure of this paper is as follows: The section 2 introduces literature survey of various existing papers, section 3 introduces the proposed system, section four explains the experimental results and finally section five concludes the agenda with future work suggestions.

2 Literature Survey

This section comprises of the findings related to our topic. It is basically an evaluative report of information found in the literature relevant to Recommendation Systems based on Soil, Crop, Fertilizers, Insurance, loans. The systems existing are Crop recommendation system, Soil based fertilizer recommendation system, Query Analysis and crop recommendation system, Recommendations with hadoop framework. These systems aim at singular elements such as recommendations only for crop, or fertilizers, or may be some subsidies and insurances for farmers.

1. In, Crop Selection Method to Maximize Crop Yield Rate using Machine Learning [2], the research centers its focus to build a recommendation system that can collect raw data for environmental factors like soil, weather parameters from experienced farmers, agricultural researchers and other stake holders. Based on these parameters, structures are studied and crop is recommended to the farmers. Statistical data analysis and predictive modeling are incorporated in order to anticipate a suitable crop accordingly.Technique named Crop Selection Method (CSM) is used to solve crop selection problem and maximize net yield rate of crop over season and achieves maximum economic growth.
2. In, Web based recommendation system [3], the process focuses on the use of data mining techniques to recommend the farmers regarding crops, crop rotation and identification of appropriate fertilizer. The system uses random forest algorithm for the crop recommendation, and have considered Year of Cultivation of Resultant Crop ,Market Price of Resultant Crop ,Output/Area Ratio of Resultant Crop as the 3 factors to distributed the rating. For crop rotation recommendation, authors have used FP tree matching frequent pattern observed during past cultivation. Also for fertilizer recommendation, Sufficiency approach is used to check the nutritional values and approaches possible combination of fertilizers to meet the crop requirements and the combination with lowest cost of fertilization will be recommended.
3. In, KrishiMantra: Agricultural Recommendation System [4], the system is used for domain knowledge and used to send recommendations to the farmers based on climate conditions and geographic data. The system shows experimental outcomes as a section of implementation of proposed architecture. The farmer types queries to the query engine, in order to get information for a specific crop. Query asked are matched to GIS data, crop knowledge domain or both, the query is transformed into a semantic web query and after performing reasoning and semantic processing, the result is sent to the mobile device of user.
4. In, Recommendation System With SVM [5], the system proposes a recommendation system for the large amount data in the form of ratings, reviews, opinions, complain, remarks, feedback, and comment about the items such as (product, event, individual and services) using SVM and collaborative filtering. GA is used as optimization technique. Here the recommendation works using hybrid filtering technique to refine different types of factors considering review generated by different reviewers.[6]

3 Proposed System

The underlying section gives a detailed representation of the design which includes the diagrammatical representation along with its explanation.

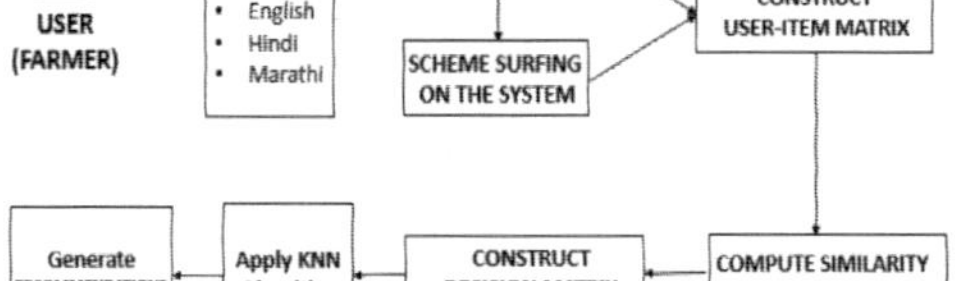

Figure 1. Block Diagram of CRSAS

The target of query analysis is to recognize the problems faced by farmers throughout the year. There is a login and registration page for farmers. Also at times farmers having probability to understand the regional language so we have included Hindi and Marathi languages with the base of English language in the user interface. This will make the interface user friendly. As there are eligibility criteria for many of the government schemes we have a profile to be filled by the farmers with basic information as the name, age, phone number, location, pan card, adhaarcard number, whether the land they cultivate is owned by the farmer or are tenants. This page makes up the important part.

	A	B	C	D
1	User ID	Scheme ID	Rating	
2	1	16	5	
3	1	8	4	
4	1	2	3	
5	1	4	1	
6	2	22	4	
7	2	9	5	
8	2	21	1	
9	3	22	3	
10	3	14	4	
11	3	15	5	
12	3	11	1	
13	4	12	2	
14	4	13	3	
15	4	16	5	

Figure 2. User Data Set

The above dataset has been taken from Kisan call center(data.gov.in). Kisan call centre is a service provided by the Government organizations for welfare of farmers. Kisan call center answer farmer's queries on a telephone call in the native languages. Kisan call centres are present in 21 different locations in the country covering all Indian states and Union Territories.

	A	B	C	D	E	F
1	schemeid	title	parameters			
2	1	Interest S	<2hectare	<60000	Financial	
3	2	Micro Irrig	<5hectare	<20000	Irrigation	
4	3	Gramin Bh	<3hectare	<60000	Financial	
5	4	Prime Mir	<2hectare	<60000	Irrigation	
6	5	Mission o	>2hectare	<30000	Horticulture	
7	6	National F	>2hectare	>30000	Marketing	
8	7	Solar wate	<5acres	>40000	Irrigation	
9	8	Pradhan n	>=2hectar	>30000	Financial	
10	9	PM Kisan I	>=2hectar	>40000	Financial	
11	10	Livestock	>5hectare	>50000	Cattle	
12	11	Soil Healtl	>2hectare	<30000	Soil	
13	12	Soil Healtl	>5hectare	<50000	soil	
14	13	Unified N.	>5hectare	>40000	Marketing	
15	14	Integrate	<2hectare	<20000	Marketing	
16	15	Neem coa	>2hectare	>30000	Fertilizers	
17	16	Pradhan N	>2hectare	<40000	Climatic Change	
18	17	Agricultur	<2hectare	<10000	Climatic Change	
19	18	Rainfed ar	>3hectare	<40000	Climatic Change	
20	19	National N	>3hectare	>100000	Climatic Change	
21	20	National S	>3hectare	>40000	Poultry	
22	21	Scheme o	<2hectare	<60000	Poultry	

Figure 3. Schemes and categories dataset

Technologies and methodologies used for developing the proposed system are based on Machine Learning that consists of Collaborative Filtering with model based approach- knn algorithm, Cosine Similarity, Support Vector Machine and Brute algorithm implemented using python.

3.1 Preprocessing

The data is loaded into Pandas Data frame and then pivot ratings into scheme features. To have best data interpretation, data frame is pivoted as schemeid and userid columns. Null values are filled with zeros.

	A	B	C
1			
2		Scheme ID	Title
3	0	1	Interest Subvention Scheme
4	1	2	Micro Irrigation Scheme
5	2	3	Gramin Bhandaran
6	3	4	Prime Minister Krishi Sinchayee Yojana
7	4	5	Mission Of Integrated Development Horticulture

Figure 4. Schemes

3.2 Threshold Values Identification

Considering the count of schemes, users(farmers), and scheme ratings, three things has been understood:

Values of lot of user scheme matrix are zeros. The data we dealed with was sparse data, and hence we worked with scipy-sparse-matrix to avoid wastage of memory and avoid problems of overflow.[7]

	A	B	C
1	User ID	Scheme ID and Category	Rating
2	1	16 = Agricultural Marketing	5.000
3	1	8 = Water	4.000
4	1	2 = Fertilizer	3.000
5	1	4 = Financial Help	1.000
6	2	22 = Climatic Change	4.000
7	2	9 = Water	5.000
8	2	21= Climatic Change	1.000
9	3	22 = Climatic Change	3.000
10	3	14 = Agricultural Marketing	4.000
11	3	15 = Agricultural Marketing	5.000
12	3	11 = Soil	1.000
13	4	12 = Soil	2.000
14	4	13 = Soil	2.000
15	4	16 = Agricultural Marketing	4.000

Figure 5. Count Of Ratings

3.3 Modelling Recommendation Systems

The data is loaded into Pandas Data frame and then pivot ratings into scheme features.

Collaborative Filtering is a technique used in Recommender Systems. Collaborative Filtering is a method of making instinctive prognosis (filtering) about the interests of a user by collecting liking or taste information from many users(collaborating). These forecast are specific to the user, but uses information collected from many users. Uses cases of collaborative Filtering usually involve very large data sets. Collaborative Filtering systems have many forms, but many common systems can be reduced to two steps.[8]

1. Includes Users who share same rating patterns with the active user.

2. Uses the ratings from the people / user similar to step 1 to calculate a prediction for the active user.

This falls under the subtitle of user based collaborative filtering. The use case of this is the user based Nearest Neighbor Algorithm.

Another sub type is the item based Collaborative Filtering proceeds in an item-centric manner.

1. Build an item-item matrix determining the relationships between pairs of items.

2. Includes the taste of the current user by examining the matrix and matching that users data.

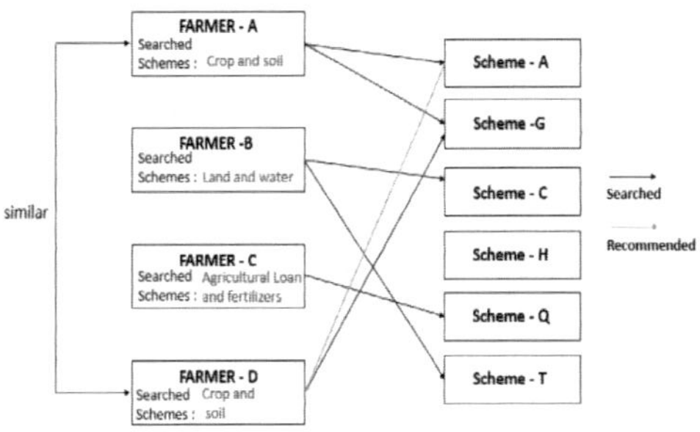

Figure 6. Collaborative Filtering Diagram

Implementing KNN algorithm:

A distance measure needed to determine the "closeness" of the particular instances. KNN uses the similar approach of classifying an object by searching its nearest neighbors and picking the most popular category among the neighbors.[9][10]
Algorithm

1. Read the input data.

2. Select X to the chosen number of neighbors

3. For every value in the data set

   (a) Find the distance between the query value and the current value for the given data set.

   (b) Sum up the distance of value and the index of the value to an ordered collection.

4. Arrange the ordered collection of distances and indices in ascending order by the distances.

5. Select the first X entries from the arranged ordered collection

6. Get the labels of the chosen X entries from collection

7. If it is classification, return the mode of the X- labels.

Following are the limitations of KNN algorithm:

1. Improper value of k reduces the performance.

2. The K Nearest Neighbour Algorithm is slow as it analysis every sample each time.

3. The algorithm is negatively affected by correlated and irrelevant features.

Optimizations in KNN algorithm:

1. We have chosen the best value of k to get optimal result.

2. We have built our own model using cosine similarity instead of methods such as Euclidean or Manhatten distance as we observed it performs better on our data because of higher variance resulting in higher accuracy along with greater classification speedup.

3. The dataset is preprocessed, simple and not correlated [11].

Another modeling algorithm taken into consideration for this project is Support Vector Machine (SVM). The machine learning algorithm is a supervised algorithm being used and implemented for classification challenges on the data sets. This algorithm is mainly used in classification problems. In this SVM algorithm, each data item is plotted as a point in n-dimensional space with each feature value being the value of a particular coordinate. Then the classification is performed by finding the hyper-plane differentiating the two classes very well.

4 Experimental Results

4.1 Analysis of Algorithms

The model has been processed with Support vector machine algorithm which yields less accuracy as compared to the KNN algorithm. After all the analysis we can conclude that k-nearest neighbors algorithm provides better accuracy and precision. The comparison table can better depict the above case [12]:

Algorithm	Accuracy	Precision
K-Nearest Neighbor	0.78	0.87
Support Vector Machine	0.62	0.75

Table 1. Comparison Table Of Algorithms

After the queries are processed and schemes are recommended based on the categories of scheme asked by the farmer. Now, the training data has high dimensionality. Instead of using Euclidean distance, we had used cosine similarity for nearest neighbor search, since Euclidean distance suffers from "curse-of-dimentionality".
The analysis of the system are done and the graphical results are displayed.

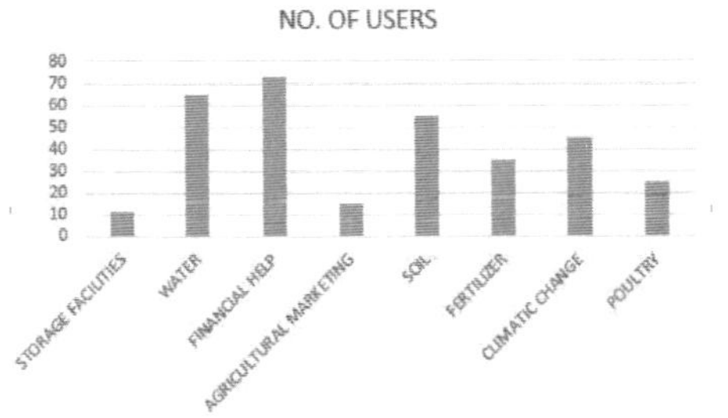

Figure 7. Graphical representation of analysis using cosine similarity

4.2 Precision and Accuracy Measure

Cosine similarity equation :

$$\text{Similarity}(A,B) = (A*B)/(|A|*|B|)$$

Accuracy : 0.7824075179015128
Precision : 0.8731884057971014

Benchmark for threshold value is k=3(considering the most appropriate value of k=sqrt(n)/2 where n is number of schemes for farmers)

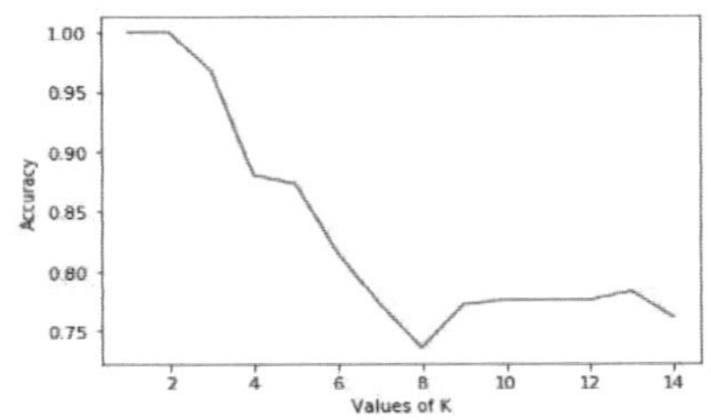

Figure 8. Precision status

5 Conclusion And Future Work

In this paper, the Query Analysis has been done using Collaborative filtering using KNN Algorithm with Gradient Ascent Singular Valued Decomposition and Support Vector Machine. After comparing the results obtained from KNN and SVM implementation, it is observed that KNN performs intuitively better. The accuracy obtained nearly stands at 87percent.Future work is aimed on working with larger data sets and advanced algorithms . The same application can be linked with other government relief facilities to provide one stop solution for farmers.

References

[1] Understanding Machine Learning: From Theory to Algorithms By: Shai Shalev-Shwartz and Shai Ben-David, 2014.

[2] Rakesh Kumar, M.P. Singh, Prabhat Kumar. Crop Selection Method to Maximize Crop Yield Rate using MachineLearning Technique.ieeexplore.ieee.org/document, 2015.

[3] Kiran Shinde , Jerrin Andrei , Amey Oke : Web Based Recommendation System for Farmers, International Journal on Recent and Innovation Trends in Computing and Communication ISSN: 2321-8169 Volume: 3 Issue: 3 1444 – 1448, 2015.

[4] Vikas Kumar, Vishal Dave, Rahul Bhadauriya, Sanjay Chaudhary : KrishiMantra: Agricultural Recommendation System , Proceedings of the 3rd ACM Symposium on Computing for Development, 2013.

[5] Sung Hwan Min and Ingoo Han : Recommender Systems Using Support Vector Machines, Proceedings of the 5th international conference on Web Engineering, 2005.

[6] Pandiyan, O. El-Hassan, A. Hassan Khamis, and P.Rajasekaran, "Ontology with SVM based diagnosis of tuberculosis and statistical analysis". International Journal of Medical and Health Sciences Research,2016 ,Vol.3, No.3, pp.37-43, ISSN(e): 2313-2752, 10.18488/journal.9/2016.3.3/9.3.37.43, 2016 Asian Medical Journals, 2016.

[7] Bailey, T. Jain, A." A note on distance-weighted k-Nearest Neighbors rules", IEEE Trans. Systems, Man, Cybernetics, 8:311-313, 1978.

[8] Breese, J.S., Heckerman, D., and Kadie, C. : Empirical Analysis of Predictive Algorithms for Collaborative Filtering. In: Proceedings of the 14th Conference on Uncertainty in Artificial Intelligence, 1998.

[9] Sadegh Bafandeh Imandoust And Mohammad Bolandraftar :Application of K-Nearest Neighbor (KNN) Approach for Predicting Economic Events: Theoretical Background ,S B Imandoust et al. Int. Journal of Engineering Research and Applications Vol. 3, Issue 5, pp.605-610, 2013.

[10] Gou, J., Du, L. Zhang, Y. amp; Xiong, T. quot;A New Distance-weighted k-nearest Neighbor Classifierquot;, Journal of Information amp; Computational Science, 9(6): 1429-1436, 2012.

[11] Hellman, M.E., quot; The nearest neighbor classification rule with a reject option quot;, IEEE Trans. Systems, Man, Cybernetics, 3: 179-185, 1970.

[12] Grčar M., Fortuna B., Mladenič D., Grobelnik M. kNN Versus SVM in the Collaborative Filtering Framework. In: Batagelj V., Bock HH., Ferligoj A., Žiberna A. (eds) Data Science and Classification. Studies in Classification, Data Analysis, and Knowledge Organization. Springer, Berlin, Heidelberg, 2000.

EEG Based Brain Computer Interfacing for Hand Assistant System Using Wavelet Transform

Dayanand Dhongade[1] and *Dr. Mukesh Patil*[2]

[1] dayananddhongade@gmail.com, DY Patil Group Ramrao Adik Institute of Technology, Nerul, Navi Mumbai
[2] mukesh.rait@gmail.com, DY Patil Group Ramrao Adik Institute of Technology, Nerul, Navi Mumbai

Abstract. Robots have been of great use to mankind for several years. In situation where human body fails to operate as per the need robot's functions in those situations quite efficiently. Electroencephalogram (EEG) controlled hand assistant makes use of EEG signals and Brain Computer Interface (BCI). EEG signals are obtained from the brain using Emotiv Insight headset, after which processing and features extraction of the signals is performed and then conditioning of signals is done as it is a low amplitude signal with additive noise. Signals processing is done on the analog signal by using wavelet transform. Wavelet transform will help to extract information from the analog signal. Then the signals are assigned with the signatures to perform the dedicated task Filtered signal is given to analog pins of Arduino Uno. With the help of inbuilt ADC available on Arduino Uno, Digital Data is also made available on the digital pins. Then through MATLAB access Arduino board. In near future if it gets similar kind of input it will understand exactly what operation to perform. Further the Robotic hand assistant can be operated as we want.

1 Introduction

The human brain begins to show the electrical activity during the embryonic period weeks. After birth, there are 1011 neurons (5*1014) synapses. The functioning and movements of all body parts is controlled by brain. After the registration of Aegean signal in all parts of the Cortex in 1943, the extensive research area started from the first year of 70th year. EEG is non-interfering and cheaper as compared to other devices. As a result, EEG is considered as most suitable one among all other. There are many things which are highly automated in this world. People who are paralyzed have to depend on others for the fulfilment of a particular task. Also there are various tasks which a scientist wants to handle but he is unable to, because of the hazards of that particular substance or chemical. Not only in such research areas, but also in areas where the human being can 't be physically present but needs to operate various important work in such areas, EEG and BCI controlled prototypes can be used. In our work, we have introduced a method in which servo motor is controlled using an EEG signal collected from the cerebral cortex area, which then artificially inserted as a biological application. The proposed project uses AF3, AF4, T7, T8, and Pz electrodes from EMOTIV INSIGHT Headset [1]. To establish this purpose, the signals from the PhysioBank ATM for EEG Motor Movements have been taken. The signals are recorded by performing various tasks out of which the selection of the first two tasks which are 1) Baseline, eyes open. 2) Baseline, eyes closed. These signals are recorded using BCI2000 system. The data is provided in EDF+ format (European Data Format) which have 64 channel output, each channel is sampled at 160 samples per second [2]. The signals are saved in .mat format for the ease of computation in MATLAB. Standard Databases undergoes the feature Extraction process which is done using Wavelet Decomposition. During Decomposition, the selection of Beta waves is done. EEG signals are often analysed in terms of the frequency bands. In terms of voluntary motor activity, 15-30 Hz range is reported which corresponds to the Alpha and Beta range. The proposed project gives the best classification in Beta range (16-31) Hz. The classified task is then sent to the Arduino via socket programming in Arduino- MATLAB interface. The task value is then mapped to the servo movement, for task 1 it rotates 90 degrees and for task 2, by 180 degrees. In this manner, the task of up and down arm movement is established.

1.1 Objective

The main and the utmost purpose of this work is to implement robotic arm that is controlled totally by the EEG signals. The Hand assistant is driven by the servo motor, which is controlled totally by the EEG signals. When the user enters any random input signal then, that signal is compared with the database using classification and the servo is then actuated according to the task classified.

1.2 Motivation

The field of EEG and BCI, widely recognized as the current challenge for Machine Learning and Neural Network, is attracting the interest of many researchers. People who are paralyzed have to depend on others for getting their work done. The proposed project makes the paralyzed people independent. The work is not limited for these people but it can be used in many areas, such as gaming, virtual reality, also in the research areas for helping scientists, to work with the hazardous materials.

2 Literature Survey

The Electroencephalography (EEG) is the process that records electrical activity of the brain. On the scalp with conductive gel electrodes are placed to obtain EEG signals. The electrical activity done due to ion exchange in brain cells and it is the measure of current flow from the summated activity of number of neurons in our brain. The EEG signals recorded after placing electrodes on scalp having the range from 0-200 micro-volts. EEG waves, also called as brain rhythms are classified according to the frequency, amplitude and shape of the scalp at which they are recorded. The EEG waveforms are mainly classified in five classes as alpha waves, beta waves, theta waves, delta waves and gamma waves. These waves are identified by frequency (Hz or cycles/sec) and amplitude.

Alpha waves were discovered by German neurologist Hans Berger. Alpha waves occur at frequencies between 8-13 Hz. The alpha waves are generally associated with relaxation and are originated from the occipital lobe of brain during wakeful relaxation while eyes are closed. During deep sleep, the alpha waves get disappear. Beta waves occur at frequencies between 13-30Hz. In alert state of the individual these waves occurred and also occurred during deep sleep. Beta wave represents alertness and tension with that it also associated with remembering the memories. Theta waves occur at frequencies between 4-7 Hz. These waves normally occur in children, but they also occur in some adults during emotional stress. The individuals having brain disorders and often in degenerative brain states these theta waves occur. Delta waves occur at frequencies between 0.5-4Hz and during very deep sleep these delta waves occur. Gamma waves have frequencies from 35Hz and above. They are most energetic waves and have the smallest amplitude. The higher frequency wave beta is more prominent when eyes are open and closed thus beta waves were considered for the further processing and feature extraction of the signals [3].

From past many years, the researchers are very curious in the field of BCI and EEG signal processing. In late, 1870, the Motor Cortex part of the Brain was discovered. Scientist applied electricity to this part of the dog's brain and it resulted in the movement of limbs [4]. The first Brain Machine Interface was invented in the year 1969 in University of Washington. The best part of this invention is monkeys were trained to move a dial using the nerve impulses which were recorded from their brain commands [5]. In 1982, scientists were able to predict in which direction a monkey's limb is moving. This was done by charging the motor cortex with electricity [6]. An unimaginable discovery took place in 1998, where a paralyzed man who cannot speak was able to do cursor movement and selecting messages from a computer menu. A paralyzed lady's brain was screwed in the motor cortex area of her brain, 2014. As a result of this, she was able to move a robotic hand with her brain [7]. From the last several decades, numerous studies have developed in BCIs with the goals ranging from providing means of communication to functional rehabilitation and in that EEG based BCI systems plays important role for communication and rehabilitation [8].

3 Proposed Methodology

The block diagram shown in Fig. 1 consists of Data Acquisition of EEG signals, EEG signal overlapping, Feature Extraction, Training Dataset Creation, Classification, Arduino- MATLAB interface and Servo Motor. The Feature Extraction is performed on the EEG signal acquired from the PhysioBank, in MATLAB. The classified task obtained from KNN classifier is mapped to the servo movements.

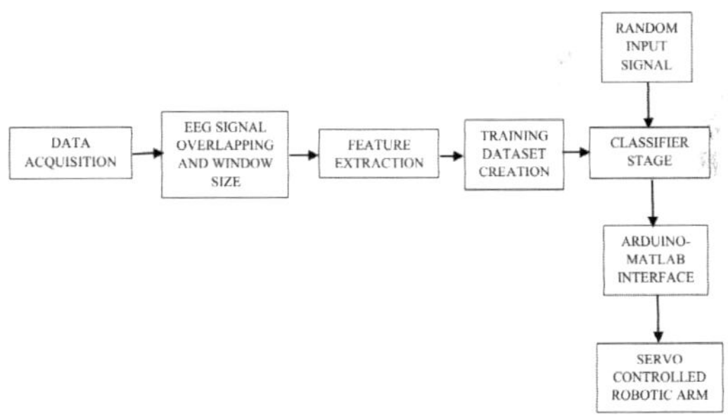

Fig. 1. Block Diagram of BCI Based Hand Assistant System

3.1 Data Acquisition

The EEG signal dataset is collected from the PhysioBank ATM. This data set consists of over 1500 one-minute EEG recording ad it is obtained from 109 volunteers. 64 channel electrode system were used to record EEG using BC2000 while subjects performing different motor tasks. The Bank mentioned four tasks, out of which for this project we opted two tasks which are-(1) Baseline, eye open and (2) Baseline, eye close. Out of the 64 channels the 5 electrodes are taken into consideration i.e., AF3, AF4, T7, T8 and Pz. The signals are saved in .mat format for the ease of computation in MATLAB for further processing, that is performing feature extraction.

3.2 EEG Signal Overlapping and Window Size

After collecting the EEG signals these signals were overlapped with window size of 750ms. The entire windowing technique and framing is applied to all the electrodes separately [9]. The first window size is the largest and it is same as size of the EEG signal. After that subsequent steps include reducing the previous window size by half and same will be repeated until getting the smallest windows size of 1 second. This is due to 160 sample/second sampling rate. The Hamming window is selected for 50 percent overlapping so that any particular information is not lost. Since we are performing overlapping and due to the spectral plot of the Hamming window, it provides the entire signal information with the best accuracy.

3.3 Feature Extraction

The important step in this work is the feature extraction. The total accuracy, the final output will be affected if the accuracy of the dataset obtained from feature extraction is not achieved. In EEG signals essential information is present at low frequency range generally between 0 to 50 Hz so multilevel wavelet decomposition was performed on EEG signals. The decomposition is multi layered indicates the frequency element and for the next process it increases the signal information. The feature extraction is done using discrete wavelet transform with 3 level of decomposition. In discrete wavelet transform dynamic scales and positions are utilized for extracting the features and defined in Eq. (1) as follows [10]:

$$DWT(j,k) = \int_{-\infty}^{\infty} x(t)\frac{1}{\sqrt{2^j}}\,\psi\,(\frac{t-2^j k}{2^j})dt \qquad (1)$$

where 2^j*k is time localization and 2^j is scale respectively, while x(t) represents the mother wavelet function. Daubechies (db4) wavelet is selected as the mother wavelet function, using sampling rate 160 sample/second EEG signals are decomposed and it provides the result into 5 bands as delta (0.5-4Hz); Theta (4-7Hz); Alpha (8-13Hz); Beta (13-30Hz); and Gamma (35-63Hz) and rest is noise. Then energy will be extracted from related frequency bands. Out of the 5 frequency band, only Beta Band is utilized. In this stage, since the work is with the Beta Waves, the selection of cd3 coefficient has been taken into consideration, which is nothing but a detailed coefficient. The most important part of this feature extraction stage is calculating the features and corresponding values mapping into the database. Features like Mean, Minimum, Variance, Standard Deviation, Entropy, Skewness, Kurtosis have been calculated for cd3 coefficient of each electrode. The Energy of wavelet coefficients is calculated for approximation and detail according to Eq. (2) as follows [11]:

$$Ek = \sum_{k=1}^{N} |Cj\,,k|^2, j \ = \ 1,\ldots.,l \qquad (2)$$

where $C_{j,\,k}$ is the detail coefficients or approximation coefficients and N denotes the number of wavelet coefficients at each level of decomposition. The energy of the wavelet packet isnormalized by comparing the energy of detail with total energy of the signal according to Eq. (3) as follows:

$$|Ek| = \frac{Ek}{\mathrm{Et}} \qquad (3)$$

The total energy E_t of the signal is calculated according to Eq. (4) as follows:

$$Et = \sum_k Ek \qquad (4)$$

This process is continued to generate the relative wavelet entropy. Wavelet entropy is used to calculate the degree of similarity between different EEG signal segments. The total wavelet entropy is calculated as per Eq. (5) as follows:

$$G(x) = -\ \sum_j Pj,k\ log\ Pj,k \qquad (5)$$

To characterize, the variability and most importantly the location of the dataset, the inclusion of skewness and kurtosis has been done. The measure of symmetry or more precisely the lack of symmetry is the skewness. A symmetricity is there between distribution and dataset if it resembles the same in both left and right from the centre point and it is expressed according to Eq. (6) as follows:

$$s = E\ \frac{(x-\mu)^3}{\sigma^3} \qquad (6)$$

where μ is the mean value of x, σ is the standard deviation value of x, and E(t) shows the expected value of the quantity t and the sample version of this population value is calculated from skewness. Kurtosis is used to measure whether the data are heavy tailed or light tailed relative to a normal distribution. If lighter the tails, then lower is the Kurtosis. Similarly, if heavier the tail, then higher is the Kurtosis. The kurtosis of a distribution is calculated according to Eq. (7) as follows:

$$k = E\ \frac{(x-\mu)^4}{\sigma^4} \qquad (7)$$

The Kurtosis is used to calculate the sample version of population value.

3.4 Training dataset Creation

For 20 subjects and for total 2 tasks, 40 samples are created in the database for total 8 features. This database is obtained automatically by running the MATLAB script, and loaded in the form of a matrix. This Dataset is used for training purpose in the classification. Any random signal is compared with this standard database.

3.5 Classification

Classification is the most important step for insuring the proper working of the system. There is a need to classify whether the task is eyes open or eyes closed. For classification of these tasks K-Nearest Neighbour classifier is used. KNN is a supervised classification method and it is a nonlinear classifier [12]. It uses class labels for training data. KNN makes prediction directly using the training dataset. It is the simple algorithm that stores training dataset of different classes or tasks and classifies new classes/tasks based on similarity measure (e.g. distance functions). In this the standard training dataset and the group matrix is provided with task labels. Further random sample is provided to the classifier and the classification is done based on distance functions. There are different types of distance functions such as Euclidean, cityblock, cosine, correlation and hamming. City block distance is used in classifier to get better accuracy of the classification. Another name for city block distance is Manhattan distance. It represents the absolute difference between co-ordinates of pair of objects. City Block distance is calculated according to Eq. (8) as follows:

$$\sum_{j=1}^{k} |aj - bj| \quad (8)$$

Based on the random input provided to the system, KNN classifier does comparison with the standard dataset and provides the output [13]. The classification between the two classes is then obtained and the information is then given as command to Arduino to control the movements of the servo motor.

3.6 Arduino MATLAB interface

The Arduino MATLAB interface is the last stage of this proposed work wherein, the computed and classified task is communicated to the Arduino via the MATLAB script. The Arduino Hardware packages are readily installed in the MATLAB R2017a. By simple connecting the Arduino board to a specific com port and mentioning the same in the MATLAB script, the servo motor is actuated according to the task. For example, for task 1 the arm rotates by 180 degrees and the wrist by 90 degrees. The rotation can be provided according to one's convenience.

4 Components

4.1 Arduino Uno Board

Arduino Uno is AT-mega328 microcontroller based board. In this work, Arduino Uno receives command on one of the 14 digital input/output pin and then on the same pin servo motor is connected. This command is crucial to Rotate the servo motors accordingly. Thus based on the classifier output servo motors are being controlled with the help of Arduino.

4.2 Servo Motor

A Servo Motor is basically a rotary mover or actuator which allows user to do precision control of linear or angular position, velocity and acceleration. Servo motors work upon a feedback system and therefore they are often referred to as motors suitable for working in Closed loop system. A servo motor has inbuilt motor, feedback circuit and motor driver. To use servo motor it needs power line, ground, and control pin. Through control pin, servo motor can be made to rotate upto 180 degrees. Therefore, a high torque servo motors are used for arm and finger movements respectively.

5 Software Implementation

The main steps for operating the robotic arm with BCI are shown in Fig. 2. The first step is to acquire the standard database from PhysioBank. After collecting the database, the signal processing is performed on it. Matlab R2017a has been used for the processing of the EEG signal and its classification. For Matlab-Arduino interfacing Support Packages of Arduino Hardware were installed on the System. This enabled the complete access of Arduino board on Matlab.

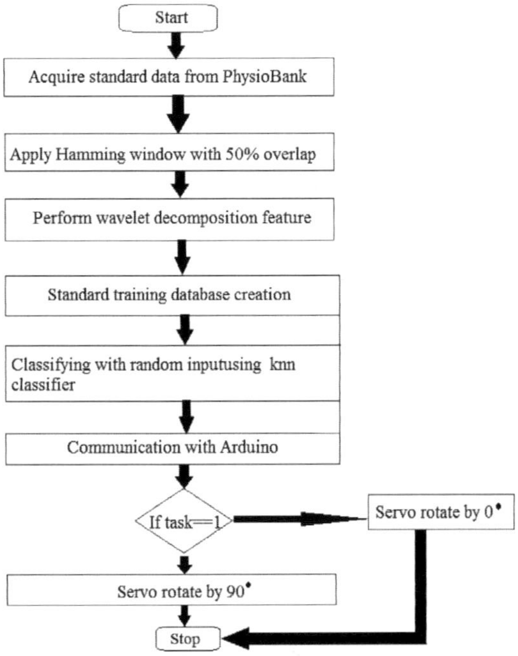

Fig. 2. System Flowchart

6 Result

The original EEG signal collected from Emotive Insight headset from the recording electrodes as shown in Fig. 3. The Emotiv Insight headset has an inbuilt EEG amplifier and ADC converter. The digitized data of EEG signal send to a computer system via Bluetooth in 2.4 GHz band. The EEG output having the frequency range of 0.2 to 45 Hz. The digitized EEG data doesn't need to be filtered as Emotive Insight headset itself contains notch filters of frequency range 50Hz and 60Hz to reject the power supply frequency.

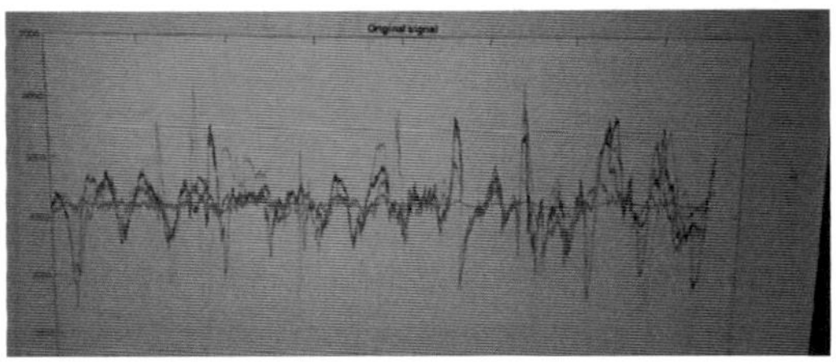

Fig. 3. Original Signal

To extract the features, the signal processing is performed on the collected data. The feature extraction is performed by using DWT. The features extracted from the EEG signals are Mean, Minimum, Variance, Standard Deviation, Entropy, Skewness, Kurtosis. The EEG signal corresponding to the different tasks is recorded and features are extracted from them. After that the classification among different tasks is done by using KNN classifier. The system is trained based on the signals collected from the Emotive Insight Headset. Based on the random input provided to the system, first the features are extracted from this input and then KNN classifier does comparison with the standard dataset and provides the output.

The output from the signal processing is then send to the digital input/output pin of Arduino onto which servo motors are connected. The interfacing of robotic arm is shown in Fig. 4. This output acts as a control command for the servo motors and the rotatory movement is performed according to the tasks.

Fig. 4. Robotic Arm

7 Conclusion

The prototype of robotic arm using BCI has been successfully developed and tested. The objective of the proposed work was to develop such a system that would help the paralyzed person work in similar fashion to a normal human being where the arm movement done by the brain signals. This system is useful for the paralyzed person whose brain functions properly. After extracting and processing EEG signals suitably, the movement of robotic arm can be designed to move in the direction according to the user brain commands. The applications of BCI are unbounded, similarly the applications and scope of improvement of proposed system is unbounded. As the number of brain commands increases, the more degree of freedom can be taken into consideration for the robotic arm movement. The same idea can be used to develop a BCI controlled Robotic leg.

References

1. Emotiv http://www.emotiv.com
2. Goldberger AL, Amaral LAN, Glass L, Hausdorff JM, Ivanov PCh, Mark RG, Mietus JE, Moody GB, Peng C-K, Stanley HE., National Library of Medicine-Circulation, *PhysioBank, PhysioToolkit,*

and PhysioNet: Components of a New Research Resource for Complex Physiologic Signals. **Circulation 2000 (June 13)**, Pages:101(23): e215–e220 (2000)

3. Schalk G., McFarland D.J., Hinterberger T., Birbaumer N., Wolpaw J.R., IEEE Transactions on Biomedical Engineering, *BCI2000: A General-Purpose Brain-Computer Interface (BCI) System*, **VOL. 51, NO. 6**, Pages: 1034-1043 (2004)
4. Charles G Gross, Journal of the History of the Neurosciences, *The Discovery of Motor Cortex and its Background,* **Vol. 16(3)**, Pages: 320-31 (2007)
5. Jerry J. Shih, Dean J. Krusienski and Jonathan R. Wolpawc, National Library of Medicine-Mayo Clin Proc., Brain-Computer Interfaces in Medicine, **Vol.87(3)**, Pages: 268–279 (2012)
6. Michael S.A. Graziano,1Charlotte S.R. Taylor,Tirin Moore, and Dylan F. Cooke, ScienceDirect- Neuron, *The Cortical Control of Movement Revisited,* **Volume 36, Issue 3,** Pages 349-362 (2002)
7. Sunny T.D., Aparna T., Neethu P., Venkateswaran J., Vishnupriya V., Vyas P.S., ICETEST, *Robotic Arm with Brain Computer Interfacing,* **Procedia Technology 24**, Pages: 1089 – 1096 (2015)
8. Ioulietta Lazarou, Spiros Nikolopoulos, Panagiotis C. Petrantonakis, Ioannis Kompatsiaris and Magda Tsolaki, Front Hum Neurosci., *EEG-Based Brain–Computer Interfaces for Communication and Rehabilitation of People with Motor Impairment: A Novel Approach of the 21st Century,* **v.12**, Pages: 12-14 (2018)
9. Chirag, Sanjeev Kumar Dhull IJSRD, *Analysis of EEG Signal Using Wavelet Transform and SVM Classifier,* **Volume-4**, Pages: 70-73 (2016)
10. Simon Haykin, Barry Van Veen, 2007 Signals and System, Second Edition John Wiley & Sons
11. Henry Candra, Mitchell Yuwono, Rifai Chai, Ardi Handojoseno, Irraivan Elamvazuthi, Hung T. Nguyen, Steven Su, nternational Conference of the IEEE Engineering in Medicine and Biology Society (EMBC), *Investigation of window size in classification of EEG-emotion signal with wavelet entropy and support vector machine* (2015)
12. Dayanand Dhongade, T.V.K.H Rao, ICIGEHT, *Classification of Sleep Disorders Based on EEG Signals by using Feature Extraction Techniques with KNN Classifier* (2017)
13. Annushree Bablani, Damodar Reddy Edla, Shubham Dodia, ICACC, *Classification of EEG data using KNN approach for concealed information test,* **Volume 143**, Pages 242-249 (2018)

ITM Web of Conferences 32, 03036 (2020) https://doi.org/10.1051/itmconf/20203203036
ICACC-2020

Supply Chain of Relief Materials using Blockchain

Jeet Bhatelia[1,*], *Sagar* Pandita[1], *Abhishek* Ajmera[1], *Narendra* Shekokar[2] and *Neha* Katre[1]

[1]Department of Information Technology, Dwarkadas J. Sanghvi College of Engineering, Mumbai, India
[2]Department of Computer Engineering, Dwarkadas J. Sanghvi College of Engineering, Mumbai, India

Abstract. Blockchain serves as an immutable ledger which allows transactions to take place in a decentralized manner. The proposed solution incorporates the use of Blockchain for Supply Chain Management of Relief Materials after a Disaster. The proposed solution also provides many additional features when compared to the current system like being tamper-proof, providing anonymity and accountability to the users. Our solution incorporates a box-in-box approach whilst keeping tabs via tamper-proof barcodes. Barcodes will be frequently scanned at designated locations. Users also have the facility to track the donated items online through a dedicated website. For blockchain infrastructure, we have used Hyperledger Fabric.

1 Introduction

Natural disasters often cause massive losses to property, people and infrastructure. The United Nations statistics show that natural disasters have cost India $80 billion over the past two decades. And when it comes to disasters, India is the worst sufferer (in terms of death & economical losses) because of high population density. Whenever disaster strikes, people all over the world try to help the people affected by sending donations & supplies. People use different ways in order to donate money online, some use links provided by government & some people use links provided by private organizations.

The problem with all these systems is that the donor does not know where his/her donated items are actually going; is it going to the disaster affected people or is it going into the pockets of corrupt officials. When the government urges people to donate money & items, they don't trust the system because of the perceived prevalence of corruption in the hierarchical government body. Even the donations that people give via online links are not accounted for; and that makes people apprehensive towards donating items. There are many fake links circulated by miscreants which dupe people into giving them their money. People want a trusted system so that they know their donations aren't being misused. The current scenario doesn't allow for traceability and accountability of the items that goes into the system. In the proposed system, a donor can track the usage of his donated items.

To do so, the ledger-based technology can be used which will bring accountability and traceability in the picture and will allow donors to see where their items really go and be assured that their donations are going in the right place. Traceability will allow backtracking of items that are allotted the category of relief material. Adulteration of data will be prevented by the decentralized peer to peer architecture of the system with backups at every node. An interface will be available to the relief camps present in the disaster affected places to request goods.

2 Literature Survey

The current system is based on the three-tier architecture. A three-tier architecture is a client-server architecture in which the user-interface, middleware, database is developed and maintained separately. [1]

These systems are based upon a central point of failure. That single point of failure makes it vulnerable to attacks involving tampering with the database.

2.1 Industry 4.0 Fostering Construction Supply Chain Management

This Paper discusses how Industry 4.0 will be responsible for the transformation of the manufacturing industry, but it will also have an impact on the construction industry and all the supply chains related to it. [2]

2.2 Chainweb P.O.W Parallel-Chain Architecture for High Throughput

PoW has problems that inhibit its ability to power a high distributed economy and is aptly criticized for its use of large amounts of electricity, and congestion fees in the form of exorbitant transaction fees. Existing Proof of Work modules are known for very low throughput, even though improvements through protocol changes have been made, none have given an ideal path towards approach the throughput levels of current payment systems. [3]

2.3 Securify: Practical Security Analysis of Smart Contract

Permission-less blockchains allow processing of smart contracts, providing foreign nodes to communicate without depending on third party handlers. Even though being potentially promising, a number of security related concerns have weakened the trust in managing money by smart contracts. To reduce issues like these, Securify, a security analyzer for Ethereum smart

* Corresponding author: jbhatelia@outlook.com

contracts that has high throughput, is autonomous, and able to decide if the business logic is vulnerable or not.[4]

2.4 Blockchain technology for enhancing supply chain resilience

This paper discusses the inner workings of blockchain technology along with its architecture. It then discusses applications of blockchain in supply chain security and the various sources of supply chain risks. It describes Blockchain enabled risk management and convergence of the blockchain with IoT. [5]

2.5 Blockchain's roles in strengthening cybersecurity and protecting privacy

This paper talks of the numerous security features of blockchain which give it an edge over existing systems. It talks about the various challenges in cybersecurity and the possible ways to circumvent them. [6]

2.6 t-Closeness: Privacy Beyond k-Anonymity and l -Diversity

Generally speaking, privacy is measured by the amount of vulnerable information about an entity. Information gain can be represented as the difference between the posterior belief and the prior belief. The originality of their approach is that they separate the information gain into two parts: from that of the whole population in the released data and that about specific individuals. [7]

2.7 Plasma: Scalable Autonomous Smart Contracts

Plasma is a work in progress software for execution of smart contracts which is scalable to a good amount of updates per second, enabling the blockchain to be able to represent a good amount of decentralized financial apps all around the world.
Plasma consists of two parts: Reforming all computation into a set of MapReduce functions, or do Proof-of-Stake token bonding on existing blockchains. [8]

2.8 Ganache

Ganache is a blockchain modelling platform for Ethereum test development that can be used to deploy smart contracts, develop dapps, and do thorough testing. [9]

2.9 Drizzle

Drizzle is an assortment of libraries that make writing dapp UI/UX much more convenient. The core of Drizzle is based on a Redux store, providing the use of Redux. [10]

- It makes adding middleware easier to the application.
- It takes care of syncing your business logic, transaction data and more. Response time is impressive as all is kept dynamic.

2.10 Hyperledger Fabric

Fabric is developed and maintained by developers all around the world. It was made keeping in mind that big organizations may be using them in future. Hyperledger Fabric is modular in nature by default bringing about flexibility, optimizing the platform for myriad use-cases like banking, insurance, healthcare, supply chain and even digital music. Fabric supports smart contracts written in languages like Java, Go and Node.js. [11]

After analysis of literature surveys, we found that we need a system that incorporates all the above mentioned blockchain related features that enables us to add integrity, transparency, accountability to the system. Centralized systems can be easily manipulated via a single-entry point. But for Decentralized systems the same manipulation needs to be done on hundreds of machines which is practically not possible, thus making it inherently more secure than centralized single point failure systems. It truly helps the donors track their product from the time of pickup to the time it reaches the Relief camp. Blockchain features an immutable digital ledger, that is extremely safe to share with 3rd parties and create transactions. This also reduces fraud, and errors. The benefits we tend to receive through blockchain will save time and several other efforts. The blockchain is impenetrable in any realistic cyber-attack and hacking. There are several potential advantages that companies acquire from the blockchain technology. Increasing the public trust through the share information policy and increasing quality. An absence of malpractice and so reducing PR risk as well for the organization at work. Hence, we are proposing a system which is based on Blockchain.

3 Proposed System Architecture

As can be seen in the below diagram, we are utilizing the platform provided by IBM, Hyperledger. This will be the core on which the blockchain and business logic will run.

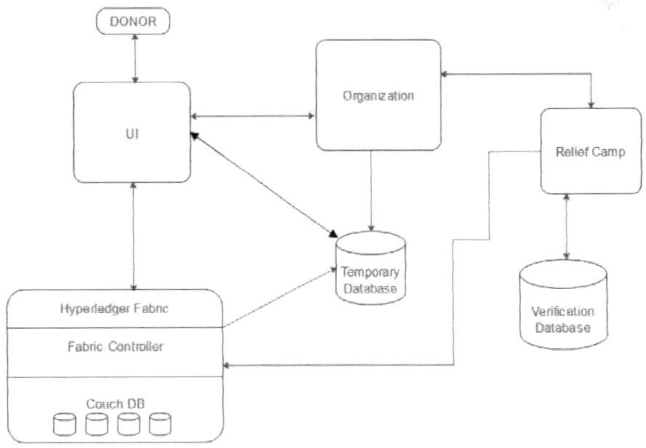

Fig. 1. Proposed System Architecture.

- The proposed system architecture consists of 4 main components and they are
  - User Interface: The User Interface and the User Experience is paramount to the system as it caters to people belonging to both ends of the spectrum. Ease of use has been kept in mind while designing the UI. The learning curve needs to be very small so that uneducated and educated people can easily

* Corresponding author: jbhatelia@outlook.com

use it. Cluttering on a page has been avoided methodically.

- Hyperledger Fabric Framework: This versatile platform provided by IBM will be at the core of the project. All back-end development and deployment will be taken care of using Fabric. A well-defined CLI has been provided for developers to create meaningful business logic (smart contract) to use in a project.
    - The Hyperledger Fabric consists of multiple components, a few of them include:
        - Controller
        - Fabric Console
        - CouchDB
    - We have also found ways to mitigate from the possible attacks on Blockchain. and they are:
        - 51% attack: Here the evil entity tries to take over the network by owning 51% of the nodes and hence enabling them to do a hard fork and take control over the network.
            - To prevent this, we will be having a central authority that will monitor the number of nodes in the network.
        - DoS Attack: It is when multiple spam nodes try to spam the honest nodes with bogus traffic and could lead to congestion of network and deny some nodes from accessing data.
            - To minimize the risk, we will change some parameters like size of block etc.
        - Sybil Attacks: This is when the attacker pretends to be many people at the same time and hence changing the integrity of the data.
            - We will incorporate strict measures in the access control system to limit such cases.
- B2B Management: The system also caters to the supply chain management side of post disaster management, this communication between two businesses can be managed on the website console.
- Relief Camps: These are the well-defined spots erected after a natural disaster for disaster affected people to go to for relief material. These camps will be kept in our database while deciding where the donated items need to go to.

The flow is as follows:

- The user accesses the portal and interacts with the UI; the user then enters the disaster to which they want to make a donation to.
- Then the user is redirected to details page where he chooses the type and quantity of item he wishes to donate. He then visits a drop-off point to donate the items.
- Meanwhile the system uses an efficient way to transfer data between the website and the database. Instead of transferring the entire table containing the items entered, a 'Tag ID' is formed – a 10-bit string which encapsulates all the information about the donated item which is stored in the database. The Tag ID can be reconstructed in a tabular form wherever required.
- At the drop-off point, the organization worker enters the donor's mobile number into the system to view the items he has entered. The worker checks the items brought by the user and matches it with the data entered.
- To ensure veracity of the items donated, the user receives a text message on his mobile phone which includes the list of items donated and an OTP which is required to conclude the transaction and only then the data is added to the Blockchain.
- Similar to above mentioned 'Tag ID', when the items are approved at the drop-off point, a Transaction ID is generated (13-bit string) which is stored in the blockchain's couchDB.
- Barcodes are stuck to each item and are read into the system via a mobile app.
- The system uses a box-in-box approach where barcodes are used to link items in boxes in a tree data-structure. The boxes in-turn are linked to the transport vehicle in a similar structure.
- The barcodes are scanned at the destination warehouse and the fabric is updated. The user can track the current location of his donated items via the website.
    - We will be using ZXing ("Zebra Crossing") barcode scanning library for decoding the barcodes.
    - For creating barcodes, we used random numbers.
- Meanwhile the relief camps can request items from the organizations by viewing item statistics of each organization.
- Our website will communicate with the Node SDK with the REST APIs we created. The Node SDK can easily communicate with Hyperledger Fabric.
- We did the Hyperledger fabric development using its version 1.4 which is currently the most stable version.

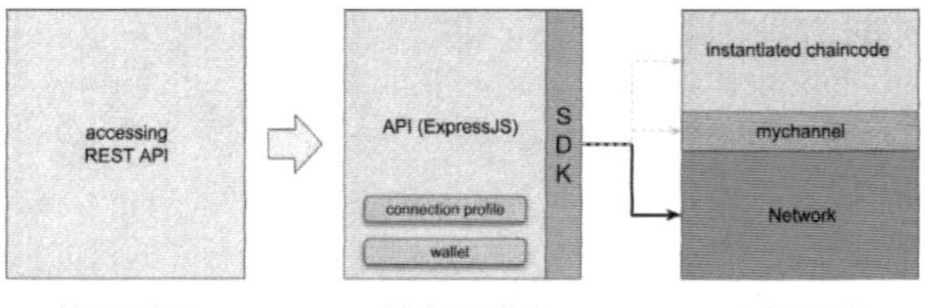

Fig. 2. Communication Architecture.

4 Features of Proposed System

- One of the major features of the proposed system is that the blockchain is immutable & it has tamper detection.
- It provides anonymity to the user.
- Even the highest level of supply chain is subject to getting hacked. Blockchain on the other hand has never been hacked. The reason is that blockchain networks are secured by several computers called

* Corresponding author: jbhatelia@outlook.com

nodes and these nodes confirm the transaction on the network.

- Other Features of the proposed system are:
  - Fault Tolerance
    - This means that since the whole system is distributed across multiple devices where the ledger is stored, thus increasing redundancy, and eliminating the Centralized architecture's single point of failure.
  - Removal of single point of failure
    - Hyperledger Fabric will use all the peers on the network, inclusive of all the organizations to replicate the ledger data. Overall, its far easier to manipulate data when its only source is a single entity. In our system it will be practically impossible for data manipulation.
  - Ease of Management
    - Once any data is added in the Hyperledger Network, it will automatically get replicated across all the participating organizations.
  - Better Authentication
    - Users who wish to donate will be able to simply login using their mobile number. An OTP will be received on their mobile, every time the user wishes to access the website, this procedure will be followed. This is a less tedious process than having passwords for each individual user who must have unique usernames. Therefore, the users do not have to remember usernames and passwords every time they want to access their website.

Table 1. Comparison between existing and proposed system.

	Existing System	**Proposed System**
Donation type	Only supports monetary donation.	Supports donation of items & money
Donor-organization consensus	Not applicable	Provided
Item tracking	Not provided	Provided
Disaster selection	Not provided	Provided
Multi-organization visibility	-	Provided
Security	Not based on Blockchain	Based on Blockchain

- From the above comparison table, we can see that the proposed system incorporates many additional features to the existing system like security, visibility, tracking. It follows a decentralized architecture instead of the existing client-server architecture.
- we conclude that the proposed system is able to plug most of the gaping holes in the current system through the use of Blockchain.
- This project's forefront idea is about bringing accountability. Comparing it with the current systems (Centralized) they are fast indeed but lack any sort of accountability towards the donor which our system provides.

5 Conclusion

In this paper, the proposed solution is customer centric and generates trust in society towards donating items for post disaster initiatives. By bringing trust, accountability and traceability in the system, it can be checked if the donated items actually reach the affected and have the donors consider it as a positive action rather than an uncertain action like we have currently wherein the third-party takes all the responsibilities without any accountability towards the donor.

REFERENCES

1. Three-Tier Architecture, https://www.techopedia.com/definition/24649/three-tier-architecture, last accessed 2019/08/21
2. P. Dallasega, IEEE Engg. Management Review, *Industry 4.0 Fostering Construction Supply Chain Management: Lessons Learned From Engineer-to-Order Suppliers*, **46(3)**, 49 (2018)
3. Chainweb, Kadena.io, **15** (to be published)
4. P. Tsankov, A. Dan, D.D. Cohen, A. Gervais, F. Bünzli, M. Vechev, arXiv:1806.01143, *Securify: Practical Security Analysis of Smart Contracts*, (2018)
5. H. Min, ScienceDirect, *Blockchain technology for enhancing supply chain resilience*, Volume **62** Issue **1**, 35 (2019)
6. N. Kshetri, ScienceDirect, *Blockchain's roles in strengthening cybersecurity and protecting privacy*, Telecommunications Volume **41**, Issue **10**, 1027 (2017)
7. N. Li, T. Li, S. Venkatasubramanian, IEEE 23rd Int. Conf. on Data Engg., *t-Closeness: Privacy Beyond k-Anonymity and l-Diversity* (2007)
8. Plasma, working draft, Plasma.io (2017)
9. Truffle Framework - Ganache, https://truffleframework.com/docs/ganache/overview, last accessed 2019/08/21
10. Truffle Framework - Drizzle, https://truffleframework.com/docs/drizzle/overview, last accessed 2019/08/21
11. Hyperledger Fabric Release Page, https://hyperledge-fabric.readthedocs.io/en/release-1.4/, last accessed 2019/08/21

* Corresponding author: jbhatelia@outlook.com

Underwater Object Detection using Tensorflow

Avinash Mahavarkar[1,3,*], *Ritika* Kadwadkar[2,**], *Sneha* Maurya[3,***], and *Mrs. Smitha* Raveendran[4,****]

[1]avinashmahavarkar@gmail.com
[2]ritika.kadwadkar1525@gmail.com
[3]snehamaurya1610@gmail.com
[4]smitha.raveendran@rait.ac.in

Abstract. Object Detection is a popular technology that detects instances within an image. In order to eliminate the barriers in Computer Vision technology due to the dissolution of the BGR(Blue-Green-Red) constituents with the increase in depth, it has been a necessity that the accuracy and efficiency of detecting any object underwater is optimum. In this article, we conduct Underwater Object Detection using Machine Learning through Tensorflow and Image Processing along with Faster R-CNN (Regions with Convolution Neural Network) as an algorithm for implementation. A suitable environment will be created so that Machine Learning algorithm will be used to train different images of the object. Open source Computer Vision has various functions which can be used for the image processing needs when an image is captured.

1 Introduction

Image processing is used to operate digital images using various algorithms. In image processing the image is in the form of two dimensional matrix on which certain procedures or algorithms are performed in order to get a favourable result. Some of these algorithms are contrast enhancement, dithering and half toning, feature detection etc. Object Detection is one of the primary applications of image processing. It is a procedure in which any stationary object or a moving object can be detected in any real time instance, an image or a video .For training the data sets machine learning plays a very important role. Machine Learning is a field within Artificial Intelligence in which the machine trains itself while adapting it to the changing environment. The trained dataset are the ones which consists of the images of objects or material which we have to detect and the tested datasets are different from the trained ones and are used for checking the accuracy of the system. 80 percent of images are used to train whereas 20 percent are used for testing. In this project, we have used Tensorflow which is an Object Detection API which uses Faster R-CNN as the machine learning algorithm . Within Tensorflow the pixels of images are in the form of matrix and operations are performed on them in order to obtain required results.There are various pre-trained models for detecting objects they are R-CNN,Mask R-CNN,YOLO (You Only Live Once) etc.However these pre-trained models have their own specified data sets, in order to make use of our self trained data we have to create a suitable environment after fine-tuning the pre-trained model. There are various applications of Tensorflow which are focused on deep learning and training. Tensorflow makes use of Python programming, hence there is utilization of respective Python version.

2 Related Work

Exploration for the need of object detection began during the 1960's.There are various traditional methods which were used for object detection such as using haar classifiers, Support Vector Machine (SVM) along with Histogram of Oriented Gradients (HOG), Oriented FAST and rotated BRIEF (ORB) feature matching etc. However these techniques did not give accurate results in case of underwater object detection. Thus the following object detection and recognition techniques proposed by different authors gave a tremendous boost within this field.

For an image to be recognized correctly its edges are taken into consideration so that a correct result is obtained.Guobo Xie and Wen Lu [18] explains as to why is edge detection important in case of image processing. They have used opencv functions to detect edges of an image by first converting it to gray scale, then by adding a filter, thresholding the obtained result thereby the output only displays the edges of an image.

Apart from edge matching feature matching is another important aspect of detecting an object in any real time instance or an image. Lie et al. [15] have proposed the SURF method for object detection in which using the algorithm which is based on feature matching technique the edge features, key points and the color resemblance of an object is been detected. However the SIFT AND SURF algorithms are patented and to use them a proper permission and license has to be issued. An alternative for these meth-

*e-mail: Mailaddressforfirstauthor
**e-mail: Mailaddressforsecondauthorifnecessary
***e-mail: Mailaddressforlastauthorifnecessary
****e-mail: Mailaddressforlastauthorifnecessary

ods is the ORB method. Ethan Rublee et al.[16] proposes in his paper the ORB (Oriented fast and Rotated Brief) feature which is an open source algorithm and two magnitudes faster as compared to SIFT and SURF however the efficiency of is compromised in this case.
Rahul Dutt Sharma et al. [14] explains in his work about the subtraction of background within a real time object so as to find the correct result. It uses a three frame differencing which uses a AND operator and an OR operator this is because only the AND operator cannot detect the objects with a moving frame as a result an OR operator is used so as to detect the moving objects unlike the two frame differencing which uses only AND operator.
Xiu Li et al[8] proposed in their research paper about the detection of various fish species underwater.LifeCLEF Fish dataset along with a video dataset from Fish4knowledge were used in training the data and the machine learning algorithm used was Fast R-CNN.
J. Kim and S. Yu[9] designed a SONAR based ROV which used a convolution based neural network in order to detect object at a distance. It comprised of a main AUV with a small ROV to travel to distant places underwater.
Hai Huang et al [10] proposed underwater marine detection using the Faster R-CNN algorithm which has a greater mAP (Mean Average Precision) as compared to other CNN algorithms they took into account data augmentation as Faster R-CNN requires mass labelled samples of images.
R. Phadnis et al[10] have introduced a custom designed algorithm which would keep a track of objects within a specific diameter so as to prevent the wastage of time if any object is lost.
Zhe Chan et al.[13] have explained the use of an artificial collimated light source so as to avoid various problems of object detection underwater. A collimated light source have parallel rays of electromagnetic radiation and thus has lowest degree of dispersion. Its aim is to focus the artificial light on the object directly such that it collimates directly on the object.
Jonathan Huang et al. [17] in the paper proposed mentions about all the tensorflow models or machine learning algorithms which are available for object detection underwater. It explains about SSD, YOLO, CNN, RCNN Faster RCNN etc. The detailed explanation of all these algorithms their advantages and disadvantages are mentioned, their accuracy percentages, their working, etc. are all included in their publication.
Our project involves underwater object detection using Tensorflow with Faster R-CNN algorithm model as our builging block. The survey based on the Faster RCNN algorithm is from the Shaoqing Ren et al [6] publication in which a detailed explanation of the working of Faster RCNN has been mentioned along with the important aspects of the algorithm and is proven to be the most accurate among the different convolution neural networks.
Sai, B Sasikala, T.[11] have proposed a paper based on object detection and their count within an image using the tensorflow object detection API. It used the Faster R-CNN algorithm same as proposed in this paper.However in this paper we have taken into account the underwater object detection concept.

3 Object Recognition

3.1 Phases of object recognition

The object detection and recognition algorithms are basically used in order to find the presence of an object, its movement and orientation within an image or real time instance. For an object to be detected and recognised the algorithm should be able to determine the presence of an object or multiple objects. Object recognition includes the following phases: preprocessing, feature extraction, feature selection, modeling, matching, and positioning [1] . The various algorithms based on feature matching are ORB, Speeded Up Robust Features (SIFT), Scale Invariant Feature Transform (SURF) etc. However these techniques have low efficiency in characterising various objects since it uses the features of an object to detect its presence.Therefore many object detection algorithms were introduced in order to overcome the drawbacks of these techniques and they are CNN,R-CNN,YOLO etc.Every algorithm within itself has its pros and cons.The most commonly used object detection and recognition algorithms are YOLO and Faster R-CNN.

3.2 Tensorflow and faster R-CNN

In this paper, underwater object detection using Tensorflow in order to train the system and Faster R-CNN as a machine learning algorithm for detection and implementation has been proposed.

3.2.1 Faster R-CNN

The basis of Faster R-CNN starts from understanding as to what is CNN(Convolution Neural Network). CNN has flourished within the applications of deep learning in case of image or video processing. A CNN consists of 4 layers - Convolution layer, Relu layer, Pooling layer and Flattening layer. The convolution layer consists of a filter used for navigation, this filter keeps fluttering over an image and makes calculation of every pixel. Relu layer has a Relu activation function used for eliminating the negative values and rounding them off to zero . Within the pooling layer, using feature map size reduction, only important parameters are considered. The flattening layer is used for the conversion of matrix into a single vector.The Convolutional and the Pooling Layer, together form the i-th layer of a CNN. The layers could be increased depending upon as to how much efficiency we need and how complex the systems are however the cost of computation increases accordingly. However the CNN algorithm is an image classification algorithm and in order to detect objects and recognize them a few modifications have to be done such as drawing the box around certain objects detected in front of a background etc.We simply cannot use use the CNN layers followed by an FC layer to do the same as the number

 https://doi.org/10.1051/itmconf/20203203037

of objects at the output are not bounded to a specific number. Girshick et al. [3] introduced a region-based CNN (R-CNN) for object detection. In this method the image is divided in a certain number of recommended regions. The ubiquitous procedure of the working of an R-CNN algorithm is from the gathered input images, region proposals are extracted. Every proposal is thus elapsed through the CNN to compute the features so that the regions can be correctly classified. However the training time in this case goes until 83 hours. In order to overcome this problem, Fast R-CNN was introduced. The only difference between R-CNN and Fast R-CNN is that instead of dividing the image into regions initially it is divided after applying CNN. The training time required for this algorithm is 9 hours. The faster R-CNN requires less training time that is about 4 hours,hence it is more efficient and accurate as compared to the previous two generations of CNN based algorithms. In figure 1, the steps which are followed as per the faster R-CNN algorithm to find objects in an image are mentioned. The basic building block of a faster R-CNN

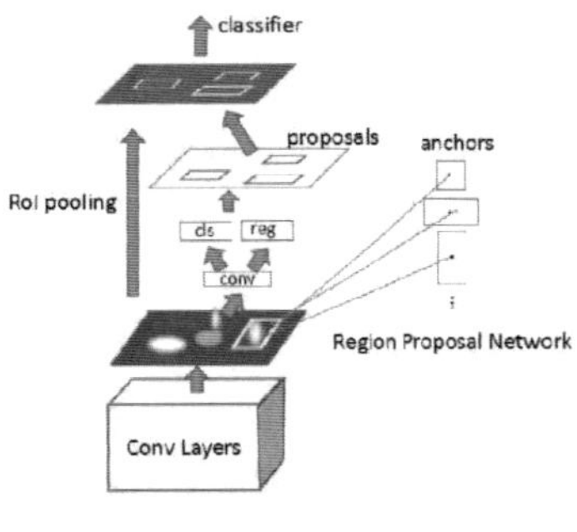

Figure 1. R-CNN Algorithm[6]

network is a Regional proposal Network (RPN) unlike R-CNN and Fast R-CNN which uses a selective search algorithm which makes the algorithm slower. An RPN can be defined as a platform that proposes the convolution features of any image or an instance within a video.The core of RPN is to detect different sizes of objects with different sizes of anchors. [7] It takes into account the boundary features of an object and by custom training the images RPN could be used in order to increase the efficiency of the output as it generates a supreme quality region of proposal with the increasing number of images. There are two steps which are in the Faster R-CNN they are: shared bottom convolutional layers, a region proposal network (RPN) and a region-of-interest (ROI) based [4] classifier.In this case the complete image is fed to the Convolution neural network.This network generates a convolution feature map which is comprised of the bottom convolution layers. The region proposal is predicted within an image. Based on this, RPN creates a respective object proposal, after which the Region of interest classifier estimates the label from a feature point which is gathered by ROI-pooling.Thus the classes of the object is recognized with respect to the trained images in the dataset. As you can see from the results table it is clear that the Faster R-CNN algorithm has the lowest test time i.e 0.2 seconds this is because of the creation of RPN instead of using the selective search algorithm. The accuracy of the system is also increased.

3.2.2 Tensorflow

Tensorflow is an Object detection API which has an open source library for machine learning.It is used to detect multiple objects in real-time video streams.[5] The system is borne from real-world experience in conducting research more than one hundred machine learning projects throughout a wide range of Google products. [2] In this project, we have utilized the Tensorflow 1.14 version. TensorFlow uses dataflow graphs to represent computation, shared state, and the operations that mutate that state. [2] It can be used as an interface between the training models and the machine learning algorithms used for object detection in our case.There are various models available in tensorflow they are keras, resnet, mobilenet, inception and delf. These pre-trained models utilizing algorithms like R-CNN,Faster R-CNN, Fast R-CNN, YOLO etc. We can also create our own model and train them for object detection. The preliminary dataset which tensorflow uses is COCO (Common Objects in Context) which is compatible with all types of GPU's, handsets, CPU's,TPU's. Along with these tensorflow also supports transfer learning which helps us define our own classes in pretrained models thus eliminating the use of large datasets.However we can train a custom based database also, Tensorflow avails the feature of a custom trained model. The below flowchart in figure 2 represents the step by procedure of using a pre-trained models for detection of objects underwater

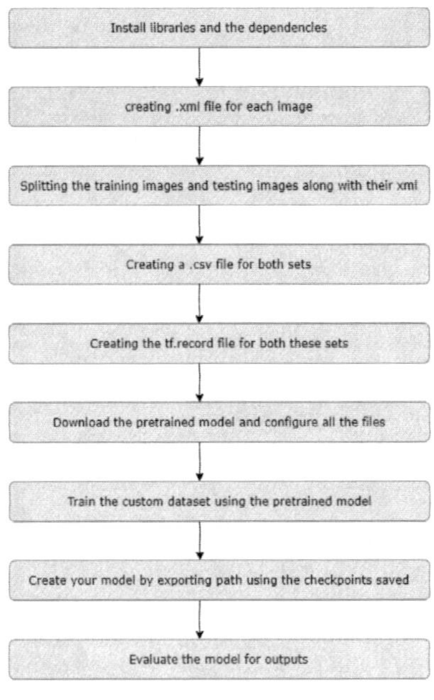

Figure 2. Tensorflow object detection flowchart to train models[6]

 https://doi.org/10.1051/itmconf/20203203037

4 Experimental Results

4.1 Underwater Setup

We have used a predefined dataset to detect an object underwater.In Tensorflow we initiate a call regarding whichever dataset is required. We have used COCO dataset for our observations. This particular dataset consists of over 80 classes, 80000 training images and 40000 validation images which keep getting updated automatically. At Ramrao Adik Institute of Technology, we have an underwater tank setup which is used for research purposes. We have used this setup for performing our experiment.Figure 3 shows the image of the tank setup. In the tank, a camera is connected to the system.The camera used is a Super Hi Vision 2 Million Pixels CMOS camera. The Camera is flexible and is waterproof with a 8.5mm diameter. Due to its small size we can inspect areas under water, gaps and holes.The camera captures real time images with objects detected in it. The system used has Intel i5-8265U 1.8GHz processor with an 8GB installed RAM. One of the important aspect of our project is using the correct GPU. Our system has NVIDIA GEFORCE MX250, with the help of this version of GPU object detection was efficiently carried out.

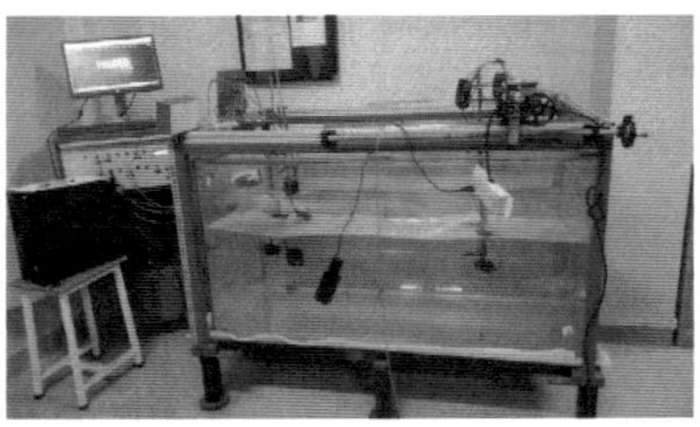

Figure 3. Tank setup

Further, we put objects like Toothbrush, Cup, Bottle, Clock, etc in the tank. To test the efficiency of this experiment, we performed this in unclean water and where the source of light was less. As the water was impure and illumination was minimum, objects were still recognized efficiently. Whenever an object is present in the proximity of the camera, a bounding box appears on the screen and it also indicates the extent of feature that is matched with the trained images in percentage.

4.2 Results

So as we can see the system is able to execute the task of object detection and recognition using tensorflow and machine learning. Faster R-CNN was used in this project which in return increased the accuracy of the system. These are the results which we procured as shown in figure 4. Even in filthy water the camera is able to detect objects with an accuracy of percentages shown in the image result. The comparison of the results with other CNN algorithm are mentioned in table 1 which relates the accuracy of the system with accuracy of the training images.

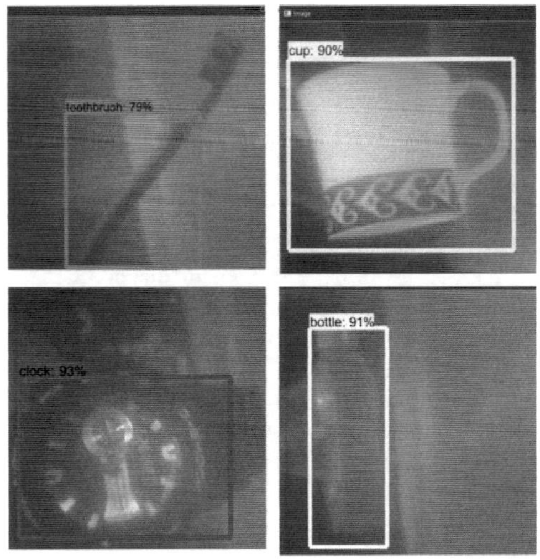

Figure 4. Objects detected under water

5 Conclusion

In this paper, we proposed the Faster R-CNN algorithm with Tensorflow for the underwater object detection. The algorithm used in our case was the Faster R-CNN algorithm which uses Regional proposal regions as the basic building block because of which the test time of detection is reduced since an RPN takes into account the boundary features of an object. By using a trained dataset it was clear that the accuracy of the system was optimal. However by using a custom trained dataset the accuracy and efficiency can be increased further more as the RPN is capable of generating a supreme quality region of proposal. Because of various effects such as dehazing, scattering of light and RGB color disappearance it becomes more and more difficult to detect objects.However by using such machine learning algorithms and proper training of images within the datasets these problems can be resolved to great extent.

Table 1. Results

Method	Test time	Training accuracy	Op accuracy
CNN	0.452 s	98.19 %	96.54 %
R-CNN	49 s	96.72 %	94.67 %
Fast R-CNN	2.3 s	97.98 %	95.68 %
Faster R-CNN	0.2 s	97.65 %	96.31 %

6 Future Work

The improvement we are trying to achieve in this project is that we are testing to add our own custom trained dataset to the model rather than using the default one. We are facing difficulties related to compatibility of the system and the various packages installed for tensorflow. After successfully attaining the same we will be able to detect the objects which we train leading to the increased efficiency of the system.

References

[1] Research on underwater object recognition based on YOLOv3 Hongbo Yang1 • Ping Liu1 • YuZhen Hu1 • JingNan Fu1

[2] TensorFlow: A System for Large-Scale Machine Learning Martín Abadi, Paul Barham, Jianmin Chen, Zhifeng Chen, Andy Davis, Jeffrey Dean, Matthieu Devin, Sanjay Ghemawat, Geoffrey Irving, Michael Isard, Manjunath Kudlur, Josh Levenberg, Rajat Monga, Sherry Moore, Derek G. Murray, Benoit Steiner, Paul Tucker, Vijay Vasudevan, Pete Warden, Martin Wicke, Yuan Yu, and Xiaoqiang Zheng, Google Brain

[3] R. B. Girshick, Donahue, T. Darrel, and J. Malik. *R*ich feature hierarchies for accurate object detection and semantic segmentation. In CVPR, pages 580–587, 2014

[4] Domain Adaptive Faster R-CNN for Object Detection in the Wild Yuhua Chen1 Wen Li1 Christos Sakaridis1 Dengxin Dai1 Luc Van Gool1,2 1Computer Vision Lab, ETH Zurich 2VISICS, ESAT/PSI, KU Leuven

[5] R. Phadnis, J. Mishra and S. Bendale, "Objects Talk - Object Detection and Pattern Tracking Using TensorFlow," 2018 Second International Conference on Inventive Communication and Computational Technologies (ICICCT), Coimbatore, 2018, pp. 1216-1219.

[6] Faster R-CNN: Towards Real-Time Object Detection with Region Proposal Networks Shaoqing Ren Kaiming He Ross Girshick Jian Sun.

[7] X. Chen, Qiang Guo, Shuohao Li and Jun Zhang, "Holistic Vertical Regional Proposal Network for scene text detection," 2017 2nd International Conference on Image, Vision and Computing (ICIVC), Chengdu, 2017, pp. 72-77.

[8] Fast Accurate Fish Detection and Recognition of Underwater Images with Fast R-CNN Xiu Li, Min Shang, Hongwei Qin, Liansheng Chen.

[9] J. Kim and S. Yu, "Convolutional neural network-based real-time ROV detection using forward-looking sonar image," 2016 IEEE/OES Autonomous Underwater Vehicles (AUV), Tokyo, 2016, pp. 396-400.

[10] Faster R-CNN for marine organisms detection and recognition using data augmentation Hai Huanga, Hao Zhoua, Xu Yang , Lu Zhang , Lu Qi, Ai-Yun Zang.

[11] Sai, B Sasikala, T.. (2019). Object Detection and Count of Objects in Image using Tensor Flow Object Detection API, 542-546.

[12] R. Phadnis, J. Mishra and S. Bendale, "Objects Talk - Object Detection and Pattern Tracking Using TensorFlow," 2018 Second International Conference on Inventive Communication and Computational Technologies (ICICCT), Coimbatore, 2018, pp. 1216-1219.

[13] Underwater Object Segmentation Based on Optical Features Zhe Chen 1 ID , Zhen Zhang 1, Yang Bu 2, Fengzhao Dai 2, Tanghuai Fan 3 and Huibin Wang 1,*

[14] Optimized Dynamic Background Subtraction Technique for Moving Object Detection and Tracking 1 Rahul Dutt Sharma, 2 Shubh Lakshmi Agrwal, 3 Sandeep K. Gupta, 4 Anil Prajapati .

[15] Learning SURF Cascade for Fast and Accurate Object Detection Jianguo Li, Yimin Zhang

[16] ORB: an efficient alternative to SIFT or SURF Ethan Rublee Vincent Rabaud Kurt Konolige Gary Bradski

[17] Speed/accuracy trade-offs for modern convolutional object detectors Jonathan Huang Vivek Rathod Chen Sun Menglong Zhu Anoop Korattikara Alireza Fathi Ian Fischer Zbigniew Wojna Yang Song Sergio Guadarrama

[18] TensorFlow: A system for large-scale machine learning, Matthieu Devin, Sanjay Ghemawat, Geoffrey Irving, Michael Isard, Manjunath Kudlur, Josh Levenberg, Rajat Monga, Sherry Moore, Derek G. Murray, Benoit Steiner, Paul Tucker, Vijay Vasudevan, Pete Warden, Martin Wicke, Yuan Yu, and Xiaoqiang Zheng

https://doi.org/10.1051/itmconf/20203203038

Integrity and Authenticity of Academic Documents Using Blockchain Approach

Mukul Rane[1,*], *Shubham* Singh[2,**], *Rohan* Singh[3,***], and *Vidhate* Amarsinh[4,****]

[1]Ramrao Adik Institute of Technology, Nerul
[2]Ramrao Adik Institute of Technology, Nerul
[3]Ramrao Adik Institute of Technology, Nerul
[4]Ramrao Adik Institute of Technology, Nerul

Abstract. Blockchain has a strong capacity to monitor and retain educational records. The paperless future has yet to become a reality, even with the ability to digitally generate documents. Physical copy of records are still regularly printed which makes them susceptible to document fraud. Thus, the issue of fake certificates and academic records has risen drastically. In this paper, we have made a reliable verification method to avoid academic frauds. The idea presented here is developed over Hyperledger. The University or The Educational Institute is responsible for issuing the certificates, mark-sheets, transcripts, etc. and mining it over the blockchain. The student is provided with the hash number which is the reference number. This number serves the reference of the data. The Organization or the Industry Personal using the hash number checks for the integrity of the submitted document. The present study discusses about importance of block chain and it's applicability especially for the applications like verification of Academic Records.
Keywords- Blockchain, Hyperledger, Academic Record Verification, Secure Hash Algorithm (SHA-256)

1 Introduction

Each corporation has critical information that demands protection. The current centralized storage system is the one that requires preservation of the information residing on the single system. Alternately, unless the content changed in the system the revised file is obtained by anyone who has to be stopped from doing so. Blockchain technology lets enterprises save the contents in every network-connected device. With such an approach a file can never be easily changed to store information [11]. For instance, whenever a file is changed in a system, it can never be updated on all network services since each service has its own version preserved in a database defined as a decentralized and distributed ledger [1]. Because the data contained in blocks and then each block is ultimately connected to another forming a block chain, the network is known as a blockchain [2]. The primary use of this application would be to prohibit participants or associations of external parties from entering into a contract. Digital currencies like Ethereum, Bit-coin, etc. emerged with the support of blockchain technology [3]. This can be the potential method of making a contract that involves only creator and recipient, excluding third parties. A contract can occur as a result of transfer of money, certification etc.

A blockchain is simply a digital log ledger which stores theoretically all types of information, such as payments, agreements, and occurrences. The processing of data occurs along a peer-to-peer platform, and is stored in electronic chunks sequentially [4]. Blockchain is rendered open, stable, decentralized despite nearly limitless storage capacity by such simple functionality [2]. Blockchain employs the hashing principle. The "hash" is a block fingerprint which takes into consideration all concerned data and logs. In short, a hash cryptography function considers an source sequence and renders it a special n-digit sequence [5]. The members on a network maintain their separate ledgers as well as other documents using conventional approaches for documenting logs and monitoring assets. This conventional approach can be costly, partly because it requires mediators paying their support for commissions. Due to problems in implementing negotiations and the proliferation of reporting needed to maintain multiple ledgers it is obviously inefficient. It is also insecure because when a centralized infrastructure is breached due to mismanagement, cyber attack, or a mere error, this affects the entire corporate network. Blockchain has a list of key attributes to overcome or boost standard approach: agreement, provenance, referential integrity and permanence. Every relevant members make choices by agreement, all stakeholders should consent to a contract being legitimate throughout this phase. Such objective is accomplished by bringing acceptance architectures into effect-infrastructure imposes the criteria whereby contracts can take place, or perhaps the sharing of objects that take place. Origin ensures audiences are mindful of whether the object derive from and the possession has changed significantly. No

*e-mail: rane.mukul@gmail.com
**e-mail: singh.shubham.16ce1034@gmail.com
***e-mail: rohansingh8174@gmail.com
****e-mail: vidhate.amarsinh@gmail.com

individual will, with absoluteness, tamper with a contract once it has been reported to the log. When a settlement is in mistake, the inconsistency should be replaced with something like a new transaction, and both transactions will then be clear [1]. A single common ledger essentially offers one way to ascertain the possession of an object or the conclusion of a transfer.

The existing Student Management System requires constant assembly between schools and organisations. With centralized data storage methods, the current university system is not successful. Student Management System can be applied to avoid the abuse of student information which is the most relevant blockchain application. The ledger application or blockchain framework uses its attributes such as confidentiality, atomicity and collaborative way of preserving information to establish a strong pavement for Student Management System implementation [6].

Academic databases are used globally, from the recipient's perspective, a valuable trait for entities promising for grants, employment, and overall teaching and research traction. Our academic database management software are generally largely geographically decentralized, require additional and un-trivial techniques for accessing records, are inefficient in several situations, and generally do not meet academic outcomes. Hence there is a need for a technology which encounters the forgery of the Academic Records and maintain the integrity of documents.

2 Literature Review

In this paper we presume that student records are stored in blockchain network form. Consider a situation in which one student has entered another educational institution. Student Managent System allows the students to validate the international or new university certificates. The paper indicates that the student has a wallet containing the certificates or details about the finished courses [7].

Once the student is about to enter a university of higher education, the institution will join the network and will validate the student's certificates. The 2-2 multi authentication protocol is used for verification process. The paper addresses the existing information disparity between the colleges and employer companies, an inadequate student credit scheme. Blockchain technology can help ensure accountability, validity and applicability of knowledge [8].

Smooth collaboration between students, academic institutions and employer organizations is achieved, enhancing the use and accountability of educational and job organisations. The paper explains an implementation of blockchain technology which is a trust-free framework called Bitcoin. A Peer-to-Peer network framework is suggested for money exchange. There is no need to identify peers because, in their interest, they can still quit and join the network. Blocks that are a transaction record are formally accepted or confirmed by casting a vote with the peer's CPU. The consensus mechanism will implement any rules and incentives the are required [9].

Using technologies like OCR, cryptographic hashing, digital signatures and 2D barcodes the integrity of the hardcopy documents was verified. Although forgery detection and integrity assurance was achieved the techniques involved were expensive and paperless environment was fully not achieved[10].

In this paper, they have used private permissioned blockchain instead of public blockchain as private permissioned blockchain gives higher performance, cost effectiveness as well as privacy. The main advantage of this paper is that in this the system is open and can be extended to any record type according to the specifics requirements of individual institutes. The drawback of the system is that it is only directed towards academic institutes. Other organizations and industries are not included[11].

3 Problem Statement

Presently the Student Management System is not secure against the document forgery. Fake documents as well as certificates are still being used at various levels. Hence we need a system which not only ensures the integrity of the documents but also maintains the authenticity. This proposed methodology proposes a system which is to be developed over a consortium blockchain. The issuing authority uploads the data by mining a block in the blockchain. Transparency is maintained as the end-user i.e. the industries or corporate officials can check for the integrity of document mentioned.

4 Proposed Methodology

Firstly the College or University authority issues the certificate, marksheet, transcript or any other document for the student and uploads it over the blockchain. After uploading the document, a hash key will be generated corresponding to that document. The student whenever submits

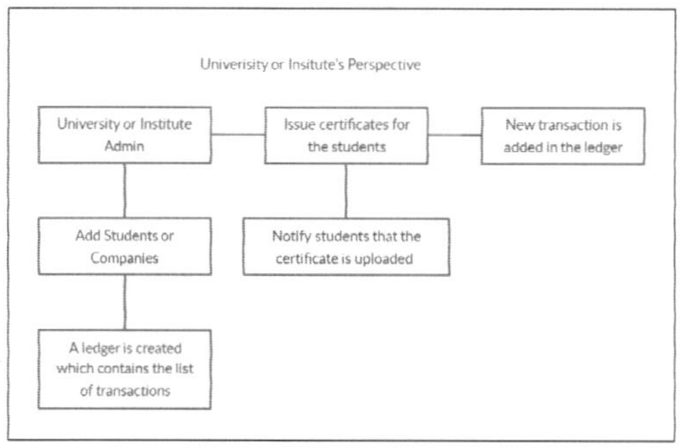

Figure 1. Block Diagram -Part 1

the document can also provide the hash number or the reference number to the Company which completely eliminates the need of the physical presence of the document and it also maintains the integrity of the document.

The Company or the Industry Personal can verify the document by just comparing the hash number or the reference number which is provided by the issuing authority. The approach comprises of dual main processes which are

 https://doi.org/10.1051/itmconf/20203203038

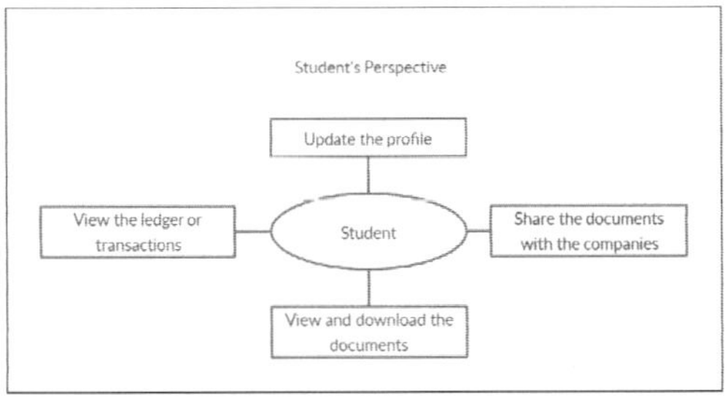

Figure 2. Block Diagram -Part 2

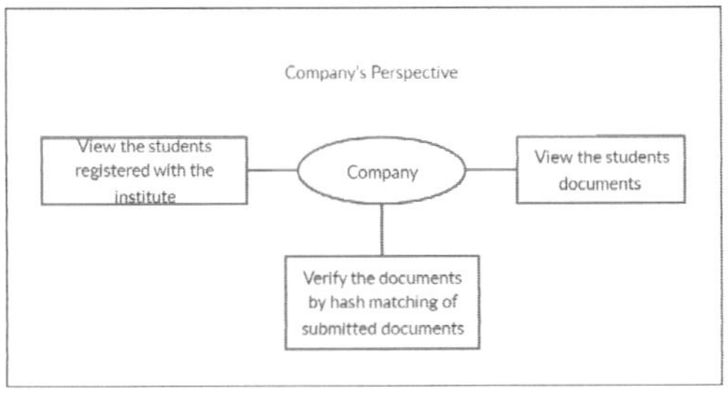

Figure 3. Block Diagram -Part 3

process generation and process validation.

• Generation Process: In this process, if the student wants to upload his documents, he will contact the co-ordinator. The co-ordinator will then log into the registration system to initiate the transaction. Then the co-ordinator will get all the relevant information of the student and the documents that student wants to upload. The documentation like the student's name, the title of the certification, the grade, the time-stamp, etc. is the block's content, using integer 9 computation. The block is ultimately tested using cryptographic strategies by previously selected nodes from the channel. The block is marked and attached to the blockchain system, such that all the users can reach the very similar chain, so that every node individually creates its very own example and indeed the hash is computed using the above process.

• Validation Process: Only after the records were produced, processed and released, the receiver can avail oneself of the same records in different situations, i.e. seeking employment, enrolling for assets etc. While these records are presented, they should be confirmed to evaluate if they have retained their credibility. Clients can post either a digital version, or a printed version paper. When displaying a paperback report, the report should first be scanned for a electronic copy to be accessed. The hash produced during the first step is used to commence the verification process [12]. The hash is determined contrasted to the one used in the actual file(retrieved through blockchain). If the analogy fails, this implies that the text has been changed. Although the checksum of every text label is computed, the hash value is also considered which helps in determining the forged text [5].

Algorithm required in this system:

SHA256: Tasks within the cryptographic computation of SHA256 are conducted onto terms which are 32-bit long using 8 terms of functioning variables such as P, Q, R, S, T, U, V and W which are of 32-bit. The term size of SHA256 measurement is, therefore, 32 bits. The characteristics for such functioning elements are determined for every computation and the SHA256 Cryptographic hash function has indeed been completed this process continues up to 64 cycles. Rationally, it should be remembered under all circumstances that certain changes in the SHA256 hashing computation are done with modulo 232.From here on out, the recipient will transform most of the increments described in the above material as increments conducted modulo 232 SHA256 also provide a 256-piece IV that is set for the main message square. A transitive digest message accumulated towards the completion of the preliminary 64 cycles filling in there as the square for the text. Post 64 iterations of the text pressure power and measurement extension, a midway message condensation of 256 bits is distributed along such lines. Once you have hashed the entire text squares, you get an advantage on 256 bits that is the last text analysis of the knowledge file. Therefore, the SHA256 cryptographic computation is virtually similar to a square figure with something like a 256-piece text square scale as well as a 512-piece key (data obstruction) penetrated into 64-bit 32-bit cycles keys using the text scheduler in each of the 64 cycles of such an example [13].

5 Implementation and Results

The current Student Management System is not efficient as providing fake documents is a big issue which is being faced. The verification of this fake documents if done is a hectic process as no dedicated system is present and it has to be done manually.

Figure 4. Admin Uploads Files of the students.

Hence if done manually, it requires at the least one day however if done for many students it can even last for

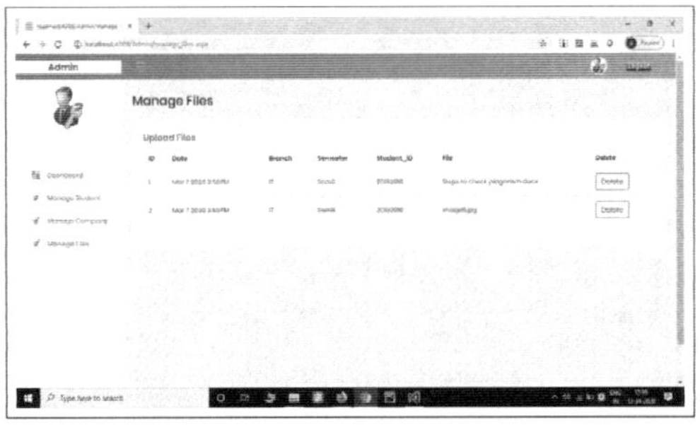

Figure 5. Admin can manage the uploaded files by deleting it.

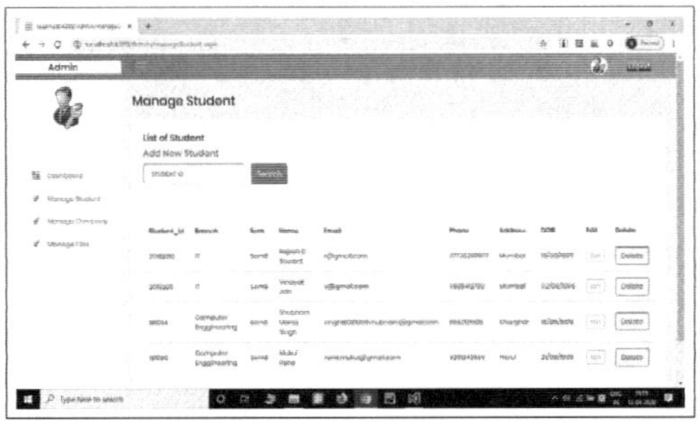

Figure 6. Admin can add students as well as Companies

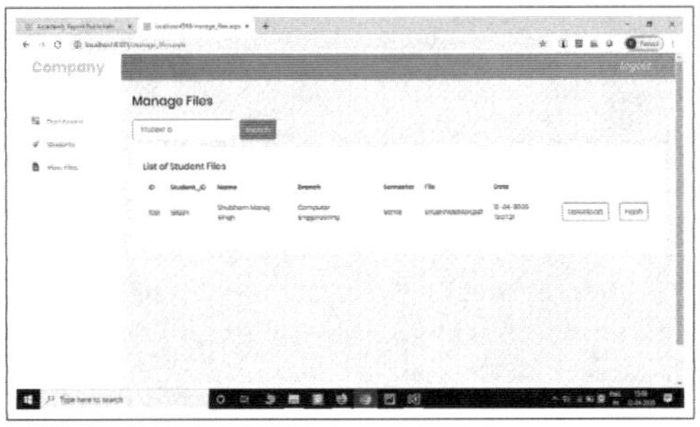

Figure 7. Companies can view the files which are uploaded over the site.

weeks which is really a time consuming process. Previously, a case had been observed where a slot of students who were about to join a company were required to verify the documents submitted during the background check. The authority concerned for verifying the documents had to contact the institute and put the joining of the slot on hold until the documents were verified. This process took few days for completion and the students had to wait until then. Including the faculty from institute and the verifying authority everyone were fully involved in this task which is tedious and soporific. By adapting to the proposed system, the time taken to verify the documents would be reduced to few minutes. The model has been tested on a group of students and it was reviewed to be reliable and fast.

After surveying a group of 100 students who had no such

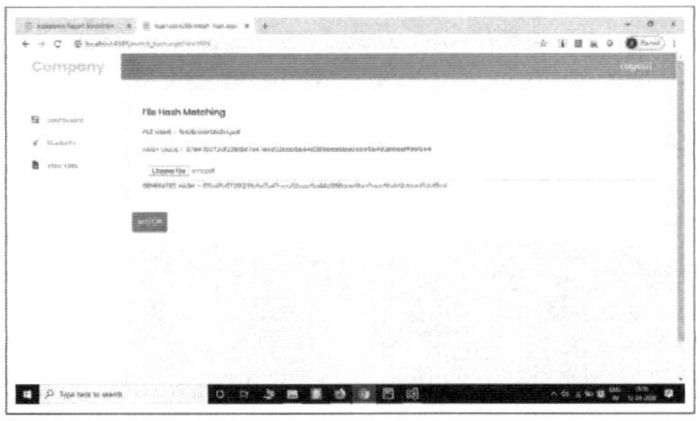

Figure 8. Company can compare hash value of files for ensuring the integrity

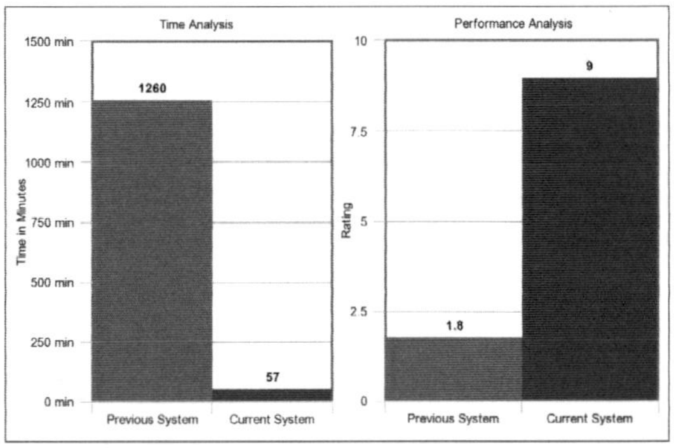

Figure 9. Analysis Graph

reliable system for verification of their documents, they had to provide the hard-copy of the original documents and move from one desk to another for completing this process which was really a hectic and frustrating process. Although if the process is done online there is no security as the documents could be edited and there is no tamper proof mechanism into use. In the same case the companies has to handle the huge crowd and perform the document verification on time but actually verifying the documents by making any call or over any other mode of communication is time consuming as sometimes the faculty is too busy to handle this request. The blockchain application has added an extra level of security as editing the documents is impossible here, thereby assuring the documents to be tamper proof. To verify our claim, we have surveyed 100 students to provide their feedback on both the systems. Average rating given to the previous system was 1.8 while our proposed system got 9. They found our system very user-friendly, time efficient and responsive.

6 Conclusion

This idea or program pays lip service to the transition problem and introduces a framework for checking college records among colleges and universities. Utilizing Hyperledger like a proprietary approved blockchain, offers higher output, benefit-effectiveness, including confidentiality contrasted with approaches for shared blockchain.

The program is indeed flexible and may be applied towards any form of records as per the specifications of every other organization. Although our system gives a convenient-to-use and reliable approach, ubiquity by various institutions is necessary to attain the mass momentum needed. Even if this is primarily aimed at academia, it would be easily adapted by including institutions seeking to verify potential job seekers' qualifications. The program can also be modified to exploit and modify current solutions, like serving as something of a network broker (i.e. cross border and global).

It is proposed to use blockchain in the student management system to preserve student information using blocks and also to accept student accomplishments and university qualifications. This idea can be implemented in upcoming time by suggesting a method to create a fully functional system that includes attendance, student marks, receipts for student payments towards the university.

7 Future Work

The further enhancement of the proposed methods can be focused on the following ideas for ensuring better performance and widespread applicability of the application. Firstly, the proposed system is implemented only for single institute. Hence, this system can be scaled to other institutes. More participants would be able to use our system. Secondly, notifications can be given to the student whose document has been uploaded over the Blockchain. This notification can be as an email or text message over mobile phone.

References

[1] O Nathan and P Alex Sandy. *"Decentralizing privacy using blockchain to protect personal data"*. SPW 2015 IEEE (2015).

[2] P.S.G. Aruna Sri and D.I. Bhaskari. *"A study on blockchain technology"* IJET(2018).

[3] J. Sidhu *"Syscoin: A peer to peer electronic cash system with blockchain-based services for e-business"*. IEEE(2017).

[4] K. Jay and A. Akutsu. *"The blockchain-based digital content distribution system"*. ICBDC IEEE(2015).

[5] Bart Preneel. *"Cryptographic Hash Functions: Theory and Practice"*. Springer-Verlag Berlin Heidelberg 2010).

[6] Sushmita Ruj and Kwok-yan Lam. *"A Blockchain framework for insurance processes"*. BSC, IEEE (2018).

[7] Aida Kamiali, Kristjan Koi and Marjan Heriko. *"Eductx: a blockchain-based higher education credit platform"*. IEEE ACCESS (2018).

[8] Gill green, Qin Liu and Hongming Zhu *"Education-industry cooperative system based on blockchain"*. HOTICN 2018, IEEE (2018).

[9] Satoshi Nakamoto. *"Bitcoin: a peer-to-peer electronic cash system"*.

[10] A Permissioned Blockchain-Based System for Verification of Academic Records *"https://ieeexplore.ieee.org/document/8763831"*

[11] Proposing a Blockchain-based Solution to Verify the Integrity of Hardcopy Documents *"https://ieeexplore.ieee.org/document/8601200"*

[12] M. Nakasumi. *"Information sharing for supply chain management based on block chain technology"*. IEEE CBS 2017.

[13] Matsui M., Zuccherato R.J. *"Security Analysis of SHA-256 and Sisters"*. Springer, Berlin, Heidelberg, 2004.

ITM Web of Conferences **32**, 03039 (2020) https://doi.org/10.1051/itmconf/20203203039
ICACC-2020

A scene perception system for visually impaired based on object detection and classification using CNN

Lalita Moharkar[1,*] , *Sudhanshu* Varun [2], *Apurva* Patil [3] , and *Abhishek* Pal [4]

[1]Assistant professor, Xavier Institute of Engineering, Mumbai, India
[2] Student of Electronics and Telecommunication Department, Xavier Institute of Engineering, Mumbai, India
[3] Student of Electronics and Telecommunication Department, Xavier Institute of Engineering, Mumbai, India
[4] Student of Electronics and Telecommunication Department, Xavier Institute of Engineering, Mumbai, India

Abstract. In this paper we have developed a system for visually impaired people using OCR and machine learning. Optical Character Recognition is an automated data entry tool. To convert handwritten, typed or printed text into data that can be edited on a computer, OCR software is used. The paper documents are scanned on simple systems with an image scanner. Then, the OCR program looks at the image and compares letter shapes to stored letter images. OCR in English has evolved over the course of half a century to a point that we have established application that can seamlessly recognize English text. This may not be the case for Indian languages, as they are much more complex in structure and computation compared to English. Therefore, creating an OCR that can execute Indian languages as suitably as it does for English becomes a must. Devanagari is one of the Indian languages spoken by more than 70% of people in Maharashtra, so some attention should be given to studying ancient scripts and literature. The main goal is to develop a Devanagari character recognition system that can be implemented in the Devanagari script to recognize different characters, as well as some words.

1. Introduction

In recent years, handwriting recognition has been one of the fascinating and demanding fields of research in the field of image processing and pattern recognition. It significantly contributes to the development of an automation method and in various applications, it can enhance the interaction between humans and machine. Several research works focused on new technologies and methods that would reduce the processing time while providing greater accuracy in recognition. Handwritten Indian script (Devanagari) is a tough task due to the different characteristics of these scripts, such as their broad character collection, complex form, presence of modifiers, presence of compound characters and character similarity. Devanagari script is mostly useful for the purpose of writing and recording most Indian languages including Hindi, Marathi, Sindhi, Nepali, Sanskrit, Konkani, Maithili, etc. One of Indian script's defining features is its variety of sounds that it must support. As there's usually a letter in Indian languages for each of the phonemes, the collection of alphabets appears to be very large. Devanagari developed through various transformations from the ancient Brahmi script. India's official Hindi national language, written in the Devanagari alphabet, has more than 500 million speakers. The subsequent characteristics will regulate the complex nature of the Devanagari script. The main idea is to train a model with thousands of images containing Devanagari scripts in it and make computer understands every letter and word by running the image over and over through the machine learning algorithms which will then be used to recognize when and when these same words or letters can be handwritten or printed on a machine. So making it much faster and more efficient as the number of such documents increases over the time. This can also be trained to recognize and study antique scripts and literature. We will be introducing an offline method for handwritten recognition of Devanagari characters in this project. Offline character recognition is a method where the letters / words to be recognized are in the form of scanned documents that are stored in the greyscale format. Later this scanned data is passed through certain stages that are essential for the identification of superior characters. Postprocessing steps to prepare images.

2. Major Steps

These steps have been successfully implemented. Once these steps have been successfully implemented on every image present in the image data set next we need to develop algorithms that's can be used to train and test the model and later predict how well the model has been trained and then we install the library for voice output.

Handwriting character Recognition Technology has been refining with the help of pattern recognition and image processing for a few decades. Various software computing methods that are used in other types of pattern and image recognition can as well be used for Devanagari character recognition.

These are the following Steps:

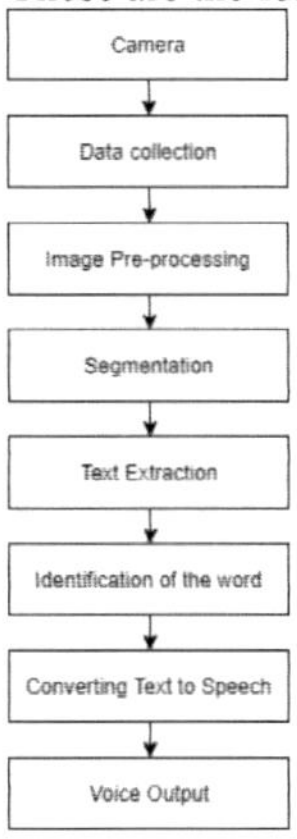

Fig. 1. Steps wise representation

2.1 Camera

The Pi camera module is a light weight, compact camera. It communicates with Pi via the serial interface protocol for the MIPI camera. It is usually used in image processing, in machine learning or in project surveillance. It is widely used in surveillance drones since camera payload is very small. Among these modules Pi can also use regular USB webcams that are used in conjunction with computers. Pi camera is used to take the image and preprocessing is done using python.

2.2 Data Collection

we have generated and stored the database by making 10 different people to write few selected words and then we scanned those words and cropped the images and labeled the images of handwritten data

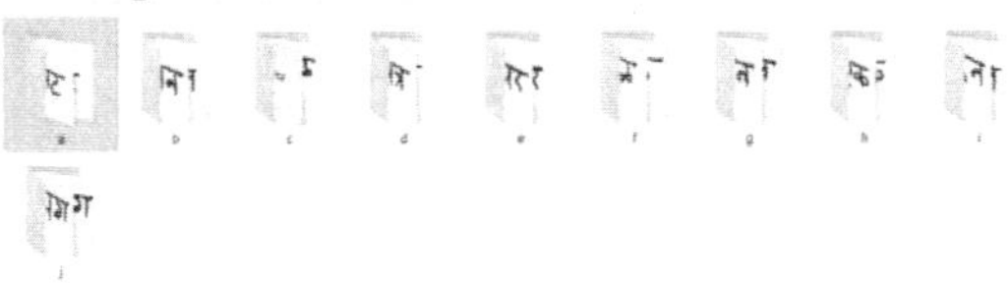

Fig. 2 . Folders of Dataset of Alphabet-wise words

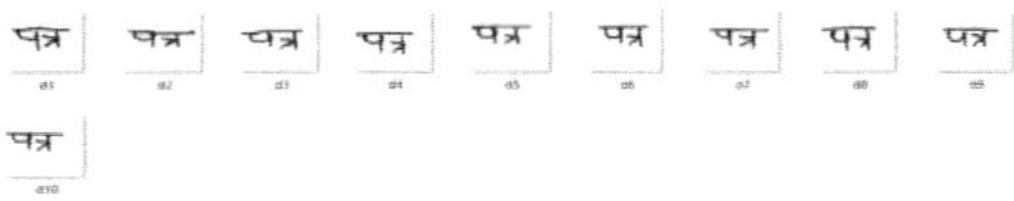

Fig. 3 . Handwritten Dataset of one person

2.3 Image Pre-processing

Pre-processing consists of all the operation that needs to be done on a scanned image to improve its efficiency, so that when the actual processing is finished, less noise is present in the image.

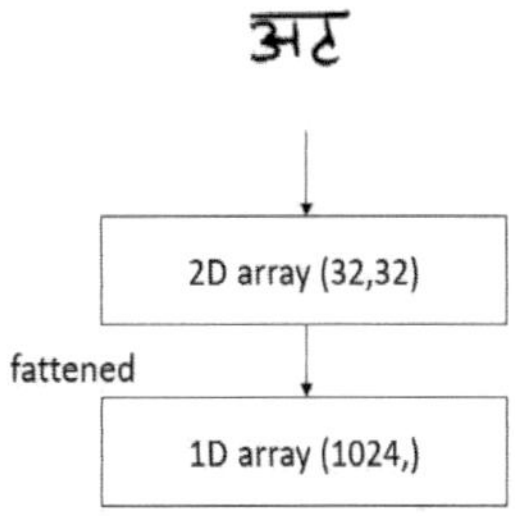

Fig. 4. Image Pre-processing

2.4 Segmentation

A sequence image of characters in the segmentation stage is decomposed into sub-images of individual character. In the proposed system, the pre-processed input image is segmented into isolated characters using a marking process to assign a number to each character. This labeling provides information on the number of characters that appear in the illustration. For the classification and reconnaissance level, each individual character is uniformly resized into 90X60 pixels.

2.5 Text Extraction

At this point all the critical features necessary for good character recognition is extracted. If the extraction of the function takes place more precisely we get better output so this is an important stage.

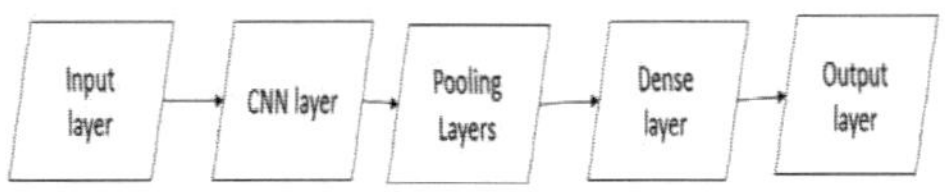

Fig. 5. Text Extraction

2.6 Identification Of Words

This stage is used for the recognition decision making segment taking advantage of the features previously extracted. It uses feed forward convolutional neural networks with several hidden layers. Such as the thick layers and the peak pooling.

2.7 Converting Text to speech

Pyttsx is a speech library cross-platform text that is independent of a platform. The key benefit of using this

 https://doi.org/10.1051/itmconf/20203203039

library for the conversion from text to speech is that it operates offline. Pyttsx however only supports Python 2.x. Therefore, we will see pyttsx3 that is modified to work with the same code on both Python 2.x and Python 3.x. The installation command is **pip install pyttsx3**

3. Literature review

According to [1] The paper describes an off-line handwritten alphabetical character recognition system which uses multilayer feed forward neural network. To extract the features of the handwritten alphabets, a new method, called, diagonal-based extraction function is implemented. Fifty data sets are used for training the neural network, each containing 26 alphabets written by different people, and 570 different handwritten alphabetic characters are used for testing. The proposed recognition system performs quite well yielding higher levels of accuracy in recognition compared to the systems using traditional horizontal and vertical extraction methods. This system will be suitable for conversion into structural text form of handwritten documents and recognition of handwritten names. Two approaches chosen to build the reconnaissance system for the Neural Network are trained using the methods of horizontal and vertical extraction of features. A simple, off-line English alphabet character recognition system using a new type of extraction feature, namely extraction of the diagonal feature, is proposed. Two approaches are chosen to build the Neural Network recognition system using 54 features and 69 features. The neural network recognition system is trained using the horizontal and vertical extraction methods to compare the recognition efficiency of the proposed diagonal method of extraction of features. There are six different networks of recognition built up. According to [2] The failures in identifying written Devanagari characters are primarily due to incorrect touching or damaged character segmentation. Because of the upper and lower Devanagari text modifiers, several portions of two consecutive lines can also overlap. According to [3] Handwritten character recognition is currently attracting researchers ' attention due to possible applications in assisting users with blind and visually impaired technology, interaction between human and robot, automatic data entry for business documents, etc. In this work , we propose a technique for recognizing D evanagari handwritten characters using deep convolutio nary neural networks (DCNN), one of the deep-learning community's recent techniques.According to [4] Handwritten Devanagari ancient manuscript recognition system was introduced using the extraction techniques of statistical features. Intersection points, open endpoints, centroid, horizontal peak extent, and vertical peak extent characteristics are extracted in the extraction process of feature. In this work, the Convolutional Neural Network, Linear Network, Multilayer Perceptron, RBF-SVM, and random forest techniques are considered for classification. Various techniques of extraction and classification of features are considered and compared with the recognition of basic characters segmented from ancient manuscripts in Devanagari.4 features are extracted for the recognition of those characters. These characteristics are intersection and open endpoints, centroid, horizontal peak, and vertical peak range. Use all possible combinations of those features. Five classifiers were used by the authors, namely MLP, Neural Network, CNN, RBF-SVM, and Random Forest. According to [5] In this thesis, we analyse the problems and challenges for Indic scripts with automatic handwritten word recognition.We addressed the latest Unicode encoding standard and why we selected a single Unicode character as our basic recognition unit. Finally, we spoke about the problems that make HWR more difficult as opposed to Latin for Indic scripts (more characters, less real data).

4. Why is CNN important?

Neural Networks were the greatest invention of the human mind by creating a network which possesses qualities similar to those of the human brain and allows for thinking machines. Machines think, learn, and perform tasks that only with the help of these neural networks are possible for the one human. With the aid of Convolutional Neural Networks, the form of a neural network that has enabled machines to visualize images and distinguish one from another has become possible. Convolutional neural networks allow machines to perceive the world as human beings and thus become an essential principle for learning when working in computer vision. Computer vision has made computers perform several of those impossible tasks that were once managed and performed only by humans. Computer vision used in surveillance, medical imaging system, navigation, inspection has enabled computers to be smart enough to detect what's going on in the world, just like human eyes. Now computers too have eyes like humans and with the help of convolutional neural networks this is all possible. Convolutional Neural Networks are integrated into machines inspired by the neurons in human brains to provide eyes to machines and allow them for visual imaging. With the aid of Convolutional Neural Networks embedded in the system, visual imagery, video recognition, object detection- all have become possible.

https://doi.org/10.1051/itmconf/20203203039

5. Flow chart

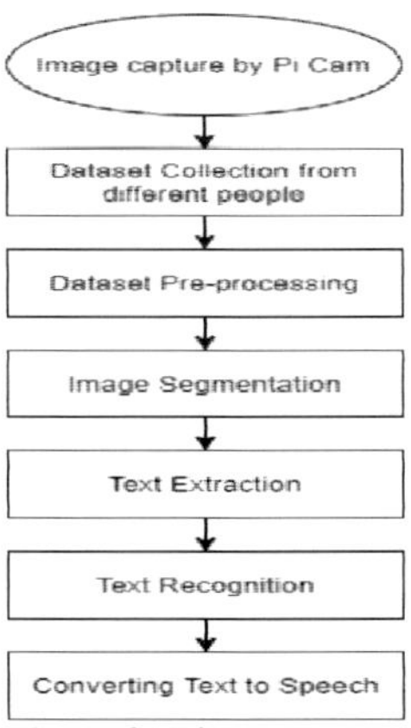

Fig. 6. Flowchart

6. Proposed Method

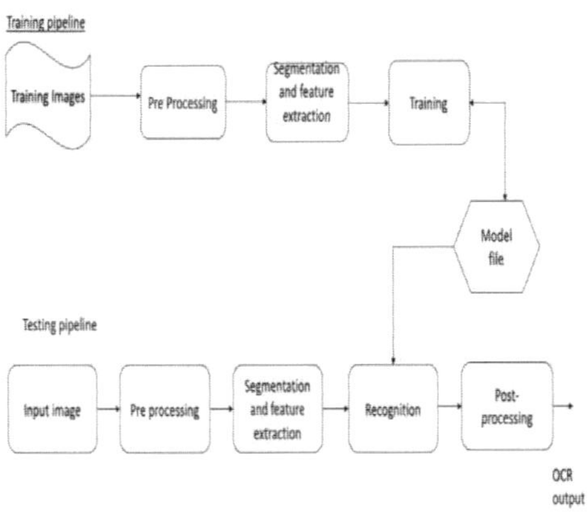

Fig. 7. Block Diagram

6.1 Convolutional Neural Networks

The Convolutional Neural Network (CNN or ConvNet) is a biologically based machine-leaning architecture that can learn from experiences such as traditional multilayer neural networks. ConvNets consists of several layers of overlapped tiling arrays of small neurons such that the original image is best represented. ConvNets is commonly used for identification of photographs and videos. Three key types of layers are used to create a ConvNet architecture .

6.1.1 Convolution Layer:

Convolution is the first layer where features are extracted from an input image. Convolution preserves the relation between pixels by using small squares of input data to learn image features. It is a mathematical operation that involves two inputs such as a matrix of images and a filter or kernel.

6.1.2 Max-Pooling Layer:

Section of pooling layers will lower the number of parameters when the images are too large. Spatial pooling also known as subsampling or down sampling which reduces each map's dimensionality but retains important information.

6.1.3 Fully-Connected Layer:

Fully connected layers are an essential component of the Convolutional Neural Networks (CNNs), which have proven to be very effective in the identification and classification of computer vision images. The CNN process begins with convolution and pooling, the image is broken down into features and analyzed separately. The product of this process feeds into a fully connected neural network structure, which drives the final decision on the classification. This article provides a thorough review of CNNs, how their architecture works and how it relates to computer vision deep learning applications in real world.

7. Results

```
   ...: model.save("DevaModel1.h5")
Using TensorFlow backend.
Found 78200 images belonging to 46 classes.
Found 13800 images belonging to 46 classes.
Model: "sequential_1"
```

Layer (type)	Output Shape	Param #
conv2d_1 (Conv2D)	(None, 30, 30, 32)	320
max_pooling2d_1 (MaxPooling2	(None, 15, 15, 32)	0
conv2d_2 (Conv2D)	(None, 13, 13, 64)	18496
max_pooling2d_2 (MaxPooling2	(None, 7, 7, 64)	0
dropout_1 (Dropout)	(None, 7, 7, 64)	0
flatten_1 (Flatten)	(None, 3136)	0
dense_1 (Dense)	(None, 128)	401536
dense_2 (Dense)	(None, 64)	8256
dense_3 (Dense)	(None, 46)	2990

```
Total params: 431,598
Trainable params: 431,598
Non-trainable params: 0
```

Fig. 8. CNN Architecture Implementation

```
Epoch 45/50
31/31 [==============================] - 1s 40ms/step - loss: 0.4474 -
accuracy: 0.8724 - val_loss: 0.3232 - val_accuracy: 0.9449
Epoch 46/50
31/31 [==============================] - 1s 38ms/step - loss: 0.4412 -
accuracy: 0.8531 - val_loss: 0.1570 - val_accuracy: 0.9357
Epoch 47/50
31/31 [==============================] - 1s 40ms/step - loss: 0.4528 -
accuracy: 0.8612 - val_loss: 0.3362 - val_accuracy: 0.9469
Epoch 48/50
31/31 [==============================] - 1s 40ms/step - loss: 0.3818 -
accuracy: 0.8796 - val_loss: 0.1314 - val_accuracy: 0.9622
Epoch 49/50
31/31 [==============================] - 1s 42ms/step - loss: 0.4044 -
accuracy: 0.8765 - val_loss: 0.1751 - val_accuracy: 0.9469
Epoch 50/50
31/31 [==============================] - 1s 44ms/step - loss: 0.3647 -
accuracy: 0.8827 - val_loss: 0.2465 - val_accuracy: 0.9551
```

Fig. 9. Training the Model

We have used a Convolutional Neural Network (CNN) model in this approach. Thus, we train it using the above-mentioned pre-processed dataset. Fig.8. represents the implementation of the architecture of the Convolutional Neural Network (CNN). The layers are present as mentioned in Fig.8. The model is trained as observed from Fig.9.

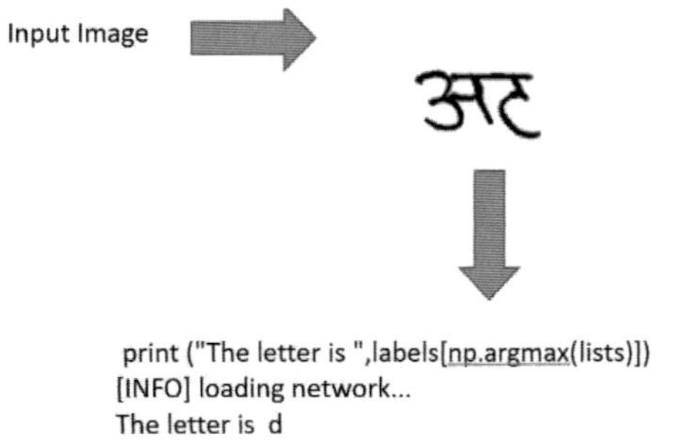

Fig. 10. Output of the Trained Model

Fig. 10. represents the output of the model after training. After the input image is provided, the model gives the respective output.

8. Conclusion

The images can be captured from the Pi cam and we can use it through the Python code for testing in the raspberry pi and then, after the text of the image is identified, we get the output in the form of sound. We proposed a CNN based method for devanagari text recognition and later convert it into speech. The accuracy obtained to recognize the text image for the dataset prepared is 94-95% using CNN as shown in Fig.10. The proposed CNN effectively learns quality related features and achieved the state-of-the-art performance.

9. Future Work

The dataset can be modified to obtain better results. The presented architecture of the Convolutional Neural Network (CNN) is optimum. But we would also try modifying the layers of the Convolutional Neural Network (CNN) which may lead to a better result. The accuracy of the model can be further increased. This can be implemented using Raspberry Pi and can be converted into a complete application which can help the visually impaired people.

10. References

[1] J. Pradeep , E. Srinivasan and S. Himavathi , IJCSIT, "*Diagonal Based Feature Extraction for Handwritten Alphabets Recognition System Using Neural Network*" , **Vol 3, No 1**, (2011)

[2] A. S. Ramteke, M. E. Rane , IJSER, *"A Survey on Offline Recognition of Handwritten Devanagari Script"* **Volume 3** (2012)

[3] M. Jangid and S. Srivastava, J.IMAGE "*Handwritten Devanagari Character Recognition Using Layer-Wise Training of Deep Convolutional Neural Networks and Adaptive Gradient Methods"* (2018)

[4] S. Narang, M K. Jindal and M. Kumar, IAC , "*Devanagari ancient documents recognition using statistical feature extraction techniques"* (2019)

[5] K. Dutta, IIITH, *"Handwritten Word Recognition for Indic & Latin scripts using Deep CNN-RNN Hybrid Networks"* (2019)

CROWD ABNORMAL BEHAVIOUR DETECTION USING DEEP LEARNING

Riddhi Sonkar[1,3,*], *Sadhana* Rathod[2,**], and *Renuka* Jadhav[3,***] *Deepali* Patil[4,****]

[1]Department of Information Technology, Ramrao Adik Institute of Technology,Navi Mumbai, India
[2]Department of Information Technology, Ramrao Adik Institute of Technology,Navi Mumbai, India
[3]Department of Information Technology, Ramrao Adik Institute of Technology,Navi Mumbai, India
[4]Department of Information Technology, Ramrao Adik Institute of Technology,Navi Mumbai, India

Abstract. Crowd analysis has become an extremely famous research point in the territory of computer vision. Computerized examination of group exercises utilizing reconnaissance recordings is a significant issue for public security since it permits the identification of hazardous groups and where they're going. We all see how many problems are faced because of the crowd. In our country, many terrorists are there. They plant a bomb in a crowded area which causes a lot of injuries. Thieves are mostly found or always leave in crowded areas so they can easily get an advantage of the crowd. In that situation, crowd analysis is very important. This paper presents the design of the deep learning architecture that provides control over the crowd behavior that will help to avoid violence or any other act which occurs because of the crowd which causes harmful effects to the society. So we are proposing a system that detects abnormal behavior of crowds using deep learning techniques.

Keywords— Crowd analysis, pre-processing, object tracking, CCTV, Machine Learning, CNN, event behavior recognition.

1 Introduction

A crowd is countless individuals assembled in a scattered or uncontrollable manner. It is a gathering of individuals assembled in a specific area. Crowds vary in various situations, for example, the crowd in a sanctuary will be unique in relation to the crowd in a shopping zone. The setting where the word 'crowd' is utilized shows the kind of gathering as far as size, duration, composition, inspiration, cohesion, and nearness of people.

Nowadays, so as to ensure social security, video surveillance frameworks whose equipment cost is low, have been broadly applied out in the public places, for example, air terminals, metro stations, traffic intersections, and schools, and so on. In any case, the greater part of the current video surveillance frameworks are simply utilized as a record framework, which can't identify and dissect an unusual occasion naturally, and it is inconceivable for an individual to watch the screen consistently. [1]

Since the observing offices are ordinarily mounted out in the public places, abnormal events discovery in crowd has been basic and has become another region of enthusiasm for the wise checking framework look into network the outcomes might be utilized for public security purposes [2].

Then again, traditional methods for individual behavior analysis can't be suitable for crowded scenarios due to the occlusion phenomenon. Video surveillance in packed territories is getting progressively huge for public security. Analyzing these crowd behaviors is crucial so any basic circumstance can be controlled before it turns out to be more serious. Videos of crowded scenes present testing issues in computer vision [3]. Video surveillance assumes an essential job in the present society in guaranteeing security in the region where huge quantities of individuals are relied upon to accumulate. An expansion in security threats has utilized surveillance systems in practically all the region. For instance, CCTV cameras are installed in the roads, shopping edifices, temples, stadiums, and so on., to guarantee security. Crowd behavior analysis encourages from numerous points of view to all the more likely comprehend crowd elements and related individuals behavior create reconnaissance or crowd control systems, organize and compose open spaces and improve computer animation models utilized with regards to video games or special effects.

The structure of society has become more complex than it used to be. The people living in society have become intolerant towards sensitive issues persisting in society [4]. This has led to increased instances of public violence. Moreover, the weak security measures have made violence break out in the crowd easier. The present practice is physically checking video takes care of from a few sources. Video analytic permits the the automatic detection of events of interest, however it faces numerous difficulties as a result of non-inflexible crowd movements and impediments. The algorithms developed for rigid ob-

*e-mail: riddhisonkar20@gmail.com
**e-mail: sadhanarathod98@gmail.com
***e-mail: renuka24jadhav@gmail.com
****e-mail: deepali.patil@rait.ac.in

https://doi.org/10.1051/itmconf/20203203040

jects are ineffectual in managing crowds. The aim of this work is to develop a system which can classify normal and abnormal behaviors in crowds using a real-time video surveillance system to monitor crowded urban environments using machine algorithm techniques [5]. This system provides rein in crime because the recorded footage is substantial evidence against the criminal and because of crowd analysis will help security agencies to stop the crowd criminal activities like riot etc.

2 Review of Literature

Numerous works have been done related to the crowd behavior analysis using different machine learning techniques. The datasets, algorithms, methods used by the authors and observed results along with the future scope are carried out in finding out efficient methods of crowd abnormal behavior detection with different types of crowded scenes. Here research on crowd behavior analysis has been carried out for several years. This section gives information of the existing system available and gives information of the various techniques used.

Lazaros Lazaridis. [1] proposed new techniques for the detection and characterization of unusual behavior in dense crowd for example the approach used to create the crowd density heat-maps, the extraction of the related optical flow. But when talking about Abnormal behavior detection it should cover the weather condition, lightning condition and camera angle but it is difficult to gather genuine information with abnormal behavior in dense crowds and that's why it will not give the more accurate results.

Vishwa Patel. [2] used object based behavior reorganization method which is transfer on the information on the people that structure the group, which was trying for denser situations. It is just reasonable for low and moderately crowded scenes. So they additionally utilized the second methodology that is all holistic approach regards the crowd as a solitary element, with the goal that the tracking issue is not a challenge. This subsequent methodology is progressively suitable for denser scenes, yet it can't identify abnormal behavior effectively.

Krutika Rohit. [6] presents behavior label distribution method, that can be used for solving problems of mixed behavior. By using behavior label distribution archived public security and safety. But this technique contains so many steps like giving sequence numbers and labels to every behavior and then analyzing the abnormal behavior. This process is time consuming and this system is not real time so that it is not much efficient to handle critical situations.

Swathi H Y. [7] discussed the various techniques utilized for recognizing unusual crowd behavior viz., crowd density estimation, tracking, motion detection and behavior recognition/understanding. They likewise examined the issues in crowd analysis and the answers for these issues. This work is their initial phase in the research of crowd behavior analysis, there are a few issues despite everything being confronted in regards to the efficiency, effectiveness, robustness of the automated surveillance systems for crowd analysis.

Dongping Zhang. [8] proposed another technique for crowd motion behavior detection that is SIFT flow innovation is used for identifying the movement data from the two adjacent frames in the video arrangements, at that point the weighted direction histogram which assumes the job of a factual estimation for the SIFT flow is taken as the contribution for the HMM model.

Marc Van Droogenbroeck. [9] presented a widespread sample based background subtraction algorithm, called ViBe, which consolidates three creative strategies i.e. classification model, background pixel model, neighboring pixel model.

Yong Shean Chong. [10] Used a novel system for representing video information by a lot of basic highlights, which are implied naturally from a long video film through a deep learning approach. In particular, a deep neural network made out of a measure of convolutional autoencoders was utilized to process video frames that caught uncommon structures in information, which gathered, make the video representation. This representation is taken care of into a measure of convolutional brief autoencoders to become familiar with the regular temporal patterns. Right now, neural network in that, all data sources and yields are autonomous from one another.

R. Mehran. [11] proposed another algorithm for discovery and confinement of abnormalities present in crowded scenes recordings by utilizing the SFM association power in blend with the Particle crowd Optimization. This work lies in presenting the enhancement of the social force and performing molecule shift in weather conditions to acquire the improved association power as per the fundamental optical flow field. The entire irregularity detection/localization process is completed with no learning stage. This infers the proposed strategy is very appropriate for genuine situations.

Weiming Hu. [12] introduced a review of ongoing improvements in visual reconnaissance inside a general handling structure for visual observation frameworks. The best in class of existing strategies in each key issue is depicted with the emphasis on the following errands: recognition, following, comprehension and depiction of practices, individual recognizable proof for visual reconnaissance, and intelligent observation utilizing numerous cameras. With respect to the discovery of moving items, it includes ecological demonstrating, movement division and article grouping. Three systems for movement division are tended to: foundation subtraction, fleeting differencing, and optical stream.

But still, there is a need to detect abnormal activity of crowds at an early stage so that it will help us to prevent problems faced because of the crowd. That motivates us to build a system which detects abnormal behavior of crowds.

3 Proposed Methodology

The proposed system consists of planning and executing the system which secured the answers for the existing system required. The task additionally includes an extensive assessment of the system, and is to give proficient security to Urban by building up an Unsupervised Abnormal Crowd Behavior Detection system. We developed a system which can characterize normal and abnormal behaviors in crowds utilizing a constant video observation system and using CNN algorithm to analyze monitoring crowded urban environments.

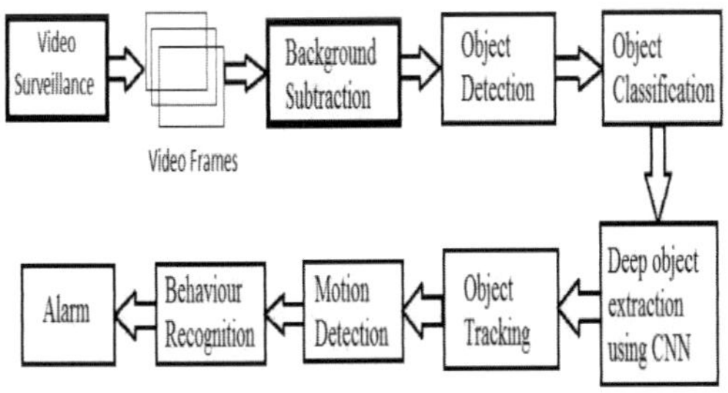

Figure 1. Proposed System

Initially, we did an analysis of existing systems that are available, but after analysis we came to know that there is a need for some real-time system that may overcome the drawbacks of an existing system. So we started research and we found that only CNN is not comfortable for real time behaviour detection so that we use both CNN and KNN in proposed system.

When we give video input i.e. video surveillance to the system, it is converted into video frames which are in ".jpg" format. Background subtraction is a technique for isolating out closer view components from the background and is finished by creating a frontal area veil. This technique is utilized for recognizing progressively moving objects from static cameras. Background subtraction procedure is significant for object tracking. There are a few methods for Background subtraction, we are using ViBe algorithm for that. Then it will detect and classify and track the object. CNN algorithm is used to deep object extraction. Deep object extraction is use for identify human begins in frame. We use KNN for calculate position difference between 2 sequence frames of object. On the bases of euclidean distance we track the object. Then it will analyze the motion of objects on the bases of 3 parameters i.e. speed, angle, direction. Using these parameters if the motion of object is beyond the threshold then it is recognize as abnormal behavior. If the behavior is abnormal then it delivers an alarm. The threshold is changes according to application.

4 Algorithms

Algorithms used to build the proposed system are described as follows:

4.1 ViBe

ViBe is a universal sample-based background subtraction algorithm. Background subtraction is the way toward isolating out frontal area objects from the Background during a sequence of video outlines. sequence subtraction is a generally utilized methodology for discovery of moving objects from static cameras[9]. This methodology varies from those dependent on the traditional conviction that the most seasoned qualities ought to be supplanted first. At long last, when the pixel is seen as a major aspect of the foundation, its worth is proliferated away from plain sight model of a neighboring pixel. We depict our strategy in full subtleties and contrast it with other foundation subtraction strategies [13]. Productivity figures show that our strategy outflanks later and demonstrated cutting edge techniques regarding both calculation speed and recognition rate. We likewise examine the presentation of a downscaled variant of our calculation to irrefutably the base of one examination and one byte of memory for each pixel. It gives the idea that even such an improved adaptation of our calculation performs superior to standard procedures.

4.2 Convolutional Neural Network (CNN)

Convolutional neural networks are most useful with very large data sets, large numbers of features and complex classification tasks. A Convolutional Neural Network (CNN) is a type of neural network algorithm that is also used in deep learning and it comprised one or more layers. The CNN algorithm is designed to take images as an input to train the system to give the predictions. It builds the features from the various groups of pixels. CNN's are simpler to prepare and have numerous less parameters than completely associated with the systems with a similar number of hidden units. Convolutional neural systems comprise of an input layer, an output layer, and hidden layer operations.

A neural system comprises of a few distinct layers, for example, the information layer, in any event one concealed layer, and a yield layer. They are best utilized in object discovery for perceiving examples, for example, edges, shapes, hues, and surfaces. The shrouded layers are convolutional layers right now neural system which acts like a channel that initially gets input, changes it utilizing a particular example/include, and sends it to the following layer. With more convolutional layers, each time another information is sent to the following convolutional layer, they are changed in various ways. For instance, in the first convolutional layer, the channel may distinguish shape/shading in a locale, and the following one might have the option to close the item it truly is , and the last convolutional layer may characterize the article as a pooch. Essentially, as an ever increasing number of layers the info experiences, the more refined examples the future ones can identify.

For a frame t, the output highlight of 5th convolution layer is a 6h6h256 vector. In a standard CNN, the high-dimensional convolution highlights are normally taken care of to fully connected layers for dimensionality decrease, and then input to a classifier. Be that as it may, in FCN, there are no completely associated layers, and we are not preparing a classification task. So we dispose of heavy classifier, for example SVM, and utilize a novel strategy for dimensionality decrease as well as abnormal recognition.

We encode the high-dimensional convolution includes as a set of binary codes by iterative quantization (ITQ) [13]. ITQ is a proficient unsupervised method for learning binary codes in huge scope picture assortments. ITQ reduces the dimensionality of information by PCA first, at that point finds a rotation of zero-centered data to limit the quantization blunder of mapping this information to binary codes. Preparing the ITQ costs not as much as preparing a classifier, and we can extend the identification task simpler dependent on the binary codes.

4.3 K-Means

K-Means clustering algorithm is an unaided algorithm and it is utilized to section the intrigue zone from the foundation. It groups, or segments the given information into K-clusterd or parts dependent on the K-centroids. The algorithm is utilized when you have unlabeled data(i.e. information without characterized classes or gatherings). The objective is to discover certain gatherings dependent on a closeness in the information with the quantity of gatherings group to by K.

A K-Means clustering algorithm is used for motion detection of the objects which are detected by CNN. We created the cluster of objects pixels. Then we calculate the difference between the position of that object and calculated Euclidean distance on the bases of that we set the threshold value for detecting abnormal behavior of the crowd.

Knn is used to calculate the points distance between two image frame in sequence to track the motion of moving objects.

5 Results

Success of intensive learning network training is subject to the presence of enormous datasets. Large buildings, commented on with the mark of ground truth, the dataset is over the top expensive because of the need of human time and exertion. A decent Dataset needed to detect unusual phenomena in crowded scenes be different, occupying every single imaginable part of the issue; And fine annotate. It should cover different seasons Conditions, power conditions, different camera angles and Crowd density. Furthermore, due to legal and confidentiality rules it is incredibly hard to gather genuine information with unusual behavior in dense crowds. After analyzing some of the most well known datasets related to abnormal crowd behavior, we conclude the UMN dataset [15]: this dataset includes panic congestion behavior in a non-reasonable way. Novel violent [16]: By comparing this dataset with UMN, which is progressively reasonable however it needs crowd density.

The proposed network gives better results than those reported in the literature. Table-I [1] is a confusion matrix of existing system which uses Density Heat maps and Optical Flow for Abnormal behavior detection in crowd scenes. On the basis of confusion matrix the accuracy of existing system is 77.08% Whereas Table-II is confusion of proposed system. On the basis of confusion matrix the accuracy of proposed system which is based on convolutional neural network and K-Means algorithm is 80.79%.

Table 1. CONFUSION MATRIX OF THE EXISTING METHOD [1]

Actual/Predicted	Actual	Predicted
Actual	83.3	5.8
Predicted	37.7	61.2

Table 2. CONFUSION MATRIX OF THE PROPOSED METHOD

Actual/Predicted	Actual	Predicted
Actual	51	3.34
Predicted	12	12

Figure 2. Some Abnormal activity is detected

Figure 3. Abnormal activity is detected

Figure 4. Abnormal Behavior is detected

References

[1] LazarosLazaridis, AnastasiosDimou, PetrosDaras, "Abnormal Behavior Detection in Crowded Scenes Using Density Heatmaps and Optical Flow" 26th European Signal Processing Conference (EUSIPCO), 2018.

[2] Vishwa Patel, Narendra Patel, MahaswetaJoshi, "A Review: Abnormal Crowd Behavior Detection Techniques" ISSN: 2321-9653; IC Value: 45.98; SJ Impact Factor: 6.887 Volume 6 Issue II,, IEEE, 2018.

[3] G.Santhiya, K.Sankaragomathi, S.Selvarani, A.Niranjan Kumar, "Abnormal Crowd Tracking and Motion Analysis" IEEE International Conference on Advanced Communication Control and Computing Technologies (ICACCCT), 2014.

[4] D. Tran, L. Bourdev, R. Fergus, L. Torresani, and M. Paluri, "Learning spatiotemporal features with 3d convolutional networks," in Computer Vision (ICCV), 2015 IEEE International Conference on. IEEE, 2015, pp. 4489–4497.

[5] J. R. Medel and A. Savakis, "Anomaly detection in video using predictive convolutional long short-term memory networks," arXiv preprint arXiv: 1612.00390, 2016.

[6] Krutika Rohit, Ms. Kinjal Mistry and Mr. JenishLavji,"A Review on Abnormal Crowd Behavior Detection " International Conference on Innovations in Information, Embedded and Communication Systems (ICIIECS),2017.

[7] Swathi H Y, Dr. H S Mohana, Dr. G Shivakumar, "Crowd Behavior Analysis: A Survey" International Conference on Recent Advances in Electronics and Communication Technology, 2017.

[8] Dongping Zhang, KaihangXu, Huailiang Feng, Ye Shen, "Abnormal Crowd Motion Behaviour Detection based on SIFT Flow " International Journal of Signal Processing, Image Processing and Pattern Recognition Vol.9, 2016.

[9] Barnich, Olivier Droogenbroeck, Marc. "ViBe: A Universal Background Subtraction Algorithm for Video Sequences. Image Processing", IEEE Transactions on. 20. 1709 - 1724. 10.1109/TIP.2010.2101613, 2011.

[10] Y. S. Chong and Y. H. Tay, "Abnormal event detection in videos using spatiotemporal auto encoder," in International Symposium on Neural Networks. Springer, 2017, pp. 189–196.

[11] R. Mehran, A. Oyama, and M. Shah, "Abnormal crowd behavior detection using social force model," in Computer Vision and Pattern Recognition, CVPR 2009. IEEE Conference on. IEEE, 2009.

[12] Weiming, H., et al., "A survey on visual surveillance of object motion and behaviors." Systems, Man, and Cybernetics, Part C: Applications and Reviews, IEEE Transactions, Vol. 34, No. 3, (2004), pp. 334-352.

[13] Barnich, Olivier; Van Droogenbroeck, Marc (2009). "ViBe: A powerful random technique to estimate the background in video sequences", IEEE International Conference on Acoustics, Speech and Signal Processing. pp. 945–948. doi:10.1109/ICASSP.2009.4959741. ISBN 978-1-4244-2353-8, 2009.

[14] Hongtao Wei1, Yao Xiao, Ruifang Li, Xinhua Liu , "Crowd abnormal detection using two-stream Fully Convolutional Neural Networks", 10th International Conference on Measuring Technology and Mechatronics Automation , 2018.

[15] Ucf web videos dataset. http://www.vision.eecs.ucf.edu/projects/rmehran/cvpr 2009/Abnormal_Crowd.htmlVI._ Downloads. 4, 7

[16] Detection of unusual crowd activity dataset. http://mha.cs.umn.edu/proj_events.shtmlcrowd. 4, 6

[17] L. Zeng, X. Xu, B. Cai, S. Qiu, and T. Zhang, "Multi-scale convolutional neural networks for crowd counting," arXiv preprint arXiv: 1702.02359, 2017.

[18] T. Hassner, Y. Itcher, and O. Kliper-Gross, "Violent flows: Real-time detection of violent crowd behavior," in Computer Vision and Pattern Recognition Workshops (CVPRW), IEEE Computer Society Conference on. IEEE, 2012, pp. 1–6, 2012.

https://doi.org/10.1051/itmconf/20203203041

Underwater Image Processing using Graphics Processing Unit (GPU)

Sayooj Ottapura[1,*], *Rahul* Mistry[2], *Jatin* Keni[3], and *Chaitanya* Jage[4]

[1]Department of Electronics Engineering, Ramrao Adik Institute of Technology, Nerul, India
[2]Department of Electronics Engineering, Ramrao Adik Institute of Technology, Nerul, India
[3]Department of Electronics Engineering, Ramrao Adik Institute of Technology, Nerul, India
[4]Department of Electronics Engineering, Ramrao Adik Institute of Technology, Nerul, India

Abstract. Image processing is a method used for enhancement of an image or to extract some useful information from the image. It is a type of signal processing in which input is an image and output may be an image or any characteristics/features associated with that image. In this paper we will be focusing on a specific type of Image Processing i.e. Underwater Image Processing. Underwater Image Processing has always faced the problem of imbalance in colour distribution and this problem can be tackled by the simplest algorithm for colour balancing. We will be proceeding with the assumption that the highest values of R, G, B observed in the image corresponds to white and the lowest values corresponds to darkness. The underwater images are majorly saturated by blue colour because of its short wavelength and in this paper, we aim to enhance the image. We proposed a colour balancing algorithm for normalizing the image. The entire process will first be carried out on a CPU followed by a GPU. We will then compare the speedup obtained. Speedup is an important parameter in the field on image processing since a better speedup can help reduce the computation time significantly while maintaining a higher efficiency.

1 Introduction

Underwater image processing has always faced numerous challenges. Physical properties of the medium i.e. impurities present in water, cause deterioration effects which are absent in the pictures taken in air. Underwater images are primarily distinguished by their low visibility since light gets extremely attenuated as it advances in the water and hence the images taken result to have poor contrast and have a presence of haze. The two main difficulties faced are absorption and scattering. In absorption, specific frequencies of light get absorbed at different depths[1]. Since blue colour has the shortest wavelength it travels the farthest, making ambient underwater environments to be dominated by a bluish hue. Scattering is any divergence from a straight-line path[2]. Scattering occurs because of the presence of suspended particles in the water and in turn drops the visibility and contrast of the captured image. Light attenuation decreases the distance of visibility in clear water by about 20 meters and in turbid water by 5 meters or less[3]. The extent of effects of absorption and scattering is decided by the number of floating particles present in the water known as "marine snow".

Underwater Image Processing can be done using either Hardware techniques or through Software techniques. The software image processing can be approached from two different perspectives: image restoration technique or as an image enhancement method.

i) The purpose of image restoration is to recover the original image from a degraded image by using models of both the images[4].

ii) Image enhancement focuses on certain criteria of the subject i.e. the image, and then produces a more visually appealing image. Image Enhancement method does not require any kind of physical model to process the image[4].

The approach that we will be discussing in the paper will be an Image enhancement method.

For the purpose of Image enhancement, we will be making use of Graphics Processing Unit (GPU). GPU is preferred over CPU because image processing algorithms typically consume a great deal of computer resources which can be easily provided by the numerous processing cores present in a GPU. Graphics processors in many technical aspects outperform other imaging acceleration methods, when compared to the fastest available Field-Programmable Gate Array (FPGA).

* Sayooj Ottapura: sayoojaugust98@gmail.com

2 Underwater Image Processing

Underwater imaging and image processing play significant roles in ocean science research. The basic purpose of the present work is to improve the quality of underwater images. A wide variety of methods are available for the purpose of image enhancement, each with its inherent advantages and disadvantages. Underwater pictures, as a natural phenomenon, have low contrast alongside showing a propensity for dominance of one colour and low sharpness.

In the year 2012, N. Shamsuddin; W.F. Wan Ahmad, B.B. Baharudin, M. Kushairi, M. Rajuddin and F. Mohd established a method on "Significance level of image enhancement techniques for underwater images". This work focused on diminishing colour[5]. In the very next year of 2013 M.S. Hitam, Wan Nural Jawahir Hj Wan Yussof, E.A. Awalludin and Z. Bachok operated on "Mixture contrast limited adaptive histogram equalization for underwater image enhancement". Here they introduced a new method known as hybrid Contrast Limited Adaptive Histogram Equalization (CLAHE) colour spaces designed specifically for enhancement of the underwater image. The technique works CLAHE on colour spaces RGB and HSV. Tentative findings suggest that the potential solution substantially increases the picture quality of underwater photographs by improving contrast, and decreases noise and errors[6].

As mentioned earlier in Section 1, underwater image processing varies widely from visual image processing, mainly due to underwater channel dysfunctions such as absorption and scattering[7, 8]. Scattering can occur in two ways:

i) Forward scattering (light deviates while it travels from the object to the camera) leads to blurry images[9].

ii) Backward scattering (the water reflects a fraction of the light to the camera before it actually reaches the objects) usually limits the contrast of the images[9].

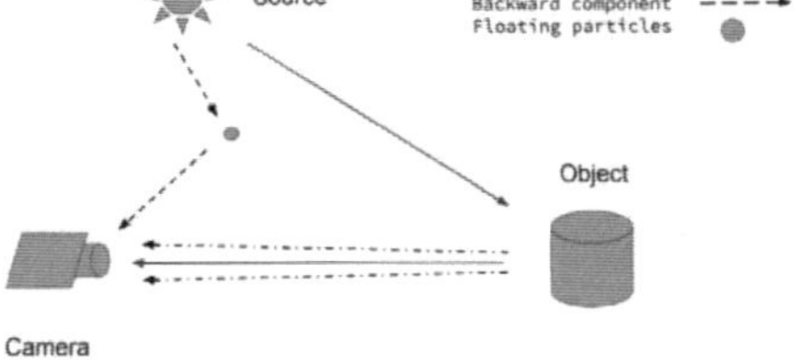

Fig. 1. The 3 elements of underwater image processing: i) the direct component (represented by a dash-dot line) ii) the forward component (represented by a straight line) and iii) the backward scatter component (represented by a dashed line)

As the images taken in underwater environment is mainly dominated by blue colour, we will be making use of a Colour Balancing Technique.

3 Image Enhancement using Graphics Processing Unit (GPU)

The Graphics Processing Unit (GPU) is widely used for real time graphics rendering in applications like high definition gaming, computer aided design software, etc[10]. GPU is becoming popular as cheap parallel supercomputer whose processing power can be utilized [11].

Even though original purpose of GPU is graphics rendering, in recent years the GPU is increasingly being used for scientific computations. GPUs are also used for general purpose computations like scientific computations, encryption/decryption etc. This type of GPUs is called as General-purpose GPUs (GPGPUs). Nowadays, GPU is used in video processing, image processing and in many more general-purpose works. Here we present an effective implementation of Simplest colour balance algorithm on the NVIDIA Tesla K80. Specifically, we showcase the effectiveness of our method by algorithm optimization. In result we display time relation between the implementation of the CPU and the GPU. We have run the algorithm using python and OpenCV on GPU[10].

Table 1. Specifications of Tesla K80.

Parameters	*Specification*
Maximum Double Precision Floating point precision	2.91 Téraflops
Maximum Single Precision Floating point precision	8.74 Téraflops
Memory Bandwidth(ECC Off)	480GB/sec
Memory size and Type	24GB GDDR5
CUDA cores	4992
Thermal solution	Passive Heatsink

Tesla K80 has two processing units. Each processing unit may be viewed as separate GPUs. So, this means Tesla K80 consists of 2 GPUs. Tesla K80 consists of 2 × 2496 cores and 2 × 12 Gigabytes of Video RAM. The operating frequency of each core is 562 MHz and the boost mode are 875 MHz[12, 13].

4 Design Implementation

In order to do the Image Enhancement process, we will be making use of the Simplest Colour Balancing (SCB) Algorithm. SCB is the Algorithm of choice because as mentioned earlier the images taken in underwater environment are majorly dominated by blue colour and so by using SCB we will be balancing out all the hues of RGB colour spectrum and thus reducing the dominance of blue making the resulting image to have an evenly balanced colour spectrum. The entire code for the algorithm is written and implemented in the Python Programming Language. The different libraries that are required in the image processing are taken from Open Computer Vision (OpenCV).

4.1 Simplest Colour Balance (SCB) Algorithm

Colour balance refers to the removal of an inherent colour bias from an image. It means balancing the intensities of each channel separately. For instance, if an image appears to be too red, it is said to have a red hue over it. Removing the red cast returns the picture to balance. Colour casts can arise from many different causes. In underwater imaging, the images are usually blue casted. There are various ways to make an image more readable and removing the colour cast which is usually blue in underwater images. Herein we propose a Simplest Colour Balance algorithm which improves readability. The SCB Algorithm does not necessarily improve the image quality. The goal here is to scale the pixel values to a range of 0 to 255[14]. However, many underwater images pixels already occupy the 0 and 255 values. To obtain a better colour improvement, a small percentage of pixels having value equal to 255 and small percentage of pixels having value equal to 0 are clipped[14]. Clipping here means setting up the quantiles, V_{max} and V_{min}. V_{min} and V_{max} are calculated by using $N \times S_1/100$ and $N \times (1 - S_2)/100 - 1$ respectively[14]. The quantiles are defined so that small proportion of pixels get the value of the quantiles. Finding the quantiles can be done by using sorting algorithm or by using histogram algorithm.

In this algorithm we have used the sorting algorithm for finding the quantiles and then normalizing it to a normal 8-bit image range. An RGB image is of 24-bit. Each channel of an image is of 8-bit. In our algorithm we are applying normalization to each channel separately. Each channel pixel values will be sorting in ascending order. Depending on the user defined saturation percentage V_{max} and V_{min} are calculated. From the left side of an original image histogram S_1% of pixels will be saturated and from the right side of the histogram that is, the pixels having a value closer to 255 are saturated to S_2%. For example, S_1=0 means there will be no pixel saturation at the beginning. S_2=3 means there will be at most $N \times S_2/100$ at the end of histogram. We cannot guarantee that exactly $N \times (S_1 + S_2)/100$ pixels get saturated because the distribution of pixel value is discrete. After a certain percent of pixel saturation is done, the image is then normalized to a specific range. Normalization is nothing but the re-scaling of real valued numeric attributes into the range between 0 and 1 in general[15]. But here the image is 8-bit so the pixel value ranges from 0 to 255. So, normalization of pixels is done for a range of 0 to 255 using the formula mentioned below[14]:

$$f(x)=[(x - Vmin)\times(max - min)]/[(Vmax - Vmin)+min] \quad (1)$$

For every pixel x, $f(x)$ will be calculated. Here 'max' and 'min' are the range of normalization. The image is scaled to [min, max].

Let's take a look at an example, consider an image having a dimension of 183 rows and 275 columns. The total number of pixels are obtained by taking product of the number of rows and number of columns. Thus, for rows and columns and hence the number of pixels is 50325 which is usually represented as 'N'. S is the saturation value which we have considered to be 2 in this example. The image will be first separated with respect to each colour channel R, G and B. Thereafter we will employ the V_{max} and V_{min} equation for each channel. Let's now calculate the value of V_{min} and V_{max} by selecting $S_1 = S_2 = 2$ and $N = 50325$.

$$V_{min} = (50325 \times 2) / 200 = 503 \quad (2)$$

$$V_{max} = \{[50325 \times (1 - 2)] / 200\} - 1 = 49821 \quad (3)$$

Now by applying the Python indexing logic we get to know that the pixel value at the index position of 503 and 49281 of the blue channel arrays is 73 and 187 respectively. Hence, the final value of V_{min} comes out to be 73 and the value of V_{max} is 187 for the blue colour channel. So, the pixel values of pixel below the 503rd pixel will be replaced by V_{min} and the pixel values of pixels above 49821st will be replaced by V_{max} for the blue colour channel. Similarly, for green channel, the value of V_{min} is 73 and the value of V_{max} is 214. The pixel values of pixel below the 503rd pixel will be replaced by V_{min} and the pixel values of pixels above 49821st will be replaced by V_{max} of the green channel. For red colour channel, the V_{min} obtained is 16 and the V_{max} value is 116. The pixel values of pixel below the 503rd pixel will be replaced by V_{min} and the pixel values of pixels above 49821st will be replaced by V_{max} for the red channel. The last step is the normalization of the processed image having a range of b = [73,187], g = [73,214] and r = [16,116]. Each channel's pixel value range will be scaled between 0 to 255 and lastly the channel will be merged.

Sorting of N pixels require $O(N \times \log(N))$ operations and a temporary duplication of the same N pixels[14].

4.2 Python Programming Language

Python is a high-level programming language. Python is object-oriented with integrated dynamic semantics for web and app development. Since Python is simple and has fairly simple and easy syntax and also supports a large number of packages and modules it is the programming language of choice for our project. The Python version used in our codes is Python 3.5. We have made use of some popular Python modules such as NumPy, math, sys, time, etc.

4.3 Open Computer Vision (OpenCV)

OpenCV-Python is an open-source library basically used for computer vision assessment. Even though C and C++ are faster when compared to Python, Python is used in complex computations because of its simplicity. Another important attribute of Python is that it can be extended to

C and C++. This functionality allows us to implement complex codes in C or C++ and to build a Python wrapper which can then be used as Python modules. This holds two benefits for us:

i) Our program doesn't compromise on speed (because in actuality the C++ code is what is running in the background).

ii) Programming in Python comparatively easy.

NumPy support in OpenCV makes the mathematical calculations simpler. NumPy library is specifically designed for mathematical operations and is also highly optimised for the same. OpenCV-Python is a capable tool for speedy handling of computer vision issues. In our program we are making use of OpenCV version 4.1.2.

5 Results and Performance Evaluation

Our output yielded a good enhanced image which is removes blue cast and makes image more readable. The pixel range of the original image is from 0 to 254. The enhanced image is obtained by saturating 0.00001 pixels at the leftmost and rightmost sections of the original image. And then we normalized it to a scale of 0-255.

The Central Processing Unit(CPU) used in this paper is the Quad-core Intel i5, 8th generation processor with an average clock speed of 1.6 GHz which can be turbo boosted up to a maximum clock speed of 1.8 GHz.

The GPU of choice is the Tesla K80 having specifications as mentioned in Table 1 in Section 3.

Developing a parallel version of code enables us to run its application on large data (e.g. more pixels, a bigger physical model of system) in less amount of time. The result of successful parallelization is measured in terms of speedup. The speedup is nothing but the simple ratio of execution time on CPU to execution time on GPU. The speedup can be calculated by using formula as[16]:

Speed up = (Program exécution time on CPU) / (Program exécution time on GPU) (4)

In case if the serial version of an application executes in 150 seconds and the corresponding parallel version of the same application runs in 15 seconds, the speedup for the parallel application is 10 times[16]. Speedup is required when an algorithm consists of high computation. In case of CPU, it will provide high clock speed but a fewer threading functionality. While in GPU, as there are a greater number of cores a good multi-threading performance is obtained. In this algorithm normalization function is applied on each pixel co-ordinates which becomes effective if multiple pixel normalization is done parallelly.

Fig. 2. Original Image.

Fig. 3. Image after undergoing the Image Enhancement.

Some of the important metrics of an image to be looked up after any kind of image processing are Mean brightness, Entropy, etc. We have found out the numerical values of this metrics and have tabulated them as follows:

Table 2. Image Metrics.

Parameters	*Numerical Values*
Program execution time in CPU	0.53 seconds
Program execution time in GPU	0.02 seconds
Speedup	26.5
Mean Brightness of original image	144.24
Mean Brightness of the enhanced image	116.45
Original image's Entropy value	6.97
Enhanced images's Entropy value	7.03

Efficiency of an image processing technique is decided on the basis of its image metrics as follows [17]:

i) Smaller the value of mean brightness better is the efficiency of the image enhancement.

ii) Bigger the value of entropy, better is the enhanced image.

As we can read from Table 2, The enhanced image obtained from applying SCB Algorithm has a low brightness value and a higher entropy as compared to the original image hence our method is fairly efficient.

6 Conclusion and Future Scope

We have provided an alternative idea for enhancing the underwater images. Our approach not necessarily improves the image quality but makes it more readable. The main aim of SCB is to balance out the hue of all the colours in the RGB spectrum and thereby reducing the dominance of blue colour in underwater images. By using GPU, we have obtained a good speedup. Use of GPU also improves the improves the efficiency and reduces the computational time in case of a higher resolution image. By modifying the saturation percentage, we can also obtain a better enhanced image. However, it has been observed that at lower values of saturation certain artifacts start appearing in the resultant image thereby ruining the quality of the image. By keeping the saturation percentage to a suitable value, we can successfully obtain really good colour balanced images. Since the SCB algorithm is fairly simple to implement and as it is not resource intensive, a better speedup can be obtained using powerful GPUs. Our method of Underwater Image Processing using Simplest Colour Balancing Algorithm implemented on GPU is more efficient and takes less computational time as compared to other Underwater Image Processing Algorithms.

The Future Scope of our Image enhancement method is as follows:

i) SCB Algorithm can be implemented in real-time image processing.
ii) SCB Algorithm can be implemented in video processing followed by an implementation in real-time video processing.
iii) We can try to implement the Algorithm in Jetson TK1 and Jetson Nano GPUs.

References

1. K. Iqbal, R. Abdul Salam, A. Osman, A. Zawawi Talib, "Underwater image enhancement using an integrated color model" **34**, 2-12 (2007)
2. J. S. Jaffe, "Computer modeling and the design of optimal underwater imaging systems" **15**, 101–111 (1990)
3. R. Fattal, "Single image dehazing" 1–9 (2008)
4. W. Hou, D. J. Gray, A. D. Weidemann, G. R. Fournier, J. L. Forand, "Automated underwater image restoration and retrieval of related optical properties" **1**, 1889–1892 (2007)
5. N. Shamsuddin, W.F. Ahmad, B.B. Baharudin, M. Kushairi, M. Rajuddin, F. Mohd, "Significance level of image enhancement techniques for underwater images" **1**, 490-494 (2012)
6. M.S. Hitam, Wan Nural Jawahir Hj Wan Yussof, E.A. Awalludin, Z. Bachok, "Mixture contrast limited adaptive histogram equalization for underwater image enhancement" (2013)
7. S. Harsdorf, R. Reuter, S. Tonebon, "Contrast-enhanced optical imaging of submersible targets" **3821**, 378-383 (1999)
8. Y. Rzhanov, L. M. Linnett, R. Forbes, "Underwater video mosaicing for seabed mapping" **1**, 224-227 (2000)
9. R. Schettini, S. Corchs, "Underwater Image Processing: State of the Art of Restoration and Image Enhancement Methods" (2010)
10. Gonzales and Woods, *Digital Image Processing* **3,** (2008)
11. B. Daga, A. Bhute, A. Ghatol, "Implementation of Parallel Processing using NVIDIA GPU Framework" (2011)
12. E. Buber, B. Diri, "Performance Analysis and GPU vs CPU comparison for Deep Learning" (2018)
13. Z. Ying, G. Li, Y. Ren, R. Wang, W. Wang, "A new image contrast enhancement algorithm using exposure fusion framework" 36-46 (2017)
14. N. Limare, "IPOL Algorithm: Simplest Color Balance," http://www.ipol.im/pub/algo/lmps_simplest_color_balance/
15. S. Gopal Krishna Patro, Kishore Kumar Sahu, "Normalization: A Preprocessing Stage" (2015)
16. P. Patil, N. Singhaniya, C. Jage, V.A. Vyawahare, M.D. Patil, P.S.V. Nataraj, "GPU Computing of Special Mathematical Functions used in Fractional Calculus" **1**, 200-233 (2017)
17. M. Marino, M. Cozza and F. Bruno, "Evaluation of Underwater Image Enhancement Algorithms under Different Environmental Conditions" (2018)

 https://doi.org/10.1051/itmconf/20203203042

Concept for Mapping Carbon footprint with Change in Vegetation Cover and Population in India

Ishma Amin, Meenakshi Agarwal, Stevert Lobo, Rahul Gurnani, Prof. (Mrs.) Priya R.L (*Authors*)
Computer Department
Vivekanand Education Society's Institute of Technology
Mumbai, India
{2016.ishma.amin, 2016.meenakshi.agarwal, 2016.stevert.lobo, 2016.rahul.gurnani, priya.rl } @ves.ac.in

***Abstract*—In most of the developing countries, the increasing rate of Carbon emissions is considered as a major cause of concern. India is leading in terms of CO2 emissions as compared to other countries. The vegetation cover comprises only 24.39% of the geographic area of India. Metropolitan cities in India are witnessing rapid urbanization. The primary objective of this proposal is to identify the relationship between the increase in carbon emissions and deforestation in metropolitan cities. An additional objective is to predict the amount of afforestation required for each area to cope up with the carbon emissions over the next 25-years. It can be achieved by using statistical models like ARIMA, LSTM and machine learning techniques such as Random Forest. The proposal provides suggestions on optimal places and techniques for sustainable afforestation to the concerned authorities using artificial intelligence.**

Keywords—Carbon Footprint, Deforestation, ARIMAX, VAR, Random Forest, LSTM, k-NN imputation, MICE Imputation, time-series synchrony quantification, machine learning.

I. INTRODUCTION

Carbon footprint is used to measure the amount of greenhouse gases mainly, carbon dioxide (CO_2) released into the atmosphere by urban activities. It is normally estimated as tons of CO_2 produced every year, which can be enhanced by huge amounts of CO_2-identical gases, including methane, nitrous oxide, and other greenhouse gases.[3].

The change in demographic profile, urbanization and increase in the number of vehicles, rapid population growth and industrialization over the years, the carbon content in the atmosphere has risen at an exponential rate.

According to the survey of the Global Climate Risk Index (CRI) of 2017, India is 14th on the list of most vulnerable countries. The global ambient air quality database published by the World Health Organization (WHO) in 2018 specifies that urban areas with the highest levels of PM2.5 were situated in India. In AirVisual's 2018 World air quality report, it was mentioned that most polluted urban areas based on PM2.5 estimates on the planet are located in India.[4].

The ecosystem services provided by tree and forest cover of the country become very essential for the existence of any living being. The panel report of India State of Forest Report 2019 states that nation-wide total forest cover is 21.67% of the geographical area, whereas the tree cover is only 2.89% [5,6]. It is also estimated that Soil Organic Carbon (SOC) defines the largest carbon stack in Indian forest areas.

Existing systems relate carbon footprint and deforestation concerning a product or domain-specific industry. This research aims to calculate the net carbon content, then calculate its relationship with forest cover. This relationship will help us to determine the requirements for the future.

This paper is divided into three sections: Section A discusses the survey of this research and section B describes the proposed idea of the system. Goals of the proposed idea for reducing CO_2 emissions are discussed in section C. It also elaborates various components of proposed architecture and methodologies for determining the impact of deforestation on regional carbon footprint levels. Finally, the merits and challenges of the proposed idea are discussed with the future scope of this project.

II. RELATED WORK

The study [7] speaks to a connection between development and qualities and points. By utilizing a negative binomial relapse model, they built the connection between ranchers' ingenuity and those qualities and points which control ranchers' homestead the executive's choices just as another homestead/rancher attributes. Accordingly, the study found that ranchers who are creative win more. The study offers the initial phase in connecting maintainability esteems and development exercises [7].

The paper [8] analyses the carbon emission of the Birla Institute of Technology and Science Pilani (BITS Pilani), using the life cycle analysis (LCA) system. The immediate emanations of college possessed offices, electricity, warmth or steam, and other circuitous discharges are the results of college exercises that are the source for greenhouse gases. Different discharges are displayed in Umberto NXT Universal programming utilizing ISO 14064 guidelines. [8]

The paper [9] uses Deep neural systems that utilize stepwise linear regressions with exponential smoothing regression slopes as trend strength indicators for a given time interval. The outcomes exhibit the estimation of Deep learning ways to deal with time series analysis and show that regression gives helpful highlights to complex interdependencies, offering a straightforward marker of trends with high predictive value [9].

This paper [10] focuses on forest cover dynamics and creating a forecasting model of the Bhanupratappur Forest

Division of Kanker, Chhattisgarh, India. It uses a logistic regression model (LRM) to analyze the changes in forests caused by road constructions and expansion of settlements. This research uses data obtained through Landsat TM satellite imagery for the duration of 1990 to 2000. The model was assessed by comparing the model-predicted forest cover with the actual forest cover for 2010 [10].

This paper is intended to anticipate the influence of variables such as electricity, coal, etc. in the growth of carbon emissions. The data was obtained from the Alcohol Industry to train and test [11].

The following TABLE I depicts the comparison of various existing systems.

TABLE I. COMPARISON BETWEEN EXISTING SYSTEMS

Existing System	Proposed System
Negative binomial regression model generating relationship.[7]	The ARIMAX model is used for forecasting and formulating equations.
Deep neural networks for trend change analysis [10].	LSTM based neural networks for trend change analysis are applied.
Logistic regression model [4] and Support Vector Machine [11] for prediction	Time Series analysis is used for prediction

III. PROPOSED IDEA

The foremost objective of this research is to identify the relationship between deforestation rate and the subsequent growth of carbon footprint levels in Indian metropolitan cities. This research also tries to predict the additional vegetation cover required to cope up with the estimated deforestation rate and carbon footprint growth over the next 25-years. The block diagram of the proposed methodology is depicted as in Fig.1.

The dataset is collected from various sources which include Indian Government websites as well as NGO's. The acquired data is preprocessed to remove missing values. A relationship between Vegetation, Carbon emission and Population is computed, which helps us to determine the pattern between vegetation change and carbon emissions. The above relationship is then used to estimate the afforestation efforts required for sustenance.

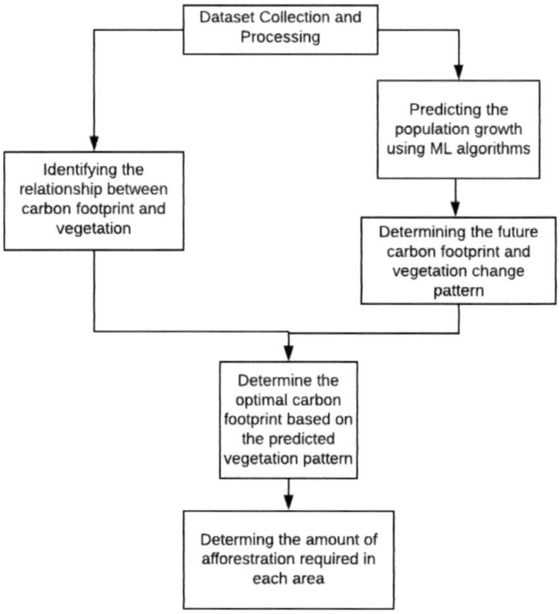

Fig. 1. Block diagram

IV. DETAILED ARCHITECTURE

This section provides a detailed explanation of the proposed idea for mapping of carbon footprint with population and vegetation cover in metropolitan regions of India. The detailed architecture of the proposed design is shown in Fig. 2.

A. Dataset Collection

This study involves the collection of data concerning vegetation cover and carbon footprint in Indian cities over the past few decades. The proposed model uses a dataset consisting of land-use statistics of India compiled from various Government sources as well as research studies specified in Table.2. Table.2 also contains details regarding the tree cover loss and carbon footprint datasets. This data encompasses the period from 2000 to 2018. Air quality data with respect to greenhouse gas emissions is collected from the Pollution Control Board's website. Multivariate Imputation by Chained Equations (MICE) is used to fill missing values by taking the multivariate nature of data into consideration. Table II. of the study provides a detailed description of data collection sources.

TABLE II. DATASET DESCRIPTION

Category	**Subcategory**	**Data source**
Land Use Statistics		
District-wise, 28 states and 7	Non-agricultural	Directorate of Economics And

union territories (Area in Hectares)	land, Barren areas, Unculturable Land, Forest Area, Geographical Area, Culturable Waste Land, Land Under Misc. Tree Crops, Mangroves, Net Sown Area, Current Fallows, Permanent Pastures, Grazing Lands	Statistics, Govt. of India(1998 - 2009) [12] Department of Agriculture, Govt. of Maharashtra (2010 - 2018) [13]
	Tree cover loss	The Global Forest Watch organization (2000 - 2018) [15, 17, 18, 19]
Carbon Footprint		
District-wise, 28 states and 7 union territories (CO_2 in metric tons)	Carbon dioxide emissions equivalent to national biomass loss	The Global Forest Watch organization (2000 - 2018) [15, 17, 18, 19]
According to air quality monitoring stations, 28 states and 7 union territories (concentrations in mg/m3)	Air quality with respect to greenhouse gas concentrations (Benzene, CO, Eth Benzene, MP Xylene, NH_3, NO, NO_2, SOx, NOx, Ozone, PM_{10})	Central Pollution Control Board, Ministry of Environment, Forest and Climate Change, Govt. of India [16]

B. Data Preprocessing

The final integrated dataset consists of 6 spatial-temporal features, namely - State, District, Vegetation Cover, % Vegetation Cover, Population and CO_2 emissions (in metric tons.) from 1998 to 2018.

The data for forest area, pasture land, orchid plantations and miscellaneous tree crops have been considered in computing vegetation cover. The percentage of vegetation cover (%V) is calculated using the formula:

$$\%V = \frac{Vegetation\ Cover}{Total\ Area} \times 100$$

Where, %V is a useful parameter for districts with fluctuating geographical boundaries. Missing values in the dataset are handled using techniques such as K Nearest Neighbours (KNN) imputation and Multiple Imputation with Chained Equations (MICE). The resulting dataset is a panel data with different districts as the cross-sections.

C. Goals

This study aims to achieve the following goals:

1) Afforestation

Identifying the relationship between carbon emission rate and deforestation can help in determining the additional vegetation cover needed to curb the carbon footprint growth. This study can furthermore suggest sustainable techniques and optimal places for afforestation in metropolitan cities.

2) Biodiversity

The biodiversity in metropolitan regions is rapidly declining due to constant deforestation. The implementation of suggested afforestation measures will help to improve biodiversity considerably. Restoration of ecosystems and habitats will help to protect several endangered species and prevent their extinction.

3) Retaining Groundwater

Trees have a fantastic capacity to assimilate and hold water. It is estimated that, as much as 1,000 tons of precipitation can be absorbed by a mature tree. However, in the absence of trees, a lot of energy is required for pumping and filtration.

4) Carbon Sequestration

As trees utilize carbon dioxide to prepare their food, afforestation can help to control CO_2 levels. A research done by EPA indicates that the shade and water vapor discharged by trees help to reduce temperatures in cities by as much as 25°C.

D. Prediction and Forecasting models

This study consists of three distinct phases. The first phase is to identify how carbon footprint growth is associated with deforestation. The second phase estimates the additional vegetation cover required over the next 25 years to cope up with the increase in carbon footprint and deforestation during that period. The third phase of this research suggests optimal techniques for sustainable afforestation according to region-specific needs. The component diagram of the proposed methodology is shown in figure 2.

1) Modelling of Carbon Footprint and Deforestation relationship (CDR)

Each feature in the final dataset can be considered as an independent time series. Techniques such as Autocorrelation function (ACF) and Partial Autocorrelation function (PACF), Causality Tests, etc. can be used to quantify the synchrony between the vegetation change (Vi) and carbon footprint/ CO2 emission (Ci) time series.

The k-NN (k - Nearest Neighbours) Intersection Algorithm can also be used to identify the relationship between Vi and Ci. The idea of this algorithm is that if an observation has k nearest neighbours in one vector representation and the same nearest neighbours in the other, the two vector representations are likely to be related. This likelihood can be calculated by the overlap of the nearest neighbours collectively for all the observations. DTW is used as the distance measure in k-NN Intersection Algorithm. [20]

Granger Causality test will be used to determine whether the time series of vegetation cover and population are useful in the forecasting of CO2. This will help to understand the cause and effect relationship between the features.

2) Estimation of required vegetation cover (Vr)

CDR identified in the first phase serves as an input in the estimation process. This phase also involves the prediction of carbon footprint growth (Cp) and variation in vegetation cover (Vp) over the next 25 years, which is based on historical time series data and population estimates.

The yearly optimal carbon footprint (Co) can then be determined for each region based on Vp and CDR. The difference between Cp and Co measures the carbon footprint (Ca) that cannot be negated by the estimated vegetation cover (Vp). Some amount of afforestation (Vr) is required to deal with Ca. Vr required for each district can be predicted with CDR and Ca.

Time series forecasting techniques such as Auto-Regressive Integrated Moving Average - X (ARIMAX) and Vector Autoregression (VAR) models will be constructed for forecasting of Cp with Vp and population as exogenous variables. LSTM based neural network and Random Forest algorithm will be used for machine learning-based estimation. Panel data estimation will be performed using Generalized Estimating Equations (GEE).

Results of the above-mentioned techniques will be evaluated and the best performing method will be selected as the forecasting model.

3) AI-based suggestions for sustainable afforestation

The objective of this phase is to provide region-specific recommendations for afforestation, based on the estimated Vr. These recommendations include tree species, forestation techniques and suitable places to carry out afforestation activities.

V. FUTURE SCOPE AND CONCLUSION

This study addresses the optimization and management of tree ecosystems in major metropolitan cities. Considering the growing population of metropolitan cities, the aim is for sustenance along with development. The above-proposed idea will be implemented in the future and develop a system for suggesting suitable areas for afforestation. A system for recommending tree species according to the terrain of the city can be coupled with the proposed system for maintaining the ecosystem.

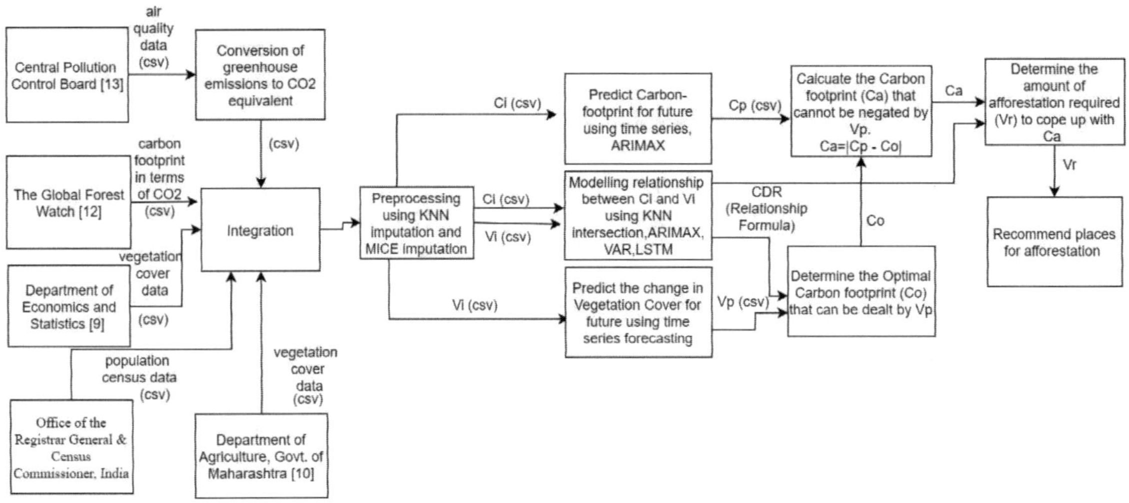

Fig. 2. Conceptual diagram

VI. REFERENCE

[1] "India's CO2 emissions are growing faster than the US' or China's" Available from: https://qz.com/india/1581665/indias-carbon-emissions-growing-faster-than-us-china-says-iea/

[2] "Has India's Forest Cover increased over the years?" Available from: https://factly.in/has-indias-forest-cover-increased-over-the-years/

[3] "Bengaluru: One tree for seven people, says an IISc study". Available from: https://www.deccanchronicle.com/lifestyle/pets-and-environment/220416/bengaluru-one-tree-for-seven-people-says-an-iisc-study.html

[4] "India:Environmental Issues" Available from: http://www.europarl.europa.eu/RegData/etudes/BRIE/2019/637920/EPRS_BRI(2019)637920_EN.pdf

[5] "India State Of Forest Report 2019 Volume-II":http://164.100.117.97/WriteReadData/userfiles/ISFR2019%20Vol-II.pdf

[6] "India State Of Forest Report 2019 Volume-I":http://164.100.117.97/WriteReadData/userfiles/ISFR2019%20Vol-I.pdf

[7] Peter Walder, Franz Sinabell, Fabian Unterlass, Andreas Niedermayr, Denisa Fulgeanu, Martin Kapfer, Michael Melcher and Jochen Kantelhardt "Exploring the Relationship between Farmers' Innovativeness and Their Values and Aims" DOI: https://doi.org/10.3390/su11205571

[8] Kuldip Singh Sangwan, Vikrant Bhakar, Vinti Arora and Prem Solanki "Measuring carbon footprint of an Indian university using life cycle assessment" DOI: 10.1016/j.procir.2017.11.111

[9] Ben Moews, J.Michael Herrmann and GbengaIbikunle "Lagged correlation-based deep learning for directional trend change prediction in financial time series" DOI: https://doi.org/10.1016/j.eswa.2018.11.027

[10] RakeshKumar, S.Nandy, ReshuAgarwal and S.P.S.Kushwaha "Forest cover dynamics analysis and prediction modeling using logistic regression model" DOI:https://doi.org/10.1016/j.ecolind.2014.05.003

[11] Chairul Saleh, Nur Rachman Dzakiyullah, Jonathan Bayu Nugroho "Carbon dioxide emission prediction using support vector machine" DOI:10.1088/1757-899X/114/1/012148

[12] Directorate of Economics And Statistics, Department of Agriculture, Cooperation and Farmers Welfare, Ministry of Agriculture and Farmers Welfare, Govt. of India. District wise land use statistics. Available from: https://eands.dacnet.nic.in/

[13] Department of Agriculture, Govt. of Maharashtra. Land Utilization Statistics. Available from: http://krishi.maharashtra.gov.in/1074/Land-Utilization-Statistics

[14] Hanqin Tian, Kamaljit Banger, Tao Bo, Vinay K. Dadhwal. "History of land use in India during 1880–2010: Large-scale land transformations reconstructed from satellite data and historical archives". DOI: https://doi.org/10.1016/j.gloplacha.2014.07.005

[15] Global Forest Watch. Forest Monitoring. Available from: https://www.globalforestwatch.org/

[16] Central Pollution Control Board, Ministry of Environment, Forest and Climate Change, Govt. of India. Air quality data. Available from: https://www.cpcb.nic.in/

[17] Hansen, M. C., P. V. Potapov, R. Moore, M. Hancher, S. A. Turubanova, A. Tyukavina, D. Thau, S. V. Stehman, S. J. Goetz, T. R. Loveland, A. Kommareddy, A. Egorov, L. Chini, C. O. Justice, and J. R. G. Townshend. 2013. "High-Resolution Global Maps of 21st-Century Forest Cover Change." Science 342 (15 November): 850–53. Data available on-line from: http://earthenginepartners.appspot.com/science-2013-global-forest.

[18] Zarin, D., Harris, N.L. 2016. Can carbon emissions drop by 50% in five years? Global Change Biology, 22: 1336-1347. doi:10.1111/gcb.13153

[19] Global Administrative Areas Database, version 3.6. Available at http://gadm.org/

[20] Arighna Roy "Quantifying relationships between two time series data sets". Available from: https://pdfs.semanticscholar.org/8824/fb4ef14f94f96a9d6799551e99a612fa7cf3.pdf

ITM Web of Conferences **32**, 03043 (2020) https://doi.org/10.1051/itmconf/20203203043
ICACC-2020

Preprocessing and Enhancement for Image Fusion using Composite Algorithm

Shirish Kulkarni[1*], and *Bhavesh* Digey[1*]
[1]Department of Instrumentation Engineering, Ramrao Adik Institute of Technology, Navi Mumbai

Abstract. A technique of alignment and removal of noise is a prominent pre-processing part of biomedical image fusion. The purpose is to evaluate and analyze visually as well as parametric findings. However, considering practical execution still there is need for improvement in pre-processing for image processing applications. Therefore, the problem of blockage and variation in scans of patients, need to be overcome by properly align and denoise input images. Therefore to design the registration algorithm in such a way, it should cover all geometric motions of biomedical images, by which it is useful to the practitioner for the detection of medical defects. Herewith we have proposed a log-polar and phase correlation composite algorithm for the registration of all geometric motions. The proposed algorithm preserves the outline portion and surface information from the images, which yields perceptible effects. This will be useful in order to take out visual data from a noisy background. Since it is shown that the results with noisy and after denoised compared visually and also parametric analysis is carried out by calculating PSNR, MSE, contrast, structural content, entropy, etc

1 INTRODUCTION

Image registration is a process of mapping a sensed image with the reference image that shares common visual information such as medical images belonging to the similar object or images of the same scene obtained from different viewpoints, or at different time instances, or sensors. However, the objective of such mapping is to match image registration, which is quintessential in many image processing applications, that incorporates a number of images for the purpose of comparison, integration. The main objective of the image registration process is to estimate the geometric transformations of the reference image IR to the sensed image, IS, where IS(x, y)= T{IR(x', y') and T is a 2-D geometric transformation that includes scale, rotation, and translation in the Cartesian coordinates. Image registration technique should comprise of geometric transformation of all motions along. There should be accountability with denoising removal of noise present in sense image due to motion artifacts before applying the transformation. The proposed method not only preserves edges and texture information from the image but also removes the noise, providing the good visual effect.

It is very important to have a low computation cost with respect to the time and load of the matrix formation. The size and correctness of the images rely on the number of samples taken into consideration. For the registration of any medical image, the scaled mapping in terms of radius and angular direction is required. This is the main cause of increases the load on computation. To increase the effectiveness and robustness of the changes, we proposed the area based Log-Polar Transformer (LPT) method. This method again increases the computational load during the mapping process. This will motivate the success of area-based LPT –PC composite algorithm this will scale up the all the geometric motion. The image registration using composite algorithm is used to get results with low computation cost.

The rest of paper is organized as follows; in the first section details of geometric actions and their methodology using Log-Polar transform and Phase correlation is explained. Literature survey is included which accomplishes work on denoising and registration. Implementation of image registration is carried out by the proposed algorithm in the consecutive section. In the next section, performance evaluation is carried on medical images (CT scan) with visual as well as parametric analysis. The last section concludes the work.

2 LITERATURE SURVEY

The various image registration approaches are proposed in the literature. The SIFT, SURF, and LPT are the major approaches. Scale Invariant Feature Transform (SIFT) enables the extraction of invariant features in a pyramidal Difference of Gaussians (DOG) and may render itself invariant to image scaling, translation, and rotation, and to some extent also invariant to

* Corresponding author: shirish.kulkarni@rait.ac.in, bhavesh.digey@rait.ac.in

illumination changes and affine [1-3]. Principal Components Analysis (PCA) is used to standardize the gradient patch, as a substitute of SIFTs sharp weighted histograms. The SIFT improves the feature matching and splits the extracted features into some sub-collections before the two images are matched [4-5].

SURF (Speeded-up Robust Features) constructs pyramids of different resolutions, uses a different method to extract feature points. It relies on the integral images for image convolutions. SURF is faster than SIFT but both aren't robust when it comes to rotation and illumination changes [6].

The similarities between the images in the frequency domain are evaluated by using the phase correlation method [7]. As compared to cross-correlation, it performs well with noise and illumination changes. The correlation method succumbs to failure when there are changes in rotation or scale between images, in such cases, Log-Polar Transform (LPT) [8-13] is widely used. Fourier-Mellin used a composite algorithm (phase correlation technique with the Log-Polar Transformation), it describes rotation and scale as translations in parameter space [14-17].

3 PROPOSED IMAGE REGISTRATION METHOD

For spinning and zooming geometric effects in image Log-Polar Transform technique is used. In this method, angular and scaling effect occurs as translation. The polar coordinates (ρ, θ) aligns with the radius and angle from the center. This approach can be evaluated by taking into consideration, logarithm of points placed in the circle (ρ). The scale transform is insensible to enlarge and pertain to scale energy spectrum distingusihes both regardless of the magnification factor. Denoising caried out in the scale domain is promising than in Fourier domain which was indicated by Moses as its importance in extracting significant information from a background of distorted images. The advantage of scale transform is that it enables us to smooth-out the spectrum without spreading the scales. It is seen that in log-polar images parameters associated with translation motion are not successfully obtained, this can be overcomed by phase correlation method.

The block diagram shown in fig. 1 is of proposed method consisting of input images to be registered, transformation for geometric motions followed by sense image aligned on the reference image to obtain a registered image. The major difference in block diagram from rest is the occurrence of image denoising using the same transform that will be used for geometric transformations.

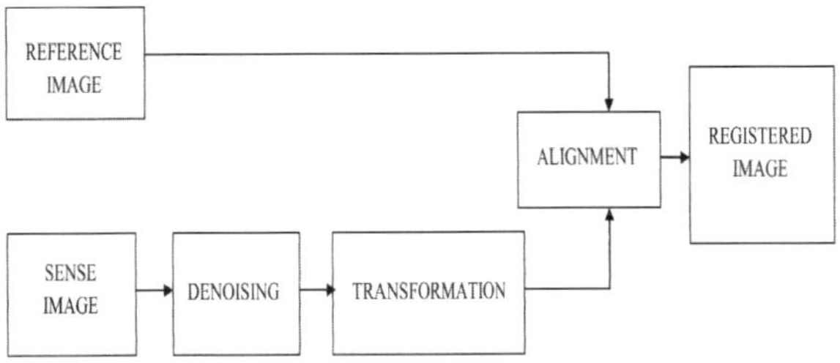

Fig 1. Block Diagram of Proposed Image Registration Technique

The proposed registration algorithm is as follow: We have two source images Ii, i = 1;2 related by a translation, rotation, and scaling.

1. Calculate the gradient as Gi=Gi(x) + j Gi(y)
2. Horizontal and Vertical boundaries are obtained using the regular Cartesian FFT by using a high pass emphasis filter.
3. Removal of noise components from the sensed image using log-polar transform.
4. Estimate rotation (θ) and scale (s) using the log-polar technique.
5. Scale up/down and de-rotate the image with respect to estimated angle.
6. Evaluate the transformation with the Phase Correlation in a frequency domain.
7. Then IFFT is taken and calculate the peaks for both cases.
8. Now for images such as reference image I^R and sense image I^s, compute Cross Power Spectrum with the reference image.
9. As in step 5, shift the image to the original position and finally, this gives a registered image.

4 RESULTS AND DISCUSSION

Performance analysis has been carried out for all four cases and the results at each case are evaluated and explained below. Image registration for chest, abdomen, lungs and head CT of four different cases are carried out and visual analysis of all four cases are shown with noise and after denoising effect shown in fig. 2,4,6,8 and 3,5,7,9 respectively. Performances of all the cases are improved with denoising effect. Hence there is a need for pre-processing before transforming sense image. Also with the parametric analysis from table 1, 2, 3 and 4, it is observed that there is an improvement in Mean Squared Error (MSE) and Peak Signal to Noise Ratio (PSNR) with denoising effect i.e there is an increase in PSNR and decrease in MSE respectively.

 https://doi.org/10.1051/itmconf/20203203043

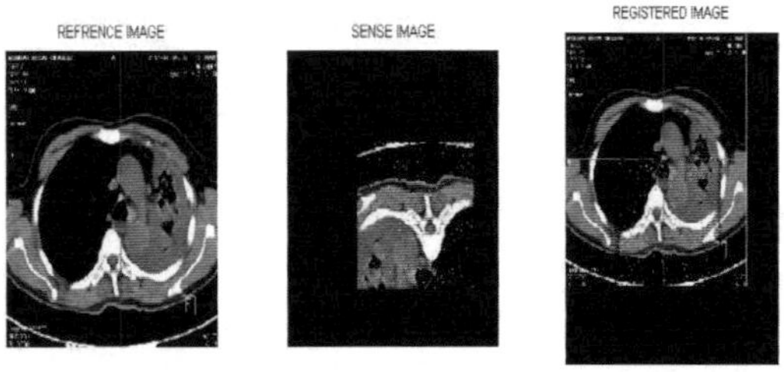

Fig 2. Image Registration for Chest CT with Noise

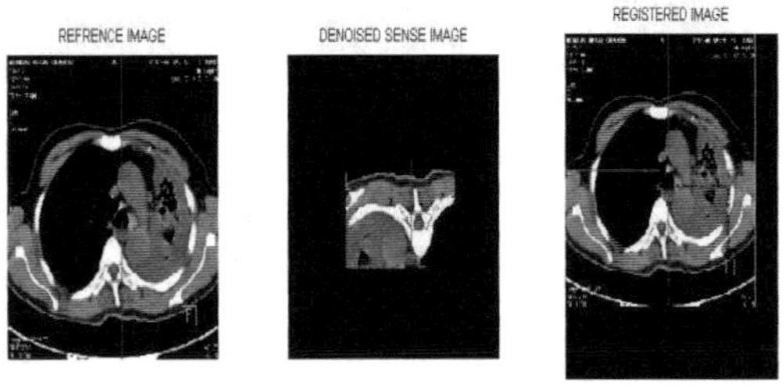

Fig 3. Image Registration for Chest CT with Denoise effect
Horizontal movement: 79, Vertical movement: 43, Rotated angle: 180°

The composite algorithm applied on Head CT has successfully registered for sense image with partial data, without exact angle shown in figure 10 and scaling effect shown in figure 11.

Table 1. Chest CT: Comparision of registered image with and without denoising effect

Sr. No.	Parameters	With Noise	With Denoising
1	Standard Deviation	96.32	96.92
2	Structural Content	2.316	2.406
3	MSE	26.26	20.59
4	PSNR	33.97	35.02
5	Contrast	1.0744	1.117
6	Entropy	4.807	4.61

Fig 4. Image Registration for Abdomen CT with Noise effect

Fig 5. Image Registration for Abdomen CT with Denoise effect
Horizontal movement: 55, Vertical movement: 51, Rotated angle: 90°

Table 2. Abdomen CT: Comparision of registered image with and without denoising effect

Sr. No.	Parameters	With Noise	With Denoising
1	Standard Deviation	66.27	66.295
2	Structural Content	2.436	2.959
3	MSE	26.261	20.592
4	PSNR	33.971	35.027
5	Contrast	1.82	1.908
6	Entropy	3.819	3.77

Fig 6. Image Registration for Lungs CT with Noise effect

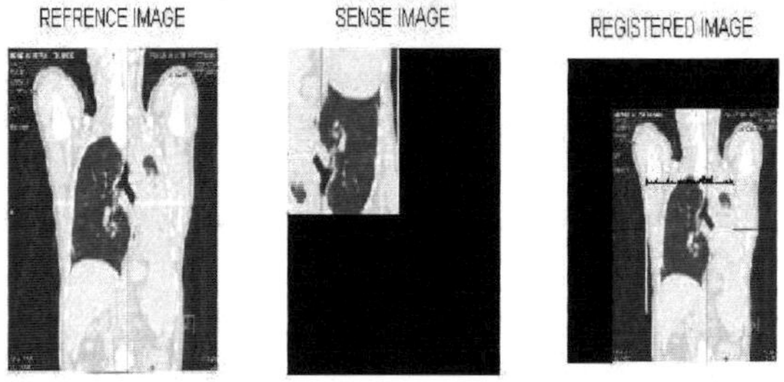

Fig 7. Image Registration for Lungs CT with Denoise effect
Horizontal movement: - 44, Vertical movement: -70, Rotated angle: 180°.

Table 3. Lungs CT: Comparision of registered image with and without denoising effect

Sr. No.	Parameters	With Noise	With Denoising
1	Standard Deviation	101.46	101.72
2	Structural Content	3.10	3.223
3	MSE	57.31	55.72
4	PSNR	30.58	30.704
5	Contrast	0.99	1.008
6	Entropy	5.37	5.189

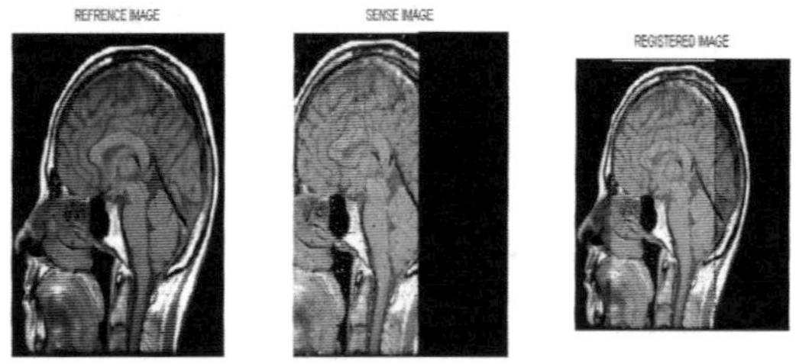

Fig 8. Image Registration for Head CT with Noise effect

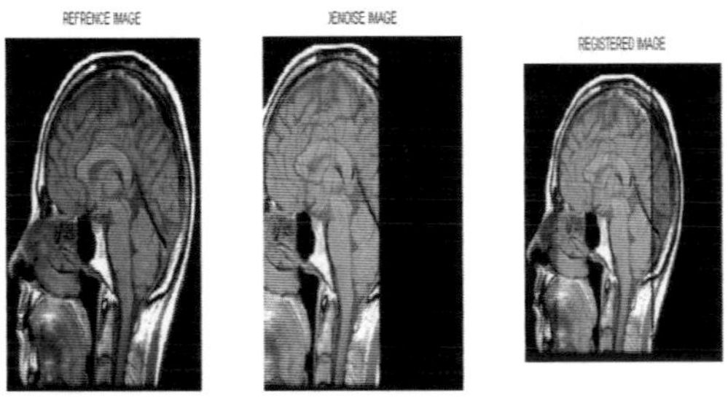

Fig 9. Image Registration for Head CT with Denoise effect Horizontal movement: 01,Vertical movement: 50, Rotated angle: 0°

Table 4. Head CT: Comparision of registered image with and without denoising effect

Sr. No.	Parameters	With Noise	With Denoising
1	Standard Deviation	78.987	80.867
2	Structural Content	0.94	0.96
3	MSE	81.386	79.458
4	PSNR	29.059	29.163
5	Contrast	1.025	1.071
6	Entropy	5.907	5.630

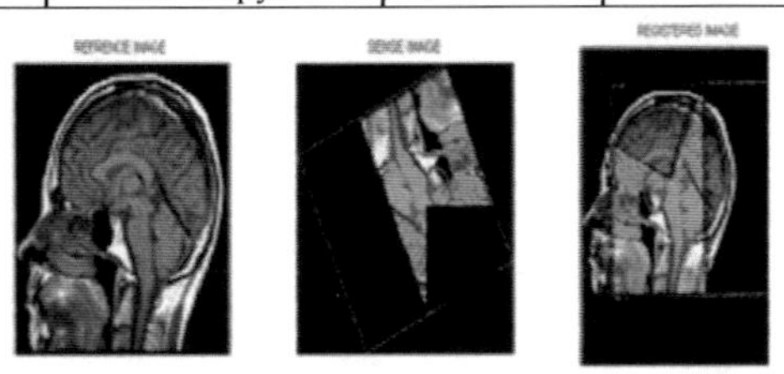

Fig 10. Image Registration for Head CT with rotation without an exact angle.
Horizontal movement: - 42, Vertical movement: 7, Rotated angle: 203°

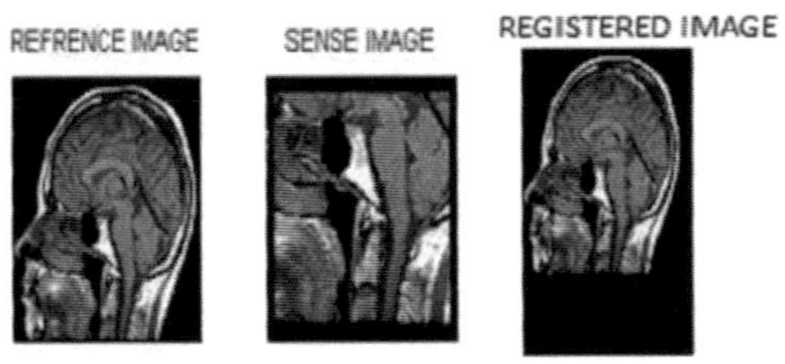

Fig 11. Image Registration for Head CT with scale. Estimated Horizontal movement 103,Vertical movement 44, Scale 1.57

5 CONCLUSION

The manuscript presents a comparison between noisy and denoised registered images of different CT images of human body organs like abdomen, chest, lungs, and head. The proposed algorithm preserves edges and texture information from the sensed CT images and also removes the noise, providing the good visual effect. This will be useful in order to take out visual data from a noisy background.

The simulated results of image registration are verified with scaling factor up to 1.57 and with any degree of rotation. The accuracy of the algorithm is verified by visual inspection of the registered image by overlaying it on a reference image. Moreover, the parametric analysis is carried out between the registered and reference images by calculating PSNR, MSE, contrast, structural content, entropy, etc.. The facility of the algorithm to improve registration parameters in presence of noise, partial data and with blurring is also confirmed. The simulated results show that this approach is highly effective.

References

1. David G. Lowe. Object recognition from local scale-invariant features, In Proceedings of the Seventh IEEE International Conference on Computer Vision, Corfu, Greece, 1999.
2. Yu-Dae Ban, Jaeyeon Lee, Dae Hwan Hwang, Yun-Koo Chung. Face Image registration methods using Normalized Cross Correlation International Conference on Control. Automation and Systems, 2008, pp.2408-2411.
3. David G. Lowe. Distinctive image features from scale-invariant key- points. International Journal of Computer Vision, 2004, (60), pp. 91-110.
4. Yan Ke and R. Sukthankar. PCA-SIFT: a more distinctive representation for local image descriptors. In Proceedings IEEE Computer Society Conference on Computer Vision and Pattern Recognition. 2004 July, 2(2), pp. 506-513.
5. Danijela Ristic-Durrant Faraj Alhwarin, Chao Wang, and Axel Grser. Improved sift features matching for object recognition. BCS International Academic Conference 2008 Visions of Computer Science. 2008, pp. 179-190.
6. Luo Juan and Oubong Gwon. A Comparison of SIFT, PCA-SIFT, and SURF. International Journal of Image Processing (IJIP). 2009, 3(4), pp. 143-152.
7. Jignesh N Sarvaiya, Dr. Suprava Patnaik, Salman Bombaywala. Image registration using Log polar transform and phase correlation. IEEE Region 10 Conference TENCON. 2009, pp. 1-5.
8. Hast, Anders. Robust and Invariant Phase Based Local Feature Matching. 22nd International Conference on Pattern Recognition (ICPR). 2014, ISSN: 1051-4651, pp. 809-814.
9. Wolberg G., Zokai S, Robust image registration using log-polar transform, In Proceeding International Conference on Image Processing, 2000 September, pp. 493-496.
10. Y.Keller, A.Averbuch, M.Israeli. Pseudo polar-based estimation of large translations, rotations, and scalings in images. IEEE Trans. on Image processing. 2005, pp. 12-22.
11. H. Liu, B. Guo, and Z. Feng. Pseudo-log-polar Fourier transforms for image registration. IEEE

Transaction Signal Processing Letters. 2006 January, 13(1), pp. 1720.
12. R. Matungka, Y. F. Zheng, and R. L. Ewing. 2D invariant object recognition using log-polar transform. In Proc. World Congress on Intelligent Control and Automation, 2008 January, pp. 223-228.
13. A. N. Myrna, M. G. Venkateshmurthy, and C. G. Patil. Detection of region duplication forgery in digital images using wavelets and log-polar mapping. In Proc. Intl. Conf. Computational Intelligence and Multimedia Applications, 2007 December, (3), pp. 371-377.
14. Xiaoxin Guo, Zhiwen Xu, Yinan Lu, and Yunjie Pang. An Application of Fourier-Mellin Transform in Image Registration. Proceedings of The Fifth International Conference on Computer and Information Technology, 2005, pp.619-623.
15. B. Srinivasa Reddy and B. N. Chatterji. An FFT-Based Technique for Translation, Rotation, and Scale-Invariant Image Registration. IEEE Trans. on Image Processing. 1996, (5), pp.1266-1271.
16. XiaoxinGuo, ZhiwenXu, Yinan Lu, and Yunjie Pang. An Application of Fourier-Mellin Transform in Image Registration. Proceedings of The Fifth International Conference on Computer and InformationTechnology, 2005, pp.619-623.
17. Y.Keller, A.Averbuch, M.Israeli. Pseudo polar-based estimation of large translations, rotations, and scalings in the image. IEEE transaction on Image processing. 2005, pp. 12-22.

Image Super-Resolution for MRI Images using 3D Faster Super-Resolution Convolutional Neural Network architecture

Vanita Mane[1,*], *Suchit* Jadhav[2,**], and *Praneya* Lal[3,***]

[1]Ramrao Adik Institute of Technology
[2]Department of Computer Engineering
[3]Mumbai, India

Abstract. Single image super-resolution using deep learning techniques has shown very high reconstruction performance over the last few years. We propose a novel three-dimensional convolutional neural network called 3D FSRCNN based on FSRCNN, which reinstates the high-resolution quality of structural MRI. The 3D neural network generates output brain images of high-resolution (HR) from a low-resolution (LR) input image. A simple design ensures less time complexity and high reconstruction quality. The network is trained using T1-weighted structural MRI images from the human connectome project dataset which is a large publicly available brain MRI database.
Index Terms—MRI, Super Resolution, SRCNN, FSRCNN

1 Introduction

Acquisition of high-resolution MRI images using effective techniques faces many obstacles. MRI or CT imaging becomes expensive as the quality of imaging increases with that the time required for the imaging also increases. There is, therefore, a need to recreate high-resolution image output from the input with low-resolution (LR) to effectively solve these problems. Super-resolution (SR) is the process of high-resolution (HR) image estimation from one or more low-resolution (LR) images.But because of its underdetermined nature SR is a challenging issue. After resolution degradation a countless number of HR images will produce the same SLR data.This drives us to solve this challenge using our thinking.The 3D scans give minute specifics as opposed to 2D models, presenting a memory consumption challenge and massive expense, making them less realistic. This motivated us to offer a solution to the difficulty of super-resolution for MRI images that are created in a 3D structure. One of the conventional methods for SR is random forest [1].It generates many trees and merges their outputs, unlike a decision tree. To implement it, the algorithm requires the much-needed varied computational power and resources for a positive outcome. Also, compared to other methods, this method does not know the mapping between images of low-resolution and high-resolution.Super Resolution Convolutional Neural Network (SRCNN) [2] shows state-of-the-art performance and reduces many steps required in conventional methods. In [3], CNN layers represent steps in SR and has outstanding performance.In [4]authors have explained about advanced deep models, high precision has been achieved for SISR, applying these models to real-world scenarios is still challenging, primarily due to massive parameters and computation. In this work, we discuss how CNNs can be used for reconstructing 3D brain MRI images with the perfect trade-off between complexity and performance. We investigate various approaches related to CNNs and finally propose a neural network called 3D Faster Super-Resolution Convolutional Neural Networks based (3D-FSRCNN) on Faster Super-Resolution Convolutional Neural Networks architecture (FSRCNN) [5].

2 Super Resolution Neural Network

2.1 Mathematical background

Super-resolution, specifically focusses at the reconstruction of HR image Y from one LR image X. It can be formulated as:

$$Y = F(x) \tag{1}$$

Where F is a transformation that reconstructs the high resolution image Y from low resolution input image X. Dong et al. [3] shows that this transformation can be achieved using Convolutional Neural Network (CNN) that minimizes difference between reconstructed and ground truth images.

2.2 Previous deep learning techniques

2.2.1 *SRCNN AND ITS LIMITATIONS*

One simple but very effective Convolutional Neural Network (SRCNN) [3] was proposed for 2D natural images that yield high performance. One approach extends the

*e-mail: vanitamane1@gmail.com
**e-mail: suchit966@gmail.com
***e-mail: praneya0028@gmail.com

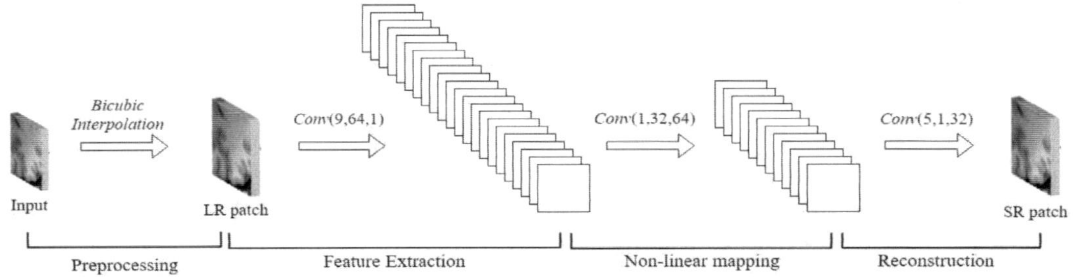

Figure 1. 3D SRCNN Architecture.

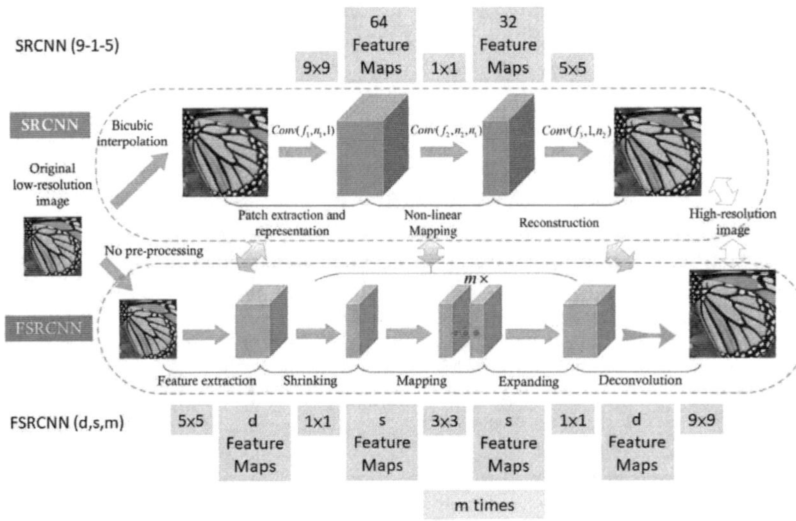

Figure 2. Comparison between SRCNN and FSRCNN [3]

idea of SRCNN and applies it to 3D brain MRI images [2] and another approach extends SRCNN to CT imaging [7], it demonstrates that 3D SRCNN successfully keeps the structure and contours in 3D MRI and CT scans. The limitation of the 3D SRCNN is that it requires more time to predict the SR scan. After analyzing the architecture of the SRCNN, it is found that there are some steps in the model which are costly. The preprocessing step while training delays the training process as it allows the input to be interpolated to the desired output size using methods such as bicubic interpolation, which is costly when we consider three-dimensional images and when testing the interpolated LR images adds further to the complexity.Also, as studied by [5] the non-linear mapping step in SRCNN is the most expensive and causes an increase in time complexity. Complexity of 3D SRCNN:

$$O(f_1^3 n_1 + n_1 f_2^3 n_2 + n_2 f_3^3) S_{HR} \quad (2)$$

Where fi and ni are size of the filter and filter number of the three layers in SRCNN respectively. SHR is the size of the output/HR image. In [2] f1 = 9, f2 = 1, f3 = 5 and n1 = 64, n2 = 32.As seen in figure 1, the complexity is dependent on the size of the HR image, and the non-linear mapping layer adds the most to the constraints of the network [5].

2.2.2 FSRCNN FOR 3D SUPER RESOLUTION

To solve these complex issues with SRCNN, [5] proposed a method to accelerate the SRCNN model called FSR-CNN. In this, the proposed 2D FSRCNN model showed a major upgrade from the previous SRCNN model. The FS-RCNN model does not have the costly interpolation step which makes it faster while training as well as while testing. One of the features of this 3D FSR- CNN model is that we can have the desired output size without interpolating the input image.Also, the non-linear mapping method in SRCNN which was found as most expensive was replaced with three steps - shrinking, mapping and expanding, reducing complexity.

In the next section, we discuss how the FSRCNN can be extended in a three-dimensional setting to produce HR brain MRI images, its architecture, and parameters related to its architecture.

2.3 Network Architecture

The 3D FSRCNN model proposed in [5] can be broken down into five parts- feature extraction, shrinking, mapping, expanding, and deconvolution as shown in Figure 2. The first four are layers of convolution while the fifth is a layer of deconvolution. We refer to a convolution layer as Conv(fi, ni, ci), and a deconvolution layer as DeConv (fi, ni, ci), where the fi, ni, ci variables represent the filter size, the number of filters and the number of channels, respectively. Since the entire network contains tens of variables, we can not analyze each one of them.Therefore, the insensitive variables are given a reasonable value in advance, leaving the sensitive variables to be unset. When a small change in the variable can have a significant effect on performance[4], we consider a variable sensitive. Such sensitive variables also reflect some important influencing factors in SR, as explained below.

Feature Extraction: This step is similar to feature extraction in SRCNN, the difference being, in FSRCNN it is done on the LR image directly rather than on interpolated image. In SRCNN, filter size (f1) was 9.As these filters are executed in SRCNN on an upscaled image, using a filter size of 5 will recover similar information as a 9 9 9 filter would in SRCNN. Thus, at this stage f1 = 5, c1 = 1 and now we need to figure out no. of filters ni. Let the ni at this layer be denoted by d as in [z]. The filter number is a sensitive variable, finally, we can represent the first layer as Conv(5, d, 1).

Shrinking: Nonlinear mapping in SRCNN follows the extraction of the feature but FSRCNN has a shrinking layer to reduce dimensionality of d. The LR features d is very large and for 3D MRI images it will be larger. Authors in [4] have used 1 1 filter to reduce computational cost. Thus, we will follow it and use 1 1 1 filter size i.e., f2 = 1 to reduce the dimension of d. The filter number n2 = s should be less than d to reduce the LR feature dimension. Thus, the second layer can be represented as Conv(1, s, d).

Non-linear mapping: This step is the most important as it maps the LR image features to the HR images. It has the most share in the super-resolution performanceAn comprehensive analysis of deep networks was conducted in [5] authors and found that retaining filter size as 3 is a great trade-off between good performance and network scale.We obey their analysis, and we maintain f3 = 3 and n3 = s. Another sensible variable is the number of layers of mapping denoted by m. So, layers of mapping can be stated as m Conv (3,s, s).

Expanding: This layer undoes the shrinking layer which reduces the LR feature dimension for computational efficiency. Generating images without expanding would generate images with poor quality. To maintain consistency [4] have used filter size f4 = 1, same as in the shrinking layer. The shrinking layer was Conv(1,d, s) so Conv(1,s, d) would be the expanding layer.

Deconvolution: This layer is responsible for upscaling and aggregating the previous features using deconvolution filters. Deconvolution may be seen as an inverse convolutionary process. As in a convolution operation stride, k outputs the 1/k number of times of the input and as the deconvolution is the inverse operation, stride k upscales the input by a factor of k. We can take advantage of this and set the phase k = n as the scaling factor, resulting in a reconstructed, upscaled HR image.By studying [2], authors of [5] have assumed that the filter size f5 should be 9 which is backed by experiments. So, the last layer can be represented as DeConv(9, 1, d) and stride of n which is set to the scaling required.
Activation:We've used the Rectified Linear Unit (ReLU) for the activation task after every convolution layer.Mathematically, It is set to R(z) = max(0, z). ReLU is the activation function most normally used in neural networks, especially in CNNs. The calculation is simple, as there are no complex calculations. Hence, the 3D FSRCNN model can take less time to train or test. This converges more rapidly. Linearity means that whenx gets big, the slope doesn't "saturate, " or plateau. It does not have the problem of the vanishing gradient than other activation functions such as sigmoid or tanh suffer. Figure 3 visualizes the ReLU activation function
Loss and Optimizer: We are following SRCNN[1] and using loss of MSE (mean square error) as cost function. The goal is to minimize the MSE between the reconstructed image Y^i and the ground truth image Yi.

Adam optimizer can be utilized to minimize the MSE loss.

$$MSE = \frac{1}{n}\sum_{0}^{n}\left(\hat{Y}i - Yi\right)^2 \tag{3}$$

Overall Architecture of the 3D FSRCNN: All the above parts are connected to form the FSRCNN as Conv(5, d, 1)-ReLU-Conv(1, s, d)-ReLU-m Conv(3, s, s)- ReLU-Conv(1, d, s)-ReLU-DeConv(9, 1, d). Authors[z] represented the FSRCNN model(d, s, m).
Complexity of 3D FSRCNN: The complexity of 3D FSRCNN model can be calculated as:-

$$O(125d^1 + sd + 27ms^2 + ds729d)S_{LR} = O(27ms^2 + 2sd + 854d)S_{LR} \tag{4}$$

If we compare the complexities of 3D SRCNN and our 3D FSRCNN, the complexity of 3D SRCNN is approximately n times the complexity of 3D FSRCNN, where n is the scaling factor in 3D FSRCNN.
Flow of the algorithm: We input the LR image into the network in the training phase, which is 1 / n the size of the ground-truth image, where n is the scaling-factor. We opt for n = 2 for our experiments. All layers process the image as explained in Figure 4, and generate an SR image as the output. The MSE loss is calculated for every SR image generated and after a batch size, backpropagation is carried out to update the weights of the network. During

 https://doi.org/10.1051/itmconf/20203203044

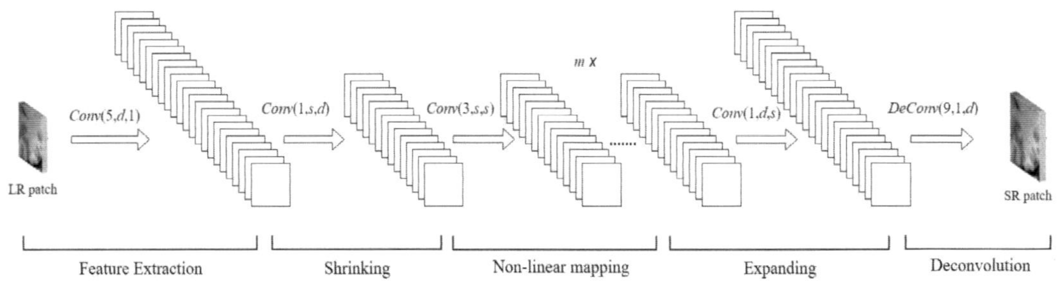

Figure 3. Proposed Architecture of 3D FSRCNN

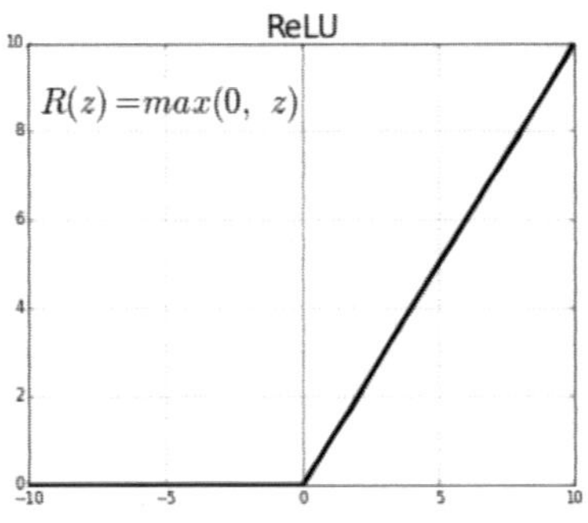

Figure 4. Visualization of ReLU Activation

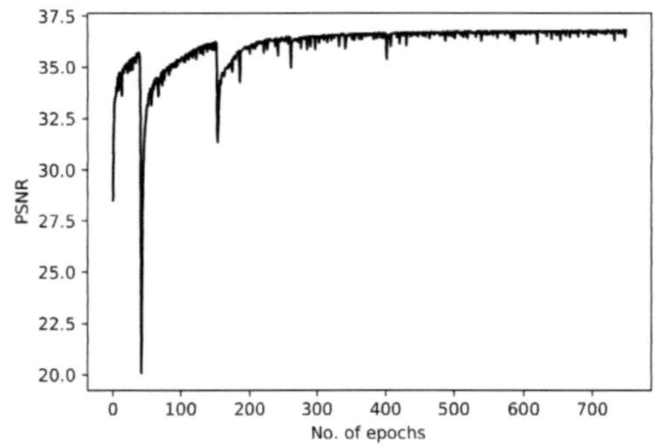

Figure 5. PSNR vs No. of epoch

the test process the test image is divided into 32 cubes and given to the 3D FSRCNN model as input. The SR images produced as output are then averaged and merged in a sliding window manner with the window shifted by half of the cube size.This dividing and merging of patches reduce the prediction time immensely. This was tested on LR images of size 128 X 160 X 160, the difference can be observed in table 1.

Table 1. Difference between prediction time

	Without Patching	With Patching
Maximum Prediction Time	229.46 s	6.86 s
Minimum Prediction Time	228.86 s	6.45 s
Average Prediction Time	228.9 s	6.73 s

2.4 Investigation of parameters

The 3D FSRCNN model, as explained above have different parameters – sensitive variables and hyperparameters. Both parameters needed experimentation and literature knowledge to decide their values. For the sensitive variable m, [6] concludes that m = 4 is the optimal value where the performance of the non-linear mapping layer is the best. Also, they have provided values d = 48, 56 and s = 12, 16 leaving us with 2 2 = 4 experiments with different combination. FSRCNN(48, 12, 4) is the smallest network but has the least performance out of all but still better than SRCNN. Table 2 gives the average loss, average PSNR for all the four combinations. We choose d = 56 and s = 12, even though the network becomes large with these values and affects the training and prediction time, the output image quality is high. Now, for hyperparameters – learning rate, momentum, epochs, batch size, we had to experiment and produce values for the same. For the learning rate, we found that lr = 0.001 was optimal in minimizing the loss at a constant rate. In many CNN implementations, momentum is set between 0.5 and 0.9, following it we set the momentum to 0.9. As seen in figure 5, after training for 750 epochs, the PSNR values seemed to become stable from the 500th epoch. Batch size had less effect on the performance, so considering the limitation of RAM, we trained our 3D FSRCNN model with batch size 32.

Table 2. Difference between prediction time

	FSRCNN(48,12,4)	FSRCNN(48,16,4)	FSRCNN(56,12,4)	FSRCNN(56,16,4)
Average Loss	23.39	19.68	19.53	**17.38**
Average PSPNR	34.93	35.61	35.71	**36.09**

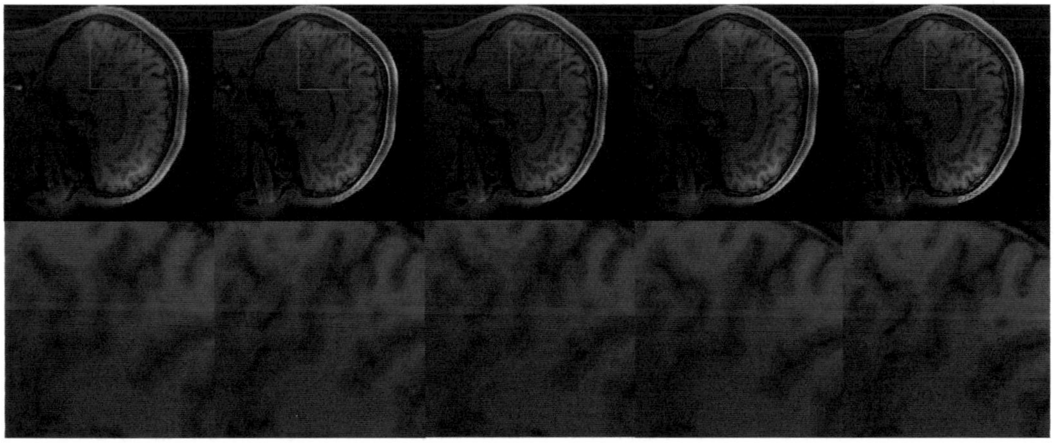

Figure 6. Illustration of 2D SRCNN, 3D SRCNN, 3D FSRCNN reconstructed results and corresponding LR and HR images.

Table 3. Comparison of SR Result

	2D SRCNN			3D SRCNN			3D FSRCNN		
	PSNR	SSIM	Time	PSNR	SSIM	Time	PSNR	SSIM	Time
Mean	33.41	0.922	3.84 s	35.75	0.942	9.82 s	37.53	0.967	6.73 s
Min	32.96	0.894	3.63 s	32.87	0.901	7.03 s	33.05	0.756	6.45 s
Max	36.76	0.939	4.06 s	39.88	0.967	12.83 s	48.40	0.975	6.86 s

3 Experiments

3.1 Dataset

To show a better generalization of the 3D FSRCNN model, a publicly available brain MRI dataset, the human connectome project[5], with 1, 113 subjects' T1 weighted anatomical images.. Those 3D images were generated using 32 channel head coil from Siemens 3 Tesla systems. The dimensions of the image are 256x320x320 with a spatial resolution of 0.7 mm isotropic. The images are in high resolution, thus, they were used as ground truth for our training.

3.2 Data Augmentation

The generation of LR MRI images is done by discarding every nth pixel from the image, where n is the scaling factor. For our purpose, the n = 2, so the LR image is downscaled by the factor of 2. HR image of dimension 256x320x320 is used to generate an LR image of dimension 128x160x160. The MRI images in the database are of size 256x320x320, processing an image with such a large size is computationally very expensive. So, we divided the MRI images into small cubes of 64x64x64. Similarly, LR images are divided into patches of 32x32x32. These patches are used for training the model instead of the whole image.

3.3 Training

We have implemented our 3D FSRCNN models using Keras with TensorFlow as backend and used some other libraries for image processing. All 3D FSRCNN models are trained on Google Colab.

4 Results and Analysis

We tested 2D SRCNN, 3D SRCNN, and 3D FSRCNN on the same data for analysis. The output of the analysis (shown in Figure 6) represent the impact on images applied by these different methods. To better understand the results, we defined it with three metrics – Peak Signal to Noise Ratio (PSNR), Structural Similarity (SSIM), and time required for reconstructing the output, two in the image domain and one in the time domain (shown in Table 3).The comparison of SR Result found that the output on 3D FSRCNN has the overall best performance impact and it outperforms the 2D SRCNN and 3D SRCNN methods.

5 Conclusion

In this research study, we represented a new deep neural network specifically designed for medical brain MRI images. We studied various super-resolution techniques, such as a 3D mDCSRN-GAN study for MRI, which claims to allow a 4-fold reduction in scanning time while maintaining the same image resolution and quality[8]. Another study re-designed the SRCNN model to explore a more effective network structure so as to increase running speed without impacting the quality[9].Based on the FSRCNN architecture, we created a 3D model which successfully reconstructs the low-resolution images with very high PSNR value. We believe that more efficiency can be gained by maintaining a proper balance between the deep network and high performance. One of the problems we came across is the increase in time complexity as the network becomes deep. A study on this topic is a potential future work. Still the results showed that our model outperforms many interpolations and deep leaning methods.

References

[1] S. Schulter, C. Leistner and H. Bischof, " Fast and accurate image upscaling with superresolution forests ", 2015 IEEE Conference on Computer Vision and Pattern Recognition (CVPR), Boston, MA, 2015, pp. 3791-3799. doi: 10.1109/CVPR.2015.7299003.

[2] C. Dong, C. C. Loy, K. He, and X. Tang, "Learning a deep convolutional network for image super-resolution ", in Computer Vision–ECCV 2014, pp. 184–199. Springer, 2014.

[3] C. Dong, C. C. Loy, K. He, and X. Tang, "Image superresolution using deep convolutional networks ", IEEE transactions on pattern analysis and machine intelligence, vol. 38, no. 2, pp. 295–307, 2016.

[4] W. Yang, X. Zhang, Y. Tian, W. Wang, J. Xue and Q. Liao, " Deep Learning for Single Image Super-Resolution: A Brief Review",in IEEE Transactions on Multimedia. doi:10.1109/TMM.2019.2919431.

[5] Dong, Chao, C.C. Loy, and Xiaoou Tang. "Accelerating the super-resolution convolutional neural network". European Conference on Computer Vision. 2016.

[6] David C. Van Essen, Stephen M. Smith, Deanna M. Barch, Timothy E.J. Behrens, Essa Yacoub, Kamil Ugurbil, for the WUMinn HCP Consortium. (2013). The WU-Minn Human Connectome Project: An overview. NeuroImage 80(2013):62-79.

[7] CT-image Super Resolution Using 3D Convolutional Neural Network by Yukai Wang, Qizhi Teng, Xiaohai He, Junxi Feng, Tingrong Zhang (Jun 2018).

[8] Yuhua Chen, Feng Shi, Anthony G. Christodoulou, Zhengwei Zhou, Yibin Xie, Debiao Li, "Efficient and Accurate MRI Super-Resolution using a Generative Adversarial Network and 3D Multi-Level Densely Connected Network",(Jun 2018).

[9] Chao Dong, Chen Change Loy, Xiaoou Tang, "Accelerating the Super-Resolution Convolutional Neural Network",(Aug 2016).

https://doi.org/10.1051/itmconf/20203203045

DROWSINESS DETECTION AND MONITORING SYSTEM

Uzair Ghole
Dept. of electronics and telecommunication
Ramrao Adik Institute of Technology, Nerul, Navi Mumbai, India.
Email id: uzairghole@outlook.com

Pravin Chavan
Dept. Of Electronics and Telecommunication
Ramrao Adik Institute of Technology, Nerul, Navi Mumbai, India.
Email id: pravinschavan6781@gmail.com

Siddharth Gandhi
Dept. Of Electronics and Telecommunication
Ramrao Adik Institute of Technology, Nerul, Navi Mumbai, India.
Email id: siddharthgandhi88@gmail.com

Rohit Gawde
Dept. Of Electronics and Telecommunication
Ramrao Adik Institute of Technology, Nerul, Navi Mumbai, India.
Email id: rohitgawde266666@gmail.com

Kausar Fakir
Dept. of electronics and telecommunication
Ramrao Adik Institute of Technology, Nerul, Navi Mumbai, India.
Email id: kausarmf@gmail.com

Abstract- **Wakefulness of a driver is an extremely important factor that needs to be continuously monitored.. A drowsy driver can be a cause of several mishaps and accidents on highways which could lead to loss of money, physical injuries, and the most important, loss of human life. Drowsiness detection system is a car safety technology that helps to prevent and thus reduce accidents caused by the driver getting drowsy. The system is designed for four-wheeler vehicles (or more) wherein the driver's fatigue or drowsiness is detected and alerts are generated. The proposed method will use a USB camera that captures the driver's face and eyes and processes the images to detect the driver's fatigue. On the detection of drowsiness, the programmed system cautions the driver through an alarm to ensure vigilance. The proposed method consists of various stages to determine the wakefulness of the driver.**

Keywords- Internet of Things, Cloud Computing, Image Processing, Machine Learning, Computer Vision

I. INTRODUCTION

- Drowsiness can be defined as a state or feeling of being lethargic; sleepiness.
- Losing attention while driving has proven to be a major cause of accidents. These mishaps can be prevented by the implementation of such a system.
- This system can provide monitoring of the state of wakefulness of the driver and also generate alerts when necessary.
- The most accurate way of detecting these factors is by using EEG signals. But, in our proposed system we will be making use of image processing techniques since such a system would be easier and more convenient to install.
- Image processing here involves multiple steps, starting from detection of a face, detection of eye position and its status. Corresponding information relevant to the main problem will be generated and further analytics will be performed to create meaningful data out of it.

II. PROBLEM DEFINITION

- Since we have successfully established the fact that drowsiness has been a major cause of road accidents, we have also need a solution to it.
- The primary aim of this system is to monitor the status of the driver and creating corresponding alerts in case of any anomaly.

III. PROTOTYPE SETUP

Hardware Components:

- Raspberry Pi 3
- USB Web Camera
- Alarm source
- Wire cables
- Power source

https://doi.org/10.1051/itmconf/20203203045

Software Components:

- Raspbian OS (and supporting bootloader)
- Computer Vision using OpenCV
- Cloud Platform

IV. APPLIED METHODOLOGY

Among all the methods under research right now, detection directly using brain waves has proven to yield the most accurate results. This system suggests a different method inspired by multiple existing methodologies. It involves measuring physical changes like body posture, the inclination of the driver's head, and wakefulness of the eye. Brain wave detection would require the driver to wear a headset for monitoring purposes every time he/she is driving. The proposed system is much more feasible and practical for implementation, without adding any prominent cost to the existing car price.

The system being non-intrusive causes no discomfort to the driver and does not affect his/her state while driving. Though external factors like light exposure could cause problems in detection but with advancing image processing techniques, and ever-improving lens qualities, this problem can surely be solved. Status of the eye will continuously be monitored and a corresponding Eyes Aspect Ratio (EAR) will be calculated. This value will be compared to a pre-defined value and alerts will be generated depending upon these comparisons.

Since micro napping could be a loophole in this system, the system will also carry a threshold value i.e. a timer will be maintained to clock the time for which the eyes remain in an undesired state.

Figure 1: Proposed Methodology

One of the applications of Computer Vision is being made use of here. We can perform a variety of facial applications, including facial recognition and even aiding in law enforcement to help detect, recognize, and track criminals. **OpenCV** provides a variety of methods to detect faces in images. All these methods are different from each other in terms of accuracy and speed. We need to identify the best suitable method for our application. Our purpose here is to detect the driver's drowsiness state, which can easily be termed as a real-time application.

Haar Cascades:

Object detection using Haar Cascade classifiers was initially proposed by Paul Viola and Michael Jones. The method makes use of machine learning technique where a cascade function is trained as a model with inputs as multiple positive and negative images. Once the model is trained, it is used to detect objects in an image. Here, the desired object is a human face.
We need our system to be quick in detecting and obtaining the desired characteristics from a given input and to assist with this **Haar Cascades** are the preferred choice.

Facial Landmarks:

Followed by the detection of faces in an image, a more complex problem is encountered, that is the detection of facial features. These features consist of the eyes, nose, mouth, and the jawline. Locating these features with respect to the each other is an important pre requisite for further calculations. We have solved this problem by plotting all the features on the face as "facial landmarks". This can be understood as a simple coordinate system wherein all the prominent features are highlighted using boundaries. The boundaries are basically a set of coordinates which can help determine the position of these features on a face. Following is an image explaining how the plotting is exactly done.

Figure 2: 68 point Facial Landmarks

V. WORKING

- Based on Raspberry Pi, the system will consist of a camera that will capture the live feed of the driver's face.
- Predefined values corresponding to the position of the eyes and other factors will be continuously compared with the upcoming values.
- The system will detect any kind of anomaly and generate an alert.
- One of the alerts would be an alarm inside the car that will generate a noise until the driver is in a healthy situation and can continue driving.
- The second alert would be in terms of a message/call to emergency contacts.
- Data that is being derived from this will be sent to a cloud platform where it will be stored, analyzed and relevant information will be generated.

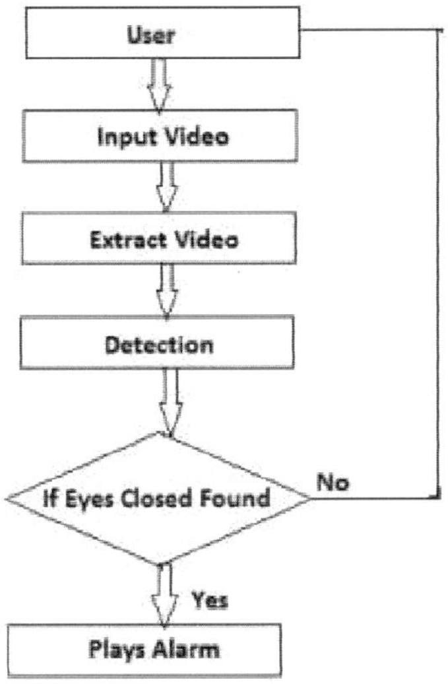

Figure 3: Flow of Operation

- The above flowchart has an entity "If eyes closed found"; briefly indicates the basic operation. This action will carry various conditions and constraints to make the system smart and foolproof.

VI. OBTAINED RESULTS

The face is detected on exposure to the web camera attached to the system. Once the face has successfully been detected, the image processing part is initiated. Various characteristics are obtained one of which is EAR: Eyes Aspect Ratio and it plays the most crucial role in determining the result with the highest possible accuracy. Following are few of the obtained results;

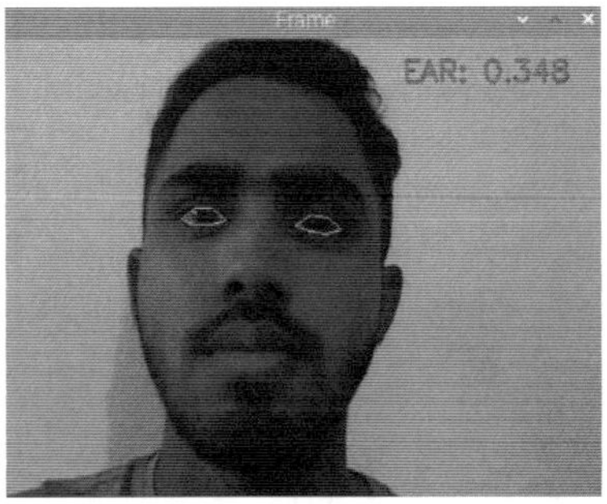

Figure 4: EAR=0.348

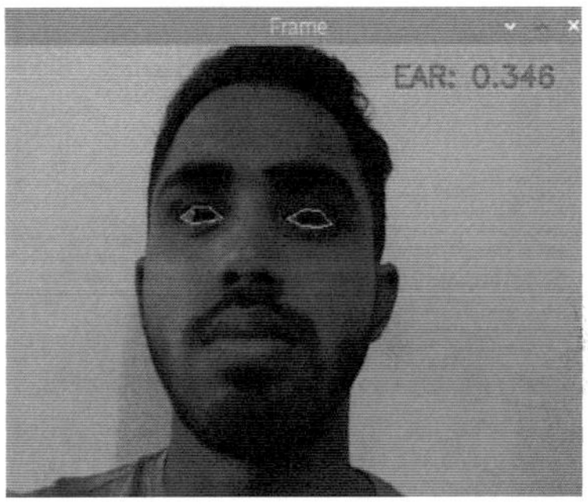

Figure 5: EAR=0.346

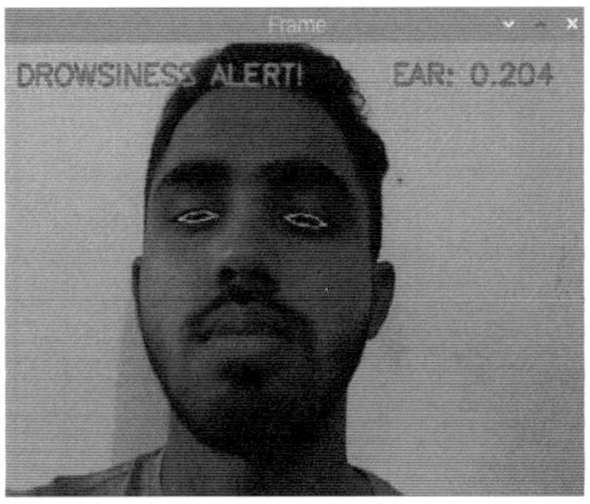

Figure 6: EAR=0.204

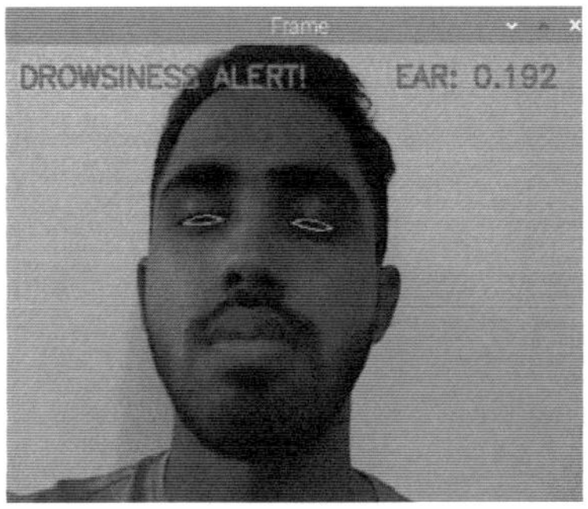

Figure 7: EAR=0.192

VII. STATISTICAL ANALYSIS

The initial model that was trained with inputs as multiple faces in different states was used to calculate an average value of the **Eye Aspect Ratio (EAR).** We obtained an average value of **"0.3"**, below which the driver's state can be determined as drowsy. Another important and probably the most critical value is then defined after calculating this average, i.e. the **number of consecutive frames** that should be considered for calculation. This value carries significance in correspondence to the real time application of the system.

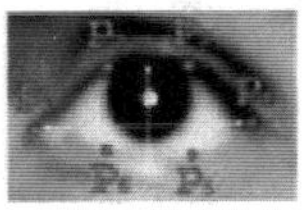

$$\text{EAR} = \frac{\|p_2 - p_6\| + \|p_3 - p_5\|}{2\|p_1 - p_4\|}$$

Figure 8: EAR Calculation

EAR	No. of Frames	State
0.348	2	Wake
0.291	3	Wake
0.218	8	Drowsy
0.210	10	Drowsy
0.310	2	Wake

The above table shows values obtained during testing of the system where the threshold value for the number of frames was "8", meaning that if EAR is less than 0.3 for 8 consecutive frames, only then will the state be determined as drowsy. If EAR goes below 0.3 for less than 8 frames, drowsiness alert will not be generated.

Following is the result of a study performed using the system over a time span of 1 month. This graph helps us understand the importance of data that can be generated using this system.

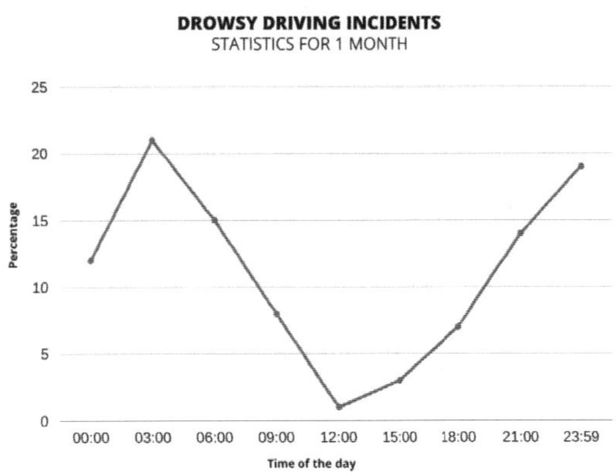

Figure 9: Percentage Distribution

VIII. CONCLUSION

Using the EAR and other characteristics the drowsiness state of the driver is detected and necessary actions are initiated. Primary action will be going off of the alarm that will cause the driver to wake up and return to a state of acceptable wakefulness. This system, if implemented properly, can help save multiple lives that are lost due to mishaps on roads. We are working towards making better and more efficient use of all the technologies being used in this project and are positive of coming up with something even more innovative.

In order to make this a complete IoT application, the data storage, corresponding analytics, and notification generation will completely be done on a cloud platform (AWS Greengrass).

IX. REFERENCES

[1] Neha Borulkar, Pravin Pandey, Chintan Davda, and Joyce Chettiar, "Drowsiness Detection and Monitoring the Sleeping Pattern using Brainwaves Technology and IoT", 2018 2nd International Conference on I-SMAC

[2] Anupama Kaushik "IOT-An Overview", International Journal of Advanced Research in Computer and Communication Engineering, Vol. 5, Issue 3, March 2016.

[3] A. Hossan, F.B.Kashem, M.M.Hasan, S.Naher and M.I.Rahman,"A smart system for driver's fatigue detection, remote notification and semi-automatic parking of vehicles to prevent road accidents," 2016 International Conference on Medical Engineering, Health Informatics and Technology.

[4] Chandraprakash Sahoo "Drowsiness Detection System", National Institute of Technology, Rourkela.

[5] Adrian Rosebrock "Drowsiness Detection using OpenCV".

[6] Paul Viola, Michael J. Jones. Rapid Object Detection using a Boosted Cascade of Simple Features. Conference on Computer Vision and Pattern Recognition (CVPR), 2001, pp. 511-518.

[7] Tereza Soukupova and Jan Cech, 21st Computer Vision Winter Workshop Luka Cehovin, Rok Mandeljc, Vitomir ˇ Struc (eds.) ˇ Rimske Toplice, Slovenia, February 3–5, 2016

[8] Road Accidents in India – 2018, Government of India, Ministry of Road Transport & Highways, Transport Research Wing.

Prediction of Fire Propagation in Forest Areas using Genetic Algorithm

Dhumal Rashmi Amol[1]

Department of Computer Engineering, Ramrao Adik Institute of Technology, Nerul, Navi Mumbai, India. 400706

Abstract. Forest fire causes significant damages to environment and living organisms. It becomes troublesome to recover from the consequences of forest fire. The early and accurate prediction of forest fire propagation in forest area will help in fire management efforts. The models required for prediction of forest fire spread requires many parameters and which are not known precisely during the emergency. So there is a need of intelligent system to model and predict the propagation of forest fire to reduce the consequences of forest fire and minimize the management efforts. In this work, we have discussed different techniques available in literature for forest fire prediction. This paper also describes the implementation and analysis of prediction of forest fire propagation using Genetic Algorithm and Geometric Semantic Genetic Programming.

Keywords: Forest Fire Danger Index, Genetic Algorithm, Geometric Semantic Genetic Programming

1 Introduction

According to United Nations Environment Program, Forest covered 30% of earths land area in 2014. Forest land is covered with trees and a place to live and survive for animals. Forests are an ecosystem for various animals and plants. Forest fire is most common and severe hazard in forests especially occur during summer. It causes a significant damage to forest wealth and also disturbing the ecology and bio-diversity of affected region. The main two causes of forest fire are natural causes and man-made causes. Man-made fires are occurred due to negligence behaviour of human being during the use of cigarette or bidi, naked flame or electric equipment's etc. Whereas natural causes like lightening put trees on fire. These kinds of fires occur in rainy season and are under control due to rain. During summer, forests become dry and lead to forest fire ignited by slight spark. Even changes in climate also influence frequency and intensity of forest fire. The increase in atmospheric temperatures and dryness creates favourable circumstances for ignition of fire. The three basic elements required for a fire to start and continue to burn are: Fuel to burn (wood, brush, lichen or any combustible material in forest), oxygen (from the air) and an ignition source (natural or man-made). The fire can't be ignited in the absence of any one of these elements.

There is a noticeable increase in forest fire across India. According to Forest Survey of India, there is huge increase in forest fire from November 2018 to February 2019.

In India most of the forest fires occur due to human activity. In the Bandipur National Park of Karnataka state of India, broke out with massive forest fire in the month of February 2019 and last for 5 days. This mainly influences the life of small animals, reptiles and birds as they are burnt and various plant species also destroyed.

The change in climate causes rise in Earth's temperature results in increase in forest fire in the regions that have no such history in past. During recent years, the fires happened in Australia in September 2019 and in California in 2018 have brought attention to wildfires across the world. These two fires destroyed millions of hectares of forests and which results in loss of habitats and food sources. This is majorly influence on the bio-diversity and ecology of affected area and need to focus on forest fire management.

The various factors influence the wild fire are listed in Table 1.

Table 1. Parameters affecting the forest fire

Parameters	Description
Wind	Change the direction of fire
Slope	Moves faster in uphill direction than downhill
Temperature	High temperature capture moisture from fuel
Humidity	Amount of water vapour in air

* rashmi.dhumal@gmail.com

Times and Seasons	Summer provides higher oxygen than winter
Fuels	Dry leaves and grass, resins, vegetation with high oil
Space between Fuels	Distance between fuels

2 Related Work

In [1], the author suggested data mining technique to predict the forest burned area. The data set used for fire spread prediction is consists of four meteorological factors such as rain, temperature, wind and humidity, which are collected through local sensors. The data mining techniques, Support Vector Machine (SVM) and given climatological factors were tested on real world data collected through local sensors. The work done in this paper was able to predict the burned areas of frequent small fires which occur in northeast region of Portugal. This was a first attempt made towards prediction of forest fire based on meteorological data. The cost of data collection is low and is real time as compared to satellite or scanner approaches. But this approach is failed in prediction of large fires. Even the data is collected on real time basis the data mining technique is applied in offline ie. after collection of data.

Perminov et al. [2] discussed the theoretical investigation was carried out for the fire spread in windy condition for crown forest. The crown forest properties like moisture content of forest fuel, bulk density, etc. are mainly contribute to estimate the spread area of forest fire. This model gives an idea about the temperature change, component concentration with respect to time and effect of other conditions on the initiation of forest fire.

In [3], the forest fire spread area was estimated using Multilayer Perceptron, Support Vector Machine, Fuzzy Logic and Radial Basis Function Networks using historical data. The total nine factors are considered which includes geographic condition, meteorological data and date and time of forest fire. The different models are implemented and evaluated their performance. The best model out of tem is Multilayer Perceptron with 65% accuracy with humidity and wind speed as an input and outputs the size of fire as small, medium and large.

Agarwal et. al. [4] discussed about the fuzzy logic based decision making technique for fuel model based forest fire. This system is similar to fire-behavioural study tool used for historical data, but can be used for real-time environmental and spatial data for fire spread prediction. Based on study of fire-behavioural model and mathematical equations the required dataset can be easily available from national databases. These databases help in appropriate selection of fuel model for a particular area. The tables associated with each image gives the essential characteristics of fuel and are used in fuzzy system for prediction of forest fire spread. This system can also be used for real-time fire spread prediction as data is available online and can be easily accessed through MATLAB commands. This system predicts the fire spread in the span of next 10 hours. This enables fire-personnel to easily handle the situation and take preventive measures. This is a first step towards real-time fire spread prediction.

In [5], author addressed the problem with propagation models based on input parameters which are difficult to identify or estimate in advance. Hence to reduce the uncertainty in the values of input parameters and to improve the prediction accuracy, a genetic algorithm based calibration technique is proposed here. The several iterations are performed to calibrate the values which increase the execution time. The multicore capabilities are applied to reduce the execution time. Three different strategies are implemented to limit the generations. The proposed work in this paper mainly focuses on time aware feature and dynamic population size. The parallel GA allows to coexist the execution of individuals from different generations improves the prediction accuracy.

In [6,9], the author discuss about the forest fire spread prediction based on intelligent system. The geometric semantic genetic programming used for fire spread prediction using meteorological data. The prediction of amount of fire spread area during forest fire is based on the relationship between climatological data, forest related data and burned area. The results obtained shows that the geometric semantic genetic algorithm is better than standard genetic algorithm.

Table 2. Parameters affecting the forest fire

	Technology Used	**Data Set Used**	**Number of Parameters**	**Predicted Spread Area**
[1]	Support Vector Machine	Real-world data collected through sensors	>12	Small
[2]	Multilayer Perceptron (MLP), Radial Basis Function Networks (RBFN), Support Vector Machines (SVM) and fuzzy logic	Historical Data	9	Small and medium
[3]	Fuzzy Logic	Topographical Data	40	Small, medium and big
[4]	Genetic Algorithm	Meteorological data	--	Small, medium and big
[5]	Geometric semantic Genetic Algorithm	Historical Data	>12	Small, medium and big

3 Description of Proposed Method

3.1. Genetic Algorithm

Genetic Programming [7,8] is a evolution technique where computer programs are represented as a set of genes that are then modified using an evolutionary algorithm known as Genetic algorithm. Genetic programming is an optimization technique which helps to produce results significantly better than traditional methods. The iterative behaviour of genetic algorithm generates better quality of results based on number of iterations and the settings of genetic algorithm.

These are evolutionary algorithms which find approximate solutions to optimization and search problems. The algorithm starts with randomly selected solutions, and then repeatedly evolves new population from it by applying various operations like crossover and mutation.

The individuals in genetic algorithm are represented by chromosomes/individuals, which is a collection of parameters within a specified range of parameters. The encoding techniques are used to represent a chromosome. There are two types of encoding techniques: value encoding and binary encoding. The initial population of individuals is generated randomly. The size of initial population is N. This size remains same for every next generation. The fitness value of each chromosome is calculated using fitness function.

3.2. Geometric Semantic Genetic Programming (GSGP)

In the genetic programming, genetic operators are applied on randomly selected individuals to evolve new child individuals. Hence these operators operate on structure or syntax of the individuals and ignore its semantic information. The syntax based genetic algorithm generates solution which is completely ignores the knowledge associated with input data which leads to incorrect design of model for particular domain where semantic of data plays an important role. The geometric semantic genetic algorithm [10] focuses on the semantic information of individuals while performing genetic operations on them.

In GSGP, the initial population is randomly generated by selecting individuals from the existing database similar to genetic algorithm. The two parent individuals P1 and P2 are randomly selected from the current generations along with random function R, whose value ranges in [0,1]. The Geometric semantic crossover generates new individual by evaluating eq.(1)

$$P_{new} = (P_1 * R) + (1-R)*P_2 \quad (1)$$

The Geometric semantic mutation operator generates new individual by selecting one random parent from current population along with random functions R1 and R2 whose value ranges in [0,1] with mutation rate 0.06

$$P_{new} = P_1 + m(R1-R2) \quad (2)$$

The implementation of Genetic algorithm is compared with geometric semantic genetic algorithm to get the best values of input parameters in the prediction of forest fire spread.

3.3. Architecture of Proposed Genetic Algorithm

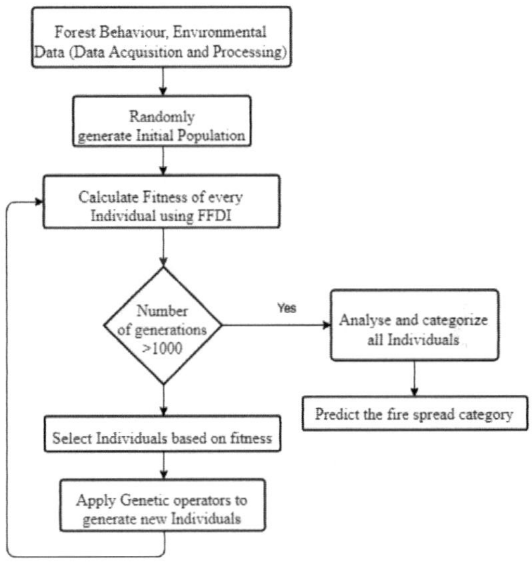

Fig. 1. Working of Genetic Algorithm.

The working of proposed system is shown in figure 1. The environmental data collected and used to randomly generate individuals of initial population. The fitness of each individual is calculated and the fittest individual is propagated to the next generation using elitism. Randomly select two individuals of current generation and apply crossover and mutation operation on them to generate new child chromosomes for next generations. The above procedure is repeated till the stopping criteria have been not reached. The stopping criterion is either the number of generations or the threshold for fitness parameter.
The proposed system, consider following parameters for forest fire spread prediction:

1. Drought factor:

Drought factor measures the availability of fuel or dryness in upper layers of soil. The value of drought factor ranges from 0 to 10. The potential of fire is low for low values of drought factor and increases the potential of fire with increased values of it. If value of drought factor is 10 indicates that there is no moisture and fuel is dry enough to initiation of fire is very high.

2. Temperature:

A temperature is a measure of heat in air mass and measured in Celsius. The increase in temperature also

https://doi.org/10.1051/itmconf/20203203046

increases the temperature of vegetation and fuel, which results in initiation of fire. The temperature also impact on the speed of wind and atmospheric stability.

3. Relative Humidity:

The amount of water vapour in air is a measure of relative humidity. It is measured in terms of percentage. The presence of the moisture in the atmosphere will affect the amount of moisture in the grass and forest fuel. The possibility forest fire spread is low when humidity is high and it increases with decrease in moisture in atmosphere.

4. Wind:

The rate of movement of air is measured as wind speed. It is measured in terms of movement of wind in distance per unit of time. It is mainly influenced by obstacles like buildings, trees etc.

In the initial population individuals/chromosomes are defined using values of above four parameters, for example [5, 26.4, 21, 4.5]. The dataset used in this study is collected from UCI, machine learning repository. The size of each population considered here is 200. The individuals from initial population are randomly selected to generate new individuals for next generation using tournament selection and modified to find best out of them to form new individuals. In every generation the fitness function to calculate Forest Fire Danger Index (FFDI) is applied to every individual and the fittest individual with maximum FFDI value, is carried forward to next generation. The stopping criterion used here is the number of generations. The system halts after 1000 generations as there are no major changes found in the initial parameters and corresponding FFDI values.

The McArthur Forest Fire Danger Indices (FFDI) [6] is used to measure the fire danger level.

$$FFDI = 2EXP\text{-}^{(-0.45 + 0.978\ ln(DF)\ -0.0345\ RH\ +\ 0.0338\ T\ +0.0234\ W)} \quad (3)$$

The value of FFDI is measured using weather variable factors such as temperature (T), relative humidity (RH), wind speed (W) and drought factor (DF). The accuracy of FFDI value depends on the accuracy of the input variables. Inaccuracy and uncertainty of these inputs may result in incorrect of the FFDI value.

4 Results and Discussion

The genetic algorithm and geometric semantic genetic algorithm are implemented on four parameters: drought factor, temperature, relative humidity and wind. In genetic algorithm, the FFDI values for fittest individual maxed out at 27 for given dataset whereas in GSGP it is maxed to 16. The population produced after given iterations was then divided into three sets according to McArthur FFDI ranges:

Low : FFDI <= 10

Medium : 10 < FFDI <= 20

High : 20 < FFDI

However the system takes a step ahead and calculates the optimal range of values for all the parameters and for all the three categories based on the above FFDI ranges defined by McArthur's formulations.

The values for input parameters in genetic algorithm are changes drastically as it randomly exchanges the values of parameters of parents based on their syntax. In geometric semantic genetic programming, the parameter values are varying smoothly to preserve the semantics of the individuals. The FFDI values calculated in GSGP are below 20 and are able to detect low to medium fire spread area affected due to forest fire.

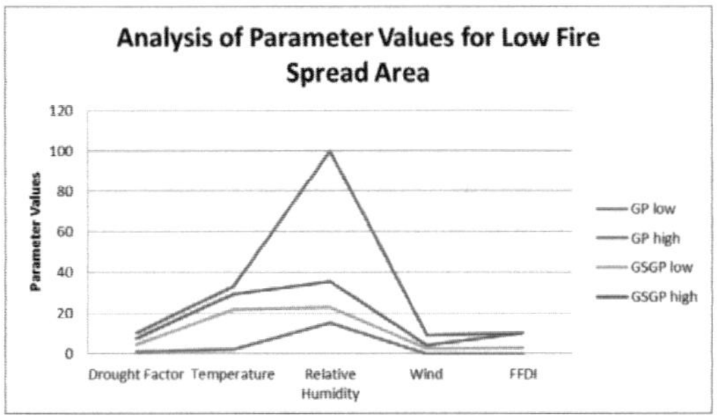

Fig. 2. Analysis of Parameter Values for Low Fire Spread Area

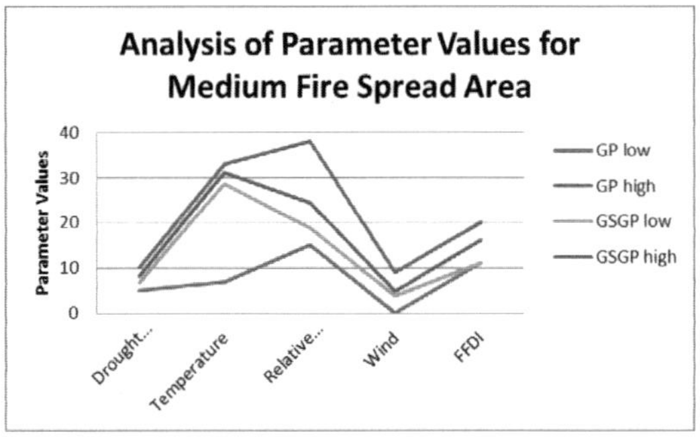

Fig. 3. Analysis of Parameter Values for Medium Fire Spread Area

Conclusion

The main aim of the proposed system is to predict fire spread area during forest fire. A genetic algorithm and geometric semantic genetic algorithm based fire spread prediction system is implemented and the result obtained shows the ranges of values for input parameters that contribute towards the initiation of fire. The system can now generate an optimal population and produce a set of ranges for each parameter considered. On the basis of the ranges, the system can predict the spread category of affected area with high accuracy. The generation of optimal population was made possible due to implementation of Geometric Semantic Genetic Algorithm. The fire spread thus, based on a reliable dataset, can be predicted accurately and quickly to enable proper fire fighting techniques. The proposed system can be implemented on real time data set captured through the sensors for more accuracy and can be compared with other predictions techniques by incorporating other factors influencing the fire spread.

References

1. P. Cortez and A. Morais. A Data Mining Approach to Predict Forest Fires using Meteorological Data. In Proceedings of the 13th EPIA 2007 - Portuguese Conference on Artificial Intelligence, December, (2007), pp512-523
2. Perminov, Valeriy, Mathematical Modeling of Crown Forest Fire Spread. Open Journal of Forestry. 2. 17-22. 10.4236/ojf.2012.21003, (2012).
3. Ozbayoglu, Murat & Bozer, Recep. Estimation of the Burned Area in Forest Fires Using Computational Intelligence Techniques. Procedia Computer Science. **12.** (2012). 282–287. 10.1016/j.procs.2012.09.070.
4. Agarwal, Jutshi & Cohen, Kelly & Kumar, Manish. (2013). Fuzzy Logic Based Real-Time Prediction Model for Wild-Land Forest Fires. AIAA Infotech at Aerospace (I at A) Conference. 10.2514/6.2013-5060.
5. Artes, Tomas & Cencerrado, Andrés & Cortés, Ana & Margalef, Tomàs. Time aware genetic algorithm for forest fire propagation prediction: exploiting multi-core platforms: Time aware genetic algorithm for forest fire propagation prediction: exploiting multi-core platforms. Concurrency and Computation: Practice and Experience. 29. 10.1002/cpe.3837. (2016).
6. Castelli, M. L. Vanneschi, And A. Popovic. 2015. Predicting Burned Areas of Forest Fires: An Artificial Intelligence Approach. Fire Ecology 11(1):106-118.
7. Koza, J.R. Genetic Programming: on the programming of computers by means of natural selection. MIT Press, Cambridge, Massachusetts, USA. (1992)
8. Koza, J.R. Human-competitive results produced by genetic programming. Genetic Programming and Evolvable Machines 11(3-4): 251-284. doi: 10.1007/s10710-010-9112-3, (2010)
9. Castelli, M., S. Silva, and L. Vanneschi. 2014. A C++ framework for geometric semantic genetic programming. Genetic Programming and Evolvable Machines 15: 19.Castro, J., T. Figueiredo, F. Fonseca, J.P. Castro, S. Nobre, and L. Pires. (2010)
10. Vanneschi, Leonardo & Castelli, Mauro & Manzoni, Luca & Silva, Sara. A New Implementation of Geometric Semantic GP and Its Application to Problems in Pharmacokinetics. 205-216. 10.1007/978-3-642-37207-0_18. (2013).

Original vs Counterfeit Indian Currency Detection

Anushka Kulkarni[1,*], *Prachi* Kedar[2,**], *Aishwarya* Pupala[3,***], and *Priyanka* Shingane[4,****]

[1]Ramrao Adik Institute of Technology,Navi Mumbai,India.
[2]Ramrao Adik Institute of Technology,Navi Mumbai,India.
[3]Ramrao Adik Institute of Technology,Navi Mumbai,India.
[4]Ramrao Adik Institute of Technology,Navi Mumbai,India.

Abstract. Currency is used to carry out not only business but also for various other transactions to get access to various services and commodities. There are a total of 7 denominations for the Indian currency each with unique features to distinguish them from each other and with various and distinct security features to prevent them from fraudulent copying. However,with the evolution of technology, there is also an increase in the ways in which fake forms of these currencies are created. These fake or counterfeit notes have various ill-effect on society. The proposed system will be used to check the genuine Indian currency notes and to find the denomination of the currency note. Comparative study for various image processing algorithms was conducted to identify and select the one which will be able to extract more prominent features,and is also better in terms of processing time,outlier rejection, efficiency in computation and in feature matching. After which a real time system is created for currency detection in real time.

1 Introduction

The evolution of technology, has lead to an increase in the ways in which fake forms of currencies are created and thus the counterfeit currency notes in the Indian market have increased. These fake or counterfeit notes have various ill-effect on society. They harm the lay man as there is no definitive way to be absolutely sure if the currency is original or fake.

This report focuses on the comparison and analysis of different image processing algorithms to find the most efficient algorithm to identify and classify real and counterfeit currency notes and to find the denomination of the currency [2].

The comparative study for various image processing algorithms was conducted to identify and select the one which will be able to extract more prominent features,and is also better in terms of processing time, outlier rejection, efficiency in computation and in feature matching.

With the rapid advancement of technology, there is also an increase in the production of counterfeit currencies, which is also making it difficult to distinguish between the real and the fake ones [1]. The proposed system will be able to recognize the currencies and classify them as real or fake.

In this approach, we will classify the fake notes using an image processing algorithm.

First, a comparative study of different image processing algorithms is performed, and then these algorithms will be implemented in the Matlab software. Based on the studies and comparison, the best algorithm for feature extraction and feature matching will be selected that extracts the maximum number of feature points, and will also perform well under different lighting conditions, and with different scaling and rotations [10].

Currently the major methods used for the classification of currency notes be it Indian or any other are either neural networks or image processing algorithms or a mixture of both [1].

Different papers have taken various different approaches to do this task and each of these existing system give us a perspective into the challenges of detecting currency as real or fake.

The many image processing algorithms that have been used each have their merits and demerits but most are found lacking in terms of it being transformed into a real time application. Most papers don't take into account the computational costs or the different processing times of these algorithms

2 Review of literature

Currently the major methods used for the classification of currency notes be it Indian or any other are either neural networks or image processing or a mixture of both [1].

Different papers have taken various different approaches to do this task and each of these existing system give us a perspective into the challenges of detecting currency as real or fake.

The many image processing algorithms that have been

*e-mail: anushkakulkarni997@gmail.com
**e-mail: prachikedar27@gmail.com
***e-mail: ashpupala12@gmail.com
****e-mail: priyanka.shingane@rait.ac.in

used each have their merits and demerits and in our paper we have analysed each of these in more detail so that we may achieve an optimal process for a real time application to do the task of identification and detection.
The following papers were referred to get background on the system requirements.
The Paper Indian Banknote Recognition using Convolutional Neural Network Shubham Mittal ,Shiva Mittal took a Deep learning based approach for the purpose of identification of denominations of Indian currency [1].
And while that method worked efficiently in real time it is to be considered that the Convolution neural networks used are computationally expensive. Neural Networks require huge amount of training data to train deep learning model from scratch.
The paper Neural Network Approach for Indian Currency Recognition by Jayant kumar Nayak, Chaitan Majhi, Apurva Kumar Srivastav, Ajaya Kumar Das - 2015 uses Neural networks to recognize and then count currency notes of different denominations in a bundle for a ROI(Region of interest) [4].
This paper had a drawback that Counterfeit currency detection was not incorporated.
Identification of Fake Notes and Denomination Recognition a paper by Archana M , Kalpitha C, Prajwal S, Pratiksha N. explained how notes could be classified based on color,dimension and identification marks(mentioned by RBI)using computer vision [6]. However it had certain demerits like Lots of pre-processing steps involved and No portable application for smartphones. Hence each of these papers offer us an insight on the varying approaches and challenges.
In our paper we have analysed each of these in more detail so that we may achieve an optimal process for a real time application to do the task of identification and detection.
In this paper the focus is on the comparison of the different image processing algorithms, their features and capabilities to analyse and judge which of them would be the most efficient in terms of working in a real time environment.
While judging the efficiency of algorithms we take into account their accuracy, computational cost, feature matching speed, scale invarience and total image matching time.It also analyses the feasibility of the deployment of the image processing algorithm in a real time environment.
This report focuses on finding the most optimal process for the task of identification of real and counterfeit currency.

3 Planning and formulation

The many image processing algorithms that have been used each have their merits and demerits but most are found lacking in terms of it being transformed into a real time application.
Most papers don't take into account the computational costs or the different processing times of these algorithms. So we have analysed each of these in more detail so that we may achieve an optimal process for a real time application to do the task of identification and detection

3.1 Understanding different algorithms

The major algorithms analysed in our paper are SIFT,SURF,ORB,FAST,BRISK and KAZE.
It is important to understand the basics of the above mentioned algorithms. We need to analyse these algorithms on the basis of their capabilities in terms of performance, timing, accuracy, computational cost, scale invarience, outlier rejection and feature matching time.
Listed below are the algorithms studied in this paper.

- SIFT - SIFT stands for Scale Invarient Feature Transform and it is one of the most foremost image processing algorithms introduced in the year 1999 [8]. It was developed by David Lowe.
  In the SIFT algorithm various points are detected and matched using the Eucledian distance In SIFT method an image is transformed into a number of feature points. All these points are unvarying to image rotation and scale.
  Also Key point locations are appropriated as maxima and minima.

- SURF - Speeded up Robust Features or the SURF in an algorithm present in computer vision that has numerous applications such as recognition, tracking, reconstruction, identification and extraction of feature points.
  It was developed by Tinne Tuytelaars, Luc Van Gool and Herbert Bay [8].
  It uses a pyramid structure technique to change the image or video capture into a coordinates.
  It is known for its speed and is quite fast when compared to its alternatives.

- ORB - Oriented FAST and rotated BRIEF (ORB) was introduced in 2011 by Ethan Rublee [9].
  It is an effective algorithm for the process of image processing and also object detection [7].
  As the name suggests it is a fusion of the two other algorithms mentioned here. These are the FAST algorithm and the BRIEF algorithm.

- FAST - Published in the year 2006 by Edward Rosten and Tom Drummond FAST is the Features from Accelerated segment test.
  The FAST image processing algorithm stands out for its speed which tends to be better than most of its comparative options. It lacks in accuracy.

- BRISK- BRISK which is the Binary Robust Invariant Scalable Keypoints is an algorithm that stands average in terms of accuracy and timing.
  However what it covers up with other points such as scale invarience and better performance with rotated

images.

- KAZE - KAZE as an feature detection image processing algorithm introduces the possibility of reduction in noise.
  The KAZE also seems to have better accuracy for rotated images.
  While the kaze feature detector works well with rotated images it has certain deficiencies.
  One such drawback is that it tends to have very high computational cost.

Further each of them are compared according to their different features and capabilities. A table listing these findings is given below:

Table 1. Analysis of Algorithms

Analysis of the different algorithms					
Features	SIFT	SURF	BRISK	KAZE	ORB
ACCURACY	Most accurate	average	Not good for rotated image	Better accuracy for rotated image	Second to sift
FEATURE MATCHING TIME	average	less than sift	Can be reduced	longer than sift	least
OUTLIER REJECTION TIME	Approx. same	Approx. same	Approx. same	Approx. same	Approx. same
TOTAL IMAGE MATCHING TIME	average	less than sift	fastest	less than sift	fastest
SCALE INVARIENCE	best	not as good as sift	Good for certain range	average	good
COMPUT. COST	half of kaze	better than sift	average	highest	least

Further the study of different research papers with regards to the timing of the algorithm has been compiled in a table as below:

Table 2. Time Comparison of Algorithms

Time Comparison of algorithms						
Referred Papers	SIFT	SURF	ORB	KAZE	FAST	BRISK
A comparative Analysis of algorithms	1.19	0.8	0.4	0.6	-	0.06
Comparison of feature extraction techniques to recognize traffic rule violations	11	3	2	-	-	-
An Improved ORB Image Feature Matching Algorithm Based on SURF	-	1.18	0.18	-	-	-
Biomedical Images Stitching Using ORB Feature Based Approach	8.01	1	0.1	-	-	-
ORB-Oriented Mismatching Feature Points Elimination	8.8	2.5	0.28	-	-	-
Analysis and Comparison of Feature Detection and Matching Algorithms for Rovers Vision Navigation	54	18	-	-	-	-
Real Time Image Mosaicing System Based on Feature Extraction Techniques	1.79	0.67	0.14	-	0.05	-
Image Feature Points Matching via Improved ORB	3.23	-	0.031	-	-	-
A Tracking Algorithm Based on ORB	0.50	0.72	0.032	-	-	-

4 Methodology

4.1 Limitations of existing systems

From the literature,after studying different papers and reports to see the various mechanisms and algorithms that

are applied for the purpose of detection of real and counterfeit Indian currency notes have certain discrepancies.
The approaches that are used have some problems as described below:

- No parameters are set to see if the note is original or just a color copy of the original.
- The time requirement of the algorithms in real time environment is not taken into consideration.
- The computational cost and the processing capabilities required are not taken into consideration.

4.2 Proposed system

The process of classification of the notes as original and counterfeit would be done using the concept of image processing.
Here we would compare the characteristics of the note with a predefined template to check if the note is real or fake and to find the denomination of the note [4].
The detection of the note is done using different security features within the note [3].
These features are:

- Secure thread
- Portrait of Mahatma Gandhi
- Watermark Of Mahatma Gandhi
- See-through register
- Latent image
- Number panel, with numerals growing from small to big size.
- Denominational numeral with Rupee Symbol
- The Ashoka Pillar emblem
- Small horizontal rectangle with numeric value of banknote
- Seven angular bleed lines

4.3 Proposed methodology

The major and relevant image processing algorithms are studied and understood. Their features are analysed.
First each of the images that are taken go through the same pre processing and cleaning methods. After this major algorithms are applied to the image in different conditions such as good lighting, bad lighting and also the quality of the note is changed [2].
This is done to see how each algorithm reacts to these changes and how it affects the results with regards to time and number of features detected. After analysing the results the most efficient and optimal process is chosen.
After this an optimal feature matcher is chosen on the basis of our system requirements. The real time system is created and it works in two phases of feature detection and feature matching to classify currency. The feature detection is done by the Orb algorithm while the phase of feature matching is done using the Brute Force Matcher.

4.4 System requirements

The implementation environment used in the project for the analysis of image processing algorithms is MATLAB software . The Matlab software was used to analyze different image processing algorithms in terms of their efficiency in finding maximum and essential feature points that will help in the classification of notes.
The specification of the pc used are: Intel Core,8 GB RAM ,3.40 Ghz. The dataset of images used in the project implementation and for analyzing different image processing algorithms is created using different denominations of Indian currency with different inclinations and lighting conditions to test the capability and efficiency of different feature identification algorithms.
For creating the real time classifying system we need Python 3, OpenCV-Python library of Python and some other python packages.

5 Design of system

5.1 System design

1. All major and relevant image processing algorithms are studied and understood.

2. After this major algorithms are applied to the image in different conditions such as good lighting, bad lighting and also the quality of the note is changed [2]. This is done to see how each algorithm reacts to these changes and how it affects the results with regards to time and number of features detected.

3. After analysing the results the most efficient and optimal process is chosen. That is the Orb algorithm is used in the real time system along with a brute force matcher.

4. The project is such that on initialization the user would encounter a home page that would help them navigate the application.

5. The user can select an image from their device and see the analysis on that image in real time that is the denomination and the genuineness.

6. The feature detection is done by the Orb algorithm on the selected image.

7. The phase of feature matching is done using the Brute Force Matcher.

5.2 Data flow diagram

The data flow diagram shows how a real time working system should be if all the optimal steps are followed. This means that the correct algorithm must be chosen which responds best to the real time working environment.

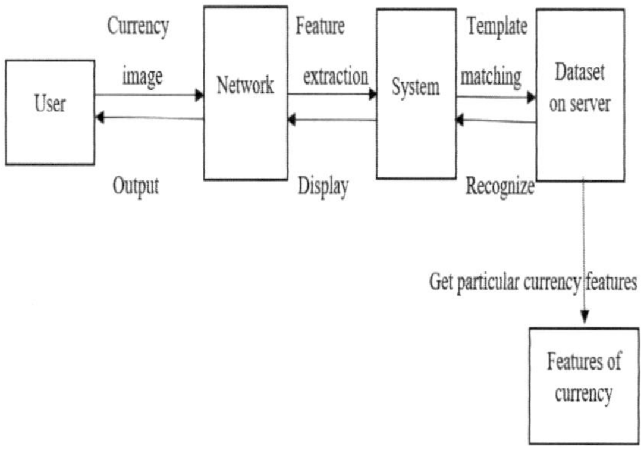

Figure 1. Data Flow Diagram

6 Experimental results

6.1 Practical implementation and analysis of algorithms

On studying the various image processing algorithms and implementing them on the currency notes in varying conditions such as good lighting and bad lighting we get to see the performance of these algorithms with regards to different parameters.

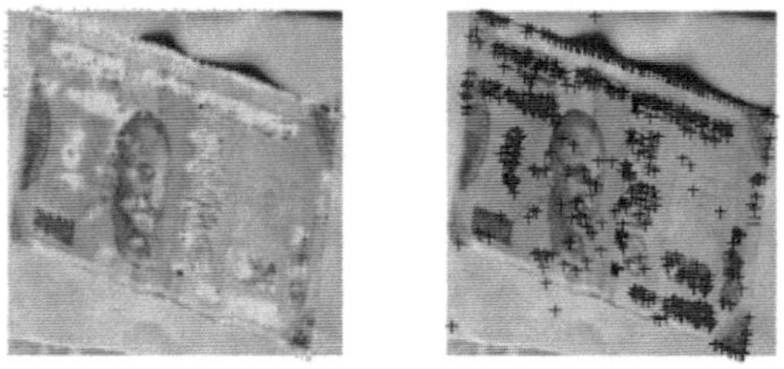

Figure 2. Sift with non crumpled currency

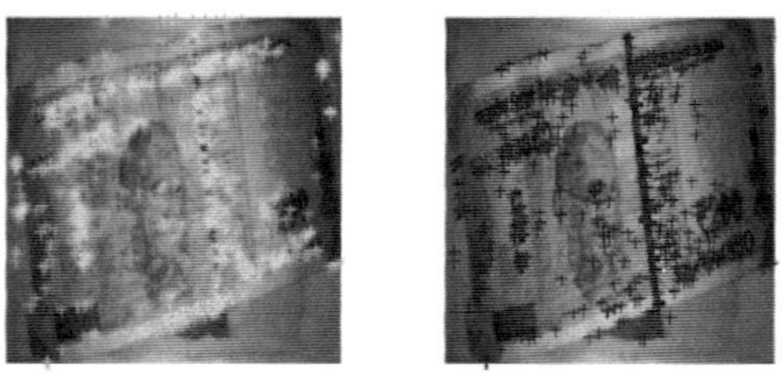

Figure 3. Sift with crumpled currency

Figure 4. ORB in good lighting

We obtain the following results in consideration to their time requirement:

Table 3. Time requirement

Algorithms	Bad light		Good light	
(Time in sec)	Crumpled	Smooth	Crumpled	Smooth
SIFT	32.58	26.7	11.42	10.57
ORB	2.73	2.71	1.61	1.58
SURF	1.47	1.57	1.71	1.59
KAZE	1.41	1.89	1.35	1.50
BRISK	1.36	1.51	1.63	1.39
FAST	1.20	1.59	1.50	1.56

Along with time requirement the algorithms are analysed for various other parameters.
The comparative study of different feature detection algorithms for their ability to discover and detect high number and high quality of features is:
KAZE <SIFT <SURF <BRISK <ORB

The order of algorithms as per their efficiency in terms of computational cost is:
KAZE <SIFT <SURF <BRISK <ORB

The order of algorithms as per their efficiency in terms of feature matching is:
SIFT <SURF <BRISK <KAZE <ORB

The efficiency of these algorithms in terms of their speed for image matching(detector-descriptor) is:
SURF <BRISK <SIFT <KAZE <ORB

6.2 Implementation of real time system and testing

The real time system that the user encounters is such that the user can select an image from their device and see the analysis on that image in real time. Here the processing happens to a still image.
The Real time System for the currency detection works to identify the denomination of the currency note and

whether the currency note is counterfeit or genuine with the use of Orb algorithm and Brute Force matcher. For the purpose of testing this system we experiment with 50 images and the resulting analysis is as follows.

Table 4. Testing of system

Currency images tested	50
Real notes	30
Fake Notes	20
True Positive	28
True Negative	18
False Positive	2
False Negative	2

Taking into consideration the above values we get an accuracy of 92 for the entire Orb based real time system.

Conclusion

After analyzing different algorithms we have discovered that SURF,SIFT and BRISK works well with large scale variations. ORB and BRISK are unvarying to affine change.
ORB is efficient algorithm able to detect large number of features. ORB performs image matching at speed as compared to other algorithms and does not compromise with the accuracy. The Orb algorithm used with Brute Force matcher proves to be efficient for currency detection in a real time system.

References

[1] S. Mittal ,S. Mittal, Indian Banknote Recognition using Convolutional Neural Network, IEEE, 3rd International Conference On Internet of Things: SIU, (2018).
[2] S. Murthy, J. Kurumathur, B.R. Reddy , Design and Implementation of Paper Currency Recognition with Counterfeit Detection, IEEE, International Conference on Green Engineering and Technologies (IC-GET), (2016).
[3] S.R. Darade , G.R. Gidaveer , Automatic Recognition of Fake Indian Currency Note, IEEE, International Conference on Electrical Power and Energy Systems (ICEPES), (2016).
[4] J.K. Nayak, C. Majhi, A. Srivastav, A. Das, Neural Network Approach for Indian Currency Recognition, IEEE ,INDICON, (2015).
[5] X. Wang, J. Zou, D. Shi, An Improved ORB Image Feature Matching Algorithm Based on SURF, IEEE, ICRAE, (2018).
[6] M. Archana, C. Kalpitha, S. Prajwal ,N. Pratiksha , Identification of Fake Notes and Denomination Recognition, IJRASET, **6**, (2018).
[7] M. Fanqing , Y. Fucheng , A Tracking Algorithm Based on ORB, IEEE, International Conference on Mechatronic Sciences, Electric Engineering and Computer, (2013) .
[8] M. Purohit, A.R. Yadav, Comparison of feature extraction techniques to recognize traffic rule violations using low processing embedded system, IEEE, International Conference on Signal Processing and Integrated Networks, (2018).
[9] C.W. Shu, X.Z. Xiao, ORB-Oriented Mismatching Feature Points Elimination, IEEE, ICPIC, (2018).
[10] H.K. Ali, A. Whitehead, Modern to Historic Image Matching: ORB/SURF an Effective Matching Technique, ISCA-CATA, (2014).
[11] Y. Qin , H. Xu , H. Chen, Image Feature Points Matching via Improved ORB, IEEE, ICPIC, (2014).

Power Consumption Optimization in IoT based Wireless Sensor Node Using ESP8266

Manushri Gowda, Jnanavi Gowda, Sahil Iyer, Manaswi Pawar, Vishal Gaikwad

Department of Electronics and Telecommunication, SIES Graduate School of Technology, Nerul, Navi Mumbai – 400706

Abstract- In this paper, we present the design and prototype implementation of a weather monitoring system for a college campus powered by a renewable energy source which is based on solar panel for remote applications. The device is powered with the help of rechargeable battery which is recharged through solar energy. Sensors are connected to the device and device uploads these sensor data on cloud with the help of Wi-Fi and internet connection. The main objective of this research is to power this device on renewable energy and continuous sensor data uploading on cloud. To keep device in running mode on battery and to save power deep sleep function of the device is used which consume very less power, which makes it sufficient to run on solar power for long time.

Keywords – Power Optimization, IoT Sensor Node, Weather station, Solar Powered Sensor Node.

1 Introduction

A weather station is a structure which is used to study the climatic conditions of a particular area. Atmospheric conditions like temperature, humidity, rainfall, pressure, wind, etc. can be measured and predicted with the help of the weather station. Weather monitoring has become very essential in recent times as it can vary in a short period of time. Hence, knowledge about it forms an important part of our day to day activities. It plays a major role in agricultural activities as it helps in determining the process of planting, harvesting and water requirements [1].

2 Literature Survey

Weather forecasting began from the early civilization. People used meteorological events to predict weather conditions. Farmers were inexperienced in the art of weather monitoring and used unreliable methods like judging the weather from the appearance of the sky and feeling the warmth in the air to carry out their predictions. Later, technology helped to replace all those conventional methods.

The earliest weather station was built in early to mid-1400s. This weather station was made up of a standard rain gauge which was used to measure rainfall. The rainfall was measured in this device using a scale which was dipped into the container. Typical weather stations that are majorly used these days are made up of heavy machinery with a number of moving parts which require regular maintenance and needs to be manually monitored and checked for signs of wear and tear. Due to manual monitoring, there is a delay in the warning of bad weather conditions. In remote areas, where there is a lack of skilled personnel these typical weather stations prove to be very expensive and in the long run are ineffective.

Meteorological departments are set up with weather stations in almost all the areas but they need a huge amount of power supply and resources to function which in turn add to the total cost of the system. On the other hand, depletion of resources is the major problem the world is facing today, so we need to find alternate ways. Excessive use of non-renewable sources of energy in today's world will exhaust the remaining amount of available energy resources at an alarming rate and make it difficult for mankind to sustain for a long period of time. Hence renewable sources of energy like wind, solar, tidal etc. should be used instead of conventional fossil fuel energy resources as much as possible.

In recent times there is an increasing shortage of natural resources so renewable sources are high in demand [2]. For today's clean economy, solar power has found a potent importance worldwide. India has become one of the cheapest producers of solar power. With the growing economy, there is a need for producing a huge amount of energy, and solar power is the best alternative for India as it has a geographical advantage. Taking advantage of India's geographical location and the existing wireless technology, we can implement weather stations by supplying power to them with the help of solar energy. The solar panels will collect the energy from the sun's radiation, convert it into electrical energy and hence provide power to the weather station for its working.

* Corresponding author: gaikwadvishal999@gmail.com

3 Proposed System

Weather conditions are highly unpredictable, hence proper knowledge about weather conditions is necessary to be prepared for any kind of calamity. Keeping this in mind, the proposed model is a weather station based on solar power, a renewable source of energy which will not pollute the environment and will use less power. It consists of a set of sensors that will monitor various weather parameters like temperature, humidity, pressure etc.

In this project we have deployed an automated weather station (AWS) powered by solar energy. AWS saves the human labour and can be placed at any remote location. It has an enclosure which will protect the circuit from rain or wind. In the past, electricity or batteries were used to power the station and thus communication links were to be established. Now renewable sources of energy such as solar energy, wind energy and turbine energy make it more efficient as well as it makes the use of wireless technology possible. We can then efficiently use this system to power an energy efficient IoTs device [7].

The basic block diagram of our system is shown in Figure 1. The sensors are connected to a Wi-Fi microchip with microcontroller capabilities. For this purpose, we use a WeMOS D1 mini which is a mini Wi-Fi board with 4 Megabyte flash memory based in ESP-8266EX. The board is connected to a rechargeable Li-ion battery which is charged via solar energy through TP-4056 charging module. This data is then uploaded to the cloud for public use [3]. This will provide data to the users without any delays. This automatic device helps us to keep track of the weather in real time.

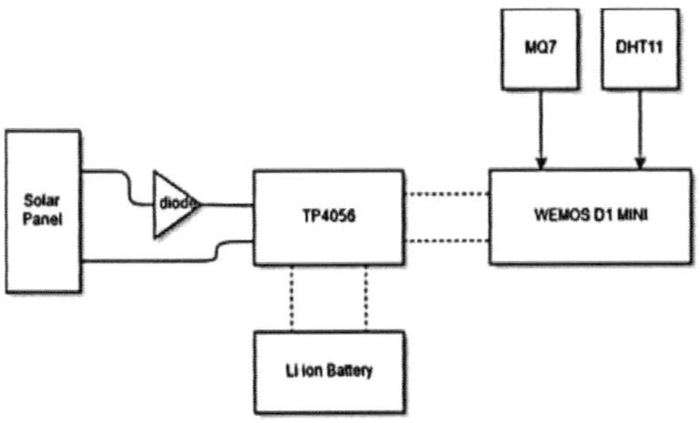

Figure.1. Block diagram of the system

4 Methodology

The main connections are shown in Figure 2. The WeMOS D1 mini module is interfaced with the various sensors namely DHT11-temperature and humidity sensor and MQ7-carbon monoxide sensor. Solar panels are located at optimum position to receive maximum sunlight. We have used a Li-ion Rechargeable Battery. This battery gets charged by the solar panel using the TP4056 charging module. The charging module TP4056 has a battery protection chip. The Wi-Fi module works on the power obtained by the Li-ion rechargeable battery. The sensor data is measured and uploaded on the Blynk App and Thinkspeak. This stage is completely powered by solar energy obtained by the solar panel.

The main part of the WeMOS board is ESP8266 chip which consumes a lot of power. Also keeping the device running for a long time will cause heating which in turn increases the temperature and will give an error in the output. To overcome these drawbacks, we use the ESP chip in deep sleep mode which is the most power efficient option.

4.1 Hardware

We have used following hardware components for the system implementation,

- WeMOS D1 MINI
  WeMOS D1 Mini is a Wi-Fi device which is based on ESP8266EX chip. It is light in weight and has a small size. It is also breadboard friendly [9].
- DHT11
  The DHT11 is a simple, low-cost digital temperature and humidity sensor.
- TP4056 Charging Module
  TP4056 is a complete constant-current/constant-voltage linear charger for single-cell lithium-ion batteries.
- MQ-7
  The MQ-7 is a carbon monoxide sensor used for sensing concentrations of Carbon Monoxide in the air.
- Solar Panel
  Photovoltaic solar panels absorb sunlight as a source of energy to generate direct current electricity.
- Li-ion Rechargeable Battery
  The 18650 is a type of rechargeable lithium-ion battery.

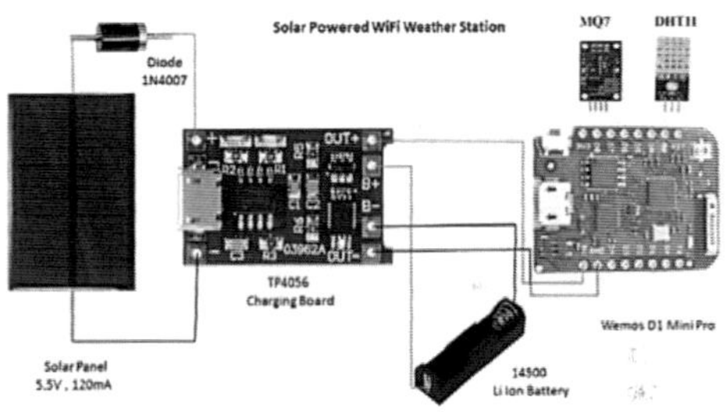

Figure.2. Connection diagram

4.2 Sleep Mode

To conserve the power of the battery we used the sleep mode technique. The ESP8266 series chip provides the three configurable sleep modes. The sleep mode is chosen by the users. The 3 sleep modes are [4]

1. MODEM SLEEP MODE
   This is used in an application that needs processor operation, for instance in PWM or I2S applications. It complies with 802.11 (U-APSD). This mode is optimized for power consumption such that the modem is stopped but Wi-Fi connection is maintained with transmission of data.
2. LIGHT SLEEP MODE
   This mode suspends the Wi-Fi modem. The CPU is put on hold and it is reactivated if required.
3. DEEP SLEEP MODE
   The projects which run on battery are efficiently implemented with the help of this mode. This mode can be used in systems wherein continuous data transmission is not required [11]. The WeMOS D1 mini module provides the deep sleep mode. It saves the battery by putting it in hibernation. We can wake up the module at regular intervals to read measurements.

https://doi.org/10.1051/itmconf/20203203048

The comparison between these three sleep modes are mentioned in below table 1.

Table.1. Difference between the 3 sleeps modes

Item		Modem-sleep	Light-sleep	Deep-sleep
Wi-Fi		OFF	OFF	OFF
System clock		ON	OFF	OFF
RTC		ON	ON	ON
CPU		ON	Pending	OFF
Substrate current		15 mA	0.4 mA	~ 20 μA
Average current	DTIM = 1	16.2 mA	1.8 mA	
	DTIM = 3	15.4 mA	0.9 mA	-
	DTIM = 10	15.2 mA	0.55 mA	

To activate deep sleep mode we have to connect the RST pin to the D0 pin as shown in figure 3. Pin D0 is not used for any other purpose.

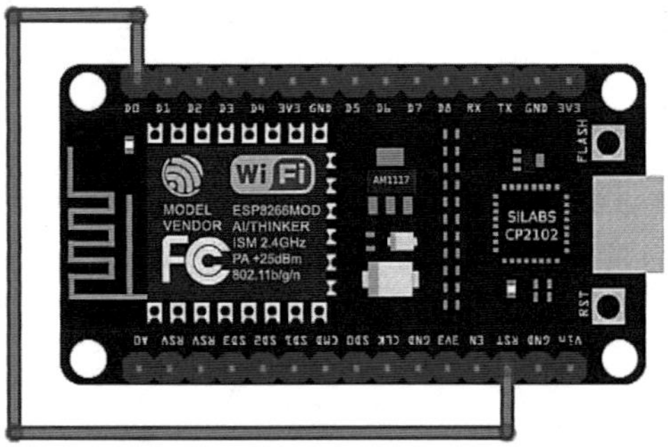

Figure.3. Connection for deep sleep mode

To wake the module manually or with an external action, we have to indicate a zero time (0). Three modes of operation are available to choose from:

- RF_DEFAULT - It is the default mode which needs to be specified. The Wi-Fi modem is enabled normally.
- RF_NO_CAL - To consume less energy an alternative version with no calibration is used. In this mode the Wi-Fi modem is activated but no calibration of the radio signal is performed.
- RF_DISABLED - In this mode the Wi-Fi modem is kept on standby. This can be used when we don't require Wi-Fi connection.

5 Experimental Results

Power is the rate of work being done or heat being transferred. Power is used to indicate the heat dissipation in a unit or individual component. The electrical power P is given

$$P = V \cdot I = I^2 \cdot R = \frac{V^2}{R}$$

where,

P is the instantaneous power measured in Watts

V is the potential difference across the component measured in Volts and

I is the current measured in Amperes.

An ampere is a unit of measure of the rate of electron flow or current in an electrical conductor. One ampere of current represents one coulomb of electrical charge (6.24 x 1018 charge carriers) moving past a specific point in one second.

mAh means milliamp hour and is a unit that measures (electric) power over time. It is commonly used to measure the energy capacity of a battery. In general, the more mAh and the longer the battery capacity or battery life.

5.1 Power consumption of the component

In this section power consumption of each component is mentioned. We have used 3.7V Li-ion battery is used. 4-5 hours of sunlight is required to completely charge the battery through the solar panel of 5-6V.

The device is put in deep sleep mode and readings are taken in an interval of 10 minutes. The power consumption of the components in normal operation is given in table 2.

Table.2. Power consumption in normal operation mode

Component	Consumption
WeMOS D1 Mini	185 mA
DHT11	0.35 mA
MQ7	150 mA
Total	**335.35 mA**

Total current consumption of the components is 335.35 mAh.

Battery capacity is 2200 mAh so the number of hours the system will work on one full charge is,

2200 mAh /335.35 mAh = 6.56 hours

The system will work continuously and data will be uploaded continuously up to 6.56 hours on full charged battery of 2200 mAh. But as battery charging is on solar energy, within 6.56 hours full battery charging is not possible, hence we have implemented sleep modes to save battery and to keep system in running condition for long duration.

The power consumption in deep sleep mode is mentioned in below table 3. If we compare table 2 and 3 then we can conclude that in sleep mode power consumption requirement is very less as compared with normal mode of operation.

Table.3. Power consumption in sleep mode

Component	Standby consumption
WeMOS D1 Mini	66μA
DHT11	60μA
MQ7	60μA
Total	186μA

As we kept 10 minutes sleep-wake cycle with a 30 second wake time, so the energy consumption budget is given as,

Wake time consumes 335.35 mA for 0.5 minutes = 167.675 mA-minutes.

Sleep time consumes 0.186 mA for 9.5 minutes = 1.767 mA-minutes.

Total consumption in 10 minutes = 169.442 mA-minutes

Thus, the average current consumption is 169.5 mA

Battery capacity is 2200 mAh, so the number of hours the system will work on one full charge is

2200/169.5 = 12.97 hours

 https://doi.org/10.1051/itmconf/20203203048

To charge a 3.7V Li-ion battery, a solar panel of voltage 5 to 6V is adequate.
Our required Solar Panel rating is = 169.5 mA at a voltage of around 5 to 6 volts.
Solar panel rating = 169.5mA x 6V = 1.017W, hence based on this we have selected solar panel with ratings as 1W / 6V.

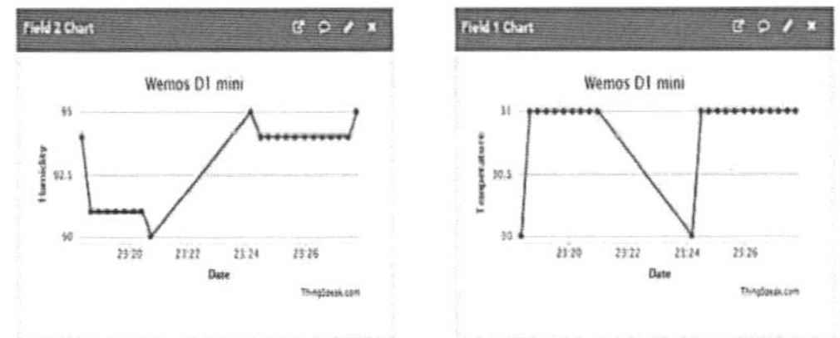

Figure.4. Sensor output on Thinkspeak

Figure.5. Implemented System Prototype

The implemented system is shown in above figure 5. This prototype is tested for few days and also checked the uploaded data on cloud.

6 Limitations

After a certain time the solar panels used as collectors will start to degrade and will need to be replaced. In extremely cloudy weather, solar panels of higher efficiency will be required.
In the long run, sensors will also need maintenance. The duration of deep sleep mode needs to be properly maintained in order to get weather readings without spending all the solar energy.

7 Conclusions

This project helped us overcome the limitations imposed by the traditional system depicted in table 4.

Table.4. Comparative analysis with the traditional system

Traditional System	**Proposed System**
Usually non-renewable resources are used to power the station, which in turn harms the ecosystem.	Solar energy is used which is much more reliable and efficient.
This system can't be deployed in remote locations.	This system can be deployed in remote areas.
High cost is incurred on its maintenance enlarging the depreciation value.	This system doesn't need frequent maintenance making the depreciation cost almost nil.
Specialization is needed to use it.	It is user friendly, can be used by laymen too.
Absence of deep sleep mode.	Deep sleep mode is implemented to reduce the power consumption

This research also successfully demonstrated that it is practically possible to power a weather monitoring system with solar power.

8 Future Scope

India has a tremendous scope to use and generate solar energy due to its geographical location. Being a tropical country, it receives solar radiation almost throughout the year. It approximately amounts to 3,000 hours of sunshine per annum. Almost each and every part of our country receives 4-7kWh of solar radiation per square meters. Our country has got a good opportunity to tap the solar power due to a high current solar power installed capacity of around 3GW.

For future work, the weather monitoring system will be further refined by including a greater number of sensors to measure different parameters such as pressure. We can use BMP 180, a digital pressure sensor which is typically used for weather forecasting [10]. We can increase productivity of the system by adding more solar panels and batteries of higher efficiency. The wake up cycle can be altered according to our convenience, so that the li-ion battery does not drain at a faster rate. Along with providing data through the cloud, we can also send alert messages when the weather conditions are not suitable.

References

1. Iswanto and Muhammad, H. "Wheatear Monitoring System with Remote Radio Frequency Wireless Communication", *International Journal of Embedded System and Application* (IJESA), Vol. **2** No. 3 September 2012.
2. Arpita Ghosh, Abhay Srivastava, Atul Patidar, C.Sandeep, Shanthi Prince,"SOLAR POWERED WEATHER STATION AND RAIN DETECTOR",2013 *Texas Instruments India Educators' Conference*.
3. R. K. Kodali and A. Sahu, "An IoT based weather information prototype using WeMos," 2016 *2nd International Conference on Contemporary Computing and Informatics (IC3I), Noida*, 2016, pp. 612-616.
4. Murugesan, Malathi & Arumugam, Gowsalya & Dhanushyaa, M & Arunachalam, Janani. (2017). HOME AUTOMATION ON ESP8266. *SSRG International Journal of Computer Science and Engineering*. 2348-8387.
5. I. Mathews, G. Kelly, P. J. King, and R. Frizzell, "GaAs solar cells for Indoor Light Harvesting," *2014 IEEE 40th Photovolt. Spec. Conf.*, pp. 510–513, 2014.
6. R. A. Kjellby, L. R. Cenkeramaddi, and T. Eirik, "Design and Prototype Implementation of Long- Range Self-powered Wireless IoT Devices," pp. 215–218, 2018.
7. R. Gunasagaran, L. M. Kamarudin, E. Kanagaraj, A. Zakaria, and A. Y. M. Shakaff, "Internet of Things : Solar

Power under Forest Canopy," *2016 IEEE Student Conf. Res. Dev., pp.* 1–4, 2016.
8. H. Sharma, A. Haque, and Z. A. Jaffery, "An Efficient Solar Energy Harvesting System for Wireless Sensor Nodes," 2018 *2nd IEEE Int. Conf. Power Electron. Intell. Control Energy Syst.*, vol. 3, pp. 461–464, 2018.
9. EINSTRONIC,"WeMos D1 Mini Series" *datasheet, EINSTRONIC, July 2017.*
10. BMP280 Sensor,"BMP280 Digital Sensor" *datasheet, Bosch, BST-BMP280-DS001-11* | Revision 1.14 | May 2015
11. *Espressif* "Low Power Solutions," datasheet, 2016.

Secure Dissemination and Protection of Raster Data using Merkle Hash Tree based Cryptowatermarking

Sangita Santosh Chaudhari

Department of Computer Engineering, Ramrao Adik Institute of Technology, Nerul, Navi Mumbai, India

Abstract. Due to rapid development in the Internet and other communication technologies, it becomes quite easy to copy and distribute multiple illegal copies of high value and sensitive data. Raster data is one of the high voluminous data and it requires huge efforts to sense and generate this data. Therefore, ownership protection as well as its integrity become one of the key problems in spatial information service. There are lot many schemes are available for watermarking and encryption individually, but if both are combined gives manifold advantages. This paper presents a cryptowatermarking scheme by combining watermarking and encryption to protect the copyright of raster data as well as to provide security dissemination level. We have proposed a scheme by employing double transposition, LSB substitution watermarking and Merkle Hash Tree for encryption and watermarking. It has been observed that the proposed scheme is not only robust against encryption attacks, but also has transparency, strongness, large data hiding capacity and correct extraction of watermark.

Keywords: Cryptowatermarking, Merkle Hash tree, Robust watermarking, Raster Data

1. Introduction

Due to rapid growth in communication technology, it becomes extremely easy to digitise data and generate other multimedia contents. It becomes easy to distribute data to multiple recipients over the Internet. However, this cause misuse of all kinds of data which is in digital format. The sensing, acquisition and pre-processing of raster data are cost and manpower intensive tasks. Also, this data is of high volume and it is sensitive sometimes. It is not advisable to store the data at any untrusted server or disseminate it directly without enforcing any safeguarding mechanism. As the data is especially important in lots of analysis applications and not freely available, it may be duplicated and distributed illegally. Therefore, copyright protection is crucial and necessary in today's era. In most of the applications, cryptographic mechanisms such as encryption and digital signatures are used to achieve confidentiality, integrity, and non-repudiation services.

All these listed security mechanisms generally help users to safeguard their data at storage and communication. Although, Watermarking is being used since years as a complementary security mechanism, it fails to secure data completely. It is mainly used for copyright protection to prove the ownership of data.

Security of raster data is required at storage and dissemination level. Watermarking and encryption techniques can be useful to do secure them at these levels. There are many different approaches/schemes are available for watermarking of raster data in spatial as well as frequency domain [1-6]. However, no one have paid attention towards security watermarked raster data at dissemination level. Attackers can use many simple manipulative attacks to tamper watermarked data. Standard algorithms AES, DES, and RSA [7] are very popular for many different types of data, but they may not be suitable for raster data due to its voluminous nature. Also, these well-known algorithms take large amount of processing time for such voluminous data. Cryptography and watermarking can be combined and can provide overall security for raster data.

In the scheme proposed by Xu et al. [8], watermarking and encryption are combined, and the watermark is embedded in the image at the time of decryption of the image. One of the major problems of this scheme is that the encrypted image does not carry watermark. Jiang and Xu [9] depicted simultaneous encryption and watermarking operations in their scheme which they proposed for remote sensing data. Enhanced Arnold scrambling is used for encryption which utilises only one key for complete image. The issue here is that If a key is known to attacker, the whole encryption system fails. Encryption and watermarking are integrated in the scheme proposed by Jiang et al. [10]. They have utilised orthogonal decomposition of remote sensing data. This scheme does not give proper output and the edges get blurred in the resultant image. Ding et al. [11] have proposed integrity authentication scheme for remote sensing images wherein they have utilised perceptual hash scheme based on deep learning concepts. PCA is used to extract the features and perceptual hash is

* Corresponding author: sangita.chaudhari@rait.ac.in

calculated on it. This will help to detect local tampering in high resolution remote sensing images. In all existing systems, complete security analysis as well as watermark robustness analysis are not done.

This paper presents the idea of combining cryptography and watermarking to secure raster data. Simple yet effective transposition cipher, LSB based watermarking and robust Merkle hash tree is combined to provide secure solution for safeguarding raster data.

The paper is organized as follows. Proposed crypto-watermarking scheme is presented in section 2. Section 3 describes error analysis measures. Experimental results are discussed in section 4. Conclusions are drawn in section 5.

2. Proposed Cryptowatermarking Scheme

Remote sensing images includes Multispectral, hyperspectral, active/passive microwave, LIDAR images and aerial photographs etc. Due to the enhanced computing power and large number of applications capable to use these data, its demand is increased dramatically. Digital watermarking and cryptography are complementary to each other and used separately from many years to achieve copyright protection and security, but when combined as Cryptowatermarking results in vary robust and secure solution to safeguard the precious data. Simple yet strong and secure solution is proposed to provide to achieve protection and secure dissemination of remote sensing data.

In the proposed Cryptowatermarking scheme, two stage transposition cipher, least significant bit (LSB) based watermarking on zigzag pattern matrix, Merkle hash tree-based indexing of the encrypted image and RSA digital signature are effectively combined to make it robust and strong. These cipher when used as individual are prone to attacks. However, proper cascading of these ciphers makes the overall system robust and strong and it is impossible to break the security provided by this scheme.

It is a common practice in communication systems to use secure hash algorithms to verify the integrity of content transferred over insecure communication channel. The employment of secure hash algorithms enables user to securely disseminate the content over the Internet. Typically, algorithms such as Secure Hash Algorithm (SHA) and Message Digest (MD) have been used to check the content integrity after receiving the entire data from sender. The Merkle hash tree (MHT) can be used to verify content delivered from sender. MHT is a binary tree that organizes hashes hierarchically. Figure 6.1 illustrates MHT having 8 objects O1 to O8 representing leaf nodes of a tree. A node N contains hash value hN which is computed as: if N is a leaf node then hN = H(O1) otherwise hN = H(hN:lc || hN:rc). Here, N:lc and N:rc are left and right child of N respectively, and "||" represents concatenation of two binary strings. The complete tree is formed using iterative hashing. Finally, root of the MHT is signed by the data owner using public key digital signature scheme. Here, each O_i corresponds to 8x8 non overlapping block of encrypted watermarked raster data.

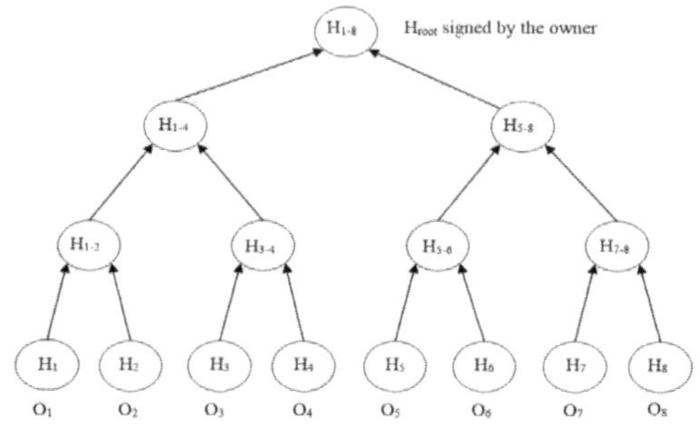

Fig. 1. Merkle Hash Tree (MHT)

Algorithm 1 and Algorithm 2 shows the Cryptowatermarking and decrpyowatermarking process respectively.

Algorithm 1: Cryptowatermarking
Input: *MxN* Raster Data (*R*), Binary Watermark(*W*), private key of sender(*S.Pr*)
Output: Encrypted Watermarked Raster Data (*EWR*), signature (*SG.EWR*)

1. For each of the bands (*R, G* and *B*) of input Raster Data(R) repeat the following process:
   1.1 Shift even rows by EK_{SR} mod *M.*
   // EK_{SR} is selected in such a way that EK_{SR} is relatively prime to *M.*
   1.2 Shift even columns by EK_{SC} mod *N.*
   // EK_{SC} is selected in such a way that EK_{SC} relatively prime to *N.*
   1.3 Perform watermarking on the Raster Data (*SR*) generated in step 1.2
   (i) Divide the Raster Data (*SR*) into 8x8 non overlapping blocks
   (ii) Read the block data using zigzag reading pattern and substitute LSB bit of each element on the pattern by each pixel of binary watermark in sequence.
   (iii) Repeat the procedure by embedding binary multiple time till all non-overlapping blocks are covered.
   1.4 Shift odd rows by OK_{SR} mod *M*
   //OK_{SR} is selected in such a way that OK_{SR} is relatively prime to M.
   1.5 Shift odd columns by OK_{SC} mod *N.*
   // OK_{SC} is selected in such a way that OK_{SC} is relatively prime to N.
   1.6 Concatenate all the resultant bands to get Encrypted watermarked Raster Data (*EWR*)
2. Perform signature generation on *EWR* generated in step 1.6
   2.1 Divide *EWR* into 8x8 non overlapping bocks
   2.2 Construct Merkle Hash tree and calculate hash of root
   2.3 Sign the hash of root by private key of sender to get signature (*SG.EWR*)

Algorithm 2: Decrpyowatermarking

Input: Encrypted Watermarked Raster Data (*EWR*), signature (*SG.EWR*), Public key Sender (*S.Pu*)
Output: *MxN* Decrypted Raster Data (*DR*), Extracted Binary Watermark(*W'*)

1. Perform signature verification for the received data *EWR*
   1.1 Divide R into 8x8 non overlapping bocks
   1.2 Construct Merkle Hash tree and calculate hash of root
   1.3 Verify the signature using public key of sender(*S.Pu*). Successful verification denotes intact data whereas unsuccessful verification indicates tampering of data in communication.
2. If signature verification is successful go to step 3 else notify sender to resend the data.
3. For each of the bands (R, G and B) of EWR repeat the following process:
   3.1 Shift odd columns by OK_{Sc} mod N.
   3.2 Shift odd rows by OK_{SR} mod M.
   3.3 Extract the watermark from the Raster Data generated in step 3.2.
      (i) Divide the Raster Data (SR) into 8x8 non overlapping blocks.
      (ii) Read the block data using zigzag reading pattern and extract LSB bit of each element from each element on zigzag pattern.
      (iii) Repeat the procedure of LSB bit extraction for all non-overlapping blocks to get the binary watermark (*W'*)
   3.4 Shift even columns by EK_{SC} mod *N*.
   3.5 Shift even rows by EK_{SR} mod *M*.
4. Concatenate all the resultant bands to obtain Decrypted Raster Data (*DR*)

Two stage transposition ciphers employed in the schemes provide good diffusion whereas the watermarking process itself provides good confusion and hence making the scheme robust. The encrypted and watermarked raster data is divided in to 8x8 blocks. All the pixels in 8x8 blocks are concatenated and represents one object. All the blocks are represented in object as concatenation of all pixels in corresponding blocks. They can be treated as leaf node of MHT (figure 1). Hash of the root is calculated using bottom up hashing approach and finally root is signed by sender with his private key. Sender sends the key set as {*S.Pu*, EK_{SC}, EK_{SR}, OK_{SC}, OK_{SR}, *M*, *N*, *size of watermark*} to the receiver. Encrypted watermarked data (EWR) along with the calculated signature (*SG.EWR*) is also sent to receiver. RSA digital signature is used to generate signature on EWR.

At receiver side, receiver first verifies the signature *SG.EWR*. Successful verification indicates tamperproof communication of encrypted watermarked data, else the sender is requested to send the data again. Decryption and watermark extraction are carried out as per the steps illustrated in Algorithm 2 and the required keys received from sender.

3. Evaluation Measures

Normalised correlation is used to indicated similarity between original watermark (W_k) and extracted watermark (W_k'). It is evaluated using equation 1. A Complete similarity is indicated by a coefficient with value one. Normalised correlation ranges between 0 to 1.

$$NC = \frac{\sum_k (w_k \cdot w_k')}{\sqrt{\sum_k (w_k')^2}} \quad (1)$$

Equation 2 shows the Entropy (E) of an image I where $P_r(\alpha_i)$ is the probability of occurrence of the grey level α_i and *G* is the total number of grey levels. Entropy is a measure indicating randomness of the pixels in the encrypted image. The value of entropy is 8 if every pixel has equal probability in encrypted image. It shows complete randomness in the output image. Low value makes the encrypted image susceptible to various statistical attacks.

$$E(I) = \sum_{i=1}^{G} p_r(\alpha_i) \log_2(p_r(\alpha_i)) \quad (2)$$

4. Results and Discussion

The proposed Cryptowatermarking system is evaluated using various remote sensing images of varying sizes. Figure 2 shows 6 such images 1 to 6 of sizes 1280x1280, 1600x1080, 800x800, 960x840, 760x640 and 640x640 respectively. The watermark of size 100x50 pixels is used for watermarking. In the experiment, different keyset for double transposition cipher is used as shown in Table 1. Encrypted watermarked raster data and decrypted raster data are shown in figure 3 and 4. The original watermark and extracted watermark are shown in figure 5. The corresponding normalized coefficient between original and extracted watermark is obtained as one. SHA 256 is used for hashing in Merkle Hash Tree and RSA digital signature is employed for signing the root of Merkle Hash Tree. Public modulus(n) is considered as "*d94d889e88853dd89769a18015a0a2e6bf82bf356fe14f251fb4f5e2df0d9f9a94a68a30c428b39e3362fb3779a497eceaea37100f264d7fb9fb1a97fbf621133de55fdcb9b1ad0d7a31b379216d79252f5c527b9bc63d83d4ecf4d1d45cbf843e8474babc655e9bb6799cba77a47eafa838296474afc24beb9c825b73ebf549*" and public exponent (*e*) is considered as *10001*. Private exponent (*d*) was calculated using values of *n* and *e*.

Encryption and decryption results are highly dependent on the order of ciphers and proper usage of utilized key space. Cryptosystem is said to be secure if the image cannot be decrypted correctly even if there is a change in sequence of ciphers and keys. Keys used here are more sensitive they should be relatively prime to number of pixels in rows and columns. Decryption many are not successful if there is a small change in the keys used in encryption and decryption.

https://doi.org/10.1051/itmconf/20203203049

In cryptography, it is very crucial to design the algorithms which provides robustness against all the attacks like brute force and statistical attacks. One of the best ways to check the security of the image security algorithm is histogram analysis. When histogram of encrypted image is uniform, it becomes difficult to get information from image and thus launching statistical attacks. As Merkle hash tree, hashing and digital signature are used, it is difficult to launch an attack and compromise key or raster data.

Table 1. Keyset for double transposition cipher

Image	EK_{SR}	OK_{SR}	EK_{SC}	OK_{SC}
Sat_Image1	347	991	103	1173
Sat_Image2	563	1093	1051	163
Sat_Image3	401	191	571	73
Sat_Image4	199	311	31	839
Sat_Image5	47	419	541	313
Sat_Image6	463	557	13	97

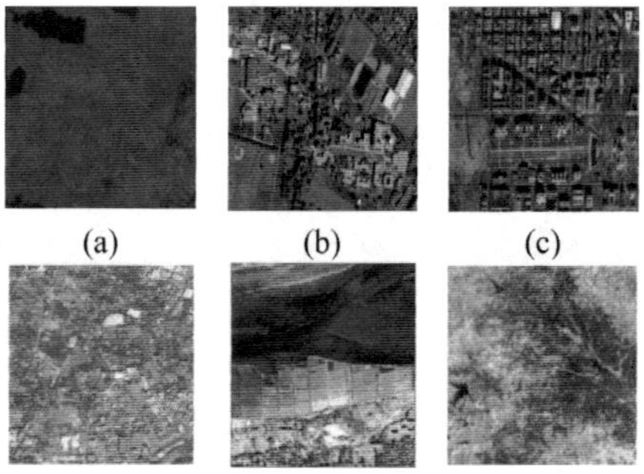

(a) (b) (c)
(d) (e) (f)

Fig. 2. Original Raster Data: (a) Sat_Image1; (b)Sat_Image2; (c)Sat_Image3; (d) Sat_Image4; (e)Sat_Image5; (f) Sat_Image6

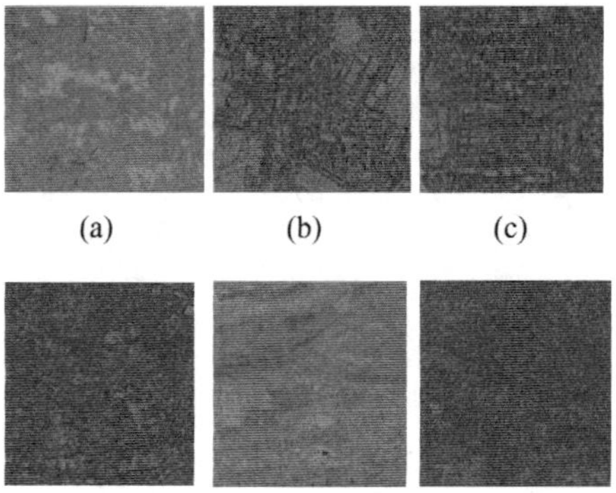

(a) (b) (c)
(d) (e) (f)

Fig. 3. Encrypted Watermarked Raster Data: (a) EWSat_Image1; (b)EWSat_Image2; (c)EWSat_Image3; (d) EWSat_Image4; (e)EWSat_Image5; (f) EWSat_Image6

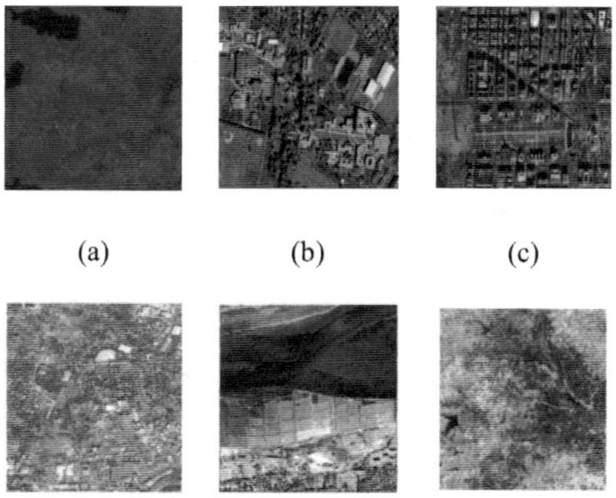

(a) (b) (c)
(d) (e) (f)

Fig. 4. Decrypted Raster Data: (a) DSat_Image1; (b)DSat_Image2; (c)DSat_Image3; (d) DSat_Image4; (e)DSat_Image5; (f) DSat_Image6

(a) (b)

Fig. 5. (a) Original Watermark, and (b) Extracted watermark with NC=1

Double transposition cipher and watermarking algorithm provides exceptionally good diffusion and confusion in the encrypted watermarked image. Histogram analysis can be used to check confusion and diffusion of the proposed scheme. Figure 6 shows the RGB histogram of both the original and encrypted watermarked raster data. From the figure, it is observed that the histogram of the encrypted watermarked data is nearly uniformly distributed, and very different from the histogram of the original data and hence there will be no clue from the encrypted watermarked image to launch statistical attack on resultant data in the proposed scheme. Entropy for encrypted watermarked data are shown in Table 2 and it is observed that it is nearly equal to 8 which shows that the scheme is robust against statistical attacks.

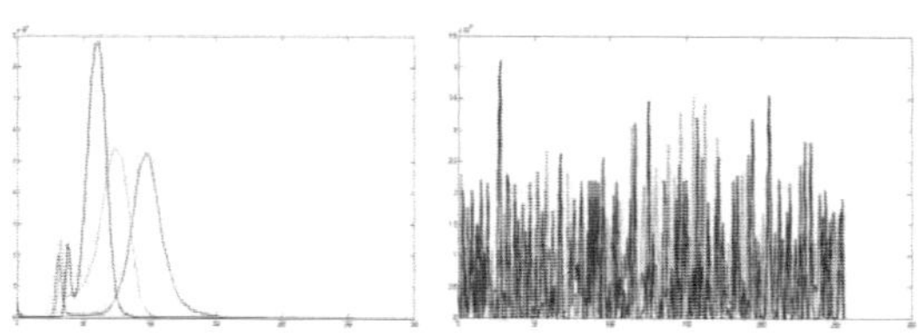

(a) (b)

Fig. 6. Histogram Analysis (a) Original Raster Data (Sat_Image1), and (b) Encrypted watermarked Raster Data

https://doi.org/10.1051/itmconf/20203203049

Table 2. Entropy of Encrypted Raster Data

Image	Entropy
EWSat_Image1	7.9990
EWSat_Image 2	7.9904
EWSat_Image 3	7.9900
EWSat_Image 4	7.9921
EWSat_Image 5	7.9981
EWSat_Image 6	7.9823

Perceptual quality of the image can be checked using peak to signal noise ratio (PSNR). If its value is small, image quality is poor and vice versa. From table 3, it is observed that the proposed system results into small PSNR values thus resulting into true randomness in the encrypted image.

Table 3. PSNR of Encrypted Raster Data

Image	PSNR
EWSat_Image1	12. 7021
EWSat_Image 2	12.2600
EWSat_Image 3	12.0306
EWSat_Image 4	11.9327
EWSat_Image 5	12.3943
EWSat_Image 6	12.2846

5. Conclusion

In this paper, we have proposed cryptowatermarking, a combination of watermarking and encryption to provide copyright protection for raster data and for secure dissemination copyrighted raster data. During transmission, Merkle Hash tree-based encryption and RSA digital signature helps in preventing attacks and data loss. Watermark can be efficiently extracted at receiver side which can be used to prove ownership of the data. The proposed scheme satisfies the security of encryption, the invisibility and robustness against various brute force and statistical attacks.

References

[1] M. Barni, F. Bartolini, V. Cappellini, E. Magli, and G. Olmo. Near-lossless digital watermarking for copyright protection of remote sensing images. IEEE International Geoscience and Remote Sensing Symposium (2002).

[2] Y. Chauhan, P. Gupta, and K. Majumder. Digital Watermarking of Satellite Images, India Conference on Computer Vision, Graphics, and Image Processing (2002).

[3] T. Hemalatha, V. Joevivek, K. Sukumar K. Soman. Robust watermarking of remote sensing images without the loss of spatial information, 10th ESRI India User Conference (2009).

[4] B. Kumari and V. Rallabandi. Modified patchwork-based watermarking scheme for satellite imagery, Signal Processing (2008).

[5] P. Zhu, and C. Chen, A copyright protection watermarking algorithm for remote sensing image based on binary image watermark, International Journal Light and Electron Optics (2013).

[6] B. Ziegeler, H. Tamhankar, J. Fowler, and L. Bruce. Wavelet-Based watermarking of remotely sensed imagery tailored to classification performance, IEEE Workshop on Advances in Techniques for Analysis of Remotely Sensed Data (2003).

[7] B. Schneier. Applied cryptography. Wiley (1995).

[8] Y. Xu, Z. Xu, and Y. Zhang. Content security protection for remote sensing images integrating selective content encryption and digital fingerprint, Journal of Applied Remote Sensing (2012).

[9] L. Jiang, and Z. Xu, Commutative encryption and watermarking for remote sensing image, International Journal of Digital Content Technology, and its Applications (2012).

[10] L. Jiang, Z. Xu, and Y. Xu. A new comprehensive security protection for remote sensing image based on the integration of encryption and watermarking, IEEE International Geoscience and Remote Sensing Symposium (2013).

[11] K. Ding, Z. Yang, Y. Wang, and Y. Liu. An improved perceptual hash algorithm based on u-net for the authentication of high-resolution remote sensing image. Applied Sciences (2019).

ITM Web of Conferences **32**, 03050 (2020) https://doi.org/10.1051/itmconf/20203203050
ICACC-2020

Identification of Anthracnose Disease in Mango Plant Using Clustering and Gray level Co- occurrence Matrix

Mamata Gawand[1,*], *Soumya* Gowda[2], *Sonali* Hnade[3], *Pooja* Mahadik[4], and *Prajakta* Dere[5]

[1] Ramrao Adik Institute of Technology ,Electronics and Telecommunication department, Nerul, India
[2] Ramrao Adik Institute of Technology ,Electronics and Telecommunication department, Nerul, India
[3] Ramrao Adik Institute of Technology ,Electronics and Telecommunication department, Nerul, India
[4] Ramrao Adik Institute of Technology ,Electronics and Telecommunication department, Nerul, India
[5] Ramrao Adik Institute of Technology ,Electronics and Telecommunication department, Nerul, India

Abstract. The aim of this paper is to help farmers to identify disease without observing each and every mango plant by eyes. Farmers can use the pesticides according to the leaf disease identified. For identification of this leaf disease K-means clustering and GLCM (Gray level co-occurrence matrix) technique are used. Affected areas of the leaf are identified more accurately by using K-means clustering. GLCM is used to get the texture features which help for identifying the mango leaf disease. The signs of the diseases on the leaf should be identified at the early for the growth of productivity in mango plant, for this leaf disease identification is important.

1 INTRODUCTION

India is the largest producer of "mangoes" which means farmers require frequently monitoring of the large scale of mango crop field. To reduce the usage of pesticides, accurately, early diagnosis is necessary. It is also important to identify the proper disease. This will reduce the cost of buying pesticides and eliminate the use of pesticides. This paper concentrates on anthracnose disease found in mango plant. Diseases in mango plant are anthracnose, alternarnia, and bacterial blight.

1. Anthracnose is most common serious diseases in mango plant. This fungal disease cause the development of dark, sunken spot or lesions. This disease is seed borne and carry over on crop residue in the soil. This fungal is spread in water droplets and worse in warm, humid weather.[1]

2. Alternarnia leaf spot symptoms first appear as small, brownish circular spot on surface of the leaves. Later on, high concentration of brown, black spot occurs evenly over the mango leaf. This disease can be controlled by regular field spray program including copper based fungicides.[2]

3. Bacterial blight is also known as apical bud necrosis (mango). This disease affects most of the parts plant including the trunk, branches, shoots, buds, flowers, leaves and fruits. Regularly removing the infected twigs, branches and fruits, and disinfecting working tools will help in preventing the disease.[2]

In this paper for identifying the disease in mango plant MATLAB software is used. For better result the image is acquired from digital camera. For segmentation K-means clustering is used and GLCM is used for the features extraction.

1.1 K-Means clustering

K-means is a centric based algorithm in which cluster size can be changed. Using k-means algorithm random two centres or pixels are selected from the infected leaf. The centres represent the faulty and faultless regions of the leaf. This is done to identify the infected part of the leaf. Clustering is a technique to form number of groups of objects. K-means clustering treats each object as having a location in space. It finds partitions such that objects within each cluster are as close to each other as possible, and as far as possible from objects in other clusters. [6]

1.2 Gray level co-occurrence matrix (GLCM)

GLCM techniques (gray level co-occurrence matrix) is used for obtaining texture features such as Homogeneity, Energy, Contrast, and Correlation. The statistic features in feature extraction obtained are standard deviation, kurtosis, variance, skewness, root mean square (RMS), entropy, mean, inverse difference matrix (IDM)[1]. The difference matrix element P(i,j|d,ɵ) contains the second order mathematical probability values for changes between gray levels'i' and 'j' at a exacting displacement distance and at a particular angle(ɵ).

* Corresponding author: author@e-mail.org

https://doi.org/10.1051/itmconf/20203203050

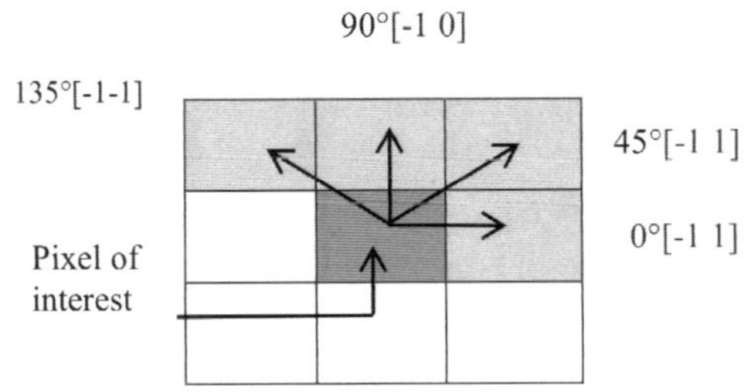

Figure 1. Gray Level Co-occurrence Matrix Angle

Typically GLCM are calculated at four different angles: 0, 45, 90, and 135 degree as shown in figure 1. For each angles different distances can be used d=1, 2, 3 , etc., and the size of GLCM of 8 bit image: 256*256 (2^8). 4 features can be calculated from each GLCM. The features are used for texture calculation. Statistical features are required for disease identification.

2 METHODOLOGY

The algorithm design is as shown in the figure 2. The steps taken at each phase are mentioned and they are briefly explained in the sections below. The whole algorithm design can be divided into four phases.

2.1. Image Acquisition:

Camera is used to acquire mango leaf image. Acquired image is RGB that is red, green and blue. The captured image is resize.

2.2 Image Pre-processing

Pre-processing method is used to enhance the input image of leaf for image conversion and filtration of noise.

2.2.1 Contrast enhancing

After capturing the image next step is to apply the blur soften method. Blurring of the image means each pixel of the image gets spread over. When we capture the image some noise is there so blurring the image used to remove some amount of noise. It will help to detect the affected area. Sharpening of the image can be reduced by using blurring of image. Limits to stretch contrast computes the lower and upper limits that can be used for contrast stretching grayscale or RGB image. The limits are returned in lowhigh. By default, the limits specify for bottom 1% and for top 1% of all pixel values.

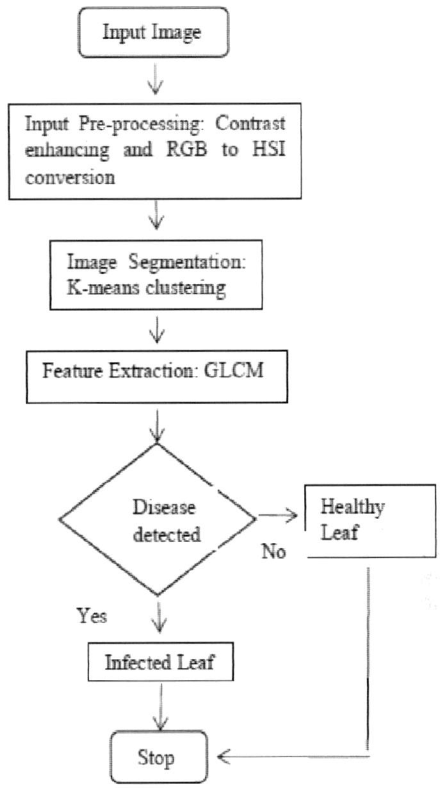

Figure 2. Algorithm of Leaf Disease Identification

2.2.2. Converting the image from RGB to HSI:

Conversion of RGB to HSI is helpful for the colour description. RGB stands the colors in the form of red, green, blue and HSI is the hue saturation intensity. RGB is group of primary colors.

To calculate the intensity average value of RGB is taken.

$$(1/3)*(R+G+B) \qquad (1)$$

The colors are the unique features in this method which can be classified for translation of RGB to HSI.

$$\theta = \cos^{\wedge}{-1}\left\{\frac{\frac{1}{2}[(R-G)+(R-B)]}{\left[(R-G)^{\wedge}2+(R-G)(G-B)^{\wedge}\frac{1}{2}\right]}\right\} \qquad (2)$$

$$H = \theta \ \text{if}\ B<G \qquad (3)$$

$$H = 360-\theta \ \text{if}\ B>G \qquad (4)$$

$$S = 1-(3/(R+G+B)\ [\min(R, G, B)] \qquad (5)$$

$$I = (1/3)(R+G+B) \qquad (6)$$

 https://doi.org/10.1051/itmconf/20203203050

The computation statistics are evaluated using GLCM function and later can be used in objective analysis of Image processing.

The infected portions of the leaves are classified based on the RGB images. The Otsu's threshold is observed and calculated based on the intensities and threshold values The HSI model of the image is used in segmenting the portion of the image [2].

2.3 Image Segmentation:

Image segmentation is used for easier analysis of image. In image segmentation, K-means clustering is used for dividing the images into clusters. One part of cluster contain image which shows diseased part of the leaf. In this image is dividing into three clusters for better segmentation result.

2.3.1Image segmentation using K-means clustering

K-means clustering is used for segmentation. The image is converted from RGB colour space to L*a*b* space. The L*a*b* space consists of a luminosity layer 'L*', chromaticity layer 'a*' and 'b*. All the colour information is in the 'a*' and 'b*' layers.[6]

In this we are using various size of clusters like 3, 6, 8 and 10. Also we are using various co-occurrence angle for the clusters size like 45°, -45°, 30°, 60°, 90° and 180°. The better result of cluster size is getting in the 45°, 60°, 90°and 180° angle. 45° angle of cluster size 3 gives best results. Using this result of clusters we get the better result of GLCM.

2.4 Feature Extraction

2.4.1 Feature extraction using GLCM:

The method of feature selection as well as extraction is very important in this application. The disease can be identified and better result can be observed with respect to features. The detection of diseases are shown with the colour distribution in the image like hardness and roughness in the texture of the image. This shows the infected areas of the leaf.

In this we are using different co-occurrence angles. By changing the angles the cluster output and the GLCM output is changes. Different 13 features like mean, variance, standard deviation (SD), root mean square (RMS), smoothness, contrast, inverse difference movement (IDM) etc. are getting using the GLCM output. The affected area in percentage is shown in the command window. In this paper we are focused on the GLCM for the better result.

3 RESULT

Various leafs from the mango plants is collected. The leaf image is firstly converted into the HSI format. Using the resultant image different size of clusters are obtained. From the cluster image different features like mean, entropy, smoothness, contrast etc., are derived. The features are displayed using the GUI. Using this features leaf disease is detected. After analysis the various clusters of image are observed and whether the leaf is healthy or unhealthy is observed. The affected area is shown in the command window in percentage. In following cases the affected area is 15.0015%. The results of disease identification are shown in four cases.

Figure 3: Input image

The input image is taken from the digital camera is shown in figure 3. This image is mango plant leaf. This leaf has Anthracnose disease.

Figure 4. Contrast enhanced image of the input image

After taking input image the contrast of the image is enhanced as shown in figure 4. It simply highlight the features of the image.

 https://doi.org/10.1051/itmconf/20203203050

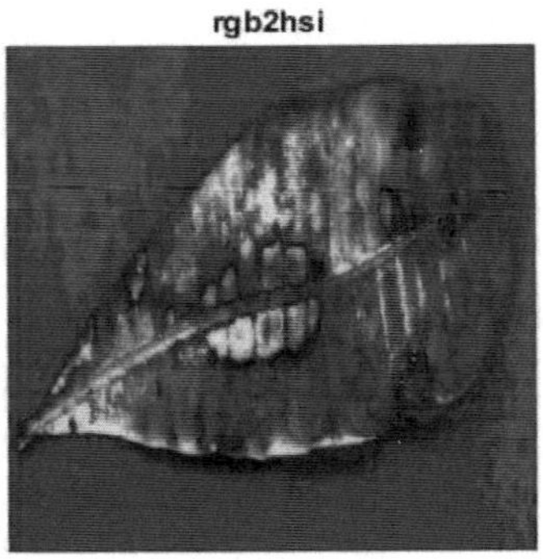

Figure 5. RGB to HSI of the input image

The RGB image is converted into the HSI image as shown in figure 5. HSI image is used in segmenting the portion of the image.

Case 1: The k-means cluster size 3 and co-occurrence angle 45° is taken for simulation.

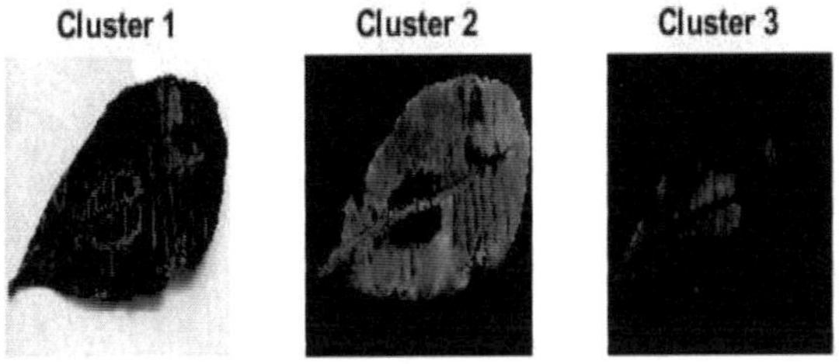

Figure 6. Cluster size 3 and 45 °co-occurrence angle

The figure 6 shows the clusters of size 3. From this clusters output we have to select the cluster number which shows the smallest disease. As compared to input image in this the cluster 2 shows the smallest disease.

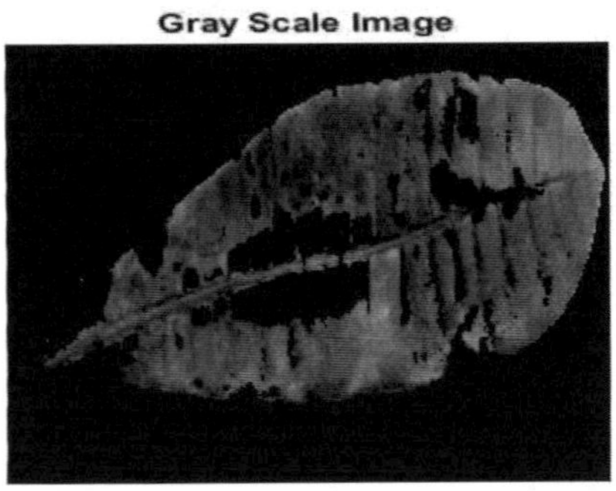

Figure 7. Gray scale image using cluster 2 and 45°co-occurrence angle

From figure 6 the cluster 2 image is transformed into the Gray scale image as shown in the figure 7. In which the disease part is more highlighted using the gray scale image and that image is used for the feature extraction using GLCM.

Case 2: The cluster size 3 and co-occurrence angle 60° using k-means clustering method.

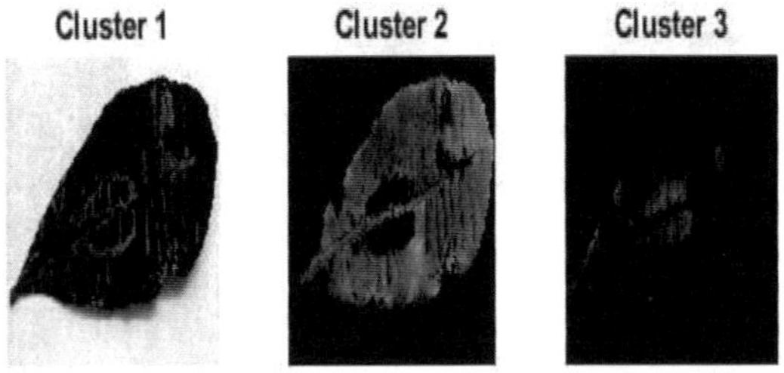

Figure 8. Cluster size 3 and 60°co-occurrence angle

The figure 8 shows the clusters of size 3. As compared to input image cluster 2 shows the smallest disease.

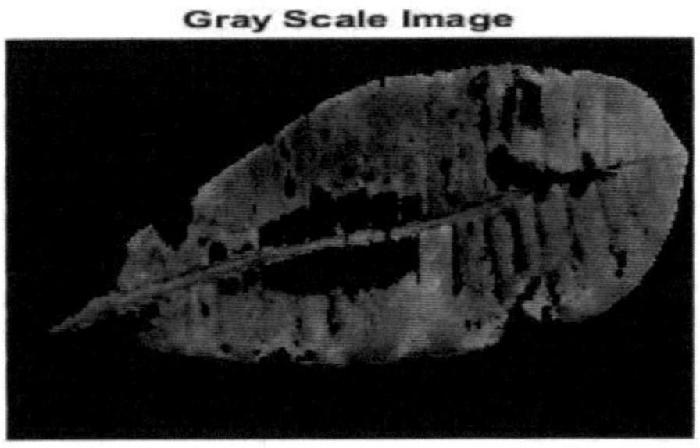

Figure 9. Gray scale image using cluster 2 and 60°co-occurrence angle

From the figure 8 the cluster 2 image is transformed into the Gray scale image as shown in the figure 9. In which the disease part is more highlighted using the gray scale.

Case 3: The cluster size 3 and co-occurrence angle 90° using k-means clustering method.

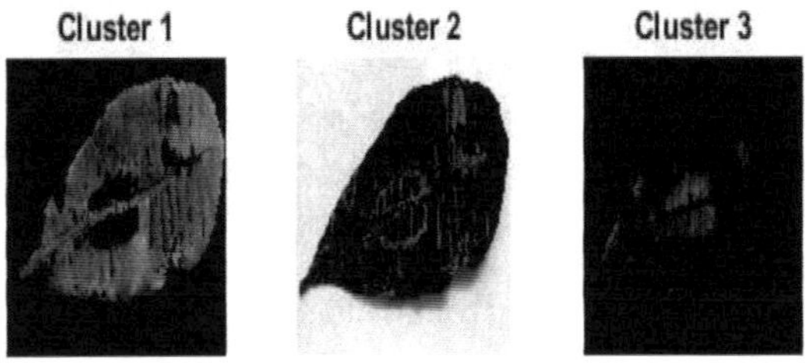

Figure 10. Cluster size 3 and 90 °co-occurrence angle

https://doi.org/10.1051/itmconf/20203203050

Figure 10 shows the clusters of size 3. As compared to figure 3, the cluster 1 shows the smallest disease.

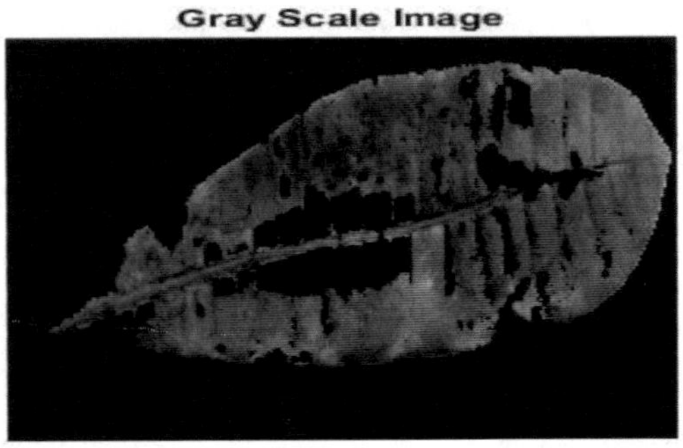

Figure 11. Gray scale image using cluster 1 and 90°co-occurrence angle

From figure 10, the cluster 1 image is transformed into the Gray scale image as shown in the figure 11. In which the disease part is more highlighted using the gray scale.

Case 4: The cluster size 3 of co-occurrence angle 180° using k-means clustering method.

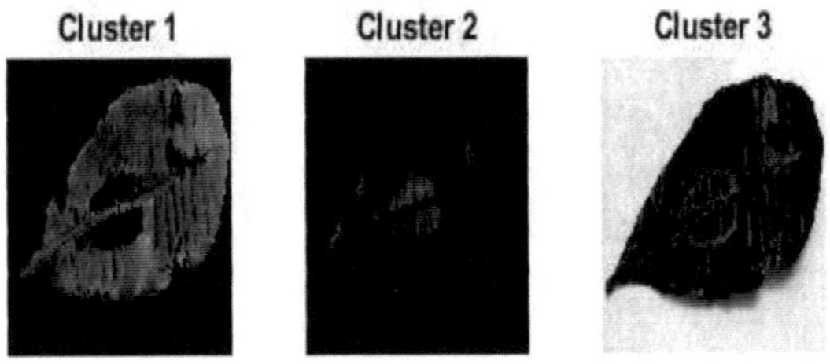

Figure 12. Cluster size 3 and 180 °co-occurrence angle

The figure 12 shows the clusters of size 3. As compared to input image in this the cluster 1 shows the smallest disease.

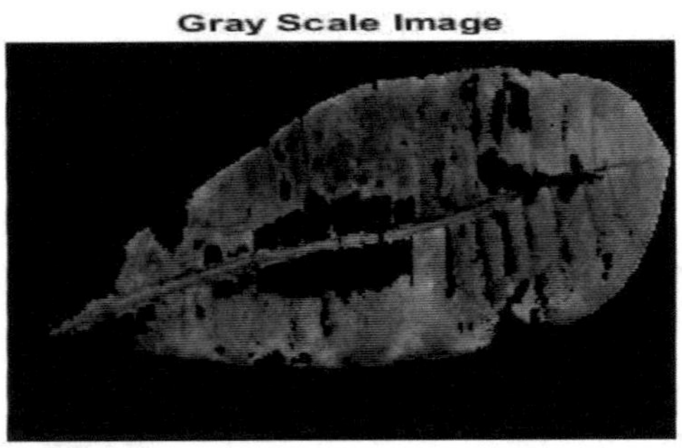

Figure 13. Gray scale image using cluster 1 and 180°co-occurrence angle

From the figure 12 the cluster 1 image is transformed into the Gray scale image as shown in the figure 13. In which the disease part is more highlighted using the gray scale.

Case 1 gives best results.

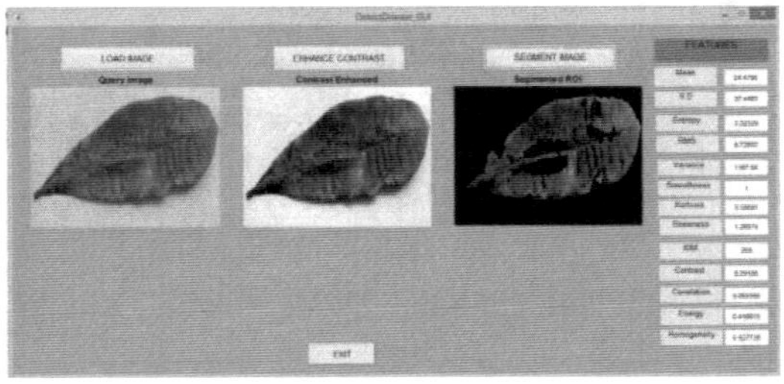

Figure 14. Segmented image from cluster 2 and extracted features using GLCM

After selecting the cluster 2 of co-occurrence angle 45° the segmented image is shown in GUI window as shown in figure 14. The features are extracted using gray level co-occurrence matrix method are shown in window as shown in figure 14. Using this features we classified the type of disease and accuracy.

In following table 1 the feature extraction formulas are given, using that formulas the values of the 13 features are calculated.

Table 1: Features Extraction Formulas and their values from Cluster size 3 of cluster 2 for co-occurrence matrix

No	Features	Formula	values
1	Contrast	$\sum n \sum m \|n-m\|2\ p(n, m, d, \theta)$	0.29185
2	Correlation	$\sum_{n,m} \frac{(n-\mu)(m-\mu)p(n,m)}{n\sigma_n,\ \sigma_m m}$	0.865556
3	Energy	$\sum n \sum m\ p(n, m, d, \theta)2$	0.416815
4	Homogeneity	$\sum n \sum m \frac{p(n,m,d,\theta)}{(1+\|n-m\|)}$	0.927735
5	Mean	$\frac{1}{(M)} Y_i$	24.4796
6	Standard Deviation	$\frac{1}{(M)} \sum_{(Y_i-\mu)} 1/2$	37.4463
7	Entropy	*-sum (p.*log2 (p))*	3.32329
8	RMS	$\sqrt{(Y1)^2+(Y2)^2+\cdots+(Yn)^2}/N$	8.72952
9	Variance	$\frac{1}{(M)} \sum (Y_i-\mu)^2$	1167.84
10	Kurtosis	$\frac{\frac{1}{N}\sum_{j=1}^{M}(Y_j-Y)^4}{(\frac{1}{N}\sum_{j=1}^{N}(Y_j-Y)^2))\hat{}2}$	3.38699
11	Skewness	$\frac{\frac{1}{M}\sum_{j}^{M}=(Y_j-Y)^3}{(\frac{1}{M}\sum_{j=1}^{M}(Y_j-Y')^2)\hat{}3/2}$	1.26074
12	IDM	$\sum_n \sum_m \frac{1}{1+(n-m^2)} p(n,m)$	255
13	Smoothness	*1-(1/(1+a))*	1

4 Conclusion

By K means clustering and GLCM technique the disease is identified at its initial stage. Thus pest control tools can be used to work out the problem. This paper is focused on using Co-occurrence method for getting accurate image of clusters and for the feature extraction. In this paper we are using altered size of clusters like 3, 6, 8 and 10. In cluster size 3 we get better results as compared to the other size of clusters. In the cluster size 3 disease is identified. Also we are using different theta angles like 45°, -45°, 30°, 60°,90°, and 180°. The better results are obtained in 45°, 60°, 90°, and 180°. In this paper we are using co-occurrence angle 45° and cluster size 3. In GLCM output, the part of the disease is highlighted. It only detect the infected area in the leaf.

References

1. G. S.Tumang ,Pests and Diseases Identification in Mango using MATLAB , IEEE, (2019)
2. S.A.Hussain,R.Hasan,S. J. Hussain ,Classsification and Detection of Plant Disease using Feature Extraction Methods,IJAER ,pp.4219-4226, **13**,Number 6,(2018).
3. G. Bhogade, R. Mawal, A. Patil, S. R. Desai,Leaf Disease Identification using Image Procesing, IJESC, **7**, Issue Number 5,(2017)
4. J. Sethupathy, Veni S., OpenCV Based Disease Identification of Mango Leaves, IJET,Oct- ,Volume8,Number5, DOI:10.21817/ijet/2016/v8i5/160805417(2016).
5. Saradhambal.G, Dhivya.R, Latha.S., ,R.Rajesh, Plant Disease Detection And Solution Using Image Classification, International Journal of Pune and Applied Mathematics,**119**,Number 14,pp879-884(2018)
6. S.Raut, A. Fulsunge ,Plant Disease Detection in Image Processing Using MATLAB,IJIRSET,**6**,Issue Number 6, DOI:10.156 80/IJIRSET.2017.0606034(2017)

Hardware Implementation of Sobel Edge Detection Algorithm

Ankita Pujare[1], *Priyanka* Sawant[2], *Hema* Sharma[3], and *Khushboo* Pichhode[4]

[1]email: ankitapujare304@gmail.com
[2]email: priyankasawant623@gmail.com
[3]email: hemasharma81298@gmail.com
[4]email: khushboo.pichhode@rait.ac.in

Abstract. In the fields of image processing, feature detection, the edge detection is an important aspect. For detection of sharp changes in the properties of an image, edges are recognized as important factors which provides more information or data regarding the analysis of an image. In this work coding of various edge detection algorithms such as Sobel, Canny, etc. have been done on the MATLAB software, also this work is implemented on the FPGA Nexys 4 DDR board. The results are then displayed on a VGA screen. The implementation of this work using Verilog language of FPGA has been executed on Vivado 18.2 software tool.
Keywords – FPGA, Image Processing, MATLAB, Edge detection.

1 Introduction

Image processing is a process to carry out some algorithms on a picture , thus to obtain an intensified image and to abstract helpful charactreristics from an image. In this process image is taken as input and characteristics that we want to extract are obtained as output. The approach for finding the margins of an objects in an image is simply referred as edge detection. It operates by diagnosing discontinuities in the intesity of light. In fields like digital image processing, machine vision and computer vision the edge detection method is utilized for extraction of features and segmentation of an image [1].

FPGA is a microcircuit which will be programmed within the area after manufacturing. FPGAs have greater potential application than, programmable ROM (PROM) chips. Because of their structure is in spatial and paralellel way, they are used in real time image processing as implementation platform [2].

The aim of this work is to analyze SOBEL and CANNY edge detection algorithms. The Sobel algorithm is applicable in image processing and computer vision, where it works on the method of approximation of derivative of an image. It is named after Irwin Sobel and Gary Feldman. Sobel algorithm checks the image horizontally and vertically and compute a discrete approximation to the derivative of each pixel. The gradient vector is the result of Sobel operator is stored at respective pixel of image matrix. The image is convolved with the kernal matrix and stores the value of gradient at corrosponding pixel. It is hence comparatively economical in means of calculations. On the contrary , the derivative results that it generates are comparatively unprocessed [3].

The Canny edge detector is a multi-stage detection algorithm which can detect broad range of edges with supresion of noise in an images. In 1986 it is discovered by John. F. Canny. He has given a theory of computation of edge detection with the explaination of why the technique works [4].

Canny Edge Detector is considered to be the most efficient edge detector. The canny edge detector is a multistage edge detection algorithm. The steps are Preprocessing, Calculating gradients, Nonmaximum suppression, Thresholding with hysterysis. The two key parameters of the algorithm are an upper threshold and a lower threshold. The upper threshold is used to mark edges that are definitely edges. The lower threshold is to find faint pixels that are actually a part of an edge [1].

The significant increase in processing speed is the major motivation behind hardware image processing. FPGA based design is inherently parallel in nature. FPGA has logic gates, large memory, fast transceivers, analog interfaces, and multicore processors. Due to this the speed of execution increases and it consumes low power too [5].

The primary objective of this work is to match various sorts of edge detection algorithms, analyze the results and find the efficient edge detection algorithm. The aim of finding out sharp changes in intensity of image is to collect significant events. Because of parallel processing the simulation speed is more.

In this work we are implementing digital image processing algorithms. It allows different types of algorithms to be executed on the input file whereas analog image processing doesn't allow so much. It restricts the problems like the of noise and unwanted signal which generally occurs in processing. In this work we are using FPGA boards which have many advantages like faster time to plug , parallel task performance, adaptibility, real time applications.

The rest of the paper is organized as follows. In section 2 literature survey of detection of edge using Sobel and Canny operator is discussed. In section 3 basic concept of edge detection algorithms like Robert Cross Operator, Sobel Operator, Prewitt Operator, Canny Operator is presented briefly. In section 4, flowchart of our work is given. In Section 5, the MATLAB results of sobel, canny and prewitt operators are given along side the implementation of Sobel algorithm on FPGA and therefore the output obtained on VGA screen. Finally, in section 6 we analyze the results and conclusions.

2 Literature Survey

In [6] the authors have applied edge detection algorithm on images taken by Binocular Microscope. In [7] the authors have implemented Sobel and Canny algorithms on X-ray images of teeth to find its edges. In [8] the author applied various types of edge detection algorithm in Robot assembly system and compared the results. In [9] the edges of license plate has been compared using different image enhancement filters. The objective of [10] is to provide an algorithm for obtaining the edges in medical field. In [11] authors have applied efficient edge detection on real time video processing using FPGA. In [12] authors have implemented parallel architecture of Sobel edge detection in FPGA. [13] deals with model based approach by performing edge detection using FPGA. In [14] authors have implemented real time canny edge detection using FPGA. In [15] authors have implemented of real time color image edge detection.

In [16] by sensing the data from forward looking optical and active W-band radar sensors, the boundaries of road and lane has been detected automatically. In [17] author described the detection and coding of visually important edges which leads to a new edge detection system. [18] deals with edge detection SAR images for road network extraction. [19] distinguishes the surface temprature by applying edge detection on the satellite images. In [20] authors have implemented Fuzzy sets of X-ray images by detecting the edges . [21] deals with mathematical morphology of medical images. [22] uses Xilinx system generator for implementing FPGA on MRI image filtering and tumor characteristics. [23] uses fusion of colors and edge information to detect and locate the people in video image. [24] describes scan line approximation by detecting the edge. In [25] based on unsupervised classification of edge authors have implemented detection of text in an image.

3 Edge detection algorithms

To identify and locate sudden changes in an image, the edge detection method is used.In simple words it is used to determine local change in the intensity of an image or the gradient of an image intensity. In image processing areas edge detection is an elemntary mechanism used to get the characteristics or data from the pixel. The process of edge detection has been used by object recognition, target tracking, segmentation, data compression, image reconstruction and so on. The original image is transformed into edge image by using edge detection method by introducing grey effect in the image [26].

The different kinds of edge detection algorithms are explained as follows:

3.1 Robert Cross Operator

To perform simple, easy and quick to compute gradient of an image, the Robert Cross Algorithm is generally used.This operator utilizes a pair of 2X2 convolution masks (1). One kernel or mask is rotated by 90 degrees of other. Thus it calculates the value of gradient by using diagonal direction approach.The approximated absolute value of the gradient is shown in the result at each pixel [27].

$$G_x = \begin{bmatrix} -1 & 0 \\ 0 & 1 \end{bmatrix} \quad G_y = \begin{bmatrix} 0 & -1 \\ 1 & 0 \end{bmatrix} \tag{1}$$

3.2 Sobel Operator

Gradient of thr image intensity ia calculated by Sobel operator at each pont. In first derivative of an image, the sobel operator searches for maximum and minimum gradient values. The gradient has certain magnitude as well as direction. The value of gradient of the pixel is then calculated in a black and white image. It uses 2 kernels with 2 directions i.e. x and y [28].

They are also known as convolution masks. If A is the image matrix and horizontal and verical kernels which carry out the convolution are G_x and G_y shown in (2).

$$G_x = \begin{bmatrix} -1 & 0 & 1 \\ -2 & 0 & 2 \\ -1 & 0 & 1 \end{bmatrix} \quad G_y = \begin{bmatrix} -1 & -2 & -1 \\ 0 & 0 & 0 \\ 1 & 2 & 1 \end{bmatrix} \tag{2}$$

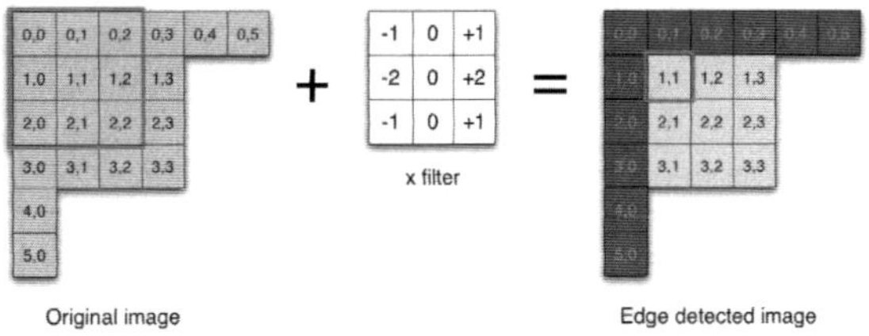

Figure 1. Sobel operator [29] .

3.3 Prewitt Operator

Prewitt operator has the same equation that are used by sobel operator with the constant c=1. The mask for Prewitt operator is shown in (3) . It is analogous to Sobel operator.It is computationally less expensive and faster method for edge detection. These operators are only applicable for noiseless and well contrasted image.Thus it is sensitive to noise, and are imprecise [30].

$$G_x = \begin{bmatrix} 0 & 1 & 1 \\ -1 & 0 & 1 \\ -1 & -1 & 0 \end{bmatrix} \quad G_y = \begin{bmatrix} -1 & -1 & 0 \\ -1 & 0 & 1 \\ -1 & -1 & 0 \end{bmatrix} \tag{3}$$

 https://doi.org/10.1051/itmconf/20203203051

3.4 Canny Operator

The objective of Canny Edge Detection Algorithm is to reduce the amount of noise present in detected image. It is the optimal algorithm among the all algorithms mentoined above. The three main characteristics of the canny edge detection are as follows:

- Low error rate: Non-edge should not be appeared in detected image or edge occurring in image should not be missed.
- Good Localization: The distance between the actual edge and detected edge must be less.
- Single Response: There shouldn't be many responses for a single edge [31].

The process of canny edge algorithm is divided into four steps:

1. Smoothing: The removal of noise or unwanted signal from an image is called as Smoothing.For this purpose Gaussian filter is applied. The Gaussian filter with size 5x5 is used to filter out the unwanted edges or signal. The filter is convolved with an image matrix to reduce the effect of false detection.
2. Finding gradient: To find out the value of gradient of pixel, canny edge detector uses any operator like prewitt, robert or sobel. In both horizontal and vertical direction, it calculates the value of first derivative and returns to that corresponding pixel. Along with edge gradient, direction of an edge has taken under consideration.
3. Non maximum suppression: Appearance of sharp and thin lines in detected image corresponds to the greater efficiency. Thus this step is used for edge thinning purpose. According to the third criteria, single edge must have single response. Thus this process removes the unwanted pixels which should not be appeared as an edge.
4. Hysteresis: Mostly all edge detection operators use only one threshold but canny uses double threshold. To store the high gradient value pixel and remove the low gradient value pixel in order to get the more accurate real edges, double threshold is used named as upper and lower. The edges that are going to express or supress is defined by two thresholds and conditions for that are as follows:

   - The edge will express only if its value is more than upper threshold.
   - The edge will suppress only if its value is less than lower threshold.
   - If the pixel value lies in between two thresholds i.e. upper and lower, then edge will only expressed if it is connected to another edge which has higher value of pixel than upper threshold [7].

4 Flow chart

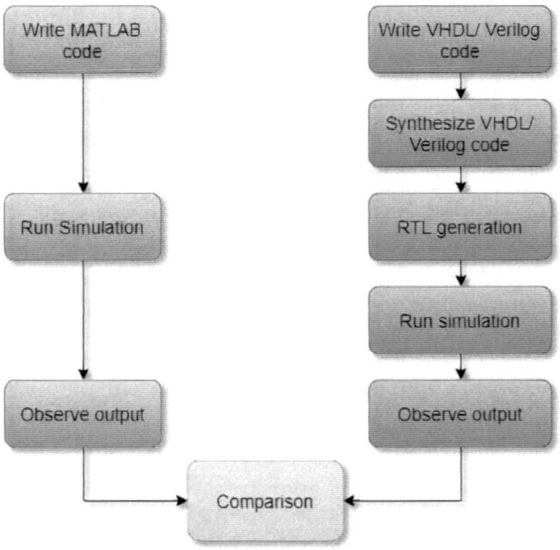

Figure 2. Flow chart.

Our work is divided in two parts as follows:

1. MATLAB simulation:

   In this part firstly we have written Matlab code for Sobel and Canny algorithms. Using that code we run the simulation on MATLAB software. After this step we got output for SOBEL and CANNY. We observed the outputs and compared the results of both the algorithms.

2. FPGA implementaion:

   In this part we have written Verilog code for Sobel algorithm in Vivado software tool. For Image Processing on FPGA following steps are executed as shown in Figure 3.

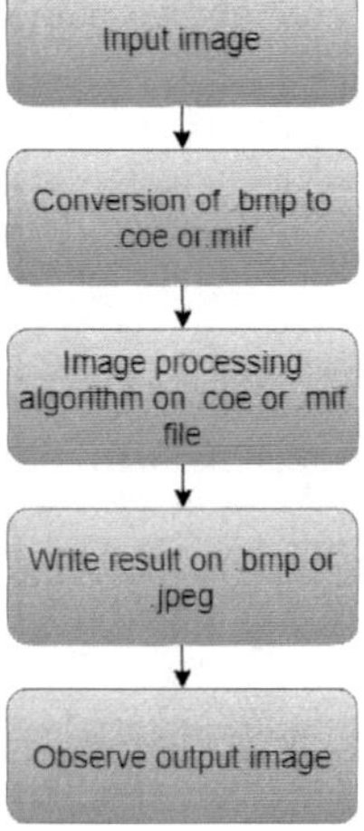

Figure 3. Processing of Image using FPGA.

https://doi.org/10.1051/itmconf/20203203051

Firstly we have to convert original image file which is in jpeg or bmp format in coe, mif or txt format. For our project we have converted jpeg file into coe file. After this image processing algorithm is applied on the image. The output file is again converted into jpeg or bmp format to see the output.

After this step we have sythesized the Verilog code for Sobel algorithm on Vivado software tool and generated RTL design. Then we implemented it on Nexys 4 DDR FPGA board. Then we observed the output on VGA screen and comapred with the MATLAB output.

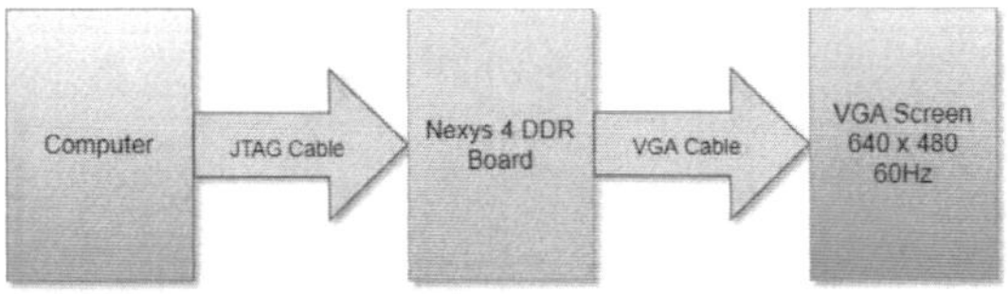

Figure 4. Block diagram of the work.

Figure 4 shows the block diagram of the work. In computer Verilog code for edge detection is run using Vivado software tool. It is then transferred to Nexys 4 DDR Board using JTAG cable. After successfully implementing the code the output is obtained on VGA screen through VGA Cable.

5 Result

5.1 MATLAB Result

The original image is shown in Figure 5. Sobel, Canny and Prewitt edge detection operator simulation outputs are shown in Figure 6, Figure 7 and Figure 8 respectively.

Figure 5. Original Image.

Figure 6. MATLAB result of Sobel Operator.

Figure 7. MATLAB result of Canny Operator.

Figure 8. MATLAB result of Prewitt Operator.

5.2 FPGA Result

Sobel edge detection algorithm has been implemented on FPGA using Nexys 4 DDR board and Vivado 18.1 software.

Figure 9. Interfacing of Nexys 4 DDR board with VGA.

Figure 10. Interfacing of original image with Nexys 4 DDR board.

Figure 11. Result of Sobel Operator on VGA.

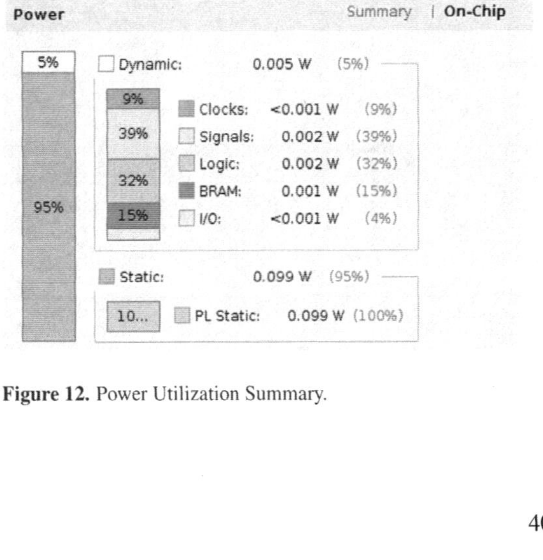

Figure 12. Power Utilization Summary.

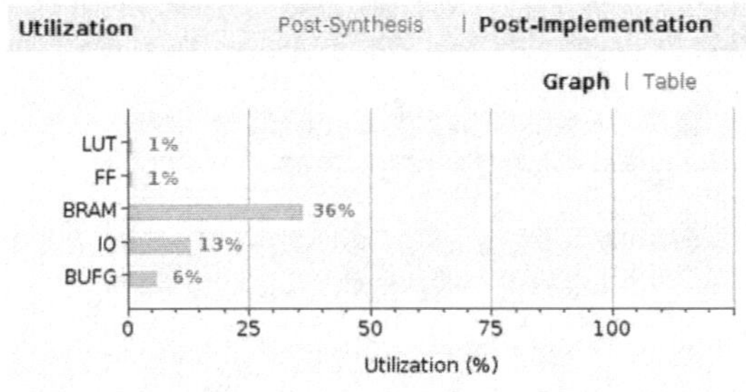

Figure 13. Device Utilization Summary.

6 Conclusion

From the MATLAB result, we have observed that Canny operator produces sharp edge with the smooth continuous pixels. Sobel and Prewitt edge detection algorithms cannot produce sharp edges as compared to Canny algorithm. From our analysis, output obtained by Canny operator is better than the output of Sobel and Prewitt edge detection operators. Also we have implemented Sobel algorithm on Nexys 4 DDR FPGA board and compared the results with MATLAB results.

6.1 Future Scope

Further we can implement this operation for Canny algorithm as well. Real time image processing is also possible using Camera.

References

[1] Anbarjafari, G. "Introduction to image processing." Digital Image Processing. University of Tartu, Tartu (2014).

[2] AlAli, Mohammad I., Khaldoon M. Mhaidat, and Inad A. Aljarrah. "Implementing image processing algorithms in FPGA hardware." 2013 IEEE Jordan Conference on Applied Electrical Engineering and Computing Technologies (AEECT). IEEE, 2013.

[3] Agrawal, Shivam S., and Amol S. Bendmali. "Enhanced Depth Video Coding for 3D videos."

[4] Dey, Nilanjan, Amira Ashour, and Prasenjit Kr Patra, eds. Feature detectors and motion detection in video processing. IGI Global, 2016.

[5] Trimberger, Stephen M., and Jason J. Moore. "FPGA security: Motivations, features, and applications." Proceedings of the IEEE 102.8 (2014): 1248-1265.

[6] H. Xiang, B. Yan, Q. Cai and G. Zou, "An edge detection algorithm based-on Sobel operator for images captured by binocular microscope," 2011 International Conference on Electrical and Control Engineering, Yichang, 2011, pp. 980-982.

[7] M. R. M. Razali, N. S. Ahmad, R. Hassan, Z. M. Zaki and W. Ismail, "Sobel and Canny Edges Segmentations for the Dental Age Assessment," 2014 International Conference on Computer Assisted System in Health, Kuala Lumpur, 2014, pp. 62-66.

[8] Balabantaray, Bunil and Jha, Panchanand and Biswal, Bibhuti. (2013). Application of Edge Detection Algorithm for Vision Guided Robotics Assembly System. Proceedings of SPIE - The International Society for Optical Engineering. 10.1117/12.2051303.

[9] Musoromy, Z., Ramalingam, S. and Bekooy, N., 2010, December. Edge detection comparison for license plate detection. In 2010 11th International Conference on Control Automation Robotics and Vision (pp. 1133-1138). IEEE.

[10] Sharma, P., Diwakar, M. and Choudhary, S., 2012. Application of edge detection for brain tumor detection. International Journal of Computer Applications, 58(16).

[11] Neoh, H.S. and Hazanchuk, A., 2004. Adaptive edge detection for real-time video processing using FPGAs. Global Signal Processing, 7(3), pp.2-3.

[12] Sanduja, V. and Patial, R., 2012. Sobel edge detection using parallel architecture based on FPGA. International Journal of Applied Information Systems, 3(4), pp.20-24.

[13] Dash, P.K., Pujari, S. and Nayak, S., 2014, February. Implementation of edge detection using FPGA and model based approach. In International Conference on Information Communication and Embedded Systems (ICICES2014) (pp. 1-6). IEEE.

[14] Gentsos, C., Sotiropoulou, C.L., Nikolaidis, S. and Vassiliadis, N., 2010, December. Real-time canny edge detection parallel implementation for FPGAs. In 2010 17th IEEE International Conference on Electronics, Circuits and Systems (pp. 499-502). IEEE.

[15] Singh, S., Saini, A.K. and Saini, R., 2012. Real-time FPGA Based Implementation of Color Image Edge Detection. International Journal of Image, Graphics and Signal Processing, 4(12).

[16] Ma, B., Lakahmanan, S. and Hero, A., 1999, October. Road and lane edge detection with multisensor fusion methods. In Proceedings 1999 International Conference on Image Processing (Cat. 99CH36348) (Vol. 2, pp. 686-690). IEEE.

[17] Robinson, G.S., 1977. Edge detection by compass gradient masks. Computer graphics and image processing, 6(5), pp.492-501.

[18] Tupin, F., Maitre, H., Mangin, J.F., Nicolas, J.M. and Pechersky, E., 1998. Detection of linear features in SAR images: Application to road network extraction. IEEE transactions on geoscience and remote sensing, 36(2), pp.434-453.

[19] Shimada, T., Sakaida, F., Kawamura, H. and Okumura, T., 2005. Application of an edge detection method to satellite images for distinguishing sea surface temperature fronts near the Japanese coast. Remote sensing of environment, 98(1), pp.21-34.

[20] Pal, S.K. and King, R.A., 1983. On edge detection of X-ray images using fuzzy sets. IEEE Transactions on Pattern Analysis and Machine Intelligence, (1), pp.69-77.

[21] Yu-Qian, Z., Wei-Hua, G., Zhen-Cheng, C., Jing-Tian, T. and Ling-Yun, L., 2006, January. Medical images edge detection based on mathematical morphology. In 2005 IEEE engineering in medicine and biology 27th annual conference (pp. 6492-6495). IEEE.

[22] Christe, S.A., Vignesh, M. and Kandaswamy, A., 2012. An efficient FPGA implementation of MRI image filtering and tumor characterization using Xilinx system generator. arXiv preprint arXiv:1201.2542.

[23] Jabri, S., Duric, Z., Wechsler, H. and Rosenfeld, A., 2000, September. Detection and location of people in video images using adaptive fusion of color and edge information. In Proceedings 15th International Conference on Pattern Recognition. ICPR-2000 (Vol. 4, pp. 627-630). IEEE.

[24] Jiang, X. and Bunke, H., 1999. Edge detection in range images based on scan line approximation. Computer vision and image understanding, 73(2), pp.183-199.

[25] Kanopoulos, N., Vasanthavada, N. and Baker, R.L., 1988. Design of an image edge detection filter using the Sobel operator. IEEE Journal of solid-state circuits, 23(2), pp.358-367.

[26] Srinivas, B. L., and K. A. Jeevan. "Edge Detection Techniques for Image Segmentation." International Journal of Innovative Research in Computer and Communication Engineering 3.7 (2015): 288-292.

[27] Umamaheswari, C., R. Bhavani, and K. Thirunadana Sikamani. "Segmentation of Tiles Image Using Various Edge Detection Techniques." International Journal of Data Mining Techniques and Applications 4.1 (2015): 10-14.

[28] Taysi, Z. Cihan, A. Gokhan Yavuz, M. Amac Guvensan, and M. Elif Karsligil. "In situ image processing capabilities of ARM-based micro-controllers." Journal of real-time image processing 9, no. 1 (2014): 111-125.

[29] Elliott, K. (2019). Sobel Algorithm. [image] Available at: http://blog.saush.com/2011/04/20/edge-detection-with-the-sobel-operator-in-ruby/ [Accessed 31 Oct. 2019].

[30] Sembok, Tengku Mohd Tegku, et al. Digital libraries: Technology and management of indigenous knowledge for global access. Springer, 2003.

[31] NM, M. Chaithra, and KV Ramana Reddy. "Implementation of canny edge detection algorithm on fpga and displaying image through vga interface." International Journal of Engineering and Advanced Technology (IJEAT) 2.6 (2013): 243-247.

Implementation of Airy function using Graphics Processing Unit (GPU)

Yugesh C. Keluskar[1], Megha M. Navada[2], Chaitanya S. Jage[3] and Navin G. Singhaniya[4]
Department of Electronics Engineering,
Ramrao Adik Institute of Technology,
Nerul, Navi Mumbai.
Email : yugeshkeluskar.yk@gmail.com[1], meghanavada@gmail.com[2], chaitanya.jage@rait.ac.in[3], navin.singhaniya@rait.ac.in[4]

***Abstract*—Special mathematical functions are an integral part of Fractional Calculus, one of them is the Airy function. But it's a gruelling task for the processor as well as system that is constructed around the function when it comes to evaluating the special mathematical functions on an ordinary Central Processing Unit (CPU). The Parallel processing capabilities of a Graphics processing Unit (GPU) hence is used. In this paper GPU is used to get a speedup in time required, with respect to CPU time for evaluating the Airy function on its real domain. The objective of this paper is to provide a platform for computing the special functions which will accelerate the time required for obtaining the result and thus comparing the performance of numerical solution of Airy function using CPU and GPU.**

Keywords*- *GPU, CPU, Airy function, Speedup.

I. INTRODUCTION

Fractional calculus (FC) is a field of mathematics that deals with derivatives and integrals of arbitrary non-integer order. It is being used in engineering domain extensively due to its ability to model real-world systems more accurately than its integer order variant. It is a topic which is around 320 years old!. The inception of this field can be attributed to a letter written to Guillaume de l'Hopital by Gottfried Leibniz in the year 1695 in which he mentions about fractional order derivatives, see [26], one can also find the foundational work of Fractional calculus in the early papers of Niels Henrik Abel [27]. But due to its mathematically intricate and cumbersome nature it remained mostly unexplored for many years until 1974 when the "First Conference on Fractional Calculus and its Applications" was held at the University of New Haven,Connecticut [28]. In recent years applications of this are growing nowadays in a rapid manner as there is a community of researchers that have came together to revive this field with the help of when advanced computing technology [1],[2]. As mentioned before using this mathematical technique, the scope of describing a real object is more accurate as compared to the classical integer-order methods. The replacement of integer orders with fractional orders has resulted into various realistic and compact model in the field of various physical, engineering, automation, biomedical, chemical engineering according to the mention made in this book [13], The function can be called a "Special Function" only when it has the ability to be useful in some applications and satisfies certain special properties. Some commonly used special functions are Gamma, Gauss Hypergeometric, Airy, Bessel,etc [2].

Airy function is the solution to Airy differential equation,which has the following form [22]:

$$\frac{d^2y}{dx^2} = xy \tag{1}$$

It has its applications in classical physics and mainly quantum physics. The Airy function also appears as the solution to many other differential equations related to elasticity, heat equation, the Orr-Sommerfield equation, etc in case of classical physics. While in the case of Quantum physics,the most well-known application of this equation is while solving WKB approximation problem [3],[24]. Taking a few steps we can arrive at the Airy Differential equation as given below. The following is the One-Dimensional Time Independent Schrödinger's equation

$$\frac{-\hbar^2}{2m}\frac{d^2\psi(x)}{dx^2} + V(x)\psi(x) = En\psi(x) \tag{2}$$

Where $\psi(x)$ is the wave-function, $\hbar$ is the reduced Planck's constant (Dirac constant), m being mass of the particle, $V(x)$ is the potential function and E is the total energy. This equation basically says that Kinetic Energy + Potential Energy = Total Energy, and that is what each term in this equation signifies. When we consider a triangular potential well i.e $V(x) = q\varepsilon x$ (q is charge of particle and ε is the electric field strength), we arrive at the following equation

For $x > 0$, $n = 1, 2, ..$

$$\frac{-\hbar^2}{2m}\frac{d^2\psi(x)}{dx^2} + q\varepsilon x\psi(x) = En\psi(x) \tag{3}$$

The above equation is the same as equation (1) with some constant terms mugging up the equation of which the Airy function is the solution. Hence we can say that for the Schrödinger equation with triangular potential well's case the solution is Airy function. However, to our knowledge, the computational complexity of such Special Mathematical Functions included in the fractional calculus increases when long time vectors are considered while implementing. It is interesting to make a platform which will allow us to speedup the performance rate and thus use it in various hardware implementations of the functions. This process cannot be automated as the definition of the function is supposed to be written from scratch by a human, hence human intervention is required. For this purpose the concept of parallel computing plays a crucial role. In parallel computing, many arithmetic and logical operations are carried out simultaneously using multi-core processors. Traditionally, parallel computing has been carried out using the CPU with a handful of cores. But, we are using the capabilities of multi-core graphics processors for parallel computing.

Even though the original purpose of GPU is for graphics rendering, in recent years the GPU is increasingly being used for scientific computations. This practice of using GPU for general purpose computations is called General Purpose Computing on Graphics Processing Unit (GPGPU) Technology. In paper [4] a parallel GPU solution of the Caputo fractional reaction-diffusion equation in one spatial dimension with explicit finite difference approximation has been provided. The optimized GPU solution obtained is faster than the optimized parallel CPU solution. So the power of parallel computing on GPU for solving fractional applications can be recognized. The paper, see [5] gives a description of the numerical approach that has been done for the evolution of algorithms which can do multiple operations in a given time, in order to solve the fractional differential equations. The procedure accepted is to fit the existing numerical schemes and to develop model parallel algorithms by utilising Parallel Computing toolbox of MATLAB. Unlike CPU, Graphics Processing Unit has parallel arrays of hundreds of smaller processors which function in parallel. We have utilised this parallel architecture of GPU to accelerate the execution of the above mentioned special function. The solution methods for fractional differential equations are not present. This absence is the main reason behind using the models of integer-order. In recent years, the field Fractional Calculus and its applications have drawn the interest of many authors.

The rest of the paper is organized as follows: In section 2, the basic concept of Airy function has been presented briefly. In section 3, a detailed explanation of GPU architecture has been written which also includes the tools for MATLAB computing with GPU. Section 4 represents the implementation steps which were performed while designing the algorithm. Finally all the results are given in section 5 and the conclusions drawn from this work are presented in section 6.

II. Basic Concept of Airy Function

The Airy function is named after Sir George Bidell Airy [3].He stumbled upon this following integral while calculating the intensity of light in the neighbourhood of a caustic. For this purpose, he introduced the function defined by the integral given below

$$W(m) = \int_0^\infty cos(\frac{\pi}{2}(w^2 - mw))dw \qquad (4)$$

which is now called the Airy function. $W(m)$ is the solution of the differential equation

$$W'' = -\frac{\pi^2}{12}mW$$

The numerical calculation of Airy function was very tricky back in those days and even nowadays it is so. But in 1838, the values of W for m varying from -4.0 to 4.0 were given by Airy and in the year it was given for values ranging from -5.6 to 5.6. The problem which arose was that the series converges slowly as m increases [3]. In 1982, a scientist named Jeffrey's introduced the notation $Ai(x)$ which is used nowadays as

$$Ai(x) = \frac{1}{\pi}\int_0^\infty cos(\frac{t^3}{2} + xt)dt \qquad (5)$$

Two linearly independent solutions of equation (1) which are real when x is real are $Ai(x)$ and $Bi(x)$. For the function $Bi(x)$, the integral representation is,

$$Bi(x) = \frac{1}{\pi}\int_0^\infty e^{\frac{-t^3}{3+xt}} + sin(\frac{t^3}{3} + xt)dt \qquad (6)$$

The solutions $Ai(x)$ and $Bi(x)$ satisfy the initial conditions

$$Ai(0) = \frac{3^{\frac{2}{3}}}{\Gamma(\frac{2}{3})} \qquad (7)$$

$$Bi(0) = \frac{3^{\frac{-1}{6}}}{\Gamma(\frac{2}{3})} \qquad (8)$$

Also the behaviour of the first kind of Airy function which is $Ai(x)$ can be described as follows:

For negative values, it has an oscillatory behaviour while for positive values, it exponentially decays. It is also observed that there is an interesting and unique smooth transition between the oscillatory behaviour and exponential decay without any abrupt change in the transition.

For the 2nd kind of Airy function $Bi(x)$ the behaviour for negative values is the same as the 1st kind but it is with a phase shift of $\frac{\pi}{2}$ and for positive values it grows exponentially. Airy function is related to Bessel Functions [25] of non integer order of first kind $J_\alpha(x)$ and to non integer order of modified Bessel function $I_\alpha(x)$ and $K_\alpha(x)$ of order $\frac{1}{3}$ which is implemented with change of the variable $\zeta = \frac{2}{3}x^{\frac{3}{2}}$. The relation between Airy functions and Bessel functions for $x > 0$ is given as

$$Ai(x) = \frac{1}{\pi}\sqrt{\frac{x}{3}}K_{\frac{1}{3}}(\frac{2}{3}x^{\frac{3}{2}}) \qquad (9)$$

$$Bi(x) = \sqrt{\frac{x}{3}}(I_{\frac{1}{3}}(\frac{2}{3}x^{\frac{3}{2}}) + I_{-\frac{1}{3}}(\frac{2}{3}x^{\frac{3}{2}})) \qquad (10)$$

For the values of $x < 0$, the functions $Ai(x)$ and $Bi(x)$ are given by

$$Ai(-x) = \sqrt{\frac{x}{9}}(J_{\frac{1}{3}}(\frac{2}{3}x^{\frac{3}{2}}) + J_{-\frac{1}{3}}(\frac{2}{3}x^{\frac{3}{2}})) \qquad (11)$$

$$Bi(-x) = \sqrt{\frac{x}{3}}(J_{\frac{1}{3}}(\frac{2}{3}x^{\frac{3}{2}}) - J_{-\frac{1}{3}}(\frac{2}{3}x^{\frac{3}{2}})) \qquad (12)$$

While computing the time required for implementation of these functions in CPU as well as GPU, the definitions of Airy function which we used were the one with Bessel and modified Bessel function (In this experiment every function was written in a different subroutine). The reason behind doing so is simple. For calculating Airy function using the integral definition we have to depend on integration techniques like Runge–Kutta–Fehlberg method to get desired accuracy [29]. Contrary to it by using Bessel functions we eliminate the use of numerical integration as the definition of Bessel functions used for computing Airy function are in terms of a power series [14]. The Bessel function of the first kind $J_\alpha(x)$ and Modified Bessel function of non-integer order $I_\alpha(x)$ and $K_\alpha(x)$ used in Airy function are defined as

$$J_\alpha(x) = \sum_{m=0}^{\infty} \frac{(-1)^m}{m!\Gamma(m+\alpha+1)} (\frac{x}{2})^{2m+\alpha}$$

$$I_\alpha(x) = (\frac{x}{2})^\alpha \sum_{k=0}^{\infty} \frac{(\frac{x^2}{4})^k}{k!\Gamma(k+\alpha+1)}$$

$$K_\alpha(x) = \frac{\pi}{2} \frac{I_{-\alpha}(x) - I_\alpha(x)}{\sin(\alpha\pi)}$$

Here Γ(x) is the Gamma Function. The Bessel functions have there applications in Fluid dynamics, Electrodynamics and mainly in Acoustics [25].

III. Graphics Processing Unit (GPU)

Graphic rendering is all about compute intensiveness and highly parallel computation. These are the features or specialization of Graphic Processor unit or GPU [6]. The process of generation of an image from a 2D or 3D model by means of computer programs is called rendering. This process needs a huge number of calculations to be performed in fraction of seconds. GPU has developed gradually into a highly parallel and multi threaded processor which consists of many cores. The computational horsepower of GPU is enormous and also it has high memory bandwidth. The floating point capability of GPU and CPU has inconsistency between them. Not only this but there are also differences between the architecture of GPU and traditional CPU. The CPU provides more resources to make single instruction execute faster, whereas the GPU makes use of hundreds of individual processing elements (cores) to execute single instruction on multiple data elements (elements in array) in parallel [2]. It is designed in such a way that more transistors are devoted to data processing rather than data caching and flow control.

To get a speedup in computation time, the applications consisting of large data sets make use of the platform of data parallel programming, the applications of processing of image and media which includes the post-process of image synthesis, video encoding and decoding, resizing of a digital image, stereo vision and automated recognition of patterns and regularities in data which maps the image blocks and pixels to parallel processing threads.It is quite obvious that a GPU will take less time for computing as compared to CPU, but the catch is to write a program by utilising special function/subroutines

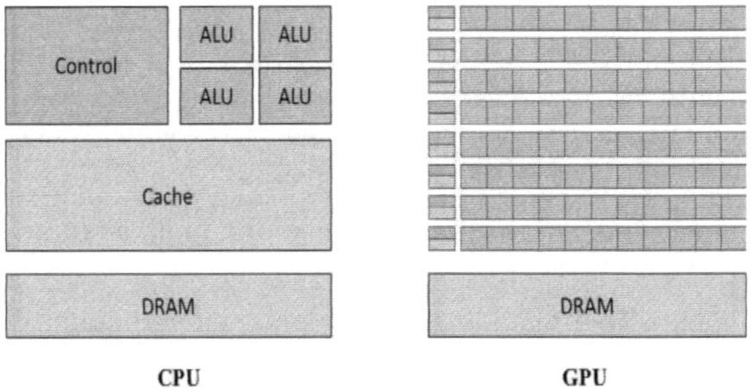

Figure 1: GPU architecture.

in such a way that it uses GPU architecture efficiently. In fact, acceleration is provided by data parallel processing for the algorithms which are present outside the field of rendering and processing of image. The GPU used in order to carry out the work represented in this paper is NVIDIA Tesla K80.

Specifications of NVIDIA Tesla K80 GPU

The following are the GPU device specifications used during computing and evaluating the Airy function.

Table I: NVIDIA Tesla K80 GPU specifications.

Parameters	Specifications
Peak Double Precision Floating point precision	2.91 Tflops
Peak Single Precision Floating point precision	8.74 Tflops
Memory Bandwidth(ECC Off)	480GB/sec
Memory size and Type	24GB GDDR5
CUDA corecores	4992
Thermal solution	Passive heat sink

Computation of GPU using MATLAB

The Matrix Laboratory, MATLAB is a programming platform constructed especially for engineers and scientists. It makes use of the MATLAB language, a matrix based language, granting the most logical expression of computational mathematics. MATLAB is used by millions of engineers worldwide. The reason behind its usage is to analyse and design the systems and products for revolutionizing our world. As MATLAB's operation is on whole matrices and arrays, it is one of the efficient ways to express computational mathematics. For envision and to obtain the insights from data, built in graphics are utilised which furthermore makes it an easy job. The desktop environment (DE) gives an opportunity to experiment, analyse and discover. These tools of MATLAB and its effectiveness are all precisely tested and constructed to work together [7]. Parallel Computing Toolbox present in MATLAB lets one to solve computationally and data-intensive problems using multi core processors like GPUs. Some of the High level constructs like parallel for loops and parallelized numerical algorithms enables us to parallelize MATLAB applications. The toolbox allows one to use the full processing power of multi core desktops by executing applications on workers that run locally [8]. The Parallel Computing Toolbox (PCT)

https://doi.org/10.1051/itmconf/20203203052

requires the NVIDIA CUDA enabled device with compute capability of 1.3 or greater [2].

IV. Design Of implementation

Some of the functions used while computing in GPU are as follows:

- gpuArray: This function is used to transfer the input data from MATLAB workspace to GPU. This function converts the array in the MATLAB workspace into a gpuArray object [8].
- gather: For transferring the data from GPU to MATLAB workspace this function is used. The gather function is used after all the operations on the data are performed by GPU.
- gpuDevice: For displaying the properties of the currently selected GPU device, the command gpuDevice is used.

Following are the steps to be followed while running a MATLAB code on GPU:

1) Start with the correct code which gives appropriate results.
2) Perform Vectorization of the code.
3) Profile the code using Run and Time function.
4) Variables should be transferred to GPU memory using gpuArray() function.
5) After the execution of code is done the output variables must be transferred to CPU memory by using gather() function.

The definitions of Airy function used while implementing it are as follows:

Ai(x) =

$$\begin{cases} \sqrt{\frac{x}{9}}(J_{\frac{1}{3}}(\frac{2}{3}x^{\frac{3}{2}}) + J_{-\frac{1}{3}}(\frac{2}{3}x^{\frac{3}{2}})) & ,x<0 \\ \frac{3^{\frac{2}{3}}}{\Gamma(\frac{2}{3})} & ,x=0 \\ \frac{1}{\pi}\sqrt{\frac{x}{3}}K_{\frac{1}{3}}(\frac{2}{3}x^{\frac{3}{2}}) & ,x>0 \end{cases}$$

Bi(x) =

$$\begin{cases} \sqrt{\frac{x}{3}}(J_{\frac{1}{3}}(\frac{2}{3}x^{\frac{3}{2}}) - J_{-\frac{1}{3}}(\frac{2}{3}x^{\frac{3}{2}})) & ,x<0 \\ \frac{3^{\frac{-1}{6}}}{\Gamma(\frac{2}{3})} & ,x=0 \\ \sqrt{\frac{x}{3}}(I_{\frac{1}{3}}(\frac{2}{3}x^{\frac{3}{2}}) + I_{-\frac{1}{3}}(\frac{2}{3}x^{\frac{3}{2}})) & ,x>0 \end{cases}$$

The following algorithm represents steps of implementation of Airy function:

1) Start with the definition of Airy function used.
2) Write a pseudo-code for the function on paper.
3) Write the actual code for the function in MATLAB and obtain the output.
4) Do the calculations of Airy function using Bessel function manually.
5) Compare the output thus obtained with that of MATLAB's result.
6) If the answer is not of the desired precision, make the necessary changes in the code.
7) Prepare a vectorized code for the same (for GPU).
8) Dump the code in GPU and thus calculate the time required for implementation.
9) On calculating the time required for the same code in CPU, obtain the Speedup parameter by using the following formula:

$$Speedup = \frac{CPUTime(T_c)}{GPUTime(T_g)} \tag{13}$$

10) Compile and analyse the results.

The Airy function is implemented on CPU and similarly on GPU by following the steps given in the above algorithm. Vectorization of code is important while implementing the function in GPU because it eliminates loops which are sequentially executed. All the operations performed on the data transferred to GPU memory are executed on GPU in parallel by using MATLAB's PCT. The above algorithm can be generalized for any function.

V. Results and Analysis

In this section a rigorous comparative study of computation time required for evaluating the Airy function on NVIDIA Tesla K80 CPU and GPU is presented. It should be taken into account that both functions (Airy function of first kind and second kind) were evaluated on total 9 test input in ascending order as shown in table 2 and 3 for 10000 times on CPU as well as GPU, and the computational time was noted down for both platforms. After that a mean was calculated for each input and listed in tables below. The reason behind doing so is to eliminate any statistical anomaly or error that might have occurred unknowingly while calculating the computation time. At last the Speedup parameter is calculated by the formula given in the algorithm described in section 4.

The following two tables present the computational time and the Speedup parameter for the purpose as discussed above. The table 2 is for $Ai(x)$ and table 3 is for $Bi(x)$. We can infer from table 2 that for $Ai(x)$ the Speedup parameter calculated using the device used in this experiment gives an improvement in computation time (for largest input) of around 2.667 times the computation time required for the CPU to evaluate the same function with the same input on GPU. This is the crux of using GPUs multi-core architecture instead of single or dual core CPUs. Similarly for $Bi(x)$ the table 3 shows that the calculated Speedup parameter is around 2.601 for the same system as mentioned above. The Speedup parameter depends on various factors that can decrease its value. As mentioned in section 2, for every function a different subroutine was used to evaluate the code, because of the complexity of the Airy function it calculates a total of 5 subroutines to evaluate the final $Ai(x)$ or $Bi(x)$ value. The function was not hardcoded (implementing Bessel and Airy functions into one single subroutine) as in real world application where this function might be used there would be an existing definition of the Bessel function.

Table II: Speedup parameter for Airy function of first kind.

Argument for $Ai(x)$	CPU Time (T_c in ms)	GPU Time (T_g in ms)	Speedup
1	0.494	0.186	2.655913978
2	0.475	0.184	2.581521739
3	0.474	0.183	2.590163934
4	0.473	0.182	2.598901099
5	0.473	0.181	2.613259669
10	0.467	0.181	2.580110497
50	0.455	0.177	2.570621469
100	0.447	0.174	2.568965517
1000	0.448	0.168	2.666666667

Table III: Speedup parameter for Airy function of Second kind.

Argument for $Bi(x)$	CPU Time (T_c in ms)	GPU Time (T_g in ms)	Speedup
1	0.468	0.191	2.450261783
2	0.463	0.190	2.436842105
3	0.461	0.189	2.439153439
4	0.460	0.185	2.486486486
5	0.457	0.184	2.483695652
10	0.453	0.180	2.516666667
50	0.450	0.176	2.556818182
100	0.447	0.173	2.583815029
1000	0.437	0.168	2.601190476

VI. Conclusion

The work which was carried out was the acceleration of computation of Airy function on GPU. The acceleration is obtained because of the presence of multiple processing cores in GPU. A validation for the function was set using MATLAB. The same code was transformed into vectorized version using Parallel Computing toolbox of MATLAB. From the results, it is observed that the computational time required for the execution is more in CPU as compared to GPU. Thus the Speedup parameter obtained is around 2 to 3 fold for Airy function when evaluated on systems with NVIDIA Tesla K80 GPU. From the results it may be concluded that Speedup parameter depends on the amount of data and number of iterations of an operation.

References

[1] V. Kiryakova, "The special functions of fractional calculus as generalized fractional calculus operators of some basic functions," Computers and Mathematics with Applications, vol. 59, no. 3, pp. 1128-1141, Feb. 2010

[2] Patil Parag,Singhaniya Navin,Jage Chaitanya,Vyawahare Vishwesh,Patil Mukesh and Paluri Nataraj. (2018). GPU Computing of Special Mathematical Functions used in Fractional Calculus. 10.2174/9781681085999118010011.

[3] Olivier Vallee and Manuel Soares - Airy function and applications in physics

[4] J. Liu, C. Gong, W. Bao, G. Tang, and Y. Jiang, "Solving the Caputo fractional reactiondiffusion equation on GPU", Discrete Dynamics in Nature and Society, Hindawi Publishing Corporation, vol. 2014, 2014.

[5] N. E. Banks, "Insights from the parallel implementation of efficient algorithms for the fractional calculus", University of Chester, United Kingdom, 2015

[6] Nvidia, CUDA C Programming Guide , Ver. 7.5, Sep. 2015. [Online]. Available: https://developer.nvidia.com/hpc

[7] "MATLAB Documentation" https://in.mathworks.com/help/matlab/

[8] Available:https://in.mathworks.com/help/parallel-computing/index.html'stid=CRUXlftnav

[9] "Predicting and Measuring Parallel Performance", February 1, 2012. [Online]. Available:https://software.intel.com

[10] "Parallel Computing", Wolfram Mathworld. [Online]. Available: http://mathworld.wolfram.com/ParallelComputing.html

[11] "Best Practices for MATLAB GPU Coding", Cornell University Center for Advanced Computing. [Online]. Available: https://www.cac.cornell.edu/matlab

[12] Ç. Uluişik and L. Sevgi, "A Tutorial on Bessel Functions and Numerical Evaluation of Bessel Integrals," in IEEE Antennas and Propagation Magazine, vol. 51, no. 6, pp. 222-233, Dec. 2009.

[13] Amparo Gil , Javier Segura , Nico M.Temme,"Numerical methods for special functions-Society for industrial and Applied Mathematics".

[14] B.K.Agarwal, Hari Prakash 2016,Quantum Mechanics,PHI,Delhi.

[15] A. K. Ghatak, R. L. Gallawa and I. C. Goyal,"Accurate solutions to Schrodinger's equation using modified Airy function," in IEEE Journal of Quantum Electronics, vol. 28, no. 2, pp. 400-403, Feb. 1992.

[16] B. Zhang, S. Xu, F. Zhang, Y. Bi and L. Huang ,"Accelerating MATLAB code using GPU:A review of tools and strategies". Artificial Intelligence, Management Science and ElectronicCommerce(AIMSEC):Dengleng, China, Aug. 2011.

[17] Fractional-order modeling of neutron transport in a nuclear reactor , by Vishwesh A.Vyawahare, P.S.V.Nataraj.

[18] G. Chen, G. Li, S. Pei and B. Wu, "High Performance Computing via a GPU" 2009 First International Conference on Information Science and Engineering, Nanjing, 2009, pp. 238-241.

[19] P. Sebah and X. Gourdon,"Introduction to the gamma function", American Journal of Scientific Research, Feb. 2002.

[20] D. W. Lozier, "NIST digital library of mathematical functions", Annals of Mathematics and Artificial Intelligence, Springer, May 2003.[Online]. Available:https://link.springer.com/article/

[21] E. Lindholm, J. Nickolls, S. Oberman and J. Montrym, "NVIDIA Tesla: A Unified Graphics and Computing Architecture," in IEEE Micro, vol. 28, no. 2, pp. 39-55, March-April 2008.

[22] Abramowitz, Milton; Stegun, Irene Ann, eds. (1983) [June 1964]. "Chapter 10". Handbook of Mathematical Functions with Formulas, Graphs, and Mathematical Tables. Applied Mathematics Series. 55 (Ninth reprint with additional corrections of tenth original printing with corrections (December 1972); first ed.). Washington D.C.; New York: United States Department of Commerce, National Bureau of Standards; Dover Publications. p. 446. ISBN 978-0-486-61272-0. LCCN 64-60036. MR 0167642. LCCN 65-12253.

[23] Digital Library of Mathematical Functions, *National Institute of Standards and Technology*, available at http://dlmf.nist.gov/.

[24] Donald A. Neamen,"Semiconductor Physics and Devices",chapter 2 - Introduction to Quantum theory of solids .

[25] K. Parand, M. Nikarya,Application of Bessel functions for solving differential and integro-differential equations of the fractional order,Applied Mathematical Modelling,Volume 38, Issues 15–16,2014,Pages 4137-4147,ISSN 0307-904X,https://doi.org/10.1016/j.apm.2014.02.001.

[26] Katugampola, Udita N. (15 October 2014). "A New Approach To Generalized Fractional Derivatives" (PDF). Bulletin of Mathematical Analysis and Applications. 6 (4): 1–15. arXiv:1106.0965. Bibcode:2011arXiv1106.0965K.

[27] Niels Henrik Abel (1823). "Oplösning af et par opgaver ved hjelp af bestemte integraler (Solution de quelques problèmes à l'aide d'intégrales définies, Solution of a couple of problems by means of definite integrals)" (PDF). Magazin for Naturvidenskaberne. Kristiania (Oslo): 55–68.

[28] Tenreiro Machado, José Kiryakova, Virginia Mainardi, Francesco. (2011). Recent history of fractional calculus. Communications in Nonlinear Science and Numerical Simulation - COMMUN NONLINEAR SCI NUMER SI. 16. 1140-1153. 10.1016/j.cnsns.2010.05.027.

[29] Kreyszig, Erwin. Advanced Engineering Mathematics. New York :Wiley, 1983.

[30] NVIDIA. (2015). TESLA K80 GPU ACCELERATOR - Board specifications [PDF file]. Available: https://www.nvidia.com/content/dam/en-zz/Solutions/Data-Center/tesla-product-literature/Tesla-K80-BoardSpec-07317-001-v05.pdf

EARLY PREDICTION MODEL FOR TYPE-2 DIABETES BASED ON LIFESTYLE

Kirti Hirnak[1,3,*], *Nikita* Chaudhari[2,**], *Akshay* Singh[3,***], and *Deepali* Patil[1,3,****]

[1]Department of Information Technology, Ramrao Adik Institute of Technology,Navi Mumbai, India
[2]Department of Information Technology, Ramrao Adik Institute of Technology,Navi Mumbai, India
[3]Department of Information Technology, Ramrao Adik Institute of Technology,Navi Mumbai, India
[4]Department of Information Technology, Ramrao Adik Institute of Technology,Navi Mumbai, India

Abstract. Nowadays diabetes has become a chronic disease that may cause many complications. There are some symptoms of diabetes such as increased appetite, blurry vision, and extreme fatigue, etc. As the increasing deformity in present years the number of diabetic patients from the whole world will reach to 642 million. Diabetes accuracy is very difficult to know so in order to cure this disease. These causes us to concentrate more there to make some changes that will reduce these numbers. So to minimize these numbers of diabetes, we researched various algorithms and methods. The proposed method focuses on extracting the attributes that gives a result in early detection of Diabetes Mellitus in patients. Various existing processes provide just a result as the patient has diabetes or not which will require the patients to visit a diagnostic centers or to a doctor. So we proposed a system based on deep learning approaches that will help to solve a serious problem. These systems take collaborative inputs from dataset to give prediction with random forest algorithm which gives more accurate results.

***Keywords*—** Diabetes Prediction, Random forest, Deep Learning, Convolutional neural network (CNN), Support Vector Machine (SVM), Data transformation.

1 Introduction

Diabetes is a common physiological health problem among humans across gender and age. Diabetes is an illness when sugar levels are high and diabetes is particularized by high blood glucose levels. This is known as hyperglycemia. In this case, the body is incompetent to produce enough insulin. Another perspective is the body cannot respond to the insulin produced. So diabetes is irretrievable; it has to be controlled.

Various types of diabetes may happen and dealing with the circumstance of diabetes relies upon the sort. All kinds of diabetes are not the cause of a person's overweight or lifestyle. In fact, some people have diabetes even before their childhood. Diabetes types are type 1 and type 2 diabetes. Type 1 diabetes which is additionally called adolescent diabetes, this sort happens when a body neglects to create insulin do type 1 diabetes people groups are insulin-subordinate. Type 2 diabetes is the most well-known diabetes as per the National Institute of Diabetes and Digestive and Kidney Diseases. Right now diabetes, the body can't utilize insulin effectively. That invigorates your pancreas to deliver more insulin until it can never again stay aware of interest. Insulin creation diminishes, which prompts high glucose. Different sorts are Gestational diabetes and prediabetes. In Gestational diabetes, this sort happens in ladies during pregnancy when the body can turn out to be less delicate to insulin. Gestational diabetes doesn't happen in all ladies and as a rule settle subsequent to conceiving an offspring. Prediabetes is a genuine well-being condition where glucose levels are higher than ordinary, yet not sufficiently high yet to be analyzed as type 2 diabetes.

A diabetes person can develop some hard complications namely heart attack and kidney failure. Globally, an estimated 463 million adults are living with diabetes, according to the latest 2019 data from the International Diabetes Federation. Diabetes prevalence is increasing rapidly; previous 2017 estimates put the number at 425 million people living with diabetes [1]. According to statistics in 2017, an estimated 8.8% of the global population has diabetes. This is likely to increase to 9.9% by the year 2045 [2]. India had a greater number of diabetics than some other nations on the planet, as per the International Diabetes Foundation. Diabetes as of now influences in excess of 62 million Indians, which is over 7.2% of the grown-up populace.

Right now, we will use the methods of deep learning, specifically - deep learning neural systems and convolutional neural systems, to propose a model for diabetes anticipation with high precision. Deep learning alludes to machine learning or it is a sub-some portion of machine learning. It is completely subject to the degree of

* e-mail: kirti50hirnak@gmail.com
** e-mail: nikitachaudhari863@gmail.com
*** e-mail: akshaysingh.mustang@gmail.com
**** e-mail: deepatli.patil@rait.ac.in

learning spoken to, significant level ideas are characterized from the low-level ideas, compared to the chain of importance of highlights, components, or ideas and the other way around [3]. It is different degrees of learning of portrayal, deliberation and breaking down the information that assists with understanding the information to be specific sound, and content, pictures. A deep learning structure comprises a multilayer perceptron with concealed layers.

The Random forest algorithm is the most acclaimed and it is an essential AI calculation. Random forest strategies give better accuracy and force. It create distinctive decision trees. Another algorithm used is Support Vector Machine. SVM is a lot of supervised AI models that are utilized in classification and relapse. The target of the support vector machine algorithm is to discover a N-dimensional space that unmistakably groups the information focuses.

2 Review Of Literature

Numerous works have been done related to the prediction of diabetes using different data mining techniques. The datasets, algorithms, methods used by the authors and observed results along with the future scope are carried out in finding out efficient methods of medical diagnosis for various types of diabetes diseases. Here research on diabetes prediction and detection has been carried out for several years.

Nahla Barakat. [4] discussed and designed an Intelligible Support Vector Machines for Diagnosis of Diabetes Mellitus. They did research on the diagnosis of diabetes mellitus by using the SVM algorithm and Rule-Extraction from SVMs. They used a dataset named as "National Survey of Diabetes data collected in Sultanate of Oman" which contains various types of samples like Fasting Venous, Oral Glucose Tolerance Test (OGTT), etc. The result of these algorithms predicts more accurate results, but there is a need for pre-prediction of diabetes to prevent or delay that disease.

Riccardo Miotto. [5] proposed the prediction of diabetes from the electronic health record. Utilized a novel framework which is called "deep patient". It was used to represent patients by a group of their general features, from a large-scale EHR database through a deep learning approach.

Ioannis Kavaliotis. [6] in this computational and structural journal, they covered aspects such as Prediction and Diagnosis, Diabetic Complications, Generic background environment, Health care, and management. They mentioned in their conclusion as in-depth exploration towards diagnosis, etipathophysiology, and treatment of diabetes mellitus have to do to prevent such disease.

Beata Strack. [7] proposed a framework dependent on the 'Wellbeing Facts database' a national information stockroom that gathers exhaustive clinical records. This dataset contains information efficiently gathered from taking an interest establishment's electronic clinical records and incorporates experience information (like a crisis, outpatient and inpatient), supplier strength, socioeconomics (like age, sex, and race), and determination and in-medical clinic mortality and emergency clinic attributes. This information is an implantation of 10 years of clinical consideration at 130 medical clinics. On this dataset they set some extraction criteria for e.g., length of the patient's stay at the medical clinic, research facility test performed, and so on as per these criteria they pick 30 days for readmission of patients to that emergency clinic. In that, they found a noteworthy connection between readmission likelihood of patients and HbA1c estimations. Toward the end they got the end as the estimation of HbA1c is required to lessen the readmission rates by giving legitimate prescriptions to every patient as per their HbA1c esteem.

Muhammad Atif Iqbal. [8] used data mining techniques that are widely used for the prediction of disease at an early stage. They performed prediction of diabetes using significant attributes with their different feature relationships are also featured. Used a variety of different tools to decide proper characteristic determination and for bunching, expectation, and affiliation rule digging for diabetes. Huge factor determination was made by the vital segment investigation technique.

Trang Pham. [9] presented DeepCare, an end-to-end deep dynamic memory neural network for personalized healthcare. This model is used to minimize extraction of required attributes from a huge dataset. DeepCare peruses clinical records, remembers ailment directions and care forms, appraises the present sickness states, and predicts the future hazard.

Akm Ashiquzzaman. [10] utilized the Neural Network and Deep Learning, an expectation framework for the malady of diabetes is introduced where the issue of overfitting is limited by utilizing the dropout strategy. A deep learning neural system is utilized where both completely associated layers are trailed by dropout layers. This model is utilized for estimating the sickness of diabetes. An epic type of profound neural system for diabetes guess with expanded precision. The yield execution of the proposed neural system appears to have beaten other condition-of-craftsmanship techniques and it is recorded as by a wide margin the best execution for the Pima Indians Diabetes Informational index.

Suyash Srivastava. [11] discussed machine learning, a part of Computerized reasoning is utilized to dissect and make the diabetes expectation model. Different scientists have likewise been done to anticipate the diabetes AI calculation, however this is an extra exertion in the exploration work dependent on a particular kind of patient in a particular network. Fake Neural System (ANN) was picked for building a model to foresee diabetes. This model is perfect for foreseeing the chance of diabetes with 92% exactness while trying with the example test information. This model can accomplish more exactness on the off chance that it trains with enormous examples preparing information later on.

But still, there is a need to predict diabetes at an early stage so that it will help us to prevent diabetes mellitus to occur in the future in the patient's life. That motivates us to build a system which predicts diabetes earlier.

3 Proposed System

Diabetic is a condition that occurs when blood glucose is too low and sugar level is too high. We proposed a model in predicting diabetes using deep learning. Deep learning is the kind of machine learning mainly based on Artificial Intelligence. The hidden layers of deep learning system do all these totally inside itself without including incidental specialists. The short portrayal of deep learning systems is given as underneath [2].

Initially, we did an analysis of existing systems that are available, but after analysis we came to know that there is a need for some real-time system that may overcome the drawbacks of an existing system. Then we searched for the dataset on which algorithms may performed. When enough information was gathered we began preprocessing information into a format that can be utilized for training purposes. When the information has been processed we start the training of our model with 70% of the complete information staying 30% will be used for testing purposes. When training of our model is finished we begin making a prediction model which will accept a few parameters as input and dependent on learning from the training informational index will give a prediction about missing parameters.

For prediction, we have used two different Algorithms Random Forest Algorithm and Support Vector Machine. In Random Forest we follow - select random samples from a given dataset, construct a decision tree for each sample and get a prediction result from each decision tree, perform a vote for each predicted result, select the prediction result with the most votes as the final prediction. While SVM follows - Generate hyperplanes which segregate the classes in the best way.

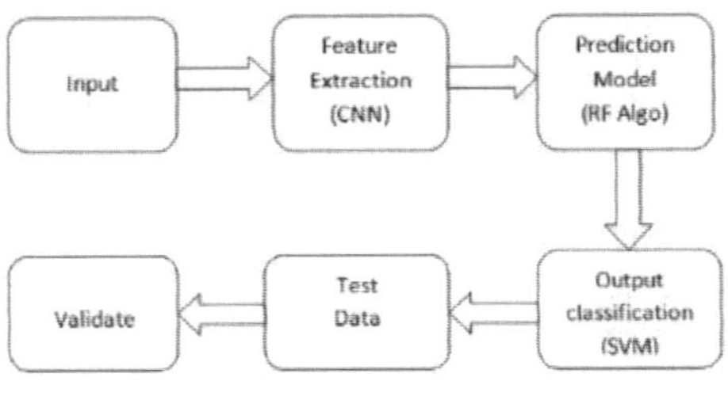

Figure 1. System flow diagram for the Deep Learning Model

Algorithms used to build the proposed system are described as follows :

3.1 Convolutional Neural Network (CNN)

A convolutional neural system (CNN) is a particular kind of artificial neural system that utilizes perceptrons, an machine learning unit calculation, for supervised learning, to break down information. CNNs have as of late been broadly utilized for some characterization and acknowledgment assignments too. In this manner, we chose these algorithm to assess their presentation for diabetes recognition to build up a choice emotionally supportive network. Extensive experiments were performed on our data set. CNN is generally made up of an input, an output layer and many hidden layers. There are 9 input layer neuron and 2 output layer neuron in proposed system. In the hidden layer 1 14 neurons and hidden layer 2 14 neurons.

3.2 Random Forest Algorithm

The Random forest algorithms is the most famous and it is a basic machine learning algorithm. Random forest techniques give better precision and power. More often than not the irregular backwoods creates better outcomes yet it is hard to enhance its exhibition and furthermore hard to deal with different sorts of information including numerical, ostensible and double information. Random forests develop different choice trees [8]. Random forest is one sort of Directed learning strategy which utilizes a gathering learning technique for characterization and relapse [16]. In Random forest, trees are run in equal so there is no collaboration between these trees while building the trees. In the Random forest technique consolidates the aftereffects of different expectations that total numerous choice trees, which is the reason it is known as a meta-estimator.

3.3 Support Vector Machine (SVM)

The Support vector machine classifies groups of data with the help of hyperplanes. It is good for binary classification of x versus other variables. SVM is a set of supervised machine learning models that are used in classification and regression. For example, if it is given two training classes, then the SVM classifier divides two clusters in a better way. For generalization purpose, one cluster should not lie closer to the data points belonging to the other cluster. It should be far away from other clusters of each type. The point occurs nearest to the margin of the classifier known as support vectors.

4 Methods and Materials

4.1 Data Preprocessing

Data preprocessing is the most important process in the data mining process. Data gathered from various sources has many missing values, null values, faulty values. These create more problems while analyzing the data. If more irrelevant and noisy data is present then it becomes difficult to apply any data mining or machine learning algorithm on such datasets. So to perform data preprocessing various tasks are performed named as: Cleaning, integration, transformation, reduction, and discretization [12].

4.2 Data cleaning

Data cleaning process comprises filling the missing qualities and expelling loud information. Loud information includes exceptions which are expelled to determine irregularities [13]. In the dataset, there are various parameters like weight, glucose, BMI, etc., which contains value as a zero. These values need to be replaced. Data cleaning replaces such values to some median values in the dataset.

4.3 Data reduction

Data reduction gets a diminished portrayal of the dataset, it is a lot liter in volume yet delivers the equivalent (or nearly the equivalent) result. Dimensionality reduction is utilized to diminish the quantity of characteristics in the dataset [14]. This task of preprocessing is used to extract required or proper attributes to the system.

4.4 Data transformation

Data transformation comprises smoothing, standardization and aggregation of information [15]. The dataset we are using has a lot of non numeric values that need to be numeric while training and model form. Converting non-numeric features into numeric. Matrix multiplication is not possible on a string, so we must convert the string to some numeric representation. Resizing inputs to a fixed size. Feed-forward neural networks and linear models have a fixed number of input nodes, so your input data always has the same size.

5 Results

The dataset used in this paper is originally taken from [7]. Wellbeing Facts is an unconstrained program offered to associations which utilize the Cerner Electronic Health Record System. The database contains parameters like age, gender, and patient ID glucose, hba1c, medical diagnosis, blood samples, etc. having total 50 parameters, which are used to predict diabetes earlier. To improve the prediction and to build a system more user-friendly we consider another dataset also which contains parameters of a patient's daily routine, diet plans, eating habits, etc. having a total 11 parameters. The combination of these parameters with previous dataset parameters gives output in a more appropriate way. This second dataset is taken from "Japan Medical Data Center (JMDC)", which is used in a medical research article [18].

Third dataset formed from the combination of above two datasets contains parameters namely Sex, Age, Blood Cholestrol, Heridatory, Smoking, Alcohol Intake, Physical Activity, Diet, Obesity, Stress, Glucose, Blood Pressure, Skin Thikness, Insuline, BMI, Medical Diagnosis and HbA1c. These are a few parameters which are really making numerous hazardous infections individuals nowadays.

Various deep learning algorithms are applied to the dataset that we used in our system and the results we get gives more accuracy than algorithms that were used in previous systems or research papers. The algorithms we ap- plied are SVM and Random Forest which build a model for training and testing separately for two separate algorithms. As a result, those models give two separate

Table 1. CONFUSION MATRIX OF SVM ALGORITHM

Actual/Predicted	Positive	Negative
True	135	1
False	3	61

Table 2. CONFUSION MATRIX OF SVM ALGORITHM (SIGMOID MODEL)

Actual/Predicted	Positive	Negative
True	126	10
False	5	59

Table 3. CONFUSION MATRIX OF RF ALGORITHM

Actual/Predicted	Positive	Negative
True	198	0
False	0	102

results but according to their accuracy system gives the prediction.

The performance of SVM and RF models can be represented by the confusion matrix on the dataset. The confusion matrix shown in Table.

SVM is a supervised machine learning model. Sup port vector machine is used to evaluate the accuracy. Results obtained from these algorithms are represented in a tabular way in the following tables. Table I represents the confusion matrix of a simple SVM algorithm. It splits the dataset into 80% of the training set and 20% testing set. Thus we get an accuracy of a normal SVM algorithm is upto 97%.

Table II represents the confusion matrix of the SVM algorithm with the sigmoidal model. As this algorithm is used for classification in our system it gives the accuracy upto 97%. SVM is used for the data points that need to be classified into groups which belong to the same groups called clusters.

Then we used the Random Forest model for predicting diabetes disease. Table III represents the confusion matrix of the RF algorithm. In the confusion matrix, we included TP, TN, FP, FN in that the case of true positive, the diabetes disease is predicted and the case of true negative, diabetes has not predicted. It splits the dataset into 70% of the training set and 30% testing set. Thus we get an accuracy of an RF algorithm us upto 100%.

6 Conclusion

Diabetes mellitus is quickly developing as one of the best worldwide wellbeing difficulties of the 21st century. Diabetes is a heterogeneous gathering of ailments. It's portrayed by the constant height of glucose in the blood. We identified and reviewed machine learning and deep learning approaches applied on diabetes research. We developed a web based system which gives the result that a patient may have diabetes or not in the future. We have arranged our preparation diabetes information to be dissected; utilizing a couple of lines of Python, we have prepared a model that is fit for anticipating whether an individual is probably going to have diabetes, giving a productive way to use clinical assets to recognize and treat the most noteworthy level of patients with diabetes. Results decide the sufficiency of the structured framework with an accomplished exactness of 97% utilizing Support Vector Machine (SVM) and by using the Random Forest Algorithm accomplished accuracy upto 100%, which provides a system with more accurate results. The advancement to this work will be suggestions that help patients to consult a doctor or some improved diet provided by system will be suitable.

References

[1] Hammoudeh, Ahmad and AlNaymat, Ghazi and Ghannam, Ibrahim and Obeid, Nadim, "Predicting Hospital Readmission among Diabetics using Deep Learning", The journal of The 5th International Symposium on Emerging Information, Communication and Networks, 2018.

[2] Goutham, Swapna and R, Vinayakumar and Kp, Soman, "Diabetes detection using deep learning algorithms", ICT Express. 4. 10.1016/j.icte.2018.10.005, 2018.

[3] Liu, Tianyi and Fang, Shuangsang and Zhao, Yuehui and Wang, Peng and Zhang, Jun.. "Implementation of Training Convolutional Neural Networks", Published on research gate article, 2015.

[4] N. Barakat, A. P. Bradley and M. N. H. Barakat, "Intelligible Support Vector Machines for Diagnosis of Diabetes Mellitus," in IEEE Transactions on Information Technology in Biomedicine, vol. 14, no. 4, pp. 1114-1120, July 2010.

[5] Miotto, Riccardo and Li, Li and Kidd, Brian, "Deep Patient: An Unsupervised Representation to Predict the Future of Patients from the Electronic Health Records" Scientific Reports. 6. 26094. 10.1038/srep26094, 2016.

[6] Ioannis Kavakiotis, Olga Tsave, Athanasios Salifoglou, Nicos Maglaveras, Ioannis Vla-Havas and Ioanna Chouvarda, "Machine Learning and Data Mining Methods in Diabetes Research" Computational and Structural Biotechnology Journal, 2017.

[7] Strack, Beata and Deshazo, Jonathan and Gennings, Chris and Olmo Ortiz, Juan Luis and Ventura, Sebastian and Cios, Krzysztof and Clore, John, "Impact of HbA1c Measurement on Hospital Readmission Rates: Analysis of 70,000 Clinical Database Patient Records", BioMed research international. 781670. 10.1155/2014/781670, 2014.

[8] Mahboob, Talha and Iqbal, Muahammad and Ali, Yasir and Wahab, Abdul and Ijaz, Safdar and Baig, Talha and Hussain, Ayaz and Malik, Muhammad and Mehdi, Muhammad and Ibrar, Salman and Abbas, Zunish, "A model for early prediction of diabetes. Informatics in Medicine Unlocked", 16. 100204. 10.1016/j.imu.2019.100204, 2019.

[9] Pham, Trang and Tran, Truyen and Phung, Dinh and Venkatesh, Svetha, "Predicting healthcare trajectories from medical records: A deep learning approach. Journal of Biomedical Informatics", 69. 10.1016/j.jbi.2017.04.001, 2017.

[10] Ashiquzzaman, Akm and Tushar, Abdul Kawsar and Islam, Dr. MD Rashedul and Shon, Dongkoo and Im, Kichang and Park, Jeong-Ho and Lim, Dong-Sun and Kim, Jongmyon, "Reduction of Overfitting in Diabetes Prediction Using Deep Learning Neural Network", Published on research gate article, 2017.

[11] Srivastava, Suyash and Sharma, Lokesh and Sharma, Vijeta and Kumar, Ajai and Darbari, Hemant, "Prediction of Diabetes Using Artificial Neural Network Approach", ICoEVCI 2018, India. 10.1007/978-981-13-1642-5-59, . 2019.

[12] Benhar H, Idri A, Fernández-Alemán J., "Data preprocessing for decision making in medical informatics: potential and analysis", World conference on information systems and technologies.p. 1208–18, 2018.

[13] Abidin NZ, Ismail AR, Emran NA., "Performance analysis of machine learning algorithms for missing value imputation", Int J Adv Comput Sci Appl ; 9:442–7, 2018.

[14] Liu, Huan and Motoda, Hiroshi , "Feature Selection for Knowledge Discovery and Data Mining", Kluwer Academic, USA. 10.1007/978-1-4615-5689-3, 2000.

[15] Malley B, Ramazzotti D, Wu J T-y, "Data preprocessing. Secondary analysis of electronic health records", Springer;. p. 115–41, 2016.

[16] VijayaKumar, K. Lavanya, B. Nirmala, I. Caroline, S, "Random Forest Algorithm for the Prediction of Diabetes", 1-5. 10.1109/ICSCAN.2019.8878802, 2019.

[17] Kaur, Harleen Kumari, Vinita, "Predictive Modelling and Analytics for Diabetes using a Machine Learning Approach. Applied Computing and Informatics", 10.1016/j.aci.2018.12.004, 2018.

[18] S. U. Amin, K. Agarwal and R. Beg, "Genetic neural network based data mining in prediction of heart disease using risk factors," 2013 IEEE Conference on Information Communication Technologies, Thuckalay, Tamil Nadu, India, pp. 1227-1231, 2013.

[19] Balaji, H. Iyenger, N Ch Sriman Narayana Caytiles, Ronnie., "Optimal Predictive analytics of Pima Diabetics using Deep Learning", International Journal of Database Theory and Application. 10. 47-62. 10.14257/ijdta..10.9.05, 2017.

https://doi.org/10.1051/itmconf/20203203054

Electronic Orientation Aid for Visually Impaired using Graphics Processing Unit (GPU)

Akshata Parab[1,1], *Rashmi* Nagare [2], *Omkar* Kolambekar[3], and *Parag* Patil[4]

[1]Department of Electronics Engineering, Ramrao Adik Institute of Technology, Nerul, India
[2]Department of Electronics Engineering, Ramrao Adik Institute of Technology, Nerul, India
[3] Department of Electronics Engineering, Ramrao Adik Institute of Technology, Nerul, India
[4] Department of Electronics Engineering, Ramrao Adik Institute of Technology, Nerul, India

Abstract. Vision is one of the very essential human senses and it plays a major role in human perception about surrounding environment. But for people with visual impairment their definition of vision is different. Visually impaired people are often unaware of dangers in front of them, even in familiar environment. This study proposes a real time guiding system for visually impaired people for solving their navigation problem and to travel without any difficulty. This system will help the visually impaired people by detecting the objects and giving necessary information about that object. This information may include what the object is, its location, its precision, distance from the visually impaired etc. All these information will be conveyed to the person through audio commands so that they can navigate freely anywhere anytime with no or minimal assistance. Object detection is done using You Only Look Once (YOLO) algorithm. As the process of capturing the video/images and sending it to the main module has to be carried at greater speed, Graphics Processing Unit (GPU) is used. This will help in enhancing the overall speed of the system and will help the visually Impaired to get the maximum necessary instructions as quickly as possible. The process starts from capturing the real time video, sending it for analysis and processing and get the calculated results. The results obtained from analysis are conveyed to user by means of hearing aid. As a result by this system the blind or the visually impaired people can visualize the surrounding environment and travel freely from source to destination on their own.

1 Introduction

Vision is the essential part of human biology, since 83% of human knowledge is perceived through eyes [3]. If that is the case, then in today's busy world it is very difficult for the visually impaired or blind people to navigate and travel alone. All regular tasks such as walking, reading, travelling, socializing are become inconvenient for visually impaired which makes their life difficult from the normal people. The traditional and oldest mobility aids for persons with visual impairments is the walking cane (also called white cane or stick) and guide dogs. However, the main pitfalls of these aids are expertise and preparation [5]. With the rapid advances in modern technology, it has given smart navigation capabilities both in the hardware and the software field. In recent years, extensive research work has been conducted to create aids for visually impaired people to interpret, guide and navigate in the surrounding environment. In this study a guidance system called Electronics Orientation Aid (EOA) is built to overcome their navigational challenges. This system allows obstacle detection and intimation of obstacle location which helps the visually impaired person to reach to the desired destination with greater awareness of the environment. The real time images of objects in the surrounding are used, and then from the captured images the objects are detected. Once the object has been identified, the user will be given some specifics such as what the object is, its location, whether or not it is a hindrance. Audio instructions are also given for the above mentioned information that will be heard by the visually impaired people, ensuring that they could visualize the objects in front and its location. As the capturing of the images and the processing has to be quick and in real time, there is a need to use the Graphics Processing Unit (GPU). Use of GPU speeds up the process of object detection and recognition. Thus using EOA, the user can travel on their own from source to destination with more ease.

This paper is organized as follows: Section I introduces the cause of this work and the brief study of literature is done in Section II is the motivation which led to the idea of this work. Section III defines the hardware organization of the entire project which will focus on the communication between different sub-systems included in our work. Similarly Section IV defines the design implementation of the system. The YOLO V3 algorithm used in EOA is explained in Section V. Section VI shows the detailed working mechanism of our study while the results are showcased in Section VII. Finally Section VIII concludes the work mentioning the future work in Section IX.

[1] Akshata Parab: parabakshata27sp@gmail.com

 https://doi.org/10.1051/itmconf/20203203054

2 Literature Survey

The visually impaired are the people who can lose vision permanently or temporarily. These people cannot see, read or write like normal people. According to the World Health Organization (WHO), 285 million people worldwide experience visual impairment, 39 million are blind and 246 have low sense of vision. Hence these people require an assistance by which they can visualize the outside world and live a normal life. Various research papers like "Wearable object detection system for the blind" by Alessandro Dionisi, Emilio Sardini, Mauro Serpelloni [11] and "A mobility aid for the blind with discrete distance indicator and hanging object detection" [2] explained the need to design a system which will provide an assistance to the visually impaired people to navigate freely from the source to destination with no or minimal help. Blind people are always dependent on others to cross road or to reach a particular address. Therefore, we build a system called EOA that will help them to carry out their activities like normal people to some extent. Various algorithms and measurements were studied from different papers like "Object Detection Based on YOLO Network" [2], "Real Time Object Detection, Tracking, and Distance and Motion Estimation based on Deep Learning: Application to Smart Mobility" [19] etc. that encouraged us to select the correct algorithm to carry out our work. This led us to complete our project with better understanding and guided us throughout the journey.

3 Hardware Organisation

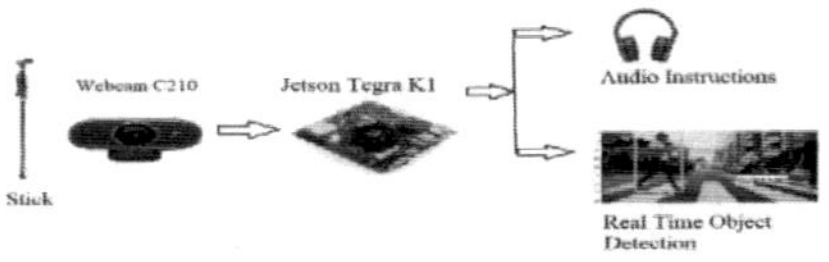

Figure 1. Flowchart depicting the hardware used in the work.

A. NVIDIA Jetson Tegra K1 (TK1): Jetson Tegra K1 is the first embedded graphics processor from NVIDIA. This is similar to modern GPU desktop with advanced features, but still uses less power (less than 6 W). The NVIDIA Jetson TK1 is a full featured package, which includes an integrated TK1 platform. This board gives us the power to utilize 192 CUDA cores for different technical applications such as robotics, computer vision, healthcare, automation, medicine and so on [7]. This board is supported by developer-friendly Ubuntu Linux software environment. The reason for choosing Jetson TK1 for our work includes its low power consumption, compact size and weight, parallel processing capability, etc. B. Logitech Web Camera: The webcam used in our work is Logitech C210. This camera is used to capture the real time video or image and send the captured images to jetson board for further analysis. The Logitech Webcam C210 features the ability to record 640x480 resolution in a 16:9 wide screen ratio with specification of 1.3 MP. This device offers impressive 720p resolution.

C. Bluetooth Headphones: After detection of the object, recognition of object and its location the final important task in this work is to convey this information to user in form of audio. For this we need bluetooth earphones or headphones that the visually impaired person will wear. Any bluetooth headphones pairable with Jetson TK1 can be used. In our project we have used bluetooth earphones that will be wirelessly connected to Jetson TK1. The purpose of using bluetooth earphones and not the wired is to reduce the hassle and make the design easy to carry.

4 Design Implementation

Computer vision is a field in which images can be captured, stored, analysed and understood. Here, the output is in the form of identification or mathematical measurements. The motive behind doing this is to make the necessary decisions based on the highly dynamic real time data and its analysis.

Computer vision is a field where understanding of human vision can be duplicated. Often referred to as image analysis [16]. The idea is to use computer vision for object detection, that could probably help the blind to visualize the surrounding environment better, using Image-to-Text and Text-to-Voice, without any complex hardware [18].

A. Object detection: Object detection is a computer vision operation that detects the images/videos and creates bounding boxes around them to locate that object. The annotated text on the bounding box can be translated into voice response and the fundamental positions of the objects can be provided from the perspective of the person's location. By recognizing the front objects and making them aware of the danger, the object sensing module in the system will help the blind to also provide a safe route to reach the destination [3].

B. Various algorithms for Object Detection: There are three main Object detection Algorithms and they are as follows:

Region-CNN (R-CNN): To solve the problem of selecting large number of regions, Ross Girshick et al. proposed a method is used to extract 2000 regions from an image called as region proposals. So, now instead of classifying huge no. of regions RCNN works only with 2000 regions. These 2000 region proposals are

https://doi.org/10.1051/itmconf/20203203054

generated using selective search algorithm [1]. 2000 region of proposals are bounded into square and fed into a convolutional neural network that produces a 4096 dimensional feature vector output.

Single Shot Detector (SSD): Object detection and classification tasks are performed in a single forward network pass. Multi Box bounding box regression technique is used in this. This method strikes a great balance between speed and precision. It runs a convolutionary network on an input image only once and computes a feature map. It predicts bounding boxes after multiple convolutionary layers in order to hold the scale. [2].

You Only Look Once (YOLO): Object detection is a task of computer vision involving the localisation of one or more objects within an image and the classification of each object in the image. It is a difficult computer vision function that includes both efficient position of objects to locate and draw a bounding box around each object in an image, and classification of objects to determine the appropriate type of object that has been identified. The solution involves a single deep neural network (originally a GoogleNet version, later revised and renamed DarkNet based on VGG).

4.1.1 You Only Look Once (YOLO):

YOLO is one of the quickest algorithms to detect objects. YOLO trains entire images and increases detection efficiency directly. All the earlier algorithms used to classify the object in the image using regions. Parts of the image which contain the object are highly likely. In YOLO the bounding boxes and class probabilities for these cases are determined by one single convolutionary network. YOLO's very quick. We simply run our CNN on a picture in order to forecast detections [3].

You Only Look Once (YOLO)[10], the computer vision device capable of detecting a range of objects in one image, with an accuracy similiar to RetinaNet, but with higher inferiority than with other existing systems, such as SS[11], R-FCN[12] and FPN FRCN[13]. Its speed makes it one of the most suitable real-time object detection systems used in systems such as robotic operations [4]. The algorithm processes the entire image, not only the region of its inferences, which reflects the overall context of the image, thus making it less likely to detect background content in an object, which enables its inferences to contemplate the overall significance of the image. YOLO has a unique, jointly trained pipeline. In contrast to other systems with different components, such as Faster RCNN [12], which must be training separately. It is widely used in real-time applications due to its tremendous speed. YOLO was one of the most popular algorithms for object detection. Some important things to know are:

YOLO takes an image and divides it into SxS grid, where S is a natural number.

Each pixel in the image causes a finite number (5 in our case) of boundary box estimates. The pixel is responsible for predicting when the centre of the object is found. Of all the boxes found, it is responsible for identifying only one object and the other identifiers are rejected.

It predicts C conditional class probabilities (one per class for the likeliness of the object class).

Total detections to be done per image= $SXS\ ((B * 5) + C)$
Where SXS = total number of images yolo divides the Input
B is the Number of Bounding boxes detected in the image.
For each bounding box, 5 elements are detected: Detected Objects, Centre coordinates(x, y), Height and Width, Confidence percentage.

C =Conditional probability for Number of Classes.

For example, if the image is divided in a $2x2$ grid, and 10 boxes are predicted with 3 classes (Bat, Ball, Gloves), we will have $2 * 2(10 * 5 + 3)$ predictions= 212 predictions.

4.2.1 Different Versions of YOLO:

YOLO requires a Neural Network framework for training and in this case we have used DarkNet.

YOLOv1: Version 1 has total 26 layers, with 24 Convolution Layers followed by two Fully Connected layers. The biggest problem with YOLOv1 is its inability to find the smallest things. Latter, 2 more versions for YOLO released.

YOLOv2: After each Conv layer there are batch normalization layers. Compared to YOLO v1 it has 30 layers. Introducing the anchor boxes. Anchor boxes are pre-defined boxes that a user gives the network an idea of how many things should be received on Darknet. A set of training materials should be used to calculate it. There is no fully connected layer. Of training photos from 320-608, fixed sizes were taken. Many labels can be given to same things, but still the problem with many symbols.YOLOv2 was still not efficient for small objects.

YOLOv3: In YOLOv3 there are 106 layers neural networks. The most important feature of YOLOv3 is that it makes detection at three different scales. It is fully conventional such that the output is obtained by applying 1x1 kernal on feature map.

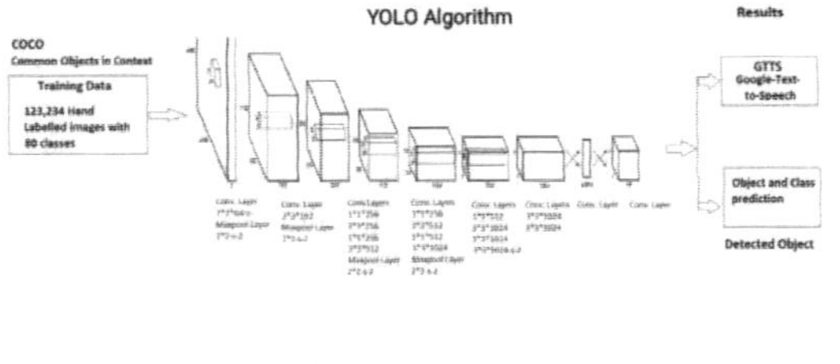

Figure 2. Flowchart depicting the YOLO Algorithm

4.1 YOLO Algorithm for Object Detection

- YOLO algorithm which passes the image through the complexities of a neural network architecture called Darknet [2].
- . Darknet is a neural C and CUDA based open source network architecture that is simple and easy to use and supports computation for CPU and GPU systems.
- In this proposed system YOLOv3 model which is more enhanced and complex is used.
- A pre-trained model Common Objects In Context (COCO) dataset is trained on yolov3 [1].
- Also, the python cv2 package has a method to setup Darknet from yolov3.cfg file.
- OpenCV is the computer vision library/ framework that we will be using to support our YOLOv3 algorithm. OpenCV has inbuilt support for Darknet Architecture [14].
- Darknet Architecture is a pre-trained 80 class platform. Our goal is to identify objects using Python language with Darknet (YOLOv3) in OpenCV.
- The input from the camera is used to feed images to this professional model at 3 frames/run.
- Then there is the calculation of various things such as identification of the detected object from the 80 class of the trained model. The measurement of the objects position is determined by its co-ordinates. This helps us to find where the object lies exactly. For example, "top/mid/bottom" or "left/centre/right".

Further the text is send to the Google-Text-To-Speech API using gTTs package

5 Working Mechanism

The working starts with the web camera. This camera captures the real time images. In other words, live video is read and is converted to individual frames. These frames are further analysed by Jetson TK1 board. From each frame the objects are detected. For the task of object detection the YOLO algorithm is used. If, objects are present in particular frame, the objects are captured and are passed through the layers of neural networks on which the YOLO algorithm works. The time for which the camera should record the video can be varied, and accordingly the frames will be captured. In our work we have kept 3 frames per shot, which collectively takes 28-35 seconds approximately. The 3 frames are read one after the other in continuation. The duration of object detection and recognition for each frame depends on how many objects are detected. If less number of objects are in front, then analysis period of particular frame will be short, if many objects are present then accordingly the period will increase. The captured images are transferred from one layer to another. This filters region of interest from the frame, where the object is present. Once the object is obtained, is compared with the COCO data set which is trained to identify 80 objects. This data set helps to identify the object which the user would be unaware of. Along with the identification, the position of that object is also calculated with respect to the centre of the frame i.e. whether the object is at top of the frame or mid or bottom. Similarly, if it lies at the right of frame or centre or left [19]. The accuracy of the detection is also mentioned. This shows how correctly the image is identified. This all calculations are done by mathematical formulas and equations. However, the distance of the object from the camera is calculated manually. The next and most important part of the system is the hearing mechanism. Without this the entire system would not be helpful for user. So now, all the detected objects along with their position, precision, distance is narrated to the user via bluetooth headphones. As a result, user will be more aware of the obstructions in front of them.

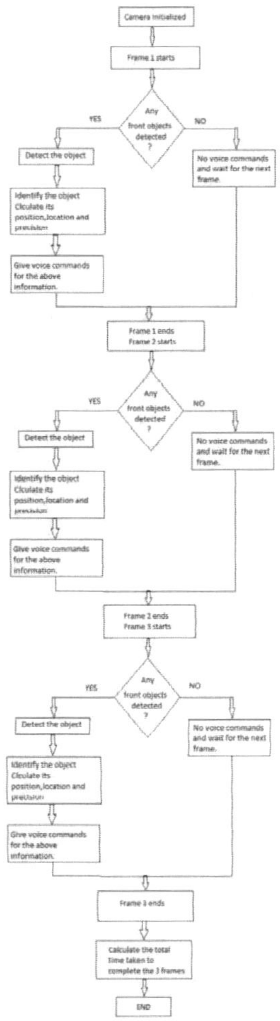

Figure 3.Working Mechanism Flowchart.

After the 3 frames are detected, identified, audio commands are given the total time is calculated. This total time

 https://doi.org/10.1051/itmconf/20203203054

represents the time from which Frame 1 has started to the end of the Frame 3 including giving of the audio commands. This time factor is of utmost important because this actually proves if this system will be useful to the blind person or not. Considering if this time factor came out to be very long then it would be of no use to the user as by that time another new object would come on the path of the blind person and accidents may happen. So any delay in any process can put the life of the visually impaired in danger. Hence, the time taken should be as small as possible. For this, we are using GPU. With GPU the process of detection becomes fast and subsequently all the process will be rapid giving quick responses and fast audio commands to the visually impaired or the blind person.

6 Results

After taking a number of trials we could capture and detect various objects along with their position and precision. The results are shown below:

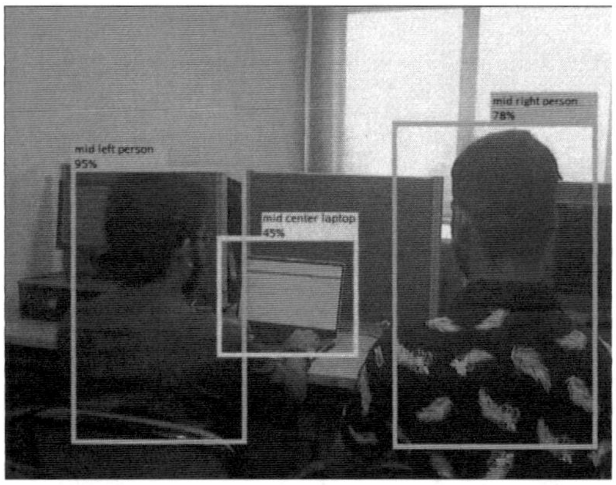

Figure 4. The output of YOLO algorithm for Frame-1.

Figure 5. The output of YOLO algorithm for Frame-2.

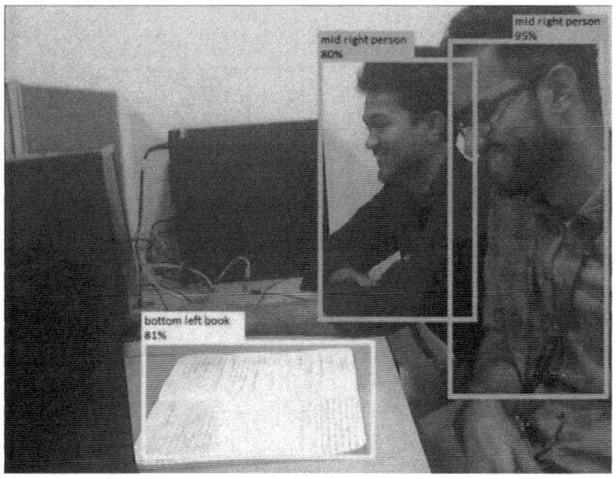

Figure 6. The output of YOLO algorithm for Frame-2.

The table below shows the analysis of the obtained results that gives the clear picture of our working.

Sr. No.	Detected Object	Position	Accuracy	Range
1	Person	Mid Left	90%	3.5 feet
2	Person	Mid Right	78%	3 feet
3	Laptop	Mid Centre	45%	4.1 feet

Table I. The summary of output generated for frame 1.

Sr. No.	Detected Object	Position	Accuracy	Range
1	Person	Mid Left	92%	5.4 Feet
2	Bottle	Mid Left	79%	7.1 Feet
3	TV monitor	Top Right	88%	7.2 Feet

Table II. The Summary of output generated for frame 2.

Sr. No.	Detected Object	Position	Accuracy	Range
1	Person	Mid Right	95%	2.2 Feet
2	Book	Bottom Left	87%	2.4 Feet
3	Person	Mid Right	80%	2.6 Feet

Table III. The summary of output generated for frame 3.

As soon as the camera is initialized, it starts recording. From Figure 4 it is observed that the algorithm has detected 3 objects which are as follows: 1 person, 1 bottle and 1 TV monitor. All 3 are located at different positions. As shown in figure 4, 1 person is located at the bottom of the horizontal axis and at centre of the vertical axis. Secondly, the bottle is at the middle of the horizontal axis and to the left of the vertical axis. Lastly the TV monitor lies at the top of the horizontal axis and to the left of the vertical axis. All these positions are determined considering the distance of the object with respect to the centre co-ordinates. For Frame-2 all these objects along with their positions are detected which is tabulated in the Table II. The output also showcases the precision. This indicates the accuracy with which the algorithm has detected the objects from the image. For the Frame-2, we get the precision for the object person as 92% which tells that the detected object is 96% truly a person. Similarly, object bottle is 79% correctly detected and the precision of the object TV monitor as per detection is 88%. The next important factor of this work is the distance. Distance is very important as it is the prime parameter which will determine the maximum distance from which object can be detected and recognized. This distance is the distance of the object from the camera. The camera will be mounted on the stick and the objects will be in front. Here, for Frame-2 the person is at the distance of 5.4 feet from the camera, the bottle is at the distance of 7.1 feet while the TV monitor is at the distance of 7.2 feet. All these distances are measured manually. Now, all this information is converted into audio. As an output, the user will be able to hear the class/identity of the object along with its position. So for example in case of Frame-2, the user will be able to hear the following audio: *"Bottom Centre Person", "Mid Left Bottle", "Top left TV monitor".*

All this will be heard one after the other in continuation with no breaks in between. After the audio for this frame is heard, again the next frame begins and again the objects are detected, analysed and the audio for that frame is heard.

Thus the overall flow of the project is summarized as follows:

1) Camera is initialized.

2) Frame-1 is started at t =0.

3) For Frame-1, objects are detected, the class of the object is identified along with its location and precision.

4) The audio of the above mentioned information is heard by the visually impaired.

5) Frame-2 starts repeating the same steps as that for Frame-1, giving the corresponding audio output.

6) Finally, at the end of the Frame-3 we get the total time taken by the process to complete 3 frames. Here, Frame3 ends at t =28.29 seconds.

The time measurement is with the help of Time Module of python. This enables initializing a timer using start and stop commands as per requirement. The total time refers to the time from which the camera is initialized to capture the image till the time at which the 3rd frame ends. So at t =0 the Frame-1 starts and the Frame-3 ends its detection at t =28.29 seconds. As the objects are detected it is immediately converted to audio through text-to-speech. So this time is the combination of the object detection, object identification and hearing of the audio.

It can be understood that time factor should be as small as possible. Because "time" factor reflects how long it will take for the user to get the audio. Therefore, it is very important that the entire process right from the object detection, object identification, position identification till conveying audio instructions to user has to be faster. As camera feeds the frames to the algorithm continuously, the fast processing ensures that there are no latencies in the output generated. The faster, continuous and latency free output means hassle free commutation of user. This is achieved by use of parallel processing power of GPU.

Identification, position identification till conveying audio instructions to user has to be faster. As camera feeds the frames to the algorithm continuously, the fast processing ensures that there are no latencies in the output generated. The faster, continuous and latency free output means hassle free commutation of user. This is achieved by use of parallel processing power of GPU.

7 Conclusion

The purpose of EOA is to guide the visually impaired user for the hassle free commutation experience. In this work, we have used OpenCV and tensor flow for capturing the images and Object detection respectively. Through YOLO V3 and Darknet the objects along with their position are identified. The work also focuses on generation of the results in minimum time possible which reduces the output latency. The Graphics Processing Unit (GPU) with its parallel processing capability is a useful tool for this purpose. Therefore, our aim is to create device that will provide artificial eyes to the visually impaired people. As a result this is an aimed combination of several subsystems that collectively make EOA for assistance of user and making their commutation safe [22]. Adding further we can add various features like night vision or safe path for overcoming the obstacles in front of them. Also we can use Raspberry Pi or Jetson Nano. This will not only reduce the overall cost of the system but will also make the system optimize and compact. This will make it easy and handy for the visually impaired people to carry anywhere.

References

1. M. H. Putra, Z. M. Yussof, K. C. Lim, S. I. Salim "Convolutional Neural Network for Person and Car Detection using YOLO Framework", Journal of Telecommunication, Electronic and Computer Engineering,2014.

2. C. Liu, Y. Tao, J. Liang, K. Li and Y. Chen, "Object Detection Based on YOLO Network", IEEE 4th Information Technology and Mechatronics Engineering Conference (ITOEC), Chongqing, China,2018.
3. Esteban Reyes, Cristopher Gomez, Esteban Norambuena, Javier Ruizdel-Solar, "Near Real-Time Object Recognition for Pepperbased on Deep Neural", Computer Science book series (LNCS, volume 11374) ,2018.
4. Mohammad Javad Shafiee, Brendan Chywl, Francis Li, Alexander Wong, "Fast YOLO: A fast you only look once system for real-time embedded object detection in video", 2017.
5. Anupam Sobti, Chetan Arora, M. Balakrishnan, "Object Detection in Real-Time Systems: Going Beyond Precision", IEEE Winter Conference on Applications of Computer Vision (WACV), 1020-1028, 2018.
6. Michal Irani and P. Anandan, "Unified Approach to Moving Object Detection in 2D and 3D Scenes", IEEEXplore, June 1998.
7. Joseph Redmon, Santosh Divvala, Ross Girshick, Ali Farhadi, "You Only Look Once: Unified, Real-Time Object Detection", Proceedings of the IEEE conference on computer vision and pattern recognition, 779-788, 2016.
8. Martin Simony, Stefan Milzy, Karl Amendey, Horst-Michael Gross, "Complex-YOLO: An euler-region-proposal for real-time 3d object detection on point clouds", The European Conference on Computer Vision (ECCV) Workshops, 2018.
9. Rachel Huang, Jonathan Pedoeem, CuixianChen, "YOLO-LITE: A realtime object detection algorithm optimized for non-GPU computers", IEEEXplore,2018.
10. Zhihuan Wu, Xiangning Chen, Y Gao, Y Li, ""Rapid target detection in high resolution remote sensing images using Yolo model", International Archives of the Photogrammetry (ISPRS), Remote Sensing and Spatial Information Sciences, Volume XLII-3, 2018.
11. Alessandro Dionisi, Emilio Sardini, Mauro Serpelloni, "Wearable object detection system for the blind", IEEE International Instrumentation and Measurement Technology Conference Proceedings, 1255-1258, 2012.
12. Niranjan Debnath, Jaya Bharati Thangiah, Shamala Pararasaingam, Syed Abdul Kader Aljunid, "A mobility aid for the blind with discrete distance indicator and hanging object detection", IEEE Region 10 Conference (TENCON), 664-667, 2004.
13. M Naveen Kumar, K Usha, "Voice based guidance and location indication system for the blind using GSM, GPS and optical device indicator", International Journal of Engineering Trends and Technology (IJETT), 2013.
14. S. Guennouni, A. Ahaitouf and A. Mansouri, "Multiple object detection using OpenCV on an embedded platform", Third IEEE International Colloquium in Information Science and Technology (CIST), Tetouan, 2014.
15. S. Mane and S. Mangale, "Moving Object Detection and Tracking Using Convolutional Neural Networks", Second International Conference on Intelligent Computing and Control Systems (ICICCS), Madurai, India, 2018.
16. S. Hayat, S. Kun, Z. Tengtao, Y. Yu, T. Tu and Y. Du, "A Deep Learning Framework Using Convolutional Neural Network for MultiClass Object Recognition", IEEE 3rd International Conference on Image, Vision and Computing (ICIVC), Chongqing, 2018.
17. P. Strumillo, "Electronic interfaces aiding the visually impaired in environmental access, mobility and navigation", 3rd International Conference on Human System Interaction, Rzeszow, 2010.
18. Asha G. Hagargund, SharshaVanria Thota, Mitadru Bera, Eram Fatima Shaik, "Image to Speech Conversion for Visually Impaired", International Journal of Latest Research in Engineering and Technology (IJLRET) ISSN: 2454-5031.
19. Z. Chen, R. Khemmar, B. Decoux, A. Atahouet and J. Ertaud, ""Real Time Object Detection, Tracking, and Distance and Motion Estimation based on Deep Learning: Application to Smart Mobility", Eighth International Conference on Emerging Security Technologies (EST), Colchester, United Kingdom, 2019.
20. P. R. Patil, M. D. Patil and V. A. Vyawahare, "Acceleration of hough transform algorithm using Graphics Processing Unit (GPU)," 2016 International Conference on Communication and Signal Processing (ICCSP), Melmaruvathur,pp. 1584-1588, 2016.
21. Parag Patil, Navin Singhaniya, Chaitanya Jage, Vishwesh A Vyawahare, Mukesh D Patil, PSV Nataraj, "GPU Computing of Special Mathematical Func-tions used in Fractional Calculus", Frontiers in Fractional Calculus, Vol. 199, 2018.
22. Chikane, Sameer and Patil, Parag and Singhaniya, Navin and Jage, Chaitanya and Patil, Mukesh and Vyawahare, Vishwesh, "HumanLike Interpretation of Lines Using Embedded GPU", Conference on Technologies for Future Cities (CTFC), 2019.
M.D. Patil, P.S.V. Nataraj, "GPU Computing of Special Mathematical Functions used in Fractional Calculus" **1**, 200-233 (2017) .

https://doi.org/10.1051/itmconf/20203203055

Seasonal performance estimation of thin film photovoltaic technology

Akshay Nichinte[1,*], *Vishwesh* Vyawahare[2,**], and *Dhiraj* Magare[3,***]

[1,2,3]Department of Electronics Engingneering, Ramrao Adik Institute of Technology, Navi Mumbai, India

Abstract. The performance of photovoltaic (PV) module in the environment can be improved by considering the seasonal effects. In this paper, the effect of seasonal variations of Amorphous-Silicon/thin film photovoltaic technology in different seasons has been presented for National Institute of Solar Energy (NISE), Gurgaon site in India. It has been observed that, the estimation efficiency and output power of a-Si technology using module temperature is well match to measured efficiency and output power. This study is mainly very important in India because of the each season's variation effect on different PV technology will be useful for large scale project assessment.

1 Introduction

The module temperature (T_m) of the solar photovoltaic (PV) is more affects to the module efficiency and output power of large solar plant system. This could be because of this module temperature that affects, the performance of PV system will automatically degrades.

For assess the feasibility of any installation, the energy produce from PV array is most applicable parameter. For overall energy production modelling, modules required to be observed during different seasons for the effect of atmosphere [1]. The main point of view of this paper is, to study the estimation of seasonal variation effect on a a-Si/thin film technology under Indian atmospheric conditions. In seasonal variation, the efficiency and power for a-Si/thin film technology is taken for analysis. The Indian climate is so much different than any other countries with various seasonal patterns. There are mainly three seasons in India: summer, monsoon and winter each has different effect on the spectrum.

An experimentally setup for testing the amorphous silicon/thin film technology, a weather station and Current-Voltage (I-V) scanner for this technology is set at National Institute of Solar Energy (NISE), Gurgaon, India, coordination with Advanced Institute for development of Industrial Science and Technology (AIST), Japan and department of New and Renewable Energy (MNRE), Government of India. The photograph for a-Si/thin film technology PV test setup in Fig. 1. This PV test setup has four major components like photovoltaic array, data logger with PV analyzer and related software for communication and analysis [2].

*e-mail: anichinte@gmail.com
**e-mail: vishwesh.vyawahare@rait.ac.in
***e-mail: dhiraj.magare@rait.ac.in

2 Methodology

The module operating temperature (T_m) is very major parameter while estimating the efficiency and output power because it directly affects to photovoltaic module output performance. To find out the accurate coefficients, mathematical module temperature model is very essential to operate and improve performance of solar PV module for a particular site. The amorphous-silicon/thin film technology modules are very sensitive to seasonal variation, while comparing with other technologies. In below Table 1, the given mathematical module temperature model has been taken for further estimation because it gives more accurate results in case of calculated module temperature coefficients for the site.

The coefficients calculated for this module temperature mathematical model using linear regression analysis model. This analysis is the part of data analysis tool, in which Least squares method are used for given site data [3]. Based on module temperature of a-Si/thin film technology, it is easy to calculate seasonal variation using efficiency and power formula which is given in equations (1) and (2) respectively. The module temperature (T_m) of a-Si placed important role for estimation of efficiency and power. The module temperature graphs of a-Si/thin film technology for both seasons (monsoon and clear sky day) which is shown Fig. 2 and 3.

Figure 2 shows the graph of time versus module temperature of a-Si thin film technology for 12th July (monsoon day) with time period of 10.00 am to 3.00 pm. The level of this temperature for this particular seasonal day is suddenly drop on around 12.00 pm to 2.00 pm noon because of cloud effects in monsoon day. At other side in Fig. 3, shows graph module temperature variations for clear sky day.

The PV module efficiency is under the standard test condition (STC) at a temperature of 25°C. The STC magnitudes are used in the estimation and measurement of the

Figure 1. Outdoor test set up of a-Si/thin film PV technology module at NISE, Gurgaon, India [2].

Table 1: Calculated coefficients and their RMSE, along with coefficients of reported model [3].

Model Format	Reference	PV Technology	RMSE	Calculated coefficients				Reported model coefficients			
				a	b	c	d	a	b	c	d
(T_m = a* T_a+b* G_t+c* V_w+d)	[3]	a-Si	4.38	7.2	0.021	1.07	-1.98	4.3	0.028	0.94	-1.52

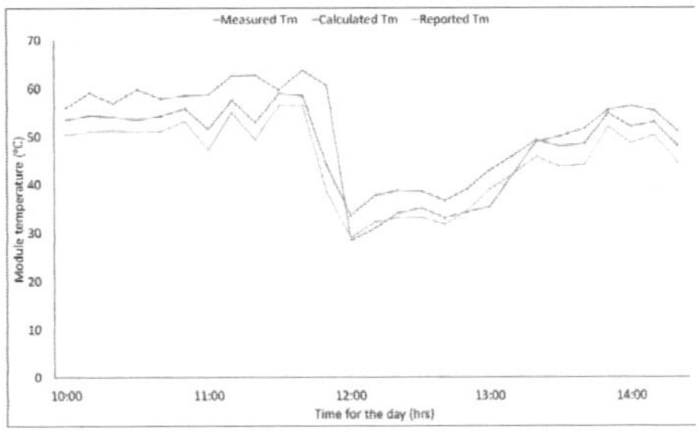

Figure 2. Module temperature graph for monsoon day 12th July of a-Si PV technology.

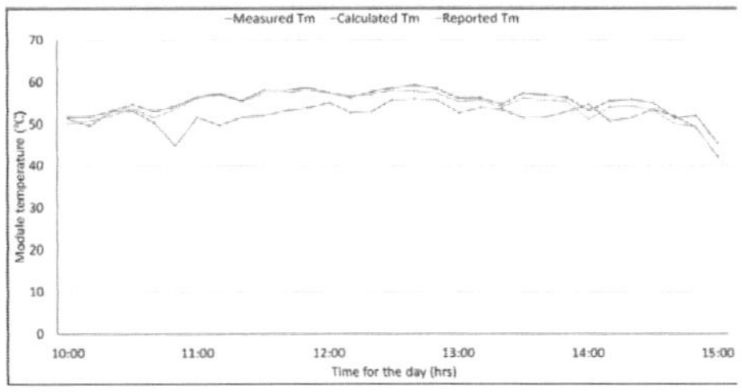

Figure 3. Module temperature graph for clear sky day 12th Oct of a-Si PV technology.

PV module performance, which helps in examine the output energy of PV systems. Although, due to environmental parameters variations STC does not occur under actual field conditions. Thus, the deviation in performance of the photovoltaic module from STC may be occur [4].

The below standard equations (1) and (2) respectively, of efficiency and output power has taken for the estimation [5].

The simplify expression for electrical efficiency,

$$\eta_c = \eta_{Tref}[1 - \beta_{ref} (T_c - T_{ref})] \quad (1)$$

This equation is represents the traditional linear expression for the photovoltaic electrical efficiency [6]. Where, η_c is the cell efficiency, η_{Tref} is electrical efficiency at temperature T_{ref}, β_{ref} is the efficiency correction coefficient for temperature (C^{-1}) and T_c is cell/module temperature. In this equations, the values of η_{Tref}, Area of module, β_{Tref} as well as T_{ref} has been taken from [4] [7]. The values of η_{Tref} and β_{ref} are normally given by the PV manufacturer. However, they can be obtained from laboratory tests also.

The expression for output power is,

$$P = \eta_c A\, G_T \quad (2)$$

In this expression, P is the output power of solar cell/module, A is the area in (m^2) of the module, G_T is the solar radiation and η_c is the calculated efficiency of solar module.

3 Results and Discussion

The mathematical model (T_m = a* T_a+b* G_t+c* V_w+d) from Table 1 of module temperature for a-Si/thin film technology has been used for the estimation of efficiency is listed in the Table 2.

The calculated efficiency of a-Si/thin film technology for monsoon day and clear sky day and their (%) difference which is taken between calculated average and measured average efficiency in (%) is shown in Table 2. The estimation and analysis, the calculated average and measured average efficiency for 12th July is 6.962 % and 6.993 % respectively; for 12th Oct is 7.091 % and 7.026 % obtained respectively. The (%) deviation in average calculated and measured power of a-Si/thin film technology for monsoon day and clear sky day and their % difference is shown in Table 3. The estimation and analysis, the (%) deviation in average calculated power and average measured power for 12th July is 71.686 and 72.832 respectively; for 12th Oct is 18.426 and 18.413 obtained respectively. The output efficiency graphs of monsoon day and clear sky day which is shown in Fig. 4 and Fig. 5 respectively. Then the output power graphs of a-Si/thin film technology for monsoon day and clear sky day which is shown in Fig. 6 and Fig. 7.

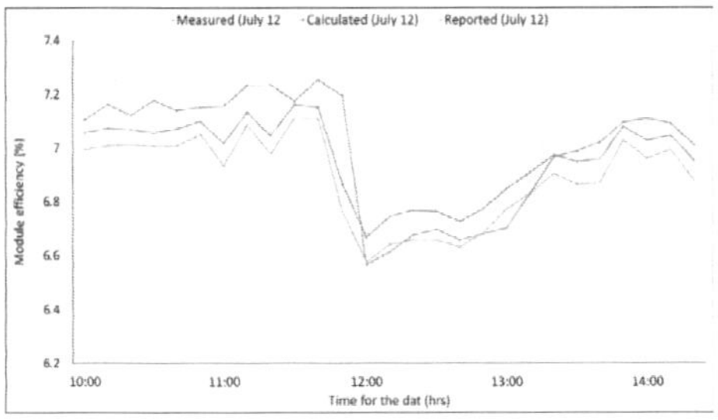

Figure 4. Efficiency for monsoon day, 12th July of a-Si PV technology.

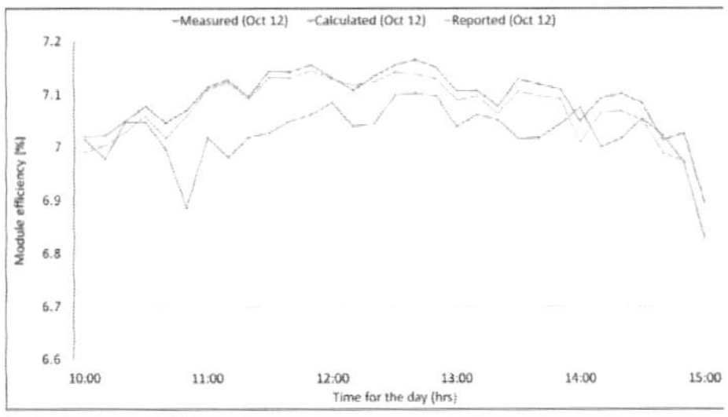

Figure 5. Efficiency for clear sky day, 12th Oct of a-Si PV technology.

Figure 4 shows the graph of time versus module efficiency of a-Si thin film technology for 12th July (monsoon day) with time period of 10.00 am to 3.00 pm. The level of this efficiency for this particular seasonal day is suddenly drop on around 11.00 pm to 12.00 pm noon, because of cloud effects in monsoon day. At other side in Fig. 5, there is efficiency graph respect to sunny hours, because of the solar panel absorb more radiation in this season.

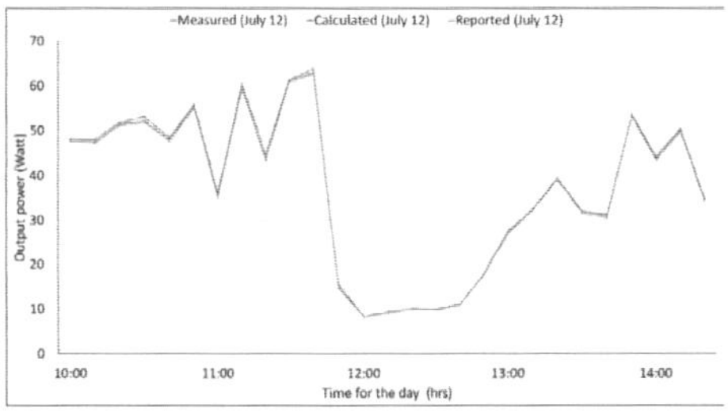

Figure 6. Output power for monsoon day, 12th July of a-Si PV technology.

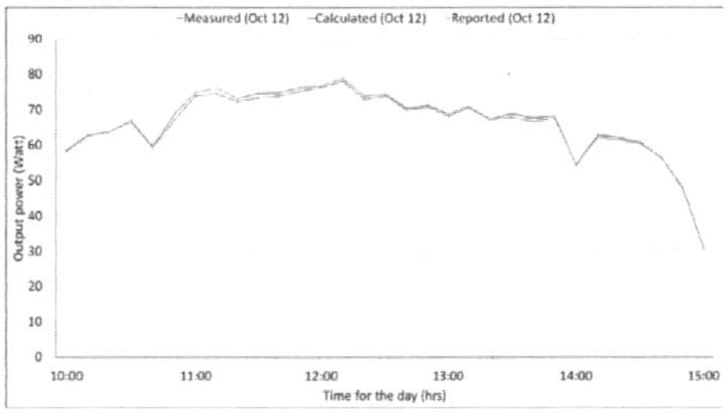

Figure 7. Output power for clear sky day, 12th Oct of a-Si PV technology.

Figure 6 shows the graph of time versus output power of a-Si thin film technology for 12th July (monsoon day) with time period of 10.00 am to 3.00 pm. The level of this power for this particular seasonal day is suddenly drop on around 12.00 pm to 2.00 pm noon because of its dropping efficiency and global irradiance (G_t). At other side in Fig. 7 shows, obtained power in this seasonal day.

The effect of seasonal variation of a-Si/thin film technology is shown in Fig. 8 and Fig. 9 for efficiency as well as output power respectively for the given site. The amorphous-silicon/thin film technology PV modules are very sensitive to seasonal variations as compared to module operating temperature. This gives the information about variations in three seasons. The graph plotted for particular representative day of each season, efficiency and output power is shown in Fig. 8 and Fig. 9.

4 Conclusions

This paper presents the relative seasonal effects on Amorphous-Silicon/thin film technology module under Indian environment. In addition, it has been successfully

https://doi.org/10.1051/itmconf/20203203055

Table 2: Calculated photovoltaic module efficiency for a-Si/thin film technology module.

Sr. No.	PV technology	Area of module in (m^2)	Date	Calculated avg. efficiency in %	Measured avg. efficiency in %	β_{ref} in %	η_{Tref} in %	% Diff. between calculated and measured Efficiency
1	Amorphous silicon	1.15	12 July	6.962	6.993	0.30	6.5	0.031
2		1.15	12 Oct	7.091	7.026	0.30	6.5	0.065

Table 3: Calculated photovoltaic module power for a-Si/thin film technology module.

Sr. No.	PV technology	Area of module in (m^2)	Date	% Deviation in avg. calculated power	% Deviation in avg. measured power	β_{ref} in %	η_{Tref} in %	% Diff. between calculated and measured power
1	Amorphous silicon	1.15	12 July	71.686	72.823	0.30	6.5	1.137
2		1.15	12 Oct	18.426	18.413	0.30	6.5	0.013

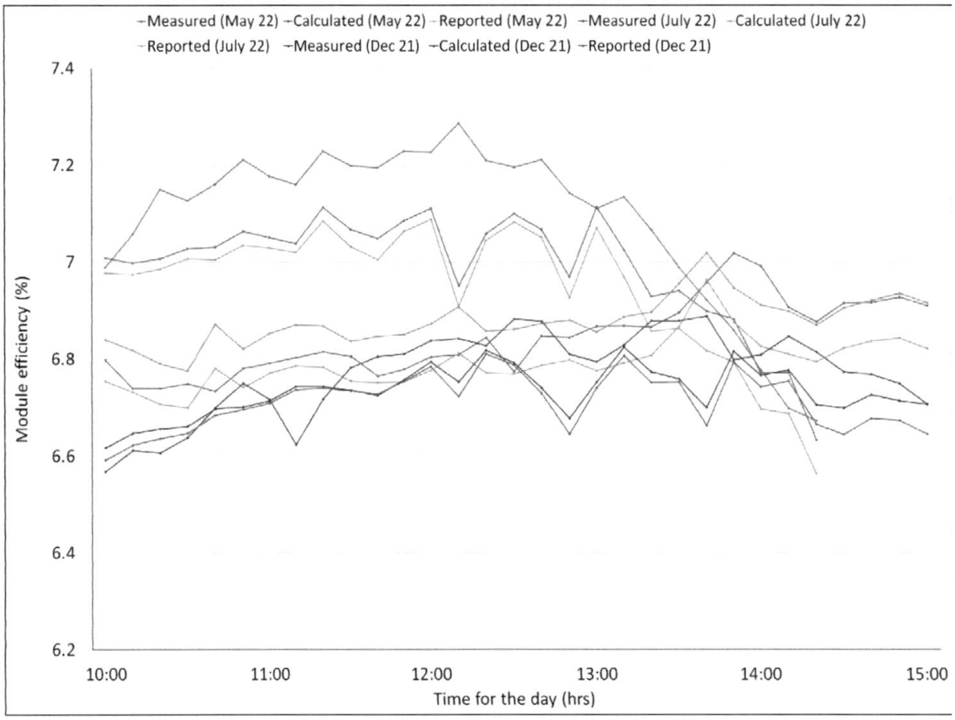

Figure 8. Seasonal module efficiency variation for Amorphous-Silicon PV technology.

estimates the efficiency and output power of Amorphous-Si/thin film technology for National Institute of Solar Energy (NISE), Gurgaon, India. It has been observed from analysis that a-Si/thin film technology is sensitive to variation in season during all seasonal days. It is happened due to strong spectral effects, that affect performance of a-Si technology. The (%) difference for calculated and measured of a-Si/thin film technology for monsoon and clear sky day in efficiency is 0.031 % and 0.065 % respectively, while (%) difference in output power are 1.137 % and 0.013 % respectively.

Acknowledgment

The authors would like to thank Advanced Industrial Science and Technology (AIST), Japan.

Nomenclature

a = ambient temperature coefficient
b = irradiance coefficient, W/m^2
c = wind speed coefficient, m/s
d = intercept
T_c/ T_m = cell or module temperature, °C
G_t = irradiance at tilted plane, W/m^2
T_a = ambient temperature, °C

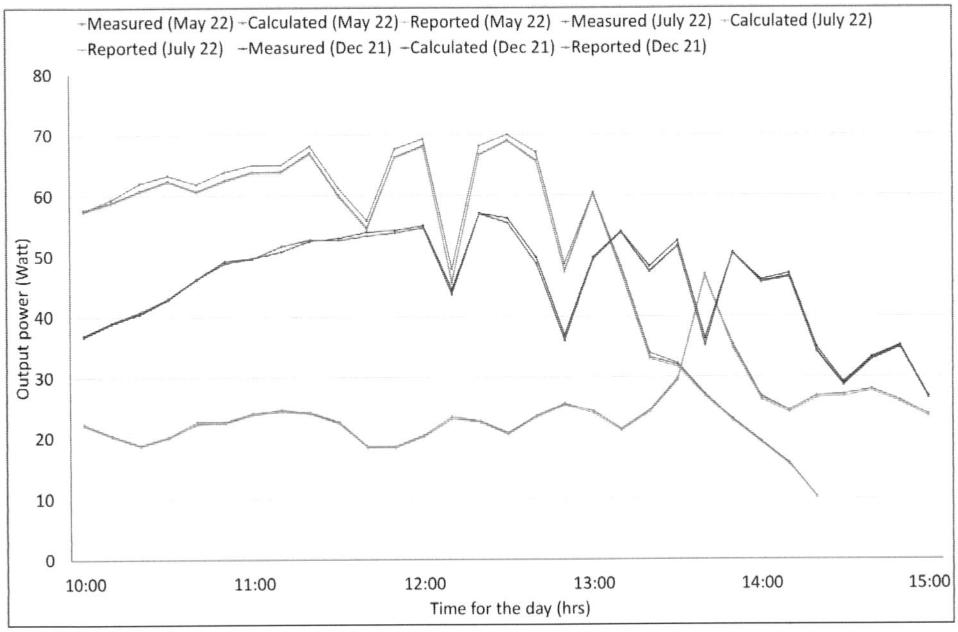

Figure 9. Seasonal module output power variation for Amorphous-Silicon PV technology.

V_w = wind speed, m/s

T_{ref} = temperature at reference condition, °C

Greek Symbols

η_c = cell or module efficiency

η_{Tref} = electrical efficiency for temperature T_{ref}

β_{ref} = Temperature coefficient for correction of efficiency (C^{-1})

References

[1] Magare, D. B., Sastry, O. S., Gupta, R., Betts, T. R., Gottschalg, R., Kumar, A., ... Singh, Y. K. "Effect of seasonal spectral variations on performance of three different photovoltaic technologies in India." International Journal of Energy and Environmental Engineering, vol. **7(1)**, 93-103.(2015). doi:10.1007/s40095-015-0190-0.

[2] Magare, D., Sastry, O. S., Gupta, R., Kumar, A., and Sinha, A., "Data Logging Strategy of Photovoltaic (PV) Module Test Beds," 27th European Photovoltaic Solar Energy Conference (EU PVSEC), Frankfurt, Germany, Sept. 24-28, pp. 3259-3262, (2012).

[3] Nichinte, A. S., Vyawahare, V. A., Magare, D. B., (2020)."Estimation and Comparison of Module Temperature Model Coefficient for Different PV Technology Module." 3rd International Conference on Communication System, Computing and IT Application CSCITA (Accepted), (2020).

[4] Magare, D., Sastry, O., Gupta, R., Mohammed, H., Bora, B., & Singh, Y. "Estimation of operating condition frequency distribution and power prediction by extending application of IEC 61853-1 standard for different technology photovoltaic modules." Journal of Renewable and Sustainable Energy, vol. **10(3)**,(2018). 033507. doi:10.1063/1.5023084

[5] Skoplaki, E., Boudouvis, A. G., & Palyvos, J. A. "A simple correlation for the operating temperature of photovoltaic modules of arbitrary mounting." Solar Energy Materials and Solar Cells, vol. **92(11)**, 1393-1402, (2008). doi:10.1016/j.solmat.2008.05.016

[6] Evans, D.L., Florschuetz, L.W., "Cost studies on terrestrial photovoltaic power systems with sunlight concentration." Solar Energy vol. **19**, 255–262, 1977.

[7] Skoplaki, E., & Palyvos, J. A. "Operating temperature of photovoltaic modules: A survey of pertinent correlations." Renewable Energy, vol. **34(1)**, 23–29, (2009). doi:10.1016/j.renene.2008.04.009

AUTHOR INDEX

AUTHOR INDEX

AUTHOR INDEX